C000302107

1,000,000 Books

are available to read at

Forgotten Books

www.ForgottenBooks.com

Read online
Download PDF
Purchase in print

ISBN 978-1-5281-0683-2
PIBN 10914430

This book is a reproduction of an important historical work. Forgotten Books uses state-of-the-art technology to digitally reconstruct the work, preserving the original format whilst repairing imperfections present in the aged copy. In rare cases, an imperfection in the original, such as a blemish or missing page, may be replicated in our edition. We do, however, repair the vast majority of imperfections successfully; any imperfections that remain are intentionally left to preserve the state of such historical works.

Forgotten Books is a registered trademark of FB &c Ltd.
Copyright © 2018 FB &c Ltd.
FB &c Ltd, Dalton House, 60 Windsor Avenue, London, SW19 2RR.
Company number 08720141. Registered in England and Wales.

For support please visit www.forgottenbooks.com

1 MONTH OF FREE READING

at

www.ForgottenBooks.com

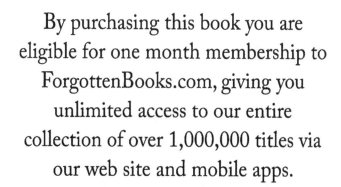

By purchasing this book you are eligible for one month membership to ForgottenBooks.com, giving you unlimited access to our entire collection of over 1,000,000 titles via our web site and mobile apps.

To claim your free month visit:

www.forgottenbooks.com/free914430

* Offer is valid for 45 days from date of purchase. Terms and conditions apply.

English
Français
Deutsche
Italiano
Español
Português

www.forgottenbooks.com

Mythology Photography **Fiction** Fishing Christianity **Art** Cooking Essays Buddhism Freemasonry Medicine **Biology** Music **Ancient Egypt** Evolution Carpentry Physics Dance Geology **Mathematics** Fitness Shakespeare **Folklore** Yoga Marketing **Confidence** Immortality Biographies Poetry **Psychology** Witchcraft Electronics Chemistry History **Law** Accounting **Philosophy** Anthropology Alchemy Drama Quantum Mechanics Atheism Sexual Health **Ancient History** **Entrepreneurship** Languages Sport Paleontology Needlework Islam **Metaphysics** Investment Archaeology Parenting Statistics Criminology **Motivational**

OF THE

American Baptist Home Mission Society,

PRESENTED BY THE

EXECUTIVE BOARD

AT THE

ANNIVERSARY HELD IN TROY, N. Y.,

MAY 13th, 14th, and 15th, 1853,

WITH

THE TREASURER'S REPORT AND OTHER DOCUMENTS.

ASTOR LIBRARY
NEW-YORK.

NEW-YORK:
PUBLISHED AT THE AMERICAN BAPTIST HOME MISSION ROOMS, NO. 354 BROOME STREET.
HOLMAN, GRAY & CO., PRINTERS, CORNER CENTRE AND WHITE STREETS.
1853.

ACT OF INCORPORATION.

AN ACT TO INCORPORATE THE AMERICAN BAPTIST HOME MISSION SOCIETY, PASSED APRIL 12, 1843, AND AMENDED FEBRUARY 9, 1849.

The People of the State of New-York, represented in Senate and Assembly, do enact as follows:

§ 1. All such persons as now are, or may hereafter become members of the American Baptist Home Mission Society, formed in the City of New-York, in the year one thousand eight hundred and thirty-two, shall be, and hereby are constituted a body corporate, by the name of the American Baptist Home Mission Society, for the purpose of promoting the preaching of the Gospel in North America.

§ 2. This Corporation shall be capable of taking, holding, or receiving any property, real or personal, by virtue of any devise or bequest contained in any last will or testament of any person

NAME.

I. This Society shall be called the American Baptist Home Mission Society.

OBJECT.

II. The object of this Society shall be to promote the preaching of the gospel in North America.

MEMBERSHIP.

III. The Society shall be composed of Annual Delegates, Life Members and Life Directors. Any Baptist church, in union with the denomination, may appoint a delegate for an annual contribution of ten dollars, and an additional delegate for each additional thirty dollars. Thirty dollars shall be requisite to constitute a member for life; and one hundred dollars paid at one time, or a sum which, in addition to any previous contribution, shall amount to one hundred dollars, shall be requisite to constitute a director for life.

OFFICERS.

IV. The Officers of the Society shall be a President, two Vice-Presidents, a Treasurer, an Auditor, a Corresponding Secretary, and a Recording Secretary, whom the Society shall annually elect by ballot.

MANAGERS AND EXECUTIVE BOARD.

V. The Officers and Life Directors shall meet immediately after the Annual Meeting of the Society, and elect fifteen Managers, residing in the city of New-York, or its vicinity, who, together with the Treasurer, Auditor, and Corresponding and Recording Secretaries, shall constitute an Executive Board to conduct the business of the Society; and shall respectively continue to discharge their official duties until superseded by a new election. Five members of the Board shall be a quorum for the transaction of business.

POWERS AND DUTIES OF THE EXECUTIVE BOARD.

VI. The Executive Board shall have power to appoint its own meetings; elect its own Chairman and Recording Secretary; enact its own By-Laws and Rules of Order, provided always, that they be not inconsistent with this Constitution; fill any vacancies which may occur in their own body, or in the offices of the Society during the year; and, if deemed necessary by two-thirds of the members present at a regular meeting, convene special meetings of the Society. They shall establish such Agencies as the interests of the Society may require; appoint Agents and Missionaries; fix their compensation; direct and instruct them concerning their particular fields and labors; make all appropriations to be paid out of the treasury; and present to the Society at each annual meeting a full report of their proceedings during the current year.

DESIGNATED FUNDS.

VII. All moneys or other property contributed and designated for any particular missionary field, shall be so appropriated, or returned to the donors, or their lawful agents.

TREASURER.

VIII. The Treasurer shall give bonds to such amount as the Executive Board shall think proper.

ELIGIBILITY TO APPOINTMENT.

IX. All the Officers, Managers, Missionaries and Agents of the Society, shall be members in good standing in regular Baptist churches.

ANNUAL MEETING.

X. The Society shall meet annually, at such time and place as the Executive Board shall appoint.

ALTERATIONS OF THE CONSTITUTION.

XI. No alteration of this Constitution shall be made without an affirmative vote of two-thirds of the members present at an annual meeting; nor unless the same shall have been proposed in writing, and the proposition sustained by a majority vote, at a previous annual meeting, or recommended by the Executive Board.

STATED MEETINGS FOR 1853-54.

Of the Executive Board—Thursday before the first Wednesday in each month.

" " Committee on Agencies and Finance— The day previous to that of the Board.

" " Committee on Missions—The Tuesday preceding.

BY-LAWS OF THE BOARD.

1. All meetings shall be opened with prayer.
2. All Committees shall be nominated by the presiding officer, and approved by the Executive Board, unless otherwise specially ordered.
3. No moneys shall be paid out of the Treasury but by order of the Executive Board.
4. All resolutions, if required, shall be presented in writing.

ORDER OF BUSINESS.

1. Reading the minutes of the last meeting.
2. Treasurer's Report.

[redacted]

5. Reports of Select Committees.
6. Unfinished Business.

[redacted]

MINUTES OF THE TWENTY-FIRST ANNIVERSARY

OF THE

American Baptist Home Mission Society,

HELD IN THE

MEETING-HOUSE OF THE FIRST BAPTIST CHURCH,

TROY, NEW-YORK, MAY 13th, 14th and 15th, 1853.

THE meeting was called to order by Rev. B. M. HILL, Corresponding Secretary, as neither of the presiding officers was present; when, upon motion, Rev. LELAND HOWARD was elected President *pro tem.*, and, in the absence of Rev. EDWARD LATHROP, Rev. J. R. STONE, of New-York, was chosen Recording Secretary, *pro tem.*

Prayer was offered by Rev. E. L. MAGOON, of New-York.

Ministering and other brethren present, not members of the Society, were invited to participate in our deliberations.

By resolution, the business sessions of the body were fixed for 9 o'clock, A. M., 3 o'clock, P. M., and 7½ o'clock, in the evening. The hours of adjournment were made 12 o'clock, M., and 5 o'clock in the afternoon.

Committees were appointed, as follows:

On Credentials of Delegates.—Rev. brn. A. D. GILLETTE, of New-York; N. A. REED, Massachusetts; E. ANDREWS, Pennsylvania; L. HAYDEN, Vermont; A. H. GRANGER, Maine.

On Nomination of Officers.—Rev. brn. E. L. MAGOON, of New-York; WM. REID, Connecticut; G. P. NICE, New-Jersey; J. E. CHESSHIRE, Rhode Island; W. P. PATTISON, New York.

On Arrangements for Public Services.—Rev. brn G. C. Baldwin, of New-York; J. G. Warren, New-York; G. W. Patch, Massachusetts; N. P. Foster, New-Hampshire; J. S. Ladd, New-York.

The Treasurer presented his Report, with the Auditor's Certificate, by the hand of the Assistant Secretary, J. R. Stone.

Upon motion of Rev. D. D. Pratt, of New-Hampshire, seconded by Rev. Wm. P. Pattison, of New-York, it was—

Resolved, That the Treasurer's Report be accepted and printed.

This resolution was sustained by Rev. brn. James Schofield, of Illinois; W. Reid, Connecticut; Daniel Dye, Wisconsin; S. Chase, Michigan; J. H. Walden, and E. L. Magoon, of New-York.

After prayer by Rev. Charles Willet, of Connecticut, the Society adjourned.

AFTERNOON SESSION.

At three o'clock the Society was called to order. Prayer was offered by Rev. M. G. Hodge, of New-York.

The Corresponding Secretary presented a brief abstract of the Annual Report of the Executive Board.

[redacted]

Upon the recommendation of the Executive Board, after full discussion, the 11th Article of the Constitution was altered so as to read thus:

"No alteration of this Constitution shall be made without an affirmative vote of two-thirds of the members present at an annual meeting; nor unless the same shall have been proposed in writing, and the proposition sustained by a majority vote, at a previous annual meeting, or recommended by the Executive Board."

Upon motion of Rev. O. AYER, of New-Hampshire, it was voted to entertain, at the next Annual Meeting, a proposition to add these words to the 11th Article of the Constitution, viz.:

"Of which they [the Board] shall have given notice one year previously."

At the recommendation of the Committee on Public Services, it was voted to make the Reports of the Committee on Obituaries, and the Committee on "The Far West," the subjects for consideration this evening.

The Board also submitted, through the Corresponding Secretary, a proposition to explain the 2d Article of the Constitution, so as to have it understood to comprise all the usual means employed for preparing the way, and securing a place, for the effective and uninterrupted preaching of the Gospel: pending which the Society adjourned.

Prayer by Rev. J. S. BACKUS, of New-York.

EVENING SESSION.

The meeting was opened with devotional services. Prayer by Rev. W. F. NELSON, of Massachusetts.

In accordance with previous arrangements, the Report of the Committee on Missions in the Far West was read by Rev. E. L. MAGOON, of New-York.

Its acceptance was moved by Rev. C. WILLET, of Connecticut, and seconded by L. D. BOONE, M. D., of Illinois, with appropriate observations. After further remarks from Rev. W. F. NELSON, of Massachusetts, Rev. LEWIS RAYMOND, of Illinois, and Rev. E. L. MAGOON, it was accepted and ordered to be printed. (See page 62.)

The Committee on Obituaries reported through Rev. A. D. GILLETTE.

On motion of Rev. S. CHASE, of Michigan, seconded by Rev. M. L. FULLER, of New-York, the Report was accepted. (See page 66.)

Rev. J. ALDRICH, of Massachusetts, led the Society in prayer.

Rev. E. L. MAGOON, of New-York, presented two communications addressed to the Society, one from Messrs. ISAAC NEWTON, W. W. TODD, and J. DOWLEY, Esqs.; and the other, from the Board of the American and Foreign Bible Society, tendering rooms for the local business of the

Society in the Bible House, Nassau Street, to be secured rent free in perpetuity.

Upon motion of Rev. S. A. Corey, of New-York, seconded by Rev. N. A. Reed, of Massachusetts, it was—

Resolved, That the communications to this Society from the American and Foreign Bible Society, and from Messrs. Newton and others, relating to the offer of rooms to this Society, be referred to a Committee to be appointed by the chair, to report to-morrow.

The Society then adjourned.

SATURDAY MORNING.

The Society assembled at 9 o'clock. The President, *pro tem.*, in the chair.

Rev. William Grant, of New-York, led in prayer.

The Minutes of Friday were read and approved.

The following brethren, nominated by the chair, were confirmed as the Committee on the Communications in regard to Rooms, viz.: Rev. Messrs. Wm. Reid, N. B. Baldwin, E. E. L. Taylor, J. S. Backus, and R. W. Martin, Thomas Wattson, D. M. Wilson, L. D. Boone, Smith Sheldon, Samuel Griggs, and J. S. Brown, Esqs.

[redacted]

quently it was announced that, with very great unanimity, the Society had made choice of the officers whose names are on the 14th page.

The Committee on Missions in the Great Central Valley, presented their Report through the chairman, Rev. J. M. PECK, D. D., which was accepted. (See page 59.)

The following resolution, presented by Rev. C. M. FULLER, and seconded by Rev. M. L. FULLER, was adopted:

Whereas, The American Baptist Home Mission Society, in its designs of mercy in spreading the Gospel over North America, is calculated to perpetuate the rights of conscience and the civil and religious liberty of our republic: Therefore,

Resolved, That we recommend to the Secretary of our Board, that he send a circular to the Churches, requesting them to make a special collection on the Sabbath before the 4th of July, or some other Sabbath designated by the Churches where they do not celebrate the Day specially for that purpose, to be placed at the disposal of the Board for the erection of houses of worship in the newly settled parts of our country; and each pastor to preach a sermon on the subject of church extension.

The hour of adjournment having arrived, on motion, the rule in relation to the close of the Sessions was suspended for half an hour.

The Committee, of which Rev. WM. REID was chairman, presented two Reports—that of the minority being signed by two of the brethren.

Upon motion of Rev. THOMAS ARMITAGE, seconded by Rev. L. F. BEECHER, D. D., both reports were laid upon the table.

After prayer by Rev. S. ILLSLEY, of New-York, adjourned.

SATURDAY AFTERNOON SESSION.

At 3 o'clock the Society assembled, and engaged in prayer with Rev. E. J. Scott, of New-York.

The Minutes of the Morning Session having been read, the subject under consideration at the time of adjournment was taken up, when, upon motion, after full discussion, the first resolution proposed by the Committee was adopted, viz.:

Resolved, That the interests of the Society require the selection of a new location for the transaction of its business.

Upon motion of Prof. M. B. ANDERSON, the following resolutions were presented as a substitute for the others reported by the Committee, and were adopted, viz.:

Resolved, That the Board of the Home Mission Society be directed to rent immediately suitable Rooms for their accommodation, provided that pledges be given that the expense shall not be defrayed from the Society's general treasury.

Resolved, That the Board be authorized to raise a fund for the purchase of suitable rooms for the Society, at an expense not exceeding forty thousand dollars, at the earliest opportunity within two years.

The Report of the majority, as thus amended, was accepted. (See page 68.)

Upon motion of Rev. Dr. Beecher, of Albany, N. Y., it was

Resolved, That the thanks of this Society be most cordially presented to the gentlemen and brethren who have so generously tendered the free use, in perpetuity, of Rooms in the Bible House, Nassau Street, New-York.

Rev. E. E. L. Taylor, of Brooklyn, N. Y., offered the following resolution, which was adopted:

Resolved, That the most grateful thanks of the Society be presented to the membership and corporation of the First Baptist Church, for the gratuitous use of the rooms in Broome-Street for so many years past.

The Report of the Committee on Financial Affairs was read by Rev. E. E. L. Taylor; which, with its resolutions appended, upon motion of Rev. J. Aldrich, of Massachusetts, seconded by Rev. J. W. Parkhurst, of Massachusetts, was accepted. (See page 55.)

Rev. L. Tracy, of Vermont, presented the Report of the Committee on the Grand Ligne Mission. This was accepted. (See page 66.)

Upon motion of Rev. Thomas Armitage, of New-York, it was—

Resolved, That a vote of thanks be tendered to the First Baptist Church, and other citizens of Troy, for the hospitalities extended to this Body.

Rev. N. A. Reed, of Massachusetts, moved the following resolution, which was adopted:

[redacted]

PUBLIC RELIGIOUS EXERCISES.

Saturday Evening was occupied in Public Services of an intensely interesting character, in accordance with the recommendation of the Committee of Arrangements.

The exercises were conducted by Rev. JONATHAN ALDRICH, of Massachusetts.

Prayer was offered by Rev. J. GIRDWOOD, of Massachusetts.

Effective Addresses were made by Rev. brethren NARCISSE CYR, of the Grand Ligne Mission; LOUIS CHARRON, of Enosburg, Vt.; JAMES TANNER, of Pembina, Minnesota; M. E. BELINA CZECHOWSKI, a converted French Pole, formerly a Roman Catholic Priest; J. M. PECK, D. D., of Illinois; and A. D. GILLETTE, of New-York.

A collection was taken for the Canadian Mission, amounting to $45.44.

The meeting was closed with prayer by Bro. TANNER.

Lord's Day Morning, Rev. D. SHEPARDSON, of Cincinnati, Ohio. preached from John iv: 35, 36.

Rev. S. B. SWAIM, of Worcester, Massachusetts, preached in the Afternoon from 1 Samuel v: 1—4.

These sermons were highly appropriate to the occasion, and were listened to by crowded assemblies.

In the Evening, Bro. ESH-QUE-GO-NE-BI, or JAMES TANNER, was ordained to the work of the Gospel Ministry, in accordance with the action of an Ecclesiastical Council, called by the authority of the Church in St. Paul, Minnesota, and held in New-York, May 11th. Brethren L. RAYMOND, of Illinois; J. ALDRICH, of Massachusetts; G. C. BALDWIN, of New-York; J. M. PECK, of Illinois, and B. M. HILL, the Corresponding Secretary, performed the various parts of the service. Previous to the Ordination, bro. Tanner gave a brief statement of his religious experience, call to the ministry, and doctrinal views; and made an earnest, eloquent appeal for the Gospel and its institutions among his Indian brethren.

Thus closed the last, and, perhaps, the most interesting Anniversary that the American Baptist Home Mission Society ever held.

Dr. **THE AMERICAN BAPTIST HOME MISSION SOCIETY**

1853.	To Cash paid Missionaries for Salaries, ...	$32,340 92
	" Cash paid Agents for Salaries, Traveling Expenses, Postage, &c., ...	5,786 05
	" Cash paid Salaries of Secretaries and Clerks, .	2,809 33
	" Cash paid for Stationery, Postage, and incidental Expenses, ...	242 60
	" Cash paid for paper and printing of Home Mission Record, and incidental expenses on same, ...	1,227 80
	" Cash paid for paper and printing Annual Report, Certificates, Blanks, &c., ...	505 65
	" Cash paid Taxes on land donated to the Society,	16 44
	" Discount on uncurrent funds, and counterfeit	

IN ACCOUNT WITH CHAS. J. MARTIN, TREASURER. *Cr.*

1853.			
	By Balance from last year, ...		6,115 63
	" Cash proceeds of note, (contributed last year,) .		300 00
	" Interest, received on funds temporarily invested, ...	89 67	
	" Interest received on Bond and Mortgage, (a special investment by direction of the donor, Theron Fisk,)	52 50	
			142 17
	" Net proceeds of $2,000, U. S. Stock, sold at 9 per cent. premium, less brokerage, . . .		2,175 00
	" Amount received for subscriptions to Home Mission Record, ...		1,015 75
	" Amount of designated funds for Meeting-houses,		679 50
	" Amount of Contributions, Legacies, &c., received from 1st April, 1852, to 31st March, 1853, ...	42,192 51	
	Of which this amount is in bills receivable not yet matured, . . .	1,150 00	
			41,042 51
			$51,470 56
March 31	By Balance, ...	$4,465 98	
	Subject to drafts of Cor. Secretary already issued upon the Treasurer, and liable to immediate presentation, amounting to, .	3,511 47	
			$954 51

CHARLES J. MARTIN, *Treasurer.*

This is to certify that I have examined the foregoing account, together with the vouchers connected therewith, and find the same correct. The balance in the hands of Charles J. Martin, Esq., Treasurer, in cash, is Four Thousand Four Hundred and Sixty-five 98-100 Dollars. He also holds bills receivable, Thirteen Hundred and Ten Dollars. He has in his possession the following securities belonging to the Society, viz.: Certificate of Stock in the Corn Exchange Bank, New-York, for Two Thousand Dollars; Brooklyn City Bond, bearing interest at six per cent., payable 1st January, 1863, for Five Hundred Dollars; also a Bond and Mortgage, (a special investment by direction of the donor,) the interest only to be used by the Society, principal of which is Fifteen Hundred Dollars.

NEW-YORK, *April 1st*, 1853. GARRAT N. BLEECKER, *Auditor.*

OFFICERS OF THE SOCIETY

AND

EXECUTIVE BOARD.

OFFICERS.

PRESIDENT.

HON. ISAAC DAVIS, LL.D., Worcester, Massachusetts.

VICE-PRESIDENTS.

WILLIAM COLGATE, Esq., New-York.
JOHN P. CROZER, Esq., Chester, Pa.

TREASURER.

CHARLES J. MARTIN, Esq., New-York.

AUDITOR.

GARRAT N. BLEECKER, Esq.,* New-York.

CORRESPONDING SECRETARY.

REV. BENJAMIN M. HILL New-York.

ANNUAL REPORT.

It is required by the Constitution of the American Baptist Home Mission Society that its Executive Board shall present, "at each Annual Meeting, a full report of their proceedings during the current year." In attempting the performance of that duty at this time, the Board would first of all gratefully recognize the hand of our gracious God in their preservation, and the enjoyment of numerous tokens of his favor in enabling them to perform the labor assigned them.

DEATHS.

A solemn bereavement in the course of the year renders this recognition more than ordinarily appropriate and necessary. One of their official associates has been stricken down by the hand of death. The Rev. MORGAN J. RHEES, D. D., was an able and useful member of the board. His faithfulness in the discharge of every duty, and his wisdom and kindness in council were highly appreciated; the loss of them is deeply regretted. His decease, while we regard it as a sore affliction, warns us of the waning light of our own day, and the necessity of our improving its rapidly fleeting hours in the more faithful performance of our duty. It is fitting to the occasion also to mention the decease of others who have been connected with the Society. Death has largely executed his commission among the Directors and Members of the Society, three of the former and twenty-one of the latter having been called from the labors of earth.* Among the number were eleven ministers of the Gospel, two of whom were missionaries of the Society ; and ten females, two of whom were ministers' wives. Four of the individuals were present at the last anniversary in Cleveland. Besides these, another missionary, who was not a member, has also fallen. Obituary notices of all have been given in the *Home Mission Record.*

DIRECTORS AND MEMBERS FOR LIFE.

One hundred and seventy-one names which, up to the beginning of the year, were represented on the lists of Directors and Members of the Society as deceased, are [redacted] persons, namely: Deacon Joshua A. Burke, Barnum M. Howard, Alanson Stewart, and Miss Eliza Skaats, of New York; Mrs. Sarah B. Peirce, of Massachusetts; and Arnold Whipple, of Rhode Island. Balances of bequests heretofore mentioned have been received from the Executors of James Vanderpool, of New Jersey; Asa H. Trueman, of New York; and John Everett, of Michigan; and a payment in part of a legacy in advance from Theron Fisk, of New York.

CHANGES IN THE EXECUTIVE BOARD.

Several changes in the Executive Board have occurred during the year. The Rev. John T. Seeley removed from the City of New York, and H. P. Freeman, Esq., on account of a change in his business relations, found it inconvenient to perform the duties of a member, and resigned. These two vacancies were filled by the election of Rev. Henry Davis and Rev. A. D. Gillette; but, unexpectedly, Brother Davis, shortly after his appointment, also removed, and Rev. Dr. Rhees deceased. The vacancies thus created were supplied by the appointment of Rev. J. R. Stone and Rev. Thomas Armitage.

ASSISTANT SECRETARY.

The extension of the Society's operations has produced a corresponding increase of routine business in the Mission Rooms, which, with an onerous correspondence, and the labor of editing the publications of the Society, left an insufficient amount of time for personal communication with those whose business often demanded it. The investigation of subjects, frequently requiring uninterrupted application and patience, could be made only at unseasonable hours; and the promotion of important interests, making absence at a distance from the city necessary, could rarely be attempted. For these reasons, the appointment of an Assistant to the Corresponding Secretary has been for some time deemed unavoidable, and has at length been consummated. Early in the year, Rev. Henry Davis was appointed to that station, and commenced his services; but on more mature reflection, he considered it his duty to resume a pastoral relation, and resigned. Rev. J. R. Stone was immediately afterwards elected, and has since then discharged the duties of the post. Those duties are to edit the *Home Mission Record*, to conduct a portion of the correspondence, to collect funds in the City of New York and its vicinity, and occasionally to visit public missionary bodies, and transact important business abroad. The measure, it is believed, will prove productive of much advantage to the Society.

[redacted]

two-thirds of the members present at an annual meeting, nor unless the same shall have been proposed in writing, and the proposition sustained by a majority vote at a previous annual meeting, or recommended by the Executive Board."

FINANCIAL AFFAIRS.

The following is a summary and practical view of the financial affairs of the Society during the past year, and of their condition at the present time:

Balance from last year's account	$6,115 63
Cash receipts from all sources	45,354 93
Making the total amount of cash in the Treasury for the year ending 31st March, 1853	51,470 56
The total amount of disbursements for the same period, was	47,004 58
Leaving a balance in the Treasury of	4,465 98
Subject to drafts afloat and liable to immediate presentation	3.511 47
Actual balance at control of the Society	954 51
The total liabilities of the Society on 31st March, 1853, amounted to	36,007 78
And the available resources at the same period were	8,115 98
Showing a balance against the Society at the close of the year of	27,891 80
Of the above amount of cash receipts, there were in contributions, legacies and donations	41,042 51
Being an increase over the amount received from the same sources last year of	8,228 35
Of the above amount of liabilities, there are due to missionaries, for services performed up to the 1st of April, and liable to immediate demand	1,713 36
Add for Drafts upon the Treasurer, afloat at the same date as above	3,511 47
In addition to the above, the amounts falling due each month for services performed, from April 1st to July 1st, will make an aggregate of	9,917 29
Making the total amount	$15,142 12
Or an aggregate at the rate of $60,000 per annum.	

Additions to the amount of liabilities must, necessarily, be made each month, as heretofore, by the appointment of missionaries, fully equalling and probably exceeding the amount heretofore appropriated in the corresponding quarter of the year.

This shows that the receipts for the ensuing year should be much more liberal than heretofore, and that the necessity for it, being predicated upon the action of the Society a year ago, gives the Board an unusual claim to the notice and aid of the Society.

It should be known that every dollar of the balance of cash reported as being in the Treasury on the 31st of March, was paid in on that day; that it constituted half the amount of receipts for the entire month, and is more than one-tenth of the amount of donations for the whole year.

At the last anniversary of the Society a Resolution was passed to "encourage the Executive Board, in the prosecution of the great work committed to them, to expend sixty thousand dollars during the coming year." It was based upon proper evidence of the necessity for that amount in providing for the known exigencies of the home field, and it passed by an unanimous vote, in a full session. It was, therefore, regarded as a pledge of the Society to amply and promptly sustain the Board in a [redacted] rely on any ground of encouragement, except that which could be realized in a sufficiently replenished treasury. Their necessities called loudly for "material aid," and, until it was received, it became their duty to curtail and even discontinue their appropiations. Their course may have proved a disappointment to some of their friends,—perhaps a serious discouragement to many who besought their aid in time of necessity; but they have the consolation to believe that it has preserved the high and, hitherto, unquestioned credit of the Society, and prevented many embarrassments to its financial transactions for the ensuing year.

MISSIONARY OPERATIONS.

The missionary operations of the Society have been extended as much as its ability would admit, and a portion of the year more so. Believing that the great importance of the home mission field had become more justly appreciated than formerly, arrangements were made, early in the year, for carrying out, in a judicious manner, the benevolent suggestions of the Society. Important stations were selected; ministers were appointed to occupy them, and appropriations were made for their necessary support. The effect at the stations generally was encouraging, and good fruit has appeared in various forms. Those arrangements were accompanied by certain providential events, which, while in some instances they called for an unusual expenditure of funds, were specially cheering as clearer indications of the duty of the Society to lengthen their cords and stretch forth the curtains of their habitation. Among those events were specific openings of important positions in California and Oregon, for the immediate occupancy of our missionaries, and affecting solicitations from Indian tribes in New Mexico to be favored with preachers and teachers. The efforts for the first class of those claims, though successfully commenced, were cut short by the failure of the needful amount of means. Those of the other class were carried out only by a new distribution of the missionaries previously in the field, and by some unexpected resources for the support of one of them at his station.

It is deeply to be regretted that, on account of an insufficient supply for the treasury, several points on the Pacific coast now remain unoccupied by our ministers; and that fair opportunities for promoting important interests in our Zion, are thereby deferred for much time to come, if not entirely lost to us.

Although much embarrassed by the disappointment of justifiable anticipations in the early part of the year, the Board have exerted themselves, as opportunity and means allowed, to follow up previous efforts to spread [redacted] throughout many local communities, and a liberal spirit has been evinced in aiding to send the gospel of salvation to the ends of the earth. A pleasing advance of the cause of Christ, through the instrumentality of the Society, is manifest in that region, and encourages still greater effort for the future.

MISSIONS ON THE PACIFIC COAST.

Various changes in our arrangements for Oregon have occurred since our last anniversary. The population which had concentrated in the villages, has been reduced by the operation of the law which gives a farm to those who actually occupy it for a series of years. To secure their title to those farms, many have removed from the villages. In the mean time the general population of the Territory has rapidly increased by immigration, and spread itself through the fertile regions of that far western country. This has created an unexpected demand for a large portion of the ministers to accompany the people to the valleys and plains selected for their residences. To meet this demand, two missionaries who had bestowed their principal attention upon educational interests in Oregon City, have removed to other places. Another is laboring as an Exploring Agent and general itinerant in all the Territory.

This field is one of the most inviting to experienced and faithful ministers. Many such would find their condition improved and their usefulness increased, by proceeding to it at once on their own account, and there are just claims on this Society for several others.

The condition of our mission in California has improved during the year. The number of missionaries is greater, some of the most important cities are now well supplied, and the prospect of general success is more encouraging than at our last anniversary. Plans are arranged for the occupancy of other cities, as soon as adequate means are placed at the disposal of the Board. That very gratifying results would speedily follow the consummation of those plans, scarcely admits of a doubt, and seems to invite to unusually liberal contributions, from all who feel really interested in the religious welfare of that great and growing State.

MISSION TO RATIONALISTS, ROMAN CATHOLICS AND PAGANS.

In our country are large numbers of Europeans, who, for various reasons have made their homes among us, and to a great extent have assumed the rights of citizenship. Those from the British islands soon become diffused throughout the community, and, except in the religious interests of a portion of them, are gradually identified with our native citizens. They are easily reached by evangelical effort, and many of them voluntarily enter [redacted] lower grade of morals and a more degraded vassalage to popery; while, in a neighboring Province and upon our very borders, the same evils, in a somewhat modified form, exist, and are ever ready to contribute their baleful influence on our educational and religious interests.

Still more recently a distant heathen nation has sent its representatives by thousands, to mingle with the population of a far western State; thus adding to the amount of paganism which has too long existed among the aboriginal tribes of our country, but augmenting its power as a moral element by its oriental novelties. Deep seated in all those moral elements are concealed the seeds of plants, poisonous as the fabled upas, but alluring as the verdant banian tree. The everlasting welfare of these foreigners' souls, and the protection of the moral interests of the great American family, obviously suggest the employment of religious influences for their special benefit. Hence the Board have, to a limited extent, followed the example of their predecessors for several years, in the employment of missionaries who use the languages familiar to those foreigners. The total number of such missionaries the past year was 13, of whom 6 use the French, 3 the German, 1 the Swedish, and 3 the Spanish languages. One of the Germans uses the French and a dialect of the Swiss also.

Those missionaries have labored faithfully among the people to whom they have been respectively sent. The French among the Canadian Catholics and immigrants in Illinois; the German, Swede and Swiss in the valley of the Mississippi; and the Spanish in New Mexico.

THE GERMAN MISSION.

The German mission has been prosecuted under many disadvantages, but it has also been attended with success enough to warrant continued efforts, and to render them as much more efficient as possible. With probably about three millions of this class of foreigners already in the country, and large accessions anticipated immediately, it is evident that special effort for their evangelization is requisite, particularly as among them is found to a very great extent the rationalism—the deadly infidelity which aims at the subversion of all that is dear in the social and religious relations of American Christians.

What are three or four missionaries of the cross among so many enemies of Jesus?

THE GRANDE LIGNE MISSION.

The missionaries of the Grande Ligne stations in Canada hold on their way with commendable zeal, and are cheered by a good degree of success. Their operations are more systematized than formerly, and nearly all

[redacted]

the most advanced military post in the Territory, and Rev. Mr. Smith remains at Santa Fe.

Until the introduction of our missionaries into this Territory, the people, whose religion is a low form of Romanism, had received but little attention from the Roman Catholics of this country or of Europe. Since that period, however—especially since the people have manifested a desire for the light of truth, much effort has been put forth to subject them to the restraints of popery through the ministrations of foreign ecclesiastics and teachers. Of late, an arrogant disposition has been manifested by these ecclesiastics to apply those restraints to our missionaries also. And although the iron rod of persecution has not yet been violently employed, the well known voice of the universal persecutor has been uttered in tones of denunciation and threatening. But our brethren, unmoved by the futile attempts to intimidate them, calmly pursue their evangelical labors, knowing that New Mexico is not Rome, and Romanism is not the established religion of New Mexico. The Board hold themselves ready to reïnforce the stations of that Territory as events may render it evidently necessary.

INDIAN MISSION.

The past year has produced a new feature in the operations of the Society. Certain Indian tribes applied for a participation in its benefits, and have been encouraged. The chief men of some Pueblos or Indian villages, in New Mexico, appeared desirous that a missionary should take up a residence among their people, and a compliance with their desire being favored by gentlemen in the territory, acquainted with their disposition, habits and customs, it was granted. Early in the year Rev. S. Gorman offered himself to labor among them, and being found properly qualified for the service, was appointed. He reached his field in September, and immediately commenced his labors. His reports evince a good degree of personal encouragement. When he has acquired the language, he will have access to other Pueblos where the same dialect is used.

Rev. Mr. Shaw, formerly stationed at Albuquerque, was also induced, by many representations of the utility of the measure, to attempt to promote the religious welfare of the Navajos—a tribe of uncivilized Indians; and as he could accomplish all that was proposed, and at the same time avail himself of a chaplaincy at the military post of Fort defiance, which is situated in the midst of that people, he consented to their request.

The recent date of his entrance into that field does not allow the formation of any decided opinion of the probable success of the measure.

Soon after the last named movement, an event occurred [redacted] qualified to preach in the English, French, and Chippewa languages.

In each of these steps the Board believe they were guided by the hand of Divine Providence, and wait with much expectation for valuable results.

A CHINESE MISSION.

Among others who have left their native land to become permanent or temporary residents in ours are some forty thousand Chinese. They are chiefly found in California, and, without doubt, will be joined by many others every year. From the commencement of immigration by this people, it has been a favorite plan of the Board to secure a proper missionary to labor among them, and much effort has been made to accomplish the object. We regret to add, as yet without success. It is not difficult to see that, aside of the great advantage which, with the Divine blessing, would accrue from such means to individuals of that peculiar race while upon our shores, detached in a great measure from the associations, prejudices, and restraints of their countrymen in China, and surrounded by the enlightening associations of American civilization, much benefit would result, in the creation of various facilities to foreign mission effort, for the introduction and diffusion of Christianity throughout the Chinese empire. The difficulties to surmount in such an undertaking are neither few nor small; but the object is too important to be neglected, and the command of Christ to his disciples to teach all nations, is too imperative to be slighted in such a connection. It is hoped that another year will produce better success.

SUMMARY OF LABORS AND RESULTS.

The number of missionaries and agents in the employment of the Society the past year, and whose names appear in the Missionary Table accompanying this Report, is 179. Of that number, 118 were in commission April 1st, 1852. The remaining 61 were new appointments, made at different periods of the year. From eight of the latter no reports have been received, or were due at the close of the past missionary year. Two quarterly reports, due on the 1st of April, failed to reach us. Three other ministers are under appointment whose labors commenced after the 31st of March, the close of the year, and are not enumerated with the above. Eight who were under appointment some portion of the year need no further aid from the Society, and cease to be considered its missionaries.

The missionaries have been distributed as follows: In Canada (West) 2; Grande Ligne Stations, Canada (East), 6; Pennsylvania 3; Delaware 2; Ohio 2; Michigan 9; Indiana 35; Illinois 33; Wisconsin 36; Iowa 22; Minnesota 4; Oregon 3; California 3; New Mexico 4. Besides whom, 9 collecting agents have been employed the whole or a portion of the year.

The number of States and Territories occupied is 13. The number of stations and out-stations supplied is 500; and the aggregate amount of time bestowed upon the field is equal to that of one man for 116 years.

The missionaries report the baptism of 1025 persons; the organization of 59 churches; and the ordination of 30 ministers. Twelve houses of worship have been completed, and thirty are in progress of building.*

---

* In addition to the above, the missionaries report the following:

Sermons preached	16.473	Sabbath Schools in the Churches	221
Lectures and Addresses	1,470	Bible Classes	114
Pastoral Visits	28,636	Number of Teachers	1,479
Prayer and other Meetings attended	8.757	Number of Scholars	10,685
Signatures to Temperance Pledge	380	Volumes in S. S. Libraries	28,400
Miles travelled in discharge of duty	142,335	Stations were M. Con. of Prayer is observed	83

The churches, aided by the Society, have contributed to the usual objects of Christian benevolence $4298.08, besides about $15,473 for the support of their ministers.

Two of the three ministers under appointment, to commence labors from or after April 1st, are designated for Illinois or Iowa, and the other for North-western Minnesota.

ENLARGED POWERS NEEDED.

The rapid pace of human progress in our country appears to require the sanction of the Society for more diversified operations, tending to the more speedy establishment of gospel institutions in important places.

The language of the second article of the Constitution of the Society, if strictly construed, may appear to some to limit those operations to the single object of aiding ministers of the gospel in the discharge of the ordinary duties of the ministry, while to others it may seem equally clear that they should include whatever instrumentalities of a kindred nature may be found essential to the speedier success of these duties. This last view, in the opinion of the Board, is sustained by the peculiar circumstances in which our missionaries often find themselves in the new states and territories, especially when under the necessity of promoting the building of places of worship, or in the performance of various other pioneer work.

The day has passed for delaying the organization of religious instrumentalities in our frontier places until an advanced period of their progress. In that progress the elements of moral evil may become elaborated and diffused throughout the social atmosphere, and work death to the bodies and souls of men. The true policy of the Society is to preöccupy those places. The establishment and perpetuation of moral influences follow only in the train of vital, active Christianity. But such a policy cannot be successfully used unless based upon broad and comprehensive principles, and maintained by liberal provision for its annual contingencies. The development of religious energy in young churches, like that of physical energy in young children, is soonest and best produced under the firm support and safe guidance of a parental arm. The aid of the older churches of the land bestowed early and freely upon the young branches of Christ's family, usually insures a healthful, vigorous growth.

Such a policy is no novelty. It has long been acted upon, and produced rare and rich fruit. Among other forms in which it has been exhibited, that which is denom-

In the denomination with which this Society is connected, no such organization exists; and if it were otherwise, it is apprehended that its benevolence could but rarely reach the churches and villages for which the Society labors. It is believed that, with the facilities of the Board to obtain reliable information, and their numerous appliances for insuring judicious expenditures of funds, a smaller amount would be requisite for the establishment of churches in many places, if it were admitted that the object of such an organization is included in their constitutional duties, and if the treasury were supplied with the requisite funds.

THE NECESSITIES OF THE ENSUING YEAR.

The free diffusion of the gospel in our country is essential to its real welfare; and as the Home Mission organization is essential to the diffusion of the gospel in the new states and territories, its efforts should never be suffered to languish. True religion and sound policy require the perpetuation and increase of all the moral influence which the home missionary can exert. So far as this Society is concerned, it should dispense with none of its stations and none of its missionaries, only as they are rendered independent of missionary support by its efficient efforts. To sustain only the number at present supported, will require as large an amount of money as was paid into the treasury during the year just closed. To increase them will require more. To increase them to the full extent of applications addressed to the Board, would require nearly double that amount. It has been ascertained by a survey of the general field, and calculations based on reliable information and experience, that to provide for new claims, which it is very important should be *immediately* satisfied, would require not less than $22,000 more than the receipts of last year.

Without mentioning many prominent places in the valley of the Mississippi, from whence such claims originate, it seems indispensable to call into the service of the Society an able German minister, to act as an Exploring Agent and Evangelist among the Germans of the North Western States. Seven other missionaries are needed in Oregon and California without delay, one of whom should labor among the Chinese ; and should exigencies require it, one or more should proceed to New Mexico. These will prove expensive appointments, requiring a large proportion of the amount already named. But of their utility and advantage to the cause there can be no question. The great importance of the stations in those regions, the astonishing rapidity with which they are becoming populated, and the affecting insufficiency of religious influences among them, demand an early and that perisheth; young and feeble churches, springing into existence in the bosom of new and promising communities, must suffer the distress of blighted hope; and immortal souls must be abandoned to their rebellion against God, if not to the fearful retributions of eternity. In proportion as ability is bestowed upon the Society, good and faithful ministers will be enabled to bear among the destitute the unsearchable blessings of the gospel, young churches will be enabled to diffuse around them the spiritual influences which instrumentally work the salvation of men and the reformation of the world. The Society is pledged in the fear of God to promote its great object faithfully. Its past history shows how faithfully its pledge has been redeemed and what confidence may be reposed in its future efforts. But it shows also the insufficiency of the means with which it has labored, where the responsibility rests for any degree of failure to accomplish what may have been expected of it, and where that responsibility must rest under the same circumstances hereafter.

CONCLUSION.

The Executive Board, in surrendering their official appointment, congratulate the Society on account of the prosperous condition of its missionary stations, as far as they have been established, and desire to express their thankfulness to God for his providential and gracious dealings with them, while, with fervent hope for the greater prosperity and efficiency of the Society, they most earnestly commend it and its operations to the more liberal support and earnest prayers of its patrons.

BENJAMIN M. HILL,

Corresponding Secretary.

MISSIONARY TABLE.

NAMES OF AGENTS AND MISSIONARIES.	POST OFFICE ADDRESS.	FIELD OF LABOR.						Cont. to Benevolent objects.	ADDITIONAL FACTS REPORTED.
CANADA (EAST.)	GRANDE LIGNE MIS.								
Narcisse Cyr	Montreal	French Canadians in M.						-----	Some conversions. Among them a Catholic Priest.
" "	"	" " "	Nov. 1,					-----	Is much encouraged.
L. Normandeau	St. Johns	Grande Ligne and vicinity.	Nov. 1,					37 34	Field enlarging and pastor encouraged.
" "	"	" " "	Nov. 1,					69.26	
Louis Roussy	"	St. Marie de Monnoir	Nov. 1,					------	Meeting-house completed.
" "	"	Fort George, St. Greg., &c.	Nov. 1,					------	Several Conversions. Baptisms deferred for a short time.
Hubert Tetrau	Milton, Montreal Dis.	Salem, Berea, and vicinity.	Nov. 1,					------	The gospel makes more progress out of the neighborhoods of the Catholic Priests.
" "	" " "	" " "	Nov. 1,					------	Increased opposition from the Priests.
Theodore Lafleur	St. Pie	St. Pie and vicinity	Feb. 1,					21 50	Gospel making encouraging progress.
" "	"	" "	Nov. 1,					37 00	
Charles Roux	St. Johns	Napierville and vicinity.	April 1,					------	
" "	"	" "	Nov. 1,					------	A great jubilee has been kept to arouse the feelings of the people against Protestants. Bibles and Testaments been burned.
CANADA (WEST.)									
J. E. Ryerson	St. Catharines	St. Catharines	May 1, 1851	13	1	8		10 00	Revival. Require no further aid.
Robert Boyd	London	London	Oct. 1, 1851	26	1	----		32 00	Cause advancing, but ch. pecuniarily weak.
NEW HAMPSHIRE.									
Oren Tracy	Concord	Collecting Agent	April 1,	52		----	---	-----	Labored in New Hampshire and Vermont.
" "	"	" "	April 1,	----		----	---	-----	Re-appointment.
MASSACHUSETTS.									
J. W. Parkhurst	Newton Centre	Collecting Agent	April 1,	52			---	------	Massachusetts.

NAMES OF AGENTS AND MISSIONARIES.	POST OFFICE ADDRESS.	FIELD OF LABOR.	Date of Commission	Months Commis'd.	Weeks labor reported.	Stations supplied.	Baptized.	Received by letter.	Scholars in S. School.	Cont. to Benevolent objects.	ADDITIONAL FACTS REPORTED.
J. W. Parkhurst	Newton Centre	Collecting Agent	April 1, 1853	12							Re-appointment.
NEW-YORK.											
C. M. Fuller	Pike, Wyoming Co.	Collecting Agent	April 1, 1852	12	43						Labored in Maine and New Jersey.
" "	" "	" "	April 1, 1853	12							Re-appointment.
David Searl	Springville	Collecting Agent	April 1, 1852	6	24						Agent in Western N. Y.
Henry Davis	Sennett, Cayuga Co.	Collecting Agent	April 1, 1852	12	26						Labored in Central N. Y. Resigned.
James S. Ladd	New York	Collecting Agent	April 1, 1852	12	52						Labored in New York, Ct., and Pa.
" "	" "	" "	April 1, 1853	12							Re-appointment.
Charles A. Fox	Binghamton	Collecting Agent	April 1, 1852	12	42		2				Labored in Pa. and New York. Resigned.
Isaac Butterfield	Oswego	Collecting & Explor'g Agt.	Oct. 1, 1852	6	17						Labored in Mich., in New York. Resigned.
NEW JERSEY.											
J. G. Collom	Mt. Holly	Collecting & Explor'g Agt.	April 1, 1853	12							A new appointment.
PENNSYLVANIA.											
P. M. Weddell	Pittsburgh	South Pittsburgh	June 1, 1852	12	39	2	50	13	60	19 63	Debt on meeting-house embarassing. Revival.
T. J. Cole	Brownsville	Brownsville and vicinity	Dec. 1, 1852	12	13	1		6	60	15 87	Congregation large and enlarging.
N. Burwell	West Greenville	West Greenville & vicinity	Nov. 1, 1852	12	13	4					A new field ; no church organized. Baptists building a meeting-house.
DELAWARE.											
J. P. Walter	Dover, Kent Co.	Dover and vicinity	Oct. 1, 1851	12	16	1	9		21		Prospects encouraging. Pastor resigned.
" "	" "	New Castle and Kent Co.	Nov. 1, 1852	12	13						Work preliminary to providing a permanent station or stations.
D. A. Nichols	" "	Dover and vicinity	July 1, 1852	6	23	2			30		Finished meeting-house. Church in an improved state.
" "	"	" "	Jan. 1. 1853	12	13				31		Meets strong opposition to Bapt. sentiments.

NAMES OF AGENTS AND MISSIONARIES.	POST OFFICE ADDRESS.	FIELD OF LABOR.	Date of Commission	Months Commis'd.	Weeks labor reported.	Stations supplied.	Baptized.	Received by letter.	Scholars in S. School.	Cont. to Benevolent objects.	ADDITIONAL FACTS REPORTED.
OHIO.											
D. B. Cheney	Columbus	Columbus	May 1, 1851	12	13	1	2	3	180	------	Need no further aid.
S. L. Collins	Steubenville	Steubenville	May 1, 1851	12	13	2	--	----	----	1 00	Declension. Pastor left the field.
E. H. Burr	Massillon	Massillon and vicinity	Oct. 1, 1851	12	13	1	--	----	97	------	Pastor resigned.
J. W. B. Tisdale	Canton	Canton and vicinity	April 1, 1852	12	30	6	2	6	65	1 00	Building meeting-house. Congregations large and prospects encouraging. Pastor resigned.
W. W. Sawyer	Troy, Miami Co.	Troy and vicinity	April 1, 1852	12	52	1	15	16	100	50 15	Sunday School interesting. Revival.
S. M. Brower	Wapakoneta	Anglaize Association	Oct. 1, 1852	12	26	3	17	2	----	102 00	Three chs. in his field build'g meet'g houses.
Wm. Sedwick	Adamsville	Meig's Co	Jan. 1, 1853	3	4	----	9	----	----	------	A temporary service to explore new fields.
A. M. Torbet	Canton	Canton and vicinity	Dec. 1, 1852	4	17	1	15	3	120	------	Finished meeting-house. Revival.
G. C. Sedwick	Morrist'n, Belmont Co.	Morristown and Ebenezer	Jan. 1, 1853	12	13	4	26	----	80	------	Revival at M. Good state of religion at E.
C. A. Clark	Cleveland	Coll. and Exploring Agent	Oct. 1, 1852	6	15	----	9	----	----	------	Labored in Ohio.
MICHIGAN.											
Lyman H. Moore	Marshall	Marshall and vicinity	Nov. 1, 1851	12	52	5	3	8	120	30 00	Completed M. H. in M. The church is gaining influence, and promise for the future is now bright.
" "	"	"	Nov. 1, 1852	12	13	8	--	4	----	------	Religious meetings interesting and increasing in interest.
Edward Anderson	Kalamazoo	Kalamazoo and vicinity	April 1, 1852	12	12	1	--	2	90	14 50	Pastor resigned on account of ill health.
Aaron Potter	Albion, Calhoun Co.	Albion and vicinity	Dec. 1, 1851	12	52	1	2	13	90	65 74	Discipline been necessary for the prosperity of the church.
" "	"	"	Dec. 1, 1852	12	13	----	--	----	50	13 65	Nothing special.
W. G. Johnson	Yorkville, Kalamazoo	Yorkville	April 1, 1852	12	52	2	3	5	60	33 00	Revival at an outstation. Dismissed several to form another church.
G. V. Ten Brook	Hillsdale	Hillsdale and Jonesville	July 1, 1851	12	10	4	1	----	----	4 37	Pastor resigned.
" "	Centreville	Centreville and vicinity	Oct. 1, 1852	12	26	3	5	3	----	2 00	Church encouraged and are building a M. H.
Supply Chase	Northville	Lake Superior Country	------------	....	4	----	--	----	----	------	A temporary service to explore the Lake Superior country. Furnished important information.
Samuel Haskell	Kalamazoo	Kalamazoo and vicinity	Sept. 1, 1852	12	26	1	10	17	----	63 66	Revival. Arranging to build a new M. H.
P. C. Dayfoot	Lansing	Lansing and vicinity	Oct. 1, 1852	12	26	5	--	4	23	------	A new station. Infidelity prevalent.
INDIANA.											
Timothy R. Cressy	Indianapolis	Indianapolis	June 1, 1851	12	11	1	--	7	165	18 00	Left for another field of labor.

NAMES OF AGENTS AND MISSIONARIES.	POST OFFICE ADDRESS.	FIELD OF LABOR.	Date of Commission	Months Commis'd.	Weeks labor reported.	Stations supplied.	Baptized.	Received by letter.	Scholars in S. School.	Cont. to Benevolent objects	ADDITIONAL FACTS REPORTED.
J. D. Meeson	Fort Wayne	Fort Wayne	May 1, 1851	12	13	1	9	....	54	13 25	Revival. Pastor left the state.
John Jones	Belleville	Indianapolis Association	Dec. 1, 1851	12	26	....	3	....	....	11 00	Deceased.
Ira C. Perrine	Herman, Ripley Co.	Whitewater Association	Nov. 1, 1851	12	39	17	20	20	308	214 60	Organized a church at one station. Building a meeting house at Lawrenceville.
" "	" "	Whitewater Valley Ass.	Nov. 1, 1852	12	13	4	3	3	....	37 00	Prospects encouraging at all his stations. Rossburgh church building a meeting house.
Wm. Chaffee	Blackford	Hartford and vicinity	June 1, 1852	6	20	1	..	1	40	30 22	Prospects considered encouraging.
" "	"	New Corydon and Hartford	Dec. 1, 1852	12	13	3	..	....	....	7 00	Religious condition of the churches encouraging.
Joseph A. Dixson	Evansville	Evansville and vicinity	Sept. 1, 1851	12	26	1	..	1	75	126 00	Religion in a low state. Sunday school interesting.
" "	"	" "	Sept. 1, 1852	12	26	1	4	3	85	306 50	Cause encouragingly progressing
John G. Kerr	Attica, Fountain Co	Attica and vicinity	Jan. 1, 1852	12	4	2	..	....	....	3 50	Resigned to take an agency for Franklin College.
A. S. Ames	Orland, Steuben Co.	Orland and vicinity	Mar. 1, 1852	12	52	4	43	11	120	88 00	Revival. Church need no further aid.
H. C. Skinner	Huntington	Huntington	Feb. 1, 1852	12	34	1	1	....	100	31 55	Declension. Congregation the largest in the place. Pastor resigned and removed to another field.
N. V. Steadman	Evansville	Indiana	April 1, 1852	12	52	....	..	1	....	......	Exploring agent and general itinerant.
" "	"	"	April 1, 1853	12	....	....	..	....	....	......	Reappointment.
Prentice T. Palmer	Waveland	Freedom Association	Nov. 1, 1851	12	39	7	11	3	280	162 00	Parkerism has been the prevalent system; correct sentiments beginning to prevail.
" "	"	" "	Nov. 1, 1852	12	13	....	3	4	....	34 90	A very large field.
Jas. M. Maxwell	Plymouth, Marshall co	Plymouth and Marshall	Nov. 1, 1851	12	39	6	..	8	60	49 48	Himself and family been sick.
" "	" "	" "	Nov. 1, 1852	12	13	7	1	1	20	6 00	Cause gradually advancing.
John Reece	Shelbyville	Shelbyville and Mt. Gilead	Oct. 1, 1851	12	26	3	..	....	40	80 00	Building meeting house at Shelbyville.
" "	"	" "	April 1, 1853	12	....	....	..	....	....	......	
Michael White	Indianapolis	Stony Creek & Pipe Creek	Nov. 1, 1851	12	35	5	4	36	115	86 63	A destitute region for 100 miles needing the cultivation of our Society.
William Sym	Jeffersonville	Jeffersonville and vicinity	Jan. 1, 1852	12	26	2	..	....	75	......	Religion in a low state. Pastor left.
Abel Johnson	Warren, Huntington co	Warren and Bluffton	Jan. 1, 1852	12	39	5	1	....	90	16 41	Cause in its infancy. Church at Bluffton purchased a lot for a meeting house.
David S. French	Covington	Tippecanoe Association	April 1, 1852	12	52	....	44	15	....	200 00	Cause advancing and more laborers wanted.
" "	"	" "	April 1, 1853	12	....	....	..	....	....	......	A re-appointment.
Eli Rees	Brookville, Franklin co	Brookville and vicinity	May 1, 1852	12	39	1	4	5	....	......	Good religious interest; a church formed.
Edwin C. Brown	Wabash	Wabash	Aug. 1, 1852	12	13	2	..	1	....	30 00	Resigned on account of ill health.
J. D Crabs	Claysville	Paoli and vicinity	April 1, 1852	12	52	1	3	15	25	3 65	Finished meeting house at Mt. Pleasant.
R. H. Cook	Goshen, Elkhart Co.	Goshen and vicinity	April 1, 1852	12	52	....	..	9	....	16 50	Prospects encouraging at G.
Jas. B. Allyn	Bluffton, Wells Co.	Trinity, Olive Branch, &c.	April 1, 1852	12	52	4	..	3	85	12 93	People beginning to feel the importance of a settled ministry.
Frederick Snyder	Terre Haute	Terre Haute	July 1, 1852	12	35	1	2	19	60	100 00	Himself and family suffered from sickness.

NAMES OF AGENTS AND MISSIONARIES.	POST OFFICE ADDRESS.	FIELD OF LABOR.	Date of Commission	Months Commis'd.	Weeks labor reported.	Stations supplied.	Baptized.	Received by letter.	Scholars in S. School.	Cont. to Benevolent objects.	ADDITIONAL FACTS REPORTED.
Wm. M. Davis	Greencastle, Putnam co	Greencastle	Sept. 1, 1852	12	26	1	22	6	30	4 75	Revival and prospects encouraging.
Wm. McCoy	New Philadelphia	Little York (¼ of the time)	Nov. 1, 1852	12	3¼	1	2	2	----	------	Nothing special.
R. M. Parks	Bedford	Bedford Association	Nov. 1, 1852	12	13	10	2	4	----	50 00	A large and destitute field. Building five meeting houses!
T. N. Robertson	Orleans, Orange Co.	Bedford Association	Nov. 1, 1852	12	13	10	--	7	----	50 00	Cause of missions on the increase. Two churches building meeting houses.
Asa Marsh	Blairsville	Evansville Association	Dec. 1, 1852	12	11	8	--	----	----	------	Very little practical godliness in his field.
Wm. M. Cornell	Boonville	Evansville Association	Dec. 1, 1852	12	----	----	--	----	----	------	Quarterly report not received.
Jas. Babcock	Rochester	Fulton Co	Oct. 1, 1852	12	26	4	48	11	71	125 00	Revivals in three of his congregations.
William Leet	Connersville	Connersville and Rushville	Nov. 1, 1852	12	13	4	--	----	----	50 00	Nothing special.
William Gillaspy	Dudley Town	Brownstown Association	Mar. 1, 1853	12	----	----	--	----	----	------	A new appointment; no report due.
Sidney Dyer	Indianapolis	Indianapolis	Nov. 1, 1852	12	13	1	4	11	130	90 50	Good state of religion in the church.
A. G. Newgent	Bennettsville	Bethel Association	Dec. 1, 1852	12	13	4	15	----	120	------	Church at Pekin nearly completed. M. H.
J. W. Nye	Lawrenceville	Pipe Creek and Manchester	Feb. 1, 1853	12	----	----	--	----	----	------	A new appointment. Report not due.
ILLINOIS.											
B. E. S. Kupfer	Highland	Germans in Madison Co.	May 1, 1851	12	13	----	--	----	----	25 00	Meets with much opposition from open infidelity and the ungodliness of nominal christians.
" "	"	" "	May 1, 1852	12	[illegible]	----	--	----	----	------	
Frederick Ketcham	Rock Island	Rock Island	June 1, 1851	12	13	3	4	5	100	75 00	Completed meeting house.
" "	"	"	June 1, 1852	12	39	2	2	4	100	5 00	Basis for permanent prosperity becoming broader and stronger.
J. Edminster	Byron, Ogle Co.	Byron, White Rock, &c.	May 1, 1851	12	13	7	--	----	110	------	Field too large for profitable cultivation.
" "	" "	" "	May 1, 1852	12	39	----	--	3	114	15 40	Interesting S. School—the best in the place.
Silas Tucker	Napierville	Napierville	April 1, 1851	12	13	1	2	4	60	3 00	Ask for no further aid to sustain their pastor.
A. J. Fuson	Flat Rock	Crawford and Clark Cos.	Oct. 1, 1851	12	26	9	30	10	208	55 55	Organized churches at two outstations; completed M. H. at Liberty. Revivals in two chs.
Charles Button	Dundee, Kane Co	Dundee and vicinity	July 1, 1851	12	13	1	--	----	35	17 00	"Spiritual Manifestations" leading some astray.
" "	"	" "	July 1, 1852	12	39	----	18	4	40	32 59	Progressing. Congregations large and attentive.
Niles Kinne	St. Charles	St. Charles and vicinity	July 1, 1851	12	13	3	--	2	60	1 82	Sickness in his family.
" "	"	" "	July 1, 1852	12	39	2	--	1	51	22 09	Many and peculiar obstacles to pure religion.
Augustus B. Cramb	Metamora	Metamora and vicinity	July 1, 1851	12	26	5	--	----	55	1 80	Needs another missionary in his field.
" "	"	" "	Nov. 1, 1852	12	13	2	--	4	35	------	Revival.
A. G. Eberhart	Edgington	Rock Island Association	June 1, 1851	12	13	6	3	11	155	10 25	Nothing special.
" "	Moline	Edgington and Moline	June 1, 1852	12	39	----	24	4	40	8 00	Revival at Moline. Need a meeting house. Completed meeting house at Edgington.

NAMES OF AGENTS AND MISSIONARIES.	POST OFFICE ADDRESS.	FIELD OF LABOR.	Date of Commission	Months Commis'd.	Weeks labor reported	Stations supplied	Baptized	Received by letter.	Scholars in S. School.	Cont. to Benevolent objects.	ADDITIONAL FACTS REPORTED.
H. S. Deppe	Steels Mills	Itinerant among Germans	Mar. 1, 1852	12	34	5	14			26 15	Devoted to his work.
Thomas Powell	Mount Palatine	Illinois	April 1, 1852	12	53						General Itinerant and Exploring Agent.
" "	"	"	April 1, 1853	12							Reappointment.
W. S. Goodno	Aurora, Kane Co.	Aurora and vicinity	May 1, 1851	12	13	1	2	1			Progress made. Pastor left the field.
J. H. Kruger	Peoria	Germans in P. and vicinity	Oct. 1, 1851	12	26	1					Organized a German Baptist church.
" "	"	"	Oct. 1, 1852	12	26					16 00	Some opposition because he refuses to sprinkle infants.
T. L. Breckenridge	Freeport	Freeport and vicinity.	Oct. 1, 1851	12	26	3	2	4	50		Require no further aid. Pastor left the field.
" "	La Salle	La Salle and vicinity	Nov. 1, 1852	12	13	1	1	3			Organized a church. Congregation increas'g.
C. D. Merit	Chillicothe	Chillicothe	July 1, 1851	12	13	4		4	70	30 55	Prospects flattering at all his outstations.
I. D. Newell	Batavia	Batavia	Nov. 1, 1851	12	13	2		4	30		Pastor resigned for another field.
" "	Aurora, Kane Co.	Aurora and vicinity	May 1, 1852	12	39	3	4	26	60	3 75	Meeting house nearly completed. Revival.
W. D. H. Johnson	Greenville, Bond Co.	Greenville and vicinity	Oct. 1, 1851	12	26	5		3	13	27 95	Secular and religious interest of the church encouraging. Building a meeting house.
" "	"	"	Oct. 1, 1852	12	26					54 80	Nothing special.
G. S. Bailey	Pekin, Tazewell Co.	Pekin and vicinity	Nov. 1, 1851	12	39	3	12	3	200	91 80	Sunday School deeply interesting. Cause progressing. Secured lots for a M. H.
" "	"	"	Nov. 1, 1852	12	13	2	2	3	125		Church trying to make arrangements to build a M. H.
Nelson Alvord	Decatur	Decatur and Taylorsville	Oct. 1, 1851	12	24	2		4	100	34 25	Church at Taylorsville building a M. H.
" "	Chillicothe	Chillicothe and vicinity	Dec. 1, 1852	12	13	2					Congregations large for the place.
J. W. Riley	Charleston	Bloomfield Association	Feb. 1, 1852	12	52	4	17	13		200 00	Organized a church at one station. Prayer meetings well attended and cause progress'g.
" "	"	"	Feb. 1, 1853	12							
J. R. Ford	Shoal Creek, Clinton co	Vandalia Association	Dec. 1, 1851	12	39	9	4	10	75	70 35	Field too large. Will supply fewer stations and be supported without further aid from us.
Lyman Palmer	Galena	Galena	Dec. 1, 1851	6	8	1			122		A temporary arrangement.
Asahel Chapin	"	"	June 1, 1852	12	39	2	6	14	171		Making great effort to build a meeting house.
J. M. Scrogin	Delavan, Tazewell Co.	Delavan and vicinity	Mar. 1, 1852	12	22	3	4		70		Building meeting house. Pastor suddenly deceased.
H. E. Hempsted	Belleville	Belleville and vicinity	Feb. 1, 1852	12	26	1	2	2	50	5 00	Declension.
S. F. Holt	Warrenville	Downers Grove ½ of time	April 1, 1852	12	17	2	14	2	62	3 00	Building a meeting house.
John Higby	Newark	Newark and vicinity	April 1, 1852	12	52	3	39	8	75	24 00	Revival. Building a meeting house at one station.
D. L. Phillips	Jonesborough	Chester ½ of the time	April 1, 1852	12	10	1	1				Finished a neat meeting house.
Henry G. Weston	Peoria	Peoria, Cass and Mason cos.	July 1, 1852	12	13						Preached to large congregations at several stations, organized two churches, but resigned his commission to return to the pastoral office at Peoria.

NAMES OF AGENTS AND MISSIONARIES.	POST OFFICE ADDRESS.	FIELD OF LABOR.	Date of Commission	Months Commis'd.	Weeks labor reported.	Stations supplied.	Baptized.	Received by letter.	Scholars in S. School.	Cont. to Benevolent objects.	ADDITIONAL FACTS REPORTED.
E. Scofield	Danby, Du Page Co.	Babcock's Grove, &c.	Aug. 1, 1852	12	26	2	--	1	----	11 00	A new field, religion in a low state. Sunday School suspended during the winter.
H. H. Richardson	Cairo	Alexander and Jackson Cos	Oct. 1, 1852	12	23	9	1	5	----	41 35	One church commenced a meeting house. Field too large to cultivate to advantage.
G. Palmquist	Rock Island	Swedes in Rock Island &c	Feb. 1, 1853	12	----	----	--	----	----	------	Report not due.
M. B. Kelly	Chester	Chester and vicinity	Feb, 1, 1853	12	----	----	--	----	----	------	Quarterly report not due.
J. V. Allinson				12	----	----	--	----	----	------	Field not designated. A new appointment.
WISCONSIN.											
James Delany	Ozaukee	Wisconsin	April 1, 1852	12	52	----	--	----	----	------	General Itinerant and Exploring Agent.
" "	"	"	April 1, 1853	12	----	----	--	----	----	------	Re-appointment.
William Cornell	Mayville, Dodge Co.	Mayville and vicinity	June 1, 1851	12	13	4	--	----	20	------	Church in prosperity. Pastor resigned.
Peter Conrad	Baraboo, Sauk Co.	Baraboo and vicinity	Oct. 1, 1851	12	26	5	7	2	25	2 18	Religion advancing on his field.
Abner Lull	Sheboygan Falls	Sheboygan Falls, &c.	Sept. 1, 1851	12	26	3	8	1	95	15 00	Pastor encouraged by increased union in the church.
" "	"	" "	Sept. 1, 1852	12	26	2	1	1	50	2 60	Church numerically reduced by removals.
Denis Mulhern	Ozaukee	Ozaukee and vicinity	May 1, 1851	12	13	1	--	1	40	------	Deeper feeling under the preaching of the gospel than usual. Church increasing in numbers.
" "	"	" "	May 1, 1852	12	30	----	2	3	----	8 50	
O. J. Dearborn	Janesville	Janesville	Oct. 1, 1851	12	26	1	7	18	80	9 04	Will support their pastor without further aid.
Joseph L. Irvin	Scott, Sheboygan Co.	Scott and Cascade	Dec. 1, 1851	12	20	3	3	2	60	------	Nothing special.
" "	" "	" "	Dec. 1, 1852	12	13	6	--	6	----	------	Embarassments in the way of present success.
Caleb Blood	Darlington	Avon and vicinity	July 1, 1851	12	13	1	2	3	70	------	Left for another station.
" "	Geneva	Geneva and vicinity	July 1, 1852	12	30	2	3	7	85	7 25	Religious state of the church encouraging.
N. E. Chapin	Beaver Dam	Beaver Dam and vicinity	June 1, 1852	12	30	3	9	4	30	20 69	Contracted for building a meeting house.
Edward L. Harris	Beloit	Beloit and vicinity	Mar. 1, 1852	12	22	2	8	11	100	78 67	Ch. harmonious and prospects encouraging.
" "	"	" "	Mar. 1, 1853	12	----	----	--	----	----	------	Report not due.
Perly Work	Sheboygan	Sheboygan	Sept. 1, 1851	12	26	5	6	5	100	19 00	Church in a good religious condition, but embarrassed by meeting house debt.
" "	"	" "	Sept. 1, 1852	12	26	3	2	7	200	24 50	In many respects made progress.
Thomas M. Symonds	Green Bay	Green Bay	June 1, 1851	12	26	4	4	2	60	5 25	Cause encouragingly progressing. Pastor suddenly deceased.
S. Cornelius, Jr.	Fond du Lac	Fond du Lac, &c.	May 1. 1851	12	13	1	--	----	50	------	Building meeting house.
" "	"	" "	May 1, 1852	12	30	----	3	3	----	------	Religion in that region in a low state. M. H. slowly progressing for want of funds.
Thomas Reese	Thompsonville	Raymond and Ives Grove.	April 1, 1852	12	26	3	--	----	33	4 80	Pastor resigned and left for another field.
A. Hamilton	Newark, Wash. Co.	Newark and vicinity	Nov. 1, 1851	12	26	3	5	----	30	------	Progressing but embarrassed by unhappy differences in the church.

NAMES OF AGENTS AND MISSIONARIES.	POST OFFICE ADDRESS.	FIELD OF LABOR.	Date of Commission	Months Commis'd.	Weeks labor reported.	Stations supplied.	Baptized.	Received by letter.	Scholars in S. School.	Cont. to Benevolent objects.	ADDITIONAL FACTS REPORTED.
A. Hamilton	Newark, Wash. Co.	Newark and West Bend	Nov. 1, 1852	12	13	3	--	----	40	------	Trials have humbled and purified the church. Prospects now encouraging.
W. J. Chapin	Aztalan, Jeff. Co.	Aztalan and vicinity	Oct. 1, 1851	12	26	5	1	3	30	4 07	Prospects encouraging. S. School interest'g.
" "	"	" "	Oct. 1, 1852	12	26	8	--	1	26	------	Repaired meeting house.
S. Dearborn	Lowell, Dodge Co.	Lowell and vicinity	July 1, 1851	12	13	1	--	----	40	------	Meetings well attended. An increasing interest in regard to the state of public morals.
" "	"	" "	July 1, 1852	12	39	----	--	----	----	------	Nothing special.
William Clack	Argyle, Lafayette Co.	Argyle and York Prairie	Dec. 1, 1851	12	39	2	--	1	8	22 00	State of religion not flattering.
William H. Card	La Crosse	La Crosse and vicinity	Nov. 1, 1851	12	39	1	2	13	40	------	M. H completed. Ch. in prosperous condit'n.
" "	"	" "	Nov. 1, 1852	12	13	----	15	1	45	------	Revival.
D. E. Bowen	Watertown, Jeff. Co.	Watertown and vicinity	May 1, 1852	12	39	3	8	14	66	6 50	Revival at an outstation; church at Watertown purchased a lot upon which to build a meeting house.
" "	"	" "	May 1, 1853	12	----	----	--	----	----	------	Re-appointment.
G. W. Freeman	Whitewater	Whitewater	Jan. 1, 1852	12	39	4	2	13	50	12 50	Church paid meeting house debt. Require no further aid.
Thomas S. Griffith	Milwaukee	Milwaukee	Feb. 1, 1852	12	52	1	3	15	285	174 12	Need no further aid.
Samuel T. Catlin	Willowriver	Willowriver, &c.	May 1, 1852	12	39	3	2	2	82	------	Organized a church and nearly completed a meeting house. Baptist influence widely prevalent in the place. Good religious feeling in the church.
Harman Ellis	Lake Mills	Lake Mills, &c.	June 1, 1852	12	39	2	--	----	25	------	Prospects favorable but labors under embarrassments.
James Andem	Neenah, Winnebago Co	Neenah and vicinity	July 1, 1852	12	39	1	4	8	15	------	Prospects not encouraging.
William McKee	Omro, Winnebago Co.	Omro and Oshkosh	June 1, 1852	12	39	4	1	6	10	3 00	More attention given to preaching.
John Hinton	Kenosha,	Kenosha and vicinity	May 1, 1852	12	39	1	--	2	54	21 50	Good attendance on preaching. "Spiritual rappings" having a baneful influence on the young.
David Matlock	Lancaster	Lancaster and vicinity	Aug. 1, 1852	12	26	3	22	10	80	16 25	Finished meeting house. Cause advancing throughout his field.
James Squier	East Troy	East Troy and vicinity	Aug. 1, 1852	12	26	4	--	----	48	15 00	Condition of the church improved.
Salmon Morton	Darlington	Darlington and vicinity	Oct. 1, 1852	12	26	2	--	----	20	------	A large and an inviting field.
Watson Clark	Green Bay	Green Bay	Sept. 1, 1852	12	8	3	--	----	50	------	Church preparing to build a meeting house.
Thomas Bright	Elkhorn	Elkhorn and vicinity	Nov. 1, 1852	12	13	5	--	----	----	------	Organized a ch. and prospects encouraging.
Anthony Case	Waushara	Waushara and vicinity	Oct. 1, 1852	12	26	4	--	----	35	------	A new and an important field.
D. D. Read	Columbus	Columbus and Portage	Dec. 1, 1852	12	13	3	--	----	40	26 00	A new field, promising good results.
M. D. Miller	Madison	Madison and vicinity	Jan. 1, 1853	12	13	1	--	----	----	------	Purchased desirable lots for a meeting house, and prosecuting plans for building a house with vigor.
J. A. Pool	Monroe	Monroe and vicinity	Mar. 1, 1853	12	----	----	--	----	----	------	A new appointment. Report not due.

NAMES OF AGENTS AND MISSIONARIES.	POST OFFICE ADDRESS.	FIELD OF LABOR.	Date of Commission	Months Commis'd	Weeks labor reported.	Stations supplied.	Baptized.	Received by letter.	Scholars in S. School	Cont. to Benevolent objects.	ADDITIONAL FACTS REPORTED.
IOWA.											
B. F. Brabrook	Davenport	Iowa	April 1, 1852	12	52						General Itinerant and Exploring Agent.
" "	"	"	April 1, 1853	12							Severely and dangerously sick during the last quarter. Re appointment.
William Elliott	Brighton	Brighton and Fairfield	Sept. 1, 1851	12	26	6	23	2	40	6 00	Church organized at one of his stations. Revival at an outstation.
" "	"	Brighton and Richland	Sept. 1, 1852	12	26		49	4	55	4 00	Revival at Glasgow, an outstation.
lihu Gunn	Keokuk, Lee Co.	Keokuk and vicinity	Nov. 1, 1851	12	39	2	3	3	60		Completed meeting house. Congregation and Sunday School increasing.
" "	"	" "	Nov. 1, 1852	12		3	17	19	120		Revival at an out station.
'illiam A. Wells	Muscatine	Muscatine, &c.	April 1, 1852	12	52	3	22	19	160	21 00	Church increasing in spirituality. Revival.
ohn Williams	Marion, Linn Co	Marion and vicinity	Sept. 1, 1851	12		3					Resigned his commission.
ohn Bates	Cascade	Cascade and vicinity	June 1 1851	12			1	4	20		Meeting house progressing.
" "	"	" "	June 1, 1852	12	39			1		10 00	Progressing
ram Burnett	Mt. Pleasant	Mt. Pleasant and vicinity	June 1, 1851	12		3	18	4	35	3 00	Organized a church at an out station.
" "	"	" "	June 1, 1852	12	39	4	16	12			Revival.
'illiam H. Turton	Farmington	Farmington and vicinity	Oct. 1, 1851	12	26	1			35		Finished lecture room.' Pastor been sick.
" "	"	" "	Oct. 1 1852	12	26	3	3			5 00	Revival. Candidates are received for baptism.
J. A. Nash	Fort Des Moines	Fort Des Moines, &c.	Dec. 1 1851	12	39	1	7	6	50		Prospects of the cause flattering in his region.
" "	"	" "	Dec. 1 1852	12	13	3					The Baptist cause decidedly on the increase.
George Scott	Maquoketa	Maquoketa, &c.	Oct. 1 1851	12		3	1	1		13 00	Encouragingly progressed during the year.
" "	"	" "	Oct. 1, 1852		26		1	4	25	12 9½	Church revived. Pastor been sick.
A. Russell Belden	Iowa City	Iowa City	Dec. 1, 1851	12	30	1	4	7	130		Rapid and healthy growth of church and congregation in all things except spirituality.
" "	"	" "	Dec. 1, 1852	12	13				100		Pastors health been poor.
G. W. Bond	Knoxville	Marion and Monroe Cos.	Oct. 1, 1851	12	26	4	1	5		50 00	Organized a church at one station.
" "	"	Knoxville and vicinity	Oct. 1, 1852	12	26	4		1			Nothing special.
B. B. Arnold	Three Rivers, Polk co.	Blakesburg, Three Riv's, &c	Oct. 1, 1851	12	20	2	6	19			Organized a church at one station. Revival at Blakesburg.
" "	"	Pleasant Grove, &c.	Oct. 1, 1852	12	26	9	4	10	68		Will soon organize a ch. at one of his stations.
Edward O. Towne	Bonaparte	Bonaparte and vicinity	Nov. 1, 1851	12	39	1	5	11			Building a meeting house.
" "	"	" "	Nov. 1, 1852	12	13	5			130	10 00	Revival at an out station; converts not baptized yet.
Isaac Leonard	Burlington	Rock Spring and vicinity	Nov. 1, 1851	12	36	8	3	1	60	5 75	Church much revived and more interest manifested by the people.
" "	"	Rock Spring and Augusta	Dec. 1, 1852	2	13		13			7 76	Revivals at two stations.
John C. Ward	Marion, Linn Co.	Marion and vicinity	Sept. 1, 1852	12	26	2	2	4	75	3 00	Made an effort to pay debts on meeting house.
Edward M. Miles	Davenport	Second Church, Davenport	June 1, 1852		39	2		10	60	10 00	Ch. revived. Prayer meetings well attended.
Elijah Evans	Apple Grove	West Union and Monroe	Aug. 1, 1852		26	3	2	7	40		Organized a church at an out station.
C. D. Farnsworth	Colesburgh	Colesburgh and vicinity	Aug. 1, 1852	12	26	4	3	4			Organized a church at one station. Revival.

NAMES OF AGENTS AND MISSIONARIES.	POST OFFICE ADDRESS.	FIELD OF LABOR.	Date of Commission	Months Commis'd.	Weeks labor reported	Stations supplied.	Baptized.	Received by letter	Scholars in S. School.	Cont. to Benevolent objects.	ADDITIONAL FACTS REPORTED.
Israel C. Curtis	Pella	Pella and vicinity	Oct. 1, 1852	12	26	5	1	3	40	......	Attentive congregations at all his stations.
D. H. Paul	Le Clair	Camanche and Le Clair	Oct. 1, 1852	12	26	4	..	6	50	12 75	Field too large for one man and asks for another.
Watson Clark	Keosauqua	Keosauqua	Sept. 1, 1852	12	18	4	..	6	80	......	Improved state of religious interest.
MINNESOTA TER.											
Julius S. Webber	Stillwater	Stillwater & Willow River	June 1, 1851	12	13	8	..	....	20	5 00	Pastor encouraged.
" "	"	Stillwater, &c.	June 1, 1852	12	39	5	1	....	25	8 35	Preparing to build a meeting house.
Timothy R. Cressy	St. Paul	St. Paul and vicinity	June 1, 1852	12	39	....	2	20	50	......	Prospects encouraging.
Lyman Palmer	St. Anthony	St. Anthony, &c.	Dec. 1, 1851	12	31	1	..	7	30	......	Infidelity prevalent.
" "	"	" "	Dec. 1, 1852	12	13	2	..	2	....	......	Religious interest increasing.
E. W. Cressy	St. Anthony	Hennepin Co.	Oct. 1, 1852	12	26	....	..	....	....	40 00	Encouraged with his field of labor. Organized a church.
James Tanner, or Eah kue go ne bi	Pembina	Pembina & Chippewa In.	....	12	....	....	..	....	....	......	A new appointment and new field.
NEW MEXICO.											
Hiram W. Read	Albuquerque	Albuquerque &c	Aug. 1, 1852	12	26	....	..	....	....	......	Has done much in religious conversation with individuals and in distributing tracts. Asks for more missionaries.
Lewis Smith	Santa Fe	Santa Fe and vicinity	Aug. 1, 1851	12	26	1	..	....	10	......	Congregations unusually large & interesting. Priests prevented the people hearing him preach at Los Vegos.
" "	"	" "	Aug. 1, 1852	12	26	....	..	....	7	15 57	Commenced preaching in Spanish and has succeeded in forming a permanent congregation of Mexicans.
J. Milton Shaw	Albuquerque	Albuquerque, &c	Dec. 1, 1851	12	39	....	..	....	....	......	Mrs. S. been dangerously sick. Not successful in establishing a promising stati:n. Removed to Fort Defiance.
Samuel Gorman	Laguna	Pueblo Indians	Oct. 1, 1852	12	13	....	..	....	....	1 25	Labors altogether preliminary.
OREGON.											
Ezra Fisher	Oregon City	Portland and other places.	April 1, 1851	12	13	4	..	....	16	......	Laboring with efficiency.

NAMES OF AGENTS AND MISSIONARIES.	POST OFFICE ADDRESS.	FIELD OF LABOR.	Date of Commission	Months Commis'd.	Weeks labor reported.	Stations supplied.	Baptized.	Received by letter.	Scholars in S. School.	Cont. to Benevolent objects.	ADDITIONAL FACTS REPORTED.
E. Scofield	Danby, Du Page Co.	Babcock's Grove, &c.	Aug. 1, 1852	12	26	2	..	1	....	11 00	A new field, religion in a low state. Sunday School suspended during the winter.
H. H. Richardson	Cairo	Alexander and Jackson Cos	Oct. 1, 1852	12	23	9	1	5	....	41 35	One church commenced a meeting house. Field too large to cultivate to advantage.
G. Palmquist	Rock Island	Swedes in Rock Island &c	Feb. 1, 1853	12	....	....	..	....	....	......	Report not due.
M. B. Kelly	Chester	Chester and vicinity	Feb, 1, 1853	12	....	....	..	....	....	......	Quarterly report not due.
J. V. Allinson	....	....	....	12	....	....	..	....	....	......	Field not designated. A new appointment.
WISCONSIN.											
James Delany	Ozaukee	Wisconsin	April 1, 1852	12	52	....	..	....	....	......	General Itinerant and Exploring Agent.
" "	"	"	April 1, 1853	12	....	....	..	....	....	......	Re-appointment.
William Cornell	Mayville, Dodge Co.	Mayville and vicinity	June 1, 1851	12	13	4	..	....	20	......	Church in prosperity. Pastor resigned.
Peter Conrad	Baraboo, Sauk Co.	Baraboo and vicinity	Oct. 1, 1851	12	26	5	7	2	25	2 18	Religion advancing on his field.
Abner Lull	Sheboygan Falls	Sheboygan Falls, &c	Sept. 1, 1851	12	26	3	8	1	95	15 00	Pastor encouraged by increased union in the church.
" "	"	" "	Sept. 1, 1852	12	26	2	1	1	50	2 60	Church numerically reduced by removals.
Denis Mulhern	Ozaukee	Ozaukee and vicinity	May 1, 1851	12	13	1	..	1	40	......	Deeper feeling under the preaching of the gospel than usual. Church increasing in numbers.
" "	"	" "	May 1, 1852	12	39	....	2	2	....	8 50	
O. J. Dearborn	Janesville	Janesville	Oct. 1, 1851	12	26	1	7	18	80	9 04	Will support their pastor without further aid.
Joseph L. Irvin	Scott, Sheboygan Co.	Scott and Cascade	Dec. 1, 1851	12	39	3	3	2	60	......	Nothing special.
" "	" "	" "	Dec. 1, 1852	12	13	6	..	6	....	......	Embarassments in the way of present success.
Caleb Blood	Darlington	Avon and vicinity	July 1, 1851	12	13	1	2	2	70	......	Left for another station.
" "	Geneva	Geneva and vicinity	July 1, 1852	12	39	2	3	7	85	7 25	Religious state of the church encouraging.
N. E. Chapin	Beaver Dam	Beaver Dam and vicinity	June 1, 1852	12	39	3	9	4	30	20 50	Contracted for building a meeting house.
Edward L. Harris	Beloit	Beloit and vicinity	Mar. 1, 1852	12	52	2	8	11	100	78 67	Ch. harmonious and prospects encouraging.
" "	"	" "	Mar. 1, 1853	12	....	....	..	....	....	......	Report not due.
Perly Work	Sheboygan	Sheboygan	Sept. 1, 1851	12	26	3	6	5	100	19 00	Church in a good religious condition, but embarrassed by meeting house debt.
" "	"	" "	Sept. 1, 1852	12	26	3	2	7	200	24 30	In many respects made progress.
Thomas M. Symonds	Green Bay	Green Bay	June 1, 1851	12	26	4	4	2	60	5 25	Cause encouragingly progressing. Pastor suddenly deceased.
S. Cornelius, Jr.	Fond du Lac	Fond du Lac, &c.	May 1. 1851	12	13	1	..	....	50	......	Building meeting house.
" "	"	" "	May 1, 1852	12	39	....	3	3	....	......	Religion in that region in a low state. M. H. slowly progressing for want of funds.
Thomas Reese	Thompsonville	Raymond and Ives Grove	April 1, 1852	12	26	3	..	....	88	4 80	Pastor resigned and left for another field.
A. Hamilton	Newark, Wash. Co.	Newark and vicinity	Nov. 1, 1851	12	39	3	5	....	50	......	Progressing but embarrassed by unhappy differences in the church.

NAMES OF AGENTS AND MISSIONARIES.	POST OFFICE ADDRESS.	FIELD OF LABOR.	Date of Commission	Months Commis'd.	Weeks labor reported.	Stations supplied.	Baptized.	Received by letter.	Scholars in S. School.	Cont. to Benevolent objects.	ADDITIONAL FACTS REPORTED.
A. Hamilton	Newark, Wash. Co.	Newark and West Bend	Nov. 1, 1852	12	13	3	--	--	40	--	Trials have humbled and purified the church. Prospects now encouraging.
W. J. Chapin	Aztalan, Jeff. Co.	Aztalan and vicinity	Oct. 1, 1851	12	26	5	1	3	30	4 07	Prospects encouraging. S. School interest'g.
" "	"	" "	Oct. 1, 1852	12	26	3	--	1	26	--	Repaired meeting house.
S. Dearborn	Lowell, Dodge Co.	Lowell and vicinity	July 1, 1851	12	13	1	--	--	40	--	Meetings well attended. An increasing interest in regard to the state of public morals.
" "	"	" "	July 1, 1852	12	39	--	--	--	--	--	Nothing special.
William Clack	Argyle, Lafayette Co.	Argyle and York Prairie	Dec. 1, 1851	12	39	2	--	1	8	22 00	State of religion not flattering.
William H. Card	La Crosse	La Crosse and vicinity	Nov. 1, 1851	12	30	1	2	13	40	--	M. H completed. Ch. in prosperous condit'n.
" "	"	" "	Nov. 1, 1852	12	13	--	15	1	45	--	Revival.
D. E. Bowen	Watertown, Jeff. Co.	Watertown and vicinity	May 1, 1852	12	39	3	8	14	60	6 50	Revival at an outstation; church at Watertown purchased a lot upon which to build a meeting house.
" "	"	" "	May 1, 1853	12	--	--	--	--	--	--	Re-appointment.
G. W. Freeman	Whitewater	Whitewater	Jan. 1, 1852	12	39	4	2	13	50	13 50	Church paid meeting house debt. Require no further aid.
Thomas S. Griffith	Milwaukee	Milwaukee	Feb. 1, 1852	12	52	1	3	15	285	174 12	Need no further aid.
Samuel T. Catlin	Willowriver	Willowriver, &c.	May 1, 1852	12	39	3	2	2	82	--	Organized a church and nearly completed a meeting house. Baptist influence widely prevalent in the place. Good religious feeling in the church.
Harman Ellis	Lake Mills	Lake Mills, &c.	June 1, 1852	12	39	2	--	--	25	--	Prospects favorable but labors under embarrassments.
James Andem	Neenah, Winnebago Co	Neenah and vicinity	July 1, 1852	12	39	1	4	8	15	--	Prospects not encouraging.
William McKee	Omro, Winnebago Co.	Omro and Oshkosh	June 1, 1852	12	39	4	1	6	10	3 00	More attention given to preaching.
John Hinton	Kenosha,	Kenosha and vicinity	May 1, 1852	12	39	1	--	2	54	21 50	Good attendance on preaching. "Spiritual rappings" having a baneful influence on the young.
David Matlock	Lancaster	Lancaster and vicinity	Aug. 1, 1852	12	26	3	22	10	80	16 25	Finished meeting house. Cause advancing throughout his field.
James Squier	East Troy	East Troy and vicinity	Aug. 1, 1852	12	26	4	--	--	48	15 00	Condition of the church improved.
Salmon Morton	Darlington	Darlington and vicinity	Oct. 1, 1852	12	26	2	--	--	20	--	A large and an inviting field.
Watson Clark	Green Bay	Green Bay	Sept. 1, 1852	12	8	3	--	--	50	--	Church preparing to build a meeting house.
Thomas Bright	Elkhorn	Elkhorn and vicinity	Nov. 1, 1852	12	13	5	--	--	--	--	Organized a ch. and prospects encouraging.
Anthony Case	Waushara	Waushara and vicinity	Oct. 1, 1852	12	26	4	--	--	35	--	A new and an important field.
D. D. Read	Columbus	Columbus and Portage	Dec. 1, 1852	12	13	3	--	--	40	25 00	A new field, promising good results.
M. D. Miller	Madison	Madison and vicinity	Jan. 1, 1853	12	13	1	--	--	--	--	Purchased desirable lots for a meeting house, and prosecuting plans for building a house with vigor.
J. A. Pool	Monroe	Monroe and vicinity	Mar. 1, 1853	12	--	--	--	--	--	--	A new appointment. Report not due.

[redacted]RY TABLE.

[redacted] of ...ssion	Months Commis'd	Weeks labor reported.	Stations supplied.	Baptized.	Received by letter.	Scholars in S. School.	Cont. to Benevolent objects.	ADDITIONAL FACTS REPORTED.
[redacted], 1851	12	39	1	..	....	....	......	Some conversions. Among them a Catholic Priest.
[redacted], 1852	12	13	....	..	....	....	......	Is much encouraged.
[redacted], 1851	12	39	1	..	....	....	37 34	Field enlarging and pastor encouraged.
[redacted], 1852	12	13	2	..	....	45	69.26	
[redacted], 1851	12	39	8	..	....	....	......	Meeting-house completed.
[redacted], 1852	12	13	....	..	....	....	......	Several Conversions. Baptisms deferred for a short time.
[redacted], 1851	12	39	3	..	....	....	......	The gospel makes more progress out of the neighborhoods of the Catholic Priests.
[redacted], 1852	12	13	....	2	....	....	......	Increased opposition from the Priests.
[redacted], 1852	9	39	1	7	....	30	21 50	Gospel making encouraging progress.
[redacted], 1852	12	13	....	..	....	30	37 00	
[redacted], 1852	7	30	4	..	....	....	......	
[redacted], 1852	12	13	....	..	....	....	......	A great jubilee has been kept to arouse the feelings of the people against Protestants. Bibles and Testaments been burned.
[redacted] 1851	12	13	1	20	8	40	10 00	Revival. Require no further aid.
[redacted] 1851	12	26	1	6	....	130	32 00	Cause advancing, but ch. pecuniarily weak.
[redacted], 1852	12	52	....	..	....	....	......	Labored in New Hampshire and Vermont.
[redacted], 1853	12	....	....	..	....	....	......	Re-appointment.
[redacted], 1852	12	52	....	..	....	....	......	Massachusetts.

NAMES OF AGENTS AND MISSIONARIES.	POST OFFICE ADDRESS.	FIELD OF LABOR.	Date of Commission	Months Commis'd.	Weeks labor reported	Stations supplied.	Baptized.	Received by letter	Scholars in S. School.	Cont. to Benevolent objects	ADDITIONAL FACTS REPORTED.
Israel C. Curtis	Pella	Pella and vicinity	Oct. 1, 1852	12	26	5	1	3	40	......	Attentive congregations at all his stations.
D. H. Paul	Le Clair	Camanche and Le Clair	Oct. 1, 1852	12	26	4	..	6	50	12 75	Field too large for one man and asks for another.
Watson Clark	Keosauqua	Keosauqua	Sept. 1, 1852	12	18	4	..	6	80	......	Improved state of religious interest.
MINNESOTA TER.											
Julius S. Webber	Stillwater	Stillwater & Willow River	June 1, 1851	12	13	8	..	....	20	5 00	Pastor encouraged.
" "	"	Stillwater, &c.	June 1, 1852	12	39	5	1	....	25	8 35	Preparing to build a meeting house.
Timothy R. Cressy	St. Paul	St. Paul and vicinity	June 1, 1852	12	39	....	2	20	50	......	Prospects encouraging.
Lyman Palmer	St. Anthony	St. Anthony, &c.	Dec. 1, 1851	12	31	1	..	7	30	......	Infidelity prevalent.
" "	"	" "	Dec. 1, 1852	12	13	2	..	2	....	......	Religious interest increasing.
E. W. Cressy	St. Anthony	Hennepin Co.	Oct. 1, 1852	12	26	....	..	....	....	40 00	Encouraged with his field of labor. Organized a church.
James Tanner, or Esh kue go ne bi	Pembina	Pembina & Chippewa In.	....	12	....	....	..	....	....	......	A new appointment and new field.
NEW MEXICO.											
Hiram W. Read	Albuquerque	Albuquerque &c	Aug. 1, 1852	12	26	....	..	....	....	......	Has done much in religious conversation with individuals and in distributing tracts. Asks for more missionaries.
Lewis Smith	Santa Fe	Santa Fe and vicinity	Aug. 1, 1851	12	26	1	..	....	10	......	Congregations unusually large & interesting. Priests prevented the people hearing him preach at Los Vegos.
" "	"	" "	Aug. 1, 1852	12	26	....	..	....	7	15 57	Commenced preaching in Spanish and has succeeded in forming a permanent congregation of Mexicans.
J. Milton Shaw	Albuquerque	Albuquerque, &c	Dec. 1, 1851	12	39	....	..	....	....	......	Mrs. S. been dangerously sick. Not successful in establishing a promising stati n. Removed to Fort Defiance.
Samuel Gorman	Laguna	Pueblo Indians	Oct. 1, 1852	12	13	....	..	....	....	1 25	Labors altogether preliminary.
OREGON.											
Ezra Fisher	Oregon City	Portland and other places	April 1, 1851	12	13	4	..	....	16	......	Laboring with efficiency.

[redacted]

of ...sion	Months Commis'd.	Weeks labor reported.	Stations supplied.	Baptized.	Received by letter.	Scholars in S. School.	Cont. to Benevolent objects.	ADDITIONAL FACTS REPORTED.
1851	12	13	1	2	3	180	......	Need no further aid.
1851	12	13	2	..	....	....	1 00	Declension. Pastor left the field.
1851	12	13	1	..	....	97	......	Pastor resigned.
1852	12	30	6	2	6	65	1 00	Building meeting-house. Congregations large and prospects encouraging. Pastor resigned.
1852	12	52	1	15	16	100	50 15	Sunday School interesting. Revival.
1852	12	26	3	17	2	....	102 00	Three chs. in his field build'g meet'g houses.
1853	3	4	....	9	....	....	......	A temporary service to explore new fields.
1852	4	17	1	15	3	120	......	Finished meeting-house. Revival.
1853	12	13	4	26	....	80	......	Revival at M. Good state of religion at E.
1852	6	15	....	9	....	....	......	Labored in Ohio.
1851	12	30	5	3	8	120	30 00	Completed M. H. in M. The church is gaining influence, and promise for the future is now bright.
1852	12	13	3	..	4	....	......	Religious meetings interesting and increasing in interest.
1852	12	13	1	..	2	90	14 50	Pastor resigned on account of ill health.
1851	12	30	1	2	13	90	65 74	Discipline been necessary for the prosperity of the church.
1852	12	13	....	..	....	50	13 65	Nothing special.
1852	12	52	2	3	5	60	33 00	Revival at an outstation. Dismissed several to form another church.
1851	12	10	4	1	....	....	4 37	Pastor resigned.
1852	12	26	3	5	3	....	2 00	Church encouraged and are building a M. H.
....	....	4	....	..	....	....	......	A temporary service to explore the Lake Superior country. Furnished important information.
1852	12	26	1	10	17	....	63 66	Revival. Arranging to build a new M. H.
1852	12	26	5	..	4	23	......	A new station. Infidelity prevalent.
1851	12	11	1	..	7	165	18 00	Left for another field of labor.

EXPLANATION OF THE MISSIONARY TABLE.

PAGES 36-46.

The parallel columns shew:

1. The names of agents and missionaries, and the States in which they reside.
2. The Post-office address of agents and missionaries.
3. The fields of labor occupied by agents and missionaries.
4. The dates at which the appointments commence.
5. The number of months for which the appointments are respectively made.
6. The number of weeks labor reported as having been performed during an appointment.
7. The number of stations and outstations supplied.*
8. The number of persons baptized by the missionaries within the time of appointment.
9. The number received by letter.
10. The number of scholars in Sabbath schools under the care of missionaries.†
11. The amount contributed to benevolent objects.
12. Additional facts reported concerning the state and progress of the churches.‡

NOTES.

* Stations are churches or villages regularly supplied on the Lord's-day, and are indicated in column 3. Outstations are places where the missionaries have *stated* appointments for preaching more or less frequently at other times than the Lord's-day.

† In new places where Union schools are established, the number of scholars connected with Baptist families only are reported.

‡ In many cases two lines appear for the same missionary, extending through all the columns. In such cases the second line indicates a re-appointment of the missionary and the dates in column 4 determine to which appointment or year the statistics and remarks on the different lines belong. A particular notice of those dates is necessary to a proper understanding of certain changes which appear against the names of some individuals.

Blairsville	Evansville Association	Dec. 1, 1852	12	11	8	--	----	----	------	
Boonville	Evansville Association	Dec. 1, 1852	12	----	----	--	----	----	------	
Rochester	Fulton Co	Oct. 1, 1852	12	26	4	48	11	71	125	00
Connersville	Connersville and Rushville	Nov. 1, 1852	12	13	4	--	----	----	50	00	Nothing
Dudley Town	Brownstown Association	Mar. 1, 1853	12	----	----	--	----	----	------	
Indianapolis	Indianapolis	Nov. 1, 1852	12	13	1	4	11	130	90	50
Bennettsville	Bethel Association	Dec. 1, 1852	12	13	4	15	----	120	------		Church a
Lawrenceville	Pipe Creek and Manchester	Feb. 1, 1853	12	----	----	--	----	----	------	
Highland	Germans in Madison Co	May 1, 1851	12	13	----	--	----	----	25	00
"	" "	May 1, 1852	12	39	----	--	----	----	------	
Rock Island	Rock Island	June 1, 1851	12	13	3	4	5	100	75	00
"	"	June 1, 1852	12	39	2	2	4	100	5	00	for
Byron, Ogle Co	Byron, White Rock, &c.	May 1, 1851	12	13	7	--	----	110	------	
"	" "	May 1, 1852	12	39	----	--	8	114	15	40
Napierville	Napierville	April 1, 1851	12	13	1	2	4	60	3	00	for nc
Flat Rock	Crawford and Clark Cos	Oct. 1, 1851	12	26	9	30	10	208	55	55
Dundee, Kane Co	Dundee and vicinity	July 1, 1851	12	13	1	--	----	35	17	00
"	" "	July 1, 1852	12	39	----	18	4	40	32	59
St. Charles	St. Charles and vicinity	July 1, 1851	12	13	3	--	2	60	1	82
"	" "	July 1, 1852	12	39	3	--	1	51	22	99
Metamora	Metamora and vicinity	July 1, 1851	12	26	5	--	----	55	1	80
"	" "	Nov. 1, 1852	12	13	2	--	4	35	------	
Edgington	Rock Island Association	June 1, 1851	12	13	6	3	11	155	10	25
Moline	[illegible]	[illegible]	[illegible]	[illegible]						

Names of Agents and Missionaries.	Post Office Address.	Field of Labor.	Date of Commission	Months Commis'd.	Weeks labor reported.	Stations supplied.	Baptized.	Received by letter.	Scholars in S. School.	Cont. to Benevolent objects.	Additional Facts Reported.
H. S. Deppe	Steels Mills	Itinerant among Germans	Mar. 1, 1852	12	34	5	14	----	----	26 15	Devoted to his work.
Thomas Powell	Mount Palatine	Illinois	April 1, 1852	12	52			----	----	------	General Itinerant and Exploring Agent.
" "	"	"	April 1, 1853	12	----	----	--	----	----	------	Reappointment.
W. S. Goodno	Aurora, Kane Co.	Aurora and vicinity	May 1, 1851	12	13	1	2	1	----	------	Progress made. Pastor left the field.
J. H. Kruger	Peoria	Germans in P. and vicinity	Oct. 1, 1851	12	26	1	--	----	----	------	Organized a German Baptist church.
" "	"	"	Oct. 1, 1852	12	26	----	--	----	----	16 00	Some opposition because he refuses to sprinkle infants.
T. L. Breckenridge	Freeport	Freeport and vicinity.	Oct. 1, 1851	12	26	3	2	4	50	------	Require no further aid. Pastor left the field.
" "	La Salle	La Salle and vicinity	Nov. 1, 1852	12	13	1	1	3	----	------	Organized a church. Congregation increas'g.
C. D. Merit	Chillicothe	Chillicothe	July 1, 1851	12	13	4	--	4	70	30 55	Prospects flattering at all his outstations.
I. D Newell	Batavia	Batavia	Nov. 1, 1851	12	13	2	--	4	30	------	Pastor resigned for another field.
" "	Aurora, Kane Co.	Aurora and vicinity	May 1, 1852	12	39	3	4	26	60	3 75	Meeting house nearly completed. Revival.
W. D. H. Johnson	Greenville, Bond Co.	Greenville and vicinity	Oct. 1, 1851	12	26	5	--	3	13	27 95	Secular and religious interest of the church encouraging. Building a meeting house.
" "	"	"	Oct. 1, 1852	12	26	----	--	----	----	54 80	Nothing special.
G. S. Bailey	Pekin, Tazewell Co.	Pekin and vicinity	Nov. 1, 1851	12	39	3	12	3	200	91 80	Sunday School deeply interesting. Cause progressing. Secured lots for a M. H.
" "	"	"	Nov. 1, 1852	12	13	2	2	3	125	------	Church trying to make arrangements to build a M. H.
Nelson Alvord	Decatur	Decatur and Taylorsville	Oct. 1, 1851	12	24	2	--	4	100	34 25	Church at Taylorsville building a M. H.
" "	Chillicothe	Chillicothe and vicinity	Dec. 1, 1852	12	13	2	--	----	----	------	Congregations large for the place.
J. W. Riley	Charleston	Bloomfield Association	Feb. 1, 1852	12	52	4	17	13	----	200 00	Organized a church at one station. Prayer meetings well attended and cause progress'g.
" "	"	"	Feb. 1, 1853	12							
J. R. Ford	Shoal Creek, Clinton co	Vandalia Association	Dec. 1, 1851	12	39	9	4	10	75	70 35	Field too large. Will supply fewer stations and be supported without further aid from us.
Lyman Palmer	Galena	Galena	Dec. 1, 1851	6	8	1	--	----	122	------	A temporary arrangement.
Asahel Chapin	"	"	June 1, 1852	12	39	2	6	14	171	------	Making great effort to build a meeting house.
J. M. Scrogin	Delavan, Tazewell Co.	Delavan and vicinity	Mar. 1, 1852	12	22	3	4	----	70	------	Building meeting house. Pastor suddenly deceased.
H. E. Hempsted	Belleville	Belleville and vicinity	Feb. 1, 1852	12	26	1	2	2	50	5 00	Declension.
S. F. Holt	Warrenville	Downers Grove ½ of time	April 1, 1852	12	17	2	14	2	62	3 00	Building a meeting house.
John Higby	Newark	Newark and vicinity	April 1, 1852	12	52	3	39	8	75	24 00	Revival. Building a meeting house at one station.
D. L. Phillips	Jonesborough	Chester ½ of the time	April 1, 1852	12	10	1	1	----	----	------	Finished a neat meeting house.
Henry G. Weston	Peoria	Peoria, Cass and Mason cos	July 1, 1852	12	13	----	--	----	----	------	Preached to large congregations at several stations, organized two churches, but resigned his commission to return to the pastoral office at Peoria.

	...Rock Island &c	Feb. 1, 1853	12	----	----	--	----	----	------	Report n
Chester	Chester and vicinity	Feb. 1, 1853	12	----	----	--	----	----	------	Quarterl
			12	----	----	--	----	----	------	Field no
Ozaukee	Wisconsin	April 1, 1852	12	88	----	--	----	----	------	General l
"	"	April 1, 1853	12	----	----	--	----	----	------	Re appoi
Mayville, Dodge Co.	Mayville and vicinity	June 1, 1851	12	18	4	--	----	20	------	Church i
Baraboo, Sauk Co.	Baraboo and vicinity	Oct. 1, 1851	12	26	5	7	2	25	2 18	Religion
Sheboygan Falls	Sheboygan Falls, &c	Sept. 1, 1851	12	26	8	8	1	95	15 00	Pastor et church
"	" "	Sept. 1, 1852	12	25	2	1	1	50	2 60	Church n
Ozaukee	Ozaukee and vicinity	May 1, 1851	12	13	1	--	1	40	------	Deeper fe gospel lumber
"	" "	May 1, 1852	12	30	----	2	2	----	8 50	
Janesville	Janesville	Oct. 1, 1851	12	26	1	7	18	80	9 04	Well supp
Scott, Sheboygan Co.	Scott and Cascade	Dec. 1, 1851	12	30	8	3	2	60	------	Nothing
" "	" "	Dec. 1, 1852	12	13	6	--	6	----	------	Embarass
Darlington	Avon and vicinity	July 1, 1851	12	13	1	2	2	70	------	Left for a
Geneva	Geneva and vicinity	July 1, 1852	12	30	2	3	7	85	7 25	Religious
Beaver Dam	Beaver Dam and vicinity	June 1, 1852	12	30	3	9	4	30	20 59	Contracte
Beloit	Beloit and vicinity	Mar. 1, 1852	12	53	2	8	11	100	78 67	Ch. harm
"	" "	Mar. 1, 1853	12	----	----	--	----	----	------	Report nc
Sheboygan	Sheboygan	Sept. 1, 1851	12	26	3	6	5	100	19 00	Church in barrass
"	" "	Sept. 1, 1852	12	26	3	2	7	200	24 50	In many r
Green Bay	Green Bay	June 1, 1851	12	26	4	4	2	60	5 25	Cause en sentlenl
Fond du Lac	Fond du Lac, &c.	May 1, 1851	12	13	1	--	----	50	------	Building r
"	" "	May 1, 1852	12	30	----	3	3	----	------	Religion i slowly p
Thompsonville	Raymond and Ives Grove	April 1, 18..	12	..	.			..	. ..	R

NAMES OF SOCIETIES.	POST OFFICE ADDRESS.	TREASURERS.	Anniversary of 1846.	Anniversary of 1847.	Anniversary of 1848.	Anniversary of 1849.	Anniversary of 1850.	Anniversary of 1851.	Anniversary of 1852.	Anniversary of 1853.	Total amount from each.
Female Mission Society	Bedford, N. Y	Miss R. A. Platt						23 16		21 39	44 55
Sunday School of First Church	Camden, N. J							10 00			10 00
Female Mission Society, Union Church	Jersey City, N. J	Mrs L. Colby						32 00	30 00	50 00	112 00
Female Mission Society of Middle street	Portsmouth, N. H							12 50			12 50
Sunday School of Amity street	New York							30 00	70 00	50 00	150 00
Sunday School of Central Church	Brooklyn					100 00		31 80	30 00		161 80
Sunday School of Pierrepont street	do							50 00	75 00		125 00
Female Mite Society	West Dedham, Mass								11 00		11 00
Weekly Contributor's Society	Framingham, Mass								34 00		34 00
Sewing Society	Norwich, N. Y								12 80		12 80
Female Mission Society	New Boston, N. H								30 00		30 00
Female Mission Society	Watertown, Mass								23 42		23 42
Ladies' Mission Society	Ashland, Mass								12 00		12 00
Sunday School of Fifth Church	Providence, R. I								18 00		18 00
Sunday School	Valley Falls, R. I	A Babcock							15 63		15 63
Salem street Sunday School	Reading, Mass								20 00		20 00
Sunday School of Tenth Church	Philadelphia								90 00		90 00
Youth's Comstock Mission Society of Olive Branch Church	New York	R. C. McCormick, Jr							70 00		70 00
Society of Inquiry, University	Lewisburg, Pa	D. Merrell								24 00	24 00
Female Mission Society, Berean Church	New York									15 00	15 00
Ladies' Mission Society	Deep River, Ct									137 14	137 14
Ladies' Mission Society of Second Church	Danbury, Ct									18 00	18 00
Ladies' Mission Society of First Church	Hartford, Ct	Mrs R. M. Burdick								35 22	35 22
Ladies Mission Society, South Church	Hartford, Ct	Mrs. J. N. Murdock								80 00	80 00
Ladies' Benevolent Society	Burnt Hills, N. Y									10 00	10 00
Female Mission Society	Millington, N. J									22 36	22 36
Sunday School	Clinton, Mass									30 00	30 00
Ladies' Mission Society	Chatham, Mass									21 00	21 00
Female Mission Society	Abington, Mass									14 25	14 25
Female Mission Society, Central Church	Poughkeepsie, N. Y									20 00	20 00
Sunday School No. 6, Ludlow st	New York	R. R. Peterson								60 00	60 00
Sunday School, Strong Place Church	Brooklyn, N. Y									25 00	25 00
Female Mission Society, North Church	Troy, N. Y									42 00	42 00
Ladies' Second Church	Plainfield, N. J									30 00	30 00

NAMES OF AGENTS AND MISSIONARIES.	POST OFFICE ADDRESS.	FIELD OF LABOR.	Date of Commission	Months Commis'd.	Weeks labor reported.	Stations supplied.	Baptized.	Received by letter.	Scholars in S. School.	Cont. to Benevolent objects.	ADDITIONAL FACTS REPORTED.
IOWA.											
B. F. Brabrook	Davenport	Iowa	April 1, 1852	12	52						General Itinerant and Exploring Agent.
" "	"	"	April 1, 1853	12							Severely and dangerously sick during the last quarter. Re appointment.
William Elliott	Brighton	Brighton and Fairfield	Sept. 1, 1831	12	26	6	23	2	40	6 00	Church organized at one of his stations. Revival at an outstation.
" "	"	Brighton and Richland	Sept. 1, 1852	12	26		49	4	55	4 00	Revival at Glasgow, an outstation.
Elihu Gunn	Keokuk, Lee Co.	Keokuk and vicinity	Nov. 1, 1851	12	39	2	3	3	60		Completed meeting house. Congregation and Sunday School increasing.
" "	"	" "	Nov. 1, 1852	12	13	3	17	19	120		Revival at an out station.
William A. Wells	Muscatine	Muscatine, &c.	April 1, 1852	12	52	3	22	19	160	21 00	Church increasing in spirituality. Revival.
John Williams	Marion, Linn Co	Marion and vicinity	Sept. 1, 1851	12	6	3					Resigned his commission.
John Bates	Cascade	Cascade and vicinity	June 1, 1851	12	13		1	4	20		Meeting house progressing.
" "	"	" "	June 1, 1852	12	39			1		10 00	Progressing
Hiram Burnett	Mt. Pleasant	Mt. Pleasant and vicinity	June 1, 1851	12	13	3	18	4	35	3 00	Organized a church at an out station.
" "	"	" "	June 1, 1852	12	39	4	16	12			Revival.
William H. Turton	Farmington	Farmington and vicinity	Oct. 1, 1851	12	26	1			35		Finished lecture room.' Pastor been sick.
" "	"	" "	Oct. 1, 1852	12	26	3	3			5 00	Revival. Candidates are received for baptism.
J. A. Nash	Fort Des Moines	Fort Des Moines, &c.	Dec. 1, 1851	12	39	1	7	6	50		Prospects of the cause flattering in his region.
" "	"	"	Dec. 1, 1852	12	13	3					The Baptist cause decidedly on the increase.
George Scott	Maquoketa	Maquoketa, &c.	Oct. 1, 1851	12	16	3	1	1		13 00	Encouragingly progressed during the year.
" "	"	" "	Oct. 1, 1852	12	26		1	4	25	12 9[illegible]	Church revived. Pastor been sick.
A. Russell Belden	Iowa City	Iowa City	Dec. 1, 1851	12	39	1	4	7	130		Rapid and healthy growth of church and congregation in all things except spirituality.
" "	"	" "	Dec. 1, 1852	12	13				100		Pastors health been poor.
G. W. Bond	Knoxville	Marion and Monroe Cos.	Oct. 1, 1851	12	26	4	1	5		50 00	Organized a church at one station.
" "	"	Knoxville and vicinity	Oct. 1, 1852	12	26	4		1			Nothing special.
B. B. Arnold	Three Rivers, Polk co.	Blakesburg, Three Riv's,&c	Oct. 1, 1851	12	26	2	6	19			Organized a church at one station. Revival at Blakesburg.
" "	"	Pleasant Grove, &c.	Oct. 1, 1852	12	26	9	4	10	68		Will soon organize a ch. at one of his stations.
Edward O. Towne	Bonaparte	Bonaparte and vicinity	Nov. 1, 1851	12	39	1	5	11			Building a meeting house.
" "	"	" "	Nov. 1, 1852	12	13	5			130	10 00	Revival at an out station; converts not baptized yet.
Isaac Leonard	Burlington	Rock Spring and vicinity	Nov. 1, 1851	12	36	8	3	1	60	5 75	Church much revived and more interest manifested by the people.
" "	"	Rock Spring and Augusta	Dec. 1, 1852	12	13		18			7 75	Revivals at two stations.
John C. Ward	Marion, Linn Co.	Marion and vicinity	Sept. 1, 1852	12	26	2	2	4	75	3 00	Made an effort to pay debts on meeting house.
Edward M. Miles	Davenport	Second Church, Davenport	June 1, 1852	12	39	2		10	60	10 00	Ch. revived. Prayer meetings well attended.
Elijah Evans	Apple Grove	West Union and Monroe	Aug. 1, 1852	12	26	3	2	7	40		Organized a church at an out station.
C. D. Farnsworth	Colesburgh	Colesburgh and vicinity	Aug. 1, 1852	12	26	4	3	4			Organized a church at one station. Revival.

Names of Agents and Missionaries.	Post Office Address.	Field of Labor.	Date of Commission	Months Commis'd.	Weeks labor reported	Stations supplied.	Baptized.	Received by Letter	Scholars in S. School.	Cont. to Benevolent objects.	Additional Facts Reported.
Israel C. Curtis	Pella	Pella and vicinity	Oct. 1, 1852	12	26	5	1	3	40	......	Attentive congregations at all his stations.
D. H. Paul	Le Clair	Camanche and Le Clair	Oct. 1, 1852	12	26	4	--	6	50	12 75	Field too large for one man and asks for another.
Watson Clark	Keosauqua	Keosauqua	Sept. 1, 1852	12	18	4	--	6	80	......	Improved state of religious interest.
MINNESOTA TER.											
Julius S. Webber	Stillwater	Stillwater & Willow River	June 1, 1851	12	13	8	--	----	20	5 00	Pastor encouraged.
" "	"	Stillwater, &c.	June 1, 1852	12	39	5	1	----	25	8 35	Preparing to build a meeting house.
Timothy R. Cressy	St. Paul	St. Paul and vicinity	June 1, 1852	12	39	----	2	20	50	......	Prospects encouraging.
Lyman Palmer	St. Anthony	St. Anthony, &c.	Dec. 1, 1851	12	31	1	--	7	30	......	Infidelity prevalent.
" "	"	" "	Dec. 1, 1852	12	13	2	--	2	----	......	Religious interest increasing.
E. W. Cressy	St. Anthony	Hennepin Co.	Oct. 1, 1852	12	26	----	--	----	----	40 00	Encouraged with his field of labor. Organized a church.
James Tanner, or Esh kue go ne bi	Pembina	Pembina & Chippewa In.	....	12	----	----	--	----	----	......	A new appointment and new field.
NEW MEXICO.											
Hiram W. Read	Albuquerque	Albuquerque &c	Aug. 1, 1852	12	26	----	--	----	----	......	Has done much in religious conversation with individuals and in distributing tracts. Asks for more missionaries.
Lewis Smith	Santa Fe	Santa Fe and vicinity	Aug. 1, 1851	12	26	1	--	----	10	......	Congregations unusually large & interesting. Priests prevented the people hearing him preach at Los Vegos.
" "	"	" "	Aug. 1, 1852	12	26	----	--	----	7	15 57	Commenced preaching in Spanish and has succeeded in forming a permanent congregation of Mexicans.
J. Milton Shaw	Albuquerque	Albuquerque, &c	Dec. 1, 1851	12	39	----	--	----	----	......	Mrs. S. been dangerously sick. Not successful in establishing a promising stati:n. Removed to Fort Defiance.
Samuel Gorman	Laguna	Pueblo Indians	Oct. 1, 1852	12	13	----	--	----	----	1 25	Labors altogether preliminary.
OREGON.											
Ezra Fisher	Oregon City	Portland and other places	April 1, 1851	12	13	4	--	----	16	......	Laboring with efficiency.

	Oregon City, &c.	Sept. 1, 1851	12	39	4	..		83	Labors nectic to an
	Vicinity of Oregon City	Sept 1, 1851	12	26	----	..			Labors statio
San Jose	San Jose and Santa Clara.	Sept. 1, 1851	12	26	5	1		77	Laborin labor
" "	" "	Sept. 1, 1852	12	26	----	.		40	Receive
San Francisco	Pine st. Ch. San Francisco	Sept. 1, 1852	12	26	1	2	12	45	Church treasu build
Stockton	Stockton	Feb. 1, 1853	12		----	.			Report

EXPLANATION OF THE MISSIONARY TABLE.

PAGES 36-46.

The parallel columns shew:

1. The names of agents and missionaries, and the States in which they reside.
2. The Post-office address of agents and missionaries.
3. The fields of labor occupied by agents and missionaries.
4. The dates at which the appointments commence.
5. The number of months for which the appointments are respectively made.
6. The number of weeks labor reported as having been performed during an appointment.
7. The number of stations and outstations supplied.*
8. The number of persons baptized by the missionaries within the time of appointment.
9. The number received by letter.
10. The number of scholars in Sabbath schools under the care of missionaries.†
11. The amount contributed to benevolent objects.
12. Additional facts reported concerning the state and progress of the churches.‡

NOTES.

* Stations are churches or villages regularly supplied on the Lord's-day, and are indicated in column 3. Outstations are places where the missionaries have *stated* appointments for preaching more or less frequently at other times than the Lord's-day.

† In new places where Union schools are established, the number of scholars connected with Baptist families only are reported.

‡ In many cases two lines appear for the same missionary, extending through all the columns. In such cases the second line indicates a re-appointment of the missionary and the dates in column 4 determine to which appointment or year the statistics and remarks on the different lines belong. A particular notice of those dates is necessary to a proper understanding of certain changes which appear against the names of some individuals.

STATE CONVENTIONS

AND

GENERAL ASSOCIATIONS IN THE UNITED STATES,

With the Names and Post Office Address of the Corresponding Secretaries; the Time and Place of their Anniversaries for 1853; the number of Missionaries employed, and amount of Receipts into their Treasuries, for 1852, including Balances of the previous year.

STATES.	CORRESPONDING SECRETARIES.	POST OFFICE ADDRESS.	PLACE OF ANNIVERSARY.	Time of Anniversary	No. of Missionaries	Amount of Receipts for Dom. Miss. in 1852.
Maine	A. H. Granger	Warren	Saco	June 15	22	2947 60
New Hampshire	H. D. Hodge	N. Sanbornton		Oct. 19	9	1765 15
*Vermont						
*Massachusetts	W. H. Shailer	Brookline		Oct. --		3827 00
Rhode Island	Henry Jackson	Newport	Providence	June 21	14	1701 54
Connecticut	E. Cushman	Deep River	Norwich	June 14	8	1427 23
New York	T. O. Lincoln	Utica	Watertown	Oct. 12	51	9434 29
New Jersey	J. M. Carpenter	Jacobstown	New Brunswick	Oct. 25	22	2945 65
Pennsylvania	G. I. Miles	Philadelphia	Philadelphia	Nov. 16	32	5679 59
Maryland	Franklin Wilson	Baltimore	Washington, D.C	Nov. 5	10	2436 21
Virginia			Fredericksburg	June 3		
North Carolina	[illegible]	Milton	[illegible]	Oct. 13	15	961 25

AGGREGATE CONTRIBUTIONS FROM ALL THE STATES, SINCE 1832.

STATES.	Total Amount to 1845.	1846	1847	1848	1849	1850	1851	1852	1853	Total for each State.
Canada	327 65	864 70	692 67	734 11	710 79	809 57	463 84	193 63	189 19	4966 15
Maine	2717 40	--------	--------	--------	500 00	--------	37 00	56 39	622 31	3933 10
New Hampshire	3083 42	528 41	242 50	343 81	50 50	625 88	419 17	1104 77	1487 00	7885 46
Vermont	1718 95	673 95	184 00	257 51	222 80	1015 75	471 98	505 17	494 71	5544 82
Massachusetts	22,313 30	1474 20	3333 03	4791 22	4022 07	5357 73	6717 06	8497 51	7974 56	64,480 64
Rhode Island	5118 45	852 35	669 56	1683 33	1545 76	2427 57	1188 66	2874 55	687 87	17,048 10
Connecticut	11,628 71	1186 03	1042 31	1072 06	1480 46	1261 34	2032 59	2490 31	3052 58	25,236 39
New York	65,772 95	6520 49	7142 38	6871 19	6614 15	7723 20	10,666 47	13,706 43	16,951 07	141,968 33
New Jersey	4851 29	1695 85	1429 27	1890 90	2724 80	2408 67	2518 29	2179 01	3419 94	23,118 02
Pennsylvania	4520 81	528 47	529 86	707 43	1556 89	1606 11	1606 98	1973 75	2252 91	5282 21
Delaware	161 20	--------	--------	158 36	60 00	228 94	203 00	168 00	157 90	1137 40
Maryland	2019 81	30 25	5 00	--------	--------	--------	15 50	--------	--------	2070 56
District of Columbia	953 12	--------	10 00	--------	--------	30 00	5 00	37 31	5 00	1040 43
Ohio	1010 45	114 81	30 84	30 50	29 45	153 52	241 88	656 62	732 48	3000 55
Michigan	337 50	29 50	13 25	172 89	556 21	610 60	1011 80	866 75	634 43	4232 93
Indiana	28 75	8 10	22 05	11 11	8 50	26 35	290 22	774 38	1669 44	2838 90
Illinois	668 09	477 63	766 50	1136 69	594 90	704 74	1329 98	1230 97	1675 93	8585 43
Wisconsin	20 10	15 63	124 00	72 15	88 06	58 85	181 91	170 09	274 87	1005 66
Iowa	83 56	41 00	120 03	62 12	93 24	162 77	171 95	396 67	278 05	1409 39
Minnesota	--------	--------	--------	--------	--------	--------	1 00	2 25	55 85	59 10
Missouri	266 82	--------	--------	--------	--------	--------	--------	2 00	--------	268 82
Kentucky	273 88	--------	10 00	20 50	--------	--------	--------	--------	--------	304 88
Virginia	9152 56	159 44	5 85	7 30	--------	--------	5 00	--------	--------	9330 15
North Carolina	5000 02	391 67	--------	--------	--------	--------	--------	--------	--------	5391 69
South Carolina	8362 95	135 15	--------	--------	--------	--------	--------	--------	30 00	8528 10
Georgia	9529 33	--------	1331 87	--------	--------	--------	--------	30 00	--------	10,891 20
Alabama	493 08	--------	--------	--------	--------	--------	--------	--------	--------	493 08
Florida	157 82	--------	15 00	--------	--------	--------	--------	--------	--------	172 82
Mississippi	1899 66	--------	--------	--------	--------	--------	--------	--------	--------	1899 66
Tennessee	477 85	--------	8 25	--------	--------	--------	--------	--------	--------	486 10
Louisiana	79 00	--------	--------	--------	--------	--------	--------	--------	--------	79 00
Arkansas	50	--------	--------	50 55	18 15	--------	--------	--------	--------	118 70
Texas	--------	--------	--------	--------	--------	--------	--------	--------	--------	--------
California	--------	--------	--------	--------	--------	--------	50 00	150 50	70 00	270 50
Oregon	--------	--------	--------	--------	--------	--------	30 00	--------	51 50	81 50
New Mexico	--------	--------	--------	--------	--------	--------	--------	62 10	94 42	156 52
Aggregates for each period	163,028 98	15,727 63	17,728 72	20,068 73	20,876 73	25,201 09	29,648 28	38,114 16	42,872 01	$373,266 33

4

NNUAL CONTRIBUTIONS SINCE 1845.

REASURERS.	Anniversary of 1846.	Anniversary of 1847.	Anniversary of 1848.	Anniversary of 1849.	Anniversary of 1850.	Anniversary of 1851.	Anniversary of 1852.	Anniversary of 1853.	Total amount from each.
W. Cauldwell...	348 21	230 00	267 51	330 84	185 65	293 42	142 72	......	1798 35
elps............	31 94	30 00	......	25 00	30 00	70 12	30 00	50 00	287 06
Theall.........	18 00	17 23	30 00	32 50	30 79	......	113 70	60 00	382 22
. Randolph.....	222 23	216 19	512 12	768 02	800 00	798 50	594 08	780 00	4691 14
....	32 00	30 00	40 62	12 00	......	......	......	......	114 62
ry Colgate......	......	133 00	147 02	156 71	......	56 00	128 30	......	621 03
....	......	......	......	50 00	......	87 00	41 50	50 00	228 50
....	40 00	100 00	150 00	75 00	110 00	60 00	30 00	230 00	795 00
orne	......	60 00	60 00	60 00	......	60 00	180 68	......	420 68
....	30 00	30 00	30 00	30 00	20 00	40 00	30 00	20 00	230 00
P. Brush........	50 00	100 00	100 00	60 00	100 00	90 00	60 00	150 00	710 00
....	......	30 00	120 50	90 00	60 00	60 00	90 00	60 00	510 50
....	......	......	30 00	30 00	......	100 00	......	......	100 00
. Todd..........	15 00	......	15 00	30 00	......	60 00	......	80 00	200 00
G. Beckwith....	129 00	160 00	200 00	150 00	136 67	141 00	185 52	83 00	1175 19
I. Fessenden, Sec	41 00	30 00	20 00	25 00	30 00	......	30 00	27 00	204 00
rgaret S. Foster,	75 00	138 00	150 00	150 00	75 00	245 00	191 84	220 21	666 05
M. Waterman..	......	85 00	......	100 00	......	100 00	......	50 00	335 00
elle.............	......	......	......	100 00	100 00	88 25	78 37	......	366 62
chel Knox	......	30 00	36 00	30 00	30 30	......	......	......	126 30
....	9 30	16 37	7 30	10 98	66 00	2 88	2 87	......	66 70
nstock, Sec.....	......	......	100 00	50 00	40 00	......	27 03	32 00	249 03
A. Butler.......	100 00	......	......	135 00	......	......	......	......	235 00
inner....	30 00	......	30 00	30 00	......	......	......	......	90 00
....	......	50 00	150 00	......	30 00	......	30 00	......	260 00
....	25 00	30 00	90 00	......	37 00	......	......	......	182 00
....	......	......	......	41 48	125 00	......	......	......	166 48
....	......	......	......	230 00	30 00	......	10 00	......	270 00
oler.............	......	......	......	......	188 00	188 00	188 00	222 00	564 00
rts..............	......	......	50 00	50 00	15 00	......	......	......	337 00
....	......	......	......	......	......	15 45	......	......	15 45
....	......	33 72	......	......	......	40 38	......	......	74 10
....	......	......	......	......	......	30 00	......	......	30 00
....	......	......	......	......	......	14 00	......	......	14 00
....	......	......	......	......	......	30 25	......	......	30 25
....	......	......	......	......	......	20 00	21 60	......	41 60
....	......	......	......	......	......	16 28	......	......	16 28

NAMES OF SOCIETIES.	POST OFFICE ADDRESS.	TREASURERS.	Anniversary of 1846.	Anniversary of 1847.	Anniversary of 1848.	Anniversary of 1849.	Anniversary of 1850.	Anniversary of 1851.	Anniversary of 1852.	Anniversary of 1853.	Total amount from each.
Female Mission Society	Bedford, N. Y	Miss R. A. Platt						23 16		21 30	44 46
Sunday School of First Church	Camden, N. J							10 00			10 00
Female Mission Society, Union Church	Jersey City, N. J	Mrs L. Colby						32 00	30 00	50 00	112 00
Female Mission Society of Middle street	Portsmouth, N. H							12 50			12 50
Sunday School of Amity street	New York							30 00	70 00	50 00	150 00
Sunday School of Central Church	Brooklyn					100 00		31 80	30 00		161 80
Sunday School of Pierrepont street	do							50 00	75 00		125 00
Female Mite Society	West Dedham, Mass								11 00		11 00
Weekly Contributor's Society	Framingham, Mass								34 00		34 00
Sewing Society	Norwich, N. Y								12 80		12 80
Female Mission Society	New Boston, N. H								30 00		30 00
Female Mission Society	Watertown, Mass								23 42		23 42
Ladies' Mission Society	Ashland, Mass								12 00		12 00
Sunday School of Fifth Church	Providence, R. I								18 00		18 00
Sunday School	Valley Falls, R. I	A Babcock							15 63		15 63
Salem street Sunday School	Reading, Mass								20 00		20 00
Sunday School of Tenth Church	Philadelphia								90 00		90 00
Youth's Comstock Mission Society of Olive Branch Church	New York	R. C. McCormick, Jr							70 00		70 00
Society of Inquiry, University	Lewisburg, Pa	D. Merrell								24 00	24 00
Female Mission Society, Berean Church	New York									15 00	15 00
Ladies' Mission Society	Deep River, Ct									187 14	187 14
Ladies' Mission Society of Second Church	Danbury, Ct									18 00	18 00
Ladies' Mission Society of First Church	Hartford, Ct	Mrs R. M. Burdick								35 22	35 22
Ladies Mission Society, South Church	Hartford, Ct	Mrs. J. N. Murdock								80 00	80 00
Ladies' Benevolent Society	Burnt Hills, N. Y									10 00	10 00
Female Mission Society	Millington, N. J									22 36	22 36
Sunday School	Clinton, Mass									30 00	30 00
Ladies' Mission Society	Chatham, Mass									21 00	21 00
Female Mission Society	Abington, Mass									14 25	14 25
Female Mission Society, Central Church	Poughkeepsie, N. Y									20 00	20 00
Sunday School No. 6, Ludlow st	New York	R. B. Peterson								60 00	60 00
Sunday School, Strong Place Church	Brooklyn, N. Y									25 00	25 00
Female Mission Society, North Church	Troy, N. Y									42 00	42 00
Ladies' Second Church	Plainfield, N. J									30 00	30 00

LIST OF LEGACIES,

PAID TO THE SOCIETY SINCE ITS ORGANIZATION.

1834	Dea Josiah Penfield, Savannah, Ga., per Rev. H. O. Wyer	$1250 00
1835	Mrs Clarissa Long, Shelburn, Mass., per W. Wilder, Esq., Ex'r	37 50
"	William Powers, Hebron, N. H., per Rev. I Merriam	100 00
"	Miss Maria Curtis, Southbridge, Mass., per Rev. E. Going	200 00
"	Mrs Jemima Elliott, Hampton, Ct., per Rev. J. Payne, Exr.	100 00
1836	Mrs Betsey Sprague, Attleboro', Mass., per Mr. A. Reed, Executor	461 25
"	Robert Rogers, Esq , Newport, R. I.	25 00
"	Ebenezer Boyd, Providence, R. I	10 00
1839	Mrs Abigail Marshall, New York, per Mr. Schofield, Executor	702 17
"	Mrs Margaret Pugsley, Dutchess Co., N. Y., per Miss Cornelia Pugsley	280 00
"	Mrs Irene Coats, New York, per Alfred Decker, Esq	250 00

[redacted]

1847	L. Crossman, Elbridge, N. Y., in advance	30 00
1848	William Jones, Iowa City, Iowa, per G. W. Hampton, Esq., Executor	25 00
"	Hon. James Vanderpool, Newark, per B. Vanderpool, Esq., Executor	1000 00
"	Miss Susan Farrar, Keene, N. H., per Rev. G. Robins	10 00
"	Mrs. Eunice Nicholls, Cambridge, Mass., per E. Mansfield, Executor	500 00
"	Mrs. Hannah Carleton, Portland, Me., per Rev. G. J. Carleton, Administrator	500 00
1849	Mr. Samuel R. Stelle, Piscataway, N. J., per Lewis R. Stelle, Esq., Executor	200 00
"	Mrs. Phebe Gale, East Bennington, Vt., per Executor of Estate of S. Harmon	25 00
"	Mr. William Reynolds, Boston, Mass., per J. H. Duncan, Esq., and Mrs. Susan D. Reynolds, Executors, in land not sold	
"	Josiah Lyman, Andover, Ct., per N. B. Lyman, Executor	50 00
"	John J. Martin, Montgomery, N. Y., M. Bookstaver, Executor	1000 00
"	Mrs. Martha Howe, West Boylston, Mass., per Messrs. E. J. Howe & Co.	50 00
"	A. H. Reed, Sweden, N. Y., per Rev. D. Searl	13 00
"	Asa H. Trueman, Owego, N. Y., E. Trueman, Executor	248 00
1850	George D. James, Amenia, N. Y., J. K. Mead and N. Rose, Executors	100 00
"	John Everett, Manchester, Mich., per F. Everett	70 00
"	Jacob Whitman, Belvidere, Ill., in part, per N. Crosby, Esq.	100 00
"	Jonas Taylor, Boston, Mass	12 50
"	Miss Rebecca Thompson, Amenia, N. Y., per A. B. Capwell	801 00
"	Joanna Minot, Boston, Mass., per E. Mears and I. Parker, Executors	100 00
"	Claudius F. Brown, Arkwright, N. Y., per David Barrell	150 00
"	Miss Anna Roe, Egremont, Mass., per R. B. Brown, Executor	50 00
1851	David Schauber, Burnt Hills, N. Y., per J. & D. M. Schauber, Executors	10 00
"	Woolcot Griffin, Gouverneur, N. Y., per O. L. Barnum, Executor	100 00
"	Joseph Flanders, Brooklyn, N. Y., per Mrs. Eliza A. Flanders and Benj. Flanders	500 00
"	William Williams, New York, per John Allan, Executor	400 00
"	Ely Wiley, South Reading, Mass	50 00
1852	Miss Pharozene C. Kelly, Hopkinton, N. H., per John Page	50 00
"	Jonathan W. Ford, Boston, Mass	100 00
"	Theron Fisk, Warsaw, N. Y., in advance, in part	1500 00
"	Joshua A. Burke, Brooklyn, N. Y., per Mrs. E. & W. A. Burk	350 00
"	Miss Eliza Skaats, New York, in part, per G. N. Bleecker, Executor	1000 00
"	Barnum M. Howard, Sweden, N. Y., per H. M. Howard, Executor	20 00
1853	Alanson Stewart, Liberty, N. Y., per W. W. Murphy	5 00
"	Mrs. Sarah B. Peirce, Middleboro', Mass	100 00
"	Arnold Whipple, Providence, R. I., per Mrs. P. Whipple, Executrix	200 00

IMPORTANT WHEN WILLS ARE MADE.

LEGACIES are sometimes diverted from the purposes of testators, on account of technical informalities, especially in the devising clause. The following form of bequest has been approved by high legal authority, to which we solicit the careful attention of those friends who kindly intend to place the Society among their legatees, as one which, if followed, will secure to us the favors intended.

FORM OF A BEQUEST TO THE SOCIETY.

I give and bequeath to the American Baptist Home Mission Society, formed in New York in the year eighteen hundred and thirty-two, the sum of —— dollars for the purposes of said Society.

DECENNIAL CENSUS FOR ILLINOIS,

Showing the Counties in the State and their Population; the number of Baptist Churches organized, their number of Members; and the number of Church Edifices erected in each County up to the year 1840 and from 1840 to 1850.

	1840.				1850.			
COUNTIES.	Population.	Churches.	Members.	Ch. edifices.	Population.	Churches.	Members.	Ch. Edifices.
Adams	14476	6	206	4	26537	8	454	6
Boone	1705	2	131	1	7627	4	416	1
Brown	4183	1	14	----	7223	1	30	----
Bureau	3067	3	62	----	5494	4	153	3
Champaigne	1475	1	71	----	2697	2	53	1
Clark	7453	2	----	----	9576	4	110	2
Crawford	4422	1	----	1	7136	3	75	2
De Kalb	1697	----	----	----	27544	1	31	----
De Witt	3247	1	20	----	5002	2	46	3
Fulton	13142	1	66	1	12276	3	240	1
Green	11951	5	293	3	13488	5	223	3
Hancock	9946	2	37	1	4753	4	188	2
Henderson	New	1	10	----	4601	2	70	1
Henry	1260	1	11	----	3810	----	----	----
Jersey	4535	2	166	----	7502	4	265	2
Jasper	1472	----	----	----	13198	1	26	----
Knox	7060	1	63	----	13280	2	98	----
La Salle	9348	2	40	1	7813	8	293	5
Lawrence	7092	1	----	----	6132	1	32	1
Lee	2035	1	55	----	5289	3	104	1
Logan	2333	1	30	----	5128	2	46	1
McDonough	5308	1	78	1	7702	4	171	2
Marshall	1849	----	----	----	5181	1	30	----
Mercer	2352	1	14	----	5255	2	22	2
McLean	6566	4	122	1	10551	5	149	3
Ogle	3479	----	----	----	10020	3	75	----
Peoria	6153	4	74	----	17550	4	232	1
Pike	11728	11	352	8	18820	9	406	8
Putnam	2131	1	58	----	3968	2	87	1
Schuyler	6972	1	39	----	10428	2	113	2
Stephenson	2809	----	----	----	11951	2	97	1
Stark	1573	1	19	----	3732	3	61	1
Tazewell	7221	2	66	----	12054	3	145	2
Warren	6739	3	55	1	8232	3	193	2
Winnebago	4609	3	73	----	11731	5	372	1
Woodforce	New	----	----	----	4452	2	108	1
36 Counties.	181888	67	2255	23	387733	112	5225	62

REMARKS.

The above Table was compiled by Rev. H. G. Weston, of Peoria. Illinois. It cost him a great deal of time and labor; especially as many of his correspondents manifested indifference and neglect. But it is hoped that hereafter additions and corrections, if necessary, will be obtained so as to render it, with the others published with our Annual Reports, still more valuable for the future history of the Home Mission Society.

REPORT OF COMMITTEES

ON TOPICS PRESENTED IN THE ANNUAL REPORT OF THE EXECUTIVE BOARD.

AT TROY, N. Y., MAY 13th, 14th AND 15th, 1853.

REPORT OF THE COMMITTEE ON FINANCE.

Presented through Rev. E. E. L. Taylor, of Brooklyn, N. Y., Chairman.

Your Committee appointed to consider the Financial part of the Report of the Board beg leave to submit the following;

The entire Receipts of the Treasurer during the year appear by his Report to be $45,354.93, exclusive of the balance in the Treasury, April 1st, 1852. Of this amount only $41,042.51, were received in contributions, legacies and donations being but $3,228.35, increase over and above the receipts of the previous year.

This result your Committee are compelled to view with unaffected dissatisfaction. To them it is a source of deep mortification, as well as of regret, that a year commenced with such fair promises, and intelligent *pledges*, a year of almost unexampled prosperity in a commercial point of view, and so marked by noble and *enlarged* liberality among philanthropists and Christians of every name, (as the receipts of all the benevolent institutions of the land show,) that during such a favored year, this Home Mission Society, with claims such as it has never before urged upon the American Zion, with new *nations* to evangelize, —whose evangelization would be the harbinger of the evangelization of heathen nations—should present so small an increase over its previous receipts, and thus, apparently indicate the grossly inadequate view of the responsibilities which God in his holy providence has thrown upon our denomination connected with Home Evangelization.

Your Committee are compelled to feel that under such a mortifying aspect of the Society's *finances*, it becomes them to pause and carefully inquire into the *cause* of such a deficiency of adequate and *promised* resources to meet the rapidly augmenting claims pressed upon her. Delinquency exists, and is chargeable *somewhere*. We meet at our Anniversaries, enjoy a jubilee over the relative importance and grandeur of our work, insist that a vast deal more ought and *must* be raised the coming year, separate with the unanimous resolution that it shall be done, and reässemble the next year to wonder that others have not done it, and yet again resolve in a similar manner with the past—"Resolve and re-resolve and die the same." All this time our country is progressing in vice and infidelity, as it is in population, wealth and power with fearful rapidity and thousands are annually pressing over the precipice of death and eternal ruin, unsaved by our benevolence. 'Tis time some "jury of inquest" be summoned over this wholesale destruction of immortal souls, and the guilt of this criminal neglect be made to fall upon and to be *felt* by the party in the fault here. Either it is to be found upon your Board of Managers, upon the Secretaries, and the Agents of the Society, and if found *there*, dismissal, and disgrace should be the slightest punishment; or else it stains the christian integrity and character of the Pastors or Churches, or *both*, located in New England, New York, Pennsylvania, New Jersey, Ohio, and Delaware. Upon some one or more of these parties must it be found. For no man in his christian senses can feel that with *such* an inviting field, as the Great West alone possesses, thrown open for this Society to cultivate, with such heathenish destitution as portions of this vast field furnish, with the numerous and affecting Macedonian cries for *help* rung in our ears, with the commission of the Church, "*beginning at Jerusalem*," still acknowledged as binding upon her, we are at all adequately meeting our responsibility to savingly bless American citizens and American heathen in their imploring destitution.

If your Board has properly surveyed the field of this Society's operations, and acted with sufficient discretion and intelligence in the selection of her Agents; if the Secretaries and Agents, with a comprehensive view of their duties, and a zeal commensurate with the importance of our country's evangelization, have

But neither your Board, the Secretaries, nor the Agents, are the possessors or *coiners* of that "Material Aid," necessary to the vigorous prosecution of this our appropriate work. If they were, it would be cheerfully tendered, and the Treasury never complain of exhaustion; while the voice of many a faithful missionary would be heard, where now no sound of the Gospel has ever reverberated.

Where then, friends of the Home Mission Society, is this criminal delinquency to be found? If not with the Board nor your salaried Agents it can lie nowhere but upon the Constituency of the Society. Upon the *Churches* and *their Pastors*, to a greater or less extent, we solemnly believe it to be chargeable, and may be traced to the following as among, at least, the more prominent causes of our past failures.

1. A low and unworthy standard as to the requisite amount to be expended in the Society's operations. No man ever accomplished anything noble or worthy his immortal being, with a low and unworthy standard before him. One reason why so many of the present churches of our denomination are so ineffective, and have attained no higher or more commanding social, intellectual, and moral position in community, is attributable to the narrow, contracted policy, and the illiberal, unworthy standard which they have adopted. With no lofty aspirations, no worthy sense of the high and holy position which the great Head of the Church has assigned to his sacramental host, they have remained "feeble in Israel," unknown and *unfelt*. But when, in any instance, they have taken a broad and intelligent view of "the high vocation wherewith they have been called," and in reliance upon God, have determined to do something worthy of Christian men and servants of the Most High God, in elevating the standard of the Cross, Heaven has proportionably blessed their efforts, and given a signal rebuke to the mean, niggardly policy and standard of the unbelieving, narrow-minded discipleship of Christ. "He that deviseth liberal things, by liberal things shall stand." So, while we talk only of our thousands and few tens of thousands, for this great work of evangelizing North America, and raise our standard no higher than this, we contract the already contracted souls of too many in our churches, and accomplish but half what might be even more easily accomplished with a becoming gospel standard. To reach, therefore, any worthy point as a denomination, in this great work of Christianizing our native land, the churches must be first brought to feel that, while they "expect great things from God," they must "attempt great things *for God*." Till they catch the inspiration of this sentiment, in all our Home Mission operations, we shall fail of doing any thing worthy of ourselves, and much less of the Master, who has left us the best example of sacrifice for country and for humanity.

2. *A Want of System* in their contributions to this specific object, is another prolific cause of so small receipts from a large share of our giving churches. Much has been written upon this point within the past few years, and we would with greater effect, in its bearings upon the cause of Home Missions. We can only say that when trusted by any church and pastor to a single annual effort, as where collections are taken at all, it is to be feared it more generally is trusted—it can never be reliable as to *amount*. A stormy Lord's day, an unexpected call

for some other object of benevolence occurring in close proximity with the collection for Home Missions,—necessarily, under such arrangements, materially affects the contributions, and must leave the Treasury fitful and uncertain as to its supplies.

If, however, *every one*, in all our churches, as was done in the primitive church, pastor and people, rich and poor, should be individually addressed to "lay by him in store as God has prospered him" for this object; and the Monthly Concert should become universally observed, as to both "prayers and alms," with reference no less to *Home* than to Foreign Mission work, (as your Committee think most just and important), we can hardly doubt that the American Baptist Home Mission Society would be longer called upon to complain of an exhausted Treasury; but compelled the rather to seek out *the men* to occupy the high places of the field which your funds would supply.

3. Again, a third cause of this delinquency, is the want of an adequate and intelligent survey on the part of many pastors and churches of the full *extent*, *destitution*, and *promise* of the great field opened for the Society's cultivation. The pecuniary resources of the constituency of this Society, which embraces the membership of the Baptist congregations North, it is believed, have never been increased more rapidly than during the past three years. During this period the Territory occupied as our missionary ground has almost quadrupled, while the increase of our receipts has been only a little over $15,000, or one-third of the present income of the Society. California with a golden territory of square miles sufficiently large to cover twenty-seven states like Massachusetts, and

the Society has been in operation during the past year than this, and none will be found more important if it is wisely employed in the future.

In hastily closing, therefore, their Report, already extended beyond the ordinary limits of similar reports, your Committee would propose, in view of the present demands upon the Treasury, and also from the new and most important feature now introduced into the working system of the Society, whereby aid in the erection of Meeting-houses over the field of our operations, as well as support for Christian School Teachers, is hereafter to be expected from its funds, the following Resolutions—

1. That the standard of this Society for its annual receipts and expenditures should not be hereafter less than any one of our benevolent organizations; and that to the attainment of this, we instruct our Board to steadily aim, in the appointment of its Agencies.

2. That all our Agents and Pastors of the churches, be earnestly recommended to secure more *systematic* as well as *enlarged* benevolence from the churches and congregations, in behalf of the Home Mission Society.

3. That the churches be specially requested and *urged* to take a sufficient number of the *Home Mission Record*, to supply every family connected with them, with a monthly copy of its issues.

REPORT OF MISSIONS IN THE VALLEY OF THE MISSISSIPPI.

Presented through the Chairman, Rev. J. M. Peck, D.D., of Illinois.

This great Central Valley of North America has been, from the organization of the society, and must be for many years to come, our principal Missionary field. And Divine Providence seems to have pointed out this middle section of our common country, as a field whereon the great contest, at this period of the world's history between truth and error, holiness and sin, should be waged, and the victory won. Here are congregating adherents of all the diversified forms of a corrupt and spurious Christianity, and of the infidel liberalism of modern Europe, together with the vicious and reckless of every class.

And here too, are men of high-souled honor, unflinching patriotism, quick in discerning every insidious encroachment against civil and religious liberty. Common sense, shrewdness, and habits of watchful observation are among the elements of character in a large proportion of the people.

And then, in about the same proportion to the whole population as in these Atlantic States, are to be found the true disciples of Christ, girding on their armour and marshalling their battalions, resolved to "do or die" in the service of the great Captain of their salvation.

Viewed as a system of operations in relation to the kingdom of Christ, and the amount of expenditure, the success of this society in that field has scarcely a parallel in modern efforts. But viewed in relation to the vast increase of population, the growth of cities and villages, the extent of new territory over which the people have spread within twenty years, and the supply in no measure has been equal to the demand.

For every church raised up in that field by missionary labor, and placed in circumstances to sustain the institutions of the Gospel, ten might now be raised up and made a strong post in the next ten years.

For every house of worship built through missionary labor in a year gone by, by a judicious and more economical mode, twenty church-houses might be erected every year in future. And in every department of christian action there is the same prospect of enlargement by increasing the means and instrumentalities employed. That portion of the Great Valley of the Mississippi which comes within the practical operations of this Society is in itself a great field, and would be well deserving the undivided attention of the managers; but other fields, equally important, come under the supervision of the Society, and cannot be neglected.

The results of the labors of this Society in the Mississippi since its formation, may be comprehended, summarily, but very imperfectly, in the following items:

1st. Liberating many worthy ministers from the embarrassment of secular affairs in providing for the indispensable wants of their families, and enabling them to devote themselves wholly to the work whereunto God had called them. This has produced excellent effects on other ministers, who continued to sustain ministerial education, and aiding the churches in looking out and bringing forward young men whom God designates to that work—all owe you much.

6th. From the commencement of Home Mission efforts in that Valley, there has been a gradual, silent, and powerful influence on churches, ministers, and the whole population, that cannot be expressed with sufficient brevity in this report. Careful observers of the changes produced in a quarter of a century, can appreciate in some measure the character and extent of this influence. Long confirmed habits in the ministers and churches have been changed; the anti-mission party in every state has degenerated in efficiency, and lessened in numbers, until further aggressive opposition to that class, would really have the aspect of persecution. Remaining yet disconnected from all modern benevolent associations, many of their ministers and churches have become active and successful evangelists in their own way, and are gradually training the churches to the duty of aiding their pastors, that they be more entirely devoted to the work of the ministry.

7th. The Reports of this Society contain but very partial statements of Home Mission labors and their fruits in the Mississippi Valley. They are a faithful record of what this Society has done, so far as its own missionaries have personally labored. And in the Appendix annually given, something may be found of the doings of Conventions and General Associations in each state. But behind these in nearly all the states of the Mississippi Valley, a system of missionary operations is carried on, which in the aggregate would exceed by far all the reported labors of this Society.

The Associations in their local character, sustain one or more itinerant missionaries within their own districts. We will give a single illustration from one State that will show the working of this system:

In Missouri during 1848–49, there were twenty itinerant missionaries employed in the district Associations. And yet the General Association of that State employed for a greater or less period some fifteen more. Three of these men in eighteen months, without interfering with their labors in protracted meetings, or lessening in any degree the value or the number of their sermons, raised $49,000, to establish a Baptist College in that state.

To all this we add, that in many organized bodies there are adopted measures to ascertain and give credit for the voluntary labors of itinerant evangelists not under special appointments. In 1838, counting their work at 75 cents *per diem*, in the old Baptist Convention of Illinois, the amount of such labor exceeded the value of $2,000. The same system is now continued in Southern Illinois with the most happy results. Within the memory of some of your Body, destitute churches were visited monthly, and itinerant labors were performed in destitute settlements in this and other Atlantic States.

But in the Mississippi Valley, the influence and labors of the Home Mission Society have been wide and effectual in bringing out this class of laborers. Their voluntary efforts should be regarded as the legitimate fruits of the Home Mission organization amongst Baptists.

In conclusion. the Committee would say that our denomination are under the highest obligations to thank God and take courage in the Home Mission cause. His providence watches incessantly over the destinies of this continent, and on his grace we may confidently rely for success and victory in the great contest with every spiritual foe.

REPORT OF THE COMMITTEE ON THE FAR WEST.

Presented through the Chairman, Rev. E. L. Magoon, of New York.

YOUR Committee would invite special attention to our territories in the remote North-West, and indicate certain strange features which may nevertheless be deemed encouraging therein. These are found in the character, contrast, and condition of the people.

First, their character. Of all political associations, colonies and newly peopled territories are the most original. They possess most mind, exert most energy, and at the outset, lay broad and rugged foundations of states, which subsequently may become superbly polished, but are seldom or never enhanced in strength. Every segment of the great circle of American Commonwealths is marked now with the special tone of its first tint, and so will doubtless continue for centuries to come. The fountain characterises the stream, and not the stream the fountain.

Greeks, Normans, and New Englanders, stand first on the scale of great [redacted] principle that moulds and unites them. The rough and knotty oak is more inflexible than the sleek poplar, and more obdurate to axe or plane; and yet one could well prefer its solidity for a ship's keel, or its polish for a parlor door. The primary good quality of our emigrant population is strength; raw material, that remains a thing of intrinsic substance and worth, when the shavings are removed. The firmest and most aspiring minds move first and farthest, as in all great upheavings from earth's central fires, the profoundest substratum of foundation granite shoots to the top.

Secondly, note *the contrasted traits* of territorial elements. Bacon, speaking of colonies as being amongst ancient, primitive, and heroical works, says, "It is a shameful and unblessed thing, to take the scum of people, and wicked condemned men, to be the people with whom you plant. And not only so, but it spoileth the plantation; for they will ever live like rogues, and not fall to work, but be lazy, and do mischief, and spend victuals, and be quickly weary, and then certify over to their country to the discredit of the plantation." This warning would be pertinent to the communities under consideration, were they generally composed of the refuse of our race, and sunk to the degraded level of an effeminate and uniform type. But of all people on the face of earth this is least true of the new men of the new world. Like the woodland giants they fell, the prairies they subdue, the rivers they traverse, and the towering barriers they overleap; each one is characterised by bold features of his own, rugged substance of most diversified and striking forms. In this contrast, apparently so wide and conflicting, there is unity of the most intimate and auspicious kind; as in a mountainous region, the heads that are highest and therefore most remote, frown least with envy, pour richest treasures at each others feet, and dwell forever in sublime fellowship upon the firmest and compactest base.

The strangest contrast in our newer states and largest territories results from the fact, that they are peopled in not very unequal proportions by the historic and non-historic tribes of mankind. Thither the remotest descendants of a common stock are drawn by kindred motives, and there they coalesce in similar pursuits. Oriental and occidental, northerner and southerner, melt and mingle in the same ardor, like opposite metals in the burning magnificence of Corinth, and thus form an amalgam of the richest texture and most enduring worth, out of which fabrics may be fashioned for every realm of beauty, grandeur, and use. Taken separately, and in their native localities, these elements are less valuable; but their transportation to the arena of their mutual struggle and assimilation transforms them into a new aspect, and imparts to them a vastly increased worth. The impatient aspirant from the mother states will wear out his ancestral small-clothes before he reaches the interior of the great West; and, if blessed with an ordinary capacity for expansion, will happily outgrow many of his insignificant notions and leave them behind. Thenceforth he will feel that the bed of his juvenile repose is shorter than that he can stretch himself upon it, and the covering is narrower than that he can wrap himself in it. The European once away from the dwarfing influence of puny tradition and conventional insipidity, that inexorable tyrant of feeble minds, will speedily swell to the fascinating majesty which through every unfolding scene he hastens to enjoy with ennobling throbs of a deeper, higher, wider, mightier life. The indigenous, or Indian element gains on the side of artificial culture, as much as the Caucasian has been fortified by unsophisticated strength. Pigments and feathers are removed from the outside of his head, while art, literature, and morality, blend their humanizing adornments within. The attire of civilization descends over the whole person, and already he develops many qualities of a man. The Asiatic, the fourth and feeblest generic component in this mighty aggregate, the attenuated East linked to the massy West, and interfusing its timid sensibility with herioc force, is no longer what he was in tropical climes. An adult baby from China, for example, with tinsel slippers, cerulean breeches, and three feet of superfluous tail dangling from his greased scalp, laid aside for boots from Lynn, shirts from Lowell, and christian clothing in general from slop-shops in New York, has the demon of caste completely out of him thereby. Artificers who furnish the inside or outside of man in this land, put so much republican and christian nationality into their handy work, that it imparts virtue at the slightest touch, and emancipates from vassalage the most abject. No citizens amongst us conform so minutely to our national customs, and habitually diffuse the spirit of freedom they are zealous to defend, as the offspring of refugees from tyranny, superstition, and want. The advantage gained to the patriot and philanthropist, who may gather the benificiaries of his wisdom and goodness on the free and unbounded domain of our own institutions, is immense.

We have glanced at the general character of the population now spreading over the great North-West, and at the bold contrast of aspect and elements seen on every hand. Let us now

Thirdly, contemplate for a moment, *our duty* in the light of *their condition.* The myriads at present gathering near the shores of the Pacific, and with whom we have especially to do as a missionary body, consist of three classes; aliens, pagans, and heathenised Christians the most degraded and impracticable of all. This rapidly enlarging body is already immense, and its motion, of necessity, must continue perpetual; but, while its corruption may not be ranker than the same fallen nature in other climes, it is still fearfully depraved, and no mass of filth was ever large enough to work itself pure. The fountain filled with blood drawn from Immanuel's veins, must irrigate this field, or nothing but desolation will be produced thereon. Human enterprise is often productive of efficient inventions; but every one of these on the land and on the sea, aside from the one unalterable way of salvation, is an increased facility of death. Human bodies and souls are mangled and murdered in denser throngs and more expeditious modes, than in days of old, and that is all that can be said in praise of unsanctified skill.

All great and enduring nations have signalized their wisdom, and insured their growth, by copiously planting colonies of vigorous germs, and fostering them with generous aid. With a native population overflowing a whole continent, with fleets careering over every sea, burthened with tributaries from every land, and with such resources for secure growth as no other nation under heaven ever could command, it is clearly our duty to kindle beacons along the Atlantic and Pacific borders, such as from Greece gleamed not on the Mediterranean or Euxine shores, and Roman eagles never saw as they flew from the balmy Adriatic to Northern seas. It is not our purpose or province to plant the colonies of Mammon, nor even those of Minerva and Apollo, but the colonies of Christ. Christendom in her most aggressive days was animated with this ambition, and if we fail to exemplify their fidelity, the very heathens will rise up in the judgment against us, and condemn us. For they, when they sent out their children to new territories, deemed it their first and highest duty to hallow the new-born state by consecrating it to their national god, feeling that the tie of a common religion was the most intimate and enduring bond between the mother country and its progeny. Every other vestige of such communities may have passed away, as at Paestum, but the depth of that primitive devotion is indicated by the mighty fanes which still rear their heads towards heaven, "fashioned to endure the assaults of time with all his hours," suggesting that the diviner sentiments in man are so akin to eternity, that the monuments even of a false religion outlast every other memorial of its age and people.

In the joy excited by the discovery of America, the chief delight with all devout minds was, that a new province would thus be added to the dominion of Christ. This is expressed in all patents for the occupation of territories here; for instance, in that of one of the very first settlements made under the auspices of religious men. James the First gave his approval to "so noble a work, which may by the providence of God hereafter tend to the glory of His Divine Majesty, in propagating the Christian religion to such people as yet live in darkness and miserable ignorance of the true knowledge and worship of God."

Our Father in heaven has mercifully committed to our acceptance and use the glorious Gospel of his Son, a regenerative force to renew, light to guide, power to bind and protect the nations. Enlightened and impelled by this, a village in the oldest commonwealth and a cabin in the newest settlement will be the same to our view, and will share alike in our beneficent zeal, so far as we are enabled to benefit both. But the mighty regions far spreading beneath the declining sun, and all glowing with golden hopes, claim our devoutest and most active solicitude. The early and only extended journey of Him on whom all our hopes depend was westward, and such has ever been the increased development of his love and power. From Asia to Europe, from Europe to America, and from the rocky icy shore, where Salvation first greeted day rising from the stormy Atlantic, to mountain range beyond mountain range, empire valley beyond empire valley, clime beyond clime—the diameter of a world—to where the mightier Pacific hymns prophetic glories round the cradle of the mightiest human destinies rapidly consummating, His voice perpetually resounds,—"I am the light of the world!" Soon great voices will be heard proclaiming that the kingdoms of this world are become the kingdoms of our Lord and of His Christ. In view of our immediate duty, and assured of final triumph, we only add, as the captain of the armies of Israel said, on the eve of a great and decisive battle against the children of Ammon, "Be of good courage, and let us play the men for our people, and for the cities of our God, and the Lord do that which seemeth him good."

REPORT OF THE COMMITTEE ON THE GRANDE LIGNE MISSION.

Presented through the Chairman, Rev. L. Tracy, of New Hampshire.

The Committee, favored with the latest intelligence from the Grande Ligne Mission, are able to report encouragingly with respect to this important field. There are now laboring in connection with the Mission five ordained ministers, one licentiate, six teachers, and three colporteurs, all of whom except three, are French Canadians, and have been converted through the instrumentality of the Mission.

There are four organized churches, numbering at present, notwithstanding a great loss by emigration into the United States and by death, 170 members. The congregations number over 400, and the Protestant population under evangelical influence is about 1,000.

The two boarding institutions contain 35 boys and 18 girls, and the five primary schools afford the means of instruction to 130 scholars, who are not only taught the common branches of education, but are instructed in the truths of that blessed book which is able to make wise unto salvation.

The press, the great moral power of the age, is also employed in the cause of the truth with increasing success. The "Semeur Canadian," the only French protestant periodical published on the continent of America, has attained a good circulation. It is taken in about 150 parishes or villages, and reaches some 3000 individuals, one-half of whom are Roman Catholics of the educated class.

While we would gladly give utterance to sentiments of regret and respect, in reference to each of the loved ones, of whom death has bereaved us, the space to which we are limited forbids. When we journeyed last year to our anniversaries in Cleveland, SALLIE KNOWLES CROZER, of Pennsylvania, and a life director, made one of our happy circle. and gave to our society the charms of her youthful loveliness, and gentle piety. In September, she departed, and is not, for God hath taken her, and her sepulchre was the first to adorn the cemetery near her father's residence beside the church edifice his munificence erected, and in whose services and Sabbath school she so delighted, and was so eminently useful.

Some who were missionaries, and others, friends and patrons of our society, are missed from our midst. For the merciful interposition of divine goodness which smoothed their passage to the tomb, and irradiated their pathway with a light so pure and glorious, we would record our devout acknowledgements, as well as for the assurance that in a higher sphere where the Master called for them, not one of their estimable qualities will be lost. Many bereaved families and churches experience divine consolation, and in the assurance of our mutual sufferings, may our sympathies be also blended. May our Heavenly Father from whom cometh every good and every perfect gift, sanctify to us and to kindred organizations of christian benevolence this dispensation, and stimulate us all to trim our lamps and gird our loins anew, for more thorough and earnest devotion to the duties devolving upon us. May we reverently bow before His footstool, and say, from the heart, "*The will of the Lord be done.*"

One of the departed belonged to the Executive Board—of him we trace a few lines indicative of his useful life:—

REV. MORGAN JOHN RHEES, D.D., late pastor of the First Baptist Church in Williamsburgh, New York, had occupied his last pastorate less than three years, yet he had won the truest affection of his people, the entire confidence and respect of his brethren in the ministry, and the community where he resided. Rarely has it been our lot to be on terms of intimacy with a man who more truly represented the character of a good minister of Jesus Christ, who in all public and private relations commanded more fully our confidence and christian love.

Mr. Rhees was born in Somerset, western Pennsylvania, October 25th, 1802. After two years, his father, Rev. Morgan Rhees, died, and his mother removed to Philadelphia, where at the age of fifteen he entered upon a preparation for commercial life, having pursued classical studies up to that time in the school of Mr. James Ross. It appears, however, that his tendency towards professional life was so strong, that he nearly prepared himself for the practice of Law, during intervals of labor in the counting house.

Admitted early to the Philadelphia bar, he entered upon practice, with prospects of distinction both in legal and political life. After nearly three years, he became the subject of religious hopes, and joined the First Baptist Church under the care of Rev. William T. Brantley, D.D. After a brief struggle with convictions and worldly interests, he entered upon Theological studies under his pastor, and in a little while elevated himself to the gospel ministry.

About this time, the cause of temperance was assuming a distinct agency for good—he engaged in its service in the State Society, and labored in its behalf with energy and zeal. His devotion to this cause continued through life, wherever his services were required.

Mr. Rhees became pastor of the Baptist Church in Trenton, New Jersey, and continued eleven years, when he resigned, much to the regret of the people in that city, and became Corresponding Secretary of the American Baptist Publication Society, in Philadelphia. With invigorated health he resigned the duties which he had performed with fidelity, and became pastor of the Baptist Church in Wilmington, Del., where he remained eight years. Each church he served was enlarged and strengthened; and hoped that his usefulness might be prolonged many years. But God in wisdom said to him, "*Come up higher*," and he now fills a sphere of activity and joy, more absorbing and delightful than any he ever filled on earth.

An able and useful man cut down in the meridian of his years, with the glow of the conflict yet in his eye, sword in hand and armor on, seems to us mortals a waste of power. In our bereavement we assert that,

> "The good die first,
> While those whose hearts are dry as summer dust,
> Burn to the socket"

The Lord doth all things well. To him we submit, conscious of his ability to fill all the vacancies occasioned by his calling his servants home to the enjoyment of their reward. In the church of his care, in the various associations he

[redacted]

Messrs. Newton, Todd and Dowley, a Committee of donors, &c., respectfully report, That it appears from these letters that a number of brethren and friends of our denomination have united in raising a subscription of fifty-five thousand dollars, for the purpose of purchasing a property in Nassau street, in the city of New York. That they propose to have the same conveyed as a donation to the American and Foreign Bible Society; that they have determined and provided, that the American Baptist Home Mission Society may have suitable rooms and accommodations in the building for permanent occupancy, and free from rent; and that legal effect is to be given to these provisions in favor of this Society, in the conveyance of the property to the Bible Society, who have already taken possession of the premises:

That the letter from the Committee declares, that they have provided for and directed this tender, and cordially invite the Society to accept of it; and that the letter from the American and Foreign Bible Society conveys a copy of the resolutions of that Society, making a formal tender of the above, and their assurance that they will make the requisite legal instrument to carry it into effect:

That while the acknowledgements of the Society are due to the generosity of the First Baptist Church and Society, which for more than ten years has furnished them their present Rooms at a nominal rent, and to the brethren and friends who have made the proposal now under consideration, they believe that the propriety of a removal from their present location is a conclusion generally acquiesced in:

That they are exceedingly desirous that this matter should receive the harmonious and unanimous action of the Society, and that its peace, prosperity and usefulness, may know no other change than progress.

They, therefore, recommend to the Society the following resolutions:

Resolved, That the interests of the Society require the selection of a new location for the transaction of its business.

Resolved, That the Board of the Home Mission Society be directed to rent immediately suitable rooms for their accommodation, *provided* that pledges be given that the expense shall not be defrayed from the Society's general Treasury.

Resolved, That the Board be authorized to raise a fund for the purchase of suitable rooms for the Society, at an expense not exceeding forty thousand dollars, at the earliest opportunity within two years.

DECENNIAL CENSUS FOR MICHIGAN,

Showing the Counties in the State and their population; the number of Baptist Churches organized; their number of members; and the number of Church Edifices erected in each County up to the year 1840 and from 1840 to 1850.

COUNTIES.	1840. Population.	Churches.	Members.	Ministers.	1850. Population.	Churches.	Members.	Ministers.	Meeting houses erected.
Allegan	1783	1	20	1	5127	2	115	3	2
Barry	1078	....	....	....	5072	2	50	3	....
Berrian	5011	1	20	1	11417	2	258	3	2
Branch	5715	2	75	2	12472	6	238	3	2
Calhoun	10599	5	215	5	15165	7	543	6	4
Cass	5710	3	73	2	10906	8	379	5	3
Chippewa	534	1	15	1	898	1	27	1	1
Clinton	1614	1	45	1	5102	3	78	4	1
Eaton	2379	1	21	1	7058	4	85	5	....
Genesee	4268	2	80	2	12031	5	198	4	....
Hillsdale	7240	4	198	3	16159	10	471	6	4

[redacted]

DIRECTORS FOR LIFE.

BY VIRTUE OF A CONTRIBUTION OF ONE HUNDRED DOLLARS OR MORE.

Ackerman, John, Dobbs Ferry, N. Y.
Adams, Rev. Paul S., Newport, N. H.
Adsit, Rev, Samuel, Jr., Sennet, N. Y.
Akerly, Richard C , New-York.
Aldrich, Rev. Jonathan, Middleborough, Ms.
Alger. Henry, Cleveland, Ohio.
Alvord, Rev. Nelson, Chillicothe, Ill.,
Anderson, Rev. Thomas D., Roxbury, Mass.
Anderson, M. B., New-York.
Archer, Ezekiel, New-York.
Armstrong, Rev. James D., Baltimore.
Atwell, Rev. G. B., Pleasant Valley, Conn.
Averill, Rev. Alexander M., Newton Centre, Ms.
Ayre, Rev. Oliver, Claremont, N. H.
Babcock, Rev. Rufus, D. D., Poughkeepsie, N.Y.
Bacheller, Jonathan, Lynn, Mass.
Bailey, Benjamin D., Providence.
Bailey, Rev. Gilbert S., Pekin, Ill.
Bailey, Rev. Joseph A., Essex, Ct.
Ballard, Rev. Joseph, Brooklyn, N. Y.
Balen, Peter, Brooklyn, N. Y.
Banks, Jacob, Sculltown, N. J.
Banvard, Rev. Joseph, West Cambridge, Ms.
Barnaby, Rev. James, West Harwich, Mass.
Barker, Rev. Enoch M., Hightstown, N. J.
Barrell, Rev. Almond C., Le Roy, N. Y.
Bates, V. J., Providence.
Beecher, Rev. Luther F. D. D., Albany, N. Y.
Beecher, Mrs. Mary C., Albany, N. Y.
Belcher, Rev. Joseph, D. D., Philadelphia.
Bennet, Rev. Ira, Pike, N. Y.
Binney, Rev. J. G., Augusta, Ga.
Binney, Mrs. Juliet P., " "
Bishop, Nathan, Boston.
Blain, Rev. John, Charlestown, Mass.
Bliss, Rev. George R , Lewisburg, Pa.
Bly, Rev. William T., Berwick, Ill.
Bolles, Matthew, jr., Boston.
Bosworth, Rev. George W , S. Boston.
Bowles, Rev. Ralph H., Tariffville, Ct.
Bradford, Rev. S. S., Pawtucket, R I.
Brant, Randolph C., Rochester, N. Y.
Brayton, Rev. Jonathan, Centrevillee, R. I.
Brayton, Philip F., Providence.
Brooks, Iveson L., Hamburg, S. C.
Brown, Rev. J. Newton, Philadelphia.
Burlingham, Rev. A. H., Boston.
Burgess, Rev. J. J., Providence, R. I.
Bump, Nathaniel, Providence.
Burke, William, Rochester, N. Y.
Burke, Abraham C. Brooklyn, N. Y.
Butcher, Washington, Philadelphia.
Butterfield, Rev Isaac, Oswego, N. Y.
Byram, Rev. B. P., Amesbury, Mass.
Caldicott, Rev. T. F., D. D.. Charlestown, Mass.
Carleton, Rev. George J., Newton Centre, Ms.
Carleton, Mrs. Jane T., Newton Centre, Mass.
Carpenter, Rev. Mark, West Springfield, Mass.
Caswell, Rev. Alexis, Providence.
Caswell, Rev. Lewis E., Boston.
Chace, Prof. George I., Providence, R. I.
Challis, Rev. James M., Roadstown, N. J.
Chandler, John H., Bankok, Siam.
Chandler, Mrs. Helen M , Bankok, Siam.
Chaplin, Rev. Jeremiah, West Dedham, Mass.
Chaplin, Rev. Adoniram J.. Dover Plains, N. Y.
Cheney, Rev. David B., Philadelphia.
Child, Mrs. Sophronia L., Philadelphia.
Choules, Rev. John O , D. D., Newport, R. I.
Church, Rev. Pharcellus, D. D., Montreal, Can.
Church, Mrs. Chara E., Montreal, Can.
Clarke, Rev. Elbert W., China, N. Y.
Clarke, Rev. Minor G., Philadelphia.
Clapp, Benjamin, Franklindale, N. Y.
Cogswell, Rev. Wilson, Providence.
Cooke, Joseph J., Providence.
Cookson, Rev. John, England.
Cole, Rev. Jirah D., Chicago, Ill.
Colgate, William, New-York.
Colgate, Mrs. Jane, New-York.
Colver, Rev. Nathaniel, Detroit, Mich.
Collins, Rev. Samuel A., Rehoboth, Mass.
Collom, Rev. J. G., Mt. Holly, N. J.
Conant, John, Brandon, Vt.
Cone, Rev. Spencer H , D. D., New-York.
Cone, Mrs. Sally Wallace, New-York.
Cone, Edward Winfield, New-York.
Cone, Spencer Wallace, New-York.
Corwin, Rev. Jason, Washington, Ill.
Cottrell, Thomas, Greenwich, N. Y.
Covell, Rev. Lemuel, New-York.
Cramb, Rev. Augustus B., Metamora, Ill.
Crane, Rev. W. C., Hernando, Miss.
Crane, William, Baltimore.
Crane, James C., Richmond, Va.
Crosby, William B , New-York.
Crozer, John P., Chester, Pa.
Crozer, Mrs. Sarah L., Chester, Pa.
Crozer, Miss Margaret K., Chester, Pa.
Crozer, Miss Elizabeth, Chester, Pa.
Cushman, Rev. Elisha, Deep River, Ct.
Dagg, Rev John L., Penfield, Ga.
Damon, Mrs. Catharine, Ashby, Mass.
Davies, John M., Newark, N. J.
Davis, Rev. Henry, Columbus, Ohio.
Davis, Hon. Isaac, Worcester, Mass.
Davis, Mrs. Mary H. E., Worcester, Mass.
Day, Rev. Henry, Ashland, Mass.
Day, Prof Henry, Providence, R. I.
Devan, Rev. Thomas T., Lyons, France.
Devan, Mrs. Emma E., Lyons. France.
Dickinson, Rev. Edmund W., Lewisburg, Pa.

Webb, Rev. G. S., New-Brunswick, N. J.
Welch, Rev. B. T., D. D., Brooklyn, N. Y.
Welch, Rev. J. O., Providence.
Wheelock, Rev. Alonzo, Elbridge, N. Y.
Wheeler, Rev. Osgood C., Sacramento, Cal.
Whidden, Randall, Calais, Me.
Whittemore, A. F., Essex, Ct.
White, Rev. J. S., West Wrentham, Mass.
Whitehead, James M., New-York.
Whiting, Rev. Niles, Bloomfield, Ct.
Whiting, Miss Martha, Charlestown, Mass.
Whitney, Ezra S., Brooklyn, N. Y.
Wightman, Rev. F., Wethersfield, Ct.
[illegible]an, Rev. Palmer G., Lyme, Ct.
Wilbur, [illegible]a, Boston.
Wildman, Rev. N., Lebanon, Ct.
Willard, Rev. F. A., South Danvers,
Willett, Rev. Charles, New-London, C
Williams, David S., Fayetteville, N. C
Williams, Richard P., Essex, Ct.
Williams, Rev. William R., D.D., New
Wilson, Francis L., Catskill, N. Y.
Wilson, Daniel M., Newark, N. J.
Wilson, Mrs. Hannah M., Newark, N.
Wilson, Mrs. Caroline T., Plainfield,
Withers, John, Alexandria, D. C.
Winegar, Rev. R., Jr., Baldwinsville,
Winterton, William, New-York.
Wooster, Rev. Henry, Deep River, Ct
Wyckoff, William H., New-York.

MEMBERS FOR LIFE.

BY VIRTUE OF A CONTRIBUTION OF THIRTY DOLLARS.

Abbott, Rev. Elisha L., Arracan, Asia.
Ackley, Rev. Alvin, Greenport, N. Y.
Adams, Miss Priscilla S., New-York.
Adams, Mrs. Mary, West Killingly, Ct.
Adams, Rev. S. W. Cleveland, Ohio.
Adams, Miss Caroline, New-York.
Adams, Albert, Augusta, Ga.
Adams, Joseph H., Williamsburgh, N. Y.
Adams, Mrs. Mary, Williamsburgh, N. Y.
Adams, Jedediah, New-York.
Adams, Van Rensselaer, Deckertown, N. J.
Adams, Rev. J. N. Butternuts, N. Y.
Adsit, Mrs. Maria J., Sennett, N. Y.
Ainsworth, Rev. S. C., Brookfield, N. Y.
Akerly, Mrs. Priscilla E., New-York.
Akerly, George B., New-York.
Akerly, William Henry, New-York.
Albro, Mrs. Hannah Hill, New-York.
Alden, Rev. John, Westfield, Mass.
Aldrich, Warren, Lowell, Mass.
Alexander, Calvin, Shelburne Falls, Mass.
Allen, Russell, Shelby, N. Y.
Allen, Walter, New-York.
Allen, Ethan, Worcester, Mass.
Allen, Rev. Marvin, Detroit, Mich.
Allen, Rev. N. T., Groton Bank, Ct.
Allen, Rev. John, Groton, Mass.
Allen, Mrs. Lorena, New York.
Allen, Benjamin, Seekonk, Mass.
Allen, Thomas, Wilmington, Del.
Allen, Rev. Thomas, Tavoy, Burmah.
Aller, Amos, Brooklyn, N. Y.
Aller, Mrs. Amos, Brooklyn, N. Y.
Allin, George, Brooklyn, N. Y.
Alger, Mrs Suson, Cleveland, Ohio.
Almond, John P., Bostwick Mills, N. C.
Ambler, Rev. E C., Millington, N. J.
Ambler, M[illegible], Mrs. Almira, Millington, N.
Ambler, [illegible]nie[illegible] Starr H., Millington, N. J.
Amsburg, [illegible]abez, Norwich, Ct.
Andem, Rev [illegible] James, Neenah, Wis.
Amory, Peter B., [illegible] New-York.
Amory, Mrs. Anna [illegible] A., M., New-York.
Anderson, William T[illegible], Princeton, N.
Anderson, Mrs. Cathari[illegible]ne J., Prince
Anderson, John T., Verdo[illegible]n, Va.
Anderson, Peter, New-York[illegible] Eng
Anderson, J. S., Stonington, [illegible] Ct.
Anderson, William, Hoboken, [illegible] N. J.
Andrews, William, Providence.
Andrews, Mrs. Delilah, Providence
Andrews, Mrs. Wm., Providence.
Andrews, Ebenezer T., Boston.
Angier, Rev Aaron, Elbridge, N. Y.
Angus, Charles Benton, N. Y.
Archibald, Rev. Thos. H., East Greenwic
Archer, Charles O., New-York.
Ardis, Rev Henry Z., Zalofa, Fa.
Armitage, Rev. Thomas, New-York.
Appleton, George, Haverhill, Mass.
Appleton, James, Sonora, Cal.
Arents, Stephen, Brooklyn, N. Y.
Armstrong, Rev. Andrew, Lambertville,
Armstrong, Mrs. M S., Lambertville, N.
Arnold, Mrs Mary N., Attleboro, Mass.
Arnold, Mrs Frances R., Providence
Arnold, Rev. Benjamin B., Three Rivers,
Arnold, Miss Phebe, Jay, N. Y.
Ashley, Elisha, Poultney, Vt.
Atkinson, Taylor B., West Philadelphia,
Atwood, Lewis, Pawtucket, R. I
Austin, H., Tarborough, N C.
Austin, Edward, New York
Avery, Mrs Clara, New-York.

Merit, Rev. Columbus D., Henry, Ill.
Merriam, Jonathan, Newton Centre, Mass.
Messenger, Rev. Edward C., West Medway, Ms.
Milbank, Samuel, jr., New-York.
Miller, John A., Little Falls, N. J.
Miller, Pardon, Providence.
Miner, Mrs. Henrietta Wilson, Newark, N. J.
Mitchell, Isaac R., San Francisco, Cal.
Moore, Rev. Isaac, Plainfield, N. J.
Morton, Rev. Charles, Penn Yan, N. Y
Mulford, Rev. Clarence W. Holmdale, N. J.
Munn, Stephen B., New-York.
Munn, William H., New-York.
Murdock, Rev. J. N., Hartford, Ct.
Murphy, Rev. John C., New-York.
Muzzy, Rev. Lawson, Pulaski, N. Y.
Neale, Rev. Rollin H., D. D., Boston.
Newell, Asa, Providence.
Newton, Isaac, New-York.
Nichols, Joseph O., Newark, N. J.
Norris, William, Newark, N. J.
Northam, Rev. G., Norming Grove, Va.
Olcott, Rev. James B., Parma, N. Y.
Packer, Rev. D., Mount Holly, Vt.
Parker, Rev. J. W., D. D., Cambridgeport, Mass.
Parker, Rev. Carlton, Wayne, Me.
Parker, Rev. S. S., Paterson, N. J.
Parkhurst, Rev. John, Chelmsford, Mass.
Parkhurst, Rev. J. W., Newton Centre, Mass.
Parks, Rev. Norman, Perry, Ill.
Parmelee, Rev. D. S., New-York.
Pattison, Rev. R. E., D.D., Newton Centre, Mass.
Pattison, Rev. Wm. P., Auburn, N. Y.
Paul, Albert, Hastings, N. Y.
Peck, Rev. John M., D. D., Lebanon, Ill.
Perkins, Rev. Aaron, Hamilton, N. Y.
Perkins, Rev. G. B. Cleveland, Ohio.
Phelps, Rev. S. Dryden, New-Haven, Ct.
Philips, Rev. Daniel W., South Reading, Mass.
Pier, Sylvester, New-York.
Pigsley, Rev. Welcome, Metamora, Ill.
Platt, Nathan C., New-York.
Plummer, John L., Roxbury, Mass.
Pollard, Rev. Andrew, Taunton, Mass.
Pratt, Rev. D. D., Nashua, N. H.
Prevaux, Rev. Francis E., San Francisco, Cal.
Price, Rev. Jacob, Edwardsburg, Mich.
Rathbone, John F, Albany, N. Y.
Raymond, Rev. Robert R., Syracuse, N. Y.
Read, James H., Providence.
Reed, Rev. Nathan A., Winchester, Mass.
Reid, Rev. William, Bridgeport, Ct.
Remington, Rev. Stephen, Philadelphia.
Richardson, Thomas, Boston.
Richardson, Rev. J. G., Lawrence, Mass.
Richmond, Rev. J. L, Union, N. Y.
Roberts, Charles L. New-York.
Rollinson, Rev. William, San Francisco, Cal.
Sanderson, Rev. A., Littleton, Mass.
Sarles, Rev. John W., Brooklyn, N. Y.
Sawyer, Rev. Reuben, Chester, Vt.
Searl, Rev. David, Springville, N. Y.
Seeley, Rev. John T., Dundee, N. Y.
Serrell, John J., New-York.
Serrell, Mrs. Mary Eliza, New-York.
Shadrach, Rev. W., Lewisburg, Pa.
Shailer, Rev. N. E, Deep River, Ct.
Shailer, Rev. Julius S., Roxbury, Mass.
Shailer, Rev. Davis T., North Becket, Mass.
Shailer, Rev. William H., Brookline, Mass.
Shardlow, Samuel, New-York.
Sharp, Rev. Daniel, D. D., Boston.
Shaw, Thomas, Boston.
Shedd, Rev. Philander, Penn Yan, N. Y.
Shepardson, Rev. D., Cincinnati, Ohio.
Sherwood, Rev. A., Upper Alton, Ill.
Skinner, Charles W., Hertford, N. C.
Skinner, John L., Windsor, Vt.
Smith, Gordon, Essex, Ct.
Smith, Rev. S. F., Newton Centre, Mass.
Smith, Rev. Henry F., Hastings, N. Y.
Smith, Mrs. Sarah B. Hastings, N. Y.
Smitzer, Rev. John, Delhi, N. Y.
Sommers, Rev. Charles G., New-York.
Spencer, O, Salt Lake, Utah Ter.
Spencer, William B., Phenix, R. I.
Stanwood, Rev. Henry, Rush, N. Y.
Steward, Rev. Ira R, New-York.
Stockbridge, Rev. Joseph, New-York.
Stockbridge, Rev. John C., Providence, R. I.
Stow, Rev. Baron, D. D., Boston.
Stow, Rev. Phineas, Boston.
Stowell, Nathaniel, Worcester, Mass.
Stubberts, Rev. William F. S., Malden, Mass.
Swan, Rev. Jabez L., New-London, Ct.
Swaim, Rev. Samuel B., Worcester, Mass.
Taggart, Rev. Joseph W., New-York.
Taylor, Rev. J. B., Richmond, Va.
Taylor, Rev. E. E. L, Brooklyn, N. Y.
Taylor, Stewart M., New-York.
Taylor, Daniel G., New-York.
Teasdale, Rev. T. C., D. D., Washington, D. C.
Thomas, Mrs. Catharine W., New-York.
Thomas, Mrs. Margaret L., New-York.
Thomas, Cornelius W., New-York.
Thomas, Augustus, New-York.
Thompson, Mrs. Huldah E., New-London, Ct.
Tingley, Rev. T. C., West Boylston, Mass.
Tinsley, Rev. Isaac, Charlottesville, Va.
Timmons, John M., Effingham, S. C.
Torian, Thomas, Halifax, Va.
Tracy, William, New-York.
Tracy, Rev. Leonard, Burlington, Vt.
Train, Rev. Arthur S. Haverhill, Mass.
Tryon, Mrs. Louisa J, Houston, Texas.
Tucker, Rev. Elisha, D. D, Chicago, Ill.
Tucker, Rev Levi, D. D., Boston.
Tucker, Daniel N., New-York.
Tucker, Rev. Anson, Lafayette, Ia.
Tucker, F, Stony Creek, Va.
Tufts, Mrs. Mary, Fitchburg, Mass.
Turpin, Mrs Mary A., Augusta, Ga.
Turpin, William H., Augusta, Ga.
Valentine, David T., New-York.
Vanderveer, John, Moorestown, N. J.
Verrinder, Rev. Wm., Jersey City, N. J.
Walthall, Rev. Joseph S., Richmond, Va.
Washington, Col. John M., Portsmouth, N. H.
Wattson, Thomas, Philadelphia.
Wayland, Rev. Francis, D. D., Providence.

Betts, Rev Platt, East Chatham, N. Y.
Bevan, Rev. Isaac, Reading, Pa.
Beverly, Miss Elizabeth, New-York.
Biddle, Samuel S., Newbern, N C.
Biddle, Rev. William P. Newbern, N. C.
Biddle, Rev. William, Brookfield, Ct.
Bidgood, Mrs. L., Hargrove's, Va.
Bigelow, Rev. John R., New-York.
Bigelow, Mrs. Eunice P., New-York.
Billings, Rev. John, Mt. Vernon, Me.
Billings, Mrs. Betsey, Mt. Vernon, Me.
Billingslea, Dr. C., Montgomery co., Ala.
Biglow, John B., Brooklyn, N. Y
Biglow, Franklin H., Brooklyn, N Y.
Biglow, Mrs. Charlotte, Brooklyn, N. Y.
Bird, Rev. John, Lloyd's, Essex co., Va.
Bishop, Jesse, Cleveland, Ohio.
Blackwell, P. Brooklyn, N. Y
Blackenton Sanford, North Adams, Mass.
Blain, Mrs. Amy A., Charlestown, Mass.
Blake, Aaron, Chelsea, Mass.
Blake, Jonathan, Brooklyn, N. Y.
Blanding, Dr. S., Columbia, S. C.
Blackmer, rah, Wheatland, N. Y.
Bleecker, Garrat N., New-York.
Bleecker, Mrs. Caroline, New-York.
Bleecker, Mrs. Jane, New-York.
Bleecker, George W. Brooklyn, N. Y.
Bliss, Elijah J Brooklyn, N Y
Bliss, Erastus L., North Adams, Mass.
Blodgett, James D., Haverhill, Mass.
Blodgett, Loring B., Cortlandville, N. Y.
Blood, Isaiah, Ballston Spa N Y
Blood, Cyrus G., Davenport, Iowa.
Blood, A. P., Ballston, N. Y
Bloodgood, ames, Springville, N. Y.
Blunt, Mrs. B., Edenton, N. C.
Bly, Mrs. Lydia, Ticonderoga, N. Y.
Boardman, Thomas, Amesbury, Mass.
Boardman, Wm. G., Albany, N Y.
Bogart, Rev. Wm., Pittsfield, Mass.
Bokee, Hon. David A., Brooklyn, N Y.
Bolles, James G., Hartford, Ct.
Boomer, Rev. James C., Chelmsford, Mass.
Bond, Lewis, Windsor, N C.
Bond, Leonard, New-York.
Bond, Rev. George W., Knoxville, Iowa.
Bonham, Daniel, Berryville, Va.
Boone, Dr. Levi D., Chicago, Ill.
Boone, Mrs. L. D., Chicago, Ill.
Booth, Miss Lydia, Poughkeepsie, N. Y.
Borden, Lawdwick, Fall River, Mass.
Borden, Isaac, do do
Borden, Charles do do
Borden, Joseph, do do
Borden, Cook, do do
Bosson, George P., Chelsea, Mass.
Bosson, Benjamin P. Chelsea, Mass.
Bostick, Elisha, Bostick's Mills, N. C.
Bostick, Elijah, do do
Bostick, Tristam, do do
Bostick, Benj. R., Robertsville, S. C.
Bostick, Mrs. Jane A., Robertsville, S. C.
Boswell, Davis, Stilesville, Ia.
Bosworth, William M., East Poultney, Vt.
Bottom, Nathan H., Shaftsbury, Vt.
Bottom, Mrs. Peace, Shaftsbury, Vt.
Boughton, James, New-York.
Boughton, Rev. N., Delavan, Wis.
Boutelle, Miss Sylvia, East Cambridge, Mass.
Bouton, Mrs. Sarah M., New-York.
Bowen, John, New-York.
Bowen, Henry, Ch li Centre, N. Y.
Bowen, David M., Canton N. J.
Bowen, Miss Lydia M., Providence.
Bowen, Rev. William, Hancock, Mass.
Bowen, William New-York.
Bowen, Mrs. A. K. Cortlandville, N. Y.
Bower, Rev. William, Westboro, Mass.
Bower, Rev. acob, Manchester Il
Bowers, Rev. C M., Clintonv lle, Mass.
Bowers, Mrs. Hannah D., Seekonk, Mass.
Boyakin, Rev. Wm. F., Carrollton, Ill.
Boyce, Peter, Green Point, N. Y.
Boyce, Mrs. Albina, Providence.
Boyd, Rev. Robert, London, Canada.
Boyden, Addison, South Dedham, Ms.
Brabrook, Rev B. F Davenport, Iowa.
Brabrook, M Lucy A., Davenport, Iowa.
Brabrook, Alfred, Taunton, Mass.
Brabrook, Joseph A., Lowell, Mass.
Bradford, W R., Boston.
Bradford John, Wilm ngton, Del.
Brainerd, Samuel, Haverhill Mass.
Brainerd, Mrs. Samuel, Haverhill, Mass.
Branch, Rev. Nicholas Springvale, Me.
Branch, Rev. William, Williamsville, N. Y.
Bradley, Collins, Mt. Vernon, Mich.
Brantly, Rev. William T., Augusta, Ga.
Bray, Joseph M., Brooklyn, N. Y.
Brayton, Philip, Phenix, R. I.
Brayton, Mrs. Mary Ann, Quidnic, R. I.
Briggs, Arnold, Fairhaven, Vt.
Briggs, Rev. Avery, Rock Island, Ill.
Breed, Rev Joseph B. Woonsocket, R. I.
Breed, Mrs. Frances A. C., Woonsocket, R. I.
Brewer, Mrs. Elizabeth, New-York.
Bridgens, Miss Mary Ann, Brooklyn, N. Y.
Bridgewood, Mrs. Jane, Williamsburgh, N. Y.
Brierly, Rev. Benj., San Francisco, Cal.
Brigham Sylvester, Dover, Ill.
Bright, Rev. T Elkhorn, Wis.
Brisbane, Rev. Wm. H., Cheviot, O.
Brisbane, Miss Maria, Charleston, S. C.
Briscoe, Sally C., Va.
Broaddus, Rev. William F., Versailles, Ky.
Broaddus, Mrs. Mary A Versailles, Ky.
Brockett, Rev. Pierpont, Hartford, Ct.
Brockway, Mrs. Elizabeth, Broadalbin, N. Y.
Britton, W. G., Britton's X Roads, N. C
Bromley, Isaac, Norwich, Ct.
Bromley, Rev. Henry, Port Jefferson, N. Y.
Bromley, Mrs. Jane M., Port Jefferson, N. Y.
Brouner, Mrs. Sarah, New-York.
Brouwere, Vermilyea T., Dundee, N. Y.
Bronson, Rev. Asa, Fall River, Mass.
Bronson, Rev. Benjamin F Methuen, Mass.
Bronson, Mrs. A C., Methuen, Mass.
Bronson, Miss Aydee A., Townsend, Mass.
Brooks, Rev. Kendall, Eastport, Me.
Browe, E. S. New-Brunswick, N. J.

Brower, Davis E., Philadelphia.
Brown, W. S., Britton's X Roads, N. C.
Brown, Josiah, Haverhill, Mass.
Brown, J. S., Shelburne Falls, Mass.
Brown, Hon. Wm. B., Spencerport, N. Y.
Brown, Edward L., Brooklyn, N. Y.
Brown, Mrs. Susan A., Brooklyn, N. Y.
Brown, Rev. Amasy, South Gardner, Mass.
Brown, Rev. Dana, Nashua, N. H.
Brown, Rev. E. T. Wooster, O.
Brown, Andrew, Middletown, N. J.
Brown, Geo W., New-York.
Brown, Miss Fanny, Westerly, R. I.
Brown, Hugh H., Providence.
Brown, Rev. E. C. Bath, N. Y
Brown, Rev. F. G., West Townsend, Mass.
Brown, Rev. Wm. L., Westboro, Mass.
Brown, Rev. Joseph P., Moosup, Ct.
Brown, Mrs. Emily M. A., Fauquire, Va.
Brown, Mrs. O. B., Washington, D. C.
Brown, Mrs. Elizabeth E., Aylett's Va.
Brown, Miss Ann F., Providence.
Brown, Mrs Maria S., New-York.
Brown, Mrs, Mary F., Keene, N. H.
Brown, Mrs. Isaac, Haverh ll, Mass.
Brown, Rev. J. F Spread Eagle, Pa.
Brown, Rev. Philip P., Holland Patent, N. Y.
Brown, Rev. William, Eaton, N Y
Brownell, Rev. E. W East Hillsdale, N Y.
Brownson, Rev. I. K., Chittenango, N. Y.
Bruen, George H., Newark, N. J
Bruen, Mrs. George H., Newark, N. J.
Bruce, Benjamin G., New-York.
Bruce, Silas, Townsend, Mass.
Brumley, Dewey, Norwich, Ct.
Brush, George P., New-York.
Brush, Mrs. Susan G., New-York.
Brusle, William A., New-York.
Brusle, Mrs. Elizabeth, New-York.
Bryant, George, Williamsburgh, N Y.
Bryant, Mary A., Chelsea, Mass.
Bryant, Elizabeth D., Chelsea, Mass.
Buckbee, Rev. C. A New-York.
Buckbee, Mrs Laura G., New-York.
Bucknell, Wm. jr., Ph ladelphia
Bucknell, Miss Levinia Louise, Philadelphia.
Bucknell, Mrs. Harriet M., Philadelphia.
Bucknall, Ebenezer G., Newark, N. J.
Bucknall, Miss Elizabeth, Newark, N. J.
Buckner, Mrs. Sarah T., Baltimore.
Budlong, ames E. Providence.
Budlong, Mrs. Rebecca S. C., Providence.
Budd, Francis F., Williamsburgh, N. Y.
Buel, Rev. Rufus F., Greece.
Buel, Mrs. Mary J., Greece.
Buffinton, Benjamin, Fall River, Mass.
Bullard, Rev. Joseph A., Ware, Mass.
Bullock, George, Utica, N. Y.
Bulkley, Rev. Justus, erseyville, Ill.
Bulkley, Mrs. Harriet, Jerseyville, Ill.
Bunnell, Rev. W. B., Yates, N Y.
Bunnell, Mrs. Elizabeth E., Yates, N. Y.
Burbank, Mrs. Irene, New-York.
Burbank, Wellman, Chelsea, Mass.
Burdick, Perrin, New-York.
Burger, William H., New-York.
Burger, Mrs. Rebecca T., New-York.
Burgess, Alexander, Providence.
Burke, Mrs Louisa S. Rochester, N. Y.
Burke, Miss Emma, Brooklyn, N Y.
Burke, Mrs. Elizabeth, Brooklyn, N. Y.
Burnett, Rev. C. C., Worcester, Mass.
Burnett, Charles C., Worcester, Mass.
Burnett, Mrs. Maria M., Suffield, Ct.
Burnett, Eli S., West Philadelphia.
Burnett, Rev. Hiram, Mt. Pleasant, Iowa.
Burr, James T Columbus, Ohio.
Burroughs, James M., Marlton, N. J.
Burroughs, Caleb G., Providence.
Burroughs, Rev. David, Amherst, N. H.
Burroughs, Rev. J. C. Chicago, Ill.
Burrows, Rev. Baxter, Grafton, Vt.
Burrows, Rev. J. L., Philadelphia.
Burrows, John R. Providence.
Burt, T. M., Kinderhook, N. Y
Burt, Edwin C., Brooklyn, N Y.
Burt, Mrs. Edwi C., Brooklyn, N. Y.
Burt, ames, Brooklyn, N. Y.
Burt, John W., Brooklyn, N. Y.
Burt, James M., Brooklyn, N. Y.
Burt, Wm. A., Mount Vernon, Mich.
Burt, William, Mount Vernon, Mich.
Burt, Wells, Mount Vernon, Mich.
Burtt, Rev. Joseph M., North Tewksbury, Mass.
Butler, Rev. John, Lewiston, Me.
Butcher, Mrs. Mary, Philadelphia.
But Mrs. Sarah, Lansingburg, N. Y.
Butts, Mrs Sarah A., Cleveland, Ohio.
Butts, Mrs. Elizabeth, Boston.
Byron, Wm. H., Milwaukee.
Cady Edwin, Danville, Iowa.
Caillhopper, Rev. F T Allowaystown, N. J.
Calder, John, Providence.
Callom, Mrs. Mary N, Sing Sing, N. Y.
Capron, Rev. Orion H. Tyringham, Mass.
Capron, Miss Rebecca S. Worcester, Mass.
Capwell, Albert B., Brooklyn, N. Y.
Capwell, Mrs Julia A., Brooklyn, N. Y.
Card, Rev. Wm H, La Cross, Wis
Card, Rev Henry S., Hinsdale, N. Y
Carleton, Miss Frances, Newton Centre, Ms.
Carleton, Miss Emelina H., Newton Centre, Ms.
Carleton, G R Newton Centre, Ms.
Carleton, Judson, Newton Centre, Ms.
Carleton, Howard, Newton Centre, Ms.
Carleton, Wm H., Newton Centre, Ms.
Carlton, Stephen Lowell, Mass.
Carraway, Mrs. H., Kingston, N. C.
Carew, Miss Emma H, New York.
Carew, Mrs Margaret N., New-York
Carroll, Mrs Sarah A S., Washington, N. C.
Carpenter, Daniel T, Pawtucket, R I.
Carpenter, Mrs. Elizabeth, Pawtucket, R. I.
Carpenter, Miss Lydia, Pawtucket, R. I.
Carpenter, Rev. Calvin G Phelps, N. Y.
Carpenter, Rev J M., Jacobstown, N. J.
Carpenter, Rev. Burton B. Griggsville, Ill.
Carpenter, James, New-York.
Carpenter, J. H, Willimantic, Ct.
Carmer, Henry, Griggsville, Ill.

Carr, Rev. Samuel J., Mansfield, Mass.
Carr, Alexander W., Rowley, Mass.
Carter, Mrs. Sarah, Richmond, Va.
Carter, Miss Mary, New-York.
Carr, Joseph, Charlestown, Mass.
Carver, Mrs. Relief E., Nunda, N. Y.
Case, Rev. Zenas, Adam's Basin, N. Y.
Case, Alonzo, Jordon, N. Y.
Caswell Mrs Esther Lois, Providence.
Caswell, Miss Martha S., Charlestown, Mass.
Cauldwell, Mrs. Cornelius, New-York.
Cauldwell, Miss Elizabeth, New-York.
Cauldwell, Ebenezer, New-York.
Cauldwell, Henry W., New-York.
Cauldwell, Mrs Susan W., New-York.
Cauldwell, Miss Anne Jane, New-York.
Cauldwell, Mrs. Ann, Whitesboro, N. Y.
Cauldwell, Mrs. Ann B., New-York.
Cavis, John, Lowell, Mass.
Chace, George I, Providence.
Chaffin, Rev. Aaron W., Danvers Mills, Mass.
Chalfant, Jacob M., Wilmington, Del.
Challiss, Mrs. Lydia Roadstown, N. J.
Challis, John, Salem, N. J.
Chambers, Azariah, Marion, N. C.
Chamberlin, Edward, Boston, Mass.
Chambers, John, Pemberton, N. J.
Champlin, Henry N.
Chapel, R. S., Brooklyn, N. Y.
Chapman, Allen A., Baltimore.
Chapman Rev John S., Tobehanna, N. Y.
Chapman, William H, New York.
Chapman, J. M.
Chapman Henry F., New-York.

Clark, Mrs. Juliet, Marlborough, N. H.
Clark, Miss E., Beaufort, S. C.
Clark, Mrs. M. G., Philadelphia.
Clark, Mrs. Elizabeth, New-York.
Clark, Miss Sallie Cone, New-York.
Clark, Miss Clarissa, Deep River, Ct.
Clark, Miss Eliza, Syracuse, N. Y.
Clark, Teresa B., Lakeville, N. Y.
Clark, Rev. C. A., Cleveland, O.
Clark, Henry, Plantsville, Ct.
Clarke, Rev. Henry, Pittsfield, Mass.
Clarke, Rev. John, Esquessing, C. W.
Clarke, William, Syracuse, N. Y.
Cleaves, Rev. F. E., Lowell, Mass.
Clement, Wm. T., Shelburne Falls, Mass.
Clopton, Rev. James C., Lynchburg, Va.
Clopton, Mrs. M., New-Kent, Va.
Coburn, Rev. J. M., Brunswick, Me.
Cobb, Mrs. Sarah, M., Brooklyn, N. Y.
Coburn, Charles, Fall River, Mass.
Cocke, Charles L., Richmond, Va.
Cockran, Justen, Lowell, Mass.
Coffin, Rev. Jas. L., Tyrone, N. Y.
Cogswell, B F., Brooklyn, N. Y.
Coggeshall, John, jr., New-Bedford, Mass.
Coggeshall, Mrs. Elizabeth, New-Bedford, Mass.
Cogswell, Mrs. Mary, Haverhill, Mass.
Coit, Miss Elizabeth, New-London, Ct.
Colby, Rev. Lewis, New-York.
Colby, Hon. Anthony, New-London, N. H.
Colby, Mrs. Eliza A., New-London, N. H.
Colby, Isaac, Salem, Mass.
Colby, Gardener, Newton, Mass.
Colburn, Rev. Alfred, Boston.

[redacted]

Condit, Miss Sarah E., New-York.
Cone, Spencer H., jr., New-York.
Cone, Miss Kate E., New-York.
Cone, Miss Amelia M., Philadelphia.
Conklin, Mrs. Ann, New-York.
Conover, Robert Petersburgh. Ill.
Conrad, Rev. Peter, Delton, Wis.
Converse. Rev. Otis, Grafton, Mass.
Cook, Mrs. Patience, Richmond, N. H.
Cook, Henry G., New-York.
Cook, Rev. Samuel, Dunbarton, N. H.
Cook, Lewis, Plantsville, Ct.
Cook, Wm. W., Whitehall, N. Y.
Coolidge, Mrs. Caroline G., Brookline, Mass.
Coolidge. William, Bouckville, N. Y.
Coolidge, John, Watertown. Mass.
Coolidge. Mrs. Mary S., Watertown, Mass.
Coolidge. Josiah, Cambridge, Mass.
Cooper, William, New-York.
Cooper, Edwin, Hoboken, N. J.
Cooper, Rev. Warren, Boylston, Mass.
Cooper, Eliphalet, New-Haven, Ct.
Cooper. Charles, New-York.
Corbett. O. G., Brooklyn, N. Y.
Corey. Rev. D. G., Utica, N Y.
Corlies, Briton, Philadelphia.
Cornell, A. C., Broadalbin, N. Y.
Cornell, Thomas, Rondout, N. Y.
Cornwell. Rev. William E., Norristown, Pa.
Corning, Ephraim, Brooklyn, N. Y.
Corwin, R. G., Lebanon, Ohio.
Cottrell, Mrs. Mary, Battenville, N. Y.
Cottrell, Miss Mary, Union Village, N. Y.
Cowan, Mrs. Hannah, New-York.
Cowdin, Mrs. Aurinda G., Fitchburg, Mass.
Cowles, Mrs. Rebekah, Claremont, N. H.
Cowles, Miss Juliette R., Claremont, N. H.
Cox, Rev. Morgan R., Seaville, N. J.
Cox, Mrs. Mary B., Seaville, N. J.
Cox, Miss Mary, New-York.
Cox, Mrs. Achsah Imlaystown, N. J.
Coxey, James, West Philadelphia, Pa.
Coy, Silvanus B., West Dedham, Mass.
Crabs, Rev. J. D., Claysville, Ia.
Craig, Rev. A. M., Britain's ✕ Roads, N. C.
Craig, Charles A , Bridgeport, Ct.
Cramer, Geo. W., Troy, N. Y.
Crane, Richard M., Newark, N. J.
Crane, Henry F., Rehoboth, Mass.
Crane, Miss Sarah H., Rehoboth, Mass.
Crane, Rev. Origin, Weston, Mass.
Crane, Rev. Daniel M., N. Hampton, Mass.
Crane, Mrs. Mary L , New-York.
Crane, Rev. W. I., Adrian, Mich.
Crandall, Mrs. J. A., Petersburg. N. Y.
Crandall, Rev. Nelson, South Hannibal, N. Y.
Crawford, Mrs. Almira A., Brooklyn, N. Y.
Crawford, Mrs. Charlotte, New-York.
Crawford, Ira. Poughkeepsie, N. Y.
Creath, Rev. Thomas B., Jarrott's. Va.
Creathe, Rev. J. W. D., Fantharpe's, Texas.
Crenshaw, Dr. W. M., Forrestville, N. C.
Cressy, Rev. Timothy R., St. Paul, Min.
Cresswell, Rev. Samuel J., Philadelphia.
Crocker, Gurdon, New-London, Ct.
Crocker, William A., New-York.
Crossman, Nathan, Elbridge, N. Y.
Croysdale, Abram, Paterson, N. J.
Crooker, Josiah F., Providence.
Crumb, Rev. J. W., Clifton Park, N. Y.
Crumb, Mrs. R. F., Clifton Park, N. Y.
Cruser, Holger, Brooklyn, N. Y.
Culp, Theophilis, New-York.
Culver, Mrs. Susan, New-London, Ct.
Cummings, Mrs. Daniel, Chelsea, Mass.
Cummings, Mrs. Abigail, Cambridge, Mass.
Cummings, George, Cambridge, Mass.
Cummings, Rev. E. E., Pittsfield, N. H.
Cummings, Mrs. Emily C., Amherst, Mass.
Cunningham, Rev. O., Middlefield, Mass.
Curry, John, Hamburg, S. C.
Curry, Mrs. Harriet, Hamburgh, S. C.
Curren, Rev. Joseph, Evansburg, Pa.
Currier, Rev. Joshua, La Motte, Iowa.
Cutler, Micajah, Lynn, Mass.
Curtis, Rev. William, Columbia, S. C.
Curtis, Rev. T. T., Tuscaloosa, Ala.
Curtis, Rev. William B., Utica, N. Y.
Curtis, Mrs. Elizabeth. Aurora, Ia.
Cushing, Samuel T., Boston.
Cusick, Rev. James, Brantford, C. W.
Cushman, Frederick A., New-York.
Cushman, Mrs. Charlotte E., Deep River, Ct.
Cushman, Mrs Elizabeth, Deep River, Ct.
Cutting, Rev. S. S., Framingham, Mass.
Cutting, Mrs. Elizabeth B., Framingham, Mass.
Dabney, Mrs. E. T., Jackson, Va.
Dagg, Mrs. John L., Pennfield, Ga.
Dakin, Rev. H. R., Pultney, N. Y.
Dale, Rev. H. S., Lebanon. Ohio.
Dalrymple. James, Bridgeton, N. J.
Damon, Rev. J. B., Lake Village, N. H.
Dana, John B., Cambridge, Mass.
Danelson, Mrs. Jemima, Brooklyn, N. Y.
Danforth, Rev. G. F., South Dartmouth, Mass.
Daniels, Mrs. E. E., Wyoming, N. Y.
Daniels, Rev. Harrison, Wyoming, N. Y.
Daniels, Mrs. Dexter, Providence.
Daniels, J. H.
Daniels, Clark, New-London, Ct.
Dannat, Mrs. Susannah J., New-York.
Dannat, Miss Mary C., New-York.
Darby, Rev. C. Central Green, N. Y.
Darrow, Rev. George R., Providence.
Davant, R. J., Gillisonville, S. C.
Davenport, Joshua, New-York.
Davies, Mrs. Alice S. H., Newark, N. J.
Davis, Mrs. Eliza H., Columbus, Ohio.
Davis, Miss Mary E., Worcester, Mass.
Davis, Edward L., Worcester, Mass.
Davis, Joseph E., Worcester, Mass.
Davis, Miss Sarah M., Worcester, Mass.
Davis, Miss Anna E., Worcester, Mass.
Davis, Miss Alice W., Worcester, Mass.
Davis, W , Strebane, N. C.
Davis, Evan. New-York.
Davis, Reuben P., Waltham, Mass.
Davis, Walter G., New-York.
Davis, Rev. Jonathan. Monticello, S. C.
Davis, Rev. C. B., Paris, Me.

Davis, Mrs. Louisa G., Paris, Me.
Davis, Rev. John, Yarmouth, Nova Scotia.
Davis, Rev Thomas, Wantage, N. J.
Davis, Rev. Judson, Ira, N. Y.
Davis, Lydia, Haverhill, Mass.
Davis, Mrs. Harriet M Nashua, N. H.
Davy, Miss Bertha, New-York.
Dawley, Joseph E., Fall River, Mass.
Day, H. W., Boston, Mass.
Day, John, New-York.
Day, Mrs. Fidelia, Haverhill, Mass.
Dayton, Morgan H New-York
Dean, H. J., Spartanburg, S. C.
Dean, Jirah, Flat Brook, N. Y.
Dean, Rev. Wm , Hong Kong, China.
Dean, Esther G., North Adams, Mass.
Dearborn, Rev Shelburn, Lowell, Wis.
Dearborn, Mrs. Emeline L., Lowell, Wis.
Decker, Alfred, New-York.
Decker, M Kesiah R., New-York.
Decker, Abel, New-York.
Decker Mrs. Abigail, New-York.
Decker, Miss Mary A. New-York.
Decker, Matthew Rahway, N. J.
Decker, William P, Hami ton, N. Y.
De La Montange, Miss lia, New-York.
Delle Torre, Joseph, New-York.
Demerest, Miss Jane, New-York.
Demarest, Samuel C Boston.
Demarest, Silas, New-York.
Deming, Amos, Savoy, Mass.
Deming, Mrs. El za J Cleveland, Ohio.
Denike, Abram, New-York.
Denike, Mrs. Adeline, New-York.
Dennis, Mrs. Elizabeth, New-York.
Dennis, Richard, Lowell, Mass.
Dennison, Charles W Boston.
Denison, Rev. Erastus, West Tisbury, Mass.
Denison, Mrs. Prudence, do do
Denison, Mrs. la, Skaneatles, N. Y.
Denison, Rev. Nathan, Skaneatles, N. Y.
Denison, Mrs. Amelia E , Deep River, Ct.
Devore, Mrs. Catharine, Edgefield, S. C.
Deweese, Samuel, West Philadelphia.
Dewey Wm G., Mystic, Ct.
Dewey, J hn H. Manchester, N. Y.
Dewhurst, Eli, Lowell, Mass.
Dewitt, Rev. J. V Virgal, N. Y
Dickinson, Mrs Caroline A., Lewisburgh, Pa.
Dickinson, Wm. W., Golandsville, Va.
Dimmock, Rev. Anth'y V Baldwinsville, Mass.
Dispeau, Mrs. Lucinda, Grafton, Mass.
Dixson, Rev. Joseph A., Evansville, Ia.
Doan, Ezra, Hudson, N. Y.
Doane, Miss Rachel F., Danvers, Mass.
Doby, John, Sen., Edgefield, S. C.
Dodge, Mrs. Eliza P., New-York.
Dodge, Rev Orrin, Ballston Spa, N. Y.
Dodge, Rev. Ebenezer, New-London, N. H.
Dodge, Solomon H Cambridge, Mass.
Dodge, Miss Hannah A., Townsend, Mass.
Dodge, Mrs Alice C., Haverhill, Mass.
Dodson, Rev. Elijah, Woodburn, Ill.
Dole, Mrs. Lydia T., Haverhill, Mass.
Doolittle, Mrs. Amanda, New-York.
Doolittle, Rev. H. D., So. Williamstown, Mass.
Donald, J. W., East Cambridge, Mass.
Dongan, Mrs. Lucretia, New-York.
Dorrance, Samuel B., Brooklyn, N. Y.
Douglass, Henry, Bethel, N. Y
Douglas, George, Gorham, N Y
Dougherty, George T., New-York.
Dowlin, Mrs. Maria S., New-York.
Dowlin, Miss Mary J., New-York.
Dowling, Rev. Thomas, Agawam, Mass.
Dowling, Mrs. Rebecca, New-York.
Dowley, John, New-York.
Downey, Rev. Francis, Whiteby, Pa.
Downing, J., Colerain, N. C.
Downs, Mrs. Harriet B , Malden, Mich.
Doyen, Mrs. A. F Haverh ll, Mass.
Drake, Ephraim, Plainfield, N. J
Drake, Mrs. A L , Plainfield, N. J.
Drake, Rev. George, New-Brunswick, N. J.
Driver, Rev. Thomas, Lynn, Mass.
Dubois, Richard, Canton, N J.
Dudley, John L., Baltimore.
Dugan, William T Brooklyn, N. Y.
Dugan, M Eliza, Brooklyn, N. Y.
Duncan, Hon. James H. Haverhill, Mass.
Duncan, Mrs. James H., Haverhill, Mass.
Duncan, Mrs. Samuel, Haverhill, Mass.
Duncan, Mrs E. E., Jackson, Va.
Duncan, Rev. H. A. Coosawhatchie, S. C.
Dunlap, Abraham B., Brooklyn, N. Y
Dunlap, Mrs. Eliza, Brooklyn, N. Y
Dunlap, Rev. James, Jacksonville, Ill.
Dunn, Rev. Andrew, Winchendon, Mass.
Dunn, Alexander, New-Brunswick, N. J.
Du Pre, Mrs. S. P Darlington, S. C.
Dupont, Alfred, Wilmington, Del.
Durant, Clark, Albany, N Y
Durbrow, W lliam, New-York.
Durfee, Sandford, Warwick, R. I.
Durkin, John, New-York.
Duryea, Levi, New-York.
Duryea, Mrs. Sarah New-York.
Dusenbury, Rev. Francisco, Etna, N. Y.
Duvall, Mrs. J., Mitchell's, Va.
Dye, Rev. Daniel, Lafargeville, N Y
Dye, Rev. Enoch P North Brookfield, N. Y.
Eastman, Lycurgus, Griggsville, Ill.
Eastman, Rev. Samuel, Burlington Wis.
Earl, Rev. Samuel H., New-York.
Eaton, Rev. George W D. D., Hamilton, N. Y.
Eaton, R. C., Springville, N Y.
Eaton, Rev. Horace, Wilton, N. H.
Eaton, Ezra, Boston, Mass.
Eddy, Rev. H New-York.
Eddy, Rev. Daniel C., Lowell, Mass.
Eddy, Mrs Sarah D , New-Bedford, Mass.
Eddy, Miss Ann E. N New-Bedford, Mass.
Eddy, ohn S., Providence, R. I.
Edgecomb, Albert, Mystic River, Ct.
Edington Mrs. Charlotte M., New-York.
Edmon, Thomas, Pemberton, N. J
Edmond, Francis, Newton Mass.
Edmonds, Miss Sarah E Ph ladelphia,
Edwards, Robert, New-York.
Edwards, Mrs. Robert, New-York.

Edwards, Rev. B. A., Watertown, Mass.
Edwards, John F., Brookline, Mass.
Edwards, Ivary, Lowell, Mass.
Eldridge, James, Williamstown, Mass.
Elgreen, Mrs. Ann, New-York.
Ellege, Rev. Jesse, Barry, Ill.
Elliott, Rev. Charles, Baldwinsville, N. Y.
Ellis, Rev. John, Norwalk, Ct.
Ellis, Mrs. Mary, Norwalk, Ct.
Elliott, Rev. William, Brighton, Iowa.
Ellsworth, Lewis, Napierville, Ill.
Elmer, Ebenezer, Bridgeton, N. J.
Ely, Henry D., Holmdel, N. J.
Emmons, Mrs. Sarah, Deep River, Ct.
English, Henry H., Philadelphia.
English, Isaac, Salem, N. J.
Eschman, Rev. John, New-York.
Eschman, Mrs. Magdalene, New-York.
Estee, Rev. Sidney A., York, N. Y.
Estep, Rev. Dr. James, Library, Pa.
Estes, A. B., Lower Three Runs, S. C.
Estes, Miss H. S., do do
Estes, Mrs. E. A., do do
Evans, Silas J., Cincinnati, Ohio
Evans, Mrs. S. E., Society Hill, S. C.
Evans, Reuben, Amesbury, Mass.
Evans, Dr. Joseph T., New-York.
Evans, Mrs. Clarissa H., New-York.
Evans, Mrs. Mary, New-York.
Eveleigh, Mrs. Mary D., Brooklyn, N. Y.
Eveleth, Samuel, Boston.
Everts, Rev. William W., Louisville, Ky.
Everett, Rev. Samuel, North Leverett, Mass.
Everett, David, New-London, N. H.
Everett, B. C., Philadelphia.
Everett, Miss Elizabeth, New-York.
Fails, David, South Dedham, Mass.
Failing, Josiah, Portland, Oregon.
Failing, Henry, Portland, Oregon.
Failing, Miss Elizabeth A., Portland, Oregon
Fairbrother, Lewis, Pawtucket, R. I.
Fales, Joseph T., Burlington, Iowa.
Fales, Oliver, West Philadelphia, Pa.
Falkner John B., Malden, Mass.
Fargo, Rev. Isaac, Romulus, N. Y.
Farish, T. Gulf, N. C.
Farnsworth, Hon. Joseph D., Fairfax, Vt.
Farnsworth, Dr. James H. Fairfax, Vt.
Farrington, David, Trumansburgh, N. Y.
Farwell, Isaac, Watertown, Mass.
Farwell, Mrs. Sarah A., Watertown, Mass.
Farr, Asa, Lowell, Mass.
Farr, Miss Mary Louisa, Hastings, N. Y.
Farrar Mrs. Susan P., Jackson, Va.
Farquharson, James, Williamsburgh, N. Y.
Faskelt, Horace B., North Adams, Mass.
Fay, Rev. Eliphas, Poughkeepsie, N. Y.
Feller, Mad. Henrietta, St. Johns, Ca. E.
Felton, R., Hertford, N. C.
Felton, Cader, Hertford, N. C.
Felton, Mrs. Mary, Hertford, N. C.
Fennel, Rev. George, Harrel's Store, N. C.
Fennell, Owen, Wilmington, N. C
Ferrier, Joh M., New-York.
Ferrell, Miss Mary Ann, New-York.
Ferris, Mrs. Hannah L., New-York.
Fickling F. W Gillisonville, S. C.
Field, Thomas F., Brooklyn, N. Y
Field, Mrs. Thomas F., Brooklyn, N. Y.
Field, Thomas S., Hoboken, N. J.
Field, Rev. Samuel W., Providence.
Field, Mrs. Lavinia F., Taunton, Mass.
Field, Chas. H., Taunton, Mass.
Field, Mrs. Elizabeth H., Providence.
Fife, Rev. James, Charlottesville, Va.
Fifield, William, East Poultney, Vt.
Fillio, Rev. Nelson, Battle Creek, Mich.
Fillio, Mrs. Phidelia, Battle Creek, Mich.
Finch Miss Sarah A., Red Oak Grove, Va.
Fish, Rev. Joel W Racine, Wis.
Fishback, Mrs. Sophia, Jeffersonton, Va.
Fisher, Mrs. Ann L., New-York.
Fisher, Rev. Abiel, Manchaug, Mass.
Fisher, Rev. Ezra, Oregon City, Oregon.
Fisher, Rev Otis, Pavilion, Ill.
Fisher, Isaac, West Townsend, Vt.
Fisk, Theron, Warsaw, N. Y.
Fisk, Willard, New-York.
Fitch, Dr. William, Stamford, Ct.
Fitzgerald, Miss Joanna, New-York.
Fithian, Samuel C Greenwich, N. J.
Fitts, William, Worcester, Mass.
Flanders, Rev. Charles W Concord, N. H.
Flanders, Mrs. M. H. L., Concord, N H.
Flanders, Timothy C., Haverhill, Mass.
Flanders, Melvin, Haverhill, Mass.
Fleet, James R., Brewington, Va.
Fleet, Dr. B. King and Queen C. H., Va.
Fleischman, Rev. Konrad A., Philadelphia.
Fletcher, Rev. Simon, Sandy Hill, N. Y.
Fletcher, Rev. Leonard, New-Orleans.
Fletcher, Rev. Horace, Townsend, Vt.
Fletcher, Mrs. Mary Amenia, N. Y.
Flinn, Mrs. E A. E., Darlington, S. C.
Flint, Brayton, Novi, Mich.
Flint, Mrs. Mary C., Novi, Mich.
Flint, Lorin, Novi, Mich.
Fogg, Rev. Samuel F., Lowell, Mass.
Foley, Thomas W., Providence.
Folwell, Job W Defiance, Ohio.
Forbes, George W., Bridgeport, Ct.
Forbes, Gustavus, Boston, Mass.
Forbes, Rev. M., Middlesex, N. Y
Forbush Rev. Jonathan E. S., Danvers, Mass
Forby, Wm. F., Brooklyn, N. Y.
Force, Lyman, Alta, N. Y
Ford, Isaac, Philadelphia.
Ford, Mrs. H. Philadelphia.
Ford, Mrs. Mary, Harvey's Store, Va.
Foreman, Miss Mary E., Hightstown, N. J.
Forrester, Mrs. Elenora, New-York.
Forristall, Mrs. Lucy, Boston.
Foster, William, West Dedham, Mass.
Foster, Mrs. Sarah K., Evansville, Ia.
Foster, Rev. J. C., Brattleboro. Vt.
Foster, Joseph, sen., Salem, N.
Forsyth, Russell, Livingston, N. Y.
Forsyth, Mrs. Sarah, Livingston, N. Y.
Forsyth, Miss Emily H., Albany, N Y.
Fox, Rev. Norman, Ballston, N. Y.
Fox, Rev. Charles A., Waverley, Pa

Fox, Albert R., Sand Lake, N. Y.
Fox, Charles. New-York.
Frasee, Ezra, Rahway. N. J.
Frasee, Mrs. Mary, Rahway, N. J.
Francis, Robert, Newington. Ct.
Francis, Mrs. Lydia D., Newington, Ct.
Francis, Norman, New-York.
Francis, Mrs. Hannah C., New-York.
Francis, John S., New-York.
Frayzer, Rev. Herndon, Twymann's, Va.
Freas, Rev. Daniel I, Salem, N. J.
Freeman, Rev. T. G., Natchez, Miss.
Freeman, Rev. Joseph, Cavendish, Vt.
Freeman, Rev. G. W., Waupun, Wis.
Freeman, Thomas W., Augusta. Ga.
Freeman, Elisha, Worcester, Mass.
Freeman, Henry P., Williamsburg. N Y.
French, George R, Wilmington, N. C.
French, Stephen L., Fall River, Mass.
French, Mrs Hannah, Haverhill, Mass.
Frinke, William S., Taylorville, Ill.
Fripp, E., Beaufort, S. C.
Fripp, Mrs. Ann H., Beaufort, S. C.
Frisby, Mrs. Lucy M., New-Haven, Ct.
Frost, James, Wake Forest, N. C.
Fulcher, Richard, Three Rivers, Mich.
Fuller, George, Troy, N. Y.
Fuller, Nathan L., New-York.
Fuller, Dr. Henry M, Beaufort, S. C.
Fuller, Rev. Martin Luther, Mooers, N. Y.
Fuller, Mrs. Achsah Smith, Pike, N. Y.
Fuller, Cyrenius M, jr, Pike, N. Y.
Fuller, Miss Elizabeth, Baltimore.
[redacted]

George, Mrs. Elizabeth C., Culpepper, Va.
German, Joseph, Beekman, N. Y.
Gibbs, Mrs. Eliza Ann, Newark, N. J.
Gibson, Rev. A., East Greene, N. Y.
Gifford, Rev Isaac S., Bedford, N. Y.
Gifford, Mrs Annie, Bedford, N. Y.
Gignilliat, W. R., Darian, Ga.
Gill, Miss Mary, Pottsville, Pa.
Gill, Miss Mary Ann, Philadelphia.
Gillett, Ashael, Rose, N. Y.
Gillman, Miss Ellen W., Roadstown, N. J.
Gilman, George H., New-York.
Gilman, David Roadstown, N. J.
Gilbert, J B., Hartford, Ct.
Giles, Alfred E., Boston.
Gilpatrick, Rev. James, Topsham, Me.
Girdwood, Rev. John, New-Bedford, Mass.
Girdwo d, Mrs. Mary, New-Bedford, Mass.
Glass, George W, Honeoye Falls, N. Y.
Glover, Charles S., New-York.
Goadby, Rev. John, Poultney, Vt.
Goddard, Jabez, York, N. Y.
Goddard, Mrs Elizabeth, York, N. Y.
Goddard, Benjamin, Worcester, Mass.
Going, Mrs. Nancy B., Columbus, Ohio.
Going, Rev. Ezra, Greenville, Ohio.
Going, J., Aurora, N. Y.
Godfry, Abel, Sennett, N. Y.
Godfrey, Edward J., New-York.
Godfrey, Mrs. Anna, Brooklyn, N. Y.
Goldthawit, Nathan, Worcester, Mass.
Goldy, John, Imlaystown, N. J.
Goldy, Mrs. Emily, Imlaystown, N. J.
[redacted]

Green, Mrs. Cornelia E., Providence.
Green, Miss Frances Mary, Providence.
Green, Mrs. Mary, New-York.
Green, Rev. John, Florida, Mass.
Green, Rev. Charles H., West Townsend, Vt.
Green, Rev. Jonathan R., Derby, Vt.
Green, Spencer, Rutland, Vt.
Green, Ralph, Three Rivers, Mass.
Green, Rev. Thomas H., Springport, N. Y.
Greenleaf, Rev. Calvin, Perry, Ill.
Greenleaf, Amos C., New-York.
Greenwood, Simeon A., Worcester, Mass.
Grenell, Mrs. Eliza, Fairport, N Y.
Gregory, Miss Clarissa, New-York.
Gregory, Rev. S., Lisbon, N Y.
Gregory, Rev. Truman, Richville, N. Y.
Griffin, Nathaniel L., Edgefield, S. C.
Griffin, Edwin, New-York.
Griffith, Mrs. Thomas S. Milwaukee, Wis.
Griggs, Samuel, Rutland, Vt.
Griggs, Mrs. Abigail S., Rutland, Vt.
Griggs, David R., Brookline, Mass.
Griggs, Seth D., Belchertown, Mass.
Grimley, Rev. Joseph I., Marlborough, N. Y.
Grimshaw, Miss Martha, New-York.
Grinnell, Mrs. Mary B., New-Bedford, Mass.
Griswold, Harry, Racine, Wis.
Gross, Rev. Alva, Lafayette, Ill.
Grose, Rev. Henry L., Galway, N. Y.
Grow, Rev. James, Thompson, Ct.
Guild, Rev. John B., East Thompson, Ct.
Guild, Mrs. Julia A., East Thompson, Ct.
Guilford, Rev. Wm M., Stirling, Mass.
Gunn, Rev. Elih Keokuk, Iowa.
Grammon, William, Newark, N. J.
Gurney, Mrs. Martha, Boston.
Gurr, Rev. C. G., Harlem, N Y.
Guy, Rev. A., South New-Berlin, N Y.
Gwathney, Mrs. E. T., Aylette, Va.
Hadaway, John T., Chelsea, Mass.
Haddock, Henry, Lynn, Mass.
Haff, Rev. H. H., East Schuyler, N. Y.
Hagar, William, Jr., Brooklyn, N. Y.
Hague, Rev. John B, Hudson, N. Y.
Hague, Rev. James, Newark, N J.
Hall, Gabriel D. Greenwich, N J.
Hall, Mrs. Mary A., Greenwich, N. J.
Hall, Enoch, Worcester, Mass.
Hall, Abner, Wallingford, Ct.
Hall, Herbert, New-York.
Hall, Rev. King S., Lake Village, N. H.
Hall, Rev. Abijah, Jr Hamilton, N. Y.
Hallsted, Mrs. Jane C., New-York.
Hamilton, Rev. Alexander, Newark, Wis.
Hamilton, John, Jr., Fredonia, N. Y
Hammond, Augustus, Pittsford, Vt
Hammond, Mrs. Mary, Pittsford, Vt.
Hammond, Miss Mary F Pittsford, Vt.
Hansford, Dr. Joseph H, Nantucket, Mass.
Hansell, F Standish, Philadelphia.
Hansell, Mrs. Emma, Philadelphia.
Harding, Rev. Theodore Horton, N Scotia.
Harger, Mrs. Hannah, Saratoga Springs, N Y.
Harger, Mrs Hannah, Chatham Corners, N. Y.
Harrimount, Wm. S., New-Haven, Ct.
Harrington, Wm, Worcester, Mass.
Harrington, Mrs. Adeline, Worcester, Mass.
Harrington, Adam, Shrewsbury, Mass.
Harrington, Stukely S., Akron, N. Y.
Harrington, Rev. Daniel, Batavia, N Y.
Harrington, Adam, Shrewsbury, Mass.
Harriott, John V., Brooklyn, N. Y.
Harris, Rev. John, Milton, Mich.
Harris, Rev Edward L, Beloit, Wis.
Harris, Rev. Wm. B., Cold Spring (L. I.), N. Y.
Harris, Rev George W., Detroit, Mich.
Harris, Mrs. Elizabeth J., Va.
Harris, Mrs. Sarah, Philadelphia.
Harris, Isaac, New-London, Ct.
Harris, Thomas J., Claremont, N. H.
Harris, Douglas W New-London, Ct.
Harmon, Mrs. Elizabeth, N. Bennington, Vt.
Harmon, Rawson, Wheatland, N. Y.
Harrison, Mrs. Camilla M., Charles City, Va.
Harrison, Rev. J. C., Easton, Pa.
Hatch, Charles G., Shelby, N. Y.
Hatch, Rev. S., Lansingburgh, N. Y.
Hatch, Ira, Union Village, N. Y.
Harlow, Robert H., Boston, Mass.
Hartshorn, Jonas, Worcester, Mass.
Hart, Henry B., Portland, Me.
Hartwell, John B. Providence, R. I.
Harvey, Hezekiah, New-York.
Harvey, Rev. Alfred, Burnt Hills, N. Y.
Hasay, Miss Angeline, New-York.
Haskell, Dr. George, Rockford, Ill.
Haskell, Rev. Samuel, Kalamazoo, Mich.
Hasegood, Miss S. F. Gillisonville, S. C.
Hastings, Andrew F., Brooklyn, N. Y.
Hastings Mrs. Andrew F., Brooklyn, N Y.
Haswell, Rev James M., Amherst, Burmah.
Haswel Mrs. Jane M Amherst, Burmah.
Hatt, Joel, Orange, N. J.
Hatt, Mrs. Sophia, New-York.
Hatfield, Robert G., New-York.
Hatfield, Mrs Charlotte S. New-York.
Hathaway, Miss Mary, New-York.
Hathaway, Charles F., Watertown, Mass.
Haviland, Mrs. Joanna, New-York.
Haviland, Miss Mary Ann, New-York.
Haviland, William C., New-York.
Hawes, Rev. Josiah, New-Sharon, Me.
Hawks, Isaac, Shelburne Falls, Mass.
Hawley, Mrs Rebecca, New-York.
Hawley, D. F., Bristol Ct.
Hayden, Rev. Lucian, Saxton's River, Vt.
Hayden, Mrs Caroline S., Saxton's River, Vt.
Haynes, Mrs. S. B Va.
Haynes, Rev. Hiram, Preston Hollow, N. Y.
Haynes, Rev. Dudley C. Philadelphia.
Hays, John P. New-York.
Hazen, Rev. Henry C, Throopsville, N. Y.
Heald, Rev. Albert, East Washington, N. H.
Healy, Ebenezer, Sennett, N. Y.
Healy, Mrs. Amia, Sennett, N Y.
Healy, F. W., Sennett, N. Y
Heath, Rev. Amasa, Adams Village, N. Y.
Hedden, William, Orange, N. J.
Hepburn, Rev. James, Stamford, Ct.
Hendrick, Rev. Joel, East Smithfield, Pa.

Herrington, Chester, Clifton Park, N. Y.
Heron, Miss Isabella, New-York.
Hervey, Rev. Nathaniel, Westboro', Mass.
Heustis, Mrs. Ann, New-York.
Hewett, Mrs. Rhoda Elizabeth, New-York.
Hewit, Edmund, Galway, N. Y.
Hickman, Mrs. E., New-Albany, Ia.
Hickok, Austin, Jay, N. Y.
Higbie, Alanson, Penfield, N. Y.
Hill, Mrs. Harriet D., New-York.
Hill, Miss Harriet R., New-York.
Hill, Mrs Mary, Miller's, Va.
Hill, Mrs. Lydia Ann, Carmel, N. Y.
Hill, David Jayne, Carmel, N. Y.
Hill, Mrs Rebecca, Essex, Ct.
Hill, Rev. William, Kane, Ill.
Hill, Samuel P., Charlestown, Mass.
Hill, Amos, Jr., West Cambridge, Mass
Hill, Rev. I N., Dover Plains, N. Y.
Hill, Leander J., Brockport, N. Y.
Hill, Henry S., East Cambridge, Mass.
Hill, Mrs Eleanor, New-York.
Hillman, William, New-York.
Hillman, Mrs. Catharine, New-York.
Hills, Mrs. Deborah, Haverhill, Mass.
Hine, Simmons, New-Haven, Ct.
Hinton, A. G., Pittsborough, N. C.
Hires, Mrs Catharine, New-Market, N J.
Hiscox, Rev. Edward, T., New-York.
Hiscox, Mrs C. O., New-York
Hitchcox, Sheldon, Suffield, Ct.
Hoar, Lewis, Warren, R. I.
Hoar, John R., Warren, R. I.
[redacted]

Horton, Mrs. Ann A., Taunton, Mass.
Horton, Danforth, Fall River, Mass.
Hosken, Rev. Charles H., London, England.
Hough, Clement, Lebanon, N. H.
Hough, Alanson H., Essex, Ct.
Houghton, C. W., Williamsburgh, N. Y.
Houghton, J., Milton, Mass.
Houghton, Rev. G. W., New Hackensack, N. Y.
Hovey, Mrs. Elizabeth, Cambridge, Mass
Hovey, Rev. Alvah, Newton Centre, Mass.
How, Calvin F., Brooklyn, N. Y.
Howe, J. S., Methuen, Mass.
Howe, Phineas, Newton Centre, Mass.
Howell, David, Southport, N. Y.
Howes, Samuel C., Chatham, Mass.
Howard, Rev. Johnson, Dover, N. Y.
Howard, Mrs. Lucy M., Rutland, Vt.
Howarth, Mrs. Helen, Salisbury, Mass.
Hoyt, Miss Harriet E., Brooklyn, N. Y.
Hubatcheck, Joseph, New-York.
Hubbard, Mrs. Mary R., Deep River, Ct.
Hubell, Alrich, Utica, N. Y.
Hudgens, Mrs. Rebecca Y., Hampton, Va.
Hull, Mrs. Maria, New-York.
Hull, Charles, Danbury, Ct.
Hulse, Smith, Dundee, N. Y.
Hughson, Levi P., Oswego, N. Y.
Humphrey, Hon. Friend, Albany.
Hunt, Rev. John, Richmond, N. H.
Hunt, Mrs. N., Sharon, Ct.
Hunt, Miss Eliza, New-York.
Huntley, Rev. George W., Wellsville, N. Y.
Huntington, Mrs. Philip, Haverhill, Mass.
[redacted]

Jaudon, Mrs. Sarah T., Robertsville, S. C.
Jaycox, Mrs. Fanny M., Cold Spring, N. Y.
Jeffery, Rev. Reuben, Albany, N. Y.
Jeffres, J. M., Red Oak Grove, Va.
Jencks, Rev. Erasmus N., Farmridge, Ill.
Jencks, Miss Maria, Pawtucket, R. I.
Jenks, Gideon, Brookfield, Mass.
Jenks, J. W. P., Westboro', Mass.
Jenkins, Mrs. Susannah, New-York.
Jenkins, Rev. J. S., Coatesville, Pa.
Jenkins, Miss Rebecca, New-York.
Jennett, John, Halifax, C. H., Va.
Jennings, Mrs. Susan C., Worcester, Mass.
Jennings, Mrs. Marcia, Deep River, Ct.
Jeril, Rev. T., Lebanon, N. Y.
Jerrard, Rev. Richard, Morrisana. N. Y.
Jeter, Rev. J. C., Beaver Dam, S. C.
Jewett, Rev. Milo P., Marion, Ala.
Jewett, Rev. Daniel. Farmington, Iowa.
Jimmerson, Robert J., New-York.
Johnson, Rev. William B., D.D., Edgefield, S. C.
Johnson, Mrs. Henrietta, Edgefield, S. C.
Johnson, William, North East, Pa.
Johnson, Mrs. Sarah S., North East, Pa.
Johnson, Mrs. Louisa M., Lynn, Mass.
Johnson, James, Brooklyn, N. Y.
Johnson, Robert, Newark, N. J.
Johnson, Rev. Solomon B., St. Louis, Mo.
Johnson, Rev. George J., Burlington, Iowa.
Johnson, Mrs. George J., Burlington, Iowa.
Johnson, Rev. Hezekiah, Oregon City, Oregon.
Johnson, Albert B., Willistown, Pa.
Johnson, Edward, New-York.
Johnston, Andrew, Newark, N. J.
Johnston, Mrs. Robert, Newark, N. J.
Jones, Rev. Stephen, Norwalk, Ohio.
Jones, Mrs. Stephen, do. do.
Jones, Rev. John, Willistown, Pa.
Jones, Mrs. Deborah, Willistown, Pa.
Jones, Mrs. Ann T., Williamsburgh, Va.
Jones, Eliza T., Tavern, P. O., Pa.
Jones, Mrs. Margaret, New-York.
Jones, Mrs. Eliza W., New-Brunswick, N. J,
Jones, Mrs. Elizabeth, Macedon, N. Y.
Jones, David, New-York.
Jones, Mrs. Sarah, New-York.
Jones, Mrs. Mary, New-York.
Jones, Mrs. Rhoda. Smithville, N. Y.
Jones, Miss Catharine L., Philadelphia.
Jones, Rev. Joseph H., Frederick City, Md.
Jones, Rev. David N., Richmond, Va.
Jones, Rev. Matthew, Stephentown. N. Y.
Jones, Rev. Theophilus, Hatboro', Pa.
Jones, Rev. Isaac D., Flemingville, N. Y.
Jones, John B., Roxbury, Mass.
Jones, William G., Wilmington, Del.
Jones, Washington. Wilmington, Del.
Jones, William M , New-York.
Jones, Mrs. Margaretta V., New-York.
Jones, Rev. J. W., Paterson, N. Y.
Jones, Howard M., Providence, R. I.
Jordan, Philana D., Columbia, Ohio
Jordon, Mrs. Esther, Brooklyn, N. Y.
Joslin, Joseph, East Poultney, Vt.
Joyce, Miss Sarah W., Worcester, Mass.
Judd, Rev. Truman O., Fairhaven, Ct.
Judson, Mrs. Emily C., Hamilton, N. Y.
Justice, David, Forestville, N. C.
Justin, Rev. Ira, Richmond, N. Y.
Kain, Charles, Marlton, N. J.
Kain, Mrs. Sarah, Marlton, N. J.
Kain, Rev. Charles, Jr., Mullica Hill, N. J.
Kain, Mrs. Maria, Mullica Hill, N. J.
Keely, Rev. George, Haverhill, Mass.
Keely, Mrs. George, Haverhill, Mass.
Keely, John, Haverhill, Mass.
Keely, Mrs. John, Haverhill, Mass.
Keely, Rev. Thomas E., Kingston, Mass.
Keen, William W., West Philadelphia.
Keen, Mrs. Susan B., West Philadelphia.
Keen, George B., West Philadelphia.
Keen, William W. J., West Philadelphia.
Keen, Charles B., West Philadelphia.
Keeney, William H., New-London, Ct.
Keeney, Rev. Curtis, New-London, Ct.
Kelly, Mrs. Joan, Elmira, New-York.
Kelley, Mrs. Catharine, New-York.
Kelley, Mrs. Eli, New-York.
Kelley, James D., Pittsfield, N. H.
Kelton, George, Salem, N. J.
Kemp, Sylvester A., Florida, Mass.
Kendrick, Silas N., Detroit, Mich.
Kendrick, Mrs. Fanny, Detroit, Mich.
Kendrick, Adin, East Poultney, Vt.
Kendrick, Rev. A. C., D.D., Rochester, N. Y.
Kendrick, Mrs. Ann, Hamilton, N. Y.
Kennan, Mrs. Eliza, Thompsonville, Va.
Kent, Henry P., Suffield, Ct.
Kerr, John, Yanceyville, N. C.
Kerr, James N., Dixon, Ill.
Kerfoot, Mrs. Maria C., Upperville, Va.
Kerfoot. Mrs. Harriet E., Battletown, Va.
Ketcham, Charles F., Brooklyn, N. Y.
Ketcham, Miss Sarah A., New-York.
Ketchum, Rev. Jonathan, Farmersville, N Y.
Key, Mrs. A., Fife's, Va.
Keyes, Mrs. Lydia L., North East, N. Y.
Keyes, Miss Sarah E , North East. N. Y.
Keyser, Rev. Charles, Wallingford, Ct.
Kimball, Mrs. Edward, Haverhill, Mass.
Kimball, Rufus, Haverhill, Mass.
Kimball, Mrs. Rufus, Haverhill, Mass.
Kincaid, Rev. Eugenio, Ava, Burmah.
Kindel, Job, Pemberton, N. J.
King, Daniel K., Port Byron, N. Y.
Kingman, Martin, New-York.
Kingman, Miss Augusta E., New York.
Kingsbury, Rev. Arnold, Fredonia, N. Y.
Kingsford, Rev. Edward, D.D., Richmond, Va.
Kingsland, Mrs. Sarah Jane, New-York,
Kingsley, Rev. A. C., Parma Centre, N. Y.
Kirk, Robert, New-York.
Kone, Louk, Maulmain, Burmah.
Knapp, Rev. Henry R., Willimantic, Ct.
Knapp, Mrs. Mary, Willimantic, Ct.
Knight, Daniel N., Brooklyn, N. Y.
Knight, Jonathan, Worcester, Mass.
Knowles, Levi, Philadelphia.
Knowles, Mrs. Susan E., Providence.
Knowlton, Miss Sarah J., North Chatham, N.Y.

Knowlton, D. A., Freeport, Ill.
Knowlton, Edwward, Florida, Mass.
Knowlton, Hezekiah, Beverly, Mass.
Knox, Miss Rachel, Hillsdale, N. Y.
Kyle, Miss Mary, New-York.
Lamont, Mrs. Anna, New-York.
L'Amoureaux, Mrs. Nancy, S. Hadley, Mass.
Ladd, Rev. James S., New-York.
Lafever, Reuben, Reading Centre, N. Y.
Lafleur, Rev. Theodore, St. Pie, Canada East.
LaGrange, Mrs. John E., Hillsdale, N. Y
Lagrange, Rev. John E., Beekmanville, N. Y.
Laing, Miss Jane, New York.
Lake, Mrs Eleanor E., New-York.
Lamb, Rev. R. P., Sardinia, N. Y.
Lamson, Rev. William, Portsmouth, N. H.
Lane, Lewis, New-York.
Lane, Maltby G., New-York
Lane, Mrs. Mary F., Va.
Laning, Mrs. Julietta, Owego, N. Y.
Langley, Mrs. Harriet N., Providence.
Lavery, Miss Mary, Brooklyn, N. Y.
Lawrence, P. P., Washington, N. C.
Lawrence, William S., New-York.
Lawton, George, Waltham, Mass.
Lea, Mrs. Elizabeth, Yanceyville, N. C.
Lea, Hon Luke A., Washington, D. C.
Leach, Rev. Berian N., New-York.
Leach, Rev. D. F., Harpersville, N. Y.
Leask, Mrs. Margaret, New-York.
Lee, George, North Bristol, N. Y.
Lee, Mrs. Amanda, North Bristol, N. Y.
Lee, Miss Ann Mollan, New-York.
Leggett, Rev. William, Owasco, N. Y.

Locke, Mrs. Sarah B., Watertown, Mass.
Logan, Rev. John, Ill.
Logan, James, Pemberton, N. J.
Long, E. J., Boston, Mass.
Long, William, Shelburne Falls, Mass.
Loring, Samuel H., Boston.
Loring, Mrs. James, Boston.
Lowe, Mrs. Harriet N., Salem, N. J.
Love, Rev. H. T., North Adams, Mass.
Love, John, New-York.
Lovell, George, Osterville, Mass.
Ludlow, John R., New-York.
Lull, Rev. Abner, Sheboygan Falls, Wis.
Luther, Job, Providence.
Luther, Gardner, Seekonk, Mass.
Lyman, Nathan, Andover, Ct.
Lyon, Jesse, Fitchburg, Miss.
Lyon, Cyrus, York, N.Y.
Lyon, Mrs. Mary, York, N. Y.
Lyon, Miss Rebecca, Plainfield, N. J
Lyon, Rev. Daniel D., Jewett City, Ct.
Lyon, Rev. Joel, Bergen, N. Y.
Lyon, Mrs. Caroline P., Chatham, Mass.
Lyon, Mrs. Merrick, Providence, R. I.
Lyon, Rev. A. S., Chatham, Mass.
Lynt, Odell D., Hastings, N. Y.
Lytle, Andrew, New-York.
McAllister, Mrs. E., Fayetteville, N. C.
McBride, Miss Jane Ann, New-York.
McCarthy, Rev. William, Newport, N. Y.
McCormick, R. C., New-York.
McCormick, Mrs. Sarah M., New-York.
McCoy, John, Charleston, Ia.
McCullen, Miss Sarah, New-York.

[redacted]

Magoon, Miss Ella Louise, New-York.
Mahoney, Rev. Henry W., Piedmont, S. C.
Mallary, Rev. S. S., Pawtucket, R. I.
Mallory, Rev. Almond O., Boston Centre, N. Y.
Mallory, Rev. James, Lagrange, N. Y.
Mandeville, Stephen, New-York.
Mandeville, Mrs. Mary, New-York.
Mandeville, Miss Phebe B., New-York.
Mandeville, George, New-York.
Mansfield, Edward, South Reading, Mass.
Mangam, William D., New-York.
Mangam, Mrs. Sarah Ann, New-York.
Mangam, Edgar B., New-York.
Mangum, Rev. Daniel, Pagesville, S. C.
Manning, Rev. Edward, Cornwall, N. S.
Manton, Rev. Joseph R., Providence.
March, Peter S., New-York.
Marchant, Henry, Jr., Providence.
Marchant, Miss Mary W., Providence.
Marsall, Rev. J. F., Columbia, S. C.
Marsall, Rev. Andrew, Savannah, Ga.
Marsh, Rev. Asa, Evansville, Ia.
Marsh, Rev. Leonard G., New-York.
Marsh, Benjamin, Newport, R. I.
Marsh, Enoch, Hudson, N. H.
Marshall, Rev. Samuel, Ohio.
Marshall, William, Fitchburg, Mass.
Marshall, Albert, Holden, Mass.
Marshall, Miss Mary Ann, New-York.
Marston, Rev. S. W., East Brookfield, Mass.
Martin, William R., New-York.
Martin, Mrs. Charles J., New-York.
Martin, Mrs. Mary C., New-York.
Martin, Miss Mary, New-York.
Martin, Alfred, New-York.
Martin, Mrs. Harriet W., New-York.
Martin, Miss Mary Ann, New-York.
Martin, Miss Sarah, New-York.
Martin, Henry L., New-York.
Martin, Stelle R., New-York.
Martin, Francis, New-York.
Martin, Reana, New-York.
Martin, Rev. Sandford S., Tremont, Ill.
Martin Peter, Philadelphia.
Martin, M. D., Bristol, Ct.
Martin, Mrs. Sarah Ann, New-York.
Mason, Mrs Sarah R., Chelsea, Mass.
Mason, Augustus F., Chelsea, Mass.
Mason, Mrs. Roxanna L., West Swanzey, N. H.
Mason, Mrs. D C Fuller, Sandusky, N. Y.
Mason, Rev. James O., Greenwich, N. Y.
Mason, Mrs. J. O., Greenwich, N. Y.
Mason, George, Providence.
Mason, Charles, New York.
Mason, John M. G., Philadelphia
Mason, Arnold G., Bridgeport, Ct.
Mason, Mrs. Arnold G., Bridgeport, Ct.
Mason, R. B., Webster, N. Y.
Mason, Rev. S. R., Lockport, N. Y.
Mason, Rev. J T, Galeville, N Y.
Mason, Pethuel, Somerville, N. J.
Mason, Charles, New-York.
Massay, Rev. Joseph T, Bellingham, Mass.
Masters, Mrs. William, Webster, Mass.
Mastin, John S., New-York.
Mather, Lucreas, Fairport, N. Y.
Mather, Mrs. Mary A., Deep River, Ct.
Mathews, Rev. George, Athol, Mass.
Mathews, Mrs. Elizabeth, Athol, Mass.
Matteson, Rev. N. H., Preston City, Ct.
Maul, Rev. William, Plainfield, N. J.
Maul, Mrs. Sarah Ann, Plainfield, N. J.
Maxwell, B., Shelburne Falls, Mass.
Maynard, Walter, Three Rivers, Mass.
Mead, John, Troy, N. Y.
Mead, William, Lowell, Mass.
Meads, Rev. George W., Vienna, N. Y.
Meech, Rev. Wm. W., North Lyme, Ct.
Meech, Levi, North Lyme, Ct.
Meech, Rev Levi, Preston, Ct.
Medbury, Rev. Nicholas, Newburyport, Ms.
Medbury, Viall, Seekonk, Mass.
Meeker, Aaron B., Elizabethtown, N. J.
Meeson, Rev. J. D., Bloomfield, N. J.
Merchant, James H., New-York.
Merchant, Mrs. Amanda M., New-York.
Meriam, Otis, Chelsea, Mass.
Merrell, Joseph, New-York.
Merrell, Charles, Malden, Mass.
Merrett, Thomas W., Somerset, N. Y.
Merrill, Joseph, Hudson, N. H.
Merriam, Rev. Asaph, Boulton, Mass.
Merrill, Joseph, Lowell, Mass.
Metcalf, Rev. Whitman, Springville, N. Y.
Mershon, Mrs. Meliona S., New-York.
Mi-shv-ki-no-di-no-i-kno (Mrs. James Tanner), Pembina, Min. Ter.
Micou, Rev. John, Jr., Louisville, Mi.
Mikels, Rev. William S., Sing Sing, N. Y.
Milbank, Miss Elizabeth, Plainfield, N. J.
Milbank, Miss Eliza W., Plainfield, N. J.
Milbank, Miss Sarah C., Plainfield, N. J.
Milbank, Miss Mary W., Plainfield, N. J.
Milbank, Mrs. Mary W., New-York.
Milbank, Miss Mary A., New-York.
Milbank, Miss Emma Louisa, New-York.
Milbank, Miss Anna Elizabeth, New-York.
Milbank, L. Ainsworth, New-York.
Milbank, Charles A., New-York.
Middleton, John, New-York.
Miles, Abial, New-York.
Miles, Mrs. Anna, New-York.
Miles, Rev. George I., Philadelphia.
Miles, Rev. Edward M., Davenport, Iowa.
Millard, George, North Adams, Mass.
Millard, S. S., Penfield, N. Y.
Millard, Barzilla, Penfield, N. Y.
Miller, Rev. Harvey, Meriden, Ct.
Miller, Mrs. Sarah R., Meriden, Ct.
Miller, Mrs. Abigail, New-York.
Miller, Miss Amanda, Banksville, Ct.
Miller, Mrs. Nancy, New-London, Ct.
Miller, Miss Anicartha, New-York.
Miller, John B., Sumpterville, S. C.
Miller, James H., Philadelphia.
Miller, Charles Moriah, N. Y.
Miller, Rev. D. Henry, Yonkers, N. Y.
Miller, Rev. U. B., Medina, Mich.
Miller, Mrs. Martha, Middletown, Ct.
Miller, Mrs. Ann Eliza, Providence.

Mills, Rev. Peletiah W., Springville, N. Y.
Milne, John C., Fall River, Mass.
Milner, Alfred A., New-York.
Milner, Mrs Alfred A., New-York.
Miner, Rev. Bradley, Providence, R. I.
Miner, Rev. Martin, Walcott, Ct.
Miner, Rev. Absalom, Waukesha, Wis.
Miner, Rev. Cyrus, Preston, Ct.
Miner, Rev. S G., Canton, Ill.
Miner, Rev. Erastus, Mystic, Ct.
Miner, Francis S., New-York.
Miner, A. B., Italy Hill, N. Y.
Miner, Nathaniel, Jerseyville, Ill.
Mingus, Miss Julia Ann, New-York.
Mitchell, Rev. George H., Wagontown, Pa.
Mitchell, Mrs. Phebe H., Wagontown, Pa.
Mixter, George, East Lyme, Ct.
Moadon, Gilbert F., Port Jarvis, N. Y.
Montgomery, William, Danbury, Ct.
Montgomery, Mrs. Susan, Danbury, Ct.
Montgomery, S. B., Danbury, Ct.
Montague, Rev. Oreb, Warsaw, N. Y.
Moon, John, New-York.
Moore, Dr. G. C., St. John's, N. C.
Moore, Mrs. Julia, St. John's, N. C.
Moore, Mrs. Theodosia M., St. Louis, Mo.
Moore, James Milton, Pa.
Moore, Francis W., New-York.
Moore, Rev. Lyman H., Marshall, Mich.
Moore, Rev. W. W., Albany, N. Y.
Moore, Rev. George C., New-York.
Moore, James Wilmington, Del.
Morgan, William, Brooklyn, N. Y.
Morgan, Miss Harriet, Brooklyn, N. Y.
[redacted]

Mustin, John, Philadelphia.
Myers, Mrs. Anna R., Philadelphia.
Myers, Jr., James, New-York.
Mylne, Rev. William, Pemberton, Va.
Napier, Rev. Robert, Mizpah, S. C.
Neale, Mrs. Melissa Y., Boston.
Nelson, Rev. Caleb, Enfield, N. Y.
Nelson, Rev. Wm. F., Greenfield, Mass.
Newcomb, Butler, Cedarville, N. J.
Newell, Andrew H., Brookline, Mass.
Newell, Mrs. Asa, Providence, R. I.
Newland, D., Stillwater, N. Y.
Newland, Rev. C. A., Coopers Plains, N. Y.
Newton, Mrs. Sally, Albany.
Newton, William, Worcester, Mass.
Newton, Rev. Calvin, Worcester, Mass.
Newton, Rev. Baxter, North Leverett, Mass.
Newton, Miss Frances M., New-York.
Nice, Rev. William J., Imlaystown, N. J.
Nice, Mrs. Elizabeth A., Imlaystown, N. J.
Nice, Rev. George P., Somerville, N. J.
Nichols, Miss Hannah, Bridgeport, Ct.
Nichols, Reuben, Kingston, N. Y.
Nicholson, A. M., Bostick Mills, N. C.
Nicholas, Rev. D. A., Phoenixville, Pa.
Nicholas, Rev. Noah, Rutland, Vt.
Niel, James R., Brooklyn, N. Y.
Noble, Mrs. Margaret, Brooklyn, N. Y.
Normandeau, Mrs. C. A., St. John, C. E.
Northam, E., Rockingham, N. C.
Northam, George, Va.
Norton, Charles C., New-York.
Norton, Rev. Noah, Brunswick, Me.
Norton, Newbery, Agawam, Mass.
[redacted]

Palmer, Mrs. William, East Lyme, Ct.
Palmer, Rev. Lyman, St. Anthony. Min.
Palmer, Rev. Prentice T., Waveland, Ia.
Palmer, Ephraim, New-Hartford, N. Y.
Parke, Rev. F. S., Cheshire, Mass.
Parker, Miss Lavinia M., Suffield, Ct.
Parker, Asa, Essex, Ct.
Parker, Joel B., Fredonia, N. Y.
Parker, Rev. A., Sturbridge, Mass.
Parker, Rev. William, Philadelphia.
Parker, Rev. A., Coventry, N. Y.
Parker, David O., Worcester, Mass.
Parker, Lydia P., Allen, Mich.
Parmlee, Mrs. Syrena, New-York.
Parmly, Rev. W. H., Burlington, N. J.
Parmely, Rev. Levi, Westchester, Pa.
Parrish, Warren, Mendon, N. Y.
Parkhurst, John, Fitchburg, Mass.
Parshley, John, New-Haven, Ct.
Parsons, Silas, Swanzey, N. H.
Parsons, Mrs. Patience, Swanzey, N. H.
Parsons, William, Medford, Mass.
Pasco, Rev. Cephas, Egremont, Mass.
Patch, Rev. George W., Marblehead, Mass.
Patterson, Mrs. Mary, Chapel Hill, N. C.
Patterson, Mrs. Lucy A., New-York.
Paulin, Mrs. Ann, Salem, N. J.
Payne, Miss Amanda, Amenia, N. Y.
Peak, John, Boston, Mass.
Peacock, Rev. John, Bradford, N. H.
Peck, Mrs. Nancy M., Owego, N. Y.
Peck, John, Clifton Park, N. Y.
Peck, Abijah, Jr., Clifton Park, N. Y.
Peck, Rev. David A., Rutland, Wis.
Peck, James W., Brooklyn, N. Y.
Peck, Rev. Daniel, South Jackson, Mich.
Peckham, Rev. S. H., Ledyard, Ct.
Peeples, Rev. Darling, Barnwell, S. C.
Peeples, Edward H., Lawtonville, S. C.
Pegg, Roger, New-York.
Pember, Ashel, New-London, Ct.
Pember, Mrs. Mary, New-London, Ct.
Penny, Rev. William, Uniontown, Pa.
Perego, Mrs. Margaret, New-York.
Pendleton, Rev. G. W., Colchester, Ct.
Pendleton, Miss Jane G., Colchester, Ct.
Pennypacker, John, Wilmington, Del.
Perine, Joseph, Plainfield, N. J.
Perine, Mrs. Sarah, Plainfield, N. J.
Perkins, Jabez, Topsham, Me.
Perkins, Rev. Nehemiah M., Waterbury, Ct.
Perkins, George, Amesbury, Mass.
Perry, Valentine, Macedon, N. Y.
Person, Rev. Ira, Concord, N. H.
Peterson, Rev. J. F., Richardson's, S. C.
Peterson, Richard E., New-York.
Peterson, Mrs. Deborah V., New-York.
Peterson, Samuel F., Philadelphia.
Pettengill, Daniel, Haverhill, Mass.
Pettis, Harvey E., Greenwich, N. Y.
Pettigrew, Rev. Wm. J., Pittsburgh, Pa.
Pew, John, Gloucester, Mass.
Phares, Rev. M. B., Vernon, Ia.
Phelps, Humphrey, New-York.
Phelps, John, Owego, N. Y.
Phelps, Mrs. Sophia Emilia, New-Haven, Ct.
Phelps, William, New-York.
Phelps, Miss Julia Adelaide, New-York.
Philleo, Calvin, Providence.
Phillips, George H., Troy, N. Y.
Phillips, Rev. W., Providence.
Phillips, Rev. David L., Jonesboro', Ill.
Phillips, Rev. Wm. F., Freedom, N. Y.
Phillips, Rev. James M., Noank, Ct.
Phillips, Dr. Samuel B., New-York.
Phillips, Rev. W. C., Canandaigua, N. Y.
Phillips, Mrs. Ann, New-York.
Phillips, Mrs. Theodosia, Norristown, Pa.
Phillips, Peter, Rondout, N. Y.
Philbrook, Rev. Abel, Pittsgrove, N. J.
Phippen, Rev. George, Tyringham, Mass.
Pier, Mrs. Deborah, New-York.
Pierce, Rev. Benj., Londonderry, Vt.
Pierce, Philo, Bristol, Ct.
Pierce, Mrs. Patty B., Nunda, N. Y.
Pierson, David, East Avon, N. Y.
Pike, Jonathan, Providence.
Pike, Mrs. Jonathan, Providence, R. I.
Pike, Miss Ann E., Providence.
Pike, Mrs. Matilda, New-York.
Pike, Miss Catharine E., New-York.
Pillsbury, Rev. Phineas, Ill.
Pinney, Mrs. Mary, Owego, N. Y.
Piper, John G., Canton, Ill.
Platt, G. W., New-York.
Platt, Mrs. Jane D., New-York.
Platt, Rev. B. F., Catskill, N. Y.
Plumb, William, Morrisiana, N. Y.
Plummer, Mrs. Jane, New-York.
Plymer, Mrs. Eliza, New-York.
Pointer, J. R., Cincinnati, Ohio.
Poole, Rev. A. W., Woodland, La.
Pouler, Seth, Lowell, Mass.
Poland, W. C., Boston.
Poland, Rev. James W., Goffstown Centre, N. H.
Pollard, Mrs. Elizabeth, Taunton, Mass.
Polhamus, H. A., New-York.
Pomroy, Rev. Samuel, North Copake, N. Y.
Pond, William, New-York.
Porter, Rev. Lemuel, Pittsfield, Mass.
Porter, Mrs. Welthea M., Pittsfield, Mass.
Post, Mrs. Sarah, New York.
Post, Alanson H., Hinesburg, Vt.
Post, Levi.
Post, Joy, Essex, Ct.
Post, John, Saline, Mich.
Potter, Rev. Charles W., Cromwell, Ct.
Potter, Rev. Aaron, Albion, Mich.
Powell, Rev. Thomas, Mt. Palatine, Ill.
Powell, Miss Sarah P., Mt. Palatine, Ill.
Powell, Rev. Peter, Marlton, N. J.
Powell, Mrs. Nancy, Powelton, N. C.
Powless, Mrs. Anna Maria, Hoboken, N. J.
Pratt, Rev. Samuel C., Lowell, Mass.
Pratt, Rev. James H., Bloomfield, N. J.
Pratt, Daniel, Brooklyn, N. Y.
Pratt, Oliver T., New-York.
Prescott, Abraham, Concord, N. H.
Price, William M., Brooklyn, N. Y.
Pryor, Rev. John, D. D., Cambridge, Mass.

Probyn, Mrs Ann
Prowitt, Henry M., Norwalk, Ct.
Purinton, Rev D B. Fellowship, Va.
Purify, Rev George W. Chapel Hill, N. C.
Purify, Mrs Lucinda, Chapel Hill, N. C.
Purify, Rev Nicholas, Washington, D C
Purington, William F. Prattsburgh, N Y.
Purington, Mrs Rhoda Jane, Prattsburgh, N.Y.
Purser, Mrs. Mary, Brooklyn, N Y.
Putnam, Rev. Daniel, Eaton, N Y.
Putnam, Mrs. Clarinda, Eaton, N. Y.
Quincy, Josiah, Rumney, N H.
Radcliff, Joshua, Haverhill, Mass.
Rafferty, Mrs Susan A, New-York.
Rand, Rev Aaron, New-York
Rand, Mrs M E Hathaway, New York.
Rand, John W, Louisville Ky
Rand, Rev Thomas Ireland, Mass.
Randall, Mrs Mary, New-York.
Randall, Mrs Mary, Mystic River, Ct
Randall, Mrs Maria, Mystic River, Ct.
Randolph, Mrs Huldah, New York.
Randolph, Mrs Sarah F, New-Market, N. J.
Randolph, Joseph F, New-York.
Randolph, Samuel, Plainfield, N J.
Randolph, Peter F, New-York.
Rankin, Mrs Sarah, Reading, Pa.
Rankin, Mrs. Eliza, Reading, Pa.
Rankin, Peter, Phœnixville, Pa
Ranney, E W., New-York.
Rassel, Rev Caleb, Smithfield, Pa
Rathbone, Lewis, Albany, N Y.
Rathbone, Mrs Mary A, Albany, N Y
Rathbone, Thomas R, Providence, R I.
[redacted]

Remsen, George, Brooklyn, N. Y.
Remster, Benjamin, Canton, N. J.
Reynolds, Mrs Mary, New-York.
Reynolds, Rev. John E, Perth, Amboy, N. J.
Reynolds, Abraham M., Newark, N. J.
Rhees, Mrs. Grace W., Williamsburg, N. Y.
Rhodes, G, Lawtonville, S C.
Rice, Rev. A., Stoneville, S. C.
Rice, Mrs Mary, Orleans, N. Y.
Rice, Josiah, Worcester, Mass.
Rich, Joseph C, Penfield, N. Y.
Richards, Rev John M., Germantown, Pa.
Richards, Rev. Humphrey, Dorchester, Mass.
Richards, Mrs. Eunice J, Dorchester, Mass.
Richards, Rev. William C, Lynn, Mass.
Richards, Mrs. Eliza G, Lynn, Mass.
Richards Joel, Claremont, N. H.
Richards, William H, Philadelphia.
Richards, William H, Jr, Philadelphia.
Richards, Edwin S, Philadelphia.
Richards, Joseph L, Philadelphia.
Richards, Zalmon, Washington, D C.
Richards, Henry, Fall River, Mass.
Richards, Truman, Brooklyn, N. Y.
Richardson, Rev. Daniel F., Hanover, N. H.
Richardson, William T., Cambridge, Mass.
Richardson, Thomas S. Brooklyn, N. Y.
Richardson, Mrs. Ann, Boston, Mass.
Richardson, Freeman, Auburn, N. Y.
Richardson, Rev John, South Berwick, Me.
Richmond, Miss Maryetta, Hillsdale, N Y
Richmond, Rev John L, Indianapolis, Ia.
Richmond, Rev. Nathaniel, Pendleton, Ia.
Rider, Charles C, Roxbury, Mass
[redacted]

Rodgers, Rev. Ebenezer, Upper Alton, Ill.
Roe, Rev. Charles H., Belvidere, Ill.
Rogers, Rev. Joseph D., Berlin, N. Y.
Rogers, Enos, Chatham, Mass.
Rogers, Mrs. Eliza D., Providence.
Rogers, Miss Eleanor F., Providence.
Rogers, Richard, New-London, Ct.
Rogers, Rev. J. B., Hornby, N. Y.
Rogers, Dr. Alexander W., Paterson, N. J.
Rollin, Rev. J. B., Tonawanda, N. Y.
Roney, Rev. William, Willistown, Pa.
Roof, Milton, New-York.
Rose, Mrs. Olive E., Troy, N Y.
Ross, Rev. Arthur A., Pawtucket, R. I.
Rowan, Phineas, Philadelphia.
Rowe, John K., Baltimore.
Royal, Rev. William, Winterseat, S. C.
Rue, Rev. Joshua E., Scotch Plains, N. J.
Rugg, George W., Worcester, Mass.
Runyon, Richard E., New-Brunswick, N. J.
Runyon, Hon. Peter P., New-Brunswick, N. J.
Runyon, Daniel, New-Brunswick, N. J.
Runyon, Renne D., New-Market, N. J.
Runyon, Mrs. Isabella, New-York.
Russell, William, Yanceyville, N. C.
Russell, Rev. Abm. A., Stockbridge, Mass.
Russell, Rev. Rutherford, Deep River, Ct.
Russell, Samuel P., Chester, Ct.
Ryland, Rev. Robert, Richmond College, Va.
Sabin, Rev. Alvah, Georgia, Vt.
Saddington, Thomas B., Williamsburgh, N. Y.
Safford, Mrs. Sarah B., Salem, Mass.
Sage, William, Rochester, N. Y.
Sage, Orrin, Rochester, N. Y.
Salisbury, William D., New-York.
Samson, Rev. George W., Washington, D. C.
Samson, I. K., Brooklyn, N. Y.
Sams, Dr. Lewis R., Beaufort, S. C.
Sanborn, Seth J., Lowell, Mass.
Sands, Ezra, Philadelphia.
Sandys, Rev. Edwin, Pittsfield, Mass.
Sanford, Rev. Miles, Gloucester, Mass.
Sanxay, Mrs. Agnes, New-York.
Sarjeant J., Salisbury Mills, Mass.
Sargent, Solon, Haverhill, Mass.
Sarles, Mrs. Cornelia A., Brooklyn, N. Y.
Satterlee, L. R., Rochester, N. Y.
Saunders, Mrs. Harriet, Nuttsville, Va.
Savage, Moses B., Brooklyn, N Y.
Savage, Mrs. Moses B., Brooklyn, N. Y.
Savage, Rev. Edward, Pawtucket, R. I
Savage, Rev. Eleazer, Kendall, N. Y.
Sawyer, Rev. William, Hamburgh, N. Y.
Sawyer, Mrs. H. N., Manchester, N. H.
Sawyer, Moses W., Malden, Mass.
Sawyer, David, Haverhill, Mass.
Sawyer, Rev. Isaac, Manchester, N. H.
Sawyer, Rev. Conant, Lowville, N Y
Sawin, Rev. Addison, A., Bristol, Vt.
Schoolcraft, John L., Albany.
Schofield, Rev. James, Freeport, Ill.
Scott, Robert, Amesbury, Mass.
Scott, John, Columbia, S. C.
Scott, Rev. James, Newburgh, N. Y.
Scott, Mrs. Cornelia S. Newburgh, N. Y.
Scott, Rev. Ebenezer J., Newfane, N. Y.
Scott, Rev. George, Maquoketa, Iowa.
Scott, Rev. Jacob R., Portland, Me.
Scribner, Mrs Maria, New-York.
Seabrook, Mrs. Anna, Middletown N. J.
Sealch, Joseph, jr., New-York.
Seage, Rev. John, Port Richmond, N. Y.
Sears, Miss Harriet H., New-York.
Seaver, Rev. Horace, Chelsea, Mass.
Secomb, E. R., Brookline, Mass.
Seecomb, Mrs Adeline G., Brookline, Mass.
Sedwick, Rev W., Adamsville, Ohio.
Seeley, Mrs. John T., Dundee, N. Y.
Seeley, Rev. Jesse N., Atlanta, Geo.
Seeley, Mrs. Agnes Jane, Atlanta, Ga.
Selleck, Rev. Lewis, Dover, N. Y.
Serrell, Miss Mary C., New-York.
Shailer, Mrs. Catharine P., Roxbury, Ma.
Shailer, Mrs. Sarah, Deep River, Ct.
Shailer, Mrs. Ann, Deep River, Ct.
Shailer, Mrs. Elizabeth, Brookline, Ms.
Shailer, Hezekiah, Suffield, Ct.
Shattuck, Levi H., Somerville, N. J.
Sharp, William B., Wilmington, Del.
Sharp, James M., New-York.
Sharp, Miss Julia D., New-York.
Shaw, Charles, Providence.
Shaw, Miss Harriet N., Providence.
Shaw, Rev. J. Milton, Fort Defiance, N. M.
Shaw, Mrs. Rhoda, New-York.
Shaw, Miss Mary A., New-York.
Sheardown, Rev. T. S., Homersville, N Y.
Shearman, Francis, New-York.
Shed, Charles.
Sheffield, Mrs. Mary, Stamford, Ct.
Sheffield, Thomas S., Brooklyn, N. Y.
Sheldon, Gaylor, Albany.
Sheldon, Smith, do.
Shenston, Joseph W., New-York.
Sheppard, Rev. William, Bridgeton, N. J.
Sheppard, Isaac, Bridgeton, N. J.
Sheppard, John M., Mintonsville, N. C.
Shepardson, Ansel, Fairfax, Vt.
Sherman, William N., Wickford, R. I.
Sherman, Mrs. Mary M., Wickford, R. I.
Sherwin, E. B., Shelburne Falls, Mass.
Sherwood, Walker, Easton, Ct.
Sherwood, Mrs. Lydia, Weston, Ct.
Sherwood, Rev. D. W., Mattewan, N. Y.
Shotwell, Rev. Samuel R., Whitesboro, N. Y.
Showalter, J. B., Willistown, Pa.
Shuck, Rev. J L., Shanghai, China
Sibell, Mrs. Sarah, New York.
Sibley, Rev Clark, New-Hampton, N. H.
Silkworth, Samuel O., New-York.
Silliman, Ezra, Bridgeport, Ct.
Silliman, Mrs Ezra, Bridgeport, Ct.
Silliman, Ebenezer, Southport, Ct.
Silliman, Rev. Gershom, Helena, Ill.
Silliman, Nathaniel L., Easton, Ct.
Silliman, Rev. Harvey, Harmony, N. Y.
Silliman, Stephen, Bridgeport, Ct.
Sims, Maurice P., Canton, N. J.
Simmons, Miss Eliza, Reading, Pa.
Simmons, Mrs. Mary Eliza, Providence.

Simpson, Joseph P., New-York.
Sistare, Mrs. Abby, New-London, Ct.
Skelding, A. Eugene, Greenwich, Ct.
Skinner, E. B., Hertford, N. C.
Skinner, Charles W., do.
Skinner, Mrs. Anna, Hertford, N. C.
Skinner, H. P., Hudson, N. Y.
Skinner, Mrs. Phebe B., Hudson, N. Y.
Skinner, Rev. H. C., Logansport, Ia.
Slack, Thomas, Brooklyn, N. Y.
Slade, Zaccheus, Newbern, N. C.
Slater, Mrs. S. L., Providence.
Slater, Rev. Franklin A., New-Rochelle, N. Y.
Slater, Mrs. Sophrania E. H., do.
Slaughter, James M., Baltimore.
Sleeper, Rev. George, Canton, N. J.
Slote, Henry L., New-York.
Smalley, George C., Brooklyn, N. Y.
Smalley, Henry, New-Brunswick, N. J.
Smith, Rev. Francis, Providence.
Smith, Mrs. M. G., Providence.
Smith, Asa F., New-Eng. Village, Mass.
Smith, Mrs. B. S. W., New-Eng. Village, Ms.
Smith, Rev. Harry, East Aurora, N. Y.
Smith, Mrs. Lydia W., East Aurora, N. Y.
Smith, Samuel, Salem, N. J.
Smith, Mrs. Sarah B., Salem, N. J.
Smith, Miss Ruth Ann, New-York.
Smith, Mrs. William H., Brooklyn, N. Y.
Smith, Mordecai, Brooklyn, N. Y.
Smith, John H., Brooklyn, N. Y.
Smith, Henry W., Brooklyn, N. Y.
Smith, Augustus, do.
[redacted]

Smith, Rev. Rufus, Brookline, Vt.
Smith, Jesse H., New-England Village, Mass.
Smith, Mrs. Mary White, Newton, Mass.
Smith, Rev. James W., Lowell, Mass.
Smith, Mrs. Jane, Troy, N. Y.
Snelling, Miss Priscilla, Chelsea, Mass.
Sniffin, Mrs. Sarah Ann, New-York.
Snowden, Mrs. Eliza, New-York.
Snow, Mrs. Abba S., Rehoboth, Mass.
Snow, Edwin M., Providence, R. I.
Souders, Mrs. Catharine B. L., Frazer's Pa.
Sommers, Mrs. Eliza B., New-York.
Southwood, Rev. William, Ayletts, Va.
Southworth, James E, Brooklyn, N. Y.
Southworth, Mrs. James E., Brooklyn, N. Y.
Southworth, John, Penfield, N. Y.
Sowers, Mrs. Mary E., Battletown, Va.
Sowers, Mrs. Elizabeth, Milwood, Va.
Sparks, Rev. Peter, Newark, N. J.
Spaulding, Isaiah, Chelmsford, Mass.
Spaulding, Daniel B., Stoningtonboro', Ct.
Spaulding, Rev. Silas, Clockville, N. Y.
Spaulding, Rev. Amos F., Boston.
Spaulding, Mrs. Carrie E., E. Cambridge, Mass.
Spear, Rev. Philetus B., Hamilton, N. Y.
Speer, Abraham, Jeddo, N. Y.
Speir, John, Brooklyn, N. Y.
Speir, Mrs. Elizabeth, Brooklyn, N. Y.
Speir, Miss Susan B., Brooklyn, N. Y.
Spencer, D., Brooklyn, N. Y.
Spencer, Robert Little, Plymouth, Va.
Spencer, Rev. Horace, Reeds Corners, N. Y.
Spencer, Elijah, Moodus, Ct.
[redacted]

Stevens, B. H., Essex, Ct.
Stevens, Thomas, Saratoga Springs, N. Y.
Stewart, Rev. Henry G., Seekonk, Mass.
Stickney, Rev. James M., Toulon, Ill.
Stickney, Mrs. J. M., Toulon, Ill.
Stickney, Samuel, Watertown, Mass.
Stillman, O M., Westerly, R. I.
Stillman, Mrs. F. G., Westerly, R. I.
Stillwoll, Albert G., Providence
Stillwell, Mrs. Lydia J Providence.
Stillwell, Charles M., Providence.
Stillwell, Frank B., Providence.
Stimson, Rev. H. K., Clifton, N. Y.
Stockbridge, Mrs. J. G., Providence.
Stocks, Thomas, Greensboro, Ga.
Stockwell, Amos W., Chickopee, Mass.
Stokes, Mrs. Caroline, New-York.
Stites, Rev. Thomas S., Dennis Creek, N. J.
Stone, Rev. Marcus, Norwich, N. Y.
Stone, Rev. James R., New-York.
Stone, Mrs. Gertrude, E. M., New-York.
Stone, Mrs. Dumaris, Swanzey, N. H.
Stone, Eben, Newton, Mass.
Storey, Simeon N., Worcester, Mass.
Storey, James Arnot, Williamsburgh, N. Y.
Storms, Andrew, New-York
Stout, Charles B., New-York.
Stout, Rev. D. B., Middletown, N. J.
Stout, Mrs. L. M. Louisa, C. H., Va.
Stow, Mrs. Baron, Boston.
Stowell, Rev. A. H., Saratoga Springs, N. Y.
Stowell, Mrs. A. H., Saratoga Springs, N. Y.
Stratton, Samuel T., Philadelphia.
Street, Miss Mary Ann, New-York.
Strickland, James L., New-London, Ct.
Strong, Myron, Rochester, N. Y
Stewart, Benjamin, N., Lowell, Mass.
Sturges, Rev. William, Marlborough, N. Y.
Sulley, James, Canton, Ill.
Sully, Mrs. Ann, Canton, Ill.
Sunderlin, Eli, Tyrone, N. Y
Sunderlin, Rev. Alonzo, Dundee, N. Y.
Sunderlin, Horace, Sennett, N. Y.
Sunderlin, Mrs. Margaret, Sennett, N. Y.
Sunderlin, Daniel W., Wayne, N. Y.
Sutton, George, New-York.
Sutton, Mrs. Elizabeth, Britton's ✕ Roads, N.C.
Swaim, Hon. Thomas, Pemberton, N. J.
Swaim, Mrs. Mary, Pemberton, N J.
Swaim, Rev. T., Flemington, N. J.
Swaim, Mrs. Eliza M., Flemington, N. J.
Swaim, Rev. A. M, Leominster, Mass.
Swaim, Samuel N., Worcester, Mass.
Swaim, Mrs. Aurora D. Worcester, Mass.
Swaim, Rev. P. M. Rockville, Ia.
Swain, Joshua, Dennis Creek, N J.
Swan, Mrs. Laura, New-London, Ct.
Swany, Andrew F., New-York.
Swany, Thomas, Brooklyn, N. Y.
Sweet, Joel, Tivoli, Ill.
Sweepson, Mrs. V B., Yanceyville, N. C.
Swick, Rev. Benjamin R. York, N. Y.
Sykes, Rev. James N South Boston, Mass.
Sym, Rev. William, Springfield, Ill.
Symonds, Newton, Reading, Mass.
Taft, Mrs. Mary, Anthony's Village, R. I.
Taggart, Mrs. Harriet M., New-York.
Taggart, William M., New-York.
Tanner, Mrs. Elizabeth F., Spring Garden, Va.
Tanner, Cyrus S., Sennett, N. Y
Tanver, William, Sennett, N. Y.
Tanner, Miss Margaret, Pambina, Min. Ter.
Tapley, Joseph, Lowell, Mass.
Tapley, Joseph W., Lowell, Mass.
Tattersall, Wm. K., New-York.
Taylor, William H., New-York.
Taylor, John G., Middleton, N. J.
Taylor, Jeremiah B., New-York.
Taylor, Mrs. Laura, New-York.
Taylor, Miss Emily, New-York.
Taylor, Miss Ann Jane, New-York.
Taylor, Miss Louisa, New-York.
Taylor, Mrs Sarah A., New-York.
Taylor, Mrs. E. E. L., Brooklyn, N. Y.
Taylor, Miss Harriet Hill, Troy, N Y.
Taylor, Mrs. Maria B., Lawtonville, S. C.
Taylor, Mrs. Dimis, York, N. Y.
Taylor, Rev. Thomas R., Camden, N. J.
Taylor, Rev. Alfred H., Norwich, Ct.
Taylor, Rev. Thomas, Jacksonville, Ill.
Taylor, Rev. David, Ovid, N. Y.
Taylor, Samuel, W., E. Cambridge, Mass.
Taylor, Daniel Webster, New-York.
Taylor, Rev. O. D., Perrington, N. Y.
Taylor, Henry C., Granville, Ohio.
Teasdale, Rev. John, Ill.
Tefft, Willard, Union Village, N Y.
Temple, James H Chillicothe, Ill.
Terry, Mrs. A. N., Spring Garden, Va.
Thatcher, Mrs Elizabeth R.
Thayer, Thomas M., Gouveneer, N. Y.
Thayer, Lewis, Worcester, Mass.
Theall, Mrs. Jane, New-York.
Theall, Miss Susan, New-York.
Thigpen, Rev. Samuel, Raymond, Mi.
Thistle, Mrs. Hannah, New-York.
Thomas, Thomas, New-York.
Thomas, Mrs. Isabella, New-York.
Thomas, Moses, Ballston, Spa, N. Y.
Thomas, James H. New-York.
Thomas, Rev. David E., Zanesville, Ohio.
Thomas, Mrs. Eliza Ann, New-York.
Thomas, Mrs. Mary, Brooklyn, N Y
Thomas, Mrs. Almira S, Brandon, Vt.
Thompson, Mrs. Ann E., New-York.
Thompson, Mrs. S. S. Pittsborough, N. C.
Thompson, Rev. Richard, Poughwade, N. Y.
Thompson, Rev. Charles, Iowa City, Iowa.
Thompson, L., Britton's ✕ Roads, N. C.
Thompson, Benjamin M Harlem, N Y
Thompson, Rev. Sherman B., East Otto, N. Y.
Thompson, Mrs. Serena, New-York.
Thornton, Rev. V R. Public Square, Ga.
Thurston, Henry, Brooklyn, N. Y.
Thurber, Edmund, Providence.
Thurber, Charles, Worcester, Mass.
Ticknor, William D. Boston.
Tiebout, Adam T., Brooklyn, N. Y.
Tiebout, Mrs. Jane, Brooklyn, N. Y.
Tilden, Rev. Chester, North Lyme, Ct.

Tillinghast, Charles E., Providence.
Tilton, Rev. Josiah H., Holden, Mass.
Tindall, Samuel L., Wilmington, Del.
Tinkham, Rev. D., Centre White Creek, N. Y.
Titchener, Henry, Binghamton, N. Y.
Titus, F. J., Middletown, Ohio.
Titus, Rev. S. W., Gorham, N. Y.
Tobey, Rev. Zalmon, Pawtucket, R. I.
Todd, Rev. William, Stevensville, Va.
Todd, Drake P., New-York.
Todd, William W., New-York.
Todd, Mrs William W., New-York.
Todd, Mrs. Angeline M., New-York.
Tolan, Rev. Wm B., Rahway, N. J.
Tolman, Rev. John N., Upper Alton, Ill.
Tolman, Thomas, Philadelphia.
Tolman, Mrs Mary, Philadelphia, Pa.
Tolman, Miss Martha, Boston.
Toplif Rev. C. H., Charlestown, Mass.
Torbet, Rev. Andrew M., Canton, Ohio.
Torian, Elijah, Halifax. C. H., Va.
Townsend S. P., New York
Townsend, Miss Naomi, New-York.
Townsend Rev. G. N., Reading, Mass.
Townsend, Mrs. Louisa L., Brooklyn, N. Y.
Townsend, Rev. B. C., Manchester, N. Y.
Tracy, Lucius H., New-London, Ct.
Tracy, Rev. Orren, Concord, N. H.
Tracy, Mrs Marcia B., Concord, N. H.
Tracy, Miss Susan M., Concord, N. H.
Train, Mrs A. S., Haverhill, Mass.
Travis, Simeon S., New-York.
Trevor, John B., Philadelphia.
Tripp, Mrs Susan, New Bedford, Ms.
[redacted]

Tustin, Rev. Josiah P., Savannah, Geo.
Tustin, John D., Camden, N. J.
Tuthill, Joseph, Brooklyn, N. Y.
Tuttle, Aaron, Littleton, Mass.
Tuxbury, Isaac, Salisbury Mills, Mass.
Twiss, Rev. Daniel F., Spotswood, N. J.
Tyler, Roswell R., Middlesex, N. Y.
Tyler, Mrs. Lucy, Deep River, Ct.
Ulyat, Rev. William C., Norwalk, Ct.
Ulyat, William, New-York.
Underhill, Rev. Charles H., Peekskill, N. Y.
Underhill, P. S., Brooklyn, N. Y.
Underhill, Mrs. Catharine M., Brooklyn, N. Y.
Van Arsdale, Dr. Henry, New-York.
Van Deboe, Adam, Claverack, N. Y.
Van Der Werken, Mrs. Jenet, New-York.
Van Derlip, George M., New-York.
Van Derlip, Mrs. Grace, New-York.
Vanderveer, Mrs. Ann, Moorestown, N. J.
Vail, J. E., Brooklyn, N. Y.
Valentine, Rev. Andrew M., W. Henrietta, N.Y.
Valentine, Elijah F., Cambridge, Mass.
Van Horn, Hon. James, Newfane, N. Y.
Vanest, Abraham, Hightstown, N. J.
Van Nostrand, Miss Mary Ann, New-York.
Van Marter, John, Brooklyn, N. Y.
Vann, Samuel A., New-Haven, Ct.
Van Sant, T. J., Williamsburgh, N. Y.
Van Valkenburgh, John, Williamsburgh, N. Y.
Vassar, Matthew, Poughkeepsie, N. Y.
Vernon, Samuel, Brooklyn, N. Y.
Vernon, Thomas, Brooklyn, N. Y.
Verstile, Mrs. Rebecca E., Savannah, Ga.
Vinal, Wm. D., Lowell, Mass.
[redacted]

Walker, Amos, Pontiac, Mich.
Wallace, Miss Eliza, Brooklyn, N. Y.
Wallace, Jonathan, Fort Covington, N. Y.
Walters, Jacob, Wilmington, Del.
Walton, Joel, Va.
Walton, Jesse, Augusta, Ga.
Walton, Rev. L., Chestnut Hill, Pa.
Ward, Uzal D., New-York.
Ward, Willard, Worcester, Mass.
Wardner, Rev. Chauncey, Covert, N. Y.
Wardner, Mrs. Margaret A., Covert, N. Y.
Ware, Dr. R. J., Montgomery co., Ala.
Warn, Mrs. Sarah M., Sennett, N. Y.
Warn, Mrs. Mary, Sennett, N. Y.
Warner, Dr. Ransom, New York.
Warnock, Miss Elizabeth, New York.
Warren, Mrs. Diantha O., West Potsdam, N. Y.
Warren, Rev. Patrick, Baltimore.
Warren, Rev. Benjamin, Ransomville, N. Y.
Warren, Rev. J. G., Troy, N. Y.
Warren Rev. Edwin R., Thompson, Ct.
Warren, Benjamin I., Williamsburgh, N. Y.
Warren, Moses, Cambridge, Mass.
Warren, Mrs. Grace, Cambridge, Mass.
Warriner, Rev. Norman, Harding, Ill.
Warriner, Rev. R. L., Preston, N. Y.
Washburn, Rev. R. A., Union Village, N. Y.
Washington, Mrs. Elizabeth, Newbern, N. C.
Wasson, Mrs. Clarissa, Albany.
Waters, Mrs. Elizabeth A., Brookline, Mass.
Watts, Mrs. Emma, New-York.
Watts, Charles Henry, New-York.
Wattson, Mrs. Mary B., Philadelphia.
Wattson, Miss Elizabeth, Philadelphia.
Wattson, Rev. W. H., West Acton, Mass.
Watson, George, New York.
Watson, James, Brooklyn, N York.
Watkinson, Wm. E., Philadelphia.
Waterbury, Rev. J. H., Elizabethtown, N. J.
Waterman, Nathan, Jr., Providence.
Way, Rev. Samuel P., Poolville, N. Y.
Waterbury, Miss Martha, Williamsburg, N Y.
Wayland, Mrs. H. S. H., Providence.
Wayland, Francis, Jr., Worcester, Mass.
Weaver, Rev. C. S., Suffield, Ct.
Webb, Mrs. Maria, New Brunswick, N. J.
Webb, Rev. Abner, Belleville, N. Y.
Webb, Rev. W. R., Jordan, N. Y.
Webb, Daniel, Le Roy, N. Y.
Webb, Rev. J. N., Fort Covington, N. Y.
Webster, Phineas, Haverhill, Mass.
Webster, Mrs. Phineas, Haverhill, Mass.
Webster, Rev. Amos, Newton, U. Falls, Mass.
Webster, Rev. S. B., Norwalk, Ohio.
Welch, Mrs. B. T., Brooklyn, N. Y.
Welch, Rev. James E., Hickory Grove, Mo.
Weld, Mrs. Lucy, New-York.
Wells, Mrs. Elizabeth, New-York.
Wells, Rev. Alfred, Vernon, N. Y.
Wells, Rev. Wm. A., Muscatine, Iowa.
Wemple, Abraham A., Schenectady, N. Y.
West, John, Brooklyn, N. Y.
West, Mrs. Ann, Brooklyn, N. Y.
West, John G., Williamsburg, N. Y.
West, Willoughby W., York, N. Y.
West, Rev Hezekiah, Mecklenburg, N. Y.
Weston, Rev. Henry G., Peoria, Ill.
Weston, Mrs. Henry G., Peoria, Ill.
Weston, Mrs. Hetty, Lynn, Mass.
Wescott, Rev Isaac, New-York.
Westervelt, John, Williamsburgh, N. Y.
Westover, Rev. John T., Kenosha, Wis.
Wetherbee, Ephraim, Broadalbin, N. Y.
Wethern, George M., Lowell, Mass.
Wetterau, Mrs. Frances, New York.
Wheat, Rev. A. C., Philadelphia.
Wheat, Mrs. Priscilla P., Philadelphia.
Wheaton, Reuben, Wilmington, Del.
Wheelock, Mrs. E. M, Elbridge, N. Y.
Wheelock, S. B., Greenwich, N. Y.
Wheeler, Mrs. Elizabeth H., Sacramento, Cal.
Wheeler, Miss Melvina P., Sacramento, Cal.
Wheeler, Rev. Benjamin, Plaistow, N. H.
Wheeler, Nelson, Providence, Mass.
Wheeler, Lucius, New-York.
Wheeler, Rev. S. S., New-York.
Wheeler, Mrs. Mary B., New-York.
Wheeler, Rev. Benjamin, Randolph, Mass.
Whidden, Mrs. Sarah, Calais, Me.
Whilden, Rev. B. W., Camden, S. C.
Whipple, Henry, Malone, N. Y.
White, Rev. Samuel, Port Richmond, N. Y.
White, Mrs. E., Port Richmond, N. Y.
White, Miss Martha D., Marcus Hook, Pa.
White, Miss Lydia, Haverhill, Mass.
White, Thomas, Brooklyn, N. Y.
White, Samuel S., Whiteville, N. Y.
White, Harvey, Mount Holly, Vt.
White, Thomas P., Bridgeport, Ct.
White, Joseph, Winchenden, Mass.
White, Beza L., Taunton, Mass.
White, Ebenezer, Newton, Mass.
White, Ebenezer B., Williamsburgh, N. Y.
White, Mrs. Mary, New-York.
White, Samuel, Bordentown, N. J.
Whitehead, Samuel, New Brunswick, N. J.
Whitehead, Mrs. Emeline V., New York.
Whitehead, Artemas K., New-York.
Whitehead, John W., New-York.
Whitehead, Linus P., New York.
Whittemore, Joseph, New York.
Whitford, H. G., Willington, Ct.
Whitman, Charles S., Belvidere, Ill.
Whitman, Hiram, Belvidere, Ill.
Whitman, Alva, Mich.
Whitman, John C., Sennett, N. Y.
Whitney, Miss Harriet, New-York.
Whitney, Mrs. Betsey, Worcester, Mass.
Whitney, Bennet, Bridgeport, Ct.
Whittier, Leonard, Haverhill, Mass.
Whittier, Mrs. Leonard, Haverhill, Mass.
Whittier, Miss Abby, Haverhill, Mass.
Whitney, Raymond, North Fairfield, Ohio.
Whitney, Mrs. E. S. Brooklyn, N. Y.
Whitney, Eben, Norwalk, Ct.
Wight, Leonard B., Wales, Mass.
Wightman, Rev. J. G., Groton, Ct.
Wiggins, Rev. J. W., Farmerville, N. Y.
Wilbur, Mrs Sally, East Avon, N. Y.
Wilbur, Curtis, Troy, N. Y.

Wilbur, Rev. O., Lowville, N. Y.
Wilcox, Rev. J. F., Springfield, Mass.
Wilcox, Mrs. Louisa S., Springfield, Mass.
Wilcox, Abraham, Shelburne Falls, Mass.
Wilder, John N., Albany.
Wilder, Mrs. Delia A., Albany.
Wilder, Rev. Sydney, North Norwich, N. Y.
Wildman, Mrs. Roxey S., Lebanon, Ct.
Wilkins, Rev. Stephen, New-York.
Wilkins, Rev. Andrew, Tyrone, N. Y.
Wilkinson, Rev. Wm., Drummondville, C. W.
Willard, Rev. George A., Warwick Neck, R. I.
Willard, Lucius A., Providence.
Willard, Mrs. Polly, Pawlet, Vt.
Willard, Mrs. Nancy, Jonesborough, Ill.
Willard, Rev. C. M., Harvard, Mass.
Willard, Hon. Levi, Keene, N. H.
Willett, Miss Sarah, New-York.
Willett, Mrs. Charles, New-London, Ct.
Williams, Mrs. Elizabeth S., Fayetteville, N. C.
Williams, Mrs. Charity S., Fayetteville, N. C.
Williams, Mrs. Mary M., Fayetteville, N. C.
Williams, Polly M., Rockport, Ohio.
Williams, Francis B., New-York.
Williams, Rev. David S., Cumberland, N. C.
Williams, Rev. William B., Williamsville, N. Y.
Williams, Mrs. Eunice, Deep River, Ct.
Williams, Rev. John, Marion, Iowa.
Williams, Rev. C. C., Plainfield, N. J.
Williams, Rev. B. S., Plymouth, N. Y.
Williams, Mrs. William R., New York.
Willingham, Thomas, Lawtonville, S. C.
Willington, Miss Catharine, Watertown, Mass.
Willis, Rev. Samuel B., Maryland, N. Y.
[redacted]

Wisner, Mrs. Sarah, Mount Morris, N. Y.
Wisner, Mrs. Adaline, Elmira, N. Y.
Wisham, Samuel, Moorestown, N. J.
Wiswell, Mrs. C. A., West Troy, N. Y.
Witherwax, Dr. J. M., Davenport, Iowa.
Withall, John, Henrietta, N. Y.
Witherbee, John B., Jamaica Plains, Mass.
Withington, Elijah, Williamsburg, N. Y.
Withington, Mrs. M., Williamsburg, N. Y.
Wolcott, Mrs. Mary S., New-York.
Wolcott, Mrs. Naomi, Rochester, N. Y.
Wollaston, Joshua, Wilmington, Del.
Wood, Mrs. J. S. Hertford, N. C.
Wood, Mrs. Mary E. Hertford, N. C.
Wood, Rev. N. N., Alton, Ill.
Wood, Jennings J., Speedwell, S. C.
Wood, George, Springfield, Ill.
Wood, Joseph T., Westboro', Mass.
Woodbridge, William A., New-York.
Woodbury, William W., Suffield, Ct.
Woodbury, Rev. John, Templeton, Mass.
Woodruff, Mrs. Innocent, Albany.
Woodward, Rev. Jonas, Parma, N. Y.
Woodward, Mrs. Eliza, Parma, N. Y.
Woodward, Mrs. Mary D., Middlesex, Va.
Woodward, Sylvester, Lowell, Mass.
Woolsey, Rev. James J., Norwalk, Ct.
Wooster, Mrs. Aurelia R., Deep River, Ct.
Worth, Rev. Edmund, Fisherville, N. H.
Worthington, S., Springfield, Mass.
Wright, Rev. David, North Colebrook, Ct.
Wright, Mrs. Abigail, North Colebrook, Ct.
Wright, William J., Hargrove's, Va.
Wright, Theodore, New-York.
[redacted]

LIST OF DECEASED

DIRECTORS AND MEMBERS FOR LIFE.

1833-4.

DIRECTOR.

Cobb, Nathaniel R., Boston, Mass.

MEMBERS.

Barrett, Rev. Thomas, Webster, Mass.
Chase, Rev. John, Brookfield, Mass.

1834-5.

MEMBER.

Lasell, Rev. J. E., Harvard, Mass.

1835-6.

DIRECTORS.

Foster, Rev. E., Amesbury, Mass
Freeman, Rev. E. W., Lowell, Mass.
Jacobs, Rev. Bela, Cambridge, Mass.

MEMBER.

Martin, Rev. A R., Staten Island, N. Y.

1836-7.

DIRECTOR.

Trask, Rev. Wm. G., Taunton, Mass.

1837-8.

DIRECTOR.

Davis, Rev. Gustavus F., Hartford, Ct.

MEMBERS.

Blain, Miss Mary E., Syracuse, N. Y
Holroyd, Rev. John, Danvers, Mass.
Kitts, Rev. T. J., Philadelphia.
Ludlow, Rev. Peter, New-York.
Starkweather, Oliver, Pawtucket, R. I.

1838-9.

DIRECTORS.

Crawford, Rev. Luther, Brooklyn, N. Y.
Knowles, Rev. James D., Newton, Mass.

MEMBERS.

Banner, Rev. Job B., Sutton, Mass.
Smalley, Rev. Henry, Cohansey, N. J.
Vaughn, Rev. Ashley, Natchez, Miss.

1839-40.

DIRECTOR.

Bolles Rev. Matthew, D. D., Boston.

MEMBERS.

Blain, Mrs. Lucy, Syracuse, N. Y.
Hubbell, Rev. Elisha D., Clifton Park, N. Y.
Sheppard. Rev. Joseph, Mount Holly, N. J.

1840-41.

DIRECTORS.

Chesman, Rev. Daniel, Lynn, Mass.
Hammond, Rev. O. T., Florida.
Shute, Rev. Caleb B., Boston.

MEMBERS.

Chaplain, Rev. J., Hamilton, N. Y.
Dodge, Rev. O. A., Lexington, Mass.
Hunting, Mrs. Dorcas, Corinth, Me.
McAllister, Charles, Fayetteville, N. C.
Nourse, Rev. Peter, Ellsworth, Me.
Stearns, Rev. Silas, Bath, Me.
Williams, Elizabeth, Society Hill, S. C.
Williams, A., Elizabeth City, N. C.

1841-2.

DIRECTOR.

Brown, Nicholas, Providence, R. I.

MEMBERS.

Colgate, John, New-York.
Eaton, Martin, Petersburg, Va
Hill, Frederick M., New-York.
Leonard, Rev. Zenas L., Sturbridge, Mass
Lipscomb, Mrs. Martha Louisa, C. H., Va.
Mercer, Rev Jesse, Washington, Geo.
Miles, Joseph, Milesburgh, Pa.

1842-3.

MEMBERS.

Gear, Rev. Hiram, Marietta, Ohio.
Towell, Mrs. E. B., Sandy Bottom, Va.
Vanderpool, Hon. James, Newark, N. J

1843-4.

DIRECTORS.

Cooper, Thomas, Eatonton, Geo.
Linsley, Rev. James H., Stratford, Ct.
Middleton, Rev. John, Geneva, N. Y.

MEMBERS.

Pickens, Mrs. Margaret Eliza, Edgefield, S. C.
Rankin, Henry, Reading, Pa.
Wasson, J. G., Albany, N. Y.

1844-5.

DIRECTORS

Armstrong, Rev John, Columbus, Miss.
Coolidge, James D., Madison, N. Y.
Going, Rev Jonathan, D. D, Granville, Ohio
Miller, Rev William G., Essex, Ct.

MEMBERS.

Adams, Mrs. Mary, New-York.
Belden, Charles D., New-York.
Birdsall, Rev. John O., Perrysburg, Ohio.
Carney, Richard, Portsmouth, Va.
Colgate, George, New-York.
McIntosh, Mrs. Mary, Philadelphia.

1845-6.

MEMBERS.

Cauldwell, Mrs. Maria, New-York.
Hall, Rev. Wilson, Beaufort, S. C.
Jones, Mrs. J. Leavitt, Bangkok, Siam.
Lathrop, Rev. Lebbeus, Samptown, N. J.
Marshall, Joseph H., Nashville, Tenn.
Mitchell, Rev. John, Hoosick, N. Y.
Randall, Mrs. Mary E., Woburn, Mass.
Reynolds, Joseph, Norwich, Ct.

1846-7.

DIRECTORS.

Bacheller, Mrs. Mary, Lynn, Mass.
Devan, Mrs. Lydia, Canton, China.
Everts, Rev. Jeremiah B., Washington, N. Y.

[redacted]

MEMBERS.

Allen, Mrs. Eliza C., New-York.
Brouner, Rev. Jacob H., New-York.
Chamberlin, Hinds, Le Roy, N. Y.
Jencks, Mrs. Caroline B, Bankok, Siam
Ludlam, John H, New-York.
Naylor, Rev. J. G., Portsmouth, N. H.
Peck, Rev. Abijah, Clifton Park, N. Y.
Shaw, Oliver, Providence, R. I.
Wayland, Rev. F., Sr., Saratoga Springs, N. Y.
Wildman, Rev. Daniel, Lebanon, Ct.
Williams, Rev. Daniel, New-York.

1849-50.

DIRECTORS.

Allen, Rev. Ira M., New-York.
Bradford, Rev. Z., Providence, R. I.
Estes, Rev. Elliott, Lower Three Runs, S. C.
Milbank, Charles W., New-York.
Peck, Rev. John, New-Woodstock, N. Y.
Train, Rev. Charles, Framingham, Mass.
Wilson, James, New-York.

MEMBERS.

Baillie, Jonathan, Parham's Store, Va.
Barker, Rev. Luke, New-York.
Brockway, C., Broadalbin, N. Y.
Brown, William, Parham's Store, Va.
Cate, Rev. George W., Barre, Mass.
Corning, Mrs. Nancy, Brooklyn, N. Y.
Cox, Charles, Rahway, N. J.
Crawford, Rev. D. B, Antioch, Miss.

[redacted]

McLaren, Finley, Le Roy, N. Y.
Munn, Mrs. Sarah P., New-York.
Ormsby, Rev. John. Knox's Corners, N. Y.
Parker, Amasa, W., Lowell, Mass.
Postley, Charles, New-York.
Randall, Jedediah, Portersville, Ct.
Snook, John, Fort Gibson, N. Y.
Todd, William H., New-York.
White, Thomas, Philadelphia.

1851-2.

DIRECTORS.

Dodge, Rev. Daniel, Philadelphia.
Hatt, Mrs. Mary I., Hoboken, N. J.
Meritt, Rev. W. H, Chapel Hill, N. C.
Sherman, Rev. O. J., Peoria, Ill.

MEMBERS.

Bolles, Rev. D. C., Southbridge, Mass.
Chase, Amos, Haverhill, Mass.
De Graffemied, Mrs. S., Crosbyville, S. C.
Farnsworth, Rev. B. F., Nashville, Tenn.
Gibbs, Mrs. Betsy H., Sullivan, N. H.
Goodell, A., Sommersworth, N. H.
Hall, Rev. Daniel, New-York.
Jones, Mrs. Susan, Newbern, N. C.
Lathrop, Mrs. Jane E., New-York.
Manning, Rev. Benjamin, Brookfield, Mass.
Martin, Mrs. R. W., New-York.
Remington, Mrs. Eliza Ann, New-York.
Rider, Miss Olive P., Suffield, Ct.
Shuck, Mrs. Eliza G., Shanghai, China.
Stone, Mrs. Sarah A, New-York.
Tucker, Mrs. Levi, Boston, Mass.
Whitman, Rev. S. S., Madison, Wis.

1852-3.

DIRECTORS.

Brown, Rev. O. B, Washington, D. C.
Crozer, Miss Sallie K, Chester, Pa.
Rhees, Rev. Morgan J., D. D., Williamsb'h, N Y

MEMBERS.

Adams, Mrs. Cornelia C, Cleveland, Ohio.
Ashley, Mrs. Hannah, Poultney, Vt.
Bellamy, Mrs. Eliza, Arcadia, N. Y.
Boynton, Mrs. Ruth, North Springfield, Vt.
Cosner, Rev. Henry, Lyndon, Ill.
Fant, Rev. Ephraim, Halselville, S. C.
Goodliff, James, New-York.
Haskell, Rev. Daniel, Hamilton, N. Y.
Haynes, Rev. Arus, M. D, New-York.
Jones, Rev. John, Belleville, Ia.
Maghee, Mrs. Ann C., New-York.
Maginnis, Rev. John, D D., Rochester, N. Y.
Miner, Mrs. Mary Jane, New-York.
Owen, Rev. E. D., Madison, Ia.
Shipley, Simon G., Boston.
Symonds, Rev. Thomas M., Green Bay, Wis.
Turner, Mrs. Grace, New-London, Ct.
Weeks, Miss Ann, New-York.
Wise, Miss Harriet, W., New-Russia, N. Y.
Wolcott, Epaphroditus, Rochester, N. Y.
Woodruff, Rev. Seth, New-Albany, Ia.

☞ Some of the preceding names may be erroneously dated, as the precise year of their decease was not reported to us. We are anxious to have this list as perfect as possible, and hereby request surviving friends of the deceased to send us the necessary corrections.

CONTENTS.

PAGE.

ANNUAL REPORT.

[redacted]

TWENTY-SECOND REPORT

OF THE

American Baptist Home Mission Society,

PRESENTED BY THE

EXECUTIVE BOARD

AT THE

ANNIVERSARY HELD IN PHILADELPHIA,

MAY 11th, 12th, 13th, and 14th, 1854,

WITH

THE TREASURER'S REPORT AND OTHER DOCUMENTS.

NEW YORK:
PUBLISHED AT THE AMERICAN BAPTIST HOME MISSION ROOMS, No. 354 BROOME ST.
HOLMAN, GRAY & CO., PRINTERS, COR. CENTRE AND WHITE STREETS.
1854.

ACT OF INCORPORATION.

AN ACT TO INCORPORATE THE AMERICAN BAPTIST HOME MISSION SOCIETY, PASSED APRIL 12, 1843, AND AMENDED FEBRUARY 9, 1849.

The People of the State of New York, represented in Senate and Assembly, do enact as follows:

§ 1. All such persons as now are, or may hereafter become members of the American Baptist Home Mission Society, formed in the City of New York, in the year One Thousand Eight Hundred and Thirty-two, shall be, and hereby are, constituted a body corporate, by the name of the American Baptist Home Mission Society, for the purpose of promoting the preaching of the Gospel in North America.

[redacted]

CONSTITUTION.

NAME.

I. THIS Society shall be called the AMERICAN BAPTIST HOME MISSION SOCIETY.

OBJECT.

II. The object of this Society shall be to promote the preaching of the Gospel in North America.

MEMBERSHIP.

III. The Society shall be composed of Annual Delegates, Life Members and Life Directors. Any Baptist church, in union with the denomination, may appoint a delegate for an annual contribution of ten dollars, and an additional delegate for each additional thirty dollars. Thirty dollars shall be requisite to constitute a member for life; and one hundred dollars paid at one time, or a sum which, in addition to any previous contribution, shall amount to one hundred dollars, shall be requisite to constitute a director for life.

OFFICERS.

IV. The Officers of the Society shall be a President, two Vice-Presidents, a Treasurer, an Auditor, a Corresponding Secretary, a Financial Secretary, and a Recording Secretary, whom the Society shall annually elect by ballot.

MANAGERS AND EXECUTIVE BOARD.

V. The Officers and Life Directors shall meet immediately after the Annual Meeting of the Society, and elect fifteen Managers, residing in the city of New York, or its vicinity, who, together with the Treasurer, Auditor, and the Secretaries, shall constitute an Executive Board to conduct the business of the Society; and shall respectively continue to discharge their official duties until superseded by a new election. Seven members of the Board shall be a quorum for the transaction of business.

POWERS AND DUTIES OF THE EXECUTIVE BOARD.

VI. The Executive Board shall have power to appoint its own meetings; elect its own Chairman and Recording Secretary; enact its own By-Laws and Rules of Order, provided always, that they be not inconsistent with this Constitution; fill any vacancies which may occur in their own body or in the offices of the Society during the year; and, if deemed necessary by two-thirds of the members present at a regular meeting, convene special meetings of the Society. They shall establish such Agencies as the interests of the Society may require; appoint Agents and Missionaries; fix their compensation; direct and instruct them concerning their particular fields and labors; make all appropriations to be paid out of the treasury; and present to the Society at each annual meeting a full report of their proceedings during the current year.

DESIGNATED FUNDS.

VII. All moneys or other property contributed and designated for any particular Missionary field, shall be so appropriated, or returned to the donors, or their lawful agents.

TREASURER.

VIII. The Treasurer shall give bonds to such amount as the Executive Board shall think proper.

ELIGIBILITY TO APPOINTMENT.

IX. All the Officers, Managers, Missionaries, and Agents of the Society, shall be members in good standing in regular Baptist churches.

ANNUAL MEETING.

X. The Society shall meet annually, at such time and place as the Executive Board shall appoint.

ALTERATIONS OF THE CONSTITUTION.

XI. No alteration of this Constitution shall be made without an affirmative vote of two-thirds of the members present at an annual meeting; nor unless the same shall have been proposed in writing, and the proposition sustained by a majority vote, at a previous annual meeting, or recommended by the Executive Board.

STATED MEETINGS FOR 1854–55.

Of the Executive Board—Thursday before the first Wednesday in each month.

" " Committee on Missions—The day previous to that of the Board.

" " Committee on Agencies and Finance—The Tuesday preceding.

BY-LAWS OF THE BOARD.

1. All meetings shall be opened with prayer.
2. All Committees shall be nominated by the presiding officer, and approved by the Executive Board, unless otherwise specially ordered.
3. No moneys shall be paid out of the Treasury, but by order of the Executive Board.
4. All resolutions, if required, shall be presented in writing.

ORDER OF BUSINESS.

1. Reading the minutes of the last meeting.

5. Reports of Standing Committees.

[redacted]

MINUTES OF THE TWENTY-SECOND ANNIVERSARY

OF THE

American Baptist Home Mission Society,

HELD IN PHILADELPHIA,

May 11th, 12th, 13th, and 14th, 1854.

The Society met on Thursday the 11th of May, at 3 o'clock, P.M., in the Meeting-house of the Spruce-street Baptist Church, and was called to order by the President, Hon. Isaac Davis, LL.D., of Worcester, Mass.

Rev. Dr. Caldicott, of Massachusetts, read the hymn commencing,

> "O Zion, tune thy voice,
> And raise thy hands on high,"

which was sung by the congregation; after which prayer was offered by Rev. A. Armstrong, of New Jersey.

The President then congratulated the Society upon the remarkable success attending its efforts since its organization, and exhorted to devout gratitude to God, and to increased zeal in behalf of the Home Mission cause.

Ministering and other brethren present, not members of the Society, were invited to participate in its deliberations.

On motion of Rev. N. B. Baldwin, of Pa., the time for commencing and closing the sessions of each day, was fixed as follows:

To commence at 9 A.M., and at 3 and 7½ P.M. To adjourn at 12 M., and 5 P.M.

On motion of Hon. J. M. Linnard, of Pa., it was unanimously *resolved*, that all committees be appointed by the President, without the confirmation of the Society, unless specially ordered otherwise.

The Chair announced the following committees:

On Credentials of Delegates—Rev. brn. I. R. STEWARD, of N. Y., T. S. GRIFFITHS, Pa., S. W. MILES, N. H., J. BELCHER, Me., and G. W. HARRIS, Mich.

On Nomination of Officers—Rev. brn. T. F. CALDICOTT, D.D., Mass., J. L. HODGE, D.D., N. Y., J. WHEATON SMITH, Pa., L. H. MOORE, Mich., and E. W. BARKER, N. J.

On Arrangements for Public Exercises—Rev. brn. M. G. CLARK, D. B. Cheney, J. H. Kennard, Pa.; E. LATHROP, N. Y., and N. B. BALDWIN, Pa.

The Treasurer, CHARLES J. MARTIN, Esq., of New York, presented his report, with the Auditor's certificate; which, on motion of JOHN HANNA, Esq., and seconded by WILSON JEWELL, M.D., of Pa., was accepted, and ordered to be printed.

The proposition of Rev. O. AYER, of N. H., to amend the 11th article of the Constitution (see Minutes of 1853, page 7) was taken up, and, upon motion of Rev. J. DOWLING, D.D., indefinitely postponed.

On the recommendation of the Executive Board, the 4th article of the

[redacted]

the income of which to be annually applied toward the salaries of the Secretaries."

The subject was referred to a committee consisting of Rev. N. A. Reed, of Mass., Hon. J. M. Linnard, Pa., and J. E. Southworth, Esq., N. Y.

After prayer by Rev. J. Belcher, D.D., the Society adjourned.

EVENING SESSION.

The meeting was opened with prayer by Rev. Samuel Baker, D.D., of N. Y., and the hymn

"Come Holy Spirit, Heavenly Dove,
With all Thy quickening powers," &c.

The Annual Report of the Executive Board was read by the Corresponding Secretary.

Upon motion of Rev. R. H. Neale, D.D., of Mass., seconded by Rev. J. E. Chesshire, of R. I., the Report was accepted and ordered to be printed.

The President then, upon motion, announced the following committees, and the Society adjourned:

On Finance—Messrs. W. Jewell, M.D., Pa., Hon. Anthony Colby, N. H., Wm. Bucknell, Esq., Pa., W. Winterton, Esq., N. Y., Rev. W. C. Child, Mass.

Grand Ligne Mission—Rev. Messrs. M. Cyr, Canada, A. P. Mason, Mass., T. Clark, Ct., J. L. Burrows, Pa., and O. Ayer, N. H.

Indian Missions—Rev. Messrs. S. Dyer, Ia., S. Catlin, Minnesota, J. Aldrich, Mass., R. Jeffrey, N. Y., and R. J. Wilson, Ct.

Missions in the Far West—Rev. Messrs. O. C. Wheeler, California, E. W. Dickenson, Pa., W. Dean, D.D., China, J. G. Oncken, Germany, and Prof. P. B. Spear, N. Y.

Missions in the Great Central Valley—Rev. Messrs. D. B. Cheney, Pa., E. W. Cressy, Min., J. A. Dixon, Ia., J. A. Goodhue, Ct., and C. N. Chandler, N. Y.

Obituary Notices—Rev. Messrs. J. Belcher, D.D., Pa., O. T. Walker, Ct., A. S. Patton, N. J., E. B. Eddy, Mass., and E. N. Jenks, Ill.

Church Edifice Fund—Rev. Messrs. M. G. Clarke, Pa., J. P. Barnett, Ia., S. J. Drake, N. J., J. T. Seeley, N. Y., and Thomas Wattson, Esq., Pa.

FRIDAY MORNING, MAY 12TH.

The Society met at 9 o'clock for devotional services. Rev. DANIEL ELDRIDGE, of N. Y., in the chair. After singing, Rev. ELON GALUSHA, of N. Y., engaged in prayer, and was followed at the Throne of Grace, by Rev. brethren F. MERRIAM, of Me., O. DODGE, of N. Y., I. BEVAN, of Pa., J. M. CHALLIS, of N. J., and N. B. BALDWIN, of Pa.; Revs. J. H. KENNARD, of Pa., and F. MERRIAM, made a few remarks, showing the great necessity of increased prayer in the Missionary enterprise, and especially in connection with liberal contributions.

At 10 o'clock, the hour appointed for business, Hon. ISAAC DAVIS resumed the chair, and the Minutes of Thursday were read and approved.

On motion of Rev. S. S. CUTTING, it was

Resolved, That the Executive Board be empowered to hold a meeting immediately for the transaction of necessary business.

The Special Committee to whom was referred so much of the Annual Report as relates to the raising of a permanent Fund of $25,000, reported through Rev. N. A. REED, of Mass., Chairman. The Report was unanimously adopted, together with the following resolution:

[redacted]

Rev. F. G. BROWN, of Mass., moved that Bro. SOUTHWORTH'S resolution be laid upon the table, with reference to the appointment of a Committee to Report on the whole matter. Bro. BROWN'S resolution was laid on the table.

Pending the discussion on Bro. SOUTHWORTH'S resolution, the Society adjourned.

Prayer by Dr. CALDICOTT, of Mass.

AFTERNOON SESSION.

President in the Chair. Prayer by Rev. G. C. BALDWIN, D.D., of New York.

On motion of Rev. S. W. FIELD, of R. I., it was

Resolved, That the vote upon Bro. SOUTHWORTH'S motion be taken at fifteen minutes before 4 o'clock.

Rev. T. G. WRIGHT, of N. J., proposed the following amendment to Mr. SOUTHWORTH'S resolution, viz:

"Provided an equally desirable lease, whether in regard to permanency, commodiousness and convenience, or all together, cannot be secured in the present location."

The amendment was seconded by Rev. J. HATT, of N. J., and adopted by the Society.

The resolution as amended was then adopted, without an opposing vote.

The Committee on Credentials reported, through Rev. I. R. STEWARD, of N. Y., that the following brethren had been duly appointed as delegates to this body, by their respective churches: namely,

Rev. F. KETCHAM, Ill., Rev. A. S. COLE, N. Y., Rev. WM. ARTHUR, N. Y., Rev. J. SHEPHERDSON, Mass., Rev. J. N. CHASE, N. H., and Bro. JOHN S. BROWN, N. H.

The Report was adopted.

The Committee on Nomination of Officers reported through Rev. T. F. CALDICOTT, D.D., of Mass., a ballot for officers for the ensuing year.

Hon. J. M. LINNARD, of Pa., THOMAS WATTSON, Esq., of Pa., and WM. BUCKNELL, Esq., of Pa., were appointed a Committee to collect, assort, and count the votes for officers.

The Tellers reported that each person named on the ballot presented by the Committee on Nomination was elected. (See page 16.)

Rev. J. BELCHER, D.D., of Pa., reported in behalf of the Committee on Obituaries; the report was adopted, and ordered to be printed in the Minutes. (Page 60.)

Rev. N. B. Baldwin, of Pa., Rev. B. M. Hill, of New York, and Rev. R. H. Neal, D.D., of Mass., made a few remarks upon the virtues of the deceased Life Directors, and Life Members, and Rev. G. W. Samson, of D. C., led in prayer.

Rev. S. Dyer, of Ind., presented the Report of the Committee on Indian Missions, and accompanied it with a speech; he was followed by Rev. S. T. Catlin, of Min., and the Report was adopted, and ordered to be printed with the Minutes. (Page 61.)

Adjourned by singing the Doxology.

FRIDAY EVENING.

Society met at 15 minutes before 8 o'clock.

President in the Chair. Prayer by Rev. N. Cyr, of the Grand Ligne Mission.

Rev. O. C. Wheeler, of Cal., presented the Report of the Committee [redacted]

After singing, Rev. J. S. Backus, of N. Y., Rev. J. E. Chesshire, of R. I., Rev. J. Aldrich, of Mass., Rev. A. W. Sunderlin, of N. Y., Rev. J. G. Oncken, of Germany, and Rev. F. Ketchum, of Illinois, led in prayer.

Rev. O. C. Wheeler, of Cal., followed with remarks on the necessity of more laborers in California.

The Society came to order for business at 10 o'clock. President in the Chair.

The Corresponding Secretary called the attention of the Society to that part of the Annual Report which relates to the Church Edifice Fund; when,

On motion, that portion of the Report was referred to the consideration of the special meeting appointed for this afternoon.

The Committee on the Grand Ligne Mission reported, through Rev. N. Cyr, of Canada. Rev. H. C. Fish, of N. J., moved the adoption of the Report, in a brief address, and was followed by Rev. Dr. Dowling, of Pa.; whereupon the Report was adopted, and ordered to be printed with the Minutes. (Page 73.)

Dr. Jewell, of Pa., presented the Report of the Committee on Financial Affairs, which, on motion of Rev. J. E. Rue, of N. J., was adopted, and ordered to be printed. (Page 78.)

Rev. D. G. Corey, of N. Y., offered the following resolution, which was carried:

Resolved, That the Executive Board be instructed to recommend in the Next Annual Report, such a change in the fifth article of the Constitution as shall allow the Society to have a voice more directly in the election of the Board of Managers.

Rev. S. Ilsley, of N. Y., offered the following, which was carried:

Resolved, That a vote of thanks be tendered to the Spruce street Baptist Church, and to the several other Baptist Churches of this city, and also to the citizens of Philadelphia, for the truly generous hospitalities which they have extended to this body.

On motion of Rev. G. C. Baldwin, D.D., of N. Y., it was

Resolved, That a committee of four be appointed to coöperate with other religious societies, to endeavor to effect a general arrangement whereby the fare on the various railroads and steamboats leading to the place of our next anniversary, may be obtained at a reduced price, and report through the denominational papers.

Rev. G. C. Baldwin, D.D., of N. Y., Rev. T. F. Caldicott, D.D., of Mass., Rev. S. S. Cutting of N. Y., and Rev. D. B. Cheney, of Pa., were appointed said committee.

On motion, the Society adjourned *sine die*. Prayer by Rev. J. Dowling, D.D., of Pa.

MEETING OF LIFE DIRECTORS AND OFFICERS.

Immediately after the adjournment of the Society, the Life Directors and Officers present proceeded to organize for the election of the Executive Board.

J. P. Crozer, Esq., of Pa., was called to the Chair.

Rev. O. B. Judd, of N. Y., moved that a committee of three be appointed to nominate the Board of Managers for the ensuing year. The resolution was adopted, and

Rev. A. P. Mason, of Mass., Rev. J. T. Seeley, of N. Y., and Hon. J. M. Linnard, of Pa., were appointed as the Committee.

On motion of Rev. J. L. Hodge, D.D., of N. Y., it was

Resolved, That when the Committee report, we proceed to vote by ballot.

The Nominating Committee reported a ballot for the Board of Managers, when, on motion, their report was accepted.

Wm. Winterton, Esq., of N. Y., and Thomas Wattson, Esq., of Pa., were appointed tellers.

[redacted]

Rev. S. S. CUTTING, of N. Y., offered the following resolution, which was passed unanimously:

Resolved, That the thanks of this Society are hereby presented to the Hon. ISAAC DAVIS, President, for the promptness, dignity, and impartiality with which he has presided on this occasion.

Adjourned. Prayer by Rev. M. WARDER, of Ky.

The Sabbath was occupied with three interesting services, though two of the brethren who had been engaged to preach before the Society were not present. Rev. Dr. DEAN, of China, occupied the morning hour, Rev. S. DRYDEN PHELPS, of New Haven, Ct., preached in the afternoon, and Rev. O. C. WHEELER, of California, in the evening.

[redacted]E AMERICAN BAPTIST HOME MISSION SOCIETY

To Cash paid Missionaries for Salaries, ...	$39,651 49
" Cash paid Agents for Salaries, Travelling Expenses, Postage, &c., ...	5,357 92
" Cash paid for Stationery, design for Diploma plate, Postages, and Incidental Expenses, . .	411 15
" Cash paid Salaries, Secretaries, and Clerks, . .	3,642 66
" Cash paid for paper and printing of Home Mission Record, and expenses on same, ...	1,607 02
" Cash paid for paper and printing Annual Report, Sermon, Certificates, Blanks, &c., ...	717 71
" Cash paid Taxes on land donated to the Society,	23 65
" Cash paid discount on uncurrent funds, and counterfeit money received on account of donations, &c., ...	67 65
" Cash paid on account of designated funds for Meeting-houses, ...	5,249 59
[redacted] to E. Loomis and E. Hanks [redacted] . .	31 76
[redacted]	

IN ACCOUNT WITH CHAS. J. MARTIN, TREASURER. *Cr.*

1854.	By Balance from last year, ...		$4,465 98
	" Cash proceeds of notes (contributed last year),		1,150 00
	" Cash interest and dividends received on sundry temporary investments, ...	$180 00	
	" Cash interest received on Bonds and Mortgages (a special investment by direction of the donor),	140 00	320 00
	" Cash amount received for subscriptions to Home Mission Record, ...		1,360 45
	" Cash amount of designated Funds for Meeting-houses, ...		5,678 83
	" Cash amount received for Educational purposes,		581 75
	" Cash from American Baptist Publication Society for Indian Hymn Books, ...		65 57
	" Cash amount of Contributions, Legacies, &c., received from 1st April, 1853, to 31st March, 1854,	$50,054 93	
	Of which this amount is in bills receivable not yet matured,	947 25	49,107 68
			$62,730 26
March 31	By Balance, ...	$4,302 71	
	Subject to drafts of Cor. Secretary already issued upon the Treasurer, and liable to immediate presentation, amounting to,	3,021 39	$1,281 32

CHARLES J. MARTIN, *Treasurer.*

This is to certify that I have examined the foregoing account, together with the vouchers connected therewith, and find the same correct. The balance in the hands of Charles J. Martin, Esq., Treasurer, in cash, is Four Thousand Three Hundred and Two 71-100 Dollars. He also holds bills receivable, Eleven Hundred and Seven 25-100 Dollars. He has in his possession the following securities, viz.: Certificate of Stock in the Corn Exchange Bank, New York, for Two Thousand Dollars; Brooklyn City Bond, bearing interest at six per cent., payable Jan. 1, 1868, for Five Hundred Dollars; also Two Bonds and Mortgages (a special investment by direction of the donor), the interest only to be used by the Society, the principal of which bonds is Two Thousand Five Hundred Dollars.

ROBERT THOMPSON, Jr., *Auditor.*

NEW YORK, *April 1st*, 1854.

OFFICERS OF THE SOCIETY

AND

EXECUTIVE BOARD.

OFFICERS.

PRESIDENT.

HON. ISAAC DAVIS, LL.D., Worcester, Massachusetts.

VICE-PRESIDENTS.

WILLIAM COLGATE, Esq., New York.
JOHN P. CROZER, Esq., Chester, Pa.

TREASURER.

CHARLES J. MARTIN, Esq., New York.

[redacted]

ANNUAL REPORT.

At each anniversary of the American Baptist Home Mission Society, it has been the mournful duty of its Executive Board to make mention of those whose names were enrolled in the lists of its membership or official affinities, but whose connection with it had been sundered by the hand of death. Occurrences during the past year require the repetition of the duty at this time. It is an appropriate introduction to the Annual Report of the Board. Familiar countenances present attract our attention, stimulate our friendly greetings, cheer our hearts, revive our Christian affection, and aid to prepare us for the important deliberations and fraternal coöperation demanded by our work of benevolence. But there are others on which we have looked as familiarly heretofore, for which we now look in vain. We feel our need of their counsels, their examples, their wisdom, their energy, their piety. But they are not here. God has taken them. Revered names rush upon our memories, but the forms with which they were identified are hidden from our sight, and are awaiting the dawn of that day when they shall hear the voice of the Son of God and live.

Among this number is one who for five successive years served the Society in the responsible office of Auditor, and in the faithful discharge of whose duty as such, in the wise counsels he imparted and the liberal benefactions he bestowed, the Board were uniformly encouraged. As an officer of the Society and member of the Executive Board, Garrat Noel Bleecker enjoyed the highest esteem of his associates, and his removal from among them in less than half a month after his last election was painfully unexpected and afflictive.

Hon. Friend Humphrey, also, whose heart was in the work of Christian benevolence, and whose hand was always ready to promote it, now sleeps in Jesus. He was a member for life and an officer of the Society from the time of its organization. Twelve years he served as a Vice-President, and two years subsequently as President.

Another, once associated with the Board, has likewise heard the summons of the king of terrors and passed pel, and four were ministers' wives. Their names will be found in our list of deceased members for the year.*

Thus, year after year, old and tried associates in our missionary work pass away, leaving us to follow up their labors in behalf of Zion and our fallen world. Let us follow them up with diligence, patience, and faith.

DIRECTORS AND MEMBERS FOR LIFE.

Fifty-nine names have been added to the list of directors and five hundred and eighty-two to that of members. The total number of the former is now 451, and of the latter 3,368.

CHANGE IN THE EXECUTIVE BOARD.

Robert Thompson, Jr., Esq., was elected by the Executive Board to fill the vacancy occasioned by the decease of Garrat N. Bleecker, Esq.

LEGACIES.

Legacies have been received from the estates of the following named persons: Miss Esther Ann Blakely, of Vermont; Miss Fanny McGilvreay, of New-Hampshire; Mrs. Lucretia Goddard and Dea. Daniel Cummins, of Massachusetts; P. F. Brayton and Mrs. Mary Leuce, of Rhode Island; Mrs. L. D. Gale, of the District of Columbia; and Edward Rogers, of Illinois. A balance in advance has also been paid by Theron Fisk, Esq., of New-York.

PROPOSED AMENDMENT OF THE CONSTITUTION.

On account of the annual increase of the Society's business, it became necessary, two years ago, to add an Assistant Secretary to the operative force of the Mission

* Among those names will be seen that of Col. J. M. Washington, who was swept overboard from the unfortunate steamer San Francisco in December last. He was in command of the military forces in New Mexico in 1849, and it was in consequence of his representations and urgent request, that Rev. H. W. Reed, on his arrival at Santa Fé, while pursuing his journey to California at that time, was induced to remain and commence a *mission in New Mexico.*

Rooms. Since that time the increase has continued at a greater ratio, and the business has been more systematically arranged into distinct departments. It has now become so much augmented as to render it desirable that both the labor and responsibility of transacting it should be divided between the officers who have the charge of those departments. To effect this object, the Board recommend an alteration of the fourth article of the Constitution, so as to read as follows: The officers of the Society shall be a President, two Vice-Presidents, a Treasurer, an Auditor, a Corresponding Secretary, a Financial Secretary, and a Recording Secretary, whom the Society shall annually elect by ballot; and of the fifth article, by striking out the words "Corresponding and Recording," and substituting the word "the."

times of embarrassment; it would diminish to a very small amount the already reasonable percentage deducted from the annual receipts for contingent expenses, and it would relieve the management of the business from objections brought by some against benevolent societies generally. The Board, therefore, recommend that the Society encourage an effort to raise a fund of Twenty-five thousand dollars, to be permanently invested; the income of which to be annually applied towards the salaries of the Secretaries.

FINANCIAL AFFAIRS.

We here present a general summary of the Society's financial transactions for the past year, and a statement of its present fiscal condition and prospects:

Balance from last year's account,		$4,465 98
Cash receipts from all sources, viz.:—		
For the General purposes of the Society,	$50,577 68	
" Church Edifice Fund,	5,678 83	
" Educational Objects,	647 32	
" Home Mission Record,	1,360 45	—58,264 28
Making the total amount of cash in the Treasury for the year ending 31st March, 1854,		62,730 26
Of the above amount received for Missionary purposes, there were in contributions, legacies and donations,	49,107 68	
Being an increase over the amount of receipts from the same sources last year of	8,066 17	
The total amount of disbursements for the same period was:—		
For General purposes,	$49,883 99	
" Church Edifices,	5,249 59	
" Educational Objects,	686 95	
" Home Mission Record,	1,607 02	
" Special Investment, by order of the Donor, the interest only to be used,	1,000 00	—58,427 55
Leaving a balance in the Treasury of		4,302 71
Subject to drafts afloat, and liable to immediate presentation,	3,021 39	
Due to Missionaries for services performed up to the 1st of April, and liable to be demanded immediately,	2,316 77	—5,338 16
Showing a deficiency in the Treasury to meet the liabilities due on the 1st of April last, of		1,035 45
The Liabilities of the Society, April 1st, 1854, were as follows, viz:—		
For General purposes,	$39,733 77	
" Church Edifice appropriations,	137 15	—39,870 92
The available resources are:—		
For General objects,	$7,400 35	
" Church Edifice Fund, &c.,	349 61	— 7,749 96
Showing a balance against *the Society, at the close of the year*, of		$31,620 96

It is gratifying to perceive from the foregoing, that the claims of the Home Mission cause are gradually coming to be more adequately considered and more fully appreciated; though the aggregate of receipts still falls below the mark aimed at, even two years ago, and far short of the amount necessary to have enabled the Board to enlarge their operations so rapidly and widely as Divine Providence has presented favorable opportunities, and openings of rare, rich promise.

It is true that the balance reported in the hands of the Treasurer, at the close of the fiscal year, would seem at first to indicate that our operations require less money than we are wont to receive; but it should be distinctly understood, that more than four thousand dollars of this sum, were received on the very day our accounts were closed; and that the receipts of March alone were nearly

In another part of this Report is presented a carefully drawn statement of the prospective wants of your treasury, for the current year. To make such appropriations as are thus demanded, judiciously, or even safely, the Board must anxiously watch the monthly receipts, for a corresponding increase over those of the preceding twelvemonth. They hear the cries of the destitute for help, and of the shivering for shelter, while the urgent voice of God bids them hasten the means of relief; but they have no miraculous power to multiply bread for the faint and perishing, nor can they furnish the full tale of bricks without the requisite materials.

HOME MISSION HOUSE.

At the last anniversary, resolutions were passed instructing the Executive Board relative to changing their place of business. By one of them they were "directed to rent, immediately, suitable rooms for their accommodation, provided that pledges be given that the expense shall not be defrayed from the Society's general treasury." Measures were immediately adopted to carry the resolution into effect. Means were provided by individuals for the payment of the rent, and the only suitable place which could be obtained at that season of the year was conditionally engaged by the committee appointed for the purpose. Its occupancy however, was declined by the Board, partly because of a difference of opinion concerning its suitableness and location, and partly because it was thought more advantageous to attempt the immediate purchase of a building, to which the removal might be permanent.

Another resolution provided, "that the Board be authorized to raise a fund for the purchase of suitable rooms for the Society, at an expense not exceeding forty thousand dollars, at the earliest opportunity within two years."

Guided much by the discussion of the subject at the last anniversary, it was at first considered by a majority of the Board as the intention of the resolution to authorize the actual purchase of a building, provided the funds in the treasury for general purposes were not used in payment. Preliminary arrangements were therefore commenced and prosecuted with some prospect of success; but, on a closer examination of the resolution, doubts were created in some minds, whether its language was sufficiently authoritative to meet the legal necessities connected with an actual purchase for the Society. The whole subject was, therefore, deferred, with the hope that it could be more satisfactorily disposed of within the two years allowed by the resolution. These considerations, measure, to commence operations according to its provisions, wherever it can be done with most advantage to the cause at large. Great necessity on the part of several churches seemed to require an effort in their behalf, without waiting for the details of the regular plan to be perfected. A considerable amount, therefore, has been collected and disbursed for their benefit, and arrangements have been made for the prospective aid of several others. The total amount thus collected is $5,678 83, nearly all of which has been applied to the aid of eleven churches. Besides these, appropriations to the amount of $14,035 have been made in the form of loans and donations, payable after they are collected, and the collection is now going on, chiefly in the States where the churches are respectively located.

Of the whole number of churches aided, two have completed and paid for their houses of worship, and it is expected that three others will enjoy the same happiness within a short period. One house, in New Mexico, has been finished, but has a balance of debt remaining upon it.

Applications for aid from the Fund are numerous, and much profit would arise to the general cause if favorable responses could be made to a considerable number of them. Several of them, at important central points, present much evidence of immediate and pressing necessity, requiring some twenty-eight thousand dollars within the current year, which, expended under the precautions of our system, would probably prove the foundation of great and lasting good.

MISSIONARY OPERATIONS.

Various considerations have required that the Missionary operations of the past year should be conducted with much reference to prominent localities in different portions of our field, and to the extending frontier settlements of our country. Great and rapid changes in the condition and influence of western cities and villages have been effected, and new ones, destined to much importance in a few years, have been founded by the multiplication of Railroads; all of which demand immediate attention. At some central positions, churches, formerly weak, have been strengthened, and others are beginning to realize the benefit of our aid.

A mission among the Chinese in California has not yet been commenced. Many difficulties have arisen to retard, but we trust not to finally prevent the accomplishment of this important object. It is worthy of being cherished, and it is hoped that success will, ere long, attend our efforts to promote it. With this exception, the plans of the Board for spreading the gospel have been as successful new appointments. Two quarterly reports, due on the 1st April, failed to reach us. Ten, who were under appointment some portion of the year, need no further aid from the Society.

Seven collecting agents have also been employed the whole or a portion of the year, and, for a few weeks, two special agents for purposes connected with the Church Edifice Fund.

The Missionaries were distributed as follows: In Canada (West), 1; Canada (East), 8; New York (near Canada), 1; Pennsylvania, 6; Delaware, 2; Ohio, 9; Michigan, 8; Indiana, 28; Illinois, 34; Wisconsin, 35; Iowa, 23; Minnesota, 8; Oregon, 4; California, 4; New Mexico, 4.

Twenty-one of the number preach in the following foreign languages: French, 8; French and German, 1; French and Polish, 1; Swedish, 1; Swedish, Danish, and Norwegian, 1; German, 3; Dutch, 1; Spanish, 2; Spanish, and Pueblo, 1; Spanish and Navajo Indian, 1; Chippewa and French, 1.

The number of States and Territories occupied is 14. The number of stations and out-stations supplied, is 612; and the aggregate amount of time bestowed upon the field, according to the reports received, is equal to that of one man for 137 years and 18 weeks.

The Missionaries report the baptism of 1322 persons; the organization of 67 churches, and the ordination of 30 ministers. Twenty-two church edifices have been completed, and 24 are in progress of building.*

Of the number baptized, more than 100 are known to

* In addition to the above, the Missionaries report the following:

Sermons preached	20,077	Sabbath Schools in the Churches	254
Lectures and Addresses	2,008	Bible Classes	95
Pastoral Visits	36,299	Number of Teachers	1,619
Prayer and other Meetings attended	10,479	Number of Scholars	10,785
Signatures to Temperance Pledge	763	Volumes in S. S. Libraries	30,330
Miles travelled in discharge of duty	170,240	Stations where M. C. of Prayer is observed	131

Roman Catholics or Lutherans.
ved to have
was reported

the establishment of the gospel in every city and settlement of that portion of our field. Not one of them, in all that lovely heritage, should be surrendered to infidelity or superstition; not one should be left under the influence of the powers of darkness, as an unrestrained moral evil in the land.

THE FAR WEST.

Our Missions on the Pacific coast present enlarged claims on the attention of the Board. Their importance is in no degree diminished, but in every respect increased, and various causes will hereafter continue to increase it. The operation of the general land law in Oregon is favorable to the settlement of that Territory by an industrious and intelligent class of inhabitants, and such, in great numbers, have availed themselves of the large bounty of the general Government, in providing for themselves valuable and permanent homes. But owing to the limited extent of many of the valleys in which those homes are selected, the vast area over which they are spread, and the legal necessity for actual occupancy of the lands in order to a proprietorship in them, the local communities are very numerous, and often small and widely separated from each other. Due care for the religious interests of a people, under such circumstances, requires a larger proportion of ministers than usual, and it is just cause of gratification to learn that several have accompanied the emigrants to that region. The number, however, is inadequate to the demands of such a field even by itinerant services, and there are central positions of much importance, for the supply of which our friends look with earnestness to the Board. Two ministers have been appointed to that Territory during the year. One of them has reached it and entered upon his labors, the other was arrested in his journey by an afflictive Providence, which may delay his departure for some time.

To the Missionary company in California, one minister has been added, who is at present laboring at Marysville. Another was appointed, with the expectation that he would have reached his field ere this time, but he also is detained by domestic affliction.

Our friends in that State have exhibited much liberality in assuming, at an early period, the support of the ministers who have gone out under the patronage of the Society, and have encouraged us, by formal pledges, to expect valuable contributions towards the support of others. It is believed that the proportion of Baptist Church members in California is as large as that of any other denomination of evangelical Christians, while the

Testament model, and the ordinances of Baptism and the Lord's Supper have been administered in Albuquerque; a church edifice has been erected and opened for worship in Santa Fé; the gospel is extensively preached in the Territory; the Bible and religious publications are freely circulated; a spirit of inquiry exists among the people; and some appear to be seriously seeking the true way of salvation. And these events have occurred where, until our Missionaries recently commenced their labors, naught of religion was known but the dark and cruel rites of gross paganism, and as dark, if not as cruel impositions of a degrading Romanism.

No additions have been made to our Missionary force in that territory the past year, but it has become necessary to send additional men, as assistants to those now there, and to fill at least one vacancy which is likely to occur. It is important, also, that arrangements be made for the establishment of a school, of an elevated character, in that Territory, at no distant day.

THE GRANDE LIGNE MISSION.

The labors of our Missionaries of the Grandė Ligne Stations continue to be attended by the Divine blessing, and their salutary influence is evidently deepening and extending among the people. A disposition to investigate the subject of Bible religion is widely extending. The Station at Montreal appears to be well selected and occupied, and from it proceeds an evangelical influence which promises great benefits to the people of that city and the entire region around it. Two missionaries have been added to the number previously in that field, but one, heretofore under appointment, finds the climate too severe for his health, and will leave his station. The churches are becoming more enlightened in respect to Christian duties, and are evidently more liberal in performing them.

INDIAN MISSIONS.

The Board have endeavored to promote the welfare of those Indian tribes which seem to have been providentially cast upon their attention, and are encouraged to persevere.

At the Pueblo of Laguna, in New Mexico, Brother Gorman has toiled amidst many difficulties arising from the uncivilized condition of the people, and the influence of a religion derived from two corrupt sources,—the Aztec idolatries and Roman Catholic traditions. He has succeeded, however, in establishing a station among them, and has erected, chiefly with his own hands a building the labors of the Missionary, when he shall have become better acquainted with their language.

An assistant for this station is very much needed, and the Board have recently appointed one whom they believe to be suitably qualified for the labor it requires.

The station among the Chippewas at Pembina, in Minnesota, is not yet perfectly organized. Brother James Tanner, the Missionary, returned to that place from his tour in the United States, last autumn, but after consultation with some chiefs of the tribe, and influential American residents, he decided to return immediately to St. Paul to expedite the transportation to his station of farming implements, books and school apparatus, which he had collected and stored at that place, as they were deemed essential to the success of his general plans. This object was accomplished through the kind offices of the Governor of the Territory and other friends, though it required of the Missionary a journey on foot, amidst the frost and snow of that high northern latitude, of some five hundred miles, and with but two attendants. On his journey homeward, the same distance, he was unattended, except by his faithful dogs, and experienced increased severity of weather in a more advanced period of the winter. But God was with him, and he safely reached his home. The anxiety of the Indians to receive instruction from him appears to be singularly great. An associate Missionary for this station has been appointed, and it is presumed he will enter upon his duties in the course of the ensuing summer.

PROSPERITY CREATING NECESSITY.

After several years of Home Mission effort, it was said in one of our Annual Reports, "Much has been accomplished, but, comparatively, the work is but just begun."

The same is true to-day. The very successes of the Society have unceasingly expanded the area of its operations, and created additional necessity for its efforts. Much more so the great increase of population in all the older States of the West; the rapid organization of new ones; the foreign origin of a large class of our present population; the immense augmentation of the same class now anticipated; the wide-spread influence of anti-republican politics, and anti-christian religion; and the growing boldness and zeal with which encroachments upon our civil and religious liberties are attempted. While, therefore, we have reason to congratulate the Society because of the happy commencement of the effort and its success thus far, it is to be hoped that stimulus to patient continuance in well-doing may be seen and felt in all the [redacted]

Much attention must be bestowed upon the rapidly increasing foreign population. The political sympathy which freely offers them an ample asylum from civil and religious oppression, is never perfect till they are taught the nature and proper use of true civil and religious freedom. The pity that weeps over their ignorance, their superstition, or their infidelity is not conformed to Christ's, unless accompanied by the benevolence which will attempt to gather them beneath the soul-sanctifying and saving influences of the gospel as a hen gathereth her chickens under her wings. And much more should be done for those who were originally aliens from our national commonwealth, but by military conquest have been made our fellow-citizens. If it were really necessary to graft them into the olive-tree of our body politic, justice demands that with us they should partake of its root and fatness. Their claim to whatever is valuable in our free institutions, and our obligations as American Christians to invite and even to urge them to come in and share them with us, especially the higher and holier blessings of the gospel feast, are indisputable.

Nor should the red men who linger on our frontiers be overlooked, especially when their cry for clearer knowledge of the "Great Spirit" is providentially wafted to our ears. They ask us for bread—the bread of life. While we possess their former hunting-grounds and fields, and they are, literally, strangers and wanderers in their fathers' ancient inheritance, shall we send them empty away, or shall we not rather heed their cry and cheerfully fill them with the good things of the kingdom of Christ?

But to promote these interests the Board are powerless without the active and efficient coöperation of the ministers and churches. Some of the ministers are needed personally to labor in the field. Our Divine Master has declared that such as do so "are worthy of their hire," and to those who contribute that hire he has constituted it a greater blessing to "give than to receive."

MEN AND MEANS FOR THE ENSUING YEAR.

To attempt the accomplishment of what actually claims the attention of the Board, the ensuing year, the entire number of missionaries now in the field should be retained in active service, and to these should be added, as the very least number, 36 others to occupy new places. Such places are now ready and waiting for 4 ministers in Oregon; 5 in California; 4 in New Mexico; 7 in Minnesota; 6 in Iowa; 4 in Illinois; 2 in Indiana; 1 in Ohio; 2 among the Sioux Indians: and 1 among the Chippewas.

treasury on the 31st of March ($4,302 71), which is applicable to the support of Missionaries, we find the amount of contributions needed for Missionary purposes the ensuing year to be $75,397 29.

It is very desirable that, in addition to this amount, the treasury should be supplied with about $2,000, designated by the donors for educational purposes; and a further sum of $300 for the expense of transporting books and school apparatus to various stations. Such aid is much needed at stations in Minnesota, New Mexico, and other points where Missionaries labor among foreigners, but the ordinary funds of the Society are unavailable for those purposes. To all of which should be added $28,000 for the Church Edifice Fund, making the aggregate of $103,397 29 needed for the ensuing year.

This estimate is the result of careful calculation, based on proper data. The amount proposed for additional effort may appear large, but it should be borne in mind that two-thirds of it is for Missions on the Pacific coast and New Mexico, the outfits and travelling expenses to which are as large as those required for foreign stations, and that the annual support of Missionaries, when there, exceeds those at foreign stations. The great advance in the cost of living everywhere makes the remainder of the estimate necessary. Missionaries of the Society cannot perform the heavy services required on inadequate salaries. They who preach the gospel should live of the gospel.

CONCLUSION.

It is cause of encouragement that the churches appear to be awaking from deep slumber on the subject of Home Missions, and that our country holds a more prominent place in their prayers and contributions; but to discern clearly her dangers and wants, thorough wakefulness and vigilance are indispensable.

The time has come when American Christians, in view of the numerous forms of corrupt religion and subtle infidelity prevalent in the land, and of the strong tendencies among the people to forget God, have solemn reason to bear their country before the throne of grace as one of the chief burdens of their prayers, and to accompany those prayers with such liberal pecuniary offerings as will prove their estimate of her happy institutions, and the spiritual welfare of her population, to be more precious than gold. If civil and religious liberty in the United States become impaired, what is all the world besides? If the gospel of Jesus Christ becomes less than the controlling element of our country's influence upon the nations, it will have been [redacted] and providences to wield it against the strongest enemies of the gospel.

May the members of this Society and all the disciples of Jesus Christ be assisted to lift up their eyes and behold that the fields are white for the harvest, and that it is their duty and privilege, as it will be for their usefulness, to enter it and reap.

By order of the Executive Board.

BENJAMIN M. HILL,

Corresponding Secretary.

[redacted]

TABLE.

Weeks labor reported.	Stations supplied.	Baptized.	Received by Letter.	Scholars in S. School.	Cont. to Benevolent Objects.	ADDITIONAL FACTS REPORTED.
39	1	1				Some seeking a better religion than Popery.
13						Is much encouraged in his labors.
39	2	13		52	41 56	Special indications of the Divine presence.
13	3	8		42	15 71	
39	3	11				Many Catholics looking favorably to the Gospel.
13	8				12 50	Church improving in contributions for the support of the cause.
39	1					Some progress and some opposition.
13	1			10		One recently converted from Romanism.
39		5		30	13 00	Signs of a revival.
13	3			30		The church improving in religious spirit.
39	4	6		20	17 37	
13					5 18	The church progressing gradually.
4	5				14 50	
13	3					A new field. Some families favorable to the Gospel.
26	8	27	1	180	14 00	A new and encouraging German Mission.—Finished meeting-house at B.
52		3				Labored in Maine, New Hampshire, and Vermont.
						Re-appointment.
52						Massachusetts.

NAMES OF AGENTS AND MISSIONARIES.	POST OFFICE ADDRESS.	FIELD OF LABOR.	Date of Commission	Months Commis'd.	Weeks labor reported.	Stations supplied.	Baptized.	Received by Letter.	Scholars in S. School.	Cont. to Benevolent Objects.	ADDITIONAL FACTS REPORTED.
J. W. Parkhurst	Newton Centre	Collecting Agent	April 1, 1854	12							Re-appointment.
NEW YORK.											
G. M. Fuller	Pike, Wyoming Co.	Collecting Agent	April 1, 1853	12	52						Labored in New Jersey and New York.
" "	" "	" "	April 1, 1854	12							Re-appointment.
James S. Ladd	New York	Collecting Agent	April 1, 1853	12	52						Labored in Rhode Island and Connecticut.
" "	" "	" "	April 1, 1854	12							Re-appointment.
G. A. Clark	Auburn	Collecting Agent	April 1, 1853	12	52						Central New York.
" "	"	" "	April 1, 1854	8							Re-appointment.
William Sawyer	White's Corners	Collecting Agent	April 1, 1853	12	35						Western New York.
" "	" "	" "	April 1, 1854	12							Re-appointment.
M. B. Czechowski	Mooers, Clinton Co.	French in M. and vicinity.	July 1, 1853	12	39	4	5	6			A French Mission. Revival. Church preparing to build a meeting-house.
J. M. Walden	Dunkirk	Agt. for Ch. Edifice Fund.									
NEW JERSEY.											
J. G. Collom	Mount Holly	Collecting Agent	April 1, 1853	12	50						Pennsylvania.
" "	" "	" "	April 1, 1854	12							Eastern Pa. and a part of New Jersey.
J. E. Rue	Hightstown	Exploring Agent	April 1, 1854	12							A new appointment for West Pa.
PENNSYLVANIA.											
P. M. Weddell	Pittsburgh	South Pittsburgh	June 1, 1852	12	13	2	2	3	70	7 00	
" "	"	" "	June 1, 1853	12	30		3	4	130	58 37	Congregations good, but no particular religious interest manifested.
T. J. Cole	Brownsville	Brownsville	Dec. 1, 1852	12	30	2		6	126	12 42	Discipline been necessary, and the effect beneficial.
" "	"	"	Dec. 1, 1853	12	13				70	24 50	Laying the foundation of a well-disciplined and efficient church.
N. Barwell	West Greenville	West Greenville, &c.	Nov. 1, 1852	12	39	4		3	106	19 88	Church building meeting-house.
" "	" "	" "	Nov. 1, 1853	12	13	5		2			Meeting-house progressing.
John White	Sharpsburg	Centreville, &c.	June 1, 1853	12	39	1	1	1	75	29 98	Church in harmony and the congregation increasing.

[redacted]

Weeks labor reported.	Stations supplied.	Baptized.	Received by Letter.	Scholars in S. School.	Cont. to Benevolent Objects.	ADDITIONAL FACTS REPORTED.
9	4	3	....	50	......	
13	1	..	7	....	......	A new station. Arranging to build a meeting-house.
39	....	..	....	....	......	Interesting meetings at an out-station. Remodelling meeting-house at that station.
21	1	..	....	20	25 75	Pastor encouraged, notwithstanding an Anti-baptist influence.
52	2	..	10	....	30 00	Need no further aid.
26	3	31	9	230	121 20	Three churches building meeting-houses.
26	....	16	2	260	100 00	One other church building meeting-houses.
11	....	2	....	....	......	Labored successfully as an itinerant.
52	....	15	....	160	......	Cause progressing, and pastor encouraged.
39	4	15	4	100	77 63	Revival. Church at E. finished a meeting-house.
26	....	..	....	....	......	Exploring agent and general itinerant.
....	....	..	....	....	......	Re-appointment.
39	1	..	10	140	12 00	Organized a church. A house of worship indispensable to further success. Hope to build one.
39	4	7	9	75	13 12	Sabbath-school decreased during the winter. Congregations large, and a general religious feeling in the community.
39	1	..	3	35	......	Organized a church. Prospects encouraging. Need a meeting-house.
39	2	1	10	100	44 00	Prospects promising.
13	....	..	6	....	......	Completed meeting-house.

NAMES OF AGENTS AND MISSIONARIES.	POST OFFICE ADDRESS.	FIELD OF LABOR.	Date of Commission	Months Commis'd.	Weeks labor reported.	Stations supplied.	Baptized.	Received by Letter.	Scholars in S. School.	Cont. to Benevolent Objects.	ADDITIONAL FACTS REPORTED.
Aaron Potter	Albion	Albion and vicinity	Dec. 1, 1852	12	39	1	--	10	40	90 59	Discipline been necessary. Religion in a low state.
" "	"	" "	Dec. 1, 1853	12	18	----	2	2	20	23 48	Church in a low state. Pastor resigned.
Samuel Haskell	Kalamazoo	Kalamazoo	Sept. 1, 1852	12	26	----	8	9	----	95 20	Building a meeting-house.
" "	"	"	Sept. 1, 1853	12	26	3	3	21	----	113 70	Meeting-house progressing.
G. V. Ten Brook	Centreville	Centreville	Oct. 1, 1852	12	26	3	2	1	30	14 50	Progressing with meeting-house.
" "	"	"	Oct. 1, 1853	12	26	2	--	----	30	7 50	Meeting-house sufficiently finished to hold meetings in it.
P. C. Dayfoot	Lansing	Lansing	Oct. 1, 1852	12	26	5	1	5	50	10 07	Infidelity and other errors prevalent.
" "	"	"	Oct. 1, 1853	12	26	4	2	1	50	9 63	Church weakened by removals. State of religion somewhat revived.
Alfred Handy	Flint	Flint and vicinity	July 1, 1853	12	39	2	1	21	----	5 00	Organized a church in F. Prospects good, but need a meeting-house in order to advance.
Asher E. Mather	Romeo	Romeo and vicinity	July 1, 1853	12	39	4	36	23	30	6 00	Completed a meeting-house. Revival. Pastor cheered.
T. Z. R. Jones	Kalamazoo	Paw Paw and vicinity		12	----	----	--	----	----	------	A new appointment, and a new field.
INDIANA.											
Ira C. Perrine	Herman, Ripley Co.	White Water Valley Asso.	Nov. 1, 1852	12	39	4	2	2	----	284 30	Revival at one station and prospects good at others.
" "	" "	" " " "	Nov. 1, 1853	12	13	13	12	11	----	23 80	Systematically collect funds for the spread of the Gospel.
Wm. Chaffee	Blackford	New Corydon and Hartford	Dec. 1, 1852	12	39	3	--	----	60	35 60	
Joseph A. Dixson	Evansville	Evansville	Sept. 1, 1852	12	26	1	--	3	100	42 00	Church progressing more than statistics show.
" "	"	"	Sept. 1, 1853	12	26	----	--	3	80	151 00	Pastor suffered from ill health. State of religion more encouraging.
N. V. Steadman	Evansville	Indiana	April 1, 1853	12	52	----	--	----	----	------	Exploring agent and general itinerant.
" "	"	"	April 1, 1854	12	----	----	--	----	----	------	
Prentice T. Palmer	Waveland	Freedom Association	Nov. 1, 1852	12	39	6	14	11	----	22 70	Needs no further aid.
James M. Maxwell	Plymouth	Plymouth and Marshall	Nov. 1, 1852	12	39	8	6	8	25	10 21	Needs more ministers in his region.
" "	"	" " "	Nov. 1, 1853	12	13	10	1	----	----	------	Surrounded by opposing influences.
John Reece	Shelbyville	Shelbyville and vicinity	April 1, 1853	12	52	2	31	18	120	76 35	The church at S. building a meeting-house.
" "	"	" " "	April 1, 1854	12	----	----	--	----	----	------	
Abel Johnson	Warren	Bluffton and Warren	Jan. 1, 1853	12	52	5	1	3	60	10 00	Religious interest in W. on the increase. The field not an encouraging one.
" "	Bluffton	" " "	Jan. 1, 1854	12	18	----	--	1	----	------	Nothing special.
David S. French	Covington	Tippecanoe Association	April 1, 1853	12	52	----	88	12	----	110 00	Two churches finished meeting-houses.

[redacted]	Weeks labor reported.	Stations supplied.	Baptized.	Received by Letter.	Scholars in S. School.	Cont. to Benevolent Objects.	ADDITIONAL FACTS REPORTED.
[redacted]	13	1	1	2	----	30 00	Prospects very encouraging.
[redacted]	39	3	9	2	----	7 90	The influence of the Church increasing.
[redacted]	52	5	3	1	200	25 00	Church revived.
[redacted]	10	1	6	----	----	------	Require no further aid. The Church is thriving.
[redacted]	39	10	23	12	150	155 00	Religion on the advance in his field, and wants more laborers.
[redacted]	13	----	5	----	125	50 00	Two churches building meeting-houses.
[redacted]	39	10	19	19	104	210 00	Church at Orleans finished a meeting-house. Organized a church at Mt. Carroll.
[redacted]	13	----	19	6	55	------	Cause of Missions rapidly gaining ground.
[redacted]	39	9	--	----	50	75 00	Congregations increasing, but still a deplorable neglect of public worship.
[redacted]	13	11	--	----	----	25 00	Better attendance than heretofore and more interest manifested.
[redacted]	41	10	24	10	----	63 00	Two churches building meeting-houses. Revival. Organized a church in Pleasant Valley.
[redacted]	13	----	2	2	----	26 00	Nothing special.
[redacted]	26	4	6	8	135	59 50	Religious interest quite favorable.
[redacted]	13	4	--	14	45	185 00	Building a meeting-house at an out-station. Resigned.
[redacted]	52	6	55	16	25	86 00	Revivals in several of his churches. Require no further aid.
[redacted]	39	1	24	24	135	75 00	Need no further aid. Grateful for past favors.
[redacted]	39	4	25	12	190	153 03	Many who were anti-mission Baptists joining his churches.
[redacted]	39	4	7	5	215	30 00	Building a meeting-house.
[redacted]	52	3	3	3	100	30 95	Some progress made. Rebuilding meeting-house.
[redacted]	39	8	5	17	30	33 89	Church paid off debt on meeting-house. Prospects brightening.
[redacted]	39	10	15	7	----	30 00	Building meeting-house at one station.
[redacted]	8	2	5	4	----	23 05	Baptists numerous, but mixed up with antinomianism.
[redacted]	13	1	--	1	60	72 00	A new appointment.

NAMES OF AGENTS AND MISSIONARIES.	POST OFFICE ADDRESS.	FIELD OF LABOR.	Date of Commission	Months Commis'd.	Weeks labor reported.	Stations supplied.	Baptized.	Received by Letter.	Scholars in S. School.	Cont. to Benevolent Objects.	ADDITIONAL FACTS REPORTED.
ILLINOIS.											
Thomas Powell	Mt. Palatine	Illinois	April 1, 1853	12	52						Exploring agent and general itinerant.
" "	"	"	April 1, 1854	12							
B. E. S. Kupfer	Highland	Germans in S. Ill.	May 1, 1852	12	13		1				Labored some with the German Church in St. Louis.
F. Ketcham	Rock Island	Rock Island	June 1, 1852	12	13	2	..	10	100	45 00	Church need no further aid.
"	" "	" "	July 1, 1853	3	13						A temporary agency in the east for the Church Edifice Fund.
"	" "	Rock Island Association		12							Re-appointment to a new field.
J. Edminster	Byron, Ogle Co	Byron and vicinity	May 1, 1852	12	13	7	..	1	120		Prospects of the Church brightening.
"	" "	Byron and Brooklyn	May 1, 1853	12	39	5	2	12	75	20 50	Prospects not so encouraging.
Charles Button	Dundee	Dundee	July 1, 1852	12	13	1	1	6	60	9 00	Need no further aid.
Niles Kinne	St. Charles	St. Charles	July 1, 1852	12	13	3	1	4	53	9 76	Many and peculiar obstacles to the progress of pure religion.
" "	"	"	July 1, 1853	12	39		1	7	74	59 41	An increased attendance upon the preaching of the Word.
Augustus B. Cramb.	Metamora	Metamora and vicinity	Nov. 1, 1852	12	39	2	39	2	50	14 10	Has suffered from sickness and left the field.
A. G. Eberhart	Moline	Moline and Edgington	June 1, 1852	12	13	2			70		Resigned pastoral charge for itinerant service.
" "	"	Rock Island Association	June 1, 1853	12	39		4				Resigned as itinerant and removed to Iowa.
H. S. Deppe	Steel's Mills	Germans in Randolph and St. Clair Co's.	Mar. 1, 1853	12	52	5	39	16	60	74 00	An interesting field, where more laborers are wanted. Organized a church at Sparta.
J. H. Krüger	Peoria	German ch. in P. & vicinity	Oct. 1, 1852	12	26	1	1	7	....	5 00	Infidelity prevalent; is encouraged notwithstanding.
" "	"	" " " "	Oct. 1, 1853	12	26		..	1		5 00	Congregations increasing.
T. L. Breckenridge	La Salle	La Salle and vicinity	Nov. 1, 1852	12	39	1	5	4	30		Raising funds to build a meeting-house, and is quite successful.
" "	"	" " "	Nov. 1, 1853	12	13		..	3			
I. D. Newell	Aurora, Kane Co.	Aurora	May 1, 1852	12	13	3	56	15	60	5 67	Completed meeting-house. Revival.
" "	" "	"	May 1, 1853	12	42		..	13		59 23	Resigned to become an agent for Church Edifice Fund.
W. D. H. Johnson	Greenville	Greenville and vicinity	Oct. 1, 1852	12	26	1	..	1	125		The whole interest progressing.
" "	"	" " "	Oct. 1, 1853	12	26		..			43 00	Finished meeting-house.
G. S. Bailey	Pekin, Tazewell Co.	Pekin and vicinity	Nov. 1, 1852	12	39	2	1	5	200	16 00	Building a meeting-house.
" "	" "	" " "	Nov. 1, 1853	12	13		..		150	5 00	Enlarged the plan for their meeting-house.
Nelson Alvord	Chillicothe	Chillicothe	Dec. 1, 1852	12	39	2	..	3	75	25 00	Sunday-school flourishing. Sabbath and prayer meetings well attended.
J. W. Riley	Westfield, Clark Co	Bloomfield Association	Feb. 1, 1853	12	52	6	19	26		187 50	Meetings well attended.
Ashel Chapin	Galena	Galena	June 1, 1852	12	13	2	..		65	6 30	Encouraged by the prospect of having a meeting-house. Church more than doubled.

[redacted]

Comms'd.	Weeks labor reported.	Stations supplied.	Baptized.	Received by Letter.	Scholars in S. School.	Cont. to Benevolent Objects.	ADDITIONAL FACTS REPORTED.
12	39	....	..	13	....	10 00	Prayer-meetings well attended.
12	26	2	..	....	30	18 00	Religion at a low ebb, and membership decreased by removals.
12	26	9	15	2	85	68 70	Churches revived.
12	26	....	18	2	....	......	Sickness in his family.
12	52	2	36	10	30	20 00	Are greatly opposed by the wicked, but the work progresses.
12	....	....	..	....	....	......	Report not due.
12	52	1	40	7	45	25 45	Completed meeting-house. Prospects encouraging.
12	....	....	..	....	....	......	Report not due.
12	39	2	19	1	....	15 50	Organized a Church. Purposing to build a meeting-house. Revival.
12	....	....	..	....	....	......	
12	35	2	..	5	120	29 00	Finishing a meeting-house. Influence of the Church increasing.
12	39	4	..	3	110	69 41	Resigned.
12	26	2	..	....	50	50 00	Large congregations. Need a meeting-house.
12	26	8	..	....	....	......	Itinerant. A destitute field. Preached to large congregations.
12	13	2	1	5	100	5 00	Left the field in consequence of ill-health.
12	26	5	..	10	130	30 57	Church commenced a meeting-house.
12	22	2	..	5	30	60 62	Completed meeting-houses at both stations.
12	26	3	37	10	75	......	Paying off debts on meeting-house. Revival.
12	26	3	11	5	....	......	Church will attempt to build a meeting-house.
12	26	1	4	3	100	......	Finished meeting-house. Revival in progress.
12	13	6	..	4	30	......	Congregations increased at all of his stations.
12	13	1	..	1	60	14 00	Their house of worship usually well filled with attentive hearers.
12	52	....	..	....	....	......	Exploring agent and general itinerant.
12	....	....	..	....	....	......	Re-appointment as a general itinerant.
12	26	2	..	2	75	......	Congregations good and attentive.
13	26	1	12	2	60	52 50	Revival.
12	13	1	..	1	40	16 00	Prospects more encouraging than heretofore.
12	39	....	..	1	....	5 00	Nothing special.
12	39	6	1	....	30	2 50	Prospects encouraging at Scott, but not encouraging at Cascade.

NAMES OF AGENTS AND MISSIONARIES.	POST OFFICE ADDRESS.	FIELD OF LABOR.	Date of Commission.	Months Commiss'd.	Weeks labor reported.	Stations supplied.	Baptized.	Received by Letter.	Scholars in S. School.	Cont. to Benevolent Objects.	ADDITIONAL FACTS REPORTED.
Caleb Blood	Geneva	Geneva	July 1, 1852	12	13	2	----	----	50	----	Church weakened by removals and deaths.
N. B. Chapin	Beaver Dam	Beaver Dam	June 1, 1852	12	13	3	----	2	40	6 50	Commenced building a meeting-house.
" "	" "	" "	June 1, 1853	12	26	----	1	5	----	20 75	Meeting-house finished. Permanent advancement made.
Edward L. Harris	Beloit	Beloit and vicinity	Mar. 1, 1852	12	52	5	----	1	100	72 74	Resigns on account of ill-health.
Perly Work	Sheboygan	Sheboygan	Sept. 1, 1852	12	26	5	1	4	120	9 00	Ch. embarrassed by debt on meeting-house.
" "	"	"	Sept. 1, 1853	12	26	----	1	5	----	22 30	Uncommon and increasing interest in religion.
S. Cornelius, Jr.	Fond du Lac	Fond du Lac	May 1, 1852	12	13	1	1	----	----	----	Nothing special.
" "	" "	" "	May 1, 1853	12	20	----	1	5	50	----	Meeting-house finished.
Alexander Hamilton	Newark, Wash. Co.	Newark and West Bend	Nov. 1, 1852	12	26	3	8	5	40	2 16	Church very prosperous.
" "	Barton	Newark and Newburg	Nov. 1, 1853	12	13	----	----	2	----	----	Purchased a lot for a meeting-house.
W. J. Chapin	Astalan	Astalan and vicinity	Oct. 1, 1852	12	26	3	2	1	35	3 25	Finished meeting-house by great effort.
" "		" " "	Oct. 1, 1853	12	20	----	----	5	----	7 80	
Sherman Dearborn	Lowell, Dodge Co.	Lowell and vicinity	July 1, 1852	12	13	1	----	----	27	----	State of things more encouraging. Sunday-school interesting and profitable.
" " "	" "	" "	July 1, 1853	12	30	----	1	4	27	75 00	Organized a church at L. Revival in progress.
Wm. H. Card	La Crosse	La Crosse & Lewis Valleys	Nov. 1, 1852	12	36	3	----	4	30	18 00	Two churches nearly ready to be organized.
D. S. Bowen	Watertown, Jeff. Co.	Watertown	May 1, 1852	12	13	3	9	3	60	8 00	Revival.
" "	" "	"	May 1, 1853	12	26	3	6	2	120	17 25	Church have a lot and materials for a meeting-house. A difficult field.
Samuel T. Catlin	Hudson	Hudson and vicinity	May 1, 1852	12	13	3	----	----	60	----	Finished meeting-house. Good religious feeling in the Church.
" "	"	" " "	May 1, 1853	12	37	----	----	----	----	6 00	Church been passing through trials; but wholesome discipline has corrected evils, and they are more prosperous.
Harmon Ellis	Lake Mills, Jeff. Co.	Lake Mills	June 1, 1852	12	13	2	----	----	25	----	State of society improving.
James Andem	Neenah	Neenah and vicinity	July 1, 1852	12	13	1	----	5	15	----	Pastor encouraged. Congregation the largest in the place.
" "	"	Neenah and Green Bay	July 1, 1853	12	39	4	1	6	60	13 00	Church at Green Bay removed their locality to Howard. Prospects encouraging.
William McKee	Omro, Winnebago Co.	Omro and Oshkosh	June 1, 1852	12	13	4	1	----	10	----	Success not been all he could wish, and leaves the field.
" "	Thompsonville	Raymond and Caledonia	Sept. 1, 1852	12	26	2	----	2	25	7 00	Religious interest encouraging.
John Hinton	Kenosha	Kenosha	May 1, 1852	12	13	1	----	3	54	----	Resigned.
O. A. Hewett	Whitewater	Whitewater	July 1, 1853	12	39	5	9	----	----	----	Congregations large and attentive; but the cause is low.
David Matlock	Lancaster	Lancaster and vicinity	Aug. 1, 1852	12	19	3	1	5	30	4 55	Cause slowly but constantly advancing.
" "	"	" " "	Aug. 1, 1853	12	13	----	4	----	50	----	Pastor has been sick. Resigns his commission.
ames Squier	East Troy	East Troy	Aug. 1, 1852	12	26	2	4	1	30	7 00	Church need no further pecuniary aid.

[redacted]

Commis'd.	Weeks labor reported.	Stations supplied.	Baptized.	Received by Letter.	Scholars in S. School.	Cont. to Benevolent Objects.	ADDITIONAL FACTS REPORTED.
12	26	2	..	3	75	11 50	Sickness in his family.
12	13	3	..	4	....	6 00	
12	39	5	..	1	60	......	Congregation large and attentive.
12	13	....	..	1	....	......	Completed meeting-house.
12	26	5	1	5	100	12 00	Nothing special.
12	26	5	..	5	100	20 00	Pastor encouraged. Church passing an important crisis.
12	39	7	7	....	60	105 00	A new fie'd. Organized churches at two stations.
12	13	2	4	1	50	40 00	A good religious feeling in his churches.
12	39	1	..	....	35	19 87	Building a meeting-house.
12	13	....	..	....	....	......	Congregations large considering the place in which they have to meet.
12	52	4	38	15	....	12 00	Organized a Church at Decatur. Revival. Prospects pleasing.
12	52	4	2	5	7	4 53	A new field. Pastor much encouraged.
12	39	1	2	6	48	27 55	Church improving.
12	....	....	..	....	....	......	
12	26	3	..	....	30	......	A new field. Finds much opposition. State of society improving.
12	26	3	..	....	....	50 00	A new station. Organized a Church at P., and now want a meeting-house
12	13	....	..	....	....	25 00	Labored successfully with two Churches where there were about forty conversions.
12	26	9	6	8	110	......	Churches small but prospects promising.
12	26	7	..	6	....	......	Some encouraging prospects.
12	26	6	41	13	30	30 25	Revival at an out-station.
12	26	4	24	13	74	3 00	Organized two Churches.
12	39	3	18	8	150	......	Church at an out-station building a meeting-house.
12	13	2	..	....	120	......	Pastor on the whole encouraged.
12	13	3	3	4	170	......	Church had some trials. Pastor resigned on account of ill-health.
12	13	....	..	1	20	20 00	Meeting-house progressing.
12	39	....	..	9	....	15 00	Meeting-house completed. Congregations large.

Names of Agents and Missionaries.	Post Office Address.	Field of Labor.	Date of Commission	Months Commiss'd.	Weeks labor reported.	Stations supplied.	Baptized.	Received by Letter.	Scholars in S. School.	Cont'd. to Benevolent Objects.	Additional Facts Reported.
Hiram Barrett	Mt. Pleasant	Jefferson and vicinity	June 1, 1852	12	13	4	9	----	40	------	Building meeting-house at J. Require no further aid.
Wm. H. Turton	Farmington	Farmington	Oct. 1, 1852	12	26	5	..	2	120	24 37	Nothing special.
" "	"	"	Oct. 1, 1853	12	26	----	2	2	---	------	Opposition from the irreligious.
J. A. Nash	Fort Des Moines	Fort Des Moines	Dec. 1, 1852	12	30	3	1	5	50	31 60	Will ask no further aid. Opened a school to aid in his support.
George Scott	Maquoketa	Maquoketa and vicinity	Oct. 1, 1852	12	26	3	--	3	40	52 00	About finishing meeting-house. Church increasing in benevolence.
" "	West Union	West Union and Auburn	Oct. 1, 1853	12	26	2	1	8	----	------	Finished meeting-house at West Union. Revival in progress.
A. Russell Belden	Iowa City	Iowa City	Dec. 1, 1852	12	30	1	21	17	96	------	Revival. Prospects encouraging.
" "	" "	" "	Dec. 1, 1853	12	13	----	1	4	90	------	Prospects still flattering.
B. B. Arnold	Three Rivers	Pleasant Grove & vicinity	Oct. 1, 1852	12	30	9	5	15	109	------	Organized a Church at one of his stations, and another at one of his out-stations.
" "	" "	Hartford and Indianola	Oct. 1, 1853	12	26	6	--	6	71	------	
Edward O. Towne	Bonaparte	Bonaparte and vicinity	Nov. 1, 1852	12	38	6	16	1	130	------	Church cannot finish their meeting-house at present without becoming too heavily involved. Are united.
Denis Leonard	Burlington	Rock Spring and Augusta	Dec. 1, 1852	12	30	5	1	1	100	56 28	Long and severe sickness in his family.
John C. Ward	Marion, Linn Co.	Marion and vicinity	Sept. 1, 1852	12	26	5	--	4	75	7 00	Organized a Church at Cedar Rapids.
" "	" "	" " "	Sept. 1, 1853	12	13	----	--	1	----	------	Wife dangerously sick and himself unwell. She has since died, and he returned to N. Y.
Edward M. Miles	Davenport	2d Church, Davenport	June 1, 1852	12	13	2	--	4	50	25 00	Meeting-house progressing.
" "	"	" "	June 1, 1853	12	30	----	10	10	----	21 00	Revival. A new impulse given to the Church.
Elijah Evans	Apple Grove	West Union, &c.	Aug. 1, 1852	12	26	3	5	12	80	------	Two Churches used houses of worship.
" "	" "	Newton, &c.	Aug. 1, 1853	12	26	----	1	4	----	------	Revival at one station.
C. D. Farnsworth	Colesburgh	Colesburgh and vicinity	Aug. 1, 1852	12	26	4	8	----	90	20 00	A large and destitute field, and asks for an itinerant for that region.
" "	"	" " "	Aug. 1, 1853	12	26	6	--	10	120	------	Progressing.
Israel G. Curtis	Pella, Marion Co.	Pella and vicinity	Oct. 1, 1852	12	26	5	3	7	40	44 25	Interesting state of things at one station.
" "	" "	Aurora and Union	Oct. 1, 1853	12	13	2	5	2	----	------	Revival at Aurora. Resigns his commission.
Dwight H. Paul	Le Claire, Scott Co.	Camanche and Le Claire	Oct. 1, 1852	12	26	4	1	5	60	12 00	Finished meeting-house at Camanche.
" "	Camanche	" " "	Oct. 1, 1853	12	26	2	1	7	45	7 00	
E. Boekenoogen	Pella, Marion Co.	Hollanders in P. & vicinity	July 1, 1853	12	30	2	--	----	----	------	A progressive state of good religious feeling.
N. S. Bastion	Dubuque	Dubuque	May 1, 1853	12	30	1	1	11	45	------	Building a meeting-house.
F. O. Nelsson	Burlington	Swedes in B. and vicinity	Nov. 1, 1853	12	13	2	7	----	----	------	Labors successful amidst much opposition.
A. G. Eberhart	Muscatine	Muscatine	Dec. 1, 1853	12	----	----	--	----	----	------	A new appointment.
James Schofield	Decora	Northern Iowa	Jan. 1, 1854	12	13	----	--	----	----	2 00	A new and destitute field. Mr. S. the only Baptist minister in three adjoining counties.
J. V. De Witt	----	----	----	----	----	----	--	----	----	------	A new appointment.
Milton Sutton	Bonaparte	Bonaparte, &c.	----	12	----	----	--	----	----	------	A new appointment.

4

[redacted]

Weeks labor reported.	Stations supplied.	Baptized.	Received by Letter.	Scholars in S. School.	Cont. to Benevolent Objects.	ADDITIONAL FACTS REPORTED.
13	5	..	....	25	3 00	
39	....	..	....	....	......	Church small and feeble.
13	1	..	....	50	......	Prospects brightening, but many discouragements.
39	....	5	11	....	15 00	Spiritual condition of the Church improved. Resigned.
9	2	..	1	....	6 25	
39	3	1	8	25	7 18	Congregation declined on account of other denominations having better meeting-houses.
26	6	3	2	....	60 00	Destitute fields of much promise.
3	....	..	....	....	......	Labored on the field but a small portion of the quarter on account of his return to St. Paul for important purposes.
26	2	..	3	....	......	Church at M. are desirous of building a meeting-house.
26	11	..	....	....	49 53	A new and interesting field.
9	5	..	....	....	......	Labors preliminary as yet, but is interested in the field, and finds Baptists throughout the valley.
....	....	..	....	....	......	A re-appointment to a new field.
13	....	..	....	....	......	Exploring agent and general itinerant.
39	....	8	....	....	......	Labored with several churches with much success, and many were baptized.
52	....	..	....	....	......	Nothing special.
7	3	..	....	10	......	Commenced building a meeting-house. Pastor resigned.
13	....	..	....	....	......	Successful in his mission. College in a prosperous state considering its infancy.
....	....	..	....	....	......	A new appointment. Detained from his field on account of severe sickness in his family.

NAMES OF AGENTS AND MISSIONARIES.	POST OFFICE ADDRESS.	FIELD OF LABOR.	Date of Commission	Months Commis'd.	Weeks labor reported.	Stations supplied.	Baptized.	Received by Letter.	Scholars in S. School.	Cont. to Benevolent Objects.	ADDITIONAL FACTS REPORTED.
CALIFORNIA.											
Levi O. Grenell	San Jose	San Jose and Santa Clara	Sept. 1, 1852	12	26	2	3	9	50	......	Need no further aid.
" "	"	" " "	Sept. 1, 1853	12	26	....	2	....	....	......	Resigned the pastoral charge of the Church at San Jose.
Wm. Rollinson	San Francisco	Pine-st Ch. San Francisco	Sept. 1, 1852	12	26	1	1	6	54	815 00	Prospects very favorable. Pastor been sick.
" "	"	" " "	Sept. 1, 1853	12	26	....	1	13	....	270 00	Expect to build a meeting-house at once. Prospects very encouraging.
J. B. Saxton	Stockton	Stockton	Feb. 1, 1853	12	52	....	..	9	25	......	Organized a Church. Purchased a lot and house, and fitted it up for public worship. Prospects encouraging. Financial condition of the Church not so good as heretofore.
"	"	"	Feb. 1, 1854	12	....	....	..	....	....	......	
O. B. Stone	Marysville	Marysville	Jan. 1, 1854	12	....	....	..	....	....	......	Report not received.
S. A. Taft	......	......	......	....	....	....	..	....	....	......	Detained from his field on account of the severe sickness of his wife.
NEW MEXICO.											
Hiram W. Read	Albuquerque	Albuquerque, &c.	Aug. 1, 1852	12	26	....	..	....	14	......	School gradually gaining favor. Much of his time during the last quarter detained at home on account of Mrs. R.'s severe and dangerous illness.
" "	"	" "	Aug. 1, 1853	12	26	....	2	7	10	......	Organized a Church. Distributed many Bibles and religious books.
Lewis Smith	Santa Fé	Santa Fé	Aug. 1, 1852	12	26	....	..	....	5	......	Congregations have been large and attentive. Obliged to suspend Spanish preaching. Building a meeting-house.
" "	"	" "	Aug. 1, 1853	12	26	....	..	....	....	......	Sees no immediate fruit of his labor; general indifference to the subject of religion in his field. Finished meeting-house.
J. Milton Shaw	Fort Defiance	Fort D. & the Navajo Ind's	Dec. 1, 1852	12	52	....	..	....	....	......	Labors among the Navajoes promising.
" "	"	" " " "	Dec. 1, 1853	12	13	....	..	....	....	......	
Samuel Gorman	Laguna	Pueblo Indians	Oct. 1, 1852	12	30	....	..	....	....	1 25	An additional school started at Corera, a Mexican village, under encouraging circumstances.
" "	......	......	Oct. 1, 1853	12	13	....	..	....	....	......	Prospects more favorable at Laguna.

EXPLANATION OF THE MISSIONARY TABLE.

PAGES 40-51.

The parallel columns show:

1. The names of Agents and Missionaries, and the States in which they reside.
2. The post-office address of Agents and Missionaries.
3. The fields of labor occupied by Agents and Missionaries.
4. The dates at which the appointments commence.
5. The number of months for which the appointments are respectively made.
6. The number of weeks labor reported as having been performed during an appointment.
7. The number of stations and outstations supplied.*
8. The number of persons baptized by the Missionaries within the time of appointment.

[redacted]

STATE CONVENTIONS

AND

GENERAL ASSOCIATIONS IN THE UNITED STATES,

With the Names and Post Office Address of the Corresponding Secretaries; the Time and Place of their Anniversaries for 1854; the number of Missionaries employed, and amount of Receipts into their Treasuries, for 1853, including Balances of the previous year.

STATES.	CORRESPONDING SECRETARIES.	POST OFFICE ADDRESS.	PLACE OF NEXT ANNIVERSARY.	Time of Anniversary	No. of Missionaries	Amount of Receipts for Dom. Miss. in 1853.
Maine	L. B. Allen	Yarmouth	Bangor	June 20	30	4126 65
New Hampshire	H. D. Hodge	Sanbornton	New London	Oct. 18	17	1868 89
Vermont	John Goadby	Poultney	N'th Bennington	Oct. 4	8	2696 35
Massachusetts	George W. Bosworth	South Boston	New Bedford	Oct. 25	43	3089 32
Rhode Island	Warren Randolph	Providence			14	1935 49
Connecticut	E. Cushman	Deep River	Hartford	June 13	14	1891 05
New York	M. G. Hodge	Albany	Syracuse	Oct. 10	65	14366 02
New Jersey	J. M. Carpenter	Jacobstown	Haddonfield	Oct. 31	22	2904 59
Pennsylvania	A. Levering	Philadelphia	Pittsburgh	Oct. 25	23	5502 68
Maryland						
Virginia						
North Carolina						
*South Carolina						
*Georgia						
*Alabama						
*Mississippi	W. Carey Crane	Hernando de Soto Co.				
*Louisiana						
Texas	R. C. Burleson		Palestine	June 17	9	1769 34
*Tennessee						
*Kentucky						
Missouri	Leland Wright			May 27	13	1282 72
Illinois	W. Stockdale		Chicago	Oct. 21		1059 49
*Southern Illinois						
Indiana	H. C. Skinner	Logansport	Indianapolis	Sept. ..	18	1735 79
Ohio	D. A. Randall	Columbus	Wooster	Oct. 18	36	3605 01
Michigan	S. Graves	Kalamazoo	Niles	Oct. 13	17	1386 57
Wisconsin	J. T. Westover	Kenosha	Madison	Oct. 25	2	405 98
†Iowa	H. R. Wilbur	Mount Pleasant	Davenport	Oct. 20		
‡California	J. B. Saxton	Stockton				

Amount of Receipts reported above 49,627 89
Amount of Receipts of the H. M. Society 56,903 83

Total amount reported for Home and Domestic Mission purposes $106,531 72

* No Reports received from these States.
† Collections in these States paid directly into our Treasury.
‡ Organized last September.

ALL THE STATES, SINCE 1832.

Total for each State.
5,058
4,097
9,518
6,303
76,480
19,743
29,760
160,039
26,951
8,807
1,276
2,070
1,174
5,759
4,520
5,145
11,064
1,555
1,686
200
343
347
9,330
5,391
8,528
10,891
493
172
1,899
486
79
118

PRIMARY SOCIETIES AND THEIR ANNUAL CONTRIBUTIONS SINCE 1845.

NAMES OF SOCIETIES.	POST OFFICE ADDRESS.	TREASURERS.	Anniversary of 1846.	Anniversary of 1847.	Anniversary of 1848.	Anniversary of 1849.	Anniversary of 1850.	Anniversary of 1851.	Anniversary of 1852.	Anniversary of 1853.	Anniversary of 1854.
Stanton street F. H. M. Society	New York	Mrs. Phelps	51 94	30 00		25 00	30 00	70 12	30 00	50 00	30 00
Norfolk street do do	do	Mrs. Jane Theall	18 00	17 23	30 00	32 50	30 79		113 70	60 00	60 00
First Church do do	do	Mrs. S. F. Randolph	222 23	216 10	512 12	766 02	800 00	708 50	504 06	750 00	
Cannon Street do do	do		33 00	30 00	46 62	12 00					
Tabernacle do do	do	Miss Mary Colgate		123 00	147 02	156 71		56 00	126 30		
Ladies' Mis. Soc. of Pierrepont st. Church	Brooklyn, N. Y.					50 00		57 00	41 50	50 00	
Young Men's Mis. Soc. Stanton st. Church	New York		40 00	100 00	150 00	75 00	110 00	60 00	30 00	230 00	190 00
Young Men's Mis. Soc. First Church	Brooklyn, N. Y.	C. G. Morse		60 00	60 00	60 00		60 00	160 68		
Sunday School of Cannon street Church	New York		30 00	30 00	30 00	30 00	20 00	40 00	30 00	20 00	15 00
Sunday School of 16th street Church	do	George P. Brush	50 00	100 00	100 00	60 00	100 00	90 00	60 00	150 00	160 00
Sunday School of Norfolk street Church	do			30 00	120 50	90 00	60 00	60 00	90 00	60 00	5 00
Sunday School of 6th street Church	do				30 00	30 00		100 00			
Sunday School of Stanton street Church	do	Drake P. Todd	15 00		15 00	30 00		60 00		30 00	30 00
Western Assoc. of Ladies of First Church	Providence, R. I.	Miss A. G. Beckwith	129 00	150 00	200 00	150 00	136 67	141 00	185 52	83 00	121 85
Female Western Mission Society	Warren, R. I.	Mrs. A. M. Fessenden, Sec.	41 00	30 00	30 00	25 00	30 00		30 00	27 00	
Ladies' Home Mission Society	Philadelphia	Mrs. Margaret S. Foster	75 00	133 00	150 00	150 00	75 00	245 00	191 84	229 21	100 00
Female Mission Society of First Church	New Bedford, Mass.	Mrs. E. F. Crowell		85 00		100 00		100 00		50 00	50 00
Piscataway Home Mission Society	New Brunswick, N. J.	Isaac Stelle				100 00	100 00	88 25	78 37		
Female Mite Society	Hillsdale, N. Y.	Miss Rachel Knox		30 00	36 00	30 00	30 30				
Youth's Benevolent Society	Burlington, N. J.		9 30	16 37	7 30	10 98	66 00	2 88	2 87		
Female Mission Society of First Church	New London, Conn.	Mrs. Comstock, Sec.			100 00	50 00	40 00		27 08	32 00	
Washington st. Female Home Mis. Soc.	Buffalo, N. Y.	Mrs. E. A. Butler	100 00			125 00					
Sunday School of Baptist Church	Hudson, N. Y.	H. P. Skinner	30 00		30 00	30 00					
Ladies' Mission Society of Baldwin Place	Boston, Mass.			50 00	150 00		30 00		30 00		30 00
Young People's Mission Society	New England Village, Mass.		25 00	20 00	90 00		37 00				
Boardman Mission Society, First Church	Charlestown, Mass.					41 48	126 00				100 00
Female Charitable Soc., Pleasant st. Ch.	Worcester, Mass.					230 00	30 00		10 00		
Sunday School of First Ch., Lowell, Mass.	Lowell, Mass.	Seth Pooler					186 00	188 00	188 00	222 00	225 00
Young Men's Mis. Soc., Second Church	Rochester, N. Y.	L. Roberts			50 00	50 00	15 00				
Sunday School of South Church	Boston, Mass.							15 45			
Female Mission Society of First Church	Newark, N. J.			33 72				40 38			
Female Mite Society	Warren, R. I.							30 00			
Female Home Mission Society	Amesbury, Mass.							14 00			
Penny-a-week Society	Amesbury, Mass.							30 25			
Female Home Mission Society	Marblehead, Mass.							20 00	21 60		
Female Home Mission Society	Rowley, Mass.							16 28			
Female Mission Society	Bedford, N. Y.	Miss R. A. Platt						23 16		21 39	30 00

URERS.	Anniversary of 1846.	Anniversary of 1847.	Anniversary of 1848.	Anniversary of 1849.	Anniversary of 1850.	Anniversary of 1851	Anniversary of 1852.	Anniversary of 1853.	Anniversary of 1854.
						10 00			
						32 00	30 00	50 00	60 00
						12 50			
						30 00	70 00	50 00	
				100 00		31 80	30 00		10 00
						50 00	75 00		22 00
							11 00		
							34 00		
							12 80		
							30 00		
							23 42		
							12 00		
							18 00		
							15 63		
							20 00		
							90 00		
nick, Jr.							70 00		
								24 00	16 00
								15 00	
								137 14	138 50
								18 00	
ardick								35 22	35 42
ardock								80 00	
								10 00	9 04
								22 36	22 13
								30 00	
								21 00	
								14 25	
								20 00	19 00
								25 00	10 00
								42 00	
								30 00	
									16 00
									62 52
									151 00
									80 00
									17 68
									30 00
									3 00
									45 00

NAMES OF SOCIETIES.	POST OFFICE ADDRESS.	TREASURERS.	Anniversary of 1846.	Anniversary of 1847.	Anniversary of 1848.	Anniversary of 1849.	Anniversary of 1850.	Anniversary of 1851.	Anniversary of 1852.	Anniversary of 1853.	Anniversary of 1854.
Sunday School	Watertown, Wis.										3 00
Ladies' Ben. Soc., First Church	Worcester, Mass.										15 00
Union Miss. Sunday School	Philadelphia										10 00
Mission Sewing Circle	East Trenton, Me.										9 66
Dorcas Society, First Church	Plainfield, N. Y.										16 00
Sunday School	New Philadelphia, Ia.										5 00
Ladies' Circle	Jamaica Plains, Mass.										50 00
Society of Inquiry	Franklin College, Ia.	J. R. Osgood									4 15
Sunday School, First Church	Williamsburgh, L. I.										20 00
Ladies' H. M. S. Union Church	Boston, Mass										65 00
Sunday School, Second Church	Williamsburgh, L. I.										10 00
Sunday School, Washington Ave. Church	Brooklyn, N. Y.										15 00
Sunday School, Berean Church	New York										30 00
Fem. Miss. Soc., Pierrepont st. Church	Brooklyn, N. Y.	Mrs. J. Gibbs									33 00
Sunday School, North Church	New York										15 00
Sunday School, Central Church	Poughkeepsie, N. Y.										5 00
Sunday School, Union Church	New York										10 00
Ladies' Sewing Soc., Union Church	Pittsburgh, Pa.										30 00
Sunday School, First Church	Chicago, Ill.										30 00
Sunday School, Central Church	Chelmsford, Mass.										2 30
Young Men's Miss. Soc.	South Abington, Mass.										25 00
Judson S. S. Mission Society	Rockville, Ct.										11 11
Sunday School	Burnt Hills, N. Y.										4 00
Female Mission Society	Plymouth, Mass.										6 00
Branch Sunday School, North Church	Staten Island, N. Y.										1 00
Juvenile Mission Society	St. Charles, Ill.										1 14

LIST OF LEGACIES,

O THE SOCIETY SINCE ITS ORGANIZATION.

Josiah Penfield, Savannah, Ga., per Rev. H. O. Wyer	$1250 00
Clarissa Long, Shelburn, Mass., per W. Wilder, Esq., Executor	37 50
am Powers, Hebron, N. H., per Rev. I. Merriam	100 00
Maria Curtis, Southbridge, Mass., per Rev. E. Going	200 00
Jemima Elliott, Hampton, Ct., per Rev. J. Payne, Executor	100 00
Betsey Sprague, Attleboro', Mass., per Mr. A. Reed, Executor	451 25
t Rogers, Esq., Newport, R. I.	25 00
zer Boyd, Providence, R. I.	10 00
Abigail Marshall, New York, per Mr. Schofield, Executor	702 17
Margaret Pugsley, Dutchess Co., N. Y., per Miss Cornelia Pugsley	280 00
Irene Coats, New York, per Alfred Decker, Esq.	250 00
Elizabeth G. Moore, Hartford, Ct., per J. B. Gilbert, Esq.	200 00
aniel Tucker, Esq., Milton, Mass., per W. D. Ticknor, Esq.	2005 00
Margaret Martin, Montgomery, N. Y., per Mr. J. J. Martin, Executor	100 00
Cynthia M. Wright, Suffield, Ct., per H. Sheldon, Administrator	50 00
ephaniah Eddy, New Bedford, Mass., per Rev. H. Jackson, Executor	150 00
osiah Kendall, Groton, Mass., per F. F. Wheelock and Rev. Amasa Sanderson, ecutors	1150 00
Jane McCall, Society Hill, S. C., per John McIver, Esq.	20 00
Lydia Sweetzer, South Reading, Mass., per H. Sweetzer	324 50
Elizabeth Griffin, New York, per one of her heirs	83 34
Josiah Flint, Cornish, N. H., per Mr. A. Burnap	80 00
as Cooper, Esq., Eatonton, Ga., per Hon. M. A. Cooper, Executor	2000 00
Betsy Hutchinson, Passumpsic, Vt., per L. P. Parks, Esq.	50 00
Amos Dodge, Brighton, Macoupin Co., Ill., by his widow	30 00
ohn Ward, Warren, N. Y., per J. Northrop and A. Ward, Executors	850 50
[illegible] vden, Saybrook, Ct., per H. L. Champlin, Executor	100 00
[illegible] I., in part, per H. Hamilton and Rev. E. K. Fuller, Ex'rs.	400 00
[illegible] Rev. B. M. Saunders, Executor	1831 87
[illegible] eck	46 75
[illegible] Society	100 00
[illegible]	10 00

1848	William Jones, Iowa City, Iowa, per G. W. Hampton, Esq., Executor	25 00
"	Hon. James Vanderpool, Newark, per B. Vanderpool, Esq., Executor	1000 00
"	Miss Susan Farrar, Keene, N. H., per Rev. G. Robins	10 00
"	Mrs. Eunice Nicholls, Cambridge, Mass., per E. Mansfield, Executor	500 00
"	Mrs. Hannah Carleton, Portland, Me., per Rev. G. J. Carleton, Administrator	500 00
1849	Mr. Samuel R. Stelle, Piscataway, N. J., per Lewis R. Stelle, Esq., Executor	200 00
"	Mrs. Phebe Gale, East Bennington, Vt., per Executor of Estate of S. Harmon	25 00
"	Mr. William Reynolds, Boston, Mass., per J. H. Duncan, Esq., and Mrs. Susan D. Reynolds, Executors, in land not sold	
"	Josiah Lyman, Andover, Ct., per N. B. Lyman, Executor	50 00
"	John J. Martin, Montgomery, N. Y., per M. Bookstaver, Executor	1000 00
"	Mrs. Martha Howe, West Boylston, Mass., per Messrs. E. J. Howe & Co.	50 00
"	A. H. Reed, Sweden, N. Y., per Rev. D. Searl	13 00
"	Asa H. Trueman, Owego, N. Y., per E. Trueman, Executor	248 00
1850	George D. James, Amenia, N. Y., J. K. Mead and N. Rose, Executors	100 00
"	John Everett, Manchester, Mich., per F. Everett	70 00
"	Jacob Whitman, Belvidere, Ill., in part, per N. Crosby, Esq.	100 00
"	Jonas Taylor, Boston, Mass.	12 50
"	Miss Rebecca Thompson, Amenia, N. Y., per A. B. Capwell	801 00
"	Joanna Minot, Boston, Mass., per E. Mears and I. Parker, Executors	100 00
"	Claudius F. Brown, Arkwright, N. Y., per David Barrell	150 00
"	Miss Anna Roe, Egremont, Mass., per R. B. Brown, Executor	50 00
1851	David Schauber, Burnt Hills, N. Y., per J. & D. M. Schauber, Executors	10 00
"	Woolcot Griffin, Gouverneur, N. Y., per O. L. Barnum, Executor	100 00
"	Joseph Flanders, Brooklyn, N. Y., per Mrs. Eliza A. Flanders and Benj. Flanders	500 00
"	William Williams, New York, per John Allan, Executor	400 00
"	Ely Wiley, South Reading, Mass	50 00
1852	Miss Phœrozene C. Kelly, Hopkinton, N. H., per John Page	50 00
"	Jonathan W. Ford, Boston, Mass	100 00
"	Theron Fisk, Warsaw, N. Y., in advance	2500 00
"	Joshua A. Burke, Brooklyn, N. Y., per Mrs. E. and W. A. Burk	350 00
"	Miss Eliza Skaats, New York, in part, per G. N. Bleecker, Executor	1000 00
"	Barnum M. Howard, Sweden, N. Y., per H. M. Howard, Executor	20 00
1853	Alanson Stewart, Liberty, N. Y., per W. W. Murphy	5 00
"	Mrs. Sarah B. Peirce, Middleboro', Mass	100 00
"	Arnold Whipple, Providence, R. I., per Mrs. P. Whipple, Executrix	200 00
"	Mrs. Fanny McGilvreay, Brookline, N. H. (Annuity), per H. A. Daniels, Administrator	40 00
"	Mrs. Lucretia Goddard, Worcester, Mass., per Hon. J. Davis, Executor	300 00
"	P. F. Brayton, Providence, R. I., per A. K. Brayton	62 00
"	Mrs. L. D. Gale, Washington, D. C.	50 00
1854	Edward Rogers, Chester, Ill., per Rev. M. B. Kelly	5 00
"	Miss Esther Ann Blakely, Pawlet, Vt., per Rev. J. J. Peck	73 00
"	Daniel Cummings, Chelsea, Mass., per Eaton, Executor	1000 00
"	Mrs. Mary Leuce, Bristol, R. I., per J. F. Baars	7 50

IMPORTANT WHEN WILLS ARE MADE.

Legacies are sometimes diverted from the purposes of testators, on account of technical informalities, especially in the devising clause. The following form of bequest has been approved by high legal authority, to which we solicit the careful attention of those friends who kindly intend to place the Society among their legatees, as one which, if followed, will secure to us the favors intended.

FORM OF A BEQUEST TO THE SOCIETY.

I give and bequeath to the American Baptist Home Mission Society, formed in New York in the year eighteen hundred and thirty-two, the sum of —— dollars for the purposes of said Society.

REPORTS OF COMMITTEES

ON TOPICS PRESENTED IN THE ANNUAL REPORT OF THE EXECUTIVE BOARD,

AT PHILADELPHIA, MAY 11th, 12th, 13th, AND 14th, 1884

and all the goodliness thereof as the flower of the field; the grass withereth, the flower fadeth." It is even so. Hence, your Committee on the decease of beloved associates in this holy cause have to report that never before has Death [redacted]

But though death has thus taken from our side our beloved associates, he has effected no triumph. They yet live and are still united with us in the service of our common Lord. True, they have passed before us into another world, but "they serve him day and night continually in his temple." Death has

the conflict have left us blessed examples, and have made delightful progress in the work which engaged their energies. Our difficulties are less in number and

---

REPORT OF THE COMMITTEE ON INDIAN MISSIONS.

Presented by their Chairman, Rev. S. Dyer, of Indiana.

We are convened in a city of holy and patriotic reminiscences. It was here that the great principle of equal brotherhood was first proclaimed in that immortal document which gave our nation being as a free Republic; and here was exhibited that unparelleled instance of patriotism, which pledged "life, fortune, and sacred honor," in defence of the freedom and rights of man. But the peculiar fact which now revives in memory, is that which associates the place of our convocation with the race on whose claims your Committee have been instructed to report. While other adventurers and settlers on the Continent of America, with an almost fatal unanimity, treated the unsuspecting aborigines with thoughtless barbarity, and open disregard of truth and right; here was manifested that instance of rectitude of dealing and sacred regard for the welfare of the race, that has stamped the name of Wm. Penn among the greatest of the age, and made his treaty with the Indians one of the facts in our history to which we delight to point the eyes of admiring nations. Meeting on a consecrated spot like this, surrounded by the waters of two beautiful streams, whose names will ever tell of the Indians dwelling here, it would be indeed surprising if no attention was bestowed upon the remnant of that people, whose history is so strikingly associated with this great city.

In presenting this subject for the consideration of the Society, the first question will naturally be: "Does this work appropriately belong to the A. B. H. M. Society?" Heretofore it has been held as a part of the great field of Foreign Missions. When it was thus regarded, the Indians were far removed from the borders of civilization, isolated and comparatively unaffected by the influences of the white race. But the developments of the last decade of years have broken down all these barriers, and brought the two races into immediate juxtaposition, so that the Home Missionary and the Foreign Missionary now intermingle in their labors, and cross each others trails as they "go preaching the Gospel," in the Far West. It is no longer a "foreign field," but "home, sweet home," now extends from sea to sea. Geographically, therefore, it belongs to this Society as a part of the great home field.

uttering the Macedonian cry, "*Come over and help us;*" and the condition of all demands prompt action. The associations connected with every hill and valley of our land, re-echo this call; and who will dare longer to treat it with disregard or neglect? Let such a one, as he kneels to pray by the deserted homes and over the desecrated graves of a noble and almost extinct race, listen to the spirits of its departed ancestors, as in the last great day, they will charge home upon him: "I was hungry, and ye gave me no meat; naked, and ye clothed me not; in darkness, and ye gave me not the 'light of life,' to guide my feet in the ways of peace"; and who will take the responsibility to answer to the charge?

As to the plan of operations, your Committee are of the decided opinion, that the same general line of conduct should be pursued as in Missions to the white settlements. There has been, for no good reason, in the judgment of your Committee, a wide departure from this course in almost all efforts hitherto made to ameliorate the condition of the Indians. Unwise connections have been made with Government agents to civilize and enlighten, ere looking for the spiritual harvest of souls; and in nearly all of these instances, the results have sadly disappointed the expectations of the laborers, while the usual success has attended those Missions which have pursued the line of duty marked out in the great commission, to "preach the Gospel."

Who can stand on the bank of the "Father of Waters," and cast his eye eastward, and remember that the whole country was once the undisputed home of millions of red men, and not feel his heart swell with the deepest emotions of sadness, and his eyes overflow with sympathetic tears, for the fallen of a mighty people. Once their wigwams were clustering along the borders of every stream, and reposing in the shade of the green valleys; their canoes were the only craft cleaving the waters of our beautiful rivers, and their shouts and songs waking an echo to break the brooding stillness from the Atlantic to the "land which slopes to the Western Main." Now all, all have passed away; their canoes have yielded the highway of waters to the steam-boat, whose ceaseless reverberations now awake the echoes of their native hills; their trails and war-paths are obliterated by the iron tracery of railroads, and the locomotive screams and rattles along, where the crouching hunter sought with care the footsteps of his panting prey. Nothing is left in these fair broad lands to evidence their existence here, but the bleaching bones of their ancestors, and the verbal monuments they have erected upon our mountains and limned upon our streams.

"But though amid the forests,
There rings no hunter's shout,
Their names are on our waters,
We may not wash them out;
Their memory liveth on our hills,
And on our wave-beat shore,
Where the everlasting rivers speak
Their dialect of yore."

Could the Indian, when the white man first came to his shore, have cast his eye far down the vista of the future, and had but a glimpse of what his race was doomed to suffer by the contact, how would he have shrunk appalled at the sight, and prayed to die, ere he should become an outcast, with none to weep over his fall.

Our conceptions of Indian character have generally been in outline, having the form and lineaments of humanity, without the usual attributes of mind and heart; a piece of mere animated clay, decked out in paint and feathers, with a vampire's thirst for blood, and a demon's passion for evil. But under the genial influences of the missionary spirit, the "painted clay" begins to assume the form of well-developed manhood, entitled to the sympathies of a common brotherhood. We have no longer, when we delineate his character, to write under the etching, "This is a man," before the similitude is recognized. This is a great point gained to favor the labors in which the Society are just engaging. The Indian is no longer regarded as unyielding as a block of granite from his native mountains, and as uncontrollable as the winds which rustles through the leaves of his forest home.

The Indians have too long been left to the influence of men whose only desire was the gratification of the basest passions. They have been too far sequestered from the great highways of trade and commercial enterprise, to attract the attention of intelligent merchants and tradesmen, hence, they are visited mostly by the lowest description of traffickers, whose distance from the established restraints of justice, emboldens them to perpetrate all forms of villany to accomplish their base ends. The natural consequences of this has been to produce a wider and deeper state of demoralization than they ever knew, prior to such unholy intercourse. They have imbibed all the meaner vices, without acquiring a single virtue as an offset.

The first rays of dawning intelligence derived from the whites, which streaked the horizon of their moral sky, have been transmitted through a medium so beclouded with pestilential vapor, as to produce, in many instances, a chronic moral insensibility, forming the most formidable barrier to success in their evangelization. We, who can appreciate the temporal and spiritual benefits of a pure and enlightened christianity, ought to adopt some adequate remedy for this contagion of vice, and to impart to the hapless victims of a schooled and artful depravity, the life giving power, to reform and save. The work is ours, and it should be promptly and liberally carried forward.

REPORT OF THE COMMITTEE ON THE "FAR WEST."

Presented through their Chairman, Rev. O. C. Wheeler, of California.

Your Committee would make no invidious comparison between the different portions of the Home Mission field. In presenting their report, therefore, upon the "Far West," they make for it no other claim than appears from the following statement of facts:

The "Far West" now embraces all of our possessions upon the Pacific slope extending from the Sierra Nevada mountains on the east, to the Pacific ocean on the west, and from the thirty-second to the forty-eighth degree of north latitude; including the territories of Washington and Oregon, and the State of California. The chief elements which give importance to that field are found in—

1st. The Extent and Character of the Country.—California possesses an area of 188,981 square miles; Oregon and Washington have an area of 341,-463; making a total of 530,443 square miles. But these numbers will convey no adequate idea of the extent of territory they express, unless elucidated by a comparison with other and more familiar districts of country. Oregon and Washington contain territory enough to form *seven* states, equal in size to the seven *largest* of our northwestern states, viz., Illinois, Indiana, Ohio, Iowa, Michigan, Wisconsin, and Minnesota; or an area about equal to that embraced in the original thirteen states of our Union. California embraces an area equal to that contained in the states of Connecticut, Massachusetts, New Hampshire, Vermont, Rhode Island, New Jersey, New York, Pennsylvania, Ohio, Maryland, and Delaware. California has 970 miles of sea-coast, and Oregon 480 miles, making a total of 1,450 miles, being nearly equal to our entire Atlantic coast. Such is the *extent* of the region we denominate the "Far West"; and the resources of that region are upon a scale of equal magnitude.

The mineral wealth of those territories is of exceeding richness, and is almost inexhaustible in amount. The gold mines of California, and the immense deposits of cinnabar found through a large portion of that state, will be sources of wealth for many years, while the coal fields of Oregon and the quarries of granite and marble in California will yet afford profitable employment to thousands.

The agricultural capacities of the Pacific slope are equal to those of any portion of the world. The soil, of virgin richness, yields, with limited culture, the most liberal harvests, and is admirably adapted to nearly every variety of vegetable and farinaceous production, while all the fruits of the temperate zone, and many of tropical varieties, attain the highest perfection. Possessing such advantages, united to a genial climate and an atmosphere of unsurpassed salubrity, these states can scarcely fail to become the prosperous home of millions. Did their importance rest solely, or even chiefly, upon the deposits of gold there existing, it might lessen, and the country now teeming with life and energy might again become a solitude if time should exhaust that source of wealth. But it is not so. While the possession of such treasures gives present prosperity, the continued progress of the "Far West" depends not alone upon the continuance of its mineral wealth; its guaranty is found in its genial climate, its fertile soil, its forests and fisheries, its coal fields and quarries, and in its manufacturing and commercial facilities. The ample resources which cluster there are the material from which the wealth and power of a nation is produced.

2d. The Character and Condition of its Population.—In this respect the "Far West" possesses a character peculiar to itself. The number of the population may be set down at 350,000, but of these fully 300,000 are men. This fact stands without a parallel. Here, in a population of 350,000, we find the active element ordinarily existing in and diffused through one and a quarter millions of people! In other words, there are already as many adult males in California and Oregon as there were at the time of the last census in the five states of Connecticut, Vermont, Rhode Island, New Hampshire, and Delaware, with an aggregate population of one million, two hundred and thirty-nine thousand. The effect which this compression of vital energy must exert in intensifying the life and increasing the vigor of the community is apparent. Imagine the power, physical, mental, and moral, of four men compressed into one, and the colossal intellect and giant frame thus formed would illustrate this people in the comparison with other communities. *A nation of* MEN, in the prime of life, in the full strength of manhood's perfected powers! Nor is this all: they are, in some respects, the choice men of our land,—if not always in the loftier elements of man's moral nature, yet in the possession of those qualities which give force to communities. The timid, the indolent, the dwarfed, have seldom ventured thither; those difficulties and dangers which have stimulated the bold and adventurous spirit have deterred them, and comparatively few remain there, save men of courage, energy, and determination. Viewed in this aspect, the world presents no nobler material upon which the moulding influence of the gospel can act. As a state draws the nature of its entire life from the character of its early settlers, it is only rational to anticipate for the future of the Pacific States a life of intense energy, such as has never yet been

Politicians and philanthropists have seen in this unlooked-for immigration the means of extending the influence of liberal principles through Asia. May not the Christian see therein the means for bearing the gospel also? In a recent memorial to Congress, referring to the first-named point, the following language is employed:—"California, by the discovery of gold within her borders, has become the residence and home of people 'from out of all nations on the earth.' We see people who have long dwelt under monarchical and despotic sway, now thinking and acting under the blessings which they feel result from our free institutions, and we cannot but see that these influences will work a great revolution in the nations of the earth; and, if the golden moment is secured; if, at the appropriate moment of time, the word is fitly spoken; if our nation seizes the opportunity now offered to it,—eternity alone can reveal the blessings which this nation has it in its power to bestow upon those who come to this portion of our rich heritage from every nation of the earth.

"We believe there never has been a period in the history of any nation, when so glorious an opportunity has been given to bestow so great a boon, and to throw so humanizing and Christianizing an influence over so many people, and of so many different nations, as is now offered to the people of these United States." "The benighted of other nations are coming to us to receive those lessons that shall be borne back to those they have left behind them, for good or for evil, for freedom or for servitude, as this great country by her people and institutions instruct them."

We, occupying the stand-point of the Christian, and regarding the movements of Providence in their higher aspects, those which contemplate the moral and spiritual renovation of the world, may adopt and elevate that language. California may be made *a great Mission ground*, a point for the world-wide diffusion of loftier principles and sublimer truths than those which belong to civil polity; the principles of the *gospel*, the truths of SALVATION! Doing this, "seizing the opportunity now offered—the golden moment," effects will be produced, the influence of which will be felt in other continents. To cherish doubts of such a result would evince a narrow view of the purposes of Him who has drawn these multitudes of Pagans to our shores. It was not that, extracting the gold from our soil, they might bear it back to lavish it upon the shrines of idol deities; not for this did God draw them to a Christian land; but rather, let us believe, that they might be prepared here to aid in fulfilling His own declaration, "The idols will I utterly abolish!"

According to an estimate made by the Secretary of State for California, there were in that State, one year ago, 25,000 of Asiatics and kindred races; of these, 22,175 were Chinese; the remainder were Australians, Sandwich Islanders, Malays, Manillos, Hindostanees, &c. Since that time the number has increased, especially of Chinese; nor is it unlikely that the revolution in China will have the effect of augmenting the number of those who will be led to seek our shores. In connection with this topic, so many reflections arise, and so much of interest is associated with the probable results of this idolatrous immigration, that we scarcely know where to restrain the pen. Yet we must pass to direct attention to another feature of this field.

e Inadequacy of the Means Employed.—The combined efforts of angelical denominations upon the field do not reach much more than American population; there are scores, if not hundreds, of gorges and districts, where the gospel is seldom or never preached; while, for the *Pagan* population, the labors of a single man, located at San Francisco, he direct effort made. But by far the larger portion of that class are to nd congregated in camps throughout the mining districts, where all that learn of Christianity is derived from the conduct, oftentimes immoral and essive, of their American neighbors.

ith this view of the wants, the importance, and the promise of the field re us, let us see what we, as a denomination, are doing to meet its demands l reapits rewards; and without other design than to bring the facts vividly be- e the mind, we give a comparative table of what is being done in the leading the North-west, and in California and Oregon, using as our basis the this Society.*

ing facts are deduced: Illinois, or Indiana, of the Pacific States, has isconsin, Iowa, territory enough to give homes to all the present population of the United States, and sources of wealth sufficient to enrich them all. The success of those who have emigrated thither will continue to attract multitudes, until the dormant wealth of all that coast shall be developed, and the richest and most powerful states of our Union will be those which lie beyond the Rocky mountains. *They possess what never before has been granted to a new state* in this age—the capital to develop all the resources of the land, and to carry out the most enlarged schemes for their advancement. Already has the commercial enterprise of San Francisco reached forth the hand after that prize for which the nations of the World have striven in all ages—the commerce of the Orient, the trade of the distant East—a prize which she will surely win. And should the Japanese expedition be successful in its object (and if not now, it will one day be attained) that same commerce, occupying the vantage-ground of *position*, will be the most powerful competitor for the new and enriching trade that will at once be created. Already the commercial relations of the Pacific coast are disclosing the elements of future power.

But there is still lying incalculable wealth undeveloped, unsought, upon those distant shores. South of California, and in the possession of a people too feeble to protect themselves from the inroads of savages, and too indolent to extract the treasures from the soil, are mines of invaluable richness. And that would be a short-sighted view, which, in estimating the future progress of the "Far West," should leave out of sight the certain development of that material wealth. The Apache will not, for many years, lord it over a soil where the precious metals teem, nor will the immense grazing regions and fertile valleys of Sonora be left to his devastating inroads. Already is a strong current of emigration setting towards the *South* of the "Far West," and it is a current which will gather strength as it flows.

Such is a brief outline of the character and prospects of this great field. Upon it the Church of Christ has a mighty work to do, and it were well that, measuring it in its magnitude and importance, she should arise and gird her for the task. There, all the grand circle of institutions flowing from and founded upon the gospel are yet to be reared. Churches are to be gathered, nurtured, and built up. Church edifices are to be erected. Institutions of learning are to be founded. To bear and plant the gospel there is a work for which no pigmy's hand is fitted. Infidelity in its most boastful aspect; vice in its most open forms, there meet and mock the effort of the Christian laborer, and the truth grapples with errors of every form upon a soil where Romanism for a hundred years has been dominant, and still is powerful. The work to which God here invites us *is* a great work, and its importance should incite us to efforts commensurate alike with its magnitude, and with the far-reaching results that will follow successful labor. Our denomination has not pastors enough there to supply the churches already gathered. The materials for new churches exist, ready to be combined into efficient organization. Scattered amongst the mountains, camping in the ravines, or occupying positions of influence in the towns and inland cities of California are our own brethren; but they are, too often, as sheep without a shepherd!

We need more Missionaries for this field! We need them to reclaim those once members of our Churches, who have wandered; we need them to stand by the sick-bed of the miner, dying far from kindred and from home, to point him to riches brighter than the wealth for which he has toiled; we need them to feed the scattered members of the flock, brethren whose names stand upon *our own* Atlantic church books; we need them to seek out the thousands of young men who have rushed to those tempting shores, and who now, far from their father's house, and removed from the hallowed influences of a Christian home, are exposed to unnumbered dangers and temptations: greatly, *urgently* we need them; nor do we believe that this need can be too solemnly pondered by the ministry and the membership of our Churches.

Long as is this Report, not the half has been said which a full statement of the subject would demand; and your Committee close by expressing the conviction that the "FAR WEST" *presents a field for Missionary effort such as* GOD *opens to his people* BUT ONCE IN CENTURIES! And that, to neglect the call which His providence here makes *on us*, will result in loss to ourselves as a denomination.

towns and cities that have been planted there within the past few years are as truly destitute, and send forth as earnestly and with as great propriety the

mittee, is above all question. In possessing ourselves of the field, we must not strive so much to surprise the outposts, as to storm the fortress. When once the strongholds are taken, the field is easily won. Every efficient church, planted in one of those important positions, becomes as a foster-mother to a whole circle of churches in "regions beyond." The expenditure may be large at first, but it will bring an early and liberal return. Your Committee think that the Board should be encouraged in their endeavors to occupy these fields at the earliest practicable moment. The early settlers of a town in this valley to a very great degree, give type to the character of those who succeed them. As the owners of the soil, its natural increase in value makes them men of wealth and influence. The religious principles, therefore, that prevail in the early history of such a town, will be likely to continue in the ascendant. Hence the exceeding difficulty often experienced by your Missionaries, in laboring where the field has been preöccupied. Men whose early associations and preferences would have inclined them to our views, have formed other ecclesiastical relations, simply because others have been in advance of us in occupying such positions. While we cannot repair our past neglect, we surely ought to provide against an increase of this embarrassment in the future.

Your Committee have also noticed, with interest and approval, the efforts of your Board in behalf of our foreign population. They are aware of the difficulty in the way of the prosecution of this work, arising from the great lack of approved men adapted to this department of the field. The number of such, compared with the magnitude of the work, which in Providence is thrown upon our hands, is exceedingly small. Nor is there any immediate prospect of a large increase. Then, again, the work in its nature presents peculiar embarrassments, even if we had men enough fully to occupy the field. Over our foreign population the "man of sin" sways his iron sceptre, and infidelity in its various forms has led multitudes far away from the truth. Romanism and rationalism, have found a prolific soil among the foreign population of the Mississippi Valley, and already are they bringing forth abundantly their pernicious fruits. And yet amid all these obstacles success has hitherto attended the

REPORT OF THE COMMITTEE ON THE GRANDE LIGNE MISSION.

Presented through Rev. N. Cyr, of Montreal, Chairman.

Your Committee, knowing that the Grande Ligne Mission is pretty extensively known, would report briefly upon it, limiting themselves to the points that are calculated to throw light on this department of our field, and lead to a just appreciation of its character and merits.

This Mission was commenced at the close of 1835, amidst the French Canadians, a population thoroughly Roman Catholic, and upon which no evangelical influence had ever been brought to bear. Descendants of French colonists, the inhabitants of Lower Canada had lived two hundred years under the moulding hand of the Romish clergy, whose dominion, not in the least counteracted, as in the mother country, by the infidelity and revolutionary movements of the eighteenth century, was completely and fully established in the Valley of St. Lawrence. Their numerous Churches, Colleges, Nunneries, Hospitals, and Asylums, with their immense wealth, were both the signs and instruments of their undisputed sway. The people sat in darkness, in the region and shadow of death, and the whole country seemed as inaccessible to the Gospel, as Cape Diamond's lofty citadel is to foreign invasion. So thought even the Christians dwelling amidst the French Canadians, and consequently they made no effort to enlighten them.

But God's thoughts are not our thoughts, and His ways are not our ways. He had designs of mercy towards this people, and to fulfil these designs, He chose some of his servants in Switzerland. They came, and for the first time was preached to them the everlasting and pure Gospel of Christ.

For the first five years, there was only one minister in the field, aided by a couple of teachers. During the second five years, three other ministers, two of whom were the fruits of the Mission, entered the work, and, from that time to the present, there has been an addition of four more, three of whom are the fruits of the Mission. And now the Missionary corps consists of six ordained ministers, two licentiates, ten teachers, three colporteurs; who, in their endeavors to spread the pure knowledge of the Gospel, have to encounter one archbishop, five bishops, and five hundred and fifty priests, besides an innumerable host of nuns and teachers, who are all devoted, soul and body, to the interests and aggrandizements of their Church.

Considering the mighty obstacles in the way of truth, shall we not rejoice and bless God, the master of the harvest, in seeing already four organized churches, into which have been received 370 converted Canadians; and which number yet 200 members, notwithstanding deaths, exclusions, and immigration into the United States. Many others have been also brought to a saving knowledge of Christ, though they have not joined the Mission Churches; and we number besides over a thousand more who have abandoned the errors of Popery, and who are under the influence of the Gospel.

Your Committee think the success of last year's operations show the increased usefulness and importance of the Grande Ligne Mission. The preaching of the Gospel was maintained in twelve different places, and has proved to many the power of God unto salvation, whilst it has built up believers in their most holy faith. Never have there been so many calls for the efforts of the colporteurs, and never have they been more active or found more access to educated and influential persons.

subscription list. About two hundred Romish families take a sufficient interest in religious matters to patronize it, and that in spite of their priests. We look

[redacted]

This new regiment alone, the body-guard of Popery in Canada, cost the Propaganda of Rome some thirty thousand dollars a year, and, what is worthy of remark, we never hear them grudging money thus spent.

But the Missionaries never allowed themselves to be frightened or discouraged by these strenuous and incessant efforts, and, notwithstanding them, the prospects of the Grande Ligne Mission were never so good.

The intense desire of the people of Canada for liberal and general education, and the progress of knowledge, begin to open the way for the Gospel. The priests feel it, and would avert the impending danger, did they occupy their heretofore unassailable position. But the people begin to open their eyes and see the evils which have retarded their progress. They are less submissive to ecclesiastical authority, and in many cases are ready to oppose it. The system of tithes, which makes a rich man of every priest, and perpetuates the power of the ecclesiastical corps, is now generally discredited, and will sooner or later be abolished.

In view of these results, and of the favorable circumstances for Missionary efforts in Canada, looking at the manifestations of independence of priestly power, the progress of education, and the gradual enlightenment of the people, your Committee would praise God and encourage the Society to labor with increased earnestness and diligence in this important field, trusting that He who has already blessed his servants in Canada, will continue to smile upon their evangelistic efforts, so that they may be blessed with the privilege of planting the banner of the glorious Gospel of Christ in that benighted but highly interesting country.

REPORT OF THE COMMITTEE ON CHURCH EDIFICE FUND.

Presented by their Chairman, Rev. M. G. Clark, Philadelphia.

The Committee appointed on so much of the Annual Report as relates to the "Church Edifice Fund," have considered the subject, and beg leave to report.

With the march of improvement by which the present age is distinguished, it is not the least pleasing and encouraging fact to the intelligent Christian, that there is a desire manifesting itself in various forms to perfect and facilitate the instrumentalities of the Gospel, though it must be confessed the Church in this respect is still far behind the world.

In commerce, what increased facilities—what means of power are now employed in comparison with a few years since! Look at her vessels, her steamships—they are floating palaces, and her storehouses are princely mansions; and the country is literally interlaced with her canals and railroads, while her exchanges and banking-houses are not only swelling to enormous sizes under its influence, but they stand before us in all the beautiful adornment of skill and wealth. And this spirit is not only manifest in the higher department of commerce, but it pervades it. It is everywhere giving expansion, facility, and beauty. Running through every avenue, is seen the electric wire, as it were, setting on fire the whole *course* of *business*. And such indeed, is the spirit of the age for improvement, that the slow-plodding farmer has cause to feel its power shaping and sharpening every tool with which he digs and tills the soil.

such amazing rapidity and perfection, are only designed to give ease, rapidity, and power to business for the purpose of increasing wealth. And if it is objected that it costs too much, we have only to reply that the evidences are

ness men feel that it makes good returns. And no intelligent business man would think to succeed, if he were to go back to the old form and style of operation, especially, while all his neighbors are pushing forward their improvements.

[redacted]

divine model for the spiritual church with some good models of material churches, well located, and fitly executed. In how many towns in the older States of this Union has Providence given us the opportunity of establishing our cause in advance, even of others! but we have prejudiced the public mind by locating our house in the woods or on the mountains, instead of placing it in the midst of the people; and often, when they have been located within their reach, the figure and style have been uninviting, and their capacity entirely inadequate to the wants of the community. And the consequence has been, that other denominations have gone forward and supplied the wants of the public with good and inviting houses, located so that they could be reached without the trouble and fatigue of a pilgrimage as to some Mecca. And the masses have enjoyed these accommodations. And they have used the masses, while we, enfeebled, have either abandoned the field altogether, or have maintained a most unequal combat. This, however, we believe, has arisen in many instances, from the *want* of means at command, to carry out suitable plans; and if proper assistance could have been rendered, no doubt but the cause would have been put on a broad and firm basis; and when now it seems only in its infancy, it would have the power of mature strength.

We rejoice that within a few years the policy of locating and building our meeting-houses seems much improved, especially in our older States, and we already begin to see the advantage. But the work is only well begun as yet.

There is, however, a practical difficulty which must be met. The best way of meeting it may not be so easy. It is not to be concealed, that there are scores and hundreds of villages, and towns, and cities even, where there are either no churches or they are young and feeble, and cannot command the means at present for the erection of a house of worship, and yet a house is absolutely necessary to their very existence, or if not to their existence, to their growth and ultimate success. This is preëminently true in the newer portions of the country. And now, what shall be done? You may send a Missionary among them, but what can he do without a suitable place in which to gather the people, where he may bring them under the sound of the Gospel. He may go from house to house, and preach, and pray, but, after all, he will make but slow progress towards building up a self-sustaining church. But could you send to your Missionaries a few hundred or thousand dollars to help complete some well-begun sanctuaries,—could they know, that, if they could bring the people to do a certain part among themselves,—they were certain of the aid which would insure success,—how many a Missionary would gather fresh courage, and how many communities would rise up with a kind of supernatural power to build for themselves the house of the Lord! And with a good house once built and paid for, there are but few congregations which would need farther aid.

Your Committee, therefore, after much reflection and somewhat extended observation believe fully, that it might be a wiser policy for the present, at least, to appropriate a *portion* of the moneys contributed and donated for the spread of the Gospel, to the erection of meeting-houses. Not that they would lessen the amount for direct preaching, but would greatly increase that; while they would call the attention of the churches, and more especially their wealthy brethren, to the importance of this subject. Indeed, it must be kept constantly before them. The Christian's mind must be aroused to the imperative demand of this subject.

Your Committee rejoice in the response which has been made to your first calls in this direction. Your Report states that more than *five thousand* dollars have been collected and appropriated, under the direction of the Board, to some *eleven* churches the past year. But what is that among so many? Instead of *five thousand*, it should be twenty times that amount. We believe that, under the present rapid growth of our country, SEVENTY-FIVE OR ONE HUNDRED THOUSAND DOLLARS could be appropriated with great economy to aid in the erection of church edifices throughout our wide land.

Your Committee do not think that the plan adopted by the Board last year, and widely published to the churches, needs any change. In conclusion they would beg leave to submit the following resolutions:

Resolved, That the Board be instructed to incorporate the Church Edifice Fund as a special object for which to collect funds.

Resolved, That we will not rest until we secure at least *one hundred thousand dollars*, to be expended under the direction of the Executive Board of the Am. Bap. Home Mission Society, according to the plan and style set forth in the *Home Mission Record, Extra*, of last year.

Resolved, That the plans for raising, collecting, as well as disbursing these funds

[redacted]

It is gratifying, nay, encouraging, to perceive, from these substantial tokens of sympathy and coöperative regard, that the work and claims of the Home Mission Society are, year by year, receiving a juster consideration, and becoming more adequately appreciated. Ten years ago, the Treasurer reported but $13,401 76, as the receipts of the year 1843–4: they are now more than quadrupled.

But while your Committee would thank God for the present, and take encouragement from the past, they do but utter a truth capable of the fullest demonstration, that but few, even of its best friends, have, as yet, given to this Society a place in their affections, a remembrance in their prayers, or a prominence in their plans of liberal benefaction, to which it seems every way entitled, and whose claims to which are most vehemently urged by thousands upon thousands of the destitute and the perishing, and approved by the Lord Jesus Christ himself; while multitudes of American Baptists give but stintingly and fitfully to its Treasury.

Your Committee have been furnished with reliable data, carefully prepared, in regard to the necessities of the ensuing year; and they commend to your most serious consideration the statements presented in the Annual Report of the Board, and the plea thereupon founded.

If the Great Commission itself, and the apostolic interpretation of its binding force and practical application, are duly considered; if the test and proof and glory of the Christian Ministry be, that "to the poor the Gospel is preached"; if it be the highest dictate of wisdom and duty alike to seize upon central positions and influential nations, for the more ready and complete evangelization of the world; if there be anything worthy of regard in the signs of the times and the evident designs of Jehovah in making this not only the land of the free, but the refuge and hope of almost all the earth beside, where he is gathering a great multitude out of every nation and kindred and tongue under heaven, in answer to the prayers of His people, that they may have a free conscience, a free Church, a free Gospel, and a free Bible, with free schools and a free government; and if it be in the highest degree obligatory, and in the fullest measure, a blessed privilege to work both when and where God works; in a word, if Patriotism has any acknowledged claims, or Religion, any controlling, impelling, sovereign, consecrating power, surely no intelligent, liberal, worthy American citizen, and especially no true and earnest disciple of the blessed Master,—no grateful blood-bought child of God and heir of heaven,—no devoted and Christ-like Minister of the Cross, can refuse or hesitate to admit, that the field given to this Society to cultivate is, at this present juncture, and of right ought to be, second to none other in the world.

In conclusion, your Committee believe that thirty-six men are too few for the actual necessities of the States and Territories that are pleading for additional laborers from this Society, and that the amount mentioned in the estimate of your Board is by no means too high. That sum and more can be employed most judiciously, in merely planting choice seed in the sunniest spots, without wasting a handful of corn, or a day's labor, in unpromising places.

But how shall the receipts of your treasury be made equal to its present liabilities, and the demands that will in all probability be urgently presented ere the close of this fiscal year?

In the judgment of your Committee, a simpler faith in the Gospel and teachings of our Lord Jesus Christ—a more intelligent and complete estimate of Christian obligation and human responsibility—is the great need. This want met, all other necessities are within our reach—*men*, *means*, *money!*

Whatever will secure to all our churches, their pastors, their deacons, and their entire membership, this spirit of Missions, this, the Spirit of Christ, who, though infinitely rich, became poor for us, that we might through His poverty be made rich,—whatever will tend to produce or cherish and promote pure and undefiled religion before God and among men—is eminently worthy the prayerful regard and the practical adoption of all who sympathize in the objects and purposes of this Society.

Beyond this recommendation, your Committee would submit for your cordial and earnest approval the following resolutions:

Resolved, That the widening field, the growing work, the numerous tokens of Divine favor, the multiplying opportunities and rare openings of rich promise, which the Great Head of the Church is presenting to the American Baptist Home Mission Society, make it in the highest degree desirable, if not imperatively necessary, that the Executive Board should have at their disposal for the current year's disbursement,

DIRECTORS FOR LIFE.

BY VIRTUE OF A CONTRIBUTION OF ONE HUNDRED DOLLARS OR MORE

Ackerman, John, Dobbs Ferry, N. Y.
Adams, Rev. Paul S., Newport, N. H.
Adsit, Rev. Samuel, Jr., Sennet, N. Y.
Akerly, Richard C., New York.
Aldrich, Rev. Jonathan, Middleboro', Ms.
Alger, Henry, Cleveland, Ohio.
Alvord, Rev. Nelson, Chillicothe, Ill.
Anderson, Rev. Thomas D., Roxbury, Mass.
Anderson, M. B., LL.D., Rochester, N. Y.
Archer, Ezekiel, New York.
Armitage, Thomas, D.D., New York.
Armstrong, Rev. James D., Baltimore.
Atwell, Rev. G. B., Pleasant Valley, Conn.
Averill, Rev. Alexander M., Newton Centre, Ms.
Ayre, Rev. Oliver, Claremont, N. H.
Babcock, Rev. Rufus, D.D., New York.
Bacheller, Jonathan, Lynn, Mass.
Bacon, Mrs. Mary H., Greenwich, N. J.
Bailey, Benjamin D., Providence.
Bailey, Rev. Gilbert S., Pekin, Ill.
Bailey, Rev. Joseph A., Essex, Ct.
Ballard, Rev. Joseph, Brooklyn.
Baldwin, Rev. N. B., Philadelphia.
Balen, Peter, Brooklyn, N. Y.
Banks, Jacob, Scull town, N. J.
Banks, Mrs. Mary, Sculltown, N. J.
Banvard, Rev. Joseph, New York.
Barnaby, Rev. James, West Harwich, Mass.
Barker, Rev. Enoch M., Hightstown, N. J.
Barrell, Rev. Almond C., Le Roy, N. Y.
Batchelder, Rev. James L., Cincinnati.
Bates, V. J., Providence.
Beecher, Rev. Luther F., D.D., New York.
Beecher, Mrs. Mary C., New York.
Belcher, Rev. Joseph, D.D., Philadelphia.
Bennet, Rev. Ira, Weedsport, N. Y.
Binney, Rev. J. G., Augusta, Ga.
Binney, Mrs. Juliet P., Augusta, Ga.
Bishop, Nathan, Boston.
Blain, Rev. John, Central Falls, R. I.
Bliss, Rev. George R., Lewisburg, Pa.
Bly, Rev. William T., Berwick, Ill.
Bolles, Matthew, Jr., Boston.
Bosworth, Rev. George W., S. Boston.
Bowles, Rev. Ralph H., Tariffville, Ct.
Boyce, James, Providence.
Bradford, Rev. S. S., Pawtucket, R. I.
Brant, Randolph C., Rochester, N. Y.
Brantly, Rev. W. T., Philadelphia.
Brayton, Rev. Jonathan, Centerville, R. I.
Brayton, Samuel H., Providence.
Brayton, Lodowic M., Knightsville, R. I.
Briggs, Rev. O. W., Brooklyn.
Brooks, Iveson L., Hamburg, S. C.
Brown, Rev. J. Newton, Philadelphia.
Buckbee, Rev. Charles A., New York.
Bucknell, William, Philadelphia.
Burlingham, Rev. A. H., Boston.
Burgess, Rev. I. J., Milltown, Me.
Bump, Nathaniel, Providence.
Burke, William, Rochester, N. Y.
Burke, Abraham C., Brooklyn.
Burke, J. R., Middleboro', Mass.
Butcher, Washington, Philadelphia.
Butterfield, Rev. Isaac, Oswego, N. Y.
Byram, Rev. B. P., Amesbury, Mass.
Caldicott, Rev. T. F., D.D., Boston.
Carleton, Rev. George J., Newtown Centre, Ms.
Carleton, Mrs. Jane T., Newtown Centre, Mass.
Carpenter, Rev. Mark, West Springfie'd, Mass.
Carter, Joseph, Charlestown, Mass.
Caswell, Prof. Alexis, D.D., Providence.
Caswell, Rev. Lewis E., Boston.
Chace, Professor George I., Providence.
Challis, Rev. James M., Roadstown, N. J.
Chandler, John H., Bankok, Siam.
Chandler, Mrs. Helen M., Bankok, Siam.
Chaplin, Rev. Jeremiah, West Dedham, Mass.
Chaplin, Rev. Adoniram J., Dover Plains, N. Y.
Charlton, Rev. Frederick, Wilmington, Del.
Cheney, Rev. David B., Philadelphia.
Child, Mrs. Sophronia L., Philadelphia.
Child, Rev. William C., Framingham, Mass.
Choules, Rev. John O., D.D., Newport, R. I.
Church, Rev. P. D.D., Williamsburgh, L. I.
Church, Mrs. Charles E., Williamsburgh, L. I.
Clarke, Rev. Elbert W., China, N. Y.
Clarke, Rev. Minor G., Philadelphia.
Clapp, Benjamin, Franklindale, N. Y.
Coggeshall, Josias, Brooklyn.
Coggeshall, Mrs. Elizabeth M., Brooklyn.
Cogswell, Rev. Wilson, St. Anthony, Min.
Cooke, Joseph J., Providence.
Cookson, Rev. John, Dover, N.H.
Cole, Rev. Jirah D., Waukegan, Ill.
Colgate, William, New York.
Colgate, Mrs. Jane, New York.
Colver, Rev. Nathaniel, Detroit, Mich.
Collins, Rev. Samuel A., Rehoboth, Mass.
Collom, Rev. J. G., Mt. Holly, N. J.
Conant, John, Brandon, Vt.
Cone, Rev. Spencer H., D.D., New York.
Cone, Mrs. Sally Wallace, New York.
Cone, Edward Winfield, New York.
Cone, Spencer Wallace, New York.
Cones, James, Cincinnati.
Corwin, Rev. Jason, Washington, Ill.
Cottrell, Thomas, Greenwich, N. Y.
Covell, Rev. Lemuel, New York.
Cramb, Rev. Augustus B., Metamora, Ill.
Crane, Rev. W. C., Hernando, Miss.
Crane, William, Baltimore.
Crane, James C., Richmond, Va.
Crosby, William B., New York.

[illegible]IRECTORS FOR LIFE.

[illegible]zer, John P., Chester, Pa.
[illegible]zer, Mrs. Sarah L. Chester, Pa.
[illegible]ozer, Miss Margaret K., Chester, Pa.
[illegible]ozer, Miss Elizabeth, Chester, Pa.
[illegible]shman, Rev. Elisha, Deep River, Ct.
[illegible]agg, Rev. John L., Penfield, Ga.
[illegible]ale, Rev. H S. Lebanon, Ohio.
[illegible]amon, Mrs Catherine, Ashby, Mass.
[illegible]avies, John M., New York.
[illegible]avis, Rev Henry, Columbus, Ohio.
Davis, Hon. Isaac, Worcester, Mass.
Davis, Mrs. Mary H. E., Worcester, Mass.
Day, Rev Ambrose, Westfield, Mass.
Day, Prof. Henry, Providence.
Day, Arthur, Shaftsbury, Vt.
Devan, Rev. Thomas T., New York.
Devan, Mrs. Emma F., New York.
Dickinson, Rev. Edmund W., Pittsburg, Pa.
Dockery, Hon. A., Dockery's Store, N. C.
Dodd, Abner, Newark, N. J.
Dorrance, Rev. George W., Webster, Mass.
Douglass, Rev. William, Providence.
Douglass, James, Cavers, Scotland.
Dowling, Rev. John, D. D., Philadelphia.
Downs, Henry S., Malden, Mass
Drake, Rev. Simeon J., Plainfield, N. J.
Drummond, James P., Brooklyn.
Dunb[illegible] Rev. Duncan, Trenton, N. J.
Dunn, Rev. Lewis A., Fairfax, Vt.
Eastwood, Rev Marvin, Glens Falls, N. Y
Eaton, Rev. William H., Salem, Mass.
Eberhart, Rev. A. G., Muscatine, Ill.
Eddy, Rev. Edwin R., Beverly, Mass.
Edmand, Francis, Newton, Mass.
Edmonds, James, Jeddo, N. Y
Edwards, Alexander, South Framingham, Ms.
Eldridge, Rev. Daniel, Hartford, N. Y.
Ellis, Rev. Robert F., Alton, Ill.
Esh-kuo-go-ne-bi (Rev. J. Tanner), Pem., Min. T.
[illegible]worth, Rev. C. D., Colesburg, Iowa.
[illegible] New York.
[illegible]

Gray, Rev. F. H., [illegible]
Green, Samuel S., Providence.
Grenell, Rev. Zelotes, Honesdale, Pa
Grenell, Rev. Levi O., San Jose, California.
Griffith, Rev. Thomas S., Dubuque, Iowa.
Haddock, Henry, Lynn, Mass.
Hague, Rev. William, D.D., Albany.
Hall, Rev. J. G., Grenada, Miss.
Hall, Rev. Addison, Kilmarnock, Va.
Halsted, Benjamin, New York.
Hansell, Rev. Wm. F., Cincinnati.
Hartwell, Rev. Jesse, Marion, Ala.
Hatt, Rev. Josiah, Hoboken, N. J.
Hatt, Rev. George, New-York.
Harris, John H., Tremont, Ill.
Hill, Rev. Benjamin M., D D., New York.
Hill, Rev. Daniel T., Carmel, N. Y.
Hill, Miss Elizabeth, Carmel, N. Y.
Hill, Rev. S. P., Washington, D. C.
Hill, Samuel, South Boston, Mass.
Hill, Samuel, jr., South Boston, Mass.
Hill, William B., Chemung, Ill.
Hillman, William, New York.
Hires, Rev. William D., New Market, N. J.
Hiscox, Rev. Edward T., New York.
Hodge, Rev. James L., D.D., Brooklyn
Hotchkiss, Rev. V. R., Rochester, N. Y.
Houghton, Hon. Joab, Santa Fe, N. M.
Howard, Rev. Leland, Rutland, Vt.
Howard, Rev. William G., Rochester, N. Y.
Howe, Rev. William, Boston,
Howell, Rev. Robert B. C., D.D., Richmond, Va.
Howell, Mrs. Mary Ann M., Richmond, Va.
Huckins, Rev. James, Galveston, Texas.
Hunt, Samuel, Providence.
Hutchinson, Rev. Wm., Bustleton, Pa.
Ide, Rev. George B., D.D., Springfield, Mass.
Isley, Rev. Silas, New York.
Ives, Rev Dwight, D.D., Suffield, Ct.
Ives, Mrs. Julia A., Suffield, Ct.
Jackson, Rev. Henry, Newport, R. I.
James, Rev. Silas C., Woodburn, Ill.
[illegible] William T., New York.

DIRECTORS FOR LIFE.

Lathrop, Rev. Edward, New York.
Lawe, Rev. William, Modesttown, Vt.
Lawton, Rev. Joseph A., Erwinton, S. C.
Lea, Sidney Slade, Yanceyville, N. C.
Lea, George F., Philadelphia.
Leighton, Rev. Samuel S., N. Londonderry, N. H.
Leverett, Rev. William, New Eng. Village, Ma.
Lewis, John G., Boston.
Lewis, Isaac, New York.
Lillie, Rev. James, D.D., Montreal, Canada.
Lincoln, Hon. Heman, Boston.
Linnard, Hon. J. M., Philadelphia.
Locke, Rev. William H., Springfield, N. J.
Loxley, Rev. Benjamin R., Philadelphia.
Loomis, Rev. Hubbell, East Killingly, Ct.
Lowndes, D. F., Boston.
Lyon, Merrick, Providence, R. I.
Mabbett, Jonathan, Dover Plains, N. Y.
Maclay, Rev. Archibald, D.D., New York.
Magoon, Rev. E. L., D.D., New York.
Magoon, Mrs. E. L., New York.
Malcom, Rev. Howard, D.D., Lewisburg, Pa.
Malcom, Rev. Thomas S., Philadelphia.
Mallary, Rev. C. D., Bain's Store, Ga.
Marble, Joel, Albany, N. Y.
Marchant, Henry, Providence.
Marple, Thompson, Canton, Ill.
Martin, Benyon W., New York.
Martin, Charles J., New York.
Marshall, Rev. Enos, Pittsford, N. Y.
Massey, Rev. Joseph T., Bellingham, Mass.
Mason, Rev. Alanson P., Chelsea, Mass.
Mason, Rev. David G., West Swanzey, N. H.
Mason, Rev. Jas. O., Greenwich, N. Y.
Masters, William, Providence.
Masters, Mrs. William, Providence.
Mathes, Rev. A. P., California.
Merit, Rev. Columbus D., Henry, Ill.
Merriam, Jonathan, Newton Centre, Mass.
Messenger, Rev. Edward C., West Medway, Ms.
Milbank, Samuel, Jr., New York.
Miller, John A., New York.
Mills, Rev. Robert C., Salem, Mass.
Miner, Mrs. Henrietta Wilson, Newark, N. J.
Mitchell, Isaac R., San Francisco, Cal.
Moore, Rev. Isaac, Plainfield, N. J.
Morton, Rev. Charles, Penn Yan, N. Y.
Mulford, Rev. Clarence W., Holmdel, N. J.
Munn, Stephen B., New York.
Munn, William H., New York.
Murdock, Rev. J. N., Hartford, Ct.
Murphy, Rev. John C., New York.
Muzzy, Rev. Lawson, Pulaski, N. Y.
Neale, Rev. Rollin H., D.D., Boston.
Newell, Asa, Providence.
Newton, Isaac, New York.
Nichols, Joseph C., Newark, N.
Norris, William, Newark, N. J.
Northam, Rev. G., Norming Grove, Va.
Olcott, Rev. James B., Parma, N. Y.
Packer, Rev. D., Mount Holly, Vt.
Parker, Rev. J. W., D.D., Cambridgeport, Mass.
Parker, Rev. Carlton, Wayne, Me.
Parker, Rev. C. S., Paterson, N. J.
Parkhurst, Rev. John, Chelmsford, Mass.
Parkhurst, Rev. J. W., Newton Centre, Mass.
Parks, Rev. Norman, Perry, Ill.
Parmelee, Rev. D. S., New York.
Pattison, Rev. R. E., D.D., Waterville, Me.
Pattison, Rev. Wm. P., Auburn, N. Y.
Paul, Albert, Hastings, N. Y.
Peck, I. B., New York.
Peck, Rev. John M., D.D., Shiloh, Ill.
Perkins, Rev. Aaron, D.D., Port Jervis, N. Y.
Perkin, Rev. G. B., Cleveland, Ohio.
Phelps, Rev. S. Dryden, New-Haven, Ct.
Philips, Rev. Daniel W., South Reading, Mass.
Pier, Sylvester, New-York.
Pigsley, Rev. Welcome, Metamora, Ill.
Platt, Nathan C., New-York.
Plummer, John L., Roxbury, Mass.
Pollard, Rev. Andrew, Taunton, Mass.
Pope, Wm. C. N., New Bedford, Mass.
Pope, Mrs. Anna F., New Bedford, Mass.
Pratt, Rev. D. D., Nashua, N. H.
Prevaux, Rev. Francis E., San Francisco, Cal.
Price, Rev. Jacob, Edwardsburg, Mich.
Purser, Thomas, Brooklyn.
Rathbone, John F., Albany.
Raymond, Rev. Robert R., Syracuse, N. Y.
Read, James H., Providence.
Reed, Rev. Nathan A., Winchester, Mass.
Reid, Rev. William, Bridgeport, Ct.
Remington, Rev. Stephen, Louisville, Ky.
Richardson, Thomas, Boston.
Richardson, Rev. J. G., Lawrence, Mass.
Richmond, Rev. J. L., Union, N. Y.
Roberts, Charles L. New-York.
Rollinson, Rev. William, San Francisco, Cal.
Sanderson, Rev. A., Littleton, Mass.
Sarles, Rev. John W., Brooklyn.
Sawyer, Rev. Reuben, Chester, Vt.
Seage, Rev. John, Port Richmond, N. Y.
Searl, Rev. David, Springfield, N. Y.
Seeley, Rev. John T., Dundee, N. Y.
Serrell, John J., New York.
Serrell, Mrs. Mary Eliza, New York.
Shadrach, Rev. W., D.D., Philadelphia.
Shailer, Rev. N. E., Deep River, Ct.
Shailer, Rev. Julius S., Roxbury, Mass.
Shailer, Rev. Davis T., North Becket, Mass.
Shailer, Rev. William H., D.D., Portland, Me.
Shardlow, Samuel, New York.
Shaw, Thomas, Boston.
Shedd, Rev. Philander, Penn Yan, N. Y.
Shepardson, Rev. D., Cincinnati, Ohio.
Sherwood, Rev. A., Upper Alton, Ill.
Skinner, Charles W., Hertford, N. C.
Skinner, John L., Windsor, Vt.
Smith, Gordon, Essex, Ct.
Smith, Rev. S. F., D.D., Newton Centre, Mass.
Smith, Rev. Henry F., Banksville, Ct.
Smith, Mrs. Sarah R., Banksville, Ct.
Smith, Rev. James W., Philadelphia.
Smitzer, Rev. John, Delhi, N. Y.
Sommers, Rev. Charles G., D.D., New York.
Spencer O., Salt Lake, Utah Ter.
Spencer, William B., Phenix, R. I.
Stanwood, Rev. Henry, Rush, N. Y.
Steward, Rev. Ira R., New York.
Stockbridge, Rev. Joseph, Plainfield, N. J.
Stockbridge, Rev. John C., Boston.

MEMBERS FOR LIFE.

Stone, Rev. James R., New York.
Stout, Charles B., New York.
Stow, Rev. Baron, D D., Boston.
Stow, Rev. Phineas, Boston.
Stowell, Nathaniel, Worcester, Mass.
Stubberts, Rev. William F. S., Malden, Mass.
Swan, Rev. Jabez L., New London, Ct.
Swaim, Rev. Samuel B., Worcester. Mass.
Taggart, Rev. Joseph W., New York.
Taylor, Rev. J. B., Richmond, Va.
Taylor, Rev. E. E. L., Brooklyn.
Taylor, Stewart M., New York.
Taylor, Daniel G., New York.
Taylor, Jeremiah B., New York.
Teasdale, Rev. T. C., D.D., Washington, D. C.
Thomas, Mrs. Catherine W., New York.
Thomas, Mrs. Margaret I., New York.
Thomas, Cornelius W., New York.
Thomas, Augustus, New York.
Thompson, Mrs. Huldah E., Troy, N. Y.
Tingley, Rev. T. C., West Boylston, Mass.
Tinsley, Rev. Isaac, Charlottesville, Va.
Timmons, John M , Effingham, S. C.
Torian, Thomas. Halifax, Va.
Tracy, William, New York.
Tracy, Rev. Leonard, Burlington, Vt.
Train, Rev. Arthur S., Haverhill, Mass.
Tryon, Mrs. Louisa J., Houston, Texas.
Tucker, Daniel N., New York.

Vandervoort, John, Moorestown, N. J.
Verrinder, Rev. William, Jersey City, N. J.
Walthall, Rev. Joseph S., Richmond, Va.
Wattson, Thomas, Philadelphia.
Wayland, Rev. Francis, D.D., Providence.
Webb, Rev. G. S., New Brunswick, N. J.
Welch, Rev. B. T., D D., Brooklyn.
Welch, Rev. J. C., Providence.
Wheat, Rev. A. C., Philadelphia.
Wheelock, Rev. Alonzo, Elbridge, N. Y.
Wheeler, Rev. Osgood C., Sacramento, Cal.
Whidden, Randall, Calais, Me.
Whittemore, A. F., Essex. Ct.
White, Rev. J. [illegible] est Wrentham, Mass.
Whitehead, James M., New York.
Whiting, Rev. Niles, Norwich, Ct.
Whitney, Ezra S., Brooklyn, N. Y.
Wightman, Rev. F., Wethersfield, Ct.
Wightman, Rev. Palmer G., Lyme, Ct.
Wilbur, Asa, Boston.
Wildman, Rev. N , Lebanon. Ct.
Willard, Rev. F. A., South Danvers, Mass.
Willett, Rev. Charles, Wilkinsville, Ct.
Williams, David S., Fayetteville, N. C.
Williams, Richard F., Essex, Ct.
Williams, Rev. William R., D.D., New York.
Wilson, Francis L., Catskill, N. Y.
Wilson, Daniel M., Newark, N. J.
Wilson, Mrs. Hannah M., Newark. N. J.

MEMBERS FOR LIFE.

Allen, Thomas, Wilmington, Del.
Allen, Rev. Thomas, Tavoy, Burmah.
Aller, Amos, Brooklyn.
Aller, Mrs. Amos, Brooklyn.
Allin, George, Brooklyn.
Alger, Mrs. Susan, Cleveland, Ohio.
Almond, John P., Bostwick Mills, N. C.
Ambler, Rev. E. C., Millington, N. J.
Ambler, Mrs. Almira, Millington, N. J.
Ambler, Starr H., Millington, N. J.
Ambler, Rev. J. V., Lanesboro', Mass.
Ambler, Mrs. A. T., Lanesboro', Mass.
Amesbury, Jabez, Norwich, Ct
Amory, Peter B., New York.
Amory, Mrs. Anna M., New York.
Andem, Rev. James, Neenah, Wis.
Anderson, William T., Princeton, N. J.
Anderson, Mrs. Catharine J., Princeton, N. J.
Anderson, John T., Verdon, Va.
Anderson, Peter, New York.
Anderson, William, Hoboken, N. J.
Andrews, William, Providence.
Andrews, Mrs. Delilah, Providence.
Andrews, Mrs. Wm., Providence.
Andrews, Ebenezer T., Boston.
Andrews, George R., New York.
Angier, Rev. Aaron, Elbridge, N. Y.
Angus, Charles, Benton, N. Y.
Archibald, Rev. Thos. H., Factory Point, Vt.
Archer, Charles O., New York.
Ardis, Rev. Henry Z., Zalofa, Pa.
Armitage, Mrs. T., New York.
Appleton, George, Haverhill, Mass.
Appleton, James, Philadelphia.
Arents, Stephen, Brooklyn.
Armstrong, Rev. Andrew, Lambertville, N. J.
Armstrong, Mrs. M. S., Lambertville, N. J.
Arnold, Mrs. Mary N., Attleboro', Mass.
Arnold, Mrs. Frances R., Providence.
Arnold, Rev. Benjamin B., Three Rivers, Iowa.
Arnold, Miss Phebe, Jay, N. Y.
Arnold, Mrs. Mary, Clifton Park, N. Y.
Arthur, Rev. William, West Troy, N. Y.
Ashley, Elisha, Poultney, Vt.
Atkinson, Taylor B., West Philadelphia, Pa.
Atwood, Lewis, Pawtucket, R. I.
Atwood, Mrs. Lydia, N. Boston, N. H.
Austin, H., Tarborough, N. C.
Austin, Edward, New York.
Avery, Mrs. Clara, New York.
Avery, Rev. E. J., Worcester, Mass.
Avery, William D., Providence.
Avery, Rev. David, Stanford, Vt.
Avery, Rev. D., Tyringham, Mass.
Avery, E. J., Brookline, Mass.
Ayer, Charles B., Preston, Ct.
Ayer, Mrs. Richard, Haverhill, Mass.
Ayres, James C., Plainfield, N. J.
Ayres, Horace, Worcester, Mass.
Ayres, Mrs. Mary, New York.
Babcock, Rev. O. W., Malone, N. Y.
Babcock, John N., New Haven, Ct.
Babcock, H. S., Homer, N. Y.
Baber, Alfred, Keeseville, N. Y.
Bacheler, Rev. M., Pownall, Vt.
Backus, Rev. Jay S., New York.
Bacon, Jacob, Boston.
Bacon, Rev. William, Dividing Creek, N. J.
Bacon, Mrs. Mary L., Trumansburg, N. Y.
Bacon, Rev. Charles L., Trumansburg, N. Y.
Bacon, Miss Ann, Dorchester, Mass.
Bagby, Rev. Richard, Stevensville, Va.
Bailey, Mrs. S. W., Parham's Store, Va.
Bailey, Timothy, Malden, Mass.
Bailey, Mrs. Sarah E., Pekin, Ill.
Bailey, S. A., Utica, N. Y.
Bailey, Jonathan, Jr., Westport, N. H.
Bailey, Mrs. Caroline, Philadelphia.
Bailey, Rev. Simon B., Hopkinton, R. I.
Bailey, Mrs. Eveline, Hopkinton, R. I.
Bailie, John, New York.
Baisley, George, Bridgeport, Ct.
Baker, Mrs. Betsey, West Dedham, Mass.
Baker, Miss Betsey, West Dedham, Mass.
Baker, Allen, Providence.
Baker, Elisha W., Providence.
Baker, Benjamin F., Brookline, Mass.
Baker, Rev. John H., East Greenwich, R. I.
Baker, Rev. James, Perryville, N. J.
Baker, David, Corning, N. Y.
Baker, Garness E., New York.
Baker, Theodore, Norwalk, Ohio.
Baker, Joseph K., Jr., West Harwich, Mass.
Baker, Rev. Samuel, D.D., Williamsburgh, N. Y.
Baker, Mrs., Williamsburgh, N. Y.
Bainbridge, Rev. Samuel M., Wheatland, N. Y.
Balch, Mrs. Jane, New York.
Baldwin, Rev. George C., D.D., Troy, N. Y.
Baldwin, Mrs. Margaret D., Boston.
Baldwin, Rev. Jonathan, Elliston, N. Y.
Baldwin, Jared G., New York.
Baldwin, Mrs. Eliza, New York.
Baldwin, A. T., Brooklyn.
Baldwin, Miss Elizabeth A., New York.
Baldwin, Josephus, Nashua, N. H.
Baldwin, Mrs. Mary Ann, Nashua, N. H.
Baldwin, Mrs. Caroline E., Philadelphia.
Balen, Mrs. Ann Maria, Brooklyn.
Ballard, Rev. Enos H., Red Mills, N. Y.
Ballard, Mrs. Asenath, Brooklyn.
Ballard, Mrs. Mary Sophia, Brooklyn.
Ballou, Alexander, Blackstone, Mass.
Banks, Miss Ann Judson, Sculltown, N. Y.
Banker, Mrs. Elizabeth, Brooklyn.
Banta, Miss Emily M., New York.
Barrass, Rev. Thomas, Baptist Town, N. J.
Barber, Aaron, Waterford, C. W.
Barber, Moses, Waterford, C. W.
Barber, Abraham, Waterford, C. W.
Bardwell, R. B., Shelburne Falls, Mass.
Bardwell, Apollos, Shelburne Falls, Mass.
Bardwell, Edward, Rochester, N. Y.
Bardwell, Mrs. Jane A., Rochester, N. Y.
Barrell, David, Fredonia, N. Y.
Barrell, Mrs. Clarinda, Fredonia, N. Y.
Barker, Rev. J. G., Richmond, Va.
Barker, Mrs. Esther Ann, Poughkeepsie, N. Y.
Barker, Anson J., Taunton, Mass.
Barnhurst, Joseph, Sr., Francisville, Pa.
Barnum, Orsel G., Gouverneur, N. Y.
Barnum, S. Eli, Danbury, Ct.

MEMBERS FOR LIFE.

Barrows, Experience, Dorset, Vt.
Bars, Mrs. Sarah A.
Barter, John, Brooklyn, N. Y.
Bartlett, Rev. Daniel, China, Me.
Bartlett, Stephen, Worcester, Mass.
Bartlett, Mrs. Elizabeth J., Deep River, Ct.
Bartolette, John T., Somerville, N. J.
Barringer, Jacob P., Troy, N. Y.
Barry, S. L., Ovid, N. Y.
Bates, Mrs. Caroline C., New Bedford, Mass.
Bates, Mrs. Joanna, Providence.
Bates, Whitman, Pawtucket, R. I.
Bates, Dennis P., Lowell, Mass.
Bates, Rev. J hn, Cascade, Iowa.
Bates, Rev. L. C., Madison, N. Y.
Batey, Rev. John.
Battell, Rev. Allen E., Marshfield, Mass.
Battle, Rev. A. J., Murfreesboro', N. C.
Baugh, Dr. J. M., Petersburg, Va.
Baxter, Thomas, Penn Yan, N. Y.
Baxter, John C., New-York.
Baxter, Thomas, Detroit, Mich.
Baxter, William M., New-York.
Beam, Joseph, Brooklyn.
Beam, Mrs. Louisa, Brooklyn.
Beam, David B., Paterson, N. J.
Bean, H. L., Skaneateles, N. Y.
Beasom, W. D., Nashua, N. H.
[redacted]

Bennett, Hiram, Salem, N. J.
Bennett, Rev. Alvin, South Wilbraham, Mass.
Bennett, Rev. David, Unionville, N. Y.
Bennett, E. A., Philadelphia.
Bennett, Mrs. Judith B., Philadelphia.
Bennett, Rev. Olney, McGrawville, N. Y.
Bennett, Joseph, Manchester, N. H.
Bennett, Rev. Perry, Lebanon, Ct.
Benton, J., Saratoga, N. Y.
Benton, Mrs. Sarah, Saratoga, N. Y.
Bernard, Rev. David, Westfield, N. Y.
Bernie, Miss Anna, New-York.
Bertine, Mrs. Sarah Ann, New-York.
Bertine, James C., New-York.
Berry, Zebina E., Worcester, Mass.
Berry, Susan C., Worcester, Mass.
Berry, Ellen L., Worcester, Mass.
Betts, Rev. Platt, East Chatham, N. Y.
Bevan, Rev. Isaac, Reading, Pa.
Beverly, Miss Elizabeth, New York.
Biddle, Samuel S., Newbern, N. C.
Biddle, Rev. William, Brookfield, Ct.
Bidgood, Mrs. L., Hargrove's, Va.
Bigelow, Rev. John R., M.D., New York.
Bigelow, Mrs. Eunice P., New York.
Billings, Rev. John, Mt. Vernon, Me.
Billings, Mrs. Betsey, Mt. Vernon, Me.
Billingslea, Dr. C., Montgomery co., Ala.
[redacted]

Bonham, Daniel, Berryville, Va.
Boone, Dr. Levi D., Chicago, Ill.
Boone, Mrs. L. D., Chicago, Ill.
Booth, Miss Lydia, Poughkeepsie, N. Y.
Borden, Lodowick, Fall River, Mass.
Borden, Isaac, Fall River, Mass.
Borden, Charles, Fall River, Mass.
Borden, Joseph, Fall River, Mass.
Borden, Cook, Fall River, Mass.
Borden, Jefferson, Fall River, Mass.
Bosson, George P., Chelsea, Mass.
Bosson, Benjamin P., Chelsea, Mass.
Bostick, Elisha, Bostick's Mills, N. C.
Bostick, Elijah, Bostick's Mills, N. C.
Bostic, Tristam, Bostick's Mills, N. C.
Bostick, Benj. R., Robertsville, S. C.
Bostick, Mrs. Jane E., Robertsville, S. C.
Boswell, Davis, Stilesville, Ia.
Bosworth, William H., East Poultney, Vt.
Bosworth, George H., Fall River, Mass.
Bottom, Nathan H., Shaftsbury, Vt.
Bottom, Mrs. Peace, Shaftsbury, Vt.
Boughton, James, New York.
Boughton, Rev. N., Delavan, Wis.
Boutelle, Miss Sylvia, East Cambridge, Mass.
Bouton, Mrs. Sarah M., New York.
Bowen, John, New York.
Bowen, Henry, Chili Centre, New York.
Bowen, David M., Canton, N. J.
Bowen, Miss Lydia M., Providence.
Bowen, Rev. William, Hancock, Mass.
Bowen, William, New York.
Bowen, Mrs. A. K., Cortlandville, N. Y.
Bower, Rev. Jacob, Manchester, Ill.
Bowers, Rev. C. M., Clintonville, Mass.
Bowers, Mrs. Hannah D., Seekonk, Mass.
Boykin, Rev. Wm. F., St. Josephs, Mo.
Boyce, Peter, Green Point, N. Y.
Boyce, Mrs. Albina, Providence.
Boyd, Rev. Robert, London, Canada.
Boyden, Addison, South Dedham, Mass.
Brabrook, Mrs. Lucy A., Brookline, Mass.
Brabrook, Alfred, Taunton, Mass.
Brabrook, Joseph A., Lowell, Mass.
Bradford, W. R., Boston.
Bradford, John, Wilmington, Del.
Brainerd, Samuel, Haverhill, Mass.
Brainerd, Mrs. Samuel, Haverhill, Mass.
Branch, Rev. Nicholas, East Thompson, Ct.
Branch, Rev. William, Williamsville, N. Y.
Bradley, Collins, Mt. Vernon, Mich.
Bray, Joseph M., Brooklyn.
Brayton, Philip, Phenix, R. I.
Brayton, Mrs. Mary Ann, Centreville, R. I.
Briggs, Arnold, Fairhaven, Vt.
Briggs, Rev. Avery, Rock Island, Ill.
Briggs, Mrs. Sarah K., Fitchburg, Mass.
Breed, Rev. Joseph B., Woonsocket, R. I.
Breed, Mrs. Frances A. C., Woonsocket, R. I.
Breed, Catharine C., Lynn, Mass.
Brewer, Mrs. Elizabeth, New York.
Bridgens, Miss Mary Ann, Brooklyn.
Bridgewood, Mrs. Jane, Williamsburgh, N. Y.
Brierly, Rev. Benj., San Francisco, Cal.
Brigham, [illegible], Ill.
Brigham, Rev. [illegible], N. Y.
Bright, Rev. T., Elkhorn, Wis.
Brinkerhoff, Rev. C., Woodstown, N. J.
Brisbane, Rev. Wm. H., Cheviot, O.
Brisbane, Miss Maria, Charleston, S. C.
Briscoe, Sally C., Va.
Britton, Everett, New York.
Broaddus, Rev. William F., Versailles, Ky.
Broaddus, Mrs. Mary A., Versailles, Ky.
Brocket, Rev. Pierpont, Hartford, Ct.
Brockway, Mrs. Elizabeth, Broadalbin, N. Y.
Britton, W. G., Britton's X Roads, N. C.
Bromley, Isaac, Norwich, Ct.
Bromley, Rev. Henry, Port Jefferson, N. Y.
Bromley, Mrs. Jane M., Port Jefferson, N. Y.
Bronner, Mrs. Sarah, New York.
Brouwere, Vermilyea T., Dundee, N. Y.
Bronson, Rev. Asa, Fall River, Mass.
Bronson, Rev. Benjamin F., Methuen, Mass.
Bronson, Mrs. Anna C., Methuen, Mass.
Bronson, Miss Aydee A., Townsend, Mass.
Brooks, Rev. Kendall, Eastport, Me.
Brooks, John, Hanover, Mass.
Brooks, Mrs Elizabeth, Cambridge, Mass.
Brown, R. S., New Brunswick, N. J.
Brower, Davis B., Philadelphia.
Brown, W. S., Britton's X Roads, N. C.
Brown, Josiah, Haverhill, Mass.
Brown, J. S., Fitchburg, Mass.
Brown, Hon. Wm. R., Spencerport, N. Y.
Brown, Edward L., Brooklyn.
Brown, Mrs. Susan A., Brooklyn.
Brown, Rev. Amasy, South Gardner, Mass.
Brown, Rev. Dana, Nashua, N. H.
Brown, Rev. E. T., Wooster, O.
Brown, Andrew, Middletown, N. J.
Brown, Geo. W., New York.
Brown, Hugh H., Providence.
Brown, Rev. E. C., Bath, N. Y.
Brown, Rev. F. G., West Townsend, Mass.
Brown, Rev. Wm. L., Boston.
Brown, Rev. Joseph P., Moosup, Ct.
Brown, Mrs. Emily M. A., Fauquier, Va.
Brown, Mrs. O. B., Washington, D. C.
Brown, Mrs. Elizabeth E., Aylett's, Va.
Brown, Miss Ann F., Providence.
Brown, Mrs. Maria S., New York.
Brown, Mrs. Mary F., Keene, N. H.
Brown, Mrs. Isaac, Haverhill, Mass.
Brown, Mrs. Margaret A., Reading, Ohio.
Brown, Rev. J. F., Scotch Plains, N. Y.
Brown, Rev. Philip P., Holland Patent, N. Y.
Brown, Rev. Wm., Eaton, N. Y.
Brown, Evander M., Saratoga Springs, N. Y.
Brown, L. R., Hartford, Ct.
Brown, Joshua, New York.
Brown, Sarah H., 2d, West Townsend, Mass.
Brown, Newel, Watertown, Mass.
Brownell, Rev. E. W., East Hillsdale, N. Y.
Brownson, Rev. I. K., Chittenango, N. Y.
Bruen, George H., Newark, N. J.
Bruen, Mrs. George H., Newark, N. J.
Bruce, Benjamin G., New York.
Bruce, Silas, Townsend, Mass.
Brumley, Dorcas, Norwich, Ct.
Brush, George F., New York.

MEMBERS FOR LIFE.

Brush, Mrs. Susan G., New York.
Brusle, William A., New York.
Brusle, Mrs. Elizabeth, New York.
Bryant, George, Williamsburgh, N. Y.
Bryant, Mary A., Chelsea, Mass.
Bryant, Elizabeth D., Chelsea, Mass.
Buckbee, Mrs. Laura G., New York.
Bucknall, Ebenezer G., Newark, N. J.
Bucknell, Miss Elizabeth, Newark, N. J.
Bucknell, Wm. Jr., Philadelphia.
Bucknell, Miss Lavinia Louise, Philadelphia.
Bucknell, Mrs. Harriet M., Philadelphia.
Buckner, Mrs. Sarah T., Baltimore.
Budlong, James E., Providence.
Budlong, Mrs. Rebecca S. C., Providence.
Budlong, Miss Rebekah A., Providence.
Budd, Francis F., Williamsburgh, N. Y.
Buel, Rev. Rufus F., Greece.
Buel, Mrs. Mary J., Greece.
Buffinton, Benjamin, Fall River, Mass.
Bull, John B., New York.
Bull, Julia M., North Amherst, Mass.
Bull, Sarah H., North Amherst, Mass.
Bullard, Rev. Joseph A., Ware, Mass.
Bullock, George, Utica, N. Y.
Bulkley, Prof. Justus, Upper Alton, Ill.
Bulkley, Mrs. Harriet, Upper Alton, Ill.
Bulkley, Mrs. Harriet, Barry, Ill.
[redacted]

Butler, Sylvanus, New Haven, Ct.
Butcher, Mrs. Mary, Philadelphia.
Butler, Mrs. Sarah, Lansingburg, N. Y.
Butrick, Mrs. Harriet H., Jay, N. Y.
Butts, Mrs. Sarah A., Cleveland, Ohio.
Butts, Mrs. Elizabeth, Boston.
Byram, Mrs. Mary H., Amesbury, Mass.
Byram, Wm. H., Milwaukee, Wis.
Cady, Edwin, Danville, Iowa.
Cailhopper, Rev. F. T., Allowaystown, N. J.
Calder, John, Providence.
Call, Rev. O. B., Wayne, N. Y.
Callom, Mrs. Mary N., Sing Sing, N. Y.
Candee, John D., New Haven, Ct.
Capin, Ezekiel, Canton, Mass.
Capron, Rev. Orion H., North Hebron, N. Y.
Capron, Miss Rebecca S., Worcester, Mass.
Capwell, Albert B., New York.
Capwell, Mrs. Julia A., New York.
Card, Rev. Wm. H., La Crosse, Wis.
Card, Rev. Henry S., Hinsdale, N. Y.
Carleton, Miss Frances, Newton Centre, Mass.
Carleton, Miss Emelina H., Newton Centre, Ms.
Carleton, G. B., Newton Centre, Mass.
Carleton, Judson, Newton Centre, Mass.
Carleton, Howard, Newton Centre, Mass.
Carleton, Wm. H., Newton Centre, Mass.
Carlton, Stephen, Lowell, Mass.
[redacted]

Cauldwell, Mrs. Eliza A., New York.
Cavis, John, Lowell, Mass.
Chaffin, Rev. Aaron W., Danvers, Mass.
Chaffin, Mrs. Catherine K., Danvers, Mass.
Chalfant, Jacob M., Wilmington, Del.
Challiss, Mrs. Lydia, Roadstown, N. J.
Challiss, John, Salem, N. J.
Chambers, Amariah, Marion, N. C.
Chamberlain, Miss Sylvia Ann, Westport, N. H.
Chamberlain, Edward, Boston.
Chamberlain, Rev. J. H., South N. Berlin, N. Y.
Chambers, John, Pemberton, N. J.
Champlin, Henry N., Whitestown, N. Y.
Chapel, R. S., Brooklyn.
Chapman, Allen A., Baltimore.
Chapman, Rev. John S., Tobehanna, N. Y.
Chapman, William H., New York.
Chapman, Rev. J. M., Lexington, Ill.
Chapman, Henry, F., New York.
Chandler, Rev. Charles N., Elmira, N. Y.
Chandler, Rev. George C., Oregon City, Oregon.
Chandler, Oliver, Boston, Mass.
Chandler, William, Nashua, N. H.
Chapen, Rev. A., Galena, Ill.
Charlock, Miss Maria, New York.
Chase, Rev. Supply, Northville, Mich.
Chase, Daniel, Baltimore.
Chase, Adrian, Haverhill, Mass.
Chase, Luther, Haverhill, Mass.
Chase, Hezekiah S., Boston.
Chase, Edwin, Holyoke, Mass.
Chase, Asa, Eaton, N. Y.
Cherryman, Rev. Reuben, Richburg, N. Y.
Cheesbrough, Rev. Isaac, Haddam, Ct.
Cheesbrough, Mrs. Asenath, Haddam, Ct.
Cheshire, Rev. John Enoch, Wickford, R. I.
Cheever, William, Westboro', Mass.
Chick, Rev. J. M., Plaistow, N. H.
Child, Ezra O., Warren, R. I.
Childs, Miss Jane L., New York.
Childs, John R., Providence.
Church, Rev. Leroy, Chicago, Ill.
Church, Miss Clara O. B., Williamsburgh, N. Y.
Church, Miss Emma C., Williamsburgh, N. Y.
Church, William, Williamsburgh, N. Y.
Church, Francis P., Williamsburgh, N. Y.
Church, John A., Williamsburgh, N. Y.
Church, Rev. Isaac M., South Kingston, R. I.
Churchill, Amos, Brandon, Vt.
Clapp, Rev. Wm. S., Danbury, Ct.
Clapp, Mrs. Jane M., Danbury, Ct.
Clapp, Russell, Providence.
Clapp, Miss Jane R., Providence.
Clark, Rev. Frederick, New Orleans, La.
Clark, Rev. Norman, Marlborough, N. H.
Clark, Abel, Willimantic, Ct.
Clark, Mrs. Juliet, Marlborough, N. H.
Clark, Miss E., Beaufort, S. C.
Clark, Mrs. M. G., Philadelphia.
Clark, Mrs. Elizabeth, New York.
Clark, Miss Sallie Cone, New York.
Clark, Miss Clarissa, Deep River, Ct.
Clark, Miss Eliza, Syracuse, N. Y.
Clark, Teresa E., Lakeville, N. Y.
Clark, Rev. O. A., Auburn, N. Y.
Clark [illegible]
Clark, Mrs. John, Bridgeport, Ct.
Clarke, Rev. Henry, Pittsfield, Mass.
Clarke, Rev. John, Esquessing, C. W.
Clarke, William, Syracuse, N. Y.
Clayton, James D., Freehold, N. J.
Cleaves, Rev. F. E., Lowell, Mass.
Cleaves, Mrs. S. A., Littleton, Mass.
Clement, Wm. T., Shelburne Falls, Mass.
Clopton, Rev. James C., Lynchburg, Va.
Clopton, Mrs. M., New Kent, Va.
Coburn, Charles, Fall River, Mass.
Coburn, Rev. J. M., Manchester, N. H.
Cobb, Mrs. Sarah M., Brooklyn.
Cocke, Charles L., Richmond, Va.
Cockran, Justin, Lowell, Mass.
Coffin, Rev. Jas. L., Tyrone, N. Y.
Cogswell, B. F., Brooklyn.
Coggshall, John, Jr., New Bedford, Mass.
Coggshall, Mrs. Elizabeth, New Bedford, Mass.
Coggswell, Mrs. Mary, Haverhill, Mass.
Coyt, Miss Elizabeth, New London, Ct.
Colby, Rev. Lewis, New York.
Colby, Hon. Anthony, New London, N. H.
Colby, Mrs. Eliza A., New London, N. H.
Colby, Isaac, Salem, Mass.
Colby, Gardener, Newton, Mass.
Colby, Mrs. Mary Colgate, New York.
Colby, Benj. E., Cambridge, Mass.
Colburn, Rev. Alfred, Boston.
Cole, Rev. L. B., Lowell, Mass.
Cole, Samuel, Clifton Park, N. Y.
Cole, Mrs. Frances L., New York.
Coley, Rev. James M., Waverly, N. Y.
Colegrove, Bela H., Sardinia, N. Y.
Coleman, James B., Somerville, N. J.
Coleman, Rev. M., Elba, N. Y.
Coleman, Mrs. Sarah, Elba, N. Y.
Coleman, Rev. Zenas, Mt. Vernon, Mich.
Colgate, Cornelius C., New York.
Colgate, Edward, New York.
Colgate, James B., New York.
Colgate, William, New York.
Colgate, Miss Elizabeth, New York.
Colgate, Miss Hannah, New York.
Colgate, Miss Jane, New York.
Colgate, Miss Sarah, New York.
Collins, Miss Susan, New York.
Collom, Mrs. Mary E., Mt. Holly, N. J.
Colver, Rev. Charles K., Worcester, Mass.
Colver, Mrs. Esther B., Worcester, Mass.
Coman, Lovian O., Le Roy, N. Y.
Compton, James I., Plainfield, N. J.
Compton, Anthony, New York.
Compton, Mrs. Maria, New York.
Compton, Rev. Robert, Newton, Pa.
Compton, Wm. H., Roadstown, N. J.
Comstock, George E., New London, Ct.
Comstock, Mrs. Ann, New London, Ct.
Conant, Mrs. John, Brandon, Vt.
Conant, Rev. Thomas, Scituate, Mass.
Conant, Rev. Thomas J., D.D., Rochester, N. Y.
Conant, Levi, Boston, Mass.
Condit, Miss Sarah E., New York.
Cone, Spencer H., Jr., New York.
Cone, Miss Kate E., New York.
Cone, Miss Amelia M., Philadelphia.

Conklin, Mrs. Ann, New York.
Connver, Robert, Petersburg, Ill.
Conrad, Rev. Peter, Delton, Wis.
Converse, Rev. Otis, Grafton, Mass.
Cook, Mrs. Patience, Keene, N. H.
Cook, Henry G., New York.
Cook, Rev. Samuel, Dunbarton, N. H.
Cook, Lewis, Plantsville, Ct.
Cook, Wm. W., Whitehall, N. Y.
Cook, Mrs. Harriet M., New York.
Coolidge, Mrs. Caroline G., Brookline, Mass.
Coolidge, William, Bouckville, N. Y.
Coolidge, John, Watertown, Mass.
Coolidge, Mrs. Mary S., Watertown, Mass.
Coolidge, Josiah, Cambridge, Mass.
Coolidge, Austin J., Cambridge, Mass.
Cooper, William, New York.
Cooper, Edwin, Hoboken, N. J.
Cooper, Rev. Warren, Boylston, Mass.
Cooper, Eliphalet, New Haven, Ct.
Cooper, Charles, New York.
Corbett, O. G., Brooklyn, N. Y.
Corey, Rev. D. G., Utica, N. Y.
Corlies, Briton, Philadelphia.
Cornelius, Rev. Samuel Jr., Fond du Lac, Wis.
Cornell, A. C., Broadalbin, N. Y.
Cornell, Thomas, Rondout, N. Y.
Cornwell, Rev. William E., Norristown, Pa.
[redacted]

Crawford, Archibald, Albany.
Crawford, Mrs. Catharine, Middletown, N. J.
Creath, Rev. Thomas B., Jarrott's, Va.
Creathe, Rev. J. W. D., Fanthorpe's, Texas.
Crenshaw, Dr. W. M., Forrestville, N. C.
Cressy, Rev. Timothy R., St. Paul, Min.
Cresswell, Rev. Samuel J., Philadelphia.
Crocker, Gurdon, New London, Ct.
Crocker, William A., New York.
Crosby, Henry L., Belvidere, Ill.
Crossman, Nathan, Elbridge, N. Y.
Croysdale, Abram, Paterson, N. J.
Crooker, Josiah F., Providence.
Crumb, Rev. J. W., Clifton Park, N. Y.
Crumb, Mrs. R. F., Clifton Park, N. Y.
Cruser, Holger, Brooklyn.
Culp, Theophilus, New York.
Culver, Mrs. Susan, New London, Ct.
Cummings, Mrs. Daniel, Chelsea, Mass.
Cummings, Mrs. Abagail, Cambridge, Mass.
Cummings, George, Cambridge, Mass.
Cummings, Rev. E. E., Pittsfield, N. H.
Cummings, Mrs. Emily C., Amherst, Mass.
Cunningham, Rev. O., Middlefield, Mass.
Curry, John, Hamburg, S. C.
Curry, Mrs. Harriet, Hamburg, S. C.
Curron, Rev. Joseph, Evansburg, Pa.
Currier, Rev. Joshua, La Motte, Iowa.
[redacted]

Davis, Mrs. Eliza H., Columbus, Ohio.
Davis, Miss Mary R., Worcester, Mass.
Davis, Edward L., Worcester, Mass.
Davis, Joseph E., Worcester, Mass.
Davis, Miss Sarah M., Worcester, Mass.
Davis, Miss Anna E., Worcester, Mass.
Davis, Miss Alice W., Worcester, Mass.
Davis, W., Sarchana, N. C.
Davis, Evan, New York.
Davis, Reuben P., Waltham, Mass.
Davis, Walter G., New York.
Davis, Rev. Jonathan, Monticello, S. C.
Davis, Rev. C. E., Paris, Me.
Davis, Charles C., Preston, Ct.
Davis, Florence H., Worcester, Mass.
Davis, Isabel G., Worcester, Mass.
Davis, Mrs. Louisa O., Paris, Me.
Davis, Rev. John, Yarmouth, Nova Scotia.
Davis, Rev. Thomas, Livingston, N. J.
Davis, Rev. Judson, Ira, N. Y.
Davis, Lydia, Haverhill, Mass.
Davis, Mrs. Harriet M., Nashua, N. H.
Davy, Miss Bertha, New York.
Dawley, Joseph E., Fall River, Mass.
Day, H. W., Boston.
Day, John, New York.
Day, Mrs. Fidelia, Haverhill, Mass.
Day, Rev. Arthur, Shaftsbury, Vt.
Day, Rev. Horace G., Schenectady, N. Y.
Dayton, Morgan H., New York.
Dean, H. J., Spartanburg, S. C.
Dean, Jirah, Flat Brook, N. Y.
Dean, Rev. Wm., D.D., Hong Kong, China.
Dean, Esther G., North Adams, Mass.
Dean, Rev. E., Auburn, N. Y.
Dearborn, Rev. Shelburn, Lowell, Wis.
Dearborn, Mrs. Emeline L., Lowell, Wis.
Deats, Hiram, Cherryville, N. J.
Decker, Alfred, New York.
Decker, Mrs. Keziah R., New York.
Decker, Abel, New York.
Decker, Mrs. Abigail, New York.
Decker, Miss Mary A., New York.
Decker, Matthew, Rahway, N. J.
Decker, William P., Hamilton, N. Y.
De La Montanye, Miss Julia, New York.
Della Torre, Joseph, New York.
Demarest, Miss Jane, New York.
Demarest, Samuel C., Boston.
Demarest, Silas, New York.
Demarest, Stephen D., New York.
Deming, Amos, Savoy, Mass.
Deming, Mrs. Eliza J., Cleveland, Ohio.
Denike, Abraham, New York.
Denike, Mrs. Adeline, New York.
Dennis, Mrs. Elizabeth, New York.
Dennis, Richard, Lowell, Mass.
Dennison, Charles W., Boston.
Denison, Rev. Frederic, Westerly, R. I.
Denison, Rev. Erastus, Groton, Ct.
Denison, Mrs. Prudence, Groton, Ct.
Denison, Mrs. Silas, Skaneateles, N. Y.
Denison, Rev. Nathan, Skaneateles, N. Y.
Denison, Mrs. Amelia R., Deep River, Ct.
Denison, Miss Elizabeth, Brooklyn.

Devore, Mrs. Catharine, Edgefield, S. C.
Deweese, Samuel, West Philadelphia.
Dewey, Wm. G., Mystic, Ct.
Dewey, Joseph H., Manchester, N. Y.
Dewhurst, Eli, Lowell, Mass.
Dewitt, Rev. J. V., Marion, Iowa.
Dexter, Mrs. Jane, Brooklyn.
Dickinson, Mrs. Caroline L., Pittsburg, Pa.
Dickinson, Wm. W., Gelandeville, Va.
Dimmock, Rev. Anth'y V., Baldwinsville, Mass.
Dispeau, Mrs. Lucinda, Grafton, Mass.
Dixon, Rev. Joseph A., Evansville, Ia.
Doan, Ezra, Hudson, N. Y.
Doane, Miss Rachel F., Danvers, Mass.
Doby, John, Sen., Edgefield, S. C.
Dodge, Mrs. Eliza R., New York.
Dodge, Rev. Orrin, Ballston Spa, N. Y.
Dodge, Prof. Ebenezer, Hamilton, N. Y.
Dodge, Solomon E., Cambridge, Mass.
Dodge, Miss Hannah A., Townsend, Mass.
Dodge, Mrs. Alice C., Haverhill, Mass.
Dodge, Mrs. Jane, Brooklyn.
Dodge, H. N., Mechanicville, N. Y.
Dodson, Rev. Elijah, Woodburn, Ill.
Dole, Mrs. Lydia T., Haverhill, Mass.
Dollins, Horatio, Worcester, Mass.
Doolittle, Mrs. Amanda, New York.
Doolittle, Rev. H. D., Hoosick, N. Y.
Donald, J. W., East Cambridge, Mass.
Dongan, Mrs. Lucretia, New York.
Dorrance, Samuel B., Brooklyn.
Douglas, Henry, Bethel, N. Y.
Douglas, George, Rochester, N. Y.
Douglas, Rev. John L., Burmah.
Dougherty, George T., New York.
Dowlin, Mrs. Maria S., New York.
Dowlin, Miss Mary J., New York.
Dowling, Rev. Thomas, Agawam, Mass.
Dowling, Mrs. Rebecca, New York.
Dowley, John, New York.
Downey, Rev. Francis, Whiteby, Pa.
Downing, J., Colerain, N. C.
Downs, Mrs. Harriet B., Malden, Mich.
Downs, Miss Elizabeth, Hightstown, N. J.
Dows, Gustavus D., Lowell, Mass.
Doyen, Mrs A. F., Haverhill, Mass.
Drake, Ephraim, Plainfield, N. J.
Drake, Mrs. A. L., Plainfield, N. J.
Drake, Rev. George, New Brunswick, N. J.
Driver, Rev. Thomas, Lynn, Mass.
Dubois, Richard, Canton, N. J.
Dudley, John L., Baltimore.
Dugan, William T., Brooklyn.
Dugan, Mrs. Eliza, Brooklyn.
Dugan, William J., Brooklyn.
Dugan, Edward J., Brooklyn.
Duncan, Hon. James H., Haverhill, Mass.
Duncan, Mrs. James H., Haverhill, Mass.
Duncan, Mrs. Samuel, Haverhill, Mass.
Duncan, Mrs. E. E., Jackson, Va.
Duncan, Rev. H. A., Coosawhatchie, S. C.
Duncan, Rev. William, Orleans, Ia.
Duncan, Rev. John, Chester, Pa.
Dunlap, [illegible]
Dunlap, [illegible]
Dunlap, [illegible], Ill.

MEMBERS FOR LIFE.

Dunn, Rev. Andrew, Winchendon, Mass.
Dunn, Alexander, New Brunswick, N. J.
Du Pre, Mrs. S. P., Darlington, S. C.
Dupont, Alfred, Wilmington, Del.
Durant, Clark, Albany.
Durbrow, William, New York.
Durfee, Sanford, Warwick, R. I.
Durfee, Miss Sarah C., Providence.
Durkin, John, New York.
Durnell, James, Philadelphia.
Duryea, Levi, New York.
Duryea, Mrs. Sarah, New York.
Dusenbury, Rev. Francisco, Etna, N. Y.
Duvall, Mrs. J., Mitchell's, Va.
Dye, Rev. Daniel, Lafargeville, N. Y.
Dye, Rev. Enoch P., North Brookfield, N. Y.
Eastman, Lycurgus, Griggsville, Ill.
Eastman, Rev. Samuel, Burlington, Wis.
Earl, Rev. Samuel H., New York.
Earl, Miss Julia, Providence.
Earle, Rev. Alfred, Davisville, Pa.
Eaton, Rev. George W., D.D., Hamilton, N. Y.
Eaton, R. C., Springville, N. Y.
Eaton, Rev. Horace, Wilton, N. H.
Eaton, Ezra, Boston.
Eaton, Rev. Joseph W., Keeseville, N. Y.
Eaton, Mrs. Sarah E., Keeseville, N. Y.
Eddy, Rev. H. J., New York.
Eddy, Rev. Daniel C., Lowell, Mass.

[redacted]

Evans, Mrs. S. E., Society Hill, S. C.
Evans, Reuben, Amesbury, Mass.
Evans, Dr. Joseph T., New York.
Evans, Mrs. Czarina H., New York.
Evans, Mrs. Mary, New York.
Eveleigh, Mrs. Mary D., Brooklyn.
Eveleth, Samuel, Boston.
Everts, Rev. William W., Louisville, Ky.
Everett, Rev. Samuel, North Leverett, Mass.
Everett, David, New London, N. H.
Everett, Benjamin C., Philadelphia.
Everett, Miss Elizabeth, New York.
Fails, David, South Dedham, Mass.
Failing, Josiah, Portland, Oregon.
Failing, Mrs. Henrietta, Portland, Oregon.
Failing, Mary C., Portland, Oregon.
Failing, Henry, Portland, Oregon.
Failing, Miss Elizabeth A., Portland, Oregon.
Fairbrother, Lewis, Pawtucket, R. I.
Fairman, James, New Haven, Ct.
Fales, Joseph T., Burlington, Iowa.
Fales, Oliver, West Philadelphia, Pa.
Falkner, John B., Malden, Mass.
Fargo, Rev. Isaac, Romulus, N. Y.
Farish, T., Gulf, N. C.
Farnsworth, Hon. Joseph D., Fairfax, Vt.
Farnsworth, Dr. James H., Fairfax, Vt.
Farnsworth, Rev. C. D., Colesburg, Iowa.

[redacted]

Fishback, Mrs. Sophia, Jeffersonton, Va.
Fisher, Mrs. Ann L., New York.
Fisher, Rev. Abiel, Mansheng, Mass.
Fisher, Rev. Ezra, Oregon City, Oregon.
Fisher, Rev. Otis, Pavilion, Ill.
Fisher, Isaac, West Townsend, Vt.
Fisher, E. R., Fishkill, N. Y.
Fisk, Theron, Warsaw, N. Y.
Fisk, Willard, New York.
Fitch, Dr. William, Stamford, Ct.
Fitzgerald, Miss Joanna, New York.
Fithian, Samuel C., Greenwich, N. J.
Fitts, William, Worcester, Mass.
Flanagan, John, Philadelphia.
Flanders, Rev. Charles W., Concord, N. H.
Flanders, Mrs. M. H. L., Concord, N. H.
Flanders, Timothy C., Haverhill, Mass.
Flanders, Melvin, Haverhill, Mass.
Fleet, James R., Brewington, Va.
Fleet, Dr. B., King and Queen C. H., Va.
Fleischmann, Rev. Konrad A., Philadelphia.
Fletcher, Rev. Simeon, Sandy Hill, N. Y.
Fletcher, Rev. Leonard, New Orleans.
Fletcher, Rev. Horace, Townsend, Vt.
Fletcher, Mrs. Mary, Amenia, N. Y.
Flinn, Mrs. E. A. E., Darlington, S. C.
Flint, Brayton, Novi, Mich.
Flint, Mrs. Mary C., Novi, Mich.
Flint, Lewis, Novi, Mich.
Flower, Amelia L., Brooklyn.
Fogg, Rev. Samuel, Lowell, Mass.
Foley, Thomas W., Providence.
Folwell, Job W., Defiance, O.
Forbes, George W., Bridgeport, Ct.
Forbes, Gustavus, Boston.
Forbes, Rev. M., Middlesex, N. Y.
Forbush, Rev. Jonathan E. S., Danvers, Mass.
Forby, Wm. F., Brooklyn.
Force, Lyman, Alta, N. Y.
Ford, Isaac, Philadelphia.
Ford, Mrs. H., Philadelphia.
Ford, Henry Clay, Philadelphia.
Ford, Mrs. Mary, Harvey's Store, Va.
Foreman, Miss Mary E., Hightstown, N. J.
Forrester, Mrs. Eleanora, Williamsburgh, N. Y.
Forristall, Mrs. Lucy, Boston.
Foster, John W., Leesville, Indiana.
Foster, William, West Dedham, Mass.
Foster, Mrs. Sarah K., Evansville, Ia.
Foster, Rev. J. C., Brattleboro', Vt.
Foster, Joseph, Sen., Salem, N. J.
Forsyth, Miss Sarah S., Livingston, N. Y.
Forsyth, Russell, Livingston, N. Y.
Forsyth, Mrs. Sarah, Livingston, N. Y.
Forsyth, Miss Emily H., Albany.
Fowle, Mrs. Lucy, Boston.
Fowler, Gamaliel, Suffield, Ct.
Fox, Rev. Norman, Ballston, N. Y.
Fox, Rev. Charles A., Waverly, Pa.
Fox, Albert R., Sand Lake, N. Y.
Fox, Mrs. Mary A., Sand Lake, N. Y.
Fox, Charles, New York.
Fox, Miss Anna Eliza, New York.
France, Ezra, Rahway, N. J.
France, Mrs. Mary, Rahway, N. J.
Francis, Robert, Newington, Ct.
Francis, Mrs. Lydia D., Newington, Ct.
Francis, Norman, New York.
Francis, Mrs. Hannah C., New York.
Francis, John S., New York.
Francis, Charles King, New York.
Frayser, Rev. Herndon, Twymann's, Va.
Frees, Rev. Daniel L., Salem, N. J.
Freeman, Rev. T. G., Natchez, Miss.
Freeman, Rev. Joseph, Cavendish, Vt.
Freeman, Rev. G. W., Waupun, Wis.
Freeman, Thomas W., Augusta, Ga.
Freeman, Elisha, Worcester, Mass.
Freeman, Henry P., Williamsburgh, N. Y.
French, George R., Wilmington, N. C.
French, Stephen L., Fall River, Mass.
French, Miss Hannah, Haverhill, Mass.
French, Rev. David S., Covington, Ia.
Frink, William S., Taylorville, Ill.
Fripp, E., Beaufort, S. C.
Fripp, Mrs. Ann H., Beaufort, S. C.
Frisby, Mrs. Lucy M., New Haven, Ct.
Frost, James, Wake Forest, N. C.
Fry, John, Philadelphia.
Fulcher, Richard, Three Rivers, Mich.
Fuller, George, Troy, N. Y.
Fuller, Nathan L., New York.
Fuller, Dr. Henry M., Beaufort, S. C.
Fuller, Rev. Martin Luther, Mooers, N. Y.
Fuller, Mrs. Achsah Smith, Pike, N. Y.
Fuller, Cyrenius, M., Jr., Pike, N. Y.
Fuller, Miss Elizabeth, Baltimore.
Fuller, Rev. Edward K., Medford, Mass.
Furman, Rev. Richard, Society Hill, S. C.
Fyfe, Rev. Robert A., Milwaukee, Wis.
Fyfe, Mrs. Rebecca S., Milwaukee, Wis.
Gage, Rev. David, New Boston, N. H.
Gage, Lewis, Methuen, Mass.
Gage, A., Methuen, Mass.
Gale, Jonas R., Delavan, Ill.
Gale, Rev. Amory, Lee, Mass.
Galusha, Truman, Jericho, Vt.
Gammell, A. M., Warren, R. I.
Gardiner, Richard, Philadelphia.
Gardner, Miss Miranda B., Fulton, N. Y.
Gardner, John, Newark, N. J.
Gardner, James C., Augusta, Ga.
Gardner, Rev. Jacob, Lyme, Ct.
Gardner, Frederick, New York.
Garfield, Rev. Benj. F., Clifton Park, N. Y.
Garnett, Dorothy, Miller's, Va.
Garrett, D. H., Haddonfield, N. J.
Garnsey, Erasmus D., Burnt Hills, N. Y.
Garrison, Rev. Cantine, Chili, N. Y.
Gates, Marcus A., South Gardner, Mass.
Gates, Horace S., Norwich, Ct.
Gates, Rev. G. W., Palmyra, N. Y.
Gates, T. J., Plainfield, Ct.
Gatling, John, Eatontown, N. J.
Gault, George, Brooklyn.
Gault, Mrs. George, Brooklyn.
Gault, Miss Georgianna E., Brooklyn.
Gay, William, Hollister, Mass.
Gayler, Mrs. Anna, New York.
George, Moses B., Haverhill, Mass.
George, Samuel, Haverhill, Mass.

MEMBERS FOR LIFE.

Hine, Simmons, New Haven, Ct.
Hinton, A. G., Pittsborough, N. C.
Hires, Mrs. Catharine, New Market, N. J.
Hiscox, Mrs. C. O., New York.
Hitchcox, Sheldon, Suffield, Ct.
Hoar, Lewis, Warren, R. I.
Hoar, John B., Warren, R. I.
Hoard, Samuel, Chicago, Ill.
Hobart, James, Westford, Vt.
Hobert, Washington, Boston.
Hodge, Mrs. Sophronia P., Brooklyn.
Hodge, Rev. M. G., Albany.
Hodge, Mrs. Hancet L., Albany.
Hodges, Rev. J., Jr., East Brookfield, Mass.
Hoffman, Joseph H., Leverington, Pa.
Hogan, Miss Ellen, New York.
Holbrook, Chas. F., Worcester, Mass.
Holbrook, Samuel F., Boston.
Holcombe, Thomas, Savannah, Ga.
Holland, Lucretia E., Boston.
Holmes, Samuel C., Bedford, N. Y.
Holmes, Rev. Lewis, Edgartown, Mass.
Holmes, Mrs. Sarah, Holmdel, N. J.
Holman, Rev. Thomas, Stafford, Ct.
Holroyd, J. Manning, Providence.
Holly, Mrs. Deborah R., Bedford, N. Y.
Holt, John M., Worcester, Mass.
Holt, Caleb, Sharon, Vt.
Homes, Rev. Martin W., Orleans, N. Y.

Howe, Phineas, Newton Centre, Mass.
Howe, John W., Holden, Mass.
Howell, David, Southport, N. Y.
Howes, Samuel C., Chatham, Mass.
Howland, Emeline B., New Bedford, Mass.
Hoyt, Miss Harriet R., Brooklyn.
Hoyt, Mrs. Julia A., Brooklyn.
Hoyt, L. D., Brooklyn.
Hubatchock, Joseph, New York.
Hubbard, Mrs. Mary A., Deep River, Ct.
Hubell, Alrich, Utica, N. Y.
Hubbell, Rev. S., Urbana, N. Y.
Hudgens, Mrs. Rebecca E., Hampton, Va.
Hughson, Levi P., Oswego, N. Y.
Hull, Mrs. Maria, New York.
Hull, Charles, Danbury, Ct.
Hulse, Smith, Dunden, N. Y.
Hungerford, Levi, Cordova, Ill.
Hunt, Dr. George, Le Claire, Ill.
Hunt, Rev. John, Richmond, N. H.
Hunt, Mrs. N., Sharon, Ct.
Hunt, Miss Ellen, New York.
Hunter, William, Boston.
Hunter, Miss Elizabeth Jane, New York.
Huntley, Rev. George W., Wellsville, N. Y.
Huntington, Mrs. Philip, Haverhill, Mass.
Hurlbut, Joel, Stamford, Ct.
Hurd, Daniel, Lowell, Mass.
Hurten, Miss Ann M., New York.

Jaycox, Mrs. Fanny M., Cold Spring, N. Y.
Jeffrey, Rev. Reuben, Albany, N. Y.
Jeffries, J. M., Red Oak Grove, Va.
Jenckes, Rev. Erastus N., Farmridge, Ill.
Jenckes, Miss Maria, Pawtucket, R. I.
Jenks, Gideon, Brookfield, Mass.
Jenks, J. W. P., Middleboro', Mass.
Jenkins, Mrs. Susannah, New York.
Jenkins, Rev. J. E., Coatesville, Pa.
Jenkins, Miss Rebecca, New York.
Jennett, John, Halifax, C. H., Va.
Jennings, Mrs. Susan C., Worcester, Mass.
Jennings, Mrs. Marcia, Deep River, Ct.
Jeril, Rev. T., Lebanon, N. Y.
Jervard, Rev. Richard, Morrisania, N. Y.
Jeter, Rev. J. C., Beaver Dam, S. C.
Jewell, Aaron C., Newark, N. J.
Jewett, Rev. Milo P., Marion, Ala.
Jewett, Rev. Daniel, Farmington, Iowa.
Jimmerson, Robert J., New York.
Jimmerson, Mrs. Miranda L., New York.
Johnson, Rev. William B., D.D., Edgefield, S. C.
Johnson, Mrs. Henrietta, Edgefield, S. C.
Johnson, William, North-East, Pa.
Johnson, Mrs. Sarah S., North-East, Pa.
Johnson, Mrs. Louisa M., Lynn, Mass.
Johnson, James, Brooklyn, N. Y.
Johnson, Robert, Newark, N. J.
Johnson, Mrs. Robert, Newark, N. J.
Johnson, Rev. Solomon B., St. Louis, Mo.
Johnson, Rev. George J., Burlington, Iowa.
Johnson, Mrs. George J., Burlington, Iowa.
Johnson, Rev. Hezekiah, Oregon City, Oregon.
Johnson, Albert B., Willistown, Pa.
Johnson, Edward, New York.
Johnson, Mrs. Mary, Albany, N. Y.
Johnson, Merrick, Willington, Ct.
Johnson, Miss Jane Ann, Wilson, N. Y.
Johnston, Andrew, Newark, N. J.
Jones, Rev. Stephen, Norwalk, Ohio.
Jones, Mrs. Stephen, Norwalk, Ohio.
Jones, Rev. John, Scaville, N. J.
Jones, Mrs. Deborah, Willistown, Pa.
Jones, Mrs. Ann T., Williamsburgh, Va.
Jones, Eliza T., Tavern P. O., Pa.
Jones, Mrs. Margaret, New York.
Jones, Mrs. Eliza W., New Brunswick, N. J.
Jones, Mrs. Elizabeth, Macedon, N. Y.
Jones, David, New York.
Jones, Mrs. Sarah, New York.
Jones, Mrs. Mary, New York.
Jones, Mrs. Rhoda, Smithville, N. Y.
Jones, Miss Catharine L., Philadelphia.
Jones, Rev. Joseph H., Frederick City, Md.
Jones, Rev. David N., Richmond, Va.
Jones, Rev. Matthew, Stephentown, N. Y.
Jones, Rev. Theophilus, Hatboro', Pa.
Jones, Rev. Isaac D., Flemingville, N. Y.
Jones, John B., Roxbury, Mass.
Jones, William G., Wilmington, Del.
Jones, Washington, Wilmington, Del.
Jones, William M., New York.
Jones, Mrs. Margaretta V., New York.
Jones, Rev. J. W., Paterson, N. Y.
Jones, Howard M., Providence, R. I.
Jones, Rev. J. D. E., North Bennington, Vt.
Jones, Mrs. Abigail, New York.
Jones, Rev. A. B., Guilford, N. Y.
Jones, Rev. H. S., Smyrna, N. Y.
Jones, Rev. P. F., New York.
Jordan, Philana D., Columbia, Ohio.
Jordon, Mrs. Esther, Brooklyn, N. Y.
Jordon, True P., Lowell, Mass.
Joslin, Joseph, East Poultney, Vt.
Joyce, Miss Sarah W., Worcester, Mass.
Judd, Rev. Truman O., Fairhaven, Ct.
Judson, Mrs. Emily C., Hamilton, N. Y.
Justice, David, Forestville, N. C.
Justin, Rev. Ira, Richmond, N. Y.
Kain, Charles, Marlton, N. J.
Kain, Mrs. Sarah, Marlton, N. J.
Kain, Rev. Charles, Jr., Mullica Hill, N. J.
Kain, Mrs. Maria, Mullica Hill, N. J.
Kauffman, Mrs. Sarah, Paoli, Pa.
Keely, Rev. George, Haverhill, Mass.
Keely, Mrs. George, Haverhill, Mass.
Keely, John, Haverhill, Mass.
Keely, Mrs. John, Haverhill, Mass.
Keely, Rev. Thomas B., Kingston, Mass.
Keen, William W., West Philadelphia.
Keen, Mrs. Susan B., West Philadelphia.
Keen, George B., West Philadelphia.
Keen, William W. J., West Philadelphia.
Keen, Charles B., West Philadelphia.
Keeney, William H., New London, Ct.
Keeney, Rev. Curtis, New London, Ct.
Kelly, Mrs. Joan, Elmira, New York.
Kelley, Mrs. Catharine, N. Y.
Kelley, Mrs. Eli, New York.
Kelley, Miss Georgiana, New York.
Kelley, James D., Pittsfield, N. H.
Kelton, George, Salem, N. J.
Kemp, Sylvester A., Florida, Mass.
Kendall, H. N., St. Louis, Mo.
Kendrick, Silas N., Detroit, Mich.
Kendrick, Mrs. Fanny, Detroit, Mich.
Kendrick, Adin, East Poultney, Vt.
Kendrick, Rev. A. C., D.D., Rochester, N. Y.
Kendrick, Mrs. Ann, Hamilton, N. Y.
Kennan, Mrs. Eliza, Thompsonville, Va.
Kenworthy, Mrs. Mary, New York.
Kerr, John, Yanceyville, N. C.
Kerr, James N., Dixon, Ill.
Kerfoot, Mrs. Maria C., Upperville, Va.
Kerfoot, Mrs. Harriet E., Battletown, Va.
Ketcham, Charles F., Brooklyn, N. Y.
Ketcham, Miss Sarah A., New York.
Ketchum, Rev. Jonathan, Farmersville, N. Y.
Key, Mrs. A., Fife's, Va.
Keyes, Mrs. Lydia L., North East, N. Y.
Keyes, Miss Sarah E., North East, N. Y.
Keyes, Jesse, Almont, Mich.
Keyser, Rev. Charles, Mount Morris, N. Y.
Kidder, Horace, Penn Yan, N. Y.
Kimball, Abraham, Boston, Mass.
Kimball, Mrs. Edward, Haverhill, Mass.
Kimball, Rufus, Haverhill, Mass.
Kimball, Mrs. Rufus, Haverhill, Mass.
Kincaid, Rev. Eugenio, Ava, Burmah.
Kindel, Job, Pemberton, N. J.
King, Daniel K., Port Byron, N. Y.
King, Robert, New York.

Kingman, E. Martin, New York.
Kingman, Mrs. Eliza F., New York.
Kingman, Sumner A., New York.
Kingman, Henry W., New York.
Kingman, Miss Augusta E., New York.
Kingsbury, Rev. Arnold, Fredonia, N. Y.
Kingsford, Rev. Edward, D.D., Richmond, Va.
Kingsland, Mrs. Sarah Jane, New York.
Kinsley, Rev. A. C., Parma Centre, N. Y.
Kirk, Robert, New York.
Kone, Louk, Maulmain, Burmah.
Knapp, Rev. Henry R., Willimantic, Ct.
Knapp, Mrs. Mary, Willimantic, Ct.
Knapp, John, Bridgeport, Ct.
Knapp, Rev. A., Otselic, N. Y.
Knight, Daniel N., Brooklyn.
Knight, Mrs. D. N., Brooklyn.
Knight, Jonathan, Worcester, Mass.
Knowles, Levi, Philadelphia.
Knowles, Mrs. Susan E., Providence.
Knowlton, Miss Sarah J., North Chatham, N. Y.
Knowlton, D. A., Freeport, Ill.
Knowlton, Edward, Marion, Iowa.
Knowlton, Hezekiah, Beverly, Mass.
Knox, Miss Rachel, Hillsdale, N. Y.
Knudson, Miss Sarah Jane, Brooklyn.
Kyle, Miss Mary, New York.
Lamont, Mrs. Anna, New York.

Leggett, Rev. William [illegible]
Leland, J. A., [illegible]
Leland, Mrs. [illegible]
Lemont, Charles A. [illegible]
Lemont, Mrs. [illegible]
Leonard, Rev. [illegible]
Leonard, Mrs. [illegible]
Leonard, Rev. [illegible]
Leonard, George [illegible]
Leveed, Rev. J. K., [illegible]
Levy, Rev. Edgar M., [illegible]
Lewis, William A., New [illegible]
Lewis, Elijah, [illegible]
Lewis, Mrs. Ann, [illegible]
Lewis, [illegible]
Lewis, Mrs. [illegible]
Lewis, Rev. [illegible]
Lewis, [illegible]
Lewis, [illegible]
Lewis, Mrs. [illegible]
Lewis, [illegible]
Lewis, William, New York.
Linnard, [illegible]
Lincoln, [illegible]
Lincoln, Mrs. Abby [illegible]
Lincoln, Rev. [illegible]
Lindsay, Wm., Fall River, Mass.
Litchfield, Rev. Daniel W., Benton, N. Y.

Lyon, Mrs. Caroline F., Chatham, Mass.
Lyon, Mrs. Merrick, Providence.
Lyon, Rev. A. S., Chatham, Mass.
Lynt, Odell D., Hastings, N. Y.
Lytle, Andrew, Williamsburgh, Va.
McAllister, Mrs. R., Fayetteville, N. C.
McBride, Miss Jane Ann, New York.
McBride, Miss Ellen E., New York.
McCarthy, Rev. William, Newport, N. Y.
McClung, Miss Caroline M., Pittsburgh, Pa.
McClung, Anthony, Kingston, N. Y.
McCormick, R. C., New York.
McCormick, Mrs. Sarah M., New York.
McCoy, John, Charlestown, Ia.
McCullen, Miss Sarah, New York.
McCune, John F., Salem, N. J.
McDade, Mrs. Jane, New York.
McDaniel, Rueelin, Fayetteville, N. C.
McFarland, Rev. D., Belleville, N. Y.
McGear, Daniel L.
McGougal, George, New York.
McIntosh, William C., Philadelphia.
McIntosh, Mrs. Mary, Philadelphia.
McIver, A. M., Society Hill, S. C.
McIver, Mrs. Ann J., Society Hill, S. C.
McJannett, Mrs. Elizabeth, Brooklyn.
McKowen, John, New York.
McLallan, James, Trumansburg, N. Y.
McLallan, Mrs. Ellen, Trumansburg, N. Y.
McLean, Mrs. Mary, New London, Ct.
McLowth, Rev. Benjamin, Scipio, New York.
McMahon, Henry L., Philadelphia.
McTaggart, Daniel, Reading, Pa.
McTaggart, Mrs. Margaret, Reading, Pa.
Macdonald, Alexander, Williamsburgh, N. Y.
Macdonald, Mrs. E., Williamsburgh, N. Y.
Macdonald, Miss M. J., Williamsburgh, N. Y.
Mack, Rev. Levi M., Whiteside Corner, N. Y.
Mack, Elisha H., Weedsport, N. Y.
Maclay, Hon. William B., New York.
Maclay, Archibald, New York.
Maclay, Moses B., New York.
Mabbett, Seneca, Dover Plains, N. Y.
Mabbett, T., Brooklyn.
Madison, Almond Z., Fredonia, N. Y.
Magee, Rev. Thomas, New Brunswick, N. S.
Magee, Thomas H., New York.
Maghee, Miss Frances, New York.
Magoon, Miss Ella Louise, New York.
Magoon, Frank N. L., New York.
Mahoney, Rev. Henry W., Piedmont, S. C.
Mallary, Rev. S. S., Pawtucket, R. I.
Mallory, Rev. Almond C., Benton Centre, N. Y.
Mallory, Rev. James, Lagrange, N. Y.
Mandeville, Stephen, New York.
Mandeville, Mrs. Mary, New York.
Mandeville, Miss Phebe E., New York.
Mandeville, George, New York.
Mansfield, Edward, South Reading, Mass.
Mangam, William D., New York.
Mangam, Mrs. Sarah Ann, New York.
Mangam, Edgar B., New York.
Mangum, Rev. Daniel, Pageville, S. C.
Manning, Rev. Edward, Cornwall, N. S.
Manning, William, Boston, Mass.
Manro, Philip A., Throopsville, N. Y.
Manton, Rev. Joseph R., Providence.
Manwaring, C. S., East Lyme, Ct.
Maple, John E., Canton, Ill.
March, Peter S., New York.
Marchant, Henry, Jr., Providence.
Marchant, Miss Mary W., Providence.
Marsall, Rev. J. F., Columbia, S. C.
Marsall, Rev. Andrew, Savannah, Ga.
Marsh, Rev. Asa, Evansville, Ia.
Marsh, Rev. Leonard G., New York.
Marsh, Benjamin, Newport, R. I.
Marsh, Enoch, Hudson, N. H.
Marshall, Rev. Samuel, Ohio.
Marshall, William, Fitchburg, Mass.
Marshall, Albert, Holden, Mass.
Marshall, Mrs. Maria, Holden, Mass.
Marshall, Miss Mary Ann, New York.
Marston, Rev. S. W., East Brookfield, Mass.
Marston, Mrs. S. H., East Brookfield, Mass.
Martin, William R., New York.
Martin, Mrs. Charles J., New York.
Martin, Mrs. Mary G., New York.
Martin, Miss Mary, New York.
Martin, Alfred, New York.
Martin, Mrs. Harriet W., New York.
Martin, Miss Mary Ann, New York.
Martin, Miss Sarah, New York.
Martin, Henry L., New York.
Martin, Stelle B., New York.
Martin, Francis, New York.
Martin, Reune, New York.
Martin, Rev. Sandford S., Tremont, Ill.
Martin, Peter, Philadelphia.
Martin, M. D., Bristol, Ct.
Martin, Mrs. Sarah Ann, New York.
Marvin, George, Norwalk, Ct.
Mason, Augustus F., Chelsea, Mass.
Mason, Mrs. Sarah R., Chelsea, Mass.
Mason, Mrs. Roxanna L., West Swanzey, N. H.
Mason, Mrs. D. C. Fuller, Sandusky, N. Y.
Mason, Mrs. J. O., Greenwich, N. Y.
Mason, George, Providence.
Mason, Charles, New York.
Mason, John M. G., Philadelphia.
Mason, Arnold G., Bridgeport, Ct.
Mason, Mrs. Arnold G., Bridgeport, Ct.
Mason, E. B., Webster, N. Y.
Mason, Rev. S. R., Lockport, N. Y.
Mason, Rev. J. T., Galeville, N. Y.
Mason, Pethuel, Somerville, N. J.
Mason, Charles J., New York.
Mason, Mrs. Lavinia, New York.
Mastin, John S., New York.
Mather, Increase, Fairport, N. Y.
Mather, Mrs. Mary A., Deep River, C
Mathews, Rev. George, Athol, Mass.
Mathews, Mrs. Elizabeth, Athol, Mass.
Matteson, Rev. N. H., Preston City, Ct.
Maul, Rev. William, Plainfield, N. J.
Maul, Mrs. Sarah Ann, Plainfield, N. J.
Maxwell, B., Shelburne Falls, Mass.
Maxwell, Rev. J. M., Plymouth, Ia.
Maynard, Walter, Three Rivers, Mass.
Meacham, Miss Elizabeth, Brooklyn.
Mead, John, Troy, N. Y.

MEMBERS FOR LIFE.

Mead, William, Lowell, Mass.
Meads, Rev. George W., Vienna, N. Y.
Mears, Elijah, Boston, Mass.
Meech, Rev. Wm. W., Hamilton, N. Y.
Meech, Rev. Levi, Preston, Ct.
Meech, Levi, North Lyme, Ct.
Medbury, Rev. Nicholas, Newburyport, Ma.
Medbury, Viall, Seekonk, Mass.
Meeker, Aaron B., Elizabethtown, N. J.
Meeson, Rev. J. D., Rondout, N. Y.
Merchant, James H., New York.
Merchant, Mrs. Amanda M., New York.
Merchant, Reuben, Stillwater, N. Y.
Meriam, Otis, Chelsea, Mass.
Merrell, Joseph, New York.
Merrell, Charles, Malden, Mass.
Merrett, Thomas W., Somerset, N. Y.
Merriam, Rev. Asaph, Bolton, Mass.
Merriam, Rev. Mylon, Sharon, Mass.
Merrill, Joseph, Lowell, Mass.
Merrill, Joseph, Hudson, N. Y.
Merryfield, Miss Carrie R., Brookline, Vt.
Messer, Richard H., New London, N. H.
Meserve, Andrew J., Lowell, Mass.
Metcalf, Rev. Whitman, Nunda, N. Y.
Mershon, Mrs. Mellona S., New York.
Mi-shy-ki-no-di-no-i-kue (Mrs. James Tanner), Pembina, Min. Ter.
Mills, Stephen, Greenwich, N. Y.
Mills, Rev. [illegible] W., Springville, N. Y.
Milne, John C., Fall River, Mass.
Milner, Alfred A., New York.
Milner, Mrs. Alfred A., New York.
Miner, Rev. Bradley, Providence.
Miner, Rev. Martin, Wolcott, Ct.
Miner, Rev. Absalom, Waukesha, Wis.
Miner, Rev. Cyrus, Attica, N. Y.
Miner, Rev. S. G., Canton, Ill.
Miner, Rev. Erastus, Cold Spring, N. Y.
Miner, Francis S., New York.
Miner, A. B., Italy Hill, N. Y.
Miner, Nathaniel, Jerseyville, Ill.
Miner, Mrs. Hannah M., Norwich, N. Y.
Mingus, Miss Julia Ann, New York.
Mitchell, Rev. George H., Waynesburg, Pa.
Mitchell, Mrs. Phebe H., Waynesburg, Pa.
Mitchell, Seth, Montrose, Pa.
Mixter, George, East Lyme, Ct.
Mondon, Gilbert F., Port Jervis, N. Y.
Monroe, Rev. Wm. Y., Lexington, Ky.
Montgomery, William, Danbury, Ct.
Montgomery, Mrs. Susan, Danbury, Ct.
Montgomery, S. B., Danbury, Ct.
Montague, Rev. Oreb, Warsaw, N. Y.
Moon, John, N. Y.
Moore, Dr. G. C., St. Johns, N. C.

Mulhern, Rev. Denis, Ozaukee, Wisc.
Mumford, Rev. N., Sherburn, N. Y.
Munger, Rev. Washington, Mystic River, Ct.
Munger, Mrs. Louisa N., Mystic River, Ct.
Munger, Morgan, Stillwater, N. Y.
Munger, L. F., Le Roy, N. Y.
Munn, Mrs. Mary, New York.
Murdock, Mrs Martha B., Hartford, Ct.
Murphy, William D., New York.
Murphy, Samuel, Hoboken, N. J.
Murphy, Rev. John, Greenwich, N. J.
Mustin, John, Philadelphia.
Myers, Mrs. Anna R., Philadelphia.
Myers, James, Jr., New York.
Mylne, Rev. William, Pemberton, Va.
Napier, Rev. Robert, Mizpah, S. C.
Neale, Mrs. Melissa Y., Boston.
Nelson, Rev. Caleb, Enfield, N. Y.
Nelson, Rev. Wm. F., Greenfield, Mass.
Nelson, Simeon B., Westport, N. H.
Newcomb, Butler, Cedarville, N. J.
Newell, Andrew H., Brookline, Mass.
Newell, Mrs. Asa, Providence.
Newhall, Rev. F., Hanover, N. H.
Newland, D., Stillwater, N. Y.
Newland, Rev. C. A., Cooper's Plains, N. Y.
Newton, Mrs Sally, Albany.
Newton, William, Worcester, Mass.
Newton, Rev. Calvin, Worcester, Mass.
Newton, Rev. Baxter, North Leverett, Mass.
Newton, Miss Frances M., New York.
Newton, Mrs. Jane, Bridgeton, N. J.
Nice, Rev. William J., Imlaystown, N. J.
Nice, Mrs. Elizabeth A., Imlaystown, N. J.
Nice, Rev. George P., Somerville, N. J.
Nichols, Miss Hannah, Bridgeport, Ct.
Nichols, Reuben, Kingston, N. Y.
Nichols, Rev. D. A., Port Providence, Pa.
Nichols, Jonathan, Berlin, N. Y.
Nicholas, Rev. Noah, Rutland, Vt.
Nicholson, A. M., Bostick Mills, N. C.
Niel, James E., Brooklyn.
Noble, Mrs. Margaret, Brooklyn.
Normandeau, Mrs. C. A., Grande Ligne, C. E.
Northam, E., Rockingham, N. C.
Northam, George, Va.
Norton, Charles C., New York.
Norton, Rev. Noah, Brunswick, Me.
Norton, Newbery, Agawam, Mass.
Norris, Mrs. F. Henrietta, Brooklyn.
Norris, Mrs. Eliza D., Sanbornton, N. H.
Numan, Abraham, Troy, N. Y.
Nunn, James D., Raleigh, N. C.
Oakley, Mrs. Cassandra, New York.
Odell, Jonathan, Yonkers, N. Y.
Oldring, Henry J., New York.
Olin, Joseph, Canton, N. Y.
Olin, Benjamin, Canton, N. Y.
Olmstead, Rev. J. W., Boston.
Olney, Rev. David B., Barrington, N. Y.
Olney, Rev. Philetus, Wayne, N. Y.
Olney, James, Pawtucket, R. I.
Olney, Rev. Lafayette W., Castile, N. Y.
Oliver, Wm., Malden, Mass.
Omberson, William J., New York.
Otis, Harvey, Kingston, N. Y.
O'Brian, Miss Mary, New York.
O'Neal, Mrs. Jenett, Brooklyn.
Oncken, Rev. J. G., Hamburg, Germany.
Oncken, Mrs. Ann, Hamburg, Germany.
Osborn, Rev. J. W., Marion, N. Y.
Osgood, Miss Sarah T., Salisbury, Mass.
Osgood, Miss Jane, Salisbury, Mass.
Osgood, John, Amesbury, Mass.
Osgood, Rev. S. M., Albion, N. Y.
Page, Rev. Stephen B., Norwalk, Ohio.
Page, Abel, Haverhill, Mass.
Page, Mrs. Abel, Haverhill, Mass.
Page, Mrs. Rachael D., Hopkinton, N. H.
Paine, Rev. John, Ware, Mass.
Paine, Walter, 3d., Fall River, Mass.
Palmer, Rev. Asa H.
Palmer, Rev. Albert G., Syracuse, N. Y.
Palmer, Mrs. Amelia W., Syracuse, N. Y.
Palmer, Mrs. William, East Lyme, Ct.,
Palmer, Rev. Lyman, St. Anthony, Min.
Palmer, Rev. Prentice T., Waveland, Ia.
Palmer, Ephraim, New Hartford, N. Y.
Park, Charles C., Italy Hollow, N. Y.
Parke, Rev. F. S., Cheshire, Mass.
Parker, Miss Lavinia M., Suffield, Ct.
Parker, Asa, Essex, Ct.
Parker, Joel R., Fredonia, N. Y.
Parker, Rev. A., Fiskedale, Mass.
Parker, Rev. William, Philadelphia.
Parker, Rev. A., Coventry, N. Y.
Parker, David O., Worcester, Mass.
Parker, Lydia P., Allen, Mich.
Parks, Rev. R. M., Bedford, Indiana.
Parkhurst, John, Fitchburg, Mass.
Parmlee, Mrs. Syrena, New York.
Parmly, Rev. W. H., Burlington, N. J.
Parmely, Rev. Levi, Westchester, Pa.
Parmely, Mrs. Catharine H., Westchester, Pa.
Parrish, Warren, Mendon, N. Y.
Parshley, John, New Haven, Ct.
Parsons, Silas, Swanzey, N. H.
Parsons, Mrs. Patience, Swanzey, N. H.
Parsons, William, Medford, Mass.
Pasco, Rev. Cephas, Egremont, Mass.
Patch, Rev. George W., Marblehead, Mass.
Patterson, Mrs. Mary, Chapel Hill, N. C.
Patterson, Mrs. Lucy A., New York.
Paulin, Mrs. Ann, Salem, N. J.
Payne, Miss Amanda, Amenia, N. Y.
Payne, William W., Auburn, N. Y.
Peak, John, Boston.
Peacock, Rev. John, Bradford, N. H.
Pease, Joseph W., Lowell, Mass.
Peck, Mrs. Nancy M., Owego, N. Y.
Peck, John, Clifton Park, N. Y.
Peck, Mrs. John, Clifton Park, N. Y.
Peck, John, 2d., Clifton Park, N. Y.
Peck, Abijah, Jr., Clifton Park, N. Y.
Peck, Rev., David A., Waupaca, Wis.
Peck, James W., Brooklyn.
Peck, Rev. Daniel, South Jackson, Mich.
Peck, George B., Providence.
Peckham, Rev. S. H., Ledyard, Ct.
Peeples, Rev. Darling, Barnwell, S. C.

MEMBERS FOR LIFE.

Peeples, Edward H., Lawtonville, S. C.
Pegg, Miss Jane, New York.
Pember, Asahel, New London, Ct.
Pember, Mrs. Mary, New London, Ct.
Penny, Rev. William, Uniontown, Pa.
Penny, Rev. Thomas J., Saltsburg, Pa.
Perego, Mrs. Margaret, New York.
Pendleton, Rev. G. W., Jacksonville, Ill.
Pendleton, Mrs. Jane G., Jacksonville, Ill.
Pennypacker, John, Wilmington, Del.
Perine, Joseph, Plainfield, N. J.
Perine, Mrs. Sarah, Plainfield, N. J.
Perkins, Jabez, Topsham, Me.
Perkins, Rev. Nehemiah M., Waterbury, Ct.
Perkins, George, Amesbury, Mass.
Perry, S. G., Walpole, N. H.
Perry, Mrs. Sarah, McWilliamstown, Pa.
Perry, Valentine, Macedon, N. Y.
Person, Rev. Ira, Concord, N. H.
Persons, Rev. R., Victory, N. Y.
Peterson, Rev. J. F., Richardson's, S. C.
Peterson, Richard E., New York.
Peterson, Mrs. Deborah V., New York.
Peterson, Samuel F., Philadelphia.
Pettengill, Daniel, Haverhill, Mass.
Pettis, Harvey E., Greenwich, N. Y.
Pettit, Curtis, Wilson, N. Y.
Pettigrew, Rev. Wm. J., Pittsburg, Pa.
Pew, John, Gloucester, Mass.
Phares, Rev. M. B., Dupont, Ia.
Pinney, Mrs. Mary, Owego, N. Y.
Piper, John G., Canton, Ill.
Pitman, Rev. Joseph [illegible]
Plant, B. H., [illegible]
Platt, G. W., New York [illegible]
Platt, Mrs. Jane B., New York [illegible]
Platt, Rev. B. F., Toledo, Ohio. [illegible]
Plumb, William, [illegible]
Plummer, Mrs. Jane, New York [illegible]
Plymon, Mrs. [illegible]
Poinier, J. B., Cincinnati [illegible]
Poole, Rev. A. W., [illegible]
Pooler, Seth, Lowell, Mass. [illegible]
Poland, W. C., [illegible]
Poland, Rev. James W., Goffstown Centre,
Pollard, Mrs. Elizabeth, Taunton, Mass.
Polhamus, H. A., New York.
Pomeroy, Rev. Samuel, Hillsdale, N.
Pomroy, Wm., Middlefield, Mass.
Pond, William, New York.
Pond, Joseph A., Boston.
Porter, Rev. Lemuel, Pittsfield, Mass.
Porter, Mrs. William M., Pittsfield, Mass.
Porter, Edwin, Lowell, Mass.
Post, Mrs. Sarah, New York.
Post, Alanson H., [illegible] Vt.
Post, Levi, [illegible], N. Y.
Post, Joy, [illegible], Ct.
Post, John, [illegible], Mich.
Post, Prof. John D., Oregon City, Oregon.
Post, Peter K., Somerville, N. J.

Quimby, Mrs. Harriet, Brooklyn.
Quincy, Josiah, Rumney, N. H.
Radcliff, Joshua, Haverhill, Mass.
Rafferty, Mrs. Susan A., New York.
Rand, Rev. Aaron, New York.
Rand, Mrs. M. E., Hathaway, New York.
Rand, John W., Louisville, Ky.
Rand, Rev. Thomas, Ireland, Mass.
Rand, Cornelia B., Acton, Mass.
Randall, Mrs. Mary, New York.
Randall, Mrs. Mary, Mystic River, Ct.
Randall, Mrs. Maria, Mystic River, Ct.
Randall, Rev. Silas B., Mystic River, Ct.
Randall, Wm. Henry, Mystic River, Ct.
Randolph, Rev. Warren, Providence.
Randolph, Mrs. Huldah, New York.
Randolph, Mrs. Sarah F., New Market, N. J.
Randolph, Joseph F., New York.
Randolph, Samuel, Plainfield, N. J.
Randolph, Peter F., New York.
Randolph, Lewis, Delhi, Ill.
Randolph, Mrs. Jane Ann, Brooklyn.
Rankin, Mrs. Sarah, Reading, Pa.
Rankin, Mrs. Eliza, Reading, Pa.
Rankin, Peter, Phoenixville, Pa.
Ranney, E. W., New York.
Rathbone, Lewis, Albany.
Rathbone, Mrs. Mary A., Albany.
Rathbone, Thomas R., Providence.
Rathbun, John S., New Haven, Ct.
Rauschenbusch, Rev. August, New York.
Raymond, Rev. Lewis, Chicago, Ill.
Raynor, Samuel, New York.
Raynor, Mrs. Sarah D., New York.
Raynor, Wm. E., New York.
Reed, Mrs. Sarah, Deep River, Ct.
Reed, Rev. Hiram W., Albuquerque, N. M.
Reed, Mrs. Alzina A. J., Albuquerque, N. M.
Reed, Rev. Daniel, Medina, N. Y.
Reed, Rev. James S., Oregon City, Oregon.
Reed, Mrs. James H., Providence.
Reed, Mrs. Hannah T., Deep River, Ct.
Reed, Evans H., Townsend, Vt.
Reed, Mrs. Fanny B., Townsend, Vt.
Reed, Mrs. Sarah B. G., Winchester, Mass.
Reed, Mrs. Emeline, Chelsea, Mass.
Reed, Thomas B., New York.
Reed, Wm. B., North East, N. Y.
Reed, Mrs. Eunice, North East, N. Y.
Reed, Mrs. Mary Ann, North East, N. Y.
Reed, Rev. R. D., Truxton, N. Y.
Reed, Mrs. R. D., Truxton, N. Y.
Reed, David, Utica, N. Y.
Reed, Enos, East Cambridge, Mass.
Reed, Lewis B., New York.
Reed, Rev. Wm., Barnstable, Mass.
Rees, Rev. Wm., Sennett, N. Y.
Reid, Mrs. Dorothy, New London, Ct.
Reid, Andrew, Warren, R. I.
Relyea, Rev. Solomon S., Kingston, N. Y
Remington, Mrs. Sarah P., Louisville, Ky.
Remsen, Garret, Wilmington, Del.
Remsen, George, Brooklyn.
Remster, Benjamin, Canton, N. J.
Requa, Mrs. Elizabeth, Sing Sing, N. Y.
Reynolds, Mrs. Mary, New York.
Reynolds, Rev. John E., Perth Amboy, N. J.
Reynolds, Abraham M., Newark, N. J.
Rhees, Mrs. Grace W., Williamsburgh, N. Y.
Rhodes, G., Lawtonville, S. C.
Rice, Rev. A., Stoneville, S. C.
Rice, Mrs. Mary, Orleans, N. Y.
Rice, Josiah, Worcester, Mass.
Rich, Joseph C., Penfield, N. Y.
Richards, Rev. John M., Germantown, Pa.
Richards, Rev. Humphrey, Dorchester, Mass.
Richards, Mrs. Eunice J., Dorchester, Mass.
Richards, Rev. Wm. C., Lynn, Mass.
Richards, Mrs. Eliza G., Lynn, Mass.
Richards, Joel, Claremont, N. H.
Richards, Wm. H., Philadelphia.
Richards, Mrs. Elizabeth, Philadelphia.
Richards, Wm. H., Jr., Philadelphia.
Richards, Edwin S., Philadelphia.
Richards, Joseph L., Philadelphia.
Richards, Zalmon, Washington, D. C.
Richards, Henry, Fall River, Mass.
Richards, Truman, Brooklyn.
Richards, Miss Isabel, New York.
Richardson, Rev. Daniel F., Hanover, N. H.
Richardson, Wm. T., Cambridge, Mass.
Richardson, Thomas S., Brooklyn.
Richardson, Mrs. Ann, Boston.
Richardson, Freeman, Auburn, N. Y.
Richardson, Rev. John, South Berwick, Me.
Richmond, Miss Maryetta, Hillsdale, N. Y.
Richmond, Rev. John L., Indianapolis, Ia.
Richmond, Rev. Nathaniel, Pendleton, Ia.
Rider, Charles C., Roxbury, Mass.
Riddick, Jethro H., Sunbury, N. C.
Riddick, Nathan, Sunbury, N. C.
Riley, Rev. G. W., Paris, Ill.
Ripley, Rev. Thomas B., Portland, Me.
Ripley, Rev. S., Foxboro', Mass.
Ripley, Rev. Henry J., D.D. Newton, Mass.
Roach, Rev. E. W., Harvey's Store, Va.
Robert, Rev. Joseph T., Portsmouth, Ohio.
Roberts, E. G., Brooklyn.
Roberts, Rev. Thomas, Holmesdale, Pa.
Roberts, Rev. Philip, Jr., Salt Point, N. Y.
Roberts, Sarah, New Bedford, Mass.
Roberts, Lewis, Brooklyn.
Roberts, Mrs. E. G., Brooklyn.
Robertson, Rev. Thomas N., Orleans, Ia.
Robbins, Lewis, Upper Freehold, N. J.
Robbins, Mrs. Elizabeth, Littleton, Mass.
Robbins, Rev. Gilbert, Keene, N. H.
Robbins, Austin, Smithville, N. Y.
Robbins, Oliver, Smithville, N. Y.
Robins, Rev. Gurdon, Hartford, Ct.
Robinson, Rev. E. G., D.D., Rochester, N. Y.
Robinson, Rev. Samuel, St. John, N. B.
Robinson, Rev Daniel, Southington, Ct.
Robinson, Benjamin, Providence.
Robinson, Mrs. Maria H., Providence.
Robinson, Rev. Demas
Robinson, Wm., New York.
Robinson, Mrs. Catharine, New York.
Robinson, Mrs. Martha, Savannah, Ga.
Robinson, Reuben T., Boston.
Robinson, Edward, Arcadia, N. Y.
Rockafellow, George, Conesus, N. Y.

Rockwell, David, Plainfield, N. J.
Rockwood, Rev. Joseph M., Belchertown, Mass.
Rodgers, Rev. Ebenezer, Upper Alton, Ill.
Roe, Rev. Charles H., Belvidere, Ill.
Roe, Mrs. Mary, Belvidere, Ill.
Rogers, Rev. Joseph D., Berlin, N. Y.
Rogers, Enos, Chatham, Mass.
Rogers, Mrs. Eliza D., Providence.
Rogers, Miss Eleanor F., Providence.
Rogers, Richard, New London, Ct.
Rogers, Rev. J. B., Hornby, N. Y.
Rogers, Dr. Alexander W., Paterson, N. J.
Rogers, George W., New London, Ct.
Rollin, Rev. J. B., Tonawanda, N. Y.
Roney, Rev. Wm., Willistown, Pa.
Roof, Milton, New York.
Rose, Mrs. Olive E., Troy, N. Y.
Ross, Rev. Arthur A., Pawtucket, R. I.
Rossell, Rev. Caleb, Smithfield, Pa.
Rowan, Phineas, Philadelphia.
Rowe, John K., Baltimore.
Royal, Rev. Wm., Wintersent, S. C.
Rue, Rev. Joshua E., Hightstown, N. J.
Rugg, George W., Worcester, Mass.
Runyon, Richard E., New Brunswick, N. J.
Runyon, Hon. Peter P., New Brunswick, N. J.
Runyon, Daniel, New Brunswick, N. J.
Runyon, Renne D., New Market, N. J.
Runyon, Mrs. Isabella, New York.
Russell, William, Yanceyville, N. C.
[redacted]

Sawyer, Rev. Conant, Lowville, N. Y.
Sawyer, Enoch, Salisbury, Mass.
Sawin, Rev. Addison A., Bristol, Vt.
Scarrett, Rev. Jas. J., Middletown, N. Y.
Schoolcraft, John L., Albany.
Scofield, Rev. James, Decorah, Iowa.
Scott, Robert, Amesbury, Mass.
Scott, John, Columbia, S. C.
Scott, Rev. James, Newburgh, N. Y.
Scott, Mrs. Cornelia S., Newburgh, N. Y.
Scott, Alfred, Lowell, Mass.
Scott, Rev. Ebenezer J., Rushford, N. Y.
Scott, Rev. George, Maquoketa, Iowa.
Scott, Rev. Jacob R., Fall River, Mass.
Scott, John, Bridgeport, Ct.
Scribner, Samuel T., New York.
Scribner, Mrs. Maria, New York.
Seabrook, Mrs. Anna, Middletown, N. J.
Seaich, Joseph, Jr., New York.
Seaich, Mrs. Ellen, New York.
Seage, Rev. John, Port Richmond, N. Y.
Sears, Miss Harriet H., Orange, N. J.
Seaver, Rev. Horace, Chelsea, Mass.
See, Mrs. Sarah Ann, New York.
Seecomb, E. R., Brookline, Mass.
Seecomb, Mrs. Adeline G., Brookline, Mass.
Sedwick, Rev. W., Adamsville, Ohio.
Seeley, Mrs. John T., Dundee, N. Y.
Seeley, Rev. Jesse N., Atlanta, Geo.
Seeley, Mrs. Agnes Jane, Atlanta, Geo.
[redacted]

Sherwood, Mrs. Lydia, Weston, Ct.
Sherwood, Rev. D. W., Mattewan, N. Y.
Showalter, J. B., Willistown, Pa.
Shuck, Rev. J. L., California.
Sibell, Mrs. Sarah, New York.
Sibell, Mrs. J. William, New York.
Sibley, Rev. Clark, New Hampton, N. H.
Silkworth, Samuel O., New York.
Silliman, Ezra, Bridgeport, Ct.
Silliman, Mrs. Ezra, Bridgeport, Ct.
Silliman, Ebenezer, Southport, Ct.
Silliman, Rev. Gershom, Helena, Ill.
Silliman, Nathaniel L., Easton, Ct.
Silliman, Rev. Harvey, Harmony, N. Y.
Silliman, Stephen, Bridgeport, Ct.
Silliman, Samuel, Fairfield, Ct.
Sims, Maurice P., Canton, N. J.
Simmons, Miss Eliza, Reading, Pa.
Simmons, Mrs. Mary Eliza, Providence.
Simmons, Miss Henrietta A., Providence.
Simpson, Joseph P., New York.
Sistare, Mrs. Abby, New London, Ct.
Skelding, A. Eugene, Greenwich, Ct.
Skinner, E. R., Hertford, N. C.
Skinner, Charles W., Hertford, N. C.
Skinner, Mrs. Anna, Hertford, N. C.
Skinner, H. P., Hudson, N. Y.
Skinner, Mrs. Phebe B., Hudson, N. Y.
Skinner, Rev. H. C., Logansport, Ia.
Slack, Thomas, Brooklyn.
Slade, Zaccheus, Newbern, N. C.
Slater, Mrs. S. J., Providence.
Slater, Rev. Franklin A., New Rochelle, N. Y.
Slater, Mrs. Sophrania E. H., do
Slaughter, James M., Baltimore.
Sleeper, Rev. George, Canton, N. J.
Slote, Henry L., New York.
Smalley, George C., New York.
Smalley, Henry, New Brunswick, N. J.
Smith, Rev. Francis, Providence.
Smith, Mrs. M. G., Providence.
Smith, Charles A., Providence.
Smith, Asa F., New England Village, Mass.
Smith, Mrs. B. S. W., New Eng. Village, Mass.
Smith, Rev. Harry, East Aurora, N. Y.
Smith, Mrs. Lydia W., East Aurora, N. Y.
Smith, Samuel, Salem, N. J.
Smith, Mrs. Sarah B., Salem, N. J.
Smith, Miss Ruth Ann, New York.
Smith, Mrs. William H., Brooklyn.
Smith, Mordecai, Brooklyn.
Smith, John H., Brooklyn.
Smith, Henry W., Brooklyn.
Smith, Augustus, Brooklyn.
Smith, Mrs. Mary B., Brooklyn.
Smith, William, Winsboro', S. C.
Smith, Jonathan, New London, Ct.
Smith, Rev. Alexander, Skaneateles, N. Y.
Smith, Mrs. Priscilla B., Clarkson, Va.
Smith, Mrs Sally, Hancock, Mass.
Smith, Mrs. Mary E., Christianville, Va.
Smith, Rev. Joseph, Grafton, Mass.
Smith, Mrs. Abigail M., Grafton, Mass.
Smith, Mrs. S. L., Fayetteville, N. C.
Smith, Hamilton E., Fowlerville, N. Y.
Smith, Rev. Samuel, New York.
Smith, Alva, York, N. Y.
Smith, George H., Branchport, N. Y.
Smith, Wm., Port Rowan, Canada West.
Smith, Rev. C., Billings, New York.
Smith, John H., New York.
Smith, William W., Broadalbin, N. Y.
Smith, Rev. Andrew M., Hartford, Ct.
Smith, Rev. Justin A., Chicago, Ill.
Smith, Rev. William A., Groton, Ct.
Smith, Rev. Isaac, East Stoughton, Mass.
Smith, Rev. J. T., Bristol, Ct.
Smith, Rev. Eli B., Fairfax, Vt.
Smith, Adam, Brooklyn.
Smith, Rev. N. W., Hydeville, Vt.
Smith, Ebenezer, East Tisbury, Mass.
Smith, Mrs. Sarah A., East Tisbury, Mass.
Smith, Rev. Dexter P., Iowa City, Iowa.
Smith, Gilbert D., New York.
Smith, Daniel, Worcester, Mass.
Smith, Rev. Lewis, Santa Fé, N. M.
Smith, Jonathan, New York.
Smith, Rev. Rufus, Brookline, Vt.
Smith, Jesse H., New England Village, Mass.
Smith, Mrs. Mary White, Newton, Mass.
Smith, Mrs. Jane, Troy, N. Y.
Smith, Lucius E., Boston, Mass.
Snelling, Miss Priscilla, Snelling, Mass.
Sniffin, Mrs. Sarah Ann, New York.
Snowden, Mrs. Eliza, New York.
Snow, Mrs. Abba S., Rehoboth, Mass.
Snow, Edwin M., Providence.
Souders, Mrs. Catharine B. L., Fraser's, Pa.
Sommers, Mrs. Eliza B., New York.
Southwick, Mrs. Cynthia, Grand de Tour, Ill.
Southwick, George, Kingston, N. Y.
Southwood, Rev. William, Ayletts, Va.
Southworth, James E., Brooklyn.
Southworth, Mrs. James E., Brooklyn.
Southworth, John, Penfield, N. Y.
Sowers, Mrs. Mary E., Battletown, Va.
Sowers, Mrs Elizabeth, Milwood, Va.
Sparks, Rev. Peter, Newark, N. J.
Spaulding, Isaiah, Chelmsford, Mass.
Spaulding, Daniel B., Stoningtonboro', Ct.
Spaulding, Rev. Silas, Clockville, N. Y.
Spaulding, Rev. Amos F., Boston.
Spaulding, Mrs. Carrie E., E. Cambridge, Mass.
Spaulding, D. A., St. Louis, Mo.
Spear, Rev. Prof. P. B., Hamilton, N. Y.
Speer, Abraham, Jeddo, N. Y.
Speir, John, Brooklyn.
Speir, Mrs. Elizabeth, Brooklyn.
Speir, Miss Susan B., Brooklyn.
Spencer, D., Brooklyn.
Spencer, Robert Little, Plymouth, Va.
Spencer, Rev. Horace, Reed's Corners, N. Y.
Spencer, Elijah, Moodus, Ct.
Sperry, Marquis T., Jordan, N. Y.
Spink, Nicholas N., Wickford, R. I.
Spinning, Rev. Oscar F., Northville, N. Y.
Spinning, Mrs Clara O., Northville, N. Y.
Spivey, Aaron J., Brownsville, Tenn.
Sprague, Rev. Oliver L., Mt. Morris, N. Y.
Sproul, Rev. Samuel, Princeton, N. J.
Squires, Rev. James, East Troy, Wis.
Stahel, Caspar, Zurich, Switzerland.

MEMBERS FOR LIFE.

Stainburn, Miss Mary, New York.
Staples, John, Stratfield, Ct.
Stark, Rev. J. F., Cincinnatus, N. Y.
Stark, Mrs. Delight, Fort Covington, N. Y.
Starkweather, Rev. John W., Charleston, N. Y.
Stead, Thomas, Plainfield, N. J.
Steadman, Rev. N. V., Evansville, Ia.
Steadman, Mrs Laura J., Evansville, Ia.
Steane, Mrs. Catharine E., Williamsburgh, N. Y.
Stearns, Miss Catharine, Brookline, Mass.
Stearns, Rev. Myron N., Oregon Ter.
Stearns, Mrs. Dorcas R., Oregon Ter.
Stearns, Rev O. O., Thomaston, Me.
Stearns, Rev. Oakman S., Newark, N. J.
Stearns, Mrs. Hannah Jane, Newark, N. J.
Steele, Mrs Mehitable, Haverhill, Mass.
Stelle, Rev. Bergen, New Brunswick, N. J.
Stelle, Rev. Lewis, Old Bridge, N. J.
Stelle, Isaac, New Brunswick, N. J.
Stelle, Benjamin, Jerseyville, Ill.
Stelle, Lewis R , Paterson, N. J.
Stelle, Augustus, New Brunswick, N. J.
Steelman, Henry, Hamilton, N. Y.
Stevens, Mrs. Mariette, Deep River, Ct.
Stevens, Samson, Westford, Mass.
Stevens, Miss Phebe Almy, Providence.
Stevens, Seriah, Boston.
Stevens, B H., Essex, Ct.
Stevens, Thomas, Saratoga Springs, N. Y.

Strickland, James L., New London, Ct.
Strong, Myron, Rochester, N. Y.
Stewart, Benjamin N., Lowell, Mass.
Story, Harriet M., Norwich, Ct.
Story, Eunice M., Worcester, Mass.
Story, Clara, Worcester, Mass.
Story, Eunice H., Worcester, Mass.
Sturges, Rev. William, Marlborough, N. Y.
Sulley, James, Canton, Ill.
Sully, Mrs. Ann, Canton, Ill.
Summers, Mrs. Aaron, Bridgeport, Ct.
Sumner, George O., New Haven, Ct.
Sunderlin, Eli, Tyrone, N. Y.
Sunderlin, Rev. Alonzo W., Dundee, N. Y.
Sunderlin, Horace, Sennett, N. Y.
Sunderlin, Mrs. Margaret, Sennett, N. Y.
Sunderlin, Daniel W., Wayne, N. Y.
Sutton, George, New York.
Sutton, Mrs. Elizabeth, Britton's X Roads N. C.
Sutton, Mrs. Mary Ann, New York.
Swaim, Hon. Thomas, Pemberton, N. J.
Swaim, Mrs. Mary, Pemberton, N. J.
Swaim, Rev. T., Flemington, N. J.
Swaim, Mrs. Eliza M., Flemington, N. J.
Swaim, Rev. A. M., Leominster, Mass.
Swaim, Samuel N., Worcester, Mass.
Swaim, Mrs. Aurora D., Worcester, Mass.
Swaim, Rev. P. M., Rockville, Ia.
Swain, Joshua, Dennis Creek, N. J.
Swan, Mrs. Laura, New London, Ct.

[redacted]

Taylor, Mrs. Dimis, York, N. Y.
Taylor, Rev. Thomas R., Camden, N. J.
Taylor, Rev. Alfred H., Mansfield Centre, Ct.
Taylor, Rev. Thomas, Jacksonville, Ill.
Taylor, Rev. David, Terre Haute, Ia.
Taylor, Samuel W., E. Cambridge, Mass.
Taylor, Daniel Webster, New York.
Taylor, Rev. O. D., Perrington, N. Y.
Taylor, Henry C., Granville, Ohio.
Taylor, Mrs. Adelia P., Albion, Mich.
Teasdale, Rev. John, Upper Alton, Ill.
Tefft, Willard, Union Village, N. Y.
Temple, James H., Chillicothe, Ill.
Terry, Mrs. A. N., Spring Garden, Va.
Thatcher, Mrs. Elizabeth R.
Thayer, Thomas M., Gouverneur, N. Y.
Thayer, Lewis, Worcester, Mass.
Thayer, James H., Cambridge, Mass.
Theall, Mrs. Jane, New York.
Theall, Miss Susan, New York.
Thigpen, Rev. Samuel, Raymond, Mi.
Thistle, Mrs. Hannah, New York.
Thomas, Thomas, New York.
Thomas, Thomas, Architect, New York.
Thomas, Mrs. Isabella, New York.
Thomas, Moses, Ballston Spa, N. Y.
Thomas, James H., New York.
Thomas, Rev. David E., Zanesville, Ohio.
Thomas, Griffith, New York.
Thomas, Rev. C. A., Brandon, Vt.
Thomas, Mrs. Eliza Ann, New York.
Thomas, Mrs. Mary, Brooklyn.
Thomas, Mrs. Almira S., Brandon, Vt.
Thompson, Robert, Jr., New York.
Thompson, Mrs. Ann E., New York.
Thompson, Mrs. S. S., Pittsborough, N. C.
Thompson, Rev. Richard, Poughwade, N. Y.
Thompson, Rev. Charles, Iowa City, Iowa.
Thompson, L., Britton's X Roads, N. C.
Thompson, Benjamin M., Harlem, N. Y.
Thompson, Rev. Sherman B., East Otto, N. Y.
Thompson, Mrs. Serena, New York.
Thornton, Rev. V. R., Public Square, Ga.
Thurston, Henry, Brooklyn.
Thurber, Edmund, Providence.
Thurber, Gorham, Providence.
Thurber, Charles, Worcester, Mass.
Ticknor, William D., Boston.
Tiebout, Adam T., Brooklyn.
Tiebout, Mrs. Jane, Brooklyn.
Tilden, Rev. Chester, North Lyme, Ct.
Tilley, Mrs. Elizabeth S., New York.
Tillinghast, Jefferson, Norway, N. Y.
Tillinghast, Charles E., Providence.
Tilton, Rev. Josiah H., Lynn, Mass.
Tindall, Samuel L., Wilmington, Del.
Tinkham, Rev. D., Centre White Creek, N. Y.
Titchener, Henry, Binghamton, N. Y.
Titus, F. J., Middletown, Ohio.
Titus, Rev. S. W., Gorham, N. Y.
Tobey, Rev. Zalmon, Patuxet, R. I.
Todd, Rev. William, Stevensville, Va.
Todd, Drake P., New York.
Todd, William W., New York.
Todd, Mrs. William W., New York.
Todd, Mrs. Angeline M., New York.
Tolan, Rev. Wm. B., Rahway, N. J.
Tolman, Rev. John N., Upper Alton, Ill.
Tolman, Thomas, Philadelphia.
Tolman, Mrs. Mary, Philadelphia.
Tolman, Miss Martha, Boston.
Toplif, Rev. C. H. Charlestown, Mass.
Torbet, Rev. Andrew M., Canton, Ohio.
Torian, Elijah, Halifax C. H., Va.
Tourtellot, Abraham, Nashua, N. H.
Tousley, Charles, New York.
Townsend, S. P., New York.
Townsend, Miss Naomi, New York.
Townsend, Rev. G. N., Reading, Mass.
Townsend, Mrs. Louisa L., Brooklyn.
Townsend, Rev. B. C., Manchester, N. Y.
Tracy, Lucius H., New London, Ct.
Tracy, Rev. Oren, Concord, N. H.
Tracy, Mrs. Marcia B., Concord, N. H.
Tracy, Miss Susan M., Concord, N. H.
Train, Mrs. A. S., Haverhill, Mass.
Travis, Simeon S., New York.
Travis, Luther, Southbridge, Mass.
Trevor, John B., Philadelphia.
Tripp, Mrs. Susan, New Bedford, Ms.
Tripp, Erwin H., New York.
Tripp, Miss Sarah, New York.
Trout, Wm., Charleston, S. C.
Trow, Rev. Augustus H., Montezuma, N. Y.
Trowbridge, Wm., Sheboygan Falls, Wis.
True, Reuben, Plainfield, N. H.
True, Osgood, Plainfield, N. H.
True, Mrs. Betsey M., Plainfield, N. H.
True, Mrs. Hannah, Meriden, N. H.
Truman, Stephen S., Owego, N. Y.
Truman, Mrs. Betsey S., Owego, N. Y.
Truman, Mrs. Eleanor M., Owego, N. Y.
Trueman, Edward D., Owego, N. Y.
Tryon, Elijah, Westhaven, Vt.
Tubbs, Benjamin H. W., Dedham, Mass.
Tucker, Harwood B., Christianville, Va.
Tucker, Richard G., Stony Creek, Va.
Tucker, Rev. Silas, Napierville, Ill.
Tucker, Mrs. F. G., Stony Creek, Va.
Tucker, Mrs. Elisha, Chicago, Ill.
Tucker, James N. G., Chicago, Ill.
Tucker, Frederick D., Williamsburgh, N. Y.
Tucker, Elisha, Middleborough, Mass.
Tucker, Mrs. Sally B.
Tucker, Rev. Cyrus T., North Marshfield, Mass.
Tuly, M. F., Albuquerque, N. M.
Turley, Capt. E., Philadelphia.
Turnbull, Rev. Robert, D.D., Hartford, Ct.
Turner, Peter C., New London, Ct.
Turner, Gabriel S., Newark, N. J.
Turney, Rev. Edmund, Cincinnati.
Turney, Mrs. Caroline, Cincinnati.
Turney, J. P., Norwalk, Ct.
Turpin, Rev. John O., Aylett's, Va.
Turton, Rev. Wm. H., Farmington, Iowa.
Tustin, Rev. Josiah P., Savannah, Ga.
Tustin, John D., Camden, N. J.
Tuthill, Joseph, Brooklyn.
Tuttle, Aaron, Littleton, Mass.
Tuxbury, Isaac, Salisbury Mills, Mass.

MEMBERS FOR LIFE.

Twiss, Rev. Daniel F., Spotswood, N. J.
Tyler, Roswell R., Middlesex, N. Y.
Tyler, Mrs. Lucy, Deep River, Ct.
Ulyat, Rev. Wm. C., Norwalk, Ct.
Underhill, Rev Charles H., Peekskill, N. Y.
Underhill, P. S., Brooklyn.
Underhill, Mrs. Catharine M., Brooklyn, N. Y.
Van Arsdale, Dr. Henry, New York.
Van Deboe, Adam, Claverack, N. Y.
Van De Werken, E., New York.
Van De Werken, Mrs. Janet, New York.
Van Derlip, George M., New York.
Van Derlip, Mrs. Grace, New York.
Van Dusen Wm., Albion, N. Y.
Vanderveer, Mrs. Ann, Moorestown, N. J.
Vail, J. E., Brooklyn.
Valentine, Rev. Andrew M., W. Henrietta, N.Y.
Valentine, Elijah F., Cambridge, Mass.
Van Horn, Hon James, Newfane, N. Y.
Vanness, Cristian, New York.
Vanest, Abraham, Hightstown, N. J.
Van Marter, John, Brooklyn.
Van Marter, Mrs. Mary, E. Brooklyn.
Van, Samuel A., New Haven, Ct.
Van Sant, T. J., Williamsburgh, N. Y.
Van Valkenburgh, John, Williamsburgh, N. Y.
Vassar, Matthew, Poughkeepsie, N. Y.
Veasey, Benjamin, Brentwood, N. H.
Vernon, Samuel, Brooklyn.
[redacted]

Walker, William, Clinton, Mass.
Walker, Rev. O. B., Brookline, Me.
Walker, Amos, Pontiac, Mich.
Wallace, Miss Eliza, Brooklyn.
Wallace, Jonathan, Fort Covington, N. Y.
Walters, Jacob, Wilmington, Del.
Walton, Joel, Va.
Walton, Jesse, Augusta, Ga.
Walton, Rev. L., Chestnut Hill, Pa.
Ward, Uzal D., New York.
Ward, Willard, Worcester, Mass.
Wardner, Rev. Chauncey, Covert, N. Y.
Wardner, Mrs. Margaret A., Covert, N. Y.
Ware, Dr. R. J., Montgomery co., Ala.
Warn, Mrs. Sarah M., Sennett, N. Y.
Warn, Mrs. Mary, Sennett, N. Y.
Warner, Dr. Ransom, New York.
Warnock, Miss Elizabeth, New York.
Warren, Mrs. Diantha O., West Potsdam, N.
Warren, Rev. Patrick, Baltimore.
Warren, Rev. Benj., Ransomville, N. Y.
Warren, Rev. J. G., Troy, N. Y.
Warren, Rev. Edwin R., Thompson, Ct.
Warren, Benjamin L., Williamsburgh, N. Y.
Warren, Moses, Cambridge, Mass.
Warren, Mrs. Grace, Cambridge, Mass.
Warren, Rev. H. S. P., Madrid, N. Y.
Warriner, Rev. Norman, Harding, Ill.
Warriner, Rev. R. L., Preston, N. Y.
[redacted]

Weld, Mrs. Lucy, New York.
Weld, Aaron D., Winchester, Mass.
Welden, Asa W., New York.
Wells, Mrs. Elizabeth, New York.
Wells, Rev. Alfred, Vernon, N. Y.
Wells, Rev. Wm. A., Muscatine, Iowa.
Wemple, Abraham A., Schenectady, N. Y.
West, John, Brooklyn.
West, Mrs. Ann, Brooklyn.
West, John G., Williamsburgh, N. Y.
West, Willoughby W., York, N. Y.
West, Rev. Hezekiah, Mecklenburg, N. Y.
Weston, Rev. Henry G., Peoria, Ill.
Weston, Mrs. Henry G. Peoria, Ill.
Weston, Mrs. Hetty, Lynn, Mass.
Weston, Franklin L., Johnson's Creek, N. Y.
Wescott, Rev. Isaac, New-York.
Wescott, Jehiel, Bridgeton, N. J.
Wescott, Jehiel, Jr., Bridgeton, N. J.
Wescott, Josiah, S. Bridgeton, N. J.
Westervelt, John, Williamsburgh, N. Y.
Westover, Rev. John T., Kenosha, Wis.
Wetherbee, Ephraim, Broadalbin, N. Y.
Wetherbee, Miss Ruby, Broadalbin, N. Y.
Wethern, George M., Lowell, Mass.
Wetteran, Mrs. Frances, New York.
Wheadon, C. H., Homer, N. Y.
Wheat, Mrs. Priscilla P., Philadelphia.
Wheaton, Reuben, Wilmington, Del.
Wheelock, Mrs. E. M., Elbridge, N. Y.
Wheelock, S. B., Greenwich, N. Y.
Wheeler, Mrs. Elizabeth H., Sacramento, Cal.
Wheeler, Miss Melvina P., Sacramento, Cal.
Wheeler, Rev. Benjamin, Plaistow, N. H.
Wheeler, Nelson, Providence.
Wheeler, Lucius, New York.
Wheeler, Rev. S. S., New York.
Wheeler, Mrs. Mary B., New York.
Wheeler, Rev. Benjamin, Randolph, Mass.
Wheeler, Russell, Utica, N. Y.
Wheeler, Mrs. Ann, New York.
Whidden, Mrs. Sarah, Calais, Me.
Whilden, Rev. B. W., Camden, S. C.
Whipple, Henry, Malone, N. Y.
Whitaker, Alanson, Granville, Ill.
Whitaker, Wilson N., Philadelphia.
White, Rev. Samuel, North Shore, N. Y.
White, Mrs. E., North Shore, N. Y.
White, Mrs. Martha D., Marcus Hook, Pa.
White, Miss Lydia, Haverhill, Mass.
White, Thomas, Brooklyn.
White, Samuel S., Whiteville, N. Y.
White, Harvey, Mount Holly, Vt.
White, Thomas P., Bridgeport, Ct.
White, Mrs. Thomas P., Bridgeport, Ct.
White, Joseph, Winchendon, Mass.
White, Beza L., Taunton, Mass.
White, Ebenezer, Newton, Mass.
White, Ebenezer B., Williamsburgh, N. Y.
White, Mrs. Mary, New York.
White, Samuel, Bordentown, N. J.
White, Mrs. Sylvanus, Brooklyn.
White, Samuel, Littleton, Mass.
White, Mrs. Mary, New York.

Whitehead, Samuel, New Brunswick, N. J.
Whitehead, Mrs. Emeline V., New York.
Whitehead, Artemas K., New York.
Whitehead, John W., New York
Whitehead, Linus P., New York.
Whittemore, Joseph, New York.
Whitford, H. G., Willington, Ct.
Whitman, Charles S., Belvidere, Ill.
Whitman, Hiram, Belvidere, Ill.
Whitman, Mrs. Matilda, Belvidere, Ill.
Whitman, Alva, Mich.
Whitman, John C., Sennett, N. Y.
Whitney, Miss Harriet, New York.
Whitney, Mrs. Betsey, Worcester, Mass.
Whitney, Bennet, Bridgeport, Ct.
Whittier, Leonard, Haverhill, Mass.
Whittier, Mrs. Leonard, Haverhill, Mass.
Whittier, Miss Abby, Haverhill, Mass.
Whitney, Raymond, North Fairfield, O.
Whitney, Mrs. E. S., Brooklyn.
Whitney, Eben, Newtown, N. Y.
Wiburg, Rev. Andreas, Philadelphia.
Wight, Leonard B., Wales, Mass.
Wightman, Rev. J. G., Groton, Ct.
Wightman, Stillman K., New York.
Wiggins, Rev. J. W. Farmerville, N. Y.
Wilbur, Rev. H. R., Mt. Pleasant, Iowa.
Wilbur, Mrs. Sally, East Avon, N. Y.
Wilbur, Curtis, Troy, N. Y.
Wilbur, Rev. O., Lowville, N. Y.
Wilcox, Rev. J. F., Springfield, Mass.
Wilcox, Mrs. Louisa S., Springfield, Mass.
Wilcox, Abraham, Shelburne Falls, Mass.
Wilder, John N., Albany.
Wilder, Mrs. Delia A., Albany.
Wilder, Rev. Sydney, North Norwich, N. Y.
Wilder, Rev. William, Doylstown, Pa.
Wilder, John, Pitcher, N. Y.
Wildman, Mrs. Roxey S., Lebanon, Ct.
Wildman, Daniel, Lebanon, Ct.
Wilkins, Rev. Stephen, New York.
Wilkins, Rev. Andrew, Tyrone, N. Y.
Wilkinson, Rev. Wm., Drummondville, C. W.
Willard, Rev. George A., Warwick Neck, R. I.
Willard, Lucius A., Providence.
Willard, Mrs. Polly, Pawlet, Vt.
Willard, Mrs. Nancy, Jonesborough, Ill.
Willard, Rev. C. M., Harvard, Mass.
Willard, Hon. Levi, Keene, N. H.
Willett, Miss Sarah, New York.
Willett, Mrs. Charles, Quinebaug, Ct.
Williams, Robert, Maquoketa, Iowa.
Williams, Mrs. Elizabeth S., Fayetteville, N. C.
Williams, Mrs. Charity S., Fayetteville, N. C.
Williams, Mrs. Mary M., Fayetteville, N. C.
Williams, Polly M., Rockport, Ohio.
Williams, Francis B., New York.
Williams, Rev. David S., Cumberland, N. C.
Williams, Rev. Wm. B., Williamsville, N. Y.
Williams, Mrs. Eunice, Deep River, Ct.
Williams, Rev. John, Princeton, N. Y.
Williams, Rev. C. C., Plainfield, N. J.
Williams, Mrs. Maruna, Plainfield, N. J.

MEMBERS FOR LIFE.

Williams, Rev. D. S., Plymouth, N. Y.
Williams, Mrs. William R., New York.
Williams, W. S., Hartford, Ct.
Willingham, Thomas, Lawtonville, S. C.
Willington, Miss Catherine, Watertown, Mass.
Willis, Rev. Samuel B., Pine Plains, N. Y.
Wilson, Mrs. Catherine, New York.
Wilson, Miss Sarah E., New York.
Wilson, Mrs. Frances N., Catskill, N. Y.
Wilson, Isaac D., Society Hill, S. C.
Wilson, Clement A., Philadelphia.
Wilson, Rev. Chas. E., Holmdel, N. J.
Wilson, Mrs. Theresa, Holmdel, N. J.
Wilson, Rev. Adam, Hebron, Maine.
Wilson, Rev. W. V., Keyport, N. J.
Wilson, Jeremiah V. F., Hoboken, N. J.
Wilson, Rev. Robert J., Stoningtonboro', Ct.
Wilson, Mrs. Grace, Stoningtonboro', Ct.
Wilson, George W., Chelsea, Mass.
Wingate, Mary, Haverhill, Mass.
Wingate, Dexter B., Grafton, Mass.
Winans, Elnathan, Lima, N. Y.
Winans, Mrs. Marcy, Lima, N. Y.
Winans, Theodore, Plainfield, N. J.
Winchell, Miss Ann, New York.
Windust, Edward, New York.
Winslow, Robert F., Fond du Lac, Wis.
Winslow, Rev. Octavius, Leamington, Eng.

Wood, Ambrose, Albion, N. Y.
Woodbridge, William A., New-York.
Woodbury, William W., Suffield, Ct.
Woodbury, Rev. John, Templeton, Mass.
Woodruff, Mrs. [illegible], Albany.
Woodruff, David, Bridgeton, N. J.
Woodward, Rev. James, Parma, N. Y.
Woodward, Mrs. Eliza, Parma, N. Y.
Woodward, Mrs. Mary D., Middlebury, Vt.
Woodward, Sylvester, Lowell, Mass.
Woodward, Darwin W., Frankfort, N. Y.
Woolsey, Rev. James J., Norwalk, Ct.
Wooster, Mrs. Amelia E., Deep River, Ct.
Worth, Rev. Edmund, Gloversville, N. Y.
Worthington, G., Springfield, Mass.
Wright, Rev. David, Hartford, Ct.
Wright, Mrs. Abigail, Hartford, Ct.
Wright, William A., Clarksville, Va.
Wright, Theodore, New Haven, Ct.
Wright, Asahel B., Lowell, Mass.
Wright, Harvey, Three Rivers, Mass.
Wright, Rev. Thomas G., Newark, N. J.
Wright, Mrs. Julia A., Newark, N. J.
Wright, Rev. Amasa T., [illegible], N. Y.
Wright, Rev. Lyman, Fayetteville, N. Y.
Wright, R. A., Rochester, N. Y.
Wyckoff, Rev. Cornelius P., Weedsport, N. Y.
Wyckoff, Mrs. Cornelius P., Weedsport, N. Y.

LIST OF DECEASED

DIRECTORS AND MEMBERS FOR LIFE.

1833-4.

DIRECTOR.

Cobb, Nathaniel R., Boston, Mass.

MEMBERS.

Barrett, Rev. Thomas, Webster, Mass.
Chase, Rev. John, Brookfield, Mass.

1834-5.

MEMBER.

Lazell, Rev. J. E., Harvard, Mass.

1835-6.

DIRECTORS.

Foster, Rev. E., Amesbury, Mass.
Freeman, Rev. E. W., Lowell, Mass.
Jacobs, Rev. Bela, Cambridge, Mass.

MEMBER.

Martin, Rev. A. R., Staten Island, N. Y.

1836-7.

DIRECTOR.

Trask, Rev. Wm. G., Taunton, Mass.

1837-8.

DIRECTOR.

Davis, Rev. Gustavus F., Hartford, Ct.

MEMBERS.

Blain, Miss Mary E., Syracuse, N. Y.
Holroyd, Rev. John, Danvers, Mass.
Kitts, Rev. T. J., Philadelphia.
Ludlow, Rev. Peter, New York.
Starkweather, Oliver, Pawtucket, R. I.

1838-9.

DIRECTORS.

Crawford, Rev. Luther, Brooklyn, N. Y.
Knowles, Rev. James D., Newton, Mass.

MEMBERS.

Banner, Rev. Job B , Sutton, Mass.
Smalley, Rev. Henry, Cohansey, N. J.
Vaughn, Rev. Ashley, Natchez, Miss.

1839-40.

DIRECTOR.

Bolles, Rev. Matthew, D.D., Boston.

MEMBERS.

Blain, Mrs. Lucy, Syracuse, N. Y.
Hubbell, Rev. Elisha D., Clifton Park, N. Y.
Sheppard, Rev. Joseph, Mount Holly, N. J.

1840-1.

DIRECTORS.

Cheesman, Rev. Daniel, Lynn, Mass.
Hammond, Rev. O. T., Florida.
Shute, Rev. Caleb B., Boston.

MEMBERS.

Chaplain, Rev. J., Hamilton, N. Y.
Dodge, Rev. O. A., Lexington, Mass.
Hunting, Mrs. Dorcas, Corinth, Me.
McAllister, Charles, Fayetteville, N. C.
Nourse, Rev. Peter, Ellsworth, Me.
Stearns, Rev. Silas, Bath, Me.
Williams, Elizabeth, Society Hill, S. C.
Williams, A., Elizabeth City, N. C.

1841-2.

DIRECTOR.

Brown, Nicholas, Providence, R. I.

MEMBERS.

Colgate, John, New York.
Eaton, Martin, Petersburg, Va.
Hill, Frederick M., New York.
Leonard, Rev. Zenas L., Sturbridge, Mass.
Lipscomb, Mrs. Martha, Louisa C. H., Va.
Mercer, Rev. Jesse, Washington, Ga.
Miles, Joseph, Milesburgh, Pa.

1842-3.

MEMBERS.

Colgate, George, New York.
Gear, Rev. Hiram, Marietta, Ohio.
Towell, Mrs. E. E., Sandy Bottom, Va.
Vanderpool, Hon. James, Newark, N. J.

1843-4.

DIRECTORS.

Cooper, Thomas, Eatonton, Geo.
Linsley, Rev. James H., Stratford, Ct.
Middleton, Rev. John, Geneva, N. Y.

MEMBERS.

Pickens, Mrs. Margaret Eliza, Edgefield, S. C.
Rankin, Henry, Reading, Pa.
Wasson, J. G., Albany, N. Y.

1844-5.

DIRECTORS.

Armstrong, Rev. John, Columbus, Miss.
Coolidge, James D., Madison, N Y.
Going, Rev. Jonathan, D.D., Granville, Ohio.
Miller, Rev. Wm. George, Essex, Ct.

DECEASED MEMBERS.

MEMBERS.

Adams, Mrs. Mary, New York.
Belden, Charles D., New York.
Birdsall, Rev. John O., Perrysburg, Ohio.
Carney, Richard, Portsmouth, Va.
McIntosh, Mrs. Mary, Philadelphia.

1845-6.

MEMBERS.

Cauldwell, Mrs. Maria, New York.
Hall, Rev. Wilson, Beaufort, S. C.
Jones, Mrs. J. Leavitt, Bankok, Siam.
Lathrop, Rev. Lebbeus, Samptown, N. J.
Marshall, Joseph H., Nashville, Tenn.
Mitchell, Rev. John, Hoosick, N. Y.
Randall, Mrs. Mary E., Woburn, Mass.
Reynolds, Joseph, Norwich, Ct.

1846-7.

DIRECTORS.

Bacheller, Mrs. Mary, Lynn, Mass.
Devan, Mrs. Lydia, Canton, China.
Everts, Rev. Jeremiah B., Washington, N. Y.

MEMBERS.

Cooper, Mrs. Eliza A., New York.
Lee, Mrs. Olive, North Bristol, N. Y.
Rose, Richard, Parham's Store, Va.
[illegible] Rev. Peter, New York.
[illegible]

Brockway, C., Broadalbin, N. Y.
Brown, Wm., Parham's Store, Va.
Cate, Rev. George W., Barre, Mass.
Corning, Mrs. Nancy, Brooklyn, N. Y.
Cox, Charles, Rahway, N. J.
Crawford, Rev. D. B., Antioch, Miss.
Forrester, James M., New York.
Gale, Mrs. Phebe, East Bennington, Vt.
Harris, Rev. Wm., Nassau, N. Y.
Lewis, Rev. D. D., New Brunswick, N. J.
Payne, Mrs. Betsy, Hamilton, N. Y.
Rodgers, Rev. John, Paterson, N. J.
Roy, Rev. Wm. A., Charlotteville, Va.
Winchell, Rev. Ruben, Lockport, N. Y.

1850-1.

DIRECTORS.

Granberry, Rev. N. R., Meridian Spring, N. Y.
Graves, Rev. Hiram A., Boston, Mass.
Judson, Rev. A., D.D., Maulmain, Burmah.

MEMBERS.

Bennett, Rev. Alfred, Homer, New York.
Briggs, Rev. Ebenezer, Middleboro', Mass.
Burdick, Miss E. M., New York.
Burke, Joshua A., Brooklyn, N. Y.
Cook, Rev B., Jr., Jewett City, Ct.
Cornelius, Mrs. Rachel, Mt. Holly, N. J.
Darrow, Rev. Francis, Waterford, Ct.
Frey, Rev. J. C. F., Pontiac, Mich.
Going, Mrs. Lucy T., Columbus, O.
Humphrey, Mrs. Julia Ann, Albany, N. Y.
[illegible] Rev. Timothy, Piqua, O.
[illegible] New York.

Manning, Rev. Benjamin, Brookfield, Mass.
Martin, Mrs. R. W., New York.
Remington, Mrs. Eliza Ann, New York.
Rider, Miss Olive P., Suffield, Ct.
Shuck, Mrs. Eliza G., Shanghai, China.
Stone, Mrs. Sarah A., New-York.
Tucker, Mrs. Levi, Boston, Mass.
Whitman, Rev. S. S., Madison, Wis.

1852-3.

DIRECTORS.

Brown, Rev. O. B., Washington, D. C.
Crozer, Miss Sallie K., Chester, Pa.
Miller, Pardon, Providence.
Rhees, Rev. Morgan J., D. D., Williamsb'h, N. Y.

MEMBERS.

Adams, Mrs. Cornelia C., Cleveland, Ohio.
Ashley, Mrs. Hannah, Poultney, Vt.
Bellamy, Mrs. Eliza, Arcadia, N. Y.
Boynton, Mrs. Ruth, North Springfield, Vt.
Cosner, Rev Henry, Lyndon, Ill.
Fant, Rev. Ephraim, Halselville, S. C.
Goodliff, James, New York.
Haskell, Rev. Daniel, Hamilton, N. Y.
Haynes, Rev. Arus, M.D., New York.
Jones, Rev. John, Belleville, Ia.
Maghee, Mrs. Ann C., New York.
Maginnis, Rev. John, D D., Rochester, N. Y.
Miner, Mrs. Mary Jane, New York.
Owen, Rev. E. D., Madison, Ia.
Shipley, Simon G., Boston.
Symonds, Rev. Thomas M., Green Bay, Wis.
Turner, Mrs. Grace, New London, Ct.
Weeks, Miss Ann, New York.
Wise, Miss Harriet W., New Russia, N. Y.
Wolcott, Epaphroditus, Rochester, N. Y.
Woodruff, Rev. Seth, New Albany, Ia.

1853-4.

DIRECTORS.

Brayton, Philip F., Providence.
Sharp, Rev. Daniel, D.D , Boston.
Tucker, Rev. Levi, D.D., Boston.
Tucker, Rev. Elisha, D.D., Chicago, Ill.
Whiting, Miss Martha, Charlestown, Mass.
Washington, Col. J. M., Portsmouth, N. H.

MEMBERS.

Bleecker, Garrat N., New York.
Brabrook, Rev. B. F. Davenport, Iowa.
Burr, James T., Columbus, Ohio.
Bliss, Erastus L., North Adams, Mass.
Ball, Rev. Eli, Richmond, Va.
Biddle, Rev. Wm. P., Newbern, N. C.
Day, John, New York.
Fay, Rev. Eliphas. Poughkeepsie, N. Y.
Griffith, Mrs. Thomas S., Milwaukee, Wis.
Guild, Rev. J. R., East Thompson, Ct.
Haviland, William C., New York.
Hurlburt, Rev. Elias, Essex N. Y.
Humphrey, Hon. Friend, Albany, N. Y.
Moore, Mrs. Alvenah B., Marshall, Mich.
Newton, Prof Calvin, Worcester, Mass.
Nesbit, Mrs. Mary C. S., Burmah.
Palmer, Rev William, Norwich, Ct.
Pegg, Roger, New York.
Paddock, Mrs. Martha, Middletown, Ct.
Rue, Mrs. Emily, Scotch Plains, N J.
Shotwell, Rev. S. R., Whitesboro', N. Y.
Sheppard, Joseph, Bridgeton, N. J.
Ulyat, William, New York.
Whitney, Mrs. Emeline, Norwalk, Ct.

CONTENTS.

ANNUAL REPORT.

[redacted]

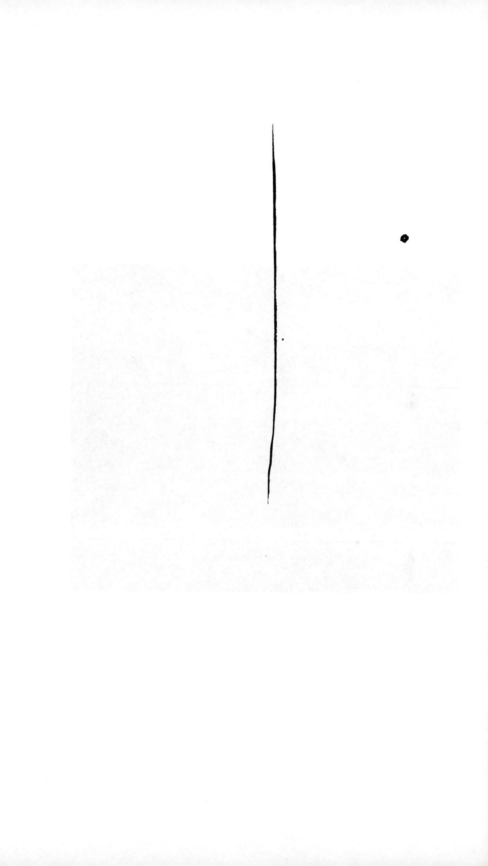

[redacted]

TWENTY-THIRD REPORT

OF THE

AMERICAN BAPTIST HOME MISSION SOCIETY,

PRESENTED BY THE

EXECUTIVE BOARD

AT THE

ANNIVERSARY HELD IN BROOKLYN,

MAY 9th, 1855,

WITH

THE TREASURER'S REPORT AND OTHER DOCUMENTS.

New York:

PUBLISHED AT THE AMERICAN BAPTIST HOME MISSION ROOMS, No. 115 NASSAU ST.

HOLMAN & GRAY, PRINTERS, COR. CENTRE AND WHITE STS.

1855.

ACT OF INCORPORATION.

AN ACT TO INCORPORATE THE AMERICAN BAPTIST HOME MISSION SOCIETY, PASSED APRIL 12, 1843, AND AMENDED FEBRUARY 9, 1849.

The People of the State of New York, represented in Senate and Assembly, do enact as follows:

§ 1. All such persons as now are, or may hereafter become members of the American Baptist Home Mission Society, formed in the City of New York, in the year One Thousand Eight Hundred and Thirty-two, shall be, and hereby are, constituted a body corporate, by the name of the American Baptist Home Mission Society, for the purpose of promoting the preaching of the Gospel in North America.

[redacted]

CONSTITUTION.

NAME.

I. THIS Society shall be called the AMERICAN BAPTIST HOME MISSION SOCIETY.

OBJECT.

II. The object of this Society shall be to promote the preaching of the Gospel in North America.

MEMBERSHIP.

III. The Society shall be composed of Annual Delegates, Life Members and Life Directors. Any Baptist church, in union with the denomination, may appoint a delegate for an annual contribution of ten dollars, and an additional delegate for each additional thirty dollars. Thirty dollars shall be requisite to constitute a member for life; and one hundred dollars paid at one time, or a sum which, in addition to any previous contribution, shall amount to one hundred dollars, shall be requisite to constitute a director for life.

OFFICERS.

IV. The officers of the Society shall be a President, two Vice Presidents, a Treasurer, an Auditor, a Corresponding Secretary, a Financial Secretary, and a Recording Secretary, whom the Society shall annually elect by ballot.

MANAGERS AND EXECUTIVE BOARD.

V. The Officers and Life Directors shall meet immediately after the Annual Meeting of the Society, and elect fifteen Managers, residing in the city of New York, or its vicinity, who, together with the Treasurer, Auditor, and the Secretaries, shall constitute an Executive Board to conduct the business of the Society; and shall respectively continue to discharge their official duties until superseded by a new election. Seven members of the Board shall be a quorum for the transaction of business.

POWERS AND DUTIES OF THE EXECUTIVE BOARD.

VI. The Executive Board shall have power to appoint its own meetings; elect its own Chairman and Recording Secretary; enact its own By-Laws and Rules of Order, provided always, that they be not inconsistent with this Constitution; fill any vacancies which may occur in their own body or in the offices of the Society during the year; and, if deemed necessary by two-thirds of the members present at a regular meeting, convene special meetings of the Society. They shall establish such Agencies as the interests of the Society may require; appoint Agents and Missionaries; fix their compensation; direct and instruct them concerning their particular fields and labors; make all appropriations to be paid out of the treasury; and present to the Society, at each annual meeting, a full report of their proceedings during the current year.

DESIGNATED FUNDS.

VII. All moneys or other property contributed and designated for any particular Missionary field, shall be so appropriated, or returned to the donors, or their lawful agents.

TREASURER.

VIII. The Treasurer shall give bonds to such amount as the Executive Board shall think proper.

ELIGIBILITY TO APPOINTMENT

IX. All the Officers, Managers, Missionaries, and Agents of the Society, shall be members in good standing in regular Baptist churches.

ANNUAL MEETING.

X. The Society shall meet annually, at such time and place as the Executive Board shall appoint.

ALTERATIONS OF THE CONSTITUTION.

XI. No alteration of this Constitution shall be made without an affirmative vote of two-thirds of the members present at an annual meeting; nor unless the same shall have been proposed in writing, and the proposition sustained by a majority vote, at a previous annual meeting, or recommended by the Executive Board.

STATED MEETINGS FOR 1855-56.

OF THE EXECUTIVE BOARD—Thursday before the first Wednesday in each month.

" " Committee on MISSIONS—The day previous to that of the Board.

" " Committee on AGENCIES and FINANCE—The Tuesday preceding.

" " Committee on CHURCH EDIFICE FUND—The Monday preceding.

BY-LAWS OF THE BOARD.

1. All meetings shall be opened with prayer.
2. All Committees shall be nominated by the presiding officer, and approved by the Executive Board, unless otherwise specially ordered.
3. No moneys shall be paid out of the Treasury, but by order of the Executive Board.
4. All resolutions, if required, shall be presented in writing.

ORDER OF BUSINESS.

[redacted]

MINUTES OF THE TWENTY-THIRD ANNIVERSARY

OF THE

American Baptist Home Mission Society,

HELD IN BROOKLYN,

May 9th, 1855.

The Society met on Wednesday, the 9th of May, 1855, in the meeting house of the Pierrepont street Baptist Church, at 10 A.M.

The meeting was called to order by WM. COLGATE, Esq., Vice President, when, after a few appropriate remarks from the Chair, in reference to the importance of prayer for Divine wisdom and the spirit of Jesus, Rev. J. C. HARRISON, of Pennsylvania, led the assembly in an address to the Throne of Grace.

Letters were read from Hon. ISAAC DAVIS, LL.D., President of the Society, and THOS. ARMITAGE, D.D., Recording Secretary, stating that they would not be able to be present, and declining a re-election to their respective offices.

Bro. SAMUEL COLGATE, of New York, was appointed Recording Secretary *pro tem.*, and Rev. A. P. MASON, of Massachusetts, Assistant Sec'y.

At this point of the proceedings, Dea. COLGATE called on the Rev. D. C. EDDY, of Mass., to take the Chair, as, from his infirmities and years, he felt inadequate to its duties.

The Chair then announced the following Committees:

On Credentials of Delegates:

Rev. brethren C. M. FULLER, of N. Y., J. S. LADD, Ct., J. W. PARKHURST, Mass., C. A. CLARK, N. Y., and J. E. RUE, N. J.

On Nomination of Officers:

Rev. br'n. E. M. Barker, of N. J., M. M. Dean, R. I., L. A. Dunn, Vt., E. E. L. Taylor, N. Y., and W. Randolph, R. I.

Ministers and other brethren present, not members of the Society, having been invited to participate in its deliberations, the invitation was accepted by the following:

Revs. C. Page, of Pennsylvania; E. F. Gurney, Jordan, N. Y.; Thos. L. Davidson, Brandford C. W.; S. Ransted, Montrose, Pa.; S. M. Woodruff, Maline, N. Y.; Emerson Andrews, Philadelphia; John R. Chase, Portsmouth Ass., N. H. Messrs. M. M. Everts, Guilford, N. Y.; James Whittemore, N. Y.; and Dolphas Bennet, Utica, N. Y.

On motion of Rev. J. R. Stone, the time of commencing and closing the sessions of each day was fixed as follows:

To commence at 9½ A.M. and at 3 and 7½ P.M.; to adjourn at 1 and 5½ P.M.

On motion it was resolved to set apart the hour of 12 o'clock, M., for the election of Officers.

In the absence of C. J. Martin, Esq., the Treasurer, Rev. J. R. Stone, the Financial Secretary, read the Treasurer's report; which, upon motion, was accepted and ordered to be printed. [See page 12.]

[redacted]

The same Committee also reported the presence of the following Life Directors and Life Members:

LIFE DIRECTORS.

Aldrich, Rev. Jonathan, Worcester, Mass.
Allin, George, Brooklyn, N. Y.
Anderson, Rev. George W., North East, N.Y.
Belcher, Rev. Joseph, D.D., Philadelphia.
Bacheller, Jonathan, Lynn, Mass.
Bailey, Rev. Joseph A., Essex, Conn.
Ballard, Rev. Joseph, Brooklyn.
Baldwin, Rev. N. B., Philadelphia.
Balen, Peter, New York.
Barker, Rev. Enoch M., Highstown, N.J.
Blain, Rev. John, Central Falls, R.I.
Bowles, Rev. Ralph H., Branford, Ct.
Boyce, James, Providence.
Brayton, Rev. Jonathan, Centerville, R.I.
Brown, Rev. J. Newton, D.D., Philadelphia.
Bruce, John M., New York.
Budlong, James E., Providence, R.I.
Burt, John W., Brooklyn.
Cheesebrough, Rev. Isaac, Groton, Ct.
Colgate, William, New York.
Collom, Rev. J. G., Mt. Holly, N.J.
Conklin, William, New York.
Covell, Rev. Lemuel, New York.
Cutting, Rev. S. S., New York.
Davey, Thomas, New York.
Day, Hon. Albert, Hartford, Conn.
Devan, Rev. Thomas T., New York.
Dowling, Rev. John, D.D., Philadelphia.
Drake, Rev. Simeon J., Plainfield, N.J.
Dunn, Rev. Lewis A., Fairfax, Vt.
Fish, Rev. Henry C., Newark, N J.
Fuller, Rev. Cyrenius M., Pike, N.Y.
Gibbs, Rev. John W., New York.
Gillette, Rev. A. D., New York.
Hatt, Rev. Josiah, Morristown, N.J.
Hill, Rev. Benjamin M., D.D., New York.
Hiscox, Rev. Edward T., New York.
Hodge, Rev. James L., D.D., Brooklyn.
Ide, Rev. George B., D.D., Springfield, Mass.
Ilsley, Rev. Silas, Brooklyn.
Kelly, Samuel R., Brooklyn.
Ladd, Rev. James S., New York.
Lathrop, Rev. Edward, D.D., New York.
Leonard, Rev. Lewis G., Cambridgeport, Mass.
Magoon, Rev. E. L., D.D., New York.
Martin, Runyon W., New York.
Mason, Rev. Alanson P., Chelsea, Mass.
Middleditch, Rev. Robert T., Red Bank, N.J.
Miller, John A., New York.
Murdock, Rev. J. N., D.D., Hartford, Ct.
Newton, Isaac, New York.
Nice, Rev. G. P., Somerville, N.J.
Parker, Rev. S. S., Patterson, N. J.
Parkhurst, Rev. J. W., Newton Centre, Mass.
Parmly, Rev. Wheelock H., Jersey City.
Pattison, Rev. Wm. P., Auburn, N.Y.
Phelps, Rev. S. Dryden, D D., New Haven, Ct.
Pierce, Rev. S. E., Gloucester, Mass.
Platt, Nathan C., New York.
Price, William M., Brooklyn.
Reed, Rev. Nathan A., Wakefield, R I.
Reid, Rev. William, New London, Ct.
Richmond, Rev. J. L., Milton, Pa.
Roberts, Lewis, Brooklyn.
Rollinson, Rev. William, San Francisco, Cal.
Salisbury, William D., New York.
Samson, J. K., Brooklyn.
Seaver, Rev. Horace, New York.
Silliman, Rev. H., Mystic River, Ct.
Silliman, Mrs. Elizabeth P., Mystic River, Ct.
Smith, Rev. Henry F., Banksville, Ct.
Southworth, James E., Brooklyn.
Stearns, Rev. Oakman S., Newark, N.J.
Steward, Rev. Ira R., New York.
Stockbridge, Rev. John C., Boston.
Stone, Rev. James R., New York.
Swaim, Rev. Samuel B., West Cambridge, Mass.
Taylor, Rev. E. E. L., Brooklyn.
Taylor, Jeremiah B., New York.
Thomas, C. W., Hastings, N. Y.
Todd, William W, New York.
Welch, Rev. B. T., D.D., Newtonville, N.Y.
Whitehead, James M., New York.
Willard, Rev. F. A., South Danvers, Mass.
Willett, Rev Charles, Wilkinsville, Ct.
Wilson, Daniel M., Newark, N.J.
Winterton, William, New York.

LIFE MEMBERS.

Ambler, Rev. E. C., Weart's Corners, N. J.
Amsbury, Jabez, Norwich, Ct.
Appleton, James, Sing Sing, N. Y.
Avery, Rev. David, Southwick, Mass.
Bainbridge, Rev. S. M., Wheatland, N. Y.
Baker, Rev. J. James, Perryville, N. J.
Baker, Rev. Samuel, D.D., Williamsburgh, N. Y.
Ballard, Mrs. Joseph, Brooklyn.
Battell, Rev. Allen E., Marshfield, Mass.
Belden, Rev. Joseph, Freehold, N. J.
Bellamy, Rev. R. K., Chickopee Falls, Mass.
Benedict, David, D.D., Pawtucket, R. I.
Biglow, F. H., Brooklyn.
Bolles, James G., Hartford, Ct.

Bond, Rev. Emmons P., New Britain, Ct.
Bromley, Dewey, Norwich, Ct.
Bruce, John M., Jr., New York.
Brown, Rev. Amasa, Concord, N. H.
Brown, Rev. Wm. L., Boston.
Brown, Rev. Joseph P., Moosup, Ct.
Brown, Rev. J. F., Scotch Plains, N. J.
Chesshire, Rev. John Enoch, Wickford, R. I.
Chick, Rev. J. M., Groton, Mass.
Clark, Rev. N. Judson, Southington, Ct.
Clark, Mrs. Caroline D., Southington, Ct.
Clark, Rev. C. A., Auburn, N. Y.
Corwin, Rev. David, Gloversville, N. Y.
Crane, Richard M., Elizabethtown, N. J.
Day, Horatio E., Hartford, Ct.
Dean, Rev. M. M., Warren, R. I.
Denison, Rev. Erastus, Groton, Ct.
Denison, Mrs. Prudence, Groton, Ct.
Dodge, Rev. Orrin, Brooklyn.
Draper, Rev. J., North Bennington, Vt.
Duncan, Rev. John, Camden, N. J.
Eddy, Rev. Daniel C., Lowell, Mass.
Evans, Rev. Charles, Brooklyn.
Field, Rev. Samuel W., Providence.
Foster, Rev. J. C., Brattleboro', Vt.
Fuller, Rev. Edward K., Reading, Mass.
Gale, Rev. Solomon, Columbus, N. J.
Gardner, Rev. Jacob, Lyme, Ct.
Gault, George, Brooklyn.
[redacted]

Martin, William R., New York.
Martin, Roune, New York.
Mason, Pothuel, Somerville, N. J.
Meech, Rev. Wm. W., Preston, Ct.
Merchant, James H., New York.
Merriam, Rev. Mylon, Sharon, Mass.
Mikels, Rev. Wm. S., Sing Sing, N. Y.
Miller, Rev. Harvey, Meriden, Ct.
Miller, Charles, Morrisania, N. Y.
Nelson, Rev. Wm. F., Greenfield, Mass.
Nice, Rev. William J., Imlaystown, N. J.
Phillips, Rev. James M., Moodus, Ct.
Post, Peter K., Somerville, N. J.
Pratt, Rev. James H., Bloomfield, N. J.
Randolph, Rev. Warren, Providence.
Raynor, Samuel, New York.
Remington, Rev. S., Brooklyn.
Richardson, Thomas S., Brooklyn.
Robins, Rev. Gurdon, Hartford, Ct.
Rue, Rev. Joshua E., Hightstown, N. J.
Savage, Moses B., Brooklyn.
Sheldon, Smith, New York.
Simpson, Joseph P., New York.
Smith, Rev. William A., Groton, Ct.
Smith, Rev. J. T., Bristol, Ct.
Smith, Rev. Lewis, Trenton, N. J.
Spratt, Rev. G. M., Lewisburgh, Pa.
Sproul, Rev. Samuel, Princeton, N. J.
Stimson, Rev. S. M., Binghamton, N. Y.
[redacted]

On motion of Rev. J. G. WARREN, this matter was referred to a Committee of five, with instructions to report at 3½ o'clock, P.M.

Rev. br'n. J. G. WARREN, of N. Y., S. B. SWAIM, Mass., E. M. BARKER, N. J., S. M. STIMSON, N. Y., and J. N. MURDOCK, Conn., were appointed that Committee.

Prayer by Rev. W. REID, of Ct. Adjourned.

AFTERNOON SESSION.

The President called the Society to order at 3 o'clock, and Prayer was offered by Rev. J. ALDRICH, of Mass.

Rev. H. LINCOLN, of Jamaica Plains, presented a memorial from Rev. br'n. BARON STOW, D.D., T. F. CALDICOTT, D.D., H. LINCOLN and others, residing in Boston and vicinity, in reference to the removal of the Rooms from Nassau street, which was referred to the Committee who were charged with the consideration of this subject.

The hour for the special order of the day not having arrived, a few extracts from the Annual Report of the Board were read by the Corresponding Secretary, which, upon motion, were accepted.

The Committee to whom was referred the Special Report of the Board and other papers, relating to the removal of Rooms, reported through their Chairman, when,

On motion, the Report was accepted. Pending the consideration of the propositions presented by the Committee, various resolutions were offered as substitutes both by Rev. S. S. CUTTING, and Rev. B. M. HILL; when it was

Resolved, That the Report of the Committee, and all the papers relating to this subject, be referred to a Committee of seven, to report in the evening, directly after the conclusion of the Annual Report of the Executive Board.

The following were appointed that Committee:

Rev. brethren J. G. WARREN, New York; S. B. SWAIM, Massachusetts; E. M. BARKER, New Jersey; S. M. STIMSON, New York; J. N. MURDOCK, Connecticut; S. S. CUTTING, New York; S. J. DRAKE, New Jersey.

Adjourned with prayer, by Rev. D. C. HAYNES, of Pennsylvania.

EVENING SESSION.

President in the Chair. Prayer by Rev. JOHN GIRDWOOD, of Mass.

The Corresponding Secretary then presented the Annual Report in full, which, upon motion of Rev. E. L. MAGOON, D.D., seconded by Rev. C. M. FULLER, was accepted, and ordered to be printed.

The Committee on Rooms not being ready to report, Rev. D. C. Eddy, of Mass., in accordance with a previous arrangement and by request of the Society, then delivered an address, taking for his subject the power and growth of Romanism in this Country, and connected therewith the claims of Home Missions.

The Committee to whom were referred the papers relating to Rooms, then presented their Report, which was accepted. On motion of Rev. H. Lincoln, of Mass., seconded by Rev. A. D. Gillette, of N. Y., its recommendations were adopted without debate, and Messrs. brethren Ebenezer Cauldwell, Thomas Thomas, John B. Durbrow, John M. Ferrier William T. Dugan, and George Gault, were appointed a special Committee to execute and carry out its provisions and instructions.

The Report of this Committee is on page 95.

Whereupon the congregation arose and sang

"Praise God from whom all blessings flow,
Praise Him all creatures here below,
Praise him above ye heavenly host,
Praise Father, Son and Holy Ghost."

Rev. Harvey Miller, of Ct., then delivered an address on the work

[redacted]

MEETING OF LIFE DIRECTORS AND OFFICERS.

A meeting of the Life Directors and Officers was held immediately after the Society adjourned, for the election of the Board of Managers, the President, ALBERT DAY, Esq., in the Chair.

On motion, it was resolved to appoint Rev. brethren E. LATHROP, of New York, S. DRYDEN PHELPS, of Ct., JOSIAH HATT, of New Jersey, J. C. STOCKBRIDGE of Mass, and THOMAS WATSON, Esq., of Pa., a Committee to nominate suitable persons to compose the Board of Managers for the ensuing year; and that the election be by ballot.

The Committee on Nomination having retired, returned and reported a ballot composed intentionally of names that did not belong to the Board of either of the Bible Societies.

Rev. R. H. BOWLES, of Ct., and R. W. MARTIN, Esq., of New York, served as Tellers, and upon their Report the Chairman declared the entire Ticket, as nominated by the Committee elected, and the persons named, Managers for the year 1855–6. [See page 14.]

The meeting, then, at a late hour, adjourned.

Dr. THE AMERICAN BAPTIST HOME MISSION SOCIETY

1855.	To Cash paid Missionaries for Salaries		$37,584 75
	" Cash paid Agents for Salaries, Traveling expenses, postage, etc.		7,683 72
	" Cash paid for Stationery, Postage, and Incidental Expenses		261 85
	" Cash paid Salaries, Secretaries, and Clerks, ...	$4,094 41	
	Less amount of Interest from Contingent Fund, ...	92 91	
			4,001 50
	" Cash paid for paper and printing of Home Mission Record, and expense on the same, ...		2,145 07
	" Cash paid for paper and printing Annual Report, Certificates, Blanks, etc., ...		772 77
	" Cash paid taxes on land donated to the Society,		8 64
	" Cash paid discount on uncurrent funds, and counterfeit money received on account, in donations,		

[redacted]

IN ACCOUNT WITH CHAS. J. MARTIN, TREASURER. *Cr.*

1855.	By Balance from last year.		$4,302 71
	" Cash proceeds of note (contributed last year),.		947 25
	" Cash interest on dividends received on sundry temporary investments, ...	$240 00	
	" Cash interest received on Bonds and Mortgages (a special investment by direction of the donor), . . .	180 44	
			420 44
	" Cash amount received for subscription to Home Mission Record, ...		1,330 53
	" Cash amount received for Church Edifice Funds, ...	4,360 30	
	" Cash legacy for Church Edifice Funds, ...	106 30	
			4,466 60
	" Cash amount received for Educational purposes,		56 50
	" Cash received from the estate of Garrat N. Bleecker, per E. Cauldwell and W. F. Van Wagenen, Esqs., executors; legacy to be invested on bond and mortgage, the interest of which to be applied towards the salaries of the officers at the rooms, ...		6,000 00
	" Cash amount of contributions, etc., received from April 1, 1854, to March 31, 1855, ...	$42,917 84	
	" Cash sundry legacies, do. do. .	2,104 46	
			45,022 30
	" Cash borrowed, secured by hypothecation of Corn Exchange Bank Stock, and Brooklyn City Bond		1,800 00
			$64,346 33
March 31,	By Balance, ...		$140 48

CHARLES J. MARTIN, *Treasurer.*

AUDITOR'S CERTIFICATE.

This is to certify that I have examined the foregoing account, together with the vouchers connected therewith, and find the same correct. The balance in the hands of Charles J. Martin, Esq., Treasurer, is one hundred and forty 48 100 dollars.

He has in his possession the following securities, viz.: Certificate of Stock in the Corn Exchange Bank, New York, for $2,000, subject to a loan thereon of $1,400; Brooklyn City Bond, bearing interest six per cent., payable 1st January, 1863, for $500, subject to a loan thereon of $400; two Bonds and Mortgages (a special investment by direction of the donor), the interest only to be used by the Society, the principal of which bonds is $2,500; also a Bond and Mortgage for $6,000, the legacy of the late Garrat N. Bleecker, the interest of which to be applied towards the salaries of the officers at the rooms. New York, 1st April, 1855.

SMITH SHELDON, *Auditor.*

OFFICERS OF THE SOCIETY

AND

EXECUTIVE BOARD.

OFFICERS.

PRESIDENT.

HON. ALBERT DAY, Hartford, Connecticut.

VICE PRESIDENTS.

WILLIAM COLGATE, Esq., New York
JOHN P. CROZER, Esq., Chester, Pa.

TREASURER.

CHARLES J. MARTIN, New York.

AUDITOR.

SMITH SHELDON, New York.

Annual Report.

THE Executive Board of the American Baptist Home Mission Society present their twenty-third Annual Report, with gratitude to the Benefactor of men for their experience of his goodness through the past missionary year. Death has not, as often heretofore, invaded their circle. The officers and managers have all been mercifully preserved, and they are not aware of more than two deaths among the company of their missionaries. An amiable lad, however, employed in the Mission Rooms, to whom all had become warmly attached, was suddenly removed from among us. The missionaries were Rev. Lyman Hutchins, of Wisconsin, and Rev. Nathan Denison, formerly of the State of New York. The last one had been but a short time on his field in Illinois, and was cut down in the midst of his strength and usefulness. But of the members and directors for life a larger number has fallen. Of the former, thirty-seven, and of the latter, four have died; of whom fifteen were ministers of the Gospel, and five were ministers' wives. These all died, we trust, in faith, having confessed that they were strangers and pilgrims on the earth, and have gone to possess the better country, which they sought—that is, the heavenly. Their names are recorded in our list of deceased members.

DIRECTORS AND MEMBERS FOR LIFE.

In the course of the past year an addition of 70 names has been made to our list of directors, and 4 have died, making the present number 517. The addition to the number of members has been 578; but 37 have died, and 32 have been constituted directors, making the total number at present 3877.

LEGACIES.

Of the receipts of the last year, upwards of eight thousand dollars were in legacies—a considerable larger amount than has been received from the same source in any previous year; which shows an increased appreciation of the cause of Home Missions among the people—an appreciation which swells in their hearts and sends forth a gush of warm sympathy and love, as the realities of eter-

[redacted]

CONTINGENT FUND.

Provision was made at the last anniversary for gradually creating a Contingent Fund of twenty-five thousand dollars, the principal of which would constitute a safeguard to the financial credit of the Society in emergencies, and the interest to be used in payment of the secretaries' salaries, thus providing effectual means of reducing the percentage on the annual receipts used in payment of contingent expenses. The arrangement was based on the fact, unofficially known to some members of the Board about two years ago, that the late much-respected auditor, Garrat Noel Bleecker, had made a liberal bequest in favor of the Society for those specific purposes. We are happy in being able now to say that the legacy, amounting to six thousand dollars, was paid early in the year, and was immediately invested in an undoubted mortgage on real estate. It is a valuable nucleus around which, it is hoped, may be gathered, in due time, the deficient amount proposed for the fund, and is an admirable example of Christian benevolence and forethought, well worthy of the imitation of all possessing means and disposed to promote the important objects contemplated in the plan. The consummation of the plan will form a noble monument to the memory of the individuals from whom it may be derived.

CHURCH EDIFICE FUND.

It would be specially gratifying to the Board if circumstances allowed them to report satisfactory progress in creating the fund for building church edifices, as heretofore proposed, but a series of unpropitious events have disappointed their hopes. Much delay was experienced in the selection of a suitable agent to solicit funds, and after such an one was appointed he was unexpectedly prevented, several months, by domestic affliction, from entering upon the duties of his appointment, and, for various reasons, continued but a short time. Having rendered good service in one or two specific cases, he considered it his duty to resign, and the Board reluctantly acquiesced in the measure.

Something, however, has been done in carrying out the design of the Church Edifice Fund. Voluntary contributions, for the benefit of particular churches, and others to be appropriated at the discretion of the Board, have been received, in all amounting to the sum of $4466.60, all of which has been appropriated for the specified purpose, some of it in the form of loans drawing a small interest, and will eventually become a portion of the fund. The legacy of the Hon. Friend Humphrey was specifically designated for this fund.

ledo, in Ohio, has, with rare energy and self-denial, succeeded in inclosing a good building, but it remains unfinished and useless for want of funds. The small and interesting church in Albuquerque, in New Mexico, the first and only one in that dark portion of our field, have the offer of a valuable plot of land as a donation from a generous-minded gentleman not connected with our denomination, if a church edifice is erected on it within a given period, but there is danger of its soon being lost, because the means of building cannot be obtained.

ALTERATION OF THE CONSTITUTION.

The Executive Board were instructed, at the last meeting of the Society, to recommend such a change in the fifth article of the Constitution as shall allow the Society to have a voice more directly in the election of the Board of Managers. This subject, though often discussed before, has received renewed attention. As the instruction is imperative, leaving the Board no discretion in deciding as to the expediency of such a change, they have no alternative but to present such a form as would, if adopted, accomplish the object in view. This they conceive could be done by striking out of the article, as it now stands, the words: "The Officers and Life Directors shall meet immediately after the annual meeting of the Society, and," and substitute the words: 'The Society shall also annually,'—leaving the remainder of the article as it is. It would then read thus, '5th, The Society shall also annually elect fifteen managers,' &c., &c.

But the Board can only present this plan of alteration for the consideration of the Society. They do not recommend its adoption, for the following reasons:

The manner in which the change was proposed, though, probably, inadvertent, appears to be an evasion of the

11th article of the Constitution, which points out with great precision the manner in which alterations of that Instrument may be made on the motion of an individual member, that is, by the presentation of the alteration desired, in a specific form, which, if accepted by a major vote of the Society, is to stand one year subject to the consideration of the Society and then to be adopted only by a vote of two thirds of the members present at the next anniversary. In the present instance the specific form of the change proposed has not been under consideration for a year, nor even presented by the mover. It is now presented for the first time.

Again. A change may be voluntarily recommended by the Executive Board, but then it is supposed to be the result of careful investigation and based upon good and sufficient reasons; but in the present case, it is not volun-

[redacted]

Thus. The provision of the Fifth Article, sought to be changed, as it now stands, was adopted at the original organization of the Society, and was based on the following considerations.

1st. The Third Article requires the sum of $100 of such persons as shall be entitled to Life Directorship, while it provides for Life Membership by the payment of only $30, and for annual membership a much smaller amount. The larger amount requisite for directorship was adopted, doubtless, with considerable reference to the necessities of the treasury, and was intended as a special means of replenishing it; but the proposed change would give both classes of members an equal right with directors, and therefore destroy that motive to enlarged liberality, and thus unfavorably effect the annual contributions to the treasury.

2d. It was considered proper and right by the original founders of the Society that individuals who were disposed to contribute the amount requisite for a directorship should enjoy some equivalent privilege or right, hence they were invested with the right of acting with the officers elected by the popular vote in the selection of managers. No other special right is, or ever has been, allowed them. The proposed change would destroy that right and the remaining motive to secure the directorship.

3d. It is to be presumed that many if not all the present life directors paid the requisite amount of money to become such on the consideration contained in the Constitution that the election of managers should devolve on them in conjunction with certain officers. Simple justice therefore demands their protection in the exercise of this vested right, until some satisfactory equivalent is devised and conferred upon them.

4th. Propositions have been made heretofore in the

Executive Board and meetings of the Society for some change like that now proposed, and, after much discussion, have been overruled or withdrawn, on the ground that the interests of the Society would be injured, or not at all benefited by the change.

In view of all which considerations the Executive Board respectfully recommend that the proposed change be indefinitely postponed.

HOME MISSION ROOMS.

At the last anniversary of the Society the Executive Board were authorized and instructed to engage suitable rooms in a building in Nassau Street, in the city of New York, erected by certain Baptist brethren, and to enter upon the use of the same as soon as such rooms should be granted to the Society on a durable lease, free from rent, [redacted]

Balance from last year's account,		$4,302 71
Cash receipts from all sources, viz.:—		
For the General purposes of the Society,	$48,189 99	
" Church Edifice Fund,	4,466 00	
" Educational Objects,	56 50	
" Home Mission Record,	1,330 53	
Special Fund for the support of Secretaries, the interest only to be used,	6,000 00	60,043 62
Making the total amount of cash in the Treasury for the year ending 31st March 1855,		64,346 33
Of the above amount received for Missionary purposes, there were in contributions, legacies and donations,	45,969 56	
Being less than the amount of receipts from the same sources last year,	3,138 13	
The total amount of disbursements for the same period was:—		
For General Purposes,	$51,406 79	
" Church Edifices,	4,572 18	
" Educational Objects,	30 37	
" Home Mission Record,	2,145 07	
" Special Investment, by order of the Donor,	6,000 00	
" Returned funds, paid by mistake,	51 44	64,206 85
Leaving a balance in the Treasury of	140 48	
To which add for Bank Stock, and Brooklyn City Bonds, par value,	2,500 00	2,640 48
Due for drafts, outstanding, liable to immediate presentation,	4,847 68	
Draft for a Church Edifice Appropriation,	1,005 07	
Due to Missionaries for services performed up to the 1st of April, and liable to be demanded immediately,	2,318 54	
Due on Loans, secured by Stocks of the Society,	1,800 00	9,971 29
Showing a deficiency in the Treasury to meet the liabilities due on the 1st of April, of		7,330 81
The total Liabilities of the Society, April 1st, 1855, were	$45,307 13	
The available resources were,	840 48	
Showing a balance against the Society, at the close of the year, of	44,466 65	

We have said that this exhibit of our financial matters is gratifying. By comparison with our early fears, and perhaps with the fiscal statements of many other benevolent societies, it is so. But when we recall our numerous declinatures to enter opening, promising fields; the words of discouragement and disheartening delay uttered to numerous parties; the necessities that have compelled a deaf ear to many an earnest entreaty even for a renewed commission, notwithstanding the high hopes that were raised at our last Anniversary; and with all these occasions of sadness, remind ourselves that the Lord of the harvest, whom we serve, has the most indisputable right to the gold and silver of the whole earth, and to the cattle on its ten thousand hills—that the Great Head of the Church has given to Baptists a worldly portion scarcely inferior to that possessed by any other denomination of his sacramental host, in this country ; and that both the providence of God and his written Word urge upon us the claims of Home Missions as with a voice of seven thunders, assuring us that what is done to prevent the overflowing of superstition, infidelity, and barbarism, into our Central Valleys, and over our Pacific slopes, must be done quickly—surely we have abundant reason for sorrow, thoughtfulness and earnest consideration ; while, in the name and help of the first Great Missionary, the Author, the Exemplar, and the Friend of Home Missions, who, though once rich, for our sakes became poor that we through his poverty might be made rich and make others [redacted] and even the present balance on hand, but $140 48, is borrowed money. This, not because our receipts have been so very small, as that our liabilities have been so numerous and imperative.

We would, in this connection, remind the patrons of the Society how very important it is to send in their contributions as early in the fiscal year as possible. The liabilities of the Society are maturing constantly, so that every month requires from $4,000 to $6,000 in cash, or its equivalent. Of course, unless the requisite funds are in hand when our drafts fall due, the Treasurer must raise the amount on temporary loans, paying the necessary interest, or protests and disgrace can not be avoided. Another expedient has been rendered necessary, the past year, partly by the difficulty of obtaining loans on call, but chiefly if not altogether by the fact that our receipts have not been sufficiently large and prompt, month by month.. Our missionaries have, in many instances, been given drafts that were payable, not at sight, nor ten days after, as usual, but thirty, and even sixty days after presentation. This was better than protested paper, it is true, but it made many a Missionary's family sad, and doubtless spoiled some sermons.

Elsewhere you will have presented estimates and necessities for the ensuing year. It is sufficient to say here that our field is as wide as our Country, our opportunities and our calls to duty are as numerous as are her upstarting villages and growing centres of population, industry and thrift. We can be limited only by our resources.

MISSIONARY OPERATIONS.

The missionary operations of the Society have been more circumscribed than in the previous year. Guided by the unanimous vote of the Society at its last meeting, the Board, in the early part of the year, freely increased the number of appointments, but failing to realize a corresponding increase of receipts into the treasury, a change of policy became necessary, and a system of retrenchment was substituted. Since then, nearly all applications for new appointments have been declined, or temporarily deferred, in hope that means would be supplied to justify favorable responses; but the report of an over-drawn treasury at the close of the year furnishes our reason for stating that those applications yet remain deferred. For the last six months only 10 new appointments have been made. Of these, 3 were substitutes for missionaries who had removed from places of too much importance to remain destitute, 3 were for Kansas, Nebraska, and New Grenada, and 3 were for stations in Oregon and California, which could be supplied by ministers already in those

[redacted]

prospects of rearing up a self-sustaining church in a few years. A minister appointed for Oregon City, and mentioned in our last report as being detained from embarking, on account of domestic affliction, has since lost his health, and abandoned the idea of proceeding.

Two missionaries under appointment last year in California, are still continued, and are accomplishing much, in building up the cause of Christ. Another has been added to the number, in the person of a member of one of the churches in that State, who is well and favorably known to the Board, and who, in view of the importance of the field and the necessity of its immediate cultivation, relinquished profitable employment in a secular profession, to engage in the work of a Gospel minister. Another minister, appointed more than a year ago, whose journey to that State was prevented by the hand of Divine Providence, would have been sent forward but for the continuance of that providence. The undertaking is considered as abandoned for the present. Still another appointment was made the past year, but with no better result.

The church at Stockton, under the care of the Rev. J. B. Saxton, who has been sustained by the Society, has become sufficiently able to assume his entire support, and are now enjoying encouraging prospects of greater success.

NEW MEXICO.

One minister has been added to the missionary company in New Mexico, and a converted native is employed as an assistant. A vacancy occurred in the station at Santa Fé, by the return of Rev. Mr. Smith to the Eastern States, which is temporarily supplied by the new missionary, Rev. F. Tolhurst. Rev. Mr. Read is at present the only missionary whose labor is chiefly devoted to the Mexican population. His field is very extensive, embracing nearly the southern half of the Territory on both sides of the Rio Grande. The church at Albuquerque is under his care, where some Americans reside and attend his ministry. He has baptized 3 persons, who, we have reason to believe, are Mexicans ; but the particulars have not reached us.

The Word of God appears to be taking root in New Mexico. Public worship is better attended than formerly, and, in Santa Fé especially, by the most respectable and influential people ; while a general interest in the institutions of evangelical religion seems to extend gradually among all classes.

NEW TERRITORIES.

Since the last anniversary the Territories of Kansas and Nebraska have been organized and opened to the occupancy of emigrants, and large numbers of a good class of ness in preaching the Gospel and teaching a school, and the Divine blessing has attended his labors. His interpreter, José Sanun, has renounced the superstitions of Romanism, and, having given satisfactory evidence of being regenerated by the Holy Spirit, has been baptized and become a member of the Church in Albuquerque. Since that event he has exhibited great devotedness to the cause of Christ; acting as an interpreter to Brother Gorman when needed, and as a preacher among his countrymen at other times. Having the confidence of the people to a great degree—among whom he is, evidently, very useful—the Board have made provision for his continued labors. A daughter of Brother Gorman has likewise been brought to the knowledge of the truth as it is in Christ, whom also he has baptized. The attention of the Pueblos to the services of the sanctuary is improving, the congregations numbering from 100 to 300 persons. This success increases the opposition of the priests to our missionary, but the Governor is his friend; affords him abundant protection, and manifests deep personal interest in his labors for the good of the people.

Rev. J. M. Shaw as yet continues at Fort Defiance, where he is perfecting himself in the knowledge of the Navajo dialect, under the instruction of the best teacher he can obtain.

An attempt was made in the course of the year to establish a station at Zuni, the most populous Pueblo in the territory, situated favorably for him to labor advantageously among the people of that place, and at the same time bestow all the attention that would be really necessary and practicable for some time upon the Indians of the Navajo and Appaché tribes. In this, however, he was defeated by the intrigues of men of corrupt minds, whose traffic with the Indians would probably be unfavorably affected by such an arrangement. The good seed sown among these tribes, however, seems to have found a lodgment in good ground, and it is hoped will soon exhibit signs of life and fruitfulness.

Brother Shaw was strengthened a small portion of the year by the co-operation of Rev. F. Tolhurst, who was sent out under the appointment of the Board, but, from a cause already mentioned, that arrangement was necessarily interrupted for the present.

The station at Pembina, in Minnesota Territory, has been discontinued on account of hostilities between the Chippewa Indians residing in that region, and their neighbors, the Sioux. To remedy this unexpected interruption, the Board contemplated the establishment of a station at Winnepeg, more remote from the theatre of their wars, among another band of Chippewas ; but having been

[redacted]

inhabitants, a large portion of whom are emancipated slaves. It is a pleasant and healthy spot. Here a missionary of the Laight Street Church, in New York, has been laboring a few years under many disadvantages, steadfastly devoting himself to the work of the ministry, supporting himself chiefly by his own hands, and steadily rejecting repeated appointments to the highest civil offices in the government of the Island, with ample salary for his support. God has blessed his labors. The people, who, on his arrival there, were ignorant and unbelieving, have been reformed in their domestic and social habits, and many of them are transformed in the spirit of their minds; a church of near 300 members has been gathered; they have built a good church edifice and a school house, both of which are paid for by their own contributions; and now there are not more than ten or twelve residents of the Island but are attendants upon public worship. But to preserve these advantages it became necessary that the missionary should be relieved from all secular employments which might interfere with his ministry, and at his desire and the recommendation of the church in Laight Street, he has been adopted as the missionary of the Society; thus giving us an opportunity to occupy an advanced post near the southern boundary of our general field. Thus our Zion is stretching forth the curtains of her habitation.

SUMMARY OF LABORS AND RESULTS.

The number of missionaries and agents employed during the past year is 179. Of that number, 140 were in commission April 1st, 1854. The remaining 39 were new appointments. Three quarterly reports, due on the 1st April, failed to reach us. Eleven who were under appointment some portion of the year, need no further aid from the Society.

Eight collecting agents have also been employed the

whole or a portion of the year, and, for a few weeks, three special agents for purposes connected with the Church Edifice Fund.

The Missionaries were distributed as follows: In Canada (West), 1; Canada (East), 9; New York (near Canada), 1; Pennsylvania, 7; Delaware, 1; Ohio, 8; Michigan, 7; Indiana, 22; Illinois, 28; Wisconsin, 38; Iowa, 21; Minnesota, 10; Oregon, 4; California, 4; New Mexico, 6; Kansas, 2.

Twenty-one of the number preach in the following foreign languages: French, 8; French and German, 1; French and Polish, 1; Swedish, 1; Swedish, Danish, and Norwegian, 1; German, 3; Dutch, 1; Spanish, 2; Spanish and Pueblo, 1; Spanish and Navajo Indian, 1; Chippewa and French, 1.

The number of States and Territories occupied is 15.

The churches aided by the Society contributed to the usual objects $5,183 49, besides about $21,300 for the support of their own ministers.

In addition to the Missionaries already mentioned, two others have been appointed, whose labors were to commence after the 31st of March.

THE NECESSITIES OF THE ENSUING YEAR.

The experience of the Executive Board goes to show that, however much may be properly expended in any year, in spreading the gospel in our country, it inevitably creates necessity for a larger amount in following years. In the language of a homely adage, though in a better sense than usually marks its use, "the more we do the more we may do." A single conquest by the soldiers of the Cross increases the area of the battle-field and the necessity for means of other conquests. Our duty is to bring all, if possible, into subjection to Christ. It is a warfare in which there is no discharge.

The field now ready for our operations presents necessity for the employment of a larger number of missionaries than have ever received our commission in a single year. There are points, in a condition to receive immediate attention, which could not be profitably supplied with less than 54 able ministers in addition to those now in the field. More than one third of them are in Oregon, California, New Mexico, Kansas and Nebraska. The probability of being able to obtain such a number of missionaries may be seen in the facts that 14 deferred regular applications are now on file at the Mission Rooms, and 13 others are awaiting such a state of our treasury as would justify calling on the applicants for regular forms; while quite as many informal applications have been discouraged because of the certain inability of the Board to comply with

$52,000. The amount requisite to 50 men needed in their respective them there one year, is about $35,000. the overdrawn amount which should be lay, make an aggregate of $88,800, as the their woes. Drawn by the powerful attractions of our country, hundreds of thousands anually reach our shores, and widely diffuse the pernicious influences of foreign religion and morals among the people. Especially is this the case in the new States and Territories, where, far removed from the domestic restraints and social examples under which they were educated, the hopeful youth and vigorous manhood of our native homes have preceded them, and where those influences are exerted with augmented power. There, with amazing rapidity, the immigrant population continually spreads itself to limits of prodigious expansion, erecting new villages and cities; establishing new and rapid means of communication between them, and promulgating new forms of error and falsehood, by new and popular agencies, skillful in deceit, and destructive in moral influence. The work of the Home Mission Society is to introduce and establish among them the glorious Gospel of the blessed God, including all those evangelical instrumentalities which enlighten minds, save souls, exalt nations, and promote the glory of God.

This work we are now specially urged to perform, not only by the constitutional design of our organization, but also by the loud and reiterated claims of flocks of Christ's sheep and lambs in the wilderness, where they are surrounded by prowling wolves; of feeble bands of his disciples congregated in cities and villages, where stealthy and bitter enemies lurk; and of dependent ministers who, without staff or scrip or purse, are there, or longing to be there in obedience to the heavenly call, as shepherds of the flock, as defenders of the truth, as preachers of righteousness and peace.

In view of such high, holy, heaven-born motives to active, vigorous, and efficient benevolent agency, all mere local policy or selfish considerations, all personal feeling or pride of opinion, sink into utter insignificancy, and demand of all, the willing, unreserved, and untiring dedication to the great object of our Association, of the utmost talent, influence and piety, we possess. The deferred claims of those who have so long waited for a litle aid should be satisfied ; the hopes of the multitude, now seeking at our hands the bread of life, must be realized ; and we ought to be willing to crucify the world and self, to qualify ourselves to more effectually bestow upon the people the unsearchable riches of Jesus Christ. Our ascended Lord and Master commands it, his people expect it, and our consciences should know no peace till, sinking in the dark deep sea of everlasting oblivion, all differences and alienations which threaten the peace of Zion, we stand together against the powers of darkness and death, a band of brethren, united, powerful and active in building up the

[redacted]

EXPLANATION OF THE FOLLOWING MISSIONARY TABLE.

The parallel columns show:

1. The names of Agents and Missionaries, and the States in which they reside.
2. The post-office address of Agents and Missionaries.
3. The fields of labor occupied by Agents and Missionaries.
4. The dates at which the appointments commence.
5. The number of months for which the appointments are respectively made.
6. The number of weeks' labor reported as having been performed during an appointment.
7. The number of stations and out-stations supplied.*
8. The number of persons baptized by the Missionaries within the time of appointment.
9. The number received by letter.
10. The number of scholars in Sabbath-schools under the care of Missionaries.†
11. The amount contributed to benevolent objects.
12. Additional facts reported concerning the state and progress of the Churches.‡

* Stations are churches or villages regularly supplied on the Lord's-day, and are indicated in column 3. Out-stations are places where the Missionaries have *stated* appointments for preaching more or less frequently at other times than the Lord's-day.

† In new places, where Union schools are established, the number of scholars connected with Baptist families only are reported.

‡ In many cases two lines appear for the same Missionary, extending through all the columns. In such cases the second line indicates a re-appointment of the Missionary, and the dates in column 4 determine to which appointment or year the statistics and remarks on the different lines belong. A particular notice of those dates is necessary to a proper understanding of certain changes which appear against the names of some individuals.

Y TABLE.

[illegible]	Months Commis'd.	Weeks labor reported.	Stations supplied.	Baptized.	Received by Letter.	Scholars in S. School.	Cont. to Benevolent Objects.	ADDITIONAL FACTS REPORTED.
[illegible]	12	39	1				------	Enjoys tokens of God's favor, amid many discouragements and much opposition.
[illegible]	12	13	....				------	Truth advancing.
[illegible]	12	39	1				31 45	Progress being made.
[illegible]	12	13	----				5 47	
[illegible]	12	39	8				85 75	Two persons renounced Romanism.
[illegible]	12	13	3				29 00	Several families favorably disposed towards the Gospel.
[illegible]	12	39	3				------	Making some progress.
[illegible]	12	39	3				14 00	The fire at Grand Ligne has embarrassed his operations.
[illegible]		13	----				12 00	Some tokens of the Divine presence. Con-

Names of Agents and Missionaries.	Post Office Address.	Field of Labor.	Date of Commission	Months Commis'd.	Weeks labor reported.	Stations supplied.	Baptized.	Received by Letter.	Scholars in S. School.	Cont. to Benevolent Objects.	Additional Facts Reported.
NEW HAMPSHIRE.											
Oren Tracy	Concord	Northern New England	April 1, 1854	12	52*		1				Collecting Agent.
" "	"	" " "	April 1, 1855	12							Re-appointed.
MASSACHUSETTS.											
J. W. Parkhurst	Newton Centre	Massachusetts	April 1, 1854	12	52		8				Collecting Agent.
" "	" "	" "	April 1, 1855	12							Re-appointed.
CONNECTICUT.											
J. S. Ladd	New York City	Connecticut & Rhode Isl'd.	April 1, 1854	12	52						Collecting Agent.
"	" "	" " "	April 1, 1855	12							Re-appointed.
NEW YORK.											
C. M. Fuller	Pike, Wyoming co.	Eastern New York and N. J.	April 1, 1854	12	52						Collecting Agent.
"	" " "	" " "	April 1, 1855	12							Re-appointed.
C. A. Clark	Auburn	Central New York	April 1, 1854	12	52						Collecting Agent.
"	"		April 1, 1855	12							Re-appointed.
Wm. Sawyer	White's Corners	Western New York	April 1, 1854	12	52						Collecting Agent.
"	" "	" "	April 1, 1855	12							Re-appointed.
M. B. Czechowski	Mooers	French Catholics	July 1, 1853	12	13	7	5				Completed a Meeting-house.
" "	"	" "	July 1, 1854	12	39		9				Suffered some persecution. Baptized eight Catholics, of whom one had been a Priest, and is now a preacher of the Gospel.
J. H. Walden	Brockport	Western New York	Dec. 1, 1853	12	10						Agent for Church Edifice Fund.
NEW JERSEY.											
J. G. Collom	Mount Holley	East Penn. and part of N. J.	April 1, 1854	12	52						Collecting Agent.
" "	" "	" " "	April 1, 1855	12							Re-appointed.
J. E. Rue	Scotch Plains	West Penn., &c., &c.	April 1, 1854	12	52						Collecting Agent.
"	" "	" "	April 1, 1855	12							Re-appointed.

Months Commis'd.	Cont. to Benevolent Objects.	ADDITIONAL FACTS REPORTED.
12	27 50	Have improved their Meeting-house.
12	2 50	People suffered from "hard times."
12	31 00	Prospects good for future prosperity. Has resigned.
12	6 90	Meeting-house progressing. Been greatly afflicted with sickness and death in his family.
12	.....	Declension. Want of union and harmony.
12	.....	Has resigned.
12	70 17	Cause advancing slowly but permanently.
12	50 00	Preparing to build a Meeting-house.
12	5 43	Has had a revival at one station, and prospects encouraging.
12	......	thing discouraging.
12	26 03	
12	00	Been sick. Cause advancing under his labors.
12	00	Encouraging prospects.
12	00	Completed a neat house of worship at one of his stations.
12		Explori Collecting agent.

Names of Agents and Missionaries.	Post Office Address.	Field of Labor.	Date of Commission	Months Commis'd	Weeks labor reported.	Stations supplied.	Baptized.	Received by Letter.	Scholars in S. School.	Cont. to Benevolent Objects.	Additional Facts Reported.
S. B. Page	Cleveland	Ohio city, (formerly)	May 1, 1854	12	39	1	3	14	180	29 66	Preparing to build a Meeting-house. Work progressing. Revival.
MICHIGAN.											
Lyman H. Moore	Marshall	Marshall	Nov. 1, 1853	12	30	3	4	16	150	101 00	Had a revival. Sent out a colony to form a new church.
" "	"	Michigan	Nov. 1, 1854	12	9	----	..	----	----	......	Agent for Church Edifice Fund.
Samuel Haskell	Kalamazoo	Kalamazoo	Sept. 1, 1853	12	26	3	3	13	265	70 00	Meeting-house progressing.
" "	"	"	Sept. 1, 1854	12	26	----	1	8	----	99 80	Prospects encouraging.
G. V. Ten Brook	Centreville	Centreville	Oct. 1, 1853	12	26	2	--	5	40	20 64	Church growing in favor with God and man.
" "	"	"	Oct. 1, 1854	12	26	4	..	6	----	12 00	Acquiring strength. Meetings interesting.
P. C. Dayfoot	Lansing	Lansing	Oct. 1, 1853	12	26	4	4	3	60	9 63	Need a Meeting-house. Some trials and difficulties.
Alfred Handy	Flint	Flint and vicinity	July 1, 1853	12	13	3	1	1	----	10 00	Prospects encouraging, but need a Meeting-house very much.
" "	"	" "	July 1, 1854	12	39	----	1	13	40	5 00	Want help for their church edifice.
A. E. Mather	Romeo	Romeo	July 1, 1853	12	13	3	4	3	100	......	Church prospering and increasing in strength.
" "	"	"	July 1, 1854	12	39	----	3	4	----	28 27	Church united and growing.
T. Z. R. Jones	Paw Paw	Paw Paw and vicinity	April 1, 1854	12	52	4	4	5	80	88 50	Church revived and strengthened. Secured a good Meeting-house and paid for it.
INDIANA.											
Ira C. Perrine	Hermon, Ripley Co.	White Water Valley Ass'n.	Nov. 1, 1853	12	39	13	51	13	230	270 68	Things look prosperous. Built a Meeting-house at Connersville.
" "	" " "	" " " "	Nov. 1, 1854	12	13	----	16	5	----	97 48	
Joseph A. Dixson	Evansville	Evansville	Sept. 1, 1853	12	9	1	3	5	120	84 00	Resigned because of ill health. Church in good condition. Meeting-house progressing.
N. V. Steadman	Evansville	Indiana	April 1, 1854	12	52	----	--	----	----	......	Exploring Agent and general Itinerant.
" "	"	"	April 1, 1855	12	----	----	--	----	----	......	Re-appointed.
J. M. Maxwell	Plymouth	Plymouth, Marshall, &c.	Nov. 1, 1853	12	9	10	1	2	----	5 50	Resigned and left the field.
John Reece	Shelbyville	Shelbyville and vicinity	April 1, 1854	12	52	1	3	5	123	56 25	Meeting-house nearly finished.
Abel Johnson	Bluffton	Bluffton and Warren	Jan. 1, 1854	12	52	2	--	6	150	3 71	Things encouraging. Need no further aid.
David S. French	Covington	Tippecanoe Association	April 1, 1854	12	52	----	20	15	----	......	Has resigned his commission on account of wife's ill health.
Eli Rees	Brookville	Brookville and vicinity	May 1, 1853	12	13	1	7	1	----	87 50	Prospering and promising.

[redacted]	Months Commis'd.	Weeks labor reported.	Stations supplied.	Baptized.	Received by Letter.	Scholars in S. School.	Cont. to Benevolent Objects.	ADDITIONAL FACTS REPORTED.
[redacted]	12	26	1	....	....	....	1 50	Resigned and left for warmer climate.
	12	34	2	....	....	....	20 00	Prospects encouraging for raising a good ch.
	12	39	....	100	24	125	165 00	Two churches built Meeting-houses. Three churches had revivals.
	12	34	1	40	32	55	21 45	Prospects good. Need no further aid.
	12	26	11	....	....	....	25 00	Encouragements at three of his stations.
	12	39	1	8	11	....	103 24	Hoping on and laboring. Encouraged.
	12	13	1	....	4	40	25 25	Church become self-supporting.
	12	13	....	13	....	....	37 50	No very special display of Divine power.
	12	34	2	31	5	....	87 50	Revival.
	12	26	6	17	5	....	103 06	Large and destitute field. Revival.
	12	26	1	13	2	85	24 50	Church strengthened. Revival.
	12	22	5	....	4	....	62 50	Cause advancing. Obstacles yielding.
	12	26	1	2	5	48	......	Place afflicted with sickness. Revival.
	12	39	3	....	7	....	......	Been sick. Religious prospects of field more promising.
	12	39	1	9	10	....	7 50	Building a Meeting-house.
[redacted]								
	12	52	....	....	....	....	......	Exploring Agent and General Itinerant.
	12	....	....	....	....	....	......	Been sick.
	12	39	8	....	....	....	200 00	Field important and promising.
	12	13	2	1	....	....	......	Leaves the field.
	12	39	1	1	....	75	......	Organized a church. Completed a Meeting-house. Prospects encouraging.
	12	13	3	....	5	110	25 25	Health poor.
	12	26	....	....	....	....	45 64	Resigned.
	12	39	6	39	3	120	......	Preaches to German and English churches. One church completed a Meeting house, another building one. Cause prosperous.
	12	26	1	1	....	....	20 00	Some conversions.
	12	26	....	....	3	....	......	Church decreased by removals.
	12	39	1	11	4	....	17 20	Building a good Meeting-house. Pastor been sick.
	12	17	....	....	....	....	......	Labored in New York. Resigned.
	12	26	1	....	....	24	......	Requires no further aid.
	12	39	5	5	3	200	137 00	Organized a church at an out-station.

NAMES OF AGENTS AND MISSIONARIES.	POST OFFICE ADDRESS.	FIELD OF LABOR.	Date of Commission	Months Commis'd.	Weeks labor reported.	Stations supplied.	Bap'ized.	Received by Letter.	Scholars in S. School.	Cont. to Benevolent Objects.	ADDITIONAL FACTS REPORTED.
Gilbert S. Bailey	Pekin, &c.	Pekin, &c.	Nov. 1, 1854	12	13	----	3	3	150	17 00	Meeting-house progressing. Suffer interruptions until it is completed.
Asahel Chapin	Galena	Galena	June 1, 1853	12	13	2	1	4	72	10 00	Progressing with Meeting-house. Baptists looked upon more favorable in that city.
" "	"	"	June 1, 1854	12	39	----	2	1	60	8 00	Meeting-house nearly completed.
H. H. Richardson	Thebes	Cairo and other places	Oct. 1, 1853	12	13	9	--	----	140	------	Resigned.
G. Palmquist	Rock Island	Swedes in Rock Island, &c.	Feb. 1, 1854	12	39	2	14	3	25	23 00	Encouraging state of religious prosperity. Resigns to labor in New York City.
M. B. Kelly	Chester	Chester and vicinity	Feb. 1, 1854	12	39	1	7	----	50	------	Discouragements. Resigned.
J. V. Allison	Mt. Carroll	Mt. Carroll	May 1, 1853	12	13	----	4	----	32	25 00	Crippled in their efforts on account of having no Meeting-house.
" "	"	"	May 1, 1854	12	39	1	1	10	70	------	Building a Meeting-house.
S. S. Martin	Delavan	Delavan	May 1, 1853	12	13	3	--	----	120	7 00	Finished a Meeting-house.
"	"	"	May 1, 1854	12	39	----	--	6	175	22 35	State of religion not encouraging.
Samuel M. Brown	Woodstock	Woodstock	Aug. 1, 1853	12	26	2	--	----	60	50 00	Nothing special.
Thomas Stokes	Duncanton	Carmi and vicinity	Oct. 1, 1853	12	26	8	--	----	----	10 00	Organized a Church.
" "	"	" " "	Nov. 1, 1854	12	13	----	--	----	----	------	Nothing special.
John Young	Bristol	Somanauk and vicinity	Aug. 1, 1853	12	13	5	5	2	160	26 00	Meeting-house nearly completed.
" "	"	Bristol	Nov. 1, 1854	12	39	3	7	----	100	------	Ch. trying to sustain their Pastor. Resigns.
J. F. Childs	Lockport, Will Co.	Lockport and Joliet	Aug. 1, 1853	12	26	2	1	----	----	13 25	Congregations enlarged.
" "	" " "	" " "	Aug. 1, 1854	12	13	----	1	2	40	8 00	Ch's in union and harmony. Pastor resigns.
W. D. Clark	Ottawa	Ottawa	Sept. 1, 1853	12	24	3	10	15	175	13 00	Need no further aid.
" "	Joliet	Lockport and Joliet	Nov. 1, 1854	12	13	2	--	10	45	------	No remarks.
Ira H. Rees	Urbana	Urbana and vicinity	Oct. 1, 1853	12	9	3	7	1	----	------	Resigns on account of ill health.
I. S. Mahan	Wethersfield	Wethersfield	Jan. 1, 1854	12	39	4	24	4	30	28 59	Revival. Needs no further aid.
John N. Tolman	Decatur, Macon Co.	Decatur	Jan. 1, 1854	12	39	3	5	17	75	40 00	Take regular monthly col's for Mission cause.
" "	"	"	Jan. 1, 1855	12	13	----	--	4	30	30 00	No remarks.
J. M. Cochran	Batavia	Batavia	April 1, 1854	12	52	2	2	13	----	117 89	Prospects encouraging.
C. D. Merit	Metamora	Metamora, &c.	July 1, 1854	12	39	3	6	8	60	30 00	One Church completed Meeting-house and another commenced one. Prospect good.
E. N. Jencks	Brimfield	Brimfield	July 1, 1854	9	39	3	11	4	75	12 70	Revival. Church completed a Meeting-house.
Nathan Denison	Mendota	Mendota and Earlville	Oct. 1, 1854	12	9	2	--	----	----	------	Organized a Church. Suddenly deceased after arriving on the field.
O. L. Barber	Chester	Chester	Nov. 1, 1854	12	13	1	--	----	35	------	Prospects of the Church flattering.
WISCONSIN.											
James Delany	Ozaukee	Wisconsin	April 1, 1853	13	52	----	--	----	----	96 69	General itinerant. Labored with some success in interesting but destitute fields.

[illegible]	Months Commis'd.	Weeks labor reported.	Stations supplied.	Received by Letter.	Scholars in S. School.	Cont. to Benevolent Objects.	ADDITIONAL FACTS REPORTED.
54	12	....			....	......	Re-appointment.
53	12	26			80	12 50	Church in a prosperous state.
54	12	26			75	15 00	Health poor. Nothing special.
53	12	13			42	......	Discontinues his labors at O.
53	12	13			....	41 89	Revival.
54	12	39			75	44 78	Lit. and Theo. Institution located in Beaver Dam. Town increasing in population and enterprise.
53	12	24			100	26 15	Labored a short time as agent for Church Edifice Fund.
54	12	26			....	24 10	Encouraged.
53	12	13			70	......	Congregation increasing.
54	12	39			....	15 00	Church weakened by removals, but are united and progressing in efficiency.
53	12	39			....	9 60	Church feeble. Striving to build a Meeting-house.
54	12	13			....	......	Meeting-house slowly advancing.
53	12	39			14	5 00	Need no further aid.
53	12	13			40	......	Church increasing.
54					....	6 00	Contemplate building a Meeting-house.
53					....	......	Leaves the field.
53					63	......	Leaves the field.
54					....	......	A very destitute region. Will form Sunday-schools. Is interested in his field.
53					110		during the year. Need

NAMES OF AGENTS AND MISSIONARIES.	POST OFFICE ADDRESS.	FIELD OF LABOR.	Date of Commission	Months Commis'd.	Weeks labor reported.	Stations supplied.	Baptized.	Received by Letter.	Scholars in S. School.	Cont. to Benevolent Objects.	ADDITIONAL FACTS REPORTED.
A. Knapp	Johnstown Centre	Johnstown Centre, &c.	June 1, 1854	12	39	7	1	6	40	......	Nothing special. Pastor resigned.
Evan S. Thomas	Omro	Omro and vicinity	June 1, 1854	12	39	4	8	11	35	6 50	Church revived. Building a Meeting-house.
T. B. Rogers	Prescott	Prescott, Wis. and Douglass &c., Minnesota Territory.	Nov. 1, 1854	12	13	2	--	3	----	......	Attentive congregations.
Thomas Brandt	Kenosha	Kenosha	May 1, 1854	12	----	----	--	----	----	......	A new appointment.
James Andem	Neenah	Neenah and Green Bay	July 1, 1853	12	13	2	--	3	30	......	Organized a church at Appleton.
Wm. McKee	Thompsonville	Raymond &c.	Sept. 1, 1853	12	26	----	--	----	40	......	Congregations large and attentive.
"	"	" "	Sept. 1, 1854	12	26	3	2	1	----	15 40	Some attention to the Gospel.
C. A. Hewett	Whitewater	Whitewater &c.	July 1, 1853	12	13	1	10	----	----	......	Improved state of things in the church.
Salmon Morton	Sun Prairie	Bird s Corners	Dec. 1, 1853	12	39	4	1	2	30	17 19	Nothing special.
Thomas Bright	Elkhorn	Elkhorn and vicinity	Nov. 1, 1853	12	39	1	24	3	60	......	Revival. Indications encouraging.
" "	"	" " "	Nov. 1, 1854	12	13	----	--	----	----	......	Nothing special.
Anthony Case	Waushara, Dodge Co.	Waushara	Oct. 1, 1853	12	26	5	--	8	75	......	Church need no further aid. Pastor resigns.
D. D. Read	Columbus	Columbus and Portage	Dec. 1, 1853	12	39		--	----	----	......	Pastor resigns to take charge of the University. Churches in a good state.
M. D. Miller	Madison	Madison	Jan. 1, 1854	12	39	1	1	10	35	......	Finished Meeting-house. Prospects of the church never more encouraging.
" "	"	"	Jan. 1, 1855	12	13	----	--	----	4	......	Difficult to promote spirituality during the winter—the gay season.
John A. Pool	Monroe	Monroe, Decatur, &c.	M'ch 1, 1854	12	26	5	1	3	50	......	Congregations large.
Joseph Bowman	Lodi, Columbia Co.	Lodi, West Point, &c.	M'ch 1, 1854	12	52	2	--	5	20	......	Church united. Pastor afflicted.
" "	" " "	" " "	M'ch 1, 1855	12	----	----	--	----	----	......	Re-appointment.
J. T. Westover	Kenosha	Kenosha	May 1, 1853	12	13	1	22	1	48	31 94	Revival.
" "	"	"	May 1, 1854	12	39	----	9	9	80	89 25	Painted and repaired their Meeting-house.
Platt Betts	Utica, Winnebago Co.	Utica and vicinity	Aug. 1, 1853	12	13	3	--	----	----	55 00	Left the field.
E. W. Cressy	Prescott, Pierce Co.	Prescott and vicinity	Oct. 1, 1854	12	23	----	--	....	36	55 00	Nothing special.
Joel W. Fish	Geneva	General itinerant	Dec. 1, 1853	12	39	----	1	----	----	94 63	Labored a part of the time among the destitute. A part of the time in Revivals.
"	"	" " "	Dec. 1, 1854	12	13	----	--	----	----	53 25	Is much encouraged in his labors.
IOWA.											
William Elliott	Brighton	Brighton and Glasgow	Sept. 1, 1853	12	24	4	3	3	40	......	Church at Glasgow building a Meeting-house.
Elihu Gunn	Keokuk	Keokuk	Nov. 1, 1853	12	39	2	28	11	150	......	Nothing special.
" "	"	"	Nov. 1, 1854	12	14	----	--	5	100	......	No remarks.
John Bates	Cascade	Cascade	June 1, 1853	12	13	1	14	5	50	......	Revival. Asks for no further aid.

Months Commis'd.	Weeks labor reported.	Stations supplied.	…ived by …tter.	…chool.	Cont. to Benevolent Objects.	ADDITIONAL FACTS REPORTED.
[illegible]					15 96	Nothing special.
					8 00	A difficult field.
					......	Church afflicted in the death of one of its
						prominent members.
					20 00	Resigned.
					......	Resigns. Church will sustain pastor hereafter
						without further aid.
					......	Revival. Organized a church at H. Build-
						ing a Meeting-house.
					12 25	Revival at an out-station
					25 00	Prospects encouraging. Benton church build-
						ing a Meeting-house.
					23 20	Progressing with Meeting-house.
					53 10	Revival.
					......	Revival.
					......	Nothing special.
					......	Been sick.
					[illegible]	Left the field.
						his connection with the Society for the

Names of Agents and Missionaries.	Post Office Address.	Field of Labor.	Date of Commission	Months Commiss'd.	Weeks labor reported.	Stations supplied.	Baptized.	Received by Letter.	Scholars in S. School	Cont. to Benevolent Objects.	Additional Facts Reported.
MINNESOTA.											
Julius S. Webber	Stillwater	Stillwater, &c.	June 1, 1853	12	13	5		5	80		Good attention to preaching.
" "	"	"	June 1, 1854	12	26						Resigns.
Timothy R. Cressy	St. Paul	St. Paul	June 1, 1853	12	13	1					Leaves St. P. for another field.
" " "	"	Southern Minnesota	June 1, 1854	12	39					20 36	Immigration pouring in.
Lyman Palmer	St. Anthony	St. Anthony	May 1, 1853	12	13	2		25			Prospects in many respects encouraging.
" "	"	"	May 1, 1854	12	39		10	23		47 00	Revival. Improving the interior of Meeting-house.
James Tanner	Pembina	Chippewa Indians	Nov. 1, 1853	12	32	5					Fighting between the Sioux and Chippewas. Mission discontinued.
T. B. Rogers	St. Anthony	Minneapolis	Oct. 1, 1853	12	26	3		3			Prospects at M. encouraging. Left to explore among the Indians with reference to laboring among them. Returned and labors at Prescott, Wis.
L. Atkinson	St. Anthony	Anoka, Itaska, &c.	Oct. 1, 1853	12	26	11		9	18	60 00	A large field. Some progress made.
"	Anoka	" "	Oct. 1, 1854	12	26	7			8		Is encouraged.
Wilson Cogswell	Shakapee City	Shakapee and vicinity	Dec. 1, 1853	12	43	7			30	23 00	Organized a church and Sunday-school. School interesting.
" "	" "	" " "	Dec. 1, 1854	12	13	6			26		Large attendance at his meetings, but have no proper place in which to hold them.
A. A. Russell	Minneapolis	Minneapolis, &c.	July 1, 1854	12	39	4		15	15	50 00	Prospects good. Arranging to build a Meeting-house.
F. O. Nelson	St. Paul	Swedes in Minn.	Nov. 1, 1854	12	13	1	2				Organized a church on the Rock River.
A. M. Torbet	St. Paul	St. Paul	Oct. 1, 1854	12	22	1	6	10			Church paid debt on Meeting-house. Pastor encouraged. Good feeling in the church.
NEBRASKA.											
W. W. Keep	Fontanelle	Fontanelle and vicinity		12							A new appointment.
KANSAS.											
Wm. W. Hall	Lawrence	Lawrence, &c.	Oct. 1, 1854	12	26	2					Enc'ged. Will probably soon organize a ch.
J. Gillpatrick		Field not fixed	Nov. 1, 1854	12	13						Exploring Agent. Is encouraged.

[redacted]

Months Commiss'd.	Weeks labor reported.	Stations supplied.	Baptized.	Received by Letter.	Scholars in S. School.	Cont. to Benevolent Objects.	ADDITIONAL FACTS REPORTED.
12	26	----	--	----	----	------	Nothing special.
12	26	----	--	4	----	------	Cause more prosperous. Several conversions in addition to those baptiz d.
12	26	----	--	----	----	------	Public labors among the native population broken up by the opposition of the Priests. American congregation recently assumed an encouraging aspect. Mr. S. retired from the Mission.
12	26	----	--	----	----	------	Embarrassments in his work.
12	----	----	--	----	----	------	Two quarterly reports due.
12	52	----	3	----	3	4 00	Preaches to an attentive congregation varying from one hundred to three hundred.
12	13	----	--	----	----	------	Opposition from the Priests. Encouraging indications.
9	----	----	--	----	----	------	A Baptized Indian employed as an assistant to Mr. Gorman.
12	26	----	--	----	----	------	Prospects encouraging. Does not trust in appearances, but in God.
12	13	----	16	1	25	3 75	Revival in Oregon City.
12	52	----	--	----	----	------	Labored with two churches where there was a large number of hopeful conversions and twenty-three in addition baptized by the two Pastors. Successful in settling a church difficulty.
12	39	----	--	----	----	------	Itinerates, and successfully engaged as Principal of the infant College.
12	----	----	--	----	----	------	Quarterly report failed to reach us.
12	----	----	--	----	----	------	A new field and a new appointment. Quarterly report not due.

NAMES OF AGENTS AND MISSIONARIES.	POST OFFICE ADDRESS.	FIELD OF LABOR.	Date of Commission	Months Commiss'd.	Weeks labor reported.	Stations supplied.	Baptized.	Received by Letter.	Scholars in S. School.	Cont. to Benevolent Objects.	ADDITIONAL FACTS REPORTED.
CALIFORNIA.											
Wm. Rollinson	San Francisco	Pine st. Ch.	M'ch 1, 1854	12	52	1	5	14	80	362 00	Good state of feeling in the church and prayer meetings largely attended.
"	"	Bush street, late Pine street Church	M'ch 1, 1855	12							Completed a Meeting-house.
J. B. Saxton	Stockton	Stockton	Feb. 1, 1854	12	52	1	8	13	30		Revival. All the interests of the church prosperous. Need no further aid.
O. B. Stone	Nevada	Marysville and Nevada	Jan. 1, 1854	12	52	2	1	11	20	125 00	Organized a church at Marysville. Completed a Meeting-house at Nevada.
"	"	Nevada	Jan. 1, 1855	12	13						Trials have existed, but are being removed.
H. H. Rhees	Ione Valley	Ione Valley	M'ch 1, 1855	12							A new appointment. Report not due.
NEW GRENADA.											
Philip Livingston	St. Andrews	St. Andrews	May 1, 1855	12							A new appointment and a new field.

4

STATE CONVENTIONS

AND

GENERAL ASSOCIATIONS IN THE UNITED STATES,

With the Names and Post Office Address of the Corresponding Secretaries; the Time and Place of their Anniversaries for 1855, the number of Missionaries employed, and amount of Receipts into their Treasuries, for 1854, including Balances of the previous year.

STATES.	CORRESPONDING SECRETARIES.	POST OFFICE ADDRESS	PLACE OF NEXT ANNIVERSARY.	Time of Anniversary	No. of Missionaries	Amount of Receipts for Dom. Miss. in 1854.
Maine	J. B. Foster	Portland		June 17	34	$4311 83
New Hampshire	H. D. Hodge	Sanbornton	Newton	Oct. 17	17	1502 43
Vermont	John Goadby	Poultney	Addison	Oct. 3	10	1857 05
Massachusetts	George W. Bosworth	South Boston	Woburn	Oct. 31	35	3758 50
Rhode Island	Warren Randolph	Providence	Warren	April 30	14	1821 58
Connecticut	E. Cushman	Deep River	Middletown	June 10	10	1910 81
New York	C. W. Hewes	Lansingburg	Binghamton	Oct. 9	54	12407 43
New Jersey	J. M. Carpenter	Jacobstown	Piscataway	Oct. 30	16	2308 29
Pennsylvania	T. Wheaton Smith	Philadelphia	Pittsburg	Oct. 24	37	7474 66
*Maryland						
*Virginia						
*North Carolina						

AGGREGATE CONTRIBUTIONS FROM ALL THE STATES, SINCE 1832.

STATES.	Total Amount to 1845.	1846.	1847.	1848.	1849.	1850.	1851.	1852.	1853.	1854.	1855.	Total for each State.
Canada	$327 65	$864 70	$602 67	$734 11	$710 79	$809 57	$453 84	$183 68	$160 19	$91 91	$145 23	$5,203 29
Maine	2,717 40	----	----	----	500 00	----	37 00	56 39	622 31	104 66	173 16	4,270 92
New Hampshire	3,083 42	528 41	242 50	343 81	50 50	625 88	419 17	1,164 77	1,457 00	1,602 60	1,875 47	11,393 58
Vermont	1,718 95	673 95	184 00	257 51	222 80	1,015 75	471 98	506 17	494 71	758 58	1,511 10	7,814 50
Massachusetts	22,313 30	1,474 20	3,333 03	4,791 22	4,022 07	5,357 73	6,717 06	8,497 51	7,974 56	12,005 92	8,265 73	84,752 50
Rhode Island	5,118 45	852 35	669 56	1,683 33	1,545 76	2,427 57	1,188 68	2,574 55	687 87	2,695 78	2,287 45	22,031 33
Connecticut	11,128 71	1,186 03	1,042 31	1,072 06	1,480 46	1,251 34	2,032 59	2,490 31	3,052 58	4,529 96	4,285 70	24,052 05
New York	65,772 95	6,520 49	7,142 38	6,871 19	6,614 15	7,723 20	10,066 47	13,706 43	16,951 07	18,071 49	20,169 13	180,228 95
New Jersey	4,851 29	1,195 85	1,419 27	1,890 90	2,724 80	2,408 67	2,518 20	2,179 01	3,419 94	3,833 51	3,463 63	30,415 16
Pennsylvania	4,520 81	528 47	529 56	707 43	1,556 89	1,606 11	1,005 98	1,973 75	2,252 91	3,024 90	3,530 82	21,837 93
Delaware	161 20	----	----	153 36	60 00	228 94	203 00	163 00	167 90	138 92	67 88	1,344 20
Maryland	2,019 81	30 25	5 00	----	----	----	15 50	----	----	----	----	2,070 56
District of Columbia	953 12	----	10 00	----	----	80 00	6 00	37 31	5 00	134 00	30 00	1,204 43
Ohio	1,010 45	114 81	30 84	30 50	29 45	153 52	241 88	656 62	732 48	2,758 60	3,226 67	8,985 82
Michigan	337 50	29 50	13 25	172 89	556 21	610 60	1,011 80	866 75	634 43	287 74	574 60	5,095 27
Indiana	28 75	8 10	22 05	11 11	8 50	26 35	290 22	774 38	1,069 44	2,306 79	2,101 50	7,247 19
Illinois	668 09	477 63	766 50	1,136 69	594 90	704 74	1,329 98	1,230 97	1,675 63	2,470 52	1,799 70	12,864 65
Wisconsin	20 10	15 63	124 50	72 16	88 06	58 35	181 91	170 09	274 87	549 71	625 90	2,181 27
Iowa	83 56	41 00	120 03	62 12	93 24	162 77	171 95	396 67	278 05	277 10	332 58	2,019 07
Minnesota	----	----	----	----	----	----	1 00	2 25	55 85	141 46	405 35	605 91
Missouri	266 82	----	----	----	----	----	----	2 00	----	75 00	215 00	558 82
Kentucky	273 68	----	10 00	20 50	----	----	----	----	----	42 25	----	346 63
Virginia	9,152 56	159 44	5 85	7 30	----	----	5 00	----	----	----	23 75	9,353 90
North Carolina	5,000 02	391 67	----	----	----	----	----	----	----	----	----	5,391 69
South Carolina	8,362 95	135 15	----	----	----	----	----	----	30 00	----	----	8,528 10
Georgia	9,529 33	----	1,331 87	----	----	----	----	30 00	----	----	----	10,891 20
Alabama	493 08	----	----	----	----	----	----	----	----	----	30 00	523 08
Florida	157 82	----	15 00	----	----	----	----	----	----	----	----	172 81
Mississippi	1,899 66	----	----	----	----	----	----	----	----	----	----	1,899 66
Tennessee	477 85	----	8 25	----	----	----	----	----	----	----	----	486 10
Louisiana	79 00	----	----	----	----	----	----	----	----	----	----	79 00
Arkansas	50	----	----	50 55	18 15	----	----	----	----	----	----	118 70
Texas	----	----	----	----	----	----	----	----	----	----	----	----
California	----	----	----	----	----	----	50 00	150 50	70 00	20 00	225 00	515 50
Oregon	----	----	----	----	----	----	30 00	----	51 50	159 12	59 33	299 95
New Mexico	----	----	----	----	----	----	----	62 10	94 42	7 38	20 00	183 90
Aggregates for each period	163,028 98	15,727 63	17,728 72	20,068 73	20,876 73	25,201 09	29,648 28	38,114 16	42,872 01	59,903 83	55,545 40	$494,907 41

NUAL CONTRIBUTIONS SINCE 1845.

ASURERS.	Previous to 1849.	Anniversary of 1849.	Anniversary of 1850.	Anniversary of 1851.	Anniversary of 1852.	Anniversary of 1853.	Anniversary of 1854.	Anniversary of 1855.	Total.
s	$81 94	$25 00	$30 00	$75 12	$30 00	$50 00	$30 00	----	316 06
	65 23	32 50	30 79	----	113 70	60 00	60 00	$70 00	432 22
Randolph	950 54	768 02	800 00	798 50	594 08	780 00	----	300 00	4,990 14
	102 62	12 00	----	----	----	----	----	10 00	124 62
Colgate	280 02	156 71	----	56 00	128 30	----	----	----	620 03
	----	50 00	----	87 00	41 50	50 00	----	----	228 50
ll	290 00	75 00	110 00	60 00	30 00	230 00	190 00	200 00	1,185 00
se	120 00	60 00	----	60 00	180 68	----	----	----	420 00
	90 00	30 00	20 00	40 00	30 00	20 00	15 00	----	245 00
Brush	250 00	60 00	100 00	90 00	60 00	150 00	160 00	----	970 00
	150 50	90 00	60 00	60 00	90 00	60 00	5 00	----	515 16
	30 00	30 00	----	100 00	----	----	----	----	160 00
Todd	30 00	30 00	----	60 00	----	80 00	80 00	20 00	300 00
Beckwith	479 00	150 00	136 67	141 00	185 52	83 00	121 85	145 00	1,442 04
Fessenden, Sec.	101 00	25 00	30 00	----	30 00	27 00	----	22 00	235 00
aret S. Foster.	358 00	150 00	75 00	245 00	191 84	229 21	100 00	206 70	1,356 05
Crowell	85 00	100 00	----	100 00	----	50 00	50 00	----	385 00
le	----	100 00	100 00	88 25	78 37	----	----	----	366 62
el Knox	66 00	30 00	30 30	----	----	----	----	13 02	139 32
	32 97	10 98	66 60	2 88	2 87	----	----	----	115 70
stock, Sec.	100 00	50 00	40 00	----	27 03	32 00	----	----	249 03
Butler	100 00	135 00	----	----	----	----	----	----	235 00
iner	60 00	30 00	----	----	----	----	----	30 00	120 00
	200 00	----	30 00		30 00	----	30 00	30 00	390 00
	145 00	----	37 00		----	----	....	----	182 00
	----	41 48	125 00		----	----	100 00	100 00	366 48

NAMES OF SOCIETIES.	POST OFFICE ADDRESS.	TREASURERS.	Previous to 1849.	Anniversary of 1849.	Anniversary of 1850.	Anniversary of 1851.	Anniversary of 1852.	Anniversary of 1853.	Anniversary of 1854.	Anniversary of 1855.	Total.
Sunday-school of First Church	Camden, N. J.		----	----	----	$10 00	----	----	----	----	$10 00
Female Mission Society, Union Church	Jersey City, N. J.		----	----	----	32 00	$30 00	$50 00	$60 00	$75 00	247 00
Female Mission Society of Middle street	Portsmouth, N. H.		----	----	----	12 50	----	----	----	----	12 50
Sunday-school of Amity street	New York		----	----	----	30 00	70 00	50 00	----	----	150 00
Sunday-school of Central Church	Brooklyn		----	100 00	----	31 80	30 00	----	10 00	----	171 80
Sunday-school of Pierrepont street	do		----	----	----	50 00	75 00	----	22 00	----	147 00
Female Mite Society	West Dedham, Mass.		----	----	----	----	11 00	----	----	----	11 00
Weekly Contributor's Society	Framingham, Mass.		----	----	----	----	34 00	----	----	----	34 00
Sewing Society	Norwich, N. Y.		----	----	----	----	12 80	----	----	----	12 80
Female Mission Society	New Boston, N. H.		----	----	----	----	30 00	----	----	30 00	60 00
Female Mission Society	Watertown, Mass.		----	----	----	----	23 42	----	----	----	23 42
Ladies' Mission Society	Ashland, Mass.		----	----	----	----	12 00	----	----	----	12 00
Sunday-school of Fifth Church	Providence, R. I.		----	----	----	----	18 00	----	----	----	18 00
Sunday-school	Valley Falls, R. I.	A. Babcock	----	----	----	----	15 63	----	----	----	15 63
Salem street Sunday-school	Reading, Mass.		----	----	----	----	20 00	----	----	----	20 00
Sunday-school of Tenth Church	Philadelphia		----	----	----	----	90 00	----	----	90 00	180 00
Youth's Comstock Mission Society of Olive Branch Church	New York	R. C. McCormick, Jr.	----	----	----	----	70 00	----	----	----	70 00
Society of Inquiry, University	Lewisburg, Pa.	S. W. Zeigler	----	----	----	----	----	24 00	16 00	10 00	50 00
Female Mission Society, Berean Church	New York		----	----	----	----	----	15 00	----	----	15 00
Ladies' Mission Society	Deep River, Ct.		----	----	----	----	----	137 14	138 50	----	275 64
Ladies' Mission Society of Second Church	Danbury, Ct.		----	----	----	----	----	18 00	----	30 00	48 00
Ladies' Mission Society of First Church	Hartford, Ct.	Mrs. R. M. Burdick	----	----	----	----	----	35 22	35 42	32 77	103 41
Ladies' Mission Society, South Church	Hartford, Ct.	Mrs. J. N. Murdock	----	----	----	----	----	80 00	----	2 00	82 00
Ladies' Benevolent Society	Burnt Hills, N. Y.		----	----	----	----	----	10 00	9 04	8 43	27 47
Female Mission Society	Millington, N. J.		----	----	----	----	----	22 36	22 13	84 00	128 49
Sunday-school	Clinton, Mass.		----	----	----	----	----	30 00	----	----	30 00
Ladies' Mission Society	Chatham, Mass.		----	----	----	----	----	21 00	----	----	21 00
Female Mission Society	Abington, Mass.		----	----	----	----	----	14 25	----	----	14 25
Female Mite Society, Central Church	Poughkeepsie, N. Y.	Miss Booth	----	----	----	----	----	20 00	19 00	15 00	54 00
Sunday-school, Strong Place Church	Brooklyn, N. Y.		----	----	----	----	----	25 00	10 00	----	35 00
Female Mission Society, North Church	Troy, N. Y.		----	----	----	----	----	42 00	----	51 00	93 00
Ladies' Second Church	Plainfield, N. J		----	----	----	----	----	30 00	----	----	30 00
Sunday School of First Church	Fall River, Mass.		----	----	----	----	----	----	16 00	----	16 00
Society of Inquiry	Madison University, N. Y.	W. T. Potter	----	----	----	----	----	----	62 52	29 00	91 52
Sunday-school of First Church	Boston, Mass.		----	----	----	----	----	----	151 00	150 00	301 00
Sunday-school of First Church	Albany, N. Y.		----	----	----	----	----	----	30 00	----	30 00
Ladies' Sewing Circle	Athol, Mass.		----	----	----	----	----	----	17 68	----	17 68
Female Mite Society	Clifton Park, N. Y.		----	----	----	----	----	----	30 00	----	30 00
Judson Society of Inquiry	Rochester University, N. Y.		----	----	----	----	----	----	3 00	----	3 00
Sunday-school of Third Church	Philadelphia		----	----	----	----	----	----	45 00	----	45 00

[illegible]	Previous to 1840.	Anniversary of 1849.	Anniversary of 1861.	Anniversary of 1862.	Anniversary of 1863.	Anniversary of 1864.	Anniversary of 1865.	Total.
						$3	----	$3 00
						15	----	15 00
						10	----	10 00
						9	----	9 66
						16	----	16 00
						5	----	5 00
						50	----	50 00
						4	----	4 15
						20	----	20 00
						65	----	65 00
						10	----	10 00
						15	----	15 00
						30	----	30 00
						23	----	23 00
						15	----	15 00
						5	----	5 00
						10	----	10 00
						30	----	30 00
						30	----	30 00
						2	4 05	6 35
							----	25 00
							----	11 11
							----	4 00
							8 00	14 00
							----	1 00
							----	1 14
							30 00	30 00
							16 50	16 50
							6 00	6 00
							100 00	100 00
							4 32	4 32
							7 17	7 17
							5 00	6 00
							30 10	30 10

NAMES OF SOCIETIES.	POST OFFICE ADDRESS.	TREASURERS.	Previous to 1849.	Anniversary of 1849.	Anniversary of 1850.	Anniversary of 1851.	Anniversary of 1852.	Anniversary of 1853.	Anniversary of 1854.	Anniversary of 1855.	Total.
Sunday-school	West Plattsburg, N. Y.		----	----	----	----	----	----	----	$3 60	$3 60
Sunday-school, Trenton and Lamberton Ch.	Trenton, N. J.		----	----	----	----	----	----	----	12 50	12 50
Sunday-school of First Church	Cincinnati, O.		----	----	----	----	----	----	----	40 00	40 00
Sunday-school	Bennington, Vt.		----	----	----	----	----	----	----	5 00	5 00
Sunday-school	North Dorchester, Mass.		----	----	----	----	----	----	----	10 00	10 00
Baptist Sunday-school	Reading, Pa.		----	----	----	----	----	----	----	19 00	19 00
Ladies' Benevolent Society	Hudson, N. H.		----	----	----	----	----	----	----	30 00	30 00
Female Mission Society	Jericho, Vt.		----	----	----	----	----	----	----	10 00	10 00
Sunday-school of First Church	New London, Ct.		----	----	----	----	----	----	----	14 00	14 00
Sunday-school	Schuylkill Falls, Pa.		----	----	----	----	----	----	----	13 27	13 27
Sunday-school	Bristol, Pa.		----	----	----	----	----	----	----	5 00	5 00
Ladies' Home Mission Society	Taunton, Mass.		----	----	----	----	----	----	----	20 00	20 00
Benevolent Mite Society	Jefferson and Gilboa, N. Y.		----	----	----	----	----	----	----	10 00	10 00
Female Benevolent Society	Middlefield, N. Y.		----	----	----	----	----	----	----	13 00	13 00
Female Mite Society	Maryland, N. Y.		----	----	----	----	----	----	----	4 42	4 42
Sunday-school	do		----	----	----	----	----	----	----	2 34	2 34
Sunday-school	Waterville, N. Y.		----	----	----	----	----	----	----	10 00	10 00
Female Mission Society	Claremont, N. H.		----	----	----	----	----	----	----	11 50	11 50
Ladies' Home Mission Society	Newburyport, Mass		----	----	----	----	----	----	----	30 00	30 00
Ladies' Home Mission Society	Ludlow, Vt.		----	----	----	----	----	----	----	16 00	16 00
Female Mission Society	Charlestown, N. Y		----	----	----	----	----	----	----	4 28	4 28
Female Mission Society	Preston Hollow, N. Y.		----	----	----	----	----	----	----	5 25	5 25
Female Mission Society	Westerloo, N. Y.		----	----	----	----	----	----	----	10 00	10 00
Female Mission Society	Rensselaerville N. Y.		----	----	----	----	----	----	----	6 75	6 75
Ladies' Home Mission Society	Haverhill	Julia M. P. Brown	----	----	----	----	----	----	----	15 00	15 00
Sunday-school, Bloomingdale Church	New York		----	----	----	----	----	----	----	60 15	60 15
Female Mite Society	East Hillsdale, N. Y.	Mrs. Betsey Pomeroy	----	----	----	----	----	----	----	5 00	5 00
High st. Sunday-school	Providence, R. I.		----	----	----	----	----	----	----	30 00	30 00
Sunday-school, Academy st.	New Haven, Ct.		----	----	----	----	----	----	----	30 00	30 00
Sewing Society	South Pittsburg, Pa.		----	----	----	----	----	----	----	16 00	16 00
Sunday-school, Strong Place	Brooklyn		----	----	----	----	----	----	----	75 00	75 00
Female Mission Society	Redstone, Pa.		----	----	----	----	----	----	----	5 00	5 00
Sunday-school	Bloomfield, Ct.		----	----	----	----	----	----	----	3 00	3 00
Ladies Mission Society	Willington, Ct.		----	----	----	----	----	----	----	25 50	25 50
Sunday-school	Pleasant Valley, Ct.		----	----	----	----	----	----	----	3 17	3 17
Sunday-school, Washington st.	Boston, Mass.		----	----	----	----	----	----	----	7 17	7 17
Female Mission Society, Calvary Church	New York	Mrs. G. N. Bleecker	----	----	----	----	----	----	----	330 00	330 00
Church Sunday-school	Rahway, N. J.		----	----	----	----	----	----	----	30 00	30 00
Union Mission Sunday-school	Philadelphia		----	----	----	----	----	----	----	10 00	10 00

LIST OF LEGACIES,

PAID TO THE SOCIETY SINCE ITS ORGANIZATION.

1834	Dea. Josiah Penfield, Savannah, Ga , per Rev. H. O. Wyer	$1250 00
1835	Mrs Clarissa Long, Shelburne, Mass., per W. Wilder, Esq., Executor	37 50
"	William Powers, Hebron, N H , per Rev. I Merriam	100 00
"	Miss Maria Curtis, Southbridge, Mass., per Rev. E. Going	200 00
"	Mrs. Jemima Elliott, Hampton, Ct , per Rev. J. Payne, Executor	100 00
1836	Mrs. Betsey Sprague, Attleboro', Mass , per Mr A. Reed, Executor	451 25
"	Robert Rogers, Esq., Newport, R. I.	25 00
"	Ebenezer Boyd, Providence, R. I.	10 00
1839	Mrs. Abigail Marshall, New York, per Mr. Schofield, Executor	702 17
"	Mrs. Margaret Pugsley, Dutchess Co., N. Y., per Miss Cornelia Pugsley	280 00
"	Mrs. Irene Coats, New York, per Alfred Decker, Esq.	250 00
1841	Mrs. Elizabeth G. Moore, Hartford, Ct., per J. B. Gilbert, Esq.	200 00
1842	Nathaniel Tucker, Esq., Milton Mass , per W. D. Ticknor, Esq.	2005 00
1843	Mrs. Margaret Martin, Montgomery, N. Y , per Mr J. J. Martin, Executor	100 00
"	Miss Cynthia M. Wright, Suffield, Ct , per H. Sheldon, Administrator	50 00

1849	Mr. Samuel R. Stelle, Piscataway, N. J., per Lewis R. Stelle, Esq., Executor	200 00
"	Mrs. Phebe Gale, East Bennington, Vt., per Executor of Estate of S. Harmon	25 00
"	Mr. William Reynolds, Boston, Mass., per J. H. Duncan, Esq., and Mrs. Susan D. Reynolds, Executors, in land not sold at Toledo, Ohio	
"	Josiah Lyman, Andover, Ct., per N. B. Lyman, Executor	50 00
"	John J. Martin, Montgomery, N. Y., per M. Bookstaver, Executor	1000 00
"	Mrs. Martha Howe, West Boylston, Mass., per Messrs. E. J. Howe & Co.	50 00
"	A. H. Reed, Sweden, N. Y., per Rev. D. Searl	13 00
"	Asa H. Trueman, Owego, N. Y., per E. Trueman, Executor	248 00
1850	George D. James, Amenia, N. Y., J. K. Mead and N. Rose, Executors	100 00
"	John Everett, Manchester, Mich., per F. Everett	70 00
"	Jacob Whitman, Belvidere, Ill., in part, per N. Crosby, Esq.	160 00
"	Jonas Taylor, Boston, Mass.	12 50
"	Miss Rebecca Thompson, Amenia, N. Y., per A. B. Capwell, Esq.	801 00
"	Joanna Minot, Boston, Mass., per E. Mears and I. Parker, Executors	100 00
"	Claudius F. Brown, Arkwright, N. Y., per David Barrell	150 00
"	Miss Anna Roe, Egremont, Mass., per R. B. Brown, Executor	50 00
1851	David Schauber, Burnt Hills, N. Y., per J. & D. M. Schauber, Executors	10 00
"	Woolcot Griffin, Gouverneur, N. Y., per O. L. Barnum, Executor	100 00
"	Joseph Flanders, Brooklyn, N. Y., per Mrs. Eliza A. Flanders and Benj. Flanders	500 00
"	William Williams, New York, per John Allan, Executor	400 00
"	Ely Wiley, South Reading, Mass.	50 00
1852	Miss Pharozene C. Kelly, Hopkinton, N. H., per John Page	50 00
"	Jonathan W. Ford, Boston, Mass.	100 00
"	Theron Fisk, Warsaw, N. Y., in advance	2500 00
"	Joshua A. Burke, Brooklyn, N. Y., per Messrs. E. and W. A. Burke	850 00
"	Miss Eliza Skaats, New York, in part, per G. N. Bleecker, Executor	1000 00
"	Barnum M. Howard, Sweden, N. Y., per H. M. Howard, Executor	20 00
1853	Alanson Stewart, Liberty, N. Y., per W. W. Murphy	5 00
"	Mrs. Sarah B. Peirce, Middleboro', Mass.	100 00
"	Arnold Whipple, Providence, R. I., per Mrs. P. Whipple, Executrix	200 00
"	Mrs. Fanny McGilvreay, Brookline, N. H. (Annuity), per H. A. Daniels, Administrator	40 00
"	Mrs. Lucretia Goddard, Worcester, Mass., per Hon. I. Davis, Executor	300 00
"	P. F. Brayton, Providence, R. I., per A. K. Brayton	62 00
"	Mrs. Elizabeth Gale, Washington, D. C.	50 00
1854	Edward Rogers, Chester, Ill., per Rev. M. B. Kelly	5 00
"	Miss Esther Ann Blakely, Pawlet, Vt., per Rev. J. J. Peck	73 00
"	Daniel Cummings, Chelsea, Mass., per Mr. Eaton, Executor	1000 00
"	Mrs. Mary Leuce, Bristol, R. I., per J. F. Baars	7 50
"	D. Valentine, Washington, Pa., per H. W. Wilson, Executor	239 80
"	Willis L. Eaton, East Weare, N. H., per J. L. Eaton, Executor	100 00
"	Asa Read, Attleboro', Mass., per Amos M. Read, Executor	1000 00
"	Friend Humphrey, Albany, N. Y., per his son, Executor	106 30
"	George Corbett, Worcester, Mass.	8 00
"	Mrs. Abby Arnold, Centreville, R. I., per W. A. Arnold	95 00
"	Garrat N. Bleecker, New York, per E. Cauldwell and W. F. Van Wagener, Executors	6000 00
"	Dr. John Goodell, Auburn, N. Y. in part	71 66
"	Eunice Shepardson, Belleville, N. Y.	70 00
"	Mrs. Mary Johnson, Albany, N. Y., per Chas. Pohlman	10 00
"	Charles H. Nichols, Boston, Mass., in part, in advance	50 00
"	Mrs. Olive Stowell, Le Roy, N. Y., per R. Bell	10 00
"	David Trull, Lowell, Mass., per J. Fox	100 00
1855	Roger Pegg, New York, per Mr. Coe, Executor	100 00
"	John Goodell Jr. Woodstock, N. Y., in part, per Mrs. Maria H. Goodell, Executrix	54 00
"	Mrs. Frances Thompson, Alabama, N. Y.	50 00
"	Miss Mercy Hayden, Grafton, Mass., per Rev. J. Smith	20 00
"	Thomas S. Murray, Newhope, Pa.	30 00
"	Wm. S. Ward, Salem, Mass.	100 00

DECENNIAL CENSUS FOR INDIANA,

Showing the Counties in the State and their Population ; the number of Members in each County ; Population of County-seats and the number of Members in each.

This Table was compiled by Rev N. V. Steadman, our Exploring Agent in Indiana. It cost him a great deal of time and labor especially as many of his correspondents manifested indifference and neglect. But it is hoped that hereafter additions and corrections, if necessary, will be obtained so as to render it, with the others published with our Annual Reports, still more valuable for the future history of the Home Mission Society

COUNTIES.	1840. Population.	Members.	County-seat Population.	Members.	1850. Population.	Members.	County-seat Population.	Members.
Adams	2,264	....	....	....	5,797	....	....	....
Allen	5,942	...	....	....	16,919	120	....	....
Bartholomew	**10,042**	....	....	....	12,428	280	....	....
Benton	....	....	....	....	1,144	17	....	....
Blackford	1,226	....	....	....	2,860	68	....	....
Boone	8,121	....	....	....	11,631	57	....	....
Brown	2,364	....	....	....	4,846	45	....	....
[illegible]	[illegible]				[illegible]	[illegible]		

COUNTIES.	1840. Population.	1840. Members.	1840. County-seat Population.	1840. Members.	1850. Population.	1850. Members.	1850. County-seat Population.	1850. Members.
Madison	8,874	129	----	----	12,375	46	----	----
Marion	16,080	----	----	----	24,103	593	----	----
Marshall	1,651	----	----	----	5,348	26	----	----
Martin	3,875	----	----	----	5,941	56	----	----
Miami	3,048	----	----	----	11,304	162	----	----
Monroe	10,143	----	----	----	11,286	483	----	----
Montgomery	14,438	108	----	----	18,084	290	----	----
Morgan	10,741	----	----	----	14,576	35	----	----
Noble	2,702	----	----	----	7,946	251	----	----
Ohio	----	----	----	----	5,308	40	----	----
Orange	9,602	----	----	----	10,809	266	----	----
Owen	8,359	----	----	----	12,106	559	----	----
Park	13,499	----	----	----	14,968	262	----	----
Perry	4,655	347	----	----	7,268	265	----	----
Pike	4,769	127	----	----	7,720	43	----	----
Porter	2,162	----	----	----	5,234	71	----	----
Posey	9,683	9	----	----	12,549	----	----	----
Pulaski	561	----	----	----	2,595	----	----	----
Putnam	16,843	----	----	----	18,615	375	----	----
Randolph	10,684	----	----	----	14,725	38	----	----
Ripley	10,392	308	----	----	14,820	455	----	----
Rush	16,456	50	----	----	16,445	124	----	----
St. Joseph	6,425	----	----	----	10,954	130	----	----
Scott	4,242	----	----	----	5,885	263	----	----
Shelby	12,005	329	----	----	15,502	527	----	----
Spencer	6,305	141	----	----	8,616	123	----	----
Stark	149	----	----	----	557	----	----	----
Steuben	2,575	----	----	----	6,104	170	----	----
Sullivan	8,315	----	----	----	10,141	197	----	----
Switzerland	9,920	174	----	----	12,932	381	----	----
Tippecanoe	13,724	----	----	----	19,377	187	----	----
Tipton	----	----	----	----	3,532	50	----	----
Union	8,017	----	----	----	6,944	185	----	----
Vanderburg	6,250	----	----	----	11,414	24	----	----
Vermilion	8,274	----	----	----	8,661	35	----	----
Vigo	12,076	----	----	----	15,289	543	----	----
Wabash	2,755	----	----	----	12,138	52	----	----
Warren	5,656	----	----	----	7,387	17	----	----
Warrick	6,321	95	----	----	8,811	97	----	----
Washington	15,269	----	----	----	17,040	470	----	----
Wayne	23,290	----	----	----	25,320	21	----	----
Wills	1,822	----	----	----	6,151	83	----	----
White	1,832	----	----	----	4,761	21	----	----
Whitley	1,237	----	----	----	5,191	50	----	----
	685,866	3,226			988,416	186,92		

Population 1800, 4,875; 1810, 24,520; 1820, 147,178; 1830, 343,031; 1840, 685,866; 1850, 988,416.

STATISTICS OF ASSOCIATIONS.

ABBREVIATIONS: Dis Dissolved: F. M. Free Mission.

ASSOCIATIONS.	1850. No. Chur's.	1850. No. Min'rs.	1850. No. Mem's.	1854. No. Chur's.	1854. No. Min'rs.	1854. No. Mem's.
Bedford	20	10	882	21	9	1,049
Bethel	10	6	719	15	6	943
Brownstown	13	7	405	17	9	756
Coffee Creek	17	10	1,049	17	8	1,108
Currie's Prairie	15	9	969	17	9	1,151
Elkhart River	15	9	738	22	18	995
Evansville	6	3	206	8	10	297
Flat Rock	31	14	1,765	31	10	1,930
Freedom	8	8	423	11	6	679
Huntington	19	5	621	14	4	840
Indianapolis	17	9	946	21	14	1,619
Judson	22	8	633	31	9	1,854
Laughery	24	18	1,120	21	15	980
Liberty	7	2	206	Dis.	Dis.	Dis.
Little Pigeon	7	1	205	9	2	261
Long Run	8	5	385	8	5	410
Madison	20	10	1,496	18	5	1,302
N. E. Indiana	20	9	506	F. M.	F. M.	550
Northern Indiana	14	13	607	16	18	792
Salamonia River	15	8	289	----	----	366
Sand Creek	14	11	751	18	9	689
Tippecanoe	12	6	666	13	6	867
[illegible]	[illegible]	[illegible]	[illegible]	[illegible]	[illegible]	[illegible]

SPECIAL REPORT

OF THE

EXECUTIVE BOARD ON ROOMS,

TO THE AMERICAN BAPTIST HOME MISSION SOCIETY,

Presented May 9th, 1855.

THE Committee, appointed by the Executive Board of the Society, by resolution of the 26th April, 1855, to prepare a statement to be presented at the Anniversary, in regard to the removal of the Society to the rooms in Nassau street, have the honor to present the following report:—

They propose to state the action of the Board, under the resolutions of the Society instructing such removal, with the reasons that influenced it, and the action that the Board have since taken in regard to this subject. They believe it to be of sufficient importance to be worthy the careful attention of the Society, and to call for a candid and complete narration of the whole subject, although special statements, with some of the documents, have been already published; these they have embodied where appropriate.

In April, 1853, the Board and the Society received a communication from a Committee of the American and Foreign Bible Society, informing them that the property in Nassau street, procured for that Society, would be subject to certain provisions, among which was one that the Bible Society should furnish to our own and certain other societies suitable rooms and accommodations for their business purposes, to be held by them permanently, and free from rent, provided they were accepted within two months after tender. This communication was accompanied by another from the Corresponding Secretary of the Bible Society, making a tender of the rooms to this Society, pursuant to the above provision. Upon the subject introduced in these communications, our Society, at its anniversary in Troy in May, 1853, passed the following resolutions:—

1st. *Resolved*, That the interests of the Society require the selection of a new location for the transaction of its business.

2d. *Resolved*, That the Board of the Home Mission Society be directed to rent immediately suitable rooms for their accommodation, provided that

Whereas, a large number of Ba
other places, have purchased a v
Nassau street, and extending to the with th
of providing rooms without the expense of rent, for the use of a
connected with the Baptist denomination: the said premises

expired, the limitation was waived, and the offer was intended to have the force and effect of the original tender, and was intended to include just as convenient and commodious apartments as we reasonably required, that in all respects it might be as satisfactory as it was sincere.

The same committee who had addressed the Real Estate Committee of the Bible Society sent a like communication, under same date, to the chairman of the board of Trustees of the First Baptist Church. The Trustees answered on the twenty-eighth of June. After alluding to the proviso accompanying the resolution, they said it was necessary that they should be informed of the commodiousness and convenience of the rooms referred to, and the character and advantages of the lease offered, so that they might be able to decide whether they were prepared to make an offer equally eligible; they requested to be furnished with a copy of the lease offered, containing a description of the rooms in question. The committee of our Board replied on the fifth of July that they could not transmit the information desired without the violation of an implied obligation to the other party, whose terms they must suppose were for their own consideration and guidance only, and that their only duty was to ascertain what rooms were available in each case, and on what terms; that, with this information before them, the Executive Board might exercise their best and most impartial judgment. They renewed the request for the information desired. As no response was received, this request was repeated on the twenty-sixth day of August. On the twelfth of September the Trustees wrote that it was evidently the design of the Society to afford the First Church and other friends an opportunity to offer, either in the present premises or on premises in the same locality, a lease of rooms, equally eligible in every respect as that which might be offered in the building in Nassau street. In accordance with this intention, they asked a copy or an exact description of the lease offered to us in Nassau street, stating, that when they received this they would inform us whether they could offer one equally eligible. To this the Committee of the Board rejoined on the thirteenth of September, 1854, stating that it was not in their power to answer all the questions of the Trustees, because the necessary papers had not been executed, yet that they were willing to answer all the essential items of inquiry, as matter of Christian courtesy; that an offer had been made them of a durable lease, with suitable provisions, free from rent, of a suite of rooms on the second floor of the building on Nassau street, and minutely described the number, size and connection of the rooms, with their character and conveniences.

The Committee on Rooms made their report to the Executive Board on the fourteenth of September, as follows:—

REPORT OF COMMITTEE ON ROOMS.

The undersigned, appointed on the first of June last a special committee to take into consideration the instructions of the American Baptist Home Mission Society, respecting suitable rooms for the occupancy of this Board, respectfully report:

That they addressed a communication to the Trustees of the First Baptist Church of this city, on the fourteenth of June, and another of the same tenor and date to Nathan C. Platt, Esq., in whom resides the fee of the property, at 115 and 117 Nassau street, referred to in the Society's instructions, transmitting the preamble and resolution passed at Philadelphia with the proviso attached; and respectfully asked of each party what accommodations they would give to our Society for the use of the Executive Board and the transaction of its necessary and local business, in accordance with the intentions and force of said resolution. As the result of the correspondence thus commenced, your committee would state that Mr. Platt, who now holds the property, subject to the uses designed by the donors, offers to give us in his own name a durable lease with proper provisions, of about one half of the available space of the second floor of the Nassau street building, comprising five rooms, numbered 5, 6, 7, 8 and 9, and free of rent, in consideration of the fact, "that it was the comprehensive and benevolent design of the originators of this edifice, and of the subscribers to the fund which has resulted in its erection, to provide suitable rooms for the permanent use of several societies, of which the American Baptist Home Mission Society was a prominent one. Mr. Platt also assures your committee that the offer is intended to include just as convenient and commodious apartments as our Society reasonably requires; that in all respects it may be as satisfactory to us as it is sincere." The accommodations thus offered consist of the following apartments: fronting on Nassau street, over No. 115, is a large room measuring 20 by 22 feet, with three windows; on Theatre alley, or the street in the rear, is another room, 20 by 23½ feet; connecting these are two others, one measuring 6¼ by 24 feet, and the other, 6½ by 26⅔, receiving their light from side windows into the interior court of the building; adjoining the rear of these long side rooms is a smaller one, 6½ by 10⅓ feet in measurement. These rooms are all con-

The Committee appointed to procure a lease of rooms tendered to this Society in Nassau street, respectfully report:—

That they found the title of the property in Nassau street to be in Nathan C. Platt, under an agreement to convey the same to the Bible Society, according to the terms set forth in the original subscription. It was, therefore, necessary that a lease should proceed from Mr. Platt, with the concurrence of the Board of the Society. We have, therefore, procured such a lease, and with it a parallel covenant on the part of the Board, both lawfully executed under instructions from the Board to that effect. The lease is for the longest usual period, and both the lease and the covenant recognize as the ground on which they rest, the original donations for the building. This is specially true in the case of the covenant, which fully recites the designs of the donors, and states that in fixing a period of twenty-one years as the duration of the lease (since *as a lease* it must have some period), it expressly disclaims any design to fix limitations to the obligation to carry into effect the stipulated purposes of the property. The considerations stated are recognized as surviving the determination of the lease, and as constituting at that time, in conscience and in equity, a claim for use on the part of the Home Mission Society as valid as that which now exists, and is made the basis of the present documents.

J. E. SOUTHWORTH, *Chairman.*

This report was accepted, and both the Lease and Covenant approved.

The following resolution was at that time unanimously passed by the Board:

Resolved, That in obeying the instructions of the American Baptist Home Mission Society, passed in May last, viz., to enter into our just and lawful possession and occupancy of rooms in Nassau street, which friends and members of this Board and Society have procured for us, by liberal contributions for that express purpose, we sincerely repudiate the idea that in so doing we are influenced in the least degree, so far as we can know our motives, by any preference for, or prejudice against, any other Christian organization in New York or elsewhere. We sincerely affirm that, being in bondage to no man, or set of men, we act in this matter as members and friends of the Home Mission Society, in the fear of God and the love of souls, for whom Christ died, as we trust he died for us.

The Lease and Covenant were subsequently duly executed and delivered to the Society, and the Board removed into the building on Nassau street during the ensuing month.

The Board respectfully submit, that in this action they have obeyed the instructions of the Society.

These instructions were positive to engage and enter upon the use of rooms in a building designated in the resolution, as soon as they were granted on a durable lease, free from rent, provided they could not secure in the location on Broome street a lease equally desirable, in regard to permanence, commodiousness and convenience, or all together.

They have been unable to secure even an offer from the First Church of *any tenure* of *any kind* in their building. They have taken rooms far superior in commodiousness and convenience to any that their former location could possibly have afforded; and in regard to permanency they have obtained more than a durable lease; they have obtained an occupancy, free from rent, for twenty-one years, the longest usual term of a lease, based upon end made in their favor by the donors of the Nassau s recognized by the Bible Society as being in full force, and s mination of the lease.

The First Baptist Church required a copy, or an exact lease offered in Nassau street, before they would make any o position thus assumed, taking the decision of the questi hands, was regarded by the Board as unjust and unwarran to those who had made an offer, and infringing upon the fre of the Board.

The meetings of the Board for the consideration of this s and the First Church was always represented there; all th sessed by the Board was open to them. In addition, as a the committee furnished them with all the details of the off they possessed. That offer, in respect to permanency, lease, which was all the Board were instructed to engage. the Board, accepting this offer, they appointed a committe completion of the lease; the Bible Society had courteously r any limit to the permanency of their grant, until, through the wishes of this Board should be made known; and which it was settled was the result of conferences between most judicious and satisfactory under the circumstances of years in the present or any future property, and, at the expiration of that time, still to acknowledge the full original force and effect of the provision.

"In the negotiations between the two Committees, which resulted in giving the foregoing form to these documents, there were some points which were regarded on both sides as settled. *First*, That the Home Mission Society came into the rooms upon the basis of the original provision of the donors, which the Bible Society had renewed, and to which they had subjected their new building; that there existed, therefore, no unequal relation between them, for their wants, although in a different measure, were equally embraced in the design. *Second*, That this provision, set in order, and re-affirmed in the covenant, gave them a moral claim to their rooms, which, in itself, was sufficient between Societies whose constituents are the same denomination, and receive their support year by year.

"They were also embarrassed by restrictions arising from the circumstances of the case.

"In the first place, the resolutions of the Home Mission Society had required a lease, and conformity to their instructions required such a form to the documents, and a lease involved necessarily a term of years. Whatever might be their own judgment as to the most judicious and satisfactory form, they could not free themselves from this restriction, and a lease was accordingly required from us.

"*Secondly*, In the present condition of the property, with the subscription still in arrears, and the building still to be paid for, it was necessary to preserve the power to mortgage the property. Since the lease is without rent, and the actual yearly value of the rooms is so large, if it were fixed for a long term of years, the market value of the property would be greatly impaired, and might involve serious practical difficulties.

"It was, therefore, concluded that, under existing circumstances, it became necessary that the provision of the donors should be recognized as the basis of the agreement, that the rights of ownership over the property should not be impaired, and that the instrument should be a lease, or some document of like effect. It was necessary further, that the lease should be made 'permanent' or 'durable'; the simple meaning of these words when applied to a lease was the longest usual term of such a tenure; this term of twenty-one years, in the present or a future building, was agreed to as sufficient, leaving the provisions subsisting thereafter in full force."

In regard to the commodiousness and convenience of their new location, the Board are of the opinion that their rooms and accommodations are all that the Society requires, and that they are proportionately equal to those enjoyed by any other Society in the city. They are open and at hand for the judgment of every member of the Society. The permanency of their occupancy is made only to depend upon the permanency of the Bible Society, and the ultimate and complete success of one of the noblest enterprises in the history of our denomination. Their confidence in this permanence they have not seen a suggestion to weaken; the world will need the Bible Society as long as it does any Society; the spirit that prompts large benevolence is the same spirit that alone can bless it; and in the entire absence of any apparent cause of apprehension, we can do no more than trust the God of the Bible.

Pending the general consideration of this subject, several questions were raised, upon which the Board reached the following conclusions:

First, Their powers under the Resolutions of the Society.—Of the Troy Resolutions in 1853, the first, to wit: "that the interests of the Society require the selection of a new location for the transaction of its business," was a general expression of the opinion of the Society upon the question, and of governing force, except as afterwards limited. The second directed a temporary removal, but had not been acted upon for a reason reported to and accepted by the Society. The third was an authority to raise a fund for the purchase of rooms, etc., and was still in force as an authority, but was of no obligation. We had reported to the Society that, by reason of a doubt whether its language was sufficiently authoritative to meet the legal necessities of the case, we had taken no action on the subject. In respect to the fund for the purchase, the Resolutions were permissive; as to a change of location they were *positive* and *directory*. The objections against them were, that they were not the best and most practicable either as a temporary or a permanent measure. At Philadelphia, in 1854, the Society, leaving their authority to raise a fund still unrevoked, provided for the immediate and permanent location of the Society. Understanding that rooms in the building in Nassau-street were available, without any charge on the general treasury, their Resolutions carried out the directory part of the Resolutions of 1853, by requiring a removal to that building, upon the conditions, first, that it be without rent, which was similar to the proviso of 1853; second, that it be on a durable lease, because the Board had represented the disadvantages of any merely temporary changes; and third, that a lease equally desirable in the respects named could not be secured in [redacted] its advantages had been weighed and decided on by the Society, and the responsibility of sacrificing these, in a course of disobedience to the Society, was more than we could assume.

Third, The measure of what was called an "independent" location—a location separate from either Nassau or Broome-street—was declined because, since it would have been a direct departure from the instructions of the Society in a direction not indicated by any of its directory resolutions, we would be justified in preferring it over an offer, which so fully and satisfactorily answered the very letter of the Society's instructions, only by the most cogent reasons, and by the unquestionable advantages and specific completeness of the proposition. So far from such being the case, we were not informed of any special disposition or attempt to undertake the raising of the fund for the purchase of a property for the Society. Nearly two years had elapsed since this subject had been before us, and the friends of such a measure had enjoyed abundant time and opportunity to perfect it; no surprise or exigency had prevented their giving to the measure this seal of entire good faith and reliability, without which they had no reason to expect us to assume the responsibility of a decision. There were no arguments in favor of the measure which the Society had not heard. The only proposition which came before us, as such, was one from four or five gentlemen of the first standing, who proposed to subscribe one hundred dollars each for the term of two or three years, provided twelve hundred dollars were raised in like manner, for the purpose of paying the rent of rooms to be hired by the Society, with a verbal understanding that it should be completed. We cannot speak with greater certainty, as the proposal was not formally presented to or filed with the Board. Weeks elapsed, from the time this was first spoken of and our final action, without seeing it perfected; and had the reasons in favor of such a measure been wholly convincing, it was not presented in such a practicable and certain form, as to justify us in assuming the danger and responsibility of preferring it to the offer then pending, and of disobeying the Society.

Fourth, The Board were aware that the use of the word "lease" in the Resolutions would suggest that of "tenant", and that an unfavorable impression might arise if the matter were not well considered. Apart from the general question, of what influence the two Societies may have upon each other, there is, in this case, no disadvantage growing out of the relation of "tenant" as such. In real property a tenant for years is the next estate in kind to the tenant in fee or owner. He holds in as ample a manner as the owner, subject to the limitations of time, rent, etc. The power of the landlord depends only on such limitations, by which the tenant is subject to summary ejectment, an increased or an onerous rent, etc. These do not apply in the present case, as the rent is nominal, and only inserted to make a legal consideration; and the property is held free from the burden of taxes and expenses that fall upon the owner.

During the consideration of the form of the lease, it was strongly urged, that it would be better that the Society, instead of a lease, should take the rooms upon some simple resolution, or a covenant by the Bible Society, recognizing and affirming the provision made in our favor by the donors of the property; that this would make an equitable claim, which, between the Societies, composed mainly of the same constituents, and governed by religious principle, would be sufficient; that a violation of such a covenant would present such a breach of good faith and honor, as would react strongly in favor of the party who suffered by it. Influenced by the force of this view, and instructed by the resolutions of the Society to take a lease, the only legal grant applicable, we have combined the advantages of both, by agreeing upon instruments, which acknowledge the force of the provision on which our claim is founded, and give us a term of twenty-one years in the present, and to guard against possibility of accident, in any future building of the Bible Society.

We had, therefore, no other and no better course to pursue than to obey the instructions of the Society.

At the time of the removal, two members of the Board presented a protest against the choice of the location in Nassau-street, setting forth the grounds on which the protest was based. A degree of importance has attached to this action from the fact, that these two brethren have publicly and in writing declared that they could not consent to go with us to the new location, "under any circumstances." They have since, with five others, prepared a constitution and plan of organization for a new Union, and made the customary arrange-

the Committee examined what there was of substance in the objections urged against the removal. The Board had published a statement of facts to correct the mistakes and inconclusive positions of the protest, and to vindicate their own good faith and consistency; yet, with a disposition to regard these objections not solely for what of soundness or merit there was in them, but also for what consequences might ensue from urging them upon public attention; or rather with a disposition, apart from and above all this, to seek the continued advancement of the Society; this Committee, in February, 1855, reported to the Board the following Resolution, which was adopted:

Whereas, There exists a diversity of opinion among the friends of the Society as to its present location, in consequence of which the harmony of the Society is disturbed; and, whereas, it is supposed that sufficient sums could be procured from our brethren and friends to secure an eligible building, to be held by the Society, free from incumbrances; therefore,

Resolved, That, if it be found, after a full understanding of the tenure by which the Society now holds and may continue to hold the possession of these rooms, that in remaining here its unity cannot be preserved, we recommend that the Society remove to an independent location, provided that a suitable building can be obtained, free from incumbrances, and without drawing from the Society's treasury for general purposes.

Apart from the consequences that have ensued from the public withdrawal of two of our number, and their action in pressing it upon the public attention, it may be questioned whether there is any reason for dissatisfaction with our present location. We have rooms, abundantly commodious and convenient for all the present and, so far as we can see, the future requirements of the Society. We are free from rent, and from the risks, burdens, cares and expenses usual to owners of property. We hold the rooms by a claim far superior, stronger and more advantageous than any by which we have heretofore held rooms, and in legal right inferior to absolute ownership only; we have a strong hold upon the affections of the hundreds of brethren and friends who have intentionally united in providing these advantages for us. Our position in respect to location and everything incident thereto, is only to be surpassed by becoming owners ourselves; and is entirely satisfactory, except so far as it is sought to derive from this very location reasons to disturb our harmony. The argument by which these are set forth, though often divided without increasing its force, seems to be comprehended in the general proposition, that by remaining in our present location we lose our freedom and independence, and become a subordinate party in a partisan combination, and in the hostility which is alleged to exist between the Bible Society and the Bible Union.

In respect to the two brethren who have publicly protested against the action of the Board, united others with them, made public these charges against the Board and their requirements of the Society, under the alternative of disunion, and opposition to the Society, we beg leave to say,—

That with the state of affairs between them and the Bible Society, which they make the basis of their action, this Society has no business. We can, however, with justice, take knowledge of the fact that the Bible Society, in reply to them, claim to stand upon their old-established principles and position, claim that there are no real principles involved, no real grounds for collsiion, and that there is in fact no other hostility than is unnecessarily provoked by the Bible Union, in pursuing toward them the same aggressive course which now raises this question among us; and that they disavow any interference with us in any way. With respect to ourselves, and our alleged partisan combination against the two brethren, and those they speak for, we do not deem it requisite to reply, or to vindicate ourselves. Our actions, as we have stated, have been in obedience to the positive instructions of the Society. If the Society prefer that the members of their Executive Board should not be members of the Board of any other Society, they have the power in their own hands; we do not wish to stand in the way of its harmony and prosperity.

Whether the position taken by the minority is right, whether the principles and causes of the difficulty they set out are real ones, whether their complaints are well grounded, whether the questions they put at issue have any merit in them, and whether, as reasonable men and as Christians, they are justified in the attitude they take and the alternative they present to us, and whether their action in its results can affect us, must be left to the Society to determine. If they are not right, the Society must also determine how far these questions can be disregarded.

If a disturbance of harmony is simply recognized as an existing fact, without inquiry into the causes, it should be considered what limits are to be set to action on that ground.

enter, even for the purpose of setting the truth and the right before our own friends; that we never had more need to give our undivided attention to the work of Home Missions, preserve the unity and advance the prosperity of our Society, keeping a proper regard to principles, and the wisdom of our actions, that we may not condemn ourselves; we can all unite in seeing reasons enough to determine upon a course still open to us, and more advantageous to us than our present position, and that is, the purchase of a property of our own.

At the time of the passage by the Board of the resolutions we have already quoted, in February, 1855, it was, in the words of the preamble, stated as the grounds of the Resolution, that it was supposed that sufficient sums could be procured from our brethren and friends to secure a home for the Society. This expectation has since been strengthened, and there are recent indications of a probable near accomplishment of the object. The great advantage that would result to the Society, could a valuable property be secured for it, should not be lost sight of. The example of the Bible House is distinctly before us, as an illustration of the benefits we should derive from a like movement. They do not need any special exposition. The Resolution of 1853, authorizing the raising of a fund for the purchase of a property, is in force up to the present Anniversary, and the Society, having now a permanent home in Nassau Street, may enjoy it or leave it at their option. The Resolutions both of 1853 and 1854, with this exception, having been carried out and accomplished, this remains the only feature of the plan expressed in these Resolutions yet to receive attention, and it will be desirable to continue such an authority in force.

The Bible Society have publicly declared that we should receive their cordial congratulation on any new advantages that might arise to lead us to a change, and that we will carry with us their sincere co-operation and sympathy; that they have no desire injuriously to affect our freedom and independence, or to place any impediment in the way of our entire freedom of action. We are persuaded that our removal will not sever or impair the equality and the sincere fraternal relations that have heretofore been cherished, and still exist between us.

In conclusion, the Board respectfully submit that they have in good faith, and with exactness, carried out the specific instructions of the Society, in the removal to Nassau Street, and in a form the most judicious and practicable under the circumstances of the case: and they respectfully recommend to the Society to give authority to raise a fund for the purchase of a property, for the use and occupation of the Society, and for such other steps as may be proper to give efficiency and success to the measure.

ADDRESS OF REV. D. C. EDDY,

OF MASSACHUSETTS.

Mr. President.—I am requested to move the acceptance of the report, and accompany the motion with a few remarks. I do this with pleasure, from the conviction that of all the great organizations which are designed to evangelize the world, none have stronger claims upon us, and none plead with more earnestness, than that whose plans have been developed in the document now read to us.

The Foreign Missionary movement, Sir, among American Baptist churches, takes its date at the year 1812—that notable year, when the departed Judson gave himself as a missionary-offering to a denomination of small resources, limited ability, but which had inscribed on its banners, " One Lord, one Faith, one Baptism." At that time there was no Missionary Union; the old Triennial Convention had not been formed, and the Home Mission Society was priests; covered over with the rust of superstitions, centuries old; fettered with prejudices which the very agonies of death do not dissolve. They form a heathenism in the midst of Christianity; a despotism in the midst of a democracy; a dark mass, floating in golden sunlight; a crown of thorns hanging on the brow of Mercy.

To the burning, quenchless desire to save the lost, and bring a revolted world to God, there are added now the love of country, and all the instincts of self-preservation. The question now is, not "Shall we leave the heathen in distant India to perish without the Gospel?" but, "Shall we ourselves be overwhelmed by error and darkness?" Not, "Shall we erect churches within sight of the pagodas of Hindostan?" but, "Shall we save our own churches?" That dreadful ecclesiastical despotism which has darkened all the prospects of continental Europe, which has ever been a most bitter foe of liberty and man, is building its altars, erecting its cathedrals, and obtaining empire on our shores. That same infidelity which has settled on German scholarship, and made midnight in the land of the Universities, is establishing its presses and forming its secret clubs all through the mighty West; and even pagan idolatry, crossing over from China, is casting its gods and erecting its shrines on the golden-sanded shores of the Pacific. The very enemies that Christianity went out to meet half a century ago have come to us, and throng around our altars and firesides.

We may not feel less interest in the millions of India; we may not contribute less for the nations of Europe; but we must not forget our own land, which has a mighty mission to accomplish among the nations of the earth, and which is being rapidly populated with the half-starved thousands of other lands, by whom the principles of civil liberty were never understood, and to whom the Bible is a proscribed and forbidden book. The heathen are at our own doors; they come

> "From Greenland's icy mountains,
> And India's coral strand;"

they speak the language of the ancient Jew and the descendants of Ishmael, and embrace all ranks, from the Ethiopian slave to the robed and titled Ecclesiastic who sits in his Episcopal palace, amid the smoke of incense, planning the subjugation of the nation.

We must look to the Home Mission enterprise as our only safety from this in-rushing flood. Political organizations may check certain evils which float upon the surface of society, and save us from momentary calamities which threaten our free institutions and even jeopard the existence of the Republic; but no political movement, however well planned, is deep enough to accomplish the object.

Laws may be made, ecclesiastical tenures may be fixed, school funds may be saved from diversion, but no statute can check the growth of Romanism, or stay the tide of Infidelity. The Society which carries the Bible in its hand; which sends the colporteur and the missionary; which scatters books and tracts; which establishes sabbath schools; which is written all over with the names of Christ—the Home Mission Society can, under God alone, effect the mighty purpose.

A single glance only is needed to show us the extent of the field, the magnitude of the work, and the imperative necessity of immediate action. The Papal church, which for twelve centuries has been the chief antagonist of Christianity, is making rapid strides in the Western States, and the peculiar work of the Home Mission Society is to meet and subdue this foe. Twenty years ago there was in this country no archbishop, now there are seven; then there were fourteen bishops, now there are nearly 40; then there were fourteen dioceses, now there are nearly fifty; then there were 262 churches, now there are nearly 2,000; then there were 327 priests, now there 1,800; then the membership was small and weak, now it numbers several millions, and every day swells the aggregate.

Nor has Popery changed materially in the transplanting. Hers is the same arrogant, despotic, hateful system that it was when the catacombs of Rome were her dungeons; when human gore was never wiped from her inquisitorial rack; when the Mamartine prison was full of her defenceless victims, and when the sweetest cup she ever drank, sweeter than the bacchanalian wine, was filled to the brim with the tears and blood of martyrs. She has the same hate to the blessed Bible, to all the means of illumination, to liberty of conscience and the blessings of Republican government. The language she holds to-day, amid the blazing light of the nineteenth century, is the identical lan-

—"In vain you look into the Scriptures for a full, clear, and succinct statement of faith and practice. Articles of doctrine are scattered without order; their meaning is hidden under obscurity of language; the advance of the inquirer is arrested by apparent contradictions, and seldom do any two readers agree in the same decision. Of all the possible forms under which a perfect and complete rule of faith could have been published, the New Testament is the most incongruous and confused, and what no sensible man would ever have adopted. We ought not to attribute to the wisdom of God that which is unworthy of the wisdom of man."

This is not the opinion of mere irresponsible editors alone. The Council of Trent, not one single dogma of which has the Church of Rome ever denied, declares that "the indiscriminate translation of the Bible will cause more evil than good." Pius VII. declares Bible Societies to be the most crafty device by which the very foundations of religion are undermined. Gregory XVI., as late as 1844, declares with vehemence:—"Among the many attempts which the enemies of Catholicism are daily making in our age to seduce the faithful, the efforts of those Bible Societies are conspicuous which labor to disseminate the books of the Holy Scriptures translated into the vulgar tongue, consigning them to the private interpretations of each, pretending to popularize the holy pages, and render them intelligible to persons of any condition—to the most loquacious woman, to the light-headed old man, to the wordy caviller."

The gouty old man who now sits on the Seven Hills, Pius IX., conscious that his power to curse is gone, and that his arm to destroy is palsied, goes back toward the dark ages, and catches up the bulls of licentious and drunken Gregory, and re-affirms them. There is scarcely a pope from Boniface III. down through all the Hildebrands and Borgias, to the present pontiff, who has not condemned, proscribed and banished either the Bible, or those who have loved its truth.

In accordance with these decisions of high authorities, the Romish Church in America is endeavoring to wrest from our hands the beloved volume. In several cases the book has been burned in our streets, the spite of priests extending to the very paper and print, and Protestants have witnessed the blasphemous auto-da-fé. Priests and presses, conclaves and mobs have all combined to quench the light of the Gospel, and blast the hopes of men. The spirit of the whole church is crowded into a single sentence, from the official organ of Bishop Hughes, which declares that "the Bible Society is the deepest scheme ever laid by Satan, in order to delude the human family, and bring them to his eternal possession."

We next find this Church with its battle-axe striking at our glorious free school system, which has done so much to adorn and elevate our nation. It is not enough that she must take the Bible from the parent; she endeavors to take the school-book from the child.

O. A. Brownson, in a late number of his Review, says:—"Our enemies rely upon godless schools, State education, as a means of checking the progress of Catholicity. We must admit they have laid their plans with infernal skill.

The result will not meet their anticipations, however. The Catholic world has been directed to this subject by those who to rule over us; and a struggle, which will end in victory for begun between Catholicity and the State, to see who will have

Says the New Orleans Catholic Messenger:—"Public schools rights; and those who advocate them, such as they now are, w ers of the holy faith which they received from their fathers."

The Shepherd of the Valley, a Catholic paper printed in St "This teaching every one to read is bearing its fruit in our own elsewhere, and a very unwholesome kind of fruit it appears to

The Chicago Tablet says to the parent that has a child at a "Take him away. Better let him never know how to write his n way through the plainest paragraph of a newspaper, or perfo calculation, than become the bond and chained slave of Sat the last day of accounts to curse you in all the unavailing repe terness of final despair. Take him away, if you do not wish yo tormented with the spectre of a soul, which God has given trust, surrendered to the great enemy of mankind. Take him him be a boor, a hewer of wood and drawer of water,—let him of the enlightened age,—let him be accounted by lettered infide only an ignorant Papist—rather than incur the anger of his of his soul. Take him away, let what will be the consequence

The Freeman's Journal says that "infidelity now reigns

In the Secunda Secundæ of Aquinas used at Maynooth College, we find the following teaching: "Those heretics who continue in their error after the second reproof are not only to be consigned to the sentence of excommunication, but also to the secular princes, to be exterminated. If the forgers of money, or other malefactors, are justly consigned to immediate death by secular princes, much more do heretics, immediately after they are convicted of heresy, deserve, not only to be excommunicated, but also justly to be killed."

In the same college are studied the works of Cardinal Bellarmine, in the third book of which occurs the following doctrine of Rome: "Heretics can justly be excommunicated, and therefore put to death. Knowing that fools may not be wanting who may believe them, and by whom they may be supported, if you confine them in prison or send them into exile, they corrupt the neighborhood by their speeches and books; therefore the only remedy is to send them forthwith to their own place. It is often useful to the men themselves who are put to death to die, when it is evident they always become worse; nor is it probable that they will ever be restored to a sane mind. All these reasons persuade us that heretics ought to be put to death."

But this you say is in Europe; there is no Maynooth here. But Aquinas and Bellarmine are text books in all the Catholic Colleges in America, and their teachings are indorsed by every Bishop and priest. Archbishop Kenrick has the effrontery to say that "heresy and unbelief are crimes, and in Christian countries, as in Italy and Spain, where all the people are Catholic, and where the Catholic religion is an essential part of the laws of the land, *they will be punished as other* CRIMES." The same high authority declares: "Catholicism will one day rule in America; and then religious freedom will be at an end." Bishop O'Connor, of Pittsburg, says:—"Religious liberty is merely endured, until its opposite can be carried into execution without peril to the Catholic world."

Here in these statements freely and boldly uttered by the highest authorities in the Romish Church, we have a view—a full-length portrait of the religio-political system, which threatens to sweep away all we love as patriots, and all on earth we venerate as Christians. And to make her conquests sure, all the immense power and patronage of Rome are being brought to bear upon those very fields which the Home Mission Society has taken to cultivate. For this she opens her coffers and pours out her treasures like water; for this she sends her Jesuits to draw their slimy track down our rivers, across our prairies and through our cities; for this she has thrust her advocates into Cabinets and halls of Legislation, into places of honor, and offices of trust. Her efforts to Romanize America, put to the blush all our efforts to save the land to Christianity and Christ. The amounts of money sent to this country from poverty-stricken Europe, and scattered all through the West, show how sincere Rome is in her determination to uproot the Protestant faith in this country, and prove what she is willing to do, to bring it like a slave to the feet of the sovereign pontiff. There came to this country in the year 1839, $160,000; in 1840, $163,000; in 1842, $177,000; in 1843, $175,000; in 1844, $150,000; in 1845,

$160,000; in 1846, $250,000. Since the year 1838, an average of nearly $200,000 has been annually received by papists in America, according to their own statistics.

Go anywhere, enter any city, and you mark the newly-erected cathedral pile, ornamented by the glittering but dead crucifix of Romanism. Enter any village where are a few miserable, squalid families, living in filth and poverty, and there you find a priest. Enter any home of a popish family, and there are prayer-books, rosaries, and the usual evidences of popish devotion. The father may be intemperate, the mother may be a vixen, the children may be dissolute, but the Church has an influence in that home. You behold on all sides the efforts of Rome to prostrate this nation. The evidences are on the walls of cathedrals, and in the hovels of poor Irish and German emigrants. It is spoken by Bishop and Archbishop; it is scattered in popish prints all over the land, and he who runneth may read.

Nor does the Church labor without hope of success. She looks to the day, (God grant it may never come!) when the sacred host shall be elevated at the altar of the Episcopal Church; when popish priests shall harangue the people from the pulpits of Baptist sanctuaries; when the knees of superstitious devotees shall press the pavement of Presbyterian houses of worship;—the day when the school-houses shall be closed; the day when the press, now free, shall be placed under the ban of ecclesiastical censorship; when all the interests of great empires shall be held by the jewelled hand of the pope, who sits

[redacted]

Bishop England, in a letter to his holiness the Pope, wrote :—" Within thirty years the Protestant heresy will come to an end. If we can secure the West and South, we will take care of New England." This same dignitary said to his Catholic brethren at Vienna: "All that is necessary is money and priests to subjugate the mock liberties of America."

And what says the highest Catholic authority in this country on this point. Bishop Hughes, at the General Council, held in Baltimore a few years since, after stating that within five years, the churches, priests and laity of the Romish communion had more than doubled, indulges in the following strain of remark :—" It is not expected that there will be another national Council held in this country for ten years. Those of us who shall live to see it, will behold by that time a development of the Church's power, beyond what the most sanguine would dare now to predict."

This is what Rome says from her ever-working presses, from her Gothic pulpits, from her courts of conscience, from her tribunals of blood. And it depends on the Home Mission enterprise, under God, to say whether she shall, or shall not, be successful. Talk not of political organizations! I admit all the good they are able to do, but they cannot drive back the waves of mingled skepticism and superstition which are rolling upon us like a flood. Talk not of statute law! I acknowledge its supremacy, but it cannot arrest the tide of emigration, or prevent the erection of cathedral prison-houses. Party politics however pure, carries nothing but the popular will; the law carries nothing but the statute book. And what can popular will or the statute book do to undermine a system at whose thunders thrones have crumbled down; at whose touch, towers of might have tottered; at whose stroke, crowns have fallen off; at whose behest, monarchs have been driven into exile; at whose curse, whole nations have shrunk back with terror? From party politics and statute law, we turn to the Home Mission enterprise, which goes forth with the Bible; which is older than Romanism; stronger than the Church; more infallible than the Pope;—the Home Mission Society, which preaches to the ignorant and the learned a Gospel which, in its infancy 1800 years ago, shook the fane of Diana, the Ephesian goddess; which in three centuries subjugated the Roman Empire; which snatched the servants of God out of the Mamartine prison, and gave them honorable places in Cæsar's household; which tore the cross from the wet and bloody soil of Calvary, and inscribed it upon the banners of the conquering Constantine. Yes, we look to the Home Mission enterprise, which preaches a Gospel that stirred the heart of Luther in the dark days of the sixteenth century; which marched triumphantly to Rome, burning the Pope's bulls in every city through which it passed; which dug down beneath the very foundations of Popery, and made such excavations there, that it has been a leaning tower ever since, and the Pope, who walks amid its galleries, feels the trembling beneath his feet, as the waves of truth come dashing against its base, or surging through its halls.

And has this great Society, with such an instrumentality at her command, with such an evil to oppose, with such tremendous responsibilities resting upon her, any time to spend in contending, brother against brother, about bricks and mortar, localities and depôts; in wrangling over men, means, and modes, when the foe cometh in like a flood? Has she energies to withdraw from the great battle of the age, to spend in strife with her own friends; can she afford to spike her guns, or turn them in upon her garrison; or withdraw the sentinels from her walls; or leave the defences unguarded, while, with her banner torn and trailing in the dust, her great work undone, Zion is in a state of insubordination and anarchy?

But I must close. Briefly, imperfectly, have I endeavored to present "the field and the foe"—the field, a great country, all covered with cities arising as if by magic; a country of boundless resources, every step of whose history is marked by peculiar and striking providences; a country filling up with incongruous materials which need a moulding influence, and many portions of which are destitute of all the ordinary means of spiritual illumination. It is a field crushed and trodden by no tyrant's heel; swept by no ecclesiastical despotism, but one like our own prairies, unhedged and luxuriant, blooming with the magnolia, and inviting the laborer's hand. Such a field never was opened before. The disciples who went to Antioch, Athens, Alexandria and Rome, had no such openings as are found every where from the mountains of New York to the shores of the Pacific.

And the foe:—a Church drunken with blood; a Church which has received [redacted] of God? See you those vast territories through which echoes no voice of him who bringeth glad tidings? They are arguments. See you new States, new cities, new towns, all swelling with human life? They are arguments. See you the efforts of papal priests and pagan idolaters? They are arguments. Listen to the music of heaven! Behold the golden gates! Gaze along the celestial streets, and mingle with the angel throng! Heaven is a splendid argument! Hear the groans of the lost! Look down into the pit, witness the smoke of torment which ascendeth up for ever; understand the meaning of the worm that never dies, and mingle with the spirits of the damned! Hell, too, is a terrible argument!

But there is another argument There stands the Cross! There hangs the bleeding Christ, suspended between two worlds that both may gaze upon him. The darkened sun, the bursting graves, the shaking earth, the rending vail, are all affected by that argument. It convinces Satan that his cause is lost; it moves also the infinite mind of God. There is in that cross the logic of eternal truth, the persuasiveness of atoning blood, and the rhetoric of unbidden tears. O, can we sit down to wrangle within sight of that cross, while those mild lips are saying, "Father forgive them!" Can we be indifferent to the cause of our perishing fellow-men, while every tear, every groan, and every drop of blood declares, "O, sinner, I do this for thee!"

We stand to-day amid stupendous motives to Home Mission labors. They utter never a word, but they plead eloquently with us. Our religion, dearer to us than life; our patriotism, of which we boast; our love of country, which has never been impeached; all are motives to this divine work. With their eloquent lips, and their beseeching looks, they plead with us, and say:—

"Go, ye messengers of God,
Like the beams of morning fly;
Take the wonder-working rod,
And lift the banner cross on high."

ADDRESS OF REV. HARVEY MILLER,

OF CONNECTICUT.

Mr. Chairman.—I rise to second the acceptance of the Report to which we have listened this evening, believing that the views which it advocates, and the recommendations which it urges, have their basis in an intelligent and comprehensive survey of the field and work to which they relate; and that they are eminently moderate and just.

I need not apprise you, that this Society has for many years been sending its agents and its publications to our churches and homes, and soliciting, with importunate urgency, our sympathy and our earnest prayers for its objects, together with our pecuniary contributions, and our labors, so far as we can give them: and they have asked, in unequivocal terms, for our choicest men [redacted]

Society, to which it bends all its energies—in simple but sublime recognition of those great truths taught by the cross of Jesus,—viz.,—the utter ruin of man as a sinner. "For if one died for all, then were all dead:" "And that man may be saved by the sacrifice of Christ:" "Christ hath redeemed us from the curse of the law, being made a curse for us:" "Whom God hath set forth to be a propitiation, through faith in his blood—that he might be just, and the justifier of him which believeth in Jesus." The convictions which govern its action might be embodied in the conclusion of a Romanist Bible-reader, of whom we have heard. When for the first time he had access to the Word of God, he read for a long time in silence in the midst of his family, and at length exclaimed, "If this book is true, we are wrong!" Having resumed his reading, he at length again broke silence by saying, "If this book is true, we are lost!" But after a third and more protracted perusal, he joyfully exclaimed, "If this book is true, we may be saved!" All other truths are of secondary importance, and all other interests are trifling compared with salvation.

But, Sir, this Society does not practically ignore any real interest of man, considered individually or socially, with regard to his physical, intellectual or moral necessities. The founders and patrons of this Society have, as accurately as others, estimated the nature and extent of every human interest. And to them, as much as to any other class of men, belongs the sentiment, which anciently drew such applause when uttered in the Roman Theatre: "We are men—and are deeply concerned in all that belongs to men." And in devotion to the one object of the Society, they find scope for the exercise of every right feeling towards men, and for the operation of their influence in all the appropriate departments of human endeavor, fully aware, from history and observation, that the influence of the Gospel is absolutely essential to the highest development of man, in his social and civil relations, in his intellectual and moral nature. Hence it will appear, that the work thus proposed is eminently congenial with the purest patriotism, the widest philanthropy, and the loftiest piety.

Sir, we do know that man is not shorn of his manhood by subjection to "the powers of the world to come." He is in no sense debased by communion with the God of glory, and by moral conformity to the image of his Son. He cannot be unfitted for his relations and duties to human society because he is "made meet for the inheritance of the saints in light." And we know this by the plainest induction of facts. We cannot fail to see, that the nations in which the Gospel has been most fully preached, and exerted the widest influence, are, at this hour, in art, in science, in commerce, in government and in morals, the foremost nations on the face of the earth. Will any pretend that New-England is behind her neighbors in any essential particular, because of the predominance of the religious element over the masses of her population, from its earliest history? Or, to cite a single fact bearing on the general argument, I need hardly remind you, that, while our almshouses are filled with paupers, and our prisons with criminals, and a great proportion of these were bred in

foreign lands, yet the children of old Bible-reading, catechising, se
Scotland are not to be found in either class or place. Little affini
for pauperism or crime. And while the Scot tells us, with instin
country, that his is "no' a very great country, but of muckle pith
no man, I presume, will dare to say that the Gospel, which has b
ally and powerfully preached there, from the days of John Kn
present time, has done aught to weaken her pith, or to quenc
No, sir; while the Gospel grasps the highest interests of the lif
does not disdain, but rather fosters the subordinate interests of
now is. And vast and varied are those incidental benefits which
Hall would say,—thus scatters by the way, in her march to

Thus, Sir, I repeat, that the work proposed and prosecuted by
appeals with commanding power, to all true patriots, genuine lo
country—and to all true philanthropists, sincere lovers of mank
speak to a Christian audience; to those who, duly awake to all
objects, yet "glory only in the cross of our Lord Jesus Christ;"
the dread significance of that ancient inquiry, "What shall it profi
shall gain the whole world, and lose his own soul?" I speak to thos
supposed to sympathize with the Redeemer in his travail of soul
of lost men, and whose ruling desire it must therefore be, that m
the Gospel and "believe to the saving of the soul." And to such
this Society commends itself by all that is dear and by all that

an immortal world, give it strong claims upon my generous regards. Indeed, to disregard the interests of this Home Field would involve much of the unmitigated baseness of neglecting to provide for one's own family. He who allows the elements of evil to operate here, unchecked by such agencies as he can employ; and suffers it to lack the elements of good which he can impart or sustain in it, practically gives his consent that his posterity shall take their chance for this life and the next in circumstances of unspeakable peril. He virtually refuses to place them on a vantage ground of priceless importance—to throw around them safeguards, which, under God, might insure their temporal and eternal welfare. I insist that such a one does, in effect, welcome the elements and agents of evil to do their worst; to riot and ravage, at will, among the homes of our land, and the homes of his children!

But on the ground of opportunity, involved in it as a Home Field, the friends of this Society may base a powerful plea for it claims. "To do good to all men, as we have opportunity," is an apostolic maxim. The opportunity defines at once the nature and the extent of our obligation to beneficent action. And it can be made to appear, that this field affords to us opportunity to do good, in greater variety and measure, than any other, and perhaps than all others. Some of these may claim our attention hereafter. But I speak now particularly of our location in it, of ready communication with all parts of it; and the directness and power with which we may operate upon it. Sir, we are on the field: no oceans need be crossed, no strange inhospitable deserts passed, nor hostile tribes encountered, to reach the scene of our operations. The whitened fields are before us; and we may reap if we will. The channels of influence are opened at our very doors, extending to the remotest borders of the land, through which the tide of blessings may be poured. And more, the streams of blessing are already flowing, and we may swell their volume, and accelerate their flow. "Others have labored," and we may, we must, or prove recreant at once to man and to God, "enter into their labors," and prosecute their holy work. We may speak from our own homes, and our voices may be heard over the Alleganies, across the mighty prairies of the West, and echo down the Pacific slope, to the dwellers in Oregon and California. Figures apart, our influence on this land may be direct, immediate, and mighty through God, and beneficent as mighty. Thus in the fact of opportunity we have the ground of claims immensely great, as urged upon us by the Home field.

But it is worthy of special consideration that it has some of the features of a foreign mission. Our population is no longer one speaking wholly a common language. We have much to do with men of foreign birth, and of strange tongues, now transplanted to our own shores. They have become constituent parts of our population. We need men who can speak to them, "in their own tongues wherein they were born, the wonderful works of God." But this requires missionaries speaking nearly every language of Europe. Had we here this evening a delegation from each of the nations now largely represented by dwellers upon our own soil, and should all of them speak to us in their vernacular, we should have a lively illustration of the confusion of tongues at Babel. It is pleasant to know that this Society has cared for them, and made the fullest provision in their power to meet their moral wants. Their missionaries have preached in some twelve different languages during the past year.

But more than this, we have among us the natives of India. China, the strange land of unnumbered myriads, until of late walled around with impassable barriers, has not merely been entered by our foreign missionaries, but she has sprung a-leak, and poured upon our shores some 25,000 of her swarthy children.

How earnestly were the eyes of Christendom formerly turned upon that inaccessible land, in quest of some access to its deluded population! But now God tests our sincerity, our love and faith, by placing them at our doors and bidding us "to speak" to them the words of eternal life. The children of Confucius are sent to the disciples of Him of Nazareth, to learn of them wiser maxims than those of their great Teacher, viz., "Words whereby they may be saved." How wonderful is this! Or, rather, have we not become so *sated* with wonders, that we are nearly incapable of impression from what is morally marvellous? Doctor L. Bacon is reported to have said in some anniversary address, some years since, that he could remember the time when he did not expect that he should ever see "a live Catholic." But, sir, who of us did expect to live to see the time when there would be tens of thousands of "live Chinamen" in our land, accessible to the sound of the Gospel? O, had we the

And if it is an awful thing that the servants of Christ have been so long in conveying the gospel to a few of the millions of other lands, who shall estimate the enormity of the neglect if we fail to bless those whom God has sent to our very doors?

But the claims of this field must be estimated not simply from its relations to us as a home field, nor from its relations to other lands, but from the magnitude of the work required. No one can regard it, on the most cursory view, as other than a vast work to secure the preaching of the gospel to the population of our country; and I now speak of those portions of it which are comparatively destitute. But the Reports of this and kindred societies are fitted to give us deeper impressions of this than could arise from a cursory view of it. You cannot fail to notice that they uniformly represent it as a field rapidly enlarging—multiplying its necessities, and involving increasing obligations. Now to one who has any definite idea of the extent of the field which has been claiming our endeavors during the past twenty years, there is something formidable, positively alarming in the idea of its further enlargement—alarming, I mean, in the responsibility which must correspond with its extent, and with our ability to furnish the needful supplies. To a considerate mind there is something startling, something oppressive—almost insupportable in the fact that divine Providence bids us in tones of commanding authority to cultivate that field. The harvest is so great, and the laborers available so few, that despondency would seem pardonable in any but the firmest spirits, fortified by the strongest faith. I am here reminded of the sadness of the senior Secretary during an interview in 1838. Much pleasure had been anticipated in the interview at the Rooms; and I had intended to lay before him the claims of certain parts of the State of Michigan, with the wants of which I had become partially acquainted, during a residence in it of two years. I found him in conversation with a gentleman from another Western State, in relation to its destitution. And he seemed so burdened with the pressing calls of the vast field, and the utter inadequacy of the means at the control of the Society, that the pleasure of the meeting was marred for me, and I could say little of the claims which I had designed to urge.

It is manifest that the wants of the field have never been met at any period since the organization of the Society. And, more than this, the Society has never been enabled to approximate very nearly to the performance of that share of the needful work for which the denomination has been responsible, by virtue of the numbers and ability which God has given it. Large regions of rich promise have been left wholly unoccupied, not simply by ourselves, but by every other class of evangelical laborers; and meantime they have been accessible to every form of error and of evil. Hence, were the demands precisely the same as twenty years since, and Oregon, and California, and New Mexico, and other vast regions, had few or no claims upon us, I should say that the plea of the Society for the supplies they have specified, is based in perfect truth, and all-sufficient moderation. And I insist that this sum, though exceeding the amount yet furnished in any single year, is not sufficiently large to be particularly creditable to the many ten thousands who are called upon to contribute it. It would be far from exhausting their resources, or, as I fear, from fairly meeting their responsibilities. With the most judicious application of this amount, large regions (we should think them such at the East) would remain destitute, and their moral wants would cry in piteous tones for Christian love and bounty to come to their rescue. Could Paul speak of such an outlay, for such a cause, from such a people, I doubt not he would call in tones of fraternal entreaty, and of Apostolic authority, for an enlargement of our faith, and zeal, and liberality. And James, were he to speak, passing by a magnificent outlay, as we may think it, for Home Missions, would give us sundry sharp and pregnant hints touching the worthlessness of a faith which hath not characteristic and corresponding works.

But we are reminded of a widening field; one already greatly transcending the limits in preceding remarks. And taking into view the millions now embraced in our population, and the multiplied millions who at the present ratio of increase must people this land at no distant day, we are overcome by the impressions thence derived of the mighty interests which are at stake, and which must be decided within a few years. The statistics of this subject, reliable as they are, for aught I can see, are fitted to stun if not to crush one. They bewilder by their vastness. They even oppress the imagination. Unless Providence shall interpose a check to the causes now in operation, this vast land must be peopled. But the territory already peopled is so vast, that all New England of our foreign commerce. And perhaps the most striking thing connected with these astonishing results, is the brief period during which they have been achieved. And from the past we must judge of the future.

But this conducts us to one of the most startling considerations, viz.: the amazing rapidity with which the population of the West increases. Take, for illustration, some of their cities. In twenty-three years, Chicago became the home of fifty thousand inhabitants. Sir, since I began preaching, the whole population of that city could have been seated in my vestry. But that population is now computed at about seventy thousand. In twenty years, St. Louis passed from four thousand to sixty thousand, and has now ninety thousand. Cincinnati, settled within the memory of some now living, numbers one hundred and sixty thousand; yet Boston, we are told, was two hundred years in raising her population to fifty thousand!

At the present rate of progress, the population of the Western Valley proper, would, at no distant period, equal that of China. But supposing the rate to be reduced to the smallest ratio fairly conceivable in the case, and still the numbers who must dwell there are positively enormous.

Now, from this consideration, who does not see an argument of momentous force, for timely endeavors, to season this mighty mass with the salt of divine truth. There is imminent danger that the field will grow beyond our grasp; that we shall not keep pace in our supply with the mighty strides of its advancing necessity. It were a question of momentous import, whether we are not already so far behind that we cannot overtake the tide of population as it rolls onward. But it is not a question whether this can be done if we delay much longer, or if we move forward only at our present rate. Let the disproportion between the demand and the supply increase a little longer, and we may despair of gaining our object.

From such considerations, we may estimate the magnitude of the work assigned to the churches of our land, and the proportion of that work which God binds upon the churches of our own denomination. And we cannot hesitate to say that our churches are morally bound to pour into the treasury of this Society three times the annual amount which they have contributed in any former year. And besides, a "Fund for church edifices should be raised of not less than fifty thousand dollars." The examples of other kindred societies in these particulars should be regarded as admonitory to ourselves. The fund for this purpose, which we greatly need, and which from our ability we ought to raise, has already been raised by several of the Evangelical denominations.

And the same holds true of the demand for faithful preachers of the Gospel. The call for such is piteous and affecting as that from Macedonia to Paul in the vision of the night. And there is something astounding in the fact, that men of God so generally fail to hear or to regard this call. One can hardly avoid the conclusion, that the will overrides the judgment and the conscience in such cases. Doctor Lyman Beecher complained of this some years since, in an anniversary address at New Haven. It might be inferred from his announcement, that Eastern men would not hear a call from God for the West, unless Gabriel should put his trump beneath heaven's blue concave and blow a blast which would make "the hollow deep of hell resound," and start the sheeted dead from their sepulchres. O, sir, is it not pitiful, that scores of ministers, in manhood's prime, will linger in the East—gentlemen at large, so far as regards ministerial labor—"in quest of a vacancy," as the polite phrase is, or at best, in circumstances where they rather vegetate than live to purpose, when, within the limits of three days' travel, they might find fields as vacant of Christian laborers as the Prince of Darkness himself could desire, yet promising, under liberal culture, harvests which an angel would deem it a privilege to reap; harvests which would gloriously repay a life-time of toil, and for the gathering of which it were a privilege to die.

But the work prosecuted by the Society has claims upon our regards, from the dangers which threaten our land in all its great interests, politically, morally, and religiously considered. These are such as are incident to a new country, with its toils, privations, and destitutions—where the supply of physical wants becomes for a time a matter of absorbing interest—and in the absence of the means of social, intellectual and moral culture; where the old ties of established society are all ruptured; where new society must be formed by strangers from various sections of the country, having among themselves almost as many points of repulsion as of attraction. Add to this the strange heterogeneous elements of a foreign immigration—embracing the children of

The other extreme is that of vain confidence,—a groundless security. The latter has more generally prevailed of late. But, with more courage than formerly, I still see no ground for confidence but in the large and devout application of the means of evangelization. The agents and instruments of evil are numerous and powerful, and ever as active as their master would have them. And our safety lies not in indolent security. We may be sure that mischief will not die a natural death, and that Satan will not resign the struggle for predominance in this land without working all the enginery of hell—not without pouring out upon it the very dregs of the infernal pit. Give these various forms of error time to fortify and intrench themselves upon our soil, and they will be found as difficult to dislodge as the Russians at Sebastopol.

But as yet, there are grounds of hope in our case. We have all the needful means of evangelization, and every advantage for their application. We have a free Bible, and "the word of God is not bound." We have a free pulpit, whence the powerful word may sound out over all the land. We have a free press, and prolific beyond all precedent. Ours is a reading people, and we have unexampled opportunity to bring to bear upon the masses the hallowed influence of a religious literature. And by all these mighty agencies, we can assail the popular mind untrammelled, nay, protected by the civil power. Let these be applied, in humble yet trustful dependence upon God,—let them be interfused with the constituent elements of new society in the West, and we may anticipate the grandest results. We do not theorize nor declaim in such announcements. We have a noble example of the experiment in point, and the world has done homage to its fruits. I refer to the Puritan emigration which settled New England. They brought the Bible as well as the axe and the plough; and reared the sanctuary and school-house along with their own dwellings. And, after the example of the Supreme Being, six days they labored and did all their work, and they rested the seventh day and hallowed it. And as the results of this experiment, they have given to the world the model of a more perfect civilization than the world had before seen. They constructed a society which has conferred upon its members generally a heritage of more rich and varied benefits, than had ever before been given to mortals. Hence we judge that if the various instruments of civil, intellectual and moral culture before named, be duly applied, the future history of our country may be glorious beyond example. We do believe, Sir, that such a field and such opportunities were never before given to men, since "the morning stars sang together and the sons of God shouted for joy."

But who, Sir, can estimate the extent of the calamity, if such opportunity should be lost, and the enterprise of subjecting this continent to Christ should fail, and the present splendid promise should suffer disastrous eclipse? And what symbols of mourning would be suited to such an event? We are reminded of the inquiries of the great modern master of rhetoric, concerning the fitting obsequies of a lost soul. But the inquiries should become yet more impassioned when we contemplate the immortal destinies of myriads of souls.

The language of that powerful paragraph is not adequate to such an occasion: —"It would not suffice for the sun to vail his light, and the moon her brightness, to cover the ocean with mourning, and the heavens with sackcloth—nor, were the whole fabric of nature to become animated and vocal, would it be possible for her to utter a groan so deep or a cry so piercing, as would express the magnitude and extent of such a catastrophe." And, Sir, should we contribute or constructively consent to such a result, posterity with its million voices would bitterly curse our apathy,—hell would hold a jubilee, and be moved from beneath to meet us, in our fall!

We may well believe that such an opportunity as is now given us, if once lost, can never be repeated. Is it not too much to hope that such an experiment can ever be renewed? And the next twenty-five or fifty years may be the crisis in our national history, whose consequences shall be felt by millions for weal or woe to the latest period of time.

And are we duly mindful of the fact, that we are suffered, if we will, to bend our energies to this great enterprise, while the energies of Europe are tasked for baleful war? How affecting the contrast! O, while millions of her treasure shall be expended, and the blood of her sons, by scores of thousands, shall be poured out like water, in murderous conflict; may not more than fragments of our bounty be consecrated to the bloodless victories of the Cross? And may not this Society be enriched and strengthened for its noble work, by at least the additions to its means for which it pleads in the name of our [redacted]

REPORT OF SPECIAL COMMITTEE ON ROOMS.

ADOPTED BY THE SOCIETY, MAY 9, 1855.

The Committee to whom was referred the Special Report of the Executive Board on Rooms, with various documents and resolutions relating to the same, beg leave to report:—

Your Committee find the special report referred to, a very carefully drawn document, reciting the history of the measures which have resulted in the occupation of the present rooms, under the instructions of the Society, and setting forth both the dissatisfaction which has arisen in consequence of such occupancy, and the remedy which the Board would suggest. This remedy and the grounds of it are thus stated, in the following preamble and resolution passed by the Board in February of the present year:

Whereas, There exists a diversity of opinion among the friends of the Society, as to its present location, in consequence of which the harmony of the Society is disturbed; and, whereas, it is supposed that sufficient sums could be procured from our brethren and friends to secure an eligible building, to be held by the Society, free from incumbrances; therefore,

Resolved, That if it be found, after a full understanding of the tenure by which the Society now holds and may continue to hold the possession of these rooms, that in remaining here its unity cannot be preserved, we recommend that the Society remove to an independent location, provided that a suitable building can be obtained, free from incumbrances, and without drawing from the Society's treasury for general purposes.

Your Committee concurring in general in the measures here suggested, and believing that no question so immaterial in itself as the rooms for a Society's business, whatever the merits of such question, should be allowed to become the occasion of division among brethren, and a hinderance to the great work of home evangelization, but should be adjusted by such a yielding of preferences mutually, as accords with the self-sacrificing spirit of the Gospel; and, further, in the belief that such an adjustment accords with the views both of the Executive Board of this Society as above expressed, and of the Board of the Society from which the lease is derived, as set forth in their published acts, recommend, in order to a final and satisfactory adjustment of these differences, the adoption of the following resolution:

Resolved, That this Society will remove its place of business to another location, the property of which shall be vested in this Society; and that the following shall be the methods and conditions for the attainment of this result, viz.: Ebenezer Cauldwell, Thomas Thomas, John B. Durbrow, John M. Ferrier, William T. Dugan, and George Gault, are hereby constituted and appointed a Committee, with power to solicit and receive donations and subscriptions, without expense to the Treasury of the Society, for the purchase or erection of a suitable building; and to purchase or erect the same.

The location shall be south of Canal Street, in the city of New York, in a central and accessible situation, and the rooms shall be, as nearly as may be, equally commodious and convenient with those now occupied by the Society.

The Committee are not limited as to the amount of money to be raised and expended for this object; but the total cost of the property procured and ready for use shall not exceed double the amount of money actually received or subscribed, and the Committee shall be satisfied that the rents arising from such parts of the building as are not wanted for the uses of the Society, will pay the annual interest and expenses, and eventually extinguish the debt.

Whenever rooms are so furnished to this Society, the Executive Board are hereby authorized and instructed to remove from the present location, and to enter upon the possession and use of the same.

Your Committee further recommend that the Special Report of the Board referred to above be accepted, and printed with the Minutes.

All which is respectfully submitted.

DIRECTORS FOR LIFE.

BY VIRTUE OF A CONTRIBUTION OF ONE HUNDRED DOLLARS OR MORE.

Ackerman, John, Dobbs Ferry, N. Y.
Adams, Rev. Paul S., Newport, N. H.
Adsit, Rev. Samuel, Jr., Auburn, N. Y.
Akerly, Richard C., New York.
Aldrich, Rev. Jonathan, Worcester, Mass.
Alger, Henry, Cleveland, Ohio.
Allin, George, Brooklyn, N. Y.
Alvord, Rev. Nelson, Minneapolis, Min. Ter.
Anderson, Rev. Thomas D., Roxbury, Mass.
Anderson, M. B., LL D., Rochester, N. Y.
Anderson, Rev. George W., North East, N. Y.
Archer, Ezekiel, New York.
Armitage, Rev. Thomas, D.D., New York.
Armstrong, Rev. James D., Baltimore.
Askeen, William, Cincinnati, O.
Atwell, Rev. G. B., Pleasant Valley, Conn.
Averill, Rev. Alexander M., Newton Centre, Ms.
Ayre, Rev. Oliver, Claremont, N. H.
Babcock, Rev. Rufus, D.D., New York.
Bacheller Jonathan, Lynn, Mass.
Bacon, Mrs. Mary H., Greenwich, N. J.
Bailey, Benjamin D., Providence, R. I.
Bailey, Rev. Gilbert S., Pekin, Ill.
Bailey, Rev. Joseph A., Essex, Ct.
Ballard, Rev. Joseph, Brooklyn.
Baldwin, Rev. N. B., Philadelphia.
Balen, Peter, New York.
Banks, Jacob, Scull town, N. J.
Banks, Mrs. Mary, Sculltown, N. J.
Banks, Miss Ann Judson, Sculltown, N. J.
Banvard, Rev. Joseph, New York.
Barnaby, Rev. James, Newburyport, Mass.
Barker, Rev. Enoch M., Highstown, N. J.
Barrell, Rev. Almond C., Albion, N. Y.
Batchelder, Rev. James L., Cincinnati, O.
Bates, V. J., Providence, R. I.
Beecher, Rev. Luther F., D.D., New York.
Beecher, Mrs. Mary C., New York.
Belcher, Rev. Joseph, D.D., Philadelphia.
Bennet, Rev. Ira, Weedsport, N. Y.
Binney, Rev. J. G., D.D., Washington, D. C.
Binney, Mrs. Juliet P., Washington, D. C.
Bishop, Nathan, Boston.
Blain, Rev. John, Central Falls, R. I.
Bliss, Rev. George R., Lewisburg, Pa.
Bly, Rev. William T., Berwick, Ill.
Boardman, W. G., Albany, N. Y.
Bolles, Matthew, Jr., Boston.
Borden, Jefferson, Fall River, Mass.
Bosworth, Rev. George W., Portland, Me.
Bowles, Rev. Ralph H., Branford, Ct.
Boyce, James, Providence.
Bradford, Rev. S. S., Pawtucket, R. I.
Brant, Randolph C., Rochester, N. Y.
Brantly, Rev. W. T., Georgia.
Brayton, Rev. Jonathan, Centerville, R. I.
Brayton, Samuel H., Phenix, R. I.
Brayton, Lodowick M., Knightsville, R. I.
Briggs, Rev. O. W., Brooklyn.
Brooks, Iveson L., Hamburg, S. C.
Browere, Vermilyea T., Dundee, N. Y.
Brown, Rev. J. Newton, D.D., Philadelphia.
Bruce, John M., New York.
Buckbee, Rev. Charles A., New York.
Bucknell, William, Philadelphia.
Budlong, James E., Providence, R. I.
Burlingham, Rev. A. H., Boston.
Burgess, Rev. I. J., Milltown, Me.
Bump, Nathaniel, Providence.
Burke, William, Rochester, N. Y.
Burke, Abraham C., Brooklyn.
Burke, J. R., Middleboro', Mass.
Burt, John W., Brooklyn.
Burt, E. C., Brooklyn.
Burroughs, Rev. J. C., Chicago, Ill.
Butcher, Washington, Philadelphia.
Butterfield, Rev. Isaac., Oswego, N. Y.
Byram, Rev. B. P., Amesbury, Mass.
Caldicott, Rev. T. F., D.D., Boston.
Carleton, Rev. George J., Newtown Centre, Ms.
Carleton, Mrs. Jane F., Newtown Centre, Mass.
Carpenter, Rev. Mark, West Springfield, Mass.
Carter, Joseph, Charlestown, Mass.
Caswell, Prof. Alexis, D D., Providence.
Caswell, Rev. Lewis E., Boston.
Chace, Professor George I., Providence.
Challis, Rev. James M., Roadstown, N. J.
Chandler, John H., Bankok, Siam.
Chandler, Mrs. Helen M., Bankok, Siam.
Chaplin, Rev. Jeremiah, West Dedham, Mass.
Chaplin, Rev. Adoniram J., Bennington, Vt.
Charlton, Rev. Frederick, Wilmington, Del.
Cheesebrough, Rev. Isaac, Groton, Ct.
Cheney, Rev. David B., Philadelphia.
Child, Mrs. Sophronia L., Brooklyn.
Child, Rev. William C., Framingham, Mass.
Choules, Rev. John O., D.D., Newport, R. I.
Church, Rev. P., D.D., New York.
Church, Mrs. Chara E., New York.
Clarke, Rev. Elbert W., China, N. Y.
Clarke, Rev. Minor G., Philadelphia.
Clapp, Benjamin, Franklindale, N. Y.
Coggeshall, Josias, Brooklyn.
Coggeshall, Mrs. Elizabeth M., Brooklyn.
Cogswell, Rev. Wilson, St. Anthony, Min.
Cooke, Joseph J., Providence.
Cookson, Rev. John, Morrisania, N. Y.
Cole, Rev. Jirah D., Waukegan, Ill.
Colgate, William, New York.
Colgate, Mrs. Jane, New York.

MEMBERS FOR LIFE.

Bond, Mrs. Mary, New Britain, Ct.
Bonham, Daniel, Berryville, Va.,
Bonney, W. F, Eaton, N. Y.
Boono, Dr. Levi D., Chicago, Ill
Boone, Hon. L. D., Chicago, Ill.
Borden, Lodowick, Fall River, Mass.
Borden, Isaac, Fall River, Mass.
Borden Charles, Fall River, Mass
Borden, Joseph, Fall River, Mass.
Borden, Cook, Fall River, Mass.
Bosson, George P., Chelsea, Mass.
Bosson, Benjamin P., Chelsea, Mass.
Bosson, Miss Mary, Chelsea, Mass.
Bostick, Elisha, Bostick's Mills, N. C
Bostick, Elijah, Bostick's Mills, N. C.
Bostick, Tristam, Bostick's Mills, N. C
Bostick, Benj. R., Robertsville, S. C.
Bostick, Mrs. Jane A, Robertsville, S. C.
Boswell, Davis, Stilesville, Ia.,
Bosworth, William M., East Poultney, Vt.
Bosworth, George H., Fall River, Mass.
Bottom, Nathan H., Shaftsbury, Vt.
Bottom, Mrs. Peace, Shaftsbury, Vt.
Boughton, James, New York.
Boutelle, Miss Sylvia, East Cambridge, Mass
Bouton, Mrs. Sarah M., New York.
Bowen, John, New York.
Bowen, Henry, Chili Centre, New York.
Bowen, David M., Canton, N. J.
Bowen, Rev. William, Hancock, Mass.
Bowen, William, New York.
Bowen, Mrs. A. K., Cortlandville, N Y.
Bowen, Henry A., Natic, R. I.
Bower, Rev. Jacob, Manchester, Ill.
Bowers, Rev. C. M., Clintonville, Mass.
Bowers, Mrs. Hannah D., Seekonk, Mass.
Boyakin, Rev. Wm. F., Portland, Oregon.
Boyce, Rev. Peter, Green Point, N. Y.
Boyce, Mrs. Albina, Providence.
Boyd, Rev. Robert, Hamilton, Canada.
Boyd, John, Albany, N. Y.
Boyden, Addison, South Dedham, Mass.
Brabrook, Mrs. Lucy A., Davenport, Iowa.
Brabrook, Alfred, Taunton, Mass.
Brabrook, Joseph A., Lowell, Mass.
Bradish, Levi J., Jamaica Plains, Mass.
Bradford, W. R., Boston.
Bradford, John, Wilminglon, Del.
Bradley, Mrs. Enoch, Haverhill, Mass.
Brainerd, Samuel, Haverhill, Mass.
Brainerd, Mrs. Samuel, Haverhill, Mass.
Branch, Rev. Nicholas, East Killingly, Ct.
Branch, Rev. William, Williamsville, N. Y.
Brandt, Rev. Thomas, Waukesha, Wis.
Bradley, Collins, Mt. Vernon, Mich.
Bray, Joseph M., Brooklyn.
Brayton, Philip, Phenix, R. I.
Brayton, Mrs. Harriett, Phenix, R. I.
Brayton, Mrs. Ruth, Phenix, R. I.
Brayton, Mrs. Betsey, Phenix, R. I.
Brayton, Mrs. Mary Ann, Centreville, R. I.
Breed, Rev. Joseph B, Woonsocket, R. I.
Breed, Mrs. Frances A. C., Woonsocket, R. I.
Breed, Catherine C., Lynn, Mass
Brewer, Mrs. Elizabeth, New York.
Bridgens, Miss Mary Ann, Brooklyn.
Bridgewood, Mrs. Jane, Williamsburgh, N. Y.
Brierly, Rev. Benjamin, San Francisco, Cal.
Brigham, Sylvester, Dover, Ill.
Brigham, Rev. J. H., Scipio, N. Y.
Briggs, Arnold, Fairhaven, Vt.
Briggs, Rev. Avery, Rock Island, Ill.
Briggs, Mrs. Sarah H., Fitchburg, Mass.
Briggs, Harris, Coventry, N. Y.
Bright, Rev. T., Elkhorn, Wis.
Brinkerhoff, Rev. O., Toulon, Ill.
Brisbane, Rev. Wm. H. Cheviot, O.
Brisbane, Miss Maria, Charleston, S. C.
Briscoe, Sally C., Va.
Britton, Everett, New York.
Brockett, Alvah, Salisbury, N. Y.
Brockett, Asahel, Bristol, Ct.
Broaddus, Rev. Wm. F., D.D., Versailles, Ky.
Broaddus, Mrs. Mary A., Versailles, Ky.
Broadhead, Mrs. Ann, New York.
Brocket, Rev. Pierpont, Hartford, Ct.
Brockway, Mrs. Elizabeth, Broadalbin, N. Y.
Britton, W. G., Brittons ⋈ Roads, N. C.
Bromley, Isaac, Norwich, Ct.
Bromley, J. Breed, Norwich, Ct.
Bromley, Dowey, Norwich, Ct.
Bromley, Rev. Henry, New York.
Bromley, Mrs. Jane M, New York.
Brouner, Mrs. Sarah, New York.
Bronson, Rev. Asa, Fall River, Mass.
Bronson, Rev. Benjamin F., Methuen, Mass.
Bronson, Mrs. Anna C, Methuen, Mass.
Bronson, Miss Aydee A., Townsend, Mass.
Brooks, Dea. Kendall, Roxbury, Mass.
Brooks, Rev. Prof. Kendall, Portland, Me
Brooks, John, Hanover, Mass.
Brooks, Mrs. Elizabeth, Cambridge, Mass
Browe, E. S., New Brunswick, N. J.
Brower, Davis E, Doylestown, Pa.
Brown, W. S., Britton's ⋈ Roads, N. C
Brown, Josiah, Haverhill, Mass.
Brown, J. S., Fitchburg, Mass.
Brown, Edward L., Brooklyn.
Brown, Mrs. Susan A., Brooklyn.
Brown, Rev. Amasa, Concord, N. H.
Brown, Rev. Dana, Nashua, N. H.
Brown, Rev. E. T., Wooster, O.
Brown, Andrew, Middletown, N. J.
Brown, Geo. W., New York.
Brown, Hugh H., Providence.
Brown, Rev. E. C., Bath, N. Y.
Brown, Rev. F. G., West Townsend, Mass
Brown, Rev. Wm. L., Watertown, Mass.
Brown, Rev. Joseph P., Moosup, Ct.
Brown, Daniel, Sempronius, N. Y.
Brown, Miss Harriet, Norwich, N. Y.
Brown, Rev. J., Springfield, O.
Brown, Mrs. Emily M. A., Fauquier, Va.
Brown, Mrs. O. B., Washington, D. C.
Brown, Mrs. Elizabeth E., Aylett's, Va.
Brown, Miss Ann F., Providence.
Brown, Mrs. Mary F., Keene, N. H.
Brown, Mrs. Isaac, Haverhill, Mass.
Brown, Mrs. Margaret A., Reading, Ohio.
Brown, Rev. J F., Scotch Plains, N. J.
Brown, Rev. Philip P., Holland Patent, N. Y.
Brown, Rev. Wm., Eaton, N. Y.
Brown, Evander M., Saratoga Springs, N. Y
Brown, L R, Hartford, Ct.

Holmes, Rev. Lewis, Edgarton, Mass.
Hotchkiss, Rev. V. R., Rochester, N. Y.
Houghton, Hon. Joab, Santa Fe, N. M.
Howard, Rev. Leland, Rutland, Vt.
Howard, Rev. William G., D.D., Rochester, N. Y.
Howe, Rev. William, Boston.
Howell, Rev. Robert B. C., D.D., Richmond, Va.
Howell, Mrs. Mary Ann M., Richmond, Va.
Huckings, Rev. James, Galveston, Texas.
Hunt, Samuel, Providence.
Hutchinson, Rev. Wm., Bustleton, Pa.
Ide, Rev. George B., D.D , Springfield, Mass.
Ilsley, Rev. Silas, Brooklyn.
Ives, Rev. Dwight, D.D., Suffield, Ct.
Ives, Mrs. Julia A., Suffield, Ct.
Ives, Mrs. Hope, Providence.
Jackson, Rev. Henry, D. D., Newport, R. I.
James, Rev. Silas C., Bunker Hill, Ill.
James, William T., New York.
James, Israel E., Philadelphia.
Jameson, William H., Boston.
Jameson, Rev. Thorndike C., Boston.
Jayne, David, Philadelphia.
Jennings, Rev. John, Fitchburg, Mass.
Jeter, Rev. J. B., D.D , Richmond, Va.
Johnson, Rev. W. D. H., Greenville, Ill.
Jones, Rev. Henry V., New Brunswick, N. J.
Jones, Rev. P. F., New York.
Jones, Rev. John D. E., Worcester, Mass.
Judd, Rev. Orrin B , LL.D., New York.
Kelly, Samuel R., Brooklyn.
Keen, Wm. W., Philadelphia.
Kempton, Rev. George, New Brunswick, N. J.
Kennard, Rev. J. H., Philadelphia.
Kendall, Mrs. Betsy, Littleton, Mass.
Kent, Henry P., Suffield, Ct.
Kent, Mrs. Jane S., Suffield, Ct.
Keyes, Rev. Charles B., Westfield, N. Y.
Ladd, Rev. James S., New York.
Larcombe, Richard J., New York.
Latham, Daniel, New London, Ct.
Latham, Mrs. Delia Ann, New London, Ct.
Latham, Daniel D., New London, Ct.
Lane, Rev. Benjamin I., Newburyport, Mass.
Lathrop, Rev. Edward, D.D., New York.
Laws, Rev. William, Modesttown, Va.
Lawton, Rev. Joseph A., Erwinton, S. C.
Lea, Sidney Slade, Yanceyville, N. C.
Lee, George F., Philadelphia.
Leighton, Rev. Samuel S., West Townsend, Mass.
Leonard, Rev. Lewis G., Cambridgeport, Mass.
Leverett, Rev. William, New Eng. Village, Ms.
Lewis, John G., Boston.
Lewis, Isaac, New York.
Lewis, Mrs. Mary, New York.
Lillie, Rev. James, D.D., Montreal, Canada.
Lincoln, Hon. Heman, Boston.
Linnard, Hon. J. M., Philadelphia.
Linnard, Mrs. Anna, Philadelphia.
Locke, Rev. William E., Springfield, N. J.
Loxley, Rev. Benjamin R., Philadelphia.
Loomis, Rev. Ebenezer, Norwich, Ct.
Lumsden, D. F., Boston.
Lyeth, Richard J., Hastings, N. Y.
Lyon, Merrick, Providence, R. I.
Mabbet, Jonathan, Dover Plains, N. Y.
McIntosh, Wm. C., Philadelphia.
Maclay, Rev. Archibald, D.D., New York.
Magoon, Rev. E. L., D.D., New York.
Magoon, Mrs. E. L., New York.
Malcom, Rev. Howard, D.D., Lewisburg, Pa.
Malcom, Rev. Thomas S., Philadelphia.
Mallary, Rev. C. D., Rain's Store, Ga.
Marble, Joel, Albany, N. Y.
Marchant, Henry, Providence.
Maple, Thompson, Canton, Ill.
Martin, Runyon W., New York.
Martin, Charles J., New York.
Marshall, Rev. Enos, Pittsford, N. Y.
Massey, Rev. Joseph T., Bellingham, Mass.
Mason, Rev. Alanson P., Chelsea, Mass.
Mason, Rev. David G., West Swanzey, N. H.
Mason, Rev. Jas. O., Greenwich, N. Y.
Masters, William, Providence.
Masters, Mrs. William, Providence.
Mather, Rev. A. P , California.
Merit, Rev. Columbus D., Henry, Ill.
Merriam, Jonathan, Newton Centre, Mass.
Messenger, Rev. Edward C., West Medway, Ms.
Middleditch, Rev. Robert T., Red Bank, N. J.
Milbank, Samuel, Jr., New York.
Miller, John A , New York.
Miller, Rev. D. Henry, Yonkers, N. Y.
Mills, Rev. Robert C., Salem, Mass.
Miner, Mrs. Henrietta Wilson, Newark, N. J.
Mitchell, Isaac R., Sandwich Islands.
Moore, Rev. Isaac, Plainfield, N. J.
Morton, Rev. Charles, Corning, N. Y.
Mulford, Rev. Clarence W., Flemington, N. J.
Munn, Stephen B., New York.
Munn, William H., New York.
Murdock, Rev. J. N., D.D., Hartford, Ct.
Murphy, Rev. John C., New York.
Muzzy, Rev. Lawson, Pulaski, N. Y.
Neale, Rev. Rollin H., D.D., Boston.
Newell, Asa, Providence.
Newton, Isaac, New York.
Nice, Rev. G. P., Somerville, N. J.
Nicholas, Joseph O., Newark, N. J.
Norris, William, Newark, N. J.
Northam, Rev. G., Norminy Grove, Va.
Olcott, Rev. James B , Parma, N. Y.
Packer, Rev. D , Mount Holly, Vt.
Parker, Rev. J. W., D.D., Cambridgeport, Mass.
Parker, Rev. Carlton, Wayne, Me.
Parker, Rev. S. S., Southbridge, Mass.
Parkhurst, Rev. John, Chelmsford, Mass.
Parkhurst, Rev. J. W., Newton Centre, Mass.
Parks, Rev Norman, Perry, Ill.
Parmelee, Rev D. S , New York.
Parmly, Rev. Wheelock H., Jersey City, N. J.
Pattison, Rev. R. E., D D , Waterville, Me.
Pattison, Rev. Wm. P , Auburn, N. Y.
Patton, Rev. Alfred S., Hoboken, N. J.
Paul, Albert, Hastings, N. Y
Peck, J. B., New York.
Peck, Rev. John M , D.D., Shiloh, Ill.
Perkins, Rev. Aaron, D D., Salem, N. J.
Perry, Rev. G. B., Cleveland, O.
Perry, Simeon N., Walpole, N. H.
Phelps, William, New York.
Phelps, Rev. S. Dryden, D.D., New Haven, Ct.
Philips, Rev. Daniel W., South Reading, Mass.
Pier, Sylvester, New York.

DIRECTORS FOR LIFE.

Pierce, Rev S. E., Gloucester, Mass.
Pigsley, Rev Welcome, Metamora, Ill.
Platt, Nathan C., New York
Plummer, John L., Roxbury, Mass
Pollard, Rev. Andrew, Taunton, Mass,
Pope, Wm G E, New Bedford, Mass.
Pope, Mrs Anna F, New Bedford, Mass.
Porter, Rev Lemuel, D D, Pittsfield, Mass.
Post, Reuben, Essex, Ct.
Pratt, Rev. D. D, Nashua, N H.
Prevaux, Rev Francis E, San Francisco, Cal.
Price, Rev. Jacob, Edwardsburg, Mich
Price, William M., Brooklyn
Purington, Rev Wm. F, Plattsburgh, N. Y.
Purser, Thomas, Brooklyn
Randall, Rev S B, Mystic River, Ct.
Rathbone, John F, Albany.
Raymond Rev Robert R, Syracuse, N. Y
Read, James H, Providence
Roding, Rev C W, Beverly, Mass
Reed, Rev Nathan A, Wakefield, R I.
Reid, Rev William, New London, Ct.
Remington, Rev Stephen, Brooklyn.
Richards, Rev William C, New York.
Richardson, Thomas, Boston.
Richardson, Rev J G, Newburyport, Mass.
Richmond, Rev. J L, Milton, Pa
Roberts, Charles L, New York
Roberts, Lewis, Brooklyn.
Robinson, James L., Hastings, N Y.
Rollinson, Rev. William, San Francisco, Cal.
[redacted]

Southworth, James E, Brooklyn.
Spencer, O., Salt Lake, Utah Ter.
Spencer, Obadiah, Essex, Ct.
Spencer, D., Brooklyn.
Spencer, William B., Phenix, R. I.
Sproul, Rev. Samuel, Princeton, N. J.
Stanwood, Rev. Henry, Rush, N. Y.
Stearns, Rev. Oakman S., Newark, N. J.
Steward, Rev Ira R., New York.
Stockbridge, Rev. Joseph, Plainfield, N. J.
Stockbridge, Rev. John C., Boston.
Stone, Rev. James R., New York.
Stout, Charles B., New York.
Stow, Rev Baron, D.D., Boston.
Stow, Rev. Phineas, Boston,
Stowell, Nathaniel, Worcester, Mass.
Stubberts, Rev. William F. S., Malden, Mass.
Swan, Rev Jabez L., New London, Ct.
Swaim, Rev. Samuel B., West Cambridge, Mass
Taggart, Rev. Joseph W., New York.
Tanner, Rev. James, Pembina, Min. Ter.
Taylor, Rev J. B., Richmond, Va.
Taylor, Rev E. E. L, Brooklyn.
Taylor, Stewart M., New York.
Taylor, Daniel G., New York.
Taylor, Jeremiah B., New York.
Teasdale, Rev. T. C., D.D., Washington, D. C.
Thomas, Mrs. Catherine W., New York.
Thomas, Mrs Margaret I., New York.
Thomas, Cornelius W., New York.
Thomas, Augustus, New York.
[redacted]

White, Rev. J. S., West Wrentham, Mass.
Whitehead, James M., New York.
Whitney, Ezra S., Brooklyn.
Wightman, Rev. F., Wethersfield, Ct.
Wightman, Rev. Palmer G., East Lyme, Ct.
Wilbur, Asa, Boston.
Wildman, Rev. N., Lebanon, Ct.
Wilkins, Rev. Stephen, New York.
Willard, Rev. F. A., South Danvers, Mass.
Willett, Rev. Charles, Wilkinsville, Ct.
Williams, David S., Fayetteville, N. C.
Williams, Richard P., Essex, Ct.
Williams, Rev. William R., D.D., New York.
Wilson, Francis L., Catskill, N. Y.
Wilson, Daniel M., Newark, N. J.
Wilson, Mrs. Hannah M., Newark, N. J.
Wilson, Mrs. Caroline T., Plainfield, N. J.
Wilson, Rev. Robert J., Stoningtonboro', Ct.
Winegar, Rev. R., Jr. Baldwinsville, N. Y.
Wines, Rev. Wm. H., Boston.
Winterton, William, New York.
Withers. John, Alexandria, D. C.
Wooster, Rev. Henry, Deep River, Ct.
Wooster, Henry C., Essex, Ct.
Wright, Rev. Thomas G., Westport, N. Y.
Wyckoff, William H., New York.

MEMBERS FOR LIFE.

BY VIRTUE OF A CONTRIBUTION OF THIRTY DOLLARS.

Abbott, Stephen, Southbridge, Mass.
Achilles, H. L., Albion, N. Y.
Ackley, Rev. Alvin, Greenport, N. Y.
Adair, William N., Somerville, N. J.
Adams, Miss Priscilla S., New York.
Adams, Mrs. Mary, West Killingly, Ct.
Adams, Rev. S. W., Cleveland, Ohio.
Adams, Miss Caroline, New York.
Adams, Albert, Augusta, Ga.
Adams, Joseph H., Williamsburg, N. Y.
Adams, Mrs. Mary, Williamsburg, N. Y.
Adams, Jedediah, New York.
Adams, Van Rensselaer, Deckertown, N. J.
Adams, Rev. J. N., Croton, N. Y.
Adams, Clark, Greenwich, N. Y.
Adlam, Rev. S., Newport, R. I.
Adsit, Mrs. Maria J., Sennett, N. Y.
Ainsworth, Rev. S. C., Brookfield, N. Y.
Akerly, Mrs. Priscilla E., New York.
Akerly, George B., New York.
Akerly, William Henry, New York.
Albro, Mrs. Hannah Hill, New York.
Alden, Rev. John, Westfield, Mass.
Alden, Rev. Wm. H., North Attleboro', Mass.
Aldrich, Warren, Lowell, Mass.
Alexander, Calvin, West Halifax, Vt.
Allen, Rev. Benoni, Cambridge, O.
Allen, Russell, Shelby, N. Y.
Allen, Walter, New York.
Allen, Ethan, Worcester, Mass.
Allen, Rev. Marvin, Detroit, Mich.
Allen, Rev. N. T., Natic, R. I.
Allen, Rev. John, Groton, Mass.
Allen, Mrs. Lorena, New York.
Allen, Benjamin, Seekonk, Mass.
Allen, Joel, East Smithfield, Pa.
Allen, Nathaniel, Brookline, Me.
Allen Alanson, Fair Haven, Vt.
Allen, Mrs. Jane, Fair Haven, Vt.
Allen, Joseph G., Lockland, Ohio.
Allen, Rev. L. B., Yarmouth, Me.
Allen, Thomas, Wilmington, Del.
Allen, Rev. Thomas, Tavoy, Burmah.
Aller, Amos, Brooklyn.
Aller, Mrs. Amos, Brooklyn.
Alger, Mrs. Susan, Cleveland, Ohio.
Almond, John P., Bostwick Mills, N. C.
Ambler, Rev. E. C., Weart's Corners, N. J.
Ambler, Mrs. Almira, Weart's Corners, N. J
Ambler, Starr H., Weart's Corners, N. J.
Ambler, Rev. J. V., Lanesboro', Mass.
Ambler, Mrs. A. T., Lanesboro', Mass.
Ames, Samuel, New York.
Ames, Robert W., Roxbury, Mass.
Amsbury, Jabez, Norwich, Ct.
Amory, Peter B., New York.
Amory, Mrs. Anna M., New York.
Andem, Rev. James.
Anderson, William T., Princeton, N. J.
Anderson, Mrs. Catharine J., Princeton, N. J.
Anderson, John T., Verdon, Pa.
Anderson, Peter, New York.
Anderson, William, Hoboken, N. J.
Anderson, Rev. Edward, Milford, N. H.
Andrews, William, Providence.
Andrews, Mrs. Delilah, Providence.
Andrews, Mrs. Wm., Providence.
Andrews, Ebenezer T., Boston.
Andrews, George R., New York.
Angus, Charles, Benton, N. Y.
Archibald, Rev. Thos. H., Factory Point, Vt.
Archibald, Mrs. Susan W. T., Manchester, Vt.
Archer, Charles O., New York.
Ardis, Rev. Henry Z., Zalofa, Fa.
Armitage. Mrs. T., New York.
Appleton, George, Haverhill, Mass.
Appleton, James, Philadelphia.
Arents, Stephen, Brooklyn.
Armstrong, Rev. Andrew, Lambertville, N. J.
Armstrong, Mrs. M. S., Lambertville, N. J.

MEMBERS FOR LIFE.

Arnold, Mrs. Mary N., Attleboro', Mass.
Arnold, Mrs. Francis R., Providence.
Arnold, Rev. Benjamin B., Three Rivers, Iowa.
Arnold, Miss Phebe, Jay, N. Y.
Arnold, Mrs. Mary, Clifton Park, N. Y.
Arnold, Israel, Providence.
Arthur, Rev. William, West Troy, N. Y.
Ashley, Elisha, Poultney, Vt.
Atkins, Lloyd, Bristol, Ct.
Atkinson, Taylor B., West Philadelphia, Pa.
Atwood, Lewis, Pawtucket, R. I.
Atwood, Mrs. Lydia N., Boston, N. H.
Austin, Edward, New York.
Austin, Samuel, Suffield, Ct.
Avery, Mrs. Clara, New York.
Avery, Rev. E. J., Worcester, Mass.
Avery, William D., Providence.
Avery, Rev. David, Southwick, Mass.
Avery, Rev. D., Tyringham, Mass.
Avery, E. J., Brookline, Mass.
Ayer, Charles B., Preston, Ct.
Ayer, Mrs. Richard, Haverhill, Mass.
Ayers, James C., Plainfield, N. J.
Ayres, Horace, Worcester, Mass.
Ayres, Mrs. Mary, New York.
Babcock, Rev. O. W., Milford, N. Y.
Babcock, John N., New Haven, Ct.
Babcock, H. S., Homer, N. Y.
Baber, Alfred, Keeseville, N. Y.
Bachelor, Rev. M., Pownall, Vt.
Backus, Rev. J. S., New York.
[redacted]

Balch, Mrs. Jane, New York.
Baldwin, Rev. George C., D.D., Troy, N. Y.
Baldwin, Mrs. Margaret D., Boston.
Baldwin, Rev. Jonathan, Elliston, N. Y.
Baldwin, Jared G., New York.
Baldwin, Mrs. Eliza, New York.
Baldwin, A. T., Brooklyn.
Baldwin, Miss Elizabeth A., New York.
Baldwin, Josephus, Nashua, N. H.
Baldwin, Mrs. Mary Ann, Nashua, N. H.
Baldwin, Mrs. Caroline E., Philadelphia.
Balen, Mrs. Ann Maria, Brooklyn.
Ball, Rev. John, Dixon, Ill.
Ball, Rev. Mason, North Amherst, Mass.
Ball, Julia M., North Amherst, Mass.
Ball, Sarah E., North Amherst, Mass.
Ballard, Rev. Enos H., Red Mills, N. Y.
Ballard, Mrs. Asenath, Brooklyn.
Ballard, Mrs. Mary Sophia, Brooklyn.
Ballard, Rev. J. B., New York.
Ballard, Zaccheus, Webster, Mass.
Bancros, Lemuel, Granville, Mass.
Ballou, Alexander, Blackstone, Mass.
Banker, Mrs. Elizabeth, Brooklyn.
Banta, Miss Emily M., New York.
Barrass, Rev. Thomas, Baptist Town, N. J.
Barrass, Mrs. Mary Ann, Baptist Town, N. J.
Barber, Aaron, Waterford, C. W.
Barber, Moses, Waterford, C. W.
Barber, Abraham, Waterford, C. W.
Barber, Rev. Bradford H., Charlestown, N. Y.
[redacted]

MEMBERS FOR LIFE.

Battle, Rev. A. J., Murfreesboro', N. C.
Baugh, Dr. J. M., Petersburg, Va.
Baxter, Thomas, Penn Yan, N. Y.
Baxter, John C., New York.
Baxter, Thomas, Detroit, Mich.
Baxter, William M., New York.
Beagle, Henry, Philadelphia.
Beam, Joseph, Brooklyn.
Beam, Mrs. Louisa, Brooklyn.
Beam, David B., Paterson, N. J.
Bean, H. L., Skaneateles, N. Y.
Beasom, W. D., Nashua, N. H.
Beatson, Miss Helen, New York.
Beaver, J. M., Hillsborough, N. C.
Beebe, Alexander M., LL.D., Utica, N. Y.
Beebe, Warren, Brooklyn.
Beebe, Mrs. Charlotte, Brooklyn.
Beecher, Miss Mary C., New York.
Beattie, Rev. W. Q., Bennettsville, N. C.
Beck, Rev. John J., Coosawhatchie, S. C.
Beck, Rev. Levi G., Doylestown, Pa.
Beckwith, Miss Abby G., Providence.
Beckwith, Elisha W., Norwich, Ct.
Beckwith, Jason, New London, Ct.
Beckwith, Ezra S., New London, Ct.
Beckwith, Nathan, Upper Red Hook, N. Y.
Beckwith, Elisha, Waterford, Ct.
Belcher, Rev. James, Oldtown, Me.
Belden, Rev. Joseph, Freehold, N. J.
Belden, Rev. A. Russell, Iowa city, Iowa.
Belden, Mrs. Mary Ann, Meriden, Ct.
Belknap, Rev. Appleton, Jeffrey, N. H.
Bell, Edward, Willimantic, Ct.
Bell, Miss Jane Ann, Willimantic, Ct.
Bellamy, Rev. David, Mt. Morris, N. Y.
Bellamy, Rev. R. K., Chickopee Falls, Mass.
Beman, Mrs. Rebecca S., Deep River, Ct.
Beman, Miss Charlotte, Deep River, Ct.
Beman, Mrs. Samantha, Brooklyn, N. Y.
Bemis, Miss Elizabeth H., Worcester, Mass.
Beeman, Rev. James M., Dickinson, N. Y.
Bemrose, Mrs. Elizabeth M., New York.
Bendall, George, Coman's Well, Va.
Benedict, Uriah, Central Falls, R. I.
Benedict, Stephen, Pawtucket, R. I.
Benedict, Rev. David, D.D., Pawtucket, R. I.
Benedict, Miss Cornelia E., Providence.
Benedict, Rev. N. D., Waywasing, N. Y.
Benedict, Mrs. Nancy, New York.
Benedict, Rev. E. L., Pitcher, N. Y.
Benjamin, W. P., New London, Ct.
Benjamin, B. M., Rochester, N. Y.
Bennett, Rev. Cephas, Tavoy, Asia.
Bennett, Joseph E., Manchester, N. H.
Bennett, Hiram, Salem, N. J.
Bennett, Rev. Alvin, South Wilbraham, Mass.
Bennett, Rev. David, Unionville, N. Y.
Bennett, E. A., Philadelphia.
Bennett, Mrs. Judith B., Philadelphia.
Bennett, Rev. Olney, Walesville, N. Y.
Bennett, Joseph, Manchester, N. H.
Bennet, Rev. Perry, Cold Spring, N. Y.
Benton, J. Saratoga, N. Y.
Benton, Mrs. Sarah, Saratoga, N. Y.
Benton, Rev. George W., Granville, Ill.
Bernard, Rev. David, Westfield, N. Y.
Bernie, Miss Anna, New York.
Bertine, Mrs. Sarah Ann, New York.
Bertine, James C , New York.
Berry, Zebina E., Worcester, Mass.
Berry, Susan C., Worcester, Mass.
Berry, Ellen L., Worcester, Mass.
Betts, Rev. Platt, East Chatham, N. Y.
Betts, Philander, Danbury, Ct.
Bevan, Rev. Isaac, Reading, Pa.
Beverly, Miss Elizabeth, New York.
Bickford, Rev. M. L., Waltham, Mass.
Biddle, Samuel S., Newbern, N. C.
Biddle, Rev. William, Chesterfield, Ct.
Bidgood, Mrs. L. Hargroves', Va.
Bigelow, Rev. John R., M.D., New York.
Bigelow, Mrs. Eunice P., New York.
Bigelow, John R., Brooklyn.
Bigelow, Mrs. Catharine, Brooklyn.
Bigelow, Franklin H., Brooklyn.
Bigelow, Miss Nancy H., Brooklyn.
Bigelow, Mrs. Charlotte, Brooklyn,
Billings, Rev. John, Mt. Vernon, Me.
Billings, Mrs. Betsey, Mt. Vernon, Me.
Billingslea, Dr. C., Montgomery Co., Ala.
Bingham, Luther, Fort Wayne, Ia.
Bingham, Miss Margaret E., Camillus, N. Y.
Bird, Rev. John, Lloyd's, Essex Co., Va.
Birdsey, Mrs. Rebecca C., Meriden, Ct.
Bishop, Jesse, Cleveland, Ohio.
Bishop, James W. A., Philadelphia.
Blackwell, J. P., Brooklyn.
Blackenton, Sanford, North Adams, Mass.
Blain, Mrs. Amy A., Central Falls, R. I.
Blake, Aaron, Chelsea, Mass.
Blake, Jonathan, Brooklyn.
Blake, David B., Providence.
Blake, Ezekiel, Chickopee Falls, Mass.
Blanding, Dr. S., Columbia, S. C.
Blackmer, Jirah, Wheatland, N. Y.
Bleecker, Mrs. Caroline, New York.
Bleecker, Mrs. Jane, New York.
Bleecker, George W., Brooklyn.
Blessing, John, Xenia, O.
Bliss, Elijah J., Brooklyn.
Blodgett, James D., Haverhill, Mass.
Blodgett, Mrs. James D , Haverhill, Mass.
Blodgett, Loring B., Cortlandville, N. Y.
Blood, Isaiah, Ballston Spa., N. Y.
Blood, Cyrus G , Davenport, Iowa.
Blood, A. P., Ballston, N. Y.
Bloodgood, James, Springville, N. Y.
Bloomer, Lewis, Ovid, N. Y.
Blunt, Mrs. R., Edenton, N. C.
Bly, Mrs. Lydia, Ticonderoga, N. Y.
Boardman, Thomas, Amesbury, Mass.
Boardman, George Dana, Newton Centre, Mass.
Bodine, Miss Mary Hudson, N. Y.
Bogart, Rev. Wm., Pittsfield, Mass.
Bokee, Hon. David A., Brooklyn.
Bolles, James G., Hartford, Ct.
Boomer, Rev. James C., Chelmsford, Mass.
Bond, Lewis, Windsor, N. C.
Bond, Leonard, New York.
Bond, Rev. George W., Knoxville, Iowa.
Bond, Rev. E. P., Aurora, Ia.
Bond, Rev. Emmons P., New Britain, Ct.

MEMBERS FOR LIFE.

Bord, Mrs. Mary, New Britain, Ct.
Bonham, Daniel, Berryville, Va.
Bonney, W. I., L[illegible]ton, N. Y.
Boone, Dr. Levi D., Chicago, Ill.
Boone, Hon. L. D., Chicago, Ill.
Borden, Lodowick, Fall River, Mass.
Borden, Isaac, Fall River, Mass.
Borden, Charles, Fall River, Mass.
Borden, Joseph, Fall River, Mass.
Borden, Cook, Fall River, Mass.
Bosson, George P., Chelsea, Mass.
Bosson, B[illegible]man P., Chelsea, Mass.
Bosson, Miss Mary, Chelsea, Mass.
Bostick, Elisha, Bostick's Mills, N. C.
Bostick, Elijah, Bostick's Mills, N. C.
Bostick, Tristam, Bostick's Mills, N. C.
Bostick, Benj. R., Robertsville, S. C.
Bostick, Mrs. Jane A., Robertsville, S. C.
Boswell, Dav[illegible], Stilesville, Ia.
Bosworth, William M., [illegible] Poultney, Vt.
Bosworth, George H., Fall River, Mass.
Bottom, Nathan H., Shaftsbury, Vt.
Bottom, Mrs. P[illegible], Shaftsbury, Vt.
Boughton, James, New York.
Boutelle, Miss Sylvia, East Cambridge, Mass.
Bouton, Mrs. Sarah M., New York.
Bowen, John, New York.
Bowen, Henry C., [illegible], New York.
Bowen, David M., Canton, N. J.
Bowen, Rev. William, H[illegible], Mass.
Bowen, William, New York.
Bowen, Mrs. A. K., Cortlandville, N. Y.
Brierly, Rev. Benjamin, San Francisco, Cal.
Brigham, Sylvester, Dover, Ill.
Brigham, Rev. J. H., Scipio, N. Y.
Briggs, Arnold, Fairhaven, Vt.
Briggs, Rev. Avery, Rock Island, Ill.
Briggs, Mrs. Sarah H., Fitchburg, Mass.
Briggs, Harris, Coventry, N. Y.
Bright, Rev. T., Elkhorn, Wis.
Brinkerhoff, Rev. C., Toulon, Ill.
Brisbane, Rev. Wm. H., Cheviot, O.
Brisbane, Miss Maria, Charleston, S. C.
Briscoe, Sally C., Va.
Britton, Everett, New York.
Brockett, Alvah, Salisbury, N. Y.
Brockett, Asahel, Bristol, Ct.
Broaddus, Rev. Wm. F., D.D., Versailles, Ky.
Broaddus, Mrs. Mary A., Versailles, Ky.
Broadhead, Mrs. Ann, New York.
Brocket, Rev. Pierpont, Hartford, Ct.
Brockway, Mrs. Elizabeth, Broadalbin, N. Y.
Britton, W. G., Brittons X Roads, N. C.
Bromley, Isaac, Norwich, Ct.
Bromley, J. Breed, Norwich, Ct.
Bromley, Dewey, Norwich, Ct.
Bromley, Rev. Henry, New York.
Bromley, Mrs. Jane M., New York.
Brouner, Mrs. Sarah, New York.
Bronson, Rev. Asa, Fall River, Mass.
Bronson, Rev. Benjamin F., Methuen, Mass.
Bronson, Mrs. Anna C., Methuen, Mass.
Bronson, Miss Aydee A., Townsend, Mass.
Brooks, Dea. Kendall, Roxbury, Mass.

Brown, Joshua, New York.
Brown, Sarah H., 2d, West Townsend, Mass.
Brown, Newel, Watertown, Mass.
Brown, Mrs. Mary W. Watertown, Mass.
Brown, Mrs. Josiah, Haverhill Mass.
Brownell, Rev. E. W. East Hillsdale, N. Y.
Brownson, Rev. I. K., Chittenango, N. Y.
Bruen, George H. Newark, N.
Bruen, Mrs. George H Newark, N. J.
Bruce, Benjamin G. New York.
Bruce, Silas, Townsend, Mass.
Bruce, John M., Jr., New York.
Brush, Mrs. Susan G., New York.
Brusle, William A., New York.
Brusle, Mrs. Elizabeth, New York.
Bryant, George, Williamsburgh, N. Y.
Bryant, Mary A., Chelsea, Mass.
Bryant, Elizabeth D., Chelsea, Mass.
Buck, David S., Cambridge, Mass.
Buckbee, Mrs. Laura G., New York.
Bucknall, Ebenezer G. Newark, N. J.
Bucknell, Miss Elizabeth, Newark, N. J.
Bucknell, Wm., Jr., Philadelphia.
Bucknell, Miss Lavinia Louisa, Philadelphia.
Bucknell, Mrs. Harriet M., Philadelphia.
Buckner, Mrs. Sarah T., Baltimore.
Budlong, Mrs. Rebecca S. C Providence.
Budlong, Miss Rebekah A., Providence.
Budd, Francis F., Williamsburgh, N. Y.
Buel, Rev. Rufus F., Greece.
Buel, Mrs. Mary J., Greece.
Buffinton, Benjamin, Fall River, Mass.
Bull, John B., New York.

Bull, Sarah E., North Amherst, Mass.
Bullard, Rev. Joseph A., Ware, Mass.
Bullock, George, Utica, N. Y.
Bulkley, Prof. Justus, Upper Alton, Ill.
Bulkley, Mrs. Harriet, Upper Alton, Ill.
Bulkley, Mrs. Harriet, Barry, Ill.
Bunnell, Rev. W. B., Pekin, Ill.
Bunnell, Mrs. Elizabeth E. Pekin, Ill.
Burbank, Mrs. Irene, New York.
Burbank, Wellman, Chelsea, Mass.
Burd, Elisha, Baptist Town, N. J.
Burdick, Perrin, New York.
Burger, William H., New York.
Burger, Mrs. Rebecca T New York.
Burgess, Silvanus, Providence.
Burgess, Alexander, Providence.
Burke, Mrs. Louisa S., Rochester, N. Y.
Burke, Miss Emma, Brooklyn.
Burke, Mrs. Elizabeth, Brooklyn.
Burnett, Rev. C. C., Worcester, Mass.
Burnett, Mrs. Maria M., Worcester, Mass.
Burnett, Eli S., West Philadelphia.
Burnett, Rev Hiram Mt. Pleasant, Iowa.
Burns, William, Philadelphia.
Burr, David M., Gloversville, N. Y.
Burr, Mrs. Emily C., Gloversville, N. Y.
Burr, Mrs. James H., Gloversville, N. Y.
Burroughs, James M Marlton, N. J.
Burroughs, Caleb G., Providence.
Burroughs, Rev. David, Amherst, N. H.
Burrows, Rev. Baxter, Grafton, Vt
Burrows, Rev. J. L., D D., Richmond, Va.
Burrows, John R., Providence
Burt, T. M., Kinderhook, N. Y.
Burt, Mrs. Edwin C., Brooklyn.
Burt, James, Brooklyn.
Burt, James M., Brooklyn.
Burt, Wm. A., Mount Vernon, Mich.
Burt, William, Mount Vernon Mich.
Burt, Wells, Mount Vernon, Mich.
Burt, Rev. Joseph M., North Tewksbury, Mass.
Burton, Rev. Nathan S., Granville, O.
Burton, Mrs. Sarah J Granville, O.
Burton, Rev. Hardin Bryantsville, Ia.
Butcher, Mrs. Mary, Philadelphia.
Butler, Rev. John, Lewiston, Me.
Butler, Rev. G. W. Shirley, Mass.
Butler, Sylvanus, New Haven, Ct.
Butler, Mrs. Sarah, Lansingburg, N. Y.
Butler, William C., Brooklyn, N. Y
Butrick, Mrs. Harriet H., Jay, N. Y.
Butts, Mrs. Sarah A., Cleveland, Ohio.
Butts, Mrs. Elizabeth, Boston.
Byram, Mrs. Mary H. Amesbury, Mass
Byram, Wm. H., Milwaukee, Wis.
Cady, Rev. Edgar, South New Berlin, N. Y.
Cady, Edwin, Danville, Iowa.
Cailhopper, Rev. F. T., Camden, N. J.
Calder, John, Providence.
Callender, Rev. N Laporte, Pa.
Call, Rev. O. B., Weston, N. Y.
Callom, Mrs. Mary N., Sing Sing, N. Y.
Campbell, Rev. T. B., East Avon, N. Y.
Candee, John D., New Haven, Ct.
Capen, Barnabas, Sharon, Mass.
Capin Ezekiel, Canton, Mass.
Capron, Miss Rebecca S., Worcester, Mass
Capron, John, Albany, N. Y
Capron, Rev. Barton, Preble, N. Y.
Capwell, Albert B., New York.
Capwell, Mrs. Julia A., New York.
Card, Rev. Wm. H., La Cross, Wis.
Card, Rev. Henry S., Hinsdale N. Y.
Carleton, Miss Frances, Newton Centre, Mass.
Carleton, Miss Emelina H., Newton Centre, Ms.
Carleton, G. R., Newton Centre, Mass.
Carleton, Judson, Newton Centre, Mass.
Carleton, Howard, Newton Centre, Mass.
Carleton, Wm. H., Newton Centre, Mass.
Carlton, Stephen, Lowell, Mass.
Carraway, Mrs. H., Kingston, N. C.
Carew, Miss Emma H., New York.
Carew, Mrs. Margaret N., New York.
Carroll, S. W. Norwich, Ct.
Carroll, Mrs. Sarah A. S. Washington, N. C
Carpenter, Daniel T Pawtucket, R. I.
Carpenter, Mrs. Elisabeth, Pawtucket, R. I
Carpenter, Miss Lydia, Pawtucket, R. I.
Carpenter, Rev. Calvin G Phelps, N. Y.
Carpenter, Rev. J M., Jacobstown, N. J.
Carpenter, Mrs. Sarah F., Jacobstown, N. J.
Carpenter, Rev. Burton B., Griggsville, Ill.
Carpenter, James, New York.
Carpenter, J. H., Willimantic, Ct.
Carmer, Henry, Griggsville, Ill.
Carr, Rev. Samuel J., Mansfield, Mass.
Carr, Alexander W., Rowley, Mass.
Carr, Rev. L. C., Lockland, O.

MEMBERS FOR LIFE.

Carr, Joseph, Charlestown, Mass.
Carrol, L. W., Norwich, Ct.
Carter, Mrs. Sarah, Richmond, Va.
Carter, Miss Mary, New York.
Carter, Edward, Troy, N. Y.
Carter, Benjamin A., Boston, Mass.
Caruthers, Rev. Isaac, Holton [illegible], Ia.
Caruthers, William, Salisbury, Mass.
Carver, Mrs. Rob[illegible] E., [illegible], N. Y.
Cary, Theron, Middletown, Ct.
Case, Rev. Zenas, Adam's Basin, N. Y.
Case, Alonzo, Jordan, N. Y.
Case, Miss Julia, Cassville, N. Y.
Casler, Rev. L., Springhill, N. Y.
Caswell, Mrs. Esther Lois, Providence.
Caswell, Miss Martha S., Charlestown, Mass.
Catlin, Rev. Samuel T., St. Croix Falls, Mis.
Catlin, Mrs. Julia F., St. Croix Falls, Mis.
Cauldwell, Mrs. Cornelius, New York.
Cauldwell, Miss Elizabeth, New York.
Cauldwell, Ebenezer, New York.
Cauldwell, Henry W., New York.
Cauldwell, Mrs. Susan W., New York.
Cauldwell, Miss Adelaide, New York.
Cauldwell, Mrs. Ann, [illegible], N. Y.
Cauldwell, Mrs. Ann B., New York.
Cavis, John, Lowell, Mass.
Cell, Rev. Jeremiah, Aurora, Ia.
Chace, Joseph D., Cortlandville, N. Y.
Chaffee, Asa, Seekonk, Mass.
Chaffin, Rev. Aaron W., Danvers, Mass.
Chaffin, Mrs. Catherine K., Danvers, Mass.
Cherryman, Rev. Reuben, Richburg, N. Y.
Chesebrough, Mrs. Asenath, Haddam, Ct.
Chesshire, Rev. John Enoch, Wickford, R. I.
Cheever, William, Westboro', Mass.
Chick, Rev. J. M., South Groton, Mass.
Child, Ezra O., Warren, R. I.
Child, Henry W., Warren, R. I.
Child, Shubael P., Warren, R. I.
Childs, Miss Jane L., New York.
Childs, John E., Providence.
Childs, Mrs. Jennett, Deep River, Ct.
Church, Rev. Leroy, Chicago, Ill.
Church, Miss Clara O. B., Williamsburg, N. Y.
Church, Miss Emma C., Williamsburg, N. Y.
Church, William, Williamsburg, N. Y.
Church, Francis P., Williamsburg, N. Y.
Church, John A., Williamsburg, N. Y.
Church, Rev. Isaac M., South Kingston, R. I.
Churchill, Amos, Hubbardton, Vt.
Clapp, Rev. Wm. S., Danbury, Ct.
Clapp, Mrs. Jane M., Danbury, Ct.
Clapp, Russell, Providence.
Clapp, Miss Jane R., Providence.
Clark, Rev. Frederick, New Orleans, La.
Clark, Rev. Norman, Marlborough, N. H.
Clark, Abel, Willimantic, Ct.
Clark, Mrs. Juliet, Marlborough, N. H.
Clark, Miss E., Beaufort, S. C.
Clark, Mrs. M. G., Philadelphia.
Clark, Mrs. Elizabeth, New York.
Clark, Miss Sallie Cone, New York.

[redacted]

Colby, Hon. Anthony, New London, N. H.
Colby, Mrs. Eliza A., New London, N. H.
Colby, Isaac, Salem, Mass.
Colby, Gardner, Newton, Mass.
Colby, Mrs. Mary Colgate, New York.
Colby, Benj. E., Cambridge, Mass.
Colburn, Rev. Alfred, Boston.
Cole, Rev. L. B., Lowell, Mass.
Cole, Samuel, Clifton Park, N. Y.
Cole, Mrs. Frances L., New York.
Cole, Mrs. Susan, Waterloo, N. Y.
Cole, Mrs. Jemima P., Plainfield, N. J.
Coley, Rev. James M., Waverly, N. Y.
Colegrove, Bela H., Sardinia, N. Y.
Coleman, James B., Somerville, N. J.
Coleman, Rev. M., Elba, N. Y.
Coleman, Mrs. Sarah, Elba, N. Y.
Coleman, Rev. Zenas, Mt. Vernon, Mich.
Colgate, Cornelius C., New York.
Colgate, Edward, New York.
Colgate, James B., New York.
Colgate, William, New York.
Colgate, Miss Elizabeth, New York.
Colgate, Miss Hannah, New York.
Colgate, Miss Jane, New York.
Colgate, Miss Sarah, New York.
Collins, Miss Susan, New York.
Colman, John B., Williamsburg, N. Y.
Collom, Mrs. Mary E., Mt. Holly, N. J.
Colver, Rev. Charles K., Worcester, Mass.
Colver, Mrs. Esther E., Worcester, Mass.
Coman, Levina C., Le Roy, N. Y.
Compton, James L., Plainfield, N. J.
Compton, Anthony, New York.
Compton, Mrs. Maria, New York.
Compton, Rev. Robert, Newton, Pa.
Compton, Wm. H., Readstown, N. J.
Comstock, George R., New London, Ct.
Comstock, Mrs. Ann, New London, Ct.
Conant, Mrs. John, Brandon, Vt.
Conant, Rev. Thomas, Scituate, Mass.
Conant, Rev. Thomas J., D.D., Rochester, N. Y.
Conant, Levi, Boston, Mass.
Condit, Miss Sarah E., New York.
Cone, Spencer H., Jr., New York.
Cone, Miss Kate E., New York.
Cone, Miss Amelia M., Philadelphia.
Conklin, Mrs. Ann, New York.
Conover, Robert, Petersburg, Ill.
Conrad, Rev. Peter, Delton, Wis.
Converse, Rev. Otis, Grafton, Mass.
Converse, Chas. E., Jamaica Plains, Mass.
Cook, Mrs. Patience, Keene, N. H.
Cook, Henry G., New York.
Cook, Lewis, Plantsville, Ct.
Cook, Wm. W., Whitehall, N. Y.
Cook, Mrs. Harriet M., New York.
Cooke, Rev. Samuel, Newton, N. H.
Coolidge, Mrs. Caroline G., Brookline, Mass.
Coolidge, William, Brockville, N. Y.
Coolidge, John, Watertown, Mass.
Coolidge, Mrs. Mary S., Watertown, Mass.
Coolidge, Josiah, Cambridge, Mass.
Coolidge, Austin J., Cambridge, Mass.
Cooper, William, New York.
Cooper, Edwin, Hoboken, N. J.
Cooper, Rev. Warren, Boylston, Mass
Cooper, Eliphalet, New Haven, Ct.
Cooper, Charles, New York.
Corbett, O. G., Brooklyn, N. Y.
Corey, Rev. D. G., Utica, N. Y.
Corlies, Briton, Philadelphia.
Cornelius, Rev. Samuel, Jr., Fond du Lac, Wis.
Cornell, A. C., Broadalbin, N. Y.
Cornell, Thomas, Rondout, N. Y.
Cornwell, Rev. William E., Norristown, Pa.
Corning, Ephraim, Brooklyn.
Corwin, R. G., Lebanon, Ohio.
Corwin, Rev. David, Gloversville, N. Y.
Corwith, Mrs. Catherine F., New York.
Cotterell, Mrs. Mary, Battenville, N. Y.
Cotterell, Miss Mary, Union Village, N. Y
Covey, Rev. Walter, Jefferson, N. Y.
Cowan, Mrs. Hannah, New York.
Cowdin, Mrs. Aurinda G., Fitchburg, Mass.
Cowles, Mrs. Rebekah, Claremont, N. H.
Cowles, Miss Juliette E., Claremont, N. H.
Cowles, Jas. Albert, Claremont, N. H.
Cox, Rev. Morgan R., New Brunswick, N. J.
Cox, Mrs. Mary B., New Brunswick, N. J.
Cox, Miss Anna, New Brunswick, N. J.
Cox, Miss Mary, New York.
Cox, John W., Mt. Holly, N. J.
Cox, Miss Achsah, Imlaystown, N. J.
Cox, Miss Abigail, New York.
Coxey, James, West Philadelphia, Pa.
Coy, Sylvanus B., West Dedham, Mass.
Crabs, Rev. J. D., Claysville, Ia.
Craig, Rev. A. M., Britton's ⋈ Roads, N. C.
Craig, Charles A., Bridgeport, Ct.
Craig, Mrs. Charles A., Bridgeport, Ct.
Crain, Miss Harriet M., Westport, N. H.
Cramer, Geo. W., Troy, N. Y.
Cramer, John, Brooklyn.
Cramer, Mrs. Margaret S., Troy, N. Y.
Crane, Richard M., Newark, N. J.
Crane, Henry F., Rehoboth, Mass.
Crane, Miss Sarah H., Rehoboth, Mass.
Crane, Rev. Origin, Weston, Mass.
Crane, Rev. Danzel M., N. Hampton, Mass.
Crane, Mrs. Mary L., New York.
Crane, Rev. W. I., Adrian, Mich.
Crandall, Mrs. J. A., Petersburg, N. Y.
Crandall, Rev. Nelson, South Hannibal, N. Y.
Crandall, Rev. B., Springport, N. Y.
Crandall, Mrs. J. Sophronia, Providence, R. I.
Cranston, B. T., Norwich, Ct.
Crawford, Mrs. Almira A., Brooklyn.
Crawford, Mrs. Charlotte, N. Y.
Crawford, Ira, Poughkeepsie, N. Y.
Crawford, Samuel H., Philadelphia.
Crawford, Archibald, Albany.
Crawford, Mrs. Catherine, Middletown, N. J.
Creath, Rev. Thomas B., Jarrott's, Va.
Creathe, Rev. J. W. D., Fanthorpe's, Texas.
Crenshaw, Dr. W. M., Forrestville, N. C.
Cressy, Rev. Timothy R., St. Paul, Min.
Cresswell, Rev. Samuel J., Philadelphia.
Crey, Joel, Jerseyville, Ill.
Crocker, Gurdon, New London, Ct.
Crocker, Albert G., New London, Ct.

Crocker, William A., New York.
Crosby, Henry L., Belvidere, Ill.
Crosby, Nathaniel, Janesville, Wis.
Cross, Francis W., Lowell, Mass.
Crossman, Nathan, Elbridge, N. Y.
Croysdale, Abram, Paterson, N. J.
Crooker, Joseph F., Providence.
Crum, Rev. J. W., Middletown Point, N. J.
Crumb, Mrs. R. F., Middletown Point, N. J.
Cruser, Holger, Brooklyn.
Cuno, Theophilus, New York.
Culver, Miss Susan, New London, Ct.
Cummings, Mrs. Daniel, Chelsea, Mass.
Cummings, Mrs. Abigail, Cambridge, Mass.
Cummings, George, Cambridge, Mass.
Cummings, Rev. E. E., Concord, N. H.
Cummings, Miss Emily C., Amherst, Mass.
Cummings, Miss Ellen, Chelsea, Mass.
Cunningham, Rev. O., Middlefield, Mass.
Curry, John, Hamburg, S. C.
Curry, Mrs. Harriet, Hamburg, S. C.
Curran, Rev. Joseph, Lanesboro, Pa.
Currier, Rev. Joshua, La Motte, Iowa.
Cutler, Micajah, Lynn, Mass.
Cutler, William D., Meriden, Ct.
Cutt[illegible], Rev. William, Columbia, S. C.
Curtis, Rev. T. T., Marion, Ala.
Curtis, Rev. William B., Utica, N. Y.
Curtis, Mrs. Elizabeth, Aurora, Ia.
Curtis, Ezra, Bridgeport, Ct.
Curtis, Mrs. Ezra, Bridgeport, Ct.
Cushing, Samuel T., Boston.

Davis, Edward L., Worcester, Mass.
Davis, Joseph E., Worcester, Mass.
Davis, Miss Sarah M., Worcester, Mass.
Davis, Miss Anna E., Worcester, Mass.
Davis, Miss Alice W., Worcester, Mass.
Davis, W., Strebane, N. C.
Davis, Reuben P., Waltham, Mass.
Davis, Walter G., New York.
Davis, Rev. Jonathan, Monticello, S. C.
Davis, Charles C., Preston, Ct.
Davis, Florence H., Worcester, Mass.
Davis, Isabel, G., Worcester, Mass.
Davis, Mrs. Louisa G., Paris, Me.
Davis, Rev. John, Yarmouth, Nova Scotia.
Davis, Rev. Thomas, Deckertown, N. J.
Davis, Rev. Judson, Ira, N. Y.,
Davis, Lydia, Haverhill, Mass.
Davis, Mrs. Harriet M., Nashua, N. H.
Davis, Levi, Davenport, Iowa.
Davis, Rev. R., Waveland, Ia.
Davis, Rev. Amos S., Richmondville, N. Y.
Davis, Russel, Preston City, Ct.
Davis, Hon. George R., Troy, N. Y.
Davy, Miss Bertha, New York.
Dawley, Joseph E., Fall River, Mass.
Day, H. W., Boston.
Day, John, New York.
Day, Mrs. Fidelia, Haverhill, Mass.
Day, Rev. Arthur, Shaftsbury, Vt.
Day, Rev. Horace G., Schenectady, N. Y.
Day, Horatio E., Hartford, Ct.
Dayton, Morgan H., New York.

[redacted]

Denison, Mrs. Amelia E., Deep River, Ct.
Denison, Miss Elizabeth, Brooklyn.
Devore, Mrs. Catharine, Edgefield, S. C.
Deweese, Samuel, West Philadelpia.
Dewey, Wm. G., Mystic, Ct.
Dewey, Joseph H., Manchester, N. Y.
Dewhurst, Rev. Eli, Bradford, Me.
Dewitt, Rev. J. V., Marion, Iowa.
Dexter, Mrs. Jane, Brooklyn.
Dickinson, Mrs. Caroline A., Pittsburg, Pa.
Dickinson, Wm. W., Golandsville, Va.
Dimmock, Rev. Anth'y V., Baldwinsville, Mass.
Dispeau, Mrs. Lucinda, Grafton, Mass.
Detson, Benjamin, Methuen, Mass.
Dixson, Rev. Joseph A., Evansville, Ia.
Doan, Ezra, Hudson, N. Y.
Doane, Miss Rachel F., Danvers, Mass.
Doby, John, Sen., Edgefield, S. C.
Dodge, Mrs. Eliza P., New York.
Dodge, Miss Mary, New York.
Dodge, Rev. Orrin, Brooklyn.
Dodge, Prof. Ebenezer, Hamilton, N. Y.
Dodge, Solomon H., Cambridge, Mass.
Dodge, Miss Hannah A., Worcester, Mass.
Dodge, Mrs. Alice C., Haverhill, Mass.
Dodge, Mrs. Jane, Brooklyn.
Dodge, H. N., McGrawville, N. Y.
Dodson, Rev. Elijah, Woodburn, Ill.
Dole, Mrs. Lydia T., Haverhill, Mass.
Dollim, Horatio, Worcester, Mass.
Doolittle, Mrs. Amanda, New York.
Doolittle, Rev. H. D., Hoosick, N. Y.
Doolittle, Johnson, Wallingford, Ct.
Doolittle, Hart, Pleasant Valley, Ct.
Donald, J. W., East Cambridge, Mass.
Dongan, Mrs. Lucretia, New York.
Dorrance, Samuel B., Brooklyn.
Doty, Miss Selima P., Hitchcockville, Ct.
Douglas, Henry, Bethel, N. Y.
Douglas, George, Rochester, N. Y.
Douglas, Rev. John L., Burmah.
Dougherty, George T., New York.
Dowlin, Mrs. Maria S., New York.
Dowlin, Miss Mary J., New York.
Dowling, Rev. Thomas, Tolland, Ct.
Dowling, Mrs. Rebecca, New York.
Dowley, John, New York.
Downer, Rev. William B., Cazenovia, N. Y.
Downey, Rev. Francis, Whiteby, Pa.
Downing, J., Colerain, N. C.
Downs, Mrs. Harriet B., Malden, Mich.
Downs, Mrs. Elizabeth, Hightstown, N. J.
Dows, Gustavus D., Lowell, Mass.
Doyen, Mrs. A. F., Haverhill, Mass.
Drake, Ephraim, Plainfield, N. J.
Drake, Mrs. A. L., Plainfield, N. J.
Drake, Rev. George, New Brunswick, N. J.
Draper, Jonathan, J. N., Bennington, Vt.
Driver, Rev. Thomas, Lynn, Mass.
Dubois, Richard, Canton, N. J.
Dudley, John L., Baltimore.
Dugan, Wm. T., Brooklyn.
Dugan, Mrs. Eliza, Brooklyn.
Dugan, William J., Brooklyn.
Dugan, Edward J., Brooklyn.
Duncan, Hon. James H., Haverhill, Mass.
Duncan, Mrs. James H., Haverhill, Mass
Duncan, Mrs. Samuel, Haverhill, Mass.
Duncan, Mrs. E. E., Jackson, Va.
Duncan, Rev. H. A., Coosawhatchie, S. C.
Duncan, Rev. William, Orleans, Ia.
Duncan, Rev. John, Camden, N. J.
Dunlap Abraham B., Brooklyn.
Dunlap, Mrs. Eliza, Brooklyn.
Dunlap, Rev. James, Jacksonville, Ill.
Dunn, Rev. Andrew, Winchendon, Mass.
Dunn, Alexander, New Brunswick, N. J.
Du Pre, Mrs. S. P., Darlington, S. C.
Dupont, Alfred, Wilmington, Del.
Durant, Clark, Albany.
Durbrow, William, New York.
Durfee, Sanford, Warwick, R. I.
Durfee, Miss Sarah C., Providence.
Durham, Nicholas O., Wearts Corners, N. J.
Durkin, John, New York.
Durnell, James, Philadelphia.
Duryea, Levi, New York.
Duryea, Mrs. Sarah, New York.
Dusenbury, Rev. Francisco, Etna, N. Y.
Duvall, Mrs. J., Mitchell's, Va.
Dwelle, Alphonso, Union Village, N. Y.
Dwelle, Mrs. Alphonso, Union Village, N. Y.
Dye, Rev. Daniel, Lafargeville, N. Y.
Dye, Rev. Enoch P., North Brookfield, N. Y.
Eastman, Lycurgus, Griggsville, Ill.
Eastman, Rev. Samuel, Burlington, Wis.
Earl, Rev. Samuel H., New York.
Earl, Miss Julia, Providence.
Earle, Rev. Alfred, Davisville, Pa.
Eaton, Rev. George W., D D., Hamilton, N Y
Eaton, R. C., Springville, N. Y.
Eaton, Rev. Horace, Wilton, N. H.
Eaton, Ezra, Boston.
Eaton, James L., Worcester, Mass.
Eaton, Mrs. Mary S., Worcester, Mass.
Eaton, Mrs. Job, Haverhill, Mass.
Eaton, Mrs. Sarah E., Keesville, N. Y.
Eddy, Rev. H. J., New York.
Eddy, Rev. Daniel C., Lowell, Mass.
Eddy, Mrs. Sarah D., New Bedford, Mass.
Eddy, Miss Ann E. N., New Bedford, Mass.
Eddy, John S., Providence, R. I.
Eddy, Mrs. Sarah J. S., Beverly, Mass
Eddy, Richard E., Boston.
Edgecomb, Albert, Mystic River, Ct.
Edington, Mrs. Charlotte M., New York
Edman, Thomas, Pemberton, N. J.
Edminster, Rev. J., Peoria, Ill.
Edmond, Francis, Brookline, Mass.
Edmond, Mrs. Emily S., Brookline, Mass.
Edmond, Francis B., Brookline, Mass.
Edmonds, Miss Sarah E., Philadelphia.
Edwards, Robert, New York.
Edwards, Mrs. Robert, New York.
Edwards, Miss Mary, New York.
Edwards, Rev. B. A., Watertown, Mass
Edwards, John F., Brookline, Mass.
Edwards, Ivory, Lowell, Mass.
Eldridge, Smith, Boston.
Eldridge, James, Williamstown, Mass.
Elgreen, Mrs. Ann, New York.
Elkin, Rev. David, Bryantsville, Indiana.

Lilege, Rev. Jesse, [illegible] Id.
Elliott, Rev. Charles, Ogdensburgh, N. Y.
Elliott, Edward G., Washington, D. C.
Elliott, Rev. William, Brighton, Iowa.
Elliott, Rev. S. L., Wallingford, Vt.
Elliott, Mrs. Sarah C., Wallingford, Vt.
Elliott, Rev. M., Steelesville, Ia.
Elliott, Mrs. Mary O. I., Mason Village, N. H.
Elliott, Samuel H., Providence.
Ellis, Theodore W., South Hadley Falls, Mass.
Ellis, Mrs. Mary, Norwalk, Ct.
Ellis, Anna, Brooklyn.
Ellsworth, Lewis, Naperville, Ill.
Ely, Henry D., Holmdel, N. J.
Ely, Mrs. Lucy, [illegible], N. J.
Emery, Thomas, Cincinnati, Ohio.
Emmons, Mrs. Sarah D., Deep River, Ct.
English, Henry H., Philadelphia.
English, Isaac, Salem, N. J.
English, Mrs. Hannah P., Beverly, Mass.
Eschman, Rev. John, Racine, Wis.
Eschman, Mrs. Magdalene, Racine, Wis.
Estee, Rev. Sidney A., [illegible], N. Y.
Estep, Rev. Dr. James, Liberty, Pa.
Estes, A. B., Lower Three Runs, S. C.
Estes, Miss H. S., Lower Three Runs, S. C.
Estes, Mrs. E. A., Lower Three Runs, S. C.
Evans, Silas J., Louisville, Ky.
Evans, Mrs. S. E., Society Hill, S. C.
Evans, Reuben, Amesbury, Mass.
Evans, Dr. Joseph T., New York.
Evans, Mrs. [illegible] H., New York.
Felton, Cader, Hertford, N. C.
Felton, Mrs. Mary, Hertford, N. C.
Felton, Rev. George D., Granville, Mass.
Fennell, Rev. George, Harrel's Store, N. C.
Fennell, Owen, Wilmington, N. C.
Ferrier, John M., New York.
Ferrell, Miss Mary Ann, New York.
Ferris, Mrs Hannah L., New York.
Ferris, O., Wilson, N. Y.
Ferris, Samuel M., Columbia, O.
Fickling, F. W., Gillisonville, S. C.
Field, Thomas F., Brooklyn.
Field, Mrs. Thomas F., Brooklyn.
Field, Thomas S., Hoboken, N. J.
Field, Mrs. Lavina F., Taunton, Mass.
Field, Mrs. Elizabeth H., Providence.
Field, Rev. Samuel W., Providence.
Field, Chas H., Taunton, Mass.
Field, George A., Taunton, Mass.
Field, Miss Ann M., Taunton, Mass.
Field, Miss Hannah E., Taunton, Mass.
Field, Miss Elsie M., Westport, N. H.
Field, Rev. Moses, Flat Brook, N. Y.
Fife, Rev. James, Charlottesville, Va.
Fife, Mrs Margaret W., Charlottesville, Va.
Fifield, Mrs. Catharine, Pawtucket, R. I.
Fifield, William, East Poultney, Vt.
Fillio, Rev. Nelson, Battle Creek, Mich.
Finch, Miss Sarah A., Red Oak Grove, Va.
Finch, George W., New York.
Fish, Rev. Joel W., Geneva, Wis.
Fish, J. L. A., Newton, Mass.

[redacted]

Foley, Thomas W., Providence.
Folwell, Job W., Defiance, Ohio.
Forbes, George W., Bridgeport, Ct.
Forbet, Gustavus, Boston.
Forbes, Rev. M., Middlesex, N. Y.
Forbush, Rev. Jonathan E., S. Danvers, Mass.
Forby, Wm. F., Brooklyn.
Force, Lyman, Alta, N. Y.
Ford, Isaac, Philadelphia.
Ford, Mrs. H., Philadelphia.
Ford, Henry Clay, Philadelphia.
Ford, Mrs. Amanda, Philadelphia.
Ford, Mrs. Mary, Harvey's Store, Va.
Foreman, Miss Mary E., Hightstown, N. J.
Forrester, Mrs. Elenora, Williamsburg, N. Y.
Forristall, Mrs. Lucy, Boston.
Foskett, Rev. Horace B., Cordaville, Mass.
Foster, John W., Leesville, Indiana.
Foster, William, West Dedham, Mass.
Foster, Mrs. Sarah K., Evansville, Ia.
Foster, Rev. J. C., Brattleboro', Vt.
Foster, Mrs. Abby A., Brattleboro', Vt.
Foster, Mrs. Martha, Cambridge, Mass.
Foster, Joseph. Sen., Salem, N. J.
Forsyth, Miss Sarah S., Livingston, N. Y.
Forsyth, Russell, Albany, N. Y.
Forsyth, Mrs. Sarah, Albany, N. Y.
Forsyth, Miss Emily H., Albany, N. Y.
Forsyth, Rusell, Jr., Albany, N. Y.
Fowle, Mrs. Lucy, Boston.
Fowler, Gamaliel, Suffield, Ct.
Fox, Rev. Norman, Ballston, N. Y.
Fox, Rev. Charles A., Waverly, Pa.
Fox, Mrs. Julia A., Waverly, Pa.
Fox, Albert R., Sand Lake, N. Y.
Fox, Mrs. Mary A., Sand Lake, N. Y.
Fox, Charles, New York.
Fox, Miss Ann Eliza, New York.
Frasee, Ezra, Rahway, N. J.
Frazee, Mrs. Mary, Rahway, N. J.
Francis, Robert, Newington, Ct.
Francis, Mrs. Lydia D., Newington, Ct.
Francis, Norman, New York.
Francis, Mrs. Hannah C., New York.
Francis, Charles King, New York.
Frayser, Rev. Herndon, Twymann's, Va.
Freas, Rev. Daniel J., Salem, N. J.
Freeman, Rev. T. G., Natchez, Miss.
Freeman, Rev. Joseph, Cavendish, Vt.
Freeman, Rev. G. W., Horicon, Wis.
Freeman, Thomas W., Augustus, Ga.
Freeman, Elisha, Worcester, Mass.
French, George R., Wilmington, N. C.
French, Stephen L., Fall River, Mass.
French, Miss Hannah, Haverhill, Mass.
French, Mrs. Moses E., Haverhill, Mass.
French, Rev. David S., Covington, Ia.
Frink, William S., Taylorville, Ill.
Fripp, E., Beaufort, S. C.
Fripp, Mrs. Ann H., Beaufort, S. C.
Frisby, Mrs. Lucy M., New Haven, Ct.
Frost, James, Wake Forest, N. C.
Frost, Joseph, Chanceville, N. J.
Fry, John, Philadelphia.
Fulcher, Richard, Three Rivers, Mich.
Fuller, George, Troy, N. Y.
Fuller, Nathan L., New York.
Fuller, Dr. Henry M., Beaufort, S. C.
Fuller, Rev. Martin Luther, Mooers, N. Y.
Fuller, Mrs Achsah Smith, Pike, N. Y.
Fuller, Cyrenins M., Jr., Pike, N. Y.
Fuller, Miss Elizabeth, Baltimore.
Fuller, Rev. Edward K., Reading, Mass.
Furguson, Rev. S. U., Plymouth, N. Y.
Furman, Rev. Richard, Society Hill, S. C.
Fyfe, Robert A., Milwaukee, Wis.
Fyfe, Mrs. Rebecca S., Milwaukee, Wis.
Gage, William W., Woburn, Mass.
Gage, Rev. David, New Boston, N. H.
Gage, Lewis, Methuen, Mass.
Gage, A., Methuen, Mass.
Gage, G. W., Methuen, Mass.
Gale, Jones R., Delavan, Ill.
Gale, Rev. Amory, Lee, Mass.
Gale, Rev. Solomon, Columbus, N. J.
Galusha, Truman, Jericho, Vt.
Gammell, A. M., Warren, R. I.
Gardiner, Richard, Philadelphia.
Gardner, Miss Miranda B., Fulton, N. Y.
Gardner, John, Newark, N. J.
Gardner, James C., Augusta, Ga.
Gardner, Rev. Jacob, Lyme, Ct.
Gardner, Frederick, New York.
Garfield, Rev. Benjamin F., Clifton Park, N. Y.
Garnett, Dorothy, Miller's, Va.
Garnett, Rev. Wm., Broadalbin, N. Y.
Garrett, D. H., Haddonfield, N. J.
Garnsey, Erasmus D., Burnt Hills, N. Y.
Garnsey, Mrs. Erasmus D., Burnt Hills, N. Y.
Garrett, Samuel, Rock Hill, Ohio.
Garrison, Rev. Cantine, Chili, N. Y.
Gates, Marcus A., South Gardner, Mass.
Gates, Horace S., Norwich, Ct.
Gates, Rev. G. W., Palmyra, N. Y.
Gates, T. J., Plainfield, Ct.
Gatling, John, Eatontown, N. J.
Gault, George, Brooklyn.
Gault, Mrs. George, Brooklyn.
Gault, Miss Georgianna E., Brooklyn.
Gay, William, Hollister, Mass.
Gaylor, Mrs Anna, New York.
George, Moses D., Haverhill, Mass.
George, Samuel, Haverhill, Mass.
George, Mrs Elizabeth C., Culpepper, Va.
German, Joseph, Beekman, N. Y.
Gibbs, Mrs. Eliza Ann, Newark, N. J.
Gibson, Rev. A., East Greene, N. Y.
Gifford, Rev. Isaac S., Bedford, N. Y.
Gifford, Mrs. Annis, Bedford, N. Y.
Gignilliat, W. R., Darien, Ga.
Gilbert, Wm. J., Middletown, Ct.
Gilbert, Isaac H., Providence.
Gill, Miss Mary, Pottsville, Pa.
Gill, Miss Mary Ann, Philadelphia.
Gillette, Mrs. Hannah J., New York.
Gillett, Ashael, Rose, N. Y.
Gillett, Nehemiah, Danbury, Ct.

MEMBERS FOR LIFE.

Gillman, Miss Ellen W., Roadstown, N. J.
Gilman, George H., New York.
Gilman, David, Roadstown, N. J.
Gilman, Mrs. John, Newburyport, Mass.
Gilbert, J. B., Hartford, Ct.
Giles, Alfred E., Boston.
Gilpatrick, Rev. James, Kansas.
Girdwood, Rev. John, New Bedford, Mass.
Girdwood, Mrs. Mary, New Bedford, Mass.
Gladding, Miss Lydia M., Providence.
Glass, George W., Honeoye Falls, N. Y.
Glover, Charles S., New York.
Goadby, Rev. John, Poultney, Vt.
Goddard, [illegible], York, N. Y.
Goddard, Mrs. Elizabeth, York, N. Y.
Goddard, Benjamin, Worcester, Mass.
G[illegible], Mrs. Nancy B., Columbus, Ohio.
G[illegible], Rev. Ezra, Greenville, Ohio.
G[illegible] J., Aurora, N. Y.
Godfrey, Abel, [illegible], N. Y.
Godfrey, Edward J., New York.
Godfrey, Mrs. Anna, Brooklyn.
Goldthwait, Nathan, Worcester, Mass.
G[illegible], John, Imlaystown, N. J.
G[illegible], Mrs. [illegible], Imlaystown, N. J.
Goodale, Rev. Joseph A., Suffield, Ct.
Goodhue, [illegible] C., New Boston, N. H.
Goodnow, Joseph, Charlestown, Mass.
Goodrich, Nathan F., [illegible], Ct.
Goodwin, Charles T., New York.
Goodwin, Rev. Thomas, Salem, N. J.
G[illegible], Rev. I. R., [illegible], N. H.
Green, David C., Providence.
Green, Arnold, Providence.
Green, Miss Frances Mary, Providence.
Green, Mrs. Mary, New York.
Green, Rev. John, Chester Village, Mass.
Green, Rev. Charles H., West Townsend, Vt.
Green, Rev. Jonathan R., Derby, Vt.
Green, Spencer, Rutland, Vt.
Green, Ralph, Three Rivers, Mass.
Green, Rev. Thomas H., Springport, N. Y.
Greenleaf, Rev. Calvin, Perry, Ill.
Greenleaf, Amos C., New York.
Greenleaf, John, Cambridge, Mass.
Greenleaf, Mrs. Elizabeth H., Cambridge, Mass.
Greenwood, Simeon A., Worcester, Mass.
Grenell, Mrs. Eliza, Honesdale, Pa.
Grenell, Mrs. C. Amelia, Newark, N. Y.
Gregory, Miss Clarissa, New York.
Gregory, Rev. S., Lisbon, N. Y.
Gregory, Uriah, Weston, Mass.
Gregory, Rev. Truman, Lee, Ill.
Griffin, Nathaniel L., Edgefield, S. C.
Griffin, Edwin, New York.
Griffin, James T., Rochester, N. Y.
Griffith, Rev. B., Philadelphia.
Griffiths, A. W., M. D., Philadelphia.
Griffiths, John J., New York.
Griggs, Samuel, Rutland, Vt.
Griggs, Mrs. Abigail S., Rutland, Vt.
Griggs, David R., Brookline, Mass.
Griggs, Seth D., Belchertown, Mass.

[redacted]

Hall, Mrs. Mary A., Greenwich, N. J.
Hall, Enoch, Worcester, Mass.
Hall, Abner, Wallingford, Ct.
Hall, Herbert, New York.
Hall, Rev. King S., Lake Village, N. H.
Hall, Rev. Abijah, Jr., Baldwinsville, N. Y.
Hall, David, 3d, Skaneateles, N. Y.
Hall, Abiathar, Fall River, Mass.
Hall, Hannah, Haverhill, Mass.
Hall, Mrs. Clarissa, Wallingford, Ct.
Hallsted, Mrs. Jane, C., New York.
Hamblet, Miss Mira C., West Swanzey, N. H.
Hamilton, Rev. Alexander, Barton, Wis.
Hamilton, John, Jr., Fredonia, N. Y.
Hamilton, Miss Ann, New London, Ct.
Hammond, Augustus, Pittsford, Vt.
Hammond, Mrs. Mary, Pittsford, Vt.
Hammond, Miss Mary F., Pittsford, Vt.
Hammond, William, Dorchester, Mass.
Hammond, James, M., Stillwater, N. Y.
Hanaford, Dr. Joseph H., Nantucket, Mass.
Hanaford, Mrs. J. H., Nantucket, Mass.
Hanaford, Howard A., Nantucket, Mass.
Hand, Joseph H., Bridgeport, Ct.
Hanly, Aaron, Peach Orchard, N. Y.
Hanna, John, Philadelphia.
Hansell, F. Standish, Philadelphia.
Hansell, Mrs. Emma, Philadelphia.
Hapgood, Miss S. F., Tunbridge, Vt.
Harding, Rev. Theodore, Horton, N. Scotia.
Hardwick, Wm., Jamaica Plains, Mass.
Harger, Mrs. Hannah, Chatham Corners, N. Y.
Harlow, Robert H., Boston.
Harmon, Rawson, Wheatland, N. Y.
Harmon, Mrs. Elizabeth N., Bennington, Vt.
Harmon, Mrs. David P., Haverhill, Mass.
Harper, Richard L., Boston.
Harrimount, Wm. S., New Haven, Ct.
Harrington, Wm., Worcester, Mass.
Harrington, Mrs. Adeline, Worcester, Mass.
Harrington, Stukely S., Akron, N. Y.
Harrington, Rev. Daniel, Batavia, N. Y.
Herrington, Adam, Shewsbury, Mass.
Harris, Rev. John, Milton, Mich.
Harris, Rev. Edward L., Delavan, Wis.
Harris, Rev. Wm. B., Cold Spring, (L. I.) N. Y.
Harris, Rev. George W., Detroit, Mich.
Harris, Mrs. Elizabeth J., Va.
Harris, Mrs. Sarah, Philadelphia.
Harris, Isaac, New London, Ct.
Harris, Thomas J., Claremont, N. H.
Harris, Douglas W., New London, Ct.
Harris, Henry, New London, Ct.
Harris, George, Plainville, Ct.
Harris, Mrs. Charlotte, New London, Ct.
Harrison, Mrs. Camilla M., Charles City, Va.
Harrison, Rev. J. C., Easton, Pa.
Harrison, Henry C., Philadelphia.
Hatch, Charles G., Shelby, N. Y.
Hatch, Rev. S., Lansingburgh, N. Y.
Hatch, Ira, Union Village, N. Y.
Hartshorn, Jonas, Worcester, Mass.
Hart, Henry B., Portland, Me.
Hartwell John B., Providence.
Harvey, Hezekiah, New York.
Harvey, Rev. Alfred, Woodstown, N. J.
Haskell, Dr. George, Rockford, Ill.
Haskell, Rev. Samuel, Kalamazoo, Mich.
Haskin, Mrs. Pamela, New York.
Hastings, Andrew F., Brooklyn.
Hastings, Mrs. Andrew F., Brooklyn.
Haswell, Rev. James M., Amherst, Burmah.
Haswell, Mrs. Jane M., Amherst, Burmah.
Hasey, Miss Angeline, New York.
Hatt, Joel, Orange, N. J.
Hatt, Mrs. Sophia, New York.
Hatt, Miss Annie Isabelle, Hoboken, N. J.
Hatfield, Robert G., New York.
Hatfield, Mrs. Charlotte S., New York.
Hathaway, Miss Mary, New York.
Hathaway, Charles F., Watertown, Mass.
Haviland, John, New York.
Haviland, Mrs Joanna, New York.
Haviland, Miss Mary Ann, New York.
Hawes, Rev. Josiah, New Sharon, Me.
Hawks, Isaac, Shelburne Falls, Mass.
Hawks, Mrs. Eliza H., North Bennington, Vt.
Hawley, Mrs. Rebecca, New York.
Hawley, D. F., Bristol, Ct.
Hayden, Rev Lucien, Saxton's River, Vt.
Hayden, Mrs. Caroline S., Saxton's River, Vt.
Hayden, John, Middlefield, N. Y.
Hayhurst, Rev. L. W., Ballston Spa, N. Y.
Haynes, Mrs. S. B., Va.
Haynes, Rev. Hiram, Preston Hollow, N. Y.
Haynes, Rev. Dudley C., Philadelphia.
Hay, Alexander, Greenwich, N. Y.
Hayes, Seth, Cromwell, Ct.
Hays, John P., New York.
Hazard, Simeon, Newport, R. I.
Hazen, Mrs. Emily N., Throopsville, N. Y.
Hazen, Rev. Henry C., Throopsville, N. Y.
Heafford, Samuel, Essex, Ct.
Heald, Rev. Albert, East Washington, N. H.
Healy, Ebenezer, Sennett, N. Y.
Healy, Mrs. Amia, Sennett, N. Y.
Healy, P. W., Sennett, N. Y.
Heart, Mrs Almira, Boston.
Heath, Rev. Amasa, Adams Village, N. Y.
Heath, Morgan, Greenwich, N. Y.
Hedden, William, Orange, N. J.
Hedden, Mrs. C F., Manchester, N. H.
Hedges, Daniel, Penn Yan, N. Y.
Hepburn, Rev. James, Stamford, Ct.
Hendlon, Miss Henrietta, New York.
Hendlon, Mrs. Anna S. Q., New York.
Hendrick, Rev. Joel, East Smithfield, Pa.
Hendrick, John M., New Haven, Ct.
Hendrickson, Rev. G F., Towner's Station, N Y
Henley, James W., New York.
Henley, Mrs. James W., New York.
Henry, Rev. Foster, Tyringham, Mass.
Hera, Rev. Edwin R., Hereford, Md.
Heritage, Jason, Moorestown, N. J.
Herrick, Mrs. Sam'l. D., Beverly, Mass.
Herrington, Chester, Clifton Park, N. Y.
Heron, Miss Isabella, Williamsburgh, N. Y.
Heron, Thomas F., Williamsburgh, N. Y.
Heron, William S., Williamsburgh, N. Y.
Hervey, Rev. Nathaniel, Westboro', Mass.
Heustis, Mrs. Ann, New Brunswick, N. J.

Hewit, Edmund, Galway, N. Y.
Hewitt, Chas. E., New London, Ct.
Heywood, Ellen, Jaffrey, N. H.
Hickman, Mrs. E., New Albany, Ia.
Hickok, Austin, Jay, N. Y. Horn,
Hide, Mrs. Fanny, Westerly, R. I.
Higbie, Alanson, Penfield, N. Y.
Higgins N. L., Elmira, N. Y. Horto
Hiler, Thomas G., Jr. Boston. Horto
Hill, Mrs. Harriet D., New York.
Hill, Miss Harriet R., New York.
Hill, Mrs. Mary, Miller's, Va.
Hill, David Jayne, Carmel, N. Y. Houg
Hill, Mrs. Rebecca, Essex, Ct. Houg
Hill, Rev. William, Kane, Ill.
Hill, Samuel P., Charlestown, Mass. Houg
Hill, Amos Jr., West Cambridge, Mass.
Hill, Rev. I. N., Albany, N. Y. Houg
Hill, Leander J., Brockport, N. Y.
Hill, Henry S., East Cambridge, Mass. Houg
Hill, Mrs. Eleanor, New York.
Hill, Rev. Thomas, Paris, Ia.
Hill, Walter E., Boston.
Hillman, Mrs. Catharine, N. Y.
Hills, Mrs. Deborah, Haverhill, Mass. Hovey
Hine, Simmons, New Haven, Ct.
Hinton, A. G., Pittsborough, N. C.
Hires, Mrs. Catherine, Freehold, N. J.
Hiscox, Mrs. C. O., New York.
Hitchcox, Sheldon, Suffield, Ct.
Hoar, Lewis, Warren, R. I. Howe,
Hoar, John B., Warren, R. I. Howe,

Hutchinson, Rev. Elisha, Windsor, Vt.
Hutchinson, Mrs. E., Windsor, Vt.
Hutchinson, Mrs. Rebecca, New York.
Hyatt, Mrs. Mary B., Brooklyn.
Hyer, Mrs. Rebecca, New York.
Ide, Rev. John, Potsdam, N. Y.
Ingalls, N. T., Belvidere, Ill.
Ingalls, Mrs. Sarah L., Belvidere, Ill.
Ingalls, Rev. Lovell, Akyab, Arracan.
Ingalls, Charles, Methuen, Mass.
Ingals, Mrs. Sarah H., Lee Centre, Ill.
Irish, Peter D., New London, Ct.
Irish, Mrs. Sarah P., New London, Ct.
Irish, William O., New London, Ct.
Irons, Rev. Arah, Delanti, N. Y.
Ivens, Mrs. Ann, Imlaystown, N. J.
Ivers, Miss Mary, New York.
Ives, Mrs. Hope, Providence.
Ives, Eli, Meriden, Ct.
Ives, William J., Meriden, Ct.
Jackson, Mrs. M. T., Newport, R. I.
Jackson, Mrs. Jerusha A., Chelsea, Mass.
Jackson, Daniel, Westford, Vt.
Jackson, Rev. Aaron, Oyster Bay, N. Y.
Jacobus, J. L., Chicago, Ill.
Jacobs, Charles P., Goshen, Ia.
Jacobs, Wm. H., Williamsburg, N. Y.
James, Rev. Joshua J., Yanceyville, N. C.
James, Edward, Albany.
James, George, Zanesville, O.
James, Francis H., Philadelphia.
James, Rev. David, Osceola, Ill.
James, Thomas M., New Bedford, Mass.
Jamison, Alexander, Wilmington, Del.
Jameson, Mrs. Lucinda L., Boston.
Jameson, Miss Eliza, Newton, Mass.
Jaquith, Edwin, Chelsea, Mass.
Jarratt, Henry, Jarratt's, Va.
Jarratt, Nicholas, Jarratt Depot, Va.
Jastram, George B., Providence.
Jaudon, Mrs. Sarah T., Robertsville, S. C.
Jaycox, Isaac, Cold Spring, N. Y.
Jaycox, Mrs. Fanny M., Cold Spring, N. Y.
Jeffrey, Rev. Reuben, Albany, N. Y.
Jeffres, J. M., Red Oak Grove, Va.
Jefferis, Rev. David, Perkiomen, Pa.
Jencks, Rev. Erasmus N., Farmington, Ill.
Jencks, Miss Maria, Pawtucket, R. I.
Jenks, Gideon, Brookfield, Mass.
Jenks, J. W. P., Middleboro', Mass.
Jenkins, Mrs. Susanna, New York.
Jenkins, Rev. J. S., Coatesville, Pa.
Jenkins, Miss Rebecca, New York.
Jennett, John, Halifax, C. H., Va.
Jennings, Mrs. Susan C., Worcester, Mass.
Jennings, Mrs. Marcia, Deep River, Ct.
Jennings, Mrs. Betsey, Deep River, Ct.
Jeril, Rev. T., Lebanon, N. Y.
Jerome, George D., Waterford, Ct.
Jerrard, Rev. Richard, Morrisania, N. Y.
Jeter, Rev. J. C., Beaver Dam, S. C.
Jewell, Aaron C., Newark, N. J.
Jewett, Rev. Milo P., Marion, Ala.
Jewett, Rev. Daniel, Farmington, Iowa.
Jimmerson, Robert J., New York.
Jimmerson, Mrs. Miranda L., New York.
Johnson, Mathew M., Woburn, Mass.
Johnson, Rev. William B., D. D., Edgefield, S. C.
Johnson, Mrs. Henrietta, Edgefield, S. C.
Johnson, William, North-East, Pa.
Johnson, Mrs. Sarah S., North-East, Pa.
Johnson, Mrs. Louisa M., Lynn, Mass.
Johnson, James, Brooklyn, N. Y.
Johnson, Robert, Newark, N. J.
Johnson, Mrs. Robert, Newark, N. J.
Johnson, Rev. Solomon B., St. Louis, Mo.
Johnson, Rev. George J., Burlington, Iowa.
Johnson, Mrs. George J., Burlington, Iowa.
Johnson, Rev. Hezekiah, Oregon City, Oregon.
Johnson, Albert B., Willistown, Pa.
Johnson, Edward, New York.
Johnson, Mrs. Mary, Albany, N. Y.
Johnson, Merrick, Willington, Ct.
Johnson, Miss Jane Ann, Wilson, N. Y.
Johnson, Oliver, Providence.
Johnson, Ralph, Norwich, N. Y.
Johnson, Elias, Troy, N. Y.
Johnston, Andrew, Newark, N. J.
Johnston, Mrs. Andrew, Newark, N. J.
Johnston, James, Sing Sing, N. Y.
Jolls, John F., Providence.
Jones, Rev. Stephen, Norwalk, Ohio.
Jones, Mrs. Stephen, Norwalk, Ohio.
Jones, Rev. John, Seaville, N. J.
Jones, Mrs. Deborah, Seaville, N. J.
Jones, Mrs. Ann T., Williamsburg, Va.
Jones, Eliza T., Tavern P. O., Pa.
Jones, Mrs. Margaret, New York.
Jones, Mrs. Eliza W., New Brunswick, N. J.
Jones, Mrs. Elizabeth, Macedon, N. Y.
Jones, David, New York.
Jones, Mrs. Sarah, New York.
Jones, Mrs. Mary, New York.
Jones, Mrs. Rhoda, Smithville, N. Y.
Jones, Miss Catherine L., Philadelphia.
Jones, Rev. Joseph H., Frederick City, Md.
Jones, Rev. David N., Richmond, Va.
Jones, Rev. Matthew, Stephentown, N. Y.
Jones, Rev. Theophilus, Hatboro', Pa
Jones, Rev. Isaac D., Flemingville, N. Y.
Jones, John B., Roxbury, Mass.
Jones, William G., Wilmington, Del.
Jones, Washington, Wilmington, Del.
Jones, William M., New York.
Jones, Mrs. Margaretta V., New York.
Jones, Rev. J. W., Hyde Park, N. Y.
Jones, Howard M., Providence, R. I.
Jones, Rev. J. D. E., North Bennington, Vt.
Jones, J. F., East Cambridge, Mass.
Jones, Rev. T., Rock Hill, Ohio.
Jones, Rev. Edward, Brookfield, Ohio.
Jones, Mrs. Abigail, New York.
Jones, Rev. A. B., Guilford, N. Y.
Jones, Rev. H. S., Smyrna, N. Y.
Jordan, Philana D., Columbia, Ohio.
Jordon, Mrs. Esther, Brooklyn, N. Y.
Jordon, True P., Lowell, Mass.
Joslin, Joseph, East Poultney, Vt.
Joyce, Miss Sarah W., Worcester, Mass.
Judd, Rev. Truman O., Fairhaven, Ct.
Justice, David, Forestville, N. C.
Justin, Rev. Ira, Richmond, N. Y.
Kain, Charles, Marlton, N. J.

MEMBERS FOR LIFE.

Kain, Mrs. Sarah, Mariton, N. J.
Kain, Rev. Charles, Jr., Mullica Hill, N. J.
Kain, Mrs. Maria, Mullica Hill, N. J.
Kasson, Marcus A., Granville, Mass.
Kauffman, Henry, Paoli, Pa.
Kauffman, Mrs. Sarah, Paoli, Pa.
Keith, William, Boston, Mass.
Kavanagh, Michael, Lowell, Mass.
Keely, Rev. George, Haverhill, Mass.
Keely, Mrs. George, Haverhill, Mass.
Keely, John, Haverhill, Mass.
Keely, Mrs. John, Haverhill, Mass.
Keely, Rev. Thomas E., Kingston, Mass.
Keen, Mrs. Susan B., West Philadelphia.
Keen, George B., West Philadelphia.
Keen, William W. J., West Philadelphia.
Keen, Charles B., West Philadelphia.
Keeney, John, New London, Ct.
Keeney, William H., New London, Ct.
Keeney, Rev. Curtis, New London, Ct.
Kelly, Mrs. John, Elmira, New York.
Kelly, Mrs. Mary M., Brooklyn.
Kelley, Mrs. Catherine, New York.
Kelley, Mrs. Ella, New York.
Kelley, Miss Georgiana, New York.
Kelsey, James D., Pittsfield, N. H.
Kelsey, Rev. Daniel, Pittsgrove, N. J.
Kelton, George, Salem, N. J.
Kemp, Sylvester A., Florida, Mass.
Kendall, H. N., St. Louis, Mo.
Kendall, Charles S., Boston.
Kendrick, Silas N., Detroit, Mich.

Kingsbury, Rev. Arnold, Fredonia, N. Y.
Kingsford, Rev. Edward, D.D., Richmond, Va.
Kingsland, Mrs. Sarah Jane, New York.
Kingsley, Rev. A. C., Parma Centre, N. Y.
Kirk, Robert, New York.
Kone, Louk, Maulmain, Burmah.
Knapp, Rev. Henry R., Greenport, N. Y.
Knapp, Mrs. Mary, Willimantic, Ct.
Knapp, John, Bridgeport, Ct.
Knapp, Rev. A., Otselic, N. Y.
Knapp, J. E., Camillus, N. Y.
Knight, Abram, Williamsburg, N. Y.
Knight, Daniel N., Brooklyn.
Knight, Mrs. D. N., Brooklyn.
Knight, Jonathan, Worcester, Mass.
Knight, Mrs. Samuel, Haverhill, Mass.
Knight, Rev. Benjamin, Strathan, N. H.
Knowles, Levi, Philadelphia.
Knowles, Mrs. Susan E., Providence.
Knowlton, Miss Sarah J., North Chatham, N. Y.
Knowlton, D. A., Freeport, Ill.
Knowlton, Edward, Marion, Iowa.
Knowlton, Hezekiah, Beverly, Mass.
Knox, Miss Rachel, Hillsdale, N. Y.
Knudsen, Mrs. Sarah Jane, Brooklyn.
Kyle, Miss Mary, New York.
L'Amoureaux, Mrs. Nancy S., Hadley, Mass.
Ladd, Mrs. C. Ann, New York.
Lafever, Reuben, Reading Centre, N. Y.
Lafleur, Rev. Theodore, St. Pie, Canada East.
La Grange, Mrs. John E., Hillsdale, N. Y.
La Grange, Rev. John E., Beckmanville, N. Y.

[redacted]

MEMBERS FOR LIFE.

Leach, Rev. Beriah N., New York.
Leach, Rev. D. F., Harpersville, N. Y.
Leach, Rev. William, South Hanson, Mass.
Leask, Mrs. Margaret, New York.
Ledger, Mrs. Marion, Brooklyn.
Lee, George, North Bristol, N Y.
Lee, Mrs. Amanda, North Bristol, N. Y.
Lee, Miss Ann Mollan, New York.
Lee, J. A., New York.
Leicester, Mrs. Mary, New York.
Leggett, Rev. William, Owasco, N. Y.
Leland, J. A., Brooklyn.
Leland, Mrs. Caroline M , Brooklyn.
Lemont, Charles A., Chelsea, Mass.
Lemont, Mrs. Anna M., New York.
Leonard, Mrs. Mahetable, Zanesville, Ohio.
Leonard, Rev. Isaac, Burlington, Iowa.
Leonard, George E., Newton, Mass.
Leonard, Mrs. Caroline F Taunton, Mass.
Leonard, George A., New York.
Lerned, Rev. J. H., Cambridge, Mass.
Levy, Rev. Edgar M., West Philadelphia.
Lewis, William J., New York.
Lewis, Elijah, Brooklyn.
Lewis, Mrs. Ann, Brooklyn.
Lewis, Mrs. Mary B. S., Brooklyn.
Lewis, Mrs. Ann, Worcester, Mass.
Lewis, Rev. Charles C., New Shoreham, R. I.
Lewis, Rev. Lester, Middetown, Ct.
Lewis, Daniel D., Philadelphia.
Lewis, Mrs. Hannah Norwich, N. Y.
Lewis, Simeon H., Boston.
Lewis, William, New York.
Lewis, Rev. Richard, Holmesburg, Pa.
Lewis, Elijah, Norwich, N. Y.
Lewis, William B., Preston, N. Y.
Lewis, Rev. Welcome, Mansfield, Mass.
Lincoln, Rev. Thomas O., Utica, N. Y.
Lincoln, Mrs. Abby A.
Lincoln, Rev. Heman, Jamaica Plains, Mass.
Lincoln, Henry E., Boston.
Lincoln, Joshua, Roxbury M
Lindsay, Wm. Fall River, Mass.
Listemuth, Miss Caroline, Philadelphia.
Litchfield, Rev. Daniel W Benton, N. Y.
Litchfield, Electus B., Brooklyn.
Litchfield, E. D. Brooklyn
Little, George W Charlestown, Mass.
Little, J. Y Dixon, Ill.
Lifsey, Mrs. Sally, Hick's Ford, Va.
Loomis, Edwin H , Lebanon, Ct.
Locke, Mrs. Harriet N., Springfield, N. J.
Locke, Jesse A., Watertown, Mass.
Locke, Mrs. Sarah B., Watertown, Mass.
Logan, Rev. John, Ill.
Logan, James, Pemberton, N. J.
Lombard, Nathan C., Lowell, Mass.
Long, E. J., Boston, Mass.
Long, William, Shelburne Falls, Mass.
Longyear, Rev. Henry Z., Phenicia, N. Y.
Loring, Samuel H., Boston.
Loring, Mrs. James, Boston.
Lowe, Mrs. Harriet N., Salem, N. J.
Love, Rev. H. T., New York.
Love, Mrs. Catherine W., New York.
Love, John, New York.
Lovell, George, Osterville, Mass.
Lovell, Mrs. Lucy, Fall River, Mass.
Lovell, Rev. Andrew S. Bloomfield, Ct.
Lucas, Rev. Elijah, Waterford, N. Y.
Ludlow, John R., New York.
Ludlow, Mrs. Clarissa Ann, Newport, R. I.
Ludlam, David, Jr., Sing Sing, N. Y.
Lull, Rev. Abner, Sheboygan Falls, Wis.
Luther, Job, Providence.
Luther, Gardner Seekonk, Mass.
Luther, Mrs. Mary, Seekonk, Mass.
Lyman, Nathan, Andover, Ct.
Lynch, Thomas, Philadelphia.
Lyon, Jesse, Fitchburg, Mass.
Lyon, Moses G., Fitchburg, Mass.
Lyon, Cyrus, York, N. Y.
Lyon, Mrs. Mary York, N. Y
Lyon, Miss Rebecca, Plainfield, N. J.
Lyon, Rev. Daniel D., Sag Harbor, N. Y.
Lyon, Rev. Joel, Bergen, N Y
Lyon, Mrs. Caroline P., Chatham, Mass.
Lyon, Mrs. Merrick, Providence.
Lyon, Rev. A. S., Chatham, Mass.
Lynt, Odell D., Hastings, N Y
Lytle, Andrew, Williamsburgh, Va.
McAllister, Mrs. E., Fayetteville, N. C.
McBride, Miss Jane Ann, New York.
McBride, Miss Eliza H., New York.
McCarthy Rev. William, Holland Patent, N. Y.
McClung, Miss Caroline M. Pittsburg, Pa.
McClung, Anthony, Kingston, N Y
McCormick, R. C., New York.
McCormick, Mrs. Sarah M., New York.
McCoy, John, Charlestown, Ia.
McCullen, Miss Sarah, New York.
McCune, John P Salem, N. J.
McCutchen, Wm. G., Williamsburg, N. Y.
McDade, Mrs. Jane, New York.
McDaniel, Randle, Fayetteville, N. C.
McFarland, Rev. D., Oswego, N. Y.
McGear, Daniel L.
McGonagal, George, New York.
McIntosh, Mrs. Mary, Philadelphia.
McIver, A. M., Society Hill, S. C.
McIver, Mrs. Ann J., Society Hill, S. C.
McJannett, Mrs. Elizabeth, Brooklyn.
McKean, Rev John A., Philadelphia.
McKean, Mrs. Eliza J., Philadelphia.
McKewan, John New York.
McLallan, James, Trumansburg, N Y.
McLallan, Mrs. Ellen Trumansburg, N. Y.
McLean, Mrs. Mary, New London, C
McLowth, Rev. Benjamin, Scipio, New York.
McMahon, Henry L., Philadelphia.
McTaggart, Daniel, Reading, Pa.
McTaggart, Mrs. Margaret, Reading, Pa.
Macdonald, Alexander, New York.
Macdonald, Mrs. E., New York.
Macdonald, Miss M. J., New York.
Mack, Rev. Levi M., Rosendale, N. Y.
Mack, Elisha H., Weedsport, N. Y.
Maclay, Hon William B., New York.
Maclay, Archibald, New York.

MEMBERS FOR LIFE.

Maclay, Moses B., New York.
Macomber, John, Watertown, N. Y.
Mabbett, Seneca, Dover Plains, N. Y.
Mabbett, James K. Dover Plains, N. Y.
Mabbett, T., Brooklyn.
Madison, Almond Z., Fredonia, N. Y.
Magee, Rev. Thomas, New Brunswick, N. S.
Magee, Thomas H., New York.
Maghee, Miss Frances, New York.
Magoon, Miss Ella Louise, New York.
Magoon, Frank N. L., New York.
Mahoney, Rev. Henry W., Piedmont, S. C.
Main, Randall W., New York.
Mallary, Rev. S. S., Pawtucket, R. I.
Mallory, Rev. Almond C., Benton Centre, N. Y.
Mallory, Rev. James, Lagrange, N. Y.
Mandeville, Stephen, New York.
Mandeville, Mrs. Mary, New York.
Mandeville, Miss Phebe E., New York.
Mandeville, George, New York.
Mansfield, Edward, South Reading, Mass.
Mangam, William D., New York.
Mangam, Mrs. Sarah Ann, New York.
Mangam, Edgar B., New York.
Mangum, Rev. Daniel, Pageville, S. C.
Mann, Rev. Levi L., Lake Hill, N. Y.
Manning, Rev. Edward, Cornwall, N. S.
Manning, William, Boston.
Manning, Melville M., Boston.
Manro, Philip A., Throopsville, N. Y.
Manton, Rev. Joseph R., Providence.
Manwaring, C. S., East Lyme, Ct.

[redacted]

Martin, M. D., Bristol, Ct.
Martin, Mrs. Sarah Ann, New York.
Marvin, George, Norwalk, Ct.
Mason, Augustu F., Chelsea, Mass.
Mason, Mrs. Sarah R., Chelsea, Mass.
Mason, Mrs. Rosanna L., West Swanzey, N. H.
Mason, Mrs. D. C. Fuller, Sandusky, N. Y.
Mason, Mrs. J. O., Greenwich, N. Y.
Mason, George, Providence.
Mason, Charles, New York.
Mason, John M. G., Philadelphia.
Mason, Arnold G., Bridgeport, Ct.
Mason, Mrs. Arnold G., Bridgeport, Ct.
Mason, R. B., Webster, N. Y.
Mason, Rev. S. R., Cambridgeport, Mass.
Mason, Rev. J. T., Galevil e, N. Y.
Mason, Pethuel, Somerville, N. J.
Mason, Charles J., New York.
Mason, Mrs. Lavinia, New York.
Mason, Miss Sarah Elizabeth, New York.
Mason, Rev. Eddy, Sennett, N. Y.
Mason, Joseph R., Providence.
Mastin, John S., New York.
Mather, Increase, Fairport, N. Y.
Mather, Mrs. Mary A., Deep River, Ct.
Mathews, Rev. George, Athol, Mass.
Mathews, Mrs. Elizabeth, Athol, Mass.
Matteson, Rev. N. H., Preston City, Ct.
Maul, Rev. William, Plainfield, N. J.
Maul, Mrs. Sarah Ann, Plainfield, N. J.
Maxwell, B., Shelburne Falls, Mass.
Maxwell, Rev. J. M., Oswego, Ia.

[redacted]

Merrine, N. J., Reading, Pa.
Micou, Rev. John, Jr., Louisville, Mi.
Mikels, Rev. William S., Sing Sing, N. Y.
Mikels, Mrs. Lydia, Sing Sing, N. Y.
Milbank, Miss Elizabeth, Plainfield, N. J.
Milbank, Miss Eliza W., Plainfield, N. J.
Milbank, Miss Sarah C., Plainfield, N. J.
Milbank, Miss Mary W., Plainfield, N. J.
Milbank, Mrs. Mary W., New York.
Milbank, Miss Mary A., New York.
Milbank, Miss Emma Louisa, New York.
Milbank, Miss Anna Elizabeth, New York.
Milbank, L. Ainsworth, New York.
Milbank, Charles A., New York.
Middlebrook, J. Henry, New York.
Middleton, John, New York.
Miles, Abial, New York.
Miles, Mrs. Hannah, New York.
Miles, Rev. George I., Bellefonte, Pa.
Miles, Rev. Edward M., Davenport, Iowa.
Miles, Thomas, Philadelphia.
Millard, George, North Adams, Mass.
Millard, S. S., Penfield, N. Y.
Millard, Barzilla, Penfield, N. Y.
Miller, Rev. Harvey, Meriden, Ct.
Miller, Mrs. Sarah R., Meriden, Ct.
Miller, Mrs. Abigail, New York.
Miller, Miss Amanda, Banksville, Ct.
Miller, Mrs. Nancy, New London, Ct.
Miller, Miss Anicartha, New York.
Miller, John B., Sumterville, S. C.
Miller, James H., Philadelphia.
Miller, Charles, Moriah, N. Y.
Miller, Rev. U. B., Ft. Wayne, Ia.
Miller, Mrs. Martha, Middletown, Ct.
Miller, Mrs. Ann Eliza, Providence.
Miller, Lydia A., Bedford, N. Y.
Miller, Edward W., Philadelphia.
Mills, Charles H., Brooklyn, N. Y.
Mills, Stephen, Greenwich, N. Y.
Mills, Rev. Pelatiah W., Springville, N. Y.
Milne, John C., Fall River, Mass.
Milne, Rev. Alexander, Marcellus, N. Y.
Milne, Mrs. Eliza N., Marcellus, N. Y.
Milner, Alfred A., New York.
Milner, Mrs. Alfred A., New York.
Miner, Rev. Martin, Wolcott, Ct.
Miner, Rev. Absalom, Waukesha, Wis.
Miner, Rev. Cyrus, Attica, N. Y.
Miner, Rev. S. G., Canton, Ill.
Miner, Rev. Erastus, Cold Spring, N. Y.
Miner, Francis S., New York.
Miner, A. B., Italy Hill, N. Y.
Miner, Nathaniel, Jerseyville, Ill.
Miner, Mrs. Hannah M., Norwich, N. Y.
Miner, Mrs. Charles, New London, Ct.
Mingus, Miss Julia Ann, New York.
Mintch, Mrs. Phebe, Shiloh, N. J.
Mitchell, Rev. George H., Wagontown, Pa.
Mitchell, Mrs. Phebe H., Wagontown, Pa.
Mitchell, Seth, Montrose, Pa.
Mixter, Rev. George, New London, Ct.
Mondon, Gilbert F., Port Jervis, N. Y.
Monroe, Rev. William Y., Lexington, Ia.
Montgomery, William, Danbury, Ct.
Montgomery, Mrs. Susan, Danbury, Ct.
Montgomery, S. P., Danbury, Ct.
Montague, Rev. Oreb, Warsaw, N. Y.
Moon, John, New York.
Moore, Dr. G. C., St. Johns, N. C.
Moore, Mrs. Julia, St. Johns, N. C.
Moore, Mrs. Theodosia M., St. Louis, Mo.
Moore, James, Milton, Pa.
Moore, Francis W., New York.
Moore, Rev. Lyman H., Marshall, Mich.
Moore, Rev. W. W., Albany, N. Y.
Moore, Rev. George C., New York.
Moore, James, Wilmington, Del.
Moore, Enoch, Danbury, Ct.
Moore, Rev. Farris, Lee, Mass.
Morgan, William, Brooklyn.
Morgan, Miss Harriet, Brooklyn.
Morgan, David, Cleveland, Ohio.
Morgan, Hiram, Blackwoodtown, N. J.
Morgan, Joshua, Philadelphia.
Morrell, Mrs. Sarah G., Savannah, Ga.
Morrill, Geo. W., Salisbury, Mass.
Morrill, Miss Mary, Salisbury, Mass.
Morrill, Joseph, Amesbury, Mass.
Morrill, Daniel, Amesbury, Mass.
Morrill, Otis H., Lowell, Mass.
Morris, Rev. J., Hamburg, S. C.
Morris, Rev. David, New York.
Morrison, Jonathan, Brooklyn, N. Y.
Morrison, Mrs. A. Henrietta, Brooklyn, N. Y.
Morse, Enoch R., Chelsea, Mass.
Morse, K. P., Greenville, Ill.
Morse, Henry D., Haverhill, Mass.
Morton, Mrs. Susan, Corning, N. Y.
Morton, Miss Sarah B., Corning, N. Y.
Moseley, Green, Dupree's Store, Va.
Moseley, Miss S. A., Dupree's Store, Va.
Moss, Mrs. Nancy, Upperville, Va.
Mott, Miss Elizabeth, New York.
Moulthrop, Major, New Haven, Ct.
Moxley, Rev. Oel W., Richville, N. Y.
Mugg, Rev. John, Gosport, Ia.
Mulford, John, Sen., Mullica Hill, N. J.
Mulford, Charles, Salem, N. J.
Mulford, Mrs. Phebe, Roadstown, N. J.
Mulberm, Rev. Denis, Ozaukee, Wisc.
Mumford, Rev. N., Sherburne, N. Y.
Munger, Rev. Washington, Mystic River, Ct.
Munger, Mrs. Louisa N., Mystic River, Ct.
Munger, Morgan, Stillwater, N. Y.
Munger, L. F., Leroy, N. Y.
Munn, Mrs. Mary, New York.
Murdock, Mrs. Martha B., Hartford, Ct.
Murphy, William D., New York.
Murphy, Samuel, Hoboken, N. J.
Murphy, Rev. John R., Marlton, N. J.
Murray, Joseph D., New Hope, Pa.
Murray, Mrs. Margaret M., New Hope, Pa.
Mustin, John, Philadelphia.
Myers, Mrs. Ann R., Philadelphia.
Myers, James, Jr., New York.
Mylne, Rev. William, Louisa, C. H., Va.
Myrick, Albert A., Pitcher, N. Y.
Napier, Rev. Robert, Mispath, S. C.
Neale, Jeremiah, Meriden, Ct.
Nelson, Rev. Caleb, Enfield, N. Y.
Nelson, Rev. Wm. F., Greenfield, Mass.

MEMBERS FOR LIFE.

Nelson, Simeon B., Westport, N. H.
Newcomb, Butler, Cedarville, N. J.
Newcomb, Mrs. Thomas, Haverhill, Mass.
Newell, Andrew H., Brookline, Mass.
Newell, Mrs. Asa, Providence.
Newhall, Rev. F., Hanover, N. H.
Newland, D., Stillwater, N. Y.
Newland, Rev. C. A., Cooper's Plains, N. Y.
Newton, Mrs. Sally, Albany.
Newton, William, Worcester, Mass.
Newton, Rev. Calvin, Worcester, Mass.
Newton, Rev. Baxter, North Leverett, Mass.
Newton, Miss Frances M., New York.
Newton, Mrs. Jane, Bridgeton, N. J.
Nice, Rev. William J., Imlaystown, N. J.
Nice, Mrs. Elizabeth A., Imlaystown, N. J.
Nichols, Miss Hannah, Bridgeport, Ct.
Nichols, Reuben, Kingston, N. Y.
Nichols, Rev. D. A., Port Providence, Pa.
Nichols, Jonathan, Berlin, N. Y.
Nichols, Charles H., Boston.
Nicholas, Rev. Noah, Rutland, Vt.
Nicholson, A. M., Bostick Mills, N. C.
Nickerson, Hardin, Providence, R. I.
Nickels, George, Rock Hill, Ohio.
Niel, James B., Brooklyn.
Noble, Mrs. Margaret, Brooklyn.
Nolton, Miss Sarah J., Petersburgh, N. Y.
Normandeau, Mrs. C. A., Grande Ligne, C. E.
Northem, E., Rockingham, N. C.
Northam, George, Va.
Norton, Charles C., New York.
Norton, Rev. Noah, Brunswick, Me.

Page, Rev. Stephen B., Cleveland, Ohio.
Page, Mrs. Emily A. L., Cleveland, Ohio.
Page, Abel, Haverhill, Mass.
Page, Mrs. Abel, Haverhill, Mass.
Page, Mrs. Rachel D., Hopkinton, N. H.
Paine, Rev. John, Ware, Mass.
Paine, Walter, 3d, Fall River, Mass.
Palmer, Rev. Asa H.
Palmer, Rev. Albert G., Syracuse, N. Y.
Palmer, Mrs. Amelia W., Syracuse, N. Y.
Palmer, Mrs. William, East Lyme, Ct.
Palmer, Rev. Lyman, St. Anthony, Min.
Palmer, Rev. Prentice T., Waveland, Ia.
Palmer, Ephraim, New Hartford, N. Y.
Park, Elisha, Providence.
Park, Rev. Charles C., Italy Hollow, N. Y.
Parke, Rev. F. S., Cheshire, Mass.
Parker, Miss Lavinia M., Suffield, Ct.
Parker, Asa, Essex, Ct.
Parker, Joel R., Fredonia, N. Y.
Parker, Rev. A., Fiskdale, Mass.
Parker, Rev. William, Philadelphia.
Parker, Rev. A., Coventry, N. Y.
Parker, David O., Hamilton, N. Y.
Parker, Lydia P., Allen, Mich.
Parker, Rev. Harvey I., Fairfax, Vt.
Parks, Rev. R. M., Bedford, Indiana.
Parks, Mrs. Marianne C., South Berwick, Me.
Parkhurst, John, Fitchburg, Mass.
Parkhurst, G. R., Brookline, Mass.
Parmlee, Mrs. Syrena, New York.
Parmelee, Elias F., Essex, Ct.
Parmelee, Rev. J. H., Xenia, Ohio.

Peeples, Edward H., Lawtonville, S. C.
Pegg, Miss Jane, New York.
Pember, Asahel, New London, Ct.
Pember, Mrs. Mary, New London, Ct.
Penny, Rev. William, Uniontown, Pa.
Penny, Rev. Thomas J., McKeesport, Pa.
Perego, Mrs. Margaret, New York.
Pendleton, Rev. G W., Jacksonville, Ill.
Pendleton, Mrs. Jane G., Jacksonville, Ill.
Perine, Joseph, Plainfield, N. J.
Perine, Mrs. Sarah, Plainfield, N. J.
Perkins, Jabez, Topsham, Me.
Perkins, Rev. Nehemiah M, Brookline, Mass.
Perkins, George, Amesbury, Mass.
Perkins, Russel B., Meriden. Ct
Perry, Mrs. Sarah, McWilliamstown, Pa.
Perry, Valentine, Macedon, N. Y.
Person, Rev. Ira, Concord, N. H.
Persons, Rev. R., Victory, N. Y.
Peterson, Rev. J. F., Richardson's, S. C.
Peterson, Richard E., New York.
Peterson, Mrs. Deborah V., New York.
Peterson, Samuel F., Philadelphia,
Pettingill, Daniel, Haverhill, Mass.
Pettingill, Miss Charlotte, Haverhill, Mass.
Pettey, Harvey E, Greenwich, N. Y.
Pettit, Curtis, Wilson, N. Y.
Pettigrew, Rev. Wm J., Pittsburg, Pa.
Pew, John, Gloucester, Mass.
Phares, Rev. M. B., Dupont, Ia.
Phelps, Humphrey, New York. *
Phelps, John, Owego, N. Y.
Phelps, Mrs. Sophia Amelia, New Haven, Ct.
Phelps, Mrs. Mary S., New York.
Phelps, Miss Julia Adelaide, New York.
Phelps, Miss Sophronia E., New York.
Phelps, Miss Mary Amelia, New York.
Phelps, Willard, New York.
Philleo, Calvin, Providence.
Phillips, George H, Troy, N. Y.
Phillips, Rev. W., Providence.
Phillips, Rev. David L., Jonesboro', Ill.
Phillips, Rev. Wm F., Freedom, N. York.
Phillips, Rev. James N., Moodus, Ct.
Phillips, Dr. Samuel B., New York.
Phillips, Rev. W. C., Canandaigua, N. Y.
Phillips, Mrs. Ann, New York.
Phillips, Mrs. Theodosia, Morristown, N. J.
Phillips, Peter, Rondout, N. Y.
Philbrook, Rev. Abel, Pittsgrove, N. J.
Phippen, Rev. George, Tyringham, Mass.
Pier, Mrs. Deborah, New York.
Pierce, Rev. Sem, Londondery, Vt.
Pierce, Philo, Bristol, Ct.
Pierce, Mrs. Pa.ty B., Nunda, N. Y.
Pierce, John W., Boston.
Pierson, David, East Avon, N. Y.
Pike, Jonathan, Providence.
Pike, Mrs. Jonathan, Providence.
Pike, Miss Ann E., Providence.
Pike, Albert B. H., Providence.
Pike, Benj. Jr., New York.
Pike, Mrs. Francis M., New York.
Pike, Miss Catharine E, New York.
Pike, Mrs. Abby C., Taunton, Mass
Pillsbury, Rev. Phineas, Ill.
Pillsbury, John G., Lowell, Mass.
Pinney, Mrs. Mary, Owego, N. Y.
Piper, John G., Canton, Ill.
Pitcher, Miss Elizabeth, Brooklyn, N. Y.
Pitman, Rev. Joseph M., Sutton, N. H.
Plant, E. H., Plantsville, Ct.
Plant, A. P., Plantsville, Ct.
Platt, G. W., New York.
Platt, Mrs. Jane D., New York.
Platt, Rev. E. F., Toledo, Ohio.
Platt, Josiah, Stratfield, Ct.
Plumb, William, Morrisania, N. Y.
Plumb, Mrs. Cynthia G., Sterling, N. Y.
Plummer, Mrs. Jane, New York.
Plymer, Mrs Eliza, New York.
Pohlman, William, Albany, N. Y.
Poiner, J. R., Cincinnati.
Poole, Rev. A. W., Woodland, La.
Pooler, Seth, Lowell, Mass.
Poland, W. C., Boston.
Poland, Rev. James W., Goffstown Centre, N. H.
Pollard, Mrs. Elizabeth, Taunton, Mass.
Polhamus, H. A., New York.
Pomeroy, Rev. Samuel, East Hillsdale, N. Y.
Pomeroy, Mrs. Betsey, East Hillsdale, N. Y.
Pomeroy, Harvey S., York, N. Y.
Pomroy, Wm., Middlefield, Mass.
Pond, William, New York.
Pond, Joseph A., Boston.
Porter, Mrs. Welthea M., Pittsfield, Mass.
Porter, Edwin, Lowell, Mass.
Porter, Miss Charlotte, Danvers, Mass.
Post, Mrs. Sarah, New York.
Post, Alanson H., Hinesburg, Vt.
Post, Levi, Pitcher, N. Y.
Post, Joy, Essex, Ct.
Post, John, Saline, Mich.
Post, Prof. John D., Oregon City, Oregon.
Post, Peter K., Somerville, N. J.
Post, Mrs. Susan A., Deep River, Ct.
Post, James T., Jerseyville, Ill.
Potter, James, Bridgeport, Ct.
Potter, Rev. Charles W., Cromwell, Ct.
Potter, Rev. Aaron, Clarkston, Mich.
Powell, Daniel L., Schenectady, N. Y.
Powell, Rev. Thomas, Mt Palatine, Ill.
Powell, Mrs. E., Mt. Palatine, Ill.
Powell, Miss Mary E, Mt. Palatine, Ill.
Powell, Miss Sarah P., Mt. Palatine, Ill.
Powell, William T., Mt. Palatine, Ill.
Powell, Rev. Peter, Beverly, N. J.
Powell, Mrs. Nancy, Powelton, N. C.
Powers, Mrs. Amelia, New London, Ct.
Powless, Mrs. Anna Maria, Hoboken, N. J.
Pratt, Rev. Samuel C., Lowell, Mass.
Pratt, Rev. James H., Bloomfield, N. J.
Pratt, Daniel, Brooklyn.
Pratt, Oliver T., New York.
Pratt, Eli, Johnstown, Ohio.
Pratt, John C., Boston.
Prescott, Abraham, Concord, N. Y.
Preston, Levi, Greenport, N. Y.
Pryor, Rev. John, D. D., Cambridge, Mass.
Probyn, Mrs. Ann.
Prowitt, Henry M., Norwalk, Ct.
Puffer, Abel, Weedsport, N. Y.

MEMBERS FOR LIFE.

Seeley, Rev. Jesse N., Atlanta, Geo.
Seeley, Mrs. Agnes Jane, Atlanta, Geo.
Seeley, Miss Sarah Elizabeth, New York.
Seeley, Miss Ellen M., Elmira, N. Y.
Siegfried, Rev. B. Y., Washington, Ohio.
Selleck, Rev. Lewis, Dover, N. Y.
Shailer, Mrs. Catherine P., Roxbury, Mass.
Shailer, Mrs. Sarah, Deep River, Ct.
Shailer, Mrs. Ann, Deep River, Ct.
Shailer, Mrs. Elizabeth, Brookline, Mass.
Shailer, Hezekiah, Suffield, Ct.
Shailer, Bezaleel, Haddam, Ct.
Shattuck, Levi H., Somerville, N. J.
Sharp, William B., Wilmington, Del.
Sharp, Miss Julia D., New York.
Shaw, Charles, Providence.
Shaw, Miss Harriet N., Providence.
Shaw, Oliver J., Utica, N. Y.
Shaw, Rev. J. Milton, Fort Defiance, N. M.
Shaw, James M., New York.
Shaw, Mrs. Rhoda, New York.
Shaw, Miss Mary A., New York.
Sheardown, Rev. T. S., Hornellsville, N. Y.
Shearman, Francis, New York.
Shed, Charles.
Sheffield, Mrs. Mary, Stamford, Ct.
Sheffield, Thomas S., Brooklyn.
Sheldon, Gaylor, Albany.
Sheldon, Smith, New York.
Sheldon, Frederick A., Troy, N. Y.
Sheldon, L. C., Suffield, Ct.
Shenston, Joseph W., New York.
Simmons, Miss Eliza, Reading, Pa.
Simmons, Mrs. Mary Eliza, Providence.
Simmons, Miss Henrietta A., Providence.
Simmons, Rev. Henry R., Providence.
Simpson, Joseph P., New York.
Sistare, Mrs. Abby, New London, Ct.
Sizer, Amasas Jr., Meriden, Ct.
Skelding, A. Eugene, Greenwich, Ct.
Skinner, E. B., Hertford, N. C.
Skinner, Charles W., Hertford, N. C.
Skinner, Mrs. Anna, Hertford, N. C.
Skinner, H. P., Hudson, N. Y.
Skinner, Mrs. Phebe B., Hudson, N. Y.
Skinner, Rev. H. C., Wabash, Ia.
Slack, Thomas, Brooklyn.
Slade, Zaccheus, Newbern, N. C.
Slater, Mrs. S. J., Providence.
Slater, Rev. Franklin A., Rome, N. Y.
Slater, Mrs. Sophrania E. H., Rome, N. Y.
Slaughter, James M., Baltimore.
Sleeper, Rev. George, Canton, N. J.
Slote, Henry L., New York.
Smalley, George C., New York.
Smalley, Henry, New Brunswick, N. J.
Smart, James, Philadelphia.
Smiley, Mrs. William, Haverhill, Mass.
Smiley, Miss Betsey, Haverhill, Mass.
Smith, Rev. Francis, Providence.
Smith, Mrs. M. G., Providence.
Smith, Charles A., Providence.
Smith, Asa F., New England Village, Mass.
Smith, Mrs. B. S. W., New Eng. Village, Mass.

[redacted]

Smith, Mrs. Harriet A., Bristol, Ct.
Smith, Rev. Eli B., Fairfax, Vt.
Smith, Adam, Brooklyn.
Smith, Rev. N. W., Hydeville, Vt.
Smith, Ebenezer, East Tisbury, Mass.
Smith, Mrs. Sarah A., East Tisbury, Mass.
Smith, Rev. Dexter P., Iowa City, Iowa.
Smith, Gilbert D., New York.
Smith, Daniel, Worcester, Mass.
Smith, Rev. Lewis, Trenton, N. J.
Smith, Jonathan, New York.
Smith, Rev. Rufus, Brookline, Vt.
Smith, Jesse H., New England Village, Mass.
Smith, Mrs. Mary White, Newton, Mass.
Smith, Mrs. Jane, Troy, N. Y.
Smith, Lucius E., Boston, Mass.
Smith, Mrs. Elizabeth, New York.
Smith, Charles E., Fall River, Mass.
Smith, Rev. Levi, West Plattsburgh, N. Y.
Smith, Mrs. Levi, West Plattsburgh, N. Y.
Snelling, Miss. Priscilla, Snelling, Mass.
Sniffin, Mrs. Sarah Ann, New York.
Snowdon, Mrs. Eliza, New York.
Snow, Mrs. Abby S., Rehoboth, Mass.
Snow, Edwin M., Providence.
Souders, Mrs. Catharine B. L., Frazer's Pa.
Sommers, Mrs. Eliza B., New York.
Southerland, Jonas, Burnt Hills, N. Y.
Southwick, Mrs. Cynthia, Grand de Tour, Ill.
Southwick, George, Kingston, N. Y.
Southwood, Rev. William, Ayletts, Va.
Southworth, Mrs. James E., Brooklyn.
Southworth, Jas. Adelbert, Brooklyn
Southworth, John, Penfield, N. Y.
Sowers, Mrs. Mary E., Battletown, Va.
Sowers, Mrs. Elizabeth, Milwood, Va.
Sparks, Rev. Peter, Newark, N. J.
Spaulding, Isaiah, Chelmsford, Mass.
Spaulding, Daniel B., Stoningtonboro', Ct.
Spaulding, Rev. Silas, Clockville, N. Y.
Spaulding, Rev. Amos F., Boston.
Spaulding, Mrs. Carrie E., E. Cambridge, Mass.
Spaulding, D. A., St. Louis, Mo.
Spear, Rev. Prof. P. B., Hamilton, N. Y.
Speer, Abraham, Jeddo, N. Y.
Speir, John, Brooklyn.
Speir, Mrs. Elizabeth, Brooklyn.
Speir, Miss Susan B., Brooklyn.
Spelman, Thomas, Alexandria, O.
Spencer, Robert Little, Plymouth, Va.
Spencer, Elijah, Moodus, Ct.
Spencer, Rev. William H., Spencer, N. Y.
Sperry, Marquis T., Jordan, N. Y.
Sperry, Rev. O., Danville, Iowa.
Spink, Nicholas N., Wickford, R. I.
Spinning, Rev. Oscar F., Northville, N. Y.
Spinning, Mrs. Clara O., Northville, N. Y.
Spinning, Mrs. Mary, New York.
Spivey, Aaron J., Brownsville, Tenn.
Sprague, Rev. Oliver I., Mt. Morris, N. Y.
Sprague, Miss Mary E., Providence.
Spratt, Rev. George, Spread Eagle, Pa.
Squires, Rev. James, East Troy, Wis.
Stahel, Caspar, Zurich, Switzerland.
Stainburn, Miss Mary, New York.
Staples, John, Stratfield, Ct.
Stark, Rev. J. F., Cincinnatus, N. Y.
Stark, Mrs. Delight, Fort Covington, N. Y.
Starkweather, Rev. John W., East Greene, N.Y.
Stead, Thomas, Plainfield, N. J.
Steadman, Rev. N. V., Evansville, Ia.
Steadman, Mrs. Laura J., Evansville, Ia.
Steane, Mrs. Catharine E., Williamsburg, N. Y.
Stearns, Miss Catharine, Brookline, Mass.
Stearns, Rev. Myron N., Oregon Ter.
Stearns, Mrs. Dorcas R., Oregon Ter.
Stearns, Rev. O. O., Racine, Wis.
Stearns, John E., Chelmsford, Mass.
Stearns, Mrs. Hannah Jane, Newark N. J.
Stedman, Daniel M. C., Wakefield, R. I.
Steele, Mrs. Mehitable, Haverhill, Mass.
Stelle, Rev. Bergen, Cherryville, N. J.
Stelle, Mrs. Hannah B., Cherryville, N. J.
Stelle, Rev. Lewis F., Old Bridge, N. J.
Stelle, Isaac, New Brunswick, N. J.
Stelle, Benjamin, Jerseyville, Ill.
Stelle, Lewis R., Paterson, N. J.
Stelle, Mrs. Adnee, Paterson, N. J.
Stelle, Augustus, New Brunswick, N. J.
Stelle, John, Brooklyn, N. Y.
Steere, Enoch, Providence.
Steelman, Rev. Henry, Norway, N. Y.
Stevens, Mrs. Mariette, Deep River, Ct.
Stevens, Samson, Westford, Mass.
Stevens, Miss Phebe Almy, Providence.
Stevens, Seriah, Boston.
Stevens, B. H., Essex, Ct.
Stevens, Thomas, Saratoga Springs, N. Y.
Stewart, Rev. Henry G., Seekonk, Mass.
Stickney, Rev. James M., Toulon, Ill.
Stickney, Mrs. J. M., Toulon, Ill.
Stickney, Samuel, Watertown, Mass.
Stillman, O. M., Westerly, R. I.
Stillman, Mrs. F. G., Westerly, R. I.
Stillwell, Albert G., Providence.
Stillwell, Mrs. Lydia J., Providence.
Stillwell, Charles M., Providence.
Stillwell, Frank E., Providence.
Stimson, Rev. H. C., Clifton, N. Y.
Stimson, Rev. S. M., Binghamton, N. Y.
Stimson, Mrs. Louisa, Binghamton, N. Y.
St. John, Edgar, Binghamton, N. Y.
Stockbridge, Mrs. Maria, Waltham, Mass.
Stockbridge, Mrs. J. C., Boston.
Stocks, Thomas, Greensboro, Ga.
Stockwell, Amos W., Chickopee, Mass.
Stockwell, J. Q. A., Sennett, N. Y.
Stokes, Mrs. Caroline, New York.
Stites, Rev. Thomas S., Dennis Creek, N. J.
Stone, Rev. Marsena, Cincinnati.
Stone, Mrs. Gertrude E. M., New York.
Stone, Mrs. Damaris, Swanzey, N. H.
Stone, Eben, Newton, Mass.
Stone, Prof. Jas. A. B., D.D., Kalamazoo, Mich.
Stone, Rev. O. B., Nevada, Cal.
Storer, Mrs. Olive H., Hudson, N. H.
Storey, Simeon N., Worcester, Mass.
Storey, James Arnot, Williamsburg, N. Y.
Story, William F., Boston.
Storms, Andrew, New York.
Storms, Anthony D., New York.
Stout, Rev. D. B., Middletown, N. J.

MEMBERS FOR LIFE.

Stout, Mrs. L. M., Louisa C. H., Va.
Stout, Richard, New York
Stout, George H., New Brunswick, N. J.
Stout, Augustus T., New Brunswick, N. J.
Stow, Henry, New Haven, Ct.
Stow, Mrs. Baron, Boston
Stowell, Rev. A. H., Providence, R. I.
Stowell, Mrs. A. H., Providence, R. I.
Stratton, Samuel T., Philadelphia
Street, Miss Mary Ann, New York.
Strickland, James L., New London, Ct.
Strong, Myron, Rochester, N. Y.
Stewart, Benjamin N., Lowell, Mass.
Story, Harriet M., Norwich, Ct.
Story, Eunice M., Worcester, Mass.
Story, Clara, Worcester, Mass.
Story, Eunice H., Worcester, Mass.
Sturges, Rev. William, Marlborough, N. Y.
Sulley, James, Minneapolis, Min.
Sulley, Mrs. Ann, Minneapolis, Min.
Summers, Mrs. Aaron, Bridgeport, Ct.
Sumner, George O., New Haven, Ct.
Sunderlin, Lu, Tyrone, N. Y.
Sunderlin, Rev. Alonzo W., Avoca, N. Y.
Sunderlin, Horace, Sennett, N. Y.
Sunderlin, Mrs. Margaret, Sennett, N. Y.
Sunderlin, Daniel W., Wayne, N. Y.
Sutton, George, New York
Sutton, Mrs. Elizabeth, Britton's X Roads, N. C.
Sutton, Mrs. Mary Ann, New York.
Swaim, Hon. Thomas, Pemberton, N. J.
[redacted]
Tapley, Joseph, Lowell, Mass.
Tapley, Joseph W., Lowell, Mass.
Tattersall, Wm. K., New York.
Taylor, William H., New York.
Taylor, John G., Holmdel, N. J.
Taylor, Mrs. Ann R., Holmdel, N. J.
Taylor, Mrs. Laura, New York.
Taylor, Miss Emily, New York.
Taylor, Miss Ann Jane, New York.
Taylor, Miss Louisa, New York.
Taylor, Mrs. Sarah A., New York.
Taylor, Mrs. E. E. L., Brooklyn.
Taylor, Miss Harriet Hill, Troy, N. Y.
Taylor, Mrs. Maria B., Lawtonville, S. C.
Taylor, Mrs. Dimis, York, N. Y.
Taylor, Rev. Thomas R., Allegany city, Pa.
Taylor, Rev. Alfred H., Mansfield Centre, Ct.
Taylor, Rev. Thomas, Jacksonville Ill.
Taylor, Rev. David, Terre Haute, Ia.
Taylor, Samuel W., E. Cambridge, Mass.
Taylor, Daniel Webster, New York.
Taylor, Rev. O. D., Perrington, N. Y.
Taylor, Henry C., Granville, Ohio.
Taylor, Mrs. Adelia P., Albion, Mich.
Taylor, Elvin, Albany, N. Y.
Taylor, John, East Cambridge, Mass.
Taylor, John, New York.
Teasdale, Rev. John, St. Louis, Mo.
Tefft, Willard, Union Village, N. Y.
Tefft, Thomas A., Providence.
Temple, James H., Chillicothe, Ill.
[redacted]

Thurber, Charles, Worcester, Mass.
Ticknor, William D., Boston.
Tiebout, Adam T., Brooklyn.
Tiebout, Mrs. Jane, Brooklyn.
Tilden, Rev. Chester, North Lyme, Ct.
Tilley, Mrs. Elizabeth S., New York.
Tillinghast, Jefferson, Norway, N. Y.
Tillinghast, Charles E., Providence.
Tillinghast, Rev. J. A., North Kingston, R. I.
Tilson, Rev. Jonathan, Hingham, Mass.
Tilton, Rev. Charles.
Tilton, Rev. Josiah H., Lynn, Mass.
Timberman, Rev. Jacob, Stockton, N. J.
Tindall, Samuel L., Wilmington, Del.
Tingley, Miss Nancy B., Valley Falls, R. I.
Tinkham, Rev. D. Centre White Creek, N. Y.
Titchener, Henry Binghamton, N. Y.
Tirrill, Jesse, Boston, Mass.
Titus, F. J., Middletown, Ohio.
Titus, Rev. S. W. Gorham, N. Y.
Titus, Mrs. Annie C., Providence.
Tobey, Rev. Zalmon, Pawtuxet, R. I.
Todd, Rev. William, Stevensville, Va.
Todd, Drake P., New York.
Todd, Mrs. Wm. W., New York.
Todd, Mrs. Angeline M., New York.
Todd, William J., New York.
Todd, Thomas W. New York.
Tolan, Rev. Wm. B. Rahway, N. J.
Tolman, Rev. John N., Decatur, Ill.
Tolman, Thomas, Philadelphia.
Tolman, Mrs. Mary, Philadelphia.
Tolman, Miss Martha, Boston.
Tolman, Mrs. Elizabeth A. Philadelphia.
Topliff, Rev. C. H. Charlestown, Mass.
Torbet, Rev. Andrew M., St. Paul, Min. Ter.
Torian, Elijah, Halifax C. H., Va.
Tourtellot, Abraham, Nashua, N. H.
Tousley, Charles, New York.
Townsend, S. P., New York.
Townsend, Miss Naomi, New York.
Townsend, Rev. G. N., Reading Mass.
Townsend, Mrs. Louisa L., Brooklyn.
Townsend, Rev. B. C., Mecklenburg, N. Y.
Townsend, Thomas, Lynn, Mass.
Townsend, John A. Providence.
Tracy, Lucius H., New London, Ct.
Tracy, Rev. Oren, Concord, N. H.
Tracy, Mrs. Marcia B., Concord, N. H.
Tracy, Miss Susan M., Concord, N. H.
Train, Mrs. A. S., Haverhill, Mass.
Travis, Simeon S., New York.
Travis Luther, Southbridge, Mass.
Trevor, John B., Philadelphia.
Tripp, Mrs. Susan, New Bedford, Ms.
Tripp, Erwin H., New York.
Tripp, Mrs. Caroline S. H. New York.
Tripp, Miss Sarah, New York.
Trout, Wm., Charleston, S. C.
Trow, Rev. Augustus H., Montezuma, N. Y.
Trowbridge, Wm., Sheboygan Falls, Wis.
True, Reuben, Plainfield, N. H.
True, Osgood, Plainfield, N. H.
True, Mrs. Betsey M., Plainfield, N. H.
True, Mrs. Hannah, Meriden, N. H.
Truesdell, Mrs. Margerie, Hillsdale, N. Y.
Truman, Stephen S., Owego, N. Y.
Truman, Mrs. Betsey S., Owego, N. Y.
Truman, Mrs. Eleanor M., Owego, N. Y.
Trueman, Edward D., Owego, N. Y.
Tubbs, Benjamin H. W., Dedham, Mass.
Tucker, Harwood B., Christianville, Va.
Tucker, Richard G., Stony Creek, Va.
Tucker, Rev. Silas, Napierville, Ill.
Tucker, Mrs. F. G. Stony Creek, Va.
Tucker, Mrs. Elisha, Chicago, Ill.
Tucker, James N. G., Chicago, Ill.
Tucker, Frederick D., Williamsburg, N. Y.
Tucker, Elisha, Middleborough, Mass.
Tucker, Mrs. Sally B.
Tucker, Rev. Cyrus T., North Marshfield, Mass.
Tucker, Ebenezer, Cambridge, Mass.
Tucker, Mrs. I. B., Millbury Mass.
Tucker, Ebenezer, Cambridge Mass.
Tukesbury, Mrs. Mary Salisbury, Mass.
Turley, Capt. E., Philadelphia.
Turnbull, Rev. Robert, D.D., Hartford, Ct.
Turner, Mrs. Mary A. New London, Ct.
Turner, Gabriel S., Newark, N. J.
Turney, Rev. Edmund, Cincinnati.
Turney, Mrs. Caroline, Cincinnati.
Turney, J. P., Norwalk Ct.
Turpin, Rev. John O., Aylett's, Va.
Turton, Rev. Wm. H., Farmington, Iowa.
Tustin, Rev. Josiah P., Charleston, S. C.
Tustin, John D., Camden, N. J.
Tuthill, Joseph, Brooklyn.
Tuttle, Aaron, Littleton, Mass.
Tuttle, Alson, Littleton, Mass.
Tuxbury, Isaac, Salisbury Mills, Mass.
Twiss, Ira, Westville, Ct.
Twiss, Rev Daniel F., Spotswood, N. J.
Tyler, Roswell B., Middlesex, N. Y.
Tyler, Mrs. Lucy, Deep River, Ct.
Tyler, Rev. Payson, Barre, Mass.
Ulyat, Rev. Wm. C., Norwalk, Ct.
Underhill, Rev. Charles H., Peekskill, N. Y.
Underhill, P. S., Brooklyn.
Underhill, Mrs. Catharine M., Brooklyn.
Upham, E. W., East Concord, N. H.
Van Antwerp, Wm. M. Albany N. Y.
Van Arsdale, Dr. Henry New York.
Van Deboe, Adam, Claverack, N. Y.
Van De Werken, E. New York.
Van Du Werken, Mrs. Janet, New York.
Van Derlip, George M., New York.
Van Derlip, Mrs. Grace, New York.
Van Dusen, Wm., Albion, N. Y.
Vanderveer, Mrs. Ann, Moorestown, N. J.
Vail, J. E. Brooklyn.
Valentine, Rev. Andrew M., W. Henrietta, N. Y.
Valentine, Elijah F., Cambridge, Mass.
Van Horn, Hon. James, Newfane, N. Y.
Vanness, Christian, New York.
Vanest, Abraham, Hightstown, N. J.
Van Marter John, Brooklyn.
Van Marter, Mrs. Mary E., Brooklyn.
Van Osdel, John M., Chicago, Ill.
Van, Samuel A., New Haven, Ct.
Vansant, T. J., Williamsburgh, N. Y.
Van Valkenburgh, John, Williamsburgh, N. Y.
Van Wagenen, W., Frederick, New York.
Vassar, Matthew, Poughkeepsie, N. Y.

MEMBERS FOR LIFE.

Vassar, Mrs. Matthew, Poughkeepsie, N. Y.
Veasey, Benjamin, Brentwood, N. H.
Vernon, Samuel, Brooklyn.
Vernon, Thomas, Brooklyn.
Verstile, Mrs. Rebecca E., Savannah, Ga.
Vinal, Wm. D., [illegible], Mass.
Vinton, Rev. Justus H., Maulmain, Burmah.
Vinton, Mrs. Calista H., Maulmain, Burmah.
Vinton, Miss Lydia, Willington, Ct.
Volk, Henry, New York.
Volk, Mrs. E. Margaretta, New York.
Vrooman, Rev. Joseph B., Fayetteville, N. Y.
Wade, Rev. Jonathan, D. D., Tavoy, Burmah.
Wade, Mrs. Deborah B. L., Tavoy, Burmah.
Wade, Joseph, Gouverneur, N. Y.
Wade, Rev. J. M., [illegible], N. Y.
Ware, Mrs. Mercy, Brookfield, Mass.
Wakefield, Charles A., Elizabethtown, N. Y.
Wakefield, Rev. Leander, Feltonville, Mass.
Wakeman, Rev. Levi H., West Woodstock, Ct.
Walden, Rev. J. H., Dunkirk, N. Y.
Waldo, Herman, Fleming, N. Y.
Waldron, Miss Maria, New York.
Walker, Rev. Joseph, Marcus Hook, Pa.
Walker, Mrs. Elizabeth, Marcus Hook, Pa.
Walker, Miss Hannah, Marcus Hook, Pa.
Walker, Rev. G. C., Somerset, N. Y.
Walker, Mrs. Eliza H., Somerset, N. Y.
Walker, Mrs. Mary, Brookneal, Va.
Walker, John B., Madison, Ga.
Walker, Andrew, New York.
Warren, Rev. Edwin R., East Greenwich, R. I.
Warren, Benjamin L., Williamsburgh, N. Y.
Warren, Moses, Cambridge, Mass.
Warren, Mrs. Grace, Cambridge, Mass.
Warren, Rev. H. S. P., Madrid, N. Y.
Warren, Horace, Norwich, Ct.
Warren, Rev. John, Easton, Ct.
Warriner, Rev. Norman, Harding, Ill.
Warriner, Rev. R. L., West Burlington, N. Y.
Washburn, Rev. R. A., Union Village, N. Y.
Washington, Mrs. Elizabeth, Newbern, N. C.
Wasson, Mrs. Clarissa, Albany.
Waters, Mrs. Elizabeth A., Brookline, Mass.
Watters, Miss Sarah A., Philadelphia.
Watts, Mrs. Emma, New York.
Watts, Charles Henry, New York.
Watts, John, Elmira, New York.
Wattson, Mrs. Mary B., Philadelphia.
Wattson, Miss Elizabeth, Philadelphia.
Wattson, Rev. W. H., West Acton, Mass.
Watson, George, New York.
Watson, James, Brooklyn.
Watson, W. W., Springfield, Ill.
Watkins, Henry M., New York.
Watkinson, Rev. Wm. E., Manyunk, Pa.
Watkinson, Rev. Mark P., Schuylkill Falls, Pa.
Waterman, Nathan, Jr., Providence.
Way, Rev. Samuel P., Poolville, N. Y.
Waterbury, Miss Martha, Williamsburgh, N. Y.
Waterbury, Francis W., North Adams, Mass.
Wayland, Mrs. H. S. H., Providence.

Weston, Rev. Henry G., Peoria, Ill.
Weston, Mrs. Henry G., Peoria, Ill.
Weston, Mrs. Hetty, Lynn, Mass.
Weston, Franklin L., Johnson's Creek, N. Y.
Wescott, Rev. Isaac, New York.
Wescott, Jehiel, Bridgeton, N. J.
Wescott, Jehiel, Jr., Bridgeton, N. J.
Wescott, Josiah S., Bridgeton, N. J.
Wescott, Rev. Henry, Blackwoodtown, N. J.
Westcott, John, Bridgeton, N. J.
Westervelt, John, Williamsburgh, N. Y.
Westover, Rev. John T., Kenosha, Wis.
Wetherbee, Ephraim, Broadalbin, N. Y.
Wetherbee, Miss Ruby, Broadalbin, N. Y.
Wetharn, George M., Lowell, Mass.
Wetteran, Mrs. Frances, New York.
Whedon, G. H., Homer, N. Y.
Wheat, Mrs. Priscilla P., Philadelphia.
Wheaton, Reuben, Wilmington, Del.
Wheaton, Mrs. Elizabeth M., Columbus, O.
Wheelock, Mrs. E. M., Elbridge, N. Y.
Wheelock, S. B., Greenwich, N. Y.
Wheeler, Mrs. Elizabeth H., Sacramento, Cal.
Wheeler, Miss Melvina P., Sacramento, Cal.
Wheeler, Rev. Benjamin, Plaistow, N. H.
Wheeler, Nelson, Providence.
Wheeler, Lucius, New York.
Wheeler, Rev. S. S., Placerville, Cal.
Wheeler, Mrs. Mary R., Placerville, Cal.
Wheeler, Rev. Benjamin, Caldwell, N. J.
Wheeler, Russell, Utica, N. Y.
Wheeler, Mrs. Ann, New York.
Wheeler, Mrs. Mary E., North Randolph, Mass.
Wheeler, Rev. R., Grafton, Vt.
Whilden, Mrs. Sarah, Calais, Me.
Whilden, Rev. B. W., Camden, S. C.
Whipple, Harvey, Malone, N. Y.
Whitaker, Alanson, Granville, Ill.
Whitaker, Wilso N., Philadelphia.
Whitcomb, Peter, Littleton, Mass.
White, Rev. Samuel, North Shore, N. Y.
White, Mrs. E., North Shore, N. Y.
White, Mrs. Martha D., Marcus Hook, Pa.
White, Miss Lydia, Haverhill, Mass.
White, Thomas, Brooklyn.
White, Samuel S., Whiteville, N. Y.
White, Harvey, Mt. Holly, Vt.
White, Thomas P., Bridgeport, Ct.
White, Mrs. Thomas P. Bridgeport, Ct.
White, Joseph, Winchendon, Mass.
White, Ross L., Taunton, Mass.
White, Ebenezer, Newton, Mass.
White, Ebenezer B., Williamsburgh, N. Y.
White, Mrs. Mary, New York.
White, Samuel, Bordentown, N. J.
White, Mrs. Sylvanus, Brooklyn.
White, Samuel, Littleton, Mass.
White, Mrs. Mary, New York.
White, Miss Emily J., Taunton, Mass.
White, Almeth, Rahway, N. J.
Whitehead, Samuel, Chester, N. J.
Whitehead, Mrs. Emiline V. New York.
Whitehead, Artemas K., New York.
Whitehead, John W. New York.
Whitehead, Linus P., New York.
Whittemore, Joseph, New York.

Whitford, H. G., Willington, Ct.
Whiting, Rufus W., Boston.
Whitman, Charles S., Belvidere, Ill.
Whitman, Hiram, Belvidere, Ill.
Whitman, Mrs. Matilda, Belvidere, Ill.
Whitman, Spooner, Belvidere, Ill.
Whitman, Alva, Mich.
Whitman, John C., Sennett, N. Y.
Whitney, Miss Harriet, New York.
Whitney, Mrs. Betsey, Worcester, Mass.
Whitney, Dennet, Bridgeport, Ct.
Whitney, Raymond, North Fairfield, O.
Whitney, Mrs. E. S. Brooklyn.
Whitney, Eben, Newtown, N. Y.
Whittier, Leonard, Haverhill, Mass.
Whittier, Mrs. Leonard, Haverhill, Mass.
Whittier, Miss Abby, Haverhill, Mass.
Whittier, Hannah, Haverhill, Mass.
Whittier, Mrs. Rebecca, Haverhill, Mass.
Whittier, Miss Sarah P. Haverhill, Mass.
Wiburg, Rev. Andreas, Philadelphia.
Wight, Leonard R., Wales, Mass.
Wightman, Rev. J. G., Groton, Ct.
Wightman, Asa, Waterford, Ct.
Wightman, Stillman K., New York.
Wiggins, Rev. J. W. Farmerville, N. Y.
Wilbur, Rev. H. R., Mt. Pleasant, Iowa.
Wilbur, Mrs. Sally, East Avon, N. Y.
Wilbur, Curtis, Troy, N. Y.
Wilbur, Rev. O., Lowville, N. Y.
Wilcox, Rev. J. F., Trenton, N. J.
Wilcox, Mrs. Louisa S. Trenton, N. J.
Wilcox, Abraham, Shelburne Falls, Mass.
Wilcox, Allen, Wing's Station, N. Y.
Wilde, Rev. Z. P., West Boylston, Mass.
Wilder, John N. Albany.
Wilder, Mrs. Delia A., Albany.
Wilder, Rev. Sydney, North Norwich, N. Y.
Wilder, Rev. William, Chester, Pa.
Wildman, John, Pitcher, N. Y.
Wildman, Mrs. Roxey S. Lebanon, Ct.
Wildman, Daniel, Lebanon, C.
Wildman, Mrs. Sally, Danbury, Ct.
Wilkins, Rev. Andrew, Sennett, N. Y.
Wilkins, Mrs. Laura J. Sennett, N. Y.
Wilkinson, Rev. Wm. Drummondville, C. W.
Willard, Rev. George A., Warwick Neck, R. I.
Willard, Lucius A., Providence.
Willard, Mrs. Polly, Pawlet, Vt.
Willard, William B., Still River, Mass.
Willard, Mrs. Nancy, Jonesborough, Ill.
Willard, Rev. C. M., Still River, Mass.
Willard, Hon. Levi, Keene, N. H.
Willett, Miss Sarah, New York.
Willett, Mrs. Charles, Quinebaug, Ct.
Williams, Robert, Maquoketa, Iowa.
Williams, Mrs. Elizabeth S., Fayetteville, N. C.
Williams, Mrs. Charity S., Fayetteville, N. C.
Williams, Mrs. Mary M. Fayetteville, N. C.
Williams, Polly M., Rockport, Ohio.
Williams, Francis B., New York.
Williams, Rev. David S., Cumberland, N. C.
Williams, Rev. Wm. B. Williamsville, N. Y.
Williams, Mrs. Eunice, Deep River, Ct.
Williams, Rev. John, Princeton, N. Y.
Williams, Rev. C. C., Plainfield, N. J.

Williams, Mrs. M[illegible], [illegible], N. J.
Williams, Rev. Lester, West Townsend, Mass.
Williams, Rev. B. S., Plymouth, N. Y.
Williams, Mrs. William R., New York.
Williams, W. S., Hartford, Ct.
Williams, Rev. N. M., Somerville, Mass.
Willingham, Thomas, Lawtonville, S. C.
Willington, Miss Catherine, Watertown, Mass.
Willis, Rev. S. [illegible], Saugerties, N. Y.
Wilson, Mrs. Catharine, New York.
Wilson, Miss Sarah E., New York.
Wilson, Mrs. Frances N., Catskill, N. Y.
Wilson, Isaac D., Society Hill, S. C.
Wilson, Clement A., Philadelphia.
Wilson, Rev. Charles E., [illegible], N. J.
Wilson, Mrs. Theresa, Marlton, N. J.
Wilson, Rev. Adam, D. D., [illegible], Maine.
Wilson, Rev. W. V., Keyport, N. J.
Wilson, Jeremiah V. F., Hoboken, N. J.
Wilson, Mrs. Grace, Stonington, [illegible], Ct.
Wilson, George W., [illegible], Mass.
Wilson, Mrs. Martha, Riceville, N. J.
Wilson, Robert, New York.
[illegible], Mary, Haverhill, Mass.
[illegible], Dexter B., [illegible], Mass.
Winans, Elnathan, [illegible], N. Y.
Winans, Mrs. Mary, [illegible], N. Y.
Winans, Theodore, Plainfield, N. J.
Winchell, Miss Ann, New York.
Windust, Edward, New York.

Wood, Ambrose, Albion, N. Y.
Woods, Gardner, Jersey, Ohio.
Woodbridge, William A., New York.
Woodbury, William W., Suffield, Ct.
Woodbury, Rev. John, Templeton, Mass.
Woodbury, Miss Frances, Danvers, Mass.
Woodbury, Eliza A., Lynn, Mass.
Woodruff, Mrs. Innocent, Albany.
Woodruff, David, Bridgeton, N. J.
Woodward, Rev. Jonas, Parma, N. Y.
Woodward, Mrs. Eliza, Parma, N. Y.
Woodward, Mrs. Mary D., Middlesex, Va.
Woodward, Sylvester, Lowell, Mass.
Woodward, Darwin W., Franklindale, N. Y.
Woolsey, Rev. James J., Norwalk, Ct.
Woolston, Mrs. Keziah, Vincentown, N. J.
Wooster, Mrs. Aurelia R., Deep River, Ct.
Worth, Rev. Edmund, Fisherville, N. H.
Worthington, S., Springfield, Mass.
Wright, Rev. David, Hartford, Ct.
Wright, Mrs. Abigail, Hartford, Ct.
Wright, William J., Hargrove's, Va.
Wright, Theodore, New York.
Wright, Asahel B., Lowell, Mass.
Wright, Harvey, Three Rivers, Mass.
Wright, Mrs. Julia A., Westport, N. Y.
Wright, Rev. Ansell T., Dennisville, N. J.
Wright, Rev. Lyman, Norwich, N. Y.
Wright, R. A., Rochester, N. Y.
Wyckoff, Rev. Cornelius P., Weedsport, N. Y.

[redacted]

LIST OF DECEASED

DIRECTORS AND MEMBERS FOR LIFE.

1833-4.

DIRECTOR.

Cobb, Nathaniel R., Boston, Mass.

MEMBERS.

Barrett, Rev. Thomas, Webster, Mass.
Chase, Rev. John, Brookfield, Mass.

1834-5.

MEMBER.

Lazell, Rev. J. E., Harvard, Mass.

1835-6.

DIRECTORS.

Foster, Rev. E., Amesbury, Mass.
Freeman, Rev. E. W., Lowell, Mass.
Jacobs, Rev. Bela, Cambridge, Mass.

MEMBER.

Martin, Rev. A. R., Staten Island, N. Y.

1836-7.

DIRECTOR.

Trask, Rev. Wm. G., Taunton, Mass.

1837-8.

DIRECTOR.

Davis, Rev. Gustavus F., Hartford, Ct.

MEMBERS.

Blain, Miss Mary E., Syracuse, N. Y.
Holroyd, Rev. John, Danvers, Mass.
Kitts, Rev. T. J., Philadelphia.
Ludlow, Rev. Peter, New York.
Starkweather, Oliver, Pawtucket, R. I.

1838-9.

DIRECTORS.

Crawford, Rev. Luther, Brooklyn, N. Y.
Knowles, Rev. James D., Newton, Mass.

MEMBERS.

Banner, Rev. Job B., Sutton, Mass.
Smalley, Henry, Cohansey, N. J.
Vaughn, Rev. Ashley, Natchez, Miss.

1839-40.

DIRECTOR.

Bolles, Rev. Matthew, D.D., Boston.

MEMBERS.

Blain, Mrs. Lucy, Syracuse, N. Y.
Hubbell, Rev. Elisha D., Clifton Park, N. Y.
Sheppard, Rev. Joseph, Mount Holly, N J.

1840-1.

DIRECTORS.

Chesman, Rev. Daniel, Lynn, Mass.
Hammond, Rev. O. T., Florida.
Shute, Rev. Caleb B., Boston.

MEMBERS.

Chaplain, Rev. J., Hamilton, N. Y.
Dodge, Rev. O. A., Lexington, Mass.
Hunting, Mrs. Dorcas, Corinth, Me.
McAllister, Charles, Fayetteville, N. C.
Nourse, Rev. Peter, Ellsworth, Me.
Stearns, Rev. Silas, Bath, Me.
Williams, Elizabeth, Society Hill, S. C.
Williams, A., Elizabeth City, N. C.

1841-2.

DIRECTOR.

Brown, Nicholas, Providence, R. I.

MEMBERS.

Colgate, John, New York.
Eaton, Martin, Petersburg, Va.
Hill, Frederick M., New York.
Leonard, Rev. Zenas L., Sturbridge, Mass.
Lipscomb, Mrs. Martha, Louisa C. H., Va.
Mercer, Rev. Jesse, Washington, Ga.
Miles, Joseph, Milesburgh, Pa.

1842-3.

MEMBERS.

Colgate, George, New York.
Elmer, E., Bridgeton, N. J.
Gear, Rev. Hiram, Marietta, Ohio.
Towell, Mrs. E. E., Sandy Bottom, Va.
Vanderpool, Hon. James, Newark, N. J.

1843-4.

DIRECTORS.

Cooper, Thomas, Eatonton, Geo.
Linsley, Rev. James H., Stratford, Ct.
Middleton, Rev. John, Geneva, N. Y.

MEMBERS.

Pickens, Mrs. Margaret Eliza, Edgefield, S. C.
Rankin, Henry, Reading, Pa.
Wasson, J. G., Albany, N. Y.

1844-5.

DIRECTORS.

Armstrong, Rev. John, Columbus, Miss.
Coolidge, James D., Madison, N. Y.

Going, Rev. Jonathan, D.D., Granville, Ohio.
Miller, Rev. Wm. George, Essex, Ct.

MEMBERS.

Adams, Mrs. Mary, New York.
Belden, Charles D., New York.
Birdsall, Rev. John O., Perrysburg, Ohio.
Carney, Richard, Portsmouth, Va.
McIntosh, Mrs. Mary, Philadelphia.

1845-6.

MEMBERS.

Cauldwell, Mrs. Maria, New York.
Hall, Rev. Wilson, Beaufort, S. C.
Jones, Mrs. J. Leavitt, Bankok, Siam.
Lathrop, Rev. Lebbeus, Samptown, N. J.
Marshall, Joseph H., Nashville, Tenn.
Mitchell, Rev. John, Hoosick, N. Y.
Randall, Mrs. Mary E., Woburn, Mass.
Reynolds, Joseph, Norwich, Ct.

1846-7.

DIRECTORS.

Bacheller, Mrs. Mary, Lynn, Mass.
Devan, Mrs. Lydia, Canton, China.
Everts, Rev. Jeremiah B., Washington, N. Y.

MEMBERS.

Cooper, Mrs. Eliza A., New York.
Lee, Mrs. Olive, North Bristol, N. Y.
Rose, Richard, Parham's Store, Va.
Thurston, Rev. Peter, New York.

[redacted]

1849-50.

DIRECTORS.

Allen, Rev. Ira M., New York.
Bradford, Rev. Z., Providence, R. I.
Estes, Rev. Elliot, Lower Three Runs, S. C.
Milbank, Charles W., New York.
Peck, Rev. John, New Woodstock, N. Y.
Train, Rev. Charles, Framingham, Mass.
Wilson, James, New York.

MEMBERS.

Baillie, Jonathan, Parham's Store, Va.
Barker, Rev. Luke, M.D., New York.
Brockway, O., Broadalbin, N. Y.
Brown, William, Parham's Store, Va.
Cate, Rev. George W., Barre, Mass.
Corning, Mrs. Nancy, Brooklyn, N. Y.
Cox, Charles, Rahway, N. J.
Crawford, Rev. D. B., Antioch, Miss.
Forrester, James M., New York.
Gale, Mrs. Phebe, East Bennington, Vt.
Harris, Rev. William, Nassau, N. Y.
Lewis, Rev. D. D., New Brunswick, N. J.
Payne, Mrs. Betsey, Hamilton, N. Y.
Rogers, Rev. John, Paterson, N. J.
Roy, Rev. Wm. A., Charlotteville, Va.
Winchell, Rev. Reuben, Lockport, N. Y.

1850-1.

DIRECTORS.

[redacted]

LIST OF DECEASED DIRECTORS AND MEMBERS FOR LIFE.

MEMBERS.

Anderson, J S., Stonington, Ct.
Bolles, Rev. D. C., Southbridge, Mass.
Chase, Amos, Haverhill, Mass.
De Graffenried, Mrs. S. Crosbyville, S. C.
Farnsworth, Rev. B. F Nashville, Tenn.
Gibbs, Mrs. Betsey H., Sullivan, N. H.
Goodall, A., Shomersworth, N. H.
Hall, Rev. Daniel, New York.
Jones, Mrs. Susan, Newbern, N. C.
Lathrop, Mrs. Jane E., New York.
Manning, Rev. Benjamin, Brookfield, Mass.
Martin, Mrs. R. W. New York.
Remington, Mrs. Eliza Ann, New York.
Rider, Miss Olive P., Suffield, Ct.
Shuck, Mrs. Eliza G.. Shanghai, China.
Stone, Mrs. Sarah A., New York.
Tucker, Mrs. Levi, Boston, Mass.
Whitman, Rev. S. S., Madison, Wis.

1852-3.

DIRECTORS.

Brown, Rev. O. B., Washington, D. C.
Crozer, Miss Sallie K. Chester, Pa.
Miller, Pardon, Providence.
Rhees, Rev. Morgan J., D.D., Williamsburg, N.Y.

MEMBERS.

Adams, Mrs. Cornelia C Cleveland, Ohio.
Ashley, Mrs. Hannah, Poultney, Vt.
Bellamy, Mrs. Eliza, Arcadia, N. Y.
Boynton, Mrs. Ruth, North Springfield, Vt.
Cosner, Rev. Henry, Lyndon, Ill.
Furst, Rev. Ephraim, Halselville, S. C.
Goodliff, James, New York.
Haskell, Rev. Daniel, Hamilton N. Y.
Haynes, Rev. Arus, M. D., New York.
Jones, Rev. John, Belleville, Ia.
Hughes, Mrs. Ann C., New York.
Maginnis, Rev. John, D.D., Rochester, N. Y.
Miner, Mrs. Mary Jane, New York.
Owen, Rev. E. D., Madison, Ia.
Shipley, Simon G., Boston.
Symonds, Rev. Thomas M.. Green Bay, Wis.
Turner, Mrs. Grace, New London, Ct.
Walton, Rev. L., Chestnut Hill, Pa.
Weeks, Miss Ann, New York.
Wise, Miss Harriet W., New Russia, N. Y.
Walcott, Epaphroditus, Rochester, N. Y.
Woodruff, Rev. Seth, New Albany, Ia.

1853-4.

DIRECTORS.

Brayton, Philip F., Providence.
Sharp, Rev Daniel, D.D., Boston.
Tucker, Rev. Levi D.D , Boston.
Tucker, Rev. Elisha, D.D., Chicago, Ill.
Whiting, Miss Martha, Charlestown, Mass.
Washington, Col. J. M., Portsmouth, N. H.

MEMBERS.

Bleecker, Garrett N., New York.
Brabrook, Rev. B. F.. Davenport, Iowa.
Burr James T., Columbus, Ohio.
Bliss, Erastus L.. North Adams, Mass.
Ball, Rev Eli, Richmond, Va.
Biddle, Rev. Wm. P., Newbern, N. C.
Coggeshall, John, Jr.. New Bedford, Mass.
Day, John, New York.
Fay, Rev. Eliphaz, Poughkeepsie, N. Y.
Griffith Mrs. Thomas S., Milwaukee, Wis.
Gould, Rev. J. B., East Thompson, Ct.
Haviland, William C , New York.
Hurlburt, Rev. Elias, Essex, N. Y
Humphrey, Hon. Friend, Albany N. Y
Moore, Mrs. Alvenah B. Marshall, Mich.
Murray, Thomas S., New Hope, Pa.
Newton, Prof. Calvin, Worcester, Mass.
Nesbit, Mrs. Mary C. S., Burmah.
Palmer, Rev. William, Norwich, Ct.
Pegg, Roger, New York.
Paddock, Mrs. Martha, Middletown, Ct.
Rue, Mrs. Emily, Scotch Plains, N. J.
Shotwell, Rev. S. R., Whitesboro', N. Y.
Sheppard, Joseph, Bridgeton, N J.
Tryon, Elijah, West Haven, Vt.
Ulyat, William, New York.
Whitney Mrs. Emeline, Norwalk, Ct.

1854-5.

DIRECTORS.

Cone, Mrs. Sallie W., New York.
Ellis, Rev. R. F., Alton, Ill.
Kimball, Rev. C. O., Charleston, Vt.
Whiting, Rev. Niles, Norwich, Ct.

MEMBERS.

Abbott, Rev. E. L., Arracan, Asia.
Angier, Rev. Aaron, Lamoille, Ill.
Austin, H. Tarborough, N. C.
Booth, Miss Lydia, Poughkeepsie, N. Y.
Boughton, Rev. N., Delavan, Wis.
Brown, Hon. Wm. B., Spencerport, N. Y
Brush, George P., New York.
Capron, Rev. Orion H., North Hebron, N. Y.
Cauldwell, Miss Eliza A., New York.
Challis, John, Salem, N J
Cleaves, Mrs. S. A. Littleton, Mass.
Davis, Evan, New York.
Davis, Rev. C. B. Paris, Me.
Demarest, Silas, New York.
Denison, Rev. Nathan, Mendota, Ill.
Drake, Rev. Jacob, Delaware, Ohio.
Ellis, Rev. John, Norwalk, Ct.
English, Isaac, Salem, N. J.
Farr, Asa, Lowell, Mass.
Fillio, Miss Phidelia, Battle Creek, Mich.
Francis, John S., New York.
Goodliff, James T., New York.
Hewett, Mrs. Rhoda Elizabeth, New York
Hill, Mrs. Matilda Pierce, Albany, N. Y.
Hill, Mrs. Lydia Ann, Carmel, New York.
Judson, Mrs. Emily C. Hamilton, N. Y.
Martin, Francis, New York.
Miner, Rev Bradley Providence, R. I.
Neale, Mrs. Melissa Y Boston.
Oakley, Mrs. Cassandra, New York.
Pennypacker, John, Wilmington Del.
Richards, Rev Humphrey Dorchester, Mass.
Richards, Mrs. Eunice J., Dorchester, Mass.
Rodgers, Rev. Ebenezer Upper Alton, Ill.
Sharp, J Milton Williamsburg, N Y
Spencer, Rev. Horace, Reed's Corners, N. Y.
Sweet, H. H., Fredonia, N. Y.
Walker, Mrs. Jane P., Central Falls, R I.
Waterbury, Rev. J. H., Elizabethtown, N. J.

MISSIONARY BOXES.

[illegible] propose to make donations of clothing, etc., to our missionaries, [illegible] please [illegible] directions:

[illegible] DONATIONS ARE EXTRA.

[illegible] a part of the Missionarys' salary, or credited as receipts into [illegible] in the *Home Mission Record*, as extra. The mis- [illegible] Therefore, while such tokens of kindness are gratefully received [illegible] by the Board, it should not be overlooked that [illegible] unless our treasury is supplied with the full amount [illegible] If that is promptly supplied, it will, indeed, be a favor to [illegible] donations of clothing; but if, by the preparation of [illegible] be diminished, it would prove a disadvantage to [illegible]

CONTENTS OF BOXES.

[illegible] are generally good judges of the sort of articles which [illegible] for a missionary box. Nevertheless, in answer to the frequent [illegible] the liberty of suggesting that the following articles, in the or- [illegible] most frequently desired. 1. Plain, substantial wearing apparel, [illegible] 2. Bedding. 3. Stationery. 4. Theological books, and [illegible] 5. [illegible] which are useful in families.

HOME MISSION HOUSE CIRCULAR.

The following Circular has been issued extensively to friends of the Home Mission Society, and we are happy to add, is receiving favorable attention. The plan of compromise is received every where with approbation. The subscription for the purchase is gradually increasing without agency labors or special efforts, and when a few thousand dollars are added, the measure so unanimously agreed upon will be consummated. It is eminently a peace measure, promising success, and worthy of the united efforts of all our friends. We commend it to the favorable consideration of such as may not have received a Circular.

AMERICAN BAPTIST HOME MISSION ROOMS, *New York, June*, 1855.

You have, probably, been apprized of the action of the American Baptist Home Mission Society, at its Anniversary in Brooklyn, on the 9th of May last, by which a foundation was laid for a happy adjustment of differences relative to the location of its place of business; and also of that of a Convention assembled in Chicago, Ill., on the 14th of the same month, in which a hearty response to that action was given, accompanied with a pledge of co-operation in a plan of removal.

In the Society's Meeting, a Committee was appointed, to carry out the important design of purchasing or building a Home Mission House; to procure the necessary means of paying for the same, and to secure the property in fee to the Society. The Committee are employing proper means for securing a suitable place as soon as they are supplied with the needful amount of cash or reliable subscriptions. The limits within which the Society require the location to be selected; the restriction to have at command at least one half the whole amount of purchase money before buying; and other conditions required, make the duty of the Committee difficult and onerous. Nevertheless, they do not hesitate to say the objects contemplated by the Society can be realized if means are promptly supplied. It is not designed to spend a large amount of money for the purpose. Several thousand dollars are already subscribed, and a few thousand more guaranteed at once will enable them to put the Society in possession of a house, ample, in all respects, for its purposes. A portion of the amount subscribed, possibly one half, will be required as soon as the purchase is made, after which the payment of the remaining balance will, probably, be made reasonably easy.

The object is one of great importance. In its accomplishment we may hope for a renewal of the harmony and prosperity which for so many years distinguished the counsels and action of the Home Mission Society and its Executive Board; a renewal made paramount by peculiar circumstances in the Christian and secular world, and especially in our own country at the present day. Let us all put our hands to this work. It will then be easily and speedily done. Let us have the Home Mission House, where, removed from the causes of contention which lately existed and will be revived, unless this plan is carried out, we may labor for the spread of the Gospel of our Lord Jesus Christ in our great field, and consistently hope for the continuance and increase of the gracious results which our heavenly Father has heretofore bestowed.

A Subscription Paper is annexed, with the hope that you will favor the Committee with your name and a subscription of as liberal an amount as consistent; that you will circulate it among your friends as extensively as practicable, for their subscriptions also; and that you will return it to the undersigned, as requested by the Committee, within a few days.

☞ If consistent with your views of duty, please affix your subscription to the paper below, then obtain as many others among your friends as practicable, and return it by mail at an early day, as one of the restrictions of the Society in their vote requires the Committee to feel assured that they can rely on one half of the whole amount needed for the purchase before it can be made. Please address the undersigned, BENJAMIN M. HILL,

Corresponding Secretary, American Baptist Home Mission Society,

No. 115 NASSAU STREET, NEW YORK.

SUBSCRIPTION PAPER.

The undersigned promise to pay CHARLES J. MARTIN, or order, the sums subscribed against our respective names on this paper, in such installments as may be required for the purpose of buying or erecting a building in the City of New York, under the direction of a Committee appointed for that purpose by the American Baptist Home Mission Society in May, 1855, for the transaction of the business of the said Society.

Dated,

SUBSCRIBERS' NAMES.	TOWN OR CITY AND STATE.	AMOUNT.

CONTENTS

ANNUAL REPORT.

TWENTY-FOURTH REPORT

OF THE

AMERICAN BAPTIST HOME MISSION SOCIETY,

PRESENTED BY THE

EXECUTIVE BOARD

AT THE

ANNIVERSARY HELD IN NEW YORK,

MAY 9th AND 10th, 1856,

WITH

THE TREASURER'S REPORT AND OTHER DOCUMENTS.

New York:
PUBLISHED AT THE AMERICAN BAPTIST HOME MISSION ROOMS, No. 115 NASSAU ST.
MILLER & HOLMAN, PRINTERS, COR. CENTRE AND WHITE STS.
1856.

ACT OF INCORPORATION.

AN ACT TO INCORPORATE THE AMERICAN BAPTIST HOME MISSION SOCIETY, PASSED APRIL 12, 1843, AND AMENDED, FEBRUARY 9, 1849.

The People of the State of New York, represented in Senate and Assembly, do enact as follows:

§ 1.—All such persons as now are, or may hereafter become, members of the American Baptist Home Mission Society, formed in the city of New York, in the year One Thousand Eight Hundred and Thirty-two, shall be, and hereby are, constituted a body corporate, by the name of the American Baptist Home Mission Society, for the purpose of promoting the preaching of the Gospel in North America.

CONSTITUTION.

NAME.

I.—This Society shall be called the American Baptist Home Mission Society.

OBJECT.

II.—The object of this Society shall be to promote the preaching of the Gospel in North America.

MEMBERSHIP.

III.—The Society shall be composed of Annual Delegates, Life Members, and Life Directors.—Any Baptist church, in union with the denomination, may appoint a delegate for an annual contribution of ten dollars, and an additional delegate for each additional thirty dollars. Thirty dollars shall be requisite to constitute a member for life, and one hundred dollars paid at one time, or a sum which, in addition to any previous contribution, shall amount to one hundred dollars, shall be requisite to constitute a Director for Life.

OFFICERS.

IV.—The officers of the Society shall be a President, two Vice-Presidents, a Treasurer, an Auditor, a Corresponding Secretary, a Financial Secretary, and a Recording Secretary, whom the Society shall annually elect by ballot.

MANAGERS AND EXECUTIVE BOARD.

V.—The Officers and Life Directors shall meet immediately after the Annual Meeting of the Society, and elect fifteen Managers, residing in the city of New York, or its vicinity, who, together with the Treasurer, Auditor, and the Secretaries, shall constitute an Executive Board to conduct the business of the Society: and shall respectively continue to discharge their official duties until superseded by a new election. Seven members of the Board shall be a quorum for the transaction of business.

POWERS AND DUTIES OF THE EXECUTIVE BOARD.

VI.—The Executive Board shall have power to appoint its own meetings; elect its own Chairman and Recording Secretary; enact its own By-Laws and Rules of Order, provided always, that they be not inconsistent with this Constitution; fill any vacancies which may occur in their own body, or in the offices of the Society during the year; and, if deemed necessary by two-thirds of the members present at a regular meeting, convene special meetings of the Society. They shall establish such Agencies as the interests of the Society may require; appoint Agents and Missionaries; fix their compensation; direct and instruct them concerning their particular fields and labors; make all appropriations to be paid out of the treasury; and present to the Society, at each annual meeting, a full report of their proceedings during the current year.

DESIGNATED FUNDS.

VII.—All moneys or other property contributed and designated for any particular Missionary field, shall be so appropriated, or returned to the donors, or their lawful agents.

TREASURER.

VIII.—The Treasurer shall give bonds to such amount as the Executive Board shall think proper.

ELIGIBILITY TO APPOINTMENT.

IX.—All the Officers, Managers, Missionaries, and Agents of the Society, shall be members in good standing in regular Baptist churches.

ANNUAL MEETING.

X.—The Society shall meet annually, at such time and place as the Executive Board shall appoint.

ALTERATIONS OF THE CONSTITUTION.

XI.—No alteration of this Constitution shall be made without an affirmative vote of two-thirds of the members present at an annual meeting; nor unless the same shall have been proposed in writing, and the proposition sustained by a majority vote, at a previous annual meeting, or recommended by the Executive Board.

STATED MEETINGS FOR 1856-57.

OF THE EXECUTIVE BOARD—Thursday before the first Wednesday in each month.

" " Committee on MISSIONS—The day previous to that of the Board.

" " Committee on AGENCIES and FINANCE—The Tuesday preceding.

" " Committee on CHURCH EDIFICE FUND—The Monday preceding.

BY-LAWS OF THE BOARD.

1. All meetings shall be opened with prayer.
2. All Committees shall be nominated by the presiding officer, and approved by the Executive Board, unless otherwise specially ordered.
3. No moneys shall be paid out of the Treasury, but by order of the Executive Board.
4. All resolutions, if required, shall be presented in writing.
5. Whenever a vacancy occurs in the Executive Board the fact shall be entered on the Minutes, and at the next stated meeting the Board shall proceed to fill such vacancy by ballot.

[redacted]

MINUTES OF THE TWENTY-FOURTH ANNIVERSARY

OF THE

American Baptist Home Mission Society,

Held in New York, May 9th, 10th, and 11th, 1856.

THE Society met on Wednesday, the 9th of May, 1856, in the meeting house of the Oliver Street Baptist Church, at half-past 9 o'clock, A.M.

The President, Hon. Albert Day, of Connecticut, took the chair at half-past 9 o'clock, A.M., being supported by John P. Crozer, Esq., Vice-President:—when the Society was called to order, in a few appropriate remarks by the President.

The Throne of Grace was addressed by Rev. A. Kalloch, of Mass.

Rev. A. P. Mason, of Mass., was appointed Assistant Secretary for the session.

On the nomination of the President, the following Committees were appointed:

On Credentials of Delegates:—Mr. J. M. Whitehead, Rev. C. M. Fuller, Rev. J. W. Parkhurst, Rev. Joshua Fletcher, Rev. James S. Ladd.

On Nomination of Officers:—Rev. G. S. Webb, of N. J., Rev. S. M. Stimson and Rev. J. S. Backus, of N. Y., Rev. J. N. Murdock, D.D., of Conn., and Rev. S. B. Swaim, of Mass.

On Life Directors and Members present:—Rev. A. P. Mason, Mass., Rev. J. S. Holme and Rev. J. Cookson, of N. Y., Rev. S. D. Phelps, D.D., of Conn., and Thomas Wattson, Esq., of Pa.

On motion of Rev. J. Belcher, D.D., of Pa., ministers and other brethren present, not members of the Society, were invited to participate in the deliberations of the Society.

The invitation was accepted by Rev. Messrs. N. Palmer, A. Van Puttkammer, Wm. Putnam, W. C. Hubbard, S. M. Broakman, and Mr. R. F.

Parshall, of N. Y., Rev. Messrs. Sidney Dyer, Ind., N. Cyr, Canada, E. Andrews, Pa., G. W. Clark, N. J., C. W. Rees, Mich., J. F. Temple, Conn.

The time of commencing and closing the sessions of each day was fixed as follows:

To commence at half-past 9 o'clock, A.M.; at 3, and at half-past 7 o'clock, P.M.

To close at 1 o'clock, and half-past five, P.M.

On motion of Rev. E. P. Dye

Resolved, That the election of officers of the Society take place at 12 o'clock, M., this day.

The Corresponding Secretary read a letter from Charles J. Martin, Esq., Treasurer of the Society, declining a re-election.

In the absence of the Treasurer, his report was read by H. P. Freeman, Esq., which, on motion, was accepted and ordered to be printed with the Annual Report. (See pages 12, 13.)

An Abstract of the Annual Report of the Executive Board was read by the Corresponding Secretary, which also, on motion, was accepted and ordered to be printed under the direction of the Board.

The following Committees were appointed to examine and report on

AFTERNOON SESSION.

The President in the Chair. Prayer was offered by Rev. Whitman Metcalf, of New York.

The Committee appointed at the last anniversary to procure a building for the transaction of the business of the Society, made a report through Ebenezer Cauldwell, Esq., the Chairman (see Document No. 1), which, after much debate, was referred, by vote, to a Committee of seven, with instructions to confer with the Committee above mentioned, and report to-morrow morning at half-past 10 o'clock, such measures or suggestions as will, if possible, make a final disposition of the matter at the present anniversary.

On motion of Rev. W. H. Parmly,

Resolved, That, whereas, our esteemed brother Charles J. Martin, on account of other and pressing engagements, has declined a re-election; we hereby tender to him our thanks for the devotion and faithfulness with which he has discharged his duties during the eight years that he has served us as Treasurer.

Adjourned, after a prayer by Rev. S. Dyer, of Ind.

EVENING SESSION.

The Society met at half-past 7 o'clock, P. M., J. P. Crozer, Esq., Vice-President, in the Chair. Prayer was offered by Rev. J. L. Hodge, D.D., followed by other devotional exercises. After which, the President took the Chair, and the following persons were appointed to constitute the Committee of seven to consult with the Committee on Mission Rooms: Rev Messrs. J. R. Stone, R. I., W. S. Clapp, Conn., S. Remington, N. Y., Edward Bright, N. Y., S. Dyer, Ind., S. W. Adams, Ohio, J. S. Backus, N. Y.

The portion of the Annual Report of the Executive Board omitted in the morning was read by the Corresponding Secretary; the acceptance of which was moved by Rev. J. R. Stone, of Providence, R. I., and seconded by Rev. M. B. Anderson, LL.D., President of Rochester University, N. Y., accompanied by deeply interesting addresses from both brethren. The Report in full was accepted and ordered to be printed, and after prayer by Rev. Wm. Rollinson, of California, the Society adjourned.

MORNING SESSION.

Saturday, May 10th, 1856.

The Society assembled at half-past 9 o'clock, A.M. The President in the Chair. Prayer by Rev. A. M. Swaim, of Mass.

The "Minutes" of the preceding day were read and approved.

The Report of the special Committee on Missionary Operations was presented by Rev. Dr. Armitage, and was accepted by the Society. (See Document No. 5.)

The Rev. W. S. Clapp presented the Report of the special Committee on Obituaries, which was accepted. (See Document No. 6.)

On motion of Rev. Dr. Hodge, seconded by Rev. Dr. Judd,

Resolved, That no appointments to be made by this Society at its annual meetings should be anticipated by the Committee of Arrangements or the Board, unless by special instructions of the Society itself.

The Committee of seven, to confer with the Committee on a Home Mission House, appointed last year, reported through their Chairman, Rev. J. R. Stone. Two other reports were also read, one from a majority of the Committee, by Rev. J. R. Stone, and the other from a minority by Rev. Dr. Bright. The whole were accepted. (See Documents No. 2, 3, 4.)

On motion of Smith Shelden, Esq.,

Resolved, Unanimously, that the Report of the minority of the Committee be adopted

After prayer by Rev. J. W. Parkhurst, of Mass., the Society adjourned.

[redacted]

Rev. J. T. Seeley, Syracuse.
" Wm. Reid, New London, Conn.
" L. A. Dunn, Fairfax, Vt.
" A. S. Patton, Hoboken, N. J.
" B. W. Barrows, Neponset, Mass.
" John Jennings, Newton Centre, Mass.
" Edward T. Hiscox, New York.
" Lemuel Covell, New York.
" J. R. Stone, Providence, R. I.
" G. C. Baldwin, D D, Troy, N. Y.
" C. M. Fuller, Pike, N. Y.
" R. J. Wilson, Elmira, N. Y.
" H. C. Fish, Newark, N. J.
" Samuel Fish, Halifax, Vt.
" John Cookson, New York.
" Wm. Wilder, Chester, Pa.
" F. G. Wright, Westport, N. Y.
" S. W. Field, Providence, R. I.
" S. S. Parker, Southbridge, Mass.
" D. B. Cheney, Philadelphia, Pa.
" C. J. Hopkins, New York.
" J. Ballard, New York.
" Elisha Cushman, Deep River, Conn.
" L. Muzzy, Pulaski, N. Y.
" Alva Gregory, Stepney, Conn.
" Leland Howard, Rutland, Vt.
" James B. Simmons, Providence, R. I.
" L. H. Wakeman, West Woodstock, Conn.
" S. D. Phelps, D.D, New Haven, Conn.
" J. M. Challiss, Roadstown, N. J.
" H. Seaver, New York.
" A. Perkins, D.D., Salem, N. J.
" G. P. Nice, Somerville, N. J.
" Ira R. Steward, New York.
" J. Aldrich, Worcester, Mass.
" Wheelock H. Parmly, Jersey City, N J.
" W. H. Wines, Boston, Mass.
" J. W. Taggart, New York.
" Rob. T. Middleditch, Red Bank, N J.

Rev. O. B. Judd, L.L.D., New York.
" P. Stow, Boston Mass.
" R. B. C. Howell, Richmond, Va.
" Alexander M. Averill N. Cambridge, Mass.
" L. Porter, D.D., Pittsfield, Mass.
" Geo. Hatt, New York.
" Joshua Fletcher, Amenia, N. Y.
" A. H. Burlingham, Boston.
" J. W. Sarles, Brooklyn, N. Y.
" J. W. Parkhurst, Newton Centre, Mass.
" Oakman S. Stearns, Newton Centre, Mass.
" B. T. Welch, D.D., Newtonville, N. Y.
" S. J. Drake, Plainfield, N. J.
" A. L. Freeman, Camillus, N. Y.
" B. P. Byram, Amesbury, Mass.
" Joseph Belcher, D.D., Philadelphia.
" M. G. Hodge, Brooklyn, N. Y.
" J. Girdwood, New Bedford, Mass.
" Nathan A. Reed, Wakefield, R. I.
" Daniel Eldridge, Shusham, N. Y.
Wm. Ham, Providence, R. I.
Samuel Shardlow, New York.
Henry P. Freeman, Brooklyn.
P. Balen, New York.
Wm. H. Munn, New York.
M. B. Savage, Brooklyn.
Francis Edmonds, Newton Centre, Mass.
Wm. Hillman, New York.
W. W. Todd, New York.
Tho. Wattson, Philadelphia.
Albert Day, Hartford, Conn.
John M. Bruce, New York.
James M. Whitehead, New York.
J E. Southworth, Brooklyn.
John A. Miller, New York.
D M. Wilson, Newark, N. J.
Heman Lincoln, Boston, Mass.
Wm. Winterton, New York.
J. P. Crozer, Chester, Pa.

John W. Burt, Brooklyn, N. Y.

LIFE MEMBERS.

Rev. J. J. Babcock Jay, New-York.
" W. B. Tolan, Stepney, Conn.
" T. R. Taylor, Alleghany City, Pa.
" H. Westcott, Blackwoodtown, N. J.
" W. S Clapp Danbury, Conn.
" S. Haskell, Kalamazoo, Mich.
" J. H. Pratt, Bloomfield, N J.
" D. W. Sherwood, Mattewan, N. Y.
" A. C. Mallory, Benton Centre, N. Y.
" S. M Stimson, Binghamton, N. Y.
" Charles Keyser, Niagara Falls, N. Y.
" J. T. Mason, Galesville, N Y.
" R Dodge, Hamilton, N. Y.
" S. W. Adams, D D, Cleveland, O.
" Bergen Stelle, Cherryville, N. J.
" Ezra Dean, Auburn, N Y.
" T. G. Freeman, New York.
" Alfred Harvey, Woodstown, N. J.
" C. A. Clark, Stonington, Conn.
" C. N. Chandler, Fredonia.
" John Duncan Camden, N. J.
" J. M. Philips, Modus.
" R. Worth, Fisherville, N. H.

Rev. S. L. Elliot, Wallingford, Vt.
" Thos. E. Keely, Medford, Mass.
" O. Tracy, Concord, N. H.
" W. S. Mikels, Sing Sing, N. Y.
" Lewis Smith, Trenton, N. J.
" Henry Steelman, Norway, N. Y.
" Samuel White, North Shore, Staten Isl.
" J. H. Baker, East Greenwich, R. I.
" J. M. Carpenter, Jacobstown, N. J.
" T. H. Archibald, Factory Point, Vt.
" Allen Darrow, Marietta, O.
" Whitman Metcalf, Nunda, N. Y.
" L. W. Hayhurst, Balston Spa, N. Y.
" Chas. C. Norton, New York.
" J. Ellis Guild, Chatham, Mass.
" E. K. Fuller, Reading, Mass.
" W. H. King, Owego, N. Y.
" C. T. Tucker, Millbury, Mass.
" E. D. Reed, Oneida, N. Y.
" H. L. Grose, Galway, N. Y.
" W. C. Phillips, Port Byron, N. Y.
" J. A. Goodhue, South Boston, Mass.
" Conant Sawyer, Lowville, N. Y.

Rev. Samuel Baker, D.D , Williamsburgh.
" Jonathan Draper, jr., N. Bennington, Vt.
" J O. Foster, Brattleboro', Vt.
" Elijah Hutchinson, Windsor, Vt.
" C. L. Bacon, Trumansburgh, N. Y.
" B. C. Townsend, Mecklenburg, N. Y.
" J. V. Ambler, Lanesboro', Mass.
Mrs. A. T. Ambler, " "
Rev. S. S. Relyea, Kingston, N. Y.
" S. B. Allen, Yarmouth, Me.
" Otis G. Corbett, Orange, N. J.
" S. M. Osgood, Philadelphia.
" J. E. Chesshire, Keesville, N. Y.
" Wm. F. Nelson, Wickford, R. I.
" A. G Mason, Jersey City, N. J.
" J. A. Tillinghast, Allenton, R. I.
" O. W. Gibbs, Bennettsburg, N. Y.
" E. Bell, Willimantic, Conn.
" H. T. Love, New-York.
" Joseph Hodges, jr., Cambridge, Mass.
" Thos. Powell, Mount Palatine, Ill.
" D. C. Eddy, Lowell, Mass.
" A. H. Stowell, Providence, R. I.
" John Eschman, New York.
" Wm. A. Smith, Groton, Conn.
" D. Dye, Three Mile Bay, N. Y.
" Abel Haskell, Yates, N. Y.
" Asaph Merriam, Fitchburgh, Mass.
" K. E Fleishman, Philadelphia.
" Noah Hooper, Somersworth, N. H.
[redacted]

Rev. A. J. Clark, Southington, Conn.
" W. W. Meech, Preston, Conn.
" Wm. L Brown, Watertown, Mass.
" L. Hayden, Saxton's River, Vt.
" H. K. Stimson, Marion, N. Y.
" Geo. Matthews, Seekonk, Mass.
" Elihu Gunn, Keokuk, Iowa.
" E E. Cummings, D.D., Concord, N. H.
" J. C. Harrison, Easton, Pa.
" L. W. Olney, Deposit, N. Y.
" N. M. Perkins, Brookline, Mass.
" J. J. Woolsey, Norwich, Conn.
" John Goadly, East Poultney, Vt.
" S. B. Page, Cleveland, O.
" W. S. Goodno, Bordentown, N. J.
" Amasa Brown, Concord, N. H.
" Stillman B. Grant, New Haven, Conn.
" J. W. Olmstead, Boston, Mass.
" Justus Bulkley, Carrollton, Ill.
" B. Griffith, Philadelphia.
" R. F. Buel, Athens, Greece.
Joseph T. Evans, New York.
Mrs C. H. Evans, "
Mrs. Nancy S. Ham, Providence, R. I.
Samuel T. Hillman, New York.
Ralph Johnson, Norwich, N. Y.
Joseph Fales, Washington, D. C.
Wm. Fay, West Halifax, Vt.
Elias Johnson, Troy, N. Y.
Abiat Miles, Brooklyn, N Y.
[redacted]

MEETING OF LIFE DIRECTORS AND OFFICERS.

Immediately after the Annual Meeting of the Society, the Officers and Life Directors met at the call of the Corresponding Secretary, as required by the Constitution, to elect the requisite Managers.

Rev. D. B. Cheney, of Pa., was chosen Chairman, and Samuel Colgate Secretary. The Rev. I. R. Steward engaged in prayer.

On motion, Rev. Messrs. E. Lathrop, D.D., J. H. Kennard, S. D. Phelps, D.D., P. Church, D.D., and A. P. Mason, were appointed a committee to nominate suitable persons for Managers, who, after consultation, presented a list which was unanimously accepted. (See page 14.)

After prayer by Rev. J. H. Kennard, Pa., the meeting adjourned *sine die.*

SAMUEL COLGATE,
Secretary.

THE SERMONS.

On the Sabbath following the meetings for business, the Missionary Sermons were preached by Rev. J. Wheaton Smith, of Philadelphia, and Rev. J. Bulkley, of Carrollton, Ill., the first in Calvary Church, New York, in the morning, and Pierrepont Street Church, Brooklyn, in the evening; and the other in the First Church, Williamsburgh, in the morning, and Tabernacle Church, New York, in the evening. They were excellent productions, and well adapted to the occasion, and were followed by spontaneous and liberal contributions in the churches where they were delivered.

Dr. THE AMERICAN BAPTIST HOME MISSION SOCIETY,

1856.	To Cash paid Missionaries for Salaries,....................		$31,460 67
	" Cash paid Agents for Salaries, Traveling expenses, Postage, etc....................................		7,334 72
	" Cash paid for Stationery, Postage, and Incidental expenses,..		353 99
	" Cash paid Salaries, Secretaries and Clerks,...	$3,994 94	
	Less amount of interest from Contingent Fund,...	420 00	
			3,574 94
	" Cash paid for Paper and printing of *Home Mission Record*, and expenses on the same,..........................		1,609 38
	" Cash paid for Paper and printing Annual Report, Certificates, Blanks, etc.,............................		778 74
	" Cash paid Taxes on Land donated to the Society,......		28 44
	" Cash paid discount on uncurrent funds, and counterfeit		

[redacted]

IN ACCOUNT WITH CHAS. J. MARTIN, TREASURER. *Cr.*

1856.	By Balance from last year,...........................		$140 48
	" Cash, interest on dividends received on sundry temporary investments,....................	$115 00	
	" Cash, interest received on Bonds and Mortgages, a special investment, by direction of the donor,..................................	175 00	
			290 00
	" Cash, amount received for subscriptions to *Home Mission Record*,..		1,152 86
	" Cash, amount received, Church Edifice Fund,..........		2,833 56
	" Cash, amount received for Ministers' Libraries,........		20 00
	" Cash, proceeds of Twenty Shares Corn Exchange Bank Stock,..		2,030 00
	" Cash, amount of Contributions and Legacies received from April 1st, 1855, to March 31st, 1856,..........		45,074 98
			$51,541 88
March 31	By Balance,..................................	$592 93	
	Subject to drafts of Corresponding Secretary already issued upon the Treasurer, and liable to immediate presentation, amounting to,..................................	2,706 73	
	Showing a deficiency of,......................	$2,113 80	

CHARLES J. MARTIN, *Treasurer.*

AUDITOR'S CERTIFICATE.

This is to certify that I have examined the foregoing account, together with the vouchers connected therewith, and find the same correct. The balance in the hands of Charles J. Martin, Esq., Treasurer, is five hundred and ninety-two 93-100 dollars ($592 93).

He is in possession of the following securities, viz.:—One Brooklyn City Bond, bearing interest six per cent., payable 1st January 1863, for five hundred dollars; Two Bonds and Mortgages, (a special investment by direction of the donor), the interest only to be used by the Society, the principal of which bonds is two thousand five hundred dollars; also, a Bond and Mortgage for six thousand dollars, the legacy of the late Garrat N. Bleecker, the interest of which is to be applied towards the salaries of the officers of the rooms.

SMITH SHELDON, *Auditor.*

NEW YORK, April 1st, 1856.

OFFICERS OF THE SOCIETY.

AND

EXECUTIVE BOARD.

OFFICERS.

PRESIDENT.

HON. ALBERT DAY, Hartford, Connecticut.

VICE-PRESIDENTS.

WILLIAM COLGATE, Esq., New York.
JOHN P. CROZER, Esq., Chester, Pa.

TREASURER.

J. E. SOUTHWORTH, New York.

AUDITOR.

[illegible]

Annual Report.

In presenting the Twenty-fourth Annual Report of the American Baptist Home Mission Society, the Executive Board have to regret that some of its statements will shew the existence of discouraging and even humiliating circumstances in the condition of the Society, during the principal portion of the year, though it will appear also, to the praise of Divine grace, that, in other respects, much has existed of an encouraging nature.

DEATHS.

Our obituary list for the year is a long one, containing 48 names. Among them are those of 15 ministers of the Gospel, the most of whom were extensively known in our Zion as useful men, some of them eminently so. Of the number, two had sustained official relations to the Board. Rev. N. V. Steadman, of Indiana, was four years an able missionary, and four more the Exploring Agent of the Society in that State. He had accomplished much there for the advancement of the cause of missions, and finally fell, literally, in the discharge of his duty.

Rev. Spencer H. Cone, D.D., was one of the originators of the Society, and was prominent in its organization. For six years he was elected a Director, and for four years Vice-President. Nineteen years he served as a member of the executive Board, thirteen of which he presided over its deliberations, with great ability. He resigned his seat a short time previous to the last anniversary, and soon after departed to his rest.

His official and private influence were often exercised with much advantage to the pecuniary and religious interests of the Society. He loved it and rejoiced in its success. Almost with his dying breath he expressed to a friend the desires of his heart for its prosperity. May many be given us by the Giver of every good gift, who shall be worthy to receive his fallen mantle.

CHANGE IN THE EXECUTIVE BOARD.

Rev. O. S. Stearns, having removed early in the year from the vicinity of New York, resigned his seat in the Executive Board. The vacancy thus made was filled by the election of Mr. D. C. Whitman, of Newark, N. J.

[redacted]

all of them very acceptable, being the gifts of those who loved the cause of Home Missions and cherished it among the objects of their latest prayers and benefactions. The names of the testators appear in the usual list accompanying this report.

CHURCH EDIFICE FUND.

Owing to the continuance of some of the untoward circumstances mentioned in the last annual report, very little progress has been made in accumulating a Church Edifice Fund. The amount received during the year is $2,833 56, and was from voluntary donations.

The total amount now belonging to the Society, exclusive of that which was given and disbursed as donations, is $4,763. This amount has been applied to the purpose for which it was designed, in the form of loans, properly secured, drawing small interest and payable in easy installments. It has aided in the building of five Church Edifices.

The fund, small as it is, will soon become productive from the interest due on the loans, and it is desirable that it may be increased by special subscriptions, at an early day. Public opinion in its favor has been emphatic. The disadvantages resulting from delay in consummating the original plan cannot easily be computed.

FINANCIAL AFFAIRS.

A full statement of the financial affairs of the Society for the past year, would show an uninterrupted series of embarrassments, rendering new appropriations inconsistent, requiring extensive retrenchment, and creating the necessity for temporary loans. The entire subject, however, has been placed, repeatedly, before the Churches, in the columns of the *Home Mission Record*, and but little more need be added in this Report. It is proper, however, to call attention to the facts, that the amount of contributions and legacies received during the year ending March 31st, 1855, showed a falling off from the previous year of more than $3,000 ; that the balance in the treasury at the close of that year, was but $140.48 ; that the amount of liabilities for all purposes at the commencement of the present year was upwards of $45,000 ; that the contributions and legacies for the entire year, did but little more than reach that amount ; and that the general aggregate of receipts was less, each month, except the first three, than that of the corresponding periods of the previous year ; while appropriations for the continuance of missionaries on important fields, were constantly necessary, making the reduction of the amount of liabilities a [redacted]

So far, however, it will, without doubt, ever be their pleasure to go forward.

The following statement shows the financial condition of the Society on the 31st day of March, 1856.

Balance from last year's account	$140 48
Receipts from all other sources	51,401 40
Total amount of receipts during the year ending March 31, 1856	$51,541 88
Total amount disbursed, same period,	50,948 95
Balance in the Treasury, March 31	$592 93
Add Brooklyn City Bond	500 00
Total amount of resources April 1, 1856	$1,092 93
The amount due missionaries, April 1, and liable to immediate demand is	$4,874 17
Deduct amount of resources above	1,092 93
Shews a deficiency of	$3,781 24
Amount of available resources, less than last year	$5,004 45
Amount of contributions and legacies only, less than last year, not including the legacy of G. N. Bleecker, in 1854, which was for a specific purpose	1,616 86

Of the amount contributed $6,809.90 did not reach the treasury until the last week in March. This is a repetition of delay, the disadvantage of which is sorely felt by the Board, and much more so by needy applicants for aid. We commend to the consideration of the Friends of the Society the importance of avoiding such delay hereafter.

MISSIONARY OPERATIONS.

The Board are unable to employ more encouraging language respecting their missionary operations than that in their last Report.

It has been a year of retrenchment;—not sudden and violent, so as seriously to affect the prosperity of the churches dependent upon them, but gradual and easy as the interests of the Society would admit.

Very few new appointments of missionaries have been made, and those were by the special request of churches which engaged to provide means for their support.

As many commissions have been allowed to expire, without renewal, as could be without injury to the cause. A considerable number of churches heretofore aided by the Society, have assumed the entire support of their ministers, and several missionaries have voluntarily resigned their commissions. By such means the number of missionaries has been reduced about one-half. On the other hand, the labors of the missionaries have, in many respects, been successful; several have reported revivals of religion in their churches, and the fact that an unusual number of them now support their pastors without missionary aid, shows that temporal blessings also have been richly added to them.

VALLEY OF THE MISSISSIPPI.

[redacted]

that Territory, where, it is possible, he may not feel the necessity of relying on the funds of the Society for support. The Indian war has so unfavorably affected the interests of the people in the section heretofore occupied by Rev. M. N. Stearns, that he has also declined a renewal of his commission for the present. Only one missionary remains in the employment of the Society in that Territory.

In CALIFORNIA we have had four missionaries at different periods of the year, but at present there are none actually in commission, their appointments all having expired, and various circumstances having rendered unnecessary, or prevented their renewal. All except one remain on the field, and some of them may find further aid necessary.

CENTRAL TERRITORIES.

The columns of the *Home Mission Record* for the past year contain evidence of a good degree of progress in the missionary interests of NEW MEXICO. Rev. H. W. Read, attended by Rev. S. Gorman, visited certain villages of that Territory, and baptized a considerable number of Mexicans, who professed to have become believers in Jesus Christ, and desirous of admission into his visible church. The evidence they gave of a genuine work of grace in their hearts was satisfactory, and they were received as members of the church in Albuquerque.

Rev. Mr. Gorman writes encouragingly from his station, to which we will refer under another head. Rev. J. M. Shaw found it necessary on account of his wife's health, to return, last autumn, to "the States," for a few months. They were accompanied by Mrs. Read, whose health also had suffered, and, as her disease subsequently assumed a more serious aspect, she was followed in the month of March by her husband. The only missionaries remaining in the Territory are Rev. S. Gorman, his assistant, José Senun, and Rev. F. Tolhurst, who labors on a temporary arrangement, among the American residents of Santa Fé. This is one of the darkest portions of our field. In it discouragements abound. Our missionaries encounter there the soul-destroying influence of a corrupt religious system, the more corrupted because of the deep degradation into which the people have been suffered to sink, through the personal examples of their religious guides. A comparison, however, of the moral condition and religious knowledge of the people, as represented at the origin of the mission, by civil and military officers of the United States Government, with those now developed, though not in the nature of things so striking as may be found in more enlightened communities, nevertheless presents manifest evidence that it is a productive mission ; and bids as fair to

[redacted]

tion of one of the number have proved serious obstacles to the promotion of religious interests.

INDIAN MISSIONS.

Circumstances have not favored an attempt to revive the mission among the Indians of Minnesota Territory.

The Rev. J. M. Shaw, having been under the necessity of temporarily leaving his field in New Mexico, and the Rev. F. Tolhurst, originally his assistant, being employed at Santa Fé, where he has no facilities for studying the language of the Navajoes, the project of establishing a mission among that people is deferred for the present.

The Rev. S. Gorman continues his arduous labors at Laguna, assisted by Bro. José Senun, and we are gratified to learn that probably another convert from Aztec and Catholic superstition has appeared among the Pueblos, to whom our brother ministers. His influence among his countrymen, when an alien from the commonwealth of Israel, was considerable. If it can be retained in his intercourse with them as a fellow-citizen with the saints, and of the household of God, we may hope to hear of encouraging usefulness in his labors among them.

GRAND LIGNE.

The work of the Lord steadily, though gradually, progresses at the Grand Ligne stations. Many persons have severed their connection with the Roman Catholic church; converts continue to be multiplied; the churches are advancing in the knowledge of their duty; and, as they become enlightened, show much cheerfulness in their more liberal support of the Gospel. The station at Montreal is well prepared, in many respects, for enlarged operations, but suffers from the lack of a place of public worship.— Could that be obtained, much more might be hoped for from the labors of Rev. N. Cyr, the missionary who is stationed there. The Rev. J. N. Williams, who has labored as a missionary in another section of the Province, has resigned his commission on account of ill health and is now the pastor of a self-sustaining church in that city, and thus strengthens the hands of the missionary.

NEW GRENADA.

The station at St Andrews, a dependency of New Grenada, established last year, continues to share in the favors of the Lord. Our devoted missionary, Rev. Philip B. Livingston, writes of the people's advance in the knowledge of the truth and their growth in grace, in a truly cheering manner, while their very liberal contributions to the treasury of Christian benevolence, show that their religion is not limited to a mere profession. The Island, [redacted]

1; making the number of States and Territories occupied fifteen.

Of the number of missionaries employed, 19 have preached the Gospel in foreign languages, viz. German, Swedish, Danish, Norwegian, Dutch, French, Spanish, and Pueblo Indian. Nearly all of the nineteen are themselves of foreign nativity. From the reports received from the missionaries it appears that 196 stations and out-stations have been supplied, and the aggregate of time bestowed upon the field is equal to that of one man for 87 years.

The missionaries report also, the Baptism of 542 persons; the hopeful conversion of 194 others; the organization of 21 churches; the ordination of 15 ministers; the completion of 9 church edifices, and progress in building of 4 others.

The churches aided by the Society contributed during the year to the usual objects of Christian benevolence, $3,361.87, besides about $14,000 for the support of the cause of Christ among themselves.

Eighteen churches, recently aided by the Society, have determined to sustain their pastors hereafter without further drafts upon our treasury.*

---

* In addition to the above, the Missionaries report the following:

Sermons preached	11,269
Lectures and Addresses	848
Pastoral Visits	24,000
Prayer and other Meetings attended	6,403
Signatures to Temperance Pledge	171
Miles traveled in discharge of duty	137,220
Schools visited	311
Sabbath Schools in the Churches	145
Bible Classes	86
Number of Teachers	929
Number of Scholars	6,817
Volumes in S. S. Libraries	20,003
Stations where Monthly Concert of Prayer is observed	56
Preparing for the ministry	18

More particular notice of some of the items stated seems to be demanded at this time.

The number of missionaries in the field has been more or less diminished at each meeting of the Board during the year, until its close; when the number was less than half that with which the year was commenced. Hence, while the number of baptisms reported is smaller than on almost any preceding year, it is larger in proportion to the number of missionaries employed and the amount of time bestowed.

In one or two respects, the results of labor have been still more encouraging. Thus, with a greatly diminished number of missionaries, nearly as many church edifices have been completed as on any previous year, and a larger number of churches have become able to sustain their pas- [redacted] ple. But even this fails to present the whole variety and extent of their labors. Their quarterly reports show that, so far as instrumentality in spreading the Gospel is concerned, they are *men of all work*, and are employed about it in season and out of season.

They are not only friends and patrons of Sabbath Schools, but, if necessary, superintendents and teachers; they are found among the most active in all good plans of moral reform; they encourage a taste for religious literature, among their people; they promote the missionary spirit, and, often, though themselves recipients of missionary bounty, they and their churches are liberal contributors to the various treasuries of christian benevolence.—They are also most efficient distributors of the Sacred criptures and religious tracts; being, by virtue of their instruction, practical colporteurs in their respective fields; in which they enjoy the best means of learning who are really destitute and needy, and what are the most judicious methods of supplying them with the precious treasure of God's word.

In these labors, and the eminent success which has attended them hitherto, it is not difficult to perceive evidence of the Society's adaptedness to the work assigned it, and the satisfactory ground of hope for its continued success.

FUTURE EFFORT.

The comparative inaction of the past year has materially affected the means of determining particularly the necessities of the year to come. It is humiliating to admit that our movements on the field have been retrograde, and many a post of observation has been abandoned till recruited strength enables us again to advance. No friend of Home Missions, however, can be satisfied with the occupancy of a position by the Society, less commanding than that recently in our possession, while the greater expansion of the population, and the more numerous settlements in frontier regions, claiming missionary aid, call loudly for a movement in advance of any hitherto attained. Our brethren in most of the older Western States now possess the means for promoting, to a considerable extent, their Domestic Missionary interests; their qualifications for employing those means advantageously must be admitted by all. It cannot be supposed, therefore, that the Home Mission Society need to bear so large a proportion of the expense of sustaining Home Missions, as heretofore in such States, though for many years to come, it may be indispensable to answer claims which the actual ability of the State Conventions cannot.

The chief efforts of the Society will be required for the [redacted]

Thus, large districts become pre-occupied by agencies of evil, which all sincere Christians deprecate, and should prevent, if possible, by early and energetic religious efforts. There is no hazard in the assertion, that, with the ordinary blessing of God, such efforts would prevent the preponderance of those agencies, and the Gospel, with its institutions, would more than counteract them where they were introduced. Funds liberally, but judiciously, expended in aiding the few Christians who may be thrown together providentially, in supporting a minister, or in building a house of worship, will accomplish more for the establishment of religion in our frontier settlements, when first commenced, than much larger sums repeated annually, for many years, can do at a later period, when false and pernicious influences have found a lodgement among the people.

The Executive Board express no opinion as to the specific amount of funds necessary to accomplish all that may be actually advantageous and necessary the ensuing year, but they believe that the amount contributed, instead of being as now reported,—scarcely $48,000, should on no account, be less than the highest point yet reached, which, in 1854, was more than $56,500, and they as decidedly believe that a much larger amount can be judiciously expended at points on our field, where the results would be especially advantageous to the young churches already organized, or which may, hereafter, be collected, and that it would soon become so to the cause of Christian benevolence generally.

The duty of Christian men and women to supply the full amount of means necessary to spread the Gospel in all parts of our country made accessible to missionaries, needs no argument; and the Board feel that, after they have collected and diffused information respecting the destitution and promise of points requiring aid, through the regular and special agencies of the Society, it becomes a matter of individual responsibility with all the members and friends of the Society, whether the work required is performed or left undone.

They are, therefore, content to refer the subject to the consciences of their patrons, with the hope that the decision and action of every one will meet the Divine approbation in that great day when the proper stewardship of all will be proved.

By order of the Executive Board,

BENJAMIN M. HILL,
Corresponding Secretary.

EXPLANATION OF THE FOLLOWING MISSIONARY TABLE.

The parallel columns show;

1. The names of Agents and Missionaries, and the States in which they reside.
2. The post-office address of Agents and Missionaries.
3. The fields of labor occupied by Agents and Missionaries.
4. The dates at which the appointments commence.
5. The number of months for which the appointments are respectively made.
6. The number of weeks' labor reported as having been performed during an appointment.
7. The number of stations and out-stations supplied.*
8. The number of persons baptized by the Missionaries within the time of appointment.
9. The number received by letter.
10. The number of Scholars in Sabbath-schools under the care of Missionaries.†
11. The amount contributed to benevolent objects.
12. Additional facts reported concerning the state and progress of the Churches.‡

*Stations are churches or villages regularly supplied on the Lord's day, and are indicated in column 3. Out-stations are places where the Missionaries have *stated* appointments for preaching more or less frequently at other times than the Lord's day.

† In new places, where Union schools are established, the number of scholars connected with Baptist families only are reported.

‡ In many cases two lines appear for the same Missionary, extending through all the columns. In such cases the second line indicates a re-appointment of the Missionary, and the dates in column 4 determine to which appointment or year the statistics and remarks on the different lines belong. A particular notice of those dates is necessary to a proper understanding of certain changes which appear against the names of some individuals.

TABLE.

Commis'd.	Weeks labor reported.	Stations supplied.	Baptized.	Received by Letter.	Scholars in S. School.	Cont. to Benevolent Objects.	ADDITIONAL FACTS REPORTED.
3			2	--	----	------	Meets with success among the young men of Montreal.
3			-	----	----	------	Need a Meeting-house. Prospects encouraging.
3			3	----	38	4 00	Progressing.
3					20	12 00	
3			4			67 00	Several Popery and want to be lay-

Names of Agents and Missionaries.	Post Office Address.	Field of Labor.	Date of Commission	Months Commis'd.	Weeks labor reported.	Stations supplied.	Baptized.	Received by Letter.	Scholars in S. School.	Cont. to Benevolent Objects.	Additional Facts Reported.
MASSACHUSETTS.											
J. W. Parkhurst	Newton Centre	Massachusetts	April 1, 1855	12	52						Collecting Agent for the State.
"	" "	"	April 1, 1856	12							" " " "
NEW YORK.											
C. M. Fuller	Pike, Wyoming Co.	Eastern N. Y. and N. J.	April 1, 1855	12	37½						Collecting Agent for Eastern N. Y. and N. J.
"	" " "	" " " "	April 1, 1856	12							" " " " " "
James S. Ladd	New York City	Connecticut and R. I.	April 1, 1855	12	52						Collecting Agent for R. I. and Conn.
C. A Clark	Auburn	Central New York	April 1, 1855	12	52						Collecting Agent for Central N. Y.
Wm. Sawyer	White's Corners	Western New York	April 1, 1855	12	24						Collecting Agent for Western N. Y.
"	" "	" "	April 1, 1856	12							
M. B. Czechowski	Sciota	French Catholics	July 1, 1854	12	13	3	6	4			Finished Meeting-house. Organized a church at Champlain. Mission transferred to the N. Y. State Con.
J. Milton Shaw	Auburn	Connecticut and New York			23						A temporary agency during an absence from his mission field in New Mexico.
Charles Gayer	New York	French and Germans	Oct. 1, 1855	12	26	4	35	2	100	30 46	A new and encouraging French and German Mission.
NEW JERSEY.											
J. G. Collom	Mt. Holly	Penn. and S. New Jersey	April 1, 1855	12	52						Collecting Agent in Pa. and Southern N. J.
"	"		April 1, 1856	12							" " " " " "
Joshua E. Rue	Hightstown	Eastern New York, etc	April 1, 1855	12	48						Collecting Agent. Resigned on account of ill health.
PENNSYLVANIA.											
P. M. Weddell	Pittsburg	South Pittsburg	June 1, 1854	12	13	1			70	7 29	Church in a good condition. Leaves for another field.
N. Burwell	West Greenville	West Greenville	Dec. 1, 1854	12	17	2				10 00	Resigned.
L. L. Still	Freeport	Freeport and Sarentum	Sept. 1, 1854	12	26	4	6		60	46 67	A new field. Retired from it discouraged.
T. J. Penny	Strattonville	Strattonville and Clarion	Dec. 1, 1855	12	13	3			80		Finished Meeting-house.

3

Commiss'd.	Weeks labor reported	Stations supplied.	Baptized.	Received by Letter	Scholars in S. School	Con. to Benevolent Objects.	ADDITIONAL FACTS REPORTED.
12	52	----	--	----	----	------	Exploring Agent and General Itinerant.
12	26	----	--	4	----	150 00	
12	13	6	--	2	100	------	
12	13	1	1	1	76	6 50	The Church will not apply for further aid.
12	13	1	--	----	40	------	Finishing a good Meeting house.
12	39		--	----	----	------	Church prosperous in the way of securing a congregation.
12	13	1	21	7	125	48 54	Revival. Building Meeting house.
12	39	----	6	4	110	71 92	Encouragingly progressing.
12	25	4	24	1	85	------	Revival. Much encouraged.
12	13	1	--	3	80	14 00	Church prosperous. Pastor resigned.
12	26	1	3	15	265	86 59	Completed Meeting house. Require no further aid.
12	26	4	2	3	30	21 67	Need no further aid. Completed Meeting-house.
12	13	3	16	----	60	------	Church progressing with Meeting house. Resigns to remove to another field.
12	13	3	2	1	75	------	Need no further aid.
12	39	3	4	29	50	50 55	Completed Meeting-house. Pastor resigned on account of poor health.
12	13	----	1	----	----	------	An useful Exploring Ag't.; suddenly deceased.
12	39	----	7	4	250	188 86	Hereafter supported on his field.
12	0[illegible]	2	--	----	----	36 00	Congregation large. Field an important one.
12	3[illegible]	----	--	----	----	15 00	
12	26	6	3	----	66	122 87	Sabbath-schools interesting.
12	26	1	14	4	115	12 00	Church generally prosperous.
12	26	----	2	2	----	------	Encouraging indications.
12	26	5	2	5	----	84 30	Organized a Church at Middletown, where anti-mission influence has been strong.

Names of Agents and Missionaries.	Post Office Address.	Field of Labor.	Date of Commission	Months Commiss'd.	Weeks labor reported.	Stations supplied.	Baptized.	Received by Letter.	Scholars in S. School.	Cont. to Benevolent Objects.	Additional Facts Reported.
Harry Smith	Valparaiso	Valparaiso	Aug. 1, 1854	12	26	----	41	3	62	9 04	Revival.
"	"	"	Aug. 1, 1855	12	26	5	--	1	75	......	Been sick.
H. C. Skinner	Wabash	Wabash	July 1, 1854	12	13	3	--	----	----	......	Congregation attentive to preaching. Church united.
"	"	"	July 1, 1855	12	39	----	--	5	125	25 00	General declension in religion.
E. L. Millis	Attica, Fountain Co.	Attica and vicinity	June 1, 1854	12	13	1	12	----	----	......	
"	" " "	" "	June 1, 1855	12	39	----	--	6	30	14 50	Completed a Meeting-house.
J. M. Whitehead	Door Village	Northern Indiana Associa'n	Aug. 1, 1855	12	26	----	16	27	----	125 00	Revival at La Porte, which church has been nearly extinct No baptism in it, until now, for seven years.
ILLINOIS.											
Thomas Powell	Mt. Palatine	Illinois	April 1, 1855	12	30	----	1	----	----	......	Exploring Agent and General Itinerant.
" "	"	Central N. Y.	April 1, 1856	12	----	----	--	----	----	......	Collecting Agent
F. Ketcham	Richland Grove	Rock Island Association	June 1, 1854	12	13	8	--	----	----	246 86	Receives his salary hereafter on his field.
J. Edminster	Peoria	2nd Church in Peoria	May 1, 1854	12	13	1	2	2	75	22 00	Encouraged.
Niles Kinne	St. Charles	St. Charles	Jan. 1, 1855	12	52	3	--	12	100	64 15	Discipline has been necessary. Pastor left the field.
H. S. Deppe	Steelsville, Ran'ph Co.	Germans in Sparta, etc.	May 1, 1854	12	13	6	5	----	----	......	Pastor's house and furniture destroyed by fire.
J. H. Kruger	Peoria	German Church in Peoria	Oct. 1, 1854	12	26	1	1	8	----	22 75	
"	"	" " "	Oct. 1, 1855	12	26	----	2	----	----	5 00	
Gilbert S. Bailey	Pekin	Pekin and vicinity	Nov. 1, 1854	12	39	5	8	14	100	------	Meeting-house progressing. Revival at an out-station. Removed to another field.
Asahel Chapin	Galena	Galena	June 1, 1854	12	13	1	--	3	----	15 00	Completed Meeting-house.
" "		"	June 1, 1855	12	39	----	--	1	57	5 00	Church pressed by pecuniary difficulties.
J. V. Allison	Mt. Carroll	Mt. Carroll and vicinity	May 1, 1854	12	13	1	--	5	75	......	Basement of Meeting-house nearly completed.
S. S. Martin	Delavan	Delavan	May 1, 1854	12	13	1	11	----	190	45 35	Need no further aid.
Thomas Stokes	Duncanton	Carmi and vicinity	Nov. 1, 1854	12	39	6	15	----	----	......	Revival.
John Young	Bristol	Bristol, Yorkville, etc.	May 1, 1854	12	13	3	--	----	100	19 00	Health poor, and leaves the field for a more favorable climate.
W. D. Clark	Joliet	Lockport and Joliet	Nov. 1, 1854	12	39	2	1	19	50	55 00	
"	"	" "	Nov. 1, 1855	12	13	----	--	6	----	......	
John N. Tolman	Decatur, Macon Co.	Decatur	Jan. 1, 1855	12	39	1	1	5	30	50 01	Building Meeting-house.
" " "	" "	"	Jan. 1, 1856	12	13	----	--	3	----	36 95	
J. M. Cochran	Batavia	Batavia and vicinity	April 1, 1855	12	52	3	--	4	85	144 79	Meetings well attended, but a spiritual dearth generally among the churches.
"	"	" "	April 1, 1856	12	----	----	--	----	----	......	Re-appointed.

13	3	6	3	136	75 25	Church at Half Moon finished a Meeting-house. Churches will sustain their pastor without further aid.
39	1	1	5	50	8 25	Prospectively encouraging.
13	----	--	2	----	11 00	Difficulties in the church settled.
52	----	--	----	----	81 53	Labored extensively with some success among foreign immigrants.
26	1	1	1	60	15 00	Need no further aid.
13	1	--	2	100	10 95	Need no further aid.
26	3	5	3	100	31 00	Paying Meeting-house debt.
26	----	1	5	----	50 16	Progressing.
13	----	--	4	12	------	Wants ministers for [illegible] county.
39	3	[illegible]	5	20	5 26	Congregation steadily increasing. Some interest at an out-station.
13	4	--	----	50	------	Struggling to build a Meeting house.
39	4	--	6	----	7 35	Been sick.
13	----	--	----	12	1 00	Good attendance on his preaching.
39	1	--	11	100	20 00	Improved their church property. Some conversions.
----	----	--	----	----	------	
26	3	--	----	36	------	The Word heard apparently with deep interest. Left the field.
39	1	8	1	61	41 12	No further aid necessary.
30	1	--	10	----	------	Need no further aid. Pastor resigned on account of poor health.
52	2	--	----	18	6 00	
13	1	1	4	80	20 00	Progressing. Left the field.
39	----	--	----	----	36 25	Labored among the destitute and where they have but little pecuniary ability.
26	3	--	7	20	------	A growing interest in the congregation. Prospects flattering.
13	1	4	7	50	15 00	Leaves the field. Church in a good condition, and need no further aid.

NAMES OF AGENTS AND MISSIONARIES.	POST OFFICE ADDRESS.	FIELD OF LABOR.	Date of Commission	Months Commis'd.	Weeks labor reported.	Stations supplied.	Baptized.	Received by Letter.	Scholars in S. School.	Cont. to Benevolent Objects.	ADDITIONAL FACTS REPORTED.
Alexander Hamilton	Barton	Barton and West Bend	Nov. 1, 1854	12	39	1	2	4	----	40 53	Building a Meeting-house. Leaves the field for another station.
" "	Appleton	Appleton and vicinity	Dec. 1, 1855	12	13	3	--	5	30	----	Prospects encouraging.
S. Dearborn	Lowell	Lowell and vicinity	July 1, 1854	12	13	3	--	2	36	7 00	
"	"	" " "	July 1, 1855	12	39	4	--	2	----	3 97	Building a Meeting-house.
Samuel T. Catlin	St. Croix Falls	St. Croix Falls and vicinity	Oct. 1, 1854	12	13	2	--	----	24	----	An interesting field. Needs a S. School Library.
A. Gibson	Hudson, St. Croix Co.	Hudson and vicinity	June 1, 1854	12	13	5	5	3	54	15 00	
"	" "	" "	June 1, 1855	12	39	7	--	8	65	15 00	Discipline been necessary. Pastor, however, encouraged.
John Bruce	Gibbsville	Hollanders in G. etc.	Aug. 1, 1854	12	26	4	1	1	----	7 50	Organized a church.
"	"	" "	Aug. 1, 1854	12	26	----	--	1	15	32 00	Opposition from his countrymen of other denominations.
E. C. Sanders	Oshkosh, Winneb'o, Co.	Oskosh and vicinity	June 1, 1854	12	13	----	2	2	30	----	Prayer-meetings deeply interesting.
"	" "	" "	June 1, 1855	12	39	----	--	13	50	3 00	S. School growing in interest. Making preparations for building Meeting-house.
Albert D. Low	Prairie du Chien	Prairie du Chien	June 1, 1854	12	8	1	2	4	20	----	Health poor. Left the field.
John Eschman	Racine	Germans in the West	July 1, 1854	12	13	----	3	----	----	----	Cause advancing.
"	"	" "	July 1, 1855	12	26	----	6	3	20	10 00	Organized a church at Milwaukie. Church at Racine in a good condition. Left the field and returned to New York.
E. M. Lewis	Lancaster	Lancaster	June 1, 1854	12	13	3	15	2	----	----	
"	"	"	June 1, 1855	12	39	----	4	13	50	19 90	Suffered many afflictions; buried his entire family in Lancaster.
IOWA.											
Elihu Gunn	Keokuk	Keokuk	Nov. 1, 1854	12	39	----	11	16	150	----	Need no further aid.
William H. Turton	Farmington	Farmington	Oct. 1, 1854	12	26	3	--	1	----	11 50	Resigns the pastorate of the church.
B. B. Arnold	Hartford	Hartford and vicinity	Oct. 1, 1854	12	26	6	14	15	76	----	
"	"	" "	Oct. 1, 1855	12	26	----	2	9	203	----	Much interest in the prayer-meetings of the church.
Isaac Leonard	Burlington	Benton and Denmark	July 1, 1854	12	13	2	--	4	80	16 40	Benton Church building a Meeting-house.
Edward M. Miles	Davenport	2nd Church in Davenport	June 1, 1854	12	13	1	4	9	----	15 00	Church acquiring permanence.
" "	"	" "	June 1, 1855	12	30½	----	--	20	55	162 50	Church needs no further aid.
C. D. Farnsworth	Delhi, Delaware Co.	Delhi and vicinity	Aug. 1, 1854	12	26	2	17	5	31	19 85	Revival.
A. G. Eberhart	Muscatine	Muscatine	M'ch 1, 1856	12	52	----	20	20	100	63 00	Precious Revival; but leaves the field. Church need no further aid. Thirty-six additional baptisms subsequent to the report.

Weeks labor reported.	Stations supplied.	Baptized.	Received by Letter.	Scholars in S. School.	Cont. to Benevolent Objects.	ADDITIONAL FACTS REPORTED.
39	----	20	20	60	3 00	Secured a site for a Meeting-house.
13	2	--	----	----	------	Encouragingly progressing.
13	1	--	----	----	19 00	Finished Meeting-house. Need no further aid.
13	6	8	9	80	------	Revival.
39	----	4	11	----	18 24	Need no further aid after the present year.
13	1	--	4	----	------	Meeting house progressing.
39	----	4	26	175	59 00	Sunday-School greatly increased. Improvement and encouragement.
26	2	--	----	68	47 00	Leaves the field on account of ill health. Church now able to sustain a pastor.
13	----	--	----	----	40 00	
39	11	--	5	50	8 25	A large field; but one of promise and encouragement.
13	1	--	----	75	------	Resigned and removed to another field.
26	5	--	----	10	------	Need a Meeting-house.
26	7	--	1	8	------	Encouraged. Field important.
26	6	--	----	----	100 00	People urgent to have the Gospel.
39	5	--	4	30	------	Population increasing rapidly.
13	----	--	----	----	------	
13	4	--	6	30	------	Prospects promising.
39	----	23	17	35	25 00	Revival. Need a Meeting-house.
39	----	6	7	36	5 00	Organized two churches.
13	6	2	----	----	------	Prospering. Attendance good,
26	1	1	8	30	58 00	Membership much scattered.
26	----	--	4	----	------	
52	----	--	----	----	------	Exploring Agent and General Itinerant.
45	3	2	1	20	------	Some encouraging indications, but Indian war interfered with his labors.
52	1	--	3	60	------	Indian wars embarrass religious progress.

Names of Agents and Missionaries.	Post Office Address.	Field of Labor.	Date of Commission	Months Commis'd.	Weeks labor reported.	Stations supplied.	Baptized.	Received by Letter.	Scholars in S. School.	Cont. to Benevolent Objects.	Additional Facts Reported.
CALIFORNIA.											
Wm. Rollinson	San Francisco	Bush-st. Church	M'ch 1, 1855	13	46	1	2	6	80	37 00	Pastor resigned. S. School in a flourishing condition.
J. B. Saxton	Stockton	Stockton	Feb. 1, 1854	12	13	1		1	35		S. School in a flourishing condition.
O. B. Stone	Nevada	Nevada	Jan. 1, 1855	12	39	1	5	9	17		Church building a parsonage. Discipline been necessary.
H. H. Rhees	Ione Valley	Ione Valley	M'ch 1, 1854	12	39	3	3	2	40		Organized a church at an out-station. Resigned.
NEW MEXICO.											
Hiram W. Read	Albuquerque	Albuquerque	Aug. 1, 1854	12	26				10		Mrs. R. obliged to return to the States on account of ill health.
" "	"	"	Aug. 1, 1855	12	26	13	9		35		The serious state of Mrs. R.'s health has compelled him to return to the States. Has labored extensively and with success.
J. Milton Shaw	Fort Defiance	Fort Defiance and the Navajoes Indians	Dec. 1, 1855	12	7						Left the field temporarily for the States.
Sam'l. Gorman	Albuquerque	Laguna and vicinity	Oct. 1, 1854	12	26						Progressing; being not opposed as heretofore.
" "	"	" "	Oct. 1, 1855	12	26		8		10		
Jose Senum	Laguna	Assistant to Mr. G.	Jan. 1, 1854	9	39						Been useful and devoted to his work.
"	"	" "	Oct. 1, 1855	12	26						
F. Tolhurst	Santa Fe	Santa Fe	Sept. 1, 1854	12	26	1					Is encouraged. Has some inquirers.
"	"	"	Sept. 1, 1855	12	26						Preaching has been well attended.
KANSAS.											
Wm. W. Hall	Lawrence	Lawrence and vicinity	Oct. 1, 1854	12	26	5		7	36		Organized a church.
" "	"	" "	Oct. 1, 1855	12	26	3		11			Need a Meeting-house.
James Gillpatrick	Topeka	Topeka and vicinity	Nov. 1, 1854	12	39	4					Formed a church at Bloomington. Been very sick for several weeks.
" "	"		Nov. 1, 1855	12	13						Wife deceased.
NEW GRENADA.											
Philip B. Livingston	St. Andrews	St. Andrews	May 1, 1854	12	39	1	45		88	39 00	Building a Meeting-house. Organized a church at New Providence and ordained his father as pastor.

STATE CONVENTIONS

AND

GENERAL ASSOCIATIONS IN THE UNITED STATES,

With the Names and Post Office Address of the Corresponding Secretaries; the Time and Place of their Anniversaries for 18[illegible]; the number of Missionaries employed, and amount of Receipts into their Treasuries in 18[illegible], including Balances of the previous year.

STATES.	CORRESPONDING SECRETARIES.	POST OFFICE ADDRESS.	PLACE OF NEXT ANNIVERSARY.	Time of Anniversary	Number of Missionaries	Amount of Receipts for Dom. Miss. in 1854.
*Maine	----	----	----	----	----	----
New Hampshire	K. S. Hall	Lake Village	Pittsfield	----	18	$1936 61
Vermont	John Goadby	Poultney	Shaftsbury	Oct. 1	9	1838 99
Massachusetts	A. L. Spalding	East Cambridge	North Adams	Oct. 29	39	4546 46
Rhode Island	Warren Randolph	Providence	Pawtuxet	April 28	10	1368 49
Connecticut	E. Cushman	Deep River	Middletown	June 10	12	2063 00
New York	Wm. Arthur	West Troy	Penn Yan	Oct. 8	33	7159 63
New Jersey	J. M. Carpenter	Jacobstown	Hightstown	Oct. 28	15	2340 71
*Pennsylvania	J. Wheaton Smith	Philadelphia	----	----	----	----
Maryland	F. Wilson	Baltimore	Washington, D.C.	Nov. 11	14	4509 96
Virginia	H. K. Ellyson	Richmond	Lynchburg	June 29	51	6370 28
North Carolina	W. M. Wingate	Wake Forrest	Raleigh	Nov. 5	11	1845 64

[redacted]

AGGREGATE CONTRIBUTIONS FROM ALL THE STATES SINCE 1832.

STATES.	Total Amount to 1845.	1846.	1847.	1848.	1849.	1850.	1851.	1852.	1853.	1854.	1855.	1856.
Canada	$327 65	$864 70	$692 67	$734 11	$710 79	$809 57	$453 84	$183 63	$189 19	$91 91	$145 23	$143 75
Maine	2,717 40				500 00		37 00	56 39	622 31	164 66	178 16	102 44
New Hampshire	3,083 42	528 41	242 50	343 81	50 50	625 58	419 17	1,104 77	1,457 00	1,632 60	1,875 47	1,608 22
Vermont	1,718 95	673 95	184 00	257 51	222 80	1,015 75	471 98	505 17	494 71	758 58	1.511 10	1,186 84
Massachusetts	22,313 30	1,474 20	3,333 08	4,791 22	4,022 07	5.357 73	6.717 06	8,497 51	7,974 56	12,005 92	8.266 73	10 467 62
Rhode Island	5,118 45	852 35	669 56	1,683 33	1,545 76	2,427 57	1,188 66	2,874 55	687 87	2.695 78	2,247 45	2,560 07
Connecticut	11,628 71	1,186 08	1,042 31	1,072 06	1,480 46	1,251 84	2.032 59	2 490 31	3,052 58	4,529 96	4,283 70	4.047 46
New York	66,772 95	6,520 49	7,142 38	6,871 19	6,614 15	7.723 20	10,666 47	13,706 48	16,951 07	18,071 49	20,189 18	14,796 88
New Jersey	4,851 29	1,696 85	1,419 27	1,890 90	2,724 80	2,408 67	2,518 20	2.179 01	3,419 94	3.833 51	3,468 63	2,986 34
Pennsylvania	4,520 81	528 47	529 86	707 43	1,556 89	1,606 11	1,606 98	1,973 75	2,252 91	3,024 90	3,530 82	2,507 89
Delaware	161 20			153 36	60 00	228 94	203 00	168 00	167 90	138 92	67 88	103 75
Maryland	2,019 81	30 25	5 00				15 50					200 00
District of Columbia	953 12		10 00			30 00	5 00	37 31	5 00	134 00	30 00	
Ohio	1,010 45	114 81	30 84	30 50	29 45	153 52	241 88	656 62	732 48	2,758 60	3 226 67	2,708 28
Michigan	337 50	29 50	18 25	172 89	556 21	610 60	1,011 80	866 75	634 43	287 74	574 60	179 23
Indiana	28 75	8 10	22 05	11 11	8 50	26 35	290 22	774 38	1,669 44	2,306 79	2.101 50	656 72
Illinois	608 09	477 63	766 50	1,136 69	594 90	704 74	1,329 98	1,230 97	1,675 63	2.479 52	1 799 70	1,700 17
Wisconsin	20 10	15 63	124 50	72 15	88 06	58 35	181 91	170 09	274 87	549 71	625 90	418 43
Iowa	83 56	41 00	120 03	62 12	93 24	162 77	171 95	396 67	278 05	277 10	332 58	578 12
Minnesota							1 00	2 25	55 85	141 46	405 35	328 25
Missouri	266 82							2 00		75 00	215 00	
Kentucky	273 88		10 00	20 50						42 25		
Virginia	9,152 56	159 44	5 85	7 30			5 00				23 75	
North Carolina	5,000 02	391 67										
South Carolina	8,362 95	135 15							30 00			30 00
Georgia	9,529 33		1,331 87					30 00				
Alabama	493 08										30 00	
Florida	157 82		15 00									
Mississippi	1,899 66											
Tennessee	477 85		8 25									
Louisiana	79 00											
Arkansas	50			50 55	18 15							
Texas												
California							50 00	150 50	70 00	20 00	225 00	105 00
Oregon							30 00		51 50	159 12	59 33	44 98
New Mexico								62 10	94 42	7 38	20 00	
U. S. Government												435 00
New Granada												89 60
Aggregates for each period	163,028 98	15,727 63	17,728 72	20,068 73	20,876 73	25,201 09	29,648 28	38,114 16	42,872 01	59,903 83	55,545 40	47,928 54

LIST OF LEGACIES,

PAID TO THE SOCIETY SINCE ITS ORGANIZATION.

1834	Dea. Josiah Penfield, Savannah, Ga., per Rev. H. O. Wyer	$1250 00
1835	Mrs Clarissa Long, Shelburne, Mass., per W. Wilder, Esq., Executor	37 50
"	William Powers Hebron, N. H., per Rev I. Merriam	100 00
"	Miss Maria Curtis, Southbridge, Mass., per Rev. E Going	200 00
"	Mrs Jemima Elliott Hampton, Ct., per Rev. J. Payne, Executor	100 00
1836	Mrs. Betsey Sprague, Attleboro', Mass., per Mr A. Reed, Executor	451 25
"	Robert Rogers, Newport, R. I.	25 00
"	Ebenezer Boyd, Providence, R. I.	10 00
1839	Mrs. Abigail Marshall, New York, per Mr. Schofield, Executor	702 17
"	Mrs Margaret Pugsley, Dutchess Co., N. Y., per Miss Cornelia Pugsley	280 00
"	Mrs Irene Coats, New York, per Alfred Decker, Esq	250 00
[illegible]	[illegible] Hartford, Ct. [illegible]	[illegible]

1848	William Jones, Iowa City, Iowa, per G. W. Hampton, Executor	25 00
"	Hon. James Vanderpool, Newark, per B. Vanderpool, Executor	1000 00
"	Miss Susan Farrar, Keene, N. H., per Rev. G. Robins	10 00
"	Mrs. Eunice Nicholls, Cambridge, Mass., per E. Mansfield, Executor	500 00
"	Mrs. Hannah Carleton, Portland, Me., per Rev. G. J. Carleton, Administrator	500 00
1849	Mr. Samuel R. Stelle, Piscataway, N. J., per Lewis R. Stelle, Esq., Executor	200 00
"	Mrs. Phebe Gale, East Bennington, Vt., per Executor of Estate of S. Harmon	25 00
"	Mr. William Reynolds, Boston, Mass., per J. H. Duncan, Esq., and Mrs. Susan D. Reynolds, Executors, in land not sold at Toledo, Ohio	
"	Josiah Lyman, Andover, Ct., per N. B. Lyman, Executor	50 00
"	John J. Martin, Montgomery, N. Y., per M. Bookstaver, Executor	1000 00
"	Mrs. Martha Howe, West Boylston, Mass., per Messrs E. J. Howe & Co.	50 00
"	A. H. Reed, Sweden, N. Y., per Rev. D. Searl	13 00
"	Asa H. Truman, Owego, N. Y., per E. Truman, Executor	248 00
1850	George D. James, Amenia, N. Y., J. K. Mead and N. Rose, Executors	100 00
"	John Everett, Manchester, Mich., per F. Everett	70 00
"	Jacob Whitman, Belvidere, Ill., in part, per N. Crosby, Esq.	160 00
"	Jonas Taylor, Boston, Mass.	12 50
"	Miss Rebecca Thompson, Amenia, N. Y. per A. B. Capwell, Esq.	801 00
"	Joanna Minot, Boston, Mass., per E. Mears and I. Parker, Executors	100 00
"	Claudius F. Brown, Arkwright, N. Y., per David Barrell	150 00
"	Miss Anna Roe, Egremont, Mass., per R. B. Brown, Executor	50 00
1851	David Schauber, Burnt Hills, N. Y., per J. & D. M. Shauber, Executors	10 00
"	Woolcot Griffin, Governeur, N. Y, per O. L. Barnum, Executor	100 00
"	Joseph Flanders, Brooklyn, N. Y., per Mrs. Eliza A. Flanders and Benj. Flanders	560 00
"	William Williams, New York, per John Allen, Executor	400 00
"	Ely Wiley, South Reading, Mass	50 00
1852	Miss Pharozene C. Kelly, Hopkinton, N. H., per John Page	50 00
"	Jonathan W. Ford, Boston, Mass	100 00
"	Theron Fisk, Warsaw, N. Y. in advance	2500 00
"	Joshua A. Burke, Brooklyn, N. Y., per Messrs. E. and W. A. Burke	850 00
"	Miss Eliza Skaats, New York, in part, per G. N. Bleecker, Executor	1000 00
"	Barnum M. Howard, Sweden, N. Y., per H. M. Howard, Executor	20 00
1853	Alanson Stewart, Liberty, N. Y., per W. W. Murphy	5 00
"	Mrs. Sarah B. Peirce, Middleboro', Mass	100 00
"	Arnold Whipple, Providence, R. I., per Mrs. P. Whipple, Executrix	200 00
"	Mrs. Fanny McGilvreay, Brookline, N. H. (Annuity), per H. A Daniels, Administrator.	40 00
"	Mrs. Lucretia Goddard, Worcester, Mass., per Hon. I. Davis, Executor	300 00
"	P. F. Brayton, Providence, R. I., per A. K. Brayton and Rev. J. Brayton, in addition	594 87
"	Mrs. Elizabeth Gale, Washington, D. C.	50 00
1854	Edward Rogers, Chester, Ill., per Rev. M. B. Kelly	5 00
"	Miss Esther Ann Blakely, Pawlet, Vt., per Rev. J. J. Peck	73 00
"	Daniel Cummings, Chelsea, Mass., per Mr. Eaton, Executor	1000 00
"	Mrs. Mary Leuce, Bristol, R. I., per J. F. Baars	7 50
"	D. Valentine, Washington, Pa., per H. W. Wilson, Executor	239 80
"	Willis L. Eaton, East Weare, N. H., per J. L. Eaton, Executor	100 00
"	Asa Read, Attleboro', Mass., per Amos M. Read, Executor	1000 00
"	Friend Humphrey, Albany, N. Y., per his son, Executor	106 80
"	George Corbett, Worcester, Mass	8 00
"	Mrs. Abby Arnold, Centreville, R. I., per W. A. Arnold	95 00
"	Garrat N. Bleecker, New York, per E. Cauldwell and W. F. Van Wagner, Executors	6000 00
"	Dr. John Goodell, Auburn, N. Y, in part	71 66
"	Eunice Shepardson, Belleville, N. Y	70 00
"	Mrs. Mary Johnson, Albany, N. Y., per Chas. Pohlman	10 00
"	Charles H. Nichols, Boston, Mass., in part, in advance	150 00
"	Mrs. Olive Stowell Le Roy, N. Y., per R. Bell	10 00
"	David Trull, Lowell, Mass., per J. Fox	200 00

1855	Roger Pegg, New York, per Mr. Coe, Executor	100 00
"	John Goodell, Jr., Woodstock, N. Y., in part, per Mrs. Maria H. Goodell, Executrix	117 83
"	Mrs Frances Thompson, Alabama, N. Y.	50 00
"	Miss Mercy Hayden Grafton, Mass., per Rev. J. Smith	20 00
"	Joseph D Murray, Newhope, Pa.	30 00
"	W S. Ward, Salem, Mass.	100 00
"	Mrs. Lucy Bushnell, Monticello, N. Y., per Rev. Samuel White	50 00
"	W. Littlefield, Belleville, N Y	30 00
"	Mary E. Bennett, Ludlow, Vt., per Rev. N. Cudworth, Executor	111 00
"	Margaret Sherwood, New York, per E J Mattocks, Executor	50 00
"	Linus Austin, Akron, Ohio	27 00
"	Mrs —— Nelson, Peoria, Ill.	3 00
"	Mrs Margaret Davies, New York, per John M. Davies	20 00
"	Abijah Porter, Danvers, Mass., per Rev. J. W. Parkhurst	500 00
"	Jacob Morse, Sturbridge, Mass., per Mrs Sophia A. Morse	400 00
"	Andrew McCleary, Frederick City, Md., per Albert Ritchie	200 00
1856	Miss Hannah Briggs, Rock Island, Ill., per Rev. A. Briggs	50 00
"	Miss Eliza Jackson, Hamilton, N. Y., per Prof. P. B. Spear	100 00
"	Mrs. M W. Denison, Rock Island, Ill., per Rev. J. W. Denison	8 00
"	Miss Achsah Cox, Imlaystown N. J	50 00
"	Samuel Stone, Dundee, Mich., T. Babcock, Executor	30 00

DOCUMENTS

REFERRED TO IN THE "MINUTES OF THE ANNIVERSARY."

DOCUMENT No. 1.

Report of the Committee to procure a Home Mission House.

To the American Baptist Home Mission Society:

The Committee appointed at your last anniversary, held in Brooklyn, May, 1855, to purchase, or erect a building for the business purposes of this society, most respectfully report:

That, although the instructions given us for our guidance were not such as we could approve of, we entered immediately on the duties assigned us, with the hope, and expectation, that the friends of Home Missions, would contribute generously for this object, and enable us to present to you, at this anniversary, a successful and satisfactory completion of our labors. Such, we regret to say, is not the case.

The amount requisite to fulfill the instructions of the Society, and obtain a building, so located—such as would please its friends—would not be less than $18,000

We have made constant application, in person and by letter, for subscriptions, donations, and collections, resulting in our obtaining thus far, about $10,000

Many have refused to aid us in this undertaking, and some, favorably inclined, do not contribute, being doubtful of our success.

In this unsatisfactory state of the matter, we come before you.

In our opinion a location for the Home Mission Society apart from the American and Foreign Bible Society, or American Bible Union, is as important now, as it was when we were appointed, and should be consummated, soon as practicable.

If the society think it advisable to remove the restrictions now imposed on our operations (particularly that which relates to the line of Canal Street, as property below that street, is much more valuable than above) and give good evidence of their co operation in the work, we will, to the best of our ability, discharge the trust reposed in us, by the 1st of January next. Otherwise, we must respectfully request you to accept our resignations.

New York, May 5th, 1856.

EBENEZ. CAULDWELL,
THOS. THOMAS,
JOHN R. DURBROW,
JOHN M. FERRIER,
GEORGE GAULT,
WM. T. DUGAN.

DOCUMENT No. 2.

Report of the Special Committee to confer with the Committee to procure a Home Mission House.

The special Committee to whom was referred the present aspect of matters pertaining to the securing of permanent rooms for this Society, have given to the questions involved the profoundest and maturest deliberation which they could bestow; and, after a free and full conference with the Committee appointed last year, beg leave to Report:

That five of their number favor the suggestion of your Standing Committee [redacted] in their judgment shall be most for the convenience and interest of the Society.

Provided, that the total cost of such property shall not exceed double the amount of money actually received or subscribed, and the Committee shall be satisfied that the rents arising from such parts of the building as are not wanted for the uses of the Society, will pay the annual interest and expenses.

And, whenever a legal title to such property is secured and vested in the American Baptist Home Mission Society, the Executive Board are hereby authorized and instructed to remove from the present location, and to enter upon the possession and use of the same.

DOCUMENT No. 4.

Report of the minority of the Special Committee of Conference respecting a Home Mission House.

The Committee, to whom was referred the subject of an independent location for the Society, report—

That they have had an interview with the committee originally appointed to solicit subscriptions for that object, and have considered the expediency of removing the restrictions imposed in the compromise under which they have acted; and without intending to express any opinion as to the wisdom of all the original terms of that compromise, the fact is indisputable that a compromise was proposed and accepted in 1855, as the basis of "conciliation." Your committee are of the opinion therefore, that it would not be advisable to discharge the Committee on an Independent Location appointed in 1855, or to change the terms of the original agreement; and they recommend, that the subject be recommitted to the committee who have had it in charge the last year, with power to fill vacancies; and if the independent location be obtained, agreeably with the terms of the compromise, your committee believe that the result should be acceptable to all parties; and should no such location be secured by January 1st, 1857, it is the deliberate opinion of your committee that the utmost care should be taken so to adjust the arrangement for the occupancy of rooms in Nassau Street, as shall be deemed perfectly equitable by the Executive Board of the Home Mission Society—equitable in the sense of obtaining such right in the building as shall correspond with the amount of money paid towards its erection on behalf of the Home Mission Society; and in the event of the failure of both of these plans, it is also the deliberate opinion of your committee that the seat of the Society's operations should be transferred to some other city, at the next anniversary.

DOCUMENT No. 5.

Report of the Special Committee on Missionary operations, presented by Rev. Thos. Armitage, D.D.

The Committee on Missions are reminded, in presenting their report, that the primary use of such a report is to stir up the gift of God in his people, so far as that gift contemplates the propagation of the faith committed to the Church, by her Divine Redeemer. This has been measurably done already, by the rehearsal of the facts constituting the Annual Report of the Board. We might, perhaps, enhance this interest, somewhat, by a fuller reference to the greatness of our field; because that greatness is at once the result and promise of Bible Christianity on this side of the globe. For, doubtless, we shall bestir ourselves to a more thorough and earnest occupation of this immense field, in proportion to a just conception of the unmeasured scene of action it spreads before us; to our great opportunities of blessing North America with a pure Gospel; and to the corresponding success attendant upon the right improvement of those opportunities. Still, it is not an easy matter, if it be possible at all, to communicate a soul-inspiring view of the responsibilities of this Society by any presentation of naked figures, however accurate and formidable, touching the history and destinies of this Continent. Much less can this be done by any detail of facts, however elaborate, relating to the thrift, [redacted] elemental in all abiding success. No incentive to untiring activity in the Home Mission work, is worthy of comparison with the living, apostolic impulse—"the love of Christ *constraineth* us." When the churches of the Saints are influenced pre-eminently by this celestial agency, all the powers of their sanctified nature are summoned to guage their responsibility in this matter, and to meet it in the name of the Lord. Then, and then only, they feel that missions must be fostered in the warm glow of their bosoms, simply because the perpetual commission of the Saviour requires this at their hands. And this, too, irrespective of any reliance upon mere civilizing auxiliaries, and even though no temporal and material advantages were found to exist, either as companions or consequences of the diffusion of Christianity. Those churches who would form an invincible propaganda of the pure faith, must place themselves in immediate contact with the burning love of Jesus Christ for the salvation of immortal souls from the degradation of a total apostacy, and from the bitter pains of eternal death. All contemplation of religious destitution, and all motives to missionary labor, must be futile and vain, except as they keep these fearful realities of the Gospel in view. The foundations of every altar we rear, must be laid in the immutable conviction of loyalty to the bare command of Christ, and an unquenchable love to the souls he has redeemed with his blood; and then, for every sacrifice of money or men we lay upon those altars we may anticipate showers of blessing. The unpossessed land before us, is the theatre of a mysterious conflict, in which Belial combats energetically against Christ; in which sin contests every step with holiness; and the prize is the souls of men. And if we are called as the servants of Christ to unite with him against those embattled hosts who are boldly marshaled under his arch foe, let us be well armed. We are called to use those invincible weapons which are tempered with the Saviour's Spirit, and which his own arm once wielded, when he bruised the head of Satan in another and a greater contest. It must be confessed, that the Printing Press—the Electric Wires—and the various forms of Steam Power—with all the other facilities of the modern Christian Missionary, are wonderful instruments furnished by Divine Providence for resisting the subtle attacks of delusion and superstition. But in their highest capacity, they are only and emphatically "carnal weapons," and are of no efficiency whatever, unless the hands that use them are controlled by the hallowing love of him who is "mighty to save," and whose voice ever reverberates above the din of the mystic turmoil; saying, "Lo I am with you always, even to the end of the world."

No true Christian among us, can look upon the achievements of this Society without feeling new obligations of thanksgiving to that God, whose grace alone has secured them. And yet, no true Christian among us can fail of deep humiliation when he reflects upon the marvellous contrast suggested by the thought, that, if the Apostles had possessed the Printing-Press, the Electric Wires, and the various forms of Steam Power, under like circumstances with ourselves, much greater things than these would have been done:—Or, if they could now visit the earth and ply these great instrumentalities for good, in all the energy of the apostolic spirit, we should speedily witness immensely greater results than we have yet seen, or hope ever to see, in the exercise of our fullest assurance of faith. Among us, the same antagonists are to be met that they met; the same human nature is to be renovated; and the same glorious Gospel is to be preached. In a word, the great difference between them and us, aside from our greater advantages, is to be found in our comparative want of the Spirit of our Lord, and in their unreserved consecration to the salvation of men, manifested in their Christ-like self-sacrifice, in their faith and their love. Take their fields of labor and ours into the account, simply, and a mighty difference is apparent in our favor. But take their success and ours into the account, in connection with these fields of labor, and we are immediately "weighed in the balance and found wanting." The nations visited by the apostles were historically stern, and permanent in their nationality. Their prejudices were inveterate, their institutions were hoary with age, their superstitions were chronic, and their licentiousness was sanctioned as very sanctity. On the other hand, the field chosen by this Society, especially that within our own national limits, is new in its history, its patriotism, its tastes, its institutions, and its iniquities. Peculiarly favorable opportunities are thus afforded us, for the infusion of new and evangelical elements into the incipient composition of this new nation, if we would but improve them by seeking a larger measure of the Spirit of Christ. If we would but emulate esteemed him not. And when he saw them as sheep scattered abroad without a shepherd, devoted to execration and doomed to ruin, he wept for grief over the metropolis of their land, because they knew not the day of their visitation. But at the same time, as the "Lamb of God who taketh away the sin of the world," he instituted a living and diffusive religion in the place of the contracted ritualism of the Jew. He enforced upon the Gospel church the vast significancy of the prayer he had taught her to utter, "Thy Kingdom come. Thy will be done on earth, as it is in heaven," by dispatching the ministers of Jehovah to the Gentiles, for the first time in the history of the world, (bating the solitary embassy of Jonah to Nineveh,) to "preach the Gospel to every creature," from one end of heaven to the other.

Every man, then, who possesses the spirit of Christ, possesses necessarily and essentially a missionary spirit; and as his spirit takes more and more the type of the Divine Original, it will be at once, necessarily and essentially both a Home and a Foreign Missionary spirit. You cannot sever the two, unless you can divide the Spirit of Christ against itself. Nay, more than this, when the true Missionary spirit is once brought into practical exercise, the interest it takes in the Home and Foreign work, will act upon itself, reciprocally, in these two departments, as the instrument of its own revival and strength.

Your Committee, regard this spirit of love for the salvation of men, as the great first principle which underlies all proper effort and all desirable prosperity in the system of modern missions. So that it is only as we obtain an appreciative view of the ruined condition of the millions of unconverted men, who are without Gospel privileges in North America, that our operations can be maintained in perpetuity until the regenerating work is finished. There are not a few errorists and nominal Christians who imagine that our whole missionary system is the ebullition of an unrestrainable enthusiasm. They predict that sooner or later the phantom which deludes us will vanish away, and then our annual offerings of money and men will cease, and the work will be abandoned. And, truly, if we lose that spirit which palpitated in the whole frame of the great Exemplar, it may well be so. But while we maintain this, we shall be steadfast and unmoveable, always abounding in the work of the Lord. While this Spirit burns in our breasts it is impossible but that men and means should be forthcoming. And the higher and more intensely it burns, the more copiously will Zion pour her gifts at the feet of her King, and the more dense will become the throng of hewers of wood and drawers of water, which she will pour forth from her gates. The more sober, and fixed, and overwhelming, shall become the conviction that our countrymen are arrayed in daring insult against the majesty of God, and against a gentle and tender Saviour, who was rich and for their sakes became poor ; the more earnestly shall we seek their rescue from their sin and blind infatuation. When our churches shall take this view of these realities, and shall feel a commiseration for the lost, at all kindred to that of their Master and Head, they will not rest, so long as one native trail in our forests—one lowly hut on our prairies—one dingy cabin on our waters—or one loathsome cellar in our cities, remains unvisited by the herald of salvation, and unhallowed by the sovereign Spirit of grace. So long as the angels of God tread our land with an uncertain step, and with pinions quivering ready for flight from it at the first beck of a jealous God, because of the moral turpitude which assigns man to the place of the brute, and the brute to the place of man, in the scale of existence, so long we must feel unutterable solicitude for our people, pulling them out of the fire. Ordinary and every-day views of the evil nature of sin are inadequate to stir up the true spirit of missions. We must seek, and obtain in our proper measure, those vigorous and lofty views of the criminality of sin, and of its eternal consequences which were discovered in the method of its remission, when the Redeemer trod the wine-press of the wrath of God. But even where these sentiments are most laid to heart, there is great danger of losing those intense convictions of the peril of sin, if perchance, a few hundred miles stretch between us and the men we seek to save. The distance to Oregon, California, or New Mexico, is apt to impose upon our strongest perceptions, and smooth down the repulsive and alarming developments of sin in those who perpetrate it; just as a few intervening miles soften down the abrupt projections and rugged profile of our mountains. We are, therefore, under the constant necessity of struggling against a merely visionary realization of the shades of death, in which these perishing ones are shrouded; and of praying for new awakenings to the consciousness that this death-shade is pregnant with the fatal threat of Jehovah to consign [redacted] privilege, than in the case of the truly apostolic Judson. At this moment he sleeps in his coral tomb. Millions of Burman hearts call him blessed, and the surges chant his dirge until the seas shall give up its dead. But judging from his life, we may anticipate, that when he who walked with Peter on the Sea of Galilee, and rescued Paul from a grave in the Mediterranean, shall descend again to bring many missionary sons to glory; he will transmute the weeds which play around the sleeping herald into an immortal laurel for the head of that faithful servant, who will rise to meet his Saviour, and stretching forth his hands, still wet with the brine of the Indian Ocean, will find his first utterance one of thanksgiving, that he was counted worthy to preach the unsearchable riches of Christ to the Gentiles. If these apostolic servants of our Lord, have esteemed it their highest honor to make exacting sacrifices for the salvation of men, at home and abroad, how much more should we cherish the love of this work, whose privilege it is to discharge the same duty without the same suffering? Those whose salvation this Society especially seeks, are at our very doors. We may reach every part of our field with but little delay of distance, and but little danger of person or property, and the Society already possesses in itself, all the ordinary elements of success. The labor it performs annually is of the most direct and simple character for the immediate salvation of men, and is performed on a scale of economy almost unequaled when we look at the amount of work it does. No part of our field is commonly pestilential, so that our Missionaries must meet an early grave at their posts. Our operations are conducted in nine foreign languages, and yet it has not been found necessary in a single case to incur the expense of educating a missionary, in any one of these tongues, before he could enter upon his work. Much less, has it been necessary to establish seminaries, or their equivalent, for the education of all the Missionaries who preach in these foreign languages; a thing indispensably requisite in many of our Foreign mission operations. Besides all this, no extraordinary difficulties of a social or national character, and calling for extraordinary skill and fortitude, repel our exertions, or defy our perseverance. Every earnest effort which the Society has put forth from the beginning, for the diffusion of our holy principles and practices, has been met with results more than rivaling first expectations. The small expenditure of the present year, has issued in the organization of twenty new churches, and the number of churches who have become self-sustaining almost equals these figures. Each of these new churches has introduced new impulses of religious agitation into the cities, villages, or hamlets, where it has been formed, and the infallible progress of the Saviour's love thus shed abroad, must spread the saving knowledge of his name in all the regions round about.

In conclusion, your Committee would implore in behalf of the Society, an increase of prayer, and labor, and liberality. In answer to importunate prayer we may expect to see the Spirit poured out from on high, on every Mission Station in the Society, during the present year. But our supplications will partake of the veriest formality if we furnish no evidence of their fervor by giving. And labor will be as indispensable as prayer and liberality. They must all go together. When God promised to bless Israel, in going out, and in coming in, his going out was the first in order. God could not bless him in coming in until Israel had first exerted himself in going out. In like manner if we would be sharers of heavenly rain poured out upon our missions, we must first form a cloud for it by the smoke of our offerings; though that cloud be little as a human hand, and fringed only with so much wreathing incense as would cover the face of two mites. For inasmuch as prayer in this enterprise, without labor, would be enthusiasm, so both prayer and labor without liberality would be presumption. Let us, therefore, depend by faith upon an omnipotent and gracious God, while the double Gospel motto of our society shall be, "PRAY AND GIVE. PRAY AND WORK."

DOCUMENT No. 6.

Report of the Special Committee on Obituaries.

Through the haste of business at the last Anniversary the Report on Obituaries was omitted. Reference is made to this now for the purpose of stating, that four Life Directors, and *thirty-nine* Life Members died during that [redacted] purposes of grace to fill the earth with his glory, He takes not counsel of any. He has previously admonished us of the trials to be imposed on our Faith—of numerous and particular disappointments in our work, and when, in addition to these, He summons away old and tried associates in our Missionary toils, —leaving us to follow up their labors in behalf of Zion and a perishing world, we then, in our bereavement feel deeply the duty to "cease from man whose breath is in his nostrils," and if in the least we have forsaken it, to fall back again upon the Saviour's promise "Lo, *I* am with you always, even unto the end of the world"—and the end of the world is the end of the work.

The missionaries of this Society, and those who are identified with it in official relations as executives and managers, are no strangers to an anguished mind under the onerous responsibilities of their work, and the dealings of God with them while prosecuting it; and your Committee would remind them, one and all, that the promise just referred to is their first and last resort and their only firm support. The visitations of Death in removing from our ranks those whose presence seemed essential, and whose ability and piety gave them a peculiar and responsible position in the interests and management of the Society, will gather clouds of darkness over our heads: but this promise sheds light through the gloom. In its gracious consolations, we learn that there are no irreparable losses to the Church of Christ, and that the grave in claiming to its trust our companions in the work of home missions, affects by no means a triumph, but simply a removal, a transfer to eternal blessedness and joy.

The stream of Death may divide our membership between heaven and earth, but are not those "to glory gone," still with us in the memory of their illustrious examples, and the power of their good works which follow them? Do they not beckon us on to the rest they now enjoy, with the assurance of the Divine promise, that, if we are faithful unto death, we shall receive the crown of Life?" And the dead of the past year, among whom appear the shining and glorified spirits of Spencer H. Cone, N. V. Steadman, Deacon John West, and many others who wrought righteousness in the Earth, what do they say to us while our memories are yet fresh with the recollection of their wise counsels, their zealous labors, and their steadfast friendships? Do they not say, "be faithful and work while it is day; for when you come to join us in this glory, and, with unclouded vision, see the Lamb in the midst of the Throne," there will then be a consciousness that you have done but little, even under the wisest outlay of time and energies, and that Grace must crown your work at last.

And, brethren, while we know that the silence of the grave has closed over them, are we not solemnly reminded that their example, so far as they followed Christ, is all that we should cling to now? for that alone, is of any worth to us in the further prosecution of the enterprise to which in this organization we have devoted our means and energies.

The example of Spencer H. Cone, rendered so prominent by the faith, the principles, and the devotion of his life, is a legacy to this Society of no ordinary value. Let us cherish it for its conspicuous excellencies. He was one of the originators of this Society. A member of its Board for nineteen years, and for thirteen years presiding over its deliberations, he was familiar with its history, progress, and results. His heart was in the work of Home Missions, and his best wishes were conceived for it. His services in the interests of this Society were constant and long-continued.

There is a sacred charm around his example; for it is a shining representation of practical wisdom, active consistency, and holy zeal.

The departure of such a fellow-laborer and standard-bearer in our holy cause, calls for renewed and persevering efforts on our part, while we become imitators of all that is of good report in our cherished companions who have passed before us to the fulfillment of promise, and to serve God day and night continually in his temple.

Respectfully submitted.

W. S. Clapp,
Ch'm. of Committee.

[redacted]

Let those who solicit aid for new and feeble churches, either find a real Church Edifice Fund, out of which adequate help can be drawn, or let their access to churches and benevolent individuals be no longer hindered by a nominal Fund. It is not fitting, that an empty shadow should stand by and forbid the bans between want and supply.

When your Committee lift up their eyes and look on the fields, when they read the heart-stirring appeals of the needy in the West and elsewhere, when they consider the indispensableness of a house of worship to the success of a Missionary, and the apparent feasibility of the plan adopted by the Society for meeting a demand so obvious and pressing, they cannot recommend that the work be abandoned.

If they believed that the merits of this enterprise had been fully understood, and duly considered by the churches, and that the sums thus far received, were the just exponent of the judgment of the churches, and of benevolent brethren upon the subject, they would receive the verdict as one from which it were useless to appeal.

But if the public response of the last three years, can be accounted for, by a lack of the proper agencies, by any untoward events in the history of the Society, or by unusual pecuniary embarrassments, so as to warrant the belief that the will of the people has not yet been expressed, then may facts which were otherwise disheartening bear a hopeful interpretation.

So far as their knowledge extends, your committee believes this latter supposition to be true, and they are strengthened in this belief by the known success of a kindred movement in another denomination of Christians.

Perhaps the *best* time for securing this Fund is past; but it does not follow that on that account it should not be done at all. Better to work under some disadvantages than to leave the work undone.

What reason can be assigned for sending a man two thousand miles away, to preach the Gospel in a destitute town or village, and appropriating the requisite funds for his support, meantime neglecting this important question:—*Where* shall he *convene the people*, and dispense the word? If those to whom we send are unable to support the Missionary, on what grounds shall we conclude them able to provide a Sanctuary? If it be a solemn duty to aid them in the one instance, how shall we excuse ourselves in the other? A work of charity should not be defeated by being left incomplete.

But it may be said that in sustaining a missionary we only meet a temporary want, acting upon the supposition that a self-sustaining church will soon spring up—while building a house of worship is doing a work for coming years as well as for the present, and thus, perhaps, prospectively helping those who will need no help.

The actual donation of a church edifice to a people, would indeed, be liable to this objection, but such is not the plan pursued by this Society. The loan of moderate sums, for a specified time, on easy terms, to deserving applicants, is extending help only to the needy, and continuing it only during a time of need; and all experience shows, that that much desired end in all Missionary labor, a self-sustaining church, is much sooner reached with, than without, a convenient house of worship. Hence the Society's loan, causes its annual appropriations to a given locality sooner to determine.

But, as arguments and resolutions touching this subject abound on the records of the Society, your committee would conclude their report, by commending to special attention, the words of Paul to the Corinthians. "Now therefore perform the doing of it that as there was a readiness to will, so there may be a performance also out of that which ye have."

M. G. Hodge,
Ch'm of Committee.

DOCUMENT No. 8.

Proposition for the amendment of the Constitution.

The Rev. D. G. Corey proposed the following amendments to the Constitution, which were received for consideration until the next anniversary.

1st. That there be added, at the end of the 3rd article, the following words: "Life Directors shall be entitled to seats in the Executive Board, with all the privileges of members of the Board, except that of voting.

2. That the 5th article be amended by striking out all before the word "elect," in the second line, and substituting the words, "5th, At each Annual Meeting the Society shall." Also to strike out the phrase, "residing in the City of New York, or its vicinity," so that the article shall read as follows:

"5th. At each Annual Meeting the Society shall elect fifteen Managers, who, together with the Treasurer, Auditor, and the Secretaries, shall constitute an Executive Board to conduct the business of the Society; and shall respectively continue to discharge their official duties until superseded by a new election. Seven members of the Board shall be a quorum for the transaction of business.

ADDRESS OF REV. J. R. STONE,

ON MOVING THE ACCEPTANCE OF THE ANNUAL REPORT OF THE EXECUTIVE BOARD.

Mr. President:—The present fiscal condition of our Society and the statement of its receipts during the past year, as presented in this Report, must awaken mingled emotions. Grateful pleasure and devout thankfulness to God seek utterance on this occasion, because of a balance in the treasury, and a happy deliverance from *protests* and distressing pecuniary embarrassments. As when a Cunard steamer was lately preserved from destruction by an iceberg, while running in a dense fog, by a favoring Providence and by dint of the quickest and most energetic action, the vessel almost grazing the side of the formidable mountain of ice; or, as when a packet-ship escapes from a lee-shore, or sunken reef, by close-hauling every yard and putting the helm hard down; so the great ship, given us to freight and sail, has passed through imminent peril, yet thus far been kept mainly on her course. We who have seen the dangers, and pulled at the ropes, cannot but feel grateful to-night. To use another figure, we feel as the members of some business house may have felt, when notes were maturing, checks being called for, and liabilities crowding, more rapidly than their sales and collections would justify. Expenses are curtailed, unfilled orders are countermanded, new adventures are declined, and the utmost economy, prudence, and vigilance called into exercise; retrenching in every practicable method and tasking every man's abilities to the utmost; till a better state of things comes to exist. Then each partner breathes freely again, and congratulations are in place.

But these feelings are succeeded, nay, accompanied, by *sad thoughts*, and emotions of *grief*, if not of *chagrin*. A celebrated ship-master, who has commanded several of the fleetest clippers that belong to the port of New York, on a certain occasion, in the China sea, when going below at the beginning of the first officer's dog-watch, gave orders to shorten no sail without calling him, and to let him remain undisturbed in his state-room unless the topmasts should be carried away. It was about the time of the breaking up of the Monsoons, and ere an hour had passed the winds had played mischief with the spars and rigging, and the captain was suddenly called. He came to the quarter-deck in anger with himself, with the mate and all his men; while the alertness and strong arms of all were put into immediate requisition to save the ship.

We have no *reason to censure the* Board or the Officers of the Society, for the embarrassed condition of the treasury, the curtailment of its expenditures, the contraction of its policy, the withholding of its commissions, or the denials of its aid, though most imploringly asked ; for they have but obeyed the stern laws of necessity; not to say prudence and wisdom. They found the ship under a press of canvas, and with a deep water-line, this time a year ago. The Society had given directions and impetus to her course. But the sky darkened. An ominous cloud spread over one quarter of the heavens. The waves ran high, and the vessel labored heavily. The rolling of the breakers broke upon astonished ears, blanching the countenance, and saddening the heart. But one course was to be pursued, and to that all energy and skill were to be directed. Seeking divine aid, and calling for such human help as might be secured, the Board have done what they could to avert disaster and successfully prosecute the work given them to accomplish: and to-night, in presenting their Report, they desire us to unite with them in a song of praise, pitched, however, to a minor key; and ask us to consider the past only as a present encouragement and a stimulant to renewed and greater endeavors.

It is a matter of regret that the receipts for the year, just closed, should not only have proved inadequate to the Society's necessities, but have fallen off also from the previous year's aggregate. To this result, however, several causes have contributed, which need only to be named:

1.—The wide-spread pecuniary embarrassment that was felt by most of the

[redacted]

The receipts of the past year have been but little more than $50,000.—Few, if any, will deny that the Executive Board could wisely dispense $80,000; aye, $100,000, ere the first of April, 1857. The destitution of the Western valley and of the Pacific shore; the formative condition of Society in a thousand rising villages; the rapid growth and vaunting irreligion of unnumbered towns and populous cities; the millions of foreigners in our country; the tribes of Indians that rove the extreme North West and New Mexico; the emigrant sons and daughters of Eastern States, in Michigan, Wisconsin, Iowa, Kansas, California, and Oregon, surely have claims upon this Society, drawn by the Great Head of the Church himself, which one hundred thousand dollars could hardly satisfy.

That the Home Mission cause is Christ's, and the work of this Society such as the Great Commission covers and enjoins—such, therefore, as should command every Christian's sympathy and active co-operation—the 2nd article of its Constitution, as illustrated by its uniform and well-known policy, the demand for its labors, the work it is doing, and the results of its efforts, from year to year, since its organization in 1832, abundantly show.

It would seem, then, that to obtain the requisite facilities and means for prosecuting the work of the American Baptist Home Mission Society, it would be only necessary to show the friends of religion and of our country the true state of things among us, and our numerous opportunities for enlarged operations, while the mere recital of what God has enabled us to accomplish should stimulate zeal and cheer all hearts.

The draining of the Harlem Sea, in Holland, was commenced in 1839, and is but just now finished. The cost of this undertaking has been $3,400,000; most of which has been repaid by the sale of lands that have been reclaimed, amounting to 45,000 acres, enough to supply 100,000 people with the means of life. A great work, and beneficent, truly: but how immeasurably inferior both in the magnitude of its design, and the importance and value of its results, compared with the work of the Society whose Anniversary we celebrate! In twenty-four years, the American Baptist Home Mission Society has enabled nearly 2300 ministers to preach the Gospel of Jesus Christ: whose united ministrations would equal those of 95 men for 20 years each. These missionaries have directly procured the erection of 200 meeting-houses; they have organized 1000 churches, ordained more than 500 ministers, and baptized nearly 25,000 converts to Christ, and gathered them into regular churches. If one soul is beyond all earthly price, who can estimate the value of labors and results such as these? Yet, the entire disbursements of this Society, from its organization to the present time, amounts to less than $540,000! In no year have the current expenditures or receipts exceeded $60,000; a sum less than the aggregate membership of the New England Baptist churches or those of New York alone.

For the present, the expense of Missions in the West, must be mainly borne by the Churches of the Eastern and Middle States, including Ohio; and that the Baptists of these States *can* raise the amount I have named—ay, the highest sum mentioned, without any great sacrifice, will appear from the following table.

Districts.	Baptist Churches.	Church Members.	A.	A C
New England (except Maine)	623	70,000	$16,225	
New England (all the States)	922	89,800	16,400	
New York	828	87,500	20,180	
New Jersey	107	14,000	3,463	
New Eng. Central States and Ohio	26.39	250,000	46,800	

A second glance at this table, and a moment's calculation only one half the church members of New England, or of N contribute to the Treasury of this Society, the average co but two dollars each; or, if combined, but one dollar eac *per annum.* Surely this could be done if the missionary sp in all our churches.

Brethren, the great *desideratum* of our times—the grea age is, a REVIVAL OF "PURE AND UNDEFILED RELIGION," propagating itself by the spirit of holiness, and the spirit Every man of us needs to feel that he is but "a steward of that having been "baptized into Jesus Christ, he has been

But oh! *when* and *how* shall so desirable a state of things come to exist? This is a question of the greatest significance, and immense practical importance. Let us bestow upon it a few minutes' further consideration,

1.—We need a more *systematic* method of reaching all the churches of New England, the Middle States, and Ohio: and the churches of these States need a more practicable, vigorous system of operations, by which every member may have the opportunity, and the invitation to do something for the cause of Home Missions. A liberal contribution from every church, made up by the generous donations of all the members, if possible, is needed each year, as early as the first of January, and as much sooner as may be. For this the personal interest and co-operative efforts of pastors and deacons, and a given number of both brethren and sisters, are indispensable. Every one can do something; every one is bound to attempt it.

2.—How desirable soever it may be to dispense with collecting agents, and let the men who are thus employed return to the pastorate, East or West, the time has not yet come, nor does it seem to me to be so very near as many predict, when we can dispense with the work of these men. Mercantile houses and manufacturing corporations would doubtless hail with joy a state of things that would enable them to dismiss their runners and collectors; to cease the employment of posters, handbills, and other advertisements, by all which so much of their profits is absorbed, but no intelligent man of them would counsel such a course at present, for they see that such services are indispensable and in the highest degree profitable. I know a house that expended nearly $3,000 last year for advertising alone, and employed a host of agents besides; but this year they are expending for such purposes nearly twice as much; and this when there is but little, if any, competition; but the increasing sales and larger dividends abundantly justify the wisdom of their course. Now the people of God should serve their master with somewhat of the zeal and wisdom and entireness of consecration that they are wont to give to business and gain.

Besides, there are many churches that are as yet unused to systematic efforts; many without pastors who could introduce and efficiently work some good plan; and not a few others, who, if they have an excellent system in theory, allow it to become a miserable and worse than useless one, in fact; as if a double track had been built for a railroad, with turn-outs, turn-tables, dépôts, etc., but there are no fired-up locomotives, no whizzing, well-filled trains, and no dividends to the stock-holders. A church-plan that keeps agents away, and yet is not worked efficiently by any one is worse than no system; indeed it is only the fossil remains, or the *débris*, of a system. Every worthy *Society*, then, that depends upon contributions, either from churches or individuals, that would live and do a great and noble work must have agents, especially so long as others do, until Christians think, and feel, and live, as Christians should; as the early Christians did; and as the Lord Christ has both enjoined and set us example.

I remember to have read somewhere of a fire that burned for a long time upon a mountain side, consuming trees, roots, and carbonized vegetable mould, till it

reached a hidden mine of silver, which it melted a
down into the valley below, whose inhabitants were
the love of Christ shall burn down through the sol
our hearts, there will flow forth blessed streams of
channels, as in the churches of Macedonia, so that ev
tainly out of a comfortable and ample competency,
shall make a full treasury for the Home Mission Soci
now find a man who will give to the cause of Christ
cally and liberally, even when money is worth *thr*
such men are prodigies. Yet why should not ever
Jesus—every steward of God's bounties—every lov
race; why should not every one of us hold himself
less; his talents either for preaching, or teaching,
THE LORD'S? Oh! brethren, this spirit of entire,
and his cause, is what is needed, demanded, expecte

DIRECTORS FOR LIFE.

BY VIRTUE OF A CONTRIBUTION OF ONE HUNDRED DOLLARS OR MORE.

Ackerman, John, Dobbs Ferry, N. Y.
Adams, Rev. Pau S., Newport, N. H.
Adsit, Rev. Samuel, Jr., Auburn, N. Y.
Aberly, Richard C., New York.
Aldrich, Rev. Jonathan, Worcester, Mass.
Alger, Henry, Cleveland, Ohio.
Allin, George, Brooklyn, N. Y.
Alvord, Rev. Nelson, Minneapolis, Min. Ter.
Anderson, Rev. Thomas D., Roxbury, Mass.
Anderson, M. B., LL.D., Rochester, N. Y.
Anderson, Rev. George W North East, N. Y.
Archer, Ezekiel, New York.
Armitage, Rev Thomas, D.D., New York.
Armstrong, Rev. James D., Baltimore.
Arnold, Whipple A., Centreville, R. I.
Askren, William, Cincinnati, O.
Atwell, Rev. G. B., Pleasant Valley, Conn.
Averill, Rev. Alexander M., Newton Centre, Ms.
Ayer, Rev. Oliver, Claremont, N H.
Babcock, Rev. Rufus, D.D., Paterson, N. J.
Bacheller, Jonathan, Lynn, Mass.
Bacon, Mrs. Mary H., Gree wich N. J.
Bailey, Benjami D., Providence, R. I.
Bailey, Rev. Gilbert S, Metamora Ill.
Bailey, Rev. Joseph A., Waterbury, Ct.
Ballard, Rev. Joseph, Brooklyn.
Baldwin, Rev. N. B., Philadelphia.
Balen, Peter, New York.
Banks, Jacob, Salem N J.
Banks, Mrs. Mary, Salem, N. J.
Banks, Miss Ann Judson, Salem, N. J.
Banvard, Rev. Joseph, New York.
Barnaby, Rev. James, Newburyport, Mass.
Barker, Rev. Enoch M., Highstown, N. J.
Barrell, Rev. Almond C., Albion, N. Y.
Barrows, Rev. B. W Dorchester, Mass.
Batchelder, Rev. James L., Cincinnat O.
Bates, V J Providence, R. I.
Beecher, Rev. L. F., D.D., Saratoga Springs, N.Y.
Beecher, Mrs. Mary C., Saratoga Springs, N. Y.
Belcher, Rev. Joseph, D.D., Philadelphia.
Bennet, Rev. Ira, Weedsport, N. Y.
Binney Rev. J. G. D D., Washington, D. C.
Binney, Mrs. Juliet P Washington, D. C.
Bishop, Nathan, LL.D., Boston.
Blain, Rev. John, Central Falls, R. I.
Blain, Mrs. Amy An Central Falls, R. I.
Bliss, Rev. Geo. R., Lewisburg, Pa.
Bly Rev. William T Minnesota Territory.
Boardman, W G., Albany, N Y.
Boiles, Matthew Jr., Boston.
Borden, Jefferson, Fall River, Mass.
Bosworth, Rev. George W., Portland, Me.
Bowles, Rev. Ralph H., Branford, Ct.
Boyce, James, Providence.
Bradford, Rev. S. S., Pawtucket, R. I.
Brant, Randolph C., Rochester, N. Y.
Brantly, Rev. W. T, Athens, Georgia.
Brayton, Rev. Jonathan, Centreville, R. I.
Brayton Samuel H, Phenix, R. I.
Brayton, Lodowick M., Knightsville, R. I.
Briggs, Rev. O. W. Brooklyn, N Y.
Brooks, Iveson L., Hamburg, S. C.
Brokaw, Joseph, New York.
Brouwere, Vermilyea T Dundee, N. Y.
Brown, Rev. J. Newton, D.D., Philadelphia.
Bruce, John M., New York.
Buckbee, Rev. Charles A New York.
Bucknell, William, Philadelphia.
Bucknell, Mrs. Margaret K. C., Philadelphia.
Bucknell, Miss L. L., Philadelphia.
Budlong, James B., Providence.
Burlingham, Rev. A. H Boston,
Burgess, Rev I. J Milltown, Me.
Bullock, Benjamin, Philadelphia.
Bump, Nathaniel, Providence.
Burger, Wm. H., New York.
Burke, William, Rochester, N. Y.
Burke, Abraham C., Brooklyn.
Burke, J. B., Middlefield, Mass.
Burt, John W., Brooklyn.
Burt, E. C., Brooklyn.
Burroughs, Rev J. C., Chicago, Ill.
Butcher, Washington, Philadelphia.
Butterfield, Rev. Isaac, Watertown, N. Y.
Byram, Rev. B. P., Amesbury, Mass.
Caldicott, Rev. T. F. D.D., Boston.
Carleton, Rev. George J., Newton Centre, Ms.
Carleton, Mrs. Jane T., Newton Centre, Mass.
Carpenter, Rev Mark Holyoke, Mass.
Carter, Joseph, Charlestown, Mass.
Caswell, Prof. Alexis, D.D., Providence.
Caswell, Rev. Lewis E., Boston.
Chace, Prof. George I., Providence.
Challis, Rev James M., Roadstown, N. J.
Chandler, John H., Bankok, Siam.
Chandler, Mrs. Helen M., Bankok, Siam.
Chaplin, Rev. Jeremiah, West Dedham, Mass.
Chaplin, Rev. Adoniram J., Bennington, Vt.
Charlton, Rev. Frederick Wilmington, Del.
Cheesebrough, Rev. Isaac, Groton, Ct.
Cheney, Rev. David B., Philadelphia.
Child, Mrs. Sophron L., Williamsburgh, N. Y.
Child, Rev. William C., Framingham, Mass.
Church, Rev. P., D.D., New York.
Church Mrs Chara E., New York.
Clarke, Rev. Elbert W., China, N. Y.

DIRECTORS FOR LIFE.

[illegible]

[redacted]

Dana, Rev. L[illegible] A., Fairfax, Vt.
[illegible]wood, Rev. Marvin, Glens Falls, N. Y.
Eaton, Rev. William H., Milford, N. H.
Eaton, Rev. Joseph W., K[illegible]sville, N. Y.
Eberhart, Rev. A. G., M[illegible], Ill.
Eddy, Rev. Edward B., Beverly, Mass.
Edmund, Francis, Newton, Mass.
Edmonds, James, Louisville, Ky.
Edwards, Alexander, South Framingham, M
Eldridge, Rev. Daniel, Hartford, N. Y.
Eustis, Samuel W., Cincinnati.
Eustis, Henry, Cincinnati.
Evans, Rev. Charles, Brooklyn, N. Y.
Farnsworth, Rev. C. D., Colesburg, Iowa.
Farquharson, James, New York.
Fendall, Rev. E. D., Moorestown, N. J.
Field, Albert, Taunton Green, Mass.
Field, Rev. Samuel, Providence.
Fish, Rev. Henry C., Newark, N. J.
Fish, Samuel, Halifax, Vt.
Fisk, Thomas, Warsaw, N. Y.
Fitch, Austin G., Maine.
Flanders, Mrs. Eliza A., Brooklyn, N. Y.
Flanders, Benjamin, Brooklyn, N. Y.
Fletcher, Rev. Joshua, Amenia, N. Y.
F[illegible], John P., Philadelphia.
Francis, Mrs. Hannah C., New York.
Freeman, Rev. Zenas, Rochester, N. Y.
Freeman, Rev. Elijah F., Metamora, Ill.

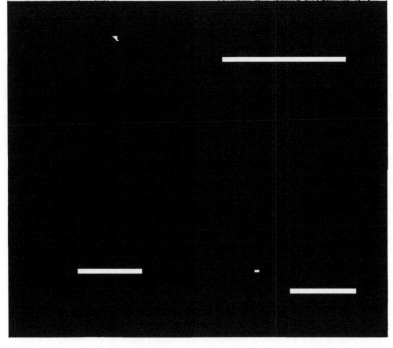

[redacted]

DIRECTORS FOR LIFE.

Harriott, John V Brooklyn.
Harris, John H., Tremont, Ill.
Hartwell, Rev. Jesse, Marion, Ala.
Hatt, Rev. Josiah, Morristown, N. J.
Hatt, Rev. George, New York.
Heath, Nathaniel, Charlestown, Mass.
Hedden, Rev. B. F. Manchester, N. H.
Hill, Rev. Benjamin M., D.D. New York.
Hill, Rev. Daniel T. Carmel, N. Y
Hill, Miss Elizabeth, Carmel, N Y
Hill, Rev. S. P., Washington, D. C.
Hill, Samuel, South Boston, Mass.
Hill, Samuel, Jr., South Boston, Mass.
Hill, Wm. B., Chemung, Ill.
Hilman, William, New York.
Hires, Rev. William D., Freehold, N. J.
Hiscox, Rev. Edward T., New York.
Hodge, Rev. James L., D.D., Newark, N. J.
Hodge, Rev. M. G. Brooklyn, N. Y
Holmes, Rev. Lewis, Edgarton, Mass.
Hopkins, Rev. Chas. J., New York.
Hopper, Samuel W Philadelphia.
Hotchkiss, Rev. V. R., Rochester, N. Y.
Houghton, Hon. Joab, Santa Fe, N M.
Howard, Rev. Leland, Rutland Vt.
Howard, Rev. William G., D.D., Rochester, N.Y.
Howe, Rev. William, Boston.
Howell, Rev. Robert B.C., D.D., Richmond, Va.
Howell, Mrs. Mary Ann M., Richmond Va.
Huckins, Rev. James, Galveston, Texas.
Hulse, Chas., Philadelphia.
Hunt, Samuel, Providence.
Hutchinson, Rev. Wm., Bustleton, Pa.
Ide, Rev George B., D.D., Springfield, Mass.
Ilsley, Rev. Silas, Essex, Ct.
Ives, Rev. Dwight, D.D., Suffield, Ct.
Ives, Mrs. Julia A., Suffield, Ct.
Jackson, Rev. Henry, D.D., Newport, R. I.
James, Rev. Silas C., Bunker Hill, Ill.
James, William T., New York.
James, Israel E., Philadelphia.
Jameson, William H., Boston.
Jameson, Rev. Thorndike C Boston.
Jayne David, Philadelphia.
Jennings, Rev. John, Newton Centre, Mass.
Jeter, Rev. J. B., D.D., Richmond, Va.
Johnson, Rev. W D. H. Greenville, Ill.
Jones, Rev. Henry V., New Brunswick, N. J.
Jones, Rev. P. F., New York.
Jones, Rev. John D. E. Worcester, Mass.
Judd, Rev. Orrin B., LL.D., New York.
Kelly, Samuel R., Brooklyn.
Keen, Wm. W., Philadelphia.
Kempton, Rev. George, New Brunswick, N. J.
Kennard, Rev. J. H., Philadelphia.
Kendall, Mrs. Betsey, Littleton, Mass.
Kent, Henry P., Suffield, Ct.
Kent, Mrs. Jane S., Suffield, Ct.
Keyes, Rev. Charles B., Westfield, N. Y.
Ladd, Rev. James S., Weedsport, N. Y.
Larcombe, Richard J., New York.
Latham, Daniel, New London, Ct.
Latham, Mrs. Delia Ann, Groton, Ct.
Latham, Daniel D., Groton, Ct.
Lane, Rev. Benjamin L, Newburyport, Mass.

Lathrop, Rev. Edward, D D., New York.
Laws, Rev. William, Modesttown, Va.
Lawton, Rev. Joseph A., Erwinton, S. C.
Lea, Sidney Slade, Yanceyville, N. C.
Lee, George F., Philadelphia.
Leighton, Rev. Sam'l S., West Townsend, Mass.
Leonard, Rev. Lewis G., Marietta, Ohio.
Leverett, Rev. William, New Eng. Village, Ms
Lewis, John G., Boston.
Lewis, Isaac, New York.
Lewis, Mrs. Mary, New York.
Lillie, Rev. James, D D., Montreal, Canada.
Lincoln, Hon. Heman, Boston.
Linnard, Hon. J. M., Philadelphia.
Linnard, Mrs Anna, Philadelphia.
Locke, Rev. William E., Springfield, N J.
Loxley, Rev. Benjamin R., Philadelphia.
Loomis, Rev. Ebenezer, Alba, Pa.
Lumsden, D. F Boston.
Lyeth, Richard J Hastings, N. Y
Lyon, Merrick, Providence, R. I.
Mabbet, Jonathan, Dover Plains, N. Y.
McIntosh, Wm. C. Philadelphia.
Maclay, Rev. Archibald, D.D New York.
Magoon, Rev. E. L., D.D. New York.
Magoon, Mrs. E. L., New York.
Malcolm, Rev Howard, D.D., Lewisburg, Pa.
Malcolm, Rev. Thomas S Philadelphia.
Mallary, Rev. C. D., Albany, Ga.
Marble, Joel, Albany, N Y.
Marchant, Henry Providence.
Maple, Thompson, Canton, Ill.
Martin, Runyon W New York.
Martin, Charles J., New York
Marshall, Rev. Enos, Pittsford, N. Y.
Massey, Rev. Joseph T., Bellingham, Mass.
Mason, Rev. Alanson P., Chelsea, Mass.
Mason, Rev. David G., West Swanzey, N. H.
Mason, Rev. Jas. O., Greenwich, N. Y.
Mason, Rev. Sumner R., Cambridge, Mass.
Masters, William Providence.
Masters, Mrs. William Providence.
Mather, Rev. A P., California.
Merit, Rev. Columbus D., Washburn, Ill.
Merriam, Jonathan, Newton Centre, Mass.
Messenger, Rev. Edward C West Medway, Ms.
Middleditch, Rev. Robert T. Red Bank, N. J
Milbank, Samuel, Jr., New York.
Miller, John A., New York.
Miller, Rev. D. Henry, Yonkers, N. Y.
Mills, Rev. Robert C., Salem, Mass.
M ner, Mrs. Henrietta Wilson, Newark, N. J.
Mitchell, Isaac R., Sandwich Islands.
Moore, Rev. Isaac, Plainfield, N. J.
Morse, Mrs. Sophia A., Sturbridge, Mass.
Morse, Jacob, turbridge, Mass.
Morton, Rev. Charles, Corning, N. Y.
Mulford, Rev. Clarence W., Flemington, N. J.
Munn, William H., New York.
Murdock, Rev. J N D.D. Hartford, Ct.
Murphy Rev. John C., New York.
Mussy, Rev. Lawson, Pulaski, N Y
Neale, Rev. Rollin H., D.D., Boston.
Newell, Asa, Providence.
Newton, Isaac, New York.

DIRECTORS FOR LIFE.

N[illegible], Rev. G. P., [illegible], N. J.
Nichols, Charles H., Boston, Mass.
Nicholas, Joseph O., Newark, N. J.
Norris, William, Newark, N. J.
N[illegible], Rev. G., [illegible], Va.
O[illegible]tt, Rev. James P., [illegible], Ill.
Pa[illegible], Rev. D., [illegible], Vt.
Parker, Rev. J. W., D.D., [illegible]geport, Me.
Parker, Rev. Carlton, Wayne, Me.
Parker, Rev. S. S., [illegible], Mass.
[illegible], Rev. John, [illegible], Mass.
P[illegible], Rev. J. W., Newton Centre, Mass.
P[illegible], Rev. Norman, [illegible], La.
[illegible], Rev. D. S., New York.
P[illegible], Rev. [illegible], [illegible] City, N. J.
Pattison, Rev. R. E., D.D., W[illegible], Me.
P[illegible], Rev. W. P., [illegible], Mich.
P[illegible], Rev. Alfred S., [illegible], N. J.
P[illegible], Albert, [illegible], N. Y.
P[illegible], J. B., New York.
P[illegible], J. E. M., D.D., [illegible].
P[illegible], Rev. A[illegible], D.D., [illegible], N. J.
P[illegible], Rev. G. B., [illegible], Ohio.
P[illegible], S[illegible] N., [illegible], N. H.
Phelps, William, New York.
Phelps, Rev. S. Dryden, D.D., New Haven, Ct.
Phillips, Rev. D. W., South Reading, Mass.
P[illegible], Sylvester, New York.
P[illegible], Rev. S. E., Glou[illegible], Mass.
[redacted]

Sarles, Rev. J. W., Brooklyn.
Savage, M. B., Brooklyn.
Sawyer, Rev. Reuben, Chester, Vt.
Seage, Rev. John, Port Richmond, N. Y.
Searl, Rev. David, Springfield, N. Y.
Sheaver(?), Rev. Horace, New York.
Seeley, Rev. John T., Syracuse, N. Y.
Serrell, John J., New York.
Serrell, Mrs. Mary Eliza, New York.
Shadrach, Rev. W., D.D., Philadelphia.
Shailer, Rev. N. E., Deep River, Ct.
Shailer, Rev. Julius S., Roxbury, Mass.
Shailer, Rev. Davis T., North Becket, Mass.
Shailer, Rev. William H., D.D., Portland, Me.
Shardlow, Samuel, New York.
Shaw, Thomas, Boston.
Shedd, Rev. Philander, Warsaw, N. Y.
Shepardson, Rev. D., Cincinnati.
Sherwood, Rev. A., Upper Alton, Ill.
Silliman, Rev. H., North Bergen, N. Y.
Silliman, Mrs. Elizabeth P., Mystic River, Ct.
Simmons, Rev. James B., Providence, R. I.
Skinner, Charles W., Hertford, N. C.
Skinner, John L., Windsor, Vt.
Slater, Horatio N., Providence, R. I.
Smith, Gordon, Essex, Ct.
Smith, Rev. S. F., D.D., Newton Centre, Mass.
Smith, Rev. Henry F., Banksville, Ct.
Smith, Mrs. Sarah B., Banksville, Ct.
[redacted]

Thompson, Mrs. Huldah E., Troy, N. Y.
Tingley, Rev. T. C., Holden, Mass.
Tinsley, Rev. Isaac, Charlottesville, Va.
Timmons, John M., Effingham, S. C.
Todd, William W., New York.
Torian, Thomas, Halifax, Va.
Tracy, William, New York.
Tracy, Rev. Leonard, Burlington, Vt.
Train, Rev. Arthur S., D.D., Haverhill, Mass.
Tryon, Mrs. Louisa J., Houston, Texas.
Tucker, Daniel N., New York.
Tucker, Rev. Anson, Lafayette, Ia.
Tucker, F., Stony Creek, Va.
Tucker, Rev. H. Holcombe, Alexandria, Va.
Tufts, Mrs. Mary, Fitchburg, Mass.
Turner, Peter C., New London, Ct.
Turpin, William H., Augusta, Ga.
Turpin, Mrs. Mary A., Augusta, Ga.
Valentine, David T., New York.
Van Antwerp, Wm. M., Albany, N. Y.
Vanderveer, John, Moorestown, N. J.
Verrinder, Rev. William, Jersey City, N. J.
Vogell, Rev. Henry C., Rome, N. Y.
Wager, James, Troy, N. Y.
Walthall, Rev. Joseph S, Newbern, N. C.
Wattson, Thomas, Philadelphia.
Wayland, Rev. Francis, D.D., Providence.
Wayland, Rev. H. Lincoln, Worcester, Mass.
Webb, Rev. G. S., New Brunswick, N. J.
Welch, Rev. B. T., D.D., Newtonville, N. J.
Welsh, Rev. J. C., Providence.
Wheat, Rev. A. C., Philadelphia.
Wheaten, John, Dorset, Vt.
Wheelock, Rev. Alonzo, Elbridge, N. Y.
Wheeler, Rev. Osgood C., Sacramento, Cal.
Whidden, Randall, Calais, Me.
Whittemore, A. F., Essex, Ct.
White, Rev. J. S., West Wrentham, Mass.
Whitehead, James M., New York.
Whitman, D. C., Newark, N. J.
Whitney, Ezra S., Brooklyn.
Wightman, Rev. F., Wethersfield, Ct.
Wightman, Rev. Palmer G, East Lyme, Ct.
Wilbur, Asa, Boston.
Wildman, Rev. N., Lebanon, Ct.
Wilkins, Rev. Stephen, Meridian, N. Y.
Willard, Rev. F. A., South Danvers, Mass.
Willett, Rev. Charles, Putnam, Ct.
Williams, David S., Fayetteville, N. C.
Williams, Richard P., Essex, Ct.
Williams, Rev. William R, D D., New York.
Wilson, Francis L., Catskill, N. Y.
Wilson, Daniel M., Newark, N. J.
Wilson, Mrs. Hannah M., Newark, N. J.
Wilson, Mrs. Caroline T., Plainfield, N. J.
Wilson, Rev. Robert J., Elmira, N. Y.
Winegar, Rev. R., Jr., Baldwinsville, N. Y.
Wines, Rev. Wm H., Boston.
Winterton, William, New York.
Withers, John, Alexandria, D. C.
Wooster, Rev. Henry, Deep River, Ct.
Wooster, Henry C., Essex, Ct.
Wright, Rev. Thomas G., Westport, N. Y.
Wyckoff, William H, New York.

MEMBERS FOR LIFE.

BY VIRTUE OF A CONTRIBUTION OF THIRTY DOLLARS.

Abbott, Stephen, Southbridge, Mass.
Abbott, Rev. S. G, Meredith Village, N. H.
Achilles, H. L., Albion, N. Y.
Ackley, Rev. Alvin, Greenport, N. Y.
Adair, William N, Somerville, N. J.
Adams, Miss Priscilla S, New York.
Adams, Mrs. Mary, West Killingly, Ct.
Adams, Rev. S. W., Cleveland, Ohio.
Adams, Rev. J., Wallingford, Ct.
Adams, Miss Caroline, New York.
Adams, Albert, Augusta, Ga.
Adams, Joseph H., Williamsburg, N. Y.
Adams, Mrs. Mary, Williamsburg, N. Y.
Adams, Jedediah, New York.
Adams, Van Rensselaer, Deckertown, N. J.
Adams, Rev. J. N., Croton, N. Y.
Adams, Clark, Greenwich, N. Y.
Adkins, Isaac K., Newport, Ohio.
Adlam, Rev. S., Newport, R. I.
Adlam, Mrs. Martha L., Newport, R. I.
Adsit, Mrs. Maria J., Auburn, N. Y.
Ainsworth, Rev. S. C., Brookfield, N. Y.
Akerly, Mrs. Priscilla E., New York.
Akerly, George B., New York.
Akerly, William Henry, New York.
Albro, Mrs. Hannah Hill, New York.
Albro, Stephen S., Newport, R. I.
Alden, Rev. John, Westfield, Mass.
Alden, Rev. Wm. H., North Attleboro', Mass.
Aldrich, Warren, Lowell, Mass.
Alexander, Calvin, West Halifax, Vt.
Allen, Rev. Benoni, Cambridge, O.
Allen, Russell, Shelby, N. Y.
Allen, Mrs. Eliza, Shelby, N. Y.
Allen, Walter, New York.
Allen, Ethan, Worcester, Mass.
Allen, Rev. Marvin, Detroit, Mich.
Allen, Rev. N. T., Jewett City, Ct.
Allen, Rev. John, Groton, Mass.
Allen, Mrs. Lorena, New York.
Allen, Benjamin, Seekonk, Mass.
Allen, Joel, East Smithfield, Pa.
Allen, Nathaniel, Brookline, Me.

[illegible], Fair Haven, Vt.
[illegible], Mrs. [illegible], Fair Haven, Vt.
[illegible], Joseph G., [illegible], Ohio.
[illegible], David, New Gloucester, Me.
[illegible], G. P., Brooklyn, N. Y.
[illegible], Rev. L. B., Yarmouth, Me.
[illegible], Wilmington, Del.
[illegible], Tavoy, Burmah.
[illegible], Brooklyn.
[illegible], Brooklyn.
[illegible], Cleveland, Ohio.
[illegible], N. C.
[illegible], West's Corners, N. J.
[illegible], Mrs. [illegible], West's Corners, N. J.
[illegible], N. J.
[illegible], Rev. J. V., [illegible], Mass.
[illegible], Mrs. [illegible], Mass.
[illegible], New York.
[illegible], Robert W., Roxbury, [illegible]
[illegible], Norwich, Ct.
[illegible], B., New York.
[illegible], Mrs. [illegible], New York.
[illegible], Rev. [illegible], North Middleboro', Mass.
[illegible], William T., [illegible], N. J.
[illegible], Mrs. [illegible], Princeton, N. J.
[illegible], John T., [illegible], Pa.
[illegible], Peter, New York.
[illegible], William, [illegible], N. J.
[illegible], Rev. Edward, Milford, N. H.
Avery, E. J., Brookline, Mass.
Avery, John, Lebanon, Ct.
Ayars, Benjamin, Greenwich, N. J.
Ayer, Charles B., Preston, Ct.
Ayer, Mrs. Richard, Haverhill, Mass.
Ayers, James C., Plainfield, N. J.
Ayers, Horace, Worcester, Mass.
Ayers, Mrs. Mary, New York.
Babcock, Rev. O. W., Gouverneur, N. Y.
Babcock, John N., New Haven, Ct.
Babcock, H. S., Homer, N. Y.
Baber, Alfred, Keeseville, N. Y.
Bachelor, Rev. M., Pownell, Vt.
Backus, Rev. J. S., New York.
Bacon, Jacob, Boston.
Bacon, Rev. William, Dividing Creek, N. J.
Bacon, Rev. Charles L., Trumansburg, N. Y.
Bacon, Mrs. Mary L., Trumansburg, N. Y.
Bacon, Miss Ann, Dorchester, Mass.
Bacon, W. A., Ludlow, Vt.
Bacon, Almon, Lyme, Ct.
Bagby, Rev. Richard, Stevensville, Va.
Bagley, S. V., New York.
Bagley, Miss Ellen, Great Falls, N. H.
Bailey, Mrs. S. W., Parham's Store, Va.
Bailey, Timothy, Malden, Mass.
Bailey, Mrs. Sarah E., Metamora, Ill.
Bailey, S. A., Utica, N. Y.
Bailey, Jonathan, Jr., Westport, N. H.
Bailey, Mrs. Caroline, Philadelphia.

[redacted]

MEMBERS FOR LIFE.

Ball, Julia M., North Amherst, Mass.
Ball, Sarah E., North Amherst, Mass.
Ballard, Rev. Enos H., Red Mills, N Y.
Ballard, Mrs. Asenath, Brooklyn.
Ballard, Mrs. Mary Sophia, Brooklyn.
Ballard, Zaccheus, Webster, Mass.
Bancroft, Henry O Granville, Mass.
Bancros, Lemuel, Granville, Mass.
Ballou, Alexander, Blackstone, Mass.
Banker, Mrs. Elizabeth Brooklyn.
Banta, Miss Emily M. New York.
Barrass, Rev. Thomas, Baptist Town, N. J.
Barrass, Mrs. Mary Ann, Baptist Town, N. J.
Barber, Aaron Waterford C. W.
Barber, Moses, Waterford, C. W
Barber, Abraham N., Waterford, C W.
Barber, Rev. Bradford H Charlestown, N. Y.
Barbour, James S., Cambridge, Mass.
Bardwell, R. B. Shelburne Falls, Mass.
Bardwell, Apollos, Shelburne Falls, Mass.
Bardwell, Jarvis B., Shelburne Falls, Mass.
Bardwell, Edward, Rochester, N. Y.
Bardwell, Mrs. Jane A Rochester N. Y.
Bardwell, E. C., Columbus, Ohio.
Barrell, Mrs. Selena, Albion, N Y.
Barrell, David, Batavia, N Y
Barrett, Mrs. Clarinda, Batavia, N. Y.
Barrett, O., Shirley, Mass.
Barker, Rev. J. G. Richmond, Va.
Barker, Mrs. Esther Ann, Poughkeepsie, N. Y.
Barker, Anson J., Taunton, Mass.
Barker, William, Lowell Mass
Barnard, Mrs. Eunice H. Sand Lake, N. Y.
Barnard, John, Muscatine, Iowa.
Barnes, John, Unio V lage, N Y
Barnes, George M., Davenport, owa.
Barnes, Rev. Wm. A., Chambersburg, Pa.
Barney, William, Albany N. Y
Barney, Mrs. Joanna, Seekonk, Mass.
Barnhurst, Joseph, Sr. Francisville, Pa.
Barnum, Ormel G., Gouverneur, N. Y.
Barnum, S. Eli, Danbury, Ct.
Barrows, Experience, Dorset, Vt.
Bar Mrs. Sarah A
Barter, John, Brooklyn N Y.
Bartlett, Rev. Daniel, Ch na, Mo.
Bartlett, Stephen Worcester, Mass.
Bartlett, Mrs. Elizabeth J., Deep River, Conn.
Bartolette, John T., Somerville, N. J.
Barringer Jacob P., Troy, N. Y.
Barry S. L., Ovid, N. Y.
Barstow, Charles, Boston.
Bates, Mrs. Caroline C, New Bedford, Mass.
Bates, Mrs. Joanna, Providence.
Bates, Whitman, Pawtucket, R. I.
Bates, Dennis P., Lowell, Mass.
Bates, Rev. John, Cascade, Iowa.
Bates, Rev. L. C., Madison, N. Y.
Bates, Rev. Ira, Centreville, R. I.
Bates, Lyma Medina, N. Y
Batey, Rev, John.
Battell, Rev. Allen E Rockport, Mass.
Battle, Rev A. J., Murfreesboro', N. C.
Baugh, Dr. J. M., Petersburgh, Va.
Baxter, Thomas, Penn Yan, N. Y.
Baxter, John C., New York.
Baxter, Thomas, Detroit, Mich.
Baxter, William M., New York
Beagle, Henry Philadelphia.
Beam, Joseph, Brooklyn.
Beam, Mrs. Louisa, Brooklyn, N. Y.
Beam, David B., Patterson, N. J.
Bean, H. L. Skaneateles, N. Y
Beasom, W D., Nashua, N H
Beattie, Rev. W. Q., Bennettsville, N. C.
Beatson, Miss Helen New York.
Beaver, J. M., Hillsborough, N. C.
Beebe, Alexander M. LL.D. Utica, N. Y.
Beebe, Warren Brooklyn, N. Y
Beebe, Mrs. Charlotte, Brooklyn, N. Y.
Beecher, Mrs. Mary C., Saratoga Springs, N. Y.
Beebee, A. M. Jr., Hamilton, N. Y.
Beck, Rev. John J., Coosawhatchie, S. C.
Beck, Rev. Levi G. Doylestown, Pa.
Beckwith, Miss Abby G., Providence.
Beckwith, Elisha W Norwich, Ct.
Beckwith, Jason, New London, Ct.
Beckwith, Ezra S., New London, Ct.
Beckwith, Clement S., New London, Ct.
Beckwith, Nathan, Upper Red, Hook, N. Y.
Beckwith, Elisha Waterford, Ct.
Belcher, Rev. James, Oldtown, Me.
Belden, Rev Joseph, Freehold, N J
Belden, Mrs. Mary Ann, Meriden, Ct.
Belknap, Rev. Appleton, Jeffrey, N. H.
Bell, Rev. Edward, Willimantic, Ct.
Bell, Miss Jane Ann, Willimantic, Ct.
Bell, Joseph, Brookfield, Ohio.
Bell, John, New York.
Bellamy, Rev. Dav d, Mt. Morris, N. Y.
Bellamy, Rev. R. K., Chicopee Falls, Mass.
Boman, Mrs. Rebecca S., Deep River, Ct.
Beman, Miss Charlotte, Deep R ver Ct.
Beman, Mrs. Samantha, Brooklyn, N Y
Bemis, Miss Elizabeth H, Worcester, Mass.
Beeman, Rev James M., Dickinson, N. Y.
Bemrose, Mrs. E izabeth M., New York.
Bendall, George, Coman's Well, Va.
Benedict, Uriah, Central Falls, R. I.
Benedict, Stephen, Pawtucket, R. I.
Benedict, Rev David, D.D., Pawtucket, R. I.
Benedict, Miss Cornelia E., Providence,
Benedict, Rev. N D., Waywasing, N. Y.
Benedict, Mrs. Nancy, New York.
Benedict, Rev. E. L. Pitcher, N Y.
Benjamin, W P New London Ct.
Benjamin, B. M., Rochester, N. Y.
Bennett, Rev. Cephas, Tavoy, Asia.
Bennett, Joseph E. Manchester, N. H,
Bennett, Hiram, Salem, N. J.
Bennett, Rev. Alvin, South Wilbraham, Mass.
Bennett, Rev. David, Unionville, N. Y.
Bennett, E. A. Philadelphia.
Bennett, Mrs. udith B Philadelpia.
Bennett, Miss Anna, Philade phia.
Bennett, Rev. Olney, Walesville, N. Y.
Bennett, Joseph, Manchester, N. H.
Bennett, Miss C. Ellen, Ludlow, Vt
Bennett, Joseph L., New London, Ct.
Bennett, Rev. Perry, Cold Spring, N. Y,
Benton, J., Saratoga, N. Y.

Benton, Mrs. Sarah, [illegible], N. Y.
Benton, Rev. George W., [illegible], Ill.
Bernard, Rev. David, [illegible], N. Y.
Bernie, Mrs. Anna, New York.
Berthe, Mrs. [illegible] Ann, New York.
Berthe, James C., New York.
Berry, Z[illegible], Worcester, Mass.
Berry, [illegible], Worcester, Mass.
Berry, Ellen L., Worcester, Mass.
Betts, Rev. Platt, [illegible], N. Y.
Betts, Philander, Danbury, Ct.
Bevan, Rev. [illegible], R[illegible], Pa.
Beverly, Miss Elizabeth, New York.
Bickford, [illegible] M. L., Waltham, Mass.
Biddle, Samuel S., Forestville, N. C.
Biddle, Rev. William, [illegible], Ct.
Belgard, Mrs. L., [illegible].
Bigelow, Rev. John S., M.D., New York.
Bigelow, Mrs. Emma P., New York.
Bigelow, John B., Brooklyn, N. Y.
Bigelow, Mrs. Catharine, Brooklyn, N. Y.
Bigelow, [illegible], Brooklyn, N. Y.
Bigelow, Miss N[illegible] H., Brooklyn, N. Y.
Bigelow, Mrs. [illegible], Brooklyn, N. Y.
Billings, Rev. John, Mt. Vernon, Me.
Billings, Mrs. B[illegible], Mt. Vernon, Me.
Billingsl[illegible], [illegible], Ala.
Bigelow, [illegible], [illegible], Vt.
Bingham, L[illegible], Fort [illegible], Ia.
Bird, Rev. John, [illegible], [illegible], Va.

[redacted]

Bonner, Rev. James C., Chelmsford, Ct.
Booth, Henry, Greenport, N. Y.
Booth, Rev. John, Fox Lake, Wis.
Bond, Leonard, New York.
Bond, Rev. George W., Knoxville, Iowa.
Bond, Rev. E. P., Aurora, Ia.
Bond, Rev. Emmons P., New Britain, Ct.
Bond, Mrs. Mary, New Britain, Ct.
Bonham, Daniel, Berryville, Va.
Bonney, W. F., Elton, N. Y.
Boone, Dr. Levi D., Chicago, Ill.
Boone, Mrs. L. D., Chicago, Ill.
Borden, Lolowick, Fall River, Mass.
Borden, Isaac, Fall River, Mass.
Borden, Charles, Fall River, Mass.
Borden, Joseph, Fall River, Mass.
Borden, Cook, Fall River, Mass.
Borland, Chauncey, Iowa City, Iowa.
Bosson, George P., Chelsea, Mass.
Bosson, Benjamin P., Chelsea, Mass.
Bosson, Mrs. Mary, Chelsea, Mass.
Bostick, Elisha, Bostick's Mills, N. C.
Bostick, Elijah, Bostick's Mills, N. C.
Bostick, Tristam, Bostick's Mills, N. C.
Bostick, Benj. R., Robertsville, S. C.
Bostick, Mrs. Jane A., Robertsville, S. C.
Boswell, Davis, Stilesville, Ia.
Bosworth, William M., East Poultney, Vt.
Bosworth, George H., Fall River, Mass.
Bottom, Mrs. Peace, Shaftsbury, Vt.

[redacted]

Bray, Joseph M., Brooklyn.
Brayton, Mrs. Harriett, Phenix, R. I.
Brayton, Mrs. Ruth, Phenix, R. I.
Brayton, Mrs. Betsy, Phenix, R. I.
Brayton, Mrs. Mary Ann, Centreville, R. I.
Brayton, Robert E., Knightsville, R. I.
Brayton, Mrs. Ruth, Knightsville, R. I.
Brayton, Mrs. Lydia, Knightsville, R. I.
Brayton, Miss Anna V., Knightsville, R. I.
Brayton, Miss Emma L. Knightsville, R. I.
Brayton, Herbert E., Phenix, R. I.
Brayton, Esther J., Phenix, R. I.
Brayton, Miss Mary E., Phenix, R. I.
Breed, Rev. Joseph B., Woonsocket, R. I.
Breed, Mrs. Frances A. C., Woonsocket, R. I.
Breed, Catharine C., Lynn, Mass.
Brenholtz, Josiah P., Reading, Pa.
Brewer, Mrs. Elizabeth, New York.
Bridgens, Miss Mary Ann, Brooklyn, N. Y.
Bridgewood, Mrs. Jane, Williamsburg, N. Y.
Brierly, Rev. Benjamin, San Francisco, Cal.
Brigham, Sylvester, Dover, Ill.
Brigham, Rev. J. H., Scipio, N. Y.
Briggs, Arnold, Fairhaven, Vt.
Briggs, Rev. Avery, Rock Island, Ill.
Briggs, Mrs. Sarah H., Fitchburg, Mass.
Briggs, Harris, Coventry, N. Y.
Bright, Rev. T., Elkhorn, Wis.
Brinkerhoff, Rev. C., Toulon, Ill.
Brisbane, Rev. Wm. H. Cheviot, Ohio.
Brisbane, Miss Maria, Charleston, S. C.
Briscoe, Sally C., Va.
Britton, Everett, New York.
Brockett, Alvah, Salisbury, N. Y.
Brockett, Asahel, Bristol, Ct.
Broaddus, Rev. William F., D.D., Versailles, Ky.
Broaddus, Mrs. Mary A., Versailles, Ky.
Broadhead, Mrs. Ann, New York.
Brockett, D. B., Salisbury, N. Y.
Brocket, Rev. Piermont, Hartford, Ct.
Brockway, Mrs. Elizabeth, Broadalbin, N. Y.
Britton, W. G., Britton's ✕ Roads, N. C.
Brokaw, Mrs. Jane Eliza K., New York.
Bromley, Isaac, Norwich, Ct.
Bromley, J. Breed, Norwich, Ct.
Bromley, Dewey, Norwich, Ct.
Bromley, Rev. Henry, Brooklyn, N. Y.
Bromley, Mrs. Jane M., Brooklyn, N. Y.
Brouner, Mrs. Sarah, New York.
Bronson, Rev. Asa, Fall River, Mass.
Bronson, Rev. Benjamin F., Methuen, Mass.
Bronson, Mrs. Anna C., Methuen, Mass.
Bronson, Miss Aydee A., Townsend, Mass.
Bronson, Rev. A., Williamstown, Mass.
Brooks, Eli T., South Brookfield, Mass.
Brooks, Dea. Kendall, Roxbury, Mass.
Brooks, Rev. Kendall, Fitchburg, Mass.
Brooks, John, Hanover, Mass.
Brooks, Mrs. Elizabeth, Cambridge, Mass.
Brouwere, Mrs. V. G., Dundee, N. Y.
Browe, E. S., New Brunswick, N. J.
Brower, Davis E., Doylestown, Pa.
Brown, W. S., Britton's ✕ Roads, N. C.
Brown, Josiah, Haverhill, Mass.
Brown, J. S., Fitchburg, Mass.
Brown, Edward L., Brooklyn, N. Y.
Brown, Mrs. Susan A., Brooklyn, N. Y.
Brown, Rev. Amasa, Concord, N. H.
Brown, Rev. Dana, Nashua, N. H.
Brown, Rev. E. T., Wooster, Ohio.
Brown, Andrew, Middletown, N. J.
Brown, George W., New York.
Brown, Hugh H., Providence.
Brown, Rev. E. C., Bath, N. Y.
Brown, Rev. F. G., West Townsend, Mass.
Brown, Rev. Wm. L., Watertown, Mass.
Brown, Rev. Joseph P., Moosup, Ct.
Brown, Daniel Sempronius, N. Y.
Brown, Oliver, Mystic River, Ct.
Brown, William, Cambridge, Mass.
Brown, Rev. Samuel M., Granville, Ill.
Brown, Miss Alice A., Auburn, N. Y.
Brown, John S., Fisherville, N. H.
Brown, Henry, Fisherville, N. H.
Brown, Miss Harriet, Norwich, N. Y.
Brown, Rev. J., Springfield, Ohio.
Brown, Mrs. Emily M. A., Fauquier, Va.
Brown, Mrs. Elizabeth E., Aylett's, Va.
Brown, Miss Ann F., Providence.
Brown, Mrs. Mary, F., Keene, N. H.
Brown, Mrs. Isaac, Haverhill, Mass.
Brown, Mrs. Margaret A., Reading, Ohio.
Brown, Rev. J. F., Scotch Plains, N. J.
Brown, Rev. Philip P., Holland Patent, N. Y.
Brown, Rev. Wm., Eaton, N. Y.
Brown, Evander M., Saratoga Springs, N. Y.
Brown, L. E., Hartford, Ct.
Brown, Samuel, Fall River, Mass.
Brown, Joshua, New York.
Brown, Sarah H., 2d, West Townsend, Mass.
Brown, Newel, Watertown, Mass.
Brown, Mrs. Mary, W., Watertown, Mass.
Brown, Mrs. Josiah, Haverhill, Mass.
Brown, Mrs. Frances J., Bedford, N. Y.
Brown, Mrs. Prudencia, Middletown, N. J.
Brownell, Rev. E. W., East Hillsdale, N. Y.
Brownson, Rev. I. K., Greenfield, Ohio.
Bruen, George H., Newark, N. J.
Bruen, Mrs. George H., Newark, N. J.
Bruce, Benjamin G., New York.
Bruce, Silas, Townsend, Mass.
Bruce, John M., Jr., New York.
Brush, Mrs. Susan G., New York.
Brusle, William A., New York.
Brusle, Mrs. Elizabeth, New York.
Bryant, George, Williamsburg, N. Y.
Bryant, Mary A., Chelsea, Mass.
Bryant, Elizabeth D., Chelsea, Mass.
Buck, David S., Cambridge, Mass.
Buckbee, Mrs. Laura G., New York.
Bucknall, Ebenezer G., Newark, N. J.
Bucknell, Miss Elizabeth, Newark, N. J.
Bucknell, Wm., Jr., Philadelphia.
Bucknell, Miss Lavinia Louisa, Philadelphia.
Bucknell, Mrs Harriet M., Philadelphia.
Buckner, Mrs. Sarah T., Baltimore.
Budlong, Mrs. Rebecca S. C., Providence.
Budlong, Miss Rebecca A., Providence.
Budd, Francis F., Williamsburg, N. Y.
Buel, Rev. Rufus F.,
Buel, Mrs. Mary J.,
Buffinton, Benjamin, Fall River, Mass.
Bull, John B., New York.
Bullard, Rev. Joseph A., Ware, Mass.

MEMBERS FOR LIFE.

[illegible]
Bull[illegible], Geo[illegible], N. Y.
Bulkley, [illegible]
[illegible]
Bulkl[illegible]
Bunnell, Rev. W. B., [illegible]
[illegible]
Burb[illegible], New York.
[illegible]
Bar[illegible], Elisha, [illegible], N. J.
[illegible], N. Y.
[illegible]
Bar[illegible], Mrs. R[illegible], New York.
[illegible]
[illegible]
[illegible], N. Y.
[illegible], N. Y.
[illegible], N. Y.
[illegible]
[illegible]
Bar[illegible], West [illegible]
Barnett, Rev. [illegible]
Barns, [illegible], Philadelphia.
[illegible], N. Y.
Burr, Mrs. [illegible], N. Y.
B[illegible], Mrs. James H., [illegible], N. Y.
[illegible], N. Y.
[illegible], N. J.
[illegible]
[illegible], Rev. [illegible]
[illegible]

C[illegible], Ezekiel, Canton, Mass.
Capron, Miss Rebecca S., Worcester, Mass.
Capron, John, Albany, N. Y.
Capron, Rev. Barton, Preble, N. Y.
Capwell, Albert B., New York.
Capwell, Mrs. Julia A., New York.
Carl, Rev. Wm. H.
Carl, Rev. Henry S., Hinsdale, N. Y.
Carleton, Miss Frances, Newton Centre, Mass.
Carleton, Miss Emelina H., Newton Centre, Ms.
Carleton, G. R., Newton Centre, Mass.
Carleton, Judson, Newton Centre, Mass.
Carleton, Howard, Newton Centre, Mass.
Carleton, Wm. H., Newton Centre, Mass.
Carlton, Stephen, Lowell, Mass.
Carew, Miss Emma H., New York.
Carew, Mrs. Margaret N., New York.
Carroll, S. W., Norwich, Ct.
Carroll, Mrs. Sarah A. S., Washington, N. C.
Carpenter, Daniel T., Pawtucket, R. I.
Carpenter, Mrs. Elizabeth, Pawtucket, R. I.
Carpenter, Miss Lydia, Pawtucket, R. I.
Carpenter, Rev. Calvin G., Phelps, N. Y.
Carpenter, Rev. J. M., Jacobstown, N. J.
Carpenter, Mrs. Sarah F., Jacobstown, N. J.
Carpenter, Rev. Burton B., Griggsville, Ill.
Carpenter, James, New York.
Carpenter, J. H., Willimantic, Ct.
Carpenter, Mrs. Martha C., Willimantic, Ct.
Carmer, Henry, Griggsville, Ill.

[redacted]

Chaffee, Asa, Seekonk, Mass.
Chaffin, Rev. Aaron W., Danvers, Mass.
Chaffin, Mrs. Catherine K., Danvers, Mass.
Chalfant, Jacob M., Wilmington, Del.
Chalfant, Mrs. Sarah E., Wilmington, Del.
Challiss, Mrs. Lydia, Roadstown, N J
Chambers, Azariah, Marion, N. C
Chamberlain, Miss Sylvia Ann, Westport, N H.
Chamberlain, Edward, Boston.
Chamberlain, Rev. J. A., South N. Berlin, N. Y.
Chambers, John, Pemberton, N. J.
Champlin, Henry N Pitcher, N. Y.
Champlin, Joseph, Jr., Wakefield, R. I.
Champlin, W illiam, New London, Ct.
Chapel, R. S., Brooklyn.
Chappel Charles, New London, Ct.
Chapman, Allen A., Baltimore.
Chapman, Rev. John S. Tobehanna, N. Y.
Chapman, William H., New York.
Chapman Henry, F., New York
Chapman, Rev. J. M., Lexington, Ill.
Chandler, Rev. Charles N., Fredonia, N. Y.
Chandler, Rev. Ge rge C., Oregon City, Oregon.
Chandler, Oliver, Boston.
Chandler, William, Nashua, N. H.
Chapin, Rev. A , Galena, Ill.
Charlock, Miss Maria, New York.
Chase, Rev. Supply, Detroit, Mich.
Chase, Daniel, Baltimore.
Chase, Adrian, Haverhill, Mass.
Chase, Luther, Haverhill, Mass.
Chase, Mrs. Amos, Haverhill, Mass.
Chase, Hezekiah S., Boston.
Chase, Edwin, Holyoke, Mass.
Chase, Asa, Eaton, N. Y
Chase, Alfred, Harwich, Mass.
Chase, Rev. A. B., Cameron, N Y.
Cherryman, Rev. Reuben, Richburg, N. Y.
Cheesebrough Mrs. Asenath, Haddam, Ct.
Cheshire, Rev. John Enoch, Keeseville, N. Y.
Cheever William, Westboro' Mass.
Chick, Rev. J. M., South Groton, Mass.
Child, Ezra O., Warren, R. I.
Child, Henry W , Warren, R. I.
Child, Shubel P., Warren, R. I.
Childs, Miss ane L New York.
Childs, John B., Providence.
Childs, Mrs. Jennett Deep River, Ct.
Chipman, J A. Boston.
Church, Rev. Leroy, Chicago, Ill.
Church, Miss Clara O. D., New York.
Church, Miss. Emma C., New York.
Church, William, New York.
Church, Frank P., New York.
Church John A., New York.
Church, Rev. Isaac M., South Kingston, R. I.
Church, Norman B. Uncasville Ct.
Churchill, Amos, East Hubbardton, Vt.
Clapp, Rev. Wm. K., Danbury Ct.
Clapp, Russell, Providence.
Clapp, Miss Jane R Providence.
Clapp, Mrs. Eliza H., Boston.
Clark, Rev. Frederick, New Orleans, La.
Clark, Rev. Norman, Marlborough, N. H.
Clark, Abel, Willimantic, Ct.
Clark, Mrs. Juliet, Marlborough, N. H.
Clark, Miss E , Beaufort, S. C.
Clark, Mrs. M. G., Philadelphia.
Clark, Mrs. Elizabeth, New York.
Clark, Miss Sallie Cone, New York.
Clark, Mrs. Louisa, South Berwick, Me.
Clark, Miss Clarissa, Deep River, Ct.
Clark, Miss Eliza, Syracuse, N. Y.
Clark, Teresa B., Lakeville, N. Y.
Clark, Rev. C. A., Auburn, N Y.
Clark, Henry, Plantsville, Ct.
Clark, Henry, Middletown, Ct.
Clark, Rev. T. W Wheatland, N. Y.
Clark, Alexander Boston.
Clark, A. S., Albany, N. Y
Clark, Mrs. John, Bridgeport Ct.
Clark, Henry, Southington, Ct.
Clark, Rev. N. Judson, Southington, Ct.
Clark, Mrs. Caro ine, Southington, Ct.
Clark, Alfred, Methuen Mass.
Clarke, Rev. Henry, Pittsfield, Mass.
Clarke, Rev. John, Esquesing C. W.
Clarke, William, Syracuse, N. Y
Clarke, John C. C., Brooklyn, N. Y.
Clayton, James D., Freehold, N. J.
Cleaves, Rev. F. E., Lowell, Mass.
Clement, Wm. T. Shelburne Falls, Mass.
Clopton, Rev. James C., Lynchburg, Va.
Clopton, Mrs. M. New Kent, Va.
Clossee, Nicholas, Door Village, Ia.
Coborn, Mrs. Hannah H., Erie, Ill.
Coburn, Charles, Fall River, Mass.
Coburn, Rev. J. M., Manchester, N. H.
Coburn, Washington L., Manchester, N. H.
Cobb, Mrs. Sarah M., Brooklyn, N. Y.
Cocke, Charles L., Richmond, Va.
Cochran, G. W. Methuen, Mass.
Cockran, Justin, Lowell Mass.
Coe, Ward, Meriden, Ct.
Coe, Tunis H., Yates, N. Y.
Coffin, Rev. James L. Big Flatts, N. Y.
Coggeshall, Mrs. Elizabeth, New Bedford, Mass.
Cogswell, B. F , Brooklyn, N. Y.
Cogswell, Mrs. Mary, Haverhill, Mass.
Coyt, Miss Elizabeth, New London, Ct.
Colby, Rev. Lewis, Jersey City, N. J.
Colby, Mrs. Eliza A. New London, N. H.
Colby, Isaac, Salem Mass.
Colby, Gardener, Newton, Mass.
Colby, Mrs. Mary Colgate, New York.
Colburn, Rev. Alfred, Boston.
Cole, Rev. L. B., Lowell, Mass.
Cole, Samuel, Clifton Park, N Y.
Cole, Mrs. Frances L., New York.
Cole, Mrs. usan, Westerloo, N Y.
Cole, Mrs. Jemima P., Plainfield, N. J.
Coley Rev. James M Waverly N. Y.
Colegrove, Bolah H Sardinia, N. Y.
Coleman, James B., Somervil e, N. J.
Coleman, Rev. M., Elba, N. Y
Coleman, Mrs Sarah, Elba, N. Y.
Coleman, Rev. Zenas, Mt. Vernon, Mich.
Colgate, Cornelius C., New York.
Colgate, Edward, New York.
Colgate, James B., New York.
Colgate, William, New York.

Colgate, Miss E[illegible], New Y.
Colgate, Miss H[illegible], New York.
Colgate, Miss Jane, New York.
Colgate, Miss Sarah, New York.
Colgrove, Uri, J[illegible], O.
Collins, Miss Susan, New York.
Colson, John B., W[illegible], N. Y.
Colby, Benj. E., C[illegible], Mass.
Colton, Mrs. M[illegible] E., Mt. Holly, N. J.
Colton, Rev. C[illegible], Worcester, Mass.
[illegible], L[illegible] O., Le Roy, N. Y.
Compton, James I., Pl[illegible], N. J.
Compton, Anth[illegible], New York.
Compton, Mrs. M[illegible], New York.
Compton, Rev. R[illegible], New[illegible], Pa.
Compton, Wm. H., Ro[illegible], N. J.
Comstock, George R., New London, Ct.
Comstock, Mrs. Ann, New London, Ct.
Comstock, C. C., New London, Ct.
Comstock, Charles F., South Lyme, Ct.
Conant, Mrs. J[illegible], P[illegible], Vt.
Conant, Rev. Thomas, S[illegible], Mass.
Conant, Rev. Thomas J., D.D., Rochester, N. Y.
Conant, Levi, Boston, Mass.
Condit, Miss Sarah E., New York.
Cone, Spencer H., Jr., New York.
Cone, Miss Kate P., New York.
Cone, Miss Amelia M., Philadelphia.
Conklin, Mrs. Ann, New York.

Corwith, Mrs. Catharine F., New York.
Cotterell, Mrs. Mary, Battenville, N. Y.
Cotterell, Miss Mary, Union Village, N. Y.
Couch, E. P., Nashua, N. H.
Covey, Rev. Walter, Jefferson, N. Y.
Cowan, Mrs. Hannah, New York.
Cowdin, Mrs. Aurinda G., Fitchburg, Mass.
Cowles, Mrs. Rebekah, Claremont, N. H.
Cowles, Miss Juliette R., Claremont, N. H.
Cowles, Jas. Albert, Claremont, N. H.
Cox, Rev. Morgan R., New Brunswick, N. J.
Cox, Mrs. Mary B., New Brunswick, N. J.
Cox, Miss Anna, New Brunswick, N. J.
Cox, Miss Mary, New York.
Cox, John W., Mt. Holly, N. J.
Cox, Miss Abigail, New York.
Coxey, James, West Philadelphia, Pa.
Coy, Sylvanus B., West Dedham, Mass.
Crabs, Rev. J. D., Claysville, Ia.
Craig, Rev. A. M., Britton's X Roads, N. C.
Craig, Charles A., Bridgeport, Ct.
Craig, Mrs. Charles A., Bridgeport, Ct.
Crain, Miss Harriet M., Westport, N. H.
Craft, Charles, New York.
Crafts, George A., Boston.
Cramer, Geo. W., Troy, N. Y.
Cramer, John, Brooklyn, N. Y.
Cramer, Mrs. Margaret S., Troy, N. Y.
Crane, Richard M., Newark, N. J.
Crane, Henry F., Rehoboth, Mass.

[redacted]

Cruser, Holger, Brooklyn, N. Y.
Cudworth, Rev. N., Ludlow, Vt.
Cudworth, Mrs. M. B., Ludlow, Vt.
Cudworth, Lydia B., Chelsea, Mass.
Culp, Theophilus, New York.
Culver, Mrs. Susan, New London, Ct.
Culver, Rev. Samuel W., Rhinebeck, N. Y.
Cummings, Mrs. Daniel, Chelsea, Mass.
Cummings, Mrs. Abigail, Cambridge, Mass.
Cummings, George, Cambridge, Mass.
Cummings, Rev. E. E., Concord, N. H.
Cummings, Mrs Emily C., Amherst, Mass.
Cummings, Miss Ellen, Chelsea, Mass.
Cunningham, Rev. O., Lebanon, Ct.
Curry, John, Hamburg, S. C.
Curry, Mrs. Harriet, Hamburg, S. C.
Curren, Rev. Joseph, Evansburg, Pa.
Currier, Rev. Joshua, La Motte, Iowa.
Curtis, Rev. Wm. Columbia, S. C.
Curtis, Rev. T. T., Marion, Ala.
Curtis, Rev. Wm. B., Newport, N. Y.
Curtis, Mrs. Elizabeth., Aurora, Ia.
Curtis, Ezra, Bridgeport, Ct.
Curtis, Mrs. Ezra, Bridgeport, Ct.
Cushing, Samuel T., Boston.
Cusick, Rev. James, Onondaga, Can.
Cushman, Frederick A., New York.
Cushman, Mrs. Charlotte E., Deep River, Ct.
Cushman, Mrs. Elizabeth, Deep River, Ct.
Cushman, Jacob R., Medfield, Mass.
Cutler, Micajah, Lynn, Mass.
Cutler, Wm. D., Meriden, Ct.
Cutler, Stephen, North Mansfield, Mass.
Cutting, Mrs. Elizabeth B., Rochester, N. Y.
Cutting, Rev. Geo. W., Hanover, N. H.
Dabney, Mrs. E. T., Jackson, Va.
Dagg, Mrs. John L., Penfield, Ga.
Daken, Rev. H. R., Pultney, N. Y.
Dale, Mrs. Amanda F., Lebanon, Ohio.
Dalrymple, James, Bridgeton, N. J.
Damon, Rev. J B., Lake Village, N. H.
Damon, Benjamin, Concord, N. H.
Damon, Isaac H., Fredonia, N. Y.
Dana, John B, Cambridge, Mass.
Danelson, Mrs Jemima, Brooklyn, N. Y.
Danforth, Rev. G. F. South Dartmouth, Mass.
Daniels, Mrs. E. E., Wyoming, N. Y.
Daniels, Rev. Harrison, Wyoming, N. Y.
Daniels, Dexter, Providence, R. I.
Daniels, Mrs. Dexter, Providence.
Daniels, Rev. J. H., Bath, Ill.
Daniels, Clark, New London, Ct.
Daniels, Thomas E., Fitchburg, Mass.
Dannat, Mrs. Susannah J., New York.
Dannat, Miss Mary C., New York.
Darby, Rev. C., Homer, N. Y.
Darrow, Rev. George R., Providence.
Darrow, Miss Julia T., Providence.
Darrow, Rev. Allen, Marietta, Ohio.
Davant, R. J., Gillisonville, S. C.
Davenport, Joshua, New York.
Davies, Mrs. Alice S. H., New York.
Davies, Mrs. Elizabeth, New York.
Davis, Miss Catharine A., Brooklyn, N. Y.
Davis, Mrs. Eliza, H., Columbus, Ohio.
Davis, Miss Mary E, Worcester, Mass.
Davis, Edward L., Worcester, Mass.
Davis, Joseph E, Worcester, Mass.
Davis, Miss Sarah M., Worcester, Mass.
Davis, Miss Anna E., Worcester, Mass.
Davis, Miss Alice W., Worcester Mass.
Davis, Florence H. Worcester, Mass.
Davis, Isabel G., Worcester, Mass.
Davis, Reuben P., Waltham, Mass.
Davis, Walter G., New York.
Davis, Charles C. Preston, Ct.
Davis, Mrs. Louisa G., Paris, Me.
Davis, Rev. John, Yarmouth, Nova Scotia.
Davis, Rev. Thomas, Deckertown, N. J.
Davis, Rev. Judson, Ira, N. Y.
Davis, Lydia, Haverhill, Mass.
Davis, Mrs. Harriet M., Nashua, N. H.
Davis, Levi, Davenport, Iowa.
Davis, Rev. R., Waveland, Ind.
Davis, Rev. Amos S, Richmondville, N. Y.
Davis, Russel, Preston City, Ct.
Davis, Hon. George R., Troy, N Y.
Davis, Rev. Joseph, Hebron, Ohio.
Davis, Joseph M., Fall River, Mass.
Davy, Miss Bertha, New York.
Dawley, Joseph E., Fall River, Mass.
Day, H. W., Boston.
Day, John, New York.
Day, Mrs. Fidelia, Haverhill, Mass.
Day, Rev. Arthur, Shaftsbury, Vt.
Day, Rev. Horace G., Schenectady, N. Y.
Day, Horatio E., Hartford, Ct.
Dayton, Morgan H., New York.
Dean, H. J., Spartanburg, S. C.
Dean, Jirah, Flat Brook, N. Y.
Dean, Rev. Wm. D.D., Wilmington, Del.
Dean, Mrs. Maria M, Wilmington, Del.
Dean, E. W., Jamaica Plains, Mass.
Dean, Rev. Myron M., Warren, R I.
Dean, Esther G., North Adams, Mass.
Dean, Rev. E., Auburn, N. Y.
Dean, Rev. R. S., Burlington, N. Y.
Dearborn, Rev. Shelburn, Lowell, Wis.
Dearborn, Mrs. Emeline L., Lowell, Wis.
Deats, Hiram, Cherryville, N J.
Decker, Alfred, New York.
Decker, Mrs. Keziah R., New York.
Decker, Abel, Yew York.
Decker, Mrs. Abigail, New York.
Decker, Miss Mary A., New York.
Decker, Matthew, Rahway, N. J.
Decker, Wm. P., Hamilton, N. Y.
De La Montague, Miss Julia, New York.
Della Torre, Joseph, Yew York.
Demarest, Miss Jane, New York.
Demarest, Samuel C., Boston.
Demarest, Stephen D., New York.
Deming, Amos, Savoy, Mass.
Deming, Mrs. Eliza J., Washington, D. C.
Deming, Mrs. Abby A., Goffstown, N. H.
Denike, Abraham, New York.
Denike, Mrs. Adeline, New York.
Dennis, Mrs. Elizabeth, New York.
Dennis, Richard, Lowell, Mass.
Dennison, Rev. Charles W., Boston.
Denison, Rev. Frederic, Norwich, Ct.

Denison, Rev. Erastus, Groton, Ct.
Denison, Mrs. Prudence, Mystic River, Ct.
Denison, Mrs. Silas, Skeneateles, N. Y.
Denison, O. J., Mendota, Ill.
Denison, Mrs. Amelia E., Deep River, Ct.
Denison, Miss Elizabeth, Brooklyn, N. Y.
Denny, John B., Norwalk, Ct.
Depew, Mrs. Sprah M., Saratoga Springs, N. Y.
Devore, Mrs. Catharine, Edgefield, S. C.
Deweese, Samuel, West Philadelpia.
Dewey, Wm. G., Mystic, Ct.
Dewey, Joseph H., Manchester, N. Y.
Dewhurst, Rev. Eli, Hampden Corners, Me.
Dewitt, Rev. J. V., Marion, Iowa.
Dexter, Mrs. Jane, Brooklyn, N. Y.
Dickerman, Samuel, Philadelphia.
Dickinson, Mrs. Caroline A., Pittsburg, Pa.
Dickinson, Wm. W., Golandsville, Va.
Dimmock, Rev. Anth'y V., Baldwinsville, Mass.
Dinsmore, Chas. M., Newton, Mass.
Dispeau, Mrs. Lucinda, Grafton, Mass.
Dotson, Benjamin, Methuen, Mass.
Dixson, Rev. Joseph A., Evansville, Ia.
Doan, Ezra, Hudson, N. Y.
Doane, Miss Rachel F., Danvers, Mass.
Doby, John, Sen., Edgefield, S. C.
Dodge, Mrs. Eliza P., New York.
Dodge, Miss Mary, New York.
Dodge, Rev. Orrin, Brooklyn, N. Y.
Dodge, Prof. Ebenezer, Hamilton, N. Y.

Dubois
Dubois
Dudle
Dugan,
Dugan,
Dunca
Dunca
Dunca
Dunca
Dunca
Dunca.
Dunlap
Dunlap
Dunlap
Dunler
Dunn,
Dunn, .
Du Pre.
Durfee,
Durfee,

Eddy, Richard E., Providence.
Eddy, Mrs. Lucy, Waterford, N. Y.
Edgecomb, Albert, Mystic River, Ct.
Edington, Mrs. Charlotte M., New York.
Edman, Thomas, Pemberton, N. J.
Edminster, Rev. J., Peoria, Ill.
Edmond, Francis, Brookline, Mass.
Edmond, Mrs. Emily S., Brookline, Mass.
Edmond, Francis B., Brookline, Mass.
Edmonds, Miss Sarah E., Philadelphia.
Edwards, Robert, New York.
Edwards, Rev. B. A., Watertown, Mass.
Edwards, John F., Brookline, Mass.
Edwards, Ivory, Lowell, Mass.
Eldridge, Smith, Boston.
Eldridge, James, Williamstown, Mass.
Elgreen, Mrs. Ann, New York.
Elkin, Rev. David, Bryantsville, Indiana.
Elledge, Rev. Jesse, Wintersett, Iowa.
Elliott, Rev. Charles, Ogdensburgh, N. Y.
Elliott, Edward G., Washington, D. C.
Elliott, Rev. William, Brighton, Iowa.
Elliott, Rev. S. L., Wallingford, Vt.
Elliott, Mrs. Sarah C., Wallingford, Vt.
Elliott, Rev. M., Stilesville, Ia.
Elliott, Mrs. Marcia O. T., Mason Village, N. H.
Elliott, L. A., Mason Village, N. H.
Elliott, Lemuel H., Providence.
Ellis, Theodore W., South Hadley Falls, Mass.
Ellis, Mrs. Mary, Norwalk, Ct.
Ellis, Anna, Brooklyn.
Ellsworth, Lewis, Napierville, Ill.
Elwell, Isaac N., Concord, N. H.
Ely, Henry D., Holmdel, N. J.
Ely, Mrs. Ann, Holmdel, N. J.
Ely, Mrs. Lucy, Jacobstown, N. J.
Ely, Horatio, Freehold, N. J.
Emery, Thomas, Cincinnati, Ohio.
Emery, Mrs. Kezia, Cincinnati, Ohio.
Emmons, Mrs. Sarah, Deep River, Ct.
English, Henry H., Philadelphia.
English, Miss Hannah P., Beverly, Mass.
English. John, Paterson, N. J.
Ensign, Chancellor, North Ridgway, N. Y.
Eschman, Rev. John, New York.
Eschman, Mrs. Magdalene, New York.
Estee, Rev. Sidney A., York, N. Y.
Estep, Rev. Dr. James, Library, Pa.
Estes, A. B., Lower Three Runs, S. C.
Estes, Miss H. S., Lower Three Runs, S. C.
Estes, Mrs. E. A., Lower Three Runs, S. C.
Evans, Silas J., Louisville, Ky.
Evans, Mrs. S. E., Society Hill, S. C.
Evans, Reuben, Amesbury, Mass.
Evans, Dr. Joseph T., New York.
Evans, Mrs. Czarina H., New York.
Evans, Rev. William E., Carbondale, Pa.
Eveleigh, Mrs. Mary D., Brooklyn, N. Y.
Eveleth, Samuel, Boston.
Everts, Rev. Wm. W., D.D., Louisville, Ky.
Everett, Rev. Samuel, North Leverett, Mass.
Everett, David, New London, N. H.
Everett, Benjamin C., Philadelphia.
Everett, Rev. William P., East Abington, Mass.
Everett, Aaron, Boston.

Fails, David, South Dedham, Mass.
Failing, Josiah, Portland, Oregon.
Failing, Mrs. Henrietta, Portland, Oregon.
Failing, Henry, Portland, Oregon.
Failing, Miss Elizabeth A., Portland, Oregon.
Fairbanks, Rev. George G., Somerville, Mass.
Fairbrother, Lewis, Pawtucket, R. I.
Fairman, James, New Haven, Ct.
Fales, Joseph T., Burlington, Iowa.
Fales, Oliver, West Philadelphia, Pa.
Falkner, John B., Malden, Mass.
Falwell, L. W., Romulus, N. Y.
Fargo, Rev. Isaac, Jr., Fairport, N. Y.
Fairchild, Stephen, M.D., Morristown, N. J.
Farish, T., Gulf, N. C.
Farnsworth, Hon. Joseph D., Fairfax, Vt.
Farnsworth, Dr. James H., Fairfax, Vt.
Farnsworth, Rev. C. D., Colesburg, Iowa.
Farnsworth, W., Fleming, N. Y.
Farr, Mrs. H. D., Albion, N. Y.
Farr, Miss Mary Louisa, Hastings, N. Y.
Farrington, David, Trumansburg, N. Y.
Farwell, Isaac, Watertown, Mass.
Farwell, Mrs. Sarah A., Watertown, Mass.
Farrar, Mrs. Susan P., Jackson, Va.
Faunce, Rev. Daniel, Somerville, Mass.
Fay, Rev. William N., West Halifax, Vt.
Feller, Mad. Henrietta, Grand Ligne, C. E.
Felton, R., Hertford, N. C.
Felton, Cader, Hertford, N. C.
Felton, Mrs. Mary, Hertford, N. C.
Felton, Rev. George D., Granville, Mass.
Fendall, Mrs E. D Moorestown, N. J.
Fennell, Rev. George, Harrell's Store, N. C
Fennell, Owen, Wilmington, N. C.
Ferguson, B., Newport, Ohio.
Ferrier, John M., New York.
Ferrell, Miss Mary Ann, New York.
Ferris, Mrs. Hannah L., New York.
Ferris, O., Wilson, N. Y.
Ferris, Samuel M., Columbia, Ohio.
Ferris, Rev. Isaac, Columbia, O.
Ferris, John M., Columbia, Ohio.
Ferris, William, Columbia, Ohio
Fickling, F. W., Gillisonville, S. C.
Field, Thomas F., Brooklyn, N. Y.
Field, Mrs. Thomas F., Brooklyn, N. Y.
Field, Thomas S., Hoboken, N. J.
Field, Mrs Lavina F., Taunton, Mass.
Field, Charles H., Taunton, Mass.
Field, George A., Taunton, Mass.
Field, Miss Ann M., Taunton, Mass.
Field, Miss Hannah E., Taunton, Mass.
Field, Mrs. Elizabeth H., Providence.
Field, Miss Elsie M., Westport, N. H.
Field, Rev Moses, Flat Brook, N. Y.
Fife, Rev. James, Charlottesville, Va.
Fife, Mrs. Margaret W., Charlottesville, Va.
Fifield, Mrs. Catharine, Pawtucket, R. I.
Fifield, William, East Poultney, Vt.
Fillio, Rev. Nelson, Battle Creek, Mich.
Finch, Miss Sarah A., Red Oak Grove, Va.
Finch, George W., New York.
Fish, Rev. Joel W., Geneva, Wis.
Fish, J. L. A., Newton, Mass.

MEMBERS FOR LIFE.

F[illegible], E. A., [illegible], N. Y.
Fish, Rev. Elisha P., H[illegible], Ct.
Fishback, Mrs. S[illegible] J., [illegible], Va.
Fisher, Mrs. Ann L., New York.
Fisher, Rev. Abel, M[illegible], Mass.
Fisher, Rev. Ezra, Oregon City, Oregon.
Fisher, Rev. Otis M., [illegible], Ill.
Fisher, Isaac, West [illegible], Vt.
Fish, Willard, New York.
Fitch, Dr. William, Stamford, Ct.
Fitzgerald, Miss Joanna, New York.
Fithian, Samuel C., Greenwich, N. J.
Fitz, William, Worcester, Mass.
Fl[illegible], Jonah, Philadelphia.
Flanders, Rev. Charles W., Concord, N. H.
Flanders, Mrs. M[illegible] L., Concord, N. H.
Flanders, Timothy C., Haverhill, Mass.
Flanders, Helen, Haverhill, Mass.
Flanders, George B., Brooklyn, N. Y.
Flanders, I. M., Nashua, N. H.
Fleet, James R., [illegible], Va.
Fleet, Dr. B., King and Queen C. H., Va.
Fleischmann, Rev. Conrad A., Philadelphia.
Fletcher, Rev. S[illegible], Sandy Hill, N. Y.
Fletcher, Rev. Leonard, New Orleans.
Fletcher, Rev. Horace, Townshend, Vt.
Fletcher, Mrs. Harriet A., Townshend, Vt.
Fletcher, Mrs. Mary, Amenia, N. Y.
Fletcher, Mrs. Sarah A., Saratoga Springs, N. Y.
Flinn, Mrs. E. A. E., Darlington, S. C.
Flint, Brayton, [illegible], Mich.
Forsyth, Miss Sarah S., Albany, N. Y.
Forsyth, Russel, Albany, N. Y.
Forsyth, Mrs. Sarah, Albany, N. Y.
Forsyth, Miss Emily H., Albany, N. Y.
Forsyth, Russell Jr., Albany, N. Y.
Fowle, Miss Lucy, Boston.
Fowler, Gamaliel, Suffield, Ct.
Fox, Rev. Norman, Ballston, N. Y.
Fox, Rev. Charles A., Waverly, Pa.
Fox, Mrs. Julia A., Waverley, Pa.
Fox, Albert R., Sand Lake, N. Y.
Fox, Mrs. Mary A., Sand Lake, N. Y.
Fox, Charles, New York.
Fox, Miss Ann Eliza, New York.
Frank, Miss Amy, Smithfield, Pa.
Frazee, Ezra, Rahway, N. J.
Frazee, Mrs. Mary, Rahway, N. J.
Francis, Robert, Newington, Ct.
Francis, Mrs. Lydia D., Newington, Ct.
Francis, Norman, New York.
Francis, Charles King, New York.
Frayzer, Rev. Herndon, Twymann's, Va.
Freas, Rev. Daniel J., Salem, N. Y.
Freeman, Rev. T. G., New York.
Freeman, Rev. Joseph, Cavendish, Vt.
Freeman, Rev. G. W., Horicon, Wis.
Freeman, Thomas W., Augusta, Ga.
Freeman, Elisha, Worcester, Mass.
Freeman, Mrs. Margaret E., Camillus, N. Y.
Freeman, Dyer, Middleboro', Mass.
French, George R., Wilmington, N. C.

Gage, A., Methuen, Mass.
Gale, Jones R., Delavan, Ill.
Gale, Rev. Amory, Lee, Mass.
Gale, Rev. Solomon, Columbus, N. J.
Gale, Rev. E., Bennington, Vt.
Galusha, Truman, Jericho, Vt.
Gammell, A. M., Warren, R. I.
Gardiner, Richard, Philadelphia.
Gardner, Miss Miranda B., Fulton, N. Y.
Gardner, John, Newark, N. Y.
Gardner, James C., Augusta, Ga.
Gardner, Rev. Jacob, Lyme, Ct.
Gardner, Frederick, New York.
Garfield, Rev. Benjamin F., Clifton Park, N.Y.
Garnett, Dorothy, Miller's, Va.
Garnett, Rev. Wm., Martindale Depot, N. Y.
Garrett, D. H. Haddonfield, N. J.
Garnsey Erasmus D. Burnt Hills, N. Y.
Garnsey Mrs. Erasmus D., Burnt Hills, N. Y.
Garret, Samuel, Rock Hill, Ohio.
Garrison, Rev. Cantine, Chili, E. Y.
Gates, Marcius A., South Gardner, Mass.
Gates, Horace S., Norwich, Ct.
Gates, Rev. G. W. Palmyra, N. Y.
Gates, T. J., Plainfield, Ct.
Gates, Cyrus, Preston, Ct.
Gatling, John, Eatontown, N. J.
Gault, George, Brooklyn, N. Y.
Gault, Mrs. George, Brooklyn, N. Y.
Gault, Miss Georgianna E., Brooklyn, N. Y.
Gay William, Hollister, Mass.
Gayer, Rev. Charles, New York.
Gayler, Mrs. Anna, New York.
George, Moses D., Haverhill, Mass.
George, Samuel, Haverhill, Mass.
George, Mrs. Elizabeth C., Culpepper, Va.
German, Joseph, Beekman, N. Y
Gibbs, Mrs. Eliza Ann, Tamaqua, Pa.
Gibbs, Rev. Oliver W., Bennettsburg, N. Y.
Gibson, Rev. A., Hudson, Wis.
Gibson, Mrs. Evelyn B., Hudson, Wis.
Gifford, Rev Isaac S, Bedford, N. Y.
Gifford, Mrs. Annis, Bedford, N. Y.
Gigniliat, W. R., Darien, Ga.
Gilbert, Wm. J., Middletown, Ct.
Gilbert, Isaac H., Providence.
Gilbert, J. B, Hartford, Ct.
Gilky, Royal, Watertown, Mass.
Gill, Miss Mary Pottsville, Pa.
Gill, Miss Mary Ann, Philadelphia.
Gillette, Mrs. Hannah J., New York.
Gillett, Asahel, Rose, N Y
Gillett, Nehemiah, Danbury, Ct.
Gilman, Miss Ellen W Roadstown, N. J.
Gilman, George H., New York
Gilman, David, Roadstown, N. J
Gilman, Mrs. John, Newburyport, Mass.
Giles, Alfred E. Boston.
Gilpatrick, Rev. James, Topeka, K. T.
Girdwood, Rev. John, New Bedford, Mass.
Girdwood, Mrs. Mary, New Bedford, Mass.
Gladding, Mrs. Lydia M., Providence.
Glass, George W Honeoye Falls, N. Y.
Gleason, Anderson, Hubbardston, Mass.
Glover, Charles S., New York.

Goadby, Rev. John, Poultney, Vt.
Goddard, Jabez, York, N. Y.
Goddard, Mrs. Elizabeth, York, N. Y.
Goddard, Benjamin, Worcester, Mass.
Going, Mrs. Nancy B., Columbus, Ohio.
Going, Rev Ezra, Greenville, Ohio.
Going, J Aurora, N Y.
Godfry, Abel, Sennett, N. Y.
Godfrey, Edward J., New York.
Godfrey, Mrs. Anna, Brooklyn, N. Y.
Goldthwait, Nathan, Worcester, Mass.
Goldy, John, Imlaystown, N J
Goldy, Mrs. Emily, Imlaystown, N J.
Gooch, Mrs Sarah J Cambridge, Mass.
Goodhue, Rev. Joseph A., uffield, Ct.
Goodhue, Ann C., New Boston, N. H.
Goodnow, Joseph, Charlestown, Mass.
Goodnough, Levi, Sudbury, Mass.
Goodrich, Nathan F Meriden Ct.
Goodwin, Charles T., New York.
Goodwin, Rev Thomas, Poughkeepsie, N. Y.
Goodno, Rev. I. R., Campton, N. H.
Goodno, Rev W. S., Bordentown, N. J.
Gonsalves, Rev. M. J., Jacksonville. Ill.
Gordon, Mrs. Elizabeth, Imlaystown, N. J.
Gordon, Abram, New London, Ct.
Gorman, Rev. Samuel, Laguna, N M.
Gorman, Miss Mary, Laguna, N M.
Gould, Joseph, Wilmington, Del.
Gould, Augustus A., M. D, Boston.
Goss, Mrs. Frances M, New York.
Gove, G. B. R., Fort Covington, N. Y.
Gowdey, David, Providence,
Granger, James N Jr., Providence.
Granger, Mrs. Ann B., Providence.
Granger, Rev. Abraham H., Providence.
Grafts, George A., Boston, Mass.
Grafton, Miss Frances, Brooklyn, N. Y.
Graham, Mrs. Susan W. Hillsboro', N. C.
Graham, James C., Jerseyville, Ill.
Grant, Rev. Daniel H., Stephentown, N. Y.
Grant, Rev. Stillman B., New Haven, Ct.
Grant, Mrs Mary S., New Haven, Ct.
Grant, Rev. William, Whitehall, N. Y.
Grant, Alexander, Providence.
Grant, Preston, Pawtucket R. I.
Grant O B., Stonington, Ct.
Graves, Rev. J M., Brighton, Mass.
Graves, C Brown's Store, N C,
Graves, Rev. Charles, Cassville, N. Y.
Graves, Rev. Samuel, Kalamazoo, Mich.
Graves, William H., Brooklyn, N. Y.
Gray, Charles F. H Pittsgrove, N. J.
Gray, William E, New York.
Gray, Mrs. Susan, Brooklyn, N Y.
Gray, Theodore H. New York.
Greene, Mrs. Lydia B., New Bedford, Mass.
Green, Russell, Providence.
Green, David C., Providence.
Green, Arnold, Providence.
Green, Miss Frances Mary, Providence.
Green, Mrs. Mary, New York.
Green, Rev. John, Chester Village, Mass.
Green, Rev. Charles H. West Townsend, Vt.
Green, Rev. Jonathan R., Derby, Vt.
Green, Spencer Rutland, Vt.
Green, Ralph, Three Rivers, Mass.

Greenleaf, John, Cambridge, Mass.
Greenleaf, Mrs Elizabeth H., Cambridge, Mass.
Greenwood, Simeon A., Worcester, Mass.
Grenell, Mrs Eliza, Port Jarvis, N. Y.
Grenell, Mrs. C. Amelia, Middletown, N. Y.
Grenell, Rufus M., Honesdale, Pa.
Gregg, Wm. Henry, Wilmington, Del.
Gregory, Miss Clarissa, New York.
Gregory, Rev. S., Lisbon, N. Y.
Gregory, Uriah, Weston, Mass.
Gregory, Rev. Truman, Lee, Ill.
Griffin, Rev. Charles, Wilmington, Del.
Griffin, Nathaniel L., Edgefield, S. C.
Griffin, Edwin, New York.
Griffin, James T., Rochester, N. Y.
Griffis, Rev. P., North Urbana, N. Y.
Griffith, Rev. B., Philadelphia.
Griffiths, A. W., M. D., Philadelphia.
Griffiths, John J., New York.
Griggs, Samuel, Rutland, Vt.
Griggs, Mrs. Abigail S., Rutland, Vt.
Griggs, David R., Brookline, Mass.
Griggs, Seth D., Belchertown, Mass.
Griggs, J. W., Boston.
Grimley, Rev. Joseph L., Unionville, N. Y.

Hall, [illegible]
Hall, [illegible]
Hamil[illegible]
Hamil[illegible]
Hamm[illegible]
Hand,
Hauly,
[illegible]

Hart, Mrs. Almira M., Boston.
Hartley, Richard W Cincinnati, Ohio.
Hatch, Charles G Shelby, N. Y
Hatch, Rev. S., Lansingburgh, N. Y.
Hatch, Ira, Union Village, N. Y.
Hartshorn, Jonas, Worcester, Mass.
Hart, Henry R. Portland Me.
Hartwell, John B., Providence.
Harvey, Hezekiah New York.
Harvey, Rev. Alfred, Woodstown, N J.
Haskell, Dr. George, Rockford, Ill.
Haskell, Rev. Samuel, Kalamazoo, Mich
Haskell, Rev. Abel, Yates, N. Y.
Haskell, Mrs. Esther, Yates, N Y.
Haskin, Mrs. Pamela, New York.
Hastings, Andrew F B ooklyn, N. Y.
Hastings, Mrs. Andrew F., Brooklyn, N. Y.
Haswell, Rev. James M., Amherst, Burmah.
Haswell, Mrs. Jane M. Amherst, Burmah.
Hasey, Miss Angeline, New York.
Hatt, Joel, Orange, N. J
Hatt, Mrs. Sophia, New York.
Hatt, Miss Annie Isabella, Morristown, N. J.
Hatfield, Robert G., New York.
Hatfield, Mrs. Charlotte S., New York.
Hathaway Luther B, Suffield, Ct.
Hathaway, Miss Mary, New York.
Hathaway, Charles F., Boston.
Hathaway, Mrs. Temperance, Boston.
Haven, Caleb, Penn Yan N Y
Havens, Robert M. Norwich, Ct.
Havens, Abraham, Freehold, N. J.
Haviland, John, New urk
Haviland, Mrs. Joanna, New York
Haviland, Miss Mary Ann, New York.
Hawes, Rev. Josiah New Sharon, Me.
Hawks, Isaac, Shelburne Falls Mass
Hawks, Mrs. El sa H North Bennington, Vt.
Hawley, Mrs. Rebecca, New York
Hawley, D. F Bristol, Ct.
Hawley, Mrs. Jane Utica, N. Y.
Hayden, Rev. Lucien, Saxton's River, Vt.
Hayden, Mrs. Caroline S. Saxton's River, Vt.
Hayden, John, Middlefield, N. Y
Hayburst, Rev. L. W., Ballston Spa, N. Y.
Haynes, Mrs. S. B., Va
Haynes, Rev. Hiram Preston Hollow, N. Y.
Haynes, Rev. Dudley C., Philadelphia.
Haynes, Mrs. L. M Norwich, N. Y.
Hay, Alexander, Greenwich, N. Y.
Hayes, Seth, Jr., Cromwell, Ct.
Hays, Seth, Colchester Ct.
Hayes, John P., New York.
Hazen, Mrs. Emily N., Throopsville, N. Y.
Hazen, Rev. Henry C., T iroopsville, N. Y.
Heafford, Samuel, Essex, Ct.
Heald, Rev. Albert, East Washington, N. H.
Healy, Ebenezer Sennett, N Y
Healy, Mrs. Amia, Sennett, N. Y.
Healy, P. W., Sennett, N. Y.
Heath, Rev. Amasa, Adams Village, N. Y.
Heath, Morgan, Greenwich, N. Y.
Heath, Moses, Flemin N. J.
Hedden, William, Orange, N. J.
Hedden, Mrs. C. F., Manchester, N. H.
Hedges, Daniel, Penn Yan, N. Y.

Hepburn, Rev James, Stamford, Ct.
Hendlen, Miss Henrietta, New York.
Hendlen, Mrs. A na S. Q., New York.
Hendrick, Rev Joe East Smithfield, Pa.
Hendrick, ohn M New Haven, Ct.
Hendrickson, Rev. G F Towner's Station, N. Y.
Henley, James W New York.
Hen ry, Mrs. James W., New York.
Henry, Rev. Foster Tyringham Mass.
Hera, Rev. Edwin R Hereford, Md.
Herbert, Mrs. Agnes D., Marlboro', N. J.
Heritage, Jason, Moorestown N. J.
Herrick Mrs. M. E., Beverley, Mass.
Herrington, Chester, Clifton Park, N. Y.
Heron, Miss sabella, Williamsburgh, N Y.
Heron, Thomas F Williamsburgh, N. Y.
Heron, William S., Williamsburgh, N Y.
Hervey, Rev Nathaniel, Westboro', Mass.
Heustis, Mrs. Ann, New Brunswick, N. J.
Hewit, Edmund, Galway, N. Y.
Hewitt, Chas. E., New London, Ct.
Hewitt, Austin D. Uncasville, Ct.
Heywood, Ellen, affrey, N. H.
Hickman, Mrs. E., New Albany, Ia.
Hicks, Mrs. Mary A n, Norwich, N. Y.
Hickok, Austin, Jay N Y
Hide, Mrs. Fanny, Westerly R. I.
Higbie, Alanson, Penfield, N. Y.
Higgins, N L Elmira, N. Y.
Hiler, Thomas G., Jr., Boston.
Hill, Mrs. Harriet D., New York.
Hill, Miss Harriet R, New York.
Hill, Mrs. Mary Miller's, Va.
Hill, David Jayne, Carmel, N Y.
Hill, Mrs. Rebecca, Essex, Ct.
Hill, Rev. William Kane, Ill.
Hill, Samuel P., Charlestown, Mass.
Hill, Amos, Jr., West Cambridge, Mass.
Hill, Rev. I. N., Bridgeport, Ct.
Hill, Leander J., Brockport, N. Y.
Hill, Henry S., East Cambridge, Mass.
Hill, Mrs. Eleanor, New York.
Hill, Rev. Thomas, Paris, Ia.
Hill, Walter E., Boston.
Hill, Ira, Newport, O.
Hillman, Mrs Catharine, New York.
Hillman, Samuel T., New York.
Hills, Mrs. Deborah, Haverhill, Mass.
Hine, Simmons, New Haven, Ct.
Hinton, A. G Pittsborough, N. C.
Hires, Mrs. Catharine, Freehold, N. J.
Hiscox, Mrs. C. O., New York.
Hitchcox, Sheldon, Suffield, Ct.
Hitchcocks, Peresh, Suffield, Ct.
Hoar, Lewis, Warren R. I.
Hoar, John R, Warren, R. I.
Hoard, Samuel, Chicago, Ill.
Hobart, James, Westford, Vt.
Hobart, Washington Boston.
Hodge, Mrs. Sophroni P., Newark, N. J.
Hodge, Mrs. Hansel L., Brooklyn, N. Y.
Hodges, Rev. J., Jr. East Brookfield, Mass.
Hoff, John, Baptist Town, N. J.
Hoff, Jeremiah, Baptist Town, N J.
Hoffman, Joseph H., Leverington, Pa.

MEMBERS FOR LIFE.

Hogan, Miss Ellen, New York.
Holbrook, Chas. F., Worcester, Mass.
Holbrook, Samuel F., Boston.
Holcombe, Thomas, Savannah, Ga.
Holland, Lucretia E., Boston.
Holland, Joab, Townshend, Vt.
Holmes, Samuel C., Bedford, N. Y.
Holmes, Mrs. Comfort, Bedford, N. Y.
Holmes, Rev. Lewis, Edgartown, Mass.
Holmes, Mrs. Sarah, Holmdel, N. J.
Holman, Rev. Thomas, West Woodstoock, Ct.
Holroyd, J. Manning, Providence.
Holly, Mrs. Deborah R., Bedford, N. Y.
Holt, John M., Worcester, Mass.
Holt, Cabel, Sharon, Vt.
Homes, Rev. Martin W., Franklin, O.
Hooper, Rev. Wm., Murfreesboro', N. C.
Hooper, Rev. Noah, Great Falls, N. H.
Hooper, Mrs. Lucy W., Great Falls, N. H.
Hope, Mrs. Amelia, Brooklyn, N. Y.
Hope, Rev. James M., Catskill, N. Y.
Hopkins, John, Bucksport, Me.
Hopkins, Ira D., Utica, N. Y.
Hopkins, William A., Providence.
Hopkins, Miss Mary E., Providence.
Hopley, John, Woburn, Mass.
Hopper, Rev. Andrew, New Providence, N. J.
Hopper, Mrs. Margaret, New Providence, N. J.
Hopper, Rev. A. M., Charlestown, Mass.
[redacted]

Howes, Samuel C., Chatham, Mass.
Howland Emeline D., New Bedford, Mas
Hoyt, Miss Harriet E., Brooklyn, N. Y.
Hoyt, Mrs Julia A., Brooklyn, N. Y.
Hoyt, L. D., Brooklyn, N. Y.
Hubatcheck, Joseph, New York.
Hubbard, Mrs. Mary R., Deep River, Ct.
Hubbell, Alrich, Utica, N. Y.
Hubbell, Rev. S., Urbana, N. Y.
Hudgens, Mrs. Rebecca Y., Hampton, Va
Hughson, Levi P., Oswego, N. Y.
Huling, Miss Frances, Saratoga Springs,
Hull, Mrs. Maria, New York.
Hull, Charles, Danbury, Ct.
Hulse, Smith, Dundee N. Y.
Hungerford, Levi, Cordova, Ill.
Hunt, Dr. George, Le Claire, Ill.
Hunt, Rev. John, Hollis, N. H.
Hunt, Mrs. N., Sharon, Ct.
Hunt, Miss Eliza, New York.
Hunt, John, Boston, Mass.
Hunt, Richard, New York.
Hunt, Edward A., New Haven, Ct.
Hunter, William, Boston.
Hunter, Miss Elizabeth Jane, New York.
Huntley, Rev. George W., Wellsville, N.
Huntington, Mrs. Philip, Haverhill, Mass
Huntington, John H., Troy, N. Y.
Huntington, Myron, Shaftsbury, Vt.
Hurlburt, Joel, Darien Depot, Ct.
[redacted]

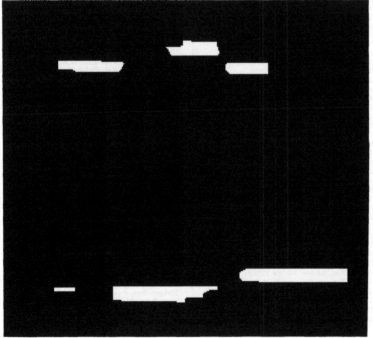

Jacoby, Mrs. B. A., Davenport, Iowa.
James, Rev Joshua J., Raleigh, N. C.
James, Edward, Albany.
James, George, Zanesville, O.
James, Francis H., Philadelphia.
James, Rev. David, Osceola, Ill.
James, Thomas M., New Bedford, Mass.
James, John, Brookfield, O.
Jamison, Alexander, Wilmington, Del.
Jameson, Mrs. Lucinda L., Melrose, Mass.
Jameson, Miss Eliza, Newton, Mass.
Janvoin, Edwin, Chelsea, Mass.
Jarratt, Henry, Jarratt's, Va
Jarratt, Nicholas, Jarratt Depot, Va.
Jastram, George B., Providence.
Jaudon, Mrs. Sarah T, Robertsville, S. C.
Jaycox, Isaac, Cold Spring, N. Y.
Jaycox, Mrs. Fanny M., Cold Spring, N. Y.
Jeffery, Mrs. Julia M., Albany, N. Y.
Jeffery, Rev. Reuben, Albany, N
Jeffress, J. M., Red Oak Grove, Va
Jefferis, Rev. David, Perkiomen, Pa.
Jencks, Rev. Erasmus N., Ottawa, Ill.
Jencks, Miss Maria, Pawtucket, R. I.
Jenks, Gideon, Brookfield, Mass.
Jenks, J. W. P, Middleboro', Mass.
Jenkins, Mrs. Susanna, New York.
Jenkins, Rev. J. S., Coatesville, Pa.
Jenkins, Miss Rebecca, New York.
Jennett, John, Halifax, C. H., Va.
Jennings, Mrs. Susan C., Worcester, Mass.
Jennings, Mrs. Marcia, Deep River, Ct.
Jennings, Mrs. Betsey, Deep River Ct.
Jeril, Rev. T., Lebanon, N. Y.
Jerome, George D., Uncasville, Ct.
Jerrard, Rev. Richard, Fond du Lac, Wis.
Jeter, Rev. J. C., Beaver Dam, S. C.
Jewell, Aaron C., Newark, N. J.
Jewett, Rev. Milo P., Poughkeepsie, N. Y.
Jewett, Rev. Daniel, Farmington, Iowa.
Jimmerson, Robert J., New York.
Jimmerson, Mrs. Miranda L., New York.
Johnson, Mathew M., Woburn, Mass.
Johnson, Rev. William B, D.D., Edgefield, S.C.
Johnson, Mrs. Henrietta, Edgefield, S. C.
Johnson, William, North East, Pa.
Johnson, Mrs Sarah S., North East, Pa.
Johnson, Mrs. Louisa M., Lynn, Mass.
Johnson, James, Brooklyn, N. Y.
Johnson, Robert, Newark, N. J.
Johnson, Mrs. Robert, Newark, N. J.
Johnson, Rev. Solomon B., St. Louis, Mo.
Johnson, Rev. George J., Burlington, Iow.
Johnson, Mrs. George J., Burlington, Iowa.
Johnson, Rev. Hezekiah, Oregon City, Oregon.
Johnson, Albert B., Willistown, Pa.
Johnson, Edward, New York.
Johnson, Mrs. Mary, Albany, N. Y.
Johnson, Merrick, Willington, Ct.
Johnson, Miss Jane Ann, Wilson, N. Y.
Johnson, Oliver, Providence.
Johnson, Ralph, Norwich, N. Y.
Johnson, Elias, Troy, N. Y.
Johnson, Mrs. Elizabeth, Philadelphia.
Johnston, Andrew, Newark, N. J.
Johnston, Mrs. Andrew, Newark N. J.
Johnston James, Sing Sing, N. Y.
Johnston, John L., Sing Sing, N. Y.
Jolls, John F., Providence.
Jones, Rev. Stephen, Norwalk, Ohio.
Jones, Mrs. Stephen, Norwalk, Ohio.
Jones, Rev. John, Seaville, N. J.
Jones, Mrs Deborah, Seaville, N. J.
Jones, Mrs. Ann T., Williamsburg, Va.
Jones, Eliza T., Tavern P. O, Pa.
Jones, Mrs. Margaret, New York.
Jones, Mrs. Eliza W., New Brunswick, N. J.
Jones, Mrs. Elizabeth, Macedon, N. Y.
Jones, David, New York.
Jones, Mrs. Sarah, New York.
Jones, Mrs Mary, New York.
Jones, Miss Catharine L., Philadelphia.
Jones, Rev. Joseph H., Frederick City, Md.
Jones, Rev. David N., Richmond, Va.
Jones, Rev. Matthew, Stephentown, N. Y.
Jones, Rev. Theophilus, Hatboro', Pa.
Jones, Rev. Isaac D., Flemingville, N. Y.
Jones, John B., Roxbury, Mass.
Jones, William G., Wilmington, Del.
Jones, Washington, Wilmington, Del.
Jones, William M., New York.
Jones, Mrs. Margaretta V., New York.
Jones, Rev. J. W., Hyde Park, N. Y.
Jones, Howard M, Providence, R. I.
Jones, Rev. J. D. E., North Bennington, Vt.
Jones, J F., East Cambridge, Mass.
Jones, Rev. T., Rock Hill, Ohio.
Jones, Rev. Edward, Brookfield, Ohio.
Jones, Mrs Abigail, New York
Jones, Rev. A. B, Guilford, N. Y.
Jones, Rev. H. S., Smyrna, N. Y.
Jordan, Elder, R. K., Richland Grove, Ill.
Jordan, Philana D., Columbia, Ohio.
Jordon, Mrs. Esther, Brooklyn, N. Y.
Jordon, True P., Lowell, Mass.
Joslin, Joseph, East Poultney, Vt.
Joyce, Miss Sarah W., Worcester, Mass.
Judd, Rev. Truman O., Fair Haven, Ct.
Justice, David, Forestville, N. C.
Justin, Rev. Ira, Richmond, N. Y.
Kain, Charles, Marlton, N. J.
Kain, Mrs. Sarah, Marlton, N. J.
Kain, Rev. Charles, Jr., Mullica Hill, N. J.
Kain, Mrs. Maria, Mullica Hill, N J.
Kasson, Marcus A., Granville, Mass.
Kauffman, Henry, Paoli, Pa.
Kauffman, Mrs. Sarah, Paoli, Pa.
Keith, William, Boston, Mass.
Kavanagh, Michael, Lowell, Mass.
Keely, Rev. George, Haverhill, Mass.
Keely, Mrs. George, Haverhill, Mass.
Keely, John, Haverhill, Mass.
Keely, Mrs. John, Haverhill, Mass.
Keely, Rev. Thomas E., Kingston, Mass.
Keen, Mrs. Susan B., West Philadelphia.
Keen, George B., West Philadelphia
Keen, William W. J., West Philadelphia.
Keen, Charles B, West Philadelphia.
Keeney, John, New London, Ct.
Keeney, William H., New London, Ct.

Keeney, Rev. Curtis, New London, Ct.
Kelly, Mrs. Joan, Elmira, N. Y.
Kelly, Mrs. Mary M., Brooklyn, N. Y.
Kelley, Mrs. Catharine, New York.
Kelley, Mrs Eli, New York.
Kelley, Miss Georgiana, New York.
Kelley, James D., Pittsfield, N. H.
Kellogg, U. H., Utica, N. Y.
Kellogg, Moses S., Chickopee Falls, Mass.
Kelsey, Rev. Daniel, Pittsgrove, N. J.
Kelton, George, Salem, N. J.
Kemp, Sylvester A., Florida, Mass.
Kemp, Nathaniel P., Jamaica Plains, Mass.
Kendall, H. N., St. Louis, Mo.
Kendall, Charles S., Boston.
Kendrick, Silas N., Detroit, Mich.
Kendrick, Mrs. Fanny, Detroit, Mich.
Kendrick, Adin, East Poultney, Vt.
Kendrick, Rev. A. C., D D., Rochester, N. Y.
Kendrick, Mrs. Ann, Hamilton, N. Y.
Kennan, Mrs. Eliza, Thompsonville, Va.
Kennard, J. Spencer, Philadelphia.
Kenworthy, Mrs. Mary, New York.
Kerr, John, Yanceyville, N. C.
Kerfoot, Mrs. Maria C., Upperville, Va.
Kerfoot, Mrs. Harriet E., Battletown, Va.
Ketcham, Charles F., Brooklyn, N. Y.
Ketcham, Rev. F., Cordova, Ill.
Ketcham, Miss Sarah A., New York.

Knigh
Knigh
Knigh
Knowl
Knowl
Knowl
Knowl
Knuds
Kyle,
L'Amo
Ladd,
La Gra
La Gra
[illegible]
[illegible]
[illegible]
[illegible]

Lee, J. A., New York.
Lee, Francis R. Trenton, N. J.
Leicester, Mrs. Mary, New York.
Leggett, Rev William, Owasco, N. Y.
Leland, J. A, Brooklyn, N. Y.
Lemont, Charles A., Chelsea, Mass.
Lemont, Mrs Ann M., New York.
Leonard, Richard, Riceville, N. J.
Leonard, Mrs. Mahetable, Zanesville, Ohio.
Leonard, Rev. Isaac, Burlington, Iowa.
Leonard, George E, Newton, Mass.
Leonard, Mrs. Caroline F., Taunton, Mass.
Leonard, George A., New York.
Lerned, Rev. J. H., Cambridge, Mass.
Levy, Rev. Edgar M., West Philadelphia.
Lewis, William J, New York.
Lewis, Elijah, Brooklyn, N. Y.
Lewis, Mrs. Ann, Brooklyn, N. Y.
Lewis, Mrs. Mary B. S., Brooklyn, N. Y.
Lewis, Mrs. Asa, Worcester, Mass.
Lewis, Rev. Charles C., Westerly, R I.
Lewis, Rev. Lester, Middletown, Ct.
Lewis, Daniel D., Philadelphia.
Lewis, Mrs. Hannah, Norwich, N. Y.
Lewis, Simeon H., Boston.
Lewis, William, New York.
Lewis, Rev. Richard, Holmesburg, Pa.
Lewis, Elijah, Norwich, N. Y.
Lewis, William B., Preston, N. Y.
Lewis, Rev. Welcome, Mansfield, Mass.
Lewis, Jr., John B., Boston.
Lincoln, Rev. Thomas O., Utica, N. Y.
Lincoln, Mrs. Abby A.
Lincoln, Rev. Heman, Jamaica Plains, Mass.
Lincoln, Henry E., Boston.
Lincoln, Joshua, Roxbury, Mass.
Linde, Frederick, New York.
Lindsay, Wm., Fall River, Mass.
Lippitt, Mrs. Elizabeth S., Cumberland, Ohio.
Lippitt, Mrs. Melinda, Hiramsburg, O.
Litchfield, Rev. Daniel W., Benton, N.Y.
Litchfield, Electus B., Brooklyn, N. Y.
Litchfield, E. D., Brooklyn, N. Y.
Little, George W., Charlestown, Mass.
Little, J. T., Dixon, Ill.
Littlefield, Jotham, Belleville, N. Y.
Lifsey, Mrs. Sally, Hick's Ford, Va.
Livermore, Rev S. T., South Livonia, N. Y.
Loomis, Asahel, Gouverneur, N. Y.
Loomis, Edwin H., Lebanon, Ct.
Lock, Rev. William, Jamestown, N. Y.
Locke, Mrs. Harriet N., Springfield, N. J.
Locke, Jesse A., Watertown, Mass.
Locke, Mrs. Sarah B, Watertown, Mass.
Lockwood, Luther G., Stratfield, Ct.
Logan, Rev. John, Ill.
Logan, James, Pemberton, N. J.
Lombard, Nathan C., Lowell, Mass.
Long, E. J., Boston, Mass.
Long, William, Shelburne Falls, Mass.
Long, William, Urbana, Ohio.
Longyear, Rev. Henry Z., Phenicia, N. Y.
Loring, Samuel H., Boston.
Loring, Mrs. James, Boston.
Love, Mrs. Harriet N., Salem, N. J.
Love, Rev. H T., New York.
Love, Mrs. Catharine W., New York.
Love, John, New York.
Lovell, George, Osterville, Mass.
Lovell, Mrs Lucy, Fall River, Mass.
Lovell, Rev. Andrew S., Bloomfield, Ct.
Lucas, Rev. Elijah, Waterford, N. Y.
Luckey, James E., Palo, Ill.
Luckey, Mrs Emma M., Palo, Ill.
Ludlow, John, R, New York.
Ludlow, Mrs. Clarissa Ann, Newport, R. I.
Ludlam, David, Jr., Sing Sing, N. Y.
Lull, Rev. Abner, Sheboygan Falls, Wis.
Luther, Job, Providence.
Luther, Gardner, Seekonk, Mass.
Luther, Mrs. Mary, Seekonk, Mass.
Lyman, Nathan, Andover, Ct.
Lynch, Thomas, Philadelphia.
Lyon, Jesse, Fitchburg, Mass.
Lyon, Moses G., Fitchburg, Mass.
Lyon, Cyrus, York, N. Y.
Lyon, Mrs. Mary, York, N. Y.
Lyon, Miss Rebecca, Plainfield, N. J.
Lyon, Rev. Daniel D., Sag Harbor, N. Y.
Lyon, Rev. Joel Sylvanus, Mich.
Lyon, Mrs. Caroline P., Chatham, Mass.
Lyon, Mrs. Merrick, Providence.
Lyon, Rev. A. S., Chatham, Mass.
Lyons, Rev. John M., Milestown, Pa.
Lynt, Odell D., Hastings, N. Y.
Lytle, Andrew, Williamsburgh, Va.
McBride, Miss Jane Ann, New York.
McBride, Miss Eliza H., New York.
McCarthy, Rev. William, Holland Patent, N.Y.
McCleos, Peter, Middletown, N. J.
McClung, Miss Caroline M., Pittsburgh, Pa.
McClung, Anthony, Kingston, N. Y.
McCormick, R. C., New York.
McCormick, Mrs. Sarah M., New York.
McCoy, John, Charlestown, Ia.
McCullen, Miss Sarah, New York.
McCune, John P., Salem, N. J.
McCutchen, Wm. G., Williamsburg, N. Y.
McDade, Mrs. Jane, New York.
McDaniel, Randle, Fayetteville, N. C.
McFarland, Rev. D., Oswego, N. Y.
McGear, Daniel L.
McGonagal, George, New York.
McIntosh, Mrs. Mary, Philadelphia.
McIver, A. M., Society Hill, S. C.
McIver, Mrs. Ann J., Society Hill, S. C.
McJannett, Mrs. Elizabeth, Brooklyn, N. Y.
McKean, Rev. John A., Philadelphia.
McKean, Mrs. Eliza J., Philadelphia.
McKewan John, New York.
McLellan, James, Trumansburg, N. Y.
McLellan, Mrs. Ellen, Trumansburg, N. Y.
McLean, Mrs. Mary, New London, Ct.
McLowth, Rev., Benjamin, Scipio, N. Y.
McMahon, Henry L., Philadelphia.
McNabb, Mrs. E., Fayetteville, N. C.
McTaggart, Daniel, Reading Pa.
McTaggart, Mrs. Margaret, Reading, Pa.
Macdonald, Alexander, New York.
Macdonald, Mrs. E., New York.

MEMBERS FOR LIFE.

Macdonald, Miss M. J., New York.
Mack, Rev. Levi M., Rosendale, N. Y.
Mack, Elisha H., Weedsport, N. Y.
Maclay, Hon. Wm. B., New York.
Maclay, Archibald, New York.
Maclay, Moses B., New York.
Macomber, John, Watertown, N Y.
Mabbett, Seneca, Dover Plains, N. Y.
Mabbett, James K., Dover Plains, N. Y.
Mabbett, T. Brooklyn, N Y.
Madison, Almond Z., Fredonia, N. Y.
Magee, Rev. Thomas, New Brunswick, N. S.
Magee, Thomas H., New York.
Maghee, Miss Frances, New York.
Magoon, Miss Ella Louise, New York.
Magoon, Frank N. L., New York.
Mahoney, Rev. Henry W., Piedmont, S. C.
Main, Randall W., New York.
Mair, Dudley, Boston.
Mallary, Rev. S. S., Pawtucket, R. I.
Mallory, Rev. Almond C., Benton Centre, N. Y.
Mallory, Rev. James, Lagrange, N. Y.
Mandeville, Stephen, Chicago, Ill.
Mandeville, Mrs. Mary, Chicago, Ill.
Mandeville, Miss Phebe E., Chicago, Ill.
Mandeville, George, New York.
Mandeville, Henry, New York.
Mansfield, Edward, South Reading, Mass.
Mangam, William D., New York.
Mangam, Edgar B., New York.

Martin, Miss Mary.
Martin,
Martin, Peter, Phila
Martin, M. D., Brist
Martin, Mrs. Sarah
Martin, George, No
Mason,
Mason, Mrs. Sarah
Mason, Mrs. Roxann
Mason, Mrs. D. C., P
Mason, Mrs. J. D., C
Mason, George, Pro
Mason, Charles, Ne
Mason, John M. G.,
Mason, Arnold G.,
Mason, R. B., Web
Mason, Mrs. Sumn
Mason, Rev. J. T.,
Mason, Pethuel, So
Mason, Charles J.,
Mason, Mrs. Lavini
Mason, Miss Sarah
Mason, Rev. Eddy,
Mason, Joseph R.,
Mason, Miss Harri

Merrett, Thomas W., Somerset, N. Y.
Merriam, Rev. Asaph. Bolton, Mass.
Merriam, Rev. Mylon. Sharon, Mass.
Merriam, Rev. Titus M., Johnson, Vt.
Merrill, Joseph, Lowell, Mass.
Merrill, Mrs. Nancy B., Hudson, N. H.
Merrill, Joseph, Hudson, N. H.
Merrill, Joseph, New York.
Merrill, Mrs. Mary F., New York.
Merryfield, Miss Carrie R., Brookline, Vt.
Messer, Richard H., New London, N. H.
Messer, Mrs. Sally S., New London, N. H.
Meserve, Andrew J., Lowell, Mass.
Metcalf, Rev. Whitman, Nunda, N. Y.
Metcalf, George P., Jamesburg, N. J.
Mershon, Mrs Mellona S., New York.
Mershon, Mrs. Marie, Trenton, N. J.
Mervine, N. J., Reading, Pa.
Micou, Rev. John, Jr., Louisville, Ky.
Mikels, Rev. William S., Sing Sing, N. Y.
Mikels, Mrs. Lydia, Sing Sing, N. Y.
Milbank, Miss Elizabeth, New York.
Milbank, Miss Eliza W., New York.
Milbank, Miss Sarah C., New York.
Milbank, Miss Mary W., New York.
Milbank, Mrs. Mary W., New York.
Milbank, Miss Mary A., New York.
Milbank, Miss Emma Louise, New York.
Milbank, Miss Anna Elizabeth, New York.
Milbank, L. Ainsworth, New York.
Milbank, Charles A., New York.
Middlebrook, J. Henry, New York.
Middleton, John, New York.
Miles, Abiel, New York.
Miles, Mrs. Hannah, New York.
Miles, Rev. George I., Bellefonte, Pa.
Miles, Rev. Edward M., Davenport, Iowa.
Miles, Thomas, Philadelphia.
Millard, George, North Adams, Mass.
Millard, S. S., Penfield, N. Y.
Millard, Barzillai, Penfield, N. Y.
Miller, Rev. Harvey, Meriden, Ct.
Miller, Mrs. Sarah R., Meriden, Ct.
Miller, Mrs. Abigail, New York.
Miller, Miss Amanda, Bankville, Ct.
Miller, Mrs. Nancy New London, Ct.
Miller, Miss Ancartha, New York.
Miller, James H., Philadelphia.
Miller, Charles, Moriah N. Y
Miller, Rev. U B., Ft. Way e, Ia.
Miller, Mrs. Martha, Middletown, Ct.
Miller, Mrs. An Eliza, Providence.
Miller, Lydia A., Bedford, N. Y
Miller, Edward W Philadelphia.
Miller, Mrs. Mary Ann, Philadelphia.
Mills, Charles H. Brooklyn, N. Y
Mills, Stephen, Greenwich, N. Y
Mills, Rev. Pelatiah W Springville, N. Y.
Milne, John C., Fall River, Mass
Milne, Rev. Alexander, Marcellus, N. Y.
Milne, Mrs. Eliza N., Marcellus, N. Y.
Milner, Alfred A., New York.
Milner, Mrs. Alfred A. New York.
Miner, Rev. Martin, Wolcott, Ct.
Miner, Rev. Absalom, Waukesha, Wis.

Miner, Rev. Cyrus, Attica, N. Y.
Miner, Rev. S. G., Canton, Ill.
Miner, Rev. Erastus, Cold Spring, N. Y.
Miner, Rev. Noyes W., Springfield, Ill.
Miner, Francis S., New York.
Miner, A. B., Italy Hill, N. Y.
Miner, Nathaniel, Jerseyville, Ill.
Miner, Mrs. Hannah M., Norwich, N. Y.
Miner, Mrs. Charles, New London, Ct.
Miner, Ezra, North Stonington, Ct.
Mingus, Miss Julia Ann, New York.
Mintch, Mrs. Phebe, Shiloh, N. J.
Mitchell, Rev. George H., Wagontown, Pa.
Mitchell, Mrs. Phebe H., Wagontown, Pa.
Mitchell, Seth, Montrose, Pa.
Mitchell, Ellen E., Montrose, Pa.
Mitchell, Rev. Thos., Troy, Pa.
Mixter, Rev. George, New London, Ct.
Mondon, Gilbert F., Port Jarvis, N. Y.
Monroe, Rev. William Y., Lexington, Ia.
Montgomery, William, Danbury, Ct.
Montgomery, Mrs. Susan, Danbury, Ct.
Montgomery, S. P., Danbury, Ct.
Montague, Rev. Oreb, Warsaw, N. Y.
Moon, John, New York.
Moore, Dr. G. C., St. John's, N. C.
Moore, Mrs. Julia, St. John's, N. C.
Moore, Mrs. Theodosia M., St. Louis, Mo.
Moore, James, Milton, Pa.
Moore, Francis W., New York.
Moore, Rev. Lyman H., Marshall, Mich.
Moore, Rev. W. W., Albany, N. Y.
Moore, Rev. George C., New York.
Moore, James, Wilmington, Del.
Moore, Enoch, Danbury, Ct.
Moore, Rev. Farris, Lee, Mass.
Morgan, Gilbert H., Mystic River, Ct.
Morgan, William, Brooklyn, N. Y.
Morgan, Miss Harriet, Brooklyn, N. Y.
Morgan, David, Cleveland, Ohio.
Morgan, David, Sen., Allegany City, Pa.
Morgan, Hiram, Blackwoodtown, N. J.
Morgan, Joshua, Philadelphia.
Morgan, Mrs. Jane E., Russell, Mass.
Morrell, Mrs. Sarah G., Savannah, Ga.
Morrill, Geo. W Salisbury, Mass.
Morrill, Miss Mary Salisbury, Mass.
Morrill, Joseph, Amesbury Mass.
Morrill, Daniel, Amesbury, Mass.
Morrill, Otis H., Lowell, Mass.
Morris, Rev. J., Hamburg, S. C.
Morris, Rev. David, New York.
Morrison, Jonathan, Brooklyn, N. Y.
Morrison, Mrs. A. Henrietta, Brooklyn, N. Y.
Morse, Mrs. Sophia A., Sturbridge, Mass.
Morse, Enoch R. Chelsea, Mass.
Morse, K. P Greenville, Ill.
Morse, Mrs. Clara S., Charlestown, Mass.
Mortimer, George W Wilmington, Del.
Morton, Mrs. Susan, Corning, N. Y.
Morton, Miss Sarah B., Corning, N. Y.
Morton, Miss Matilda N., Corning, N. Y.
Morton, Miss Kate E., Corning, N. Y.
Moseley, Green, Dupree's Store, Va.
Moseley, Miss S. A., Dupree's Store, Va.

Moss, Mrs. Nancy, Upperville, Va.
Mott, Miss Elizabeth, New York.
Moulthrop, Major, New Haven, Ct.
Mount, David, Albany, N. Y.
Moxley, Rev Oel W., Richville, N. Y.
Mugg, Rev. John, Gosport, Ia
Mulford, John, Sen., Mullica Hill, N. J.
Mulford, Charles, Salem, N. J.
Mulford, Mrs. Phebe, Roadstown, N. J.
Mulhorn, Rev. Denis, Ozaukee, Wisc.
Mumford, Rev. N. Sherburne, N. Y.
Munger, Rev. Washington, Mystic River, Ct.
Munger, Mrs. Louisa N., Mystic River, Ct.
Munger, Morgan, Schaghticoke, N. Y.
Munger, L. F., Leroy, N. Y.
Munn, Mrs. Mary, New York.
Murdock, Mrs. Martha B., Hartford, Ct.
Murphy, William D., New York.
Murphy, Samuel, Hoboken, N. J.
Murphy, Rev John R., Marlton, N. J.
Murray, Thomas S., New Hope, Pa.
Murray, Mrs. Margarget M., New Hope, Pa.
Murray, Miss Sarah L., Boston.
Mustin, John, Philadelphia.
Myers, Mrs. Ann R., Philadelphia.
Myers, James, Jr., New York.
Mylne, Rev. William, Louisa, C. H., Va.
Myrick, Albert A., Gilbertsville, N. Y.
Napier, Rev. Robert, Mizpath, S. C.
Neale, Jeremiah, Plainville, Ct.

Northe
Norton
Norris,
Norris,
Noyes,
Numa
Nunn,
Odell,
Ogden,
Oldrin
Olin, J
Olin,
Olmst
Olney,
Olney,
Olney
Ombe
Otis,
O'Bri
Ogde

Parker, Asa, Essex, Ct.
Parker, Joel R., Fredonia, N. Y.
Parker, Rev. A., Fiskdale, Mass.
Parker, Rev. William, Philadelphia.
Parker, Rev. A., Coventry, N. Y.
Parker, David O., Hamilton, N. Y.
Parker, Lydia P., Allen, Mich.
Parker, Rev. Harvey I., Fairfax, Vt.
Parker, Miss E. R., Norwich, N. Y.
Parker, Mrs. Susan E., Boston, Mass.
Parks, Rev. R. M., Bedford, Ind.
Parks, Miss Nancy J., Great Falls, N. H.
Parks, Mrs. Marianne C., South Berwick, Me.
Parkhurst, John, Fitchburg, Mass.
Parkhurst, G. R., Brookline, Mass.
Parmelee, Mrs. Syrena, New York
Parmelee, Silas F., Essex, Ct.
Parmelee, Rev. J. H., Xenia, O.
Parmely, Rev. Levi, Elgin, Ill.
Parmely, Mrs. Catharine H., Elgin, Ill.
Parish, Warren, Mendon, N. Y.
Parshley, John, New Haven, Ct.
Parsons, Silas, Swanzey, N. H.
Parsons, Mrs. Patience, Swanzey, N. H.
Parsons, William, Medford, Mass.
Pasco, Rev. Cephas, Egremont, Mass.
Passage, Adam, Weedsport, N. Y.
Patch, Rev. George W., Marblehead, Mass.
Patrick, Charlotte M., Saratoga Springs, N. Y.
Pattengill, Rev. C. N., Westville, N. Y.
Patterson, Rev. Wm. C., East Dedham, Mass.
Patterson, Mrs. Mary, Chapel Hill, N. C.
Patterson, Mrs. Lucy A., New York.
Patton, John B.
Paulin, Mrs. Ann, Salem, N. J.
Paulin, Rev. William, Hamilton Square, N. J.
Payne, Miss Amanda, Amenia, N. Y.
Payne, William W., Auburn, N. Y.
Payne, N. B., New London, Ct.
Peak, John, Boston.
Peacock, Rev. John, Plaistow, N. H.
Peacock, Miss Ann, Plaistow, N. H.
Pearce, Rev. William, Marietta, O.
Pearson, Mrs. T. C., Ludlow, Vt.
Pease, Joseph W., Lowell, Mass.
Peck, Mrs. Nancy M., Owego, N. Y.
Peck, John, Clifton Park, N. Y.
Peck, Mrs. John, Clifton Park, N. Y.
Peck, John, 2d, Clifton Park, N. Y.
Peck, Abijah, Jr., Clifton Park, N. Y.
Peck, Rev. David A., Waupaca, Wis.
Peck, James W., Brooklyn, N. Y.
Peck, Rev. Daniel, South Jackson, Mich.
Peck, George B., Providence.
Peckham, Rev. S. H., Ledyard, Ct.
Peeples, Rev. Darling, Barnwell, S. C.
Peeples, Edward H., Lawtonville, S. C.
Pegg, Miss Jane, New York.
Pember, Asahel, New London, Ct.
Pember, Mrs. Mary, New London, Ct.
Penny, Rev. William, Uniontown, Pa.
Penny, Rev. Thomas J., Strattonville, Pa.
Perego, Mrs. Margaret, New York.
Pendleton, Rev. G. W., Jacksonville, Ill.
Pendleton, Mrs. Jane G., Jacksonville, Ill.
Percy, Everett, *Boston.*

Perine, Joseph, Plainfield, N. J.
Perine, Mrs Sarah, Plainfield, N. J.
Perkins, Jabez, Topsham, Me.
Perkins, Rev. Nehemiah M., Brookline, Mass.
Perkins, George, Amesbury, Mass.
Perkins, Russel B., Meriden, Ct.
Perkins, Elisha, Fond du Lac, Wis.
Perkins, Samuel S. Boston.
Perry, Mrs Sarah, McWilliamstown, Pa.
Perry, Valentine, Macedon, N. Y.
Person, Rev. Ira, Concord, N. H.
Persons, Rev. R., Victory, N. Y.
Peterson, Rev. J. F., Richardson's, S. C.
Peterson, Richard E., New York
Peterson, Mrs Deborah V., New York.
Peterson, Samuel F., Philadelphia.
Pettingill, Daniel, Haverhill, Mass.
Pettingill, Miss Charlotte, Haverhill, Mass.
Petteys, Harvey E., Greenwich, N. Y.
Petteys, Mrs. Helen J., Greenwich, N. Y.
Pettit, Curtis, Wilson, N. Y.
Pettigrew, Rev. Wm. J., Pittsburg, Pa.
Pew, John, Gloucester, Mass.
Phares, Rev. M. B., Dupont, Ia.
Phelps, Humphrey, New York.
Phelps, John, Owego, N. Y.
Phelps, Mrs. Sophia Emelia, New Haven, Ct.
Phelps, Mrs. Mary S., New York.
Phelps, Miss Julia Adelaide, New York.
Phelps, Miss Sophronia E., New York.
Phelps, Miss Mary Amelia, New York.
Phelps, Willard, New York.
Philleo, Calvin, Providence.
Phillips, George H., Troy, N. Y.
Phillips, Rev W., Providence.
Phillips, Rev. David L., Jonesboro', Ill.
Phillips, Rev. Wm. F., Freedom, N. Y.
Phillips, Rev. James N., Moodus, Ct.
Phillips, Dr Samuel R., New York.
Phillips, Rev. W. C., Port Byron, N. Y.
Phillips, Mrs. Ann, New York.
Phillips, Mrs. Theodosia, Morristown, N. J.
Phillips, Peter, Rondout, N. Y.
Phillips, Mrs. Zilla, North Nassau, N. Y.
Philbrook, Rev Abel, Pittsgrove, N. J.
Phippen, Rev. George, Tyringham, Mass.
Pier, Mrs. Deborah, New York.
Pierce, Rev Sem, Londonderry, Vt.
Pierce, Philo, Bristol, Ct.
Pierce, Mrs Patty B., Nunda, N. Y.
Pierce, John W., Boston.
Pierce, John N., Lowell, Mass.
Pierson, David, East Avon, N. Y.
Pike, Jonathan, Providence
Pike, Mrs Jonathan, Providence.
Pike, Miss Ann E., Providence.
Pike, Albert B. H., Providence.
Pike, Benj Jr., New York.
Pike, Mrs. Frances M., New York.
Pike, Miss Catharine E., New York.
Pike, Mrs. Abby C., Taunton, Mass.
Pillsbury, Rev. Phineas, Ill.
Pillsbury, John G., Lowell, Mass.
Pinney, Mrs. Mary, Owego, N. Y.
Piper, John G., Canton, Ill.
Pitcher, Miss Elizabeth, Brooklyn, N. Y.

Poole, Rev. A. W., Woodland, La.
Pooler, Seth. Lowell, Mass
Poland, W. C., Boston.
Poland, Rev. James W., Goffstown Centre, N.H.
Pollard, Mrs Elizabeth, Taunton, Mass.
Polhamus, H. A., New York.
Pomeroy, Rev. Samuel, East Hillsdale, N. Y.
Pomeroy, Mrs. Betsey, East Hillsdale, N. Y.
Pomeroy, Harvey S., York, N. Y.
Pomroy, Wm., Middlefield, Mass.
Pond, William, New York.
Pond, Joseph A., Boston.
Pond, Moses W., Boston.
Porter, Mrs. Welthea M., Pittsfield, Mass.
Porter, Edwin, Lowell, Mass

Putnam, R
Putnam, M
Putnam, R
Putnam, J

Quincy, Jos
Radcliff, Jo
Rafferty, M
Ramage, M

Rand, Rev.
Rand, [illegible]
Rand, John
Rand, Rev.

Read, Rev. Hiram W., Albuquerque, N. M.
Read, Mrs. Alzina A. J., Albuquerque, N. M.
Read, Rev. Daniel, Medina, N. Y.
Read, Rev. James S.
Read, Mrs. James H., Providence.
Read, George W., Fall River, Mass.
Read, Mrs. Hannah T., Deep River, Ct.
Reading, Cæzer, Flemington, N. J.
Reed, Evans H., Townsend, Vt.
Reed, Mrs. Fanny B., Townsend, Vt.
Reed, Mrs. Sarah B. G., Wakefield, R. I.
Reed, Mrs. Emeline, Chelsea, Mass.
Reed, Dr. James, Decatur, Ill.
Reed, Thomas B. New York.
Reed, Wm. B., North East, N. Y.
Reed, Miss Mary F North East, N. Y.
Reed, Mrs. Mary Ann, North East, N. Y.
Reed, Mrs Eunice, North East, N. Y.
Reed, Rev. E. D., Truxton, N Y.
Reed, Mrs. E. D., Truxton, N. Y.
Reed, David, Utica, N. Y.
Reed, Enos, East Cambridge, Mass.
Reed, Lewis B New York.
Reed, Rev. Wm. Barnstable, Mass.
Reed, Rufus, Albion, N. Y.
Reed, G. Washington, Philadelphia.
Reed, Miss Henrietta A., Boston.
Rees, Rev. Wm. Bennett, N Y
Reid, Mrs. Dorothy, New London, Ct.
Reid, Margaret Louisa. New London, Ct.
Reid, Andrew, Warren, R. I.
Reimer, Frederick, Orange, N. J
Relyea, Rev. Solomon S. Kingston, N. Y.
Remington, Mrs. Sarah P., Brooklyn, N. Y.
Remsen, Garret Wilmington, Del.
Remsen, George, Brooklyn, N Y
Remster, Benjamin, Canton, N J.
Requa, Mrs. Elizabeth, Sing Sing, N. Y.
Reynolds, Mrs. Mary, New York.
Reynolds, Rev. John E., Sedgwick, Me.
Reynolds, Abraham M., Newark, N. J.
Reynolds Stephen D., Wickford, R. I.
Rhees, Mrs. Grace W Williamsburgh, N. Y.
Rhodes, G., Lawtonville, S. C.
Rice, Rev. A., Stoneville, S. C.
Rice, Mrs. Mary, Orleans, N Y.
Rice, Josiah, Worcester, Mass.
Rice, Luther J., South Valley, N. Y.
Rich, Joseph C Penfield, N. Y.
Richards, Rev. John M., Germantown, Pa.
Richards, Rev. Wm. C., Lynn, Mass.
Richards, Mrs. Eliza G., Lynn, Mass.
Richards, Wm H. Philadelphia.
Richards, Mrs. Elizabeth, Philadelphia.
Richards, Wm. H., Jr., Philadelphia.
Richards, Edwin S., Philadelphia.
Richards, Joseph L., Philadelphia.
Richards, Miss Eleanor A., Philadelphia.
Richards, Miss Sarah A Philadelphia.
Richards, Zalmon, Washington, D. C.
Richards, Henry, Fall River, Mass.
Richards, Truman, Brooklyn, N. Y.
Richards, Miss Isabel, New York.
Richards, James, Cleveland, Ohio.
Richards, A. R., Rochester, N. Y.
Richards, Mrs Cornelia V. H., Providence.
Richardson, Rev. Daniel F., Hanover, N. H.
Richardson, Wm. T Cambridge, Mass.
Richardson, Thomas S., Brooklyn, N. Y.
Richardson, Mrs. Ann, Boston.
Richardson, Freeman, Auburn, N. Y
Richardson, Rev. John, South Berwick, Me.
Richardson, Mrs. Euphemia, Troy, N Y.
Richmond, Miss Maryetta, Hillsdale, N. Y.
Richmond, Rev. Nathaniel, Pendleton, Ia.
Rider, Charles C., Roxbury Mass.
Riddick, Jethro H., Sunbury, N. C.
Riddick, Nathan, Sunbury, N C.
Riley, Rev. G. W Paris, Ill.
Ripley, Rev. Thomas B., Portland, Me.
Ripley, Rev. S., Foxboro' Mass.
Ripley, Rev. Henry, J., D.D. Newton, Mass.
Roach, Rev. E. W. Harvey's Store, Va.
Robert, Rev. Joseph T., Zanesville, Ohio.
Roberts, E. G., Brooklyn, N. Y.
Roberts, Mrs. E. G., Brooklyn, N. Y
Roberts, Rev. Thomas, Riceville, N. J.
Roberts, Thomas, Jr., Chanceville, N. J.
Roberts, Rev. Phillip, Jr., New Rochelle, N.Y.
Roberts, Sarah, New Bedford, Mass.
Robertson, Rev. Thomas N., Orleans, Ia.
Robbins, Lewis, Upper Freehold, N. J.
Robbins, Mrs. Elizabeth, Littleton, Mass.
Robbins, Rev. Gilbert, Keene, N H.
Robbins, Austin, Smithville, N. Y.
Robbins, Oliver, Smithville, N. Y.
Robbins, Ira, Boston.
Robbins, Rev. Gurdon, Hartford, Ct.
Robbins, Charles, Providence.
Robinson, Rev. E. G., D.D., Rochester, N. Y.
Robinson, Rev. Samuel, St. John, N. B.
Robinson, Rev. Daniel, Martindale, N. Y.
Robinson, Benjamin, Providence.
Robinson, Mrs. Maria E., Providence.
Robinson, Rev. Demas.
Robinson, Wm., New York.
Robinson, Mrs. Catharine, New York.
Robinson, Mrs. Martha, Savannah, Ga.
Robinson, Reuben T. Boston.
Robinson, Edward Arcadia, N. Y
Robinson, Solomon, Webster, Mass.
Robinson, Mrs. Barbara, Tremont, Ill.
Rockafellow, George, Conesus, N. Y.
Rockwell, David Plainfield, N J.
Rockwood, Rev. Joseph M., Belchertown, Mass.
Rockwood, Mrs. Lucretia, Brooklyn, N. Y.
Roe, Rev Charles H., Belvidere, Ill.
Roe, Mrs. Mary, Belvidere, Ill.
Roel, Austin, Randolph, Mass.
Rogers, Rev. Joseph D., Berlin, N. Y.
Rogers, Enos, Chatham, Mass.
Rogers, Mrs. Eliza D., Providence.
Rogers, Miss Eleanor F., Providence.
Rogers, Richard, New London, Ct.
Rogers, Rev. J. B., Portage, Wis.
Rogers, Dr. Alexander W., Paterson, N. J.
Rogers, George W., New London, Ct.
Rogers, Richard, New London, Ct.
Rogers, Mrs. Sally, New London, Ct.

Rogers, Mrs. Phebe, Deep River, Ct.
Rogers, Gilbert, Waterford, Ct.
Rogers, Archibald, Greenwich, N. Y.
Rollin, Rev. J. B., Tonawanda, N. Y.
Roney, Rev. William, Williatown, Pa.
Roof, Milton, New York.
Rose, Mrs. Mary, Granville, Ohio.
Rose, Mrs. Olive E., Troy, N. Y.
Ross, Rev. Arthur A., Pawtucket, R. I.
Ross, Daniel V., Providence.
Rossell, Rev. Caleb., Smithfield, Pa.
Rouse, Rev. Henry H., Stamford, Ct.
Rowan, Phineas, Philadelphia.
Rowe, John K., Baltimore.
Rowell, James, Salisbury, Mass.
Royal, Rev. Wm., Wintersest, S. C.
Rue, Rev. Joshua E., Hightstown, N. J.
Rue, Joshua E., Jr., Hightstown, N. J.
Rue, Miss Mary, Hightstown, N. J.
Rugg, George W., Worcester, Mass.
Runyon, Richard E., New Brunswick, N. J.
Runyon, Hon. Peter P., New Brunswick, N. J.
Runyon, Daniel, New Brunswick, N. J.
Runyon, Elias, New Brunswick, N. J.
Runyon, Reune D., New Market, N. J.
Runyon, Ephraim, J., New Market, N. J.
Runyon, Mrs., Isabella, New York.
Rupert, Benjamin, Du Buque, Iowa.
Russell, Rev. Philemon, Canton, Mass.
Russell, William, Yanceville, N. C.

Sawyer,

Sawyer, Moses W., M
David, Have
Sawyer, Rev. Isaac, I

Sawyer, Rev. A. W.,
Scarrett, Rev. Jas. J.
Schaffer, Charles, Ph
Schoolcraft, John L.,

Scott, Robert, Amenb
Scott, John, Columb
Scott, Mrs. Cornelia
Scott, Alfred, Lowell.

Scott, Rev. Jacob R.,
Scott, John, Bridgep
Scribner, Samuel, T.,
Scribner, Mrs. Maria,
Seabrook, Mrs. Anna,
Seaich, Joseph, Jr., N
Seaich, Mrs. Ellen, N.
Seare, Miss Harriet H
See, Mrs. Sarah Ann

Sheldon, Smith, New York.
Sheldon, Frederick A., Troy, N. Y.
Sheldon, L. C., Suffield, Ct.
Sheldon, William, North East, N. Y
Shelley, Lewis E., Davenport, Iowa.
Shenston, Joseph W New York
Shepard, Russell R Worcester, Mass.
Sheperd, Sylvanus B., Salem. Mass.
Shepperd, Rev. William, Bridgeton, N. J.
Sheppard, Isaac A., Bridgeton, N J.
Sheppard, Joseph, Bridgeto N. J.
Sheppard, John M. M tonsville, N. C.
Shepardson, Ansel, Fairfax, Vt.
Shepardson, Miss J lia H., Cincinnati, Ohio.
Sherman, William N., Wickford, R. I.
Sherman, Mrs. Mary M Wickford, R. I.
Sherman, Geo. J Providence.
Sherwin, E. B., Shelbu Falls, Mass.
Sherwin, Miss Eliza, elburne Falls, Mass.
Sherwood, Walker, Easton, Ct
Sherwood, Mrs. Lydia, Weston, Ct
Sherwood, Rev. D. W., Matteawan, N. Y.
Shoemaker, Robert, Philadelphia.
Shotwell, Hugh, Brooklyn, N Y
Shotwell, Rev, J. M., Belleville, N Y.
Showalter J B., Wi listown, Pa.
Shuck, Rev. J. L., Sacramento, Cal.
Shugg, Richard, New York.
Shute, Rev. Samuel M., Alexandria Va.
Sibell, Mrs. Sarah New York.
Sibell, Mrs. J William, New York.
Sibley, Rev. Clark, New Hampton, N. H.
Silcox, Mrs. Elizabeth, New York.
Silkworth, Samuel O., N York.
Silliman, Ezra, Bridgeport, Ct.
Silliman, Erva Bridgeport Ct.
Silliman, Mrs. Ezra, Bridgeport, Ct.
Silliman, Ebenezer Southport, Ct.
Silliman, Rev. Gershom, Helena, Ill.
Silliman, Nathaniel L., Easton, Ct.
Silliman, Rev. Harvey, Harmony, N Y.
Silliman, Stephen, Bridgeport, Ct.
Silliman, Samuel, Fairfield, Ct.
Simons, Edward Woburn, Mass.
Sims, Maurice P Canton, N. J
Simmons, Miss Eliza, Reading, Pa.
Simmons, Mrs. Mary Eliza, Providence.
Simmons, Miss Henrietta A., Providence.
Simpson, Joseph P., New York.
Sinnet, Alonzo Granville, Ohio.
Sistare, Mrs. Abby, New London, Ct.
Sizer, Amasa, Jr., Meriden, Ct.
Skelding, A. Eugene, Greenwich, Ct.
Skinner, E. B., Hertford N C.
Skinner, Charles W Hertford, N. C.
Skinner, H. P., Hudson, N. Y.
Skinner, Miss Sarah R., Hudson, N. Y.
Skinner, Mrs. Phebe B., Hudson, N. Y.
Skinner, Rev. H. C., Wabash, Ia.
Slack, Thomas, Brooklyn, N. Y.
Slade, Zaccheus, Newbern, N. C.
Slate, Needham, Mansfield, Ct.
Slater, Mrs. S. J., Providence.
Slater, Rev. Franklin A., Rome, N. Y.
Slater, Mrs. Sophronia E. H., Rome, N. Y.
Slaughter, James M., Baltimore.
Sleeper, Rev George Dividing Creek, N. J.
Slote, Henry L., New York.
Slover, Mrs. Susan E., New Brunswick, N. J.
Smalley George C. New York
Smalley, Henry New Brunswick, N. J
Smart, J mes, Philadelphia.
Smart, Miss Mary A., Philadelphia.
Smart, Rev. M M., Russia, N Y
Smiley, Mrs. William, Haverhill, Mass.
Smiley, Miss Betsey, Haverhill, Mass.
Smith, Rev. Francis, Providence.
Smith, Mrs. M. G., Providence.
Smith, Charles A., Providence
Smith, Asa F New England Village, Mass.
Smith, Mrs. R. S. W N Eng. V lage, Mass.
Smith, Rev. Harry, Valparaiso, Ia.
Smith, Mrs Lydia W. Valparaiso, Ia.
Smith, Samuel, Salem, N. J
Smith, Mrs. Sarah B. Salem, N J
Smith, Mrs. Ruth Ann, New York.
Smith, Mrs. W llam H., Brooklyn, N. Y.
Smith, Mordecai Brooklyn, N. Y
Smith John H., Brooklyn, N Y
Smith, Henry W., Brooklyn. N. Y.
Smith, Augustus, Brooklyn, N. Y.
Smith, Mrs. Mary B., Brooklyn N. Y.
Smith, Mi Ada Fanny, Providence.
Smith, William, Winsboro' S. C
Smith, Jonathan, New London, Ct.
Smith, Rev. Alexander, Skeneateles, N. Y.
Smith, Mrs. Priscilla B., Clarkson, Va.
Smith, Mrs. Sally, Hancock. Mass.
Smith, Mrs Mary E., Christiansville, Va.
Smith, Rev. Joseph, Grafton, Mass.
Smith, Mrs. Abigail M., Grafton. Mass.
Smith. Mrs. S. L., Fayettev lle, N C.
Smith, Hamilton E., Fowlerville, N. Y.
Smith, Rev. Samuel, New York.
Smith, Alvah, York, N. Y.
Smith, George H Branchport, N. Y.
Smith, William, Port Rowan. Canada West.
Smith, Rev. C. Billings, Iowa City, Iowa.
Smith, John H., New York.
Smith, Rev. William W. Broadalbin, N Y.
Smith, Rev. Andrew M., Hartford, Ct.
Smith, Rev. Justin A., Chicago, Ill.
Smith, Rev. Wm. A., Groton, Ct.
Smith, Rev. Isaac, East Stoughton, Mass.
Smith, Mrs. Harriet A., Bristol, Ct.
Smith, Shubael, Colchester Ct.
Smith, Elias, New London, Ct.
Smith, Rev. Eli B., Fairfax, Vt.
Smith, Adam, Brooklyn, N. Y.
Smith, Rev N. W. Hydeville, Vt.
Smith, Ebenezer East Tisbury Mass.
Smith, Mrs. Sarah A., East Tisbury, Mass.
Smith, Rev. Dexter P Iowa City, Iowa.
Smith, Mrs Hannah B., owa City, Iowa.
Smith, Gilbert D., New York
Smith, Daniel, Worcester Mass.
Smith, Rev. Lewis, Trenton, N. J.
Smith, Jonathan, New York.
Smith, Rev. Rufus, Jericho, Vt.
Smith, Mrs. Mary E., Jericho, Vt.

Smith, Rev. C. B., Townsend, Vt.
Smith, Miss Emma F., Banksville, Ct.
Smith, Jesse H., New England Village, Mass.
Smith, Mrs. Mary White, Newton, Mass.
Smith, Mrs. Jane, Troy, N. Y.
Smith, Lucius E., Boston, Mass.
Smith, Mrs. Elizabeth, New York.
Smith, Charles E., Fall River, Mass.
Smith, Rev. Levi, West Plattsburgh, N. Y.
Smith, Mrs. Levi, West Plattsburgh, N. Y.
Smith, Rufus, Shelburne Falls, Mass.
Smith, Rev. R. T., Lyndonville, N. Y.
Snelling, Miss. Priscilla, Chelsea, Mass.
Sniffin, Mrs. Sarah Ann, New York.
Snowdon, Mrs. Eliza, New York.
Snow, Mrs. Abby S., Rehoboth, Mass.
Snow, Edwin M., Providence.
Souders, Mrs. Catharine B. L., Fraser's, Pa.
Sommers, Mrs. Eliza B., New York.
Southerland, Jonas, Burnt Hills, N. Y.
Southwick, Mrs. Cynthia, Grand de Tour, Ill.
Southwick, George, Kingston, N. Y.
Southwood, Rev. William, Ayletts, Va.
Southworth, Mrs. James E., Brooklyn.
Southworth, Jas. Adelbert, Brooklyn.
Southworth, John, Penfield, N. Y.
Sowers, Mrs Mary E., Battletown, Va.
Sowers, Mrs. Elizabeth, Milwood, Va.
Spalding, Miss H. M., Middletown, Ct.
Sparks, Rev. Peter, Newark, N. J.
Spaulding, Isaiah, Chelmsford, Mass.

Starr,
Stark
Stead,
Stead
Stean
Stearn
Stearn
Stearn
Stelle,
Stetso
Steve
Steve

Stone, A. P. Millbury, Mass.
Stone, Nathan, Jamaica Plains, Mass.
Storer, Mrs. Olive H., Hudson, N. H.
Storey, Simeon N., Worcester, Mass.
Storey, James Arnot, Williamsburg, N. Y.
Story, William F., Boston.
Story, Joseph, Boston.
Storms, Andrew, New York.
Storms, Anthony D., New York.
Stout, Rev. D. B., Middletown, N. J.
Stout, Mrs. L. M., Louisa C. H., Va.
Stout, Richard, New York.
Stout, George H., New Brunswick, N. J.
Stout, Augustus T., New Brunswick, N. J.
Stow, Henry, New Haven, Ct.
Stow, Mrs. Baron, Boston.
Stowell, Rev. A. H. Providence, R. I.
Stowell, Mrs. A. H., Providence, R. I.
Stratton, Samuel T., Philadelphia.
Street, Miss Mary Ann, New York.
Strickland, James L., New London, Ct.
Strong, Myron, Rochester, N. Y.
Stetson, J. S., New Lisbon, N. Y.
Stewart, Benjamin N., Lowell, Mass.
Story, Harriet M., Norwich, Ct.
Story, Eunice M., Worcester, Mass.
Story, Clara, Worcester, Mass.
Story, Eunice H, Worcester, Mass.
Strickland, Eliza C., New London, Ct.
Strong, Alvah, Rochester, N. Y.
Stuart, John, Greenwich, N. Y.
Sturges, Rev. William, Marlborough, N. Y.
Sulley, James, Minneapolis, Min.
Sulley, Mrs. Ann, Minneapolis, Min.
Summers, Mrs. Aaron, Bridegport, Ct.
Sumner, George O., New Haven, Ct.
Sunderlin, Eli, Tyrone, N. Y.
Sunderlin, Rev. Alonzo W., Avoca, N. Y.
Sunderlin, Horace, Sennett, N. Y.
Sunderlin, Mrs. Margaret, Sennett, N. Y.
Sunderlin, Daniel W., Wayne, N. Y.
Sutton, Mrs. Elizabeth, Britton's ✕ Roads, N. C.
Sutton, Mrs. Mary Ann, New York.
Swaim, Hon. Thomas, Pemberton, N. J.
Swaim, Mrs. Mary, Pemberton, N. J.
Swaim, Rev. T., Flemington, N. J.
Swaim, Mrs. Eliza M., Flemington, N. J.
Swaim, Rev. A. M., Leominster, Mass.
Swaim, Samuel N., West Cambridge, Mass.
Swaim, Mrs. Aurora D., West Cambridge, Mass.
Swaim, Rev. P. M., Rockville, Ia.
Swain, Joshua, Dennis Creek, N. J.
Swallow, Mrs. Almira, Boston.
Swan, Mrs. Laura, New London, Ct.
Swany, Andrew F, New York.
Swany, Thomas, Brooklyn, N. Y.
Sweet, Rev. Joel, Tivoli, Ill.
Swepson, Mrs. V. B., Yanceyville, N. C.
Swick, Rev. Benjamin R, Lima, N. Y.
Swick, Mrs. Harriet, Lima, N. Y.
Swift, William A., Boston.
Sykes, Rev. James N., South Boston, Mass.
Sym, Rev. William, Springfield, Ill.
Symes, W. J., New York.
Symonds, Newton, Reading, Mass.
Symonds, Margaret, North Salem, Mass.
Taft, Timothy, Clinton, N. Y.
Taft, Mrs. Mary, Anthony's Village, R. I.
Taggart, Mrs. Harriett M., New York.
Taggart, William M, New York.
Tandy, Rev. Lorenzo, North Middleboro', Mass.
Tanner, Mrs. Elizabeth F., Spring Garden, Va.
Tanner, Cyrus S., Sennet, N. Y.
Tanner, Mrs. C. S., Sennett, N. Y.
Tanner, William, Sennett, N. Y.
Tanner, Miss Margaret, Pembina, Min. Ter.
Tanner, Elijah, Pembina, Min. Ter.
Tanner, John, Pembina, Min. Ter.
Tanner, Mrs. Margaret, Pembina, Min. Ter.
Tanner, Edward, Min. Ter.
Tapley, Joseph, Lowell, Mass.
Tapley, Joseph W., Lowell, Mass.
Tattersall, Wm. K., New York.
Taylor, William H., New York.
Taylor, John G., Holmdel, N. J.
Taylor, Mrs. Ann B., Holmdel, N. J.
Taylor, Mrs. Laura, New York.
Taylor, Miss Emily, New York.
Taylor, Miss Ann Jane, New York.
Taylor, Miss Louisa, New York.
Taylor, Mrs. Sarah A., New York.
Taylor, Mrs. E E. L., Brooklyn, N. Y.
Taylor, Miss Harriet Hill, Troy, N. Y.
Taylor, Mrs. Maria B., Lawtonville, S. C.
Taylor, Mrs. Dimis, York, N. Y.
Taylor, Rev. Thomas R., Allegheny City, Pa.
Taylor, Rev. Alfred H., Mansfield Centre, Ct.
Taylor, Rev. Thomas, Jacksonville, Ill.
Taylor, Rev. David, Terre Haute, Ia.
Taylor, Samuel W., E. Cambridge, Mass.
Taylor, Rev. O. D., Perrington, N. Y.
Taylor, Henry C., Granville, O.
Taylor, Mrs. Adelia P., Albion, Mich.
Taylor, Elvin, Albany, N. Y.
Taylor, John, East Cambridge, Mass.
Taylor, John, New York.
Taylor, J. R., East Cambridge, Mass.
Tefft, Willard, Union Village, N. Y.
Tefft, Thomas A., Providence.
Temple, James H., Chilicothe, Ill.
Terry, Mrs. A. N., Spring Garden, Va.
Thatcher, Mrs. Elizabeth R.
Thayer, Thomas M., Gouverneur, N. Y.
Thayer, Lewis, Worcester, Mass.
Thayer, James H., Cambridge, Mass.
Theall, Mrs. Jane, New York.
Theall, Miss Susan, New York.
Thigpen, Rev. Samuel, Raymond, Mi.
Thistle, Mrs. Hannah, New York.
Thomas, Thomas, New York.
Thomas, Thomas, (architect), New York.
Thomas, Mrs. Isabella, New York.
Thomas, Moses, Ballston Spa, N. Y.
Thomas, James H., New York.
Thomas, Rev. David E., Zanesville, Ohio.
Thomas, Griffith, New York.
Thomas, Rev. C. A., D D., Brandon, Vt.
Thomas, Mrs. Eliza Ann, New York.
Thomas, Mrs. Mary, Brooklyn, N. Y.
Thomas, Mrs. Almira S., Brandon, Vt.

Thomas, Rev. Evan J., Edwardsburgh, Mich.
Thompson, Robert, Jr., New York.
Thompson, Mrs. Ann E., New York.
Thompson, Mrs. S. S., Pittsborough, N. C.
Thompson, Rev. Richard, Milton, Ct.
Thompson, Rev. Charles E., Iowa City, Iowa.
Thompson, L., Britton's X Roads, N. C.
Thompson, Benjamin M., Harlem, N. Y.
Thompson, Rev. Sherman B., Little Valley, N.Y.
Thompson, Mrs. Serena, New York.
Thompson, Mrs. Harvey, Norwich, N. Y.
Thompson, Joshua J., Mt. Holly, N. Y.
Thurston, Henry, Brooklyn, N. Y.
Thurber, Edmund, Providence.
Thurber, Gorham, Providence.
Thurber, Charles, Worcester, Mass.
Ticknor, William D., Boston.
Tiebout, Adam T., Brooklyn, N. Y.
Tiebout, Mrs. Jane, Brooklyn, N. Y.
Tilden, Rev. Chester, North Lyme, Ct.
Tilley, Mrs. Elizabeth S., New York.
Tillinghast, Jefferson, Norway, N. Y.
Tillinghast, Charles E., Providence.
Tillinghast, Rev. J. A., North Kingston, R. I.
Tilson, Rev. Jonathan, Hingham, Mass.
Tilton, Rev. Charles.
Tilton, Rev. Josiah H., Lynn, Mass.
Tilton, J. D., Meredith Village, N. H.
Timberman, Rev. Jacob, Stockton, N. J.
Tindall, Samuel L., Wilmington, Del.
Tingley, Miss Nancy B., Valley Falls, R. I.
Tinkham, Rev. D., Center White Creek, N. Y.

Tracy, Miss S
Train, Mrs. A
Travis, Luth
Treat, E. S.,
Treves, John
Tripp, Mrs. S
Tripp,
Tripp, Mrs. C
Tripp, Miss S
Trout, Wm.,
Trow, Rev. A
Trowbridge,
True, Reuben
True, Osgood,
True, Mrs. De
True, Mrs. H
Truesdell, M
Truman, Mrs.
Truman, Edw
Tryon, Miss E
Tuttle, Benja
Tucker, Harw
Tucker, Rich
Tucker, Rev.
Tucker, Mrs.
Tucker, Mrs.
Tucker, Jame
Tucker, Erwin

Upham, Silas, Weston, Mass.
Van Arsdale, Dr. Henry, New York.
Van Deboe, Adam, Olaverack, N. Y.
Van De Werken, E., New York.
Van De Werken, Mrs. Janet, New York.
Van Derlip, George M., New York.
Van Derlip, Mrs. Grace, New York.
Van Dusen, Wm., Albion, N. Y.
Vanderveer, Mrs. Ann, Moorestown, N. J.
Van Pelt, Mrs. Harriet, Port Richmond, N. Y.
Vail, J. B., Brooklyn, N. Y.
Valentine, Rev. Andrew M., W. Henrietta, N.Y.
Valentine, Elijah F., Cambridge, Mass.
Van Horn, Hon. James, Newfane, N. Y.
Van Sickler, Reuben N., Albany, N.Y.
Vanness, Christian, New York.
Vanest, Abraham, Hightstown, N. J.
Van Marter, John, Brooklyn, N. Y.
Van Marter, Mrs. Mary E., Brooklyn, N. Y.
Van Osdel, John M., Chicago, Ill.
Van, Samuel A., New Haven, Ct.
Vansant, T. J., Williamsburg, N. Y.
Van Valkenburgh, John, Williamsburg, N. Y.
Van Vleck, Rev. J., Lyndon, Ill.
Van Wagenen, W. Frederick, New York.
Van Wickle, Simon, New Brunswick, N. J.
Vassar, Matthew, Poughkeepsie, N. Y.
Vassar, Mrs. Matthew, Poughkeepsie, N. Y.
Veasey, Benjamin, Brentwood, N. H.
Vernon, Samuel, Brooklyn, N. Y.
Vernon, Thomas, Brooklyn, N. Y.
Verstile, Mrs. Rebecca E., Savannah, Ga.
Vinal, Wm. D., Lowell, Mass.
Vinton, Rev. Justus H., Maulmain, Burmah.
Vinton, Mrs. Calista H., Maulmain, Burmah.
Vinton, Mrs. Lydia, West Willington, Ct.
Volk, Henry, New York.
Volk, Mrs. E. Margaretta, New York.
Votey, Rev. Chas. A., Ovid, N. Y.
Vrooman, Rev. Joseph B., Fayetteville, N. Y.
Wade, Rev. Jonathan, D. D., Tavoy, Burmah.
Wade, Mrs. Deborah B. L., Tavoy, Burmah.
Wade, Josiah, Gouverneur, N. Y.
Wade, Rev. J. M., Williamson, N. Y.
Waite, Miss Mercy, Brookfield, Mass.
Wakefield, Charles A., Elizabethtown, N. Y.
Wakefield, Rev. Leander, Feltonville, Mass.
Wakeman, Rev. Levi H., West Woodstock, Ct.
Walden, Rev. J. H., Brockport, N. Y.
Waldo, Harman, Fleming, N. Y.
Waldron, Miss Maria, New York.
Walker, Rev. Joseph, Marcus Hook, Pa.
Walker, Mrs. Elizabeth, Marcus Hook, Pa.
Walker, Miss Hannah, Marcus Hook, Pa.
Walker, Rev. G. C., Johnson's Creek, N. Y.
Walker, Mrs. Eliza H., Somerset, N. Y.
Walker, Mrs. Mary, Brookneal, Va.
Walker, John R., Madison, Ga.
Walker, Andrew, New York.
Walker, William A., New York.
Walker, Lewis A., New York.
Walker, Michael P., New York.
Walker, Charles, Chicago, Ill.
Walker, George C., Chicago, Ill.
Walker, Rev. Wareham, Utica, N. Y.
Walker, Rev. John, Coldbrook, Mass.
Walker, Rev. William C., Willington, Ct.
Walker, Mrs. L. A., Willington, Ct.
Walker, Samuel, Roxbury, Mass.
Walker, Rev. O. T., New London, Ct.
Walker, Mrs. Velina P., New London, Ct.
Walker, William, Clinton, Mass.
Walker, Rev. O. B., Brookline, Me.
Walker, Amos, Pontiac, Mich.
Walker, Francis, Pawtucket, R. I.
Walker, Rev. James, Greenbush, N. Y.
Wallace, Mrs. Margaret, New York.
Wallace, Miss Eliza, Brooklyn, N. Y.
Wallace, Jonathan, Fort Covington, N. Y.
Walter, Rev. John P., Dover, Del.
Walters, Jacob, Wilmington, Del.
Walton, Joel, Va.
Walton, Jesse, Augusta, Ga.
Ward, Uzal D., New York.
Ward, Willard, Worcester, Mass.
Ward, William, Worcester, Mass.
Wardner, Rev. Chauncey, Covert, N. Y.
Wardner, Mrs. Margaret A., Covert, N. Y.
Ware, Dr. R. J., Montgomery co., Ala.
Warn, Mrs. Sarah M., Sennett, N. Y.
Warn, Mrs. Mary, Sennett, N. Y.
Warner, Dr. Ransom, New York.
Warnock, Miss Elizabeth, New York.
Warren, Mrs. Diantha O., West Potsdam, N. Y.
Warren, Rev. Patrick, Baltimore.
Warren, Rev. Benj., Kendall, N. Y.
Warren, Rev. J. G., Boston.
Warren, Chas. W., Utica, N. Y.
Warren, Rev. Edwin R., East Greenwich, R. I.
Warren, Benjamin I., Williamsburg, N. Y.
Warren, Moses, Cambridge, Mass.
Warren, Mrs. Grace, Cambridge, Mass.
Warren, Rev. H. S. P., Madrid, N. Y.
Warren, Horace, Norwich, Ct.
Warren, Rev. John, Easton, Ct.
Warriner, Rev. Norman, Harding, Ill.
Warriner, Rev. R. L., West Burlington, N. Y.
Washburn, Nathan W., Mt. Pleasant, Ill.
Washburn, Rev. R. A., Union Village, N. Y.
Washington, Mrs. Elizabeth, Newbern, N. C.
Wasson, Mrs. Clarissa, Albany.
Waters, Mrs. Elizabeth A., Brookline, Mass.
Watters, Miss Sarah A., Philadelphia.
Watts, Mrs. Emma, New York.
Watts, Charles Henry, New York.
Watts, John, Elmira, New York.
Wattson, Mrs. Mary B., Philadelphia
Wattson, Miss Elizabeth, Philadelphia.
Wattson, Rev. W. H., West Acton, Mass.
Watson, George, New York.
Watson, James, Brooklyn, N. Y.
Watson, W. W., Springfield, Illinois.
Watson, John, New York.
Watkins, Henry M., New York.
Watkinson, Rev. Wm. E., Manyunk, Pa.
Watkinson, Rev. Mark P., Schuylkill Fall, Pa.
Waterman, Nathan, Jr., Providence.
Way, Rev. Samuel P., Poolville, N. Y.
Waterbury, Miss Martha, Williamsburg, N. Y.

Waterbury, Francis W., North Adams, Mass.
Wayland, Mrs. H. S. H., Providence.
Wayland, Francis. Jr., Worcester, Mass.
Weaver, Rev. C. S., Norwich, Ct.
Weaver, Mrs. Diana, Norwich, Ct.
Weaver, Edwin H., Norwich, Ct.
Weaver, Mrs. Ann, Groton, Ct.
Weaver, Wanton A., New London, Ct.
Weaver, C. Arnold, New London, Ct.
Webb, Mrs. Maria, New Brunswick, N. J.
Webb, Rev. Abner, Belleville, N. Y.
Webb, Rev. W. R., Palmyra, N. Y.
Webb, Daniel, Le Roy, N. Y.
Webb, Rev. J. N., Fort Covington, N. Y.
Webb, Mrs. J. N., Fort Covington, N. Y.
Webber, Rev. Julius S., Romulusville, N. Y.
Webster, Phineas, Haverhill, Mass.
Webster, Mrs. Phineas, Haverhill, Mass.
Webster, Rev. Amos, Newton Up. Falls, Mass.
Webster, Rev. S. B., Norwalk, O.
Webster, Caleb, Lowell, Mass.
Weckerly, Daniel, Philadelphia.
Weddell, Rev. Peter M., Canton, Ohio.
Welch, Mrs. B. T., Newtonville, N. Y.
Welch, Rev. James E., Hickory Grove, Mo.
Weirick, Miss Sallie A., Logansport, Ia.
Weld, Nathaniel, Jamaica Plain, Mass.
Weld, Mrs. Lucy, New York.
Weld, Aaron D., Winchester, Mass.
Welden, Asa W., New York.
Wells, Mrs. Elizabeth, New York.
Wells, Rev. Alfred, Vernon, N. Y.

Wheeler, Rev. Benja
Wheeler, Rev. S. S., P
Wheeler, Mrs. Mary E
Wheeler, Rev. Benjam
Wheeler, Russell, Uti
Wheeler, Mrs. Ann, Y
Wheeler, Mrs. Mary E.
Wheeler, Rev. R., Graf
Whilden, Rev. B. W., (
White, Rev. Samuel, N
White, Mrs. E., North
White, Mrs. Martha D.
White, Lydia, Ha
White,
White,
White,
White,
White,
White, Joseph, Winch
White, Ezra L., Taunt
White, Ebenezer, New
White, Ebenezer B., W
White, Mrs. Mary, New
White, Samuel, Borde
White, Mrs. Sylvanus.

Wightman, Rev. J. G., Groton, Ct.
Wightman, Asa, New London, Ct.
Wightman, Stillman K., New York.
Wightman, Mrs. Emeline, Flanders, Ct.
Wightman, John, Colchester, Ct.
Wiggins, Rev. J. W., Farmersville, N. Y.
Wilbur, Rev. H. R., Mt. Pleasant, Iowa.
Wilbur, Mrs. Sally, East Avon, N. Y.
Wilbur, Curtis, Troy, N. Y.
Wilbur, Rev. O., Lowville, N. Y.
Wilcox, Rev. J. F., Trenton, N. J.
Wilcox, Mrs. Louisa S., Trenton, N. J.
Wilcox, Abraham, Shelburn Falls, Mass.
Wilcox, Allen, Wing's Station, N. Y.
Wilds, Rev. Z. P., West Boylston, Mass.
Wilder, John M., Albany.
Wilder, Mrs. Delia A., Albany.
Wilder, Rev. Sydney, North Norwich, N. Y.
Wilder, Rev. William, Chester, Pa.
Wildman, John, Pitcher, N. Y.
Wildman, Mrs. Roxey S., Lebanon, Ct.
Wildman, Daniel, Lebanon, Ct.
Wildman, Mrs. Sally, Danbury, Ct.
Wilkins, Rev. Andrew, Sennett, N. Y.
Wilkins, Mrs. Laura J., Sennett, N. Y.
Wilkinson, Rev. Wm., Drummondville, C. W.
Willard, Rev. Geo. A., Warwick Neck, R. I.
Willard, Lucius A., Providence.
Willard, Mrs. Polly, Pawlet, Vt.
Willard, Wm. B., Still River, Mass.
Willard, Mrs. Nancy, Jonesborough, Ill.
Willard, Rev. C. N., Still River, Mass.
Willard, Hon. Levi, Keene, N. H.
Willard, Mrs Anna F., South Abington, Mass.
Willett, Miss Sarah, New York.
Willett, Mrs. Charles, Quinebaug, Ct.
Williams, Charles S., Mystic River, Ct.
Williams, Robert, Brookfield, Iowa.
Williams, Mrs. Elizabeth S., Fayetteville, N. C.
Williams, Mrs. Charity S., Fayetteville, N. C.
Williams, Mrs. Mary M., Fayetteville, N. C.
Williams, Polly M., Rockport, O.
Williams, Francis B., New York.
Williams, Rev. David S., Cumberland, N. C.
Williams, Rev. Wm. B., Williamsville, N. Y.
Williams, Mrs. Eunice, Deep River, Ct.
Williams, Rev. John, Princeton, N. Y.
Williams, Rev. C. C., Plainfield, N. J.
Williams, Mrs. Marana, Plainfield, N J.
Williams, Rev. Lester, West Townsend, Mass.
Williams, Rev. B S., Plymouth, N. Y.
Williams, Mrs. William R., New York.
Williams, W. S., Hartford, Ct.
Williams, Rev. N. M., Somerville, Mass.
Willingham, Thomas, Lawtonville, S. C.
Willington, Miss Catharine, Watertown, Mass.
Willis, Rev. Samuel B, Saugerties, N. Y.
Willis, J. D. K., Chelsea, Mass.
Willis, Benjamin B., Philadelphia.
Wilson, Mrs. Catharine, New York.
Wilson, Miss Sarah E., New York.
Wilson, Mrs. Francis N., Catskill, N. Y.
Wilson, Isaac D., Society Hill, S. C.
Wilson, Clement A., Philadelphia.
Wilson, Rev. Charles E., Holmdel, N. J.
Wilson, Mrs. Theresa, Marlton, N. J.
Wilson, Rev. Adam, D.D., Paris, Me.
Wilson, Rev. W. V., Keyport, N. J.
Wilson, Jeremiah V. F., Hoboken, N. J.
Wilson, Mrs. Grace, Elmira, N. Y.
Wilson, George W., Chelsea, Mass.
Wilson, Mrs. Martha, Riceville, N. J.
Wilson, Robert, New York.
Wingate, Mary, Haverhill, Mass.
Wingate, Dexter B., Grafton, Mass.
Winans, Elnathan, Lima, N. Y.
Winans, Mrs. Marcy, Lima, N. Y.
Winans, Theodore, Plainfield, N. J.
Winchell, Miss Ann, New York.
Windust, Edward, New York.
Winslow, Robert F., Fond du Lac, Wis.
Winslow, Rev. Octavius, Leamington, Eng.
Winston, Rev. Meriwether, Richmond, Va.
Winter, Rev. Thomas, Roxborough, Pa.
Winter, Rev. John, Knoxville, Ill.
Winterton, Mrs. Mary, New York.
Wise, Miss Clarissa R., New Russia, N. Y.
Wisner, Mrs. Sarah, Mount Morris, N. Y.
Wisner, Mrs. Adaline, Elmira, N. Y.
Wisham, Samuel, Moorestown, N. J.
Wiswell, Mrs C. A., West Troy, N. Y.
Witherwax, Dr. J. M., Davenport, Iowa.
Witherwax, Mrs. Emeline B., Davenport, Iowa.
Withall, John, Henrietta, N. Y.
Witherbee, John B., Jamaica Plains, Mass.
Withington, Elijah, Morrisania, N. Y.
Withington, Mrs. M , Morrisania, N. Y.
Wolcott, Mrs. Mary S , New York.
Wolcott, Mrs. Naomi, Rochester, N. Y.
Wollaston, Joshua, Wilmington. Del.
Worrall, Rev. Thos. D., Mt. Holly, N. J.
Wood, Mrs. J. S., Hertford, N. C.
Wood, Mrs. Mary E , Hertford, N. C.
Wood, Rev. N. N., D D., Upper Alton, Ill.
Wood, Jennings J., Speedwell, S. C.
Wood, George, Springfield, Ill.
Wood, Joseph T., Westboro', Mass.
Wood, Mrs. Amelia, Brooklyn, N. Y.
Wood, Eliphalet, Honesdale, Pa.
Wood, Ambrose, Albion, N. Y.
Woods, Gardner, Jersey, Ohio.
Woods, Hiram, Nashua, N. H.
Woodbridge, William A., New York.
Woodbury, William W., Suffield, Ct.
Woodbury, Rev. John, Templeton, Mass
Woodbury, Miss Frances, Danvers, Mass.
Woodbury, Eliza A., Lynn, Mass.
Woodman, Moses, New Gloucester, Me.
Woodruff, Mrs. Innocent, Albany.
Woodruff, David, Bridgeton, N. J.
Woodward, Rev. Jonas, Parma, N. Y.
Woodward, Mrs. Eliza, Parma, N. Y.
Woodward, Mrs. Mary D., Middlesex, Va.
Woodward, Sylvester, Lowell, Mass.
Woodward, Darwin W., Franklindale, N. Y.
Woolsey, Rev. James J., Norwalk, Ct.
Woolston, Mrs. Keziah, Vincentown, N. J.
Wooster, Mrs. Aurelia R., Deep River, Ct.
Work, Rev. Perly, Sheboygan, Wis.
Worth, Rev. Edmund, Fisherville, N. H.
Worthington, S., Springfield, Mass.

MEMBERS FOR LIFE.

Wright, Rev. David, Hartford, Ct.
Wright, Mrs. Abigail, Hartford, Ct.
Wright, William J., Hargrove's, Va.
Wright, Theodore, New York.
Wright, Asahel B., Lowell, Mass.
Wright, Harvey, Three Rivers, Mass.
Wright, Mrs. Julia A., Westport, N. Y.
Wright, Rev. Ansell T., Weart's Corners, N. J.
Wright, Rev. Lyman, Norwich, N. Y.
Wright, R. A., Rochester, N. Y.
Wright, James G., Canton, N. J.
Wyckoff, Mrs. Cornelius R., Weedsport, N. Y.
Wyckoff, J. N., Brooklyn, N. Y.
Wyckoff, Mrs. Elizabeth, Brooklyn, N. Y.
Wyckoff, W. G., Middletown, N. J.
Wyckoff, Francis, Plainfield, N. J.
Wyckoff, Mrs. Sarah B., Brooklyn, N. Y.
Wyckoff, Jacob F., New York.
Wyer, Rev. Henry O., Savannah, Ga.
Wynn, Mrs. Susan, Tuckahoe, N. J.
Wynn, Benjamin F., Tuckahoe, N. J.
Yendell, Sarah, Boston.
Yeomans, Mrs. Olive, Providence.
Yeomans, Miss Mary Ann, Providence.
York, Mrs. Hannah, Haverhill, Mass.
York, C., Norwich, N. Y.
York, Mrs. Esther, Norwich, N. Y.
Young, Mrs. Sarah, Brooklyn, N. Y.
Young, Rev. George, Hatboro', Pa.
Young, Rev. Robert F., Chestnut Hill, Pa.
Young, Mrs. Maria Ann, Chestnut Hill, Pa.
Young, Robert McCarthy, New York.
Young, Rev. G. W., Antiatown, Pa.
Young, William W., Stamford, Ct.
Yuran, Mrs. S. S., Tunbridge, Vt.
Zebley, John F., New York.
Zimmerman, Edwin, New York.

LIST OF DECEASED

DIRECTORS AND MEMBERS FOR LIFE.

1833-4.

DIRECTOR.

Cobb, Nathaniel R., Boston, Mass.

MEMBERS.

Barrett, Rev. Thomas, Webster, Mass.
Chase, Rev. John, Brookfield, Mass.

1834-5.

MEMBER.

Lazell, Rev. J. E., Harvard, Mass.

1835-6.

DIRECTORS.

Foster, Rev. E., Amesbury, Mass.
Freeman, Rev. E. W., Lowell, Mass.
Jacobs, Rev. Bela, Cambridge, Mass.

MEMBER.

Martin, Rev. A. R., Staten Island, N. Y.

1836-7.

DIRECTOR.

Trask, Rev. Wm. G., Taunton, Mass.

1837-8.

DIRECTOR.

Davis, Rev. Gustavus, F., Hartford, Ct.

MEMBERS.

Blain, Miss Mary E., Syracuse, N. Y.
Holroyd, Rev. John, Danvers, Mass.
Kitts, Rev. T. J., Philadelphia.
Ludlow, Rev. Peter, New York.
Starkweather, Oliver, Pawtucket, R. I.

1838-9.

DIRECTORS.

Crawford, Rev. Luther, Brooklyn, N. Y.
Knowles, Rev. James D., Newton, Mass.

MEMBERS.

Banner, Rev. Job B., Sutton, Mass.
Smalley, Henry, Cohansey, N. J.
Vaughn, Rev. Ashley, Natchez, Miss.

1839-40.

DIRECTOR.

Bolles, Rev. Matthew, D.D., Boston.

MEMBERS.

Blain, Mrs. Lucy, Syracuse, N. Y.
Hubbell, Rev. Elisha D., Clifton Park, N. Y.
Sheppard, Rev. Joseph, Mount Holly, N. J.

1840-1.

DIRECTORS.

Chesman, Rev. Daniel, Lynn, Mass.
Hammond, Rev, O T., Florida.
Shute, Rev. Caleb B., Boston.

MEMBERS.

Chaplain, Rev. J., Hamilton, N. Y.
Dodge, Rev. O. A., Lexington, Mass.
Hunting, Mrs. Dorcas, Corinth, Me.
McAllister, Charles, Fayettteville, N. C.
Nourse, Rev. Peter, Ellsworth, Me.
Stearns, Rev. Silas, Bath, Me.
Williams, Elizabeth, Society Hill, S. C.
Williams, A., Elizabeth City, N. C.

1841-2.

DIRECTOR.

Brown, Nicholas, Providence, R. I.

MEMBERS.

Colgate, John, New York.
Eaton, Martin, Petersburg, Va.
Hill, Frederick M., New York.
Leonard, Rev. Zenas L., Sturbridge, Mass.
Lipscomb, Mrs. Martha, Louisa C. H., Va.
Mercer, Rev. Jesse, Washington, Ga.
Miles, Joseph, Milesburgh, Pa.

1842-3.

MEMBERS.

Colgate, George, New York.
Elmer E., Bridgeton, N. J.
Gear, Rev. Hiram, Marietta, Ohio.
Powell, Mrs. E. E., Sandy Bottom, Va.
Vanderpool, Hon. James, Newark, N. J.

LIST OF DECEASED DIRECTORS AND MEMB

1843-4.

DIRECTORS.

Cooper, Thomas, Eatonton, Geo.
Linsley, Rev. James H., Stratford, Ct.
Middleton, Rev. John, Geneva, N. Y.

MEMBERS.

Pickins, Mrs. Margaret, Eliza, Edgefield, S. C.
Rankin, Henry, Reading, Pa.
Wasson, J. G., Albany, N. Y.

1844-5.

DIRECTORS.

Armstrong, Rev. John, Columbus, Miss.
Coolidge, James D., Madison, N. Y.
Going, Rev. Jonathan, D.D., Granville, Ohio.
Miller, Rev. Wm. George, Essex, Ct.

MEMBERS.

Adams, Mrs. Mary, New York.
Belden, Charles D., New York.
Birdsall, Rev. John O., Perrysburg, Ohio.
Carney, Richard, Portsmouth, Va.
McIntosh, Mrs. Mary, Philadelphia.

1845-6.

MEMBERS.

Cauldwell, Mrs. Maria, New York.
Hall, Rev. Wilson, Beaufort, S. C.
Jones, Mrs. J. Leavitt, Bankok, Siam.
Lathrop, Rev. Lebbeus, Samptown, N. J.
Marshall, Joseph H., Nashville, Tenn.

Chamberlin, Hin

Shaw, Oliver, Pro
Wildman, Rev. D
Williams, Rev. D

Bradford, Rev. Z.,

Milbank, Charles
Peck, Rev. John,
Train, Rev. Charl
Wilson, James, N

Battle, Jonathan,
Barber, Rev. Luk
Brockway, G., Br

Humphrey, Mrs. Julia Ann, Albany, N. Y.
Jackson, Rev. Timothy, Piqua, Ohio.
Kelly, Mrs. Elizabeth, New York.
Kendall, Josiah, Littleton, Mass.
Logan, Rev. John, Blandenville, Ill.
Lester, David, Brooklyn, N. Y.
McLaren, Finley, Le Roy, N. Y.
Munn, Mrs. Sarah P., New York.
Ormsby, Rev. John, Knox's Corners, N. Y.
Parker, Amasa W., Lowell, Mass.
Postley, Charles, New York.
Randall, Jedediah, Portersville, Ct.
Snook, John, Port Gibson, N. Y.
Todd, William H., New York.
White, Thomas, Philadelphia.

1851-2.

DIRECTORS.

Dodge, Rev. Daniel, Philadelphia.
Batt, Mrs. Mary T., Hoboken, N. J.
Merritt, Rev. W. H., Chapel Hill, N. C.
Sherman, Rev. O. J., Peoria, Ill.

MEMBERS.

Anderson, J. S., Stonington, Ct.
Bolles, Rev. D. C., Southbridge, Mass.
Chase, Amos, Haverhill, Mass.
De Graffenried, Mrs. S., Crosbyville, S. C.
Downing, J., Colerain, N. C.
Farnsworth, Rev. B. F., Nashville, Tenn.
Gibbs, Mrs. Betsey H., Sullivan, N. H.
Goodell, A., Somersworth, N. H.
Hall, Rev. Daniel, New York.
Jones, Mrs. Susan, Newbern, N. C.
Lathrop, Mrs. Jane E. New York.
Manning, Rev. Benjamin, Brookfield, Mass.
Martin, Mrs. R. W., New York.
Miller John B., Sumterville, S. C.
Remington, Mrs. Eliza Ann, New York.
Rider, Miss Olive P., Suffield, Ct.
Shuck, Mrs. Eliza G., Shanghai, China.
Stone, Mrs. Sarah A., New York.
Tucker, Mrs. Levi, Boston, Mass.
Whitman, Rev. S. S., Madison, Wis.

1852-3.

DIRECTORS.

Brown, Rev. O. B., Washington, D. C.
Crozer, Miss Sallie K., Chester, Pa.
Miller, Pardon, Providence.
Rhees, Rev. M. J., D.D., Williamsburg, N. Y.

MEMBERS.

Adams, Mrs. Cornelia C., Cleveland, Ohio.
Ashley, Mrs. Hannah, Poultney, Vt.
Bellamy, Mrs. Eliza, Arcadia, N. Y.
Boynton, Mrs Ruth, North Springfield, Vt.
Brown, Mrs. O. B., Washington, D. C.
Carraway, Mrs. H., Kingston, N. C.
Cosner, Rev. Henry, Lyndon, Ill.
Faut, Rev. Ephraim, Halselville, S. C.
Goodliff, James, New York.
Haskell, Rev. Daniel, Hamilton, N. Y.
Haynes, Rev. Arus, M.D., New York.
Jones, Rev. John, Belleville, Ia.
Maghee, Mrs. Ann C., New York.
Maginnis, Rev. John, D.D., Rochester, N. Y.
Miner, Mrs. Mary Jane, New York.
Owen, Rev. E. D. Madison, Ia.
Shipley, Simon G., Boston.
Symonds, Rev. Thomas M., Green Bay, Wis.
Turner, Mrs. Grace, New London, Ct.
Walton, Rev. L., Chestnut Hill, Pa.
Weeks, Miss Ann, New York.
Wise, Miss Harriet W., New Russia, N. Y.
Walcott, Epaphroditus, Rochester, N. Y.
Woodruff, Rev. Seth, New Albany, Ia.

1853-4.

DIRECTORS.

Brayton, Philip F., Providence.
Sharp, Rev. Daniel, D.D., Boston.
Tucker, Rev. Levi, D.D., Boston.
Tucker, Rev. Elisha, D D., Chicago, Ill.
Whiting, Miss Martha, Charlestown, Mass.
Washington, Col. J., M., Portsmouth, N. H.

MEMBERS.

Bleecker, Garrat N., New York.
Brabrook, Rev. B. F., Davenport, Iowa.
Burr, James T., Columbus, Ohio.
Bliss, Erastus L., North Adams, Mass.
Ball, Rev. Eli, Richmond, Va.
Biddle, Rev. Wm. P., Newbern, N. C.
Coggeshall, John, Jr., New Bedford, Mass.
Day, John, New York.
Fay, Rev. Eliphas, Poughkeepsie, N. Y.
Griffith, Mrs. Thomas S., Milwaukee, Wis.
Guild, Rev. J. B , East Thompson, Ct.
Haviland, William C., New York.
Hurlburt, Rev. Elias, Essex, N. Y.
Humphrey, Hon. Friend, Albany, N. Y.
Lawrence, P. P., Washington, N. C.
Moore, Mrs. Alvah B., Marshall, Mich.
Murray, Joseph D., New Hope, Pa.
Newton, Prof. Calvin, Worcester, Mass.
Nesbit, Mrs. Mary C. S., Burmah.
Palmer, Rev William, Norwich, Ct.
Pegg, Roger, New York.
Paddock, Mrs. Martha, Middletown, Ct.
Rue, Mrs. Emily, Scotch Plains, N. J.
Shotwell, Rev. S. R., Whitesboro', N. Y.
Sheppard, Joseph, Bridgeton, N. J.
Tryon, Elijah, West Haven, Vt.
Ulyat, William, New York.
Whitney, Mrs. Emeline, Norwalk, Ct.

1854-5.

DIRECTORS.

Cone, Mrs. Sallie W., New York.
Ellis, Rev. R. F., Alton, Ill.
Kimball, Rev. C. O., Charleston, Vt.
Whiting, Rev. Niles, Norwich, Ct.

MEMBERS.

Abbott, Rev. E. L., Arracan, Asia.
Angier, Rev. Aaron, Lamoille, Ill.
Austin, H., Tarborough, N. C.
Booth, Miss Lydia, Poughkeepsie, N. Y.
Boughton, Rev. N., Delavan, Wis.
Brown, Hon. Wm. B., Spencerport, N. Y.

LIST OF DECEASED DIRECTORS AND MEMBERS

Brush, George P., New York.
Capron, Rev. Orion H., North Hebron, N. Y.
Cauldwell, Miss Eliza A., New York.
Challis, John, Salem, N. J.
Cleaves, Mrs. S. A., Littleton, Mass.
Davis, Evan, New York.
Davis, Rev. C. B., Paris, Me.
Demarest, Silas, New York.
Denison, Rev. Nathan, Mendota, Ill.
Drake, Rev. Jacob, Delaware, Ohio.
Edwards, Mrs Robert, New York.
Ellis, Rev. John, Norwalk, Ct.
English, Isaac, Salem, N. J.
Farr, Asa, Lowell, Mass.
Fillio, Mrs. Phidelia, Battle Creek, Mich.
Francis, John S., New York.
Goodliff, James T., New York.
Hewett, Mrs. Rhoda Elizabeth, New York.
Hill, Mrs. Matilda Pierce, Albany, N. Y.
Hill, Mrs. Lydia Ann, Carmel, N. Y.
Judson, Mrs. Emily C., Hamilton, N. Y.
Miner, Rev. Bradley, Providence, R. I.
Neale, Mrs. Melissa Y., Boston.
Oakley, Mrs. Cassandra, New York.
Pennypacker, John, Wilmington, Del.
Richards, Rev. Humphrey, Dorchester, Mass.
Richards, Mrs. Eunice J., Dorchester, Mass.
Rodgers, Rev. Ebenezer, Upper Alton, Ill.
Sharp, J. Milton, Williamsburg, N. Y.
Skinner, Mrs. Anna, Hertford, N. C.

Morse, Jacob, Sturbr
Munn, Stephen B., N
Pratt, Rev. D. D., Na

ME

Ballard, Rev. John
Belden, Rev. A. R., L
Bishop, William, Bl
Bottom, Hon. N. H.,
Brayton, Philip, Ph
Calam, Mrs. Mary N.,
Challiss, John, Salem
Clapp, Mrs. Jane M.,
Colver, Mrs. Esther S
Cox, Miss Achsah, In
Davis, Rev. Jonathan

Hardin, Rev. Theodo
Harris, Isaac, New L
Hazard, Simeon, New
Hunt, Dr. George, L
Jones, Mrs. Rhoda, S
Leland, Mrs. Carolin
Mangam, Mrs. Sarah
Miller, John B., Sum
Nice, Rev. W. J., Ind

CONTENTS.

[redacted]

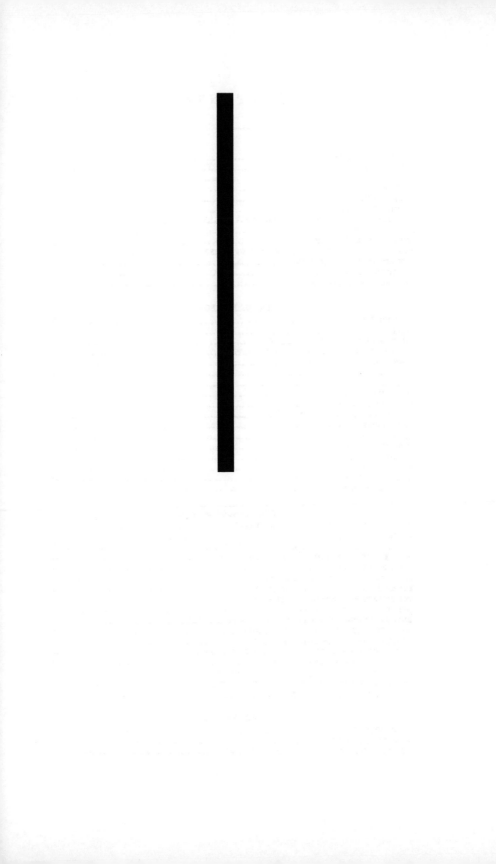

TWENTY-FIFTH REPORT

OF THE

American Baptist Home Mission Society,

PRESENTED BY THE

EXECUTIVE BOARD

AT THE

ANNIVERSARY HELD IN BOSTON,

MAY 13 AND 14, 1857,

WITH

THE TREASURER'S REPORT AND OTHER DOCUMENTS.

New York:
PUBLISHED AT THE AMERICAN BAPTIST HOME MISSION ROOMS, No. 115 NASSAU ST.,
AND PRINTED BY MILLER & CURTIS, CORNER CENTRE AND WHITE STS., N. Y.
1857.

ACT OF INCORPORATION.

AN ACT TO INCORPORATE THE AMERICAN BAPTIST HOME MISSION SOCIETY, PASSED APRIL 12, 1843, AND AMENDED, FEBRUARY 9, 1849.

The People of the State of New York, represented in Senate and Assembly, do enact as follows:

§ 1. All such persons as now are, or may hereafter become, members of the American Baptist Home Mission Society, formed in the city of New York, in the year one thousand eight hundred and thirty-two shall be, and hereby are, constituted a body corporate, by the name of the American Baptist Home Mission Society, for the purpose of promoting the preaching of the gospel in North America.

§ 2. This Corporation shall be capable of taking, holding, or receiving any property, real or

[redacted]

CONSTITUTION.

NAME.

I.—This Society shall be called the AMERICAN BAPTIST HOME MISSION SOCIETY.

OBJECT.

II.—The object of this Society shall be to promote the preaching of the Gospel in North America.

MEMBERSHIP.

III.—The Society shall be composed of Annual Delegates, Life Members, and Life Directors. Any Baptist Church, in union with the denomination, may appoint a delegate for an annual contribution of ten dollars, and an additional delegate for each additional thirty dollars. Thirty dollars shall be requisite to constitute a member for life, and one hundred dollars paid at one time, or a sum which in addition to any previous contribution, shall amount to one hundred dollars, shall be requisite to constitute a Director for Life.

OFFICERS.

IV.—The officers of the Society shall be a President, two Vice-Presidents, a Treasurer, an Auditor, Secretaries of Correspondence, and a Recording Secretary, whom the Society shall annually elect by ballot.

MANAGERS AND EXECUTIVE BOARD.

V.—The Officers and Life Directors shall meet immediately after the Annual Meeting of the Society, and elect fifteen Managers, residing in the city of New York, or its vicinity, who, together with the Treasurer, Auditor, and the Secretaries, shall constitute an Executive Board to conduct the business of the Society; and shall respectively continue to discharge their official duties until superseded by a new election. Seven members of the Board shall be a quorum for the transaction of business.

POWERS AND DUTIES OF THE EXECUTIVE BOARD.

VI.—The Executive Board shall have power to appoint its own meetings; elect its own Chairman and Recording Secretary; enact its own By-Laws and Rules of Order, provided always, that they be not inconsistent with this Constitution; fill any vacancies which may occur in their own body, or in the offices of the Society during the year; and, if deemed necessary by two-thirds of the members present at a regular meeting, convene special meetings of the Society. They shall establish such Agencies as the interests of the Society may require; appoint Agents and Missionaries; fix their compensation; direct and instruct them concerning their particular fields and labors; make all appropriations to be paid out of the treasury; and present to the Society, at each annual meeting, a full report of their proceedings during the current year.

DESIGNATED FUNDS.

VII.—All moneys or other property contributed and designated for any particular Missionary field, shall be so appropriated, or returned to the donors, or their lawful agents.

TREASURER.

VIII.—The Treasurer shall give bonds to such amount as the Executive Board shall think proper.

ELIGIBILITY TO APPOINTMENT.

IX.—All the Officers, Managers, Missionaries, and Agents of the Society, shall be members in good standing in regular Baptist Churches.

ANNUAL MEETING.

X.—The Society shall meet annually, at such time and place as the Executive Board shall appoint.

ALTERATIONS OF THE CONSTITUTION.

XI.—No alteration of this Constitution shall be made without an affirmative vote of two-thirds of the members present at an annual meeting: nor unless the same shall have been proposed in writing, and the proposition sustained by a majority vote, at a previous annual meeting, or recommended by the Executive Board.

STATED MEETI

OF THE EXECUTIVE BOARD.—Thursday before th

" " Committee on MISSIONS—The day previ

" " Committee on AGENCIES and FINANCE—

" " Committee on CHURCH EDIFICE FUND—

BY-LAWS O

1. All meetings shall be opened with prayer.
2. All Committees shall be nominated by the Board, unless otherwise specially ordered.
3. No moneys shall be paid out of the Treasury,
4. All resolutions, if required, shall be presented
5. Whenever a vacancy occurs in the Executive and at the next stated meeting the Board

MINUTES OF THE TWENTY-FIFTH ANNIVERSARY

OF THE

American Baptist Home Mission Society,

Held in Boston, Mass., May 13 and 14, 1857.

The American Baptist Home Mission Society met in the Meeting House of the Harvard Street Baptist Church, at ten o'clock, A.M.

The President, Hon. Albert Day, of Connecticut, took the chair at ten o'clock, A.M., and called the Society to order, when prayer was offered by the Rev. J. C. Harrison, of New York.

In the absence of the Recording Secretary, upon motion, A. B. Capwell, of N. Y., was appointed to act as Recording Secretary.

The following Committees were appointed, upon the nomination of the President:

***On Credentials of Delegates*:—Rev. James S. Ladd, N. Y.; Rev. L. Lewis, Conn.; Rev. J. W. Parkhurst, Mass.; Hon. J. M. Linnard, Pa.; and Rev. E. Ely, Minnesota Territory.**

***On Nomination of Officers*:—Hon. Isaac Davis, Mass.; Rev. L. F. Beecher, D.D., N. Y.; Thomas Wattson, Esq., Pa.; Rev. J. L. Hodge, D.D., N. J.; Rev. Sidney Dyer, Ind.**

***On Life Directors and Life Members present*:—P. Mason, Esq., N. J.; Rev. H. J. Eddy, Ill.; Rev. William Reid, Conn.; Rev. Henry Davis, D D., Ohio; Rev. William H. Shailer, D.D., Maine.**

On motion of the Rev. J. C. Harrison, N. Y., ministers and other brethren present, not members of the Society, were invited to participate in the deliberations of the Society.

The invitation was accepted by the Rev. E. Andrews, Pa.; Rev. B. F. Chapman, Ill.; J. C. Holt, Tenn.; Moses Curtis, Esq., Conn.; Rev. John G. Butler, Prof. Theo. Institution, N. Hampton; Rev. Isaac D. Stewart, N. H.

An abstract of the Annual Report
the Corresponding Secretary, when c
ine and report upon portions of it, as f

On Missionary Operations:—Rev
J. R. Stone, R. I.; Rev. G. P. Nice,
Rev. Charles Willet, Conn.

On the Church Edifice Fund:—

Burlingham, Rev. A. H., New York.
Byram, Rev. B. P., Amesbury, Ms.
Caswell, Rev. Lewis E., Boston, Ms.
Chaplin, Rev., Adoniram, J.
Chaplin, Rev. Jeremiah, West Dedham, Ms.
Cheney, Rev. D. B., Philadelphia, Pa.
Colver, Rev. Nathaniel, Cincinnati, Ohio.
Cookson, Rev. John, Morrisania, N. Y.
Crane, Rev. O., Scituate, Ms.
Cushman, Rev. Elisha, Deep River, Ct.
Davis, Hon. Isaac, Worcester, Ms.
Day, Rev. Henry, Philadelphia, Pa.
Day, Hon. Albert, Hartford, Ct.
Eaton, Rev. W. H., Nashua, N. H.
Eddy, Rev. E. B., Winchester, Ms.
Eldridge, Rev. Daniel, Shushan, N. Y.
Fish, Rev Henry C., Newark, N. J.
Foster, Rev. J. C., Beverly, Ms.
Fuller, Rev. C. M., Pike, N. Y.
Girdwood, Rev. John, New Bedford, Ms.
Goodhue, Rev. J. A. Boston, Ms.
Gould, Chas. D., Boston, Ms.
Hiscox, Rev. E. T., New York.
Holme, Rev. S. J., Brooklyn, N. Y.
Hodge, Rev. J. L., D.D, Newark, N. J.
Hunt, Samuel, Providence, R. I.
Ilsley, Rev Silas, Essex, Ct.
Jennings, Rev. John, Newton Centre, Ms.
Ladd, Rev. Jas. S. New York.
Leighton, Rev. S. S., West Townsend, Ms.
Linnard, J. M., Philadelphia, Pa.
Magoon, Rev. E. L., D.D., New York.
Mason, Rev. A. P., Chelsea, Ms.
Mason, Rev. S. R., Cambridgeport, Ms.
Messenger, Rev. E. C., West Medway, Ms.
Mills, Rev. R. C., Salem, Ms.
Nice, Rev. G. P., Somerville, N. J.
Nott, Rev. A. K., Kennebunkport, Me.
Parker, Rev. Carlton, Hebron, Me.
Parkhurst, Rev. John, Chelmsford, Ms.
Parkhurst, Rev. J. W., Newton Centre, Ms.
Parmly, Rev W. H., Jersey City, N. J.
Pattison, Rev. R. E., D.D., Waterville, Me.
Patton, Rev. A. S., Hoboken, N. J.
Phelps, Rev. S. D, D.D., New Haven, Ct.
Porter, Rev. Lemuel, D.D., Pittsfield, Ms.
Pryor, Rev. John, D.D., Cambridge, Ms.
Reed, Rev. Nathan A., Bristol, R. I.
Reding, Rev. C. W., Manchester, Ms.
Reid, Rev. William, New London, Ct.
Remington, Rev. S., Brooklyn, N. Y.
Richardson, Rev. J. G., Newburyport, Ms.
Ricker, Rev. Joseph, Woburn, Ms.
Sanford, Rev. Miles, North Adams, Ms.
Seeley, Rev. John T., Syracuse, N. Y.
Shailer, Rev. W. H., D.D., Portland, Me.
Shailer, Rev. N. E., Deep River, Ct.
Simmons, Rev. James B., Providence, R. I.
Stone, Rev. James R., Providence, R. I.
Stearns, Rev. O. S., Newton Centre, Ms.
Stockbridge, Rev. J. C., Boston, Ms.
Stubberts, Rev. W. F., Malden, Ms.
Southworth, James E, Brooklyn, N. Y.
Tilton, Rev. J. D., Sandbornton, N. H.
Wattson, Thomas, Philadelphia, Pa.
White, Rev. Samuel, Staten Island, N. Y.
Whitman, D. C., Newark, N. J.
Wilbur, Asa, Boston, Ms.

LIFE MEMBERS.

Allen, Rev. John, North Wrentham, Ms.
Armstrong, Rev. A. Lambertville, N. J.
Ball, Rev. Mason, North Amherst, Ms.
Ball, Julia M., North Amherst, Mass.
Baldwin, Rev. G. C., D.D., Troy, N. Y.
Barnes, Rev. W. A., Philadelphia, Pa.
Bates, Rev. L. C., Madison, N. Y.
Belcher, Rev. James, Oldtown, Me.
Bernard, Rev. David, Akron, O.
Boomer, Rev. James C., Chelmsford, Ms.
Brown, Rev. W. L., Watertown, Ms.
Brown, Rev. Joseph, Springfield, O.
Browning, Rev. Amasa, Concord, N. H.
Brooks, Kendall, Fitchburg, Ms.
Bronson, Rev. B. F., Methuen, Ms.
Bronson, Rev. A. C., Leominster, Ms.
Bronson, Rev. Asa, Fall River, Ms.
Burlingham Mrs. Emma S., New York.
Capwell, Albert B., Brooklyn, N. Y.
Carter, B. A., Boston, Ms.
Carr, A. W., Rowley, Ms.
Carr, Rev. S. J., Somerset, Ms.
Chick, Rev. J. M., South Groton, Ms.
Cheever, William, Westboro', Ms.
Colby, Gardner, Newton, Ms.
Colver, Rev. B K., Detroit, Mich.
Conover, Rev. Edward, West Troy, N. Y.
Conant, Rev. Thomas, Scituate, Ms.
Corey, Rev. D. G., Utica, N. Y.
Corwin, Rev. David, Cohoes, N. Y.
Cutler, Rev. Stephen, North Mansfield, Ms.
Cutting, Rev. Geo. W., Mason Village, N. H.
Dewhurst, Rev. Eli, Belfast, Me.
Demarest, Samuel C., Boston, Ms.
Dimmock, Rev. A. V., Baldwinsville, Ms.
Denison, Rev. A. E., Clinton, Ct.
Durbrow, John R., New York.
Dyer, Sidney, Indianapolis, Ia.
Edmund Francis, Brookline, Ms.
Fairbanks, Rev. Geo. G., Somerville, Ms.
Fuller, Rev. E. K., Reading, Ms.
Fletcher, Rev. Horace, Townsend, Vt.
Gale, Rev. Amory, Hudson, Wis.
George, Moses D., Haverhill, Ms.
Goadby, Rev John, Poultney, Vt.
Griggs, Samuel, Rutland, Vt.
Griffith, Rev. B., Philadelphia, Pa.
Granger, Rev. A. H., Providence, R. I.
Gurr, Rev. C. G, Great Falls, N. H.
Hall, Rev. King S., Lake Village, N. H.
Hall, A., Chatham, Ms.
Holmes, Rev. Lewis, Edgartown, Ms.
Hodges, Rev. Joseph, jr. Cambridge, Ms.
Harrison, Rev. J. C., Kingston, N. Y.
Hayden, Rev. L., Saxton's River, Vt.
Hooper, Rev. N., Newburyport, Ms.
Jameson, Miss Eliza, Newton Upper Falls, Ms.
Jeffrey, Rev. Reuben, Albany, N. Y.
Jenkins, Rev. J. S., Philadelphia, Pa.
Keeley, Rev. Thomas E., Medford, Ms.
Knight, Rev. Benjamin, Salem, Ms.
Lamson, Rev. Wm., Portsmouth, N. H.

Lewis, Rev. Lester, Middletown, Ct.
Lincoln, Rev. Heman, Jamaica Plain, Ms.
Lovell, Rev. A. S., Bloomfield, Ct.
Lyons, Rev. John M., Columbus, N. J.
Mason, P., Somerville, N. J.
Mace, Jeremiah, Middleboro', Ms.
Matthews, Rev. George, Seekonk, Ms.
Meech, Rev. W. W., Preston, Ct.
Merriam, Rev. Mylon, Sharon, Ms.
Merriam, Rev. F., China, Me.
Merrifield, E. P., West Wardsboro', Vt.
Nelson, Rev. W. F., Wickford, R. I.
Olney, Rev. L. W., Deposit, N. Y.
Osgood, Rev. S. M., Philadelphia, Pa.
Patch, Rev. G. W., Marblehead, Ms.
Phelps, Mrs. S. E., New Haven, Ct.
Poland, Rev. J. W., Goffstown Centre, N. H.
Putnam, John, Boston, Ms.
Randolph, Rev. Warren, Providence, R. I.
Richards, Rev. W. C., Lynn, Ms.
Remington, Mrs. Sarah P., Brooklyn, N. Y.
Ripley, Rev. S., Northboro' Ms.

On motion, the report was accepted
the Annual Report.

The Committee on Credentials rep
cepted and committee discharged.

On motion of Rev. John Pryor, D.

The Corresponding Secretary read the remaining portions of the Annual Report of the Executive Board, embracing a brief review and summary of the Society's history and work for the first quarter century of its existence, closing with the present Anniversary Meeting. After which, addresses, appropriate to the occasion, were delivered by the Rev. T. Swaim, of N. J., and the Rev. E. T. Hiscox, of N. Y.

On motion, the Annual Report was accepted and ordered to be printed under the direction of the Executive Board.

An invitation was received from the Boston Young Men's Christian Association, inviting the members of this Society, and others to visit their rooms, and tendering the free use of reading rooms, and the use of their committee rooms, for meetings, if desired.

MORNING SESSION.

May 15, 1857.

The Society assembled at half-past nine o'clock, A. M. The President in the Chair.

After singing, prayer was offered by Rev. W. H. Shailer, D.D., of Maine.

The "Minutes" of the preceding day were read and approved.

In the absence of Hon. J. H. Duncan and Rev. D. B. Cheney, Rev. E. L. Magoon, D.D., of N. Y., and John B. Durbrow, of N. Y., were appointed to fill their places on Committee on Amendments to the Constitution.

On motion of Rev. H. C. Fish, of N. J., the following resolution was unanimously passed:

Resolved, That the thanks of this body be formally returned to the Boston Young Men's Christian Association for their kind invitation to visit their rooms and make them their resort, and that we take this occasion to express to this Association our wishes for their largest success.

On motion of Rev. J. Girdwood, of Mass.,

Resolved, That the thanks of this Society be tendered to the Rev. T. Swaim, of N. J., and Rev. E. T. Hiscox, for their interesting and appropriate addresses, and that copies of them be requested for publication.

On motion of Rev. Henry Davis, D.D., of Ohio.

Resolved, That the thanks of this body be presented to the Harvard Street Church and Society, and to our brethren and friends of this city and vicinity, for the hospitality extended to us; and that we tender to the esteemed Pastor of this Church, the Rev. D. C. Eddy, our sympathies under the severe affliction which has befallen him, in the death of his only son, which has occurred during our present session.

The Committee on a Western Agency, reported, presenting for adoption the following resolution:

Resolved, That we approve the creation of a Western Agency by the Executive Board.

The Committee on Amendments
ing resolution:

Resolved, That Article 4th of the Co
words, "a Corresponding Secretary, a
the words, "Secretaries of Correspondei
4th. The officers of the Society shall be
an Auditor, Secretaries of Corresponde
Society shall annually elect by ballot."

Adopted by the following vote :

The Report of the Committee o
by Rev. J. R. Stone, R. I. The
appended thereto adopted. (See p

The hour of half-past twelve hav
prayer by Rev. J. T. Seely, of N.

AFTERN

The President called the Society
singing, prayer was offered by the

Rev. E. T. Hiscox presented the
which was adopted. (See page 54.

The Committee on the Church

MEETING OF OFFICERS AND LIFE DIRECTORS.

At a meeting of the Officers and Life Directors of the American Baptist Home Mission Society, held at the Harvard Street Baptist Church, Boston, May 15, 1857, the Hon. J. M. Linnard, of Pa., was chosen Chairman, and Rev. E. T. Hiscox, of N. Y., Secretary.

A Committee to nominate managers was appointed, consisting of Rev. N. B. Baldwin, Pa.; J. L. Hodge, D.D., N. Y.; N. A. Reed, R. I.; S. D. Phelps, D.D., Conn.; and S. Dyer, Ind.; who, after consultation, presented the following list of names, which was accepted and the persons designated were unanimously elected, viz.: (See Page 14.)

E. T. Hiscox, *Secretary.*

THE SERMON.

The Missionary Sermon was preached by Rev. Wm. T. Brantly, D.D., of Philadelphia, on Sabbath evening May 17, in the Harvard Street Church, Boston, from the 2nd Corinthians, 9th chap., 15th verse—"Thanks be to God for his unspeakable gift;" and was admirably adapted to the occasion, having a tendency to deepen the harmonious spirit which pervaded the meetings for business; to elucidate the glorious gospel of the blessed God which the missionaries of the Society bear to the destitute emigrants throughout our field, and to unite more firmly all hearts in the good work in which the Society is engaged.

At the close of the sermon a contribution of about one hundred dollars was presented by the congregation to aid the Society in its operations.

The prospects of the Society for the future were never better than now. For its success let Zion pray.

Dr. THE AMERICAN BAPT

1857. To Cash paid Missionari
" Cash paid Agents for
Postage, etc.,.....
" Cash paid Secretarie
Of which amount
interest from Sp
" Cash paid for Fuel,
dental expenses,..
" Cash paid for Paper,
Mission Record, and
" Cash paid for Paper
Certificates, Blank

IN ACCOUNT WITH JAMES E. SOUTHWORTH, TREASURER. *Cr.*

1857.	By Balance as per last Report,		$592 93
	" Cash received in Contributions and Legacies, from April 1, 1856, to March 31, 1857,		41,124 18
	" Cash received for subscriptions to *Home Mission Record*,		1,018 13
	" Cash received for Church Edifice Fund,		2.196 58
	" Cash received for Ministers' Libraries,		41 00
	" Cash received for dividends on temporary investments,	$30 00	
	" Cash received for interest on Bond and Mortgages, a special investment, by direction of the donor,	87 50	
			117 50
	" Cash received for a counterfeit bank note charged in last year's account,		10 00
	" Cash received for interest from Special Salary Fund,		420 00
			$45,520 32
March 31	By Balance,		$8,967 09

(Signed) JAMES E. SOUTHWORTH, *Treasurer.*

AUDITOR'S CERTIFICATE.

This is to certify that we have examined the foregoing account, together with the vouchers connected therewith, and find the same correct.

The balance in the hands of the Treasurer is eight thousand nine hundred and sixty-seven dollars and nine cents ($8,967.09).

(Signed) A. B. CAPWELL, } *Auditing*
D. C. WHITMAN, } *Committee.*

NEW YORK, May 12, 1857.

EXECU

O

HON. ALBERT

JOHN P. CR
J. B. SOUTH

D. C. WI

ANNUAL REPORT

OF THE EXECUTIVE BOARD OF THE AMERICAN BAPTIST HOME MISSION SOCIETY, MAY 14, 1857.

We celebrate to-day, the Twenty-fifth Anniversary of the American Baptist Home Mission Society. May we be favored with the Divine presence and guidance, so that our deliberations and decisions may prove conducive to the glory of God, and the prosperity of the important cause committed into our hands.

DEATHS.

We meet without the company of some who have heretofore regarded our anniversaries as occasions of deep interest; in the responsibilities of which they considered it their duty, and in the enjoyments of which it was their privilege, to share. They have been called up higher, to participate in the communings and happiness of "the general assembly and church of the first-born which are written in heaven."

The number of deaths, so far as we have been able to ascertain, is twenty-nine. Of these, twelve were ministers of the gospel, of whom, one, the Rev. J. G. Collom, was an agent of the Society. His services were valuable, and, stricken down as he was in the midst of arduous and successful labors, his loss is much deplored.

Of the others, one was Deacon William Colgate, of New York, an old and valued friend of the Society, and

one of its constituent mem
he was chosen Treasurer, w
advantage to the Society f
clined a re-election. Ten
of the Executive Board, and
he was annually elected as a
His counsels were always tl
died respected and belove
with him.

DIRECTORS AND

During the year, forty
Directors for life, and nin
have deceased. The total
dred and ninety-two.

To the list of members
thirty names have been a

WESTERN AGENCY.

In view of the great rapidity with which new towns and villages are springing up in the valley of the Mississippi, and of the importance of establishing churches in them, with a wise reference to expedition, economy, and efficiency, the Executive Board have decided to establish a Western Agency, and to seek some persons of requisite qualifications to enter the station, and discharge its duties, with the title of "Secretary of Correspondence."

In order to facilitate this important object, the Board propose that the 4th Article of the Constitution of the Society be altered, by striking out the words, a "Corresponding Secretary, a Financial Secretary," and substituting the words—"Secretaries of Correspondence," so that the article will read as follows: 5th. The officers of the Society shall be a President, two Vice-Presidents, a Treasurer, an Auditor, Secretaries of Correspondence, and a Recording Secretary, whom the Society shall annually elect by ballot.

HOME MISSION ROOMS.

In 1855, a committee was appointed by the Society for the purpose of endeavoring to obtain a place for the transaction of the Society's business; which committee was continued at the last anniversary, though limited in the time to accomplish the object to the first day of January, 1857. They were instructed, in case of failure, to endeavor to effect an arrangement, by which the Society would be secured in a perfectly equitable occupancy of the rooms in Nassau street, then used by the Executive Board for the purpose, under a lease from Nathan C. Platt, Esq.

No place having been obtained on the first of January, the committee proceeded to the other branch of their

duty, and made their Rep
following vote was passed

Resolved, That we deem
by lease of the rooms oc
satisfactory.

FINANC

The financial affairs of tl
indeed, by an increase of
reverse of this is the case
disbursements, as the am
time, would justify.

The following statemen
of the Society on the 31st

Balance from last year's account,......
Receipts from all sources,.................

of the Board, requiring the entire amount to have been in the treasury, to justify a favorable response.

The object in view in stating these facts, is to counteract an impression which may be formed in some minds, as has been heretofore, under similar circumstances, that our treasury is well supplied, and our necessities are sufficiently provided for.

Our conviction is, that to meet the real and immediate necessities of our western brethren, who look to this Society for aid, in their efforts to spread the gospel, the amount of means now in our possession is very insufficient; and the monthly receipts of the entire year ensuing should be increased a hundred per cent. over those of the last year.

This may be seen in the facts, that against the balance reported in the treasury, there are, already, claims falling due within the quarter ending July 1st, to the amount of $11,573 21, of which $5,385 85 will be due on the first of May; that numerous applications for aid requiring large appropriations, now await the action of the Board; and that new ones, to a considerable amount, must, as usual, be anticipated, each month.

The funds received under designation from the donors, for Church Edifices and other purposes, can be used only as designated. Thus, the amount remaining for the support of missionaries is reduced.

Owing to the increase in the distances of missionary fields, the cost of the removal of missionaries to those fields, and of supporting them when there, is very much increased.

These facts, together with that of the diminished amount of funds received into the treasury, show why the numb... of missionaries is less than formerly. ...de

As the receipts of each of the last three month... ...erly

ceeded those of earlier periods of the year, additional missionaries were appointed; and as good reasons exist for anticipating larger receipts within the ensuing twelve months, the number will probably be speedily augmented.

MISSIONARY OPERATIONS.

The missionary operations of the Society have been more encouraging, in several respects, than was anticipated at the commencement of the year. Several new missionaries have been appointed, some new stations have been established; revivals of religion have occurred at different points, and success in various forms, has attended the labors of a large proportion of the missionaries.

VALLEY OF THE MISSISSIPPI.

In the valley of the Mississippi, all the States heretofore occupied by the Society, have received attention, though a larger proportion of missionaries have been distributed at its more distant points. Several of the stations supplied are of more than ordinary importance, and some of them have made encouraging advances in ability to sustain the cause without our aid.

THE PACIFIC COAST.

Very little change has occurred in our arrangements for the supply of stations on the Pacific coast, though the consideration of that subject has recently been revived. The missionaries in California are performing their onerous duties amid difficulties peculiar to a field inhabited by a heterogeneous and ever-varying population, but, generally, with more encouraging success than formerly.

CENTRAL TERRITORIES.

The only missionaries in New Mexico, at present, are J. M. Shaw, who labors among the Mexican population, and Rev. S. Gorman, whose station is among the Pueblo Indians. They are, however, assisted by native converts, and are making steady progress in their difficult work. An amicable arrangement has recently been entered into with the Board of Managers of the American and Foreign Bible Society, by which certain colporteurs, who have been in their service in that territory a short time, are to be transferred to this Society, and employed as assistants to our missionaries. The conversion of several Mexicans appears to have imparted new hope and courage to our brethren. The force employed there, may soon be strengthened by an additional missionary, and, with the native assistants, will, probably, prove as adequate a supply for all the real necessities of that field, as any developments of Divine Providence now before us would seem to demand, or, as a judicious expenditure of missionary funds will justify; especially, when the increase and expansion of more enlightened, vigorous mind, in other territories, is so astonishingly great, and in the midst of which there are existing such active, powerful, and insidious antagonisms to the gospel of Jesus Christ, and to the civil and religious institutions of our country.

There are three missionaries in Nebraska, and one in Kansas. The number in both territories should be increased, as the state of the treasury will allow.

INDIAN MISSIONS.

The only stations among any class of Indians, occupied at present by our missionaries, is at Laguna, in New Mexico. Here Rev. S. Gorman remains in the performance of the most self-denying labors, aided by José Senun, a native assistant. At our last dates from him, a solemn crisis seemed impending at this field, which would decide whether the people would receive the gospel, or utterly reject it.

OTHER STATIONS.

At the Grande Ligne stations, and at St. Andrea, in New Granada, the progress of evangelical religion is, as heretofore, gradually on the advance.

SUMMARY OF LABORS AND RESULTS.

The number of missionaries employed during the whole of the year, is eighty-eight. Of this number, fifty-two were under appointment on the first of April, 1856, and thirty-six were new appointments. In addition to these, eight others have been appointed, whose labors commence after the first of April. The number in commission on the first of April, is seventy-one. Seven collecting agents have been employed, also, the whole, or portions of the year.

[redacted]

one hundred and forty-one others; the organization of twenty-four churches; the ordination of seventeen ministers; the completion of three church edifices, and progress in building eight others.

The churches, aided by the society, contributed during the year to the usual objects of Christian benevolence $2,576 71; besides $11,351 for the support of the cause of Christ among themselves.

Ten churches, recently aided by the Society, will sustain their pastors hereafter without missionary aid.*

REVIEW OF A QUARTER OF A CENTURY.

With the present anniversary, we are brought to the completion of a quarter of a century of the Society's history. It is, therefore, a specially suitable period for a brief review of its progress.

At the time of its organization in 1832, the State of Illinois formed the boundary of what was then considered the "far west." Michigan had but recently been organized as a territory, with but here and there a settlement. Iowa and Wisconsin were unknown, except as portions of the Missouri and North Western Territories; and, like all the regions beyond, at the North, and the West, were

* In addition to the above, the Missionaries report the following:—

Sermons preached	8,442
Lectures and Addresses	700
Pastoral Visits	21.769
Prayer and other Meetings attended	4,932
Signatures to Temperance Pledge	314
Miles traveled in discharge of duty	98,167
Schools visited	286
Sabbath Schools in the Churches	100
Bible Classes	60
Number of Teachers	549
Number of Scholars	4,993
Volumes in S. S. Libraries	13,865
Stations where Monthly Concert of Prayer is observed	50
Preparing for the ministry	9

the pastures of the buffal
Indian.

The population of the
of less than thirteen millio
were east of the Allegha
Baptist churches at the s
three hundred and twent
thousand and twenty-four.
dred and seventeen of the
fifty-three of the latter, w
The number of actual p
Much the larger portion
Sabbath labors between
sometimes more ; and no
through the week in sec
eral standard of literary a

tian reserve. Even in Ohio, the most advanced western State in missionary feeling and action, "one-half of the Baptists would have been opposed to any comprehensive scheme of benevolent effort, and much less than that proportion could have been actively enlisted in any such scheme."* "In the Annual Report of the Foreign Mission Board for 1831, the only credit from Ohio is $10 50. It was from a brother; the fruit of reading Mrs. Judson's Memoir."† The whole amount credited to all the Western States and Territories that year, was only an additional fifty dollars from Michigan, which was for the Burman Bible.

PRELIMINARY MEASURES.

It was under such circumstances, that a few brethren in Boston and its vicinity, became aware of the discredit and danger threatening the churches of the West and the East. They held frequent and anxious consultations respecting the ways and means of improving such a discouraging state of things, and finally decided upon setting on foot a religious exploration of the valley of the Mississippi. The agency for its execution was committed into the hands of Rev. Jonathan Going, than whom no better qualified man could have been selected. Through his wise and faithful performance of the duties proposed, those brethren were enabled in November, 1831, to proceed, through the medium of the Massachusetts Baptist Missionary Society, to adopt preliminary measures "to arouse the Baptist community throughout the United States, to systematic efforts in the cause of domestic missions,"‡ and to form a general Society, to whom should

* Rev. J. Stevens, 11th Report of H. M. Soc., p. 66.
† Rev. J. Stevens, 11th Annual Report H. M. Soc., page 67.
‡ Minutes Convention for Organization of the Society, page 3.

tution was prepared, which
sanctioned by a general Co
1832; by which act, existe
Baptist Home Mission Soci

THE FOUNDER

Among the hands emp
laying the foundations of t
those of Jonathan Going,
James D. Knowles, Natl
Daniel Dodge, Spencer H.

nine labored in Illinois ; four had their fields as far away as Missouri ; and one went to the, then, great distance of the State of Mississippi.

ALTERNATE PROSPERITY AND ADVERSITY.

With varied success, the Society struggled on through many difficulties, gradually extending its operations westward and southward, until the year 1845, when, on account of radical differences of opinion upon the subject of human slavery, an amicable separation took place between the members residing in the slave States and those of the free. After that period, its operations were gradually withdrawn from the slave States, and for several years past, none of its missionaries have borne its commission among them. Indeed, the necessity for it ceased by the organization and labors of a Society for Home Missions in the Southern States.

At the anniversary of the following year, the Constitution of the Society, which contained provision for inconvenient auxiliaryships, was essentially changed, freeing it from all incumbrances which had originated in such relations, and might be repeated. From that period, its progress became, each year, increasingly encouraging. Its treasury, until the last three years, became annually better supplied, and its missionary operations were expanded in an equal proportion. Its labors were extended to immigrants from foreign lands, to the French Canadians, and to the large Mexican population which has been annexed to our country ; to all of whom the gospel has been, and continues to be, preached in their native tongues, and from among whom, many have been converted to Christ, and gathered into churches.

THE PRESENT "FAR WEST."

If now, when twenty-five years have passed, we search for the "far-west," as occupied by civilized man, in one

direction, we can not stop
perior, three hundred mi
boundary of Illinois, and
point of Wisconsin ; if, ii
than the Red River of tl
miles still further. In an
the Mississippi a hundred
of St. Anthony. Journe
we must proceed hundreds
presence of the wild Indi
the Rocky Mountains. I
now, the States of Wiscoi
tories of Minnesota and K
Mexico. Still further on,
and Washington. Beyon
tence has gathered toget

and sixty-eight ministers, of which five thousand six hundred and seventy-eight churches and three thousand six hundred and ninety-four ministers are at the West. This shows that our churches and ministers have increased since 1830, in about the same ratio as the general population.

In 1830, there were, east of the Alleghanies, one thousand six hundred and eighty-eight churches, and one thousand one hundred and eighteen ministers more than at the West of that range. Now, while at the East, there are three hundred and eighty ministers more than at the West, there are at the West five hundred and eighty-two churches more than at the East. Many of the western ministers are yet secularized, or perform an irregular itinerant service, but the pastoral relation is better understood and appreciated in all the West, and is sustained at its most distant settlements.

With the exception of a few districts of limited extent, the churches possess the true missionary character, and are active and liberal in missionary effort. A large number of those which, twenty-five years ago, barred their pulpits against missionaries, and excluded from their fellowship such of their members as countenanced them, now zealously coöperate with them in spreading the gospel. The story of Pagan blindness and idolatry moves many a Baptist heart at the West, and the statement of an exhausted foreign missionary treasury brings out, if not so largely, yet, as freely, there as here, the needful offerings to replenish it. Instead of $60 50, which was the sum total of western contributions for that cause in 1831, the last Report of the Missionary Union contains acknowledgments of nearly $10,000 for the year, from the north-western States alone. No Judson's Memoirs are indispensable now, to unseal the fountain of in-

amid conflicting views of
at the disposal of the Exe
a year ago, the free-will (

A taste for useful litera
ly cultivated and sustaine
They patronize the useful
promote the sciences; th
of learning, and, what is b
mendable degree, in reve
of Jesus Christ.

THE INFLUENCE AN

While all due credit i
local means of accomplish
be assuming to assert t

whom were believed to be regenerated souls. They have organized 1011 churches, into which those baptized converts have been gathered, and ordained 534 ministers, chiefly reared up as preachers from the membership of those churches. Sabbath schools and Bible classes have been formed and sustained in all the churches supplied by by those missionaries. There are no means of ascertaining, accurately, the number of children and youths who have enjoyed the benefit of those schools, but, after making liberal allowance for deaths and disappointments in character, it can not be an exaggeration to estimate the number of men and women who have commenced an honorable career in life, with minds imbued with the teachings of God's holy word in those schools, at less than 100,000.

THE SOCIETY MAKES MISSIONARY CHURCHES.

The ministers patronized by the Society, being themselves missionaries, naturally impart a missionary character to all the churches with which they become connected. That this has been the case, is illustrated by the single fact, that during the short period of only fifteen years, in which such statistics have been embodied in their reports, the churches which have been aided by the Society, have contributed for the distribution of Bibles and Tracts, for missions at home and abroad, and for other objects of Christian benevolence, the sum of $40,743 83, or more than $2,700 per annum. Let it be clearly understood, that this amount was paid by young and feeble churches, at the very time they were themselves recipients of missionary benevolence, and that it does not include a dollar from churches sustaining the gospel independently of that benevolence. The contributions of those churches which have become thus independent, form noble columns in the Annual Reports of regular benevolent Societies.

THE SOCIETY PROMOTES MORAL REFORM.

The missionaries have established for themselves a good reputation as moral reformers. Quietly and without ostentation they have passed through the families of their respective fields, removing or correcting moral evils as they met them. Their success is seen, in one branch of moral reform, in the fact, that, since the year 1840, at least 17,257 signatures to the temperance pledge have been obtained by their unaided personal efforts.

THE SOCIETY BUILDS CHURCH EDIFICES.

They have, also, bestowed much attention upon the accommodations essential to the promotion of public worship. Uncontrollable circumstances have subjected them to an active leading agency, in the building of church edifices. Not less than 202 have been erected mainly by their exertions.

THE SOCIETY STIMULATES ACTIVITY IN OTHERS.

There are but few prominent cities or villages at the West which do not contain some evidence of the efficient influence of the Society in churches planted, houses of worship erected, or appendages of morality, benevolence, philanthrophy, and religion, established by those missionaries.

The movements of the denomination there in the direction of Christian effort, were originally induced by their counsels; the advance of the Baptist population in educational and literary interests, was, to a great extent,
influe d by their wisdom; its missionary character and
mote received the first impulse from their teachings and
men. es; what of moral and spiritual energy mark the
western churches thus far, is traceable, in no
They have, to their early training by those devoted men
24,718 pers the language of a well-informed western

man,* when speaking of its benefits to a particular State, the "Society has given light and strength; it has aroused our churches to action; it has been, in many instances, their life.†

The Annual Report of the Society, especially the Tenth and Twentieth, and the *Home Mission Record*, contain many details furnished by State Conventions and Societies; by exploring agents and missionaries, and by travelers and journalists, which substantiate these statements.

It is in vain, however, to attempt by such means, to ascertain all the fruits of the Society's operations. Such statistics must fall far short of the actual aggregate of its benefits. They are written above, and, without doubt, are wisely concealed from our present knowledge.

THE COST OF THE WORK.

The amount expended in the performances of the foregoing labors, reckoning from the organization of the Society, in 1832, is the comparatively small amount, in round numbers, of $540,000, or an average of only $21,600 per annum; the manner of making up the accounts of the Society for a large proportion of the time renders it difficult to ascertain accurately the average cost of transacting the business, but for the last five years, which are believed to have been as expensive as any preceding them, it has been, including salaries, taxes on lands, discounts on uncurrent funds, counterfeit bank bills, insurance, stationery, postage, printing, and all other incidental expenses, twenty-four and one-fifth per cent. per annum.

A FACT AND A REFLECTION.

No anniversary of the Society has ever before been held in Boston. It is a singular coincidence that it occurs here at this time, and that here, where the idea of

*Prof. J. Stevens.

† 11th Ann. Rept., page 67.

the Society had its origin
this brief sketch of the val
a quarter of a century ag
of those results cause hap
ones in whose prayers and
and may not those who u
sels, but who survive ther
on earth, and those who
their pious designs, rejoic
the success granted them
worthy to be identified w
a charity?

If, amid the changes of
the utility or advantages
come mooted questions, w
to point to its one great a

ty justified them. The Conventions of Ohio and Michigan and Illinois have thus undertaken the work of domestic missions in their respective States, and a corresponding withdrawal of Home Mission effort there has followed.

FUTURE WORK FOR THE SOCIETY.

The increase of new States and Territories has continually presented strong claims upon the benevolence of the Society, and called into requisition a large proportion of its means. Six new Territories, and one far distant new State, now present those claims; and our rapidly increasing and expanding population warns us of some two or three other Territories soon to be organized, and to which the Society's labors must be extended.

ADAPTEDNESS OF THE SOCIETY TO ITS WORK.

What the Society has done, it can with the blessing of God, repeat; and, with its acquired experience to guide, it can do more. It can keep pace better with the advance of civilization beyond the Mississippi; beyond the Missouri; beyond the Rocky Mountains; and it can duplicate its benefits wherever Territories are formed or States are organized, to the eastern shore of the Pacific Ocean; to the utmost verge of civilized society in North America, which is its appropriate field. There is no good reason to doubt its adaptedness to the performance of all the labor which is essential to the spread of the gospel in that great field, and if there were no reason to doubt the possession of requisite means for its performance, we might now joyfully anticipate the full accomplishment of the important design of the founders of the Society.

AN INCREASE OF MEANS ESSENTIAL.

Whatever may be the results of its operations hereafter, an equal amount of labor to that already performed can

the next twenty-five years ca
nor even by only the same
have been thus far in the fiel
ter of the Society for efficie
aggregate of labors and resu
tury as are now recorded, w
of circumstances now existir
ture, a large addition to the
tofore employed. But if an
have labored will require a
heretofore, how very much
the treasury be increased to
requisite addition.

EXPLANATION OF THE FOLLOWING MISSIONARY TABLE.

The parallel columns show:—

1. The names of Agents and Missionaries, and the States in which they reside.
2. The post-office address of Agents and Missionaries.
3. The fields of labor occupied by Agents and Missionaries.
4. The dates at which the appointments commence.
5. The number of months for which the appointments are respectively made.
6. The number of weeks' labor reported as having been performed during an appointment.
7. The number of stations and out-stations supplied.*
8. The number of persons baptized by the Missionaries within the time of appointment.
9. The number received by letter.
10. The number of Scholars in Sabbath-schools under the care of Missionaries.†
11. The amount contributed to benevolent objects.
12. Additional facts reported concerning the state and progress of the Churches.‡

* Stations are churches or villages regularly supplied on the Lord's day, and are indicated in column 3. Out-stations are places where the Missionaries have *stated* appointments for preaching more or less frequently at other times than the Lord's day.

† In new places, where Union-schools are established, the number of scholars connected with Baptist families only are reported.

‡ In many cases two lines appear for the same Missionary, extending through all the columns. In such cases the second line indicates a re-appointment of the Missionary, and the dates in column 4 determine to which appointment or year the statistics and remarks on the different lines belong. A particular notice of those dates is necessary to a proper understanding of certain changes which appear against the names of some individuals.

[redacted] Y TABLE.

[redacted]	Months Commiss'd.	Weeks labor reported.	Stations supplied.	Baptized.	Received by Letter.	Scholars in S. School.	Cont. to Benevolent Objects.	ADDITIONAL FACTS REPORTED.
	12	39	1	--	----	----	------	Meetings attended by Roman Catholics, and has encouraging success
	12	13	----	1	----	----	------	Progressing. Need a meeting-house.
	12	39	1	10	----	30	38 00	Usual success.
	12	13	----	--	----	----	1 50	
	12	39	1	4	----	----	112 50	Gospel making progress.
	12	13	----	--	----	----	37 50	
	12	39	1	--	----	30	------	A spirit of inquiry and prayer among the young.
	12	39	1	--	2	14	94 51	Romish Priests losing their authority over the people.
	12	13	----	--	----	15	13 50	
	12	26	8	9	4	200	28 20	Labors among the Germans. Needs no further aid.
	12	52	----	--	----	----	------	Collecting agent.
	----	----	----	--	----	----	------	Reappointment.

NAMES OF AGENTS AND MISSIONARIES.	POST OFFICE ADDRESS.	FIELD OF LABOR.	Date of Commission	Months Commis'd.	Weeks labor reported.	Stations supplied.	Baptized.	Received by Letter.	Scholars in S. School.	Cont. to Benevolent Objects.	ADDITIONAL FACTS REPORTED.
MASSACHUSETTS.											
J. W. Parkhurst	Newton Center	Massachusetts	April 1, 1856	12	52	----	--	----	----	------	Collecting agent.
" "	" "	"	April 1, 1857	----	----	----	--	----	----	------	Reappointment.
CONNECTICUT.											
A. E. Denison	Clinton	Connecticut & Rhode Isl'd.	April 1, 1857	----	----	----	--	----	----	------	Collecting agent. A new appointment.
NEW YORK.											
C. M. Fuller	Pike	Eastern N. Y. & N. J.	April 1, 1856	12	52	----	--	----	----	------	Collecting agent.
"	"	" "	April 1, 1857	12	----	----	--	----	----	------	Reappointment.
Wm. Sawyer	White's Corners	Western N. Y.	April 1, 1856	12	34	----	2	----	----	------	Collecting agent.
"	Ransomville	" "	April 1, 1857	12	----	----	--	----	----	------	Reappointment.
Joshua Fletcher	Amenia	Connecticut & Rhode Isl'd	April 1, 1856	12	45½	----	--	----	----	------	Collecting agent. Resigned.
Jas. S. Ladd	New York	New York and vicinity	April 1, 1857	12	----	----	--	----	----	------	Collecting agent, a new appointment.
Charles Randall	Auburn	Central New York	April 1, 1857	----	----	----	--	----	----	------	Collecting agent, a new appointment.
Charles Gayer	New York	French and Germans	Oct. 1, 1856	12	26	4	20	----	115	35 70	Building a meeting-house.
NEW JERSEY.											
J. G. Collom	Mount Holly	Penn. and S. New Jersey	April 1, 1856	12	39	----	--	----	----	------	Collecting agent. Deceased, December, 1856.
PENNSYLVANIA.											
Thomas J. Penny	Strattonville	Strattonville and Clarion	Dec. 1, 1855	12	26	3	--	----	90	40 96	Resigned and left the field.
A. J. Hires	Jersey Shore	Penn. and Southern N. J.	April 1, 1857	12	----	----	--	----	----	------	Collecting agent, a new appointment.

reported.	Letter.	Cont. to Benevolent Objects.	ADDITIONAL FACTS REPORTED.
		......	Resigned, and entered the pastorate of a ch.
		......	Pastor encouraged. Congregation large. Church revived.
	2	......	
	1	8 00	Progressing.
	6	41 18	S. School large and prosperous.
	5	12 00	Revival. Need no further aid.

Names of Agents and Missionaries.	Post Office Address.	Field of Labor.	Date of Commission	Months Commiss'd.	Weeks labor reported.	Stations supplied.	Baptized.	Received by Letter.	Scholars in S. School.	Cont. to Benevolent Objects.	Additional Facts Reported.
Harry Smith	Valparaiso	Valparaiso	Aug. 1, 1856	12	26		15		35	9 00	Revival.
H. C. Skinner	Wabach	Wabach	July 1, 1855	12	13	1			50	33 00	Church suffered from emigration further westward.
" "	"	"	July 1, 1856	12	39				54	9 12	
E. L. Millis	Attica	Attica	June 1, 1855	12	13	1	6	8	30		Need no further aid.
J. M. Whitehead	Westville	Northern Ia. Association	Aug. 1, 1855	12	26		50	7		125 00	Revival. No statistics of S. schools sent us.
" "	"	" "	Aug. 1, 1856	12	26		8	13		267 61	Laboring successfully.
J. G. Werthner	Evansville	Germans in E.	May 1, 1856	12	39	3	7	9			Experiences much opposition from his countrymen.
Lyman Wilder	Columbia City	Columbia City	Nov. 1, 1856	12	6½	3				3 00	A new and difficult field.
Adolphus Patze		Northern Association		12							Labors among Germans, a new appointment.
J. H. Dunlap		Huntington etc.	Feb. 1, 1857	12							A new appointment.
Sidney Dyer			April 1. 1857	12							New appointment. Agent for Church Ed. Fund.
ILLINOIS.											
J. Edminster	Peoria	Adams St. Ch.	May 1, 1856	12	39	3	1	5	150	35 57	A steady increase of interest.
"	"	" "	May 1, 1857	12							Reappointment.
J. H. Kruger	"	Germans in P.	Oct. 1. 1855	12	26	1	1				Nothing special, reported.
" "	"	" "	Oct. 1, 1856	12	26			2		5 00	
Asahel Chapin	Galena	Galena	June 1, 1855	12	13	1	4		57	5 00	Resigned, for another field.
W. D. Clark	Joliet	Joliet and Lockport	Nov. 1, 1855	12	39	2	1	23	75	40 00	Will labor with Lockport Church, and need no further aid.
J. N. Tolman	Decatur	Decatur	Jan. 1, 1856	12	39	1	2	13	45	86 40	Meeting-house progressing.
" "	"	"	Jan. 1, 1857	12	13			7		3 00	Congregations good. Prospects encouraging.
J. M. Cochran	Batavia	Batavia	April 1, 1856	12	52	3	7	6	100	89 00	Church weakened by removal further West.
" "	"	"	April 1, 1857	12							A reappointment.
F. Ketcham	Galena	Galena	June 1, 1856	12	39	1	2	3	50		Church encouraged. Paying their debt.
O. L. Barler	Chester	Chester	Nov. 1, 1855	12	39	1			50	15 30	Slow progress. A difficult field.
WISCONSIN.											
James Delany	Horicon	Horicon and Mayville	July 1, 1856	12	39	2		3	90		Mayville Ch. completed meeting-house.

Months Commis'd.	reported.	ied.	Cont. to Objects.	ADDITIONAL FACTS REPORTED.
			62	Need no further aid.
			00	Need no further aid.
				Has no church edifice.
			----	A reappointment.
			10 00	Prospects encouraging. Church united.
			00	Church gaining strength.
				Nothing special reported.
				Church progressing; spiritual condition improving.
			00	Severe cold weather unfavorable to meetings, and S. S.
			00	Need a meeting-house. Public morals improving.
			00	Encouraging in some respects.
			00	Trials in the Ch. Discipline needed.

Names of Agents and Missionaries.	Post Office Address.	Field of Labor.	Date of Commission	Months Commis'd.	Weeks labor reported.	Stations supplied.	Baptized.	Received b Letter.	Scholars in S. School.	Cont. to Benevolent Objects.	Additional Facts Reported.
Milton Sutton	Bonaparte	Bonaparte	May 1, 1855	12	13	1	9	7	80	......	Need no further aid.
Thomas S. Griffith	Du Buque	Du Buque	July 1, 1855	12	13	1	3	7	175	106 00	Encouraging.
" "	"	"	July 1, 1856	12	39	....	24	12	250	354 00	Completed meeting-house. Deep religious interest in the church.
Asahel Chapin	Vinton	Vinton and vicinity	June 1, 1856	12	39	4	1	9	40	5 00	A new field. Church making a vigorous effort to procure a M. H.
Jonas Woodward	Cedar Rapids	Cedar Rapids etc.	May 1, 1856	12	39	1	1	12	30	......	Meeting-house sufficiently advanced to be occupied for the public worship.
" "	" "	" "	May 1, 1857	12	....	....	..	....	....	......	A reappointment.
J. F. Guild	Newton	Newton and vicinity	July 1, 1856	12	39	2	..	23	25	3 28	A new field. Revival.
A. A. Sawin	Lyons	Lyons & Clinton	July 1, 1856	12	39	2	..	7	30	67 00	Organized a church at Clinton. Secured a lot for M. H. at Lyons.
A. Norelius	Ridgeport	Swedes in Boom Co.	July 1, 1856	12	39	2	..	2	16	3 45	Organized a church at Providence.
G. F. Brayton	Freeman	St. Charles	June 1, 1856	12	39	7	3	33	40	......	A new field. Procured a site for a M. H. Ch. gradually increasing.
L. M. Newell	....	....	....	....	....	....	..	....	....	......	
MINNESOTA.											
Timothy R. Cressy	Cannon City	Red Wing and vicinity	June 1, 1855	12	13	11	..	....	50	......	Nothing special reported.
" "	" "	Cannon City etc.	June 1, 1856	12	39	....	..	11	....	150 00	Organized churches at two of his stations.
Lyman Palmer	Anoka	Anoka and vicinity	Aug. 1, 1855	12	13	5	..	....	6	......	Organized a church at Anoka, and another in Brooklyn.
" "	"	" "	Nov. 1, 1856	12	13	....	..	....	12	......	Appearances hopeful. Congregations good.
L. Atkinson	"	Wright and other Counties	Oct. 1, 1855	12	26	6	..	....	....	100 00	Itinerates in new fields.
"	"	Hennepin and other Co.	Oct. 1, 1856	12	26	9	..	....	....	......	
Wilson Cogswell	Shakapee	Shakapee etc.	Dec. 1, 1855	12	52	5	..	1	60	6 00	A difficult and unpromising field.
A. A. Russell	Minneapolis	Minneapolis	July 1, 1855	12	13	2	..	5	42	17 00	Congregation increasing.
" "	"	"	July 1, 1856	12	39	....	2	13	60	47 00	Church revived and preparing to build M. H.
F. O. Nilsson	St. Paul	Scandinavians	Nov. 1, 1855	12	39	6	28	....	45	......	Revival.
" "	Scandia	"	Nov. 1, 1856	12	13	....	2	....	60	......	Prospects good and is greatly encouraged.
A. M. Torbet	St. Paul	St. Paul	Oct. 1, 1855	12	26	1	..	14	60	216 00	Need a larger M. H.
" "	"	"	Oct. 1, 1856	12	26	....	..	10	115	12 00	Church has purchased a lot, for a new church edifice.
J. L. Irwin	Saratoga	Itinerant	Sept. 1, 1858	12	26	3	..	....	....	50 00	Organized a church at Saratoga.

Months Commis'd.	Cont. to Benevolent Objects.	ADDITIONAL FACTS REPORTED.
12	......	A new field. Cong. large and increasing.
12	......	Church revived. Congregation large.
12	......	Revival. Several conversions.
12	......	Prospects encouraging at Wasioga.
12	......	A new appointment.
12	......	A new appointment.
12	......	A new appointment.
12	......	A new appointment.
12	......	A new appointment.

Names of Agents and Missionaries.	Post Office Address.	Field of Labor.	Date of Commission	Months Commis'd.	Weeks labor reported.	Stations supplied.	Baptized.	Received by Letter.	Scholars in S. School.	Cont. to Benevolent Objects.	Additional Facts Reported.
NEW MEXICO.											
J. Milton Shaw	Albuquerque	Santa Fé, etc.	Oct. 1, 1856	12	13						Several hopefully converted and waiting to be baptized. Many others inquiring the way of salvation.
Samuel Gorman	"	Laguna and vicinity	Oct. 1, 1855	12	39		4		10		Making some advances but suffers for a meeting-house.
" "	"	" "	Oct. 1, 1856	12	13						A solemn crisis. The people ready to receive or reject the gospel.
Jose Senum	"	" "	Oct. 1, 1855	12	26						An assistant to Mr. Gorman.
" "	"	" "	Oct. 1, 1856	12	13						
F. Tolhurst	Santa Fé	Santa Fé, etc.	Sept. 1, 1855	12	26						Resigned and removed to Fort Fillmore as Chaplain to U. S. Army.
CALIFORNIA.											
J. B. Saxton	San Francisco	San Francisco	July 1, 1856	12	39	1		4	40		Organized a Church of 13 members. Prospects encouraging.
O. B. Stone	Nevada	Nevada	July 1, 1856	12	39	1		2			Building a good meeting-house.
H. H. Rhees	Ione Valley	Ione Valley	Nov. 1, 1856	12	13	3	2				Need a meeting-house.
NEW GRANADA.											
Philip Livingston	St. Andrews	St. Andrews	May 1, 1855	12	13	1			86		Wife's health made it necessary for him to visit New York.
" "	"	"	May 1, 1856	12	39				95	25 20	Reappointment.

STATE CO

GENERAL ASSOCIATION

With the Names and Post Office Address of the their Anniversaries for 1857; *the number of their Treasuries, for* 1856, *including Balances*

STATES.	CORRESPONDING SECRETARIES.	PO
Maine	L. B. Allen	
New Hampshire	E. S. Hall	
Vermont	John Goadby	Poul
Massachusetts	A. F. Spalding	Calai
Rhode Island	Warren Randolph	Provi
Connecticut	E. Cushman	Deep
New York	John Smitzer	
New Jersey	J. M. Carpenter	
Pennsylvania	J. Wheaton Smith	
Maryland	F. Wilson	
Virginia	H. K. Ellyson	

AGGREGATE CONTRIBUTIONS FROM ALL THE STATES SINCE 1832.

STATES.	Total Amount to 1845.	1846.	1847.	1848.	1849.	1850.	1851.	1852.	1853.	1854.	1855.	1856.	1857.
Canada	$327 65	$864 70	$692 67	$734 11	$710 79	$800 57	$458 84	$153 63	$189 19	$91 91	$145 23	$143 75	$450 36
Maine	2,714 40				500 00		37 60	56 39	622 31	164 66	173 16	102 44	82 09
New Hampshire	3,083 42	528 41	242 50	343 81	50 50	625 88	419 17	1,104 77	1,487 00	1,632 60	1,875 47	1,608 22	1,627 09
Vermont	1,718 95	673 95	184 00	257 51	222 80	1,015 75	471 98	505 17	494 71	758 58	1,511 10	1,186 34	967 44
Massachusetts	22,313 30	1 474 20	3,333 03	4,791 22	4,022 07	5,357 73	6,717 06	8,497 51	7,974 56	12,005 92	8 205 73	10,467 62	10,176 01
Rhode Island	5,118 45	852 35	669 56	1,683 33	1,545 76	2,427 57	1,188 66	2,874 55	687 87	2,695 78	2,287 45	2,560 07	1,768 88
Connecticut	11,628 71	1,186 03	1,042 81	1,072 06	1,490 46	1,251 34	2,032 59	2,490 31	3,052 58	4,529 96	4,285 70	4,047 46	3,840 83
New York	65,772 95	6,520 49	7,142 38	6,871 10	6,614 15	7,723 20	10,666 47	13,706 43	16,951 07	18,071 40	20,189 13	14,790 88	14,855 15
New Jersey	4,861 29	1,195 85	1,419 27	1,890 90	2,724 80	2,408 67	2,518 20	2,179 01	3,419 94	3,533 51	3,463 63	2,985 34	2,498 44
Pennsylvania	4,520 81	528 47	529 86	707 43	1,556 80	1,606 11	1,605 98	1,973 75	2,252 91	3,024 90	3,530 82	2,507 89	1,594 36
Delaware	161 20			153 36	60 00	228 94	203 00	163 00	167 90	138 92	67 88	103 75	183 04
Maryland	2,019 81	30 25	5 00				15 50					200 00	
District of Col'bia	953 12		10 00			30 00	5 00	37 31	5 00	134 00	30 00		8 22
Ohio	1,010 45	114 81	30 84	30 50	29 45	153 52	241 88	656 62	732 48	2,758 60	3,226 67	2,708 28	1,065 00
Michigan	337 50	29 50	13 25	172 89	556 21	610 60	1,011 80	866 75	634 43	287 74	574 60	179 23	198 72
Indiana	28 75	8 10	22 05	11 11	8 50	26 35	290 22	774 38	1,669 44	2,306 79	2,101 50	656 72	1,317 29
Illinois	668 00	477 63	766 50	1,136 69	594 90	704 74	1,329 98	1,230 97	1,675 63	2,470 82	1,799 70	1,700 17	150 86
Wisconsin	20 10	15 63	124 50	72 15	88 06	58 35	181 91	170 00	274 87	549 71	625 90	418 43	179 19
Iowa	83 56	41 00	120 03	63 12	93 24	102 77	171 95	390 67	278 05	277 10	332 58	573 12	383 93
Minnesota							1 00	2 25	55 85	141 46	405 85	328 25	577 07
Nebraska													150 00
Kansas													5 00
Missouri	266 82							2 00		75 00	215 00		29 00
Kentucky	273 88		10 00	20 50						42 25			
Virginia	9,152 56	159 44	5 85	7 30			5 00				23 75		7 00
North Carolina	5,000 02	391 67											
South Carolina	8,363 95	135 15							30 00			30 00	20 00
Georgia	9,529 33		1,331 87					30 00					40 00
Alabama	493 08										30 00		
Florida	157 82		15 00										
Mississippi	1,899 66												
Tennessee	477 85		8 25										
Louisiana	79 00												
Arkansas	50			50 55	18 15								
Texas													
California							50 00	150 50	70 00	20 00	225 00	105 00	
Oregon							30 00		51 50	159 12	59 33	44 98	17 60
New Mexico								62 10	94 42	7 38	20 00		30 00
U. S. Government												435 00	
New Granada												89 60	25 20
Unknown													139 00
Ag. for each period	163,028 98	15,727 63	17,728 72	20,068 73	20,576 73	25,201 09	29,648 28	38,114 16	42,872 01	59 903 83	55,545 40	47 928 54	43,286 76

LIST OF LEGACIES

D TO THE SOCIETY SINCE ITS ORGAN

Josiah Penfield, Savannah, Ga., per Rev. H. O. Wyer
. Clarissa Long, Shelburne, Ms., per W. Wilder, Esq., Executor ....
lliam Powers, Hebron, N. H., per Rev. L. Merriam................
Maria Curtis, Southbridge, Ms., per Rev. E. Going...............
Jemima Elliott, Hampton, Ct., per Rev. J. Payne, Executor..........
Betsey Sprague, Attleboro', Ms., per Mr. A. Reed, Executor.....
ert Rogers, Newport, R. I..
nezer Boyd, Providence, R. I..
Abigail Marshall, New York, per Mr. Schofield, Executor............
. Margaret Pugsley, Dutchess Co., N. Y., per Miss Cornelia Pugsley .
. Irene Coats, New York, per Alfred Decker, Esq...................
. Elizabeth G. Moore, Hartford, Ct., per J. B. Gilbert ....
haniel Tucker, Milton, Ms., per W. D. Ticknor ....
. Margaret Martin, Montgomery, N. Y., per Mr. J. J. Martin, Executo
Cynthia M. Wright, Suffield, Ct., per H. Sheldon, Administrator ....
Zephaniah Eddy, New Bedford, Ms., per Rev. H. Jackson, Executor...
Josiah Kendall, Groton, Ms., per F. F. Wheelock and Rev. A. Sander
Jane McCall, Society Hill, S. C., per John McIver ....
Lydia Sweetzer, South Reading, Ms., per H. Sweetzer...............
. Elizabeth Griffin, New York, per one of her heirs ....
. Josiah Flint, Cornish, N. H., per Mr. A. Burnap....................
mas Cooper, Esq., Eatonton, Ga., per Hon. M. A. Cooper, Executor ..
Betsey Hutchinson, Passumpsic, Vt., per L. P. Parks................
. Amos Dodge, Brighton, Macoupin Co., Ill., by his widow..........
John Ward, Warren, N. Y., per J. Northrop and A. Ward, Executors.
ph H. Haydon, Saybrook, Ct., per H. L. Champlin, Executor..........
n Allen, Centerville, R. I., in part, per H. Hamilton and Rev. E. K. F
. Jesse Mercer, Wilks Co., Ga., per Rev. B. M. Saunders, Executor....
Mary Bliven, McDonough, N. Y., per Rev. John Peck ....

1849	Mr. William Reynolds, Boston, Ms., per J. H. Duncan, Esq., and Mrs. Susan D. Reynolds, Executors, in land not sold at Toledo, Ohio	
"	Josiah Lyman, Andover, Ct., per N. B. Lyman, Executor	$50 00
"	John J. Martin, Montgomery, N. Y., per M. Bookstaver, Executor	1000 00
"	Mrs. Martha Howe, West Boylston, Ms., per Messrs. E J. Howe & Co.	50 00
"	A. H. Reed, Sweden, N. Y., per Rev. D. Searl	13 00
"	Asa H. Truman, Owego, N. Y., per E. Truman, Executor	248 00
1850	George D. James, Amenia, N. Y., J. K. Mead and N. Rose, Executors	100 00
"	John Everett, Manchester, Mich., per F. Everett	70 00
"	Jacob Whitman, Belvidere, Ill., in part, per N. Crosby, Esq	160 00
"	Jonas Taylor, Boston, Ms.	12 50
"	Miss Rebecca Thompson, Amenia, N. Y., per A. B. Capwell, Esq.	801 00
"	Joanna Minot, Boston, Ms., per E. Mears and I. Parker, Executors	100 00
"	Claudius F. Brown, Arkwright, N. Y., per David Barrell	150 00
"	Miss Anna Roe, Egremont, Ms., per R. B. Brown, Executor	50 00
1851	David Schauber, Burnt Hills, N. Y., per J. & D M. Shauber, Executors	10 00
"	Woolcot Griffin, Governeur, N. Y., per O. L. Barnum, Executor	100 00
"	Joseph Flanders, Brooklyn, N Y., per Mrs. Eliza A. Flanders and Benj. Flanders	500 00
"	William Williams, New York, per John Allen, Executor	400 00
"	Ely Wiley, South Reading, Ms.	50 00
1852	Miss Pharozene C. Kelly, Hopkinton, N. H., per John Page	50 00
"	Jonathan W. Ford, Boston, Ms.	100 00
"	Theron Fisk, Esq., Warsaw, N. Y., in advance	2500 00
"	Joshua A. Burke, Brooklyn, N. Y., per Messrs. E. and W. A. Burke	350 00
Miss	Eliza Skaats, New York, in part, per G. N. Bleecker, Executor	1000 00
"	Barnum M. Howard, Sweden, N. Y., per H. M. Howard, Executor	20 00
1853	Alanson Stewart, Liberty, N. Y., per W. W. Murphy	5 00
"	Mrs. Sarah B. Peirce, Middleboro', Ms.	100 00
"	Arnold Whipple, Providence, R. I., per Mrs. P. Whipple, Executrix	200 00
"	Mrs. Fanny McGilvreay, Brookline, N. H. (Annuity), per H. A. Daniels, Administrator	40 00
"	Mrs. Lucretia Goddard, Worcester, Ms., per Hon. I. Davis, Executor	308 00
"	P. F. Brayton, Providence, R. I., per A. K. Brayton and Rev. J. Brayton, in addition	594 87
"	Mrs. Elizabeth Gale, Washington, D. C.	50 00
1854	Edward Rogers, Chester, Ill., per Rev. M. B. Kelly	5 00
"	Miss Esther Ann Blakely, Pawlet, Vt., per Rev. J. J. Peck	73 00
"	Daniel Cummings, Chelsea, Ms., per Mr. Eaton, Executor	1000 00
"	Mrs. Mary Leuce, Bristol, R. I., per J. F. Baars	7 50
"	D. Valentine, Washington, Pa., per H. W. Wilson, Executor	239 80
"	Willis L. Eaton, East Weare, N. H., per J. L. Eaton, Executor	100 00
"	Asa Read, Attleboro', Ms., per Amos M. Read, Executor	1000 00
"	Friend Humphrey, Albany, N. Y., per his son, Executor	106 30
"	George Corbett, Worcester, Ms.	8 00
"	Mrs. Abby Arnold, Centerville, R. I., per W. A. Arnold	95 00
"	Garrat N. Bleecker, New York, per E. Cauldwell and W. F. Van Wagner, Executors	6000 00
"	Eunice Shepardson, Belleville, N. Y.	70 00
"	Mrs. Mary Johnson, Albany, N. Y., per Chas. Pohlman	10 00
"	Charles H. Nichols, Boston, Ms., in part, in advance	150 00
"	Mrs. Olive Stowell Le Roy, N. Y., per R. Bell	10 00
"	David Trull, Lowell, Ms., per J. Fox	300 00
1855	Roger Pegg, New York, per Mr. Coe, Executor	100 00
"	John Goodell, jr., Woodstock, N. Y., in part, per Mrs. Maria H. Goodell, Executrix	268 25
"	Mrs. Frances Thompson, Alabama, N. Y.	50 00
"	Miss Mercy Hayden Grafton, Ms., per Rev. J. Smith	20 00
"	Joseph D. Murray, New Hope, Pa.	30 00
"	W. S. Ward, Salem, Ms.	100 00
"	Mrs. Lucy Bushnell, Monticello, N. Y, per Rev. Samuel White	50 00
"	W. Littlefield, Belleville, N. Y.	30 00
"	Mary E. Bennett, Ludlow, Vt., per Rev. N. Cudworth, Executor	111 00
"	Margaret Sherwood, New York, per E. J. Mattocks, Executor	60 00
"	Linus Austin, Akron, O.	27 00

1855 Mrs. —— Nelson, Peoria, Ill..........
" Mrs. Margaret Davies, New York, per J.
" Abijah Porter, Danvers, Ms., per Rev. J
" Jacob Morse, Sturbridge, Ms., per Mrs.
" Andrew McCleary, Frederick City, Md.,
1856 Miss Hannah Briggs, Rock Island, Ill.,
" Miss Eliza Jackson, Hamilton, N. Y., p
" Mrs. M. W. Denison, Rock Island, Ill.,
" Miss Achsah Cox, Imlaystown, N. J....
" Samuel Stone, Dundee, Mich., T. Babco
" Louisa S. Platt, Haverhill, Ma., S. Peas
" Mrs. Hannah Kent, Danversport, Ms..
" Manly Street, Holyoke, Ms..........
" Mrs. Lorain Sheldon, Suffield, Ct.......
" Mrs. Abigail Hatch, Boston, Ms., Thos.
" Interest on legacy of $550, by the late
Kelton, Executor..............
" Rev. Asel Waters, Miami, Ia., in part,

IMPORTANT WH

Legacies are sometimes diverted from t malities, especially in the devising clause high legal authority, to which we solicit the to place the Society among their legatees, intended

DOCUMENTS

REFERRED TO IN THE "MINUTES OF THE ANNIVERSARY."

DOCUMENT NO. 1.

Report of the Committee on the Church Edifice Fund.

Your committee on "the Church Edifice Fund" have attended to the duty assigned them, and beg leave to report:

One of the first wants of a recently-organized church is a house, in which to meet for the public worship of God. It is important that such a house should be centrally situated, neat, convenient, substantial, and in good architectural taste.

But, a young church, in a new region, is usually feeble. Its members are few and in moderate circumstances. Hence, when it "arises to build" it needs help. It is the object of the Home Mission Society, by its "Church Edifice Fund," to render this help. This it proposes to do, by loaning money, which is ultimately to be re turned, with moderate interest, in order to be loaned again in like manner. This is, in many respects, a wise plan, and should not altogether be laid aside.

But, a still more excellent plan has been suggested to your committee, which they take pleasure in presenting to your consideration. The plan is to go in advance of the churches, into new and important places, and their obtain suitable building lots. Some of the advantages of this plan, are as follows, viz.:—

1. The small expense of such building lots, when early secured. Sometimes they can be obtained as donations, and, when purchased, their cost is often not more than twenty dollars to one hundred. While the same "parcels of ground," in a few years may be worth thousands of dollars.

2. A central position is ready for the church as soon as it is formed. For want of such a lot, our brethren are often obliged to purchase in unsuitable places, far from the centre of population, to their great injury.

3. This valuable property will cost the newly-formed church but little, or, nothing, so that they can devote their means directly to a house for worship. If the land is given to the Society, it will be given by it, to the church. If purchased, the church will be expected, when able, to refund merely its first cost, with interest, they having all the advantage of its increased value.

4. The lot may be obtained of such a si
sold to aid them in building.

5. Great expense of time and money
may *soon* proceed to build; agents will
country for help, and brethren will not be

In view of these and similar consider
recommend

1. That "the Church Edifice Fund" be
of suitable building lots, in new places.

2. That said lots be permanently secure
on them, with such legal provisions as ma

3. That loans continue to be made to
cording to the discretion of the Board.

4. That, in addition to the usual contr
ciety, especial efforts be made to complete
been decided that this fund, if possible, sh
dollars. Your committee regret to learn
has yet been raised. They believe tha
brethren will take prompt measures to su
plan suggested, are like seed corn, in fruit
invested in building lots, now, may save t
some future day. Such investments will

their hearts have been most profoundly stirred by the urgent demand for more laborers, that comes from large States and Territories that are being rapidly filled up with enterprising, intensely active, and gain-seeking multitudes, of various languages and races, no less than by the destitution of some particular communities, the superstitions prevailing elsewhere, and the irreligion of not a few others.

The conviction has also forced itself upon your Committee, that the greatness of the work, the imperativeness of its claims, and its present pressing demands, all authorized though they are, and all emphasized by the Great Head of the Church, are not yet duly appreciated by the churches and ministers of the older States, which are, perhaps, more highly favored with the well-sustained institutions of the gospel, and the ampler enjoyment of external prosperity and elegant culture.

Till within but a few years, this wide field was little occupied and little known, except by the Indian tribes and the animals of the chase, and the few trading companies that sought their furs. Now, thousands of thriving and increasing settlements—many considerable towns, and some well-populated cities, present themselves as inviting homes to the emigrant. God has renewed the pillars of the West, bearing the inscription "*Ne plus ultra*," to the very coast of our continent. Some portion, indeed, of this vast territory, is desert, but the greater part is fertile, and a large extent is like the vale of Sidim for richness. Nor is some of it unlike the vale of Sidim in the moral aspect of its population. Many tribes of Indians that inhabit the more northern section are ignorant of the name of Jesus; those of New Mexico are sunk in the most abject form of Romanism, while in the very State of California, thousands of Chinese grope in the licentiousness of heathenism; and all these under the eyes of our own government, occupying our own national territory, a government called Christian, a territory of a Christian nation. What an extensive, inviting, pressing field for the vigorous, liberal prosecution of the glorious work of the American Baptist Home Mission Society. What is the duty of American Baptists to these benighted multitudes? How can they fail to perceive the wonderful leadings of Providence, in thus encircling within their national limits these myriads of degraded and eternity-bound souls? Long has their prayer ascended that God would bring the tribes of the earth to behold the light of His love, and to rejoice in the glory of His gospel. And not only has he blessed the labors in foreign fields, but has increased the facilities for the speedy evangelization of the nations, by bringing their representatives within our bounds, and under our own political and social influence. By the accession of New Mexico, and the emigration to California, a new day of promise dawned upon the work of missions. By the uncovering of golden grains, that had been hidden for ages, God attracted to our own shores those of distant climes, that came flocking in search of the inviting boon. Among others, some thirty thousand Chinese, it is said, have crossed the Pacific. Many of these will visit their native land again; and if they were converted to Christ, what powerful foreign missionaries would they prove, as they gathered their former associates together, and, like the woman of Samaria, declared to their neighbors the wonderful claims of the gospel. Has not God thus given us a direct avenue to the very heart of heathendom and superstition?

Our combined missionary force, now operating in the vast area of New Mexico, Nebraska, Kansas, and New Granada, numbers but ten missionaries. Brethren. What are we about? Are we fast asleep, while the meridian sunbeams are peering into our eye-lids? Shall we continue to offer stereotyped prayers—"Thy Kingdom come, and Thy will be done!" while at this most interesting, most critical, most opportune time for action, we continue to dole out the meagre pittance we have hitherto done for the great cause represented by this Society?

The operations of the past year, though not so large as sometimes, heretofore, have been owned by God, and are such as should encourage and stimulate to greater liberality, urge to renewed and more vigorous endeavors, and should awaken more earnest, importunate prayers for an adequate supply of men and means, and facilities for the proper evangelization of our entire field, so that the next year's report may mention not eighty-eight missionaries only, and $45,000 contributed to our treasury; but one hundred and fifty men, and at least $100,000.

The review of the Society's work for the twenty-five years of its history, should humble us all, that so little has been attempted, while it awakens the liveliest gratitude and devout thankfulness, as we say, "*What hath God wrought!*"

In conclusion, your Committee would submit the following resolutions as expressive of their sentiments:—

Resolved, That the cause of Home Missions is second in importance to no other department of Christian effort.

Resolved, That the West, no less than the East, greatly needs, and imperatively demands, men of strong, well-disciplined powers and executive abilities, combined with devoted, consistent piety.

Resolved, That the men whom the East can not readily give up, and whose gifts and graces are highly appreciated here, are the very men whom the West are asking for, in large numbers, and whom the West will gladly and abundantly sustain.

F. S. Stubberts,
J. R. Stone,
G. P. Nice,
D. G. Corey,
Chas. Willet.

DOCUMENT No. 3.

Report of the Committee on Obituaries.

While we record with sorrow the loss of good men, who have labored long and most successfully in the cause of Christian benevolence, and have been especially endeared to this Society by their faithfulness to its interests, we can not withhold an expression of gratitude to God, that he has given to the world such men, and to this Society such friends and advocates.

The places they filled so long and so worthily, are vacant in our midst to-day. But, still they live. They live in the grateful recollections of those who remain, and in the savor of the good works they so well performed.

While all the members of the Society who have departed this life during the past year deserve mention, there are two in particular who should receive more than a passing notice.

Deacon William Colgate, of New York, has lately ceased from his labors, and entered into rest. He was one of the constituent members of this Society. He was its first Treasurer; in which capacity he served for three years, to the great advantage of its interests. Ten years he was one of the Executive Board, and for fifteen years has filled the office of Vice-President. Highly favored and blessed with the means for doing good, above most, he received also from the same Divine source, a disposition to dispense largely of the bounties committed to his trust. We would not unduly laud the large benefactions of the wealthy, forgetful of the smaller contributions of the poor, which, though they may weigh less in the balance of the money-changer, are often of greater value in the sight of God. But we name it here, to the praise of divine grace, that William Colgate was what we are too seldom permitted to see, a rich man, serving God with all fidelity; who, while engaged in large business, and reaping large gains, had still a heart and a hand for every good work.

His last days were those of great physical suffering, but of spiritual peace and comfort. His work was done; and with composure, and in the assurance of faith, he waited the message that called him home. We loved him while living, we respect his memory now that he is gone, and mingle with our sorrow for his loss, regrets that there are so few to fill his place.

Rev. J. G. Collom was cut off in the midst of life, and called away by sudden disease, from most useful and successful labors as an agent of this Society. During the lucid intervals of his last sickness, he prayed and counseled for the still greater success and prosperity of Home Missions; and in the ravings of delirium, proved his intense devotion to the cause, by proposing impossible methods for filling an exhausted treasury, and securing abundant means for sending the gospel over all the land. But he rejoices now in the presence of his Lord, and waits the final ingathering of the ripening harvest.

We mingle our tears for the departed, with our thanksgivings for the triumphs of the gospel. May both, successes and bereavements, be sanctified to the still larger usefulness of this Society, and stimulate us to greater diligence, since the time of our departure, also, is at hand.

Respectfully submitted, on behalf of Committee,

EDWARD T. HISCOX.

[illegible] [redacted] [illegible]

[illegible] [redacted] [illegible]

[illegible] [redacted] [illegible]

[illegible]

[illegible]

DIRECTORS FOR LIFE.

BY VIRTUE OF A CONTRIBUTION OF ONE HUNDRED DOLLARS OR MORE.

Ackerman, John, Dobbs Ferry, N. Y.
Adams, Rev. Paul S., Newport, N. H.
Adsit, Rev. Samuel, Jr., Auburn, N. Y.
Akerly, Richard C., New York.
Aldrich, Rev. Jonathan, Worcester, Mass.
Alger, Henry, Cleveland, Ohio.
Allin, George, Brooklyn, N. Y.
Alvord, Rev. Nelson, Tonica, Ill.
Anable, Rev. Cortland, W. Brooklyn, N. Y.
Anderson, Rev. Thomas D., Roxbury, Mass.
Anderson, M. B., LL.D., Rochester, N. Y.
Anderson, Rev. George W., North East, N. Y.
Archer, Ezekiel, New York.
Armitage, Rev. Thomas, D.D., New York.
Armstrong, Rev. James D., Baltimore.
Arnold, Wipple A., Centreville, R. I.
Ashton, D. R., Philadelphia.
Askren, William, Cincinnati, O.
Atwell, Rev. G. B., Pleasant Valley, Conn.
Averill, Rev. Alex. M., North Cambridge, Ms.
Ayer, Rev. Oliver, Claremont, N. H.
Babcock, Rev. Rufus, D.D., Paterson, N. J.
Bacheller, Jonathan, Lynn, Mass.
Bacon, Mrs. Mary H., Greenwich, N. J.
Backus, Rev. Jay S., New York.
Bailey, Benjamin D., Providence, R. I.
Bailey, Rev. Gilbert S., Metamora, Ill.
Bailey, Rev. Joseph A., Waterbury, Ct.
Ballard, Rev. Joseph, Brooklyn.
Baldwin, Rev. N. B., Philadelphia.
Balen, Peter, New York.
Banks, Jacob, Salem, N. J.
Banks, Mrs. Mary, Salem, N. J.
Banks, Miss Ann Judson, Salem, N. J.
Banvard, Rev. Joseph, Pawtucket R. I.
Barnaby, Rev. James, Newburyport, Mass.
Barker, Rev. Enoch M., Hightstown, N. J.
Barns, John, Danversport, Mass.
Barrell, Rev. Almond C., Albion, N. Y.
Barrows, Rev. S. W., Neponset, Mass.
Batchelder, Rev. James L., Cincinnati, O.
Bates, V. J., Providence, R. I.
Beecher, Rev. L F., D.D., Saratoga Springs, N.Y.
Beecher, Mrs. M. C., Saratoga Springs, N. Y.
Belcher, Rev. Joseph, D.D., Philadelphia.
Bennet, Rev. Ira, Weedsport, N. Y.
Binney, Rev. J. G., D.D., Washington, D. C.
Binney, Mrs. Juliet P., Washington, D. C.
Bishop, Nathan, LL.D., Boston.
Blain, Rev. John, Central Falls, R. I.
Blain, Mrs. Amy Ann, Central Falls, R. I.
Bliss, Rev. George R., Lewisburg, Pa.
Bly, Rev. William T., Minnesota Territory.
Boardman, W. G., Albany, N. Y.
Bolles, Matthew, Jr., Boston.
Borden, Jefferson, Fall River, Mass.
Bosworth, Rev. George W., Portland, Me.
Bowles, Rev. Ralph H., Branford, Ct.
Boyce, James, Providence.
Bradford, Rev. S. S., Pawtucket, R. I.
Brainerd, Samuel, Haverhill, Mass.
Brant, Rev. Randolph C., Lawrence, Kansas.
Brantly, Rev. W. T., Philadelphia.
Brayton, Rev. Jonathan, Pawtucket, R. I.
Brayton, William E., Providence, R. I.
Brayton, Samuel H., Phenix, R. I.
Brayton, Lodowick M., Knightsville, R. I.
Briggs, Rev. O. W., Brooklyn, N. Y.
Brooks, Iveson L., Hamburg, S. C.
Brokaw, Joseph, New York.
Brouwere, Vermilyea T., Dundee, N. Y.
Brown, Rev. J. Newton, D.D., Philadelphia.
Bruce, John M., New York.
Buckbee, Rev. Charles A., New York.
Bucknell, William, Philadelphia.
Bucknell, Mrs. Margaret K. C., Philadelphia.
Bucknell, Miss L. L., Philadelphia.
Budlong, James E., Providence.
Burlingham, Rev. A. H., New York.
Burgess, Rev. I. J., Milltown, Me.
Bullock, Benjamin, Philadelphia.
Bump, Nathaniel, Providence.
Burger, William H., New York.
Burke, William, Rochester, N. Y.
Burke, Abraham C., Brooklyn, N. Y.
Burke, J. B., Middlefield, Mass.
Burt, John W., Brooklyn, N. Y.
Burt, E. C., Brooklyn, N. Y.
Burt, James, Brooklyn, N. Y.
Burt, James M., Brooklyn, N. Y.
Burroughs, Rev. J. C., Chicago, Ill.
Butcher, Washington, Philadelphia.
Butterfield, Rev. Isaac, Watertown, N. Y.
Byram, Rev. B. P., Amesbury, Mass.
Caldicott, Rev. T. F., D.D., Boston.
Carleton, Rev. George J., Newton Centre, Ms.
Carleton, Mrs. J. T., Newton Centre, Mass.
Carpenter, Rev. Mark, Holyoke, Mass.
Carter, Joseph, Malden, Mass.
Caswell, Prof. Alexis, D.D., Providence.
Caswell, Rev. Lewis E., Boston.
Cauldwell, Ebenezer, New York.
Chace, Prof. George L. Providence.
Challis, Rev. James M., Roadstown, N. J.
Chandler, John H., Bankok, Siam.
Chandler, Mrs. Helen M., Bankok, Siam.
Chaplin, Rev. Jeremiah, West Dedham, Mass.
Chaplin, Rev. Adoniram J., Bennington, Vt.

Charlton, Rev. Frederick, Wilmington, Del. | Dowli
Cheesebrough, Rev. Isaac, Groton, Ct.
Cheney, Rev. David B., Philadelphia. | Drake
Child, Mrs. Sophronia L., Williamsburg, N. Y.
Child, Rev. William C., Framingham, Mass.
Church, Rev. P., D D., New York.
Church, Mrs. Chara E., New York.
Clarke, Rev. Minor G., Indianapolis, Ia. | Eaton
Clapp, Benjamin, Franklindale, N. Y. | Eaton
Coggeshall, Josias, Brooklyn, N. Y. | Eberh
Coggeshall, Mrs. Elisabeth M., Brooklyn, N. Y.
Cogswell, Rev. Wilson, Shakapee, Min.
Colby, Hon. Anthony, New London, N. H.
Colby, Isaac, Concord, N. H.
Cole, Rev. Jirah D., Waukegan, Ill. | Edwa
Colgate, Mrs. Jane, New York. | Eldri
Colgate, Samuel, New York. | Endri
Colgate, Charles C., New York. | Eusti
Colgate, James B., New York.
Colver, Rev. Nathaniel, Cincinnati, O. | Evans
Collins, Rev. Samuel A., Rehoboth, Mass.
Cone, Edward Winfield, New York.
Cone, Spencer Wallace, New York. | Farn
Cones, James, Cincinnati, O. | Farqu
Conklin, William, New York. | Fonda
Cooke, Joseph J., Providence. | Field,
Cookson, Rev. John, Morrisania, N. Y.
Cooper, William, New York. | Fish,
Corwin, Robert G., Lebanon, O. | Fish,
Corwin, Rev. Jason, Darlington, Wis. | Fish.

DIRECTORS FOR LIFE.

Irs. E. Croser, Philadelphia.
lev. Thomas S., Dubuque, Iowa.
Rev. William M., Roxbury, Mass.
Henry, Lynn, Mass.
ev. William, D.D., Albany, N. Y.
mes, Newark, N. J.
. J. G., Grenada, Miss.
Addison, Kilmarnock, Va.
Benjamin, Brooklyn, N. Y.
liam, Providence, R. I.
Rev. William F., Cincinnati.
Standish F., Philadelphia.
Irs. Hannah, Saratoga Springs, N. Y.
John V., Brooklyn, N. Y.
hn H., Tremont, Ill.
Rev. Jesse, Marion, Ala.
. Josiah, Morristown, N. J.
. George, New York.
athaniel, Charlestown, Mass.
Rev. B. F., Manchester, N. H.
Benjamin M., D.D., New York.
Daniel T., Carmel, N. Y.
Elizabeth, Carmel, N. Y.
S. P., Washington, D. C.
uel, South Boston, Mass.
iel, Jr., South Boston, Mass.
iam B., Chemung, Ill.
William, New York.
r. William D., Freehold, N. J.
ev. Edward T., New York.
v. James L., D.D., Newark, N. J.
v. M. G., Brooklyn, N. Y.
Rev. Lewis, Edgarton, Mass.
Rev. Charles J., New York.
amuel W., Philadelphia.
, Rev. V. R., D.D., Rochester, N. Y.
, Hon. Joab, Santa Fe, N. M.
Rev. Leland, Rutland, Vt.
Rev. William G., D.D., Chicago, Ill.
r. William, Boston.
ev. Robert B. C., D.D., Richmond, Va.
rs. Mary Ann M., Richmond, Va.
Rev. James, Galveston, Tex.
arles, Philadelphia.
uel, Providence.
Rev. Hiram, Roxbury, Mass.
n, Rev. William, Bustleton, Pa.
George B., D.D., Springfield, Mass.
r. Silas, Essex, Ct.
Dwight, D.D., Suffield, Ct.
Julia A., Suffield, Ct.
Rev. Henry, D.D., Newport, R. I.
v. Silas C., Bunker Hill, Ill.
illiam T., New York.
uel E., Philadelphia.
William H., Boston.
Rev. Thorndike C., Mellrose, Mass.
vid, Philadelphia.
Rev. John, Newton Centre, Mass.
r. J. B., D.D., Richmond, Va.
Rev. W. D. H., Greenville, Ill.
r. Henry V., Noank, Ct.
r. P. F., New York.
v. John D. E., Worcester, Mass.
. Orrin B., LL.D., New York.
L. W., Philadelphia.

Kempton, Rev. George, New Brunswick, N. J.
Kendrick, Edward E., Albany, N. Y.
Kennard, Rev. J. H., D.D., Philadelphia.
Kendall, Mrs. Betsey, Littleton, Mass.
Kent, Henry P., Suffield, Ct.
Kent, Mrs. Jane S., Suffield, Ct.
Keyes, Rev. Charles B., Westfield, N. Y.
Ladd, Rev. James S., New York.
Larcombe, Richard J., New York.
Latham, Daniel, Groton, Ct.
Latham, Mrs. Delia Ann, Groton, Ct.
Latham, Daniel D., New London, Ct.
Lane, Rev. Benjamin I., Newburyport, Mass.
Lathrop, Rev. Edward, D.D., New York.
Laws, Rev. William, Modesttown, Va.
Lawton, Rev. Joseph A., Erwinton, S. C.
Lea, Sidney Slade, Yanceyville, N. C.
Lee, George F., Philadelphia.
Leighton, Rev. Sam'l S., West Townsend, Mass.
Leonard, Rev. Lewis G., Marietta, Ohio.
Leverett, Rev. William, New Eng. Village, Ms.
Lewis, John G., Boston.
Lewis, Isaac, New York.
Lewis, Mrs. Mary, New York.
Lillie, Rev. James, D.D., Montreal, Canada.
Lincoln, Hon. Heman, Boston.
Lincoln, Rev. B. H., South Framingham, Mass.
Linnard, Hon. J. M., Philadelphia.
Linnard, Mrs. Anna, Philadelphia.
Litchfield, E. B., Brooklyn, N. Y.
Litchfield, E. D., Brooklyn, N. Y.
Locke, Rev. William E., Springfield, N. J.
Loxley, Rev. Benjamin R., Philadelphia.
Loomis, Rev. Ebenezer, Alba, Pa.
Lumsden, D. F., Boston.
Lyeth, Richard J., Hastings, N. Y.
Lyon, Merrick, Providence, R. I.
Mabbet, Jonathan, Dover Plains, N. Y.
McIntosh, Wm. C., Philadelphia.
Maclay, Rev. Archibald, D.D., New York.
Magoon, Rev. E. L., D.D., New York.
Magoon, Mrs. E. L., New York.
Malcolm, Rev. Howard, D.D., Lewisburg, Pa.
Malcolm, Rev. Thomas S., Philadelphia.
Mallary, Rev. C. D., Albany, Ga.
Marble, Joel, Albany, N. Y.
Marchant, Henry, Providence.
Marcley, Mrs. Caroline T., Morrisania, N. Y.
Maple, Thompson, Canton, Ill.
Martin, Runyon W., New York.
Martin, Charles J., New York.
Marshall, Rev. Enos, Pittsford, N. Y.
Massey, Rev. Joseph T., Bellingham, Mass.
Mason, Rev. Alanson P., Chelsea, Mass.
Mason, Rev. David G., Keene, N. H.
Mason, Rev. Jas. O., Greenwich, N. Y.
Mason, Rev. Sumner R., Cambridgeport, Mass.
Masters, William, Providence.
Masters, Mrs. William, Providence.
Mather, Rev. A. P., California.
Merit, Rev. Columbus D., Washburn, Ill.
Merriam, Jonathan, Newton Center, Mass.
Messenger, Rev. Edward C., West Medway, Ms.
Middleditch, Rev. Robert T., Red Bank, N. J.
Milbank, Samuel, Jr., New York.
Milbank, Jeremiah, New York.
Miller, John A., New York.

Miller, Rev. D. Henry, Meriden, Ct.
Mills, Rev. Robert C., Salem, Mass.
Miner, Mrs. Henrietta Wilson, Newark, N. J.
Mitchell, Isaac R., Sandwich Islands.
Moore, Rev. Isaac, Jonesville, Mich.
Morse, Mrs. Sophia A., Sturbridge, Mass.
Morse, Jacob, Sturbridge, Mass.
Morton, Rev. Charles, Corning, N. Y.
Mulford, Rev. Clarence W., Flemington, N. J.
Munn, William H., New York.
Murdock, Rev. J. N., D D., Hartford, Ct.
Murphy, Rev. John C., New York.
Mussy, Rev. Lawson, Pulaski, N. Y.
Neale, Rev. Rollin H., D.D., Boston.
Newell, Asa, Providence.
Newton, Isaac, New York.
Nice, Rev. G. P., Somerville, N. J.
Nichols, Charles H., Boston, Mass.
Nicholas, Joseph O., Newark, N. J.
Norris, William, Newark, N. J.
Northam, Rev. G., Norminy Grove, Va.
Nott, Rev. A., Kingman, New York.
Olcott, Rev. James B., Springfield, Ill.
Packer, Rev. D., Mount Holly, Vt.
Page, Joseph, Philadelphia.
Parker, Rev. J. W., D.D., Newton Center, Ma.
Parker, Rev. Carlton, Wayne, Me.
Parker, Rev. S. S., Southbridge, Mass.

Spencer, William B., Phenix, R. I.
Sproul, Rev. Samuel, Imlaystown. N. J.
Stanwood, Rev. Henry, Kalamazoo, Mich.
Stearns, Rev. Oakman S., Newton Centre, Mass.
Steward, Rev. Ira R., New York.
Stewart, Lispenard, New York.
Stockbridge, Rev. Joseph, Plainfield, N. J.
Stockbridge, Rev. John C., Boston.
Stone, Rev. James R., Providence, R. I.
Stone, Gertrude E. M., Providence, R. I.
Stout, Charles B., New York.
Stout, Richard, New York.
Stow, Rev. Baron, D.D., Boston.
Stow, Rev. Phineas, Boston.
Stowell, Nathaniel, Worcester, Mass.
Stubberts, Rev. William F. S., Malden, Mass.
Swan, Rev. Jabez L., New London, Ct.
Swaim, Rev. Samuel B., West Cambridge, Mass.
Taggart, Rev. Joseph W., New York.
Tanner, James, Pembina, Min. Ter.
Taylor, Rev. J. B., Richmond, Va.
Taylor, Rev. E. E. L., D.D., Brooklyn.
Taylor, Stewart M., New York.
Taylor, Daniel G., New York.
Taylor, Jeremiah B., New York.
Teasdale, Rev. T. C., D.D., Washington, D. C.
Thomas, Mrs. Catharine W., New York.
Thomas, Mrs. Margaret I., New York.
Thomas, Cornelius W., New York.
Thomas, Augustus, New York.
Thompson, Mrs. Huldah E., Troy, N. Y.
Tilton, Rev. J. D., Meredith Village, N. H.
Tingley, Rev. T. C., Holden, Mass.
Tinsley, Rev. Isaac, Charlottesville, Va.
Timmons, John M., Effingham, S. C.
Todd, William W., New York.
Torian, Thomas, Halifax, Va.
Townsend, Palmer, Brooklyn, N. Y.
Tracy, William, New York.
Tracy, Rev. Leonard, Whitehall, N. Y.
Train, Rev. Arthur S., D.D., Haverhill, Mass.
Tryon, Mrs. Louisa J., Houston, Texas.
Tucker, Daniel N., New York.
Tucker, Rev. Anson, Lafayette, Ia.
Tucker, F., Stony Creek, Va.
Tucker, Rev. H. Holcombe, Alexandria, Va.
Tufts, Mrs. Mary, Fitchburg, Mass.
Turner, Peter C., New London, Ct.
Turpin, William H., Augusta, Ga.
Turpin, Mrs. Mary A., Augusta, Ga.
Valentine, David T., New York.
Van Antwerp, Wm. M., Albany, N. Y.
Vanderveer, John Moorestown, N. J.
Verrinder, Rev. William, Jersey City, N. J.
Vogell, Rev. Henry C., Rome, N. Y.
Wager, James, Troy, N. Y.
Wakeman Rev. Levi H., West Woodstock, Ct.
Walthall, Rev. Joseph S., Newbern, N. C.
Wattson, Thomas, Philadelphia.
Wayland, Rev. Francis, D D., Providence.
Wayland, Rev. H. Lincoln, Worcester, Mass.
Webb, Rev. G. S., D.D., New Brunswick, N. J.
Welch, Rev. B. T., D.D., Newtonville, N. Y.
Welsh, Rev. J. C., Providence.
Wheat, Rev. A. C., Philadelphia.
Wheaten, John, Dorset, Vt.
Wheelock, Rev. Alonzo, Elbridge, N. Y.
Wheeler, Rev. Osgood C., Sacramento, Cal.
Whidden, Randall, Calais, Me.
Whittemore, A. F., Essex, Ct.
White, Rev. J. S., West Wrentham, Mass.
White, Rev. Samuel, North Shore, N. Y.
Whitehead, James M., New York.
Whitman, D. C., Newark, N. J.
Whitney, Ezra S., Brooklyn.
Wightman, Rev. Palmer G., East Lyme, Ct.
Wilbur, Asa, Boston.
Wilder, Rev. William, Chester, Pa.
Wildman, Rev. N., Lebanon, Ct.
Wilkins, Rev. Stephen, ——, Ky.
Willard, Rev. F. A., South Danvers, Mass.
Willett, Rev. Charles, Putnam, Ct.
Williams, David S., Fayetteville, N. C.
Williams, Richard P., Essex, Ct.
Williams, Rev. William R., D.D., New York.
Wilson, Francis L., Catskill, N. Y.
Wilson, Daniel M., Newark, N. J.
Wilson, Mrs. Hannah M., Newark, N. J.
Wilson, Rev. Robert J., Elmira, N. Y.
Winegar, Rev. R., Jr., Baldwinsville, N. Y.
Wines, Rev. Wm. H., Boston.
Winterton, William, New York.
Withers, John, Alexandria, D. C.
Witherwax, J. M., Davenport, Iowa.
Woolsey, Rev. J. J., Norwalk, Ct.
Wooster, Rev. Henry, Deep River, Ct.
Wooster, Henry C., Essex, Ct.
Wright, Rev. Thomas G., Westport, N. Y.
Wyckoff, William H., New York.

MEMBERS FOR

BY VIRTUE OF A CONTRIBUTION OF TI

Abbott, Stephen, Chickopee Falls, Mass.
Abbott, Rev. S. G., Bradford, N. H.
Achilles, H. L., Albion, N. Y.
Ackley, Rev. Alvin, Greenport, N. Y.
Adair, William N., Somerville, N. J.
Adams, Miss Priscilla S., New York.
Adams, Mrs. Mary, West Killingly, Ct.
Adams, Rev. S. W., Cleveland, O.
Adams, Rev. R. J., Wallingford, Ct.
Adams, Miss Caroline, New York.
Adams, Albert, Augusta, Ga.
Adams, Joseph H Williamsburg, N. Y.
Adams, Mrs. Mary, Williamsburg, N. Y.
Adams, Jedediah, New York.
Adams, Rev. Sullivan, Shaftsbury, Vt.
Adams, Van Rensselaer, Deckertown, N. J.
Adams, Rev J. N., Croton, N. Y.
Adams, Clark, Greenwich, N. Y.
Adams, Rev. John Quincy, New York.
Adam, Mrs. Carrie E., New York.
Adkins, Isaac K., Newport, Ohio.
[illegible]

Aller, Am

Almond, J

Ambler, M
Ambler, St
Ambler, E
Ambler, M

Ames, Rol

Amsbury,
Amory, Pe
M

Anderson,
Anderson,
Anderson,
Anderson,
Anderson,
[illegible]

Austin, Samuel, Suffield, Ct.
Austin, Cornelius, Rochester, N. Y.
Avery, Mrs. Clara, New York.
Avery, Rev. E. J. Worcester, Mass.
Avery, William D., Providence.
Avery, Rev. D., Tyringham, Mass.
Avery, E. J., Brookline, Mass.
Avery, John, Lebanon, Ct.
Ayars, Benjamin, Greenwich, N. J.
Ayer, Charles B., Preston, Ct.
Ayer, Mrs. Richard, Haverhill, Mass.
Ayers, James C. Plainfield, N. J.
Ayers, Horace, Worcester, Mass.
Ayers, Mrs Mary, New York.
Babcock, Rev. O. W., Gouverneur, N. Y.
Babcock, John N, New Haven, Ct.
Babcock, H. S., Homer, N. Y.
Babcock, Rev. J. J., Jay, N. Y.
Baber, Alfred, Keeseville, N. Y.
Bachelor, Rev. M. Pownell, Vt.
Bacon, Jacob, Boston.
Bacon, Rev. William, Newport, N. J.
Bacon, Rev. Charles L., Trumansburg, N. Y.
Bacon, Mrs. Mary L., Trumansburg, N. Y.
Bacon, Miss Ann Dorchester, Mass.
Bacon, W. A. Ludlow, Vt.
Bacon, Almon, Lyme, Ct.
Bagby, Rev. Richard, Stevensville, Va.
Bagley, S. V., New York.
Bagley, Miss Ellen, Great Falls, N. H.
Bailey, Mrs. S. W., Parham's Store, Va.
Bailey, Timothy, Malden, Mass.
Bailey, Mrs. Sarah E., Metamora, Ill.
Bailey, S. A., Utica, N. Y.
Bailey, Jonathan, Jr., Bentley's Corners, N. Y.
Bailey, Mrs. Caroline, Philadelphia.
Bailey, Rev. L., New London, Ohio.
Baily, Rev. Simon B., Hopkinton, R. I.
Baily, Mrs. Eveline, Hopkinton, R. I.
Baily, Cushing, Boston.
Baillie, John, New York.
Bainbridge, Rev. Samuel M., Penn Yan, N. Y.
Bains, Edward, Philadelphia.
Baisley, George, Bridgeport, Ct.
Baker, Mrs. Betsey, West Dedham, Mass.
Baker, Miss Betsey, West Dedham, Mass.
Baker, Allen, Providence.
Baker, Elisha W., Providence.
Baker, Benjamin F., Brookline, Mass.
Baker, Rev. John H., Brand's Iron Works, R. I.
Baker, Rev. James, Perryville, N. J.
Baker, David, Corning, N. Y.
Baker, Garness E., New York.
Baker, Theodore, Norwalk, Ohio.
Baker, Joseph K., Jr, West Harwich, Mass.
Baker, Rev. Samuel, D.D., Williamsburg, N.Y.
Baker, Mrs. Elizabeth A., Williamsburg, N.Y.
Baker, John R., New York.
Baker, Harriet M., West Dedham, Mass.
Balch, Mrs. Jane, New York.
Baldwin, Rev. George C., D D., Troy, N. Y.
Baldwin, Mrs. Margaret D., Boston.
Baldwin, Rev. Jonathan, Elliston, N. Y.
Baldwin, Jared G., New York.
Baldwin, Mrs. Eliza, New York.
Baldwin, A. T., Brooklyn.
Baldwin, Miss Elizabeth A., New York.
Baldwin, Josephus, Nashua, N. H.
Baldwin, Mrs. Mary Ann, Nashua, N. H.
Baldwin, Mrs. Nancy, Nashua, N. H.
Baldwin, Mrs. Caroline E., Philadelphia.
Baldwin, Mrs. Esther J., Southfield, N. Y.
Balen, Mrs. Ann Maria, New York.
Ball, Rev. John, Dixon, Ill.
Ball, Rev. Mason, North Amherst, Mass.
Ball, Julia M., North Amherst, Mass.
Ball, Sarah E., North Amherst, Mass.
Ballard, Rev. Enos H., Red Mills, N. Y.
Ballard, Mrs. Asenath, Brooklyn.
Ballard, Mrs. Mary Sophia, Brooklyn.
Ballard, Zacheus, Webster, Mass.
Bancroft, Miss. Sarah A., Worcester, Mass.
Bancroft, Henry O., Granville, Mass.
Bancros, Lemuel, Granville, Mass.
Ballou, Alexander, Blackstone, Mass.
Banker, Mrs. Elizabeth, Brooklyn.
Banta, Miss Emily M., New York.
Batchelder, Mrs. Henry, Beverly, Mass.
Barrass, Rev. Thomas, Baptist Town, N. J.
Barrass, Mrs. Mary Ann, Baptist Town, N. J.
Barber, Aaron, Vittoria, C. W.
Barber, Mrs. Elizabeth, Vittoria, C. W.
Barber, Moses, Waterford, C. W.
Barber, Abraham N., Waterford, C. W.
Barber, Rev. Bradford H., Charlestown, N. Y.
Barbour, James S., Cambridge, Mass.
Bardwell, R. B., Shelburne Falls, Mass.
Bardwell, Apollos, Shelburne Falls, Mass.
Bardwell, Jarvis B., Shelburne Falls, Mass.
Bardwell, Edward, Rochester, N. Y.
Bardwell, Mrs. Jane A., Rochester, N. Y.
Bardwell, E. C., Columbus, Ohio.
Barrell, Mrs. Selena, Albion, N. Y.
Barrell, David, Batavia, N. Y.
Barrett, Mrs. Clarinda, Batavia, N. Y.
Barrett, O., Shirley, Mass.
Barker, Rev. J. G., Richmond, Va.
Barker, Mrs. Esther Ann, Poughkeepsie, N. Y.
Barker, Anson J, Taunton, Mass.
Barker, William, Lowell, Mass.
Barnard, Mrs. Eunice H., Sand Lake, N. Y.
Barnard, John, Muscatine, Iowa.
Barnes, John, Union Village, N. Y.
Barnes, Rev. George W., Florence, Neb. Ter.
Barnes, Rev. Wm. A., Chambersburg, Pa.
Barney, William, Albany, N. Y.
Barney, Mrs. Joanna, Seekonk, Mass.
Barnhurst, Joseph, Sr., Francisville, Pa.
Barnum, Ormel G., Gouverneur, N. Y.
Barnum, S Eli, Danbury, Ct.
Barnum, Abel S., Yates, N. Y.
Barrows, Experience, Dorset, Vt.
Bar, Mrs. Sarah A.
Barrows, Mrs. Sarah W., Dorchester, Mass.
Barter, John, Brooklyn, N. Y.
Bartlett, Rev. Daniel, China, Me.
Bartlett, Stephen, Worcester, Mass.
Bartlett, Mrs. Elizabeth J., Deep River, Ct.
Bartolette, John T., Somerville, N. J.
Barringer, Jacob P., Troy, N. Y.

Barry, S. L., Ovid, N. Y.
Barstow, Charles, Boston.
Batchelder, Mrs. Henry, Beverly, Mass.
Bateman, Mrs. Rachel, Dividing Creek, N. J.
Bates, Mrs. Caroline C., New Bedford, Mass.
Bates, Mrs. Joanna, Providence.
Bates, Whitman, Pawtucket, R. I.
Bates, Dennis P., Lowell, Mass.
Bates, Rev. John, Cascade, Iowa.
Bates, Rev. L. C., Madison, N. Y.
Bates, Rev. Ira, Centreville, R. I.
Bates, Lyman, Medina, N. Y.
Bates, Levi D., Providence.
Bates, William B., Bellingham, Mass.
Batey, Rev. John.
Battell, Rev. Allen E., Rockport, Mass.
Battle, Rev. A. J., Murfreesboro', N. C.
Baugh, Dr. J. M., Petersburgh, Va.
Baxter, Thomas, Penn Yan, N. Y.
Baxter, John C., New York.
Baxter, Thomas, Detroit, Mich.
Baxter, William M., New York.
Beagle, Henry, Philadelphia.
Beam, Joseph, Brooklyn.
Beam, Mrs. Louisa, Brooklyn, N. Y.
Beam, David B., Paterson, N. J.
Bean, H. L., Skaneateles, N. Y.
Bean, Benjamin, Olentangy, Ohio.
Bessom, W. D., Nashua, N. H.
Beattie, Rev. W. Q., Bennettsville, N. C.

Benja
Benja
Benne
Benne
Benne
Benne
Bento
Bento
Bern.
Berni
Berlin
Berlin
Berry,
Berry,

Blaisdell, Josiah C., Fall River, Mass.
Blake, Aaron, Chelsea, Mass.
Blake, Jonathan. Brooklyn, N. Y.
Blake, David B., Providence.
Blake, Ezekiel, Chicopee Falls. Mass.
Blake, Frederick. Boston, Mass.
Blanding, Dr. S. Columbia, S. C.
Blackmer, Jirah, Wheatland, N. Y.
Bleecker, Mrs. Caroline C., New York.
Bleecker, Mrs. Jane, New York.
Bleecker, George W., Brooklyn, N. Y.
Blessing, John, Xenia, O.
Bliss, Elijah J., Brooklyn, N. Y.
Bliss, Alanson. Hamilton, N. Y.
Bliss, E. J., Brandon. Vt.
Blodgett, James D., Haverhill, Mass.
Blodgett, Mrs. James D., Haverhill, Mass.
Blodgett, Loring B., Cortlandville, N. Y.
Blood, Isaiah, Ballston Spa, N. Y.
Blood, Cyrus G., Davenport, Iowa.
Blood, A P., Ballston, N. Y.
Bloodgood, James, Springville, N. Y.
Bloomer, Lewis. Ovid, N. Y.
Blunt. Mrs. R., Edenton, N. C.
Bly, Mrs. Lydia, Ticonderoga, N. Y.
Boardman, Thomas, Amesbury, Mass.
Boardman. Rev, George D, Rochester, N. Y.
Bodine, Miss Mary. Hudson, N. Y.
Bogart, Rev. Wm Pittsfield. Mass.
Boker, Hon. David A., Brooklyn, N. Y.
Bolles, James G. Hartford, Ct.
Bolles, Francis A, Niantic, Ct
Boomer, Rev. James C, Chelmsford, Ct.
Boone, Dr. Levi D., Chicago, Ill.
Boone, Mrs. L. D, Chicago, Ill.
Booth, Henry, Greenport, N, Y.
Booth, Rev, John, Fox Lake, Wis.
Bond, Leonard, New York.
Bond, Rev. G. W., Knoxville, Iowa.
Bond, Rev. E. P., Aurora, Ia.
Bond, Rev. Emmons P., New Britain, Ct.
Bond, Mrs. Mary, New Britain, Ct.
Bond, Rev. Phineas, Cornish Flat, N. H.
Bonham, Daniel, Berryville, Va.
Bonney, W. F., Eaton, N. Y.
Borden, Lodowick Fall River, Mass.
Borden, Isaac, Fall River, Mass.
Borden, Charles, Fall River, Mass.
Borden, Joseph. Fall River, Mass.
Borden, Cook Fall River. Mass.
Borland, Chauncey, Iowa City. Iowa.
Bosson, George P., Chelsea, Mass.
Bosson, Benjamin P., Chelsea, Mass.
Bosson, Miss Mary, Chelsea, Mass.
Bostick, Elisha, Bostick's Mills, N. C.
Bostick, Elijah, Bostick's Mills, N. C.
Bostick, Tristam, Bostick Mills, N. C.
Bostick, Benj. R., Robertsville, S. C.
Bostick, Mrs. Jane A., Robertsville, S. C.
Boswell, Davis, Stilesville, Ia.
Bosworth, William M, East Poultney, Vt.
Bosworth. George H., Fall River, Mass.
Bottom, Mrs. Peace, Shaftsbury, Vt.
Bottom, Mrs. Francis S., Shaftsbury, Vt.
Boughton, James, New York.
Bourne, Rev. C. C., Leesville, N. Y.
Boutelle, Miss Sylvia, East Cambridge, Mass.
Bouton, Mrs. Sarah M., New York.
Bowen, John, New York.
Bowen, Henry, Chili Center, New York.
Bowen, David M, Roadstown, N. J.
Bowen, Mrs. Elizabeth, Roadstown, N. J.
Bowen, Rev. Wm., Hancock, Mass.
Bowen, William, New York.
Bowen, Mrs. A. K., Cortlandville, N. Y.
Bowen, Henry A., Natic, R. I.
Bowen, Caleb. Seekonk, Mass.
Bower, Rev. Jacob, Manchester, Ill.
Bowers, Rev. C. M., Clintonville, Mass.
Bowers, Mrs. Anna D., Seekonk, Mass.
Boyakin, Rev. Wm. F., Portland, Oregon.
Boyce, Rev. Peter, Green Point, N. Y.
Boyce, Mrs. Albina, Providence.
Boyd, Rev. Robert, Chicago, Ill.
Boyd, John, Albany, N Y.
Boyden, Addison, South Dedham, Mass.
Boynton, J. M., North Springfield, Vt.
Brabrook, Mrs. Lucy A., Davenport, Iowa.
Brabrook, Alfred, Taunton, Mass.
Brabrook, Joseph A., Lowell, Mass.
Bracket, Prince, Webster, Mass.
Bradish, Levi J., Jamaica Plains, Mass.
Bradford, W. R., Boston.
Bradford, John, Wilmington, Del.
Bradley, Collins, Mt. Vernon. Mich.
Bradley, Mrs. Enoch. Haverhill, Mass.
Bradley, Mrs Elizabeth F., Amesbury, Mass.
Brainerd, Mrs. Samuel, Haverhill, Mass.
Branch, Rev. Nicholas. Westford, Ct.
Branch, Rev. William, Williamsville, N. Y.
Brandt, Rev. Thomas Waukesha, Wis.
Bray, Joseph M., Brooklyn, N. Y.
Brayton, Mrs. Harriet, Phenix, R. I.
Brayton, Mrs Ruth, Phenix, R I
Brayton, Mrs. Betsy, Phenix, R I.
Brayton, Mrs Mary Ann Centerville, R. I.
Brayton, Robert E., Providence, R I.
Brayton, Mrs. Ruth, Providence R I.
Brayton, Miss Emma L, Providence, R. I.
Brayton, Mrs. Lydia Knightsville, R. I.
Brayton, Miss Anna V., Knightsville, R. I.
Brayton, Herbert E., Phenix, R. I.
Brayton, Esther J, Phenix, R I.
Brayton, Miss Mary E., Phenix, R. I.
Brayton, John P., Albany, N Y.
Breckenridge, James C, West Meriden, Ct.
Breed, Rev. Joseph B., Woonsocket, R. I.
Breed, Mrs. Frances A. C., Woonsocket, R. I.
Breed Catharine C., Lynn. Mass.
Brenholtz, Josiah P., Philadelphia.
Brewer, Mrs. Elizabeth, New York.
Bridgens, Miss Mary Ann, Brooklyn, N. Y.
Bridgewood, Mrs. Jane, Williamsburg, N. Y.
Brierly, Rev. Benj., San Francisco, Cal.
Brigham, Sylvester, Cordova, Ill.
Brigham, Rev. J. H., Scipio, N. Y.
Brigham, Francis D, Feltonville, Mass.
Briggs, Arnold, Fairhaven, Vt
Briggs, Rev. Avery, Rock Island. Ill.
Briggs, Mrs. Sarah H., Fitchburg, Mass.
Briggs, Harris, Coventry, N. Y.

Briggs, Mrs. Sylvia Ann, Hinsdale, N H.
Bright, Rev. T., Elkhorn, Wis.
Brinkerhoff, Rev. C., Toulon, Ill.
Brisbane, Rev. Wm. H., Cheviot, Ohio. Brown
Brisbane, Miss Maria, Charleston, S. C. Brown
Briscoe, Sally C., Va. Brown
Britton, Everett, New York.
Brockett, Alvah, Salisbury, N. Y.
Brockett, Asahel, Bristol, Ct. Brown
Broaddus Rev. Wm. F., D.D., Versailles, Ky. Brown
Broaddus, Mrs. Mary A., Versailles, Ky.
Broadhead, Mrs. Ann, New York. Brown
Broadwell, Sherman, Morristown, N. J. Brown
Brockett, D. B., Salisbury, N. Y.
Brocket, Rev. Piermont, Hartford, Ct. Brown
Brockway, Mrs. Elizabeth, Broadalbin, N. Y.
Britton, W. G., Britton's ✕ Roads, N. C.
Brokaw, Mrs. Jane Eliza K., New York.
Bromley, Isaac, Norwich, Ct.
Bromley, J. Breed, Norwich, Ct.
Bromley, Dewey, Norwich, Ct.
Bromley, Rev. Henry, Brooklyn, N. Y. Bruen,
Bromley, Mrs. Jane M., Brooklyn, N. Y.
Bronner, Mrs. Sarah, New York.
Bronson, Rev. Asa, Fall River, Mass. Bruce,
Bronson, Rev. Benj. F., Methuen, Mass. Brush,
Bronson, Mrs. Anna C., Methuen, Mass. Brusle
Bronson, Miss Aydee A., Townsend, Mass. Brusle
Bronson, Rev. A., Williamstown, Mass.
Bronson, Rev. Asa C., Leominster, Mass.

Burke, Samuel M., Galesville, N. Y.
Burnett, Rev. C. C., Worcester, Mass.
Burnett, Mrs. Maria M., Worcester, Mass.
Burnett, Eli S., West Philadelphia.
Burnett, Rev. Hiram, Mt. Pleasant, Iowa.
Burns, William, Philadelphia.
Burr, David M., Gloversville, N. Y.
Burr, Mrs. Emily C., Gloversville, N. Y.
Burr, James H., Gloversville, N. Y.
Burr, Mrs. James, H., Gloversville, N. Y.
Burr, Miss Julia A., Gloversville, N. Y.
Burroughs, James M., Marlton, N. J.
Burroughs, Caleb G., Providence.
Burrows, Rev. David, Chester, Vt.
Burrows, Rev. J. L., D.D., Richmond, Va.
Burrows, Rev. Baxter, Grafton, Vt.
Burrows, Mrs. Lorenzo, Albion, N. Y.
Burrows, John R., Providence.
Burrows, A. B., Brockport, N. Y.
Burt, T. M., Kinderhook, N. Y.
Burt, Mrs. Edwin C., Brooklyn, N. Y.
Burt, Wm. A., Mount Vernon, Mich.
Burt, William, Mount Vernon, Mich.
Burt, Wells, Mount Vernon, Mich.
Burt, Rev. Joseph M., North Tewksbury, Mass.
Burton, Rev. Nathan S., Granville, O.
Burton, Mrs. Sarah J., Granville, O.
Burton, Rev. Hardine, Bryantsville, Ia.
Burwell, Rev. Ira D., Moriah, N. Y.
Butcher, Charles, Freehold, N. J.
Butcher, Mrs. Mary, Philadelphia.
Butler, Rev. John, Lewiston, Me.
Butler Rev. G. W., Hartford, N. Y.
Butler, Mrs. Eusebia C. S., Hartford, N. Y.
Butler, Sylvanus, New Haven, Ct.
Butler, Mrs. Sarah, Lansingburg, N. Y.
Butler, Wm. C., Plainfield, N. J.
Butrick, Mrs. Harriet H, Jay, N. Y.
Butts, Mrs. Sarah A., Washington, D. C.
Butts, Mrs. Elizabeth, Boston.
Butts, Peleg, New Bedford, Mass.
Butts, Nelson W., Albion, N. Y.
Byram, Mrs. Mary H., Amesbury, Mass.
Byron, Wm. H., Milwaukee, Wis.
Cady, Rev. Edgar, Min. Ter.
Cady, Edwin, Danville, Iowa.
Cailhopper, Rev. F. T., Camden, N. J.
Calder, John, Providence.
Calder, Mrs. John L., Providence.
Callender, Rev. N., Laporte, Pa.
Call, Rev. O. B., Weston, N. Y.
Call, John R., Boston.
Campbell, Rev. T. P., East Avon, N. Y.
Campbell, Richard, Trenton, N. J.
Candee, John D., New Haven, Ct.
Capen, Barnabas D., Sharon, Mass.
Capin, Ezekiel, Canton, Mass.
Capron, Miss Rebecca S., Worcester, Mass.
Capron, John, Albany, N. Y.
Capron, Rev. Barton, Preble, N. Y.
Capwell, Albert B., Brooklyn, N. Y.
Capwell, Mrs. Julia A., Brooklyn, N. Y.
Card, Rev. Wm. H., La Crosse, Wis.
Card, Rev. Henry B., Hinsdale, N. Y.
Carleton, Miss Frances, Newton Center, Mass.
Carleton, Miss E. H., Newton Center, Mass.
Carleton, G. R., Newton Center, Mass.
Carleton, Judson, Newton Center, Mass.
Carleton, Howard, Newton Center, Mass.
Carleton, Wm. H., Newton Center, Mass.
Carlton, Stephen, Lowell. Mass.
Carlton, Guy, Methuen, Mass.
Carew, Miss Emma H., New York.
Carew, Mrs. Margaret N., New York.
Carlisle, Charles, New Haven, Ct.
Carroll, S. W., Norwich, Ct.
Carroll, Mrs. Sarah A. S., Washington, N. C.
Carpenter, Daniel T., Pawtucket, R. I.
Carpenter, Mrs Elizabeth, Pawtucket, R. I.
Carpenter, Miss Lydia, Pawtucket, R. I.
Carpenter, Rev. Calvin G., Phelps, N. Y.
Carpenter, Rev. J. M., Jacobstown, N. J.
Carpenter, Mrs. Sarah F., Jacobstown, N. J.
Carpenter, Rev. Burton B, Griggsville, Ill.
Carpenter, James, New York.
Carpenter, J. H., Willimantic, Ct.
Carpenter, Mrs. Martha C., Willimantic, Ct.
Carmer, Henry, Griggsville, Ill.
Carr, Rev. Samuel J., Mansfield, Mass.
Carr, Alexander W., Rowley, Mass.
Carr, Rev. L. C., Moline, Ill.
Carr, Gideon S., Little Mill Creek, O.
Carr, Joseph, Charlestown, Mass.
Carr, J. C., Portsmouth, N. H.
Carr, Thomas T., Newport, R. I.
Carrol, L. W., Norwich, Ct.
Carter, Mrs. Sarah, Richmond, Va.
Carter, Miss Mary, New York.
Carter, Edward, Troy, N. Y.
Carter, Benj. A., Boston.
Caruthers, Rev. Isaac, Heltonsville, Ia.
Caruthers, William, Salisbury, Mass.
Carver, Mrs. Relief E., Nunda, N. Y.
Cary, Theron, Middletown, Ct.
Case, Rev. Zenas, Adam's Basin, N. Y.
Case, Alonzo, Jordan, N. Y.
Case, Miss Julia, Caseville, N. Y.
Castle, Augustus, Alexandria, O.
Castler, Rev. L., Hamilton, N. Y.
Caswell, Mrs. Esther Lois, Providence.
Caswell, Miss Martha S., Charlestown, Mass.
Cathcart, Rev. Wm., Mystic River, Ct.
Cathcart, Mrs. Eliza, Mystic River, Ct.
Catlin, Rev. Samuel T., St. Croix Falls, Wis.
Catlin, Mrs. Julia F., St. Croix Falls, Wis.
Cauldwell, Mrs. Cornelius, New York.
Cauldwell, Miss Elizabeth, New York.
Cauldwell, Henry W., New York.
Cauldwell, Mrs. Susan W., New York.
Cauldwell, Miss Ann Jane, New York.
Cauldwell, Mrs. Ann B., New York.
Cauldwell, Mrs. Ann, Whitesboro', N. Y.
Cavender, A. H., St. Paul, Min.
Cavis, John, Lowell, Mass.
Cell, Rev. Jeremiah, Aurora, Ia.
Chadsey, Jeremiah G., Wickford, R. I.
Chafee, Joseph D., Cortlandville, N. Y.
Chaffee, Asa, Seekonk, Mass.
Chaffin, Rev. Aaron W., Danvers, Mass.
Chaffin, Mrs. Catharine K., Danvers, Mass.

Chalfant, Jacob M., Wilmington, Del.	
Chalfant, Mrs. Sarah R., Wilmington, Del.	
Challis, Mrs. Lydia, Roadstown, N. J.	
Chamberlain, Edward, Boston.	Clark,
Chamberlain, Rev. J. A., South N. Berlin, N.Y.	Clark,
Chamberlin, John C., West Woodstock, Ct.	Clark,
Chambers, Azariah, Marion, N. C.	Clark,
Chambers, Rev. J., McConnelsville, O.	Clark,
Chambers, John, Pemberton, N. J.	Clark,
Champlin, Henry N., Pitcher, N. Y.	Clark,
Champlin, Joseph Jr., Wakefield, R. I.	Clark,
Champlin, Wm., New London, Ct.	Clark,
Chandler, Miss Sarah Flora, Boston.	Clark,
Chandler, Rev. Charles N., Elgin, Ill.	
Chandler, Rev. George C., Oregon City, Ore.,	Clark,
Chandler, Oliver, Boston.	
Chandler, Wm., Nashua, N. H.	Clark,
Chapel, R. S., Brooklyn.	Clark,
Chapin, Henry O., Chickopee Falls, Mass.	Clark,
Chapin, Rev. A., Vinton, Iowa.	Clark,
Chapman, Allen A., Baltimore.	Clark,
Chapman, Rev. John S., Tobehanna, N. Y.	Clark,
Chapman, Wm H., New York.	
Chapman, Henry F., New York.	Clark,
Chapman, Rev. J. M., Lexington, Ill.	Clark,
Chapman, Rhodes B., Providence.	Clark,
Chappel, Charles, New London, Ct.	Clark,
Charlock, Miss Maria, New York.	Clark,
Chase, Rev. Supply, Detroit, Mich.	Clark,
Chase, Daniel, Baltimore.	
Chase, Adeline, Haverhill, Mass.	Clark,

Cole, Rev. L. B., Lowell, Mass.
Cole, Samuel, Clifton Park, N. Y.
Cole, Mrs. Frances L., New York.
Cole, Mrs. Susan, Westerloo, N. Y.
Cole, Mrs. Jemima P., Plainfield, N. J.
Cole, Robert H., Southbridge, Mass.
Coley, Rev James M., Waverley, N. Y.
Colegrove, Belah H., Sardinia, N. Y.
Coleman, James B., Somerville, N. J.
Coleman, Rev. M., Elba, N. Y.
Coleman, Mrs. Sarah, Elba, N. Y.
Coleman, Rev. Zenas, Mt. Vernon, Mich.
Colgate, Cornelius C., New York.
Colgate, Edward, New York.
Colgate, William, New York.
Colgate, Miss Elizabeth, New York.
Colgate, Miss Hannah, New York.
Colgate, Miss Jane, New York.
Colgate, Miss Sarah, New York.
Colgrove, Uri, Johnstown, O.
Collins, Miss Susan, New York.
Collins, Mrs. Ann D., Haverhill, Mass.
Colman, John B., Williamsburgh, N. Y.
Colley, Benj. E., Cambridge, Mass.
Collom, Mrs. Mary E., Mt. Holly, N. J.
Colver, Rev. Charles K., Detroit, Mich.
Coman, Lovian O., Le Roy, N. Y.
Compton, James L., Plainfield, N. J.
Compton, Anthony, New York.
Compton, Mrs. Maria, New York.
Compton, Rev. Robert, Newton, Pa.
Compton, Wm. H., Roadstown, N. J.
Comstock, George R., New London, Ct.
Comstock, Mrs. Ann, New London, Ct.
Comstock C C., New London, Ct.
Comstock Charles F, South Lyme, Ct.
Conant, Mrs. John, Brandon, Vt.
Conant, Rev. Thomas, Scituate, Mass.
Conant, Rev. Thos. J., D.D., Rochester, N. Y.
Conant Levi, Boston, Mass.
Condit, Miss Sarah E., New York.
Cone, Spencer H., Jr, New York.
Cone, Miss Kate E., New York.
Conklin, Mrs. Ann, New York.
Conover, Robert, Petersburg, Ill.
Conover, Cyrenius G., Middletown, N. J.
Conover, Mrs. Rebecca M., Holmdel, N. J.
Conover, Rev. Edward, West Troy, N. Y.
Conrad, Rev. Peter, Delton, Wis.
Converse, Rev. Otis, Grafton, Mass.
Converse, Charles E, Jamaica Plains, Mass.
Converse, Jas. W., Jamaica Plains, Mass.
Converse, Joseph H., Jamaica Plains, Mass.
Cook, Lewis, Southington, Ct
Cook, Mrs. Patience, Keene, N. H.
Cook, Henry G., New York.
Cook, Lewis, Plantsville, Ct.
Cook, Wm. W., Whitehall, N. Y.
Cook, Mrs. Harriet M, New York.
Cook, John, Woodstown, N. J.
Cooke, Rev. Samuel, Newton, N. H.
Cool, Rev. Leona d, Peru, Ia.
Coolidge, Mrs. Caroline G., Brookline, Mass.
Coolidge, William, Bouckville, N. Y.
Coolidge, John, Watertown, Mass.
Coolidge, Mrs. Mary S., Watertown, Mass.
Coolidge, Josiah, Cambridge, Mass.
Coolidge, Austin J., Cambridge, Mass.
Coolidge, Joseph G., Cambridge, Mass.
Coon, Rev. Charles, Mt. Holly, Vt.
Cooper, Edwin, Hoboken, N. J.
Cooper, Rev. Warren, Boylston, Mass.
Cooper Eliphalet, New Haven, Ct.
Cooper, Charles New York.
Copp, Miss Louisa P., Danversport, Mass.
Corbett, O. G., Orange, N. J.
Corbin Pennel, Jr., West Woodstock, Ct.
Corey, Rev. D. G., Utica, N. Y.
Corlies, Britton, Philadelphia.
Corliss, Miss Sarah, Greenwich, N. Y.
Cornelius, Rev. Samuel, Jr., Winona, Min.
Cornell, A. C., Broadalbin, N Y.
Cornell, Thomas, Rondout, N. Y.
Cornell, Wm. M., Plainfield, N. J.
Cornwell Rev. William E., Princeton, N. J.
Corning, Ephraim, Brooklyn, N. Y.
Corthell, Loring, New London, Ct.
Corwin, R. G., Lebanon, Ohio.
Corwin, Rev. David, Cohoes, N. Y.
Corwin, Rev. Ira, South Bend, Ia.
Corwith, Mrs Catharine F., New York.
Cotterell, Mrs Mary, Battenville, N. Y.
Cotterell, Miss Mary, Union Village, N. Y.
Couch, E. P., Nashua, N. H.
Covey, Rev. Walter, Jefferson, N. Y.
Cowan, Mrs. Hannah, New York.
Cowdin, Mrs Aurinda G., Fitchburg, Mass.
Cowles, Mrs. Rebekah, Claremont, N. H.
Cowles, Miss Juliette R, Claremont, N. H.
Cowles, Jas. Albert, Claremont, N. H.
Cox, Rev. Morgan R., New Brunswick, N. J.
Cox, Mrs Mary B, New Brunswick, N. J.
Cox, Miss Anna, New Brunswick, N. J.
Cox, Miss Mary, New York.
Cox, John W., Mt. Holly, N. J.
Cox, Miss Abigail, New York.
Coxey, James, West Philadelphia, Pa.
Coy, Sylvanus B., West Dedham, Mass.
Crabs, Rev. J. D., Claysville, Ia.
Craig, Rev. A. M., Britton's X Roads, N. C.
Craig, Charles A., Bridgeport, Ct.
Craig, Mrs. Charles A., Bridgeport, Ct.
Crain, Miss Harriet M, Westport, N. H.
Craft, Charles, New York.
Crafts, George A., Boston.
Cramer, Geo. W., Troy, N. Y.
Cramer, John, Brooklyn, N. Y.
Cramer, Mrs. Margaret S., Troy, N. Y.
Crane, Richard M., Newark, N. J.
Crane Henry F, Rehoboth, Mass.
Crane, Miss Sarah H., Rehoboth, Mass.
Crane, Rev. Daniel M., N. Hampton, Mass.
Crane, Mrs. Mary L., New York.
Crane, Rev. W. I, Adrian, Mich.
Crane, Millen, Spring Hill, Ct.
Crandall, Henrie, Providence, R. I.
Crandall, Mrs. J. A, Petersburg, N. Y.
Crandall, Rev. Nelson, South Hannibal, N. Y.
Crandall, Rev. B., Springport, N. Y.
Crandall, Mrs. J. Sophronia, Providence, R. I.

Cruser, Holger, Brooklyn, N. Y.
Cudworth, Rev. N., Ludlow, Vt.
Mrs. M. B., Ludlow, Vt.

Day, Horatio E., Hartford, Ct.
Day, Mrs. Fanny D., Haverhill, Mass.
Dayton, Morgan H., New York.
Dean, H. J., Spartanburg, S. C.
Dean, Jirah, Flat Brook, N. Y.
Dean, Rev. Wm. D.D., Wyoming, N. Y.
Dean, Mrs. Maria M., Wyoming, N. Y.
Dean, E. W., Jamaica Plains, Mass.
Dean, Rev. Myron M., Warren, R. I.
Dean, Esther G., North Adams, Mass.
Dean, Rev. B., Auburn, N. Y.
Dean, Rev. R. S., Burlington, N. Y.
Dearborn, Rev. Shelburn, Lowell, Wis.
Dearborn, Mrs. Emeline L., Lowell, Wis.
Deats, Hiram, Cherryville, N. J.
Deats, Mrs. Rebecca, Cherryville, N. J.
Decker, Alfred, New York.
Decker, Mrs. Keziah R., New York.
Decker, Abel, New York.
Decker, Mrs. Abigail, New York.
Decker, Miss Mary A., New York.
Decker, Matthew, Rahway, N. J.
Decker, Rev. Wm. P., Evans Mills, N. Y.
De Golyer, Joseph, Troy, N. Y.
De La Montague, Miss Julia, New York.
Della Torre, Joseph, New York.
Demarest, Miss Jane, New York.
Demarest, Samuel C., Boston.
Demarest, Stephen D., New York.
Deming, Amos, Savoy, Mass.
Deming, Mrs. Eliza J., Washington, D. C.
Deming, Mrs. Abby A., Goffstown, N. H.
Denike, Abraham, New York.
Denike, Mrs. Adeline, New York.
Dennis, Mrs. Elizabeth, New York.
Dennis, Richard, Lowell, Mass.
Dennison, Rev. Charles W., Buffalo, N. Y.
Denison, Rev. Frederick, Norwich, Ct.
Denison, Rev. Erastus, Groton, Ct.
Denison, Mrs. Prudence, Mystic River, Ct.
Denison, Mrs. Silas, Skaneateles, N. Y.
Denison, O. J., Mendota, Ill.
Denison, Mrs. Amelia E., Deep River, Ct.
Denison, Miss Elizabeth, Brooklyn, N. Y.
Denny, John B., Norwalk, Ct.
Depew, Mrs. Sarah M., Saratoga Springs, N. Y.
Detson, Benj., Methuen, Mass.
Devore, Mrs. Catharine, Edgefield, S. C.
Deweese, Samuel, West Philadelphia.
Dewey, Wm. G., Mystic, Ct.
Dewey, Joseph H., Manchester, N. Y.
Dewhurst, Rev. Eli, Hampden Corners, Me.
Dewitt, Rev. J. V., Marion, Iowa.
De Wolf, D. R., Brooklyn, N. Y.
Dexter, Mrs. Jane, Brooklyn, N. Y.
Dickerman, Samuel, Philadelphia.
Dickinson, Mrs. Caroline A., Dayton, Ohio.
Dickinson, Wm. W., Golandsville, Va.
Dimmock, Rev. Anthony V., Baldwinsville, Ms.
Dinsmore, Charles M., Newton, Mass.
Dispeau, Mrs. Lucinda, Grafton, Mass.
Dixson, Rev Joseph A., Evansville, Ia.
Doan, Ezra, Hudson, N. Y.
Doan, Miss Rachel F., Danvers, Mass.
Doby, John, sen., Edgefield, S. C.
Dodge, Mrs. Eliza P., New York.
Dodge, Miss Mary, New York.
Dodge, Rev. Orrin, Brooklyn, N. Y.
Dodge, Prof. Ebenezer, Hamilton, N. Y.
Dodge, Solomon H., Cambridge, Mass.
Dodge, Miss Hannah A., Worcester, Mass.
Dodge, Mrs. Alice C., Hampton Falls, N. H.
Dodge, Mrs. Jane, Brooklyn, N. Y.
Dodge, H. N., McGrawville, N. Y.
Dodson, Rev. Elijah, Woodburn, Ill.
Dole, Mrs. Lydia T., Haverhill, Mass.
Dollim, Horatio, Worcester, Mass.
Doolittle, Mrs. Amanda, New York.
Doolittle, Rev. H. D., Hoosick, N. Y.
Doolittle, Johnson, Wallingford, Ct.
Doolittle, Hart, Pleasant Valley, Ct.
Donald, J. W., East Cambridge, Mass.
Dongan, Mrs. Lucretia, New York.
Dorrance, Samuel B., Brooklyn, N. Y.
Doty, Miss Selima P., Hitchcockville, Ct.
Douglas, Henry, Bethel, N. Y.
Douglas, George, Elgin, Ill.
Douglas, Rev. John L., Burmah.
Dougherty, George T., New York.
Dowlin, Mrs. Maria S., New York.
Dowlin, Miss Mary J., New York.
Dowling, Rev. Thomas, Tolland, Ct.
Dowling, Mrs. Rebecca, New York.
Dowley, John, New York.
Downer, Rev. Wm. B., Peterboro', N. Y.
Downey, Rev. Francis, Whiteby, Pa.
Downs, Mrs. Harriet B., Malden, Mich.
Downs, Mrs. Elizabeth, Hightstown, N. J.
Downs, Calvin, New Haven, Ct.
Dows, Gustavus D., Lowell, Mass.
Doyen, Mrs. A. F., Haverhill, Mass.
Drake, Simeon, Pittsfield, N. H.
Drake, J. C., Panama, N. Y.
Drake, Ephraim, Plainfield, N. J.
Drake, Mrs. A. L., Plainfield, N. Y.
Drake, Rev. George, New Brunswick, N. J.
Draper, Jonathan J. N., Bennington, Vt.
Driver, Rev. Thomas, Lynn, Mass.
Drown, Henry B., Providence.
Dubois, Richard, Canton, N. J.
Dubois, A. E., Randolph, Mass.
Dudley, John L., Baltimore.
Dugan, Wm. T., Brooklyn, N. Y.
Dugan, Mrs. Eliza, Brooklyn, N. Y.
Dugan, Wm. J., Brooklyn, N. Y.
Dugan, Edward J., Brooklyn, N. Y.
Duncan, Hon. James H., Haverhill, Mass.
Duncan, Mrs. James H., Haverhill, Mass.
Duncan, Mrs. Samuel, Haverhill, Mass.
Duncan, Mrs. E. E., Jackson, Va.
Duncan, Rev. H. A., Coosawhatchie, S. C.
Duncan, Rev. Wm. Orleans, Ia.
Duncan, Rev. John, Camden, N. J.
Dunham, Joseph, New Brunswick, N. J.
Dunham, Nelson, New Brunswick, N. J.
Dunklee, Mrs. Eliza A., Boston.
Dunlap, Abraham B., Brooklyn, N. Y.
Dunlap, Mrs. Eliza, Brooklyn, N. Y.
Dunlap, Rev. James, Jacksonville, Ill.
Dunlevy, Hon. A. H., Lebanon, O.

Dunn, Rev. Andrew, Weymouth, Mass.
Dunn, Alexander, New Brunswick, N. J.
Du Pre, Mrs. S. P., Darlington, S. C.
Dupont. Alfred, Wilmington, Del.
Durant, Clark, Albany.
Durbrow, William, New York.
Durbrow. John B., New York.
Durfee, Sanford, Warwick. R. I.
Durfee. Miss Sarah C., Providence.
Durham. Nicholas O., Weart's Corners, N. J.
Durham. Enos, Greenwich, N. Y.
Durkin, John, New York
Durnell. James, Philadelphia.
Duryea, Levi, New York.
Duryea. Mrs. Sarah. New York.
Dusenbury, Rev. Francisco, Etna, N. Y.
Duvall, Mrs. J., Mitchell's, Va.
Dwelle, Alphonso. Union Village, N. Y.
Dwelle, Mrs Alphonso, Union Village, N. Y.
Dye, Rev. Daniel, Three Mile Bay, N. Y.
Dye, Rev. Enoch P., North Brookfield, N. Y.
Dye, 2d Samuel, Marietta, Ohio.
Dyer, Miss Eliza J., Brooklyn, N. Y.
Dyer, Ransom B., New Haven, Ct.
Dyer, Ezra C., Cambridge, Mass.
Dyer, Mrs. Louisa C., Providence.
Eastman Lycurgus, Griggsville, Ill.
Eastman, Rev. Samuel, Burlington, Wis.
Earl, Rev. Samuel H., New York.
Earl, Mrs. George C., Providence.
Earl, Miss Julia, Providence.

hn B., Malden, Mass.
F., Romulus, N. Y.
Isaac, Jr., Fairport, N. Y.
tephen, M.D., Morristown, N. J.
ewis, McDonough, N. Y.
half, N. C.
Hon. Joseph D., Fairfax, Vt.
Dr. James H., Fairfax, Vt.
Rev. O. D., Colesburg, Iowa.
W., Fleming, N. Y.
I. D., Albion, N. Y.
Mary Louisa, Hastings, N. Y.
David, Trumansburg, N. Y.
ac, Watertown, Mass.
s. Sarah A., Watertown, Mass.
Susan P., Jackson, Va.
Charles, Athol, Mass.
r. Daniel, Somerville, Mass.
William N., Belchertown, Mass.
am, Albany, N. Y.
Henrietta, Grand Ligne, C. E.
nin, Salem, Mass.
Hertford, N. C.
or, Hertford, N. C.
Mary, Hertford, N. C.
George D., Granville, Mass.
s. E. D., Moorestown, N. J.
ard, Wallingford, Ct.
r. George, Harrell's Store, N. C.
en, Wilmington, N. C.
L., Newport, Ohio.
n M., New York.
ss Mary Ann, New York.
Hannah L., New York.
Wilson, N. Y.
uel M., Columbia, Ohio.
Isaac, Columbia, Ohio.
n M., Columbia, Ohio.
liam, Columbia, Ohio.
W., Gillisonville, S. C.
nas F., Brooklyn, N. Y.
Thomas F., Brooklyn, N. Y.
nas S., Hoboken, N. Y.
Lavina F., Taunton, Mass.
les H., Taunton, Mass.
ge A., Taunton, Mass.
Ann M., Taunton, Mass.
Hannah E., Taunton, Mass.
T., Taunton, Mass.
ly C., Taunton, Mass.
ine B., Taunton, Mass.
Elizabeth H., Providence.
Elsie M., Westport, N. H.
Moses, Flat Brook, N. Y.
ss Helen J., Great Falls, N. H.
James, Charlottesville, Va.
Margaret W., Charlottesville, Va.
Catharine, Pawtucket, R. I.
liam, East Poultney, Vt.
Nelson, Battle Creek, Mich.
s Sarah A., Red Oak Grove, Va.
rge W., New York.
Joel W., Geneva, Wis.
A., Webster, Mass.
, Pitcher, N. Y.

Fish, Rev. Elisha P., Haddam, Ct.
Fish, Frederick E., Providence, R. I.
Fishback, Mrs. Sophia, Jeffersonton, Va.
Fisher, Mrs. Ann L., New York.
Fisher, Rev. Abiel, Manchaug, Mass.
Fisher, Rev. Ezra, Washington Butte, Oregon.
Fisher, Rev. Otis, Mt. Palatine, Ill.
Fisher, Isaac, West Townsend, Vt.
Fisher, Joseph, Adamsville, Ohio.
Fisk, Willard, New York.
Fitch, Dr. William, Stamford, Ct.
Fitzgerald, Miss Joanna, New York.
Fithian, Samuel C., Greenwich, N. J.
Fitz, William, Worcester, Mass.
Flanagan, John, Philadelphia.
Flanders, Rev. Charles W., Concord, N. H.
Flanders, Mrs. M. H. L., Concord, N. H.
Flanders, Timothy C., Haverhill, Mass.
Flanders, Helvin, Haverhill, Mass.
Flanders, George S., Brooklyn, N. Y.
Flanders, I. M., Nashua, N. H.
Fleet, James R., Brewington, Va.
Fleet, Dr. B., King and Queen C. H., Va.
Fleischman, Rev. Konrad A., Philadelphia.
Fletcher, Rev. C., Tewksbury, Mass.
Fletcher, Rev. Simon, Sandy Hill, N. Y.
Fletcher, Rev. Leonard, New Orleans.
Fletcher, Rev. Horace, Townshend, Vt.
Fletcher, Mrs. Harriet A., Townshend, Vt.
Fletcher, Mrs. Mary, Southington, Ct.
Fletcher, Henry J., New York.
Fletcher, Mrs. Sarah A., Saratoga Springs, N. Y.
Fletcher, Hezekiah, Minneapolis, Min. Ter.
Flinn, Mrs. E. A. E., Darlington, S. C.
Flinn, James W., Brooklyn, N. Y.
Flint, Brayton, Novi, Mich.
Flint, Mrs. Mary C., Novi, Mich.
Flint, Lorin, Novi, Mich.
Flower, Amelia, L., Brooklyn.
Fogg, Rev. Samuel, Me.
Foland, H. H., Leesville, N. Y.
Fole, Thomas W., Providence.
Folwell, Job W., Defiance, Ohio.
Foote, Mrs. Euphemia, Tonica, Ill.
Foote, Jared, New Haven, Ct.
Forbes, George W., Bridgeport, Ct.
Forbes, Gustavus, Boston.
Forbes, Rev. M., Middlesex, N. Y.
Forbush, Rev. Jonathan E., S. Danvers, Mass.
Forby, Wm. F., Brooklyn.
Force, Lyman, Alta, N. Y.
Ford, Isaac, Philadelphia.
Ford, Mrs. H., Philadelphia.
Ford, Henry Clay, Philadelphia.
Ford, Mrs. Amanda, Philadelphia.
Ford, Miss Hannah Adelia, Philadelphia.
Ford, Mrs. Mary, Harvey's Store, Va.
Foreman, Miss Mary E., Hightstown, N. J.
Foreman, Samuel B., Wilmington, Del.
Forrestor, Mrs. Elenora, Williamsburg, N. Y.
Forristall, Mrs. Lucy, Boston.
Forrell, David, Stockholm, Sweden.
Foskett, Rev. Horace B., Cordaville, Mass.
Foster, John W., Leesville, Ia.
Foster, William, West Dedham, Mass.

oster, Mrs. Sarah K., Evansville, Ia.
oster, Rev. J. C., Beverly, Mass.
oster, Mrs. Abby A., Beverly, Mass.
oster, Mrs. Martha, Cambridge, Mass.
Foster, Joseph, Sen., Salem, N. J.
Foster, Mrs. Susan S., Keene, N. H.
Forsyth, Miss Sarah S., Albany, N. Y.
Forsyth, Mrs. Sarah, Albany, N. Y.
Forsyth, Miss Emily H., Albany, N. Y.
Forsyth, Russel, Jr., Albany, N. Y.
Fortune, John, Newport, N. Y.
Fowle, Mrs. Lucy, Boston.
Fowler, Gamaliel, Suffield, Ct.
Fox, Rev. Norman, Schenectady, N. Y.
Fox, Rev. Charles, A., Waverly, Pa.
Fox, Mrs. Julia A., Waverly, Pa.
Fox, Albert R., Sand Lake, N. Y.
Fox, Mrs. Mary A., Sand Lake, N. Y.
Fox, Charles, New York.
Fox, Miss Ann Eliza, New York.
Frank, Miss Amy, Smithfield, Pa.
Frasee, Ezra, Rahway, N. J.
Frasee, Mrs. Mary, Rahway, N. J.
Francis, Robert, Newington, Ct.
Francis, Mrs. Lydia D., Newington, Ct.
Francis, Norman, New York.
Francis, Charles King, New York.
Francis, James, Pittsfield, Mass.
Frayzer, Rev. Herndon, Twymann's, Va.
Fr... Daniel J., Salem, N. Y.
... York.

Fuller, Rev. Edward
Fullerton, Noah, S
Fulton, Rev. John
Fulton, Miss Harr
Ferguson, Rev. S.
Furman, Rev. Ric
Fyfe, Rev. Robert
Fyfe, Mrs. Rebec
Gage, William W
Gage, Rev. David
Gage, G. W., M
Gage, Lewis, M
Gage, A., Meth
Gage, Rev. Leo
Gale, Jonas R.
Gale, Rev. Am
Gale, Rev. Sol
Gale, Rev. E.
Galusha, Tru
Gammell, A.
Gardiner, Ri
M
Gardner, Jo
Gardner,
Gardner, Re
Gardner, F
Gardner, M
Garfield, R
Garnett, D
Garnett, T
Garrett, I
Garnsey,
...

Gill, Miss Mary, Pottsville, Pa.
Gill, Miss Mary Ann, Philadelphia.
Gillette, Mrs. Hannah J., New York.
Gillett, Asahel, Rose, N. Y.
Gillett, Nehemiah, Danbury, Ct.
Gillet, Simeon S. Davenport, Iowa.
Gillman, Miss Ellen W., Roadstown, N. J.
Gilman, George H., New York.
Gilman, David, Roadstown, N. J.
Gilman, Mrs. John, Newburyport, Mass.
Giles, Alfred E. Boston.
Gillpatrick, Rev. James, Topeka, K. T.
Girdwood, Mrs. Mary, New Bedford, Mass.
Gladding, John H., Providence.
Gladding, Mrs. Lydia M., Providence.
Glass, George W., Honeoye Falls, N. Y.
Gleason, Andrew, Barre, Mass.
Glover, Charles S., New York.
Glover, H. K. Cambridgeport, Mass.
Goadby, Rev. John, Poultney, Vt.
Goddard, Jabez, York, N. Y.
Goddard, Mrs. Elizabeth, York, N. Y.
Goddard, Benjamin, Worcester, Mass.
Godding, Mrs. Lucina, East Burke, N. H.
Going, Mrs. Nancy B., Greenville, Ohio.
Going, Rev. Ezra, Greenville, Ohio.
Going, J., Aurora, N. Y.
Godfrey, Edward J., New York.
Godfrey, Mrs. Anna, Brooklyn, N. Y.
Godfry, Abel Bennett, N. Y.
Goldthwait, Nathan, Worcester, Mass.
Goldthwait, Mrs. Anna, Newport, N. H.
Goldy, John, Imlaystown, N. J.
Goldy, Mrs. Emily, Imlaystown, N. J.
Gooch, Mrs. Hannah, Cambridge, Mass.
Gooch, Mrs. Sarah J., Cambridge, Mass.
Goodell, Asab, West Woodstock, Ct.
Goodhue, Ann C., New Boston, N. H.
Goodnow, Rev. M. J. Jacksonville, Ill.
Goodnough, Levi, Sudbury, Mass.
Goodrich, Nathan F., Meriden, Ct.
Goodwin, Charles T., New York.
Goodwin, Mrs. Emily G., New York.
Goodwin, Rev. Thomas, Pemberton, N. J.
Goodno, Rev. I. R., Campton, N. H.
Goodno, Rev. W. S., Bordentown, N. J.
Goodnow, Joseph, Charlestown, Mass.
Goodnow, Rev. A. W. Stamford, Vt.
Gordon, Mrs. Elizabeth, Imlaystown, N. J.
Gordon, Abram, New London, Ct.
Gorham, Mrs. Julia, New Haven, Ct.
Gorman, Rev. Samuel, Laguna, N. M.
Gorman, Miss Mary, Laguna, N. M.
Gould, Joseph, Wilmington, Del.
Gould, Augustus A., M.D., Boston.
Goss, Mrs. Frances M., New York.
Gove, G. B. R., Fort Covington, N. Y.
Gowdey, David, Providence.
Grafton, Rev. B. C. Cambridge, Mass.
Granger, James N. Jr., Providence.
Granger, Mrs. Ann B., Providence.
Granger, Rev. Abraham H., Providence.
Grafts, George A., Boston, Mass.
Grafton, Miss Frances, Brooklyn, N. Y.
Graham, Mrs. Susan W., Hillsboro', N. C.
Graham, James C., Jerseyville, Ill.
Grant, Rev. Daniel H., Stephentown, N. Y.
Grant, Rev. Stillman B., New Haven, Ct.
Grant, Mrs. Mary S., New Haven, Ct.
Grant, Rev. William Whitehall, N. Y.
Grant, Alexander, Providence.
Grant, Preston, Pawtucket, R. I.
Grant, O. B., Stonington, Ct.
Graves, Rev. J. M., Brighton, Mass.
Graves, C., Brown's Store, N. C.
Graves, Rev. Charles, Whitesboro', N. Y.
Graves, Rev. Samuel, Kalamazoo, Mich.
Graves, William H., Brooklyn, N. Y.
Graves, Rev. A. P., Truxton, N. Y.
Gray, Martin E., Willoughby, Ohio.
Gray, Charles F. H., Pittsgrove, N. J.
Gray, William E., New York.
Gray, Mrs. Susan, Brooklyn, N. Y.
Gray, Theodore H., New York.
Greaves, Joseph, Brooklyn, N. Y.
Greene, Mrs. Lydia B., New Bedford, Mass.
Greene, William C., Providence, R. I.
Greene, Mrs. Catharine, Albany, N. Y.
Green, Russell, Providence.
Green, David C., Providence.
Green, Arnold, Providence.
Green, Miss Frances Mary, Providence.
Green, Mrs. Mary, New York.
Green, Rev. John, Chester Village, Mass.
Green, Rev. Charles H., West Townsend, Vt.
Green, Rev. Jonathan R., Derby Vt.
Green, Spencer, Rutland, Vt.
Green, Ralph, Three Rivers, Mass.
Green, Rev. Thomas H., Springport, N. Y.
Green, Miss Fanny, Saratoga Springs, N. Y.
Green, Rev. James W., Albany, N. Y.
Green, John A., New York.
Greenleaf, Rev. Calvin, Griggsville, Ill.
Greenleaf, Amos C., New York.
Greenleaf, John, Cambridge, Mass.
Greenleaf, Mrs. Elizabeth H., Cambridge, Mass.
Greenwood, Simeon A. Worcester, Mass.
Greenwood, Mrs. Martha T., New London, N. H.
Greenwood, Walter, Templeton, Mass.
Grenell, Mrs. Eliza, Port Jarvis, N. Y.
Grenell, Mrs. C. Amelia, Middletown, N. Y.
Grenell, Rufus M., Rock Island, Ill.
Gregg, Wm. Henry, Wilmington, Del.
Gregory, Miss Clarissa, New York.
Gregory, Rev. S., Lisbon N. Y.
Gregory, Uriah, Weston, Mass.
Gregory, Rev. Truman, Lee, Ill.
Griffin, Rev. Charles, Wilmington, Del.
Griffin, Nathaniel L. Edgefield, S. C.
Griffin, Edwin, New York.
Griffin, James T., Rochester, N. Y.
Griffin, Reuben P., Boston, Mass.
Griffis, Rev. P., Lodi Center, N. Y.
Griffith, Rev. B., Philadelphia.
Griffiths, A. W., M. D., Philadelphia.
Griffiths, John J., New York.
Griggs, Samuel, Rutland, Vt.
Griggs, Mrs. Abigail S., Rutland, Vt.
Griggs, David R., Brookline, Mass.
Griggs, Seth D., Belchertown, Mass.
Griggs, J. W., Boston.
Grimley, Rev. Joseph L., Unionville, N. Y.

Grimshaw, Miss Martha, Arcadia, N. Y.
Grinnell, Mrs. Mary B., New Bedford, Mass.
Griswold, Harry, Racine, Wis.
Griswold, Aaron,——N. Y.
Grose, Rev. Henry L., Galway, N. Y.
Gross, Rev. Alva, Brimfield, Ill.
Groat, Thomas J., New York.
Groat, Edward, New York.
Grover, Joseph, Elmira, N. Y.
Grow, Rev. James, Thompson, Ct.
Grummon, William, Newark, N. J.
Guild, Rev. J. Ellis, Newton, Iowa.
Guild, Mrs. Julia A., East Thompson, Ct.
Guild, George M., Boston
Guild, Reuben A., Providence.
Gunn, Rev. Elihu, Keokuk, Iowa.
Gunn, George, New Haven, Ct.
Gunnison, Rev. George W., Erie, Pa.
Gurney, Mrs. Martha, Boston.
Gurney, Mrs. C. J., Woodstock, Ill.
Gurr, Rev. C. G., Great Falls, N. H.
Guy, Rev. A., Middletown, O.
Gwathney, Mrs. E. T., Aylette, Va.
Hadaway, John T., Chelsea, Mass.
Haddock, Henry, Lynn, Mass.
Hadley, Elias H., Lowell, Mass.
Hadley, Moses, Boston.
Haff, Rev. H. H., East Schuyler, Mass.
Hagan, John, Newburgh, N. Y.
Hagar, William, Jr., Brooklyn, N. Y.

Hand
Hanl
Ham
Hans
Hap
Hark
Harlo
Harm
Harm
Harpe
Harri
Harri
Harri
Harri
Harri
Harri
Harri
Harri
Harri

ray, John, Fall River, Mass.
ray, Luther B., Suffield, Ct.
ay, Miss Mary, New York.
ay, Charles F., Boston.
ay, Mrs. Temperance, Boston.
uel, Orange, N. J.
ohn, Orange, N. J.
Irs. Sophia, New York.
liss Annie Isabella, Morristown, N. J.
rout, Rev. J. B., Fall River, Mass.
Caleb, Penn Yan, N. Y.
, Robert M., Norwich, Ct.
, Abraham, Freehold, N. J.
od, John, New York.
od, Mrs. Joanna, New York.
d, Miss Mary Ann, New York.
Rev. Josiah, New Sharon, Me.
Isaac, Shelburne Falls, Mass.
Mrs. El'za H., North Bennington, Vt.
, Mrs. Rebecca, New York.
, D. F., Bristol, Ct.
, Mrs. Jane P., Utica, N. Y.
lexander, Greenwich, N. Y.
, Rev. Lucien, Saxton's River, Vt.
, Mrs. Caroline S., Saxton's River, Vt.
, John, Middlefield, N. Y.
Seth, Jr., Cromwell, Ct.
John P., New York.
rst, Rev. L. W., Ballston Spa, N. Y.
, Mrs. A. B., Va.
, Rev. Hiram, Preston Hollow, N. Y.
, Rev. Dudley C., Boston.
, Mrs. L. M., Norwich, N. Y.
Seth, Colchester, Ct.
Mrs. Emily N., Throopsville, N. Y.
Rev. Henry C., Throopsville, N. Y.
d, Samuel, Essex, Ct.
Rev. Albert, East Washington, N. H.
Ebenezer, Sennett, N. Y.
Mrs. Amia, Sennett, N. Y.
P. W., Sennett, N. Y.
Rev. Amasa, Adams Village, N. Y.
Morgan, Greenwich, N. Y.
Moses, Flemington, N. J.
, William, Orange, N. J.
, Mrs. C. F., Manchester, N. H.
, Daniel, Penn Yan, N. Y.
n, Rev. James, Stamford, Ct.
n, Miss Henrietta, New York.
n, Mrs. Anna S. Q., New York.
k, Rev. Joel, East Smithfield, Pa.
k, John M., New Haven, Ct.
hem, Rev. G. F., Towner's Station, N. Y.
, James W., Stamford, Ct.
, Mrs. James W., Stamford, Ct.
Rev. Foster, Tyringham, Mass.
ev. Edwin B., Hereford, Md.
t, Mrs. Agnes D., Marlboro', N. J.
ge, Jason, Moorestown, N. J.
k, Mrs. M. E., Beverley, Mass.
gton, Chester, Clifton Park, N. Y.
Miss Isabella, Williamsburgh, N. Y.
Thomas F., Rochester, N. Y.
William S., Rochester, N. Y.
, Rev. Nathaniel, Westboro', Mass.

Heustis, Mrs. Ann, New Brunswick, N. J.
Hewit, Edmund, Galway, N. Y.
Hewitt, Chas. E., New London, Ct.
Hewitt, Austin D., Uncasville, Ct.
Heywood, Ellen, Jaffrey, N. H.
Hick, Miss Henrietta P., New York.
Hickman, Mrs. E., New Albany, Ia.
Hicks, Mrs. Mary Ann, Norwich, N. Y.
Hickok, Austin, Jay, N. Y.
Hide, Mrs. Fanny, Westerly, R. I.
Higbie, Alanson, Penfield, N. Y.
Higgins, N. L., Elmira, N. Y.
Hiler, Thomas G., Jr., Boston.
Hill, Mrs. Harriet D., New York.
Hill, Miss Harriet S., New York.
Hill, Mrs. Mary, Miller's, Va.
Hill, David Jayne, Carmel, N. Y.
Hill, Mrs. Rebecca, Essex, Ct.
Hill, Rev. William, Kane, Ill.
Hill, Samuel P., Charlestown, Mass.
Hill, Amos, Jr., West Cambridge, Mass.
Hill, Rev. I. N., Bridgeport, Ct.
Hill, Leander J., Brockport, N. Y.
Hill, Henry S., East Cambridge, Mass.
Hill, Mrs. Eleanor, New York.
Hill, Rev. Thomas, Paris, Ia.
Hill, Walter E., Boston.
Hill, Ira, Lower Newport, Ohio.
Hill, Rev. Levi L., Hudson, N. Y.
Hill, Rev. L. D., Turner, Me.
Hillman, Mrs. Catharine, New York.
Hillman, Samuel T., New York.
Hillman, Mrs. Annes, New York.
Hills, Mrs. Deborah, Haverhill, Mass.
Hine, Simmons, New Haven, Ct.
Hinton, A. G., Pittsborough, N. C.
Hires, Mrs. Catharine, Freehold, N. J.
Hires, Rev. Allen J., Jersey Shore, Pa.
Hiscox, Mrs. C. O., New York.
Hitchcocks, Peresh, Suffield, Ct.
Hitchcox, Sheldon, Suffield, Ct.
Hixon, Charles D., Sharon, Mass.
Hoar, Lewis, Warren, R. I.
Hoar, John R., Warren, R. I.
Hoard, Samuel, Chicago, Ill.
Hobart, James, Westford, Vt.
Hobart, Washington, Boston.
Hodge, Mrs. Sophronia F., Newark, N. J.
Hodge, Mrs. Harriet L., Brooklyn, N. Y.
Hodges, Rev. J., Jr., Cambridge, Mass.
Hoff, John, Baptist Town, N. J.
Hoff, Jeremiah, Baptist Town, N. J.
Hoffman, Joseph H., Leverington, Pa.
Hogan, Miss Ellen, Williamsburgh, N. Y.
Holbrook, Chas. F., Worcester, Mass.
Holbrook, Samuel F., Boston.
Holcombe, Thomas, Savannah, Ga.
Holland, Lucretia E., Boston.
Holland, Joab, Townshend, Vt.
Holmes, Samuel C., New York.
Holmes, Mrs. Comfort, New York.
Holmes, Rev. Lewis, Edgartown, Mass.
Holmes, Mrs. Sarah, Holmdel, N. J.
Holman, Rev. Thomas, West Woodstock, Ct.
Holman, Rev. J. H., New York.

Oregon.

yd, J. Manning, Providence.
y, Mrs. Deborah R., Bedford, N. Y.
olt, John M., Worcester, Mass.
Holt, Cabel, Sharon, Vt.
Homes, Rev. Martin W., Franklin, O.
Homes, Mrs. Mary P., Phelps, N. Y.
Honeter, William, Ostrander, Ohio.
Hood, William, Danversport, Mass.
Hooper, Rev. Wm., Murfreesboro', N. C.
Hooper, Rev. Noah, Newburyport, Mass.
Hooper, Mrs. Lucy W., Newburyport, Mass.
Hope, Mrs. Amelia, Brooklyn, N Y.
Hope, Rev. James M., Cat-kill, N. Y.
Hopkins, John, Bucksport, Me.
Hopkins, Ira D., Utica, N. Y.
Hopkins, William A., Providence.
Hopkins, Miss Mary E., Providence.
Hopkins, Mrs. Hannah, Pascoag, R. I.
Hopley, John, Woburn, Mass.
Hopper, Rev. Audrew, New Providence, N. J.
Hopper, Mrs. Margaret, New Providence, N. J.
Hopper, Rev. A. M., Charlestown, Mass.
Hopper, Miss Catharine, Poughkeepsie, N. Y.
Horn, John, New York.
Hornish, Joseph H., Elizabeth, Pa.
Horr, George E., Boston.
Horr, Miss Anne, Gouverneur, N. Y.
Horton, Rev. Josephus W., Taunton, Mass.
Horton, Mrs. Anna A., Taunton, Mass.
Horton, Danforth, Fall River, Mass.
Horton, J. W., Newton, Mass.
Hosken, Rev. Charles, H. London, England.
Hotchkiss, Alfred, Plantsville, Ct.
Hotchkiss, Norman, Southington, Ct.
Hough, Clement, Lebanon, N. H.
Hough, Alanson H. Essex, Ct.
Hough, Walter, Almont, Mich.
Hough, James, Almont Mich.
Hough, Rev. Samuel, Pike, N. Y.
Hough, Mrs. Elmira L. H., Pike, N. Y.
Hough, Mrs. Ellen T., Elba, N. Y.
Houghton, C. W, Williamsburgh, N. Y.
Houghton, J., Milton, Mass.
Houghton, Rev. G. W., New Hackensack, N.Y.
House, Francis L., Mason, N. H.
Houston, A., Elmira, N. Y.
Hovey, Rev. Alvah, Newton Center, Mass.
Hovey, Wm. B., Cambridge, Mass.
How, Mrs. Myra, Haverhill, Mass.
How, Calvin F., Brooklyn, N. Y.
Howard, Rev. Johnson, Dover, N. Y.
Howard, Mrs. Lucy M., Rutland, Vt.
Howard, Mrs. Birsha S., Townshend, Vt.
Howard, Levi, Chelmsford, Mass.
Howarth, Mrs. Helen, Salisbury, Mass.
Howe, J. S. Methuen, Mass.
Howe, Christopher, Methuen, Mass.
Howe, Elizabeth D., Lynn, Mass.
Howe, Phineas, Newton Center, Mass.
Howe, John W., Holden, Mass.
Howell, James, Trenton, N. J.
Howell, David, Southport, N. Y.
Howes, Samuel C., Chatham, Mass.
Howland, Emeline D, New Bedford, Mass.
Hoyt, Miss Harriet E., Brooklyn, N. Y.
Hoyt, Mrs. Julia A., Brooklyn, N. Y.
Hoyt, L. D., Brooklyn, N. Y.
Hoyt, Rev. J. M, Cleveland, Ohio.
Hubatcheck, Joseph, New York.
Hubbard, Mrs. Mary R., Deep River, Ct.
Hubbard, Rev. W. C., Chittenango, N. Y.
Hubbell, Alrich, Utica, N. Y.
Hubbell, Rev. S., Urbana, N. Y.
Hudgens, Mrs. Rebecca Y., Hampton, Va.
Hughson, Levi P., Pulaski, N. Y.
Huling, Miss Frances, Saratoga Springs, N. Y
Hull, Mrs. Maria, New York.
Hull, Charles, Danbury, Ct.
Hulse, Smith, Dundee, N. Y.
Humphrey, Mrs. Cordelia R, Geneva, Ill.
Hungerford, Levi, Cordova, Ill.
Hunt, Rev. John, Hollis, N. H.
Hunt, Mrs. N., Sharon, Ct.
Hunt, Miss Eliza, New York.
Hunt, John, Boston, Mass.
Hunt, Richard, New York.
Hunt, Edward A., New Haven, Ct.
Hunter, William, Boston.
Hunter, Miss Elizabeth Jane, New York.
Huntley, Rev. George W., Wellsville, N. Y.
Huntington, Rev. Jay, North Bennington, Vt
Huntington, Mrs. Philip, Haverhill, Mass.
Huntington, John H., Troy, N. Y.
Huntington, Myron, Shaftsbury, Vt.
Hurlburt, Joel, Darien Depot, Ct.
Hurd, Daniel, Chicago, Ill.
Hurd, Orville, New York
Hurton, Miss Ann M., New York.
Husted, Daniel, Bridgeton, N. J.
Husted, Isaac B, Bridgeton, N. J.
Husted, Rev. W. H., Sinclearsville, N. Y.
Hutchings, Charles H., New York.
Hutchinson, Rev. Elisha, Brooklyn, N. Y.
Hutchinson, Mrs. E., Brooklyn, N. Y.
Hutchinson, Mrs. Rebecca, Brooklyn, N. Y.
Hyatt, Mrs. Mary S., Brooklyn, N. Y.
Hyer, Mrs. Rebecca, New York.
Ide, Rev. John, Potsdam, N. Y.
Ingalls, N. T., Belvidere, Ill.
Ingalls, Mrs. Sarah L., Belvidere, Ill.
Ingalls, Charles, Methuen, Mass.
Ingals, Mrs. Sarah H., Sublette, Ill.
Ingerson, Irad S., Woburn, Mass.
Inman, Rev. Thomas E., Salem, Ohio.
Iveson, Mrs. Pamelia C., Lynn, Mass.
Irish, Peter D., New London, Ct.
Irish, Mrs. Sarah P., New London, Ct.
Irish, William O., New London, Ct.
Irish, Miss Sarah E., New London, Ct.
Irons, Rev. Arah, Delanti, N. Y.
Ivens, Mrs. Ann, Imlaystown, N. J.
Ivens, Miss Helena R., Imlaystown, N. J.
Ivers, Miss Mary, New York.
Ives, Mrs. Hope, Providence.
Ives, Eli, Meriden, Ct.
Ives, William J., Meriden, Ct.
Ives, John, Meriden, Ct.
Ives, Abram, Holyoke, Mass.
Jackson, Henry, Croton, N. Y.

Jackson, Mrs. M. T., Newport, R. I.
Jackson, Mrs. Jerusha A., Chelsea, Mass.
Jackson, Daniel, Westford, Vt
Jackson, Rev. Aaron, Oyster Bay, N. Y.
Jacobus, J. L. Chicago, Il
Jacobs, Charles P. Goshen, Ia.
Jacobs, William H., Williamsburgh, N. Y.
Jacobs, William, Oxford, N. Y
Jacoby, Mrs. B. A., Davenport, Iowa.
James, Rev. Joshua J Raleigh, N. C.
James, Edward, Albany.
James, George, Zanesville, O.
James, Francis H., Philadelphia.
James, Rev. David, Osceola, Ill.
James, Thomas M., New Bedford, Mass.
James, John, Brookfield, O.
Jamison, Alexander, Wilmington, Del.
Jameson, Mrs. Lucinda L., Melrose, Mass.
Jameson, Miss Eliza, Newton, Mass.
Janvein, Edwin, Chelsea, Mass.
Jarratt, Henry, Jarratt's, Va.
Jarratt, Nicholas, Jarratt Depot, Va.
Jastram, George B., Providence.
Jaudon, Mrs. Sarah T., Kansas City, Mo.
Jaycox, Isaac, Monmouth, Ill.
Jaycox, Mrs. Fanny M., Monmouth, Ill.
Jeffery, Mrs. J lia M., Albany N Y.
Jeffery, Rev. Reuben, Albany, N. Y
Jeffress, J. M. Red Oak Grove, Va
Jefferis, Rev. David, Perkiomen Pa.
Jencks, Rev. Erasmus N Ottawa, Ill.
Jencks, Livingston, La Salle, Ill.
Jenks, Miss Maria P., Pawtucket, R. I.
Jenks, Gideon, Brookfield, Mass.
Jenks, J. W. P Middleboro' Mass.
Jenkins, Mrs. Susanna, New York.
Jenkins, Rev. J S. Coatesville, Pa.
Jenkins, Miss Rebecca, New York.
Jennett, John, Halifax, C. H., Va.
Jennings, Mrs. Susan C., Worcester, Mass.
Jennings, Mrs. Marcia, Deep River, Ct.
Jennings, Mrs. Betsey, Deep River, Ct.
Jeril, Rev. T Lebanon, N. Y.
Jerome, George D., Uncasville, Ct.
Jerrard, Rev. Richard, Fond du Lac, Wis.
Jeter, Rev. J. C., Beaver Dam, S. C.
Jewell, Aaron C. Newark, N J.
Jewell, Albert, East Green, N Y
Jewett, Rev. Milo P., Poughkeepsie, N. Y.
Jewett, Rev. Daniel, Bonaparte, Iowa.
Jimmerson, Robert J New York.
Jimmerson, Mrs. Miranda L., New York.
Johnson, Nathan M., Woburn, Mass.
Johnson, Rev. William B., D.D., Edgefield, S.C.
Johnson, Mrs. Henrietta, Edgefield, S. C.
Johnson, William, North East, Pa.
Johnson, Mrs. Sarah S., North East, Pa.
Johnson, Mrs. Louisa M. Lynn, Mass.
Johnson, James, Brooklyn, N. Y
Johnson, Robert, Newark, N J.
Johnson, Mrs. Robert, Newark, N. J.
Johnson, Rev. Solomon B., St. Louis, Mo.
Johnson, Rev. George J Burlington, Iowa.
Johnson, Mrs. George J., Burlington, Iowa.
Johnson, Rev. Benedict, West Woodstock, Ct.
Johnson, Rev. Hezekiah, Oregon City, Oregon.
Johnson, Albert B., Williamstown, Pa.
Johnson, Edward, New York.
Johnson, Mrs. Mary, Albany, N. Y.
Johnson, Merrick, Willington, Ct.
Johnson, Miss Jane Ann, Wilson, N. Y.
Johnson, Oliver, Providence.
Johnson, Ralph, Norwich, N Y
Johnson, Mrs. Mary, Norwich, N Y.
Johnson, Elias, Troy, N. Y.
Johnson, Mrs. Elizabeth, Philadelphia.
Johnson, Mrs. Catharine B., Haverhill, Mass.
Johnson, Mrs. Mehitable, Danversport, Mass.
Johnston, Andrew Newark, N. J.
Johnston, Mrs. Andrew Newark, N. J.
Johnston, James, Sing Sing, N. Y
Johnston, John L., Sing Sing, N. Y.
Johonnet, Mrs. Andrew, Providence.
Jolls, John F Providence.
Jones, Rev. Stephen, Norwalk, Ohio.
Jones, Mrs. Stephen, Norwalk, Ohio.
Jones, Rev. John, Seaville, N. J.
Jones, Mrs. Deborah, Seaville, N. J.
Jones, Mrs. Ann T Williamsburg, Va.
Jones, Eliza T Tavern P. O., Pa.
Jones, Mrs. Margaret, New York.
Jones, Mrs. Eliza W New Brunswick, N. J.
Jones, Mrs. Elizabeth, Macedon, N. Y.
Jones, David, New York.
Jones, Mrs. Sarah, New York.
Jones, Mrs. Mary, New York.
Jones, Miss Catharine L., Philadelphia.
Jones, Rev. Joseph H., Frederick City, Md.
Jones, Rev. David N., Richmond, Va.
Jones, Rev. Matthew Stephentown, N. Y.
Jones, Rev. Theophilus, Hatboro' Pa.
Jones, Rev. Isaac D., Wiltonville, N. Y.
Jones, John R., Roxbury, Mass.
Jones, W lliam G., Wilmington, Del.
Jones, Washington, Wilmington, Del.
Jones, William M., New York.
Jones, Mrs. Margaretta V. New York.
Jones, Rev. J W. Hyde Park, N. Y.
Jones, Howard M., Providence, R. I.
Jones, J. F., East Cambridge, Mass.
Jones, Rev. T Rock Hill, Ohio.
Jones, Rev. Edward, Brookfield, Ohio.
Jones, Mrs. Abigail, New York.
Jones, Rev. A. B., Guilford, N. Y.
Jones, Rev. H. S., Smyrna, N. Y.
Jones, Mrs. Clara A., Worcester, Mass.
Jones, John M., West Troy, N Y
Jordan, Elder R. K., Richland Grove, Ill.
Jordan, Philana D., Columbia, Ohio.
Jordon, Mrs. Esther Brooklyn, N Y.
Jordon, True P., Lowell, Mass.
Joslin, Joseph, East Poultney, Vt.
Joyce, Miss Sarah W., Worcester Mass.
udd, Rev. Truman O., Fair Haven, Ct.
Justice, David, Forestville, N. C.
Justin, Rev. Ira, Richmond, N. Y
Kain, Mrs. Sarah, Marlton, N. J.
Kain, Rev. Charles, Jr., Mullica Hill, N. J.
Kain, Mrs. Maria, Mullica Hill, N. J.
Kasson, Marcus A., Desoto, Wis.

Kauffman, Henry, Paoli, Pa.
Kauffman, Mrs. Sarah, Paoli, Pa.
Keith, William, Boston, Mass.
Kavanagh, Michael, Lowell, Mass.
Keely, Rev. George, Haverhill, Mass.
Keely, Mrs. George, Haverhill, Mass.
Keely, John, Haverhill, Mass.
Keely, Mrs. John, Haverhill, Mass.
Keely, Rev. Thomas E., Medford, Mass.
Keen, Mrs. Susan B., West Philadelphia.
Keen, George B., West Philadelphia.
Keen, William W. J., West Philadelphia.
Keen, Charles B., West Philadelphia.
Keeney, John, New London, Ct.
Keeney, William H., New London, Ct.
Keeney, Rev. Curtis, New London, Ct.
Kelly, Mrs. Joan, Elmira, N. Y.
Kelly, Mrs. Mary M., Brooklyn, N. Y.
Kelley, Mrs. Catharine, New York.
Kelley, Mrs. Eli, New York.
Kelley, Miss Georgiana, New York.
Kelley, James D., Pittsfield, N. H.
Kellogg, U. H., Utica, N. Y.
Kellogg, Moses S., Chickopee Falls, Mass.
Kelsey, Rev. Daniel, Pittsgrove, N. J.
Kelton, George, Salem, N. J.
Kemp, Sylvester A., Florida, Mass.
Kemp, Nathaniel P., Jamaica Plains, Mass.
Kendall, H. N., St. Louis, Mo.
Kendall, Charles S., Boston.
Kendrick, Silas N., Detroit, Mich.

Kingm
Kingm
King
Kingm
Kingsl
Kings
Kingsl
Kingsl
Kirk,
Kline,
Kone,
Knapp
Knapp
Knapp
Knap
Knap
Knigl
Knigl
Knig
Knig
Knig
Knig
Knig
Know
Knox

y, Miss Mary, Brooklyn, N. Y.
nce, A. W., Mooresville, N. Y.
nce, William S., New York.
nce, Miss Lorraine, Pine Plains, N. Y.
nce, Mrs. Abigail L., Pine Plains, N. Y.
nce, Mrs. Sarah, Poughkeepsie, N. Y.
on, James T., Newburgh, N. Y.
on, George, Waltham, Mass.
on, Mrs. George W., Waltham, Mass.
on, Rev. L., North Linklean, N. Y.
on, Samuel, Providence.
on, Mrs. Alida A., New York.
on, George F., Providence.
er, Michael, Newtown, Ohio.
Mrs. Elizabeth, Yanceyville, N. C.
Hon. Luke A., Washington, D. C.
, Elbridge G., Jamaica Plain, Mass.
, Rev. Beriah N., Middletown, Vt.
, Rev. D. F., Harpersville, N. Y.
, Rev. William, Omaha City, Neb. Ter.
, Mrs. Margaret, Brooklyn, N. Y.
r, Mrs. Marion, Brooklyn, N. Y.
George, North Bristol, N. Y.
Mrs. Amanda, North Bristol, N. Y.
Miss Ann Mollan, New York.
. A., New York.
Francis R., Trenton, N. J.
ster, Mrs. Mary, New York.
tt, Rev. William, Owasco, N. Y.
d, J. A., Brooklyn, N. Y.
nt, Charles A., Chelsea, Mass.
nt, Mrs. Ann M., New York.
rd, Richard, Riceville, N. J.
rd, Mrs. Mahetable, Zanesville, O.
rd, Rev. Isaac, Burlington, Iowa.
rd, George E., Newton, Mass.
rd, Mrs. Caroline F., Taunton, Mass.
rd, George A., New York.
rd, Halsey, West Woodstock, Ct.
l, Rev. J. H., Cambridge, Mass.
James, Wharton, O.
Rev. Edgar M., West Philadelphia.
, William J., New York.
, Elijah, Brooklyn, N. Y.
Mrs. Ann, Brooklyn, N. Y.
Mrs. Mary B. S., Brooklyn, N. Y.
Mrs. Asa, Worcester, Mass.
Rev. Charles C., Westerly, R. I.
, Rev. Lester, Middletown, Ct.
, Daniel D., Philadelphia.
Mrs. Hannah, Norwich, N. Y.
Simeon H., Boston.
William, New York.
Rev. Richard, Holmesburg, Pa.
Elijah, Norwich, N. Y.
William B., Preston, N. Y.
Rev. Welcome, Mansfield, Mass.
Jr., John B., Boston.
n, Rev. Thomas O., Utica, N. Y.
n, Mrs. Abby A.
n, Rev. Heman, Jamaica Plains, Mass.
n, Henry E., Boston.
n, Joshua, Roxbury, Mass.
n, John L., Providence.
Frederick, New York.

Lindsay, Wm., Fall River, Mass.
Linsley, Charles, New Haven, Ct.
Lippitt, Mrs. Elizabeth S., Cumberland, O.
Lippitt, Mrs. Melinda, Hiramsburg, O.
Litchfield, Rev. Daniel W., Benton, N. Y.
Little, George W., Charlestown, Mass.
Little, J. T., Dixon, Ill.
Littlefield, Jotham, Belleville, N. Y.
Lifsey, Mrs. Sally, Hick's Ford, Va.
Livermore, Rev. S. T., South Livonia, N. Y.
Lloyd, Amos, Mullica Hill, N. J.
Loomis, Asahel, Gouverneur, N. Y.
Loomis, Edwin H., Lebanon, Ct.
Lock, Rev. William, Jamestown, N. Y.
Locke, Mrs. Harriet N., Springfield, N. J.
Locke, Jesse A., Watertown, Mass.
Locke, Mrs. Sarah B., Watertown, Mass.
Lockwood, Luther G., Stratfield, Ct.
Logan James, Pemberton, N. J.
Lombard, Nathan C.
Long, E. J., Boston, Mass.
Long, William, Shelburne Falls, Mass.
Long, William, Urbana, O.
Longstreet, Mrs. Mary L., Imlaystown, N. J.
Longyear, Rev. Henry Z., Phenicia, N. Y.
Lord, Henry E., New York.
Loring, Samuel H., Boston.
Loring, Mrs. James, Boston.
Love, Mrs. Harriet N., Salem, N. J.
Love, Rev. H. T., New York.
Love, Mrs. Catharine W., New York.
Love, John, New York.
Lovell, George, Osterville, Mass.
Lovell, Mrs. Lucy, Fall River, Mass.
Lovell, Rev. Andrew S., Bloomfield, Ct.
Louther, Rev. Thos., Duncansville, Pa.
Lucas, Rev. Elijah, Waterford, N. Y.
Luckey, James E., Palo, Ill.
Luckey, Emma M., Palo, Ill.
Ludlow, John R., New York.
Ludlow, Mrs. Clarissa Ann, Newport, R. I.
Ludlam, David, Jr., Sing Sing, N. Y.
Lull, Rev. Abner, Oshkosh, Wis.
Luther, Job, Providence.
Luther, Gardner, Seekonk, Mass.
Luther, Mrs. Mary, Seekonk, Mass.
Lyle, Robert, New Brunswick, N. J.
Lyman, Nathan, Andover, Ct.
Lynch, Thomas, Philadelphia.
Lyon, Jesse, Fitchburg, Mass.
Lyon, Moses G., Fitchburg, Mass.
Lyon, Cyrus, York, N. Y.
Lyon, Mrs. Mary, York, N. Y.
Lyon, Miss Rebecca, Plainfield, N. J.
Lyon, Rev. Daniel D., Sag Harbor, N. Y.
Lyon, Rev. Joel, Sylvanus, Mich.
Lyon, Mrs. Caroline P., Chatham, Mass.
Lyon, Mrs. Merrick, Providence.
Lyon, Rev. A. S., Natick, Mass.
Lyons, Rev. John M., Milestown, Pa.
Lynt, Odell D., Hastings, N. Y.
Lytle, Andrew, Williamsburgh, Va.
McBride, Miss Jane Ann, New York.
McBride, Miss Eliza H., New York.
McCarthy, Rev. William, Holland Patent, N.Y.

McClees, Peter, Middletown, N. J.
McClung, Miss Caroline M., Pittsburgh, Pa.
McClung, Anthony, Kingston, N. Y.
McCormick, R. C., New York.
McCormick, Mrs. Sarah M., New York.
McCoy, John, Charlestown, Ia.
McCullen, Miss Sarah, New York.
McCune, John P., Salem, N. J.
McCutchen, Wm. G., Williamsburg, N. Y.
McDade, Mrs. Jane, New York.
McDaniel, Randle, Fayetteville, N. C.
McFarland, Rev. D., Oswego, N. Y.
McGear, Daniel L.
McGonagal, George, New York.
McIntosh, Mrs. Mary, Philadelphia.
McIver, A. M., Society Hill, S. C.
McIver, Mrs. Ann J., Society Hill, S. C.
McJannett, Mrs. Elizabeth, Brooklyn, N. Y.
McKean, Rev. John A., Philadelphia.
McKean, Mrs. Eliza J., Philadelphia.
McKewan, John, New York.
McLellan, James, Trumansburg, N. Y.
McLellan, Mrs. Ellen, Trumansburg, N. Y.
McLean, Mrs. Mary, New London, Ct.
McLowth, Rev. Benjamin, Scipio, N. Y.
McMahon, Henry L., Philadelphia.
McNabb, Mrs E., Fayetteville, N. C.
McTaggart, Daniel, Reading, Pa.
* McTaggart, Mrs. Margaret, Reading, Pa.
Macdonald, Alexander, New York.
Macdonald, Mrs. R., New York.

Manni
Manro
Manto
Manw
March
Marsh,
Marsto
Marsto
Martin
Martin
Martin

Miss Sarah Elizabeth, New York.
, James, Brooklyn, N. Y
Rev. Eddy, Sennett, N. Y.
, Joseph R., Providence.
George, Providence.
Miss Harriett, Boston.
William, Fall River, Mass.
', Mrs. Catharine, Bellingham, Mass.
, John, S., New York.
', Increase, Fairport, N. Y.
', Mrs. Mary A., Deep River, Ct.
rs, Rev. George, Seekonk, Mass.
rs, Mrs. Elizabeth, Seekonk, Mass.
rson, Nathan F., Providence.
on, Rev. N. H., Preston City, Ct.
Rev. William, Plainfield, N. J.
Mrs. Sarah Ann, Plainfield, N. J.
ll, B., Shelburne Falls, Mass.
ll, Rev. J. M., Oswego. Ia.
, Mrs. Eliza, Albany, N. Y.
rd, Walter, Three Rivers, Mass.
rd, Mrs. Clarissa, Corning, N. Y.
im, Miss Elizabeth, Brooklyn, N. Y.
John, Troy, N. Y.
Joshua, New York.
William, Lawrence, Mass.
John K., Amenia, N. Y.
Rev. George W., Vienna, N. Y.
Elijah, Boston.
Rev. Wm. W.. Anthony, R. I.
Mrs. Lydia, Preston, Ct.
Rev. Levi, Preston. Ct.
Levi W., Preston, Ct.
'y, Rev. Nicholas, Newburyport, Mass.
'y, Viall, Seekonk, Mass.
, Aaron B., Elizabeth, N. J
, Rev. J D., Haddonfield, N. J.
nt, James H., New York.
nt, Mrs. Amanda M , New York.
nt, Reuben, Stillwater. N. Y.
nt, Miss Mary, Stillwater, N. Y.
, Otis, Chelsea, Mass.
Mrs. Mary, Washburn, Ill.
, Charles, Malden, Mass.
, Thomas W.. Somerset, N. Y.
n, Rev. Asaph, Bolton, Mass.
n, Rev. Mylon, Sharon, Mass.
n, Rev. Titus M., Johnson, Vt.
n, Rev. Franklin, China, Me.
:, Timothy, West Willington, Ct.
Mrs. David J.. Newburyport, Mass.
Joseph, Lowell, Mass.
, Mrs. Nancy B., Hudson, N. H.
Joseph, Hudson, N. H.
Joseph, New York.
, Mrs. Mary F. New York.
J. Warren, Cambridge, Mass.
, Rev. Thomas W., Kalamazoo, Mich }
, Daniel, Worcester, Mass.
ld, Elliott P., West Wardsboro', Vt.
ld, Miss Carrie R.. Brookline, Vt.
Richard H., New London, N. H.
Mrs. Sally S., New London, N. H.
Mathew, Methuen. Mass.
, Andrew J., Lowell, Mass.
, Rev. Whitman, Nunda, N. Y.

Metcalf, George P., Jamesburg N. J.
Mershon, Mrs. Mellona S.. New York.
Mershon, Mrs. Marie, Trenton. N. J
Mervine, N. J., Reading, Pa.
Micou, Rev. John, Jr., Louisville. Miss
Miers, Mrs. Christina, Flemington, N. J.
Mikels, Rev. William S . New York.
Mikels, Mrs. Lydia, New York.
Milbank, Miss Elizabeth, New York.
Milbank, Miss Eliza W., New York.
Milbank, Miss Sarah C., New York.
Milbank, Miss Mary W., New York.
Milbank, Mrs. Mary W., New York.
Milbank, Miss Mary A., New York.
Milbank, Miss Emma Louise, New York.
Milbank, Miss Anna Elizabeth. New York.
Milbank, L., Ainsworth, New York.
Milbank, Charles A., New York.
Middlebrook, J. Henry, New York.
Middleton, John, Brooklyn, N. Y.
Miles, Abial. Brooklyn, N. Y.
Miles, Mrs. Hannah, Brooklyn, N. Y.
Miles, Rev. George I., Bellefonte, Pa.
Miles, Rev. Edward M., Davenport, Iowa.
Miles, Thomas, Philadelphia.
Millard, C. J., Boston, Mass.
Millard, George, North Adams, Mass.
Millard, S. S., Penfield, N. Y.
Millard, Barzilla. Penfield, N. Y.
Miller, Mrs. Sarah R., Meriden, Ct.
Miller, Mrs. Abigail, New York
Miller, Miss Amanda, Banksville, Ct.
Miller, Mrs. Nancy, New London, Ct.
Miller, Miss Anicartha, New York.
Miller, James H., Philadelphia.
Miller, Charles, Moriah, N. Y.
Miller, Rev. U. B , Ft. Wayne, Ia.
Miller, Mrs. Anna R.. Ft. Wayne, Ia.
Miller, Mrs. Martha, Middletown, Ct.
Miller, Mrs. Ann Eliza, Providence.
Miller, Lydia A., Bedford, N. Y.
Miller, Edward W.. Philadelphia.
Miller, Mrs. Mary Ann. Philadelphia.
Miller, Rev. John S.. Mt. Holly, N. J.
Mills, Charles H., Brooklyn. N. Y.
Mills, Stephen, Greenwich, N. Y.
Mills, Rev. Peletiah W.. Springville, N. Y.
Milne, John C , Fall River, Mass.
Milne, Rev. Alexander, Marcellus, N. Y.
Milne, Mrs. Eliza N., Marcellus, N. Y.
Milner, Alfred A., New York.
Milner, Mrs. Alfred A.. New York.
Miner, Rev. Martin, Wolcott, Ct.
Miner, Rev. Absalom, Waukesha, Wis.
Miner, Rev. Cyrus, Attica, N. Y.
Miner, Rev. S. G., Canton. Ill.
Miner, Rev. Erastus, Cold Spring, N. Y.
Miner, Rev. Noyes W.. Springfield, Ill.
Miner, Francis S., New York.
Miner, A. B., Italy Hill, N. Y.
Miner, Nathaniel, Jerseyville, Ill.
Miner, Mrs. Hannah M., Norwich. N. Y.
Miner, Mrs. Charles, New London, Ct.
Miner, Ezra, North Stonington, Ct.
Mingus, Miss Julia Ann, New York.
Mintch, Mrs. Phebe, Shiloh, N J.
Mitchell, Rev. George H., Wagontown, Pa.

MEMBERS FOR LIFE.

Mitchell, Mrs. Phebe H., Wagoontown, Pa.
Mitchell, Beth, Montrose, Pa.
Mitchell, Ellen E. Montrose, Pa.
Mitchell, Rev. Thos., Troy Pa.
Mixter, Rev. George, New London, Ct.
Mondon, Gilbert F., Port Jarvis, N. Y.
Monroe, Rev. William Y Graham, Ia.
Montgomery, W lliam, Danbury Ct.
Montgomery, Mrs Susan, Danbury, Ct.
Montgomery, S. P Danbury, Ct.
Montgomery, Wm., Jr., Danbury, Ct.
Montgomery, Miss Susan, Danbury Ct.
Montague, Rev Oreb, Warsaw, N. Y.
Moon, Joh New York.
Moore, Dr. G. C St. John's, N. C.
Moore, Mrs. lia, St. John's, N. C.
Moore, Mrs. Theodosia M., St. Louis, Mo.
Moore, James, Milton, Pa.
Moore, Francis W. New York.
Moore, Rev. Lyman H., Lansing, Mich.
Moore, Rev. W. W., Albany N. Y.
Moore, Rev. George C., New York.
Moore, James, Wilmington, Del.
Moore, Enoch, Danbury, Ct.
Moore, Rev. Farris, Lee, Mass.
Moore, Robert, Greencastle, Ia.
Morgan, Gilbert E. Mystic R ver, Ct.
Morgan, William, Brooklyn, N. Y.
Morgan, Miss Harriet, Brooklyn, N. Y.
Morgan, David, Cleveland Ohio.
Morgan, David, Sen., Allegany City, Pa.
Morgan, Hiram, Blackwoodtown, N. J.
Morgan, Joshua, Philadelphia.
Morgan, Mrs. Jane E., Russell, Mass.
Morgan, Avery, Hartford, Ct.
Morgan, Wm. P Albion, N Y
Morrell, Mrs. Sarah G., Savannah, Ga.
Morrill, Geo. W., Salisbury, Mass.
Morrill, Miss Mary, Salisbury, Mass.
Morrill, Joseph, Amesbury, Mass.
Morrill, Daniel, Amesbury, Mass.
Morris, Rev. J Hamburg, S. C.
Morris, Rev. David, New York.
Morrison, onathan, Brooklyn, N. Y.
Morrison, Mrs. A. Henrietta, Brooklyn, N. Y.
Morse, Mrs. Sophia A., Sturbridge, Mass.
Morse, Enoch R., Chelsea, Mass.
Morse, K. P., Gree ville, Ill.
Morse, Mrs. Clara S., Charlestown, Mass.
Morse, Curtis G., South Dedham, Mass.
Morse, Benjamin, ——, Iowa.
Mortimer, George W Wilmington Del.
Morton, Mrs. Susan Corn ng, N Y
Morton, Miss Sarah B., Corning, N. Y.
Morton, Miss Mat lda N., Corning, N. Y.
Morton, Miss Kate E., Corning, N. Y.
Morton, George, Brooklyn, N. Y
Mosely, Green, Dupree's Store, Va.
Mosely, Miss S. A., Dupree's Store, Va.
Moss, Lemuel, Rochester, N. Y.
Moss, Mrs. Nancy, Upperville, Va.
Mott, Miss Elizabeth, New York.
Moulthrop, Major, New Haven, Ct.
Mount, David, Albany, N. Y.
Moxley, Rev. Oel W., Richville, N. Y.

Mugg, Rev John, Gosport, Ia.
Mulford, John, Sen., Mullica Hill, N. J.
Mulford, C arles, Salem, N. J.
Mulford, Mrs. Phœbe, Roadstown, N. J.
Mulhern, Rev. Dennis, Frankfort, Wis.
Mumford, Rev. N., Desota, N. Y
Munger, Rev. Washington, Waterford, Ct.
Munger, Mrs. Louisa N Waterford, Ct.
Munger, Morgan, Schaghticoke, N. Y.
Munger, L. F., Leroy, N. Y
Munn, Mrs. Mary New York.
Murdock, Mrs. Martha B., Hartford, Ct.
Murphy, Wm. D., New York.
Murphy, Samuel, Hoboken, N. J.
Murphy, Rev. John R., Marlton, N. J.
Murray, Thomas S., New Hope, Pa.
Murray, Mrs. Margaret M., New Hope, Pa.
Murray, Miss Sarah L., Boston.
Mustin, John, Philadelphia.
Myers, Mrs. Ann R., Philadelphia.
Myers, James Jr., New York
Mylne, Rev Wm., Louisa, C H Va.
Myrick Albert A., Gilbertsville, N. Y.
Napier, Rev. Robert, Mizpath, S. C.
Neale, Jeremiah, Plainville, Ct.
Neale, Joh Southington, Ct.
Nearing, Alfred N., New York.
Nelson, Rev. Caleb, Enfield, N. Y.
Nelson, Rev Wm. F Wickford, R. I.
Nelson, Simeon B., Westport, N. H.
Newcomb, Butler, Cedarville, N. J.
Newcomb, Mrs. Thomas, Haverhill, Mass.
Newcomb, James, New London, Ct.
Newcomb, osiah T., Newport, N. J.
Newell, Andrew H Brookline, Mass.
Newell, Mrs. Asa Providence.
Newhall, Rev. Charles, Stratham, N. H.
Newland, D., Stillwater N. Y
Newland, Rev. C A., Cooper's Plains, N. Y.
Newland, Peabody, Lawrenceville, N. Y.
Newton, Mrs. Sally A bany.
Newton, Wm., Worcester, Mass.
Newton, Rev. Calvi Worcester, Mass.
Newton, Rev. Baxter, Cazenovia, N. Y.
Newton, Miss Frances M New York.
Newton, Mrs. Jane, Bridgeton N. J.
Newton, Horace B., A bany, N Y.
Nice, Mrs. Elizabeth A., Imlaystown, N. J.
Nichols, Reuben, Davenport, Iowa.
Nichols, Rev. D. A. Port Providence, Pa.
Nichols, Jonathan, Berlin, N. Y.
Nichols, Mrs. Eliza A., Boston.
Nichols, Luther W Amherst, N. H.
Nicholas, Rev. Noah, Rutland, Vt
Nicholson, A. M. Bostick Mills N C.
Nickerson, Harden, Providence, R I.
Nickels, George, Rockh ll, O.
Niel, James R., Brooklyn, N. Y.
Nilsson, Rev. Frederick O., Scandia, Min.
Nixon, George, Providence.
Noble, Mrs. Margaret, Brooklyn, N Y.
Nolton, Miss Sarah J Petersburgh, N. Y.
Norman, Miss Arnoretta D., Elmira, N. Y.
Normandeau, Mrs. C. A., Grand Ligne, C. E.
Northam E, Rockingham, N C.

Northam, George, Va.
Norton, Rev. Charles C., New York.
Norton, Rev Noah. Brunswick, Me.
Norton, Newbury, Agawam, Mass.
Norton, M. F, Cleveland, O.
Norris, Mrs. F. Henrietta, Brooklyn, N. Y.
Norris, Mrs. Eliza D, Sanbornton, N. H.
Noyes, Henry, Chelsea, Mass.
Noyes, A. D., New London, Ct.
Numan, Abraham, Troy, N. Y.
Nunn, James D., Raleigh, N. C.
Nye, Thomas, Littleton, Mass.
Oby, Mrs. Rebecca, Danversport, Mass.
Odell, Jonathan, Yonkers, N. Y.
Ogden, Joseph H., Greenwich, N. J.
Ogden, Horace E., Greenwich, N. J.
Ogden, Elmer, Greenwich, N. J.
Oldring, Henry J., Williamsburgh, N. Y.
Olin, Joseph, Lawrenceville, N. Y.
Olin, Benjamin, Canton, N. Y.
Olmsted, Rev J. W., Boston.
Olney, Rev. David B, Warsaw, N. Y.
Olney, Rev. Philetus, Barrington, N. Y.
Olney, Mrs. P., Barrington, N. Y.
Olney, James, Pawtucket, R. I.
Olney, Rev. Lafayette W., Deposit, N. Y.
Olney, Edward A. M., Kalamazo, Mich.
Olney, Wm., Malden, Mass.
Oliver, Marius, Bridgeport, Ct.
Omberson, Wm. J., New York.
Otis Harvey, Kingston, N. Y.
O'Brien, Miss Mary, New York.
O'Neal, Mrs. Jenet, Brooklyn, N. Y.
Oncken, Rev. J. G., Hamburg, Germany.
Oncken, Mrs. Ann, Hamburg, Germany.
Oncken, Miss Marg't. A., Hamburg, Germany.
Onderdonk, Peter C, New Brunswick, N. J.
Osborn, Rev. J. W., Marion, N Y.
Osgood, Miss Sarah T, Salisbury, Mass
Osgood, Miss Jane, Salisbury, Mass.
Osgood, John, Amesbury, Mass.
Osgood, Rev. S. M., Philadelphia.
Osgood, Miss Sarah Ann, Danvers, Mass.
Osgood, Miss Caroline W., Philadelphia.
Ostrander, Richard, Hoosic, N. Y.
Overstreet, Mrs. Catharine R., Providence.
Paddock, Samuel, Meriden, Ct.
Page, Rev. Stephen B., Cleveland, O.
Page, Mrs. Emily A. L., Cleveland, O.
Page, Abel, Haverhill, Mass.
Page, Mrs. Abel, Haverhill, Mass.
Page Mrs. Rachel D., Hopkinton, N. H.
Page, Henry S., Cleveland, O.
Page, Rev. C. J., New Brunswick, N. J.
Paine, Rev. John, Ware, Mass.
Paine, Walter, 3d, Fall River, Mass.
Palmer, Rev. Asa H.
Palmer, Rev. Albert G., Bridgeport, Ct.
Palmer, Mrs. Amelia W., Bridgeport, Ct.
Palmer, Mrs. Wm, East Lyme, Ct.
Palmer, Rev. Lyman, Anoka, Min.
Palmer, Rev Prentice T, Waveland, Ia.
Palmer, Ephraim, New Hartford, N. Y.
Palmer, H. K. W, Chelsea, Mass.
Palmer, Elias, New York.
Palmer, Mrs. Hannah, New York.
Palmer, Benj., Du Buque, Iowa.
Palmer, M. E., Wyoming, N. Y.
Pardee, Leonard, New Haven, Ct.
Park, Elisha, Providence.
Park, Rev Charles C., Italy Hollow, N. Y.
Parke, Rev. F. S., Cheshire, Mass.
Parker, Miss Lavinia M., Suffield, Ct.
Parker, Asa, Essex. Ct.
Parker, Joel R., Fredonia, N. Y.
Parker, Rev. A., Agawam, Mass.
Parker, Rev. Wm., Philadelphia.
Parker, Rev. A., Coventry, N. Y.
Parker, David O., Hamilton, N. Y.
Parker, Lydia P., Allen, Mich.
Parker, Rev. Harvey L., Fairfax, Vt.
Parker, Mrs. E. R. Norwich, N. Y.
Parker, Miss Susan E., Boston.
Parks, Rev. R. M., Bedford, Ind.
Parks, Miss Nancy J., Great Falls, N. H.
Parks, Mrs. Marianne C., South Berwick, Me.
Parkhurst, John, Fitchburg, Mass.
Parkhurst, G. R., Brookline, Mass.
Parmlee, Mrs. Syrena, New York.
Parmelee, Elias F., Essex, Ct.
Parmelee, Rev. J. H, Xenia, O.
Parmely, Rev. Levi, Elgin, Ill.
Parmely, Mrs. Catharine H., Elgin, Ill.
Parish, Warren, Mendon, N. Y.
Parshley, John, New Haven, Ct.
Parsons, Silas, Swanzey, N. H
Parsons, Mrs. Patience, Swanzey, N. H.
Parsons, Wm., Medford, Mass
Pasco, Rev. Cephas, Egremont, Mass.
Passage, Adam, Weedsport, N. Y.
Patch, Rev. George W., Marblehead, Mass.
Patrick, Charlotte M., Saratoga Springs, N. Y.
Pattengill, Rev. C, N., Westville, N. Y.
Patterson, Rev. Wm. C., East Dedham, Mass.
Patterson, Mrs. Mary, Chapel Hill, N. C.
Patterson, Mrs. Lucy A, New York.
Patton, John E.
Paulin, Mrs. Ann, Salem, N. J.
Paulin, Rev. Wm., Hamilton Square, N. J.
Payne, Miss Amanda, Amenia, N. Y.
Payne, Wm. W., Auburn, N. Y.
Payne, N. B., New London, Ct.
Peak, John, Boston.
Peacock, Rev. John, Plaistow, N. H.
Peacock, Eliza Ann, Plaistow, N. H.
Pearce, Rev. Wm., Marietta, O.
Pearson, Mrs. T C., Ludlow, Vt.
Pease, Joseph W., Lowell, Mass.
Peaslee, Mrs. Abigail W., Haverhill, Mass.
Peck, Mrs. Nancy M., Owego, N. Y.
Peck, John, Clifton Park, N. Y.
Peck, Mrs. John, Clifton Park, N. Y.
Peck, John, 2d, Clifton Park, N. Y.
Peck, Abijah, Jr, Clifton Park, N. Y.
Peck, Rev. David A., Waupaca, Wis.
Peck, James W., Brooklyn, N. Y.
Peck, Rev. Daniel, South Jackson, Mich.
Peck, George B., Providence.
Peckham, Rev. S. H., Ledyard, Ct.
Peeples, Rev. Darling, Barnwell, S. C.

James T., Jerseyville, Ill.
Rev. Charles B., Dover Plains, N. Y.
, James, Bridgeport, Ct.
, Rev. Charles W., Cromwell, Ct.
, Rev. Aaron, Clarkston, Mich.
, Daniel L., Schenectady, N. Y.
, Rev. Thomas, Davenport, Iowa.
, Mrs. E., Davenport, Iowa.
, Miss Sarah P., Davenport, Iowa.
, William T., Ottawa, Ill.
, Rev. Peter, Beverly, N. J.
, Mrs Nancy, Powelton, N. C.
, William, Cincinnati, Ohio.
, Mrs. Amelia, New London, Ct.
, Charles W., Bloomfield, N. J.
, Mrs. Anna Maria, Hoboken, N. J.
Rev. John, Newport, R. I.
Rev. Samuel C., Lowell, Mass.
Rev. James H., Bloomfield, N. J.
Daniel, Brooklyn N. Y.
Oliver T., New York.
Eli, Johnstown, Ohio.
John C., Boston.
Rev. John, Granville, O.
Paul, Albion, N. Y.
Miss Jennie H., Yates, N. Y.
Jeremiah, Burlington, N. Y.
, Mrs. Susan, Norwich, N. Y.
, Abraham, Concord, N. H.
, Levi, Greenport, N. Y.
, Mrs. Ann.
, Henry M., Norwalk, Ct.
, Mrs. Hannah S., New York.
Abel, Weedsport, N. Y.
Rev. George W., Chapel Hill, N. C.
Mrs. Lucinda, Chapel Hill, N. C.
Rev. Nicholas, Washington, D. C.
ton, Mrs. Rhoda Jane, Prattsburgh, N.Y.
n, Rev. D. B, Smithfield, Pa.
n, Rev. J. M., Va.
n, Rev. Lewis M., Rensselaerville, N. Y.
Miss Mary Ann Providence.
Mrs. Polly, Providence.
, Rev. Daniel, Eaton, N. Y.
, Mrs. Clarinda Eaton, N. Y.
, Rev. H. C., Greenwich, N. J.
, John, Boston.
, Mrs. Charlotte K., Danversport, Mass.
, Mrs. Augusta, Danversport, Mass.
, Mrs. Ann, Philadelphia.
Mrs. Harriet, Brooklyn, N. Y.
Josiah, Rumney, N. H.
, Joshua, Haverhill, Mass.
, Mrs. Susan A., Brooklyn, N. Y.
, Mrs. Elizabeth, Rock Hill, Ohio.
, P. A., Boston.
ev. Aaron, New York.
rs. M. E., Hathaway, N. Y.
ohn W., Warrenville, Ill.
ev. Thomas, Ireland, Mass.
ornelia E., Acton, Mass.
, Mrs. Mary, New York.
, Mrs. Mary, Mystic River, Ct.
, Mrs. Maria, Mystic River, Ct.
, Wm. Henry, Mystic River, Ct.
, Rev. D. A., Columbus, O.

Randall, Rev. Charles. Auburn, N. Y.
Randall, Benjamin, Oxford, N. Y.
Randolph, Rev. Warren, Providence.
Randolph, Mrs. Huldah, New York.
Randolph, Mrs. Sarah F., New Market, N. J.
Randolph, Joseph F., New York.
Randolph, Samuel, Plainfield N. J.
Randolph, Peter F. New York.
Randolph, Lewis, Delhi, Ill.
Randolph, Jacob D. F., Brooklyn, N. Y.
Randolph, Mrs. Jane Ann, Brooklyn, N. Y.
Randolph, David F., New Brunswick, N. J.
Randolph, Ambrose F., New Brunswick, N. J.
Randolph, John S, Somerville. N. J.
Rankin, Mrs. Sarah, Reading, Pa.
Rankin, Mrs. Eliza, Reading, Pa.
Rankin, Peter, Phœnixville, Pa
Rankin, Samuel, Rock Hill, Ohio.
Ranney, E. W., M.D., New York.
Rathbone, Lewis, Albany.
Rathbone, Mrs. Mary A., Albany.
Rathbone, Thomas R., Providence.
Rathbun, John R., New Haven, Ct.
Rawson, Elihu T., Columbus, Ohio.
Rauschenbusch, Rev. August, Mt. Sterling, Mo.
Raymond, Rev. Lewis, Sandusky, Ohio.
Raymond, Samuel G., Danbury, Ct.
Raymond. Chas P., South Norwalk, Ct.
Raynor, Samuel, New York.
Raynor, Mrs. Sarah D., New York.
Raynor, William P., New York.
Raynor, Miss Mary S., New York.
Raynor, James W., New York.
Rea, William A., Providence.
Read, Rev. Hiram W., Albuquerque, N. M.
Read, Mrs. Alzina A. J., Albuquerque, N. M.
Read, Rev. Daniel, Medina, N. Y.
Read, Rev. James S.
Read, Mrs. James H., Providence,
Read, George W., Fall River, Mass.
Read, Mrs. Hannah T., Deep River, Ct.
Read, Dr. Thomas H., Decatur, Ill.
Reading, Cæzer, Flemington, N. J.
Reed, Mrs. Sarah, Deep River, Ct.
Reed, Evans H., Townsend, Vt.
Reed, Mrs. Fanny B., Townsend, Vt.
Reed, Mrs. Sarah B. G., Bristol, R. I.
Reed, Mrs. Emeline, Chelsea, Mass.
Reed, Thomas B., New York.
Reed, Wm. B., North East, N. Y.
Reed, Mrs. Mary Ann, North East, N. Y.
Reed, Mrs. Eunice, North East, N. Y.
Reed, Miss Mary F., North East. N. Y.
Reed, Rev. E. D., Oneida, N. Y.
Reed, Mrs. E. D, Oneida, N. Y.
Reed, David, Utica, N. Y.
Reed, Enos, East Cambridge, Mass.
Reed, Lewis B., New York.
Reed, Rev. William, Barnstable, Mass.
Reed, Rufus, Albion, N. Y.
Reed, G. Washington, Philadelphia.
Reed, Miss Henrietta A., Boston.
Reed, Rev. James, Hamburg, N. Y.
Rees, John F., Sennett, N. Y.
Reese, Rev. Daniel, White Creek, N. Y.
Reid, Mrs. Dorothy, New London, Ct.

Reynolds, Stephen D., Wickford, R. I.
Rhodes, G., Lawtonville, S. C.
Rice, Rev. A., Stonsville, S. C.
Rice, Mrs. Mary Orleans, N. Y.
Rice, Josiah, Worcester, Mass.
Rice, Luther J., South Valley, N. Y.
Rich, Joseph C., Penfield, N. Y.
Rich, George B., New Haven, Ct.
Richards, Rev. John M., Germantown, Pa.
Richards, Rev. Wm. C., Lynn, Mass.
Richards, Mrs. Eliza G., Lynn, Mass.
Richards, Wm. H., Philadelphia.
Richards, Mrs. Elizabeth Philadelphia.
Richards, Wm. L., Jr., Philadelphia.
Richards, Edwin S., Philadelphia.
Richards, Joseph L., Philadelphia.
Richards, Miss Eleanor A. Philadelphia.
Richards, Miss Sarah A., Philadelphia.
Richards, Zalmon, Washington, D. C.
Richards, Henry, Fall River Mass.
Richards, Truman, Brooklyn, N. Y.
Richards, Miss Isabel New York.
Richards, James, Cleveland, Ohio.
Richards, A. R. Rochester, N. Y.
Richards, Rev. Samuel, Providence, R.
Richards, Mrs. Maria T. Providence, R. I.
Richards, Ebenezer T., Holyoke, Mass.
Richards, Mrs. Cornelia V. H., Providence.
Richardson, Rev. Daniel F., Hanover, N. H.
Richardson, Wm. T., Cambridge, Mass.
Richardson, Thomas S., Brooklyn, N. Y.
Richardson, Mrs. Ann, Boston.
Richardson, Freeman, Auburn, N. Y.
Richardson, Rev. John, South Berwick, Me.
Richardson, Mrs. Euphemia, Troy N. Y.
Richardson, Mrs. Lydia, Salem, Mass.
Richmond, Miss Maryetta, Hillsdale, N. Y.
Richmond, Rev. Nathaniel, Pendleton, Ia.
Rider, Charles C. Roxbury, Mass.
Riddick, Jethro H. Sunbury, N. C.
Riddick, Nathan, Sunbury, N. C.
Riley, Rev. G. W., Paris, Ill.

Robinson, R
Robinson, R
Robinson, Be
Robinson, M
Robinson, De
Robinson, W
Robinson, M
Robinson, Mr
Robinson, R
Robinson, E
Robinson, So
Robinson, M
Robinson, He
Rockafellow,
Rockwell, Da
Rockwood, R
Rockwood, M
Roe, Rev. Ch
Roe, Mrs. Ma
Roel, Austin,
Rogers, Rev.
Rogers, Enos
Rogers, Mrs.
Rogers, Miss
Rogers, Richa
Rogers, Rev.
Rogers, Dr. Al
Rogers, Georg
Rogers, Richa
Rogers, Mrs. S
Rogers, Danie
Rogers, Mrs. I
Rogers, Gilber
Rogers, Archil
Rollin, Rev. J.
Roney, Rev. W
Roof, Milton,
Rose, Mrs. Ma
Rose, Mrs. Oli
Rose, Northup
Ross, Rev. Art
Ross, Daniel V

George W., Worcester, Mass.
n, Richard R., New Brunswick, N. J.
n, Hon. Peter P., New Brunswick, N. J.
n, Daniel, New Brunswick, N. J.
n, Elias, New Brunswick, N. J.
n, Reune D., New Market, N. J.
n, Ephraim, J., New Market, N. J.
n, Mrs. Osee, New Market, N. J.
n, Mrs. Isabella, New York.
t, Benjamin, Du Buque, Iowa.
ll, Rev. Philemon R., Canton, Mass.
ll, William, Yanceville, N. C.
ll, Rev. Abm. A., Stockbridge, Mass.
ll, Rev. Rutherford, Deep River, Ct.
ll, Samuel P., Chester, Ct.
ll, Mrs. James, Haverhill, Mass.
l, Levi F., Cambridge, Mass.
l, Rev. Robert, Richmond College, Va.
Rev. Alvah, Georgia, Vt.
gton, Thomas B., Williamsburg, N. Y.
l, Mrs. Sarah B., Salem, Mass.
l, Morgan, Norwich, Ct.
Wm., Rochester, N. Y.
Orrin, Rochester, N. Y.
ary, Wm. D., New York.
n, Mrs. Harriet H., Brooklyn, N. Y.
n, Rev. George W., Washington, D. C.
Dr. Lewis R., Beaufort, S. C.
rn, Seth J., Manchester, N. H.
rs, Henry, Warren, R. I.
Ezra, Philadelphia.
, William H., Boston.
s, Rev. Edwin, Pittsfield, Mass.
d, Mrs. Harriet E., Norwich, N. Y.
y, Mrs. Agnes, New York.
nt, Solon, Haverhill, Mass.
nt, Adaline A., Grafton, Vt.
nt, J., Amesbury, Mass.
nt, Mrs. Betsey, Amesbury, Mass.
, Mrs. Cornelia A., Brooklyn, N. Y.
lee, L. R., Rochester, N. Y.
Matthew, New Haven, Ct.
ers, Mrs. Harriet, Nuttsville, Va.
ers, Thomas E., Lowell, Mass.
s, Moses B., Brooklyn, N. Y.
s, Mrs. Moses B., Brooklyn, N. Y.
s, Rev. Edward, Columbus, Ohio.
s, Mrs. Sarah F., Columbus, Ohio.
s, E. Payson, Columbus, Ohio.
s, Rev. Eleazer, Kendall, N. Y.
s, Mrs. Bridget, Bedford, N. Y.
s, Morgan, Little Mill Creek, Ohio.
, Rev. Addison A., Lyons, Iowa.
, Mrs. C. A. Scott, Lyons, Iowa.
, Mrs. Sarah, Cambridge, Mass.
r, Rev. Wm., Ransomville, N. Y.
r, Mrs. H. N., Manchester, N. H.
r, Moses W., Malden, Mass.
r, David, Haverhill, Mass.
r, Rev. Isaac, Manchester, N. H.
r, Rev. Conant, Canton, N. Y.
r, Enoch, Salisbury, Mass.
r, Rev. A. W., Lawrence, Mass.
r, Mrs. Maria G., Haverhill, Mass.
tt, Rev. Jas. J., Jackson, Mich.

Schaffer, Charles, Philadelphia.
Schoolcraft, John L., Albany.
Schofield, Rev. James, Rossville, Iowa.
Scott, Robert, Amesbury, Mass.
Scott, John, Columbia, S. C.
Scott, Mrs. Cornelia S., Newburg, N. Y.
Scott, Alfred, Lowell, Mass.
Scott, Rev. Ebenezer J., Rushford, N. Y.
Scott, Rev. George, Maquoketa, Iowa.
Scott, Rev. Jacob R., Rochester, N. Y.
Scott, John, Bridgeport, Ct.
Scribner, Samuel T., Danbury, Ct.
Scribner, Mrs. Maria, Danbury, Ct.
Seabrook, Mrs. Anna, Middletown, N. J.
Seaich, Joseph, Jr., New York.
Seaich, Mrs. Ellen, New York.
Sears, Miss Harriet H., New York.
See, Mrs. Sarah Ann, New York.
Seecomb, E. R., Brookline, Mass.
Seecomb, Mrs. Adeline G., Brookline, Mass.
Sedwick, Rev. W., Adamsville, Ohio.
Seeley, Mrs. John T., Syracuse, N. Y.
Seeley, Rev. Jesse N., Memphis, Tenn.
Seeley, Mrs. Agnes Jane, Memphis, Tenn.
Seeley, Miss Sarah Elizabeth, New York.
Seeley, Miss Ellen M., Elmira, N. Y.
Selleck, Mrs. Harriet B., Huntington, N. Y.
Seymour, James H., Gloversville, N. Y.
Siegfried, Rev. B. Y., Washington, Ohio.
Selleck, Rev. Lewis, Dover, N. Y.
Shailer, Mrs. Catharine P., Roxbury, Mass.
Shailer, Mrs. Sarah, Deep River, Ct.
Shailer, Mrs. Ann, Deep River, Ct.
Shailer, Mrs. Elizabeth, Portland, Me.
Shailer, Hezekiah, Suffield, Ct.
Shailer, Bezaleel, Haddam, Ct.
Shailer, Rev. Davis T., Becket, Mass.
Shank, Rev. Michael, Medina, Ohio.
Shattuck, Levi H., Somerville, N. J.
Sharp, William B., Wilmington, Del.
Sharp, Miss Julia D., Williamsburgh, N. Y.
Sharp, Mrs. Mary, Saratoga Springs, N. Y.
Sharp, Mrs. Ann, Boston, Mass.
Shaw, Charles, Providence.
Shaw, Miss Harriet N., Providence.
Shaw, Oliver J., Utica, N. Y.
Shaw, Rev. J. Milton, Albuquerque, N. M.
Shaw, James M., New York.
Shaw, Mrs. Rhoda, New York.
Shaw, Miss Mary A., New York.
Sheardown, Rev. T. S., Homerville, N. Y.
Shearman, Francis, New York.
Shed, Charles.
Sheffield, Mrs. Mary, Stamford, Ct.
Sheffield, Thomas S., Brooklyn, N. Y.
Shelden, Martin J., Suffield, Ct.
Sheldon, Gaylor, Albany.
Sheldon, Frederick A., Troy, N. Y.
Sheldon, L. C., Suffield, Ct.
Sheldon, William, North East, N. Y.
Shelley, Lewis E., Davenport, Iowa.
Shelmire, Mrs. Maria, Rochester, N. Y.
Shenston, Joseph W., New York.
Shepard, Russell R., Worcester, Mass.
Sheppard, Sylvanus B., Salem, N. J.

Shepardson, Ansel, Fairfax, Vt.
Shepardson, Miss Julia H., Cincinnati, O.
Sherman, William N., Wickford, R. I.
Sherman, Mrs. Mary M., Wickford, R. I.
Sherman, Geo. J., Providence.
Sherwin, E. B., Shelburne Falls, Mass.
Sherwin, Miss Eliza, Shelburne Falls, Mass.
Sherwood, Walker, Easton, Ct.
Sherwood, Mrs. Lydia, Weston, Ct.
Sherwood, Rev. D. W., Matteawan, N. Y.
Shoemaker, Robert, Philadelphia.
Shotwell, Hugh, Brooklyn, N. Y.
Shotwell, Rev. J. M., Mannsville, N. Y.
Showalter, J. B., Willistown, Pa.
Shubarth, Niles B., Providence.
Shuck, Rev. J. L., Sacramento, Cal.
Shugg, Richard, New York.
Shute, Rev. Samuel M., Alexandria, Va.
Sibell, Mrs. Sarah, New York.
Sibell, Mrs. J. William, New York.
Sibley, Rev. Clark, New Hampton, N. H.
Silcox, Mrs. Elizabeth, New York.
Silkworth, Samuel O., New York.
Silliman, Ezra, Bridgeport, Ct.
Silliman, Erva, Bridgeport, Ct.
Silliman, Mrs. Ezra, Bridgeport, Ct.
Silliman, Ebenezer, Southport, Ct.
Silliman, Nathaniel L., Easton, Ct.
Silliman, Rev. Harvey, Adams Basin, N. Y.

Smile
Smith
Smith
Smith
Smith
Smith
Smith
Smith
Smith
Smith
Smith
Smi

Mrs. Helen M., Greenwich, N. Y.
Allen, Gouverneur, N.Y.
Rev. C. B., Townsend, Vt.
Miss Emma F., Banksville, Ct.
Jesse H., New England Village, Mass.
Mrs. Mary White, Newton, Mass.
Mrs. Jane, Troy, N. Y.
Lucius E., Boston.
Mrs. Elisabeth, New York.
Charles E., Fall River, Mass.
Rev. Levi, West Plattsburg, N. Y.
Mrs. Levi, West Plattsburg, N. Y.
Rufus, Shelburne Falls, Mass.
Rev. R. T., Lyndonville, N. Y.
Henry N., North Chatham, N. Y.
Rev. Sherman G., East Greenwich, R. I.
Wm. B., Cherryville, N. J.
r, Miss Priscilla, Chelsea, Mass.
Mrs. Sarah Ann, New York.
n, Mrs. Eliza, New York.
Mrs. Abby S., Stonebridge, R. I.
Edwin M., Providence.
Peter, Marietta, Ohio.
, Mrs. Catharine B. L., Frazer's, Pa.
rs, Mrs Eliza B., New York.
'land, Jonas, Burnt Hills, N. Y.
ick, Mrs. Cynthia, Grand de Tour, Ill.
ick, George, Kingston, N. Y.
ood, Rev. Wm., Aylett's, Va.
orth, Mrs. James E., Brooklyn.
orth, James Adelbert, Brooklyn.
orth, John, Penfield, N. Y.
Mrs. Mary E., Battletown, Va.
Mrs. Elizabeth, Milwood, Va.
l, Rev. Lysander E., Morris, N. Y.
g, Miss H. M., Middletown, Ct.
Rev. Peter, Newark, N. J.
ng, Isaiah, Chelmsford, Mass.
ng, Daniel B., Stoningtonboro', Ct.
ng, Rev. Silas, Clockville, N. Y.
ng Rev. Amos F., Boston.
ng, Mrs. Carrie E., E. Cambridge, Mass.
ng, D. A., St. Louis, Mo.
Rev. Prof. P. B., Hamilton, N. Y.
Abraham, Jeddo, N. Y.
William, Reading, Mass.
John, Brooklyn, N. Y.
Mrs. Elizabeth, Brooklyn, N. Y.
Miss Susan B., Brooklyn, N. Y.
n, Thomas, Alexandria, O.
n, Mrs. Mary G., Granville, O.
r, Robert, Little Plymouth, Va.
r, Elijah, Moodus, Ct.
r, Rev. Wm. H., Spencer, N. Y.
r, Charles M., East Lyme, Ct.
r, Thaddeus H., Suffield, Ct.
, Marquis T., Jordan, N. Y.
, Rev. O., Danville, Iowa.
Nicholas N., Wickford, R. I.
ng, Rev. Oscar F., Northville, N. Y.
ng, Mrs. Clara O., Northville, N. Y.
ng, Mrs. Mary, New York.
n, Rev. W. D., Amanda, O.
e, Rev. Oliver I., Mount Morris, N. Y.
e, Miss Mary E., Providence.

Spratt, Rev. George, Spread Eagle, Pa.
Spratt, Rev. G. M., Lewisburg, Pa.
Sproul, Mrs. Abigail, Imlaystown, N. J.
Squires, Rev. James, East Troy, Wis.
Stahel, Casper, Zurich, Switzerland.
Stainburn, Miss Mary, New York.
Stanton, Daniel W., East Lyme, Ct.
Stanton, Reuben, South Westerloo, N. Y.
Staples, John, Stratfield, Ct.
Stark, Rev. J. F., Cincinnatus, N. Y.
Stark, Mrs. Delight, Fort Covington, N. Y.
Starkweather, Rev. John W., East Greene, N.Y.
Star, Isaiah, Wilmington, Del.
Stead, Thomas, Plainfield, N. J.
Steadman, Mrs Lura J., Evansville, Ia.
Steane, Mrs. Catharine E., Williamsburg, N.Y.
Stearns, Miss Catharine, Brookline, Mass.
Stearns, Rev. Myron N., Oregon Ter.
Stearns, Mrs. Dorcas R., Oregon Ter.
Stearns, Rev. O. O., Racine, Wis.
Stearns, Mrs. Hannah Jane, Newark, N. J.
Stedman, Daniel M. C., Wakefield, R. I.
Steele, Mrs. Mehitable, Haverhill, Mass.
Stelle, Rev. Bergen, Cherryville, N. J.
Stelle, Mrs. Hannah B., Cherryville, N. J.
Stelle, Rev. Lewis F., Old Bridge, N. J.
Stelle, Isaac, New Brunswick, N. J.
Stelle, Benjamin, Jerseyville, Ill.
Stelle, Lewis R., Paterson, N. J.
Stelle, Mrs. Adnee, Paterson, N. J.
Stelle, Augustus, New Brunswick, N. J.
Stelle, John, Brooklyn, N. Y.
Stelle, Manning, Plainfield, N. J.
Stelle, Peter R., New Brunswick, N. J.
Stelle, Samuel M., St. Louis, Mo.
Steere, Enoch, Providence.
Steelman, Rev. Henry, Sheakleyville, Pa.
Stetson, J. J., Farmington, Ill.
Stevens, Mrs. Mariette, Deep River, Ct.
Stevens, Samson, Westford, Mass.
Stevens, Miss Phebe Almy, Providence.
Stevens, Seriah, Boston.
Stevens, George W., Boston.
Stevens, B. H., Essex, Ct.
Stevens, Thomas, Saratoga Springs, N. Y.
Stevens, David, Middletown, Ct.
Stevens, John E., Chelmsford, Mass.
Stewart, Benj. N., ——, Wis.
Stewart, Rev. Henry G., Seekonk, Mass.
Stewart, Elliot, Ogden, N. Y.
Stewart, Orlando, Cambridge, Mass.
Stewart, Mrs. Hannah, Huntington, N. J.
Stickney, Rev. James M., Toulon, Ill.
Stickney, Mrs. J. M., Toulon, Ill.
Stickney, Samuel, Watertown, Mass.
Stickney, Mrs. Ann M., Fall River, Mass.
Stiles, James, Bridgeton, N. J.
Stillman, O. M., Westerly, R. I.
Stillman, Mrs. F. G., Westerly, R. I.
Stillwell, Albert G., Providence.
Stillwell, Mrs. Lydia J., Providence.
Stillwell, Charles M., Providence.
Stillwell, Frank E., Providence.
Stillwell, Lewis D., Providence.
Stimson, Rev. H. K., Marion, N. Y.

... Creek, N. J.
Stone, Rev. Marsena, Lebanon, Ohio.
Stone, Mrs Damaris, Swanzey, N. H.
Stone, Eben, Newton, Mass.
Stone, Prof J. A. B., D D., Kalamazoo, Mich.
Stone, Rev. O. B Nevada, Cal.
Stone, Miss Ann Judson, Worcester Mass.
Stone, A. F Millbury, Mass.
Stone, Nathan Jamaica Plains, Mass.
Storer, Mrs. Ol ve H., Hudson N. H.
Storer, Rev Joseph, Fisherville, N. H.
Storey, Simeon N., Worcester, Mass.
Storey, James Arnot, Williamsburg, N. Y.
Storms, Andrew, New York.
Storms, Anthony D., New York.
Story, Wm. F Boston.
Story, Joseph, Boston.
Story, Harriet M Norwich, Ct.
Story, Eunice M., Worcester, Mass
Story, Clara, Worcester, Mass.
Story, Eunice H., Worcester, Mass.
Stout, Rev. D. B., Middletown, N J.
Stout, Mrs. L. M., Louisa, C. H., Va.
Stout, George H., New Brunswick, N. J.
Stout, Agustus T New Brunswick, N. J.
Stout, Thomas, New Brunswick, N. J.
Stow, Henry Ne Haven, Ct.
Stow, Mrs. Baron, Boston.
Stowell, Rev. A. H., Providence, R. I.
Stowell, Mrs. A. H., Providence, R. I.
Stratton, Samuel T Philadelphia.
Strawn, Mrs. Mary E., Ottawa, Ill.
Street, Samuel, Holyoke, Mass.
Street, Miss Mary Ann New York.
Strickland, James L. New London, Ct.
Strickland, Eliza C., New London, Ct.
Strong, Myron, Rochester, N Y.
Strong, Alvah, Rochester, N. Y
Stuart, John, Greenwich, N. Y.
Sturges, Rev. Wm., Marlborough, N. Y.
Sulley, James, Minneapolis, Min.
Sulley, Mrs. Ann, Minneapolis, Min.
Summers, Mrs. Aaron, Bridgeport, Ct.

Taylor. John, New York.
Taylor, J. R., East Cambridge, Mass.
Taylor, William, New York.
Tefft, Willard, Union Village, N. Y.
Tefft, Thomas A., Providence.
Temple, James H., Chilicothe, Ill.
Terry, Mrs. A. N., Spring Garden, Va
Thalcher, Mrs. Elizabeth R.
Thayer, Thomas M., Gouverneur, N. Y.
Thayer, Lewis, Worcester, Mass.
Thayer, James H., Cambridge, Mass.
Theall, [illegible]rs. Jane, New York.
Theall, Miss [illegible]usan, New York.
Thigpen, Rev. Samuel Raymond, Mi.
Thistle, Mrs. Hann[illegible] New York.
Thomas, Thomas, (a[illegible]eet), New York.
Thomas, Mrs. Isabell[illegible]New Yor[illegible]
Thomas, James H., [illegible]ew York.
Thomas, Rev. [illegible]vi[illegible], E., Zanesville, Ohio.
Thomas, Griffith, New York.
Thomas, Rev. C. A., D.D., Brandon, Vt.
Thomas, Mrs Eliza Ann, New York.
Thomas, Mrs. Mary, Brooklyn, N. Y.
Thomas, Mrs. Almira S., Brandon, Vt.
Thomas, Rev. Evan J., Atlanta, Ill.
Thompson, Robert, Jr., New York.
Thompson, Mrs. Ann E., New York.
Thompson, Mrs. S. S., Pittsborough, N. C.
Thompson, Rev. Richard, Milton, Ct.
Thompson, Rev. Charles E., Iowa City, Iowa.
Thompson, L., Britton's X Roads, N. C.
Thompson, Benjamin M., Harlem, N. Y.
Thompson, Rev Sherman B., Little Valley, N. Y.
Thompson, Mrs. Serena, New York.
Thompson, Mrs. Harvey, Norwich, N. Y.
Thompson, Joshua, J., Salem, N. J.
Thompson, Richard H., Manchester, N. H.
Thompson, Horace, New Haven, Ct.
Thurston, Henry, Brooklyn, N. Y.
Thurber, Edmund, Providence.
Thurber, Gorham, Providence.
Thurber, Charles, Worcester, Mass.
Ticknor, William D., Boston.
Tiebout, Adam T., Brooklyn, N. Y.
Tiebout, Mrs. Jane, Brooklyn, N. Y.
Tilden, Rev. Chester, North Lyme, Ct.
Tilley, Mrs. Elizabeth S., New York.
Tillinghast, Jefferson, Norway, N. Y.
Tillinghast, Charles E., Providence.
Tillinghast, Rev. J. A., Allenton, R. I.
Tilson, Rev. Jonathan, Hingham, Mass.
Tilton, Rev. Charles.
Tilton, Rev. Josiah H., Lynn, Mass.
Tilton, Mrs. Abigail S. F, Meridith Village, N H.
Timberman, Rev. Jacob, Stockton, N. J.
Tindall, Samuel L., Wilmington, Del.
Tingley, Miss Nancy B., Valley Falls, R. I.
Tingley, Timothy C., Holden, Mass.
Tinkham, Rev. D., Center White Creek, N. Y.
Titchener, Henry, Binghamton, N. Y.
Tirrill, Jesse, Boston.
Titus, F. J., Middletown, O.
Titus, Rev. S. W., Gorham, N. Y.
Titus, Mrs. Annie C., Providence.
Tobey, Rev. Salmon, Pawtucket, R. I.
Todd, Rev., William, Stevensville, Va.
Todd, Drake P., New York.
Todd, Mrs. William W., New York.
Todd, Mrs. Angeline M., New York.
Todd, William J., New York.
Todd, Thomas W, New York.
Tolan, Rev. William B., Stepney Depot, Ct.
Tolman, Rev. John N., Decatur, Ill.
Tolman, Thomas, Philadelphia.
Tolman, Mrs. Mary, Philadelphia.
Tolman, Miss Martha, Boston.
Tolman, Mrs. Elizabeth A. Philadelphia.
Tonkin, Rev. Henry, Concord, N. H.
Toplif, Rev. C. H., Charlestown, Mass.
Torbet, Rev. Andrew M., St. Paul, Min. Ter.
Torian, Elijah, Halifax C. H., Va.
Tourtellot, Abraham, Nashua, N. H.
Tousley, Charles, New York.
Towle, Miss Sarah G., Newburyport, Mass.
Townsend, S. P., New York.
Townsend, Miss Naomi, New York.
Townsend, Rev. G. N., Reading, Mass.
Townsend, Mrs. Louisa L., Brooklyn, N. Y.
Townsend, Rev. B. C., Hector, N. Y.
Townsend, Thomas, Lynn, Mass.
Townsend, John A., Providence.
Tracy, Lucius H., New London, Ct.
Tracy, Rev. Oren, Concord, N. H.
Tracy, Mrs. Maria B., Concord, N. H.
Tracy, Miss Susan M., Concord, N. H.
Train, Mrs. A. S., Haverhill, Mass.
Travis, Simeon S., New York.
Travis, Luther, Southbridge, Mass.
Treat, E. S., Rochester, N. Y.
Trevor, John B., Philadelphia.
Tripp, Mrs. Susan, New Bedford, Mass.
Tripp, Ervin H., New York.
Tripp, Mrs. Caroline S. H., New York.
Tripp, Miss Sarah, New York.
Trout, William, Charleston, S. C.
Trow, Rev. Augustus H., Montezuma, N. Y.
Trowbridge, William, Sheboygan Falls Wis.
True, Reuben, Plainfield, N. H.
True, Osgood, Plainfield, N. H.
True, Mrs. Betsey M., Plainfield, N. H.
True, Mrs. Hannah, Meriden, N. H.
True, Mrs. Mary, Amesbury, Mass.
Truesdell, Mrs. Margerie, Hillsdale, N. Y.
Truman, Jonathan, Greenport, N. Y.
Truman, Stephen S., Owego, N. Y.
Truman, Mrs. Betsey S., Owego, N. Y.
Truman, Mrs. Eleanor M., Owego, N. Y.
Truman, Edward D., Owego, N. Y.
Trump, Isaac V., Somerville, N. J.
Tryon, Miss Eveline, Ballston, N. Y.
Tubbs, Benjamin H., West Dedham, Mass.
Tucker, Harwood B., Christianville, Va.
Tucker, Richard G., Stony Creek, Va.
Tucker, Rev. Silas, Galesville, Ill.
Tucker, Mrs. F. G., Stony Creek, Va.
Tucker, Mrs. Elisha, Chicago, Ill.
Tucker, James N. G., Chicago, Ill.
Tucker, Frederick D., Williamsburg, N. Y.
Tucker, Elisha, Middleborough, Mass.
Tucker, Mrs. Sally B.

Tucker, Rev. Cyrus T., Millbury, Mass.
Tucker Mrs. Sophia B., Millbury, Mass.
Tucker, Ebenezer, Cambridge, Mass.
Tukesbury, Mrs. Mary, Salisbury, Mass.
Turley, Capt. E., Philadelphia.
Turley, Mrs. Susan, Philadelphia.
Turnbull, Rev. Robert, D. D., Hartford, Ct.
Turner, Mrs. Mary A., New London, Ct.
Turner, Gabriel S., Newark, N. J.
Turner, Maria, Chelsea, Mass.
Turney, Rev. Edmund, D.D., Cincinnati.
Turney, Mrs. Caroline, Cincinnati.
Turney, J. P., Norwalk, Ct.
Turpin, Rev. John O., Aylett's, Va.
Turton, Rev. Wm. H., Farmington, Iowa.
Tustin, Rev. Josiah P., Charleston, S. C.
Tustin, John D., Camden, N. J.
Tuthill, Joseph, Brooklyn, N. Y.
Tuttle, Aaron, Littleton, Mass.
Tuttle, Alson, Littleton, Mass.
Tuxbury, Isaac, Salisbury Mills, Mass.
Twiss, Ira, Westville, Ct.
Twiss, Rev. Daniel F., Spotswood, N. J.
Tyler, Roswell R., Middlesex, N. Y.
Tyler, Mrs. Lucy, Deep River, Ct.
Tyler, Rev. Payson, Conway, Mass.
Ulyat, Rev. Wm. C., Norwalk, Ct.
Underhill, P. S., Brooklyn, N. Y.
Underhill, Mrs. Catharine M., Brooklyn, N. Y.
Updike, Miss Mary Ann, New York.

Vernon, Samu
Vernon, The
Vezutile, Mrs.
Vinal, Wm. D
Vinton, Rev.
Vinton, Mrs.
Vinton, Mrs.
Volk, Henry,
Volk, Mrs. E.
Volk, Miss E.
Votey, Rev. C
Vrooman, Re
Wade, Rev. J
Wade, Mrs. D
Wade, Josiah
Wade, Rev. J
Wald, Miss C
Waite, Miss
Wakefield, C
Wakefield, Re
Walden, Rev.
Waldo, Harm
Waldron, Mis
Wales, Sarah,
Walker, Rev.
Walker, Mrs.
Walker, Miss
Walker, Rev.
Walker, Mrs.
Walker, Mrs.

s. Mary, Sennett, N. Y.
Dr. Ransom, New York.
Benjamin L., Williamsburg, N. Y.
Miss Elizabeth, New York.
Mrs. Diantha O., West Potsdam, N. Y.
Rev. Patrick, Baltimore.
Rev. Benj., Kendall, N. Y.
Rev. J. G., Boston.
Chas. W., Utica, N. Y.
Rev. Edwin R., East Greenwich, R. I.
Moses, Cambridge, Mass.
Mrs. Grace, Cambridge, Mass.
Rev. H. S. P., Madrid, N. Y.
Horace, Norwich, Ct.
Rev. John, Easton, Ct.
Mrs. Emma, Burlington, Iowa.
Thomas, New York.
, Rev. Norman, Le Clair, Ill.
, Rev. R. L., South Valley, N. Y.
n, Nathan W., Mt. Pleasant, Ill.
a, Rev. R. A., Union Village, N. Y.
ton, Mrs. Elizabeth, Newbern, N. C.
Mrs. Clarissa, Albany.
Mrs. Elizabeth A., Brookline, Mass.
Horace, Brooklyn, N. Y.
Richard, New York.
Miss Sarah A., Philadelphia.
an, R. W., Covington, Ia.
aiah, New York.
rs. Emma, New York.
harles Henry, New York.
ohn, Elmira, N. Y.
Mrs. Mary B , Philadelphia.
Miss Elizabeth, Philadelphia.
Rev. W. H., West Acton, Mass.
George, New York.
James, Brooklyn, N. Y.
W. W., Springfield, Ill.
John, New York.
Henry M., New York.
on, Rev. Wm. E., Manyunk, Pa.
on, Rev. Mark R., Portsmouth, Va.
n, Nathan, Jr., Providence.
r. Samuel P., North Brookfield, N. Y.
. Welthy A., North Brookfield, N. Y.
ry, Miss Martha, Williamsburg, N. Y.
ry, Mrs. Mary, North Adams, Mass.
ry, Francis W., North Adams, Mass.
, Mrs. H. S. H., Providence.
, Francis, Jr., Worcester, Mass.
Rev. C. S., Norwich, Ct.
Mrs. Diana, Norwich, Ct.
Edwin H., Norwich, Ct.
Mrs. Ann, Groton, Ct.
Wanton A., New London, Ct.
C. Arnold, New London, Ct.
Daniel L., Albany, N. Y.
rs. Maria, New Brunswick, N. J.
ev. Abner, Belleville, N. Y.
ev. W. R., Dixon, Ill.
aniel, Leroy, N. Y.
ev. J. N., Fort Covington, N. Y.
rs. J. N., Fort Covington, N. Y.
ohn, Newtown, Ohio.
Rev. Julius S., Romulusville, N. Y.

Webster, Phineas, Haverhill, Mass.
Webster, Mrs. Phineas, Haverhill, Mass.
Webster, Rev. Amos, Newton Up Falls, Mass.
Webster, Rev. S. B., Norwalk, O.
Webster, Caleb, Lowell, Mass.
Webster, Rev. J. D., Green, N. Y.
Weckerly, Daniel, Philadelphia.
Weddell, Rev. Peter M., Canton, Ohio.
Welch, Mrs. B. T., Newtonville, N. Y.
Welch, Rev. James E., Hickory Grove, Mo.
Weirick, Miss Sallie A., Logansport, Ia.
Weld, Nathaniel, Jamaica Plain, Mass.
Weld, Mrs. Lucy, New York.
Weld, Aaron D., Winchester, Mass.
Welden, Asa W., New York.
Wells, Mrs. Elizabeth, New York.
Wells, Rev. Alfred, Attica, N. Y.
Wells, Rev. Wm. A., Muscatine, Iowa.
Wells, Miss Mary E., Providence, R. I.
Wemple, Abraham A., Schenectady, N. Y.
Wescott, Rev. Isaac, Gloversville, N. Y.
Wescott, Jehiel, Bridgeton, N. J.
Wescott, Jehiel, Jr., Bridgeton, N. J.
Wescott, Josiah S., Bridgeton, N. J.
Wescott, Rev. Henry, Warrenville, Ill.
Wescott, John, Bridgeton, N. J.
West, Mrs. Ann, Brooklyn, N. Y.
West, John G., Williamsburg, N. Y.
West, Willoughby W., York, N. Y.
West, Rev. Hezekiah, Mecklenburg, N. Y.
Weston, Rev. Henry G., Peoria, Ill.
Weston, Mrs. Henry G., Peoria, Ill.
Weston, Mrs. Hetty, Lynn, Mass.
Weston, Franklin L., Johnson's Creek, N. Y.
Westervelt, John, Williamsburg, N. Y.
Westover, Rev. John T., Fox Lake, Wis.
Wetherbee, Ephraim, Broadalbin, N. Y.
Wetherbee, Miss Ruby, Broadalbin, N. Y.
Wethern, George M., Lowell, Mass.
Wetterau, Mrs. Frances, New York.
Whedon, C. H., Homer, N. Y.
Wheat, Mrs. Priscilla P., Philadelphia.
Wheaton, Reuben, Wilmington, Del.
Wheaton, Mrs. Elizabeth M., Columbus, O.
Wheaton, William, Cohansey, N. J.
Wheelock, Mrs. E. M., Elbridge, N. Y.
Wheelock, S. B., Greenwich, N. Y.
Wheelock, Mrs. C. E. S., Milwaukee, Wis.
Wheeler, Mrs. Elizabeth H., Sacramento, Cal.
Wheeler, Miss Melvina, P., Sacramento, Cal.
Wheeler, Mrs. Maria N., Grafton, Vt.
Wheeler, Rev. Benj., Plaistow, N. H.
Wheeler, Lucius, New York.
Wheeler, Rev. S. S. Placerville, Cal.
Wheeler, Mrs. Mary B., Placerville, Cal.
Wheeler, Rev. Benj., Caldwell, N. J.
Wheeler, Russell, Utica, N. Y.
Wheeler, Mrs. Ann, New York.
Wheeler, Mrs. Mary E., North Randolph, Ms.
Wheeler, Rev. R., Grafton, Vt.
Whidden, Mrs. Sarah, Calais, Me.
Whilden, Rev. B. W., Camden, S. C.
Whipple, Harvey, Malone, N. Y.
Whipple, Ethan, Providence, R. I.
Whipple, Mrs. Hannah, New Boston, N. H.

Whitaker, Alanson, Granville, Ill.
Whitaker, Wm. N., Philadelphia.
Whitcomb, Peter, Littleton, Mass.
White, Mrs. E., North Shore, N. Y.
White, Mrs. Martha D., Marcus Hook, Pa.
White, Miss Lydia, Haverhill, Mass.
White, Thomas, Brooklyn, N. Y.
White, Samuel S., Whiteville, N. Y.
White, Harvey, Mt. Holly, Vt.
White, Thomas P., Bridgeport, Ct.
White, Mrs. Thomas P., Bridgeport, Ct.
White, Joseph, Winchendon, Mass.
White, Beza L., Taunton, Mass.
White, Ebenezer, Newton, Mass.
White, Ebenezer B., Williamsburg, N. Y.
White, Mrs. Mary, New York.
White, Samuel, Bordentown, N. J.
White, Mrs. Sylvanus, Brooklyn.
White, Samuel, Littleton, Mass.
White, Miss Mary, New York.
White, Miss Emily J., Taunton, Mass.
White, Almeth, Rahway, N. J.
Whitehead, Samuel, Chester, N. J.
Whitehead, Mrs. Emeline V., New York.
Whitehead, Artemas K., New York.
Whitehead, John W., New York.
Whitehead, Linus P., New York.
Whitehead, Rev. Wm. M., Frankford, Pa.
Whitehead, Rev. J. M., Westville, Ia.
Whitford, H. G., Willington, Ct.
Whitford, Mrs. ...

Wilcox, Abrah
Wilcox, Allen,
Wilde, Rev. Z.
Wilder,
Wilder, Mrs. De
Wilder, Rev. Syd
Wildman, John,
Wildman, Mrs.

Wildman, Mrs.
Wilkins, Rev. A
Wilkins, Mrs.
Wilkinson, Rev.
Willard, Rev. G
Willard, Lucius
Willard, Mrs. Pe
Willard, Wm. B.
Willard, Mrs. N
Willard, Rev. C.
Willard, Hon. L
Willett, Mrs. A
Willett, Miss S
Willett, Mrs. Ch
Williams, Charl
Williams, Rober
Williams, Mrs. E
Williams, Mrs. C
Williams, Mrs. M
Williams, Polly
Williams, Franci
Williams, Rev.

Wingate, Dexter B., Grafton, Mass.
Winans, Elnathan, Lima, N. Y.
Winans, Mrs. Marcy, Lima, N. Y.
Winans, Theodore, Plainfield, N. J.
Winchell, Miss Ann, New York.
Windust, Edward, New York.
Winslow, Robert F., Fond du Lac, Wis.
Winslow, Rev. Octavius, Leamington, Eng.
Winston, Rev. Meriwether, Richmond, Va.
Winter, Rev. Thomas, Roxborough, Pa.
Winter, Rev. John, Knoxville, Ill.
Winterton, Mrs. Mary, New York.
Wise, Miss Clarissa R., New Russia, N. Y.
Wisner, Mrs. Sarah, Mount Morris, N. Y.
Wisner, Mrs. Adaline, Elmira, N. Y.
Wisham, Samuel, Moorestown, N. J.
Wiswell, Mrs. C. A., West Troy, N. Y.
Witherwax, Mrs. Emeline B., Davenport, Io.
Withall, John, Henrietta, N. Y.
Witherbee, John B., Jamaica Plains, Mass.
Withington, Elijah, Morrisania, N. Y.
Withington, Mrs. M., Morrisania, N. Y.
Wolcott, Mrs. Mary S., New York.
Wolcott, Mrs. Naomi, Rochester, N. Y.
Wollaston, Joshua, Wilmington, Del.
Worrall, Rev. Thos. D., Lowell, Mass.
Wood, Mrs. J. S., Hertford, N. C.
Wood, Mrs. Mary E., Hertford, N. C.
Wood, Rev. N. N., D. D., Upper Alton, Ill.
Wood, Jennings J., Speedwell, S. C.
Wood, George, Springfield, Ill.
Wood, Joseph T., Westboro', Mass.
Wood, Mrs. Amelia, Brooklyn, N. Y.
Wood, Eliphalet, Honesdale, Pa.
Wood, Ambrose, Albion, N. Y.
Woods, Gardner, Jersey, Ohio.
Woods, Hiram, Nashua, N. H.
Woodbridge, William A., New York.
Woodbury, William W., Suffield, Ct.
Woodbury, Rev. John, Templeton, Mass.
Woodbury, Miss Frances, Danvers, Mass.
Woodbury, Eliza A., Lynn, Mass.
Woodman, Moses, New Gloucester, Me.
Woodruff, Mrs. Innocent, Albany.
Woodward, Rev. Jonas, Cedar Rapids, Iowa.
Woodward, Mrs. Eliza, Cedar Rapids, Iowa.
Woodward, Mrs. Mary D., Middlesex, Va.
Woodward, Sylvester, Lowell, Mass.
Woodward, Darwin W., Franklindale, N. Y.
Woodworth, Levi B., Canaan, Ohio.
Woolston, Mrs. Keziah, Vincentown, N. J.
Wooster, Mrs. Aurelia R., Deep River, Ct.
Work, Rev. Perly, Sheboygan, Wis.
Worth, Rev. Edmund, Kennebunk, Me.
Worthington, S., Springfield, Mass.
Wright, Rev. David, Hartford, Ct.
Wright, Mrs. Abigail, Hartford, Ct.
Wright, Wm. J., Hardgrove's Va.
Wright, Theodore, New York.
Wright, Asahel B., Lowell, Mass.
Wright, Harvey, Three Rivers, Mass.
Wright, Mrs. Julia A., Westport, N. Y.
Wright, Rev. Ansell T., Weart's Corners, N. J.
Wright, Rev. Lyman, Norwich, N. Y.
Wright, R. A., Rochester, N. Y.
Wright, James G., Canton, N. J.
Wyckoff, Mrs. Cornelius R., Weedsport, N. Y.
Wyckoff, J. N., Woodbridge, N. J.
Wyckoff, Mrs. Elizabeth, Woodbridge, N. J.
Wyckoff, W. G., Middletown, N. J.
Wyckoff, Francis, Plainfield, N. J.
Wyckoff, Mrs. Sarah B., Brooklyn, N. Y.
Wyckoff, Jacob F., New York.
Wyer, Rev. Henry O. Savannah, Ga.
Wynn, Mrs. Susan, Tuckahoe, N. J.
Wynn, Benjamin, F., Tuckahoe, N. J.
Yale, Levi, Augusta, N. Y.
Yendell, Sarah, Boston.
Yeomans, Mrs. Olive, Providence.
Yeomans, Miss Mary Ann, Providence.
York, Mrs. Hannah, Haverhill, Mass.
York, C., Norwich, N. Y.
York, Mrs. Esther, Norwich, N. Y.
Young, Mrs. Sarah, Brooklyn, N. Y.
Young, Rev. George, Hatbo,o', Pa.
Young, Rev. Robert F., Chestnut Hill, Pa.
Young, Mrs. Maria Ann, Chester Hill, Pa.
Young, Robert McCarthy, New York.
Young, Rev. G. W., Antistown, Pa.
Young, William W., Stamford, Ct.
Yuran, Mrs., S. S., Tunbridge, Vt.
Zebley, John F., Yew York.
Zimmerman, Edwin, New York.

LIST O

DIRECTORS AND

1833-4.

DIRECTOR.

Cobb, Nathaniel R., Boston, Mass.

MEMBERS.

Barrett, Rev. Thomas, Webster, Mass.
Chase, Rev. John, Brookfield, Mass.

1834-5.

MEMBER.

Lazell, Rev. J. E., Harvard, Mass.

1835-6.

DIRECTORS.

Foster, Rev. E., Amesbury, Mass.
Freeman, Rev. E. W., Lowell, Mass.
[illegible]

Rev. Jonathan, D.D., Granville, O.
Rev. Wm. George, Essex, Ct.

MEMBERS.

, Mrs. Mary, New York.
, Charles, D., New York.
l, Rev. John O., Perrysburg, O.
, Richard, Portsmouth, Va.
sh, Mrs. Mary, Philadelphia.

1845-6.

MEMBERS.

ell, Mrs. Maria, New York.
Rev. Wilson, Beaufort, S. C.
Mrs. J., Leavitt, Bankok, Siam.
p, Rev. Lebbeus, Samptown, N. J.
ll, Joseph H., Nashville, Tenn.
ll, Rev. John, Hoosick, N. Y.
l, Mrs. Mary B., Woburn, Mass.
ds, Joseph, Norwich, Ct.

1846-7.

DIRECTORS.

ler, Mrs. Mary, Lynn, Mass.
Mrs. Lydia, Canton, China.
, Rev. Jeremiah B., Washington, N. Y.

MEMBERS.

, Mrs. Eliza A., New York.
rs. Olive, North Bristol, N. Y.
Richard, Parham's Store, Va.
on, Rev. Peter, New York.

1847-8.

DIRECTORS.

, John J., Montgomery, N. Y.
ev. David, Reed's Creek, Ark.
son, Rev. William, New York.
Rev. Philetus B., Owego, N. Y.
Rev. Wm. M., Houston, Texas.

MEMBERS.

Joseph, New London, N. H.
Rev. George, Manchester, N. H.
Joshua, New York.
Mrs. Sarah A., Richmond, Va.
, Rev. Thomas, Newport, R. I.
Mrs. Sarah, New Woodstock, N. Y.
Rev. Linus M., Hamilton, N. Y.
son, Rev. Charles, Poughkeepsie, N.Y.
, Edwin G., Elizabeth City, N. C.
John, Hertford, N. C.

1848-9.

DIRECTORS.

ct, Rev. George, New York.
George, New York.

MEMBERS.

Mrs. Eliza C., New York.
r, Rev. Jacob H., New York.
erlin, Hinds, Leroy, N. Y.
Mrs. Caroline B. Bankok, Siam.
, John H. New York.
Rev. J. G., Portsmouth, N. H.
Rev. Abijah, Clifton Park, N. Y.
Oliver, Providence, R. I.
od, Rev. F. S., Saratoga, Springs, N. Y.
an, Rev. Daniel, Lebanon, Ct.
as, Rev. Daniel, New York.

1849-50.

DIRECTORS.

Allen, Rev. Ira M., New York.
Bradford, Rev. Z., Providence, R. I.
Estes, Rev. Elliot, Lower Three Runs, S. C.
Milbank, Charles, W., New York.
Peck, Rev. John, New Woodstock, N. Y.
Train, Rev. Charles, Framingham, Mass.
Wilson, James, New York.

MEMBERS.

Baillie, Jonathan, Parham's Store, Va.
Barker, Rev. Luke, M.D., New York.
Brockway, C., Broadalbin, N. Y.
Brown, William, Parham's Store, Va.
Cate, Rev. George W., Rowe, Mass.
Corning, Mrs. Nancy, Brooklyn, N. Y.
Cox, Charles, Rahway, N. J.
Crawford, Rev. R. B., Antioch, Miss.
Forrester, James M., New York.
Gale, Mrs. Phebe, East Bennington, Vt.
Harris, Rev. William, Nassau, New York.
Lewis, Rev. D.D., New Brunswick, N. J.
Payne, Mrs. Betsey, Hamilton, N. Y.
Rogers, Rev. John, Paterson, N. J.
Roy, Rev. Wm. A., Charlottesville, Va.
Winchell, Rev. Reuben, Lockport, N. Y.
Yancey, Algernon, Yanceyville, N. C.

1850-1.

DIRECTORS.

Granberry, Rev. N. R., Meridian Springs, Miss.
Graves, Rev. Hiram A., Boston, Mass.
Judson, Rev. A., D.D., Maulmain, Burmah.

MEMBERS.

Bennett, Rev. Alfred, Homer, N. Y.
Bond, Levi, Windsor, N. C.
Briggs, Rev. Ebenezer, Middleboro', Mass.
Burdick, Miss E. M., New York.
Burke, Joshua A., Brooklyn, N. Y.
Cook, Rev. B., Jr., Jewett City, Ct.
Cornelius, Mrs. Rachel, Mt. Holly, N. J.
Darrow, Rev. Francis, Waterford, Ct.
Davis, W. Strebane, N. C.
Frey, Rev. J. C. F., Pontiac, Mich.
Going, Mrs. Lucy T., Columbus, O.
Horn, Turner, Britton's X Roads, N. C.
Humphrey, Mrs. Julia Ann, Albany, N. Y.
Jackson, Rev. Timothy, Piqua, O.
Kelly, Mrs. Elizabeth, New York.
Kendall, Josiah, Littleton, Mass.
Logan, Rev. John, Blandenville, Ill.
Lester, David, Brooklyn, N. Y.
McLaren, Finley, Le Roy, N. Y.
Munn, Mrs. Sarah P. New York.
Ormsby, Rev. John, Knox's Corners, N. Y.
Parker, Amasa W., Lowell, Mass.
Postley, Charles, New York.
Randall, Jedediah, Portersville, Ct.
Snook, John, Fort Gibson, N. Y.
Todd, William H., New York.
White, Thomas, Philadelphia.

1851-2.

DIRECTORS.

Dodge, Rev. Daniel, Philadelphia.

Hall, Rev. Daniel, New York.
Jones, Mrs. Susan, Newbern, N. C.
Lathrop, Mrs. Jane E., New York.
Manning, Rev. Benjamin, Brookfield, Mass.
Martin, Mrs. R. W., New York.
Miller, John B., Sumterville, S. C.
Morrill, Otis H., Lowell, Mass.
Remington, Mrs. Eliza Ann, New York.
Rider, Miss Olive P., Suffield, Ct.
Shuck, Mrs. Eliza G., Shanghai, China.
Stone, Mrs. Sarah A., New York.
Tucker, Mrs. Levi, Boston, Mass.
Whitman, Rev. S. S., Madison, Wis.

1852-3.

DIRECTORS.

Brown, Rev. O. B., Washington, D. C.
Crozer, Miss Sallie K., Chester, Pa.
Miller, Pardon, Providence.
Rhees, Rev. M. J., D.D., Williamsburg, N. Y.

MEMBERS.

Adams, Mrs. Cornelia C., Cleveland, O.
Ashley, Mrs. Hannah, Poultney, Vt.
Bellamy, Mrs. Eliza, Arcadia, N. Y.
Boynton, Mrs. Ruth, North Springfield, Vt.
Brown, Mrs. O. B., Washington, D. C.
Carraway, Mrs. H., Kingston, N. C.
Cosner, Rev. Henry, Lyndon, Ill.
Fant, Rev. Ephraim, Halselville, S. C.
Goodliff, James, New York.
Haskell, Rev. Daniel, Hamilton, N. Y.
Haynes, Rev. Arus, M. D., New York.
Jones, Rev. John, Belleville, Ia.
Maghee, Mrs. Ann C., New York.
Maginnis, Rev. John, D.D., Rochester, N. Y.
Miner, Mrs. Mary Jane, New York.
Owen, Rev. E. D., Madison, Ia.
Shipley, Simon G., Boston.
Symonds, Rev. Thomas M., Green Bay, Wis.
Turner, Mrs. Grace, New London, Ct.
Walton, Rev. L., Chestnut Hill, Pa.
Weeks, Miss Ann, New York.

Griffit
Guild,
Havila
Hurlb
Humpl
Lagrar
Lawre
Moore,
Murra
Newto
Nesbit
Palme
Pegg,
Paddo
Rue, N
Shotw
Shepp
Tryon,
Ulyat,
Whitn

Cone,
Ellis,
Kimba
Whiti

Abbot
Angie
Austin
Booth,
Bough
Brown
Brush,
Capro
Cauld
Challi
Cleave
Davis,
Davis,
Dema

Hill, Mrs. Lydia Ann, Carmel, N. Y.
Judson, Mrs. Emily C., Hamilton, N. Y.
Miner, Rev. Bradley, Providence, R. I.
Neale, Mrs. Melissa Y., Boston.
Oakley, Mrs. Cassandra, New York.
Pennypacker, John, Wilmington, Del.
Porter, Edwin, Lowell, Mass.
Richards, Rev. Humphrey, Dorchester, Mass.
Richards, Mrs. Eunice J., Dorchester, Mass.
Rodgers, Rev. Ebenezer, Upper Alton, Ill.
Sharp, J. Milton, Williamsburg, N. Y.
Skinner, Mrs. Anna, Hertford, N. C.
Spencer, Rev. Horace, Reed's Corners, N. Y.
Spivey, Aaron J., Brownsville, Tenn.
Sweet, H. H., Fredonia, N. Y.
Taylor, Daniel Webster, New York.
Walker, Mrs. Jane P., Central Falls, R. I.
Waterbury, Rev. J. H., Elizabethtown, N. J.

1855-6.

DIRECTORS.

Cone, Rev. Spencer H., D.D., New York.
Choules, Rev. J. O., D.D., Newport, R. I.
Crane, James C., Richmond, Va.
Germond, George C., Williamsburg, N. Y.
Ives, Mrs. Hope, Providence, R. I.
Morse, Jacob, Sturbridge, Mass.
Munn, Stephen B., New York.
Pratt, Rev. D D., Nashua, N. H.
Purser, Thomas, Brooklyn, N. Y.

MEMBERS.

Ballard, Rev. John B., New York.
Belden, Rev. A. R., Iowa City, Iowa.
Bishop, William, Bloomington, Ill.
Bottom, Hon. N. H., Shaftsbury, Vt.
Brayton, Philip, Phenix, R. I.
Calam, Mrs. Mary N., Sing Sing, N. Y.
Challiss, John, Salem, N. J.
Clapp, Mrs. Jane M., Danbury, Ct.
Colver, Mrs. Esther B., Worcester, Mass.
Cox, Miss Achsah, Imlaystown, N. J.
Davis, Rev. Jonathan, Monticello, S. C.
Davis, Rev. Joseph, Hebron, O.
Edwards, Miss Mary, New York.
English, Isaac, Salem, N. J.
Evans, Mrs. Mary, New York.
Hardin, Rev. Theodore, Horton, N. Scotia.
Harris, Isaac, New London, Ct.
Hazard, Simeon, Newport, R. I.
Hunt, Dr. George, Le Clair, Ill.
Jones, Mrs. Rhoda, Smithville, N. Y.
Leland, Mrs. Caroline M., Brooklyn, N. Y.
Logan, Rev. John, Blandensville, Ill.

Mangam, Mrs. Sarah Ann, New York.
Miller, John B., Sumpterville, S. C.
Nice, Rev. W. J., Imlaystown, N. J.
Nichols, Miss Hannah, Bridgeport, Ct.
Purser, Mrs. Mary, Brooklyn, N. Y.
Richards, Joel, Claremont, N. H.
Richmond, Rev. J. L., Indianapolis, Ia.
Scott, Rev. James, Newburgh, N. Y.
Sheppard, Rev. Wm., Bridgeton, N. J.
Sheppard, Joseph, Bridgeton, N. J.
Smith, Z. L., Norwich, Ct.
Steadman, Rev. N. V., Evansville, Ia.
Sutton, George, New York.
Teasdale, Rev. John, St. Louis, Mo.
Thomas, Moses, Ballston Spa., N. Y.
Thornton, Rev. V. R., Public Square, Geo.
West, John, Brooklyn, N. Y.
Whitman, Hiram, Belvidere, Ill.
Wheeler, Nelson, Providence, R. I.
Wyckoff, Rev. Cornelius P., Weedsport, N. Y.

1856-7.

LIFE DIRECTORS.

Clarke, Rev. Elbert W., Arcade, N. Y.
Colgate, William, New York.
Collom, Rev. J. G., Mt. Holly, N. J.
Conant, John, Brandon, Vt.
Cramb, Rev. Augustus B., Metamora, Ill.
Flanders, Benjamin, Brooklyn, N. Y.
Granger, Rev. J. N., D.D., Providence, R. I.
Kelly, Samuel R., Brooklyn, N. Y.
Wightman, Rev. F., Wethersfield, Ct.

LIFE MEMBERS.

Beebe, Alexander M., LL.D., Utica, N. Y.
Capern, Thomas, Moorestown, N. J.
Cone, Miss Amelia M., Philadelphia.
Farnsworth, W., Fleming, N. Y.
Forsyth, Russell, Albany, N. Y.
Guest, Rev. Pitney, Canton, O.
Hovey, Mrs. Elizabeth, Cambridge, Mass.
Ingals, Rev. Lovell, Akyab, Arracan.
Kain, Charles, Marlton, N. J.
Martin, Stelle R., Rahway, N. J.
Marsh, Rev. L. G., New York.
Marshall, Rev. Andrew, Savannah, Geo.
Miller, Rev. Harvey, Meriden, Ct.
Perego, Mrs. Margaret, New York.
Phillips, Samuel B., M. D., New York.
Silliman, Rev. Gershom, Helena, Ill.
Smith, Mrs. Hannah B., Iowa City, Iowa.
Thomas, Thomas, New York.
Underhill, Rev. Charles H., Peekskill, N. Y.
Walker, Mrs. Grace W., Marcus Hook, Pa.
Woodruff, David, Bridgeton, N. J.

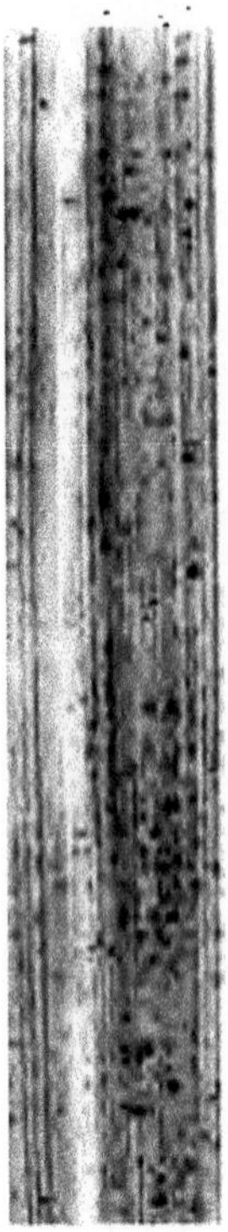

TWENTY-SIXTH REPORT

OF THE

American Baptist Home Mission Society,

PRESENTED BY THE

EXECUTIVE BOARD

AT THE

ANNIVERSARY HELD IN PHILADELPHIA,

MAY 14 AND 15, 1858;

WITH

THE TREASURER'S REPORT AND OTHER DOCUMENTS.

NEW YORK:
PUBLISHED AT THE AMERICAN BAPTIST HOME MISSION ROOMS, No. 115 NASSAU ST.,
AND PRINTED BY THOMAS HOLMAN, CORNER CENTRE AND WHITE STS., N. Y.
1858.

ACT OF INCORPORATION.

AN ACT TO INCORPORATE THE AMERICAN BAPTIST HOME MISSION SOCIETY, PASSED APRIL 12, 1843, AND AMENDED, FEBRUARY 9, 1849.

The People of the State of New York, represented in Senate and Assembly, do enact as follows:

§ 1. All such persons as now are, or may hereafter become, members of the American Baptist Home Mission Society, formed in the City of New York, in the year one thousand eight hundred and thirty-two, shall be, and hereby are, constituted a body corporate, by the name of the American Baptist Home Mission Society, for the purpose of promoting the preaching of the gospel in North America.

§ 2. This Corporation shall be capable of taking, holding, or receiving any property, real or personal, [redacted]

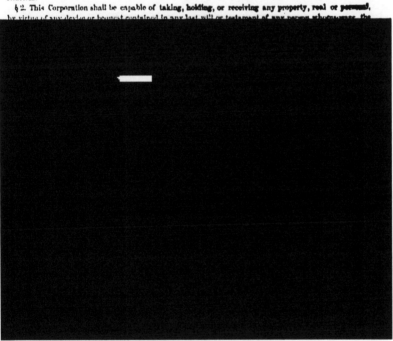

CONSTITUTION.

NAME.

I.—This Society shall be called the American Baptist Home Mission Society.

OBJECT.

II.—The object of this Society shall be to promote the preaching of the gospel in North America.

MEMBERSHIP.

III.—The Society shall be composed of Annual Delegates, Life Members, and Life Directors. Any Baptist Church, in union with the denomination, may appoint a delegate for an annual contribution of ten dollars, and an additional delegate for each additional thirty dollars. Thirty dollars shall be requisite to constitute a member for life, and one hundred dollars paid at one time, or a sum which, in addition to any previous contribution, shall amount to one hundred dollars, shall be requisite to constitute a Director for Life.

OFFICERS.

IV.—The officers of the Society shall be a President, two Vice-Presidents, a Treasurer, an Auditor, Secretaries of Correspondence, and a Recording Secretary, whom the Society shall annually elect by ballot.

MANAGERS AND EXECUTIVE BOARD.

V.—The Officers and Life Directors shall meet immediately after the Annual Meeting of the Society and elect fifteen Managers, residing in the city of New York, or its vicinity, who, together with the Treasurer, Auditor, and the Secretaries, shall constitute an Executive Board to conduct the business of the Society; and shall respectively continue to discharge their official duties until superseded by a new election. Seven members of the Board shall be a quorum for the transaction of business.

POWERS AND DUTIES OF THE EXECUTIVE BOARD.

VI.—The Executive Board shall have power to appoint its own meetings; elect its own Chairman and Recording Secretary; enact its own By-Laws and Rules of Order, provided always that they be not inconsistent with this Constitution; fill any vacancies which may occur in their own body, or in the offices of the Society during the year; and, if deemed necessary by two-thirds of the members present at a regular meeting, convene special meetings of the Society. They shall establish such Agencies as the interests of the Society may require; appoint Agents and Missionaries; fix their compensation; direct and instruct them concerning their particular fields and labors; make all appropriations to be paid out of the treasury; and present to the Society, at each annual meeting, a full report of their proceedings during the current year.

DESIGNATED FUNDS.

VII.—All moneys or other property contributed and designated for any particular missionary field, shall be so appropriated, or returned to the donors, or their lawful agents.

TREASURER.

VIII.—The Treasurer shall give bonds to such amount as the Executive Board shall think proper.

ELIGIBILITY TO APPOINTMENT.

IX.—All the Officers, Managers, Missionaries, and Agents of the Society, shall be members in good standing in regular Baptist Churches.

ANNUAL MEETING.

X.—The Society shall meet annually, at such time and place as the Executive Board shall appoint.

ALTERATIONS OF THE CONSTITUTION.

XI.—No alteration of this Constitution shall be made without an affirmative vote of two-thirds of the members present at an annual meeting: nor unless the same shall have been proposed in writing, and the proposition sustained by a majority vote, at a previous annual meeting, or recommended by the Executive Board.

STATED MEETINGS FOR 1858-1859.

OF THE EXECUTIVE BOARD.—Thursday before the first Wednesday in each month, at four o'clock P.M., during the summer months; at three o'clock P.M., in the winter months; and half-past three P.M., in the fall and spring months.

Of the Committee on MISSIONS—The day previous to that of the Board, at three o'clock P.M.

" " Committee on AGENCIES and FINANCE—The Tuesday preceding, at four o'clock P.M., in the summer months; and at three P.M., in the winter months.

Of the Committee on CHURCH EDIFICE FUND—The Monday preceding, at half-past nine A.M.

BY-LAWS OF THE BOARD.

1. All meetings shall be opened with prayer.
2. All Committees shall be nominated by the presiding officer, and approved by the Executive Board, unless otherwise specially ordered.
3. No moneys shall be paid out of the Treasury, but by order of the Executive Board.
4. All resolutions, if required, shall be presented in writing.
5. Whenever a vacancy occurs in the Executive Board, the fact shall be entered on the Minutes and at the next stated meeting the Board shall proceed to fill such vacancy by ballot.

ORDER OF BUSINESS.

1. Reading the Minutes of the last Meeting.
2. Treasurer's Report.
3. Communications of Secretaries of Cor.
4. Reports of Standing Committees.
5. Reports of Select Committees,
6. Unfinished Business.
7. New Business.

STANDING COMMITTEES.

AGENCIES AND FINANCE.	MISSIONS.	CHURCH EDIFICE FUND.
S. Sheldon, *Ch'n.*	E. E. L. Taylor, *Ch'n.*	H. P. Freeman, *Ch'n.*
Richard Stout, *Sec.*	Wheelock H. Parmly, *Sec.*	J. B. Peck, *Sec.*
L. Ballard,	A. D. Gillette,	C. W. Thomas,
Z. Ring,	M. G. Hodge,	S. K. Wightman,
E. Cauldwell,	J. S. Holme.	A. H. Burlingham.
J. E. Southworth.		

LEGACIES.

A. B. Capwell, H. C. Fish, L. Ballard,

MINUTES OF THE TWENTY-SIXTH ANNIVERSARY

OF THE

American Baptist Home Mission Society,

Held in Philadelphia, Pa., May 14, 15, and 16, 1858.

THE American Baptist Home Mission Society convened in the Meeting House of the Tenth Baptist Church, Eighth Street, at half-past ten o'clock, A.M.

The President, Hon. Albert Day, of Connecticut, being absent, Vice-President John P. Crozer, Esq., of Chester, Pa., called the Society to order; and after singing the 788th Hymn, prayer was offered by the Rev. Wm. Dean, D.D., N. Y.

The acting President briefly addressed the Society upon the important position occupied by this Society in the present juncture of affairs.

The following Committees were appointed, upon the nomination of the President:—

On Credentials of Delegates.—Rev. James S. Ladd, N. Y.; Rev. Addison A. Sawin, Iowa; Rev. Allen J. Hires, Jersey Shore, Pa.; Rev. S. M. Osgood, Philadelphia; and Rev. C. P. Sheldon, N. Y.

On Nomination of Officers.—Rev. E. E. L. Taylor, D.D., N. Y.; Hon. J. M. Linnard, Philadelphia; Rev. William Rollinson, N. J.; Rev. Baron Stow, D.D., Boston; Rev. T. R. Cressey, Minnesota.

On Life Directors and Life Members present.—Rev. S. W. Adams, D.D., Ohio; Rev. John E. Chesshire, N. Y.; Rev. G. M. Spratt, Pa.; Rev. M. G. Hodge, N. Y.; Rev. George I. Chace, R. I.

On motion of Rev. J. C. Harrison, N. Y., ministers and other brethren present, not members of the Society, were invited to participate in the deliberations of the Society.

The invitation was accepted by Rev. E. Andrews, N. Y.; Rev. August Rauschenbusch, Mo.; Rev. Charles Button, Ill.

On motion of Rev. W. H. Parmly, the following were fixed as the times of commencing and closing the sessions of each day, as follows, viz.:—

To commence at half-past nine, A.M.; at three and half-past seven o'clock, P.M. Close at half-past twelve and half-past five, P.M.

The Report of the Treasurer was presented, which was accepted, and ordered to be printed with the Annual Report.

On motion of Rev. George C. Baldwin, D.D., N. Y., seconded by Rev. A. D. Gillette, D.D.,

Resolved, That in view of the fact that the amount of the Society's receipts during the past year, so signally characterized by financial disasters, has been so nearly equal that of the preceding year, is a new and striking proof of that special care which the God of Grace and Providence has, ever since its existence, extended over the interests of this Institution.

On motion of Rev. A. A. Sawin, Iowa, seconded by Rev. W. H. Parmly, N. J.,

Resolved. That in view of the large portion of the income of the past year having been derived from legacies, a Committee of Three be now appointed to prepare a Minute on the importance of such legacies being increased both in number and amount.

The Chair appointed upon this Committee, Rev. Joseph Belcher, D.D., Pa.; Rev. A. A. Sawin, Iowa; and Rev. W. H. Parmly, N. J.

On motion of Rev. Wm. L. Nelson, of R. I., the election of Officers of the Society was made the special order for four o'clock, P.M., this day.

The Annual Report of the Executive Board, was read by the Secretary of Correspondence. Having presented that portion of the Report having reference to the death of Life Directors and

Life Members, the Secretary was requested to pause, and the Society invited to unite in prayer offered by the Rev. G. S. Webb, D.D., N. J. After singing a stanza of the hymn,

"Why do we mourn departed friends?"

and appropriate remarks by the Rev. B. T. Welch, D.D., N. Y.; Rev. Joseph Belcher, D.D., Pa.; Rev. Wm. Reid, Ct.; and Rev. A. D. Gillette, N. Y.; the Secretary resumed the reading of the Annual Report.

The following Committees were appointed to examine and report upon portions of the Report, as follows, viz.:—

On Missionary Operations.—Rev. D. B. Cheney, Pa.; Rev. B. T. Welch, D.D., N. Y.; Hon. Peter P. Runyon, N. J.; Thomas Wattson, Esq., Pa.; and Rev. J. J. Woolsey, Ct.

On Obituaries.—Rev. A. D. Gillette, D.D., N. Y.; Rev. Wm. Reid, Ct.; Rev. J. C. Harrison, N. Y.; Rev. Wm. C. Ulyatt, Ct.; and Rev. Thomas S. Malcom, Pa.

After prayer by Rev. J. H. Kennard, D.D., Philadelphia, the hour having arrived, the Society adjourned.

AFTERNOON SESSION.

After singing, prayer was offered by Rev. Z. Freeman, N. Y.

The Minutes of the Morning Session were read and approved.

The Committee on Life Directors and Members presented a written report showing forty-six Life Directors, and seventy-three Life Members present, viz.:—

LIFE DIRECTORS.

Anderson, Rev. Geo. W., Newcastle, Del.
Anderson, Rev. Thos. D., Roxbury, Mass.
Babcock, Rev. Rufus, D.D., Paterson, N. J.
Barker, Rev. Enoch, M., Beverly, N. J.
Baldwin, Rev. N. B., Philadelphia, Pa.
Barrell, Rev. A. C., Albion, N. Y.
Brown, Rev. I. Newton, D.D., Philadelphia, Pa.
Belcher, Rev. Joseph, D.D., Philadelphia, Pa.
Burlingham, Rev. A. H., New York.
Cheney, Rev. D. B., Philadelphia, Pa.
Cookson, Rev. John, Morrisania, N. Y.
Challiss, Rev. James M., Roadstown, N. J.
Chace, Prof. Geo. I., Providence, R. I.
Dean, Rev. Wm., D.D., Wyoming, N. Y.
Dunn, Rev. L. A., Fairfax, Vt.
Day, Rev. Henry, Philadelphia, Pa.
Davis, Rev. Henry, D.D., Columbus, Ohio.
Field, Rev. Samuel W., Providence, R. I.
Foster, Thomas S., Philadephia, Pa.
Freeman, Rev. Zenas, Rochester, N. Y.
Hill, Rev. Benjamin M., New York.
Hodge, Rev. M. G., Brooklyn, N. Y.
Holme, Rev. J. S., Brooklyn, N. Y.
Kennard, Rev. J. H., D.D., Philadelphia.
Ladd, Rev. James S., New York.
Lathrop, Rev. Edward, D.D., New York.
Malcom, Rev. Howard, D.D., Lewisburg, Pa.
Malcom, Rev. Thomas S., Philadelphia, Pa.
Martin, Rev. G. P., English Neighborhood, N. J.
Mason, Rev. Alanson P., Chelsea, Mass.
Morse, Rev. J. B., Orange, N. J.
Nice, Rev. G. P., Philadelphia, Pa.
Parmly, Rev. Wheelock H., Jersey City, N. J.
Reid, Rev. William, New London, Ct.
Shadrach, Rev. Wm., D.D.. Mitchell's Mills, Pa.
Stubberts, Rev. Wm. F., Malden, Mass.
Stow, Rev. Baron, D.D., Boston, Mass.
Taylor, Rev. E. E. L., D.D., Brooklyn, N. Y.
White, Rev. Samuel, Staten Island, N. Y.
Wattson, Thomas, Philadelphia.
Webb, Rev. G. S., D D., New Brunswick, N. J.
Wright, Rev. Thomas G., Wappingers Falls, N. Y.
Wright, Rev. Lyman, Norwich, N. Y.
Woolsey, Rev. James J., Norwalk, Ct.
Welch, Rev. B. T., D.D., Newtonville, N. Y.

LIFE MEMBERS.

Ambler, Rev. E. C. Woodstown, N. J.
Armstrong, Rev. Andrew, Lambertsville, N. J.
Adams, Rev. S. W., D.D., Cleveland, Ohio.
Brown, Samuel, M.D., Philadelphia, Pa.
Brown, Rev. James F., Scotch Plains, N. J.
Baker, Rev. Samuel, D.D., Williamsburg, N. Y.
Baldwin, Rev. Geo. C., D.D., Troy, N. Y.
Belden, Rev. Joseph, Bordentown, N. J.
Beck, Rev. Levi G., New Brittain, Pa.
Capwell, A. B., Brooklyn, N. Y.
Caillhopper, Rev. F. T., Camden, N. J.
Clark, Rev. N. Judson, Schuylkill Falls, Pa.
Clark, Mrs. Caroline, Schuylkill Falls, Pa.
Cathcart, Rev. Wm., Philadelphia, Pa.
Chase, Rev. J. N., New Boston, N. H.
Chesshire, John Enoch, Keesville, N. Y.
Colburn, Rev. Alfred, Providence, R. I.
Coleman, Daniel B., Trenton, N. J.
Cressey, Rev T R., Cannon City, Min.
Deats, Hiram, Cherryville, Pa.
Dewhurst, Rev Eli, Belfast, Me.
Doolittle, Rev. H D, Burnt Hill, N. Y.
Denison, Rev. A. F., Clinton, Ct.
Evans, John M, Philadelphia, Pa.
Foljambe, Rev. Sam'l W, S. Framingham, Mass.
Goodwin, Rev. Thomas, Pemberton, N. J.
Griffith, Rev. B, Philadelphia. Pa.
Hires, Rev. A. J., Woodstown, N. J.
Harrison, Henry C., Philadelphia, Pa
Harrison, Rev. John C., Kingston, N. Y.
Jeffrey, Rev R., Philadelphia, Pa.
Kennard, Rev. J, Spencer, Bridgeton, N. J.
Kain, Rev. Charles, Jr., Mullica Hill, N. J.
Levy, Rev. Edgar M., West Philadelphia, Pa.
Lee, Franklin, Philadelphia, Pa.
Mason, Pethuel, Somerville, N. J.
Murphy, Rev. John R., Marlton, N. J.
Meech, Rev. W. W., Long Plain, Mass.
Meesen, Rev. J. D., Burlington, N. J.
Mitchell, Mrs. Maria M., Boston, Mass.
Nelson, Rev. Wm. F., Wickford, R. I.
Olmstead, Rev. J. W., Boston, Mass.
Osgood, Rev. S. M., Philadelphia, Pa.
Osborne, Rev. J. W., Piqua, Ohio.
Peters, Rev. J. H., Philadelphia, Pa.
Phillips, George W., Penningtonville, Pa.
Putnam, Rev. H. C., Point Pleasant, Pa.
Runyon, Hon. Peter P., New Brunswick, N. J.
Randolph, Rev. Warren, Germantown. Pa.
Rogers, Rev. Thos. S., Clifton Park, N. Y.
Read, Rev. H. W., Falls Church, Va.
Raynor, Samuel, New York.
Richardson, Rev. D. F., Hanover, N. H.
Smart, John, Philadelphia, Pa.
Spratt, Rev. Geo. M., Lewisburg, Pa.
Sawin, Rev. A. A., Lyons, Iowa.
Smith, Rev. J. A., Chicago, Ill.
Swaine, Rev. Thomas, Flemington, N. J.
Sym, Rev. Wm., Towanda, Pa.
Stelle, Rev. Bergen, Cherryville, N. J.
Sheldon, Rev. C. P., Troy, N. Y.
Tolan, Rev. W. B., Stepney Depot, Ct.
Taylor, Rev. A. W., Hollidaysburg, Pa.
Ulyat, Rev. W. C., Norwalk, Ct.
Wilson, Rev. Jas. E., Haddonfield, N. J.
Williams, Walter S., Hartford, Ct.
Willis, B. B., Philadelphia, Pa.
Walker, Rev. Joseph, Marcus Hook, Pa.
Walker, Geo. C., Johnson's Creek, N. Y.
Walker, Mrs. E. H., Johnson's Creek, N. Y.
Williams, Rev. Lester, Jr., W. Townsend, Mass.
Wickerly, Daniel, Philadelphia.
Young, Rev. R. F., Chestnut Hill, Pa.
Young, Rev. Geo. W., Antestown, Pa.

The Committee on Credentials reported one delegate present, Rev. J. N. Chase, from the Baptist Church, New Boston, N. H.

Report accepted, and Committee discharged.

On motion of Rev. Geo. C. Baldwin, D.D., N. Y.,

Resolved, That a Committee of Five be appointed to confer with a Committee of like number from the Missionary Union, the American and Foreign Bible Society. and the Baptist Publication Society, with a view of harmonizing the efforts and operations of these several Societies, and of devising plans and measures by which the operations of said Societies may be rendered more effective, and their business attended with less expense ; and that said Committee report to this Society, at its next Annual Meeting.

On motion, a Committee of Three was appointed, consisting of Rev. Edward Lathrop, D.D., N. Y. ; James E. Southworth, Esq., N. Y., and Rev. D. B. Cheney, Pa., to nominate the Committee of Five to be appointed under the last Resolution.

The hour of four o'clock having arrived, the special order was called, when the Committee on Nomination of Officers presented their report of names of persons to fill the various offices provided for in the Constitution of the Society.

The following tellers were appointed by the President, viz.:

Rev. J. S. Holme, N. Y.; Rev. W. Randolph, Pa.; Rev. A. P. Mason, Mass.; Rev. J. B. Morse, N. J.; and Rev. Wm. Reid, Ct.

The tellers, having collected and counted the ballots, declared the following persons duly elected to the offices designated, viz.: (See page 14.)

On motion of Rev. W. F. Nelson, R. I.

Resolved, That this Society earnestly recommend to the churches and individuals proposing to aid its treasury, to forward their annual contributions, as far as possible. previous to the first day of January.

The Committee, appointed to nominate the Committee of Five on Conference, reported the following names, viz.: Rev. B. Sears, D.D., R. I.; Rev. E. E. L. Taylor, D.D., N. Y.; Hon. J. M. Linnard, Pa.; Rev. S. Bailey, D.D., Ind.; Rev. H. G. Weston, Ill. The nomination was confirmed by the Society.

Rev. J. H. Kennard, D.D., Pa., offered the following resolution which was adopted:

Resolved, That, as a Society, we survey the present amazing outpouring of the Holy Spirit throughout our country, in the conversion of sinners, with profound gratitude to God, to whom alone the praise and glory is due.

After a song of praise, prayer was offered by Rev. B. T. Welch, D.D., N. Y. Adjourned.

EVENING SESSION.

The Society reassembled, and was called to order by the President at half-past seven o'clock, P.M. The exercises of the evening were commenced by singing a song of praise. The Scriptures were read by Rev. F. Wilson, Md., and prayer offered by Rev. J. M. W. Williams, of Md.

The Secretary of Correspondence, Rev. B. M. Hill, D.D., concluded the reading of the Report of the Executive Board.

On motion of Rev. W. Shadrack, D.D., Pa., the Annual Report was accepted and ordered to be printed, under the direction of the Executive Board.

After which, addresses were delivered before the Society by Rev. George D. Boardman of Rochester, N. Y., and the Hon. Eli Thayer, M. C., from Massachusetts.

A collection was taken up in aid of the Society's funds, amounting to $54.30

After a prayer by Rev. T. R. Cressey, of Minnesota, the Society adjourned.

MORNING SESSION.

MAY 15, 1858.

The Society was called to order by the President at half-past nine o'clock, A.M. Prayer was offered by Rev. Henry Davis, D.D., of Ohio.

Minutes of the afternoon and evening sessions of the preceding day were read and approved.

On motion of W. H. Parmly, N. J.

Resolved, That the thanks of this Society be tendered to the Rev. Geo. D. Boardman and the Hon. Eli Thayer for their able, interesting, and suggestive addresses, delivered before the Society last evening.

Rev. J. Belcher, D.D., on behalf of the Special Committee upon Legacies, presented the report of that Committee, which, after full consideration, was adopted, and ordered printed with the Annual Report.

Rev. A. D. Gillette, D.D., N. Y., presented the Report of the Committee on Obituaries. After joining in prayer with Rev. Joseph Walker, Pa., the Report was adopted.

Rev. D. B. Cheney, Pa., presented the Report of the Committee on Missionary Operations, which was adopted.

On motion of E. E. L. Taylor, D.D., N. Y.

Resolved, That the thanks of this body be presented to the Tenth Baptist Church, and Society, and to our brethren of this city and vicinity, for the generous hospitality extended to them during their present Anniversary.

Rev. J. W. Olmstead, of Mass., offered the following which was adopted :

Resolved, That the Executive Board of the Society be requested to inquire as to the expediency of having its anniversary compressed within the limits of a single day.

Minutes read and approved.

After prayer by Rev. M. G. Clarke, Ind., adjourned *sine die*.

MEETING OF THE OFFICERS AND LIFE DIRECTORS.

At a meeting of the Officers and Life Directors of the American *Baptist* Home Mission Society, held at the Tenth Baptist Church,

Philadelphia, May 15, 1858; James E. Southworth, Esq., N. Y., was chosen Chairman; and A. B. Capwell, N. Y., Secretary.

A Committee to nominate Managers was appointed, consisting of Rev. D. B. Cheney, Pa.; Rev. S. W. Adams, D.D., O.; Rev. M. G. Hodge, N. Y.; and Rev. A. P. Mason, Mass.; who, after consultation, presented the following list of names, which was accepted, and the persons designated unanimously elected, viz.:— (See Page 14.)

A. B. CAPWELL, *Recording Secretary.*

THE MISSIONARY SERMON.

The Missionary Sermon was preached by Rev. Lemuel Porter, D.D., of Pittsfield, Mass., in the evening of the Lord's day, May 16, in the same church edifice where the business meetings had been held, from Psalms 126: 6—"He that goeth forth and weepeth, bearing precious seed, shall doubtless come again with rejoicing, bringing his sheaves with him." It was a very appropriate discourse, presenting "the encouragements to self-denying labor in the cause of Home Missions." Its design and tendency were to awaken more earnest and efficient coöperation on the part of ministers and churches in the work of Home Missions.

At the close of the sermon, a contribution was taken to aid the Society in its operations.

The beneficial influence of this anniversary will long be felt by those who were present to enjoy it. Their interest in the cause of Home Missions was deepened, and their hope for the improved religious condition of thousands scattered abroad at far distant points of the great West, was much encouraged. Let the earnest prayer of every friend of the Society be—"Establish thou the work of our hands upon us; yea, the work of our hands establish thou it."

amount there was received
Fund....................

" Cash paid on account of Church

" Cash paid for Fuel, Stationery
incidental expenses.........

" Cash paid for Paper, Printing
Mission Record, and inciden
same for thirteen months....

" Cash paid for Paper and Prin
Certificates, Blanks, etc.,....

" Cash paid interest on conditions

" Cash paid Taxes on Land donat

" Cash paid for Insurance.......

" Cash paid for Rent of Rooms..

" Cash paid for Discounts on U
Loss on Counterfeit Money..

" Cash paid for Printing at Anniv

" Cash paid on account of funds
by the order of the Executive

" Cash paid expense of Collecting

" Cash paid as Loaned on Bond a
amount of conditional donati
which the Society is paying i

Balance to new account..........

IN ACCOUNT WITH D. C. WHITMAN, TREASURER. *Cr.*

1858.	By Balance as per last Report........................	$8,967 09
	" Cash received in Contributions and Legacies, from April 1, 1857, to March 31, 1858........$41,045 82	
	Of which there is in a Note not paid..........75 00	
		40,970 82
	" Cash received for subscriptions to *Home Mission Record* for twelve months............................	944 87
	" Cash received for a Sunday School Library.........	5 00
	" Cash received for Church Edifice Fund............	657 00
	" Cash received for dividends on temporary investments....................................	30 00
	" Cash received for interest on Bond and Mortgage, a special investment by direction of the donor......	98 55
	" Cash received for interest from Special Salary Fund.	420 00
		$52,093 33
March 31	By Balance,..	$4,459 02

(Signed) D. C. Whitman, *Treasurer.*
Per Jas. M. Whitehead, *Clerk.*

OFFICERS.

PRESIDENT.

JOHN P. CROZER, Esq., Chest

VICE-PRESIDENTS.

J. E. SOUTHWORTH, Esq., New
J. W. MERRILL, Esq., Boston.

TREASURER.

EBENEZER CAULDWELL, Esq., N

AUDITOR.

SMITH SHELDON, New Yo

SECRETARIES OF CORRESPONDEN

REV. BENJAMIN M. HILL, New
REV. D. B. CHENEY, Philadelp

RECORDING SECRETARY.

A. B. CAPWELL, Esq., New Y

MANAGERS

Re

ANNUAL REPORT

OF THE EXECUTIVE BOARD OF THE AMERICAN BAPTIST HOME MISSION SOCIETY, MAY 14 AND 15, 1858.

THE Constitution of the American Baptist Home Mission Society, requires of the Executive Board, at each annual meeting, a full Report of their proceedings for the previous year.

In performing that duty at this time, we would gratefully acknowledge the Divine favor by which we have been happily and prosperously carried through a period of financial trouble that brought ruin to thousands of individuals, and dismay to the nations of the earth; and by which spiritual blessings have been made to follow, encouraging us, and our missionaries, and the churches to whom they minister in word and doctrine. It has been a year of signal displays of Almighty power and grace. God has "put down the mighty from their seats, and exalted them of low degree." He has made bare His arm for man's salvation. He has accomplished much of his purpose of mercy to our fallen world, and has graciously allowed this Society to be one of the honored instrumentalities of its accomplishment. Through it, many souls have been redeemed from everlasting death; churches of Jesus Christ have been gathered; the ordinances of the gospel have been administered; and foundations have been laid for the successful advance of christianity and civilization in the extreme frontier ter-

place have been made glad: an
and blossomed as the rose. It h
a fearful heart, be strong, fear
been strengthened, and feeble
firmed.

DEATHS.

It is our duty and privilege to
who have ceased to meet with us
to share the blessedness of the re

Our list of the deceased for th
have ever had occasion to write
names. Seven of them were dir
members, were ministers of the g
were among the earliest, most
friends of the Society. Two of
missionaries. Of seven, who we
had known the trials of missionar
for years, endured loneliness an
her husband's frequent absence
when living, sustained the cause
butions; and some of them, as ou

turn comes, we may disappear, as they did, like the summer cloud, whose gentle rain had fallen to refresh the parched earth beneath its onward course.

DIRECTORS AND MEMBERS FOR LIFE.

During the past year, three hundred and seven persons have been constituted members, and thirty-four Directors for life. The deaths already mentioned, together with twenty-two others in former years, but only recently reported to us, make the present number of the first named class four thousand eight hundred and seventy-eight; that of the others, six hundred and sixteen; and of both classes, five thousand four hundred and ninety-four.

CHANGES IN THE EXECUTIVE BOARD.

Rev. A. K. Nott, who was elected at the last anniversary as a Manager, declined the position, and it has been occupied by Z. Ring, Esq., by the election of the Board.

D. C. Whitman, Esq., who was elected Treasurer at the last anniversary, being required by business pursuits to be absent in Europe, resigned the office at the close of the missionary year; and Ebenezer Cauldwell, Esq., was elected to fill the vacancy. The duties of the office he has since performed.

Rev. E. L. Magoon, D.D., having removed to a distance from the city of New York, resigned his seat in the Board; and the vacancy was filled by the election of Rev. J. S. Holme.

For the same reason, Rev. J. L. Hodge, D.D., resigned also; but as it was near the anniversary of the Society, the election of his successor was not thought necessary.

ADDITIONAL SECRETARY.

The Rev. Dr. Colver, who was elected at the last anniversary as a Secretary of Correspondence, declined the

has postponed to a future period
Church Edifice Fund, for which, h
commenced.

FINANCIAL AFFA

The financial condition of the
March, was as follows :—

Balance from last year's account,......................	
Receipts from all sources,............................	
Total resources for the year ending March 31, 1858,....	
Amount disbursed in the same period,................	
Balance in the Treasury, March 31,....................	
Amount of liabilities April 1, 1858, of which $3,473 1 demand,...................................	
Balance against the Society,..........	

MARCH RECEIPT

As has been the case for some y
portion of the amount contribut
received in the month of March.
this may be found in the fact tha
have adopted systematic plans
among other measures, adjusted t
for the Society, so as to terminat
the receipt of so large a sum as is
time which is the closing month

caused a misapprehension that the treasury was rich, and unfavorably affected its replenishment. A closer examination might have shown that, large as the balance created at so late a day may have been, the amount of liabilities subject to immediate demand was as large or larger. Thus, nearly a fourth part of our receipts the past year reached the treasury in March, and, consequently, a considerable balance remained to be credited in the new account of April 1st. On the other hand, there is a heavy account of liabilities, the portion of which subject to immediate demand is but little less than that balance.

The Board have learned by serious experience that their true policy is to regulate their appropriations by the amount of funds actually in the treasury, and in that policy they enjoy the general concurrence of the Society. Such a policy forbids the appropriation of funds based on mere estimates of receipts for any given period in advance.

But ministers residing in eastern states, who are willing to remove to missionary stations in the west, find it indispensable to make their arrangements for removal some months previous to their departure. The larger number prefer to proceed in the spring, and, therefore, must make their arrangements for removal in the winter. The expense of emigration to frontier states and territories, and the support of missionary families for a year or two after, are always considerable, and sometimes very heavy; and as ministers are rarely able to encounter the expense of either without aid from the missionary treasury, it is indispensable that it be sufficiently supplied to justify the Board in encouraging their expectation of that aid, but as each month in the year, except March, usually produces claims on account of appropriations already made, sufficient to absorb the ordinary receipts, it follows that new applications for aid during a few previous months must, to a considerable extent, be deferred ; and if that supply is withheld until March, which is near the time when the missionaries should commence their journey, they must be subjected to months of suspense or abandon the plan of removal. The latter is frequently chosen from necessity. Such was the case the past year. Because of an insufficient amount of funds during the winter months, and the great uncertainty of much increase in the spring, only a few applicants could be encouraged. It will be seen, therefore, that the winter months, more than any others, are those in which the Board need to know what amount of appropriations they can safely make, or what number of missionaries they can appoint, and to what stations they can be sent.

A CHANGE SUGGESTED.

They would, therefore, respectfully suggest, that those churches which have adopted the plan of forwarding their contributions in March, would increase the efficiency of their co-operation by closing their respective Home Mission years in December, and transmitting the amount of their annual contributions immediately thereafter. Such an arrangement would prove very advantageous to the new western churches and villages, as it would secure a larger number of good ministers to enter them in the name of the Lord.

CONDITIONAL DONATIONS.

Among other modes adopted by our friends for supplying the treasury, some have made donations or legacies in advance, from time to time, with the condition that they should be entitled to interest annually, during their natural lives. The amount of those donations has reached but a few thousand dollars, but as they create a claim *for interest* until the decease of the donors, it has been deemed prudent to invest the whole on good security, and thus create a suitable resource for the payment of the interest, without using funds annually contributed. The amount thus invested, will be subject to variation by the decease of each donor; by which event the amount of their respective donations will be immediately merged in the funds of the society for general purposes.

An additional reason for making the investment, existed in the fact that an unusual proportion of receipts the past year was in the form of legacies. The amount of such receipts differs very much from year to year, and it is seldom that there are any means of estimating it correctly in advance, consequently, no reliance can be placed on legacies as available funds until they are actually deposited in the treasury. To have appropriated the whole amount, therefore, for the support of missionaries the past year, would have exposed the Board to probable embarrassment in this upon which we have now entered, unless they had perfectly good reasons to expect an equal amount of legacies within the year, or that the ordinary contributions would considerably exceed those of the year just closed. A part only of the amount, therefore, has been expended, and the balance was employed for the investment mentioned.

MISSIONARY OPERATIONS.

In laboring to extend missionary operations, the older western fields have not been overlooked, but the new and more distant states and territories have required and received a larger share of our attention. We have much to encourage the belief that the arrangement has been advantageous to the cause of Christ.

Nearly every church aided by the Society, has suffered in temporal interests, and some of them very seriously, by the financial troubles of the country; but, toward the

the powers of darkness. The revi
and continues to be, very extensive
diffused among the churches of the
and extended to California; and
been unusually efficacious even i
darkest portion of our field.

DISTRIBUTION OF MISSIO

The distribution of missionaries a
of their labors in the states a
follows:—

CANADA.

Four missionaries labored in Ca
middle of the year one of them
of Quebec, where he receives his s
of the Society. Thirteen perso
Catholics, were converted and ba
edifice was completed in this field.

NEW YORK.

One missionary was sustained in t
by funds designated for that purpose
is pastor of a French and German
in both of those languages. He

PENNSYLVANIA.

In Pennsylvania there was but one missionary. His principal effort was to finish a house of worship, and perfect the organization of a church. In this he succeeded well.

DELAWARE.

A German missionary was sustained to labor among his countrymen in Delaware. Twelve of them were baptized by him. The church have a good place of worship, and exert a good influence over the German population of the place.

OHIO.

We had only three missionaries in Ohio. Two of their churches enjoyed revivals, and all of them succeeded in paying portions of debt upon their houses of worship. Twenty-five persons were added to them by baptism.

MICHIGAN.

In Michigan there were five missionaries, who baptized thirty-nine persons. One of their churches has partly completed a house of worship. An additional minister is now under appointment for a frontier portion of this state.

INDIANA.

Twelve missionaries labored in Indiana. Four of their churches enjoyed revivals, and one hundred and fifty-five persons were added to their membership by baptism. Two churches became able to dispense with missionary aid, one completed a house of worship, and four others are preparing places for that purpose.

ILLINOIS.

In Illinois we had but six missionaries, the General Association of that great and prosperous state having undertaken to supply their destitute points. The revival influence reached four of the churches supplied by us, and forty-six persons were baptized. One church edifice was finished; three churches were building, or paying off debts incurred by building; and one become independent of missionary aid.

WISCONSIN.

The number of missionaries in Wisconsin was fourteen. Revivals were reported in three churches, and sixty baptisms in all; two churches became able to support the gospel without missionary aid; two finished houses of worship, and two were progressing in building; two more missionaries will immediately occupy stations in this state, but there are four other prominent towns and cities, and several rural districts, to which able men should be sent without delay.

IOWA.

In Iowa were seventeen missionaries in commission. Revivals were reported from four places, and eighty baptisms from all; one church dispenses with further missionary aid; five church edifices have been finished, and two others have been commenced. It is believed that, west of the Demoine River, which comprises nearly half of the vast area of this state, and in which are several important villages, there is not a Baptist minister devoted entirely to the preaching of the gospel.

MINNESOTA.

Fifteen missionaries labored in Minnesota. Two of them reported revivals at several stations, or out-stations, and forty-nine baptisms. Seventeen of the candidates were Swedes, and had been Lutherans in their native land; four church edifices were commenced, and preliminary measures taken for the commencement of others; two other missionaries have been appointed for this state, and will soon be in their fields. In three of the principal cities of Minnesota no Baptist minister labors regularly, and several considerable towns or villages are entirely without supplies. In two of these cities are churches, suffering from their lack of able, active, and devoted pastors.

NEBRASKA.

There were three missionaries in the territory of Nebraska. Two persons were baptized; another missionary is now proceeding to that field, and he should be followed, as soon as practicable, by at least four more.

KANSAS.

The disturbed state of political affairs in Kansas has been unfavorable to religious interests. Only four missionaries were sustained there, who appear to have been laying good foundations for success when more peaceful times are enjoyed. One of them has left the field, but another is under appointment, who will commence his labors within a few days, and, under more improved circumstances, some six more well qualified ministers would find important fields ready for their entrance.

NEW MEXICO.

Two missionaries and five native assistants were employed in New Mexico. A considerable number of persons were converted and renounced the Romish religion, of whom twenty-two were baptized. A new church was formed; a church edifice was well advanced toward completion, and one or two others will soon be commenced. The native assistants labored familiarly among the people wherever they could gain access to them, and their labors were blest of God as prominent means of producing these encouraging results.

CALIFORNIA.

We had three missionaries in California. They reported the commencement of revivals and the baptism of eight persons. A good house of worship has been provided by one of the churches.

there should be one or two in that t
for some time entreated to send a st
one of the principal cities of Orego
points mentioned would require al
and an addition of some thirty per c
received last year from contributions

SUMMARY OF LABORS AND

The following is a summary of lab
the stations occupied by our mission
year :—

The number of missionaries emplo
and of assistant missionaries, five
appointments. The number in com
first of March, was sixty-nine. Six
were in constant employment ; four
portion of the year, and an addition
months for the Church Edifice Fund

The number of states and territo
missionaries, is sixteen. Twenty
preached in foreign languages and c
natives of foreign lands.

The number of stations and out

Lutheranism; the hopeful conversion of four hundred and eight others; the organization of twenty-seven churches; the ordination of seventeen ministers; the partial preparation for the ministry of ten young men in their churches; the completion of twelve church edifices, and progress in building of seventeen others, by their people.

The churches aided by the Society, contributed two thousand one hundred and twenty-one dollars to the usual objects of christian benevolence, and raised for the support of the gospel among themselves, fifteen thousand one hundred and twenty-four dollars.

Seven churches, heretofore aided by the Society, have become able to support their pastors, and no longer ask aid from our treasury.*

Seven new appointments have been made, for services to commence on the first of April or soon after.

For further details respecting the missionaries, their fields, labors, and results, we respectfully refer the Society to the Missionary Table accompanying this Report.

CONCLUSION.

Although we feel assured that the labors of the year, now reported, have not been in vain, but, on the contrary,

* In addition to the above, the Missionaries report the following:—

Sermons preached	10,222
Lectures and Addresses	1,207
Pastoral Visits	23,377
Prayer and other meetings attended	7,040
Signatures to Temperance Pledge	469
Miles traveled in discharge of duty	114,777
Schools visited	288
Sabbath Schools in the churches	107
Bible Classes	63
Number of Teachers	728
Number of Scholars	6,946
Volumes in S. S. Libraries	13,343
Stations where Monthly Concert of Prayer is observed	41
Preparing for the Ministry	10

that they have produced "fruits of righteousness which are by Jesus Christ, unto the glory and praise of God," we can but regard them as comparatively small and unsatisfactory. We would not think disparagingly of a single effort put forth for the promotion of God's glory among men; much less of a single result which tends to effect that great object; but when we find ourselves surrounded on all sides with proofs of the vast magnitude and importance of the work to be performed; of the large amount and varied nature of the means and instrumentalities essential to its performance; and, above all, that the word of God bids us do with our might whatever our hands find to do in his cause; and then remember how feeble, faint, and few have been our united efforts in the promotion of home evangelization, a humiliating consciousness arises that we all, who are responsible for the performance of the work, have been unprofitable servants.

This conviction is increased when we contemplate the labors of the Society thus far, as a preparation for those of the future. A new missionary year has commenced, with an extended and difficult field to occupy, requiring a large augmentation of capable laborers, and a much increased amount of means for their support. We can not, as formerly, speak of that field as being limited, westward, by the Mississippi river. It extends beyond the Missouri; it includes the central territories, and reaches even to the far distant ocean that divides the West from the East. The vast area included within its boundaries is being filled up with an active, energetic population, far more rapidly than we of the Atlantic States ordinarily conceive. Three new States are now asking of Congress admission into the Union; and preliminary measures are in progress for the same privilege by still another. Two organized territories will do the same with but little delay, and three large districts now ask of the general government a place among the territories of the country.

A larger emigration than ever before known in our country, will probably wend its way into that vast region within the ensuing twelve months. Lines of travel have been marked out in all directions ; railroads, already commenced, are being pressed forward to speedy completion ; others are projected and endowed by government grants of land and State credit, which leave no room for doubt of their being soon extended to very distant points in the general field, facilitating a future and more numerous settlement of that wide domain.

This anticipation of the general fact does not depend simply on inferences from the past, nor mere conjecture for the future. The wave of emigration is now actually in motion, swelling its volume with each day's progress, and gaining impetus that will impel it to the most distant point fit for the uses of emigrating humanity. That entire region must and will be occupied by immortal beings, whose intellectual and moral powers will exercise an active influence for good or for evil upon each other and upon our entire country. The object of this Society is to impart a healthful tone to those powers, to influence them by the teachings of Divine inspiration in favor of christian institutions, and to win those who wield them to the love and service of Jesus Christ.

This great work of christian benevolence can not be performed without the early establishment of gospel institutions among the people. All other efforts will fail as they have ever failed. The success of these may be impeded by the lack of individual interest in the work on the part of professing christians, and of faith and prayer in the churches. For these reasons the means of effort

veringly in the work. We repea
greatly honored it as an instrumen
of men to his service, and it is
faithful continuance in well doin,
honored by him in time to come.

By order of the Execu

BE
Secreta

EXPLANATION OF THE FOLLOWING MISSIONARY TABLE.

The parallel columns show—

1. The names of Agents and Missionaries, and the States in which they reside.
2. The post-office address of Agents and Missionaries.
3. The fields of labor occupied by Agents and Missionaries.
4. The dates at which the appointments commence.
5. The number of months for which the appointments are respectively made.
6. The number of weeks' labor performed during the time reported.
7. The number of stations and out-stations supplied.*
8. The number of persons baptized by the Missionaries within the time reported.
9. The number received by letter.
10. The number of Scholars in Sabbath-schools under the care of Missionaries.†
11. The amount contributed to benevolent objects.
12. Additional facts reported concerning the state and progress of the Churches.‡

* Stations are churches or villages regularly supplied on the Lord's day and are indicated in column 3. Out-stations are places where the Missionaries have *stated* appointments for preaching more or less frequently.

† In new places, where Union-schools are established, the number of scholars connected with Baptist families only are reported.

‡ In many cases, two lines appear for the same Missionary, extending through all the columns. In such cases, the second line indicates a re-appointment of the Missionary, and the dates in column four determine to which appointment or year the statistics and remarks on the different lines belong. A particular notice of those dates is necessary to a proper understanding of certain changes which appear against the names of some individuals.

MISSIONARY TABLE.

POST OFFICE ADDRESS.	FIELD OF LABOR.	Date of Commission.	Months Commis'd.	Weeks labor reported.	Stations supplied.	Baptized.	Received by Letter.	Scholars in S. School.	Contrib. to Benevolent Objects.	AD
real...............	French in M...............	Nov. 1, 1856	12	39	1	2	..	..	100 00	Extended his
'	"	Nov. 1, 1857	12	13	....	..	..	..	......	His wife dec gressing.
le Ligne..........	Grande Ligne...............	Nov. 1, 1856	12	39	1	5		20	96 50	Removed to (without ou
arie de Monnoir...	St. Marie de Monnoir.......	Nov. 1, 1856	12	39	1	5	..	..	149 50	The cause of field.
le Ligne..........	Grande Ligne...............	Nov. 1, 1857	12	13	....	..	..	..	......	
le...............	St. Pie...................	Nov. 1, 1856	12	39	1	1	..	14	187 35	Completed a
....	"	Nov. 1, 1857	12	13	....	..	..	12	......	

Names of Agents and Missionaries.	Post Office Address.	Field of Labor.	Date of Commission.	Months Commis'd.	Weeks labor reported.	Stations supplied.	Baptized.	Received by Letter.	Scholars in S. School.	Contrib's to Benevolent Objects.	Additional Facts Reported.
CONNECTICUT.											
A. E. Denison	Clinton	Connecticut & Rhode Island.	April 1, 1857	12	52	....	..	....	....	......	Collecting agent.
NEW YORK.											
C. M. Fuller	Pike	Eastern N. Y. & N. J.	April 1, 1857	12	50	....	..	....	....	......	Collecting agent.
William Sawyer	Ransomville	Western N. Y.	April 1, 1857	12	3	....	..	....	....	......	Collecting agent. Resigned on account of ill health.
James S. Ladd	New York	New York and vicinity.	April 1, 1857	12	52	....	..	....	....	......	Collecting agent.
Charles Randall	Auburn	Central New York	April 1, 1857	12	48	....	..	....	....	......	Collecting agent.
H. West	Watkins	Western N. Y.	Sept. 1, 1857	7	30	....	..	....	....	......	Collecting agent.
Charles Morton	Corning	Eastern N. Y.	Jan. 1, 1858	12	12	....	..	....	....	......	Collecting agent.
Charles Gayer	New York	French & Ger. in N. Y. & vic.	Oct. 1, 1856	12	26	3	29	....	25	102 32	Organized a church at Morrisania.
" "	"	" "	Oct. 1, 1857	12	26	4	43	....	270	64 36	Revival in his church in New York, and need a larger M. H.
PENNSYLVANIA.											
Rev. A. J. Hires	Jersey Shore	Pa. and So. N. J.	April 1, 1857	12	52	....	..	....	....	......	Collecting agent in Pa. and S. N. Jersey.
Demas L. Clouse	West Greenville	West Greenville	Oct. 1, 1857	12	26	2	..	6	20	......	Finished a M. H. Church encouraged and revived.
DELAWARE.											
Rev. F. A. Bauer	Wilmington	Germans in W. and vicinity.	Jan. 1, 1857	12	52	3	3	2	31	6 00	Congregations gradually increasing. Purchased a suitable M. H.
" "	"	" "	Jan. 1, 1858	12	13	....	9	....	....	......	Wife deceased. Revival.

3

POST OFFICE ADDRESS.	FIELD OF LABOR.	Date of Commission.	Months Commis'd.	Weeks labor reported.	Stations supplied.	Baptized.	Received by Letter.	Scholars in S. School.	Contrib's to Benevolent Objects.	
ledo	Toledo	July 1, 1856	12	13	1	1	6	70	64 38	Church re
"	"	July 1, 1857	12	39	....	8	34	80	......	Continued
eveland	3rd Church, Cleveland	May 1, 1856	12	13	1	2	1	160	22 20	Paying off
"	" "	May 1, 1857	12	39	....	2	9	175	90 20	Sunday sc
oy	Troy	June 1, 1857	12	39	2	12	4	70	......	Church re out-stati
w Paw	Paw Paw	April 1, 1857	12	32	4	7	12	40	18 00	Revival. prosper

Names of Agents and Missionaries.	Post Office Address.	Field of Labor.	Date of Commission.	Months Commis'd.	Weeks labor reported.	Stations supplied.	Baptized.	Received by Letter.	Scholars in S. School.	Contrib's to Benevolent Objects.	Additional Facts Reported.
Harry Smith	Valparaiso	Valparaiso	Aug. 1, 1856	12	26	1	35	8	85	50	Revival. Asks for no further aid.
H. C. Skinner	Wabash	Wabash	July 1, 1856	12	13	1	1	....	55	6 00	Sabbath school interesting.
" "	"	"	July 1, 1857	12	39	....	..	....	....	30 00	Improving their M. H.
J. M. Whitehead	Westville	Northern Association	Aug. 1, 1856	12	26	....	48	25	....	142 00	Revival at W.
" "	"	Westville and vicinity	Aug. 1, 1857	12	26	3	8	....	....	......	Completed M. H. A good state of religious feeling.
J. G. Werthner	Evansville	Germans in E.	May 1, 1856	12	13	3	..	5	....	......	Himself and family sick, and left the field.
Lyman Wilder	Columbia City	Columbia City (half the time)	Nov. 1, 1856	12	19⅛	3	11	10	40	20 00	An experiment in an old pre-occupied place.
" "	" "	" "	Nov. 1, 1857	12	6⅛	....	..	2	70	3 00	Secured the lease of a good church edifice.
Adolphus Patze	La Porte	Germans in North. Assoc.	M'ch 1, 1857	12	26	8	1	....	....	......	Prospects discouraging. Resigned.
J. H. Dunlap	Port Mahon	Huntington	Feb. 1, 1857	12	39	4	8	4	100	20 00	Resigned and removed.
Sidney Dyer	Indianapolis	......	April 1, 1857	12	11	....	..	....	....	......	Agent for Church Ed. Fund. Resigned.
J. D. Crabs	Claysville	Gosport (half the time)	April 1, 1857	12	26	1	19	4	85	......	Revival.
R. H. Cook	Middlebury	Elkhart Riv. Association	June 1, 1857	12	39	13	20	11	210	......	An extensive revival. Building a M. H. at Pleasant Valley.
L. B. Chamberlin	Huntington	Huntington	Nov. 1, 1857	3	13	5	3	5	70	......	A difficult field.
" "	"	"	Feb. 1, 1857	12	....	....	..	....	....	......	
ILLINOIS.											
J. Edminster	Peoria	Adams St. Ch. in P.	May 1, 1856	12	13	3	3	3	180	......	Church revived.
" "	"	" "	May 1, 1857	12	13	....	..	....	150	......	Resigned after first quarter.
J. H. Kruger	"	Germans in P.	Oct. 1, 1856	12	13	1	..	....	....	......	Discouraged and resigned.
J. N. Tolman	Decatur	Decatur	Jan. 1, 1857	12	39	1	..	15	....	72 50	Finished M. H. Needs no further aid.
J. M. Cochran	Batavia	Batavia	April 1, 1857	12	52	3	2	2	45	88 32	Revival at an out-station.
F. Ketcham	Galena	Galena	June 1, 1856	12	13	1	15	1	80	......	Finances of the church improving.
" "	"	"	June 1, 1857	12	39	....	3	....	....	21 50	Paying off debt on M. H.
I. S. Mahan	Peoria	Adams St. Ch. in P.	Sept. 1, 1857	6	26	1	23	9	100	......	An encouraging revival.
WISCONSIN.											
James Delaney	Horicon	Horicon and Mayville	July 1, 1856	12	13	2	..	....	110	......	Cause rising from a depressed condition.

POST OFFICE ADDRESS.	FIELD OF LABOR.	Date of Commission.	Months Commis'd.	Weeks labor reported	Stations supplied.	Baptized.	Received by Letter.	Scholars in S. School.	Contrib's to Benevolent Objects.	ADI
n..............	Horicon and Mayville.......	July 1, 1857	12	39	3	..	2	70	......	Recent revival
e City..........	Portage City...............	Aug. 1, 1856	12	26	3	9	1	50	100 50	Revival. Buil
....	"	Aug. 1, 1857	12	23	....	..	6	....	......	Sickness and
ıa....	Kenosha..................	May 1, 1856	12	13	1	3	2	80	......	Asks for no fu
ıwega...........	Weyauwega................	Nov. 1, 1856	12	39	5	5	9	30	5 36	Church need a
tt.......	Prescott and vicinity.......	May 1, 1857	12	30	1	2	9	....	7 85	Church have and fitted u
on..............	Appleton..................	Dec. 1, 1856	12	39	3	1	6	40	......	Preparing to l
....	"	Dec. 1, 1857	12	13	....	..	3	....	......	Commenced b
....	Lowell....................	July 1, 1856	12	13	1	..	....	45	......	Need no furth
n....	Hudson......	June 1, 1856	12	13	8	6	8	50	19 00	Resigned. Th
Falls....	River Falls and vicinity.....	June 1, 1857	12	39	5	13	....	....	......	Organized a Several con
....	Ripon and vicinity..	Aug. 1, 1856	12	26	1	5	1	....	14 00	Revival spirit
....	" "	Aug. 1, 1857	12	26	....	2	4	80	41 95	Finished a goo
on...............	Madison..........	Dec. 1, 1856	12	39	1	..	5	60	......	The church s
....	"	Dec. 1, 1857	12	13	....	..	3	83	45 00	Repaired M. E
sh......	Oshkosh...................	Jan. 1, 1857	12	39	1	8	18	60	......	Congregations
	"	Jan. 1, 1858	12	13	....		2	50	......	Encouraging

NAMES OF AGENTS AND MISSIONARIES.	POST OFFICE ADDRESS.	FIELD OF LABOR.	Date of Commission.	Months Commiss'd.	Weeks labor reported.	Stations supplied.	Baptized.	Received by Letter.	Scholars in S. School.	Contrib's to Benevolent Objects.	ADDITIONAL FACTS REPORTED.
Jonas Woodward	Cedar Rapids	Cedar Rapids, etc.	May 1, 1857	12	39	....	14	21	100	......	Finished M. H. Revival at an out-station.
I. E. Guild	Newton	Newton	July 1, 1856	12	13	2	1	2	65	3 00	Discouraging circumstances.
" "	"	"	July 1, 1857	12	39	....	..	1	40	22 50	Severely injured, and unable to labor.
A. A. Sawin	Lyons	Lyons and Clinton	July 1, 1856	12	13	2	..	7	90	......	
" "	"	" "	July 1, 1857	12	39	....	..	6	75	......	Denied the use of school-house at Lyons. Are fitting up an eligible hall for public worship.
A. Norelius	Ridgeport	New Sweden, etc.	July 1, 1856	12	13	2	1	....	14	......	
G. F. Brayton	Freeman	St. Charles, etc.	June 1, 1856	12	13	7	..	....	40	14 00	Building a M. H.
" "	St. Charles	" "	June 1, 1857	12	22	....	1	22	62	......	Finished M. H. Resigned.
L. M. Newell	Wawkon	Wawkon and Makee	June 1, 1857	12	39	1	..	2	15	20 00	Need a suitable place for public worship.
Thomas M. Ind	Burlington	Burlington	May 1, 1857	12	39	5	25	4	116	......	Organized a church. Completed M. H. Revival.
George Scott	Strawberry Point	Strawberry Point	May 1, 1857	12	39	3	3	10	150	120 00	Finished a M. H., the only one in the county. Religious improvement in the field.
Chas. E. Brown	Vernon Springs	Vernon Springs	Aug. 1, 1857	12	26	3	2	14	30	4 00	Organized a church, and is encouraged.
P. P. Shirley	Le Clair Centre	Le Clair Centre	June 1, 1857	12	39	1	25	4	100	......	Revival. Completed M. H.
J. M. Coggshall	Burriss City	Burriss and Wapello	July 1, 1857	12	39	3	..	....	45	......	A new field. Prospects good.
G. G. Edwards	Toledo, Pierce Co.	Toledo	Sept. 1, 1857	12	26	6	..	8	....	......	A new field. Organized a church, the only one in the county.
J. H. Parmelee	St. Charles	St. Charles, etc.	Jan. 1, 1858	12	13	1	4	3	....	......	Building a M. H.
B. B. Arnold	Hartford	Hartford	M'ch 1, 1858	12	....	....	..	....	....	......	
MINNESOTA.											
Timothy R. Cressy	Cannon City	Cannon City, etc.	June 1, 1856	12	13	3	..	3	....	50 00	A lot for a M. H. given at one station, and bought one at another.
" "	" "	" "	June 1, 1857	12	39	....	6	....	....	......	Revival. Several converts.
L. Atkinson	Anoka	Hennepin and Wright Co.	Oct. 1, 1856	12	26	9	..	....	....	......	Prospect of organizing a church at one station.
F. O. Nilsson	Scandia	Scandinavians in Carver Co.	Nov. 1, 1856	12	39	5	13	3	70	15 00	Building M. H.
" "	"	" "	Nov. 1, 1857	12	13	....	4	....	60	5 00	Revival. M. H. not complete but occupied.
J. L. Irwin	Saratoga	Itinerant	Sept. 1, 1856	12	13	3	..	....	20	......	Resigned and left the field.
J. C. Hyde	Hastings	Hastings	Nov. 1, 1856	12	39	1	..	7	45	......	Church increasing slowly, but suffer by the financial pressure.
" "	"	"	Nov. 1, 1857	12	13	[illegible]	1	2	44	......	
Lyman Whitney	St. Anthony	St. Anthony	Oct. 1, 1856	12	39	1	2	3	50	......	Resigned and removed.

POST OFFICE ADDRESS.	FIELD OF LABOR.	Date of Commission.	Months Commis'd.	Weeks labor reported.	Stations supplied.	Baptized.	Received by Letter.	Scholars in S. School.	Contrib's to Benevolent Objects.	
'inona	Winona	Nov. 1, 1856	12	39	1	12	....	70	10 00	
"	"	Nov. 1, 1857	12	13	....	..	3	....	......	Church r M. H. r
shland	Ashland and Wasioga	Oct. 1, 1856	12	26	3	1	....	115	......	Organized
'asioga	Wasioga and vicinity	Oct. 1, 1857	12	26	4	..	....	....	......	Sunday s
'abashaw	Wabashaw	May 1, 1857	12	39	2	..	....	24	......	A new fie
ake City	Lake City	July 1, 1857	12	39	2	..	....	13	......	Organized
. Peter	St. Peter and Traverse	May 1, 1857	12	39	4	..	2	18	50 00	Organized
inneapolis	Minneapolis	July 1, 1857	12	39	4	5	50	115	58 51	Building
ed Wing	Red Wing	Aug. 1, 1857	12	26	1	..	2	20	......	Secured l
aribault	Faribault	Jan. 1, 1858	12	13	1	5	9	....	......	Prospects
ochester	Rochester	Aug. 1, 1857	12	26	1	..	10	48	7 00	Organized

Names of Agents and Missionaries.	Post Office Address.	Field of Labor.	Date of Commission.	Months Commis'd.	Weeks labo reported.	Stations supplied.	Baptized.	Received by Letter.	Scholars in S. School.	Contrib's to Benevolent Objects.	Additional Facts Reported.
NEW MEXICO.											
J. Milton Shaw	Albuquerque	Santa Fe, etc.	Oct. 1, 1856	12	39	....	11	....	....	......	Organized a church at Socorro. Licensed a preacher. Inquirers numerous.
" "	Socorro	Socorro	Oct. 1, 1857	12	26	....	7	....	....	......	Commenced a M. H.
Samuel Gorman	Albuquerque	Laguna and vicinity	Oct. 1, 1856	12	26	....	4	....	....	......	Roman Catholic priests troublesome.
" "	"	" "	Oct. 1, 1857	12	26	....	..	....	....	......	Books much called for.
Jose Senun	Laguna	" "	Oct. 1, 1856	12	26	....	..	....	....	......	Assistant to Rev. S. Gorman.
" "	"	" "	Oct. 1, 1857	12	26	....	..	....	....	......	Labors abundant in reading and explaining the scriptures, and suffers persecution on account of it.
Jose Maria Chavez	Peralto	Manzana, etc.	April 1, 1857	12	52	....	..	....	....	......	Unmistakable signs of the breaking of gospel light.
Romaldo Chavez			April 1, 1857	12	52	....	..	....	....	......	A Sabbath congregation meets regularly in his own house. Four persons baptized in his village. True religion gaining ground.
Jose Santos Tayes			April 1, 1857	12	52	....	..	....	....	......	Labors much. Many listen and receiving bibles and books. Error giving way to truth.
Antonio Jose Garcia	Peralto		April 1, 1857	12	52	....	..	....	....	......	Labors from house to house. Families receive him with pleasure, which heretofore excluded him.
CALIFORNIA.											
J. B. Saxton	San Francisco	San Francisco	July 1, 1856	12	13	1	..	5	40	10 00	Remodelling and improving M. H.
" "	"	"	July 1, 1857	12	39	....	6	9	60	......	Revival.
O. B. Stone	Nevada	Nevada	July 1, 1856	12	13	1	..	2	....	......	City population decreasing. Will try to sustain the cause without further aid.
H. H. Rhees	Ione Valley	Ione Valley	Nov. 1, 1856	12	39	3	2	3	....	......	Organized a church at an out-station.
" "	"	"	Nov. 1, 1857	12	13	....	..	....	....	......	Spirit of prayer in the church for a revival.
NEW GRENADA.											
Philip B. Livingston	San Andreas	San Andreas, etc.	May 1, 1856	12	13	1	10	....	95	......	Need no further aid.

Vermont	John Goadby	East Poul
Massachusetts	N. M. Perkins	Brookline
Rhode Island	Francis Smith	Providenc
Connecticut	E. Cushman	Deep Rive
New York	John Smitzer	Oneida...
New Jersey	J. M. Carpenter	Jacobstow
Pennsylvania	Isaac Bevan	Philadelpl
Maryland	F. Wilson	Baltimore
Virginia	H. K. Ellyson	Richmond
North Carolina	T. E. Skinner	Raleigh..
South Carolina	J. J. Brantly	Greenville
Georgia	J. F. Dagg	Cuthbert.
Alabama	S. S. Sherman	....
* Mississippi	L. H. Milikin	Jackson..
* Louisiana	....	....
* Texas	....	....
Tennessee	A. C. Dayton	Nashville
Kentucky	A. Broaddus	Louisville
Missouri	S. C. Major	Fayette...
Illinois	J. A. Smith	Chicago..
* Southern Illinois	....	....
Indiana	M. G. Clark	Indianapol
Ohio	D. A Randall	Columbus.
Michigan	J. E. Johnson	Jackson..
Wisconsin	J. T. Westover	Beaver Da
[illegible]	[illegible]	[illegible]

AGGREGATE CONTRIBUTIONS FROM ALL THE STATES SINCE 1832.

STATES.	Total Amount to 1845.	1846.	1847.	1848.	1849.	1850.	1851.	1852.	1853.	1854.	1855.	1856.	1857.	1858.
Canada	$327 65	$864 70	$692 67	$734 11	$710 79	$809 57	$453 84	$183 63	$189 19	$91 91	$145 23	$143 75	$450 36	$446 44
Maine	2,714 40				500 00		37 00	56 39	622 31	164 66	173 16	102 44	82 09	27 37
New Hampshire	3,083 42	528 41	242 50	343 81	50 50	625 88	419 17	1,104 77	1,487 00	1,682 60	1,875 47	1,606 22	1,627 09	1,377 14
Vermont	1,718 95	673 95	184 00	257 51	222 80	1,015 75	471 98	505 17	494 71	758 58	1,511 10	1,186 34	967 44	860 69
Massachusetts	22,313 30	1,474 20	3,333 03	4,791 22	4,022 07	5,357 73	6,717 06	8,497 51	7,974 56	12,005 92	8,265 73	10,467 62	10,176 01	11,620 98
Rhode Island	5,118 45	852 35	669 56	1,683 33	1,545 76	2,427 57	1,188 66	2,874 55	687 87	2,695 78	2,287 45	2,560 07	1,768 88	1,265 58
Connecticut	11,628 71	1,186 03	1,042 31	1,072 06	1,480 46	1,251 34	2,032 59	2,490 31	3,052 58	4,529 96	4,285 70	4,047 46	3,840 83	3,089 55
New York	65,772 95	6,520 49	7,142 38	6,871 19	6,614 15	7,723 20	10,666 47	13,706 43	16,951 07	18,071 49	20,189 13	14,796 88	14,855 15	13,950 00
New Jersey	4,851 29	1,695 85	1,419 27	1,890 90	2,724 80	2,408 67	2,518 20	2,179 01	3,419 94	3,833 51	3,463 63	2,985 34	2,498 44	2,637 69
Pennsylvania	4,520 81	528 47	529 86	707 43	1,556 89	1,606 11	1,605 98	1,973 75	2,252 91	3,024 90	3,530 82	2,507 89	1,894 36	2,277 41
Delaware	161 20			153 36	60 00	228 94	203 00	163 00	167 90	138 92	67 88	103 75	183 04	51 00
Maryland	2,019 81	30 25	5 00				15 50					200 00		
District of Col'bia	953 12		10 00			30 00	5 00	37 31	5 00	134 00	30 00		8 22	
Ohio	1,010 45	114 81	30 84	30 50	29 46	153 52	241 86	656 62	732 48	2,758 60	3,226 67	2,708 28	1,665 00	864 56
Michigan	337 50	29 50	13 25	172 89	556 21	610 60	1,011 80	866 75	634 43	287 74	574 60	179 23	198 72	284 81
Indiana	28 75	8 10	22 05	11 11	8 50	26 35	290 22	774 38	1,669 44	2,306 79	2,101 50	656 72	1,317 29	1,013 79
Illinois	668 09	477 63	766 50	1,136 69	594 90	704 74	1,329 98	1,230 97	1,675 63	2,479 52	1,799 70	1,700 17	150 86	124 54
Wisconsin	20 10	15 63	124 50	72 15	88 06	58 35	181 91	170 09	274 87	549 71	625 90	418 43	179 19	186 06
Iowa	83 56	41 00	120 03	62 12	93 24	162 77	171 95	396 67	278 05	277 10	332 58	573 12	383 92	744 96
Minnesota							1 00	2 25	55 85	141 46	405 35	328 25	577 07	647 23
Nebraska													150 00	100 00
Kansas													5 00	98 00
Missouri	266 82							2 00		75 00	215 00		29 00	15 00
Kentucky	273 88		10 00	20 50						42 25				
Virginia	9,152 56	159 44	5 85	7 30			5 00				23 75		7 00	
North Carolina	5,000 02	891 67												
South Carolina	8,362 95	135 15							30 00			30 00	20 00	
Georgia	9,529 33		1,331 87					30 00					40 00	
Alabama	493 08										30 00			
Florida	157 82		15 00											
Mississippi	1,899 66													
Tennessee	477 85		8 25											
Louisiana	79 00													
Arkansas	50			50 55	18 15									
Texas														
California							50 00	150 50	70 00	20 00	225 00	105 00		10 00
Oregon							30 00		51 50	159 12	59 33	44 98	17 60	10 00
New Mexico								62 10	94 42	7 38	20 00		30 00	5 00
U. S. Government												435 00		
New Grenada												39 60	25 20	
Unknown													139 00	
Ag. for each period	163,028 96	15,727 63	17,728 72	20,068 73	20,876 73	25,201 09	29,648 28	38,114 16	42,872 01	59,903 83	55,545 40	47,928 54	43,286 76	41,707 82

1834 Dea. Josiah Penfield, Savannah, Ga., per Rev. H. O. Wyer.
1835 Mrs. Clarissa Long, Shelburne, Mass., per W. Wilder, Esq.
" William Powers, Hebron, N. H., per Rev. I. Merriam.....
" Miss Maria Curtis, Southbridge, Mass., per Rev. E. Going.
" Mrs. Jemima Elliott, Hampton Ct., per Rev. J. Payne, Exe
1836 Mrs. Betsey Sprague, Attleboro', Mass., per Mr. A. Reed, E
" Robert Rodgers, Newport, R. I........................
" Ebenezer Boyd, Providence, R. I.......................
1839 Mrs. Abigail Marshall, New York, per Mr. Schofield, Exec
" Mrs. Margaret Pugsley, Dutchess Co., N. Y., per Miss Corr
" Mrs. Irene Coats, New York, per Alfred Decker, Esq......
1841 Mrs. Elizabeth G. Moore, Hartford, Ct., per J. B. Gilbert..
1842 Nathaniel Tucker, Milton, Mass., per W. D. Ticknor......
1843 Mrs. Margaret Martin, Montgomery, N. Y., per Mr. J. J. M
" Miss Cynthia M. Wright, Suffield, Ct., per H. Sheldon, Adı
1844 Mr. Zephaniah Eddy, New Bedford, Mass., per Rev. H. Ja
" Mr. Josiah Kendall, Groton, Mass., per F. E. Wheelock and
" Miss Jane McCall, Society Hill, S. C., per John McIver.....
" Miss Lydia Sweetzer, South Reading, Mass., per H. Sweetze
" Mrs. Elizabeth Griffin, New York, per one of her heirs....
" Dea. Josiah Flint, Cornish, N. H., per Mr. A. Burnap.....
" Thomas Cooper, Esq., Eatonton, Ga., per Hon. M. A. Coop
" Miss Betsey Hutchinson, Passumpsic, Vt., per L. P. Parks.
" Rev. Amos Dodge, Brighton, Macoupin Co., Ill., by his wi
" Mr. John Ward, Warren, N. Y., per J. Northrop and A. W
1845 Joseph H. Hayden, Saybrook, Ct., per H. L. Champlin, Ex
1846 John Allen, Centreville, R. I., in part, per H. Hamilton an
" Rev. Jesse Mercer, Wilks Co., Ga., per Rev. B. M. Saunders
" Miss Mary Bliven, McDonough, N. Y., per Rev. John Peck.
" Mrs. Betsey Haykes, Cincinnatus, N. Y., per Trustees of th
" Mrs. Charlotte Cole, Alexandria, Va., per Robert Bell, Ex
" Dea. Medad Jackson, W. Meredith, N. Y., per H. Jackson
" Mrs. Urania Grant, West Wrentham, Mass., per R. E. Edd
" Mr. Richard Dubois, Malta, N. Y., per H. J. Rodgers, Exec
1847 Dea. Saxton Bailey, Lebanon, Ct., per Executor.... .....
" Mr. Lewis Porter, Covert, N. Y., in advance, per J. McLell

849	Mr. Samuel R. Stelle, Piscataway, N. J., per Lewis R., Stelle, Esq., Executor	$200 00
"	Mrs. Phebe Gale, East Bennington, Vt., per Executor of Estate of S. Harmon	25 00
"	Mr. William Reynolds, Boston, Mass., per J. H. Duncan, Esq., and Mrs. Susan D. Reynolds, Executors in land not sold at Toledo, Ohio	
"	Josiah Lyman, Andover, Ct. per N. B. Lyman, Executor	50 00
"	John J. Martin, Montgomery N. Y., per M. Bookstaver, Executor	1000 00
"	Mrs. Martha Howe, West Boylston, Mass. per Messrs. E. J. Howe & Co.	50 00
"	A. H. Reed Sweden, N. Y., per Rev. D. Searl.	13 00
"	Asa H. Truman, Owego, N. Y., per E. Truman, Executor	248 00
850	George D. James, Amenia, N. Y., J. K. Mead and N. Rose, Executors	100 00
"	John Everett, Manchester, Mich., per F. Everett	70 00
"	Jacob Whitman, Belvidere, Ill., in part, per N. Crosby, Esq	160 00
"	Jonas Taylor, Boston, Mass.	12 50
"	Miss Rebecca Thompson, Amenia, N. Y., per A. B. Capwell, Esq	801 00
"	Joanna Minot, Boston, Mass., per E. Mears and I. Parker, Executors	100 00
"	Claudius F. Brown, Arkwright, N. Y. per David Barrell.	150 00
"	Miss Anna Roe, Egremont, Mass., per R. B. Brown, Executor	50 00
851	David Schauber, Burnt Hills, N. Y. per J. & D. M. Schauber, Executors.	10 00
"	Woolcott Griffin, Governeur, N. Y., per O. L. Barnum, Executor	100 00
"	Joseph Flanders, Brooklyn, N. Y., per Mrs. Eliza A. Flanders and Benj. Flanders	500 00
"	William Williams, New York, per John Allen, Executor	400 00
"	Ely Wiley, South Reading, Mass.	50 00
852	Miss Pharozene C. Kelly Hopkinton, N. H., per John Page	50 00
"	Jonathan W. Ford, Boston, Mass.	100 00
"	Theron Fisk, Esq., Warsaw, N. Y., in advance	2500 00
"	Joshua A. Burke, Brooklyn, N. Y., per Messrs. E. and W. A. Burke	350 00
"	Miss Eliza Skaats, New York, in part, per G. N. Bleecker, Executor	1000 00
"	Barnum M. Howard, Sweden, N. Y., per H. M. Howard, Executor	20 00
853	Alanson Stewart, Liberty, N. Y., per W. W. Murphy	5 00
"	Mrs. Sarah B. Pierce, Middleboro' Mass.	100 00
"	Arnold Whipple, Providence, R. I. per Mrs. P. Whipple, Executrix	200 00
"	Mrs. Fanny McGilvreay Brookline, N. H. (Annuity), per H. A. Daniels, Administrator	40 00
"	Mrs. Lucretia Goddard, Worcester, Mass., per Hon. I. Davis, Executor	300 00
"	P. F. Brayton, Providence, R. I. per A. K. Brayton and Rev. J. Brayton, in addition	594 87
"	Mrs. Elizabeth Gale, Washington, D. C.	50 00
854	Edward Rodgers, Chester, Ill. per Rev. M. B. Kelly	5 00
"	Miss Esther Ann Blakely Pawlet, Vt., per Rev. J. J. Peck	73 00
"	Daniel Cummings, Chelsea, Mass., per Mr. Eaton, Executor	1000 00
"	Mrs. Mary Louce, Bristol, R. I., per J. F. Baars.	7 50
"	D. Valentine, Washington, Pa., per H. W. Wilson, Executor.	239 80
"	Willis L. Eaton, East Weare, N. H., per J. L. Eaton, Executor	100 00
"	Asa Read, Attleboro' Mass., per Amos M. Read, Executor	1000 00
"	Friend Humphrey Albany, N. Y. per his son, Executor	106 30
"	George Corbett, Worcester, Mass.	8 00
"	Mrs. Abby Arnold, Centreville, R. I., per Wm. Arnold.	95 00
"	Garrat N. Bleecker, New York, per E. Cauldwell and W. F. Van Wagner, Executors	6000 00
"	Eunice Shepherdson, Belleville, N. Y	70 00
"	Mrs. Mary Johnson, Albany N. Y per Chas. Pohlman	10 00
"	Mrs. Olive Stowell, Le Roy, N. Y., per R. Bell	10 00
"	David Trull, Lowell, Mass., per J. Fox	400 00
1855	Roger Pegg, New York, per Mr. Coe, Executor.	100 00
"	John Goodell, jr., Woodstock, N. Y in part, per Mrs. Maria H. Goodell, Executrix	268 25
"	Mrs. Frances Thompson, Alabama N. Y.	50 00
"	Miss Mercy Hayden, Grafton, Mass., per Rev. J. Smith	20 00
"	Joseph D. Murray, New Hope, Pa	30 00
"	W. S. Ward, Salem, Mass.	100 00
"	Mrs. Lucy Bushnell, Monticello, N. Y., per Rev. Samuel White	50 00
"	W. Littlefield, Belleville, N. Y	30 00
"	Mary E. Bennett, Ludlow, Vt., per Rev. N. Cudworth, Executor	111 00
"	Margaret Sherwood, New York, per E. J. Mattocks, Executor	50 00

1855	Linus Austin, Akron, O.	$27 00
"	Mrs. —— Nelson, Peoria, Ill.	3 00
"	Mrs. Margaret Davies, New York, per John M. Davies	20 00
"	Abijah Porter, Danvers, Mass., per Rev. J. W. Parkhurst	500 00
"	Jacob Morse, Sturbridge, Mass., per Mrs. Sophia A. Morse	400 00
"	Andrew McCleary, Frederick City, Md., per Albert Ritchie	200 00
1856	Miss Hannah Briggs, Rock Island, Ill., per Rev. A. Briggs	50 00
"	Eunice Upham, West Woodstock, Ct., P. Corbin, jr., Executor	327 34
"	Hon. Nathan H. Bottom, Shaftsbury, Vt., per Norman Bottom, Executor	100 00
"	Miss Eliza Jackson, Hamilton, N. Y., per Prof. P. B. Spear	100 00
"	Mrs. M. W. Denison, Rock Island, Ill., per Rev. J. W. Dennison	8 00
"	Miss Achsah Cox, Imlaystown, N. J.	50 00
"	Samuel Stone, Dundee, Mich., T. Babcock, Executor	30 00
"	Louisa S. Platt, Haverhill, Mass., S. Peaslie, Executor	35 00
"	Mrs. Hannah, Kent, Danversport, Mass	100 00
"	Manly Street, Holyoke, Mass	25 00
"	Mrs. Lorain Sheldon, Suffield, Ct.	355 47
"	Mrs. Abigail Hatch, Boston, Mass., per Thos. Mair, Executor	1491 24
"	David Stanton, Penn's Neck, N. J., per George Kelton, Executor	33 00
"	Rev. Azel Waters, Miama, Ia., in part, per C. W. Morgan, Executor	92 53
1857	Mrs. Rachael Prescott, per John Crockett, Executor	100 00
"	Azariah Snow, Lunenburgh, Vt., per John Snow, Executor	15 00
"	Mrs. E. K. Babcock, Jay, N. Y., per Rev. J. J. Babcock	4 75
"	Wm. Cook, Worcester, N. Y., in advance	100 00
"	Mrs. Elizabeth Hovey, Cambridge, Mass., Geo. Cummings, Executor	3000 00
"	Hannah Godfrey, Hastings, N. Y., C. A. Wilson, Executor	10 00
"	Betsey Miller, Earlville, N. Y., per L. H. Miller	100 00
"	Mrs. Phebe Mulford, Roadstown, N. J., per I. Smalley, Executor	50 00
"	Hannah S. Trask, Fall River, Mass., R. C. Brown and Joseph Borden, Executors	402 13
"	Miss Catharine Sharp, Barre, N. Y., in part, per A. L. Daniels	400 00
"	Miss Achsah Pierce, Mohawk, N. Y., in part, per Rev. H. T. Love	117 33
"	Michael Shepard, Salem, Mass., per H. F. Shepard, Executor	1000 00
"	Cornelia A. Perry, Centre White Creek, N. Y., per Nathaniel Cottrell, Executor	300 00
"	Mrs. Eleanor Willard, Harvard, Mass	100 00
"	Sabina Bennett, West Eaton, N. Y.	14 00
"	James Nickerson, Cazenovia, N. Y.. Benjamin T. Clark, Executor	100 00
1858	Jabez Keep Cortlandville N. Y., per Rev. Henry Bowen, in part	619 00
"	Aaron Treat, North Stonington, Ct.	5 00

IMPORTANT WHEN WILLS ARE MADE.

LEGACIES are sometimes diverted from the purposes of testators on account of technical informalities, especially in the devising clause. The following form of bequest has been approved by high legal authority, to which we solicit the careful attention of those friends who kindly intend to place the Society among their legatees as one which, if followed, will secure to us the favors intended.

FORM OF A BEQUEST TO THE SOCIETY.

I give and bequeath to the American Baptist Home Mission Society, formed in New York, in the year eighteen hundred and thirty-two, the sum of —— dollars, for the purposes of said Society.

REPORTS.

REPORT ON THE MISSIONS OF THE BOARD.

The Committee appointed upon so much of the Report of the Board as relates to its missionary operations, having given such attention as they have been able to the duties assigned them, beg leave to submit the following:—

Your Committee feel, that to give anything like a just conception of the "missionary operations" of the Board, requires something more than the study of an hour. It is not merely to examine the labors of one man, or to measure the results attained of a single station. It is not simply to describe the moral wastes of one city, state, or territory. Nor is it to recite the achievements of a single year. The "missionary operations" of the Board embrace the labors of many men, cover many and widely separated towns and cities, states and territories, and reach, in their yet undeveloped results, years in the distant future. Your Committee, therefore, feel that they can do little more in their report than to state a few general facts, and suggest a few guiding principles.

The American Baptist Home Mission Society in its "missionary operations" has a history yet to be written. True, many of the records of its heroic, self-denying, pioneer laborers, may be even now beyond our reach. They live in the fruits that follow them, but their record is on high. Many of the early laborers under the patronage of this Society, have "finished their course." They were "good men and true." Upon their fields they were men of renown, and yet even with their names, but few of the present patrons of the Society are familiar. These men and others of a kindred spirit, who yet remain, have placed us, as a people, under a debt of gratitude such as we shall never be able to repay. The least we can do, is from time to time to refresh our memories with their fortitude and patience, their zeal and labor in the kingdom of Christ.

To study the "missionary operations" of the Board requires that one should go to the field of their operations. They have sown their seed beside all waters, they have planted the handful of corn upon the top of the mountain, whose fruit has long since been shaking like Lebanon. Their "missionary operations" have embraced the exploring of new territories, the opening up of new fields of labor, the planting of new preaching stations, the organizing and training of new churches, the forming of new Sunday Schools, the building of new houses of worship, and, in a word, the converting of moral wastes into fruitful fields. And that such results as these have been attained in the past, in an encouraging degree, the well-known fruits of missionary labor bear abundant testimony. Whoever will go upon the field of

fornia, Oregon, and Washington, on the West;
territories, or provinces, your missionaries have
Many precious revivals have been enjoyed, and
A goodly number of meeting-houses have been c

Moreover, so far as your Committee have be
operations" of the past year have been wisely dist
looked over the whole field, and from their point
occupy the most available portions. It may, h
the spirit that gave this Society a being, and
occupancy of the older states, such as New Y
rather has to do with the frontier, and is a pi
great destitution here, it is worthy of inquiry, wh
agencies.

Upon the whole, in looking over the "mission
has been done, your Committee have only words
tion to utter.

But there is another view to be taken of the
not been done.

Your Committee feel that the amount expe
tions" of the Board has been altogether inadequa
of the field. While something has been done
gratitude, there still "remaineth much land to be
evangelization" claims, and is worthy to receive,
benevolent efforts than has hitherto been given
awake to the importance or magnitude of the w
feel that the Board should be encouraged to u
missionary operations," in the future.

In order to this, they must seek greatly to au
They must both instruct and arouse the churches

tions." Our people have an undeveloped interest and love for home missions, they have the ability greatly to enlarge their former efforts, the cause demands it, and no time should be lost in its accomplishment.

Your Committee feel that, in conducting the "missionary operations" of the Board, great care should be taken in selecting the fields to be occupied. Centres of influence should be sought for, where there can not only be built up self-sustaining churches at an early day, but from whence the work of evangelization may be extended into the "regions round about."

And these centres of influence should be early occupied. It has been our misfortune in times past, to allow our operations to be so tardy, our occupancy of the fields so late, as greatly to hinder our success. A very slight acquaintance with the growth of new towns will suggest many reasons why our "missionary operations" should keep pace with the tide of emigration. To be too late on the field in many instances, is almost equal to a defeat.

REPORT OF THE COMMITTEE ON LEGACIES.

PRESENTED THROUGH THE REV. DR. BELCHER, OF PHILADELPHIA, CHAIRMAN.

The subject of *Legacies* to the American Baptist Home Mission Society, to which the attention of this body has been called, and on which you have directed your present Committee to report, is one of great importance, demanding the serious and prayerful consideration of every disciple of the Lord Jesus who has had the bounty of Providence committed to his hands.

The venerable apostle Peter, after having declared his zeal in present activity, adds, "Moreover, I will endeavor that you may be able, after my decease, to have these things always in remembrance." This declaration suggests, as your Committee think, the doctrine that entire devotedness to the service of Christ, both in life and death, is alike the duty and the privilege of his followers. It is pleasant to reflect on the character of the large number of our beloved friends, who, after active co-operation with us in our holy cause while they lived, have, during the past year, been called to their rest, leaving behind them evidences in death of their attachment to the church of Christ and their country, which, in a season of great commercial distress, have preserved the Board of our Society from the distressing embarrassment felt by some similar organizations. Useful in life, even after death they shall long serve the holy cause by extending the truths of "Christ's gospel," and thus saving souls from eternal ruin.

In the opinion of not a few brethren, in whose judgment we can not but repose confidence, this subject of testamentary bequests to the cause of holy benevolence has not received a due share of attention. Posthumous usefulness is not desired so generally and to so great an extent as it ought to be; and your Committee would urge on their brethren and sisters, in prospect of finally arranging their property, prayerfully to settle the question as to what proportion they should appropriate to the sacred treasury, and what department of christian usefulness it shall encourage. The history of not a few families where indolence, extravagant habits of life, and neglect of christian duties in general are shown, painfully suggest the contrast between the parents and the children, and the desirableness of compelling posterity to the habits of industry and enterprise, which shall honor alike the memories of the dead, and scatter blessings among the living. The possession of property to such an extent as to discourage industry can not be a blessing in a country like ours, while the diffusion of christianity now is sowing seed which must produce blessings for all time and eternity. Brethren, let your bequests for the benefit of your country cause the blessings of perishing sinners to hallow your memory when your spirits shall return to God, and your bodies shall rest in hope.

Your Committee, in closing their report, may be permitted to say that, on this subject, "wisdom is profitable to direct." Assuredly, in some cases, it is important that christians should be their own executors, doing good *now* while they possess the means of effecting it, remembering alike the uncertainty of life and the possibility of their friends half wishing the death of those whose usefulness is to be advanced by others after their decease. "I had got," says holy Baxter, "the just sum of a thousand pounds. Having no child, I devoted it to charity. Before my purpose was accomplished, the king caused his exchequer to be shut, and it was lost; which I mention to counsel any man that would do good, to do it speedily, and with all his might." The late excellent author of *Mammon* says on the subject, "by making your charity to consist only in testamentary bequests, you are calculating on the certainty and stability of that which has become the very emblem of change and uncertainty."

In closing their report, your Committee would urge the importance of entire consecration alike of ourselves and our possessions to the cause of him who has given himself and his infinite resources of happiness to us. In this season of vast communications of heavenly blessings, may we pray for an enlarged measure of grateful zeal, and prove more fully than ever, that "the liberal soul deviseth liberal things, and by liberal things shall he stand."

All which is respectfully submitted,

JOSEPH BELCHER,
A. SAWIN,
W. H. PARMLY.

NECESSARY PRECAUTIONS.

. It was not the design of the Society in the above Report to encourage delay on the part of any person till the arrival of the death hour, in contributing to the cause of benevolence. They believe with the poet, that

"Life is the time to serve the Lord."

And, with the inspired wise man, they would say to all, "Whatsoever thy hand findeth to do, do it with thy might." It is better, when practicable, for all the friends of benevolence to be their own executors and leave nothing after their decease for others to do in distributing their estate for benevolent purposes. But it is not always practicable, or thought of, or agreeable, to dispose of property in that way, when the claims of this world demand men's attention and resources. And it is very frequently the case that such a disposition of property is desirable *to* men when those claims are satisfied, or the approach of death renders them inoperative. When the desire and ability exist, they should be gratified. And this is what the Society would encourage.

It should not be overlooked, that, whatever is worth doing at all, should be well done, and this rule is as applicable to will-making as to anything else; and more so than to many other things, because the maker of a will can not assist in remedying any defects in his works when it has passed into the hands of his executors. Such defects often appear, especially in bequests to organized Societies. The devising clause is wrongly constructed, misnomers or errors in titles occur, and points of law are left open to litigation, trouble, and expense.

For these, and other reasons, it is always more safe and important for every person, when disposed to make a will, to obtain accurate information as to the true title of any Society he intends to benefit by a legacy. This he can do by correspondence with the proper officer of said Society, or by obtaining a copy of the Annual Report of the Society, or by consulting with some one of its prominent, active friends. He may thus feel assured that he has THE RIGHT TITLE of the Society, on which to base his devise. It is equally important to employ an *able*, experienced lawyer in drawing up the will, or at least, to consult with upon the points of law which should be guarded. Difficulties, contentions, and heart-burnings may thus be avoided, at least, so far as the construction of the document is concerned.

In order to assist those who may entertain kind intentions toward the American Baptist Home Mission Society, we append the following as an approved devising clause in the case of an ordinary legacy for its benefit :—

Form of a Bequest to this Society.

I give and bequeath to the American Baptist Home Mission Society, formed in New York, in the year eighteen hundred and thirty-two, the sum of ——— dollars, for the purposes of said Society.

OBITUARIES.

The *Committee on Obituaries*, appointed at the last anniversary of the Home Mission Society, made the following Report.

Our Society has its death roll, whose list is constantly increasing. Thus, while we are all pressing to possess the earth, we are also marching to the better land. Already the names of those of us who have fallen asleep, are told by hundreds. During the past year, "the last enemy" has made greater inroads upon us than in any preceding one.

These departed, we are not accustomed to, nor do we now, forget. For we, the living, are still one with them, the dead. They are but gone before us a little, and we are following. A narrow stream alone divides Christians on earth and the saints in glory.

Among those recently deceased are some who have long stood by us, ministers and laymen, and liberal supporters, whose names are household words, and whose late friends are all around us. Of these was the consort of our respected first Vice-President, J. E. Southworth, who, for a quarter of a century, walked with him

and served her generation; John M. Peck, D.D., pionee
west—friend of the emigrant, lover of christian mission
and on earth, whose name is indelible in the valley o
Tucker last, but one of a large family of ministers, who
all among us; R. C. McCormick, whose writing is
diplomas; Herbert Hall, Deacon of the Calvary Bapt
liberal supporter of the gospel, and one, who, as an o
purchased to himself "a good degree and great boldness

But to mention all our deceased friends by name, an
an impracticable task. Each was esteemed and respecte
be found in the list of the deceased, as published in t
Society. The fact that they were members of our bo
contributions, or those of their brethren, testifies to their
the christian regard in which they were held by those wh

Their removal from among us was the will of God, and
submission.

To surviving friends, as a society, we tender our earne
that has drunk up their spirits, starts in the silent t
brotherhood we suffer with the suffering. Though unkn
to the many friends of our friends, we here tender our co

After these, our departed brethren, we, their associa
lingering look. But they have suddenly proceeded too

DIRECTORS FOR LIFE.

BY VIRTUE OF A CONTRIBUTION OF ONE HUNDRED DOLLARS OR MORE.

Ackerman, John, Dobbs Ferry, N. Y.
Adams, Rev. Paul S., Brattleboro'. Vt.
Adsit, Rev. Samuel, Jr., Auburn, N. Y.
Akerly, Richard C., Chicago, Ill.
Alden, Rev. William H., Lowell, Mass.
Aldrich, Rev. Jonathan, Worcester, Mass.
Alger, Henry, Cleveland, Ohio.
Allin, George, Brooklyn, N. Y.
Alvord, Rev. Nelson, Tonica, Ill.
Anable, Rev. Cortland W., Brooklyn, N. Y.
Anderson, Rev. Thomas D., Roxbury, Mass.
Anderson, M. B., LL.D., Rochester, N. Y.
Anderson, Rev. George W., New Castle, Del.
Appleton, George, Haverhill, Mass.
Archer, Ezekiel, New York.
Armitage, Rev. Thomas, D.D., New York.
Armstrong, Rev. James D., Baltimore.
Arnold, Wipple A., Centreville, R. I.
Ashton, D. R., Philadelphia.
Askren, William, Cincinnati, O.
Atwell, Rev. G. B., Pleasant Valley, Ct.
Averill, Rev. Alex. M, North Cambridge, Mass.
Ayer, Rev. Oliver, Claremont, N. H.
Babcock, Rev. Rufus, D.D., Paterson, N. J.
Bacheller, Jonathan, Lynn, Mass.
Bacon, Mrs. Mary H., Greenwich, N. J.
Backus, Rev. Jay S., Syracuse, N. Y.
Bailey, Benjamin D., Providence, R. I.
Bailey, Rev. Gilbert S., Metamora, Ill.
Bailey, Rev. Joseph A., Waterbury, Ct.
Ballard, Rev. Joseph, New York.
Baldwin, Rev. N. B., Philadelphia.
Balen, Peter, New York.
Banks, Jacob, Salem, N. J.
Banks, Mrs. Mary, Salem, N. J.
Banks, Miss Ann Judson, Salem, N. J.
Banvard, Rev. Joseph, Pawtucket, R. I.
Barnaby, Rev. James, Newburyport, Mass.
Barker, Rev. Enoch M., Beverly, N. J.
Barns, John, Danversport, Mass.
Barrell, Rev. Almond C., Albion, N. Y.
Barrows, Rev. B. W., Neponset, Mass.
Batchelder, Rev. James L., Cincinnati, O.
Bates, V. J., Providence, R. I.
Beach, William, New York.
Beecher, Rev. L .F., D.D., Saratoga Springs, N.Y.
Beecher, Mrs. M. C., Saratoga Springs, N. Y.
Belcher, Rev. Joseph, D.D., Philadelphia.
Bennet, Rev. Ira, Sparta, Wis
Binney, Rev. J. G., D.D., Washington, D. C.
Binney, Mrs. Juliet P., Washington, D. C.
Bishop, Nathan, LL.D., Boston.
Blain, Rev. John, Central Falls, R. I.
Blain, Mrs. Amy Ann, Central Falls, R. I.
Bliss, Rev. George R., Lewisburg, Pa.
Bly, Rev. William T., Minnesota Territory.
Boardman, W. G., Albany, N. Y.
Bolles, Matthew, Jr., Boston.
Borden, Jefferson, Fall River, Mass.
Bosworth, Rev. George W., Portland, Me.
Bowen, Rev. Henry, Cortlandville, N. Y.
Bowles, Rev. Ralph H., Lee, Mass.
Boyce, James, Providence.
Bradford, Rev. S. S., Pawtucket, R. I.
Brainerd, Samuel, Haverhill, Mass.
Brant, Rev Randolph C., Lawrence, Kansas.
Brantly, Rev. W. T., Philadelphia.
Brayton, Rev. Jonathan, Centreville, R. I.
Brayton, William E., Providence, R. I.
Brayton, Samuel H., Phœnix, R. I.
Brayton, Lodowick M., Knightsville, R. I.
Briggs, Rev. O. W., Brooklyn, N. Y.
Brockway, Charles, Broadalbin, N. Y.
Brooks, Iveson L., Hamburg, S. C.
Brooks, Rev. Kendall, Fitchburg, Mass.
Brokaw, Joseph, New York.
Brouwere, Vermilyea T., Dundee, N. Y.
Brown, Rev. I. Newton, D.D., Philadelphia.
Bruce, John M., New York.
Buckbee, Rev. Charles A., New York.
Bucknell, William, Philadelphia.
Bucknell, Mrs. Margaret K. C., Philadelphia.
Bucknell, Miss L. L., Philadelphia.
Budlong, James E., Providence.
Burlingham, Rev. A. H., New York.
Burgess, Rev. I. J., Milltown, Me.
Bullock, Benjamin, Philadelphia.
Bump, Nathaniel, Providence.
Burger, William, New York.
Burke, William, Rochester, N. Y.
Burke, Abraham C., Brooklyn, N. Y,
Burke, J. B., Hamilton, Can.
Burt, John W., Brooklyn, N. Y.
Burt, E. C., Brooklyn, N. Y.
Burt, James, Brooklyn, N. Y.
Burt, James M., Brooklyn, N. Y.
Burroughs, Rev. J. C., Chicago, Ill.
Butcher, Washington, Philadelphia.
Butterfield, Rev. Isaac, Davenport, Iowa.
Byram, Rev. B. P., Amesbury, Mass.
Caldicott, Rev. T. F., D.D., Boston.
Carleton, Rev. George J., Newton Centre, Mass
Carleton, Mrs. J. T., Newton Centre, Mass.
Carpenter, Rev. Mark, Holyoke, Mass.
Carter, Joseph, Malden, Mass.
Caswell, Prof. Alexis, D.D., Providence.
Caswell, Rev. Lewis E., Boston
Cauldwell, Ebenezer, New York.
Chace, Prof. George I., Providence.
Challis, Rev. James M., Roadstown, N. J.
Chandler, John H., Bankok, Siam.
Chandler, Mrs. Helen M., Bankok, Siam.
Chaplin, Rev. Jeremiah, West Dedham, Mass.
Charlton, Rev. Frederick, Philadelphia.
Cheesebrough, Rev. Isaac, Groton, Ct.
Cheney, Rev. David B., Philadelphia.
Chester, Mrs. Sophronia L., Williamsburg, N. Y.
Child, Rev. William C., Roxbury, Mass.
Church, Rev. P., D.D., New York.
Church, Mrs. Chara E., New York.
Clarke, Rev. Minor G., Indianapolis, Ia.
Clapp, Benjamin, Franklindale, N. Y.
Coggeshall, Josias, Brooklyn, N. Y.
Coggeshall, Mrs. Elizabeth M., Brooklyn, N. Y.
Cogswell, Rev. Wilson, Shakapee, Min.
Colby, Hon. Anthony, New London, N. H.
Colby, Isaac, Concord, N. H.
Cole, Rev. Jirah D., Waukegan, Ill.
Colgate, Mrs. Jane, New York.
Colgate, Samuel, New York.
Colgate, Charles C., New York.
Colgate, James B., New York.
Colver, Rev. Nathaniel, D.D., Cincinnati, O.
Collins, Rev. Samuel A., Taunton, Mass.
Cone, Edward Winfield, New York.
Cone, Spencer Wallace, New York.

Cones, James, Cincinnati, O.
Conklin, William, New York.
Cooke, Joseph J., Providence.
Cookson, Rev. John, Morrisania, N. Y.
Cooper, William, New York.
Corwin, Robert G., Lebanon, O.
Corwin, Rev. Jason, Darlington, Wis.
Cottrell, Thomas, Greenwich, N. Y.
Covell, Rev. Lemuel, New York.
Crane, Rev. W. C., Hernando, Miss.
Crane, Rev. Origin, New England Village, Mass.
Crane, William, Baltimore.
Crosby, William B., New York
Crozer, John P., Chester, Pa.
Crozer, Mrs. Sarah L., Chester, Pa.
Crozer, George K., Chester, Pa.
Crozer, Robert Hall, Chester, Pa.
Cushman, Rev. Elisha, Deep River, Ct.
Cuthbert, Rev. James H., Philadelphia.
Cuthbert, Lucius, Princeton, N. J.
Cutting, Rev. S. S., Rochester, N. Y.
Dagg, Rev. John L., D.D., Penfield, Ga.
Damon, Mrs. Catharine, Ashby, Mass.
Dana, Mrs. Nancy, Boston.
Daniels, Clark, New London, Ct.
Davey, Thomas, New York.
Davies, John M., New York.
Davis, Rev. Henry, D.D., Columbus, Ohio.
Davis, Hon. Isaac, LL.D., Worcester, Mass.
Davis, Mrs. Mary H. E., Worcester, Mass.
Davis, Rev. Ebenezer S., Brooklyn, N. Y.
Day, Rev. Ambrose, Westfield, Mass.
Day, Rev. Henry, Philadelphia.
Day, Arthur, Shaftsbury, Vt.
Day, Hon. Albert, Hartford, Ct.
Decker, Alfred F., New York.
Devan, Rev. Thomas T., Nyack, N. Y.
Devan, Mrs. Emma E., Nyack, N. Y.

Fost
Glad
Glov
Gra
Gre
Gre
Gre
Gre

Hutchinson, Rev. William, Sandy Hill, N. Y.
Hyde, Rev. J. C., Hastings, Min.
Ide, Rev. George B., D.D., Springfield, Mass.
Ilsley, Rev. Silas, Essex, Ct.
Ives, Rev. Dwight, D.D., Suffield, Ct.
Ives, Mrs. Julia A., Suffield, Ct.
Jackson, Rev. Henry, D.D., Newport, R. I.
James, Rev. Silas C., Bunker Hill, Ill.
James, William T., New York.
James, Israel E., Philadelphia.
Jameson, William H., Mellrose, Mass.
Jameson, Rev. Thorndike C., Mellrose, Mass.
Jayne, David, Philadelphia.
Jennings, Rev. John, Newton Centre, Mass.
Jeter, Rev. J. B., D.D., Richmond, Va.
Johnson, Rev. W. D. H., Greenville, Ill.
Jones, Rev. Henry V., Noank, Ct.
Jones, Rev. P. F., New York.
Jones, Rev. John D. E., Worcester, Mass.
Judd, Rev. Orrin B., LL.D., New York.
Keely, John, Haverhill, Mass.
Keen, Wm. W., Philadelphia.
Kempton, Rev. George, North East, N. Y.
Kendrick, Edward E., Albany, N. Y.
Kennard, Rev. J. H., D.D., Philadelphia.
Kent, Henry P., Suffield, Ct.
Kent, Mrs. Jane S., Suffield, Ct.
Keyes, Rev. Charles B., Westfield, N. Y.
Keyser, Rev. Charles, Providence, R. I.
Ladd, Rev. James S., New York.
Larcombe, Richard J., New York.
Larcombe, Rev. Thomas, Philadelphia.
Latham, Daniel, Groton, Ct.
Latham, Mrs. Delia Ann, Groton, Ct.
Latham, Daniel D., New London, Ct.
Lane, Rev. Benjamin I., Newburyport, Mass.
Lathrop, Rev. Edward, D.D., New York.
Laws, Rev. William, Modesttown, Va.
Lawton, Rev. Joseph A., Erwinton, S. C.
Lea, Sidney Slade, Yanceyville, N. C.
Lee, George F., Philadelphia.
Leighton, Rev. Sam'l S., West Townsend, Mass.
Leonard, Rev. Lewis G., D.D., Marietta, Ohio.
Leverett, Rev. William, Newport, R. I.
Lewis, John G., Boston.
Lewis, Isaac, New York.
Lewis, Mrs. Mary, New York.
Lillie, Rev. James, D.D., Montreal, Canada.
Lincoln, Hon. Heman, Boston.
Lincoln, Rev. B. H., South Framingham, Mass.
Linnard, Hon. J. M., Philadelphia.
Linnard, Mrs. Anna, Philadelphia.
Litchfield, E. B., Brooklyn, N. Y.
Litchfield, E. D., Brooklyn, N. Y.
Locke, Rev. William E., Lancaster, Pa.
Loxley, Rev. Benjamin R., Philadelphia.
Loomis, Rev. Ebenezer, Alba, Pa.
Lumsden, D. F., Boston.
Lyeth, Richard J., Hastings, N. Y.
Lyon, Merrick, Providence, R. I.
Mabbet, Jonathan, Dover Plains, N. Y.
McIntosh, Wm. C., Philadelphia.
Maclay, Rev. Archibald, D.D., New York.
Magoon, Rev. E. L., D.D., Albany, N. Y.
Magoon, Mrs. E. L., Albany, N. Y.
Malcolm, Rev. Howard, D.D., Lewisburg, Pa.
Malcolm, Rev. Thomas S., Philadelphia.
Mallary, Rev. C. D., Albany, Ga.
Marble, Joel, Albany, N. Y.
Marchant, Henry, Providence.
Marcley, Mrs. Caroline T., Morrisania, N. Y.
Maple, Thompson, Canton, Ill.
Martin, Runyon W., New York.
Martin, Charles J., New York.
Marshall, Rev. Enos, Covert, N. Y.
Massey, Rev. Joseph T., Bellingham, Mass.
Mason, Rev. Alanson P., Chelsea, Mass.
Mason, Rev. David G., Keene, N. H.
Mason, Rev. Jas. O., Greenwich, N. Y.
Mason, Rev. Sumner R., Cambridgeport, Mass.
Masters, William, Providence.
Masters, Mrs. William, Providence.
Mather, Rev. A. P., California.
Merit, Rev. Columbus D., Washburn, Ill.
Merriam, Jonathan, Newton Centre, Mass.
Messenger, Rev. Edward C., West Medway, Ms.
Middleditch, Rev. Robert T., Red Bank, N. J.
Milbank, Samuel, Jr., New York.
Milbank, Jeremiah, New York.
Miller, John A., New York.
Miller, Rev. D Henry, Meriden, Ct.
Mills, Rev. Robert C., Salem, Mass.
Miner, Mrs. Henrietta Wilson, Newark, N. J.
Mitchell, Isaac R., Sandwich Islands.
Moore, Rev. Isaac Jonesville, Mich.
Morse, Mrs. Sophia A., Wyoming, N. Y.
Morse, Rev. J. B., North Orange, N. J.
Morton, Rev. Charles, Corning, N. Y.
Mudge, Rev. Warham, Palmyra, N. Y.
Mulford, Rev. Clarence W., Flemington, N. J.
Munn, William H., New York.
Murdock, Rev. J. N., D.D., Boston.
Murphy, Rev. John C., New York.
Muzzy, Rev. Lawson, Pulaski, N. Y.
Neale, Rev. Rollin H., D.D, Boston.
Newell, Asa, Providence.
Newton, Isaac, New York.
Nice, Rev. G. P. Somerville, N. J.
Nichols, Charles H., Boston, Mass.
Nicholas, Joseph O., Newark, N. J.
Norris, William, Newark, N. J.
Northam, Rev. G., Norminy Grove, Va.
Nott, Rev. A. Kingman, New York.
Olcott, Rev. James B., Springfield, Ill.
Packer, Rev. D., Mount Holly, Vt.
Page, Joseph, Philadelphia.
Parker, Rev. J. W., D.D., Newton Centre, Mass.
Parker, Rev. Carlton, Hebron, Me.
Parker, Rev. S. S., Southbridge, Mass.
Parker, Gilman, Danversport, Mass.
Parker, Rev. Wm., Philadelphia.
Parkhurst, Rev. John, Chelmsford, Mass.
Parkhurst, Rev. J. W., Newton Centre, Mass.
Parks, Rev. Norman, Perry, Ill.
Parmelee, Rev. D. S., New York.
Parmly, Rev. Wheelock H., Jersey City, N. J.
Patch, Abijah, Boston, Mass.
Pattison, Rev. R. E., D.D., Waterville, Me
Pattison, Rev. Wm. P., Ypsilanti, Mich.
Patton, Rev. Alfred S., Hoboken, N. J.
Paul, Albert, Hastings, N. Y.
Peck, J. B., New York.
Perkins, Rev. Aaron, D.D., Salem, N. J.
Perry, Rev. G. B., Cleveland, Ohio.
Perry, Simeon N., Walpole, N. H.
Perry, George T., Jr, Brooklyn, N. Y.
Peterson, Lemuel, Philadelphia.
Phelps, William, New York.
Phelps, Rev. S. Dryden, D.D., New Haven, Ct.
Phillips, Rev. Daniel W., South Reading, Mass.
Phillips, Rev. James M., Mystic River, Ct.
Pier, Sylvester, New York.
Pierce, Rev. S. E., Gloucester, Mass.
Pigsley, Rev. Welcome, Metamora, Ill.
Platt, Nathan C., New York.
Plummer, John L., Roxbury, Mass.
Pollard, Rev. Andrew, Taunton, Mass.
Pond, Moses, Boston, Mass.
Pope, Wm. G. E., New Bedford, Mass.
Pope, Mrs. Anna F., New Bedford, Mass.
Pope, Francis E., Danversport, Mass.
Porter, Rev. Lemuel, D.D., Pittsfield, Mass.
Porter, Isaac, Danversport, Mass.
Post, Reuben, Essex, Ct.
Potter, William H., Mystic River, Ct.
Pray, Rev. E. N., Boston, Mass.
Prevaux, Rev. Francis E., San Francisco, Cal.
Price, Rev. Jacob, Edwardsburg, Mich.
Price, William M., Brooklyn.
Pryor, Rev. John, D.D., Cambridge, Mass.

DIRECTORS FOR LIFE.

Parmelee, Rev. Wm. F., Naples, N. Y.
Randall, Rev. S. B., Mystic River, Ct.
Rathbone, John F., Albany, N. Y.
Raymond, Rev. Robert R., Brooklyn, N. Y.
Read, James H., Providence, R. I.
R[illegible], Rev. C. W., [illegible], Mass.
Reed, Rev. Nathan A., Bristol, R. I.
Ross, Rev. William, Sennett, N. Y.
Reed, Rev. William, New London, Ct.
Remington, Rev. Stephen, Brooklyn, N. Y.
Reynolds, Joseph, Aurora, N. Y.
Richards, Rev. William C., Providence, R. I.
Richardson, Thomas, Boston, Mass.
Richardson, Rev. J. G., Valley Falls, R. I.
Richmond, Rev. J. L., Mt. Vernon, Ohio.
Ricker, Rev. Joseph, Woburn, Mass.
Roberts, Charles L., New York.
Roberts, Lewis, Brooklyn, N. Y.
Roberts, A. L., Brooklyn, N. Y.
Robinson, James L., Hastings, N. Y.
Robinson, Rev. William, Rahway, N. J.
Salisbury, William D., New York.
Sampson, J. K., Brooklyn, N. Y.
Sargent, Rev. A., Littleton, Mass.
Sanford, Rev. Miles, North Adams, Mass.
Sarles, Rev. J. W., Brooklyn, N. Y.
Savage, M. B., Brooklyn, N. Y.
Sawyer, Rev. Reuben, —— N. Y.
Sage, Rev. John, White Pigeon, Mich.
Searl, Rev. Davis, Springfield, N. Y.
Sears, Rev. Barnas, D.D., Providence, R. I.
Seeley, Rev. John T., Syracuse, N. Y.
Sewell, John J., New York.
Seeley, Mrs. Mary Eliza, New York.
Shadrach, Rev. W., D.D., Philadelphia, Pa.
Shailer, Rev. N. E., Deep River, Ct.
Shailer, Rev. Julius S., Roxbury, Mass.
Stowell, Nathaniel, Worcester, Mass.
Stubberts, Rev. William F., Malden, Mass.
Swan, Rev. Jabez L., New London, Ct.
Swaim, Rev. Samuel B., West Cambridge, Mass.
Taggart, Rev. Joseph W., Detroit, Mich.
Tanner, James, Pembina, Min. Ter.
Taylor, Rev. J. B., Richmond, Va.
Taylor, Rev. E. E. L., D.D., Brooklyn, N. Y.
Taylor, Stewart M., New York.
Taylor, Daniel G., New York.
Taylor, Jeremiah B., New York.
Teasdale, Rev. T. C., D.D., Washington, D. C.
Thomas, Cornelius W., New York.
Thomas, Mrs. Catharine W., New York.
Thomas, Augustus, New York.
Thomas, Mrs. Margaret L., New York.
Thompson, Mrs. Huldah E., Troy, N. Y.
Tilton, Rev. J. D., Sandbornton, N. H.
Tingley, Rev. T. C., Scituate, Mass.
Tinsley, Rev. Isaac, Charlottesville, Va.
Timmons, John M., Effingham, S. C.
Todd, William W., New York.
Toran, Thomas, Halifax, Va.
Townsend, Palmer, Brooklyn, N. Y.
Tracy, William, New York.
Tracy, Rev. Leonard, Keene, N. H.
Train, Rev. Arthur S., D.D., Haverhill, Mass.
Tryon, Mrs. Louisa J., Houston, Texas.
Tucker, Daniel N., New York.
Tucker, Rev. Anson, Lafayette, Ia.
Tucker, F., Stony Creek, Va.
Tucker, Rev. H. Holcombe, Alexandria, Va.
Tufts, Mrs. Mary, Fitchburg, Mass.
Turner, Peter C., New London, Ct.
Turpin, Dr. William H., Augusta, Ga.
Turpin, Mrs. Mary A., Augusta, Ga.
Urann, Joseph, Boston, Mass.

[redacted]

Woolsey, Rev. J. J., Norwalk, Ct.
Wooster, Rev. Henry, Deep River, Ct.
Wooster, Henry C., Essex, Ct.
Wright, Rev. Thomas G., Wappingers Falls, N. Y.
Wright, Rev. Lyman, Norwich, N. Y
Wyckoff, William H., New York.

MEMBERS FOR LIFE.

BY VIRTUE OF A CONTRIBUTION OF THIRTY DOLLARS.

Abbott, Stephen, Chicopee Falls, Mass.
Abbott, Rev. S. G., Bradford, N. H.
Achilles, H. L., Albion, N. Y.
Ackley, Rev. Alvin, Greenport, N. Y.
Adair, William N., Somerville, N. J.
Adams, Miss Priscilla S., New York.
Adams, Mrs. Mary, West Killingly, Ct.
Adams, Rev. S. W., Cleveland, O.
Adams, Rev. R. J., Wallingford, Ct.
Adams, Mrs. Eliza J., Wallingford, Ct.
Adams, Miss Caroline, New York.
Adams, Albert, Augusta, Ga.
Adams, Joseph H., Williamsburgh, N. Y.
Adams, Mrs. Mary, Williamsburgh, N. Y.
Adams, Jedediah, New York.
Adams, Rev. Sullivan, Shaftsbury, Vt.
Adams, Van Rensselaer, Deckertown, N. J.
Adams, Rev. J. N., Croton, N. Y.
Adams, Clark, Galesville, N. Y.
Adams, Rev. John Quincy, New York.
Adam, Mrs. Carrie E., New York.
Adkins, Isaac K., Newport, Ohio.
Adlam, Rev. S., Newport, R. I.
Adlam, Mrs. Martha L., Newport, R. I.
Adalt, Mrs. Maria J., Auburn, N. Y.
Agenbroad, Rev. J. P., Minnesota.
Ainsworth, Rev. S. C., Earleville, N. Y.
Akerly, Mrs. Priscilla E., Chicago, Ill.
Akerly, George B., Chicago, Ill.
Akerly, William Henry, Chicago, Ill.
Albro, Mrs. Hannah Hill, New York.
Albro, Stephen S., Newport, R. I.
Alden, Rev. John, Northampton, Mass.
Aldrich, Warren, Lowell, Mass.
Alexander, Calvin, West Halifax, Vt.
Allds, Jotham G., Claremont, N. H.
Allen, Rev. Benoni, Cambridge, O.
Allen, Russell, Shelby, N. Y.
Allen, Mrs. Eliza, Shelby, N. Y.
Allen, Walter, New York.
Allen, Ethan, Worcester, Mass.
Allen, Rev. Marvin, Detroit, Mich.
Allen, Rev. N. T., Jewett City, Ct.
Allen, Rev. John, North Wrentham, Mass.
Allen, Mrs. Lorena, New York.
Allen, Benjamin, Seekonk, Mass.
Allen, Joel, East Smithfield, Pa.
Allen, Nathaniel, Brookline, Me.
Allen, Mrs. Mary B. M., North Sedgwick, Me.
Allen, Alanson, Fair Haven, Vt.
Allen, Mrs. Jane, Fair Haven, Vt.
Allen, Joseph G., Rockland, Ohio.
Allen, David, New Gloucester, Me.
Allen, G. P., Brockport, N. Y.
Allen, Rev. L. B., Yarmouth, Me.
Allen, Thomas, Wilmington, Del.
Allen, Rev. Thomas, Tavoy, Burmah.
Allen, Mrs. A. D., Norwalk, Ohio.
Aller, Amos, Brooklyn, N. Y.
Aller, Mrs. Amos, Brooklyn.
Alger, Mrs. Suson, Cleveland, Ohio.
Almond, John P., Bostwick Mills, N. C.
Ambler, Rev. E. S., Woodstown, N. J.
Ambler, Mrs. Almira, Woodstown, N. J.
Ambler, Starr H., Woodstown, N. J.
Ambler, Rev. J. V., Lanesboro', Mass.
Ambler, Mrs. A. T., Lanesboro', Mass.
Ames, Samuel, New York.
Ames, Robert W., Roxbury, Mass.
Ames, Erasmus D., Uncasville, Ct.
Ames, Rev. W. W., Greenfield, Mass.
Ames, Mrs. W. W., Greenfield, Mass.
Ammidown, H., Southbridge, Mass.
Amsbury, Jabez, Norwich, Ct.
Amory, Peter B., New York.
Amory, Mrs. Anna M., New York.
Andem, Rev. James, Newport, N. H.
Andem, Mrs. Emma W., Newport, N. H.
Anderson, William T., Princeton, N. J.
Anderson, Mrs. Catharine J., Princeton, N. J.
Anderson, John T., Verdon, Pa.
Anderson, Peter, New York.
Anderson, William, Hoboken, N. J.
Anderson, Rev. Edward, Milford, N. H.
Andrews, Milton, New Britain, Ct.
Andrews, William, Providence, R. I.
Andrew, Mrs. Deliah, Providence, R. I.
Andrews, Mrs. Wm., Providence, R. I.
Andrews, Ebenezer T., Boston.
Andrews, George R., New York.
Andrews, B. B., Wilson, N. Y.
Appleton, James Philadelphia, Pa.
Archer, Charles O., New York.
Archibald, Mrs. Susan W T., Manchester, Vt.
Ardis, Rev. Henry Z., Zalofa, Fla.
Arents, Stephen, Brooklyn, N. Y.
Armitage, Mrs. Thomas, New York.
Armstrong, Rev. Andrew, Lambertville, N. J.
Armstrong, Mrs. M. S., Lambertville, N. J.
Armstrong, Montgomery, New Haven, Ct.
Arnold, Mrs. Mary N., Attleboro, Mass.
Arnold, Mrs. Francis R., Providence, R. I.
Arnold, Rev. Benjamin B., Hartford, Iowa.
Arnold, Miss Phebe, Jay, N. Y.
Arnold, Mrs. Mary, Clifton Park, N. Y.
Arnold, Israel, Providence, R. I.
Arnold, A. Chapman, New London, Ct.
Arthur, Rev. William, Newtonville, N. Y.
Ash, Rev. J. R., Logansport, Ia.
Ashton, Samuel K., M.D., Philadelphia, Pa.
Atkins, Loyd, Bristol, Ct.
Atkinson, Taylor B., West Philadelphia, Pa.
Attwater, Erasmus, Throopsville, N. Y.
Atwood, Lewis, Waterbury, Ct.
Atwood, Rev. John, New Boston, N. H.
Atwood, Mrs. Lydia N., New Boston, N. H.
Austin, Edward, New York.
Austin, Samuel, Suffield, Ct.
Austin, Cornelius, Rochester, N. Y.
Avery, Mrs. Clara, New York.
Avery, Rev. E. J. Worcester, Mass.
Avery, William D., Providence, R. I.
Avery, Rev. D., Tyringham, Mass.
Avery, E. J., Brookline, Mass.

Bacon, Mrs. Mary L., Trumansburg, N. Y.
Bacon, Miss Ann, Dorchester, Mass.
Bacon, W. A., Ludlow, Vt.
Bacon, Almon, Lyme, Ct.
Bacon, Martha A., Chelsea, Mass.
Bagby, Rev. Richard, Stevensville, Va.
Bagley, S. V., New York.
Bagley, Miss Ellen, Waterboro Centre, Me.
Bailey, Mrs. S. W., Parham's Store, Va.
Bailey, Timothy, Malden, Mass.
Bailey, Mrs. Sarah E., Metamora, Ill.
Bailey, S. A., Utica, N. Y.
Bailey, Jonathan, Jr., Bentley's Corners, N. Y.
Bailey, Mrs. Caroline, Philadelphia, Pa.
Bailey, Rev. L., New London, Ohio.
Baily, Rev. Simon B., Hopkinton, R. I.
Baily, Mrs. Eveline, Hopkinton, R. I.
Baily,
Bailie,
Ba Yan, N. Y.
Ba
Ba
Ba
Baker, , Mass.
Baker, , Mass.
Baker,
Baker,
Baker, Elisha W., Providence,
Baker, Benjamin F., Brookline, Mass.
Baker, Rev. John H., East Greenwich, R. I.
Baker, Rev. James, Perryville, N. J.
Baker, David, Corning, N. Y.
Baker, Garness E., New York.
Baker, Theodore, Norwalk, Ohio.
Baker, Joseph K., Jr., West Harwich, Mass.
Baker, Rev. Samuel, D.D., Williamsburg, N.Y.
Baker, Mrs. Elizabeth A., Williamsburg, N. Y.
Baker, John R., New York.
Baker, Harriet M., West Dedham, Mass.
Balch, Mrs. Jane, New York.
Baldwin, Rev. George C., D.D., Troy, N. Y.
Baldwin, Mrs. Margaret D., Boston, Mass.
Baldwin, Rev. Jonathan, Eliston, N. Y.
Baldwin, Jared G., New York.
Baldwin, Mrs. Eliza, New York.
Baldwin, A. T. Brooklyn, N. Y.
Baldwin, Miss Elizabeth A., New York.
Baldwin, Josephus, Nashua, N. H.
Baldwin, Mrs. Mary Ann Nashua, N. H.
Baldwin, Mrs. Nancy, Nashua, N. H.
Baldwin, Mrs. Caroline E., Philadelphia

Barrett, Mr
Barrett, O.
Barker, Be
Barker, Mr
Barker, An
Barker, Wi
Barker, Mr
Barnard, M
Barnard, J.
Barnes, Jol
Barnes, Re
Barnes, Re
Barney, W.
Barney, Mr
Barnum, O
Barnum, S.
Barnum, A
Barrows, E
Barrows, M
Barter, Joh
Bartholom
Bartlett, R
Bartlett, St
Bartlett, M
Bartolette,
Barringer,
Barrass, R
Barrass, M
Barber, Aa
Barber, Mr
Barber, Mo
Barber, Ab
Barber, Mi
Barber, Re
Barry, S. I.
Barstow, C.
Bassett, Ny
Batchelder
Bateman,
Bates, Mrs.
Bates, Mrs.
Bates, Whi
Bates, Den
Bates, Rev
Bates, Rev.
Bates, Rev.
Bates, Lym
Bates, Levi
Bates, Will
Batey, Rev
Battell, Re

Beattie, Rev. W. Q., Bennettsville, N. C.
Beatson, Miss Helen, New York.
Beaver, J. M., Hillsborough, N. C.
Beebe, Warren, Brooklyn, N. Y.
Beebe, Mrs. Charlotte, Brooklyn, N. Y.
Beebe, Mrs. Lydia, Waterford, Ct.
Beecher, Mrs. Mary C., Saratoga Springs, N. Y.
Beebee, A. M., Jr., Hamilton, N. Y.
Beck, Rev. John J., Coosawhatchie, S. C.
Beck, Rev. Levi G., Doylestown, Pa.
Beckwith, Miss Abby G., Providence.
Beckwith, Elisha W., Norwich, Ct.
Beckwith, Jason, New London, Ct.
Beckwith, Ezra S., New London, Ct.
Beckwith, Clement S., New London, Ct.
Beckwith, Nathan, Upper Red Hook, N. Y.
Beckwith, Elisha, Waterford, Ct.
Beckwith, Mrs. Betsey, Albion, N. Y.
Belcher, Rev. James, Oldtown, Me.
Belden, Rev. Joseph, Bordentown, N. J.
Belden, Mrs. Mary Ann, Meriden, Ct.
Belknap, Rev. Appleton, Lyme, N. H.
Bell, Rev. Edward, South Woodstock, Ct.
Bell, Miss Jane Ann, South Woodstock, Ct.
Bell, Joseph, Brookfield, O.
Bell, John, Tarrytown, N. Y.
Bellamy, Rev. David, Mt. Morris, N. Y.
Bellamy, Rev. R. K., Chicopee Falls, Mass.
Beman, Mrs. Rebecca S., Deep River, Ct.
Beman, Miss Charlotte, Deep River, Ct.
Beman, Mrs. Samantha, Brooklyn, N. Y.
Bemis, Miss Elizabeth H., Worcester, Mass.
Beeman, Rev. James M., Dickinson, N. Y.
Bemrose, Mrs. Elizabeth M., Port Jarvis, N. Y.
Bendall, George, Coman's Well, Va.
Benedict, Uriah, Central Falls, R. I.
Benedict, Stephen, Pawtucket, R. I.
Benedict, Rev. David, D.D., Pawtucket, R. I.
Benedict, Miss Cornelia E., Providence.
Benedict, Rev. N. D., Waywasing, N. Y.
Benedict, Mrs. Nancy, New York.
Benedict, Rev. E. L., Maine, N. Y.
Benjamin, W. P., New London, Ct.
Benjamin, B. M., Rochester, N. Y.
Bennett, Rev. Cephas, Tavoy, Asia.
Bennett, Joseph E., Manchester, N. H.
Bennett, Hiram, Salem, N. J.
Bennett, Rev. Alvin, Freetown Corners, N. Y.
Bennett, Rev. David, Unionville, N. Y.
Bennett, E. A., Philadelphia.
Bennett, Mrs. Judith B., Philadelphia.
Bennett, Miss Anna, Philadelphia.
Bennett, Rev. Olney, Walesville, N. Y.
Bennett, Joseph, Manchester, N. H.
Bennett, Joseph L., New London, Ct.
Bennett, Rev. Perry, Winchester, Ill.
Bennett, Mrs. Flavilla, Bennettsville, N. Y.
Benton, Mrs. Sarah, Saratoga, N. Y.
Benton, Rev. George W., Granville, Ill.
Benton, Austin W., Jamaica Plains, Mass.
Bernard, Rev. David, Akron, Ohio.
Bernie, Miss Anna, New York.
Bertine, Miss Sarah Ann, New York.
Dertine, James C., New York.
Berry, Zebina E., Worcester, Mass.
Berry, Susan C., Worcester, Mass.
Berry, Ellen L., Worcester, Mass.
Berry, S. Homer, Norwalk, O.
Betts, Rev. Platt, Omro, Wis.
Betts, Philander, Danbury, Ct.
Bevan, Rev. Isaac, Philadelphia.
Beverly, Miss Elizabeth, New York.
Bicking, Richard, Wilmington, Del.
Bickford, Rev. M. L., Waltham, Mass.
Biddle, Samuel S., Forestville, N. C.
Biddle, Rev. William, Voluntown, Ct.
Bidgood, Mrs. L., Hargroves', Va.
Bigelow, Rev. John R., M.D., New York.
Bigelow, Mrs. Eunice P., New York.
Bigelow, John B., Brooklyn, N. Y.
Bigelow, Mrs. Catharine, Brooklyn, N. Y.
Bigelow, Franklin H., Brooklyn, N. Y.
Bigelow, Miss Nancy H., Brooklyn, N. Y.
Bigelow, Mrs. Charlotte, Brooklyn, N. Y.
Bigelow, Rev. J. F., Middleboro, Mass.
Bill, Rev. G. B., Rumney, N. H.
Bill, O. A., New Haven, Ct.
Bill, Eleazer, Willimantic, Ct.
Billings, Rev. John, Mt. Vernon, Me.
Billings, Mrs. Betsey, Mt. Vernon, Me.
Billingslea, Dr. C., Montgomery Co., Ala.
Biglow, Barna., Perkinsville, Vt.
Bingham, Luther, Fort Wayne, Ia.
Bird, Rev. John, Lloyd's, Essex Co., Va.
Birdsey, Mrs. Rebecca C., Meriden, Ct.
Birdsey, Linus, Meriden, Ct.
Birdsey, Mrs. V. A., Meriden, Ct.
Bishop, Jesse, Cleveland, O.
Bishop, James W. A., Philadelphia.
Bishop, Mrs. Caroline C., New York.
Blackford, Ephraim, New Market, N. J.
Blackledge, Jacob, Stoningtonboro', Ct.
Blackwell, J. P., Brooklyn, N. Y.
Blackinton, Sanford, North Adams, Mass.
Blackmer, Jirah, Wheatland, N. Y.
Blaisdell, Josiah C., Fall River, Mass.
Blake, Aaron, Chelsea, Mass.
Blake, Jonathan, Brooklyn, N. Y.
Blake, David B., Providence.
Blake, Ezekiel, Chicopee Falls, Mass.
Blake, Frederick D., Boston, Mass.
Blanding, Dr. S., Columbia, S. C.
Bleecker, Mrs. Jane, New York.
Bleecker, George W., Brooklyn, N. Y.
Blessing, John, Xenia, O.
Bliss, Elijah J., Brooklyn, N. Y.
Bliss, Alanson, Hamilton, N. Y.
Bliss, E. J., Brandon, Vt.
Bliss, N., Brooklyn, N. Y.
Blodgett, James D., Haverhill, Mass.
Blodgett, Mrs. James D., Haverhill, Mass.
Blodgett, Loring B., Cortlandville, N. Y.
Blood, Isaiah, Ballston Spa, N. Y.
Blood, Cyrus G., Davenport, Iowa.
Blood, A. P., Ballston, N. Y.
Bloodgood, James, Springville, N. Y.
Bloomer, Lewis, Ovid, N. Y.
Blunt, Mrs. R., Edenton, N. C.
Bly, Mrs. Lydia, Ticonderoga, N. Y.
Boardman, Thomas, Amesbury, Mass.
Boardman, Rev. George D., Rochester, N. Y.
Bodine, Miss Mary, Hudson, N. Y.
Bogart, Rev. Wm., East Galway, N. Y.
Bokee, Hon. David A., Brooklyn, N. Y.
Bolles, James G., Hartford, Ct.
Bolles, Francis, Niantic, Ct.
Boomer, Rev. James C., Chelmsford, Mass.
Boone, Dr. Levi D., Chicago, Ill.
Boone, Mrs. L. D., Chicago, Ill.
Booth, Henry, Greenport, N. Y.
Booth, Rev. John, Fentonville, Mich.
Bond, Leonard, New York.
Bond, Rev. G. W., Eugene City, Oregon.
Bond, Rev. E. P., Lawrenceburgh, Ia.
Bond, Rev. Emmons P., New Britain, Ct.
Bond, Mrs. Mary, New Britain, Ct.
Bond, Rev. Phineas, Cornish Flat, N.H.
Bonham, Rev. J. W., Lowell, Mass.
Bonham, Daniel, Berryville, Va.
Bonney, W. F., Eaton, N. Y.
Borden, Lodowick, Fall River, Mass.
Borden, Isaac, Fall River, Mass.
Borden, Charles, Fall River, Mass.
Borden, Joseph, Fall River, Mass.
Borden, Cook, Fall River, Mass.
Borland, Chauncey, Iowa City, Iowa.
Bosson, George P., Chelsea, Mass.
Bosson, Benjamin P., Chelsea, Mass.
Bosson, Miss Mary, Chelsea, Mass.
Bostick, Elisha, Bostick's Mills, N. C.

Bowen, John, New York.
Bowen, Henry, Club Centre, New York.
Bowen, David M. Roadstow , N. J.
Bowen, M[illegible] beth Roadstown, N. J.
Bowen, Rev. Wm. Hancock, Mass.
Bowen, William, New York
Bowen, Mrs. A. K., Cortlandville, N. Y.
Bowen, Henry A., Natic, R. I.
Bowen, Caleb, Seekonk, Mass.
Bower, Rev. Jacob, Kane, Ill.
Bowers, Rev. C. M., Clintonville, Mass.
Bowers, Mrs. Anna D., Seekonk, Mass.
Boyakin, Rev. Wm. F. Belleville, Ill.
Boyce, Rev. Peter, Green Point, N. Y.
Boyce, Mrs. Albi[illegible], Providence.
Boyd, Rev. Robert, Chicago, Ill.
Boyd, John, Albany, N. Y.
Boyden, Addison, South Dedham, Mass.
Boynton, J. M., North Springfield, Vt.
Brabrook, Mrs. Lucy A., Davenport, Iowa.
Brabrook, Alfred, Taunton, Mass.
Brabrook, Joseph A., Lowell, Mass.
Bracket, Prince, Webster, Mass.
Bradish, Levi J., Boston, Mass.
Bradford, W. R., Boston.
Bradford, John, Wilmington, Del.
Bradley, Collins, Mt. Vernon, Mich.
Bradley, Mrs. Enoch, Haverhill, Mass.
Bradley, Mrs. Sarah Ann S. Haverhill, Mass.
Bradley, Mrs. Elizabeth F., Amesbury, Mass.
Brainerd, Mrs. Samuel, Haverhill, Mass.
Branch, Rev. Nicholas, Westford, Ct.
Branch, Rev. William, Williamsville, N. Y.
Brandt, Rev. Thomas, Waukesha, Wis.
Bray, Joseph M., Brooklyn, N. Y.
Brayton, Mrs. Harriet, Phenix, R. I.
Brayton, Mrs. Ruth, Phenix, R. I.
Brayton, Mrs. Betsy, Phenix, R. I.
Brayton, Mrs. Mary Ann, Centreville, R. I.
Brayton, Robert E., Providence, R. I.
Brayton, Mrs. Ruth, Providence, R. I.
Brayton, Miss Emma L., Providence, R. I.
Brayton, Mrs. Lydia, Knightsville, R. I.
Brayton, Miss Anna V., Knightsville, R. I.
Brayton, Herbert E., Phenix, R. I.
Brayton, Esther J., Phenix, R. I.
Brayton, Miss Mary E., Phenix, R. I.
Brayton, John P., Albany, N. Y.
Breckenridge, James C., West Meriden, Ct.
Breed, Rev. Joseph B., Woonsocket, R. I.
[illegible]

Brockwa
Brokaw,
Bromley
Bromley
Bromley
Bromley
Bromley
Brouner,
Bronson,
Bronson,
Bronson,
Bronson,
Bronson,
Bronson,
Brooks, I
Brooks, I
Brooks, I
Brooks,
Brooks,
Brooks, I
Brooks,
Brouwer
Browe, B
Brower,
Brown, W
Brown, J
Brown, J
Brown, F
Brown, M
Brown, E
Brown, E
Brown, R
Brown, A
Brown, G
Brown, I
Brown, R
Brown, R
Brown, R
Brown, R
Brown, T
Brown, O
Brown, W
Brown, H
Brown, M
Brown, J
Brown, F
Brown, M
Brown, R
Brown, M
Brown, M

Brown, Miss Maria C., Watertown, Mass.
Brown, Mrs. Josiah, Haverhill, Mass.
Brown, Mrs. Frances J., Bedford, N. Y.
Brown, James, Boston, Mass.
Brown, Henry, New London, Ct.
Brownell, Rev. E. W., East Hillsdale, N. Y.
Brownson, Rev. I. K. Greenfield, Ohio.
Brownson, Moses, Butternuts, N. Y.
Bruen, George H., Newark, N. J.
Bruen, Mrs. George H., Newark, N. J.
Bruce, Benjamin G., New York.
Bruce, Silas, Boston, Mass.
Bruce, John M., Jr., New York.
Brush, Mrs. Susan G., New York.
Brusle, William A., New York.
Brusle, Mrs. Elizabeth, New York.
Bryant, George, Williamsburg, N. Y.
Bryant, Mary A., Chelsea, Mass.
Bryant, Elizabeth D., Chelsea, Mass.
Bryant, Harriet T., Chelsea, Mass.
Buck, David S., Cambridge, Mass.
Buckbee, Mrs. Laura G., New York.
Bucknell, Ebenezer G., Newark, N. J.
Bucknell, Miss Elizabeth, Newark, N. J.
Bucknell, Wm., Jr., Philadelphia, Pa.
Bucknell, Miss Lavinia Louisa, Philadelphia.
Bucknell, Mrs. Harriet, M., Philadelphia.
Buckner, Mrs. Sarah T., Baltimore.
Budlong, Mrs. Rebecca S. C., Providence.
Budlong, Miss Rebecca A., Providence.
Budd, Francis F., Williamsburg, N. Y.
Buel, Rev. Rufus F., Providence, R. I.
Buel, Mrs. Mary J., Providence. R. I.
Buffinton, Benjamin, Fall River, Mass.
Bull, John B., New York.
Bullard, Rev. Joseph A., Ware, Mass.
Bullard, Solomon R., Nashua, N. H.
Bullock, George, Utica, N. Y.
Bulkley, Rev. Justus, Carrollton, Ill.
Bulkley, Mrs. Justus, Carrolton, Ill.
Bulkley, Mrs. Harriet, Barry, Ill.
Bundy, Asa S., West Woodstock, Ct.
Bundy, Mrs. Hannah, West Hartwick, N. Y.
Bunnell, Rev. W. B., Tremont, Ill.
Bunnell, Mrs. Elizabeth E. Tremont, Ill.
Burbank, Mrs. Irene, New York.
Burbank, Wellman, Chelsea, Mass.
Burchard, Leonard, Brooklyn, N. Y.
Burd, Elisha, Baptist Town, N. J.
Burdick, Perrin, New York.
Burdick, V. H., Min.
Burdick, Mrs. Betsey, Greenwich, N. Y.
Burger, Mrs. Rebecca T., New York.
Burgess, Sylvanus, Providence.
Burgess, Alexander, Providence.
Burke, Mrs. Louisa S., Rochester, N. Y.
Burke, Mrs. Emma, Brooklyn, N. Y.
Burke, Mrs. Elizabeth, Brooklyn, N. Y.
Burke, Samuel M., Galesville, N. Y.
Burlingham, Mrs. Emma S., New York.
Burnett, Mrs. Maria M., Middleboro,' Mass.
Burnett, Rev. C. C., Middleboro', Mass.
Burnett, Eli S., West Philadelphia, Pa.
Burnett, Rev. Hiram, Mt. Pleasant, Iowa.
Burns, Wm., Philadelphia.
Burr, David M., Gloversville, N. Y.
Burr, Mrs. Emily C., Gloversville, N. Y.
Burr, James H., Gloversville, N. Y.
Burr, Mrs. James H., Gloversville, N. Y.
Burr, Miss Julia A., Gloversville, N. Y.
Burroughs, James M., Marlton, N. J.
Burroughs, Caleb G., Providence.
Burrows, Rev. David, Chester, Vt.
Burrows, Rev. J. L., D.D., Richmond, Va.
Burrows, Rev. Baxter, Grafton, Vt.
Burrows, Mrs. Lorenzo, Albion, N. Y.
Burrows, John R., Providence.
Burrows, A. B., Brockport, N. Y.
Burt, T. M., Kinderhook, N. Y.
Burt, Mrs. Edwin C., Brooklyn, N. Y.
Burt, Wm. A., Mount Vernon, Mich.
Burt, William, Mount Vernon, Mich.
Burt, Wells, Mount Vernon, Mich.
Burt, Rev. Joseph M., North Tewksbury, Mass.
Burton, Rev. Nathan S., Granville, O.
Burton, Mrs. Sarah J., Granville, O.
Burton, Rev. Hardine, Georgia, Ia.
Burwell, Rev. Ira D., Moriah, N. Y.
Butcher, Charles, Freehold, N. J.
Butcher, Mrs. Mary, Philadelphia.
Butler, Rev. John, Lewiston, Me.
Butler, Rev. G. W., Berlin Hights, Ohio.
Butler, Mrs. Eusebia C. S., Berlin Hights, Ohio.
Butler, Sylvanus, New Haven, Ct.
Butler, Mrs. Sarah, Lansingburg, N. Y.
Butler, Wm. C., Plainfield, N. J.
Butrick, Mrs. Harriet H., Jay, N. Y.
Butts, Mrs. Sarah A., Washington, D. C.
Butts, Mrs. Elizabeth, Boston.
Butts, Peleg, New Bedford, Mass.
Butts, Nelson W., Albion, N. Y.
Byram, Mrs. Mary H., Amesbury, Mass.
Byron, Wm. H., Milwaukee, Wis.
Cady, Rev. Edgar, Lake City, Min.
Cady, Edwin, Danville, Iowa.
Calkin, Rev. Abijah M., Cochecton, N. Y.
Cailhopper, Rev. F. T., Camden, N. J.
Calder, John, Providence.
Calder, Mrs. John L., Providence.
Callender, Rev. N., LaPorte, Pa.
Call, Rev. O. B., Mason, Mich.
Call, John R., Boston.
Campbell, Rev. T. P., East Avon, N. Y.
Campbell, Richard, Trenton, N. J.
Candee, John D., New Haven, Ct.
Capen, Barnabas D., Sharon, Mass.
Capin, Ezekiel, Canton, Mass.
Capron, Miss Rebecca S., Worcester, Mass.
Capron, John, Albany, N. Y.
Capron, Rev. Barton, Preble, N. Y.
Capwell, Albert B., Brooklyn, N. Y.
Capwell, Mrs. Julia A., Brooklyn, N. Y.
Card, Rev. Wm. H., LaCrosse, Wis.
Card, Rev. Henry S., Sandusky, N. Y.
Carleton, Miss Frances, Newton Centre, Mass.
Carleton, Miss E. H., Newton Centre, Mass.
Carleton, G. R., Newton Centre, Mass.
Carleton, Judson, Newton Centre, Mass.
Carleton, Howard, Newton Centre, Mass.
Carleton, Wm. H., Newton Centre, Mass.
Carlton, Stephen, Lowell, Mass.
Carlton, Guy, Methuen, Mass.
Carew, Miss Emma H., New York.
Carew, Mrs. Margaret N., New York.
Carlisle, Charles, New Haven, Ct.
Carpenter, Daniel T., Pawtucket, R. I.
Carpenter, Mrs. Elizabeth, Pawtucket, R. I.
Carpenter, Miss Lydia, Pawtucket, R. I.
Carpenter, Rev. Calvin G., Phelps, N. Y
Carpenter, Rev. J. M., Jacobstown, N. J.
Carpenter, Mrs. Sarah F., Jacobstown, N. J.
Carpenter, Rev. Burton B., Griggsville, Ill.
Carpenter, James, New York.
Carpenter, J. H., Madison, Wis.
Carpenter, Mrs. Martha C., Madison, Wis.
Carpenter, Elliot, Putnam, Ct.
Carmer, Henry, Griggsville, Ill.
Carr, Rev. Samuel J., Somerset, Mass.
Carr, Alexander W., Rowley, Mass.
Carr, Rev. L. C., Moline, Ill.
Carr, Gideon S., Little Mill Creek, O.
Carr, Joseph, Charlestown, Mass.
Carr, J. C., Portsmouth, N. H.
Carr, Thomas T., Newport, R. I.
Carrol, L. W., Norwich, Ct.
Carroll, S. W., Norwich, Ct.
Carroll, Mrs. Sarah A. S., Washington, N. C.
Carter, Mrs. Sarah, Richmond, Va.
Carter, Miss Mary, New York.
Carter, Edward, Troy, N. Y.

Caldwell, Mrs. Cornelius, New York.
Cauldwell, Miss Elizabeth, New York
Cauldwell, Henry W., New York
Caldwell, Mrs. Susan W., New York.
Caldwell, Miss Ann Jane, New York
Cauldwell, Mrs. Ann B., New York
Cauldwell, Mrs. Ann, Whitesboro', N. Y.
Cavender, A. H., St. Paul, Min.
Cavis, John, Lowell, Mass.
[illegible] Rev. Jeremiah, Aurora, Ia.
Chadsey, Jeremiah G., Wickford, R. I.
Chafee, Joseph D., Cortlandville, N. Y.
Chaffee, Asa, Seekonk, Mass.
Chaflin, Rev. Aaron W., Danvers, Mass.
Chaflin, Mrs. Catharine K., Danvers, Mass.
Chalfant, Jacob M., St. Paul, Min.
Chalfant, Mrs. Sarah E., St. Paul, Min.
Challis, Miss Lydia, Roadstown, N. J.
Challis, E. F., Cornish, N. H.
Chamberlain, Edward, Boston.
Chamberlain, Rev. J. A., South N. Berlin, N. Y.
Chamberlin, John C., West Woodstock, Ct.
Chambers, Azariah, Marion, N. C.
Chambers, Rev. J., McConnelsville, O.
Chambers, John, Pemberton, N. J.
Champlin, Henry N., Pitcher, N. Y.
Champlin, Joseph, Jr., Wakefield, R. I.
Champlin, Wm., New London, Ct.
Chandler, Miss Sarah [illegible], Boston.
Chandler, Rev. Charles N., Watertown, N. Y.
Chandler, Rev. George C., Oregon City, Oregon.
Chandler, Oliver, Boston.
Chandler, Wm. Nashua, N. H.
Chapel, R. S., Brooklyn.
Chapin, Henry O., Chickopee Falls, Mass.
Chapin, Rev. A., Vinton, Iowa.
Chapman, Allen A., Baltimore.
Chapman, Rev. John S., Alley,
Chapman, W. H., New York.
Chapman, Henry F., New York.
Chapman, Rev. J. M., Lexington, Ill.
Chapman, Rhodes B., Providence.
Chapman, Miss Rebecca, New Haven, Ct.
Chappel, Charles, New Loondon, Ct.
Charlock, Miss Maria, New York.
Charter, James, Boston, Mass.
Chase, Rev. Supply, Detroit, Mich.
Chase, Daniel, Baltimore.
Chase, Adrian, Haverhill, Mass.
Chase, Luther, Haverhill, Mass.
Chase, Mrs. Amos, Haverhill, Mass.

Church
Church
Church
Clapp
Clapp,
Clapp,
Clapp,
Clapp,
Clark, [illegible]
Clark, [illegible]
Clark, [illegible]
Clark, [illegible]
Clark, [illegible]
Clark, [illegible]
Clark, [illegible]
Clark, [illegible]
Clark, [illegible]
Clark,
Clark, [illegible]
Clark, [illegible]
Clark, [illegible]
Clark, [illegible]
Clark, [illegible]
Clark, [illegible]
Clark, [illegible]
Clark, [illegible]
Clark, [illegible]
Clark, [illegible]
Clark, [illegible]
Clark, [illegible]
Clark, [illegible]
Clark, [illegible]
Clark, [illegible]
Clark, [illegible]
Clark, [illegible]
Clark, [illegible]
Clark, [illegible]
Clark, [illegible]
Clark, [illegible]
Clark, [illegible]
Clarke,
Clarke,
Clarke,
Clarke,
Clayton
Cleaver
Cleaves
Cleaves
Clement
Clement

ʀev. James L., Wyocena, Wis.
all, Mrs. Elizabeth, New Bedford, Mass.
l, B. F., Brooklyn, N. Y.
l, Mrs. Mary, Haverhill, Mass.
l, Mrs. Amanda, Janesville, Wis.
iss Elizabeth, New London, Ct.
ʀev. Lewis, Cambridge, Mass.
ʀrs. Eliza A., New London, N. H.
saac, Salem, Mass.
ardner, Newton, Mass.
ʀrs Mary Colgate, New York.
, Rev. Alfred, Boston.
, Charles C., West Dedham, Mass.
v. L. B., Lowell, Mass.
muel, Clifton Park, N. Y.
s. Frances L., New York.
s. Susan, Westerloo, N. Y.
s. Jemima P., Plainfield, N. J.
bert H., Southbridge, Mass.
ʀev. James M., Waverly, N. Y.
re, Belah H., Sardinia, N. Y.
, James B., Somerville, N. J.
, Rev. M., ———, Wis.
, Mrs. Sarah, ———, Wis.
, Rev. Zenas, Mt. Vernon, Mich.
, Daniel B., Trenton, N. J.
, Cornelius C , New York.
, Edward, New York.
, William, New York.
, Miss Elizabeth, New York.
, Miss Hannah, New York.
, Miss Jane, New York.
, Miss Sarah, New York.
e, Uri, Johnstown, O.
Wm. R., Lebanon, Ohio.
Mrs. Ann D., Haverhill, Mass.
Rev. Roswell, Charlestown, N. Y.
, John B., Williamsburg, N. Y.
Benj. E., Cambridge, Mass.
Mrs. Mary E., Mt. Holly, N. J.
Rev. Charles K., Charlestown, Mass.
Lovian O., Le Roy, N. Y.
n, James I., Plainfield, N. J.
n, Anthony, New York.
n, Mrs. Maria, New York.
n, Rev. Robert, Newton, Pa.
n, Wm. H., Roadstown, N. J.
k, George R., New London, Ct.
k, Mrs. Ann, New London, Ct.
k, C. C., New London, Ct.
k, Charles F., Lyme, Ct.
Mrs John, Brandon, Vt.
Rev. Thomas, Scituate, Mass.
Rev. Thomas J., D.D., Rochester, N. Y.
Levi, Boston, Mass.
Miss Sarah E., New York.
pencer H., Jr., New York.
iss Kate E., New York.
, Mrs. Ann, New York.
, Lewis L., Paterson, N. J.
r, Mrs. Catharine S., New York.
r, Robert, Petersburg, Ill.
r, Cyrenius G., Middletown, N. J.
r, Mrs Rebecca M., Holmdel, N. J.
r, Rev. Edward, West Troy, N. Y.
, Rev. Peter, East Troy, Wis.
e, Rev. Otis, Worcester, Mass.
e, Charles E., Jamaica Plains, Mass.
e, James W., Jamaica Plains, Mass.
e, Elisha S., Malden, Mass.
e, Joseph H., Jamaica Plains, Mass.
lihu, New Brunswick, N. J.
iss Mary B., Watertown, Mass.
rs. Patience, Keene, N. H.
enry G., New York.
ewis, Plantsville, Ct.
m. W., Whitehall, N. Y.
rs. Harriet M., New York.
ohn, Woodstown, N. J.
Rev. Samuel, Concord, N. H.

Cool, Rev. Leonard, Perrysburg, Ia.
Coolidge, Mrs. Caroline G., Brookline, Mass.
Coolidge, William, Bouckville, N. Y.
Coolidge, John, Watertown, Mass.
Coolidge, Mrs. Mary S., Watertown, Mass.
Coolidge, Josiah, Cambridge, Mass.
Coolidge, Austin J., Cambridge, Mass.
Coolidge, Joseph G., Cambridge, Mass.
Coon, Rev. Charles, Mt. Holly, Vt.
Cooper, Edwin, Hoboken, N. J.
Cooper, Rev. Warren, Boylston, Mass.
Cooper, Eliphalet, New Haven, Ct.
Cooper, Charles, New York.
Cooper, Obadiah, Brooklyn, N. Y.
Copp, Miss Louisa P., North Danvers, Mass.
Corbett, O. G., Orange, N. J.
Corbin, Penuel, Jr., West Woodstock, Ct.
Cordo, Henry, H., New Brunswick, N. J.
Corey, Rev. D. G., Utica, N. Y.
Corlies, Britton, Philadelphia.
Corliss, Miss Sarah, Greenwich, N. Y.
Cornelius, Rev. Samuel, Jr., Winona, Min.
Cornell, A. C., Broadalbin, N. Y.
Cornell, Thomas, Rondout, N. Y.
Cornell, Wm. M., Plainfield, N. J.
Corthell, Loring, New London, Ct.
Corwin, R. G., Lebanon, Ohio.
Corwin, Rev. David, Cohoes, N. Y.
Corwin, Rev. Ira, South Bend, Ia.
Corwith, Mrs. Catharine F., New York.
Cotterell, Mrs. Mary, Battenville, N. Y.
Cotterell, Miss Mary, Union Village, N. Y.
Cotton, Mrs. Alma, Middletown, Ct.
Couch, E. P., Nashua, N. H.
Covey, Rev. Walter, West Meredith, N. Y.
Cowan, Mrs. Hannah, New York.
Cowdin, Mrs. Aurinda G., Fitchburg, Mass.
Cowles, Mrs. Rebekah, Claremont, N. H.
Cowles, Miss Juliette R., Claremont, N. H.
Cowles, Jas. Albert, Claremont, N. H.
Cox, Rev. Morgan R., New Brunswick, N. J.
Cox, Mrs. Mary B., New Brunswick, N. J.
Cox, Miss Anna, New Brunswick, N. J.
Cox, Miss Mary, New York.
Cox, Miss Abigail, New York.
Coxey, James, West Philadelphia, Pa.
Coy, Sylvanus B., West Dedham, Mass.
Crabs, Rev. J. D., Claysville, Ia.
Crafts, George A., South Boston, Mass.
Craig, Rev. A. M., Britton's ⋈ Roads, N. C.
Craig, Charles A., Bridgeport, Ct.
Craig, Mrs. Charles A., Bridgeport, Ct.
Crain, Miss Harriet M., Westport, N. H.
Craft, Charles, New York.
Crafts, George A., Boston.
Cramer, Geo. W., Troy, N. Y.
Cramer, John, Brooklyn, N. Y.
Cramer, Mrs. Margaret S., West Troy, N. Y.
Crane, Mrs. Fanny D., Antrim, N. H.
Crane, Richard M., Newark, N. J.
Crane, Henry F., Rehoboth, Mass.
Crane, Miss Sarah H., Rehoboth, Mass.
Crane, Rev. Danzel M., N. Hampton, Mass.
Crane, Mrs. Mary L., New York.
Crane, Rev. W. J., Adrian, Mich.
Crane, Millen, Spring Hill, Ct.
Crandall, Henrie, Providence, R. I.
Crandall, Mrs. J. A., Petersburg, N. Y.
Crandall, Rev. Nelson, South Hannibal, N. Y.
Crandall, Rev. B., Springport, N. Y.
Crandall, Mrs. J. Sophronia, Providence, R. I.
Cranston, B. T., Norwich, Ct.
Cranston, Benj. T., Jr., Providence.
Crawford, Mrs. Almira A., Brooklyn, N. Y.
Crawford, Mrs. Charlotte, New York.
Crawford, Ira, Poughkeepsie, N. Y.
Crawford, Samuel H., Philadelphia.
Crawford, Archibald, Albany.
Crawford, John B., Middletown, N. J.
Crawford, Mrs. Catharine, Middletown, N. J.

Crossman, Nathan, Elbridge, N. Y.
Croysdale, Abram, Paterson, N. J.
Crumb, Rev. J. W. Middletown Point, N. J.
Crumb, Mrs. R. F., Middletown, Point, N. J.
Cruser, Holger, Brooklyn, N. Y.
Cudworth, Rev. N., Ludlow, Vt.
Cudworth, Mrs. M. B., Ludlow, Vt.
Cudworth, Lydia. B., Chelsea, Mass.
Culp, Theophilus, New York.
Culver, Mrs. Susan, New London, Ct.
Culver, Rev. Samuel W., Vernon, N. Y.
Cummings, Mrs. Daniel, Chelsea, Mass.
Cummings, Mrs. Abigail, Cambridge, Mass.
Cummings, George, Cambridge, Mass.
Cummings, Rev. E. E., D.D., Concord, N. H.
Cummings, Mrs. Emily C., Worcester, Mass.
Cummings, Miss Ellen, Chelsea, Mass.
Cunningham, Rev. O., Lebanon, Ct.
Curry, John, Hamburg, S. C.
Curry, Mrs. Harriet, Hamburg, S. C.
Curren, Rev. Joseph, Sharpsburg, Pa.
Currier, Rev. Joshua, La Motte, Iowa.
Curtis, Rev. Wm., Columbia, S. C.
Curtis, Rev. T. T., Marion, Ala.
Curtis, Rev. Wm. B., Newport, N. Y.
Curtis, Mrs. Elizabeth, Aurora, Ia.
Curtis, Ezra, Bridgeport, Ct.
Curtis, Mrs. Ezra, Bridgeport, Ct.
Cushing, Samuel T., Boston.
Cusick, Rev. James, Onondaga, Can.
Cushman, Frederick A., New York
Cushman, Mrs. Charlotte E., Deep River, Ct.
Cushman, Mrs. Elizabeth, Deep River, Ct.
Cushman, Jacob R., Medfield, Mass.
Cutler, Micajah, Lynn, Mass.
Cutler, Wm. D., Meriden, Ct.
Cutler, Stephen, New England Village, Mass.
Cutler, Jonathan, Brattleboro, Vt.
Cutting, Mrs. Elizabeth B., Rochester, N. Y.
Cutting, Rev. Geo. W., Mason Village, N. H.
Dabney, Mrs. E. T., Jackson, Va.
Dagg, Mrs. John L., Penfield, Ga.
Daggett, Homer M., North Attleboro, Mass.
Daken, Rev. H. R., Pultney, N. Y.
Dale, Mrs. Amanda F., Lebanon, Ohio.
Dalrymple, James, Bridgeton, N. J.
Damon, Rev. J. B., Lake Village, N. H.
Damon, Benjamin, Concord, N. H.
Damon, Isaac H., Fredonia, N. Y.
Dana, John B., Cambridge, Mass.
Dane, Osgood, Romeville, Mass.

, Mrs. Eliza J., Washington, D. C.
, Mrs. Abby A., Goffstown, N. H.
Abraham, New York
Mrs. Adaline, New York.
Mrs. Elizabeth, New York.
Richard, Lowell, Mass.
n, Rev. Charles W., New York.
, Rev. Frederick, Norwich, Ct.
, Mrs. Amy M., Norwich, Ct.
, Rev. Erastus, Groton, Ct.
, Mrs. Prudence, Mystic River, Ct.
, Mrs. Silas, Skeneateles, N. Y.
, O. J., Mendota, Ill.
, Mrs. Amelia E., Deep River, Ct.
, Miss Elizabeth, Brooklyn, N. Y.
, Rev. A. E., Clinton, Ct.
John B., Norwalk, Ct.
Mrs. Sarah M., Saratoga Springs, N. Y.
Benj., Methuen, Mass.
Mrs. Catharine, Edgefield, S. C.
, Samuel, West Philadelphia, Pa.
Wm. G., Mystic, Ct.
Joseph H., Manchester, N. Y.
st, Rev. Eli, Belfast, Me.
Rev. J. V., Marion, Iowa.
, D. R., Brooklyn, N. Y.
Mrs. Jane, Brooklyn, N. Y.
Samuel, K., Central Falls, R. I.
ian, Samuel, Philadelphia.
on, Mrs. Caroline A., Dayton, Ohio.
on, Wm. W., Golandsville, Va.
k, Rev. Anthony V., Baldwinsville, Mass.
, Daniel E., Berlin, N. Y.
re, Charles M., Newton, Mass.
, Mrs. Lucinda, Grafton, Mass.
Rev. Joseph A., Evansville, Ia.
zra, Hudson, N. Y.
liss Rachel F., Danvers, Mass.
ohn, Sen., Edgefield, S. C.
Mrs. Eliza P., New York.
Miss Mary, New York.
Prof. Ebenezer, Hamilton, N. Y.
Solomon H., Cambridge, Mass.
Miss Hannah A., Worcester, Mass.
Mrs. Alice C., Hampton Falls, N. H.
Mrs. Jane, Brooklyn, N. Y.
H. N., McGrawville, N. Y.
Rev. Elijah, Woodburn, Ill.
rs. Lydia T., Haverhill, Mass.
Horatio, Worcester, Mass.
e, Rev. H. D., Burnt Hills, N. Y.
e, Johnson, Wallingford, Ct.
e, Hart, Pleasant Valley, Ct.
J. W., East Cambridge, Mass.
, Mrs. Lucretia, New York.
e, Samuel B., Brooklyn, N. Y.
e, Otis M., Greenville, Ct.
rs. Lucy, Nashua, N. H.
iss Selima P., Hitchcockville, Ct.
on, Miss Henrietta M., Moorestown, N. J.
, Henry, Bethel, N. Y.
, George, Elgin, Ill.
, Rev. John L., Burmah.
rty, George T., New York.
Mrs. Maria S., New York.
Miss Mary J., New York.
, Rev. Thomas, Tolland, Ct.
, Mrs. Rebecca, New York.
John, New York.
, Rev. Wm B., Peterboro, N. Y.
, Rev. Francis, Whitby, Pa.
Mrs. Harriet B., Malden, Mich.
Mrs. Elizabeth, Hightstown, N. J.
Calvin, New Haven, Ct.
Gustavus D., Lowell, Mass.
Mrs. A. F., Haverhill, Mass.
Simeon, Pittsfield, N. H.
J. C., Panama, N. Y.
Ephraim, Plainfield, N. J.
Mrs. A. L., Plainfield, N. J.

Drake, Rev. George, New Brunswick, N. J.
Draper, Jonathan J. N., Bennington, Vt.
Driver, Rev. Thomas, Lynn, Mass.
Drown, Henry B., Providence.
Dubois, Richard, Canton, N. J.
Dubois, A. E., Randolph, Mass.
Dudley, John L., Baltimore.
Dugan, Wm. T., Brooklyn, N. Y.
Dugan, Mrs. Eliza, Brooklyn, N. Y.
Dugan, Wm. J., Brooklyn, N. Y.
Dugan, Edward J., Brooklyn, N. Y.
Duncan, Hon. James H., Haverhill, Mass.
Duncan, Mrs. James H. Haverhill, Mass.
Duncan, Mrs. Samuel, Haverhill, Mass.
Duncan, Mrs. E. E., Jackson, Va.
Duncan, Rev. H. A., Coosawhatchie, S. C.
Duncan, Rev. Wm., Orleans, Ia.
Duncan, Rev. John, Boston, Mass.
Dunham, Jepthah, New Brunswick, N. J.
Dunham, Nelson, New Brunswick, N. J.
Dunklee, Mrs. Eliza A., Boston, Mass.
Dunlap, Abraham B., Brooklyn, N. Y.
Dunlap, Rev. James, Jacksonville, Ill.
Dunlevy, Hon. A. H., Lebanon, O.
Dunn, Rev. Andrew, Weymouth, Mass.
Dunn, Alexander, New Brunswick, N. J.
Du Pre, Mrs. S. P., Darlington, S. C.
Dupont, Alfred, Wilmington, Del.
Durant, Clark, Albany, N. Y.
Durant, Thomas P., Boston, Mass.
Durbrow, William, New York.
Durbrow, John B., New York.
Durfee, Sanford, Warwick, R. I.
Durfee, Miss Sarah C., Providence.
Durham, Nicholas O., Weart's Corners, N. J.
Durham, Enos, Greenwich, N. Y.
Durham, Anson, Greenwich, N. Y.
Durkin, John, New York.
Durnell, James, Philadelphia.
Duryea, Levy, New York.
Duryea, Mrs. Sarah, New York.
Dusenberry, Rev. Francisco, Newfield, N. Y.
Duvall, Mrs. J., Mitchell's, Va.
Dwelle, Alphonso, Union Village N. Y.
Dwelle, Mrs. Alphonso, Union Village, N. Y.
Dye, Rev. Daniel, Three Mile Bay, N. Y.
Dye, Rev. Enoch P., North Brookfield, N. Y.
Dye, 2nd, Samuel, Marietta, Ohio.
Dyer, Miss Eliza J., Brooklyn, N. Y.
Dyer, Ransom B., New Haven, Ct.
Dyer, Ezra C., Cambridge, Mass.
Dyer, Mrs. Louisa C., Providence.
Dyer, Rev. Sidney, Indianapolis, Ia.
Eastman, Lycurgus, Griggsville, Ill.
Eastman, Rev. Samuel, Burlington, Wis.
Earl, Rev. Samuel H., New York.
Earl, Mrs. George C., Providence.
Earl, Miss Julia, Providence.
Earle, Rev. Alfred, Davisville, Pa.
Earle, Rev. Joseph Fort Anne, N. Y.
Eaton, Rev. George W., D.D., Hamilton, N. Y
Eaton, R. C., Springville, N. Y.
Eaton, Rev. Horace, Dunbarton, N. H.
Eaton, Ezra, Boston.
Eaton, James L., Chicago, Ill.
Eaton, Mrs. Mary S., Chicago, Ill.
Eaton, Mrs. Job, Haverhill, Mass.
Eaton, Mrs. Sarah E., Benton City, Iowa.
Eaton, Mrs. Caroline B., Nashua, N. H.
Eaton, Zenas, South Reading, Mass.
Eddy, Rev. H. J., Bloomington, Ill.
Eddy, Mrs. Sarah D., New Bedford, Mass.
Eddy, Miss Ann E. N., New Bedford, Mass.
Eddy, John S., Providence, R. I.
Eddy, Mrs. Sarah J. S., Winchester, Mass.
Eddy, Mrs. Emily A., Providence.
Eddy, Richard E., Providence.
Eddy, Mrs. Lucy, Waterford, N. Y.
Eddy, Miss Agnes, Waterford, N. Y.
Edgecomb, Albert, Mystic River, Ct.

Elkin, Rev. David, Bryantsville, Ind.
Elledge, Rev. Jesse, Stockton, Iowa.
Elliott, Rev. Charles, Etna, N. Y.
Elliott, Edward G., Washington, D. C.
Elliott, Rev. Wm., Brighton, Iowa.
Elliott, Rev. S. L., Fairfax, Vt.
Elliott, Mrs. Sarah C., Fairfax, Vt.
Elliott, Rev. M., Stilesville, Ia.
Elliott, Mrs. Marica, O. T., Mason Village, N. H.
Elliott, L. A., Mason Village, N. H.
Elliott, Lemuel H., Providence.
Ellis, George, Dorchester, Mass.
Ellis, Theodore W., South Hadley Falls, Mass.
Ellis, Anna, Brooklyn.
Ellsworth, Lewis, Napierville, Ill.
Elwell, Isaac N., Concord, N. H.
Elwell, Isaac, Concord, N. H.
Elwell, Mrs. Elizabeth, Concord, N. H.
Ely, Henry D., Holmdel, N. J.
Ely, Mrs. Ann, Holmdel, N. J.
Ely, Miss Lucy, Clarksboro, N. J.
Ely, Horatio, Freehold, N. J.
Emery, Thomas, Cincinnati, Ohio.
Emery, Mrs. Kezia, Cincinnati, Ohio.
Emmons, Mrs. Sarah, Deep River, Ct.
English, Henry H., Philadelphia.
English, Miss Hannah P., Salem, Mass.
English, Mrs. Elizabeth J., Paterson, N. J.
Ensign, Chancellor, North Ridgway, N. Y.
Eschman, Rev. John, New York.
Eschman, Mrs. Magdalene, New York.
Estee, James, Leroy, N. Y.
Estee, Rev. Sydney A., Aurora, Ill.
Estep, Rev. Dr. James, Library, Pa.
Estes, A. B., Lower Three Runs, S. C.
Estes, Miss H. S., Lower Three Runs, S. C.
Estes, Mrs. E. A., Lower Three Runs, S. C.
Evans, John M., Philadelphia.
Evans, Silas J., Louisville, Ky.
Evans, Mrs. S. E., Society Hill, S. C.
Evans, Reuben, Amesbury, Mass.
Evans, Dr. Joseph T., New York.
Evans, Mrs. Czarina. H., New York.
Evans, Rev. Wm. E., Carbondale, Pa.
Evans, Rev. P. H., Greencastle, Ia.
Evans, Miss Anna B., New York.
Eveleigh, Mrs. Mary D., Brooklyn, N. Y.
Eveleth, Samuel, Boston.
Everts, Rev. Wm. W., D.D., Louisville, Ky.
Everett, Rev. Samuel, North Leverett Mass.

r. Harvey, Middleboro', Mass.
., John, Philadelphia.
Rev. Charles W., Concord, N. H.
Mrs. M. H. L., Concord, N. H.
Timothy C., Haverhill, Mass.
, Helvin, Haverhill, Mass
George B., Brooklyn, N. Y.
I. M., Nashua, N. H.
nes R., Brewington, Va.
B., King and Queens C. H., Va.
an, Rev. Konrad A., Philadelphia.
Rev. C., Tewksbury, Mass.
Rev. Simon, Sandy Hill, N. Y.
Rev. Leonard, New Orleans, La.
Rev. Horace, Townshend, Vt.
Mrs. Harriet A., Townshend, Vt.
Mrs. Mary, Southington, Ct.
Henry J., New York.
Mrs. Sarah A., Saratoga Springs, N. Y.
Hezekiah, Mineapolis, Min. Ter.
rs. E. A. E., Darlington, S. C.
mes W., Brooklyn, N. Y.
ayton, Novi, Mich.
s. Mary C., Novi, Mich.
rin, Novi, Mich.
Amelia, L., Brooklyn, N. Y.
v. Samuel, Me.
, Rev. Sam'l W., S. Framingham, Mass.
L. H., Leesville, N. Y.
omas W., Providence.
Job W., Defiance, Ohio.
rs. Euphemia, Tonica, Ill.
ured, New Haven, Ct.
George W., Bridgeport, Ct.
Gustavus, Boston.
Rev. M., Prattsburg, N. Y.
Rev. Jonathan E. S., Ashland, Mass.
Wm. F., Brooklyn, N. Y.
yman, Burdett, N. Y.
aac, Philadelphia.
s. H., Philadelphia.
enry Clay, Philadelphia.
s. Amanda, Philadelphia.
ac Albert, Philadelphia.
ss Elizabeth, Philadelphia.
ss Hannah Adelia, Philadelphia.
illiam, Albany, N. Y.
s. Mary, Harvey's Store, Va.
, Miss Mary E., Hightstown, N. J.
, Samuel B., Wilmington, Del.
r, Mrs. Elenora, Williamsburg, N. Y.
l, Mrs. Lucy, Boston.
David, Stockholm, Sweden.
Rev. Horace B., Tyler, Ill.
John W., Leesville, Ill.
William, West Dedham, Mass.
Mrs. Sarah K., Evansville, Ia.
Rev. J. C., Beverly, Mass.
Mrs. Abby A., Beverly, Mass.
Mrs. Martha, Cambridge, Mass.
Joseph, Sen., Salem, N. J.
Mrs. Susan S., Keene, N. H.
Miss Sarah S., Albany, N. Y.
Mrs. Sarah, Albany, N. Y.
Miss Emily H., Albany, N. Y.
Russel, Jr., Albany, N. Y.
John, Newport, N. Y.
Mrs. Lucy, Boston.
Gamaliel, Suffield, Ct.
r. Norman, Schenectady, N. Y.
r. Charles A., Waverly, Pa.
s. Julia A., Waverly, Pa.
bert R., Sand Lake, N. Y.
s. Mary A., Sand Lake, N. Y,
arles, New York.
ss Ann Eliza, New York.
Miss Amy, Smithfield, Pa.
Ezra, Rahway, N. J.
Mrs. Mary Rahway, N. J.
Robert, Newington, Ct.

Francis, Mrs. Lydia D., Newington, Ct.
Francis, Norman, New York.
Francis, Charles King, New York.
Francis, James, Pittsfield, Mass.
Frayzer, Rev. Herndon, Twymann's, Va.
Freas, Rev. Daniel J., Salem, N. Y.
Freeman, Rev. T. G., New York.
Freeman, Rev. Joseph, Cavendish, Vt.
Freeman, Rev. G. W., Fox Lake, Wis.
Freeman, Thomas W., Augusta, Ga.
Freeman, Elisha, Worcester, Mass.
Freeman, Mrs. Margaret E., Camillus, N. Y.
Freeman, Dyer, Middleboro', Mass.
Freeman, D., Webster, Mass.
French, Miss Abigail, Turner, Me.
French, George R., Wilmington, N. C.
French, Stephen L., Fall River, Mass.
French, Miss Hannah, Haverhill, Mass.
French, Mrs. Moses E., Haverhill, Mass.
French, Rev. David S., Covington, Ia.
French, Rev. Alpheus, Valparaiso, Ia.
Frescoln, Rev. Leonard, Mapleton, Ohio.
Frey, Rev. James, Jr., Perryton, Ohio.
Frickett, Rev. James, Alloway'stown, N. J.
Frink, William S., Taylorville, Ill.
Fripp, E., Beaufort, S. C.
Fripp, Mrs. Ann H., Beaufort. S. C
Frisby, Mrs. Lucy M., New Haven, Ct.
Frisk, Rev. Lars Leonard, Chicago, Ill.
Frost, James, Wake Forest, N. C.
Frost, Joseph, Chanceville, N. J.
Frost, Mrs. Lydia, Middletown, N. J.
Fry, John, Philadelphia.
Fulcher, Richard, Three Rivers, Mich.
Fuller, George, Troy, N. Y.
Fuller, Nathan L., New York.
Fuller, Dr. Henry M., Beaufort, S. C.
Fuller, Rev. M. L., Metamora, Ill.
Fuller, Cyrenius M., Jr., Pike, N. Y.
Fuller, Robert O., Cambridge, Mass.
Fuller, Mrs. Sarah, Cambridge, Mass.
Fuller, Mrs. Sarah Ann, Pike, N. Y.
Fuller, William, Suffield, Ct.
Fuller, Miss Elizabeth, Baltimore.
Fuller, Rev. Edward K., Reading, Mass.
Fullerton, Noah, South Abington, Mass.
Fulton, Rev. John, New Woodstock, N. Y.
Fulton, Miss Harriet, Carmel, N. Y.
Furguson, Rev. S. U., Plymouth, S. C.
Furman, Rev. Richard, Society Hill, S. C
Fyfe, Rev. Robert A., Toronto, Canada.
Fyfe, Mrs. Rebecca S., Toronto, Canada.
Gage, William W., Woburn, Mass.
Gage, Rev. David, Acworth, N. H.
Gage, G. W., Methuen, Mass.
Gage, Lewis, Methuen, Mass.
Gage, A., Methuen, Mass.
Gage, Rev. Leonard, West Woodstock, Ct.
Gage, Rev. L. L., Frewsburgh, N. Y.
Gale, Jonas R., Delavan, Ill.
Gale, Rev. Amory, Minneapolis, Min.
Gale, Rev. Solomon, Berlin, N. Y.
Gale, Rev. E., Bennington, Vt.
Galusha, Truman, Jericho, Vt.
Gammell, A. M., Warren, R. I.
Ganong, Aaron, Carmel, N. Y.
Gardiner, Richard, Philadelphia.
Gardner, Miss Miranda B., Fulton, N. Y.
Gardner, John, Newark, N. Y.
Gardner, James C., Augusta, Ga.
Gardner, Rev. Jacob, Lyme, Ct.
Gardner, Frederick, New York.
Gardner, Mrs. S., North Lansing, N. Y.
Garfield, Rev. Benjamin F., Meridian, N. Y.
Garnett, Dorothy, Miller's, Va.
Garnett, Rev. Wm. Lowville, N. Y.
Garrett, D. H., Haddenfield, N. J.
Garnsey, Erasmus D., Burnt Hills, N. Y.
Garnsey, Mrs. Erasmus D., Burnt Hills, N. Y.
Garret, Samuel, Rock Hill, Ohio.

Garrison, Rev. Cantine, Chili, N. Y.
Gatenby, John V., Williamsburg, N. Y.
Gates, Marcius A., South Gardner, Mass.
Gates, Horace S., Norwich, Ct.
Gates, Mrs. Laura P., Norwich, Ct.
Gates, Rev. G. W., —— Wis.
Gates, T. J., Plainfield, Ct.
Gates, Cyrus, Preston, Ct.
Gatling, John, Eatontown, N. J.
Gault, Mrs. George, Brooklyn, N. Y.
Gault, Miss Georgianna E., Brooklyn, N. Y.
Gay, William, Dedham, Mass.
Gay, George, Meriden, Ct.
Gayer, Rev. Charles, New York.
Gaylor, Mrs. Anna, Brooklyn, N. Y.
Gearhart, Mrs. Hannah M., Trenton, N. J.
George, Moses D., Haverhill, Mass.
George, Samuel, Haverhill, Mass.
George, Mrs. Elizabeth C., Culpepper, Va.
German, Joseph, Beekman, N. Y.
Germond, Mrs. Elizabeth, Williamsburg, N. Y.
Germond, Mrs. Juliana, Washington, N. Y.
Gibbs, Mrs. Eliza Ann, Lyons Farms, N. J.
Gibbs, Rev. Oliver, W., Bennettsburg, N. Y.
Gibson, Rev. A., River Falls, Wis.
Gibson, Mrs. Evelyn R., River Falls, Wis.
Gibson, Mrs. Betsey W., Owego, N. Y.
Gibson, Ely, Owego, N. Y.
Gifford, Rev. Isaac S., East Chatham, N. Y.
Gifford, Mrs. Annie, East Chatham, N. Y.
Gignilliat, W. R., Darien, Ga.
Gilbert, Wm. J., Middletown, Ct.
Gilbert, Rev. Isaac H., Bristol, Ct.
Gilbert, Mrs. Mary E., Bristol, Ct.
Gilkey, Royal, Watertown, Mass.
Gill, Miss Mary, Pottsville, Pa.
Gill, Miss Mary Ann, Philadelphia.
Gillette, Mrs. Hannah J., New York.

Griggs, David R., Brookline, Mass.
Griggs, Seth D., Belchertown, Mass
Griggs, J. W., Boston.
Grimley, Rev. Joseph J., Unionville, N. Y.
Grimshaw, Miss Martha, Arcadia, N. Y.
Grinnell, Mrs. Mary B., New Bedford, Mass.
Grinnell, Sylvia H., New Bedford, Mass.
Griswold, Harry, Racine, Wis.
Griswold, Aaron.——N. Y.
Grose, Rev. Henry L., Galway, N. Y.
Gross, Rev. Alva, Brimfield, Ill.
Grout, Thomas J., New York.
Grout, Edward, New York.
Grover, Joseph, Elmira, N. Y.
Grow, Rev. James, Thompson, Ct.
Grummon, William, Newark, N. J.
Guild, Rev. J. Ellis, Newton, Iowa.
Guild, Mrs. Julia A., East Thompson, Ct.
Guild, George M., Boston.
Guild, Reuben A., Providence.
Gunn, Rev. Elihu, Keokuk, Iowa.
Gunn, George, New Haven, Ct.
Gunn, E., Montague, Mass.
Gunnison, Rev. George W., Erie, Pa.
Gunnison, Pelatiah, Jackson, Pa.
Gurney, Mrs. Martha, Boston.
Gurney, Mrs. C J., Woodstock, Ill.
Gurr, Rev. C. G., Great Falls, N. H.
Guy, Rev. A., Middletown, O.
Gwathney, Mrs. E. T., Ayletts, Va.
Hadaway, John T., Chelsea, Mass.
Haddock, Henry, Lynn, Mass.
Hadley, Elias H., Lowell, Mass.
Hadley, Moses, Boston.
Haff, Rev. H. H., East Schuyler, Mass.
Hagan, John, Newburgh, N. Y.
Hagar, William, Jr., Brooklyn, N. Y.
Hague, Rev. John B., Hudson, N. Y.
Hall, George, Providence.
Haines, Jacob, Moorestown, N. J.
Haines, Mrs. Mary Jane, Moorestown, N. J.
Hale, William, Meriden, Ct.
Haley, Miss Emma S., Boston.
Hall, Gabriel D., Greenwich, N. J.
Hall, Mrs. Mary A., Greenwich, N. J.
Hall, Enoch, West Acton, Mass.
Hall, Almer, Wallingford, Ct.
Hall, Rev. King S., Lake Village, N. H.
Hall, Rev. Abijah, Jr., —— Ct.
Hall, David, 3rd, Skeneateles, N. Y.
Hall, Abiathar, Fall River, Mass.
Hall, Hannah, Haverhill, Mass.
Hall, Mrs. Clarissa, Wallingford, Ct.
Hall, Almer I., Wallingford, Ct.
Hallsted, Mrs. Jane C., New York.
Hallsted, James C., Waterloo, N. Y.
Ham, Mrs. Nancy S., Providence.
Hamblet, Miss Mira C., West Swanzey, N. H.
Hamilton, Rev. Alexander, Appleton, Wis.
Hamilton, John, Jr., Fredonia, N. Y.
Hamilton, Miss Ann, New London, Ct.
Hammon, Mrs. Philip, Beverly, Mass.
Hammond, Augustus, Pittsford, Vt.
Hammond, Mrs. Mary, Pittsford, Vt.
Hammond, Miss Mary F., Pittsford, Vt.
Hammond, William, Dorchester, Mass.
Hammond, James M., Chicago, Ill.
Hammond, N. O, East Cambridge, Mass.
Hanaford, Dr. Joseph H., Nantucket, Mass.
Hanaford, Mrs. J. H., Nantucket, Mass.
Hanaford, Howard A., Nantucket, Mass.
Hand, Joseph H., Bridgeport, Ct.
Hand, Rev. George, Hatboro', Pa.
Hanly, Aaron, Peach Orchard, N. Y.
Hanna, John, Philadelphia.
Hansell, Mrs. Emma, Philadelphia.
Hanson, Charles B., New Haven, Ct.
Hapgood, Miss S. F., Gillisonville, S. C.
Hardwick, Wm., Jamaica Plains, Mass.
Hardy, Jesse, Warner, N. H.
Harger, Mrs. Hannah, Chatham Corners, N. Y.
Harkness, Albert H., Providence.
Harlow, Robert H., Boston.
Harmon, Rawson, Wheatland, N. Y.
Harmon, Mrs. David P., Haverhill, Mass.
Harmon, Rev. B. F., Duck Creek, Ohio.
Harper, Richard L., Boston.
Harrimount, Wm. S., New Haven, Ct.
Harring, Mrs. Almira, East Lansing, N. Y.
Harrington, Wm., Worcester, Mass.
Harrington, Mrs. Adaline, Worcester, Mass.
Harrington, Stukely S., Akron, N. Y.
Harrington, Rev. Daniel, Battle Creek, Mich.
Harrington, Adam, Shewsbury, Mass.
Harris, Rev. John, Milton, Mich.
Harris, Rev. Edward L., Delavan, Wis.
Harris, Rev. Wm. B., Cold Spring, (L. I.) N. Y.
Harris, Rev. George W., Detroit, Mich.
Harris, Mrs. Elizabeth J., Va.
Harris, Mrs. Sarah, Philadelphia.
Harris, Thomas J., Claremont, N. H.
Harris, Henry, New London, Ct.
Harris, George, Plainville, Ct.
Harris, John, New London, Ct.
Harris, Mrs. Charlotte, New London, Ct.
Harris, Giles, New London, Ct.
Harris, Miss Mary Ann, New York.
Harris, Rev. Alfred, Bustleton, Pa.
Harris, Mrs. Phebe, Roadstown, N. J.
Harris, Tracy H., New York.
Harrison, George, Troy, N. Y.
Harrison, Mrs. Camille M., Charles City, Va.
Harrison, Rev. J. C., Kingston, N. Y.
Harrison, Henry C., Philadelphia.
Hart, Mrs. Almira M., Boston.
Hart, Henry B., Portland, Me.
Hart, Daniel H., Meriden, Ct.
Hartley, Richard W., Cincinnati, Ohio.
Hartshorn, Jonas, Worcester, Mass.
Hartwell, Rev. Foster, Westerloo, N. Y.
Hartwell, John R., Providence.
Harvey, Hezekiah, New York.
Harvey, Rev. Alfred, Perth Amboy, N. J.
Hasey, Miss Angeline, New York.
Haskell, Dr. George, Rockford, Ill.
Haskell, Rev. Samuel, Kalamazoo, Mich.
Haskell, Rev. Abel, Yates, N. Y.
Haskell, Mrs. Esther, Yates, N. Y.
Haskin, Mrs. Pamela, New York.
Hastings, Andrew F., Brooklyn, N. Y.
Hastings, Mrs. Andrew F., Brooklyn, N. Y.
Haswell, Rev. James M., Amherst, Burmah.
Haswell, Mrs. Jane M., Amherst, Burmah.
Hatch, Charles G., Shelby, N. Y.
Hatch, Rev. S., Lansingburgh, N. Y.
Hatch, Ira, Union Village, N. Y.
Hatfield, Robert G., New York.
Hatfield, Mrs. Charlotte S., New York.
Hathaway, John, Fall River, Mass.
Hathaway, Luther B., Suffield, Ct.
Hathaway, Miss Mary, New York.
Hathaway, Charles F., Boston.
Hathaway, Mrs. Temperance, Boston.
Hatt, Joel, Orange, N. J.
Hatt, John, Orange, N. J.
Hatt, Mrs. Sophia, New York.
Hatt, Miss Annie Isabella, Morristown, N. J.
Haughwout, Rev. J. B., Fall River, Mass.
Haven, Caleb, Penn Yan, N. Y.
Havens, Robert M., Norwich, Ct.
Havens, Abraham, Freehold, N. J.
Haviland, John, New York.
Haviland, Mrs Joanna, New York.
Haviland, Miss Mary Ann, New York.
Hawes, Rev. Josiah, New Sharon, Me.
Hawks, Isaac, Shelburne Falls, Mass.
Hawks, Mrs. Eliza H., North Bennington, Vt.
Hawley, Mrs. Rebecca, New York.
Hawley, D. F., Bristol, Ct.
Hawley, Mrs. Jane P., Burlington, Iowa.

[illegible] Amasa, Adams Village, N. Y.
Heath, Morgan, Greenwich, N. Y.
Heath, Rev. Moses, McKeesport, Pa.
Hedden, William, Orange, N.
Hedges, Daniel, Pen Yan, N. Y.
Hellwig, Albert A. M., Gloversville, N. Y.
Hepburn, Rev. James, Northville, Ct.
Hendlen, Miss Henrietta, New York.
Hendlen, Mrs. Anna S. Q., New York.
Hendrick, Rev. Joel, East Smithfield, Pa.
Hendrick, John M., New Haven, Ct.
Hendrickson, Rev. G. F., South Dover, N. Y.
Hendrickson, Mrs. Rachel, South Dover, N. Y.
Henley, James W., Stamford, Ct.
Henley, Mrs. James W., Stamford, Ct.
Henry, Rev. Foster, Pawtuxet, R. I.
Hera, Rev. Edwin R., Hereford, Md.
Herbert, Mrs. Agnes D., Marlboro', N. J.
Heritage, Jason, Moorestown, N. J.
Herrick, Mrs. M. E., Beverley, Mass.
Herrington, Chester, Clifton Park, N. Y.
Heron, Miss Isabella, Williamsburgh, N. Y.
Heron, Thomas F., Verndon, Ill.
Heron, William S., Rochester, N. Y.
Heustis, Mrs. Ann, New Brunswick, N. J.
Hewins, Luther G., New Bedford, Mass.
Hewins, Elijah, Sharon, Mass.
Hews, Mrs. Jane, La Porte, Ia.
Hewit, Edmund, Galway, N. Y.
Hewitt, Chas. E., New London, Ct.
Hewitt, Austin D., Uncasville, Ct.
Heywood, Ellen, Jaffrey, N. H.
Hick, Miss Henrietta P., New York.
Hickman, Mrs. E., New Albany, Ia.
Hicks, Mrs. Mary Ann, Norwich, N. Y.
Hickok, Austin, Jay, N. Y.
Hide, Mrs. Fanny, Westerly, R. I.
Higbie, Alanson, Penfield, N. Y.
Higgins, N. L., Elmira, N. Y.
Higgins, Mrs. Susan, New York.
Hiler, Thomas G., Jr., Boston.
Hill, Mrs. Harriet D., New York.
Hill, Mrs. Mary, Miller's, Va.
Hill, David Jayne, Carmel, N. Y.
Hill, Mrs. Rebecca, Essex, Ct.
Hill, Rev. William, Kane, Ill.
Hill, Samuel P., Charlestown, Mass.
Hill, Amos, Jr., West Cambridge, Mass.
Hill, Rev. I. N., Elizabeth, N. J.
Hill, Leander J., Brockport, N. Y.
Hill, Henry S., East [illegible]

Houghton, J., Milton, Mass.
Houghton, Rev. G. W., New Hackensack, N. Y.
House, Francis L., Mason, N. H.
House, Rev. A. H., Passumpsic, Vt.
Houston, A. Elmira, N. Y.
Hovey, Rev. Alvah, Newton Centre, Mass.
Hovey, Wm. B., Cambridge, Mass.
How, Mrs. Myra, Haverhill, Mass.
How, Calvin F., Brooklyn, N. Y.
Howard, Rev. Johnson, Dover, N. Y.
Howard, Mrs. Lucy M., Rutland, Vt.
Howard, Mrs. Birsha S., Townshend, Vt.
Howard, Levi, Chelmsford, Mass.
Howarth, Mrs. Helen, Salisbury, Mass.
Howe, J. S. Methuen, Mass.
Howe, Christopher, Methuen, Mass.
Howe, Elizabeth D., Lynn, Mass.
Howe, Rev. Phineas, Marshfield, Mass.
Howe, John W. Holden, Mass.
Howe, J. J., Shelburne Falls, Mass.
Howe, Jones, Boston.
Howell, James, Trenton, N. J.
Howell, David, Southport, N. Y.
Howes, Samuel C., Chatham, Mass.
Howland, Emeline D., New Bedford, Mass.
Howland, George H., Boston.
Howlett, Rev. Thos. R., New Brunswick, N. J.
Hoyt, Miss Harriet E., Brooklyn, N. Y.
Hoyt, Mrs. Julia A., Brooklyn, N. Y.
Hoyt, L. D., Brooklyn, N. Y.
Hoyt, Rev. J. M., Cleveland, Ohio.
Hubatcheck, Joseph, New York.
Hubbard, Mrs. Mary R., Deep River, Ct.
Hubbard, Rev. W. C., Chittenango, N. Y.
Hubbell, Alrich, Utica, N. Y.
Hubbell, Rev. S., Urbana, N. Y.
Hudgens, Mrs. Rebecca Y., Hampton, Va.
Hughson, Levi P., Pulaski, N. Y.
Huling, Miss Frances, Saratoga Springs, N. Y.
Hull, Mrs. Maria, New York.
Hull, Charles, Danbury, Ct.
Hulse, Smith, Dundee, N. Y
Humphrey, Mrs. Cordelia R., Geneva, Ill.
Humphrey, Rev. Edward, East Haverhill, Mass.
Hungerford, Levi, Cordova, Ill.
Hunt, Rev. John, Hollis, N. H.
Hunt, Mrs. N., Sharon, Ct.
Hunt, Miss Eliza, New York.
Hunt, John, Boston, Mass.
Hunt, Richard, New York.
Hunt, Edward A., New Haven, Ct.
Hunt, Thomas, Brooklyn, N. Y.
Hunt Mrs. Thomas, Brooklyn, N. Y.
Hunter, William, Boston.
Hunter, Miss Elizabeth Jane, New York.
Huntley, Rev. George W., Spencer, N. Y.
Huntington, Rev. Jay, North Bennington, Vt.
Huntington, Mrs. Philip, Haverhill, Mass.
Huntington, John H. Troy, N. Y.
Huntington, Myron, Shaftsbury, Vt.
Hurlburt, Joel, Darien Depot, Ct.
Hurd, Daniel, Chicago, Ill.
Hurd, Orville, New York.
Hurd, Asa, Braman's Corners, N. Y.
Hurton, Miss Ann M., New York.
Husted, Daniel, Bridgeton, N. J.
Husted, Isaac B., Bridgeton, N. J.
Husted, Rev. W. H., Sinclearsville, N. Y.
Hutchings, Charles H., New York.
Hutchinson, Rev. Elisha, Brooklyn, N. Y.
Hutchinson, Mrs. E., Brooklyn, N. Y.
Hutchinson, Mrs. Rebecca, Brooklyn, N. Y.
Hyatt, Mrs. Mary B., Brooklyn, N. Y.
Hyde, Horatio N., Watertown, Mass.
Hyer, Mrs. Rebecca, New York.
Ide, Rev. John, Princeton, Ill.
Ingalls, N. T., Belvidere, Ill.
Ingalls, Mrs. Sarah L., Belvidere, Ill.
Ingalls, Charles, Methuen, Mass.
Ingals, Mrs. Sarah H., Sublette, Ill.
Ingerson, Irad S., Woburn, Mass.
Inman, Rev. Thomas E., Salem, Ohio.
Ireson, Mrs. Pamelia C., Lynn, Mass.
Irish, Peter D., New London, Ct.
Irish, Mrs. Sarah B., New London, Ct.
Irish, William O., New London, Ct.
Irish, Miss Sarah E., New London, Ct.
Ivens, Mrs. Ann, Imlaystown, N. J.
Ivens, Miss Helena R., Imlaystown, N. J.
Ivers, Miss Mary, New York.
Ives, Eli, Meriden, Ct.
Ives, William J., Meriden, Ct.
Ives, John, Meriden, Ct.
Ives, Abram, Holyoke, Mass.
Jackson, Henry, Croton, N. Y.
Jackson, Mrs. M. T., Newport, R. I.
Jackson, Mrs. Jerusha A., Chelsea, Mass.
Jackson, Daniel, Westford, Vt.
Jackson, Rev. Aaron, Oyster Bay, N. Y.
Jackson, Mrs. Susan, Newton, Mass.
Jacobus, J. L., Chicago, Ill.
Jacobs, Charles P., Goshen, Ia.
Jacobs, William H., Williamsburgh, N. Y.
Jacobs, William, Oxford, N. Y.
Jacoby, Mrs. B. A., Davenport, Iowa.
James. Rev. Joshua J., Raleigh, N. C.
James, Edward, Albany.
James, George, Zanesville, O.
James, Francis H., Philadelphia.
James, Rev. David, Osceola, Ill.
James, Thomas M., New Bedford, Mass.
James, John, Brookfield, O.
Jamison, Alexander, Wilmington, Del.
Jameson, Mrs. Lucinda L., Melrose, Mass.
Jameson, Miss Eliza, Newton Upper Falls, Mass.
Janvoin, Edwin, Chelsea, Mass.
Jarratt, Henry, Jarratt's, Va.
Jarratt, Nicholas, Jarratt Depot, Va.
Jastram, George B., Providence.
Jaudon, Mrs. Sarah T., Kansas City, Mo.
Jaycox, Isaac, Monmouth, Ill.
Jaycox, Mrs. Fanny M., Monmouth, Ill.
Jeffery, Mrs. Julia M., Philadelphia.
Jeffery, Rev. Reuben, Philadelphia.
Jefferis, Rev. David, Perkiomen Bridge, Pa.
Jeffress, J. M., Red Oak Grove, Va.
Jencks, Rensselaer J., ——
Jencks, Rev. Erasmus N., Ottawa, Ill.
Jencks, Livingston, La Salle, Ill.
Jenks, Miss Maria P., Pawtucket, R. I.
Jenks, Gideon, Brookfield, Mass.
Jenks, J. W. P., Middleboro', Mass.
Jenkins, Mrs. Susanna, New York.
Jenkins, Rev. J. S., Philadelphia, Pa.
Jenkins, Miss Rebecca, New York.
Jennett, John, Halifax, C. H., Va.
Jennings, Mrs. Susan C., Newton, Mass.
Jennings, Mrs. Marcia, Deep River, Ct.
Jennings, Mrs. Betsey, Deep River, Ct.
Jerome, George D., Uncasville, Ct.
Jeter, Rev. J. C., Beaver Dam, S. C.
Jewell, Aaron C., Newark, N. J.
Jewell, Albert, East Green, N. Y.
Jewett, Rev. Milo P., Poughkeepsie, N. Y.
Jewett, Rev. Daniel, Bonaparte, Iowa.
Jimmerson, Robert J., New York.
Jimmerson, Mrs. Miranda L., New York.
Johnson, Nathan M., Woburn, Mass.
Johnson, Rev. William B., D.D., Edgefield, S. C.
Johnson, Mrs. Henrietta, Edgefield, S. C.
Johnson, William, North East, Pa.
Johnson, Mrs. Sarah S., North East, Pa.
Johnson, Mrs. Louisa M., Lynn, Mass.
Johnson, James, Brooklyn, N. Y.
Johnson, Robert, Newark, N. J.
Johnson, Mrs. Robert, Newark, N. J.
Johnson, Rev. Solomon B., St. Louis, Mo.
Johnson, Rev. George J., Burlington, Iowa.
Johnson, Mrs. George J., Burlington, Iowa.
Johnson, Rev. Benedict, West Woodstock, Ct.

[illegible]

Johnston, John L., Sing Sing, N. Y.
Johonnet, Mrs. Andrew, Providence.
Jolls, John F., Providence.
Jones, Nathaniel, Jr., Homer, N. Y.
Jones, Rev. Stephen, Norwalk, Ohio.
Jones, Mrs. Stephen, Norwalk, Ohio.
Jones, Rev. Jol , Seaville, N. J.
Jones, Mrs. Deborah, Seaville, N. J.
Jones, Mrs. Ann T., Williamsburg, Va.
Jones, Eliza T., Tavern P. O., Pa.
Jones, Mrs. Margaret, New York.
Jones, Mrs. Eliza W., Noank, Ct.
Jones, Mrs. Elizabeth, Macedon, N. Y.
Jones, David, New York.
Jones, Mrs. Sarah, New York.
Jones, Mrs. Mary, New York.
Jones, Miss Catharine L., Philadelphia.
Jones, Rev. Joseph H., Frederick City, Md.
Jones, Rev. David N., Richmond, Va.
Jones, Rev. Theophilus, ughtown, Pa.
Jones, Rev. saac D., Wiltonville, N. Y.
Jones, John R., Roxbury, Mass.
Jones, William G., Wilmington, Del.
Jones, Washington, Wilmington, Del.
Jones, William M., New York.
Jones, Mrs. Margaretta V., New York.
Jones, Rev. J. W., Hyde Park, N. Y.
Jones, Rev. Howard M., Schoolcraft, Mich.
Jones, J. F., East Cambridge, Mass.
Jones, Rev. T., Rock Hill, Ohio.
Jones, Rev. Edward, Brookfield, Ohio.
Jones, Mrs. Abigail, New York.
Jones, Rev. A. B., Guilford, N. Y.
Jones, Rev. H. S., Smyrna, N. Y.
Jones, Mrs. Clara A., Worcester, Mass.
Jones, John M., West Troy, N. Y.
Jones, John, Philadelphia.
Jones, Mrs. Elizabeth, Du Buque, Iowa.
Jones, E., North Leverett, Mass.
Jones, George B., Pittsburg, Pa.
Jordan, Elder R. K., Richland Grove, Ill.
Jordan, hilana D., Columbia, Ohio.
Jordon, Mrs. Esther, Brooklyn, N. Y.
Jordon, True P., Lowell, Mass.
Joslin, Joseph, East Poultney, Vt.
Joyce, Miss Sarah W., Worcester, Mass.
Judd, Rev. Truman O., Fair Haven, Ct.
Judd, Mrs. L. A. H., Fair Haven, Ct.
Justice, David, Forestville, N. C.
Justin, Rev. Ira, Richmond, N. Y.
Kain, Mrs. Sarah [illegible]

Knight, Jonathan, Worcester, Mass.
Knight, Mrs. Samuel, Haverhill, Mass.
Knight, Rev. Benjamin, Salem, Mass.
Knowles, Levi, Philadelphia.
Knowles, Mrs. Susan E., Providence.
Knowles, Isaac, New London, Ct.
Knowlton, Miss Sarah J., North Chatham, N. Y.
Knowlton, D. A., Freeport, Ill.
Knowlton, Edward, Marion, Iowa.
Knowlton, Hezekiah, Beverly, Mass.
Knowlton, I. R., Cumberland, Ohio.
Knox, Miss Rachel, Hillsdale, N. Y.
Knudsen, Mrs. Sarah Jane, Brooklyn.
Kone, Louk, Maulmain, Burmah.
Kyle, Miss Mary, New York.
L'Amoureaux, Mrs. Nancy, S. Hadley, Mass.
Lacompt, Edwin A., Boston.
Ladd, Mrs. C. Ann, New York.
Ladow, John T., Dividing Creek, N. J.
Lafever, Reuben, Reading Centre, N. Y.
Lafferty, Mrs. Hannah, Exeter, N. H.
Lafleur, Rev. Theodore, Longueieul, C. E.
La Grange, Rev. John, St. Peter, Min. Ter.
Laing, Miss Jane, New York.
Lake, Mrs. Eleanor E., New York.
Lamb, Rev. R. P., Salisbury, N. Y.
Lamb, Rev. R. G., Jackson, Pa.
Lamb, Caleb, Wyoming, N. Y.
Lamp, George E., Holyoke, Mass.
Lamon, Joseph, Crawfordsville, Ia.
Lamont, Mrs. Anna, New York.
Lamont, Samuel, Owego, N. Y.
Lamport, Hiram H., New York.
Lamson, Rev. William, Portsmouth, N. H.
Lane, Lewis, New York.
Lane, Maltby G., New York.
Lane, Mrs. Mary F., —— Va.
Lane, Calvin S., Boston.
Lane, Rev. H. F., ——
Laning, Mrs. Julietta, Owego, N. Y.
Langley, Joshua H., Providence.
Langley, Mrs. Harriet N., Providence.
Lansing, Rev. Lewis S., Morrison, Ill.
Larkins, Elihu, New Haven, Ct.
Larmore, Wm., Wyoming, N. Y.
Laster, Miss Mary Jane, Boston.
Latham, Rev. Alanson, Haddonfield, N. J.
Latham, Mrs. Charlotte, Haddonfield, N. J.
Lathrop, John M., Somerville, N. J.
Lavery, Miss Mary, Brooklyn, N. Y.
Lawrence, A. W., Mooresville, N. Y.
Lawrence, William S., New York.
Lawrence, Miss Lorraine, Pine Plains, N. Y.
Lawrence, Mrs. Abigail L., Pine Plains, N. Y.
Lawrence, Mrs. Sarah, New York.
Lawson, James T., Newburgh, N. Y.
Lawton, George, Waltham, Mass.
Lawton, Mrs. George W., Waltham, Mass.
Lawton, Rev. L., North Linklean, N. Y.
Lawton, Samuel, Providence.
Lawton, Mrs. Alida A., New York.
Lawton, George F., Providence.
Lawyer, Michael, Newtown, Ohio.
Lea, Mrs. Elizabeth, Yanceyville, N. C.
Lea, Hon. Luke A., Washington, D. C.
Leach, Elbridge G., Stoughton, Mass.
Leach, Rev. Beriah N., Middletown, Vt.
Leach, Rev. D. F., Harpersville, N. Y.
Leach, Rev. William, Omaha City, Neb. Ter.
Leask, Mrs. Margaret, Brooklyn, N. Y.
Ledger, Mrs. Marion, Brooklyn, N. Y.
Lee, George, North Bristol, N. Y.
Lee, Mrs. Amanda, North Bristol, N. Y.
Lee, Miss Ann Mollan, New York.
Lee, J. A., New York.
Lee, Francis R., Trenton, N. J.
Leicester, Mrs. Mary, New York.
Leggett, Rev. William, Owasco, N. Y.
Leland, J. A., Brooklyn, N. Y.
Lemont, Charles A., Chelsea, Mass.
Lemont, Mrs. Ann M., New York.
Leonard, Richard, Riceville, N. J.
Leonard, Thomas, Riceville, N. J.
Leonard, Mrs. Mahetable, Zanesville, O.
Leonard, Rev. Isaac, Burlington, Iowa.
Leonard, George E., Newton, Mass.
Leonard, Mrs. Caroline F., Taunton, Mass.
Leonard, George A., New York.
Leonard, Halsey, West Woodstock, Ct.
Lerned, Rev. J. H., Still River, Mass.
Lester, Samuel C., Auburn, N. Y.
Lett, James, Wharton, O.
Levy, Rev. Edgar M., West Philadelphia, Pa.
Lewis, William J., New York.
Lewis, Elijah, Brooklyn, N. Y.
Lewis, Mrs. Ann, Brooklyn, N. Y.
Lewis, Mrs. Mary B. S., Brooklyn, N. Y.
Lewis, Mrs. Asa, Worcester, Mass.
Lewis, Rev. Charles C., Westerly, R. I.
Lewis, Daniel D., Philadelphia.
Lewis, Mrs. Hannah, Norwich, N. Y.
Lewis, Simeon H., Boston.
Lewis, William, New York.
Lewis, Rev. Richard, Holmesburg, Pa.
Lewis, Elijah, Norwich, N. Y.
Lewis, William B., Preston, N. Y.
Lewis, Rev. Welcome, Mansfield, Mass.
Lewis, John B., Jr., Boston.
Lincoln, Rev. Thomas O., Utica, N. Y.
Lincoln, Mrs. Abby A.
Lincoln, Rev. Heman, Jamaica Plains, Mass.
Lincoln, Henry E., Philadelphia.
Lincoln, Joshua, Roxbury, Mass.
Lincoln, John L., Providence.
Linde, Frederick, New York.
Lindsay, Wm., Fall River, Mass.
Linsley, Charles, New Haven, Ct.
Lippit, Mrs. Elizabeth S., Cumberland, O.
Lippit, Mrs. Melinda, Hiramsburg, O.
Lippit, Christopher, Hiramsburgh, Ohio.
Litchfield, Rev. Daniel W., —— Ill.
Litchfield, Wm. B., Brooklyn, N. Y.
Litchfield, Lawrence, Jamaica Plains, Mass.
Litchfield, Nichols, Boston, Mass.
Little, George W., Charlestown, Mass.
Little, J. T., Dixon, Ill.
Little, Warren, Stamford, Ct.
Littlefield, Jotham, Belleville, N. Y.
Lifsey, Mrs. Sally, Hick's Ford, Va.
Livermore, Rev. S. T., Cooperstown, N. Y.
Lloyd, Amos, Mullica Hill, N. J.
Loomis, Asahel, Gouverneur, N. Y.
Loomis, Edwin H., Lebanon, Ct.
Lock, Rev. William, Jamestown, N. Y.
Locke, Myron, Wyoming, N. Y.
Locke, Mrs. Harriet N., Springfield, N. J.
Locke, Jesse A., Watertown, Mass.
Locke, Mrs. Sarah B., Watertown, Mass.
Locke, Edw. Coolidge, Watertown, Mass.
Lockwood, Luther G., Stratfield, Ct.
Lockwood, Mrs. Martha J., New York.
Logan, James, Pemberton, N. J.
Lombard, Nathan C.
Long, E. J., Boston, Mass.
Long, William, Shelburne Falls, Mass.
Long, William, Urbana, O.
Longstreet, Mrs. Mary L., Imlaystown, N. J.
Longyear, Rev. Henry Z., Phenicia, N. Y.
Lord, Henry E., New York.
Loring, Samuel H., Boston.
Loring, Mrs. James, Boston.
Low, Mrs. Harriet N., Salem, N. J.
Love, Rev. H. T., Brooklyn, N. Y.
Love, Mrs. Catharine W., Brooklyn, N. Y.
Love, John, New York.
Lovell, George, Osterville, Mass.
Lovell, Mrs. Lucy, Fall River, Mass.
Lovell, Rev. Andrew S., Bloomfield, Ct.
Louther, Rev. Thos., Duncansville, Pa.
Low, Mrs. Eliza G., Haverhill, Mass.

Lucas, Rev. Elijah, Stanford, N. Y.
Lucas, Mrs. Thirza, Bangall, N. Y.
Luckey, James E., Palo, Ill.
Luckey, Emma M., Palo, Ill.
Ludington, Samuel, [illegible], N. Y.
Ludlow, John R., New York.
Ludlow, Mrs. Clarissa Ann, Newport, R. I.
Ludlam, David, Jr., Sing Sing, N. Y.
Lull, Rev. Abner, Oshkosh, Wis.
Luther, Job, Providence.
Luther, Gardner, Seekonk, Mass.
Luther, Mrs. Mary, Seekonk, Mass.
Lyle, Robert, New Brunswick, N. J.
Lynch, Thomas, Philadelphia.
Lyon, Jesse, Fitchburg, Mass.
Lyon, Moses G., Fitchburg, Mass.
Lyon, Cyrus, York, N. Y.
Lyon, Mrs. Mary, York, N. Y.
Lyon, Miss Rebecca, Plainfield, N. J.
Lyon, Rev. Daniel D., Sag Harbor, N. Y.
Lyon, Rev. Joel, Owosso, Mich.
Lyon, Mrs. Caroline P., Chatham, Mass.
Lyon, Mrs. Merrick, Providence.
Lyon, Rev. A. S., Natick, Mass.
Lyons, Rev. John M., Columbus, N. J.
Lynt, Odell D., Hastings, N. Y.
Lythe, Andrew, Williamsburgh, Va.
McBride, Miss Jane Ann, New York.
McBride, Miss Eliza H., New York.
McCarthy, Rev. William, Goshen, N. Y.
McChees, Peter, Middletown, N. J.
McClung, Miss Caroline M., Pittsburgh, Pa.
McClung, Anthony, Kingston, N. Y.
McCormick, Mrs. Sarah M., New York.
McCoy, John, Charlestown, In.
McMullen, Miss Sarah, New York.
McCune, John P., Salem, N. J.
McCutchen, Wm. G., Williamsburg, N. Y.
[redacted]

Mallory, Rev. Almond C., Benton Centre, N. Y.
Mallory, Rev. James, Eden, N. Y.
Mandeville, Stephen, Chicago, Ill.
Mandeville, Mrs. Mary, Chicago, Ill.
Mandeville, Miss Phebe E., Chicago Ill.
Mandeville, George, New York.
Mandeville, Henry, New York.
Mansfield, Edward, South Reading, Mass.
Mangam, William D., New York.
Mangam, Edgar B., New York.
Mangum, Rev. Daniel, Pagesville, S. C.
Mann, Rev. Levi L., Trout Creek, N. Y.
Manning, Rev. Edward, Cornwall, N. S.
Manning, William, Boston.
Manning, Melville M., Boston.
Manning, Mrs. Rachel D., Plainfield, N. J.
Manning, Francis H., Worcester, Mass.
Manro, Philip A., Throopsville, N. Y.
Manton, Rev. Joseph R., Providence.
Manwaring, C. S., East Lyme, Ct.
Maple, John E., Canton, Ill.
March, Peter S., New York.
Marchant, Henry, Jr., Providence.
Marchant, Miss Mary W., Providence.
Marchant, Henry C., Providence.
Marsall, Rev. J. F., Columbia, S. C.
Marsh, Rev. Asa, Austin, Min. Ter.
Marsh, Benjamin, Newport, R. I.
Marsh, Enoch S., Hudson, N. H.
Marshall, Rev. Samuel, Ohio.
Marshall, Albert, Holden, Mass.
Marshall, Mrs. Maria, Holden, Mass.
Marshall, Mrs. Mary Ann, New York.
Marston, John, Saratoga Springs, N. Y.
Marston, Mrs. Marcia, Saratoga Springs, N. Y.
Marston, Rev. S. W., Greenville, Ill.
Marston, Mrs. S. H., Greenville, Ill.
Martin, William R., New York.
[redacted]

Mason, Joseph R., Providence.
Mason, George, Providence.
Mason, Miss Harriet, Boston.
Mason, William, Fall River, Mass.
Massey, Mrs. Catharine, Bellingham, Mass.
Mastin, John S., New York.
Mather, Increase, Horse Heads, N. Y.
Mather, Mrs. Mary A., Deep River, Ct.
Mathews, Rev. George, Seekonk, Mass.
Mathews, Mrs. Elizabeth, Seekonk, Mass.
Mathewson, Nathan F., Providence.
Matteson, Rev. N. H., Preston City, Ct.
Maul, Rev. William, Greenwich, N. J.
Maul, Mrs. Sarah Ann, Greenwich, N. J.
Maxwell, B., Shelburne Falls, Mass.
Maxwell, Rev. J. M., Oswego, Ia.
Mayell, Mrs. Eliza, Albany, N. Y.
Maynard, Walter, Three Rivers, Mass.
Maynard, Mrs. Clarissa, Corning, N. Y.
Meacham, Miss Elizabeth, Brooklyn, N. Y.
Mead, John, Troy, N. Y.
Mead, Joshua, New York.
Mead, William, Lawrence, Mass.
Mead, John K., Amenia, N. Y.
Meads, Rev. George W., Vienna, N. Y.
Medbery, Andrew N., Seekonk, Mass.
Meech, Rev. Wm. W., Long Plain, Mass.
Meech, Mrs. Lydia, Preston, Ct.
Meech, Rev. Levi, Preston, Ct.
Meech, Levi W., Preston, Ct.
Medbury, Rev. Nicholas, Newburyport, Mass.
Medbury, Viall, Seekonk, Mass.
Meeker, Aaron B., Elizabeth, N. J.
Meekins, Mrs. Harriet R. H., Northampton, Mass.
Meeson, Rev. J. D., Burlington, N. J.
Merchant, James H., New York.
Merchant, Mrs. Amanda M., New York.
Merchant, Miss Louise, New York.
Merchant, Reuben, Stillwater, N. Y.
Merchant, Miss Mary, Stillwater, N. Y.
Meriam, Otis, Chelsea, Mass.
Merit, Mrs. Mary, Washburn, Ill.
Merrell, Charles, Malden, Mass.
Merrett, Thomas W., Somerset, N. Y.
Merriam, Rev. Asaph, Bolton, Mass.
Merriam, Rev. Mylon, Sharon, Mass.
Merriam, Rev. Titus M., Johnson, Vt.
Merriam, Rev. Franklin, China, Me.
Merriam, Harriet N., Chelsea, Mass.
Merrick, Timothy, West Willington, Ct.
Merril, Mrs. David J., Newburyport, Mass.
Merrill, Joseph, Lowell, Mass.
Merrill, Mrs. Nancy B., Hudson, N. H.
Merrill, Joseph, Hudson, N. H.
Merrill, Joseph, New York.
Merrill, Mrs. Mary F., New York.
Merrill, J. Warren, Cambridge, Mass.
Merrill, Rev. Thomas W., Kalamazoo, Mich.
Merrill, Daniel, Worcester, Mass.
Merrill, Charles, Malden, Mass.
Merrifield, Rev. Elliott P., Tyson's Furnace, Vt.
Merrifield, Miss Carrie R., Brookline, Vt.
Meserve, Andrew J., Lowell, Mass.
Messer, Richard H., New London, N. H.
Messer, Mrs. Sally S., New London, N. H.
Messer, Matthew, Methuen, Mass.
Metcalf, Rev. Whitman, Nunda, N. Y.
Metcalf, George P., Greenfield, Mass.
Mershon, Mrs. Marie, Trenton, N. J.
Mervine, N. J., Reading, Pa.
Micou, Rev. John, Jr., Louisville, Miss.
Miers, Mrs. Christina, Flemington, N. J.
Mikels, Rev. William S., New York.
Mikels, Mrs. Lydia, New York.
Milbank, Miss Elizabeth, New York.
Milbank, Miss Eliza W., New York.
Milbank, Miss Sarah C., New York.
Milbank, Miss Mary W., New York.
Milbank, Mrs. Mary W., New York.
Milbank, Miss Mary A., New York.
Milbank, Miss Emma Louise, New York.
Milbank, Miss Anna Elizabeth, New York.
Milbank, L. Ainsworth, New York.
Milbank, Charles A., New York.
Middlebrook, J. Henry, New York.
Middleton, John, Brooklyn, N. Y.
Miles, Abial, Brooklyn, N. Y.
Miles, Mrs. Hannah, Brooklyn, N. Y.
Miles, Rev. Edward M., Davenport, Iowa.
Miles, Thomas, Philadelphia.
Miles, Mrs. Margaretta L., Philadelphia.
Millard, C. J., Boston, Mass.
Millard, George, North Adams, Mass.
Millard, S. S., Penfield, N. Y.
Millard, Barzilla, Penfield, N. Y.
Miller, Mrs. Sarah R., Meriden, Ct.
Miller, Mrs. Abigail, New York.
Miller, Miss Amanda, Banksville, Ct.
Miller, Mrs. Nancy, New London, Ct.
Miller, Miss Anicartha, New York.
Miller, James H., Philadelphia.
Miller, Charles, Moriah, N. Y.
Miller, Rev. U. B., Fort Wayne, Ia.
Miller, Mrs. Anna R., Fort Wayne, Ia.
Miller, Mrs. Martha, Middletown, Ct.
Miller, Mrs. Ann Eliza, Providence.
Miller, Lydia A., Bedford, N. Y.
Miller, Edward W., Philadelphia.
Miller, Mrs. Mary Ann, Philadelphia.
Miller, Rev. John S., Mt. Holly, N. J.
Miller, Ezra, Franklin, N. Y.
Mills, Charles H., Brooklyn, N. Y.
Mills, Stephen, Greenwich, N. Y.
Mills, Rev. Pelatiah W., Springville, N. Y.
Milne, John C., Fall River, Mass.
Milne, Rev. Alexander, Macedon, N. Y.
Milne, Mrs. Eliza N., Macedon, N. Y.
Milner, Alfred A., New York.
Milner, Mrs. Alfred A., New York.
Miner, Rev. Martin, Wolcott, Ct.
Miner, Rev. Absalom, Waukesha, Wis.
Miner, Rev. S. G., Canton, Ill.
Miner, Rev. Erastus, Cold Spring, N. Y.
Miner, Rev. Noyes W., Springfield, Ill.
Miner, Francis S., New York.
Miner, A. B., Italy Hill, N. Y.
Miner, Nathaniel, Jerseyville, Ill.
Miner, Mrs. Hannah M., Norwich, N. Y.
Miner, Mrs. Charles, New London, Ct.
Miner, Ezra, North Stonington, Ct.
Miner, Roswell S., Boston.
Mingus, Miss Julia Ann, New York.
Mintch, Mrs. Phebe, Shiloh, N. J.
Mitchell, Rev. George H., Wagontown, Pa.
Mitchell, Mrs. Phebe H., Wagontown, Pa.
Mitchell, Seth, Montrose, Pa.
Mitchell, Ellen E., Montrose, Pa.
Mitchell, Rev. Thomas, Troy, Pa.
Mitchell, Mrs. Maria M., Brockport, N. Y.
Mixter, Rev. George, New London, Ct.
Mondon, Gilbert F., Port Jarvis, N. Y.
Monroe, Rev. William Y., Graham, Ia.
Montgomery, William, Danbury, Ct.
Montgomery, Mrs. Susan, Danbury, Ct.
Montgomery, S. P., Danbury, Ct.
Montgomery, Wm., Jr., Danbury, Ct.
Montgomery, Miss Susan, Danbury, Ct.
Montague, Rev. Oreb, Whitewater, Wis.
Moon, John, New York.
Moone, Lyman, Lyndonville, N. Y.
Moore, Dr. G. C., St. Johns, N. C.
Moore, Mrs. Julia, St. Johns, N. C.
Moore, Mrs. Theodosia, M., St. Louis, Mo.
Moore, James, Milton, Pa.
Moore, Francis W., New York.
Moore, Rev. Lyman H., Lansing, Mich.
Moore, Rev. W. W., Albany, N. Y.
Moore, Rev. George C., New York.
Moore, James, Wilmington, Del.
Moore, Enoch, Danbury, Ct.

[illegible], Va.
Morrill, Geo W., Salisbury, Mass.
Morrill, Miss Mary, Salisbury, Mass.
Morrill, Joseph, Amesbury, Mass.
Morrill, Daniel, Amesbury, Mass.
Morris, Rev. J., Hamburg, S. C.
Morris, Rev. David, New York.
Morrison, Jonathan, Brooklyn, N. Y.
Morrison, Mrs. A. Henrietta, Brooklyn, N. Y.
Morse, Mrs. Sophia A., Sturbridge, Mass.
Morse, Enoch R., Chelsea, Mass.
Morse, K. P., Greenville, Ill.
Morse, Mrs. Clara S., Charlestown, Mass.
Morse, Curtis G., South Dedham, Mass.
Morse, Benjamin, —— Iowa.
Morse, Charles A., Brooklyn, N. Y.
Mortimer, George W., Wilmington, Del.
Morton, Mrs. Susan, Corning, N. Y.
Morton, Miss Sarah B., Corning, N. Y.
Morton, Miss Matilda N., Corning, N. Y.
Morton, Miss Kate E., Corning, N. Y.
Morton, George, Brooklyn, N. Y.
Mosely, Green, Dupree's Store, Va.
Mosely, Miss S. A., Dupree's Store, Va.
Moss, Lemuel, Rochester, N. Y.
Moss, Mrs. Nancy, Upperville, Va.
Mott, Miss Elizabeth, New York.
Moulthrop, Major, New Haven, Ct.
Mount, David, Albany, N. Y.
Moxley, Rev. Oel W., Richville, N. Y.
Mugg, Rev. John, Gosport, Ia.
Mulford, John, Sen., Mullica Hill, N. J.
Mulford, Charles, Salem, N. J.
Mulhern, Rev. Dennis, Frankfort, Wis.
Mumford, Rev. N., Desota, N. Y.
Munger, Rev. Washington, Waterford, Ct.
Munger, Mrs. Louisa N., Waterford, Ct.
Munger, Morgan, Schaghticoke, N. Y.
Munger, L. F., Leroy, N. Y.
Munn, Mrs. Mary, New York.
Murdock, Mrs. Martha, B., Boston, Mass.
Murphy, Wm. D., New York.
Murphy, Samuel, Hoboken, N. J.
Murphy, Rev. John R., Marlton, N. J.
Murray, Thomas S., New Hope, Pa.
Murray, Mrs. Margaret M., New Hope, Pa.
Murray, Miss Sarah L., Boston.
Mustin, John, Philadelphia.
Myers, Mrs. Ann R., Philadelphia.
Myers, James, Jr., New York.
Mylne, Rev. Wm., Louisa, C. H., Va.

Page, Mrs. Emily A. L., Cleveland, O.
Page, Abel, Haverhill, Mass.
Page, Mrs. Abel, Haverhill, Mass.
Page, Mrs. Rachel D., Hopkinton, N. H.
Page, Henry S., Cleveland, O.
Page, Rev. C. J., New Brunswick, N. J.
Page, Hale W., Fitchburg, Mass.
Page, Enos, Streetsboro', Ohio.
Paine, Rev. John, Ware, Mass.
Paine, Walter, 3d Fall River, Mass.
Palmer, Rev. Asa H.
Palmer, Rev. Albert G., Wakefield, R. I.
Palmer, Mrs. Amelia W., Wakefield, R. I.
Palmer, Mrs. Wm. East Lyme, Ct.
Palmer, Rev. Lyman, Anoka, Min.
Palmer, Rev. Prentice T., Waveland, Ia.
Palmer, Ephraim, New Hartford, N. Y.
Palmer, H. K. W., Chelsea, Mass.
Palmer, Elias, New York.
Palmer, Mrs. Hannah, New York.
Palmer, Benj., Du Buque, Iowa.
Palmer, Mrs. Eliza, Wyoming, N. Y.
Pardee, Leonard, New Haven, Ct.
Park, Elisha, Providence.
Park, Rev. Charles C., Naples, N. Y.
Parke, Rev. F. S., Broadalbin, N. Y.
Parker, Miss Lavinia M., Suffield, Ct.
Parker, Asa, Essex, Ct.
Parker, Joel R., Fredonia, N. Y.
Parker, Rev. A., Agawam, Mass.
Parker, Rev. Wm., Philadelphia.
Parker, Rev. A., Coventry, N. Y.
Parker, David O., Hamilton, N. Y.
Parker, Lydia P., Allen, Mich.
Parker, Rev. Harvey L., Fairfax, Vt.
Parker, Mrs. E. R., Norwich, N. Y.
Parker, Miss Susan E., Boston.
Parker, Jonathan, Boston.
Parks, Rev. R. M., Bedford, Ind.
Parks, Mrs. Nancy J., Great Falls, N. H.
Parks, Mrs. Marianne C., South Berwick, Me.
Parkhurst, John, Fitchburg, Mass.
Parkhurst, G. R., Brooklyn, N. Y.
Parmlee, Mrs. Syrena, New York.
Parmelee, Elias F., Essex, Ct.
Parmelee, Rev. J. H., Xenia, O.
Parmely, Rev. Levi, Elgin, Ill.
Parmely, Mrs. Catharine H., Elgin, Ill.
Parish, Warren, Mendon, N. Y.
Parshley, John, New Haven, Ct.
Parsons, Silas, Swanzey, N. H.
Parsons, Mrs. Patience, Swanzey, N. H.
Parsons, Wm., Medford, Mass.
Partridge, Henry A., Minneapolis, Min.
Pasco, Rev. Cephas, Egremont, Mass.
Passage, Adam, Weedsport, N. Y.
Patch, Rev. George W., Marblehead, Mass.
Patrick, Charlotte M., Saratoga Springs, N. Y.
Pattengill, Rev. C. N., Whitesboro' N. Y.
Patterson, Rev. Wm. C., East Dedham, Mass.
Patterson, Mrs. Mary, Chapel Hill, N. C.
Patterson, Mrs. Lucy A., New York.
Patton, John E.
Paulin, Mrs. Ann, Salem, N. J.
Paulin, Rev. Wm., Hamilton Square, N. J.
Pavy, Rev. John, Clifty, Ia.
Payne, Miss Amanda, Amenia, N. Y.
Payne, Wm. W., Auburn, N. Y.
Payne, N. B., New London, Ct.
Payne, Mrs. Betsey S., Auburn, N. Y.
Payne, Mrs. Peninah S., Auburn, N. Y.
Peak, John, Boston.
Peacock, Rev. John, Amoskeag, N. H.
Peacock, Eliza Ann, Amoskeag, N. H.
Pearce, Rev. Wm., Marietta, O.
Pearson, Rev. Ira, Ludlow, Vt.
Pearson, Mrs. T. C., Ludlow, Vt.
Pease, Joseph W., Lowell, Mass.
Peaslee, Mrs. Abigail W., Haverhill, Mass.
Peck, Mrs. Nancy M., Owego, N. Y.
Peck, John, Clifton Park, N. Y.
Peck, Mrs. John, Clifton Park, N. Y.
Peck, John, 2nd, Clifton Park, N. Y.
Peck, Abijah, Jr., Clifton Park, N. Y.
Peck, Rev. David A., Waupaca, Wis.
Peck, James W., Brooklyn, N. Y.
Peck, Rev. Daniel, South Jackson, Mich.
Peck, George B., Providence
Peckham, Rev. S. H., Ledyard, Ct.
Peckham, Wm. L., New London, Ct.
Peeples, Rev. Darling, Barnwell, S. C.
Peeples, Edward H., Lawtonville, S. C.
Peirce, Mrs. Eliza H., Williamsburgh, N. Y.
Pegg, Miss Jane, New York.
Pember, Asahel, New Haven, Ct.
Pember, Mrs. Mary, New London Ct.
Pennel, Wm. A. Granville, Ill.
Penny, Rev. Wm., Uniontown, Pa.
Penny, Rev. Thomas J., Strattonville, Pa.
Pendleton, Rev. G. W., Jacksonville, Ill.
Pendleton, Mrs. Jane G., Jacksonville, Ill.
Percy, Everett, Boston.
Perine, Joseph, Plainfield, N. J.
Perine, Mrs. Sarah, Plainfield, N. J.
Perley, John E., Boston.
Perkins, Jabez, Topsham, Me.
Perkins, Rev. Nehemiah M., Brookline, Mass.
Perkins, George, Amesbury, Mass.
Perkins, Russel B., Meriden, Ct.
Perkins, Schuyler, Little Mill Creek, O.
Perkins, Mrs. Eveline A., Meriden, Ct.
Perkins, Eliab, Fond du Lac, Wis.
Perkins, Samuel S., Boston.
Perrine, J. W., Freehold, N. J.
Perry, Mrs. Sarah, McWilliamstown, Pa.
Perry, Valentine, Macedon, N. Y.
Perry, Samuel S., Manchester, N. Y.
Persons, Rev. R., Victory, N. Y.
Peterson, Rev. J. F., Richardson's, S. C.
Peterson, Richard E., New York.
Peterson, Mrs. Deborah V., New York.
Peterson, Samuel F., Philadelphia.
Pettingill, Daniel, Haverhill, Mass.
Pettingill, Mrs. Charlotte, Haverhill, Mass.
Petteys, Harvey E., Greenwich, N. Y.
Petteys, Mrs. Helen J., Greenwich, N. Y.
Pettit, Curtis, Wilson, New York.
Pettigrew, Rev. W. J., Pittsburgh, Pa.
Pew, John, Gloucester, Mass.
Phares, Rev. M. B., Dupont, Ia.
Phelps, Humphrey, New York.
Phelps, John, Owego, N. Y.
Phelps, Mrs. Sophia Emelia, New Haven, Ct.
Phelps, Mrs. Mary S., New York.
Phelps, Miss Julia Adelaide, New York.
Phelps, Miss Sophronia E., New York.
Phelps, Miss Mary Amelia, New York.
Phelps, Willard, New York.
Philleo, Calvin, Providence.
Phillips, John M., Penningtonville, Pa.
Phillips, Geo. W., Penningtonville, Pa.
Phillips, George H., Troy, N. Y.
Phillips, Rev. W., Providence.
Phillips, Rev. David L., Jonesboro', Ill.
Phillips, Rev. W. F., Dodgeville, Wis.
Phillips, Rev. W. C., Min. Ter.
Phillips, Mrs. Ann, New York.
Phillips, Mrs. Theodosia, Morristown, N. J.
Phillips, Peter, Rondout, N. Y.
Phillips, Mrs. Zilla, North Nassau, N. Y.
Phillips, Mrs. Lester S., New London, Ct.
Philbrook, Rev. Abel, Pittsgrove, N. J.
Phippen, Rev. George, Tyringham, Mass.
Pier, Mrs. Deborah, New York.
Pierce, Rev. Sem. Londonderry, Vt.
Pierce, Philo, Bristol, Ct.
Pierce, Mrs. Patty B., Nunda, N. Y.
Pierce, John W., Boston.
Pierce, John N., Harvard, Mass.
Pierce, Mrs. Osgood, Beverly, Mass.

Piper, John G., Canton, Ill.
Piper, David, Jay, N. Y.
Pitcher, Miss Elizabeth, Brooklyn, N. Y.
Pitman, Rev. Joseph M., Sutton, N. H.
Pixley, Rev. Joseph B., Hartwick, N. Y.
Plant, F. H., Plantsville, Ct.
Plant, A. P., Plantsville, Ct.
Plant, Mrs. Cornelia, Plantsville, Ct.
Platt, W., New York.
Platt, Mrs. Jane D., New York.
Platt, Rev. E. F., Toledo, Ohio.
Platt, Josiah, Stratfield, Ct.
Platt, Daniel, Amenia, N. Y.
Platt, Abraham, New Brunswick, N. J.
Platts, Daniel, Bridgeton, N. J.
Playford, Thomas, Stamford, Ct.
Plumb, William, Pomfret, Wis.
Plumb, Mrs. Cynthia B., Evansburgh, Pa.
Plummer, Mrs. Jane, New York.
Plymer, Mrs. Eliza, New York.
Pohlman, William, Albany, N. Y.
Poiner, J. R., Cincinnati.
Poole, Rev. A. W., Woodland, La.
Pooler, Seth, Lowell, Mass.
Poland, W. [illegible], Boston.
Poland, Rev. James W., Goffstown Centre, N. H.
Pollard, Mrs. Elizabeth, Taunton, Mass.
Polhamus, H. A., New York.
Pomeroy, Rev. Samuel, West Stockbridge, Mass.
Pomeroy, Mrs. Betsey, West Stockbridge, Mass.
Pomeroy, Harvey S., York, N. Y.
Pomroy, William, Middlefield, Mass.
Pond, William, New York.
Pond, Joseph A., Boston.
Pond, Moses W., Boston.
Pope, Edward R., New Bedford, Mass.
Pope, Elizabeth Coggeshall, New Bedford, Mass.
Porter, Mrs. Welthea M., Pittsfield, Mass.
Porter, Timothy, Waterbury, Ct.
Porter, Miss Charlotte, Danvers, Mass.
Porter, Mrs. Rebecca P., Danvers Mills, Mass.
Porter, Eliza J., Danversport, Mass.
Porter, Henry S., M. D., Philadelphia.
Post, Mrs. Sarah, New York.
Post, Alanson H., Hinesburg, Vt.
Post, Levi, Pitcher, N. Y.
Post, Joy, Essex, Ct.
Post, John, Saline, Mich.
Post, Prof. John D., Oregon City, Oregon.
Post, Peter K., Somerville, N. J.

Raum, Miss Catharine, Trenton, N. J.
Rawson, Elihu T., Columbus, Ohio.
Rauschenbusch, Rev. August, Rochester, N. Y.
Raymond, Rev. Lewis, Aurora, Ill.
Raymond, Samuel G., Danbury, Ct.
Raymond, Chas P., South Norwalk, Ct.
Raynor, Samuel, New York.
Raynor, Mrs. Sarah D., New York.
Raynor, William P., New York.
Raynor, Miss Mary S., New York.
Raynor, James W., New York.
Rea, William A., Providence.
Read, Rev. Hiram W., Falls Church, Va.
Read, Mrs. Alzina A. J., Falls Church, Va.
Read, Rev. Daniel, Medina, N. Y.
Read, Rev. James S.
Read, Mrs. James H., Providence.
Read, George W., Fall River, Mass.
Read, Mrs. Hannah T., Deep River, Ct.
Read, Dr. Thomas H., Decatur, Ill.
Reading, George, New York.
Reading, Caeser, Flemington, N. J.
Reed, Mrs. Sarah, Deep River, Ct.
Reed, Evans H., Townsend, Vt.
Reed, Mrs. Fanny B., Townsend, Vt.
Reed, Mrs. Sarah B. G., Bristol, R. I.
Reed, Mrs. Emeline, Chelsea, Mass.
Reed, Thomas B., New York.
Reed, Wm. B., North East, N. Y.
Reed, Mrs. Mary Ann, North East, N. Y.
Reed, Mrs. Eunice, North East, N. Y.
Reed, Miss Mary F., North East, N. Y.
Reed, Rev. E. D., Oneida, N. Y.
Reed, Mrs. E. D., Oneida, N. Y.
Reed, David, Utica, N. Y.
Reed, Enos, East Cambridge, Mass.
Reed, Lewis B., New York.
Reed, Rev. William, Raynham, Mass.
Reed, Rufus, Albion, N. Y.
Reed, G. Washington, Philadelphia.
Reed, Miss Henrietta A., Boston.
Rees, John F., Sennett, N. Y.
Reese, Rev. Daniel, White Creek, N. Y.
Reid, Mrs. Dorothy, New London, Ct.
Reid, Margaret Louisa, New London, Ct.
Reid, Robert W., New London, Ct.
Reid, Wm. Henry, New London, Ct.
Reid, Andrew, Warren, R. I.
Reimer, Frederick, Orange, N. J.
Relyea, Rev. Solomon S., Liberty, Miss.
Remington, Mrs. Sarah P., Brooklyn, N. Y.
Remington, Mrs. Hannah, Easton, Ct.
Remsen, Garret, Wilmington, Del.
Remsen, George, Brooklyn, N. Y.
Remster, Benjamin, Canton, N. J.
Requa, Mrs. Elizabeth, Sing Sing, N. Y.
Reynolds, Mrs. Mary, New York.
Reynolds, Rev. John E., Weedsport, N. Y.
Reynolds, Abraham M., Newark, N. J.
Reynolds, Stephen D., Wickford, R. I.
Reynolds, Rev. Anderson, Harpersville, N. Y.
Rhodes, G., Lawtonville, S. C.
Rice, Rev. A., Stoneville, S. C.
Rice, Mrs. Mary, Orleans, N. Y.
Rice, Josiah, Worcester, Mass.
Rice, Luther J., South Valley, N. Y.
Rich, Joseph C., Penfield, N. Y.
Rich, George B., New Haven, Ct.
Richards, Rev. John M., Germantown, Pa.
Richards, Rev. Wm. C., Lynn, Mass.
Richards, Mrs. Eliza G., Lynn, Mass.
Richards, Mrs. Elizabeth, Philadelphia.
Richards, Wm. H., Jr., Philadelphia.
Richards, Edwin S., Philadelphia.
Richards, Joseph L., Philadelphia.
Richards, Miss Eleanor A., Philadelphia.
Richards, Miss Sarah A., Philadelphia.
Richards, Mary L., Philadelphia.
Richards, Emilie, Philadelphia.
Richards, Zalmon, Washington, D. C.
Richards, Henry, Fall River, Mass.
Richards, Truman, Brooklyn, N. Y.
Richards, Miss Isabel, New York.
Richards, James, Cleveland, Ohio.
Richards, A. R., Rochester, N. Y.
Richards, Rev. Samuel, Providence, R. I.
Richards, Mrs. Maria T., Providence, R. I.
Richards, Ebenezer T., Holyoke, Mass.
Richards, Mrs. Cornelia V. H., Providence.
Richardson, Rev. Daniel F., Hanover, N. H.
Richardson, Wm. T., Cambridge, Mass.
Richardson, Thomas S., Brooklyn, N. Y.
Richardson, Mrs. Ann, Boston.
Richardson, Freeman, Auburn, N. Y.
Richardson, Rev. John, South Berwick, Me.
Richardson, Mrs. Euphemia, Troy, N. Y.
Richardson, Mrs. Lydia, Salem, Mass.
Richmond, Miss Maryetta, Harlemville, N. Y.
Richmond, Rev. Nathaniel, Pendleton, Ia.
Rider, Charles C., Roxbury, Mass.
Riddick, Jethro H., Sunbury, N. C.
Riddick, Nathan, Sunbury, N. C.
Rigley, Henry, Albany, N. Y.
Riley, Rev. G. W., Paris, Ill.
Ripley, Rev. Thomas B., Portland, Me.
Ripley, Joseph, Hingham, Mass.
Ripley, Rev. S., Northboro', Mass.
Ripley, Rev. Henry J., D.D., Newton, Mass.
Ripley, Rev. Nathaniel, Oxford, N. Y.
Roach, Rev. E. W., Harvey's Store, Va.
Robert, Rev. Joseph T., Zanesville, Ohio.
Roberts, E. G., Brooklyn, N. Y.
Roberts, Mrs. E. G., Brooklyn, N. Y.
Roberts, Rev. Thomas, Riceville, N. J.
Roberts, Thomas, Jr., Chanceville, N. J.
Roberts, Rev. Philip, Jr., New Rochelle, N. Y.
Roberts, Sarah, New Bedford, Mass.
Roberts, Mrs. Thyrsa, Brooklyn, N. Y.
Robertson, Rev. Thomas N., Orleans, Ia.
Robbins, Lewis, Imlaystown, N. J.
Robbins, Mrs. Mary, Imlaystown, N. J.
Robbins, Mrs. Elizabeth, Littleton, Mass.
Robbins, Rev. Gilbert, Sterling, Mass.
Robbins, Austin, Smithville, N. Y.
Robbins, Oliver, Smithville, N. Y.
Robbins, Ira, Boston.
Robbins, Rev. Gurdon, Hartford, Ct.
Robbins, Charles, Providence.
Robinson, Alfred, Cooperstown, N. Y.
Robinson, Rev. E. G., D.D., Rochester, N. Y.
Robinson, Rev. Samuel, St. John, N. B.
Robinson, Rev. Daniel, Martindale, N. Y.
Robinson, Benjamin, Providence.
Robinson, Mrs. Mary E., Providence.
Robinson, Demas.
Robinson, Wm., New York.
Robinson, Mrs. Catharine, New York.
Robinson, Mrs. Martha, Savannah, Ga.
Robinson, Reuben T., Boston.
Robinson, Edward, Arcadia, N. Y.
Robinson, Solomon, Webster, Mass.
Robinson, Mrs. Barbara, Tremont, Ill.
Robinson, Henry M., Concord, N. H.
Rockafellow, George, Avoca, N. Y.
Rockwell, David, Plainfield, N. J.
Rockwood, Rev. Joseph M., New Eng. Vil., Mass.
Rockwood, Mrs. Lucretia, Brooklyn, N. Y.
Roe, Rev. Charles H., Belvidere, Ill.
Roe, Mrs. Mary, Belvidere, Ill.
Roel, Austin, Randolph, Mass.
Rogers, Rev. Joseph D., Berlin, N. Y.
Rogers, Enos, Chatham, Mass.
Rogers, Mrs. Eliza D., Providence.
Rogers, Miss Eleanor F., Providence.
Rogers, Richard, New London, Ct.
Rogers, Rev. J. B., Portage, Wis.
Rogers, Dr. Alexander W., Paterson, N. J.
Rogers, George W., New London, Ct.
Rogers, Richard, New London, Ct.
Rogers, Mrs. Sally, New London, Ct.

[illegible] John A., Granville, Mass.
Rouse, Rev. Henry H., Stamford, Ct.
Rowan, Phineas, Philadelphia.
Rowe, John K., Baltimore.
Rowe, Elwin, Keeseville, N. Y.
Rowell, James, Salisbury, Mass.
Royal, Rev. Wm., Winterseat, S. C.
Rue, Rev. Joshua E., Louisville, Ky.
Rue, Joshua E., Jr., Hightstown, N. J.
Rue, Miss Mary, Hightstown, N. J.
Rugg, George W., Worcester, Mass.
Runyon, Richard E., New Brunswick, N. J.
Runyon, Hon. Peter P., New Brunswick, N. J.
Runyon, Daniel, New Brunswick, N. J.
Runyon, Elias, New Brunswick, N. J.
Runyon, Reune D., New Market, N. J.
Runyon, Ephraim J., New Market, N. J.
Runyon, Mrs. Osee, New Market, N. J.
Runyon, Mrs. Isabella, New York.
Runyon, Isaac M., Plainfield, N. J.
Rupert, Benjamin, Du Buque, Iowa.
Russell, Rev. Philemon R., Rock, Mass.
Russell, William, Yanceville, N. C.
Russell, Rev. Abm. A., Walworth, N. Y.
Russell, Rev. Rutherford, Deep River, Ct.
Russell, Samuel P., Chester, Ct.
Russell, Mrs. James, Haverhill, Mass.
Russell, Levi F., Cambridge, Mass.
Ryland, Rev. Robert, Richmond College, Va.
Sabin, Rev. Alvah, Georgia, Vt.
Saddington, Thomas B., Williamsburg, N. Y.
Safford, Mrs. Sarah B., Salem, Mass.
Safford, Morgan, Norwich, Ct.
Sage, Wm., Rochester, N. Y.
Sage, Orrin, Rochester, N. Y.
Salisbury, Wm. D., New York.
Samson, Mrs. Harriet H., Brooklyn, N. Y.
Samson, Rev. George W., Washington, D. C.
Sams, Dr. Lewis R., Beaufort, S. C.
Sanborn, Seth J., Manchester, N. H.
Sanders, Henry, Warren, R. I.
Sanders, Jacob, Homer, N. Y.
Sanders, Mrs. Martha A., Newton Corner, N. Y.
Sands, Ezra, Philadelphia.
Sands, William H., Boston.
Sandys, Rev. Edwin, Pittsfield, Mass.
Sanford, Mrs. Harriet E., Norwich, N. Y.
Sanxey, Mrs. Agnes, Brooklyn, N. Y.
Sargeant, Adaline A., New England Village, Mass.
Sargeant, J., Amesbury, Mass.
Sargeant, Mrs. Betsey, Amesbury, Mass.

Shepardson, Rev. John, Petersham, Mass.
Shepardson, Mrs. Maria A., Petersham, Mass.
Shepardson, Ansel, Fairfax, Vt.
Shepardson, Miss Julia H., Cincinnati, O.
Sheppard, Sylvanus B., Salem, N. J.
Sheppard, Isaac A., Bridgeton, N. J.
Sheppard, Miss Jane B., Bridgeton, N. J.
Sheppard, John M., Mintonsville, N. C.
Sherman, William N., Wickford, R. I.
Sherman, Mrs. Mary M., Wickford, R. I.
Sherman, Geo. J., Providence.
Sherwin, E. B., Shelburne Falls, Mass.
Sherwin, Miss Eliza, Shelburne Falls, Mass.
Sherwood, Walker, Easton, Ct.
Sherwood, Mrs. Lydia, Weston, Ct.
Sherwood, Rev. D. W., Matteawan, N. Y.
Shoemaker, Robert, Philadelphia.
Shotwell, Hugh, Brooklyn, N. Y.
Shotwell, Rev. J. M., Mannsville, N. Y.
Showalter, J. B., Willistown, Pa.
Shubarth, Niles B., Providence.
Shuck, Rev. J. L., Sacramento, Cal.
Shugg, Richard, New York.
Shute, Rev. Samuel M., Alexandria, Va.
Sibell, Mrs. Sarah, New York.
Sibell, Mrs. J. William, New York.
Silcox, Mrs. Elizabeth, New York.
Silkworth, Samuel O., New York.
Silliman, Ezra, Bridgeport, Ct.
Silliman, Erva, Bridgeport, Ct.
Silliman, Mrs. Ezra, Bridgeport, Ct.
Silliman, Ebenezer, Southport, Ct.
Silliman, Nathaniel L., Easton, Ct.
Silliman, David, Fairfield, Ct.
Silliman, Rev. Harvey, Adams Basin, N. Y.
Silliman, Stephen, Bridgeport, Ct.
Silliman, Samuel, Fairfield, Ct.
Silliman, Louisa, Easton, Ct.
Sills, William, Willington, Ct.
Simonds, Edward, Woburn, Mass.
Sims, Maurice P., Canton, N. J.
Simmons, Miss Eliza, Reading, Pa.
Simmons, Mrs. Mary Eliza, Indianapolis, Ia.
Simmons, Miss Henrietta A., Indianapolis, Ia.
Simmons, Edward W., North East, N. Y.
Simpson, Joseph P., New York.
Simpson, Thomas, Cheviot, O.
Sinnet, Alanson, Granville, O.
Sisson, Moses H., Norwich, Ct.
Sistare, Mrs. Abby, New London, Ct.
Sizer, Amasa, Jr., Meriden, Ct.
Skelding, A. Eugene, Mianus, Ct.
Skinner, E. B., Hertford, N. C.
Skinner, Charles W., Hertford, N. C.
Skinner, H. P., Hudson, N. Y.
Skinner, Miss Sarah R., Hudson, N. Y.
Skinner, Mrs. Phebe B., Hudson, N. Y.
Skinner, Rev. H. C., Wabash, Ia.
Skinner, Mrs. Louisa R., Wabash, Ia.
Skinner, Ebenezer, Brooklyn, N. Y.
Slack, Thomas, Brooklyn, N. Y.
Slade, Zaccheus, Newbern, N. C.
Slate, Needham, Mansfield, Ct.
Slater, Mrs. S. J., Providence.
Slater, Rev. Franklin A., Keyport, N. J.
Slater, Mrs. Sophronia E. H., Keyport, N. J.
Slaughter, James M., Baltimore.
Sleath, Samuel, South Ballston, N. Y.
Sleeper, Rev. George, Dividing Creek, N. J.
Sleeper, Mrs. Narcessa B., Dividing Creek, N. J.
Slote, Henry L., New York.
Slover, Mrs. Susan E., New Brunswick, N. J.
Smalley, Henry, New Brunswick, N. J.
Smalley, Mrs. Susan M., Brooklyn, N. Y.
Smart, James, Philadelphia.
Smart, Miss Mary A., Philadelphia.
Smart, Rev. M. M., Russia, N. Y.
Smiley, Mrs. William, Haverhill, Mass.
Smiley, Miss Betsey, Haverhill, Mass.
Smith, Rev. Francis, Providence.
Smith, Mrs. M. G., Providence.
Smith, Charles A., Providence.
Smith, Asa F., New England Village, Mass.
Smith, Mrs. B. S. W., New Eng. Village, Mass.
Smith, Rev. Harry, Valparaiso, Ia.
Smith, Mrs. Lydia W., Valparaiso, Ia.
Smith, Samuel, Salem, N. J.
Smith, Mrs. Sarah B., Salem, N. J.
Smith, Mrs. Ruth Ann, New York.
Smith, Mrs. William H., Brooklyn, N. Y.
Smith, Mordecai, Brooklyn, N. Y.
Smith, John H., Brooklyn, N. Y.
Smith, Henry W., Brooklyn, N. Y.
Smith, Augustus, Brooklyn, N. Y.
Smith, Mrs. Mary B., Brooklyn, N. Y.
Smith, Miss Ada Fanny, Providence.
Smith, William, Winsboro', S. C.
Smith, Jonathan, New London, Ct.
Smith, Rev. Alexander, Skeneateles, N. Y.
Smith, Mrs. Priscilla B., Clarkson, Va.
Smith, Mrs. Sally, Hancock, Mass.
Smith, Mrs. Mary E., Christianville, Va.
Smith, Rev. Joseph, Worcester, Mass.
Smith, Mrs. Abigail M., Worcester, Mass.
Smith, Mrs. S. L., Fayetteville, N. C.
Smith, Hamilton E., Fowlerville, N. Y.
Smith, Rev. Samuel, New York.
Smith, Alvah, York, N. Y.
Smith, George H., Branchport, N. Y.
Smith, William, Port Rowan, Canada West.
Smith, Rev. C. Billings, Iowa City, Iowa.
Smith, John H., New York.
Smith, Rev. William W., Broadalbin, N. Y.
Smith, Rev. Andrew M., Hartford, Ct.
Smith, Rev. Justin A., Chicago, Ill.
Smith, Rev. Wm. A., Groton, Ct.
Smith, Rev. Isaac, Foxboro', Mass.
Smith, Mrs. Harriet A., Amherst, Mass.
Smith, Shubael, Colchester, Ct.
Smith, Eliza, New London, Ct.
Smith, Mrs. Wm. M., New London, Ct.
Smith, Rev Eli B., D D., Fairfax, Vt.
Smith, Adam, Brooklyn, N. Y.
Smith, Rev. N. W., Vershire, Vt.
Smith, Ebenezer, East Tisbury, Mass.
Smith, Mrs. Sarah A., East Tisbury, Mass.
Smith, Rev. Dexter P., Iowa City, Iowa.
Smith, Gilbert D., New York.
Smith, Daniel, Worcester, Mass.
Smith, Rev. Lewis, Hightstown, N. J.
Smith, Jonathan, New York.
Smith, Rev. Rufus, West Swanzey, N. H.
Smith, Mrs. Mary E., West Swanzey, N. H.
Smith, Mrs. Annie, Worcester, Mass.
Smith, Henry D., Worcester, Mass.
Smith, William H., Brooklyn, N. Y.
Smith, E. M., Croton, N. Y.
Smith, Rev. Edgar, East Lansing, N. Y.
Smith, Capt. Leonard, New London, Ct.
Smith, Mrs. Helen M., Greenwich, N. Y.
Smith, Allen, Gouverneur, N. Y.
Smith, Rev. C. B., Townsend, Vt.
Smith, Miss Emma F., Banksville, Ct.
Smith, Jesse H., New England Village, Mass.
Smith, Mrs. Mary White, Newton, Mass.
Smith, Mrs. Jane, Troy, N. Y.
Smith, Lucius E., Boston.
Smith, Mrs. Elizabeth, New York.
Smith, Charles E., Fall River, Mass.
Smith, Rev. Levi, North Granville, N. Y.
Smith, Mrs. Levi, North Granville, N. Y.
Smith, Rufus, Shelburne Falls, Mass.
Smith, Rev. R. T., Lyndonville, N. Y.
Smith, Henry N., North Chatham, N. Y.
Smith, Rev. Sherman G., East Greenwich, R. I.
Smith, Wm. B., Cherryville, N. J.
Smith, Albert, New York.
Smith, H. H., Davenport, Iowa.
Smith, Adoniram, North Randolph, Mass.
Smith, Edward T., Albany, N. Y.

Southworth, James Adalbert, Brooklyn, N. Y
Southworth, John, Penfield, N. Y.
Sowers, Mrs. Mary E., Battletown, Va.
Sowers, Mrs. Elizabeth, Milwood, Va
Spafford, Rev. Lysander, E., Morris, N. Y.
Spalding, Miss H. M., Middletown, Ct.
Sparks, Rev. Peter, Newark, N. J.
Spaulding, Isaiah, Chelmsford, Mass.
Spaulding, Daniel B., Stoningtonboro', Ct.
Spaulding, Rev. Silas, Clockville, N. Y.
Spaulding, Rev. Amos F., Calais, Me.
Spaulding, Mrs. Carrie E., Calais, Me.
Spaulding, D. A., St. Louis, Mo.
Spaulding, Edward, Billerica, Mass.
Spear, Rev. Prof. P. B., Hamilton, N. Y.
Spear, Abraham, Jeddo, N. Y.
Spear, William, Reading, Mass.
Speir, John, Brooklyn, N. Y.
Speir, Mrs. Elizabeth, Brooklyn, N. Y.
Speir, Miss Susan B., Brooklyn, N. Y.
Spelman, Thomas, Alexandria, O.
Spelman, Mrs. Mary G., Granville, O.
Spencer, Robert, Little Plymouth, Va.
Spencer, Elijah, Moodus, Ct.
Spencer, Rev. Wm. H., Spencer, N. Y.
Spencer, Charles M., East Lyme, Ct.
Spencer, Thaddeus H., Suffield, Ct.
Sperry, Marquis T., Jordan, N. Y.
Sperry, Rev. O., Danville, Iowa.
Spink, Nicholas N., Wickford, R. I.
Spinning, Rev. Oscar F., Butternuts, N. Y.
Spinning, Mrs. Clara O., Butternuts, N. Y.
Spinning, Mrs. Mary, New York.
Spoldon, Rev. W. D., Amanda, O.
Sprague, Rev. Oliver L., Dansville, N. Y.
Sprague, Miss Mary E., Providence.
Spratt, Rev. George, Spread Eagle, Pa.
Spratt, Rev. G. M., Lewisburg, Pa.
Sproul, Mrs. Abigail, Imlaystown, N. J.
Sproul, James, Keyport, N. J.
Squires, Rev. James, East Troy, Wis.
Stahel, Caspar, Zurich, Switzerland.
Stainburn, Miss Mary, New York.
Stanton, Daniel W., New London, Ct.
Stanton, Reuben, South Westerloo, N. Y.
Stanton, Miss Catharine, South Westerloo, N. Y.
Staples, John, Stratfield, Ct.
Stark, Rev. J. F., Clarksville, N. Y.
Stark, Mrs. Delight, Fort Covington, N. Y.
Starkweather, Rev. John W., Akron, N. Y.
Star, Isaiah, Wilmington, Del.

Irs. Baron, Boston.
, Rev. A. H., Seekonk, Mass.
, Mrs. A. H., Seekonk, Mass.
an, J. S. T., Brooklyn, N. Y.
a, Samuel T., Philadelphia.
, Mrs. Mary L., Ottawa, Ill.
Samuel, Holyoke, Mass.
Miss Mary Ann, New York.
nd, James L., New London, Ct.
nd, Eliza C., New London, Ct.
Myron, Rochester, N. Y.
Alvah, Rochester, N. Y.
John, Greenwich, N. Y.
, Rev. Wm., Marlborough, N. Y.
James, Minneapolis, Min.
Mrs. Ann, Minneapolis, Min.
rs, Mrs. Aaron, Bridgeport, Ct.
, George O., Jr., New Haven, Ct.
in, Eli, Tyrone, N. Y.
in, Rev. Alonzo W., Avoca, N. Y.
in, Horace, Sennett, N. Y.
in, Mrs. Margaret, Sennett, N. Y.
in, Ursula, Sennett, N. Y.
in, Daniel W., Wayne, N. Y.
Mrs. Elizabeth, Britton's Roads, N. C.
Mrs. Mary Ann, New York.
Hon. Thomas, Pemberton, N. J.
Mrs. Mary, Pemberton, N. J.
Rev. T., Flemington, N. J.
Mrs. Eliza M., Flemington, N. J.
Rev. A. M., Leominster, Mass.
Samuel N., West Cambridge, Mass.
Mrs. Aurora D., West Cambridge, Mass.
Rev. P. M., Rockville, Ia.
Mrs. Thirza, C., Brentwood, N. H.
Miss Louisa M., Brentwood, N. H.
Joshua, Dennis Creek, N. J.
, Mrs. Almira, Boston.
Mrs. Laura, New London.
Andrew F., New York.
Thomas, Brooklyn, N. Y.
out, Mrs. Margaret, Crescent, N. Y.
Rev. Joel, Tivoli, Ill.
Mrs. Sarah A., Troy, N. Y.
r, Albert, South Reading, Mass.
n, Mrs. V. B., Yanceyville, N. C.
Rev. Benj. R., Lima, N. Y.
Mrs. Harriet, Lima, N. Y.
William A., Boston.
Rev. James N., East Boston, Mass.
ev. Wm., Springfield, Ill.
W. J., New York.
ls, Newton, Reading, Mass.
ls, Margaret, North Salem, Mass.
John, Portage, Mich.
mothy, Clinton, N. Y.
rs. Mary, Anthony Village, R. I.
t, Mrs. Harriet M., Detroit, Mich.
t, Wm. M., Detroit, Mich.
. Daniel A., Watertown, Mass.
e, I. A., Rochester, N. Y.
Rev. Los., Barry, Mass.
, Mrs. Elizabeth F., Spring Garden, Va.
, Cyrus S., Sennett, N. Y.
, Mrs. C. S., Sennett, N. Y.
, William, Sennett, N. Y.
, Miss Margaret, Pembina, Min. Ter.
, John, Pembina, Min. Ter.
, Mrs. Margaret, Pembina, Min. Ter.
, Edward, Pembina, Min. Ter.
, Elijah, Pembina, Min. Ter.
Joseph Lowell, Mass.
Joseph W., Boston.
all, Wm. K., New York.
Wm. H., New York.
John G., Holmdel, N. J.
Mrs. Ann B., Holmdel, N. J.
Miss Sarah, Holmdel, N. J.
Mrs. Sophia, Holmdel, N. J.
James C., Holmdel, N. J.

Taylor, Mrs. Laura, New York.
Taylor, Miss Emily, New York.
Taylor, Miss Ann Jane, New York.
Taylor, Miss Louisa, New York.
Taylor, Mrs. Sarah A., New York.
Taylor, Mrs. E. E. L., Brooklyn, N. Y.
Taylor, Miss Harriet Hill, Troy, N. Y.
Taylor, Mrs. Maria B., Lawtonville, S. C.
Taylor, Mrs. Dimis, York, N. Y.
Taylor, Rev. Thomas R., Allegheny City, Pa.
Taylor, Rev. Alfred H., Hollidaysburg, Pa.
Taylor, Rev. Thomas, Jacksonville, Ill.
Taylor, Samuel W. E., Bath, Me.
Taylor, Rev. O. D., Freeport, Ill.
Taylor, Henry C., Granville, O.
Taylor, Mrs. Adelia P., Albion, Mich.
Taylor, Elvin, Albany, N. Y.
Taylor, John, East Cambridge, Mass.
Taylor, John, New York.
Taylor, J. R., East Cambridge, Mass.
Taylor, William, New York.
Taylor, Mrs. Jane B., Philadelphia.
Tefft, Willard, Greenwich, N. Y.
Tefft, Thomas A., Providence.
Temple, James H., Chillicothe, Ill.
Terrell, Holland, Albany, N. Y.
Terry, Mrs. A. N. Spring Garden, Va.
Thatcher, Mrs. Elizabeth R.
Thayer, Thomas M., Gouverneur, N. Y.
Thayer, Lewis, Worcester, Mass.
Thayer, James H., Cambridge, Mass.
Theall, Mrs. Jane, New York.
Theall, Miss Susan, New York.
Thigpen, Rev. Samuel, Raymond, Miss.
Thistle, Mrs. Hannah, New York.
Thomas, Thomas, (architect) New York.
Thomas, Mrs. Isabella, New York.
Thomas, James H., New York.
Thomas, Rev. David E., Zanesville, Ohio.
Thomas, Griffith, New York.
Thomas, Rev. C. A., D.D., Brandon, Vt.
Thomas, Mrs. Eliza Ann, New York.
Thomas, Mrs. Mary, Brooklyn, N. Y.
Thomas, Mrs. Almira S., Brandon, Vt.
Thomas, Rev. Evan J., Atlanta, Ill.
Thomas, Osmar, Streetsboro', Ohio.
Thompson, Robert, Jr., New York.
Thompson, Mrs. Ann E., New York.
Thompson, Mrs. S. S., Pittsborough, N. C.
Thompson, Rev. Charles E., Iowa City, Iowa.
Thompson, L., Britton's Roads, N. C.
Thompson, Benjamin M., Harlem, N. Y.
Thompson, Rev. Sherman B., Little Valley, N. Y.
Thompson, Mrs. Serena, New York.
Thompson, Mrs. Harvey, Norwich, N. Y.
Thompson, Joshua, J., Salem, N. J.
Thompson, Richard H., Fisherville, N. H.
Thompson, Horace, New Haven, Ct.
Thurston, Henry, Brooklyn, N. Y.
Thurber, Edmund, Providence.
Thurber, Gorham, Providence.
Thurber, Charles, Worcester, Mass.
Ticknor, William D., Boston.
Tiebout, Adam T., Brooklyn, N. Y.
Tiebout, Mrs. Jane, Brooklyn, N. Y.
Tilden, Rev. Chester, North Lyme, Ct.
Tilley, Mrs. Elizabeth S., New York.
Tillinghast, Jefferson, Norway, N. Y.
Tillinghast, Charles E., Providence.
Tillinghast, Rev. J. A., Allenton, R. I.
Tilson, Rev. Jonathan, Hingham, Mass.
Tilton, Rev. Charles.
Tilton, Rev. Josiah H., Holden, Mass.
Tilton, Mrs. Abigail S. F., Sandbornton, N. H.
Timberman, Rev. Jacob, Mansfield, N. J.
Tindall, Samuel, L., Wilmington, Del.
Tingley, Miss Nancy B., Valley Falls, R. I.
Tingley, Timothy C., North Scituate, Mass.
Tingley, Miss Emma S., North Scituate, Mass.
Tinkham, Rev. D., Centre White Creek, N. Y.

[illegible], Philadelphia.
Tolman, Miss Martha, Boston.
Tolman, Mrs. Elizabeth A., Philadelphia.
Tonkin, Rev. Henry, Concord, N. H.
Tophf, Rev. C. H., Weston, Mass.
Torbet, Rev. Andrew M., St. Paul, Min. Ter.
Torian, Elijah, Halifax C. H., Va.
Torrance, Riley, Jay, N. Y.
Tourtellot, Abraham, Nashua, N. H.
Tousley, Charles, New York.
Towle, Miss Sarah G., Newburyport, Mass.
Townsend, S. P., New York.
Townsend, Miss Naomi, New York.
Townsend, Rev. G. N., Bellingham, Mass.
Townsend, Mrs. Louisa L., Brooklyn.
Townsend, Rev. B. C., Gorham, N. Y.
Townsend, Thomas, Lynn, Mass.
Townsend, John A., Providence.
Tracy, Lucius H., New London, Ct.
Tracy, Rev. Orrin, Concord, N. H.
Tracy, Mrs. Marcia B., Concord, N. H.
Tracy, Miss Susan M., Concord, N. H.
Train, Mrs. A. S., Haverhill, Mass.
Travis, Simeon S., New York.
Travis, Luther, Southbridge, Mass.
Treat, E. S., Rochester, N. Y.
Trevor, John B., Philadelphia.
Trevor, R. M., Pittsburgh, Pa.
Tripp, Mrs. Susan, New Bedford, Mass.
Tripp, Ervin H., New York.
Tripp, Mrs. Caroline S. H., New York.
Tripp, Miss Sarah S. B., New York.
Trout, William, Charleston, S. C.
Trow, Rev. Augustus H., Montezuma, N. Y.
Trowbridge, William, Sheboygan Falls, Wis.
True, Mrs. Betsey M., Plainfield, N. H.
True, Mrs. Hannah, Meriden, N. H.
True, Mrs. Mary, Amesbury, Mass.
Truesdell, Mrs. Margerie, Hillsdale, N. Y.
Trull, Jesse L., Tewksbury, Mass.
Truman, Jonathan, Greenport, N. Y.
Truman, Stephen S., Owego, N. Y.
Truman, Mrs. Betsey, S., Owego, N. Y.
Truman, Mrs. Eleanor M., Owego, N. Y.
Truman, Edward, D., Owego, N. Y.
Trump, Isaac V., Somerville, N. J.
Tryon, Miss Eveline, Ballston, N. Y.
Tucker, Harwood B., Christianville, Va.
Tucker, Richard G., Stony Creek, Va.
Tucker, Rev. Silas, Galesville, Ill.
Tucker, Mrs. F. G., Stony Creek, Va.

Waldron, Miss Maria, New York.
Wales, Sarah, Sennett, N. Y.
Walker, Rev. Joseph, Marcus Hook, Pa.
Walker, Mrs. Elizabeth, Marcus Hook, Pa.
Walker, Miss Hannah, Marcus Hook, Pa.
Walker, Rev. G. C., Johnson's Creek, N. Y.
Walker, Mrs. Eliza H., Somerset, N. Y.
Walker, Mrs. Mary, Brookneal, Va.
Walker, John B., Madison, Ga.
Walker, Andrew, New York.
Walker, William A., New York.
Walker, Lewis A., New York.
Walker, Michael P., New York.
Walker, Charles, Chicago, Ill.
Walker, George C., Chicago, Ill.
Walker, Rev. Wareham, New York.
Walker, Rev. John, Coldbrook, Mass.
Walker, Rev. William C., Willington, Ct.
Walker, Mrs. L. A., Willington, Ct.
Walker, Samuel, Roxbury, Mass.
Walker, Rev. O. T., New London, Ct.
Walker, Mrs. Velina P., New London, Ct.
Walker, William, Clinton, Mass.
Walker, Rev. O. B., Foxcroft, Me.
Walker, Amos, Pontiac, Mich.
Walker, Francis, Pawtucket, R. I.
Walker, Rev. James, Greenbush, N. Y.
Wallace, Mrs. Margaret, New York.
Wallace, Miss Eliza, Brooklyn, N. Y.
Wallace, Jonathan, Fort Covington, N. Y.
Walter, Rev. John P., General Wayne, Pa.
Walters, Jacob, Wilmington, Del.
Walton, Joel, Va.
Walton, Jesse, Augusta, Ga.
Ward, Uzal D., New York.
Ward, Willard, Worcester, Mass.
Ward, William, Worcester, Mass.
Wardner, Rev. Chauncey, Perry, N. Y
Wardner, Mrs. Margaret A., Perry, N. Y.
Warford, Elijah, Cherryville, N. J.
Ware, Dr. R. J., Montgomery Co., Ala.
Waring, James, Jr., Fall River, Mass.
Warn, Mrs. Sarah M., Sennett, N. Y.
Warn, Mrs. Mary, Sennett, N. Y.
Warner, Dr. Ransom, New York.
Warner, Benjamin I., Williamsburg, N. Y.
Warnock, Miss Elizabeth, New York.
Warren, Mrs. Diantha O., West Potsdam, N. Y.
Warren, Rev. Patrick, Baltimore, Md.
Warren, Rev. Benjamin, Chili, N. Y.
Warren, Rev. J. G., D.D., Boston.
Warren, Charles W., Utica, N. Y.
Warren, Rev. Edwin R., East Greenwich, R. I.
Warren, Moses, Cambridge, Mass.
Warren, Mrs. Grace, Cambridge, Mass.
Warren, Rev. H. S. P., Madrid, N. Y.
Warren, Horace, Norwich, Ct.
Warren, Rev. John, Easton, Ct.
Warren, Mrs. Emma, Burlington, Iowa.
Warren, Thomas, New York.
Warriner, Rev. Norman, Le Clair, Ill.
Warriner, Rev. R. L., South Valley, N. Y.
Warriner, Mrs. Clarissa, South Valley, N Y.
Washburn, Nathan W., Mt. Pleasant, Ill.
Washburn, Rev. R. A., Andover, N. Y.
Washington, Mrs. Elizabeth, Newbern, N. C.
Wasson, Mrs. Clarissa, Albany.
Waterbury, Miss Martha, Williamsburg, N. Y.
Waterbury, Mrs. Mary, Saratoga Springs, N. Y.
Waterbury, Francis W., Saratoga Springs, N. Y.
Waterbury, N. H., Saratoga Springs, N. Y.
Waterman, Nathan, Jr., Providence.
Waterman, R. W., Covington, Ia.
Waters, Mrs. Elizabeth A., Brookline, Mass.
Waters, Horace, Brooklyn, N. Y.
Watkins, Mrs. Hannah, New York.
Watkins, Henry M., New York.
Watkinson, Rev. Wm. E., Manyunk, Pa.
Watkinson, Rev. Mark R., Portsmouth, Va.
Watrous, Richard, New York.
Watson, George, New York.
Watson, James, Brooklyn, N. Y.
Watson, W. W., Springfield, Ill.
Watson, John, New York.
Watson, Rev. D. S., Cleveland, Ohio.
Watters, Miss Sarah A., Philadelphia.
Watts, Isaiah, New York.
Watts, Mrs. Emma, New York.
Watts, Charles Henry, New York.
Watts, John, Elmira, N. Y.
Wattson, Mrs. Mary B., Philadelphia.
Wattson, Miss Elizabeth, Philadelphia.
Wattson, Rev. W. H., West Acton, Mass.
Way, Rev. Samuel P., North Brookfield, N. Y.
Way, Mrs. Welthy A., North Brookfield, N. Y.
Wayland, Mrs. H. S. H., Providence.
Wayland, Francis, Jr., Worcester, Mass.
Wead, Mrs. Nancy, Malone, N. Y.
Weaver, Rev. C. S., Norwich, Ct.
Weaver, Mrs. Diana, Norwich, Ct.
Weaver, Edwin H., Norwich, Ct.
Weaver, Mrs. Ann, Groton, Ct.
Weaver, Wanton A., New London, Ct.
Weaver, C. Arnold, New London, Ct.
Weaver, Daniel L., Albany, N. Y.
Webb, Mrs. Maria, New Brunswick, N. J.
Webb, Rev. Abner, Belleville, N. Y.
Webb, Rev. W. R., Dixon, Ill.
Webb, Daniel, Leroy, N. Y.
Webb, Rev. J. N., Fort Covington, N. Y.
Webb, Mrs. J. N., Fort Covington, N. Y.
Webb, John, Newtown, Ohio.
Webber, Rev. Julius S., Warsaw, N. Y.
Webster, Phineas, Haverhill, Mass.
Webster, Mrs. Phineas, Haverhill, Mass.
Webster, Rev. Amos, Boston, Mass.
Webster, Rev. S. B., Norwalk, O.
Webster, Caleb, Lowell, Mass.
Webster, Rev. J. D., Green, N. Y.
Weckerly, Daniel, Philadelphia.
Weddell, Rev. Peter M., Canton, Ohio.
Welch, Mrs. B. T., Newtonville, N. Y.
Welch, Rev. James E., Hickory Grove, Mo.
Weirick, Miss Sallie A., Logansport, Ia.
Weld, Nathaniel, Jamaica Plain, Mass.
Weld, Mrs. Lucy, New York.
Weld, Aaron D., Winchester, Mass.
Welden, Asa W., New York.
Weller, R. F., Albany, N. Y.
Wells, Mrs. Elizabeth, New York.
Wells, Rev. Alfred, Attica, N. Y.
Wells, Rev Wm. A., Muscatine, Iowa.
Wells, Miss Mary E., Providence, R. I.
Wells, Henry E., Greenport, N. Y.
Wemple, Abraham A., Schenectady, N. Y.
Wemple, Mrs. Mary S., Schenectady, N. Y.
Wescott, Rev. Isaac, Gloversville, N. Y.
Wescott, Jehiel, Bridgeton, N. J.
Wescott, Jehiel, Jr., Bridgeton, N. J.
Wescott, Josiah S., Bridgeton, N. J.
Wescott, Rev. Henry, Warrenville, Ill.
Wescott, John, Bridgeton, N. J.
West, Mrs. Ann, Brooklyn, N. Y.
West, John G., Williamsburg, N. Y.
West, Willoughby W., York, N. Y.
West, Rev. Hezekiah, Watkins, N. Y.
Weston, Rev. Henry G., Peoria, Ill.
Weston, Franklin L., Johnson's Creek, N. Y.
Westervelt, John, Williamsburg, N. Y
Westover, Rev. John T., East Troy, Wis.
Westover, Mrs. John T., East Troy, Wis.
Wetherbee, Ephraim, Broadalbin, N. Y.
Wetherbee, Miss Ruby, Broadalbin, N. Y.
Wethern, George M., Lowell, Mass.
Wetterau, Mrs. Frances, New York.
Whedon, C. H., Homer, N. Y.
Wheat, Mrs. Priscilla P., Philadelphia.
Wheaton, Reuben, Wilmington, Del.
Wheaton, Mrs. Elizabeth M., Columbus, O
Wheaton, John M., Columbus, O.

[illegible], Mrs. Mary [illegible], North [illegible], Mass.
W[illegible], Rev. R., Grafton, Vt.
W[illegible]n, [illegible] J., G[illegible]nwich, N. Y.
W[illegible]n, Mrs. Sarah, Ca[illegible], M
Wi[illegible]n, Rev. B. W., [illegible], S. C.
Whipple, Harvey, Malone, N. Y.
Whipple, Ethan, Providence, R. I.
Whipple, Mrs. Phebe, Providence, R. I.
Whipple, Mrs. Hannah, New Boston, N. H.
Whitaker, Alanson, Granville, Ill.
Whitaker, Wm. N., Philadelphia.
Whitcomb, Peter, Littleton, Mass.
White, Mrs. E. North Shore, N. Y.
White, Mrs. Martha D. Marcus Hook, Pa.
White, Miss Lydia, Haverhill, Mass.
White, Thomas, Brooklyn, N. Y.
White, Samuel S., Whiteville, N. Y.
White, Harvey, Mt. Holly, Vt.
White, Thomas P., Bridgeport, Ct.
White, Mrs. Thomas P., Bridgeport, Ct.
White, Joseph, Winchendon, Mass.
White, Beza L. Taunton, Mass.
White, Ebenezer Newton, Mass.
White, Ebenezer B., Williamsburg, N. Y.
White, Mrs. Mary, New York.
White, Samuel, Bordentown, N. J.
White, Mrs. Sylvanus, Brooklyn.
White, Samuel, Littleton, Mass.
White, Miss Mary, New York.
White, Miss Emily J. Taunton, Mass.
White, Almeth, Rahway, N. J.
Whitehead, Samuel, Bound Brook, N. J.
Whitehead, Mrs. Emel[illegible] V. New York.
Whitehead, Artemas K. New York.
Whitehead, John W. New York.
Whitehead, [illegible]nus P., New York.
Whitehead, Rev. Wm. M., Spread Eagle, Pa.
Whitehead, Rev. J. M., Westville, La.
Whitford, H. G., Willington, Ct.
Whitford, Mrs. Florilla, Willington, Ct.
Whiting, Rufus W., Boston.
Whitman, Charles S., Belvidere, Ill.
Whitman, Mrs. Matilda, Belvidere, Ill.
Whitman, Spencer, Belvidere, Ill.
Whitman, Alva, Mich.
Whitman, John C., Sennett, N. Y.
Whitney, Miss Harriet, New York.
Whitney, Mrs. Betsey, Worcester, Mass.
Whitney, Bennet, Bridgeport, Ct.
Whitney, Raymond, North Fairfield, O.
Whitney, Mrs. E. S., Brooklyn, N. Y.

W[illegible]
Wildm[illegible]
Wiley, J
Wiley, M
W[illegible]
Wilkins,
Wilkins[illegible]
Willard,
Willard,
Willard,
Willard,
Willard,
Willard,
Willard,
Willett,
Willett,
William[illegible]
William[illegible]
William[illegible]
William[illegible]
William[illegible]
William[illegible]
William[illegible]
William
William[illegible]
William[illegible]
William[illegible]
William
William[illegible]
William[illegible]
William[illegible]
William
William
William[illegible]
William[illegible]
William[illegible]
William[illegible]
William
Willingh[illegible]
Willingt[illegible]
Willis, [illegible]
Willis, J
Willis, [illegible]
Wilson,
Wilson,
Wilson,
Wilson,
Wilson,
Wilson,
Wilson,
Wilson,

Windust, Edward, New York.
Winslow, Robert F., Fond du Lac, Wis.
Winslow, R. Octavius, Leamington, Eng.
Winston, Rev. Meriweather, Richmond, Va.
Winter, Rev. Thomas, Roxborough, Pa.
Winter, Rev. John, Knoxville, Ill.
Winterton, Mrs. Mary, New York.
Wise, Miss Clarissa R., New Russia, N. Y.
Wisner, Mrs. Sarah, Mount Morris, N. Y.
Wisham, Samuel, Philadelphia.
Wiswell, Mrs. C. A., West Troy, N. Y.
Witherwax, Mrs. Emeline B., Davenport, Iowa
Witherwax, Miss Mary B. Davenport, Iowa.
Withall, John, Henrietta, N. Y.
Witherbee, John B., Jamaica Plains, Mass.
Withington, Mrs. M., Morrisania, N. Y.
Wolcott, Mrs. Mary S., New York.
Wolcott, Mrs. Naomi, Rochester, N. Y.
Wollaston, Joshua, Wilmington, Del.
Worrall, Rev. Thomas D., Lowell, Mass.
Wood, Lowell, M., Boston.
Wood, George W., Brooklyn, N. Y.
Wood, Mrs. J. S., Hertford, N. C.
Wood, Mrs. Mary E., Hertford, N. C.
Wood, Rev. N. N., D.D., Upper Alton, Ill.
Wood, Jennings, J., Speedwell, S. C.
Wood, George. Springfield, Ill.
Wood, Joseph T., Westboro' Mass.
Wood, Mrs. Amelia, Brooklyn, N. Y.
Wood, Eliphalet, Honesdale, Pa.
Wood, Ambrose, Albion, N. Y.
Woods, Gardner, Jersey, Ohio.
Woods, Hiram, Nashua, N. H.
Woodbridge, William A., New York.
Woodbury, William W., Suffield, Ct.
Woodbury, Rev. John, Templeton, Mass.
Woodbury, Miss Frances, Danvers, Mass.
Woodbury, Eliza A., Lynn, Mass.
Woodman, Moses, New Gloucester, Me.
Woodruff, Mrs. Innocent, Albany.
Woodward, Rev. Jonas, Cedar Rapids, Iowa.
Woodward, Mrs. Eliza, Cedar Rapids, Iowa.
Woodward, Mrs. Mary D., Middlesex, Va.
Woodward, Sylvester, Lowell, Mass.
Woodward, Darwin W., Franklindale, N. Y.
Woodworth, Levi B., Canaan, Ohio.
Woolston, Mrs. Keziah, Vincentown, N. J.
Worrall, Ellwood P., West Chester, Pa.
Wooster, Mrs. Aurelia R., Deep River, Ct.
Wooster, Hinman, Charlottte, Vt.
Work, Rev. Perley, Omeo., Wis.
Worth, Rev. Edmund, Kennebunk, Me.
Worth, J. C., Hanover, N. H.
Worthington, S., Springfield, Mass.
Wright, Rev. David, North Lyme, Ct.
Wright, Wm J., Hardgrove's Va.
Wright, Theodore, N. Y.
Wright, Asahel B., Lowell, Mass.
Wright, Harvey, Three Rivers, Mass.
Wright, Mrs. Julia A., Westport, N. Y,
Wright, Rev. Ansell T., Weart's Corners, N. J.
Wright, R. A., Rochester, N. Y.
Wright, James G., Canton, N. J.
Wright, B. H., Dover Plains, N. Y.
Wyckoff, Mrs. Cornelius R , Weedsport, N. Y.
Wyckoff,
Wyckoff,
Wyckoff, W. G., Middletown, N. J.
Wyckoff, Francis, Plainfield, N. J.
Wyckoff, Mrs. Sarah B., Brooklyn, N. Y.
Wyckoff, Jacob F., New York.
Wyer, Rev. Henry O., Alexandria, Va.
Wynn, Mrs. Susan, Tuckahoe, N. J.
Wynn, Benjamin F., Tuckahoe, N. J.
Yale, Levi, Augusta, N. Y.
Yendall, Sarah, Boston.
Yeomans, Mrs. Olive, Providence.
Yeomans, Miss Mary Ann, Providence.
York, Mrs. Hannah, Haverhill, Mass.
York, C., Norwich, N. Y.
York, Mrs. Esther, Norwich, N. Y.
Young, Mrs. Sarah, Brooklyn, N. Y.
Young, Rev. George, N. J.
Young, Rev. Robert F., Chestnut Hill, Pa.
Young, Mrs. Maria Ann, Chestnut Hill, Pa.
Young, Robert McCarthy, New York.
Young, Rev. G. W., Antistown, Pa.
Young, William W., Stamford, Ct.
Yuran, Mrs. S S., Tunbridge, Vt.
Zebley, John F., New York.
Zimmerman, Edwin, New York.

1833–4.

DIRECTOR.

Cobb, Nathaniel R., Boston, Mass.

MEMBERS.

Barrett, Rev. Thomas, Webster, Mass.
Chase, Rev. John, Brookfield, Mass.

1834–5.

MEMBER.

Lazell, Rev. J. E., Harvard, Mass.

1835–6.

DIRECTORS.

Foster, Rev. E., Amesbury, Mass.
Freeman, Rev. E. W., Lowell, Mass.
Jacobs, Rev. Bela, Cambridge, Mass.

MEMBER.

Martin, Rev. A. R., Staten Island, N. Y.

1836–7.

DIRECTOR.

Trask, Rev. Wm. G., Taunton, Mass.

1837–8.

DIRECTOR.

Davis, Rev. Gustavus F., Hartford, Ct.

MEMBERS.

Blain, Miss Mary E., Syracuse, N. Y.
Holroyd, Rev. John, Danvers, Mass.
Kitts, Rev. T. J., Philadelphia.

Bolles,

Blain,
Hubbe
Shepp

Chesm
Hamm
Shute,

Chapla
Dodge,
Huntin
McAlli
Nourse
Stearn
Willia
Willia

Brown

Colgat
Eaton,
Hill, F
Leonar

1843-4.

DIRECTORS.

Cooper, Thomas, Eatonton, Geo.
Linsley, Rev. James H., Stratford, Ct.
Middleton, Rev. John, Geneva, N. Y.

MEMBERS.

Pickins, Mrs. Margaret Eliza, Edgefield, S. C.
Rankin, Henry, Reading, Pa.
Wasson, J. G., Albany, N. Y.

1844-5.

DIRECTORS.

Armstrong, Rev. John, Columbus, Miss.
Coolidge, James D., Madison, N. Y.
Going, Rev. Jonathan, D.D., Granville, O.
Miller, Rev. Wm. George, Essex, Ct.

MEMBERS.

Adams, Mrs. Mary, New York.
Belden, Charles D., New York.
Birdsall, Rev. John O., Perrysburg, O.
Carney, Richard, Portsmouth, Va.
McIntosh, Mrs. Mary, Philadelphia.

1845-6.

MEMBERS.

Cauldwell, Mrs. Maria, New York.
Hall, Rev. Wilson, Beaufort, S. C.
Jones, Mrs. J. Leavitt, Bankok, Siam.
Lathrop, Rev. Lebbeus, Samptown, N. J.
Marshall, Joseph H., Nashville, Tenn.
Mitchell, Rev. John, Hoosick, N. Y.
Randall, Mrs. Mary E., Woburn, Mass.
Reynolds, Joseph, Norwich, Ct.

1846-7.

DIRECTORS.

Bacheller, Mrs. Mary, Lynn, Mass.
Devan, Mrs. Lydia, Canton, China.
Everts, Rev. Jeremiah B., Washington, N. Y.

MEMBERS.

Cooper, Mrs. Eliza A., New York.
Lee, Mrs. Oilve, North Bristol, N. Y.
Rose, Richard, Parham's Store, Va.
Thurston, Rev. Peter, New York.

1847-8.

DIRECTORS.

Martin, John J., Montgomery, N. Y.
Orr, Rev. David, Reed's Creek, Ark.
Parkinson, Rev. William, New York.
Peck, Rev. Philetus B., Owego, N. Y.
Tryon, Rev. Wm. M., Houston, Texas.

MEMBERS.

Colby, Joseph, New London, N. H.
Evans, Rev. George, Manchester, N. H.
Gilbert, Joshua, New York.
Jeter, Mrs. Sarah A., Richmond, Va.
Leaver, Rev. Thomas, Newport, R. I.
Peck, Mrs. Sarah, New Woodstock, N. Y.
Peck, Rev. Linus M., Hamilton, N. Y.
Van Loon, Rev. Charles, Poughkeepsie, N. Y.
Wilson, Edwin C., Elizabeth City, N. C.
Wood, John, Hertford, N. C.

1848-9.

DIRECTORS.

Benedict, Rev. George, New York.
Child, George, New York.

MEMBERS.

Allen, Mrs. Eliza C., New York.
Brouner, Rev. Jacob H., New York.
Chamberlin, Hinds, Leroy, N. Y.
Jencks, Mrs. Caroline B., Bankok, Siam.
Ludlam, John H., New York.
Naylor, Rev. J. G., Portsmouth, N. H.
Peck, Rev. Abijah, Clifton Park, N. Y.
Shaw, Oliver, Providence, R. I.
Wayland, Rev. F., Sr., Saratoga Springs, N. Y.
Wildman, Rev. Daniel, Lebanon, Ct.
Williams, Rev. Daniel, New York.

1849-50.

DIRECTORS.

Allen, Rev. Ira M., New York.
Bradford, Rev. Z., Providence, R. I.
Estes, Rev. Elliott, Lower Three Runs, S. C.
Milbank, Charles W., New York.
Peck, Rev. John, New Woodstock, N. Y.
Train, Rev. Charles, Framingham, Mass.
Wilson, James, New York.

MEMBERS.

Baillie, Jonathan, Parham's Store, Va.
Barker, Rev. Luke, M.D., New York.
Brockway, C., Broadalbin, N. Y.
Brown, William, Parham's Store, Va.
Cate, Rev. George W., Barre, Mass.
Corning, Mrs. Nancy, Brooklyn, N. Y.
Cox, Charles, Rahway, N. J.
Crawford, Rev. D. B., Antioch, Miss.
Forrester, James M., New York.
Gale, Mrs. Phebe, East Bennington, Vt.
Harris, Rev William, Nassau, N. Y.
Lewis, Rev. D. D., New Brunswick, N. J.
Lyman, Nathan, Andover, Ct.
Payne, Mrs. Betsey, Hamilton, N. Y.
Rogers, Rev. John, Paterson, N. J.
Roy, Rev. Wm. A., Charlotteville, Va.
Winchell, Rev. Reuben, Lockport, N. Y.
Yancey, Algernon, Yanceyville, N. C.

1850-1.

DIRECTORS.

Granberry, Rev. N. R., Meridian Springs, Miss.
Graves, Rev. Hiram A., Boston, Mass.
Judson, Rev. A., D.D., Maulmain, Burmah.

MEMBERS.

Bennett, Rev. Alfred, Homer, N. Y.
Bond, Levi, Windsor, N. C.
Briggs, Rev. Ebenezer, Middleboro', Mass.
Burdick, Miss E. M., New York.
Burke, Joshua A., Brooklyn, N. Y.
Cook, Rev. B., Jr., Jewett City, Ct.
Cornelius, Mrs. Rachel, Mount Holly, N. J.
Darrow, Rev. Francis, Waterford, Ct.
Davis, W., Strebane, N. C.
Frey, Rev. J. C. F., Pontiac, Mich.
Going, Mrs. Lucy T., Columbus, O.
Horn, Turner, Britton's ✠ Roads, N. C.
Humphrey, Mrs. Julia Ann, Albany, N. Y.
Jackson, Rev. Timothy, Piqua, O.
Kelly, Mrs. Elizabeth, New York.
Kendall, Josiah, Littleton, Mass.
Logan, Rev. John, Blandenville, Ill.
Lester, David, Brooklyn, N. Y.
McLaren, Finley, Le Roy, N. Y.
Munn, Mrs. Sarah P., New York.

Merritt, Rev. W. H., Chapel Hill, N. C.
Sherman, Rev. O. J., Peoria, Ill.

MEMBERS.

Anderson, J. S., Stonington, Ct.
Bolles, Rev. D. C., Southbridge, Mass.
Chase, Amos, Haverhill, Mass.
De Graffenried, Mrs. S., Crosbyville, S. C.
Downing, J., Colerain, N. C.
Farnsworth, Rev. B. F., Nashville, Tenn.
Gibbs, Mrs. Betsey H., Sullivan, N. H.
Goodell, A., Somersworth, N. H.
Hall, Rev. Daniel, New York.
Jones, Mrs. Susan, Newbern, N. C.
Lathrop, Mrs. Jane E., New York.
Manning, Rev. Benjamin, Brookfield, Mass.
Martin, Mrs. R. W., New York.
Miller, John B., Sumterville, S. C.
Morrill, Otis H., Lowell, Mass.
Remington, Mrs. Eliza Ann, New York.
Rider, Miss Olive P., Suffield, Ct.
Shuck, Mrs. Eliza G., Shanghai, China.
Stone, Mrs. Sarah, A., New York.
Tucker, Mrs. Levi, Boston, Mass.
Whitman, Rev. S. S., Madison, Wis.

1852-3.

DIRECTORS.

Brown, Rev. O. B., Washington, D. C.
Crozer, Miss Sallie K., Chester, Pa.
Miller, Pardon, Providence.
Rhees, Rev. M. J., D.D., Williamsburg, N. Y.

MEMBERS.

Adams, Mrs. Cornelia C., Cleveland, O.
Ashley, Mrs. Hannah, Poultney, Vt.
Bellamy, Mrs. Eliza, Arcadia, N. Y.
Boynton, Mrs. Ruth, North Springfield, Vt.
Brown, Mrs. O. B., Washington, D. C.
Carraway, Mrs. H., Kingston, N. C.
Conner, Rev. Henry, Lyndon, Ill.
Fant, Rev. Ephraim, Habelville, S. C.
Goodliff, James, New York.
Haskell, Rev. Daniel, Hamilton, N. Y.
Haynes, Rev. Arus, M.D., New York.

Hill, Mrs. Matilda Pierce, Albany, N. Y.
Hill, Mrs. Lydia Ann, Carmel, N. Y.
Judson, Mrs. Emily C., Hamilton, N. Y.
Miner, Rev. Bradley, Providence, R. I.
Neale, Mrs. Melissa Y., Boston.
Oakley, Mrs. Cassandra, New York.
Pennypacker, John, Wilmington, Del.
Porter, Edwin, Lowell, Mass.
Richards, Rev. Humphrey, Dorchester, Mass.
Richards, Mrs. Eunice J., Dorchester, Mass.
Rodgers, Rev. Ebenezer, Upper Alton, Ill.
Sharp, J. Milton, Williamsburg, N. Y.
Skinner, Mrs. Anna, Hertford, N. C.
Spencer, Rev. Horace, Reed's Corners, N. Y.
Spivey, Aaron J., Brownsville, Tenn.
Sweet, H. H., Fredonia, N. Y.
Taylor, Daniel Webster, New York.
Walker, Mrs. Jane P., Central Falls, R. I.
Waterbury, Rev. J. H., Elizabethtown, N. J.
Willard, Hon. Levi, Keene, N. H.

1855-6.

DIRECTORS.

Cone, Rev. Spencer H., D.D., New York.
Choules, Rev. J. O., D.D., Newport, R. I.
Crane, James C. Richmond, Va.
Germond, George C. Williamsburg, N. Y.
Ives, Mrs. Hope, Providence, R. I.
Morse, Jacob, Sturbridge, Mass.
Munn, Stephen B., New York.
Pratt, Rev. D. D., Nashua, N. H.
Purser, Thomas, Brooklyn, N. Y
Shaw, Thomas, Boston, Mass.

MEMBERS.

Ballard, Rev. John B., New York.
Belden, Rev. A. R., Iowa City, Iowa.
Bishop, William, Bloomington, Ill.
Bottum, Hon. N. H., Shaftsbury, Vt.
Brayton. Philip, Phenix, R. I.
Calam, Mrs. Mary N., Sing Sing, N. Y.
Challis, John, Salem, N. J.
Clapp, Mrs. Jane M., Danbury, Ct.
Colver, Mrs. Esther B., Worcester, Mass.
Cox, Miss Achsah, Imlaystown, N. J.
Davis, Rev. Jonathan, Monticello, S. C.
Davis, Rev. Joseph, Hebron, O.
Edwards, Miss Mary, New York.
English, Isaac, Salem, N. J.
Evans, Mrs. Mary, New York.
Fish, Rev. Elisha P., Haddam, Mass.
Hardin, Rev. Theodore, Horton, N. Scotia.
Harris, Isaac, New London, Ct.
Hazard, Simeon, Newport, R. I.
Hedden, Mrs. C. F., Manchester, N. H.
Hunt, Dr. George, Le Clair, Ill.
Jones, Mrs. Rhoda, Smithville, N. Y.
Leland, Mrs. Caroline M., Brooklyn, N. Y.
Logan, Rev. John, Blandensville, Ill.
Mangam, Mrs. Sarah Ann, New York.
Miller, John B., Sumpterville, S. C.
Miner, Rev. Cyrus, Attica, N. Y.
Nelson, Rev. Caleb, Omego Creek, N. Y.
Nice, Rev. W J., Imlaystown, N. J.
Nichols, Miss Hannah, Bridgeport, Ct.
Purser, Mrs. Mary, Brooklyn, N. Y.
Richards, Joel, Claremont, N. H.
Richmond, Rev. J. L., Indianapolis, Ia.
Scott, Rev. James, Newburg, N. Y.
Sheppard, Rev. Wm., Bridgeton, N. J.
Sheppard, Joseph, Bridgeton, N. J.
Smith, Z. L., Norwich, Ct.
Steadman, Rev. N. V., Evansville, Ia.
Stickney, Samuel, Watertown, Mass.
Sutton, George, New York.
Teasdale, Rev. John, St. Louis, Mo.
Thomas, Moses, Ballston Spa, N. Y.
Thornton, Rev. V. R., Public Square, Geo.
Tubbs, Benj. H., West Dedham, Mass.
West, John, Brooklyn, N. Y.
Whitman, Hiram, Belvidere, Ill.
Wheeler, Nelson, Providence, R. I.
Wyckoff, Rev. Cornelius P., Weedsport, N. Y.

1856-7.

DIRECTORS.

Clarke, Rev. Elbert W., Arcade, N. Y.,
Colgate, William, New York.
Collom, Rev. J. G., Mt. Holly, N. J.
Conant, John, Brandon, Vt.
Cramb, Rev. Augustus B., Metamora, Ill.
Flanders, Benjamin, Brooklyn, N. Y.
Granger, Rev. J. N., D.D., Providence, R. I.
Kelly, Samuel R., Brooklyn, N. Y.
Wightman, Rev. F., Wethersfield, Ct.

MEMBERS.

Beebe, Alexander M., L L.D., Utica, N. Y.
Capern, Thomas, Moorestown, N. J.
Cone, Miss Amelia M., Philadelphia.
Danforth, Rev. G. F., South Dartmouth, Mass.
Edmond, Mrs. Emily S., Brookline, Mass.
Farnsworth, W., Fleming, N. Y.
Forsyth, Russell, Albany, N. Y.
Graham, James C., Jerseyville, Ill.
Guest, Rev. Pitney, Canton, O.
Green, Rev. Jonathan R., Derby, Vt.
Hayes, Seth, Colchester, Ct.
Harvey, Rev. Nathaniel, Westboro', Mass.
Hovey, Mrs. Elizabeth, Cambridge, Mass.
Ingals, Rev. Lovell, Akyab, Arracan.
Kain, Charles, Marlton, N. J.
Martin, Stelle R., Rahway, N. J.
Marsh, Rev. L. G., New York.
Marshall, Rev. Andrew, Savannah, Geo.
Marshall, William, Fitchburg, Mass.
Miller, Rev. Harvey, Meriden, Ct.
Perego, Mrs. Margaret, New York.
Phillips, Samuel B., M.D., New York.
Silliman, Rev. Gershom, Helena, Ill.
Smith, Mrs. Hannah B., Iowa City, Iowa.
Thomas, Thomas, New York.
Underhill, Rev. Charles H., Peekskill, N. Y.
Walker, Mrs. Grace W., Marcus Hook, Pa.
Woodruff, David, Bridgeton, N. J.

1857-8.

DIRECTORS.

Chaplin, Rev. Adoniram J., Bennington, Vt.
Dale, Rev. Harvey S., Lebanon, Ohio.
Farquharson, Rev. James, Warren Me.
Hatt, Rev. Josiah, Morristown, N. J.
Peck, Rev. John M., D. D., Shiloh, Ill.
Seaver, Rev. Horace, New York.
Welch, Rev. J. C., Providence, R. I.

MEMBERS.

Archibald, Rev. Thomas H., Factory Point, Vt.
Ashley, Elisha, Poultney, Vt.
Barnhurst, Joseph, Sr. Francisville, Pa.
Benton, John, Saratoga, N. Y.
Brown, Mrs. Prudencia, Middletown, N. J.
Corning, Ephraim, Brooklyn, N. Y.
Cox, John W., Mt. Holly, N. J.
Crosby, Nathaniel, Janesville, Wis.
Cornwell, Rev. William E. Princeton, N. J.
Demming, Levi L., Honesdale, Pa.
Dunlap, Mrs. Eliza, New York.
Ellis, Mrs. Mary, Norwalk, Ct.
Farnsworth, Hon. J. D., Fairfax, Vt.
Fish, Rev. Elisha P., Haddam, Ct.
Fuller, Mrs. Achsah Smith, Pike, N. Y.
Gilbert, J. B., Hartford, Ct.
Grafton, Rev. Benj. C., Cambridge, Mass.

LIST OF DECEASED DIRECTORS AND MEMBERS FOR LIFE.

Hall, Herbert, New York.
Harmon, Mrs. Elizabeth, North Bennington, Vt.
Hayden, Mrs. Caroline S., New London, N. H.
Healy, Ebenezer, Sennett, N. Y.
Irons, Rev. Asah, Sheriden, N. Y.
Jerrard, Rev. Richard, Fond du Lac, Wis.
Kingman, Henry W., New York.
Lewis, Rev. Lester, Middletown, Ct.
McCormick, Richard C., New York.
Mallary, Rev. S. S., Pawtucket, R. I.
Marshall, William, Fitchburg, Mass.
Mason, Mrs. Sarah R., Chelsea, Mass.
Mears, Elijah, Boston, Mass.
Miles, Rev. George I., Muscatine, Iowa.
Mulford, Mrs. Phebe, Roadstown, N. J.
Plumer, John, Goffstown Centre, N. H.
Powell, Miss. Sarah P., Davenport, Iowa.
Rand, Rev. Thomas, Ireland, Mass.
Reed, Rev. James, Hamburg, N. Y.
Richards, William H., Philadelphia.
Russell, Rev. Caleb, Upper Middleton, Pa.
Sarles, Mrs. Cornelia A., Brooklyn, N. Y.
Scribner, Samuel T., Danbury, Ct.
Seeley, Mrs. Agnes Jane, New Frin, Ill.
Southworth, Mrs. James E., Brooklyn, N. Y.
Taylor, Rev. David, Terre Haute, Ia.
Thompson, Rev. Richard, Milton, Ct.
Todd, Mrs. William W., New York.
True, Osgood, Plainfield, N. H.
True, Reuben, Plainfield, N. H.
Twiss, Rev. Daniel F., Spottswood, N. J.
Van Valkenburgh, John, Williamsburg, N. Y.
Weston, Mrs. Hetty, Lynn, Mass.
Weston, Mrs. Henry G., Peoria, Ill.
Wightman, Rev. J. G., Groton, Ct.
Wilcox, Mrs. Louisa S., Trenton, N. J.
Withington, Elijah, Morrisania, N. Y.
Winans, Elnathan, Lima, N. Y.
Wright, Mrs. Abigail, North Lyme, Ct.

TWENTY-SEVENTH REPORT

OF THE

AMERICAN BAPTIST HOME MISSION SOCIETY,

PRESENTED BY THE

EXECUTIVE BOARD

AT THE

ANNIVERSARY HELD IN NEW YORK,

MAY 13, 14 AND 15, 1859;

WITH

THE TREASURER'S REPORT AND OTHER DOCUMENTS.

NEW YORK:
PUBLISHED AT THE AMERICAN BAPTIST HOME MISSION ROOMS, No. 115 NASSAU STREET,
AND PRINTED BY THOMAS HOLMAN, CORNER CENTRE AND WHITE STS.
1859.

ACT OF INCORPORATION.

AN ACT TO INCORPORATE THE AMERICAN BAPTIST HOME MISSION SOCIETY, PASSED APRIL 12, 1843, AND AMENDED FEBRUARY 9, 1849.

The People of the State of New York, represented in Senate and Assembly, do enact as follows:

§ 1. All such persons as now are, or may hereafter become members of the American Baptist Home Mission Society, formed in the City of New York, in the year one thousand eight hundred and thirty-two, shall be, and hereby are constituted a body corporate, by the name of the American Baptist Home Mission Society, for the purpose of promoting the preaching of the Gospel in North America.

§ 2. This corporation shall be capable of taking, holding, or receiving any property, real or personal, by virtue of any devise or bequest contained in any last will or testament of any person whomsoever, the clear annual income of which devise or bequest shall not exceed the sum of ten thousand dollars; Provided, no person leaving a wife, or child, or parent, shall devise or bequeath said Corporation more than one-fourth of his or her estate, after the payment of his or her debts; and such devise or bequest shall be valid to the extent of such one-fourth, and no such deviso or bequest shall be valid in any will which shall not have been made and executed at least two months before the death of the testator; and provided that no verbal mistake in the name of the said Corporation shall invalidate any gift, grant, devise, or legacy intended for it. The net income of said Society, arising from their real estate, shall not exceed the sum of ten thousand dollars annually.

§ 3. This Corporation shall possess the general powers, and be subjected to the provisions contained in title third of chapter eighteen of the first part of the Revised Statutes, so far as the same are applicable and have not been repealed.

§ 4. This Act shall take effect immediately.

§ 5. The Legislature may at any time modify or repeal this Act.

CONSTITUTION.

NAME.

I.—This Society shall be called the AMERICAN BAPTIST HOME MISSION SOCIETY.

OBJECT.

II.—The object of this Society shall be to promote the preaching of the Gospel in North America.

MEMBERSHIP.

III.—The Society shall be composed of Annual Delegates, Life Members, and Life Directors. Any Baptist Church, in union with the denomination, may appoint a delegate for an annual contribution of ten dollars, and an additional delegate for each additional thirty dollars. Thirty dollars shall be requisite to constitute a Member for Life, and one hundred dollars, paid at one time, or a sum which, in addition to any previous contribution, shall amount to one hundred dollars, shall be requisite to constitute a Director for Life.

OFFICERS.

IV.—The officers of the Society shall be a President, two Vice-Presidents, a Treasurer, two Auditors, Secretaries of Correspondence and a Recording Secretary, whom the Society shall annually elect by ballot.

MANAGERS AND EXECUTIVE BOARD.

V.—The Officers and Life Directors shall meet immediately after the Annual Meeting of the Society, and elect fifteen Managers, residing in the City of New York, or its vicinity, who together with the Treasurer, Auditors, and the Secretaries, shall constitute an Executive Board to conduct the business of the Society; and shall respectively continue to discharge their official duties until superseded by a new election. Seven members of the Board shall be a quorum for the transaction of business.

POWERS AND DUTIES OF THE EXECUTIVE BOARD.

VI.—The Executive Board, shall have power to appoint its own meetings; elect its own Chairman and Recording Secretary; enact its own By-Laws and Rules of Order, provided always, that they be not inconsistent with this Constitution; fill any vacancies which may occur in their own body, or in the offices of the Society during the year; and, if deemed necessary by two-thirds of the members present at a regular meeting, convene special meetings of the Society. They shall establish such Agencies as the interests of the Society may require; appoint Agents and Missionaries; fix their compensation; direct and instruct them concerning their particular fields and labors; make all appropriations to be paid out of the treasury; and present to the Society, at each annual meeting, a full report of their proceedings during the current year.

DESIGNATED FUNDS.

VII.—All moneys or other property contributed and designated for any particular Missionary field or purpose, shall be so appropriated, or returned to the donors, or their lawful agents.

TREASURER.

VIII.—The Treasurer shall give bonds to such amount as the Executive Board shall think proper.

ELIGIBILITY TO APPOINTMENT.

IX.—All the Officers, Managers, Missionaries, and Agents of the Society, shall be members in good standing in regular Baptist Churches.

ANNUAL MEETING.

X.—The Society shall meet annually at such time and place as the Executive Board shall appoint.

ALTERATIONS OF THE CONSTITUTION.

XI.—No alteration of this Constitution shall be made without an affirmative vote of two-thirds of the members present at an annual meeting; nor unless the same shall have been proposed in writing, and the proposition sustained by a majority vote, at a previous annual meeting, or recommended by the Executive Board.

STATED MEETINGS FOR 1859-60.

OF THE EXECUTIVE BOARD.—Thursday before the first Wednesday in each month, at four o'clock P. M., during the Summer months; at three P. M., in the Winter months; and half-past three P. M., in the Fall and Spring months.

OF THE COMMITTEE ON MISSIONS.—The day previous to that of the Board, at three o'clock P. M.

OF THE COMMITTEE ON AGENCIES AND FINANCE.—The Tuesday preceding, at four o'clock P. M., in the Summer months; and at three P M., in the Winter months.

OF THE COMMITTEE ON CHURCH EDIFICE FUND.—The Monday preceding, at half-past nine A. M.

BY-LAWS OF THE BOARD.

1. All meetings shall be opened with prayer.
2. All Committees shall be nominated by the presiding officer, and approved by the Executive Board unless otherwise specially ordered.
3. No moneys shall be paid out of the Treasury, but by order of the Executive Board.
4. All resolutions, if required, shall be presented in writing.
5. Whenever a vacancy occurs in the Executive Board, the fact shall be entered on the Minutes and at the next stated meeting the Board shall proceed to fill such vacancy by ballot.

ORDER OF BUSINESS.

1. Reading the Minutes of the last Meeting.
2. Treasurer's Report.
3. Communications of Secretaries of Cor.
4. Reports of Standing Committees.
5. Reports of Select Committees.
6. Unfinished Business.
7. New Business.

STANDING COMMITTEES.

AGENCIES AND FINANCE.	MISSIONS.	CHURCH EDIFICE FUND.
S. Sheldon, *Ch'n.*	E. E. L. Taylor, *Ch'n.*	H. P. Freeman, *Ch'n.*
Richard Stout, *Sec.*	Wheelock H. Parmly, *Sec.*	J. B. Peck, *Sec.*
L. Ballard,	A. D. Gillette,	S. K. Wightman,
Z. Ring,	M. G. Hodge,	F. S. Miner,
E. Cauldwell,	J. S. Holme,	D. M. Wilson.
J. E. Southworth.	H. G. Weston.	

LEGACIES.

A. B. Capwell, H. C. Fish, B. M. Hill.

MINUTES OF THE TWENTY-SEVENTH ANNIVERSARY

OF THE

American Baptist Home Mission Society,

Held in New York, May 13, 14, and 15, 1859.

The American Baptist Home Mission Society met in the meeting-house of the Calvary Baptist Church, New York City, at half-past ten o'clock, A. M., May 13, 1859.

The President, John P. Crozer, Esq., called the Society to order; and after a song of praise, prayer was offered by Rev. Thomas Roberts, N. J., and the President delivered an interesting introductory address.

The following committees were appointed, upon the nomination of the President:

On Credentials of Delegates.—Hon. J. M. Linnard, Pa.; Rev. O. Tracy, N. H.; Rev. J. W. Parkhurst, Mass.; Rev. James S. Ladd, N. Y.; Rev. Thomas Powell, Iowa.

On Nomination of Officers.—Rev. Edward Lathrop, D.D., N. Y.; Rev. M. G. Hodge, N. Y.; Rev. R. Babcock, D.D., N. J.; Rev. C. Willett, Wis.; Thos. Wattson, Esq., Pa.

On Life Directors and Life Members.—Rev. Lemuel Porter, D.D., Mass.; Rev. Harrison Daniels, N. Y.; Rev. Wm. H. Parmly, N. J.; Wm. H. Munn, Esq., N. Y.; Rev. S. D. Phelps, D.D., Ct.

On motion of Rev. Wm. H. Parmly, N. J., it was

Resolved, That ministers and other brethren present, not members of the Society, be invited to participate in our deliberations.

The invitation was accepted by Rev. S. Boothby, Lewiston, Me.; Rev. F. Daman, Bow, N. H.; Rev. Wm. N. Wilbur, Saxton River, Vt.; Rev. D. F. Carnahan, Ohio Baptist Convention; Rev. John Rounds, New Gloucester, Me.; Rev. L. F. Ames, N. Y.; Rev. A. F. Shanefelt, White Hall, Pa.

On motion of Rev. R. Babcock, D.D., N. J., the following were fixed as the times of commencing and closing the sessions of the Society, viz.:

To commence at half-past nine, A. M.; at half-past two and half-past seven o'clock, P. M., and to close at one and five o'clock, P. M.

The Report of the Treasurer was read by Ebenezer Cauldwell, Esq., N. Y., Treasurer, which was accepted and ordered to be printed with the Annual Report.

On motion of Rev. D. B. Cheney, Pa., the Committee on Nominations of Officers were directed to present their report in the form of a printed ballot, and the election of officers of the Society was made the special order for half-past eleven o'clock, A. M., to-morrow.

Rev. B. M. Hill, D.D., Secretary of Correspondence, then read portions of the Annual Report of the Executive Board, when

On motion of Rev. J. C. Stockbridge, Mass., the further reading of the Report of the Executive Board was suspended, for the purpose of bringing before the Society business of importance, to be presented for their action.

The Secretary of Correspondence thereupon presented a communication from the Executive Board, recommending certain alterations of the Constitution, as follows:

First—In the fourth article, so as to provide for *two Auditors*, instead of one, and "*a Corresponding Secretary*" instead of "Secretaries of Correspondence."

Second—That in the fifth article, the word "Auditor" be made plural, so as to correspond with the above.

Third—That in the seventh article, the words *or purpose* be inserted immediately after the words "missionary field."

The hour of adjournment having arrived, after prayer by Rev. J. C. Harrison, D.D., N. Y., the Society adjourned.

AFTERNOON SESSION.

After singing, prayer was offered by Rev. J. L. Hodge, D.D., Ct.

The committee of Conference appointed at the last annual meeting to act jointly with committees from other Societies, made a verbal report through Rev. E. E. L. Taylor, D.D., to the effect that nothing had been done, principally in consequence of the decease of Isaac Newton, Chairman of the joint committees.

The report was accepted, and the committee discharged from the further consideration of the subject referred to them.

On motion of Rev. M. G. Hodge—

Resolved, That the recommendations of the Board, touching changes in the Constitution, be referred to a committee of five, to report as soon as practicable during this session.

The amendments to the Constitution were then taken up, and the amendment of the fourth Article, striking out the words "*an Auditor*" and inserting "*two Auditors,*" was adopted.

Rev. Edward Bright, D.D., moved to refer the second amendment, to change the number of Secretaries of Correspondence to a Corresponding Secretary, back to the Executive Committee, which was carried.

The second amendment, striking out of Article fifth the word "Auditor" and inserting "Auditors," was adopted.

On motion of Rev. R. Jeffery, Pa., it was resolved that the Society now receive a communication from the committee of the Convention recently held in the meeting-house of the Oliver Street Baptist Church, N. Y. Whereupon Rev. C. N. Chandler, N. Y., from the committee, presented a series of resolutions passed by that Convention.

On motion of Rev. Wm. Reid, Ct., the resolutions were laid upon the table for the present.

The hour having arrived, the Society adjourned, after prayer by Rev. W. Shadrach, D.D., Pa.

. . . . Hotchkiss, D.D., of Roche.
and address the Society on this occasion.

The Secretary of Correspondence, R
cluded the reading of the report of the]

When, on motion of Rev. J. C. H
Annual Report was accepted and ordere
direction of the Executive Board.

Addresses were then delivered before
Wm. Cathcart, of Pa., and the Rev. C. V

After prayer by Rev. L. Porter, D
adjourned.

MORNING SESSION

The Society was called to order by t
nine o'clock, A. M. After singing, pr
Rev. George Kempton, N. Y.

The minutes of the session of the pre
approved.

The committee on Life Directors and M
report through Rev. L. Porter, D.D.,
Directors, and 195 Life Members present.

The report was accepted, and the nam
Life Members ordered to be inserted in th

LIFE DIRECTORS.

Alden, Rev. W. H., Lowell, Mass. | Barker, R
Aldrich, Rev. Jonathan, Worcester, Mass.

Covell, Rev. Lemuel, New York.
Davis, Rev. Henry, Columbus, Ohio.
Drake, Rev. S. J., Plainfield, N. J.
Davies, John M., New York.
Dunbar, Rev. Duncan, New York.
Dodge, Rev. O., Brooklyn, N. Y.
Davis, Hon. Isaac, Worcester, Mass.
Dunn, Rev. L. A., Fairfax, Vt.
Draper, Jonathan, North Bennington, Vt.
Eldridge, Rev. Daniel, Shushan, N. Y.
Everett, Erastus, Brooklyn, N. Y.
Eaton, Rev. Joseph, Benton, Iowa.
Fletcher, Rev. Joshua, Southington, Ct.
Foster, Rev. Joseph C., Beverly, Mass.
Fuller, Rev. E. K., Reading, Mass.
Gibbs, Rev. J. W., Brooklyn, N. Y.
Grenell, Rev. L. O., Honesdale, Pa.
Gault, George, Brooklyn, N. Y.
Girdwood, Rev. John, New Bedford, Mass.
Gillette, Rev. A. D., D.D., New York.
Gray, Rev. E. H., Shelburne Falls, Mass.
Halstead, Benjamin, Brooklyn, N. Y.
Husted, Rev. W. H., Gerry, N. Y.
Hodges, Rev. Joseph, Cambridge, Mass.
Howard, Rev. Leland, Rutland, Vt.
Hodge, Rev. M. G., Brooklyn, N. Y.
Holme, Rev. J. S., Brooklyn, N. Y.
Ives, Rev. Dwight, D.D., Suffield, Ct.
Lincoln, Rev. H. H., Harlem, N. Y.
Lathrop, Rev. Edward, D.D., New York.
Loxley, Rev. B. R., Philadelphia, Pa.
Linnard, Hon. J. M., Philadelphia, Pa.
Ladd, Rev. J. S., Brooklyn, N. Y.
Larcombe, Richard J., New York.
Middleditch, Rev. R. T., Red Bank, N. J.
Miller, Rev. D. Henry, Meriden, Ct.
Munn, Wm. H., New York.
Miller, John A., Brooklyn, N. Y.
Maclay, Rev. A., D.D., New York.
Malcom, Rev. Howard, D.D., Philadelphia, Pa.
Magoon, Rev. E. L., Albany, N. Y.
Mason, Rev. A. P., Chelsea, Mass.
Mills, Rev. Robert C., Salem, Mass.
Morgan Ebenezer, New London, Ct.
Mickels, Rev. W. S., New York.
Porter, Rev. Lemuel, D.D., Pittsfield, Mass.
Parmly, Rev. W. H. Jersey City, N. J.
Parker, Rev. Carlton, Hebron, Me.
Peltz, Rev. G. A., New York.
Parkhurst, Rev. J. W., Newton Centre, Mass.
Phelps, Rev. S. D., New Haven, Ct.
Peck, J. B., New York.
Pryor, Rev. J., D.D., Cambridge, Mass.
Parker, Rev. S. S., Southbridge, Mass.
Rollinson, Rev. Wm., Rahway, N. J.
Sanford, Rev. Miles, North Adams, Mass.
Stockbridge, Rev. J. C., Boston, Mass.
Sterns, Rev. O. S., Newton Centre, Mass.
Seeley, Rev. John T., Syracuse, N. Y.
Samson, J. K., Brooklyn, N. Y.
Smith, Rev. H. F., Bloomfield, N. J.
Shadrach, Rev. Wm., Philadelphia, Pa.
Taylor, Rev. E. E. L., Brooklyn, N. Y.
Tingley, Rev. T. C., North Scituate, Mass.
Turney, Rev. E., D.D., Cincinnati, Ohio.
Verrinder, Rev. Wm., Jersey City, N. J.
Vogell, Rev. Henry C., Rome, N. Y.
Wattson, Thomas, Philadelphia, Pa.
Webb, Rev. J. S., D.D., New Brunswick, N. J.
Wilder, Rev. Wm., Chester, Pa.
Willett, Rev. Chas., La Crosse, Wis.
White, Rev. Samuel, North Shore, N. Y.
Wright, Rev. Thomas G., Wappingers Falls, N.Y.
Wakeman, Rev. L. H., West Woodstock, Ct.
Wilds, Z. P., Harlem, N. Y.
Wheelock, Rev. S., Fredonia, N. Y.

LIFE MEMBERS.

Adams, Rev. R. J., Wallingford, Ct.
Ainsworth, Rev. S. C., Truxton, N. Y.
Armstrong, Rev. A. Lambertville, N. J.
Adams, Rev. S. W., Cleveland, Ohio.
Adams, Rev. J. M., Croton, N. Y.
Ambler, Rev. J. V., Lanesboro, Mass.
Abbot, Rev. S. B., Bradford, N. H.
Bickford, Rev. M. L., Waltham, Mass.
Belcher, Rev. Jas. Boston, Mass.
Barker, A. J., Taunton, Mass.
Bainbridge, Rev. S. M., Penn Yan, N. Y.
Baker, Rev. Saml., D.D., Williamsburgh, N. Y.
Bills, Rev. G. B. Hollis, N. H.
Barrell, David, Fredonia, N. Y.
Bellamy, Rev. David, Mt. Morris, N. Y.
Burwell, Rev. Ira D., Moriah, N. Y.
Bates, Dennis P., Lowell, Mass.
Brown, Rev. Jos. P., Plainfield, Conn.
Bronson, Rev. A. C., Mystic River, Conn.
Brooks, Rev. W. R., Hamilton, N. Y.
Belden, Rev. Joseph, Bordentown, N. J.
Brown, Rev. A., Concord, N. H.
Baker, Rev. J. James, Plainfield, N. J.
Bullard, Rev. J. A., Penfield, N. Y.
Babcock, Rev. H. S., Homer, N. Y.
Burton, Rev. N. S., Granville, Ohio.
Brown, Rev. Jos., Springfield, Ohio.
Baker, Rev. John H., East Greenwich, R. I.
Bronson, Rev. B. F., Woburn, Mass.
Bell, Rev. E., South Woodstock, Conn.
Brigham, Rev. E. P., Shushan, N. Y.
Burr, J. H., Gloversville, N. Y.
Beman, Mrs. S., N. Y.
Bonham, Rev. J. W., Lowell, Mass.
Brown, Rev. Wm. L., Watertown, Mass.
Cheever, Wm., Westboro', Mass.
Carr, Rev. S. J., Somerset, Mass.
Cummings, Rev. E. E., Concord, N. H.
Clark, Rev. C. A., New York.
Corey, Rev. D. G., Utica, N. Y.
Cauldwell, Susan W., New York.
Crane, Rev. W. J., Middlebury, N. Y.
Chick, Rev. J. M., Grafton, Mass.
Carr, Rev. A. W., Rowley, Mass.
Chase, Rev. G. S., Warren, R. I.
Clark, Rev. G. W., New Market, N. J.
Chesshire, Rev. John E., Keeseville, N. Y.
Carpenter, Rev. C. G., Elbridge, N. Y.
Church, Rev. Leroy, Chicago, Ill.
Capwell, A., B., Brooklyn, N. Y.
Clark, Rev. N. Judson, Philadelphia, Pa.
Clark, Mrs. N. Judson, Philadelphia, Pa.
Clark, Alfred, Matheun, Mass.
Colver, Rev. Charles K., Charlestown, Mass.
Drake, J. C., Westfield, N. Y.
Denison, Rev. A. E. Clinton, Conn.
Dey, Rev. Arthur, Half-Moon, N. Y.
Denike, Abraham, N. Y.
Dimmock, Rev. A. B., East Haddam, Ct.
Daniels, Rev. H., Wyoming, N. Y.
Dean, Rev. W., D.D., Wyoming, N. Y.
Duncan, Rev. John, Boston, Mass.
Deitz, Rev. Charles M., Imlaystown, N. J.
Duncan, Hon. James H., Haverhill, Mass.
Eaton, Rev. Geo. W., Hamilton, N. Y.
Everett, Rev. W. P., Williamsburg, N. Y.
Eddy, Rev. H. J., Bloomington, Ill.
Edwards, Rev. B. A., Plymouth, Mass.
Fox, Rev. Norman, Schenectady, N. Y.
Fletcher, Rev. H., Townshend, Vt.
Fox, Rev. C. A., Waverly, Pa.
Fitz, Rev. Wm., Hartford, Conn.
Faunce, Rev. D. W., Worcester, Mass.
Griffith, Rev. B., Philadelphia, Pa.
Goodwin, Rev. Thomas, Pemberton, N. J.
Grimley, Rev. Joseph J., Unionville, N. Y.
Gonsalves, Rev. M. J., Cal.
Gilbert, Rev. J. H., Bristol, Ct.

Horr, George E., Chicopee, Mass.
Hall, Rev. W. S., N. Y.
Hill, Philip E., Bridgewater, Mass.
Hutson, Rev. J. C., D.D., Kingston, N. Y.
Hopper, Rev. Andrew, Willington, N. J.
Hedden, Rev. Wm. D., Orange, N. J.
Haskell, Rev. A., Yates, N. Y.
Hartwell, Rev. F., New Baltimore, N. Y.
Huntington, Rev. J., North Bennington, Vt.
Ingalls, Charles, Methuen, Mass.
Johnson, Elias, Troy, N. Y.
Jeffery, Rev. R., Philadelphia, Pa.
Jenkins, Rev. J. S., Philadelphia, Pa.
Keely, Rev. Thomas E., South Danvers, Mass.
Kalloch, Rev. I. S., Boston, Mass.
Kempsey, Rev. M. C., Jersey City, N. J.
Love, John, New York.
Levy, Rev. E. M., Newark, N. J.
Lamson, Rev. William, D.D., Portsmouth, N. H.
Moore, Rev. George C., Maryborough, Can.
Mallory, Rev. J., Newtown, Ct.
Maul, Rev. Wm., Greenwich, Ct.
McKean, Rev. John A., Philadelphia.
Mason, Rev. J., Union Village, N. Y.
Moore, Rev. D., Le Roy, N. Y.
Meech, Rev. W. W., Long Plain, Mass.
Metcalf, Rev. W., Nunda, N. Y.
Morris, Rev. David, Cross River, N. Y.
Matthews, Rev. George, Seekonk, Mass.
Mason, Pethuel, Somerville, N. J.
Murphy, Rev. John R., Marlton, N. J.
Miller, Lydia A., Bedford, N. Y.
McDonald, Alexander, Williamsburgh, N. Y.
Odell, Jonathan, Yonkers, N. Y.
Osgood, Rev. S. M., Philadelphia, Pa.
Olney, Rev. L. W., Castile, N. Y.
Parker, J. R., Fredonia, N. Y.
Pasco, Rev. Cephas, North Egremont, Mass.
Pease, Rev. Wm. A., Haddam, Ct.
Putnam, Rev. H. C., Point Pleasant, Pa.
Parkhurst, Mrs. M. W., Newton Centre, Mass.
Powell, Rev. Thomas, Davenport, Iowa.

Raynor
Stowell
Sheldon
Smith,
Smith,
Scott, I
Slater,
Seeley,
Sawin,
Swick,
Slater,
Stelle,
Swaim
Sherw
Stimso
Seabro
Seeley,
Smith,
Spauld
Spinni
Story,
Storer
Sunde
Tolma
Tripp,
Tracy,
Titus,
Votey
Vassa
Westo
Wells,
Welch
Watso
Whipp
Wilde
Walke
Wilso
Walke
Wrigl
Webst
Youn
Yerke

The Committee on *Credentials of Del*
Rev. S. T. Rogers as a delegate from t
N. Y., on the payment of ten dollars

Rev. A. H. Burlingham, N. Y., offered the following:

Resolved, That in view of the manifest desire for changes in our constitution on the part of many in this Society, a committee of five be raised to consider what amendments to the constitution are desirable, and report during this session, that if approved by the majority of this body, they may be entered upon the Minutes, to be acted upon at the next annual meeting.

On motion of Rev. Nathaniel Colver, D.D., Ohio, the communication from the Oliver Street Convention was taken from the table, and referred to the same committee.

Hon. P. P. Runyon, of N. J., offered the following resolution, viz.:

Resolved, That a committee of five be appointed to inquire into any possible means or methods, by which the operations of this Society may be invigorated and extended. The inquiry of the committee to include the matter of any existing impediments in the way of such onward movement, to report at the present session.

The resolution was unanimously adopted, and the following committee appointed, viz.:—John M. Davies, Esq., N. Y.; Hon. P. P. Runyon, N. J.; Wm. Bucknell, Esq., Pa.; Rev. L. Porter, D.D., Mass.; Rev. H. G. Weston, N. Y.

The hour of half-past eleven having arrived, the special order was taken when, the committee on Nomination of Officers presented their report of names of persons to fill the various offices provided for in the constitution of the Society.

The following tellers were appointed by the President, viz.: Rev. C. K. Colver, Mass.; Rev. L. Porter, D.D., Mass.; E. K. Fuller, Vt.; Rev. John Girdwood, Mass.; who subsequently reported the following persons duly elected officers, viz.: (See page 15.)

The President nominated the following committee of five upon Amendments to the Constitution: Rev. Edward Lathrop, D.D., N. Y.; Hon. J. M. Linnard, Pa.; Hon. J. Warren Merrill, Mass.; Rev. G. S. Webb, D.D., N. J.; Rev. Wm. Dean, D.D., N. Y.

On motion of Rev. Edw. Bright, D.D., N. Y., the committee on Amendments to the Constitution were directed to report at the opening of the afternoon session.

After a song of praise, the Society listened to an address from Rev. Alexander Hamilton, a Missionary of the Society at Appleton, Wis., and also by Rev. Isaac Butterfield, Davenport, Iowa, who stated the embarrassed condition of the Church at that place.

The following resolution was offered by Rev. E. E. L. Taylor, D.D., of N. Y.:

Resolved, That the statements presented by our brother, the Rev. I. Butterfield, relative to the pecuniary condition of the Second Baptist Church in Davenport, Iowa, appeals to the *special* sympathy and *prompt* assistance on the part of the Churches and brethren at the East.

The resolution was unanimously adopted, and pledges of loans and cash received and collected amounting to $1,030.75—$600 loaned, $430.75 given.

The hour of adjournment having arrived, after prayer by Rev. Joseph Walker, of Pa., the Society adjourned.

AFTERNOON SESSION.

The President called the Society to order at half-past one o'clock, P. M. After a song of praise, prayer was offered by Rev. J. W. Kennard, D.D., Pa.

The Committee on Amendments to the Constitution presented their report as follows:

The Committee to suggest changes in the Constitution, to be submitted to the consideration of the Society unanimously present the following:

1. That the third article read as follows:

The Society shall be composed of such persons as shall be members or directors for life, at the time of the adoption of this amended Constitution, and those who are entitled to become such on the completion of payments already commenced for that purpose, and of annual members. Any regular Baptist Church, by contributing to the funds of the Society ten dollars annually may appoint one annual member; for twenty-five dollars, in addition, a second annual member; and an additional annual member for each additional fifty dollars. Individuals, also may, become annual members by the annual payment of ten dollars.

2. That the fourth article be so altered as to provide for one or more Corresponding Secretaries, instead of "Secretaries of Correspondence." And that the words, "whom the Society shall annually elect by ballot," be stricken out.

3. That the fifth article read as follows:

There shall be twelve managers, also, residing in the city of New York or its vicinity, who shall be divided by lot among themselves into two classes of six members each. The term of service of the first class shall expire in one year, and that of the second class in two years. At each annual meeting of the Society after the first *election* under this amended Constitution, one class only shall be elected for the term *of two years*, to the end that the half of the whole number of managers may be annually chosen; provided, however, that vacancies may be filled for the unexpired term. The officers and managers shall be elected by ballot, and continue to discharge their official duties until superseded by a new election.

4. That the words, "The Executive Board," at the commencement of the sixth article, be stricken out, and the following words substituted: "The Treasurer, Auditors, Recording Secretary, and Managers of the Society, shall constitute an Executive Board to conduct the business of the Society; seven of whom shall be a quorum for that purpose." And that the words, "present at a regular meeting," on the fourth and fifth lines of this article, be stricken out.

5. That the tenth article be altered by adding after the words "annually," the words, "for the election of officers and managers, and the transaction of their necessary business."

On motion of A. B. Capwell, Esq., the propositions for amending the Constitution recommended by the Committee, as amended and adopted, were sustained by a majority vote of the Society, and ordered to be entered in the Minutes and presented to the next annual meeting of the Society for their action.

John M. Davies, Esq., presented the report from the Committee on Inquiry, as follows:

Your Committee to whom was referred the question of "What can be done to increase the vigor of the efforts of the American Baptist Home Mission Society," beg leave to report:

Your Committee are gratified to know that the Society stands high in the respect and affections of Christians, and that its affairs have been managed with great fidelity and accuracy since its origin, but it is a matter of regret, when we consider the vastness of the field which it occupies, the number of persons who contribute to its funds, and the pecuniary ability which God has conferred on us as a denomination, that no more has been accomplished. Your Committee believe that greater efficiency is required in the executive department of the Society, and that this great cause, which we love, and in which we are engaged, can be greatly invigorated. They therefore respectfully suggest to this end:

1. That the entire services of the Secretary, who has this day been provisionally secured, be obtained, if possible.

2. That one of the Secretaries occupy the Western part of our country, traveling among the Churches, conducting such correspondence, and rendering such other service as may best promote the interests of Home Missions, and the other Secretary reside in New York, visit Churches and prominent individuals, oversee the editing of the Home Mission Record, secure the services of missionaries, and act with vigor at the rooms.

4. That the question of the sphere of action of the Secretaries be referred to the Executive Board.

5. In case the services of the junior Secretary cannot be obtained, the Board be authorized to fill the vacancy, by some other person until our next annual meeting.

and for their hospitalities on the occasion.

On motion of Joseph H. Reed, Esq.,

Resolved, That in the judgment of this Society dred thousand dollars to carry on its operations the pastors of our Churches be earnestly requested the accomplishment of this design.

The minutes were read and approved,

A. B. CAPWE]

EXECUTIVE BOARD.

OFFICERS.

PRESIDENT.

JOHN P. CROZER, Esq., Chester, Pa.

VICE-PRESIDENTS.

J. E. SOUTHWORTH, Esq., New York.
J. W. MERRILL, Esq., Boston.

TREASURER.

EBENEZER CAULDWELL, Esq., New York.

AUDITORS.

SMITH SHELDON, New York.
RICHARD STOUT, do.

SECRETARIES OF CORRESPONDENCE.

REV. BENJAMIN M. HILL, D.D., New York.
REV. D. B. CHENEY, San Francisco, Cal.

RECORDING SECRETARY.

A. B. CAPWELL, Esq., New York.

MANAGERS.

REV. M. G. HODGE, Brooklyn, *Chairman.*

LOOMIS BALLARD, Brooklyn, N. Y.
REV. H. C. FISH, D.D., Newark, N. J.
REV. E. E. L. TAYLOR, D.D., Brooklyn, N. Y.
S. K. WIGHTMAN, Esq., New York.
REV. W. H. PARMLY, Jersey City, N. J.
H. P. FREEMAN, Williamsburgh, N. Y.
REV. A. D. GILLETTE, D.D., New York.
J. B. PECK, New York.
Z. RING, New York.
REV. J. S. HOLME, Brooklyn, N. Y.
J. E. SOUTHWORTH, Brooklyn, N. Y.
REV. H. G. WESTON, New York.
F. S. MINER, New York.
D. M. WILSON, Newark, N. J.

RECORDING SECRETARY OF THE BOARD, AND CLERK.

JAMES M. WHITEHEAD, New York.

" Cash paid Secretary and Clerks fo
amount there was received fı
Fund $420..................

" Cash paid on account of Church I

" Cash paid for Fuel, Stationery, I
incidental expenses..........

" Cash paid for Paper, Printing an
Mission Record, and incidental ex

" Cash paid for Paper and Printin
Certificates, Blanks, &c........

" Cash paid interest on conditional d

" Cash paid Taxes on Land donated t

" Cash paid for Insurance..........

" Cash paid for Rent of Rooms.......

" Cash paid for Discounts on Uncurre
on Counterfeit Money..........

" Cash paid Anniversary Expenses....

" Cash paid on account of funds retur
the order of the Executive Board

" Cash paid the Grande Ligne Mission,
nation.........................

" Balance...........................

IN ACCOUNT WITH EBENEZER CAULDWELL, TREASURER. *Cr.*

1859.	By Balance as per last Report		$4,459 02
	" Cash received in Contributions, from April 1, 1858, to March 31, 1859	$34,470 17	
	" Cash received in Legacies for the same period	7,188 12	
			41,658 29
	" Cash received for Church Edifice Fund	$1,747 63	
	" Cash received for Interest on Loan	14 00	
			1,761 63
	" Cash received for subscriptions to *Home Mission Record*		1,174 23
	" Cash received for dividends on temporary investments		30 00
	" Cash received for interest from Special Salary Fund		420 00
	" Cash received for interest on Bond and Mortgage, a special investment by direction of the donor		87 50
	" Cash received for interest on investment to cover amount of conditional donations, for which the Society are paying interest		275 67
	" Cash received for Grande Ligne Mission, a special designation		120 00
			$49,986 34
March 31,	By Balance		$4,803 86
	Subject to drafts outstanding	$2,528 12	
	Salaries due	1,009 19	
		$3,537 31	

E. Cauldwell, *Treasurer.*

ANNUAL REPORT

OF THE EXECUTIVE BOARD OF THE AMERICAN BAPTIST HOME MISSION SOCIETY, MAY 14, 1859.

ANNUAL REPORT.

In presenting our Annual Report, we would first speak of God, in whose cause we have labored during the past year; of His forbearance with us, notwithstanding our ill deserts; of His condescension in using us for the promotion of His purpose of mercy to mankind; and of His saving grace to souls who have heard the Gospel proclaimed by this Society, through our humble agency. To His name be all the praise for this grace, and for its good fruits.

In the last report of the Board, the commencement of a work of grace, widely extended among our stations, was mentioned, and we are happy to state that the reports of missionaries show its continuance up to the close of the past missionary year. They yet speak of goodness and mercy from on high; of the gracious influences of the Holy Spirit in the regeneration of souls; of obedience to the faith by numbers of the people, and of the gathering of numerous Churches. A spiritual and moral culture has been extended over the vast prairies of the West, and beside its far-reaching water-courses, that has mellowed the hard-bound fallows of many a stubborn heart, and made fruitful in truth and righteousness many a barren mind. The same true and faithful One who called the Society into existence, and guided its progress in the period of youth and inexperience, has directed its maturer energies during the past year. He has blessed it, and made it a blessing to our fellow-man. The evidence of this has cheered us as trials have thickened in our pathway, and as fellow-laborers in the Master's vineyard have successively departed to their rest.

DEATHS.

The Board have passed through the year without experiencing the sorrows of bereavement in their official circle, but they have noticed with solemn interest, the decease of members and Directors of the Society in various parts of the land. Included in the number are seven ministers of the Gospel. We have sorrowfully enrolled all their names in the list of the deceased.

DIRECTORS AND MEMBERS FOR LIFE.

Thirty-one persons have been constituted Directors for life, of whom eleven had been previously members. Three Directors have died. The present number is six hundred and forty-four. Three hundred and sixty-one persons were constituted members for life, and twenty-four have died, leaving the present number, five thousand two hundred and five; and the total number of both classes, five thousand eight hundred and forty-eight.

FINANCIAL AFFAIRS.

It is a cause of gratification to the Board that, instead of reporting a diminished amount of donations and legacies from that of the previous year, as they have done on several former anniversaries of the Society, they can now announce an increase. The financial condition of the Society on the 31st of March was as follows:

Balance from last years' account	$ 4,459 02
Receipts from all sources	45,527 32
Total amount of resources for the year	49,986 34
Total amount of disbursements for the year	45,182 48
Amount of cash in the treasury April 1st, 1859	4,803 86
Amount due to missionaries, same date	3,537 31
Leaving a surplus of cash of	1,266 55
While the indebtedness of the Society on the first of April, falling due, and being payable in about equal monthly installments, afterwards, was	28,194 41

Of the above amount of receipts, $7,188 12 was in legacies.

MISSIONARY OPERATIONS.

The policy of selecting stations for patronage which seem most immediately important, and where efficient Churches can soonest be established, has been maintained as far as practicable the past year: but an impartial regard to the general interests of all the sections where aid was expected from the Society, and the fact that the treasury was insufficiently supplied with funds, prevented its application to many places of importance. So far as it has been applied, the results have been sufficiently encouraging to warrant its continuance and extension to other places, as fast as the replenishments of the treasury will admit.

DISTRIBUTION OF MISSIONARIES.

The distribution of missionaries was as follows: Six labored in the Province of Canada. They occupied twelve stations connected with the Grand Ligne Mission, and were successful in diffusing light amidst the surrounding darkness of Romanism. Eleven persons professed faith in Christ, and were baptized. Many others abandoned the Romish religion, and became regular attendants upon the ministry of the missionaries. The spirit of free religious inquiry is evidently spreading extensively in the Province. An excellent religious paper is published by one of the missionaries, which is doing good service among the people, including many educated and influential young men.

One German missionary, heretofore sustained in the city of New York, retained his connection with the Society only three months of the year, at which time the station under his care had reached a point of great prosperity. Lots had been purchased, and the building of a new church edifice, much larger than that previously occupied, *had been* commenced, and was progressing rapidly toward completion; a happy state of religious feeling existed among them; nineteen persons had been baptized; Sabbath Schools and places of worship had been established as out-stations, and the religious influence of the Church had become extended in several directions among the German population in the city and vicinity.

One missionary was sustained in the western part of Pennsylvania. The station was comparatively new, but he successfully labored in it, having baptized six persons, and gathered a considerable congregation.

One German missionary labored in Delaware three months when he retired from the field, and was subsequently succeeded by another, under whose pastoral care the Church became much united. Two persons were baptized.

In Ohio we had four missionaries; two of whom reported revivals in their Churches. The Church under the care of one of them, in a prominent city, has determined to dispense with further aid from our treasury. Baptism was administered to fourty-four persons at different stations, at one of which a revival was enjoyed.

Six missionaries occupied sixteen stations in Michigan. They baptized thirty-one persons, several of them the fruit of a revival, and organized four Churches. One church edifice was completed, and another commenced, and two of the Churches decided to ask no further aid in supporting their ministers.

In Indiana there were six missionaries who supplied twenty-seven stations, at three of which revivals of religion were enjoyed. Eighty-seven persons were baptized; two Churches were organized; two church edifices were completed and three commenced.

Three missionaries labored in Illinois—one of them only three months, when he resigned and removed from the place. The Church of another became sufficiently strong to support him without further aid from us. The remaining one is a French missionary, who labored in a colony of his countrymen and is yet doing good. Revivals were reported by two of the missionaries. Fifty-four persons were baptized.

In Wisconsin there were eighteen missionaries, having thirty-five stations under their care. At four of them revivals occurred. The baptism of fifty-two persons and organization of five Churches are reported. At four of the stations the building of church edifices was commenced, and one of the Churches will not ask further aid.

The number of missionaries in Iowa was twenty. They supplied seventy stations, at eight of which precious revivals were enjoyed, during which two hundred and twenty-three persons were baptized. Twenty-one Churches were organized, five houses of worship were completed, another was commenced, and one Church became self-sustaining.

There were twenty-one missionaries in Minnesota, who occupied sixty stations and baptized one hundred and thirty-six persons, chiefly the fruit of revivals at six of those stations. Fifteen Churches were organized, six places of worship were completed, and four commenced.

In Kansas there were four missionaries, who supplied fourteen stations and baptized seventeen persons. Three Churches were organized, and one church edifice was commenced.

In Nebraska there were four missionaries, having eight stations to supply. Seven persons were baptized, and two Churches organized.

Two missionaries and six assistants labored in New Mexico. Nineteen baptisms are reported. One church edifice was completed, and the building of another progressing. One native convert was added to the number of assistant missionaries, and one who had labored some time as an assistant, was licensed to preach. Much open and violent persecution was experienced by the missionaries and converts from the Romanists of that Territory, which seems, however, to have induced special inquiry on the part of many people into the doctrines of the Gospel, and it was hoped would lead to other desirable results.

Only two missionaries labored in California, but they also enjoyed tokens of the Divine presence. They baptized thirteen persons and organized a Church. One of the Churches heretofore aided by the Society will sustain their pastor without further missionary aid.

In addition to these, seven collecting agents labored all the year, and three others a few weeks each. They also report having performed a large amount of missionary labor, in destitute Churches and in aiding pastors ; one of the happy results of which was the baptism by them of forty-two persons.

SUMMARY OF LABORS AND RESULTS.

The following is a summary of labors and results at all the stations occupied by the missionaries during the past year :

One hundred and sixteen missionaries, assistant missionaries, and agents labored under the commission of the Society. Thirty-one of the number were new appointments at various periods of the year. The number in commission on the 31st of March was eighty-three. Twenty-two of the missionaries preached in foreign languages ; twenty of them were natives of foreign lands.

The number of States and Territories occupied was sixteen. The number of stations and out-stations supplied was two hundred and sixty-nine. The aggregate amount of time bestowed on the field was equal to that of one man for eighty-five and a quarter years.

fifteen church edifices; and
teen others.

The Churches aided by th
usual objects of Christian be
the support of the Gospel am
Seven Churches heretofor
become self-sustaining.*

For further details, we res
the Missionary Table accomp

THE POLICY OF PRE-O

While our summary of la
presents evidence of a degree
of the Society which should
it shows also, that we have fa
ing all that was desirable, or
of preöccupation, which is of
circumscribed within compar
that of securing possession

---

* In addition to the above, the missionaries report t

Sermons preached.........................
Lectures and Addresses.......................
Pastoral Visits.....

Double the number of missionaries who were in the entire field, could have been advantageously distributed in the ten most western States and Territories occupied; but such a distribution would have required a much greater amount of funds in our treasury, especially in the early part of the year, than we had a right to anticipate from any past experience. We preferred, therefore, to go forward in the plain, open highway of prudence, as vigorously as the means actually at command would allow, rather than by anticipating more than we might realize, to halt or stumble in the intricate and troublesome paths of financial embarrassment. The partial adoption, at an early period of our history, of the policy of preoccupation, has produced results which prove its true value. Its application to Iowa, some sixteen years ago, has placed the Churches of that State in a position of which the Society need not be ashamed. In Minnesota, where it has been more fully carried out, the results are yet more satisfactory. In that State, where less than ten years ago the desolateness of Indian occupancy prevailed, and white adventurers upon the soil could scarcely be enumerated by hundreds, with no religious influences but those of Romanism, there are now sixty-one Baptist Churches, consisting of some two thousand members, and supplied by about forty regularly laboring ministers. We may add, as a general remark, that those Churches occupy the most prominent places in the State, and those ministers are able, faithful men. Preliminary steps have already been taken by our brethren there for the execution of plans calculated to extend a sound educational and religious influence throughout the State.

This policy should be continued there so long as necessity requires it, and it should be extended with promptness and vigor to all the new States and Territories of the

Union. Should the necessary means be provided by the Society, we have no doubt the results will show the wisdom and advantage of the effort. While all the Western States will require more or less attention for several years to come, it should not be overlooked that the new ones, as they successively rise up, must, inevitably, be the most needy, and require the most prompt interposition of of our Christian benevolence. Thus Kansas is now ready for the same effort that has succeeded so well in Minnesota; and Nebraska and other Territories will soon follow in the same way.

THE CHARACTER OF ITS POPULATION.

The population of our western territory, now nearly as numerous as that of the eastern, and increasing in a greater ratio, is expanding with astonishing rapidity upon the most distant frontiers. It is a heterogeneous mass of foreigners from every quarter of the globe, and of natives of every State, and city, and hamlet in the land. We might speak of the general objects which draw them there, and the means by which they seek to secure them, but a far more serious and important subject for our consideration is found in the fact that they are immortal beings, hurrying along in their earthly career to the retributions of eternity, and that the tendencies of those objects upon their hearts and minds are to shut out spiritual light and hope, and to stifle concern for the welfare of their souls. It would dishonor us as Christians to overlook their moral condition and spiritual perils, or to neglect to follow them with the means of grace which Christ our Lord and Master has put into our hands and commanded us to bear to them. But how much more would it dishonor us to forget that in that immense number of immortals are found those who have gone from our personal companionship, our parental guidance, our Christian brotherhood, our praying circles, and our loved sanctuaries; to dwell beyond the influence of Christian institutions, to mingle with the irreligious, to be endangered by subtile infidelity, possibly to be captivated by a religion of mere form, based upon tradition and sustained by falsehood, and at last to die and lose their souls. We do not assert that moral and religious evils exist in that quarter which are unknown to ourselves; too often they are transplanted from old and impure moral fields at the east, to the more fresh and fertile soil of the west, where they vegetate with ranker growth; but we insist that they exist there in far greater proportion to the counteracting influences of true religion and pure morality, than in the Eastern States; while the force of existing religious example, as a restraint upon sin, or a corrective of bewildering desire for rapid accumulation of wealth, if operative at all, is often reduced to the smallest degree. Such are the frontier points towards which tends emigration in our country. To these proceed our countrymen and friends, and loved ones; and amidst such influences they plant themselves, and build their habitations, and create their cities with a rapidity which astonishes the world. Here, then, in a special sense, should the Gospel be sent—not tardily, after the foundations of society are laid in irreligion and error, but simultaneously with the very beginnings of social concentration; so that its hallowed influence may be felt and seen in the adjustment of the corner-stone of the foundation, and in the form and progress of the superstructure, to its completion. If it be the policy of the enemies of God to be first in such a work, shall it not be counteracted by the same policy in the Church of Christ? Is it consistent for the children of light, who labor for truth and righteousness, to allow a perpetuation of the charge of having less wisdom in such things than the children of the world? The early introduction of Christian institutions into the settlements of the West, by able, earnest ministers, sustained promptly and efficiently from a responsible source, well informed of all the interests of the general field, and enjoying the blessing of God, is the only reliable means of moulding those settlements into proper moral form, or of shaping their social character into a semblance of those which good men everywhere admire.

SOLEMN AND FRIENDLY ADVICE.

It is in this connection that we often remember the exhortation of a distinguished and far-seeing English minister, when warning his American brethren of a prominent danger of their country. "The object of your zeal must be your own country—to supply her rapidly increasing population with able, faithful ministers. . . . You must cultivate the waste places of your homestead. Think what your country is and especially what she must be—not only for the magnitude of her territory, and the multitude of her people, the vastness of her wealth, and the greatness of her power, but for the importance of her example. On your land hang, in a great measure, the future interests of the globe. Hence the unspeakable importance of your Churches concentrating, in a great measure, their religious efforts upon your country. If it were necessary, in order to supply your own people with pastors, one half of your male members should become ministers, while it should be the chief business of the other half to support them. These are my deliberate views of the duties of the Christians of America." The correctness of these views of John Angell James, is seen in the developments of the score of years since they were uttered, and is often illustrated in the details of our Society's history. Most earnestly do we ask of our friends a more particular study of those details in the light of the Society's own publications, a more *prominent* place in the exercises of the sanctuary and the monthly concert of prayer, and a deeper interest in the sympathies of ministers and people.

A WAY TO FOLLOW IT.

We might here specify numerous points which should be immediately added to our list of missionary stations, and the amount of means indispensable for their efficient cultivation ; but this cannot be specially necessary among our brethren, and might, at least in some instances, be unadvisable elsewhere. We unhesitatingly say, however, that the westward advance of civilization in our field, the claims of the needy for the Gospel at important points, and the actual necessities of many well qualified and desirable ministers, who earnestly ask the Society's aid to occupy those points, cannot be suitably provided for with a smaller amount than double that received during the year now closed. We add that, with reasonable assurance given at an early period that such an amount will be placed at the disposal of the Board within the present year, those points will be occupied with good missionaries, and in a course of profitable cultivation. We respectfully and affectionately submit to the Society whether the claims of the thousands of benighted infidel and Roman Catholic foreigners cast among us by Divine Providence, the larger number of our own unconverted kindred, the yet more numerous thousands of our impenitent countrymen, to whom it is expected that we shall send the Gospel of the grace of God, shall be promptly met, and whether an energetic, adequate co-operation of each and every member and friend shall be offered to justify the Board in an immediate attempt to meet those claims.

By order of the Executive Board,

BENJAMIN M: HILL,

Secretary of Correspondence.

1. Because it is our own. The ties by
identification which we and ours have wit
2. Because it holds and will hold such
all the historical nations, and hence we ha
or alliances can give us. We can reach
avenues of the heart. The language whi
world. The immigrating propensity of th
3. The questions of the utmost impor
on these shores—questions relating to man'

EXPLANATION OF THE FOLLO

The parallel columns show—

1. The names of Agents and Missionaries, and the Sta
2. The post office address of Agents and Missionaries.
3. The field of labor occupied by Agents and Missionar
4. The dates at which the appointments commence.
5. The number of months for which the appointments
6. The number of weeks' labor performed during the t
7. The number of stations and out-stations supplied.*
8. The number of persons baptized by the Missionaries
9. The number received by letter.
10. The number of Scholars in Sabbath Schools under tl
11. The amount contributed to benevolent objects.
12. Additional facts reported concerning the state and p

MISSIONARY TABLE.

NAMES OF AGENTS AND MISSIONARIES.	POST OFFICE ADDRESS.	FIELD OF LABOR.	Date of Commission.	Months Commis'd.	Weeks labor reported.	Stations supplied.	Baptized.	Received by Letter.	Scholars in S. School.	Contrib. to Benevolent Objects.	ADDITIONAL FACTS REPORTED.
CANADA (EAST).											
GRANDE LIGNE MISSION.											
Narcisse Cyr	Montreal	Among the French in M.	Nov. 1, 1857	12	39	1	1	....	....	200 00	Successful in distributing the Scriptures, and in other respects.
" "	"	"	Nov. 1, 1858	12	13	....	..	....	....	......	
Louis Roussy	Grande Ligne	Grande Ligne	Nov. 1, 1857	12	39	1	8	....	....	150 00	Ordinary fruits of Gospel labor. Some families leaving the Romish communion.
" "	"	"	Nov. 1, 1858	12	13	....	..	....	40	......	
T. Riendeau	St. Pie	St. Pie	Nov. 1, 1857	12	39	1	2	....	12	150 00	Encouraging progress of the Gospel. Enquiry for the truth extending in his field.
"	"	"	Nov. 1, 1858	12	13	....	..	....	....	......	The missionaries in Canada are encouraged to hope for good results from the labors of Mr. Chinaquy, a converted Roman Catholic Priest, who has recently visited and lectured in that Province.
N. Duval	St. Marie de Monnoir	St. Marie de Monnoir	Nov. 1, 1858	12	13	....	..	....	....	......	
Louis Pasche	Granby	Granby and vicinity	Nov. 1, 1858	12	13	4	..	....	....	12 00	
J. D. Rossier	Grande Ligne	Itinerant	Nov. 1, 1858	12	13	3	..	....	....	......	
NEW HAMPSHIRE.											
Oren Tracy	Concord	N. Hampshire and Vermont	April 1, 1858	12	52	....	..	....	....	......	Collecting agent for N. H. and Vermont.
P. Bond	Cornish	Maine	April 1, 1858	12	6	....	1	....	....	......	Collecting agent for Maine. Resigned.
MASSACHUSETTS.											
J. W. Parkhurst	Newton Centre	Massachusetts	April 1, 1858	12	52	....	..	....	....	......	Collecting agent for Massachusetts.

POST OFFICE ADDRESS.	FIELD OF LABOR.	Date of Commission.	Months Commis'd.	Weeks labor reported.	Stations supplied.	Baptized.	Received by Letter.	Scholars in S. School.	Contrib. to Benevolent Objects.	ADI
1.....	Connecticut and R. Island..	April 1, 1858	12	52	....	28	....	....	......	Collecting agen
....	....	April 1, 1858	12	16½	....	..	....	....	......	Collecting agen
rk...........	....	April 1, 1858	12	52	....	15	..	....	......	Collecting agen
....	Central New York........	April 1, 1858	12	52	....	..	....	....	......	Collecting agen
....	Western New York........	April 1, 1858	12	9						

Names of Agents and Missionaries.	Post Office Address.	Field of Labor.	Date of Commission.	Months Commis'd.	Weeks labor reported.	Stations supplied.	Baptized.	Received by Letter.	Scholars in S. School.	Contrib. to Benevolent Objects.	Additional Facts Reported.
OHIO.											
E. F. Platt	Toledo	Toledo	July 1, 1857	12	13	1	2	2	80	25 00	Usual prosperity. Church will sustain itself.
S. B. Page	Cleveland	Third church, Cleveland	May 1, 1857	12	13	1	20	4	160	12 50	Revival.
"	"	" "	May 1, 1858	12	39	....	2	1	....	75 62	Renewing efforts to pay church debt.
T. P. Childs	Troy	Troy and vicinity	June 1, 1857	12	13	2	7	5	....	10 00	Reduced debt on Meeting-House.
"	"	" "	June 1, 1858	12	39	....	10	2	....	3 50	Revival.
Daniel W. Morgan	Huron	Huron and vicinity	Dec. 1, 1858	12	13	1	3	....	....	37 50	Church training for usefulness.
MICHIGAN.											
Alfred Handy	Paw Paw	Paw Paw	April 1, 1858	12	52	1	8	1	40	2 00	The Church will soon complete M. H., and hereafter sustain their Pastor.
J. S. Goodman	Flint	Flint and vicinity	July 1, 1858	12	13	2	12	2	60	25 00	Trying to pay church debt. Revival.
A. J. Bingham	Allegan	Allegan and vicinity	June 1, 1857	12	13	5	2	....	60	......	Trying to overcome obstacles to progress.
" "	"	" "	June 1, 1858	12	26	2	..	3	70	13 00	Resigns. No further aid required.
John Seage	White Pigeon	White Pigeon	Dec. 1, 1857	12	39	....	1	2	62	16 50	Finished M. H. Sunday School flourishing.
" "	"	"	Dec. 1, 1858	12	13	3	..	1	70	15 00	
Lyman H. Moore	Lansing	Lansing	Jan. 1, 1858	12	39	2	6	4	25	156 25	Building a Meeting-House.
" "	"	"	Jan. 1, 1859	12	13	....	..	3	....	......	
O. B. Call	Lyons	Lyons and vicinity	Dec. 1, 1858	12	13	3	2	6	40	......	Experienced some opposition from the irreligious.
INDIANA.											
Lyman Wilder	Columbia city	Indiana	Nov. 1, 1858	5	22	....	1	....	....	......	Exploring agent for Indiana.
" "	"	"	April 1, 1859	12	....	....	..	....	....	......	" " "
H. C. Skinner	Wabash	Wabash	July 1, 1857	12	13	1	1	1	40	......	Declension in all that region.
" "	"	"	Oct. 1, 1858	12	26	....	..	....	....	......	Church united.
J. M. Whitehead	Westville	Westville and vicinity	Aug. 1, 1857	12	26	3	22	10	120	10 06	Revival in his Church, and at an out station where the Church was nearly extinct. Now they sustain a settled Pastor.
" "	"	" "	Aug. 1, 1858	12	26	....	17	6	....	16 00	Revival.
Lyman Wilder	Columbia city	Columbia city half the time.	Nov. 1, 1857	12	19½	2	2	....	20	11 86	M. H. progressing. Resigned to be Ex. Agent.
E. H. Cook	Middlebury	Elkhart River Association	June 1, 1857	12	13	13	17	....	300	58 00	Revival. Building a M. H. at one station.
"	"	" "	June 1, 1858	12	39	....	15	11	200	201 85	Finished a M. H. at Goshen. Churches more prosperous.

POST OFFICE ADDRESS.	FIELD OF LABOR.	Date of Commission.	Months Commiss'd.	Weeks labor reported.	Stations supplied.	Baptized.	Received by Letter.	Scholars in S. School.	Contrib. to Benevolent Objects.	ADDI
ton	Huntington	Feb. 1, 1858	12	52	5	12	6	75	40 07	Revival at an o
a city..........	Columbia city (half the time)	Dec. 1, 1858	12	13	3	..	.....	....	5 00	completed M. H
....	Batavia.....................	April 1, 1858	12	52	5	16	10	120	105 00	Revival. Need
....	Galena......................	June 1, 1857	12	13	1	28	3	100	......	Resigned and re
....	Sugar Creek and vicinity....	Nov. 1, 1858	12	13	2	..	....	14	......	Laboring in a Fr

Names of Agents and Missionaries.	Post Office Address.	Field of Labor.	Date of Commission.	Months Commiss'd.	Weeks labor reported.	Stations supplied.	Baptized.	Received by Letter.	Scholars in S. School.	Contrib. to Benevolent Objects.	Additional Facts Reported.
J. De Bois	Hudson	Hudson	Oct. 1, 1857	12	19	1	2	2	30	......	Removed from the field.
Ernest Tschirch	Racine	Germans in Racine	Jan. 1, 1858	12	30	2	2	3	25	48 27	An interesting field Meetings attended by Lutherans and Catholics.
" "	"	" "	Jan. 1, 1859	12	13	....	..	....	....	2 90	Is working zealously. Good results hoped for.
D. H. Cooley	Stevens' Point	Stevens' Point	June 1, 1858	12	30	1	1	10	50	302 60	Building a M. H. Several conversions.
A. W. Peck	Superior city	Superior city	Oct. 1, 1858	12	26	1	..	....	....	......	A new field. Organized a Church, and is encouraged.
Wm. Sturgeon	Frankfort	Waubeek and vicinity	Sept. 1, 1858	12	26	4	..	....	....	76 50	A new field. Encouraged to cultivate it.
Denis Mulhern	De Soto	De Soto and vicinity	Aug. 1, 1858	12	26	1	2	....	30	......	A new interest.
S. T. Catlin	Osceola Mills	Osceola Mills and Le Roy	Dec. 1, 1858	12	13	2	2	....	....	......	A new field. Is encouraged.
S. Cornelius, Jr.	Portage city	Portage city	Jan. 1, 1859	12	13	1	..	3	80	......	Finished lecture-room. Prospects improving.
IOWA.											
Thomas Powell	Davenport	Iowa	April 1, 1858	12	39	....	..	....	....	......	Resigned on account of his wife's ill health.
James Schofield	Rossville	Rossville and vicinity	April 1, 1858	12	52	6	..	....	45	86 00	Church united, but embarrassed by the "hard times."
Asahel Chapin	Vinton	Vinton	June 1, 1857	12	13	1	5	6	30	......	Church revived.
" "	"	"	June 1, 1858	12	39	....	2	8	....	5 00	Meetings well attended, and is encouraged.
Jonas Woodward	Cedar Rapids	Kingston and Cedar Rapids	May 1, 1857	12	13	....	8	2	70	24 38	Building a M. H. at an out station.
" "	"	" "	May 1, 1858	12	39	3	7	3	150	41 80	Organized a Church, and completed a M. H.
J. Ellis Guild	Newton	Newton and vicinity	July 1, 1857	12	10	1	1	....	....	......	Resigned.
A. A. Sawin	Lyons	Lyons and Clinton	July 1, 1857	12	7	2	2	2	100	......	Finished M. H. at Clinton.
L. M. Newell	Wawkon	Wawkon and Makee	June 1, 1857	12	13	2	1	....	12	......	
"	"	Wawkon and vicinity	June 1, 1858	12	39	5	..	5	18	6 30	Prayer-meetings interesting Sickness in his family.
Thomas M. Ind	Burlington	South Burlington	May 1, 1857	12	13	5	1	....	116	36 00	Influence of the Church increasing.
" "	"	" "	May 1, 1858	12	39	....	38	6	330	35 00	Church paid debt on M. H. Revival.
George Scott	Strawberry Point	Strawberry Point	May 1, 1857	12	13	3	10	18	100	50 00	Revival. Organized a Church at an out station.
"	" "	" "	May 1, 1858	12	39	9	18	12	175	......	Errors abound in the community. Church embarrassed by debt.
Charles E. Brown	Vernon Springs	Vernon Springs	Aug. 1, 1857	12	26	5	..	1	40	......	
" "	"	"	Aug. 1, 1858	12	26	....	..	5	60	......	Secured a lot for a M. H. Raising funds to build one.

POST OFFICE ADDRESS.	FIELD OF LABOR.	Date of Commission.	Months Commiss'd.	Weeks labor reported.	Stations supplied.	Baptized.	Received by Letter.	Scholars in S. School.	Contrib. to Benevolent Objects.	ADDIT
Centre........	Le Clair Centre............	June 1, 1857	12	13	4	[illegible]	6	25	......	Revivals. Fiel part of it.
"	" "	June 1, 1858	12	39	6	18	12	20	51 10	Organized Chur
....	Burriss city and Wapello...	July 1, 1857	12	13	3	..	....	10	......	Organized a Ch
....	Wapello and vicinity.......	July 1, 1858	12	39	....	..	....	9	1 25	Church revived
....	Toledo and vicinity.........	Sept. 1, 1857	12	26	5	[illegible]	3	140	2 00	Four Churches aged, but en
....	" "	Sept. 1, 1858	12	26	....	..	7	30	......	
rles............	St. Charles and vicinity.....	Jan. 1, 1858	12	39	4	[illegible]	3	....	12 00	Organized Ch
....	" "	Jan. 1, 1859	12	13	...	..	....	20	...	Some religious
d	Hartford.......	M'ch 1, 1857	12	52	3	[illegible]	2	71	24 50	Need no furthe
sa	Oskaloosa................	Aug. 1, 1858	12	26	3	..	8	60	......	Finished a M.
r city..........	Webster city..............	Nov. 1, 1858	12	13	3	[illegible]	....	....	......	Organized a Ch
oo............	Waterloo.................	Sept. 1, 1858	12	26	3	21	3	100	......	Revival.
wa............	Ottumwa	Nov. 1, 1858	12	13	2	8	9	....	......	Negotiating for
.	Central Association	Dec. 1, 1858	12	10	...	[illegible]	7	....	58 00	Successful in

NAMES OF AGENTS AND MISSIONARIES.	POST OFFICE ADDRESS.	FIELD OF LABOR.	Date of Commission.	Months Commiss'd.	Weeks labor reported.	Stations supplied.	Baptized.	Received by Letter.	Scholars in S. School.	Contrib. to Benevolent Objects.	ADDITIONAL FACTS REPORTED.
John La Grange	St. Peter	St. Peter and Traverse	May 1, 1857	12	13	4	3	....	25	......	Gaining pecuniary strength.
" "	"	" "	May 1, 1858	12	39	6	4	3	20	112 50	Building a M. H. Church suffering by "hard times," and failure of crops.
A. Norelius	Cannon Falls	Cannon Falls, etc.	April 1, 1858	12	52	....	15	2	20	3 00	Labors among Scandinavians with success.
Amory Gale	Minneapolis	Minneapolis	July 1, 1857	12	13	4	2	7	125	6 00	Resigns and leaves. The Church prospering.
Enos Munger	Lakeland	Lakeland	Aug. 1, 1857	12	26	2	..	....	36	......	Prospects encouraging.
"	"	"	Aug. 1, 1858	8	34	....	2	10	40	......	Church revived.
H. C. Hazen	Faribault	Faribault	Jan. 1, 1858	12	39	1	14	14	30	......	Building a lecture-room.
"	"	"	Jan. 1, 1859	12	13	2	..	....	45	......	Religious interest encouraging. Financial affairs discouraging.
Erastus Westcott	Rochester	Rochester	Aug. 1, 1857	12	26	2	2	14	92	2 78	Building a lecture-room on the rear of the lot designed for a M. H.
" "	"	"	Aug. 1, 1858	12	26	....	1	9	80	17 00	
Wm. C. Phillips	St. Cloud	St. Cloud	May 1, 1858	12	39	2	..	7	85	......	Church revived, and inquirers in the congregation.
Geo. W. Fuller	Chatfield	Chatfield	June 1, 1858	12	39	5	8	8	75	......	Revival, and refitting M. H.
J. F. Wilcox	Northfield	Northfield	Aug. 1, 1858	12	21	5	..	5	12	......	Finds much work to do.
A. Smith Lyon	Newport	Newport and Cottage Grove	June 1, 1858	12	39	2	..	....	....	225 00	A new field. Organized a Church at N.
Isaac Waldron	Cannon Falls	Zumbrota and Cannon Falls	Nov. 1, 1858	12	13	5	..	2	45	......	Considerable religious interest.
H. B. Slater	Saratoga	Saratoga	Oct. 1, 1858	12	26	6	8	5	....	......	Revival.
Lyman Palmer	Anoka	Anoka	Sept. 1, 1858	12	26	1	..	6	60	......	Nearly finished M. H. Good state of religious feeling.
E. F. Gurney	....	Austin	M'ch 1, 1859	12	....	....	..	....	....	......	
NEBRASKA.											
G. W. Barnes	Florence	Florence and vicinity	Sept. 1, 1857	12	26	1	2	....	25	......	An association organized for the Territory.
"	"	Cumming city and Florence	Sept. 1, 1858	12	26	....	5	....	....	......	People leaving for the "gold regions."
J. G. Bowen	Nebraska city	Nebraska city and vicinity	Dec. 1, 1857	12	39	1	..	5	60	......	Sickness so prevalent as to prevent meetings.
"	" "	" "	Dec. 1, 1858	12	13	....	..	....	25	6 00	Some favorable indications.
Lucius H. Gibbs	Plattsmouth	Plattsmouth and Rock Bluffs	Oct. 1, 1858	12	26	3	..	2	....	......	A new field. The country pecuniarily embarrassed.
John M. Taggart	Fontenelle	Fontenelle and vicinity	June 1, 1858	12	39	3	..	2	18	......	Encouraging progress.

POST OFFICE ADDRESS.	FIELD OF LABOR.	Date of Commission.	Months Commiss'd.	Weeks labor reported.	Stations supplied.	Baptized.	Received by Letter.	Scholars in S. School.	Contrib. to Benevolent Objects.	ADD
ace	Lawrence..................	April 1, 1858	12	52	1	5	8	100	100 25	Church united ill health.
worth..........	Leavenworth	Feb. 1, 1858	12	26	1	..	10	....	......	
ville	Brownville, etc...........	Dec. 1, 1857	12	39	7	..	....	26	......	Building M. H
ns.............	Doniphan county..........	April 1, 1858	12	46	5	1	14	50	......	Organized Chu couraged.
....	" "	April 1, 1859	12	....	....	..	....	....	......	
....	....	....	....	....	....	..	....	....	......	

STATE CONVENTIONS

AND

GENERAL ASSOCIATIONS IN THE UNITED STATES,

With the Names and Post Office Addresses of the Corresponding Secretaries; the Time and Place of their Anniversaries for 1859; *the number of Missionaries employed, and amount of Receipts into their Treasuries, for* 1858, *including Balances of the previous year.*

STATES.	CORRESPONDING SECRETARIES.	POST OFFICE ADDRESSES.	PLACES OF NEXT ANNIVERSARY.	Time of Anniversary.	Number of Missies.	Amount of Receipts for Do. Migs. in 1858.
Maine	N. M. Wood	Waterville	Biddeford	June 21	20	$3572 17
New Hampshire	Joseph Storer	Fisherville	Nashua	Oct. 19	11	1977 19
Vermont	John Goadby	East Poultney	Rutland	Oct. 5	13	2345 02
Massachusetts	J. Ricker	Boston	Springfield	Oct. 26	36	3944 34
* Rhode Island	Francis Smith	Providence				
Connecticut	E. Cushman	West Hartford	Hartford	June 7	9	1641 56
New York	John Smitzer	Oneida	Owego	Oct. 12	27	6513 01
New Jersey	J. M. Carpenter	Jacobstown	Lambertville	Nov. 1	16	3332 18
Pennsylvania	Isaac Bevan	Philadelphia	Upland		22	4445 37
Maryland	A. Fuller Crane	Baltimore	Newtown	Nov. 10	9	3027 75
* Virginia	H. K. Ellyson	Richmond				
* North Carolina	T. E. Skinner	Raleigh				
* South Carolina	J. J. Brantly	Greenville				
* Georgia	J. F. Dagg	Cuthbert				
* Alabama	S. S. Sherman					
Mississippi	L. H. Milikin	Jackson	Canton	May 19	2	
* Louisiana						
* Texas						
* Tennessee	A. C. Dayton	Nashville				
* Kentucky	A. Broaddus	Louisville				
* Missouri	S. C. Major	Fayette				
* Illinois	J. A. Smith	Chicago				
* Southern Illinois						
* Indiana	M. G. Clark	Indianapolis				
Ohio	D. F. Carnahan	Columbus	Urbana	Oct. 19	19	4702 24
Michigan	J. A. Clark	Adrian	Lansing	Oct. 16	10	800 97
Wisconsin	J. T. Westover	Monroe	Beaver Dam	Sept. 21	9	668 12
Iowa	T. S. Griffith	Dubuque	Oscaloosa	Oct. 8	16	2326 32
* Minnesota						
* California						
Oregon	C. H. Mattoon		Forest Grove			

Amount of Receipts reported above	$39,296 24
Amount of Receipts of the H. M. Society	49,986 34
Total amount reported for Home and Domestic Mission purposes	$89,282 58

* No Reports received from these States.

STATES.	Total Amount to 1850.	1851–
Canada	4,139 49	1,0
Maine	3,214 40	1,0
New Hampshire	4,874 52	6,5
Vermont	4,072 96	3,7
Massachusetts	41,291 55	43,4
Rhode Island	12,297 02	9,7
Connecticut	17,860 91	16,3
New York	100,644 16	79,5
New Jersey	14,990 78	15,4
Pennsylvania	9,449 57	12,3
Delaware	603 50	7
Maryland	2,055 06	
District of Columbia	993 12	2
Ohio	1,369 57	7,6
Michigan	1,719 95	3,2
Indiana	104 86	7,1
Illinois	4,348 55	8,
Wisconsin	378 79	1,
Iowa	502 72	1,4
Minnesota	....	6
Nebraska	....	...
Kansas	....	...
Missouri	266 82	[illegible]
Kentucky	304 38	
Virginia	9,325 15	
North Carolina	5,391 69	...
South Carolina	8,498 10	
Georgia	10,861 20	
Alabama	493 08	
Florida	172 82	...
Mississippi	1,899 66	...
Tennessee	486 10	...
Louisiana	79 00	...
Arkansas	69 20	...
Texas	....	...
California	....	[illegible]
Oregon	....	[illegible]
New Mexico	....	[illegible]
U. S. Government	....	...
New Granada	....	...
Unknown	....	...
Aggregate for each period	262,618 08	222,

LIST OF LEGACIES

PAID TO THE SOCIETY SINCE ITS ORGANIZATION.

1834	Dea. Josiah Penfield, Savannah, Ga., per Rev. H. O. Wyer	$1250 00
1835	Mrs. Clarissa Long, Shelburne, Mass., per W. Wilder, Esq., Executor	37 50
"	William Powers, Hebron, N. H., per Rev. I. Merriam	100 00
"	Miss Maria Curtis, Southbridge, Mass., per Rev. E. Going	200 00
"	Mrs. Jemima Elliott, Hampton, Ct., per Rev. J. Payne, Executor	100 00
1836	Mrs. Betsey Sprague, Attleboro', Mass., per Mr. A. Reed, Executor	451 25
"	Robert Rodgers, Newport, R. I.	25 00
"	Ebenezer Boyd, Providence, R. I.	10 00
1839	Mrs. Abigail Marshall, New York, per Mr. Schofield, Executor	702 17
"	Mrs. Margaret Pugsley, Dutchess Co., N. Y., per Miss Cornelia Pugsley	280 00
"	Mrs. Irene Coats, New York, per Alfred Decker, Esq	250 00
1841	Mrs. Elizabeth G., Moore, Hartford, Ct., per J. B. Gilbert	200 00
1842	Nathaniel Tucker, Milton, Mass., per W. D. Ticknor	200 50
1843	Mrs. Margaret Martin, Montgomery, N. Y., per Mr. J. J. Martin, Executor	100 00
"	Miss Cynthia M., Wright, Suffield, Ct., per H. Sheldon, Administrator	50 00
1844	Mr. Zephaniah Eddy, New Bedford, Mass.. per Rev. H. Jackson, Executor	150 00
"	Mr. Josiah Kendall, Groton, Mass., per F. E. Wheelock and Rev. A. Sanderson, Executors.	1150 00
"	Miss Jane McCall, Society Hill, S. C., per John McIver	20 00
"	Miss Lydia Sweetzer, South Reading, Mass., per H. Sweetzer	324 00
"	Mrs. Elizabeth Griffin, New York, per one of her heirs	83 34
"	Josiah Flint, Cornish, N. H., per Mr. A. Burnap	80 00
"	Thomas Cooper, Esq., Eatonton, Ga., per Hon. M. A. Cooper, Executor	2000 00
"	Miss Betsey Hutchinson, Passumpsic, Vt., per L. P. Parks	50 00
"	Rev. Amos Dodge, Brighton, Macoupin Co., Ill., by his widow	30 00
"	Mr. John Ward, Warren, N. Y., per J. Northrop and A. Ward, Executors	847 50
1845	Joseph H. Hayden, Saybrook, Ct., per H. L. Champlin, Executor	100 00
1846	John Allen, Centreville, R. I., in part, per H. Hamilton and Rev. E. K. Fuller, Executors.	400 00
"	Rev. Jesse Mercer, Wilks Co., Ga., per B. M. Saunders, Executor	1331 87
"	Miss Mary Bliven, McDonough, N. Y., per Rev. John Peck	46 75
"	Mrs. Betsey Haykes, Cincinnatus, N. Y., per Trustees of the Baptist Society	100 00
"	Mrs. Charlotte Cole, Alexandria, Va., per Robert Bell, Executor	10 00
"	Dea. Medad Jackson, W. Meredith, N. Y., per H. Jackson, and W. Stillson, Executors	1105 00
"	Mrs. Urania Grant, West Wrentham, Mass., per R. E. Eddy	20 00
"	Mr. Richard Dubois, Malta, N. Y., per H. J. Rodgers, Executor	50 00
1847	Dea. Saxton Bailey, Lebanon, Ct., per Executor	100 00
"	Mr. Lewis Porter, Covert, N. Y., in advance, per J. Mc Lellan	250 00
"	Miss Mary Havens, St. Catharine, Canada West, per E. Savage	68 98
"	Miss Amanda Hadley, Brattleboro', N. H., per Rev. J. Z. Foster	25 00
"	James Shearer, Canada West, in part, per Rev. E. Savage	151 00
"	L. Crossman, Elbridge, N. Y., in advance	30 00
1848	William Jones, Iowa City, Iowa, per G. W. Hampton, Executor	25 00
"	Hon. James Vanderpool, Newark, N. J., per B. Vanderpool, Executor	1000 00
"	Miss Susan Farrar, Keene, N. H., per G. Robins	10 00
"	Mrs. Eunice Nicholls, Cambridge, Mass., per E., Mansfield, Executor	500 00
"	Mrs. Hannah Carleton, Portland, Me., per Rev. G. J. Carleton, Administrator	500 00
1849	Mr. Samuel R. Stelle, Piscataway, N. J., per Lewis R. Stelle, Esq., Executor	200 0)
"	Mrs. Phebe Gale, East Bennington, Vt., per Executor of Estate of S. Harmon	25 00
"	Mr. William Reynolds, Boston, Mass., per J. H. Duncan, Esq., and Mrs. Susan D. Reynolds, Executors in land not sold at Toledo, Ohio	
"	Josiah Lyman, Andover, Ct., per N. B. Lyman, Executor	50 00

ADDRESS OF JOHN P. CROZER, ESQ.,

PRESIDENT OF THE SOCIETY, DELIVERED AT THE ANNIVERSARY IN NEW YORK, MAY 13, 1859.

Brethren of the Home Mission:—In meeting together this morning, my mind recurs to our last Anniversary in Philadelphia. It is one of pleasant and profitable recollection; no note of discord was touched, no unkind expression in debate escaped the lips of any speaker; harmony and love, and an earnest desire to promote the interests of the Society—I may say, the interests of Christ's kingdom—was strikingly manifest throughout. If the same spirit pervades our present anniversary, my duties as presiding officer will be easy and pleasant, and the great objects of the Home Mission Society strengthened and advanced.

It is, brethren, a cause of much satisfaction to us all; but especially so to your Board and Executive officers, that no desire, as far as I know, at least, is anywhere expressed to restrict or interfere with the Home Mission operations. In this age of advancement, modification, and changes, I think no better evidence than this is needed, to prove that our Society has the sympathy and confidence of the Baptist denomination.

The Home Mission Record presents cheering accounts, from month to month, from the occupants of the Mission stations, widely scattered through the Western States and Territories. I was gratified, when in the Home Mission rooms some months ago, in tracing upon the map, as pointed out to me by your excellent Secretary, the several stations where your missionaries labor; but though these stations are numerous, they are few, indeed, compared with the vast field upon which we should operate. Brethren, the work of missions, whether in the foreign or the home field, is a glorious work. It is well worthy our prayerful, untiring effort.

It was a grand conception in the mind of Carey and his associates, which gave birth to the Asiatic Missions; but the work of Jonathan Going and the active friends associated with him, may bear a respectable comparison in its results. The former claims the veneration and respect due to age. The other is of comparatively recent date. Foreign missions were from the first attended with a glow of enthusiasm—a sacred halo, which enveloped the work in charm—Home Mission labor was esteemed more as a plodding work. It had all the self-denial of the foreign field, without its dignity in the Christian world. These relations are now being modified; recent events have, in a measure, divested the foreign field of its charm, while the Home field is each succeeding year assuming a position of higher importance.

We may well rejoice in every effort to reclaim and evangelize a sin-ruined world—every aim to carry the Gospel and its holy influences into the remotest corners of the earth, to plant the standard of the Cross in the heathen wastes of Asia, the midnight darkness of Africa, and in the large Islands of the Oceans. I would not desire to detract from foreign missions. The work—the cause should kindle emotions of sympathy and love in every Christian heart; but, in my view, the Home Mission has preëminent claims. It is true, God has made of one blood all nations of the earth, and the souls of all these are alike precious in His sight, but the sympathies of our nature are first and strongest towards those who are around us. It begins with the family tie, and extending wider, reaches from the family connections and relations, to neighbors, associates, towns, districts, and country.

The residents of our own loved country are our brethren; bound together with us by the ties of country, and of social life. We have felt the power and influence of Christianity, infused as it now is in the laws and government under which we live, and it is our high interest and aim to secure this infusion in all after time. This we owe to the country as Christian men and patriots, and this can only be effectually done by diffusing far and wide the precepts of Christianity. The love of country, and the love of Jesus, here combine in their promptings to vigorous, untiring action for the conversion of men in our own land.

We would still recognize the truth that the increase belongs to God—vain are the best directed efforts of men unaccompanied by the Holy Spirit, yet we may expect results with almost the same certainty as effects follow causes. We may rest in faith that God will continue to smile upon, and bless our labors.

The American Baptist Home Mission Society had its origin in love: members of our Eastern Churches, floating on the wave of emigration, were scattered through the West in sparsely settled districts where a preached word was seldom heard; here your missionaries found them, and here, a nucleus happily existed, around which, through the labors of these missionaries, Churches were soon formed, many of which now hold an important and commanding influence.

Brethren, it would be profitable, could I, on the broad maps of Ohio, of Indiana, of Illinois, of Michigan, and of Wisconsin; and then across the Mississippi, of the new States and Territories, mark the points where your former and your present labors have been attended with marked and encouraging results. Could I trace in one view to the eye, or present at one glance to the mind the results—the fruits of your life as a Society—the twenty-seven years of your existence, I am sure it would cause a thrill of emotion, a holy glow of gratitude to God, that you were His instruments for so glorious a work.

Well, brethren, our Society has yet scarcely passed its childhood. It is just merging into manhood and muscular strength. It stands up before you to-day in the comely proportions of youth, health, and vigor; I love to glance at its capabilities for good. A Society formed of Baptist members who have felt the power of Divine love in their own souls, yearning, as we trust, with desires for a wide extension of this holy influence. A vast field opening up before it, extending to the shores of the Pacific Ocean. A foreign population mingling from year to year, with immigrants from the old States, are forming settlements in this wide field, far, very far beyond the power of this Society, aided by kindred societies of other evangelical denominations, to supply with the preached Word. Let us, brethren, to the utmost extent of our ability, occupy these distant stations. Let us make strenuous effort to be, under God, the instruments of planting Churches, and securing an evangelical influence in these remote settlements. God has hitherto crowned our labors with success; He will continue to smile upon them. Let us aim to acquit ourselves well as good stewards.

Brethren, I know of no gauge by which to measure the results of our Home Mission effort. The full extent and scope of its usefulness cannot be estimated by any process to which I have access. The seeds of Divine truth have been widely scattered, but, I trust, a far wider diffusion of these truths shall yet be made through our instrumentality; a rich harvest, a glorious ingathering of souls is already manifest, but the magnitude of the work; the mighty results, under God which may be in store for the Society, can only appear in all their fullness at the great day when the secrets of all hearts shall be revealed.

OPINION OF THE SOCIETY AMONG THE GREEN MOUNTAINS.

The American Baptist Home Mission Society is at the present time second to no one of our benevolent organizations in the confidence and affection of the people. While this fact may be owing to the misfortunes which have befallen others, under the administration of imperfect policy, rather than to the paramount importance of its object, yet it would be difficult to conceive of higher and juster views of benevolent obligation, than those embraced in the aims of this Society.

It is both necessary and right, morally and scripturally, that whatever be our obligation to those more remote, those around us in our own field of labor should not be neglected; and general observation proves, that if there is negligence at home, it will also extend abroad. It is a law of grace as well as of Providence, that no one can look hopefully for food where famine pinches. So we are obligated to cultivate our home interests, in order to produce bread for the starving abroad.

This high purpose has been most nobly and wonderfully accomplished by this Society in its practical operations, both in the past and present, for which it commends itself most earnestly to the continued confidence and support, and to the prayers of the Churches, and of all who desire the spread of "the glorious Gospel of the blessed God." We can contemplate with sadness but certainty, what would have been the chaotic state of religion, in our numerous Western States and Territories, but for this special agency for planting the Cross over this vast and populous extent of country.

Twenty-six years ago last April this Society was organized. Just at the time when the tide of emigration was beginning to pour such a flood of souls into the land of the prairies, and there are hundreds of Churches and tens of thousands of souls scattered over this vast paradise, now calling it blessed, as the agency by which the Gospel was preached to the pioneer. God has owned and eminently blessed it, in its noble work of planting Churches and preaching the Gospel to the destitute. It has steadily and perseveringly kept pace with the progress of civilization and the spirit of enterprise in the West, and labored to hold up in comparison with earthly treasures the better wealth of heaven. * * * * *

RELIGIOUS DESTITUTION IN IOWA.

The following extracts from the Seventeenth Annual Report of the Iowa Baptist Convention will be read with deep interest:

"There is no section of the State but that is suffering for more laborers in the Lord's harvest. One impressed with the destitution of his own locality, imagining that it is greater than any other, need only go into another region, and he finds there also, as at home, the same imperative necessity for messengers of Christ. Our population, and all the elements of social and political power are increasing with amazing rapidity. Excepting a few larger towns on the river, and isolated points here and there at wide intervals, the State may be said to be a great moral waste, whose perishing thousands are going unministered unto by the Gospel of Salvation, to the doom of the lost. We do not exaggerate, nor speak for effect, when we say that the State of Iowa is Missionary ground that, viewed either in its destitution or its promise, has few equals. Dividing the State into four sections, two east and two west of the Des Moines River, and these divided by a line drawn through the centre of the State east and west, we find a population in the southeastern section of no less than 270,000, with 41 ministers, or 1 to 6,585 persons; in the northeastern section the population is estimated at 255,000, with 25 ministers, or 1 to 10,200 persons; in the northwestern section there is an estimated population of 30,000, with two ministers, or one minister to 15,000 persons; in the southwestern section there is a population of about 190,000 and 25 ministers, or one minister to 7,600 persons. There is a great difficulty in meeting the wants of these thousands. They are scattered over wide distances, and can be collected only in small companies in cabins, and groves, and school-houses. * * * *

"If the 'sober realities' of our destitution could be realized abroad, and brethren enter these wide wastes as the Missionary goes to a heathen shore, deeply impressed with the truth that he is nearly alone, of all these thousands who love the Master, and, expecting nothing, be prepared for all things, we should have a stronger hope of the destitution around being supplied by immigration from abroad. Shall, however, these wastes be left to be possessed by infidelity? If not, how can *we* help to make the wilderness a garden. * * * * * * * * *

"The American Baptist Home Mission Society has employed more Missionaries in Iowa the last year than in any other State; and we are informed of their desire to extend their benefactions yet more generously; at the same time we are assured that instead of increase, the probabilities are that their means will be more limited than the year previous, and that they will be constrained to curtail their expenditures."

[illegible], Rev. John, Morrisania, N. Y.
Cooley, Rev. D. H., Stevens Point, Wis.
Cooper, William, New York
Corwin, Robert G., Lebanon, O.
Corwin, Rev. Jason, Darlington, Wis.
Cottrell, Thomas, Greenwich, N. Y.
Covell, Rev. Lemuel, New York.
Crane, Rev. W. C., Hernando, Miss.
Crane, Rev. Origin, New England Village, Mass.
Crane, William, Baltimore
Crosby, William B., New York.
Crozer, John P., Chester, Pa.
Crozer, Mrs. Sarah L., Chester, Pa.
Crozer, George K., Chester, Pa.
Crozer, Robert Hall, Chester, Pa.
Cushman, Rev. Elisha, East Hartford, Ct.
Cuthbert, Rev. James H., Philadelphia.
Cuthbert, Lucius, Princeton, N. J.
Cutting, Rev. S. S., Rochester, N. Y.
Dagg, Rev. John L., D.D., Penfield, Ga.
Damon, Mrs. Catharine, Ashby, Mass.
Dana, Mrs. Nancy, Boston.
Daniels, Clark, New London, Ct.
Davy, Thomas, New York.
Davies, John M., New York.
Davis, Rev. Henry, D.D., Columbus, Ohio.
Davis, Hon. Isaac, LL.D., Worcester, Mass.
Davis, Mrs. Mary H. E., Worcester, Mass.
Davis, Rev. Ebenezer S., Holland Patent, N. Y.
Day, Rev. Ambrose, Westfield, Mass.
Day, Rev. Henry, Philadelphia.
Day, Arthur, Shaftsbury, Vt.
Day, Hon. Albert, Hartford, Ct.
Decker, Alfred F., New York.
Devan, Rev. Thomas T., Nyack, N. Y.
Devan, Mrs. Emma E., Nyack, N. Y.
Dickinson, Rev. Edmund W., Dayton, Ohio.
Dockery, Hon. A., Dockery's Store, N. C.
Dodd, Abner, Newark, N. J.
Dodge, Rev. Orrin, Brooklyn, N. Y.
Dorrance, Rev. George W., Washington, D. C.
Douglass, Rev. William, Providence.
Douglass, James, Cavers, Scotland.
Dowling, Rev. John, D.D., New York.
Downs, Henry S., Iowa.
Drake, Rev. Simeon J., Plainfield, N. J.
Drummond, James P., Brooklyn, N. Y.
Dunbar, Rev. Duncan, New York.
Dunn, Rev. Lewis A., Fairfax, Vt.
Earle, Rev. Alfred, Piermont, N. Y.
Eastwood, Rev. Marvin, Glens Falls, N. Y.

Hiscox, Rev. Edward T., D.D., New York.
Hodge, Rev. James L., D.D., Bridgeport, Ct.
Hodge, Rev. M. G., Brooklyn, N. Y.
Hodges, Rev. Joseph, Cambridge, Mass.
Holme, Rev. J. S., Brooklyn, N. Y.
Holmes, Rev. Lewis, Edgerton, Mass.
Holt, Caleb, Sharon, Vt.
Hopkins, Rev. Charles J., Rondout, N. Y.
Hopper, Samuel W., Philadelphia.
Hopper, Rev. A. M., Auburn, N. Y.
Hotchkiss, Rev. V. R., D.D., Rochester, N. Y.
Houghton, Hon. Joab. Santa Fé, N. M.
Howard, Rev. Leland. Rutland, Vt.
Howard, Rev. William G., D.D., Chicago, Ill.
Howe, Rev. William, Boston.
Howell, Rev. Robert B. C., D.D., Nashville, Tenn.
Howell, Mrs. Mary Ann M., Nashville, Tenn.
Huckins, Rev. James, Galveston, Tex.
Hulse, Charles, Philadelphia.
Hunt, Samuel, Providence.
Hutchins, Rev. Hiram, Roxbury, Mass.
Hutchinson, Rev. William, Sandy Hill, N. Y.
Hyde, Rev. J. C., Winona, Min.
Ide, Rev. George B., D.D., Springfield, Mass.
Ilsley, Rev. Silas, Essex, Ct.
Ives, Rev. Dwight, D.D., Suffield, Ct.
Ives, Mrs Julia A., Suffield, Ct.
Jackson, Rev. Henry, D.D., Newport, R. I.
James, Rev. Silas C., Bunker Hill, Ill.
James, William T., New York.
James, Israel E., Philadelphia.
Jameson, William H., Melrose, Mass.
Jameson, Rev. Thorndike C., Melrose, Mass.
Jayne, David, Philadelphia.
Jennings, Rev. John, Newton Centre, Mass.
Jeter, Rev. J. B., D.D., Richmond, Va.
Johnson, Rev. W. D. H., Greenville, Ill.
Jones, Rev. Henry V., Rondout, N. Y.
Jones, Rev. P. F., New York.
Jones, Rev. John D. E., Worcester, Mass.
Judd, Rev. Orrin B., LL.D., New York.
Keely, Rev. George, Haverhill, Mass.
Keely, John, Haverhill, Mass.
Keen, Wm. W., Philadelphia.
Kempton, Rev. George, North East, N. Y.
Kendrick, Edward E., Albany, N. Y.
Kennard, Rev. J. H., D.D., Philadelphia.
Kennard, Rev. Spencer J., Bridgeton, N. J.
Kent, Henry P., Suffield, Ct.
Kent, Mrs. Jane S., Suffield, Ct.
Keyes, Rev. Charles B., Westfield, N. Y.
Keyser, Rev. Charles, Providence, R. I.
Ladd, Rev. James S., New York.
Lamb, Rev. R. P., Salisbury, N. Y.
Larcombe, Richard J., New York.
Larcombe, Rev. Thomas, Philadelphia.
Latham, Daniel, Groton, Ct.
Latham, Mrs. Delia Ann, Groton, Ct.
Latham, Daniel D., New London, Ct.
Lane, Rev. Benjamin I., Newburyport, Mass.
Lathrop, Rev. Edward, D.D., New York.
Laws, Rev. William, Modesttown, Va.
Lawton, Rev. Joseph A., Erwinton, S. C.
Lea, Sidney Slade, Yanceyville, N. C.
Lee, George F., Philadelphia.
Leighton, Rev. Sam'l S., West Townsend, Mass.
Leonard, Rev. Lewis G., D.D., Marietta, Ohio.
Lerned, Rev. John H., Harvard, Mass.
Leverett, Rev. William, Newport, R. I.
Lewis, John G., Boston.
Lewis, Isaac, New York.
Lewis, Mrs. Mary, New York.
Lillie, Rev. James, D.D., Montreal, Canada.
Lincoln, Hon. Heman, Boston.
Lincoln, Rev. B. H., South Framingham, Mass.
Linnard, Hon. J. M., Philadelphia.
Linnard, Mrs. Anna, Philadelphia.
Litchfield, E. B., Brooklyn, N. Y.
Litchfield, E. D., Brooklyn, N. Y.
Locke, Rev. William E., Lancaster, Pa.
Loxley, Rev. Benjamin R., Philadelphia.
Loomis, Rev. Ebenezer, Alba, Pa.
Lumsden, D. F., Boston.
Lyeth, Richard J., Hastings, N. Y.
Lyon, Merrick, Providence, R. I.
Mabbet, Jonathan, Dover Plains, N. Y.
McIntosh, William C., Philadelphia.
Maclay, Rev. Archibald, D.D., New York.
Magoon, Rev. E. L., D.D., Albany, N. Y.
Magoon, Mrs. E. L., Albany, N. Y.
Malcom, Rev. Howard, D.D., Philadelphia, Pa.
Malcom, Rev. Thomas S., Philadelphia.
Mallary, Rev. C. D., Albany, Ga.
Marble, Joel, Albany, N. Y.
Marchant, Henry, Providence.
Marcley, Mrs. Caroline T., Morrisania, N. Y.
Maple, Thompson, Canton, Ill.
Martin, Rev. G. P., English Neighborhood, N. J.
Martin, Runyon W., New York.
Martin, Charles J., New York.
Marshall, Rev. Enos, Covert, N. Y.
Massey, Rev. Joseph T., Bellingham, Mass.
Mason, Rev. Alanson P., Chelsea, Mass.
Mason, Rev. David G., Keene, N. H.
Mason, Rev. Jas. O., Greenwich, N. Y.
Mason, Rev. Sumner R., Cambridgeport, Mass.
Masters, William, Providence.
Masters, Mrs. Wm., Providence.
Mather, Rev. A. P., California.
Merit, Rev. Columbus D., Washburn, Ill.
Merriam, Jonathan, Newton Centre, Mass.
Messenger, Rev. Edward C., West Medway, Ms.
Middleditch, Rev. Robert T., Red Bank, N. J.
Milbank, Samuel, Jr., New York.
Milbank, Jeremiah, New York.
Miller, John A., New York.
Miller, Rev. D. Henry, Meriden, Ct.
Mills, Rev. Robert C., Salem, Mass.
Miner, Mrs. Henrietta Wilson, Newark, N. J.
Mitchell, Isaac R., Sandwich Islands.
Moore, Rev. Isaac, Jonesville, Mich.
Morgan, Capt. Ebenezer, New London, Ct.
Morse, Mrs. Sophia A., Wyoming, N. Y.
Morse, Rev. J. B., North Orange, N. J.
Morton, Rev. Charles, Corning, N. Y.
Mudge, Rev. Warham, Palmyra, N. Y.
Mulford, Rev. Clarence W., Flemington, N. J.
Munn, William H., New York.
Murdock, Rev. J. N., D.D., Boston.
Murphy, Rev. John C., New York.
Muzzy, Rev. Lawson, Pulaski, N. Y.
Neale, Rev. Rollin H., D.D., Boston.
Newell, Asa, Providence.
Nice, Rev. G. P., Philadelphia.
Nichols, Charles H., Boston, Mass.
Nicholas, Joseph O., Newark, N. J.
Norris, William, Newark, N. J.
Northam, Rev. G., Nominy Grove, Va.
Nott, Rev. A. Kingman, New York.
Olcott, Rev. James B., Springfield, Ill.
Packer, Rev. D., Mount Holly, Vt.
Page, Joseph, Philadelphia.
Parker, Rev. J. W., D.D., Newton Centre, Mass.
Parker, Rev. Carlton, Hebron, Me.
Parker, Rev. S. S., Southbridge, Mass.
Parker, Gilman, Danversport, Mass.
Parker, Rev. Wm., Philadelphia.
Parkhurst, Rev. John, Chelmsford, Mass.
Parkhurst, Rev. J. W., Newton Centre, Mass.
Parks, Rev. Norman, Perry, Ill.
Parmelee, Rev. D. S., New York.
Parmly, Rev. Wheelock H., Jersey City, N. J.
Patch, Abijah, Boston, Mass.
Pattison, Rev. R. E., D.D., Waterville, Me.
Pattison, Rev. William P., Ypsilanti, Mich.
Patton, Rev. Alfred S., Hoboken, N. J.
Paul, Albert, Hastings, N. Y.
Peck, J. B., New York.
Peck, Mrs. Mary, New York.
Peltz, Rev. George A., New York.

Pond, Moses, Boston, Mass.
Pope, Wm. G. E., New Bedford, Mass.
Pope, Mrs. Anna F., New Bedford, Mass.
Pope, Francis E., Danversport, Mass.
Porter, Rev. Lemuel, D.D., Pittsfield, Mass.
Porter, Isaac, Danversport, Mass.
Post, Reuben, Essex, Ct.
Potter, William H., Mystic River, Ct.
Pray, Rev. E. N., Boston, Mass.
Prevaux, Rev. Francis E., San Francisco, Cal.
Price, Rev. Jacob, Edwardsburg, Mich.
Price, William M., Brooklyn.
Pryor, Rev. John, D.D., Cambridge, Mass.
Purington, Rev. Wm. F., Naples, N. Y.
Randall, Rev. S. B., Mystic River, Ct.
Rathbone, John F., Albany, N. Y.
Raymond, Rev. Robert R., Brooklyn, N. Y.
Read, James H., Providence, R. I.
Reding, Rev. C. W., Manchester, Mass.
Reed, Rev. Nathan A., Middletown, N. Y.
Rees, Rev. William, Seneca Falls, N. Y.
Reid, Rev. William, New London, Ct.
Remington, Rev. Stephen, Brooklyn, N. Y.
Reynolds, Joseph, Amenia, N. Y.
Richards, Rev. William C., Providence, R. I.
Richardson, Thomas, Boston, Mass.
Richardson, Rev. J. G., Valley Falls, R. I.
Richmond, Rev. J. L. Mt. Vernon, Ohio.
Ricker, Rev. Joseph, Charlestown, Mass.
Roberts, Charles L., New York.
Roberts, Lewis, Brooklyn, N. Y.
Roberts, A. F., Brooklyn, N. Y.
Robinson, James L., Hastings, N. Y.
Rollinson, Rev. William, Rahway, N. J.
Salisbury, William D., New York.
Samson, J. K., Brooklyn, N. Y.
Sanderson, Rev. A., Littleton, Mass.
Sandford, Rev. Miles, North Adams, Mass.
Sarles, Rev. J. W., Brooklyn, N. Y.
Sather, P., Brooklyn, N. Y.
Savage, M. B., Brooklyn, N. Y.
Sawyer, Rev. Reuben, ——, N. Y.
Seage, Rev. John, White Pigeon, Mich.
Searl, Rev. David, Springfield, N. Y.
Sears, Rev. Barnas, D.D., Providence, R. I.
Seeley, Rev. John T., Syracuse, N. Y.
Serrell, John J., New York.
Serrell, Mrs. Mary Eliza, New York.
Shadrach, Rev. W., D.D., Philadelphia, Pa.
Shailer, Rev. N. E., Deep River, Ct.

Spe
Spr
Sta
Ste
Ste
Ste
Sto
Sto
Ste
Ste
Ste
Ste
Sto
Ste
Stu
Stu
Sw
Sw
Ta
Ta
Ta
Ta
Ta
Ta
Ta
Te
Th
Th
Th
Th
Th
Th
Til
Ti
Ti
Ti
To
To
To
Tr
Tr
Tr
Tr
Tu
Tu
Tu
Tu
Tu
Tu
Tu

Weaver, Wanton A., New London, Ct.
Webb, Rev. G. S., D.D., New Brunswick, N. J.
Welch, Rev B. T., D.D., Newtonville, N. Y.
Wheat, Rev. A. C., Philadelphia.
Wheaton, John, Dorset, Vt.
Wheelock, Rev. Alonzo, D D., Fredonia, N. Y.
Wheeler, Rev. Osgood C., Sacramento, Cal.
Whidden, Randall, Calais, Me.
Whittemore, A. F., Essex, Ct.
White, Rev. J. S., West Wrentham, Mass.
White, Rev. Samuel, North Shore, N. Y.
Whitehead, James M., New York.
Whitman, D. C., Newark, N. J.
Whitney, Ezra S., Brooklyn.
Whightman, Rev. Palmer G., Branford, Ct.
Wilbur, Asa, Boston.
Wilder, Rev. William, Chester, Pa.
Wilds, Rev. Z. P., Harlem, N. Y.
Wilkins, Rev. Stephen, Fort Wayne, Ia.
Willard, Rev. F., South Danvers, Mass.
Willett, Rev. Charles, La Crosse, Wis.
Williams, David S., Fayetteville, N. C.
Williams, Richard P., Essex, Ct.
Williams, Rev. William R., D.D., New York.
Wilson, Francis L., Catskill, N. Y.
Wilson, Daniel M., Newark. N. J.
Wilson, Mrs. Hannah M., Newark, N. J.
Wilson, Rev. Robert J., Elmira, N. Y.
Winegar, Rev. R., Amsterdam, N. Y.
Wines, Rev. Wm. H., Tarrytown, N. Y.
Winterton, William, New York.
Withers, John, Alexandria, D. C.
Witherwax, J. M., Davenport, Iowa.
Woolsey, Rev. J. J., Norwalk, Ct.
Wooster, Rev. Henry, Deep River, Ct.
Wooster, Henry C., Essex, Ct.
Wright, Rev. Thomas G., Wappingers Falls, N. Y.
Wright, Rev. Lyman, Norwich, N. Y.
Wyckoff, William H., LL.D., New York.

MEMBERS FOR LIFE.

BY VIRTUE OF A CONTRIBUTION OF THIRTY DOLLARS.

Abbott, George, Boston.
Abbott, Mrs. H. O., Antrim, N. H.
Abbott, Stephen, Chicopee Falls, Mass.
Abbott, Rev. S. G., Bradford, N. H.
Abrams, Rev. Geo. W., Braman's Corners, N. Y.
Achilles, H. L., Albion, N. Y.
Ackley, Rev. Alvin, Greenport, N. Y.
Adair, William N., Somerville, N. J.
Adams, Miss Priscilla S., New York.
Adams, Mrs. Mary, West Killingly, Ct.
Adams, Rev. S. W., Cleveland, O.
Adams, Rev. R. J., Wallingford, Ct.
Adams, Mrs. Eliza J., Wallingford, Ct.
Adams, Miss Caroline, New York.
Adams, Albert, Augusta, Ga.
Adams, Joseph H., Williamsburgh, N. Y.
Adams, Mrs. Mary, Williamsburgh, N. Y.
Adams, Jedediah, New York.
Adams, Rev. Sullivan, Shaftsbury, Vt.
Adams, Van Rensselaer, Deckertown, N. J.
Adams, Rev. J. M., Croton, N. Y.
Adams, Clark, Galesville, N. Y.
Adams, Rev. John Quincy, New York.
Adams, Mrs. Carrie E., New York.
Adkins, Isaac K., Newport, Ohio.
Adlam, Rev. S., Newport, R. I.
Adlam, Mrs. Martha L., Newport, R. I.
Adsit, Mrs. Maria J., Auburn, N. Y.
Agenbroad, Rev. J. P., Prairie du Chien, Wis.
Ainsworth, Rev. S. C., Truxton, N. Y.
Akerly, Mrs. Priscilla E., Chicago, Ill.
Akerly, George B., Chicago, Ill.
Akerly, William Henry, Chicago, Ill.
Albro, Mrs. Hannah Hill, New York.
Albro, Stephen S., Newport, R. I.
Alden, Rev. John, Northampton, Mass.
Aldrich, Warren, Lowell, Mass.
Alexander, Calvin, West Halifax, Vt.
Allds, Jotham G., Claremont, N. H.
Allen, Rev. Benoni, Cambridge, O.
Allen, Russell, Shelby, N. Y.
Allen, Mrs. Eliza, Shelby, N. Y.
Allen, Walter, New York.
Allen, Ethan, Worcester, Mass.
Allen, Rev. Marvin, Detroit, Mich.
Allen, Rev. N. T., Jewett City, Ct.
Allen, Rev. John, North Wrentham, Mass.
Allen, Mrs. Lorena, New York.
Allen, Benjamin, Seekonk, Mass.
Allen, Joel, East Smithfield, Pa.
Allen, Nathaniel, Brooklin, Me.
Allen, Mrs. Mary B. M., North Sedgwick, Me.
Allen, Alanson, Fair Haven, Vt.
Allen, Mrs. Jane, Fair Haven, Vt.
Allen, Joseph G., Rockland, Ohio.
Allen, David, New Gloucester, Me.
Allen, G. P., Brockport, N. Y.
Allen, Rev. L. B., Yarmouth, Me.
Allen, Thomas, Wilmington, Del.
Allen, Rev. Thomas, Tavoy, Burmah.
Allen, Mrs. A. D., Norwalk, Ohio.
Allen, Alexander H., Delphi, N. Y.
Allen, Mrs. Catharine A., Willingsville, N. Y.
Aller, Amos, Brooklyn, N. Y.
Aller, Mrs. Amos, Brooklyn, N. Y.
Alger, Mrs. Susan, Cleveland, Ohio.
Almond, John P., Bostwick's Mills, N. C.
Ambler, Rev. E. C., Woodstown, N. J.
Ambler, Mrs. Almira, Woodstown, N. J.
Ambler, Starr H., Woodstown, N. J.
Ambler, Rev. J. V., Lanesboro', Mass.
Ambler, Mrs. A. T., Lanesboro', Mass.
Ames, Samuel, New York.
Ames, Robert W., Roxbury, Mass.
Ames, Erasmus D., Uncasville, Ct.
Ames, Rev. W. W., Greenfield, Mass.
Ames, Mrs. W. W., Greenfield, Mass.
Ames, Mrs. Mary S., Salem, Mass.
Ammidown, H., Southbridge, Mass.
Amsbury, Jabez, Norwich, Ct.
Amory, Peter B., New York.
Amory, Mrs. Anna M., New York.
Andem, Rev. James, Jericho, Vt.
Andem, Mrs. Emma W., Jericho, Vt.
Anderson, William T., Princeton, N. J.
Anderson, Mrs. Catharine J., Princeton, N. J.
Anderson, John T., Verdon, Pa.
Anderson, Peter, New York.
Anderson, William, Hoboken, N. J.
Anderson, Rev. Edward, Milford, N. H.
Andrews, Milton, New Britain, Ct.
Andrews, William, Providence, R. I.
Andrews, Mrs. Deliah, Providence, R. I.
Andrews, Mrs. Wm., Providence, R. I.

[illegible]
Arnold, Mrs Frances R., Providence, R. I.
Arnold, Rev. Benjamin B., Hartford, Iowa.
Arnold, Miss Phebe, Jay, N. Y.
Arnold, Mrs. Mary, Clifton Park, N. Y.
Arnold, Israel, Providence, R. I.
Arnold, A. Chapman, New London, Ct.
Arthur, Rev. William, Newtonville, N. Y.
Ash, Rev. [illegible] R., Logansport, [illegible]a.
Ashton, Samuel K., M.D., Philadelphia, Pa.
Atkins, Loyd, Bristol, Ct.
Atkins, Roswell, Bristol, Ct.
Atkinson, Taylor B., West Philadelphia, Pa.
Atwater, Erasmus, Throopsville, N. Y.
Atwood, Lewis, Waterbury, Ct.
Atwood, Rev. John, New Boston, N. H.
Atwood, Mrs. Lydia N., New Boston, N. H.
Austin, Edward, New York.
Austin, Samuel, Suffield, Ct.
Austin, Cornelius, Rochester, N. Y.
Avery, Mrs. Clara, New York.
Avery, Rev. E. J., Worcester, Mass.
Avery, William D., Providence, R. I.
Avery, Rev. D., Tyringham, Mass.
Avery, E. J., Brookline, Mass.
Avery, John, Lebanon, Ct.
Ayer, Charles B., Preston, Ct.
Ayer, Mrs. Richard, Haverhill, Mass.
Ayers, James C., Plainfield, N. J.
Ayers, Horace, Worcester, Mass.
Ayers, Mrs. Mary, New York.
Ayers, Benjamin, Greenwich, N. J.
Babcock, Rev. O. W., Gouverneur, N. Y.
Babcock, John N., New Haven, Ct.
Babcock, H. S., Homer, N. Y.
Babcock, Rev. J. J., Jay, N. Y.
Baber, Alfred, Keeseville, N. Y.
Bachellor, Mrs. Abbey A., Haverhill, Mass.
Bachelor, Rev. M., Pownal, Vt.
Bacon, Jacob, Boston, Mass.
Bacon, Rev. William, Newport, N. J.
Bacon, Rev. Charles L., Trumansburg, N. Y.
Bacon, Mrs. Mary L., Trumansburg, N. Y.
Bacon, Miss Ann, Dorchester, Mass.
Bacon, W. A., Ludlow, Vt.
Bacon, Almon, Lyme, Ct.
Bacon, Martha A., Chelsea, Mass.
Bagby, Rev. Richard, Stevensville, Va.
Bagley, S. V., New York.
Bagley, Miss Ellen, Waterboro Centre, Me.
Bailey, Mrs. S. W., Parham's Store, Va.

Bake
Bake
Bake
Balc
Bald
Bald
Bald
Bald
Bald
Bald
Bald
Bald
Bald
Bald
Bald
Bald
Bald
Bale
Ball,
Ball,
Ball,
Ball,
Balla
Balla
Balla
Ball
Banc
Banc
Banc
Bang
Ball
Bank
Bant
Bar,
Bart
Bart
Bar
Bar
Bar
Bar
Bar
Bar
Bar
Bar
Bar
Bar
Bar
Barl
Barl
Bar

Barrows, Mrs. Sarah W., Dorchester, Mass.
Barter, John, Brooklyn, N. Y.
Bartholomew, Jacob, Philadelphia, Pa.
Bartlett, Rev. Daniel, China, Me.
Bartlett, Stephen, Worcester, Mass.
Bartlett, Mrs. Elizabeth J., Deep River, Ct.
Bartollette, John T., Somerville, N. J.
Barringer, Jacob P., Troy, N. Y.
Barrass, Rev. Thomas, Baptist Town, N. J.
Barrass, Mrs. Mary Ann, Baptist Town, N. J.
Barber, Aaron, Vittoria, C. W.
Barber, Mrs. Elizabeth, Vittoria, C. W.
Barber, Moses, Waterford, C. W.
Barber, Abraham N., Waterford, C. W.
Barber, Miss Charlotte, New Haven, Ct.
Barber, Rev. Bradford H., Charleston, N. Y.
Barry, S. L., Ovid, N. Y.
Barstow, Charles, Boston.
Bassett, Nymphas, Shelbyville, Ia.
Batchelder, Mrs. Henry, Beverly, Mass.
Bateman, Mrs. Rachel, Dividing Creek, N. J.
Bates, Mrs. Caroline C., New Bedford, Mass.
Bates, Mrs. Joanna, Providence.
Bates, Whitman, Pawtucket, R. I.
Bates, Dennis P., Lowell, Mass.
Bates, Rev. John, Cascade, Iowa.
Bates, Rev. L. C., Groton, N. Y.
Bates, Rev. Ira, Centreville, R. I.
Bates, Lyman, Medina, N. Y.
Bates, Levi D., Providence.
Bates, William B., Pawtucket, R. I.
Batey, Rev. John.
Battell, Rev. Allen E., West Townsend, Mass.
Battle, Rev. A. J., Murfreesboro', N. C.
Baugh, Dr. J. M., Petersburgh, Va.
Baxter, Thomas, Penn Yan, N. Y.
Baxter, John C., New York.
Baxter, Thomas, Detroit, Mich.
Baxter, William M., New York.
Beagle, Henry, Philadelphia.
Beam, Joseph, Brooklyn, N. Y.
Beam, Mrs. Louisa, Brooklyn, N. Y.
Beam, David B., Paterson, N. J.
Bean, H. L., Skaneateles, N. Y.
Bean, Benjamin, Ostrander, Ohio.
Beason, W. D., Nashua, N. H.
Beattie, Rev. W. Q., Bennettsville, N. C.
Beatson, Miss Helen, New York.
Beaver, J. M., Hillsborough, N. C.
Beebe, Mrs. Charlotte, Brooklyn, N. Y.
Beebe, Mrs. Lydia, Waterford, Ct.
Beecher, Mrs. Mary C., Saratoga Springs, N. Y.
Beebee, A. M., Jr., Hamilton, N. Y.
Beck, Rev. John J., Coosawhatchie, S. C.
Beck, Rev. Levi G., New Britain, Pa.
Beckwith, Miss Abby G., Providence.
Beckwith, Elisha W., Norwich, Ct.
Beckwith, Jason, New London, Ct.
Beckwith, Ezra S., New London, Ct.
Beckwith, Mrs. Ezra S., New London, Ct.
Beckwith, Clement S., New London, Ct.
Beckwith, Nathan, Upper Red Hook, N. Y.
Beckwith, Elisha, Waterford, Ct.
Beckwith, Mrs. Betsey, Albion, N. Y.
Belcher, Rev. James, Oldtown, Me.
Belden, Rev. Joseph, Bordentown, N. J.
Belden, Mrs. Mary Ann, Meriden, Ct.
Belknap, Rev. Appleton, Lyme, N. H.
Bell, Rev. Edward, South Woodstock, Ct.
Bell, Miss Jane Ann, South Woodstock, Ct.
Bell, Joseph, Brookfield, O.
Bell, John, New York.
Bellamy, Rev. David, Mt. Morris, N. Y.
Bellamy, Mrs. Lucy A. C., Mt. Morris, N. Y.
Bellamy, Rev. R. K., Chicopee Falls, Mass.
Beman, Mrs. Rebecca S., Deep River, Ct.
Beman, Miss Charlotte, Deep River, Ct.
Beman, Mrs. Samantha, Brooklyn, N. Y.
Bemis, Miss Elizabeth H., Worcester, Mass.
Beeman, Rev. James M., Dickinson, N. Y.
Bemrose, Mrs. Elizabeth M., Port Jarvis, N. Y.
Bendall, George, Coman's Well, Va.
Bendernagel, John, New York.
Benedict, Stephen, Pawtucket, R. I.
Bendict, Rev. David, D.D., Pawtucket, R. I.
Benedict, Miss Cornelia E., Providence.
Benedict, Rev. N. D., Wawarsing, N. Y.
Benedict, Mrs. Nancy, New York.
Benedict, Rev. E. L., Maine, N. Y.
Benjamin, W. P., New London, Ct.
Benjamin B. M., Rochester, N. Y.
Bennett, Rev. Cephas, Tavoy, Asia.
Bennett, Joseph E., Manchester, N. H.
Bennett, Hiram, Fulton City, Ill.
Bennett, Rev. Alvin, Freetown Corners, N. Y.
Bennett, Rev. David, Unionville, N. Y.
Bennett, E. A., Philadelphia.
Bennett, Mrs. Judith B., Philadelphia.
Bennett, Miss Anna, Philadelphia.
Bennett, Rev. Olney, Preston, N. Y.
Bennett, Joseph, Manchester, N. H.
Bennett, Joseph L., New London, Ct.
Bennett, Rev. Perry, Winchester, Ill.
Bennett, Mrs. Flavilla, Bennettsville, N. Y.
Benton, Mrs. Sarah, Saratoga, N. Y.
Benton, Rev. George W., Granville, Ill.
Benton, Austin W., Jamaica Plains, Mass.
Bernard, Rev. David, Akron, Ohio.
Bernie, Miss Anna, New York.
Bertine, Miss Sarah Ann, New York.
Bertine, James C., New York.
Berry, Zebina E., Worcester, Mass.
Berry, Susan C., Worcester, Mass.
Berry, Ellen L., Worcester, Mass.
Berry, S. Homer, Norwalk, O.
Beston, Rev. F., Cheshire, Mass.
Betts, Rev. Platt, Omro, Wis.
Betts, Philander, Danbury, Ct.
Bevan, Rev. Isaac, Philadelphia.
Beverly, Miss Elizabeth, New York.
Bicking, Richard, Wilmington, Del.
Bickford, Rev. M. L., Waltham, Mass.
Biddle, Samuel S., Forestville, N. C.
Biddle, Rev. William, Voluntown, Ct.
Bidgood, Mrs. L., Hargroves', Va.
Bigelow, Rev. John R., M.D., New York.
Bigelow, Mrs. Eunice P., New York.
Bigelow, John B., Brooklyn, N. Y.
Bigelow, Mrs. Catharine, Brooklyn, N. Y.
Bigelow, Franklin H., Brooklyn, N. Y.
Bigelow, Miss Nancy H., Brooklyn, N. Y.
Bigelow, Mrs. Charlotte, Brooklyn, N. Y.
Bigelow, Rev. J. F., Middleboro, Mass.
Bill, Rev. G. B., Rumney, N. H.
Bill, O. A., New Haven, Ct.
Bill, Eleazer, Willimantic, Ct.
Billings, Rev. John, Mt. Vernon, Me.
Billings, Mrs. Betsey, Mt. Vernon, Me.
Billingslea, Dr. C., Montgomery Co., Ala.
Biglow, Barna, Perkinsville, Vt.
Bingham, Luther, Fort Wayne, Ia.
Bird, Rev. John, Lloyd's, Essex Co., Va.
Birdsey, Mrs. Rebecca C., Meriden Ct.
Birdsey, Linus, Meriden, Ct.
Birdsey, Mrs. V. A., Meriden, Ct.
Bishop, Charles, New London, Ct.
Bishop, Jessie, Cleveland, O.
Bishop, James W. A., Philadelphia.
Bishop, Mrs. Caroline C., New York.
Blackford, Ephraim, New Market, N. J.
Blackledge, Jacob, Stoningtonboro', Ct.
Blackwell, J. P., Brooklyn, N. Y.
Blackinton, Sanford, North Adams, Mass.
Blackmer, Jirah, Wheatland, N. Y.
Blackmer, John, Greece, N. Y.
Blaisdell, Josiah C., Fall River, Mass.
Blake, Aaron, Chelsea, Mass.
Blake, Jonathan, Brooklyn, N. Y.
Blake, David B., Providence.
Blake, Ezekiel, Chicopee Falls, Mass.

Bloodgood, James, Springville, N. Y.
Bloomer, Lewis, Ovid, N. Y.
Blunt, Mrs. R., Edenton, N. C.
Bly, Mrs. Lydia, Ticonderoga, N. Y.
Boardman, Thomas, Amesbury, Mass.
Bodine, Miss Mary, Hudson, N. Y.
Bogart, Rev. Wm., East Galway, N. Y.
Bokee, Hon. David A., Brooklyn, N. Y.
Bolles, James G., Hartford, Ct.
Bolles, Francis, Niantic, Ct.
Bolton, Rev. A., Jordanville, N. Y.
Boomer, Rev. James C. Chelmsford, Mass
Boone, Dr. Levi D., Chicago, Ill.
Boone, Mrs. L. D. Chicago, Ill.
Booth, Henry, Greenport, N. Y.
Booth, Rev. John, Fentonville, Mich.
Booth, Abel A., Eaton, N. Y.
Bond, Leonard, New York.
Bond, Rev. G. W., Eugene City, Oregon.
Bond, Rev. E. P., Lawrenceburgh, Ia.
Bond, Rev. Emmons P., New Britain, Ct.
Bond, Mrs. Mary, New Britain, Ct.
Bond, Rev. Phineas, Cornish Flat, N. H.
Bonham, Rev. J. W., Lowell, Mass.
Bonham, Daniel, Berryville, Va.
Bonney, W. F., Eaton, N. Y.
Borden, Lodowick, Fall River, Mass.
Borden, Isaac, Fall River, Mass.
Borden, Charles, Fall River, Mass.
Borden, Joseph, Fall River, Mass.
Borden, Cook, Fall River, Mass.
Borland, Chauncey, Iowa City, Iowa.
Bosson, George P., Chelsea, Mass.
Bosson, Benjamin P., Chelsea, Mass.
Bosson, Miss Mary, Chelsea, Mass.
Bostick, Elisha, Bostick's Mills, N. C.
Bostick, Elijah, Bostick's Mills, N. C.
Bostick, Tristam, Bostick's Mills, N. C.
Bostick, Benj. R., Robertsville, S. C.
Bostick, Mrs. Jane A., Robertsville, S. C.
Boswell, Davis, Stilesville, Ia.
Bosworth, William M., East Poultney, Vt.
Bosworth, George H., Fall River, Mass.
Bosworth, William, Greenwich, N. Y.
Bottum, Mrs. Peace, Shaftsbury, Vt.
Bottum, Mrs. Frances S., Shaftsbury Vt.
Bottum, Elijah, Shaftsbury, Vt.
Bottum, Nathan, Shaftsbury, Vt.
Boughton, James, New York.
Bourne, Rev. C. C., Leesville, N. Y.

Bronson, Rev. Asa, Stonington, Ct.
Bronson, Rev. Benj. F., Woburn, Mass.
Bronson, Mrs. Anna C., Woburn, Mass.
Bronson, Miss Aydee A., Townsend, Mass.
Bronson, Rev. A., Williamstown, Mass.
Bronson, Rev. Asa C., Mystic River, Ct.
Bronson, Mrs. Marinda, Stonington, Ct.
Brooks, Samuel, Sen., Cornwall, N. Y.
Brooks, Eli T., South Brookfield, Mass.
Brooks, Dea. Kendall, Roxbury, Mass.
Brooks, Miss Mary, Fitchburg, Mass.
Brooks, John, Hanover, Mass.
Brooks, Mrs. Elizabeth, Cambridge, Mass.
Brooks, Rev. Walter R., Hamilton, N. Y.
Brooks, Alpheus, Bridgeton, N. J.
Browe, Rev. E. S., Riceville, N. J.
Brower, Davis E., Doylestown, Pa.
Brown, W. S., Britton's Cross Roads, N. C.
Brown, Josiah, Haverhill, Mass.
Brown, J. S., Fitchburg, Mass.
Brown, Edw. L., Brooklyn, N. Y.
Brown, Mrs. Susan A., Brooklyn N. Y.
Brown, Rev. Amasa, Concord, N. H.
Brown, Rev. Dana, Nashua, N. H.
Brown, Rev. E. T., Wooster, Ohio.
Brown, Andrew, Middleton, N. J.
Brown, George W., New York.
Brown, Hugh H., Providence.
Brown, Rev. E. C., Prairie City, Ill.
Brown, Rev. F. G., West Townsend, Mass.
Brown, Rev. Wm. L., Watertown, Mass.
Brown, Rev. Joseph P., Moosop, Ct.
Brown, Daniel, Sempronius, N. Y.
Brown, Oliver, Mystic River, Ct.
Brown, William, Cambridge, Mass.
Brown, Rev. Samuel M., Granville, Ill.
Brown, Miss Alice A., Auburn, N. Y.
Brown, John S., Fisherville, N. H.
Brown, Henry H., Fisherville, N. H.
Brown, Miss Harriet, Norwich, N. Y.
Brown, Rev. J., Springfield, Ohio.
Brown, Mrs. Emily M. A., Fauquier, Va.
Brown, Mrs. Elizabeth E., Aylett's, Va.
Brown, Miss Ann F., Providence, R. I.
Brown, Mrs. Mary F., Keene, N. H.
Brown, Mrs. Isaac, Haverhill, Mass.
Brown, Mrs. Margaret A., Reading, Ohio.
Brown, Rev. J. F., Scotch Plains, N. J.
Brown, Rev. Philip P., Madison, N. Y.
Brown, Rev. Wm., Hartford, N. Y
Brown, Evander M., Saratoga Springs, N. Y.
Brown, L. R., Hartford, Ct.
Brown, Samuel, M.D., Philadelphia, Pa.
Brown, Joshua, New York.
Brown, Sarah H., 2nd, West Townsend, Mass.
Brown, Newel, Watertown, Mass.
Brown, Mrs. Mary, W. Watertown, Mass.
Brown, Aaron, Lorraine, N. Y.
Brown, Mrs. Lucretia, Fisherville, N. H.
Brown, Mrs. Maria C., Watertown, Mass.
Brown, Mrs. Josiah, Haverhill, Mass.
Brown, Mrs. Frances J., Bedford, N. Y.
Brown, James, Boston, Mass.
Brown, Henry, New London, Ct.
Brown, Miss A. Matilda, New London, Ct.
Brown, Mrs. Sophia C., Fisherville, N. H.
Browne, Rev. Addison, Tyringham, Mass.
Brownell, Rev. E. W., West Rupert, Vt.
Brownson, Rev. I. K., Greenfield, Ohio.
Brownson, Moses, Butternuts, N. Y.
Bruen, George H., Newark, N. J.
Bruen, Mrs. George H., Newark, N. J.
Bruce, Benjamin G., New York.
Bruce, Silas, Boston, Mass.
Bruce, John M., Jr., New York.
Brush, Mrs. Susan G., New York.
Brusle, William A., New York.
Brusle, Mrs. Elizabeth, New York.
Bryant, George, Williamsburgh, N. Y.
Bryant, Mary A., Chelsea, Mass.

Bryant, Elizabeth D., Chelsea, Mass.
Bryant, Harriet T., Chelsea, Mass.
Bryant, James, Dorchester, Mass.
Buck, David S., Cambridge, Mass.
Buckbee, Mrs. Laura G., New York.
Bucknell, Ebenezer G., Newark, N. J.
Bucknell, Miss Elizabeth, Newark, N. J.
Bucknell, Wm., Jr., Philadelphia, Pa.
Bucknell, Miss Lavinia Louisa, Philadelphia.
Bucknell, Mrs. Harriet M., Philadelphia.
Buckner, Mrs. Sarah T., Baltimore.
Budlong, Mrs. Rebecca S. C., Providence.
Budlong, Miss Rebecca A., Providence
Budd, Francis F., Williamsburgh, N. Y.
Buel, Rev. Rufus F., Providence, R. I.
Buel, Mrs. Mary J., Providence, R. I.
Buel, Rev. A. P., Bordentown, N. J.
Buffinton, Benjamin, Fall River, Mass.
Bull, John B., New York.
Bullard, Rev. Joseph A., Ware, Mass.
Bullard, Solomon R., Nashua, N. H.
Bullock, George, Utica, N. Y.
Bullock, Rev. A. D., Palmer Depot, Mass.
Bulkley, Rev. Justus, Carrollton, Ill.
Bulkley, Mrs. Justus, Carrollton, Ill.
Bulkley, Mrs. Harriet, Barry, Ill.
Bundy, Asa S., West Woodstock, Ct.
Bundy, Mrs. Hannah, West Hartwick, N. Y.
Bunnell, Rev. W. B., Tremont, Ill.
Bunnell, Mrs. Elizabeth E., Tremont, Ill.
Bunnell, Miss Alwilda, Williamsburgh, N. Y.
Burbank, Mrs. Irene, New York.
Burbank, Wellman, Chelsea, Mass.
Burbank, Asa L., Worcester, Mass.
Burchard, Leonard, Brooklyn, N. Y.
Burd, Elisha, Baptist Town, N. J.
Burdick, Perrin, New York.
Burdick, V. H., ———, Min.
Burdick, Mrs. Betsey, Greenwich, N. Y.
Burger, Mrs. Rebecca T., New York.
Burgess, Sylvanus, Providence.
Burgess, Alexander, Providence.
Burke, Mrs. Louisa S., Rochester, N. Y.
Burke, Mrs. Emma, Brooklyn, N. Y.
Burke, Mrs. Elizabeth, Brooklyn, N. Y.
Burke, Samuel M. Galesville, N. Y.
Burlingham, Mrs. Emma S., New York.
Burnett, Mrs. Maria M., Middleboro', Mass.
Burnett, Rev. C. C., Middleboro', Mass.
Burnett, Eli S., West Philadelphia, Pa.
Burnett, Rev. Hiram, Mt. Pleasant, Iowa.
Burns, Wm., Philadelphia, Pa.
Burr, David M., Gloversville, N. Y.
Burr, Mrs. Emily C., Gloversville, N. Y.
Burr, James H., Gloversville, N. Y.
Burr, Mrs. James H., Gloversville. N. Y.
Burr, Miss Julia A., Gloversville, N. Y.
Burr, Harvey W., Gloversville, N. Y.
Burroughs, James M., Marlton, N. J.
Burroughs, Caleb G., Providence, R. I.
Burrows, Rev. David, Chester, Vt.
Burrows, Rev. J. L., D.D., Richmond, Va.
Burrows, Rev. Baxter, Grafton, Vt.
Burrows, Mrs. Lorenzo, Albion, N. Y.
Burrows, John R., Providence, R. I.
Burrows, A. B., Brockport, N. Y.
Burt, T. M., Kinderhook, N. Y.
Burt, Mrs. Edwin C., Brooklyn, N. Y.
Burt, William, Mount Vernon, Mich.
Burt, Wells, Mt. Vernon, Mich.
Burt, Rev. Joseph M., North Tewksbury, Mass.
Burton, Rev. Nathan S., Granville, O.
Burton, Mrs. Sarah J., Granville, O.
Burton, Rev. Hardine, Georgia, Ia.
Burwell, Rev. Ira D., Moriah, N. Y.
Bushnell, Geo. W., Winthrop, Ct.
Butcher, Charles, Freehold, N. J.
Butcher, Mrs. Mary, Philadelphia, Pa.
Butler, Rev. John, Lewiston, Me.
Butler, Mrs. Eusebia C. S., Berlin Heights, Ohio.

Calkin, Rev. Abijah M., Cochecton, N. Y.
Calhopper, Rev. F. T., Camden, N. J.
Calder, John, Providence, R. I.
Calder, Mrs. John L., Providence, R. I.
Callender, Rev. N., LaPorte, Pa.
Call, Rev. O. B., Lyons, Mich.
Call, John R., Boston, Mass.
Cameron, John A., Thurso, Can.
Campbell, Miss Mary, New York.
Campbell, Rev. T. P., East Avon, N. Y.
Campbell, Rev. Charles, Milestown, Pa.
Campbell, Mrs. Charles, Milestown, Pa.
Campbell, Richard, Trenton, N. J.
Candee, John D., New Haven, Ct.
Capen, Barnabas D., Sharon, Mass.
Capin, Ezekiel, Canton, Mass.
Capron, Miss Rebecca S., Worcester, Mass.
Capron, John, Albany, N. Y.
Capron, Rev. Barton, Preble, N. Y.
Capwell, Albert B., Brooklyn, N. Y.
Capwell, Mrs. Julia A., Brooklyn, N. Y.
Card, Rev. William H., LaCrosse, Wis.
Card, Rev. Henry S., Sandusky, N. Y.
Carleton, Miss Frances, Newton Centre, Mass.
Carleton, Miss E. H., Newton Centre, Mass.
Carleton, G. R., Newton Centre, Mass.
Carleton, Judson, Newton Centre, Mass.
Carleton, Howard, Newton Centre, Mass.
Carleton, William H., Newton Centre, Mass.
Carleton, Stephen, Lynn, Mass.
Carlton, Guy, Methuen, Mass.
Carew, Miss Harriet, New York.
Carew, Mrs. Margaret N., New York.
Carew, William Henry, New York.
Carlisle, Charles, New Haven, Ct.
Carpenter, Daniel T., Pawtucket, R. I.
Carpenter, Mrs. Elizabeth, Pawtucket, R. I.
Carpenter, Miss Lydia, Pawtucket, R. I.
Carpenter, Rev. Calvin G., Phelps, N. Y.
Carpenter, Rev. J. M., Jacobstown, N. J.
Carpenter, Mrs. Sarah F., Jacobstown, N. J.
Carpenter, Rev. Burton B., Griggsville, Ill.
Carpenter, James, New York.
Carpenter, J. H., Madison, Wis.
Carpenter, Mrs. Martha C., Madison, Wis.
Carpenter, Elliot, Putnam, Ct.
Carmer, Henry, Griggsville, Ill.
Carr, Rev. Samuel J., Somerset, Mass.
Carr, Alexander W., Rowley, Mass.
Carr, Rev. L. C., Moline, Ill.

Caul
Caul
Caul
Cav
Cav
Cell,
Cha
Chat
Chal
Chat
Chat
Chal
Chal
Chal
Cha
Cha
Cha
Cha
Cha
Cha
Cha
Cha
Cha
Cha
Cha
Cha
Cha
Cha
Cha
Chaj
Cha
Chaj
Chaj
Chaj
Chaj
Chaj
Chaj
Chaj
Chaj
Chaj
Cha
Cha
Cha
Cha
Cha
Cha
Cha
Cha
Cha
Cha

Child, Henry W., Warren, R. I.
Child, Shubel P., Warren, R. I.
Childs, Miss Jane L., New York.
Childs, John E., Providence, R. I.
Childs, Mrs. Jennet, Deep River, Ct.
Chipman, J. A., Boston, Mass.
Church, Rev. Leroy, Chicago, Ill.
Church, Miss Clara O. B., New York.
Church, Miss Emma C., New York.
Church, William, New York.
Church, Frank P., New York.
Church, John A., New York.
Church, Rev. Isaac M., South Kingston, R. I.
Church, Norman B., Uncasville, Ct.
Churchill, Amos, East Hubbardton, Vt.
Churchill, John B., St. Johnsville, N. Y.
Clapp, Ozias, Boston, Mass.
Clapp, Rev. Wm. S., New York.
Clapp, Russell, Providence, R. I.
Clapp, Miss Jane R., Providence, R. I.
Clapp, Mrs. Eliza H., Boston, Mass.
Clapp, Rev. Warren B., Dover, N. H.
Clark, Rev. Frederick, New Orleans, La.
Clark, Rev. Norman, Ira, Vt.
Clark, Mrs. Juliet, Ira, Vt.
Clark, Abel, Willimantic, Ct.
Clark, Mrs. Betsey Ann, Bedford, N. Y.
Clark, Philo W., North East, N. Y.
Clark, Mrs. Sarah M., New Brunswick, N. J.
Clark, Miss E., Beaufort, S. C.
Clark, Mrs. M. G., Indianapolis, Ia.
Clark, Mrs. Elizabeth, New York.
Clark, Miss Sallie Cone, New York.
Clark, Miss Martha, New York.
Clark, Mrs. Louisa, South Berwick, Me.
Clark, Miss Clarissa, Deep River, Ct.
Clark, Miss Eliza, Syracuse, N. Y.
Clark, Teresa B., Lakeville, N. Y.
Clark, Mrs. Ann, DeWitt, Iowa.
Clark, Mrs Thomas, Westfield, N. J.
Clark, Rev. C. A., Homer, N. Y.
Clark, Henry, Middletown, Ct.
Clark, Rev. T. W., Wheatland, N. Y.
Clark, Alexander, Boston, Mass.
Clark, A. S., Albany, N. Y.
Clark, Mrs. John, Bridgeport, Ct.
Clark, Henry, Southington, Ct.
Clark, Rev. N. Judson, Schuylkill Falls, Pa.
Clark, Mrs. Caroline, Schuylkill Falls, Pa.
Clark, Alfred, Methuen, Mass.
Clark, Edward, Sheldrake, N. Y.
Clark, Lyman, Meriden, Ct.
Clark, David, Putnam, Ct.
Clark, George, Chelsea, Mass.
Clark, Rev. George W., New Market, N. J.
Clarke, Rev. Henry, Pittsfield, Mass.
Clarke, Rev. John, Esqueesing, C. W.
Clarke, William, Syracuse, N. Y.
Clarke, John C. C., Brooklyn, N. Y.
Clayton, James D., Freehold, N. J.
Cleaver, Isaac A., Spread Eagle, Pa.
Cleaves, Rev. F. E., Fitchburg, Mass.
Cleaves, Mrs. Kate, Fitchburg, Mass.
Cleaves, Samuel, Portsmouth, N. H.
Cleghorn, Rev. Adams, Belleville, N. Y.
Clement, Wm. T., Shelburne Falls, Mass.
Clement, Rev. Joshua, Post Mills, Vt.
Clopton, Rev. James C., Lynchburg, Va.
Clopton, Mrs. M., New Kent, Va.
Closse, Nicholas, Door Village, Ia.
Coburn, Hannah H., Erie, Ill.
Coburn, Charles, Fall River, Mass.
Coburn, Rev. J. M., Manchester, N. H.
Coburn, Mrs. Lydia P., Manchester, N. H.
Coburn, Washington L., Manchester, N. H.
Cobb, Mrs. Sarah M., Brooklyn, N. Y.
Cocke, Charles L., Richmond, Va.
Cochran, G. W., Methuen, Mass.
Cockran, Justin.
Coe, Ward, Meriden, Ct.
Coe, Tunis H., Yates, N. Y.
Coffin, D. B., N. Newton, Mass.
Coffin, Rev. James L., Wyocena, Wis.
Coggeshall, Mrs. Elizabeth, New Bedford, Mass.
Cogswell, B. F., Brooklyn, N. Y.
Cogswell, Mrs. Mary, Haverhill, Mass.
Cogswell, Mrs. Amanda, Janesville, Wis.
Coyt, Miss Elizabeth, New London, Ct.
Colby, Rev. Lewis, Cambridge, Mass.
Colby, Mrs. Eliza A., New London, N. H.
Colby, Isaac, Salem, Mass.
Colby, Gardner, Newton, Mass.
Colby, Mrs. Mary Colgate, New York.
Colby, Mrs. Emily F., Hennicker, N. H.
Colburn, Rev. Alfred, Providence, R. I.
Colburn, Charles C., West Dedham, Mass.
Cole, Rev. L. B., Lowell, Mass.
Cole, Samuel, Clifton Park, N. Y.
Cole, Mrs. Frances L., New York.
Cole, Mrs. Susan, Westerloo, N. Y.
Cole, Mrs. Jemima P., Plainfield, N. J.
Cole, Robert H., Southbridge, Mass.
Cole, Mrs. Lucy B., Beverly, Mass.
Coley, Rev. James M., Waverly, N. Y.
Colgrove, Belah H., Sardinia, N. Y.
Coleman, James B., Somerville, N. J.
Coleman, Rev. M, ———, Wis.
Coleman, Mrs. Sarah, ———, Wis.
Coleman, Rev. Zenas, Mt. Vernon, Mich.
Coleman, Daniel B., Trenton, N. J.
Colesworthy, Rev. George, Greenfield, Mass
Colgate, Cornelius C., New York.
Colgate, Edward, New York.
Colgate, William, New York.
Colgate, Miss Elizabeth, New York.
Colgate, Miss Hannah, New York.
Colgate, Miss Jane, New York.
Colgate, Miss Sarah, New York.
Colgrove, Uri, Johnstown, O.
Collett, Wm. R., Lebanon, Ohio.
Collins, Mrs. Ann D., Haverhill, Mass.
Collins, Rev. Roswell, Charlestown, N. Y.
Collins, William S., Davenport, Iowa.
Colman, John B., Williamsburg, N. Y.
Colley, Benj. E., Cambridge, Mass.
Collom, Mrs. Mary E., Mt. Holly, N. J.
Colver, Rev. Charles K., Charlestown, Mass.
Coman, Lovian O., Le Roy, N. Y.
Combs, Wm. S., Imlaystown, N. J.
Comey, J. F., Brooklyn, N. Y.
Compton, James I., Plainfield, N. J.
Compton, Anthony, New York.
Compton, Mrs. Maria, New York.
Compton, Rev. Robert, Newton, Pa.
Compton, Wm. H., Roadstown, N. J.
Comstock, George R., New London, Ct.
Comstock, Mrs. Ann, New London, Ct.
Comstock, C. C., New London, Ct.
Comstock, Charles F., Lyme, Ct.
Conant, Mrs. John, Brandon, Vt.
Conant, Rev. Thomas, Scituate, Mass.
Conant, Rev. Thomas, J., D.D., Rochester, N. Y.
Conant, Levi, Boston, Mass.
Condit, Miss Sarah E., New York.
Cone, Spencer H., Jr., New York.
Cone, Miss Kate E., New York.
Conklin, Mrs. Ann, New York
Conklin, Lewis L., Paterson, N. J.
Conklin, George, Amenia, N. Y.
Conover, Mrs. Catharine S., New York.
Conover, Robert, Petersburg, Ill.
Conover, Cyrenius G., Middletown, N. J.
Conover, Mrs. Rebecca M., Holmdel, N. J.
Conover, Rev. Edward, West Troy, N. Y.
Conrad, Rev. Peter, East Troy, Wis.
Converse, Rev. Otis, Worcester, Mass.
Converse, Charles E., Jamaica Plains, Mass.
Converse, James W., Jamaica Plains, Mass.
Converse, Elisha S., Malden, Mass.
Converse, Joseph H., Jamaica Plains, Mass.

Coolidge, Josiah, Cambridge, Mass.
Coolidge, Austin J., Cambridge, Mass.
Coolidge, Joseph G., Cambridge, Mass.
Coon, Rev. Charles, Mt. Holly, Vt.
Cooper, Edwin, Hoboken, N. J.
Cooper, Rev. Warren, Boylston, Mass.
Cooper, Eliphalet, New Haven, Ct.
Cooper, Charles, New York.
Cooper, Obadiah, Brooklyn, N. Y.
Copp, Miss Louisa P., North Danvers, Mass.
Corbett, O. G., Orange, N. J.
Corbett, Mary S., Orange, N. J.
Corbin, Penuel, Jr., West Woodstock, Ct.
Cordo, Henry A., New Brunswick, N. J.
Corey, Rev. D. G., Utica, N. Y.
Corliss, Britton, Philadelphia, Pa.
Corliss, Miss Sarah, Greenwich, N. Y.
Cornelius, Rev. Samuel, Jr., Fond du Lac, Wis.
Cornwell, A. C., Broadalbin, N. Y.
Cornell, Thomas, Rondout, N. Y.
Cornell, Miss Mary A., Rondout, N. Y.
Cornell, Paul D., Auburn, N. Y.
Cornell, Wm. M., Plainfield, N. J.
Corthell, Loring, New London, Ct.
Corwin, R. G., Lebanon, Ohio.
Corwin, Rev. David, Cohoes, N. Y.
Corwin, Rev. Ira, South Bend, Ia.
Corwith, Mrs. Catharine F., New York.
Cotterell, Mrs. Mary, Battenville, N. Y.
Cotterell, Miss Mary, Union Village, N. Y.
Couch, E. P., Nashua, N. H.
Covey, Rev. Walter, West Meredeth, N. Y.
Cowan, Mrs. Hannah, New York.
Cowdin, Mrs. Aurinda G., East Templeton, Mass.
Cowles, Mrs. Rebekah, Claremont, N. H.
Cowles, Miss Julliette R., Claremont, N. H.
Cowles, James Albert, Claremont, N. H.
Cox, Rev. Morgan R., New Brunswick, N. J.
Cox, Mrs. Mary B., New Brunswick, N. J.
Cox, Miss Anna, New Brunswick, N. J.
Cox, Miss Mary, New York.
Cox, Miss Abigail, New York.
Coxey, James, West Philadelphia, Pa.
Coy, Sylvanus B., West Dedham, Mass.
Craba, Rev. J. D., Claysville, Ia.
Crafts, George A., South Boston, Mass.
Craig, Rev. A. M., Britton's Cross Roads, N. C.
Craig, Charles A., Bridgeport, Ct.
Craig, Mrs. Charles A., Bridgeport, Ct.
Crain, Miss Harriet M., Keene, N. H.

Cra
Cre
Cre
Cre
Cre
Cre
Cre
Cro
Cro
Cro
Cro
Cro
Cro
Cru
Cru
Cro
Cru
Cru
Cru
Cre
Cru
Cru
Cru
Cud
Cud
Cud
Cul
Cul
Cum
Cum
Cum
Cum
Cum
Cum
Cum
Cun
Car
Car
Car
Car
Curt
Curt
Curt
Curt
Curt
Curt
Curt
Cush
Cush
Cush

Dalrymple, James, Bridgeton, N. J.
Dalrymple, Rev. W. H., Nashua, N. H.
Damon, Rev. J. B., Lake Village, N. H.
Damon, Benjamin, Concord, N. H.
Damon, Isaac H., Fredonia, N. Y.
Dana, John B., Cambridge, Mass.
Dane, Osgood, Somerville, Mass.
Danelson, Mrs. Jemima, Brooklyn, N. Y.
Danelson, James E., Brooklyn, N. Y.
Danforth, Mrs. Susan B., North Danvers, Mass.
Daniels, Mrs. E. E., Wyoming, N. Y.
Daniels, Rev. Harrison, Wyoming, N. Y.
Daniels, Dexter, Providence, R. I.
Daniels, Mrs. Dexter, Providence, R. I.
Daniels, Rev. J. H., Bath, Ill.
Daniels, Thomas E., Fitchburg, Mass.
Daniels, Mrs. Florida, Ridgeway, N. Y.
Dannat, Mrs. Susannah J., New York.
Darby, Rev. C., Homer, N. Y.
Darrow, Rev. George R., West Boylston, Mass.
Darrow, Miss Julia T., West Boylston, Mass.
Darrow, Rev. Allen, Norwalk, Ohio.
Darrow, Mrs. Sarah, Norwalk, Ohio.
Davant, R. J., Gillisonville, S. C.
Davenport, Joshua, New York.
Davenport, Joseph P., New York.
David, Thomas, Hiramsburgh, Ohio.
Davies, Mrs. Alice S. H., New York.
Davies, Mrs. Elizabeth, New York.
Davis, Mrs. Eliza H., Columbus, Ohio.
Davis, Miss Mary E., Worcester, Mass.
Davis, Edward L., Worcester, Mass.
Davis, Joseph E., Worcester, Mass.
Davis, Miss Sarah M., Worcester, Mass.
Davis, Miss Anna E., Worcester, Mass.
Davis, Miss Alice W., Worcester, Mass.
Davis, Florence H., Worcester, Mass.
Davis, Isabel G., Worcester, Mass.
Davis, Mrs. George W., Haverhill, Mass.
Davis, Reuben P., Waltham, Mass.
Davis, Walter G., New York.
Davis, Charles C., Preston, Ct.
Davis, Mrs. Harriet F., Preston, Ct.
Davis, Mrs. Louisa G., Paris, Me.
Davis, Rev. John, Yarmouth, Nova Scotia.
Davis, Rev. Thomas, Deckertown, N. J.
Davis, Rev. Judson, Mexico, N. Y.
Davis, Lydia, Haverhill, Mass.
Davis, Mrs. Harriet M., Nashua, N. H.
Davis, Levi, Davenport, Iowa.
Davis, Rev. R., Waveland, Ind.
Davis, Francis T., Parkesburg, Pa.
Davis, Rev. Amos S., Whitesides Corners, N. Y.
Davis, Russel, Preston City, Ct.
Davis, Hon. George R., Troy, N. Y.
Davis, Stilman S., Nashua, N. H.
Davis, Joseph M., Fall River, Mass.
Davis, Jacob, Dorchester, Mass.
Davis, Clark, Minerville, N. Y.
Davis, Eden, Webster, Mass.
Davis, Harriet H., Dorchester, Mass.
Davis, John F., Brooklyn, N. Y.
Davy, Miss Bertha, New York.
Dawley, Joseph E., Fall River, Mass.
Dawson, J. C., Philadelphia.
Day, H. W., Boston.
Day, John, New York.
Day, Mrs. Fidelia, Haverhill, Mass.
Day, Rev. Arthur, Athens, N. Y.
Day, Rev. Horace G., Schenectady, N. Y.
Day, Horatio E., Hartford, Ct.
Day, Mrs. Fanny D., Haverhill, Mass.
Day, Charles J., New York.
Dayton, Morgan H., New York.
Dean, H. J., Spartanburg, S. C.
Dean, Jirah, Flat Brook, N. Y.
Dean, Rev. Wm., D.D., Wyoming, N. Y.
Dean, Mrs. Maria M., Wyoming, N. Y.
Dean, E. W., Roxbury, Mass.
Dean, Rev. Myron M., Boston, Mass.
Dean, Esther G., North Adams, Mass.
Dean, Rev. E., Auburn, N. Y.
Dean, Rev. R. S., Montezuma, N. Y.
Dean, Hon. Peter W., Grafton, Vt.
Dearborn, Samuel S., Jamaica Plains, Mass.
Dearborn, Rev. Shelburn, Lowell, Wis.
Dearborn, Mrs. Emeline L., Lowell, Wis.
Deats, Hiram, Cherryville, N. J.
Deats, Mrs. Rebecca, Cherryville, N. J.
Decker, Alfred, New York.
Decker, Mrs. Keziah R., New York.
Decker, Abel, New York.
Decker, Mrs. Abigail, New York.
Decker, Miss Mary A., New York.
Decker, Matthew, Rahway, N. J.
Decker, Rev. Wm. P., Evans' Mills, N. Y.
Decker, Mrs. Julia S., Evans' Mills, N. Y.
De Golyer, Joseph, Troy, N. Y.
De Golyer, Mrs. Antoinette, Troy, N. Y.
Deitz, Rev. Chas. M., Imlaystown, N. J.
De La Montague, Miss Julia, New York.
Della Torre, Joseph, New York.
Demarest, Miss Jane, New York.
Demarest, Samuel C., Boston.
Demarest, Stephen, D., New York.
Demerest, Nicholas, New York.
Deming, Amos, Savoy Mass.
Deming, Mrs. Eliza J., Washington, D. C.
Deming, Mrs. Abby A., Goffstown, N. H.
Denike, Abraham, New York.
Denike, Mrs. Adaline, New York.
Dennis, Mrs. Elizabeth, New York.
Dennis, Richard, Lowell, Mass.
Dennison, Rev. Charles W.
Denison, Rev. Frederick, Norwich, Ct.
Denison, Mrs. Amy H., Norwich, Ct.
Denison, Rev. Erastus, Groton, Ct.
Denison, Mrs. Prudence, Mystic River, Ct.
Denison, Mrs. Silas, Skaneateles, N. Y.
Denison, O. J., Mendota, Ill.
Denison, Mrs. Amelia E., Deep River, Ct.
Denison, Mrs. Elizabeth, Brooklyn, N. Y.
Denison, Rev. A. E., Clinton, Ct.
Denny, John B., Norwalk, Ct.
Depew, Mrs. Sarah M., Saratoga Springs, N. Y.
Detson, Benj., Methuen, Mass.
Devore, Mrs. Catharine, Edgefield, S. C.
Deweese, Samuel, West Philadelphia, Pa.
Dewey, Wm. G., Mystic, Ct.
Dewey, Joseph H., Manchester, N. Y.
Dewhurst, Rev. Eli, Hampton Corners, Me.
Dewitt, Rev. J. V., Marion, Iowa.
De Wolf, D. R. Brooklyn, N. Y.
Dexter, Mrs Jane, Brooklyn, N. Y.
Dexter, Samuel K., Central Falls, R. I.
Dickerman, Samuel, Philadelphia.
Dickinson, Mrs. Caroline A., Dayton, Ohio.
Dickinson, Wm. W., Golandsville, Va.
Dimmock, Rev Anthony V., Baldwinsville, Mass.
Dineson, Daniel E., Berlin, N. Y.
Dinsmore, Charles M., Newton, Mass.
Dispeau, Mrs. Lucinda, Grafton, Mass.
Dixson, Rev. Joseph A., Evansville, Ia.
Doan, Ezra, Hudson, N. Y.
Doan, Miss Rachel F., Danvers, Mass.
Doby, John, Sen., Edgefield, S. C.
Dodge, Mrs. Eliza P., New York.
Dodge, Miss Mary, New York.
Dodge, Prof. Ebenezer, Hamilton, N. Y.
Dodge, Solomon H., Cambridge, Mass.
Dodge, Miss Hannah A., Worcester, Mass.
Dodge, Mrs. Alice C., Hampton Falls, N. H.
Dodge, Mrs Jane, Brooklyn, N. Y.
Dodge, H. N., McGrawville, N. Y.
Dodson, Rev. Elijah, Woodburn, Ill.
Dole, Mrs. Lydia T., Haverhill, Mass.
Dollim, Horatio, Worcester, Mass.
Doolittle, Rev. H. D., Burnt Hills, N. Y.
Doolittle, Johnson, Wallingford, Ct.
Doolittle, Hart, Pleasant Valley, Ct.

..., New York.
Dowley, John, New York.
Downer, Rev. Wm. B., Peterboro', N. Y.
Downey, Rev. Francis, Whitely, Pa.
Downs, Mrs. Harriet B., Malden, Mich.
Downs, Miss Elizabeth, Hightstown, N. J.
Downs, ...vin, New Haven Ct.
Dows, Gustavus ..., Lowell, Mass.
Doyen, Mrs. A. F., Haverhill, Mass.
Drake, Simeon, Pittsfield, N. H.
Drake, J. C., Panama, N. Y.
Drake, Ephraim, Plainfield, N. J.
Drake, Mrs. A. L., Plainfield, N. J.
Drake, Rev. George, New Brunswick, N. J.
Drake, Mrs. Caroline M., Xenia, Ohio.
Draper, Jonat... N. Bennington, Vt.
Driver, Rev. Thomas, Lynn, Mass.
Drown, Henry B., Providence, R. I.
Dubois, Richard, Canton, N. J.
Dubois, ... E., Randolph, Mass.
Dudley, John L., Baltimore, Md.
Dugan, Wm. T., Wabashaw, Minn.
Dugan, Mrs. Eliza, Wabashaw, Minn.
Dugan, Wm. J., Wabashaw, Minn.
Dugan, Edward, Wabashaw, Minn.
Duncan, Hon. James I., Haverhill, Mass.
Duncan, Mrs. James H., Haverhill, Mass.
Duncan, Mrs. Samuel, Haverhill, Mass.
Duncan, Mrs. E. F., Jackson, Va.
Duncan, Rev. H. A., Coosawhatchie, S. C.
Duncan, Rev. Wm., Orleans, la.
Duncan, Rev. John, Boston, Mass.
Dunham, Nelson, New Brunswick, N. J.
Dunklee, Mrs. Eliza A., Boston, Mass.
Dunlap, Abraham B., Brooklyn, N. Y.
Dunlap, Rev. James, Jacksonville, Ill.
Dunlevy, Hon. A. H., Lebanon, O.
Dunn, Rev. Andrew, Weymouth, Mass.
Dunn, Alexander, New Brunswick, N. J.
Du Pre, Mrs. S. P., Darlington, S. C.
Dupont, Alfred, Wilmington, Del.
Durant, Clark, Albany, N. Y.
Durant, Thomas P., Boston, Mass.
Durbrow, Wm. New York.
Durbrow, John B., New York.
Durfee, Sanford, Warwick, R. I.
Durfee, Miss Sarah C., Providence, R. I.
Durham, Nicholas O., Weart's Corners, N. J.
Durham, Enos, Greenwich, N. Y.
Durham, Anson, Greenwich, N. Y.
Durkin, John, New York

Eat...
Eat...
Eato...
Eddy
Eddy
Eddy
Eddy
Eddy
Eddy
Eddy
Eddy
Eddy
Eddy
Eddy,
Edgec...
Eding...
Edma...
Edmin...
Edma...
Edmo...
Edmo...
Edmo...
Edmo...
Edwar...
Edwar...
Edwar...
Edwar...
Egbert
Elder,
Eldridg...
Eldridg...
Elgree...
Elledge
Ellicott
Elliott,
Elliott,
Elliott,
Elliott,
Elliott,
Elliott,
Elliott,
Ellis, L...
Ellis, G...
Ellis, Th...
Ellis, A...
Ellis, Ja...
Ellswor...
Elwell,
Elwell,
Elwell,

Estep, Rev. Dr. James, Library, Pa.
Estes, A. B., Lower Three Runs, S. C.
Estes, Miss H. L., Lower Three Runs, S. C.
Estes, Mrs. E. A., Lower Three Runs, S. C.
Evans, Rev. George, Richmondville, N. Y.
Evans, John M., Philadelphia, Pa.
Evans, Silas J., Louisville, Ky.
Evans, Mrs. S. E., Society Hill, S. C.
Evans, Reuben, Amesbury, Mass.
Evans, Dr. Joseph F., New York.
Evans, Mrs. Czarina H., New York.
Evans, Rev. William E., Carbondale, Pa.
Evans, Rev. P. H., Greencastle, Ia.
Evans, Miss Anna B., New York.
Evans, Thomas J., Lowell, Mass.
Eveleigh, Mrs. Mary D., Brooklyn, N. Y.
Eveleth, Samuel, Boston, Mass.
Everts, Rev. Wm. W., D.D., Louisville, Ky.
Everett, Rev. Samuel, North Leverett, Mass.
Everett, David, New London, N. H.
Everett, Benj. C., Philadelphia.
Everett, Rev. Wm. P., Williamsburgh, N. Y.
Everett, Aaron, Boston.
Everett, Rev. Wm., Macon, Geo.
Everett, William, Brooklyn, N. Y.
Failing, Josiah, Portland, Oregon.
Failing, Mrs. Henrietta, Portland, Oregon.
Failing, Henry, Portland, Oregon.
Failing, Miss Elizabeth A., Portland, Oregon.
Fails, David, South Dedham, Mass.
Fairbanks, Rev. George G., Somerville, Mass.
Fairbrother, Lewis, Pawtucket, R. I.
Fairman, James, New Haven, Ct.
Fales, Joseph T., Burlington, Iowa.
Fales, Oliver, West Philadelphia, Pa.
Falkner, John B., Malden, Mass.
Falwell, L. W., Romulus, N. Y.
Fargo, Rev. Isaac, Jr., Fairport, N. Y.
Fairchild, Stephen, M.D., Morristown, N. J.
Fairchild, Lewis, McDonough, N. Y.
Farish, T., Gulf, N. C.
Farnam, Mrs. Jane D., Concord, N. H.
Farnsworth, Dr. James H., Fairfax, Vt.
Farnsworth, Rev. C. D., Colesburgh, Iowa.
Farnsworth, Mrs. E. S., New London, Ct.
Farr, Mrs. H. D., Albion, N. Y.
Farr, Miss Mary Louisa, Hastings, N. Y.
Farrington, David, Trumansburg, N. Y.
Farwell, Isaac, Watertown, Mass.
Farwell, Mrs. Sarah A., Watertown, Mass.
Farrar, Mrs. Susan P., Jackson, Va.
Farrar, Rev. Charles, Chester, Vt.
Faunce, Rev. Daniel, Worcester, Mass.
Fay, Rev. William N., Belchertown, Mass.
Feary, William, Albany, N. Y.
Fellows, Miss Kate, New Haven, Ct.
Feller, Mad. Henrietta, Grand Ligne, C. E.
Felt, Benjamin, Salem, Mass.
Felton, R., Hertford, N. C.
Felton, Cader, Hertford, N. C.
Felton, Mrs. Mary, Hertford, N. C.
Felton, George D., Granville, Mass.
Fendall, Mrs. E. D., Moorestown, N. J.
Fenn, Hubbard, Wallingford, Ct.
Fennell, Rev. George, Harrell's Store, N. C.
Fennell, Owen, Wilmington, N. C.
Ferguson, B., Newport, Ohio.
Ferrier, John M., New York.
Ferrell, Miss Mary Ann, New York.
Ferris, Mrs. Hannah L., New York.
Ferris, O., Wilson, N. Y.
Ferris, Samuel M., Columbia, Ohio.
Ferris, Rev. Isaac, Columbia, Ohio.
Ferris, John M., Columbia, Ohio.
Ferris, William, Columbia, Ohio.
Fickling, F. W., Gillisonville, S. C.
Field, Thomas F., Brooklyn, N. Y.
Field, Mrs. Thomas F., Brooklyn, N. Y.
Field, Thomas S., Hoboken, N. J.
Field, Mrs. Lavinia F., Taunton, Mass.
Field, Charles H., Taunton, Mass.
Field, George A., Taunton, Mass.
Field, Miss Ann M., Taunton, Mass.
Field, Miss Hannah E., Taunton, Mass.
Field, Wm. T., Taunton, Mass.
Field, Fanny C., Taunton, Mass.
Field, Adeline B., Taunton, Mass.
Field, Mrs. Elizabeth H., Providence.
Field, Miss Elsie M., Westport, N. H.
Field, Rev. Moses, Flat Brook, N. Y.
Fieldin, Miss Helen J., Great Falls, N. H.
Fife, Rev. James, Charlottesville, Va.
Fife, Mrs. Margaret W., Charlottesville, Va.
Fifield, Mrs. Catharine, Pawtucket, R. I.
Fifield, William, East Poultney, Vt.
Fillio, Rev. Nelson, Battle Creek, Mich.
Finch, Miss Sarah A., Red Oak Grove, Va.
Finch, George W., New York.
Fish, Rev. Joel W., Geneva, Wis.
Fish, J. L. A., Webster, Mass.
Fish, E. A., Pitcher, N. Y.
Fish, Frederick E., Providence, R. I.
Fish, Mrs. Ann Judson, Webster, Mass.
Fishback, Mrs Sophia, Jeffersonton, Va.
Fisher, Mrs. Ann L., New York.
Fisher, Rev. Abiel, Manchaug, Mass.
Fisher, Rev. Ezra, Washington Butte, Oregon
Fisher, Rev. Otis, Mt. Palatine, Ill.
Fisher, Isaac, West Townsend, Vt.
Fisher, Joseph, Adamsville, Ohio.
Fisher, Rev. Hiram H., Burlington Flatts, N. Y.
Fisher, Rev. Geo., Galway Village, N. Y.
Fisher, Mrs. Emily, Galway Village, N. Y.
Fisk, Willard, New York.
Fitch, Dr. William, Stamford, Ct.
Fitch, Rev. H., New Lisbon, N. Y.
Fitzgerald, Miss Joana, New York.
Fithian, Samuel C., Greenwich, N. J.
Fitz, William, Hartford, Ct.
Fitts, Rev. Harvey, Middleboro', Mass.
Flanagan, John, Philadelphia, Pa.
Flanders, Rev. Charles W., Concord, N. H.
Flanders, Mrs. M. H. L., Concord, N. H.
Flanders, Mrs. Mary E., Concord, N. H.
Flanders, Benjamin H., Boston, Mass.
Flanders, Timothy C., Haverhill, Mass.
Flanders, Helvin, Haverhill, Mass.
Flanders, George B., Brooklyn, N. Y.
Flanders, I. M., Nashua, N. H.
Fleet, James R., Brewington, Va.
Fleet, Dr. B., King and Queens C. H., Va.
Fleischman, Rev. Konrad A., Philadelphia, Pa.
Fletcher, Rev. C., Tewksbury, Mass.
Fletcher, Rev. Simon, Sandy Hill, N. Y.
Fletcher, Rev. Leonard, New Orleans, La.
Fletcher, Rev. Horace, Townshend, Vt
Fletcher, Mrs. Harriet A., Townshend, Vt.
Fletcher, Mrs. Mary, Southington, Ct.
Fletcher, Henry J., New York.
Fletcher, Mrs. Sarah A., Saratoga Springs, N. Y.
Fletcher, Hezekiah, Minneapolis, Min.
Flinn, Mrs. E. A. E., Darlington, S. C.
Flinn, James W., Brooklyn, N. Y.
Flint, Brayton, Novi, Mich.
Flint, Mrs. Mary C., Novi, Mich.
Flint, Lorin, Novi, Mich.
Flint, George, Lyme, N. H.
Flower, Amelia L., Brooklyn, N. Y.
Floyd, Mrs. Abbey, Beverly, Mass.
Fogg, Rev. Samuel, Me.
Foljambe, Rev. Sam'l W., S. Framingham, Mass.
Foland, H. H., Leesville, N. Y.
Fole, Thomas W., Providence, R. I.
Folwell, Job W., Defiance, Ohio.
Foote, Mrs. Euphemia, Tonica, Ill.
Foote, Jared, New Haven, Ct.
Forbes, George W., Bridgeport, Ct.
Forbes, Gustavus, Boston, Mass.
Forbes, Rev. M., Prattsburgh, N. Y.
Forbush, Rev. Jonathan E. S., Ashland, Mass.

Forrester, Mrs. [illegible], Williamsburgh, N. Y.
Forristall, Mrs. Lucy, Boston, Mass.
Forrell, David, Stockholm, Sweden.
Fosdick, William, Nashua, N. H.
Foskett, Rev. Horace B., Tyler, Ill.
Foster, John W., Leesville, Ill.
Foster, William, West Dedham, Mass.
Foster, Mrs. Sarah K., Evansville, Ia.
Foster, Rev. J. C., Beverly, Mass.
Foster, Mrs. Abby A., Beverly, Mass.
Foster, Mrs. Martha, Cambridge, Mass.
Foster, Joseph, Sen., Salem, N. J.
Foster, Mrs. Susan S., Keene, N. H.
Forsyth, Miss Sarah S., Albany, N. Y.
Forsyth, Mrs. Sarah, Albany, N. Y.
Forsyth, Miss Emily H., Albany, N. Y.
Forsyth, Russel, Jr., Albany, N. Y.
Fortune, John, Newport, N. Y.
Fowle, Mrs. Lucy, Boston, Mass.
Fowler, Gamaliel, Suffield, Ct.
Fox, Rev. Norman, Schenectady, N. Y.
Fox, Rev. Charles A., Waverly, Pa.
Fox, Mrs. Julia A., Waverly, Pa.
Fox, Albert R., Sand Lake, N. Y.
Fox, Mrs. Mary A., Sand Lake, N. Y.
Fox, Charles, New York.
Fox, Miss Ann Eliza, New York.
Frank, Miss Amy, Smithfield, Pa.
Frazee, Ezra, Rahway, N. J.
Frazee, Mrs. Mary, Rahway, N. J.
Francis, Robert, Newington, Ct.
Francis, Mrs. Lydia D., Newington, Ct.
Francis, Norman, New York.
Francis, Charles King, New York.
Francis, James, Pittsfield, Mass.
Frayzer, Rev. Herndon, Twymann's, Va.
Freas, Rev. Daniel J., Salem, N. Y.
Freeman, Rev. T. G.
Freeman, Rev. Joseph, Cavendish, Vt.
Freeman, Rev. G. W., Fox Lake, Wis.
Freeman, Thomas W., Augusta, Ga.
Freeman, Elisha, Worcester, Mass.
Freeman, Mrs. Margaret E., Ann Arbor, Mich.
Freeman, Dyer, Middleboro', Mass.
Freeman, D., Webster, Mass.
French, Miss Abigail, Turner, Me.
French, George R., Wilmington, N. C.
French, Stephen L., Fall River, Mass.
French, Miss Hannah, Haverhill, Mass.
French, Mrs. Moses E., Haverhill, Mass.
French, Rev. David S., Covington, Ia.

Fult
Fulte
Furg
Furn
Fyfe,
Fyfe,
Gage
Gage
Gage
Gage
Gage
Gage
Gage
Gale,
Gale,
Gale,
Gale
Gale,
Galu
Gam
Gano
Gard
Gard
Gard
Gard
Gard
Gard
Gard
Garfi
Garn
Garn
Garre
Garn
Garn
Garre
Garri
Gater
Gates
Gates
Gates
Gates
Gates
Gates
Gatlin
Gault
Gault
Gay,
Gay,
Gayer
Gayle
Gaarh

Gignilliat, W. R., Darien, Ga.
Gilbert, Wm. J., Middletown, Ct.
Gilbert, Rev. Isaac H., Bristol, Ct.
Gilbert, Mrs. Mary E., Bristol, Ct.
Gilkey, Royal, Watertown, Mass.
Gill, Miss Mary, Pottsville, Pa.
Gill, Miss Mary Ann, Philadelphia.
Gillette, Mrs. Hannah J., New York.
Gillett, Asahel, Rose, N. Y.
Gillett, Nehemiah, Danbury, Ct.
Gillet, Simeon S., Davenport, Iowa.
Gilman, Miss Ellen W., Roadstown, N. J.
Gilman, George H., New York.
Gilman, David, Roadstown, N. J.
Gilman, Mrs. John, Newburyport, Mass.
Giles, Alfred E., Boston, Mass.
Gilpatrick, Rev. James.
Girdwood, Mrs. Mary, New Bedford, Mass.
Gladding, John H., Providence, R. I.
Gladding, Mrs. Lydia M., Providence, R. I.
Glass, George W., Honeoye Falls, N. Y.
Gleason, Andrew, Barre, Mass.
Glover, Charles S., New York.
Glover, H. K., Cambridgeport, Mass.
Goadby, Rev. John, East Poultney, Vt.
Goddard, Mrs. Elizabeth, York, N. Y.
Goddard, Benjamin, Worcester, Mass.
Godden, Miss Mary E., Lowell, Mass.
Godding, Mrs. Lucina, East Burke, N. H.
Going, Mrs. Nancy B., Greenville, Ohio.
Going, Rev. Ezra, Greenville, Ohio.
Going, J., Aurora, N. Y.
Godfrey, Edward J., New York.
Godfrey, Mrs. Anna, Brooklyn, N. Y.
Godfry, Abel, Sennet, N. Y.
Goldthwait, Nathan, Worcester, Mass.
Goldthwait, Mrs. Anna, Newport, N. H.
Goldy, John, Imlaystown, N. J.
Goldy, Mrs. Emily, Imlaystown, N. J.
Goldy, Miss Sarah, Imlaystown, N. J.
Gooch, Mrs. Hannah, Cambridge, Mass.
Gooch, Mrs. Sarah J., Cambridge, Mass.
Gooch, Nathan G., Cambridge, Mass.
Goodell, Asah, West Woodstock, Ct.
Goodhue, Ann C., New Boston, N. H.
Gonsalves, Rev. M. J., San Francisco, Cal.
Goodnough, Levi, Sudbury, Mass.
Goodrich, Nathan F., Meriden, Ct.
Goodwin, Charles T., New York.
Goodwin, Mrs. Emily G., New York.
Goodwin, Rev. Thomas, Pemberton, N. J.
Goodno, Rev. I. R., Campton, N. H.
Goodno, Rev. W. S., La Salle, Ill.
Goodnow, Joseph, Charlestown, Mass.
Goodnow, Rev. A. W., Stamford, Vt.
Goodnow, Mrs. Jennie F., Boston, Mass.
Gordon, Mrs. Elizabeth, Trenton, N. J.
Gordon, Abram, New London, Ct.
Gordon, Adoniram J., Providence, R. I.
Gorham, Miss Ellen J., Elbridge, N. Y
Gorham, Mrs. Julia, New Haven, Ct.
Gorman, Rev. Samuel, Santa Fe, N. M.
Gorman, Miss Mary, Santa Fe, N. M
Gould, Joseph, Wilmington, Del.
Gould, Augustus A., M.D., Boston, Mass.
Goss, Mrs. Frances M., New York.
Gove, G. B. R., Fort Covington, N. Y.
Gowdey, David, Providence, R. I.
Granger, James N., Jr., Providence, R. I.
Granger, Mrs. Ann B., Providence, R. I.
Granger, Rev. Abraham H., Providence, R. I
Grafton, Miss Frances, Brooklyn, N. Y.
Graham, Mrs. Susan W., Hillsboro', N. C.
Grant, Rev. Daniel H., Stephentown, N. Y.
Grant, Rev. Stillman B., New London, Ct.
Grant, Mrs. Mary S., New Haven, Ct
Grant, Rev. William, Whitehall, N. Y
Grant, Alexander, Providence, R. I.
Grant, Preston, Pawtucket, R. I.
Grant, O. B., Stonington, Ct.
Graves, Rev. J. M., Newton, Mass.
Graves, C., Brown's Store, N. C.
Graves, Rev. Charles, Eaton, N. Y.
Graves, Rev. Samuel, Kalamazoo, Mich.
Graves, William H., Brooklyn, N. Y.
Graves, Rev. A. P., Lacon, Ill.
Gray, Martin E., Willoughby, Ohio
Gray, Charles F. H., Pittsgrove, N.
Gray, William E., New York.
Gray, Mrs. Susan, Brooklyn, N. Y.
Gray, Theodore H., New York.
Greaves, Joseph, Brooklyn, N. Y.
Green, Russell, Providence, R. I.
Green, David C., Providence, R. I.
Green, Arnold, Providence, R. I.
Green, Miss Frances Mary, Providence,
Green, Mrs. Mary, New York.
Green, Rev. John, Westfield, Mass.
Green, Rev. Charles H., Hydeville, Vt.
Green, Mrs. Sarah E., Hydeville, Vt.
Green, Spencer, Rutland, Vt.
Green, Ralph, Three Rivers, Mass.
Green, Rev. Thomas H., Ogdensburgh, N. Y.
Green, Alma C., Troy, N. Y.
Green, Miss Fanny, Saratoga Springs, N. Y.
Green, Rev. James W., Albany, N. Y.
Green, John A., New York.
Green, Edward F., Brookfield, Ohio.
Greene, Mrs. B., New Bedford, Mass.
Greene, William C., Providence, R. I.
Greene, Mrs. Catharine, Albany, N. Y.
Greenleaf, Rev. Calvin, Griggsville, Ill.
Greenleaf, Amos C., New York.
Greenleaf, John, Cambridge, Mass.
Greenleaf, Mrs. Elizabeth H. Cambridge, Mass.
Greenwood, Simeon A., Worcester, Mass.
Greenwood, Samuel, New London, N. H.
Greenwood, Mrs. Martha T., New London, N. H.
Greenwood, Walter, Templeton, Mass.
Grenell, Mrs. Eliza, Port Jarvis, N. Y.
Grenell, Mrs. C. Amelia, Honesdale, Pa
Grenell, Rufus M., Rock Island, Ill.
Gregg, William Henry, Wilmington, Del.
Gregory, Miss Clarissa, New York.
Gregory, Rev. S., New Lisbon, N. Y.
Gregory, Uriah, Weston, Mass.
Gregory, Rev. Truman, Lee, Ill.
Griffee, Peter, Philadelphia, Pa.
Griffin, Rev. Charles, Wilmington, Del.
Griffin, Nathaniel L., Edgefield, S. C
Griffin, Edwin, New York.
Griffin, James T., Rochester, N. Y.
Griffin, Reuben P., Boston, Mass.
Griffis, Rev. P., Lodi Centre, N. Y.
Griffith, Rev. B., Philadelphia, Pa.
Griffiths, A.W., M.D., Philadelphia, Pa.
Griffiths, John J., New York.
Griggs, David R., Brookline, Mass.
Griggs, Seth D., Belchertown, Mass.
Griggs, J. W., Boston, Mass.
Grimley, Rev. Joseph J., Unionville, N. Y.
Grimshaw, Miss Martha, Arcadia, N. Y.
Grinnell, Mrs. Mary B., New Bedford, Mass
Grinnell, Sylvia H., New Bedford, Mass.
Griswold, Harry, Racine, Wis.
Griswold, Aaron, ——, N. Y.
Grose, Rev. Henry L., Galway, N. Y
Gross, Rev. Alva, Brimfield, Ill.
Grout, Thomas J., New York
Grout, Edward, New York.
Grover, Joseph, Elmira, N. Y.
Grow, Rev. James, Thompson, Ct
Grummon, William, Newark, N. J.
Guild, Rev. J., Ellis, Newton, Iowa.
Guild, Mrs. Julia A., East Thompson, Ct.
Guild, George M., Boston, Mass.
Guild, Reuben A., Providence, R. I
Gunn, Rev. Elihu, Keokuk, Iowa
Gunn, George, New Haven, Ct.
Gunn, E., Montague, Mass.

Hagar, William, Jr., Brooklyn, N. Y.
Hague, Rev. John B., Hudson, N. Y.
Hall, George, Providence R. I.
Haines, Jacob, Moorestown, N. J.
Haines, M . Mary Jane, Moorestown, N. J.
Haines, Chalkey, Marlton, N. J.
Hale, William, Meriden, Ct.
Haley, Miss Emma S., Boston, Mass.
Hall, Gabriel D. Greenwich, N J.
Hall, Mrs. Mary A., Greenwich, N. J.
Hall, Enoch, West Acton, Mass.
Hall, Almer, Wallingford, Ct.
Hall, Rev. King S., Lake Village, N. H.
Hall, Rev. Abijah, Jr., ——, Ct.
Hall, David, 3rd, Skaneateles, N. Y.
Hall, Abiathar, Fall River, Mass.
Hall, Hannah, Haverhill, Mass.
Hall, Mrs. Clarissa, Wallingford, Ct.
Hall, Almer I., Wallingford, Ct.
Hall, Rev. W. S., New York.
Hallsted, Mrs. Jane C., New York.
Hallsted, James C. Waterloo, N. Y.
Ham, Mrs. Nancy S., Providence, R. I.
Hamblet, Miss Mira C., West Swanzey, N. H.
Hamilton, Rev. Alexander, Appleton, Wis.
Hamilton, John, Jr., Fredonia, N. Y.
Hamilton, Miss Ann, New London, Ct.
Hammon, Mrs. Philip, Beverly, Mass.
Hammond, Augustus, Pittsford, Vt.
Hammond, Mrs. Mary, Pittsford, Vt.
Hammond, Miss Mary F., Pittsford, Vt.
Hammond, William, Dorchester, Mass.
Hammond, James M., Chicago, Ill.
Hammond, N. O., East Cambridge, Mass.
Hanaford, Dr. Joseph H., Beverly, Mass.
Hanaford, Mrs. J. H., Beverly, Mass.
Hanaford, Howard A., Beverly, Mass.
Hancox, Richard, Williamsburgh, N. Y.
Hand, Joseph H., Bridgeport, Ct.
Hand, Rev. George Hatboro', Pa.
Hanly, Aaron, Peach Orchard, N. Y.
Hansell, Mrs. Emma, Philadelphia, Pa.
Hanson, Charles B., New Haven, Ct.
Hapgood, Miss S. F., Gillisonville, S. C.
Hardwick, Wm., South Boston, Mass.
Hardy, Jesse, Warner, N. H.
Harger, Mrs. Hannah, Chatham Corners, N. Y.
Harkness, Albert H., Providence, R. I.
Harlow, Robert H., Boston, Mass.
Harmon, Rawson, Wheatland, N. Y.
Harmon, Mrs. David P., Haverhill, Mass.

Gignilliat, W. R., Darien, Ga.
Gilbert, Wm. J., Middletown, Ct.
Gilbert, Rev. Isaac H., Bristol, Ct.
Gilbert, Mrs. Mary E., Bristol, Ct.
Gilkey, Royal, Watertown, Mass.
Gill, Miss Mary, Pottsville, Pa.
Gill, Miss Mary Ann, Philadelphia.
Gillette, Mrs. Hannah J., New York.
Gillett, Asahel, Rose, N. Y.
Gillett, Nehemiah, Danbury, Ct.
Gillet, Simeon S., Davenport, Iowa.
Gilman, Miss Ellen W., Roadstown, N. J
Gilman, George H., New York.
Gilman, David, Roadstown, N. J.
Gilman, Mrs. John, Newburyport, Mass.
Giles, Alfred E., Boston, Mass.
Gilpatrick, Rev. James.
Girdwood, Mrs. Mary, New Bedford, Mass.
Gladding, John H., Providence, R. I.
Gladding, Mrs. Lydia M., Providence, R. I.
Glass, George W., Honeoye Falls, N. Y.
Gleason, Andrew, Barre, Mass.
Glover, Charles S., New York.
Glover, H. K., Cambridgeport, Mass.
Goadby, Rev. John, East Poultney, Vt.
Goddard, Mrs. Elizabeth, York, N. Y.
Goddard, Benjamin, Worcester, Mass.
Godden, Miss Mary E., Lowell, Mass.
Godding, Mrs. Lucina, East Burke, N. H.
Going, Mrs. Nancy B., Greenville, Ohio.
Going, Rev. Ezra, Greenville, Ohio.
Going, J., Aurora, N. Y.
Godfrey, Edward J., New York.
Godfrey, Mrs. Anna, Brooklyn, N. Y.
Godfry, Abel, Sennet, N. Y.
Goldthwait, Nathan, Worcester, Mass.
Goldthwait, Mrs. Anna, Newport, N. H.
Goldy, John, Imlaystown, N. J.
Goldy, Mrs. Emily, Imlaystown, N. J.
Goldy, Miss Sarah, Imlaystown, N. J.
Gooch, Mrs. Hannah, Cambridge, Mass.
Gooch, Mrs. Sarah J., Cambridge, Mass.
Gooch, Nathan G., Cambridge, Mass.
Goodell, Asah, West Woodstock, Ct.
Goodhue, Ann C., New Boston, N. H.
Gonsalves, Rev. M. J., San Francisco, Cal.
Goodnough, Levi, Sudbury, Mass.
Goodrich, Nathan F., Meriden, Ct.
Goodwin, Charles T., New York.
Goodwin, Mrs. Emily G., New York.
Goodwin, Rev. Thomas, Pemberton, N. J.
Goodno, Rev. I. R., Campton, N. H.
Goodno, Rev. W S., La Salle, Ill.
Goodnow, Joseph, Charlestown, Mass.
Goodnow, Rev. A. W., Stamford, Vt.
Goodnow, Mrs. Jennie F., Boston, Mass.
Gordon, Mrs. Elizabeth, Trenton, N. J.
Gordon, Abram, New London, Ct.
Gordon, Adoniram J., Providence, R. I.
Gorham, Miss Ellen J., Elbridge, N. Y
Gorham, Mrs. Julia, New Haven, Ct.
Gorman, Rev. Samuel, Santa Fe, N. M.
Gorman, Miss Mary, Santa Fe, N. M
Gould, Joseph, Wilmington, Del.
Gould, Augustus A., M.D., Boston, Mass
Goss, Mrs. Frances M., New York.
Gove, G. B. R., Fort Covington, N. Y
Gowdey, David, Providence, R. I
Granger, James N., Jr., Providence, R. I.
Granger, Mrs. Ann B., Providence, R. I.
Granger, Rev. Abraham H, Providence, R. I
Grafton, Miss Frances, Brooklyn, N. Y.
Graham, Mrs. Susan W, Hillsboro', N. C
Grant, Rev. Daniel H., Stephentown, N. Y.
Grant, Rev. Stillman B., New London, Ct.
Grant, Mrs. Mary S., New Haven, Ct
Grant, Rev. William, Whitehall, N Y
Grant, Alexander, Providence, R. I.
Grant, Preston, *Pawtucket, R. I.*
Grant, O B., Stonington, Ct.

Graves, Rev. J. M., Newton, Mass.
Graves, C, Brown's Store, N. C.
Graves, Rev. Charles, Eaton, N. Y.
Graves, Rev. Samuel, Kalamazoo, Mich.
Graves, William H., Brooklyn, N. Y.
Graves, Rev. A. P., Lacon, Ill.
Gray, Martin E., Willoughby, Ohio
Gray, Charles F. H., Pittsgrove, N.
Gray, William E., New York.
Gray, Mrs. Susan, Brooklyn, N. Y.
Gray, Theodore H., New York.
Greaves, Joseph, Brooklyn, N. Y.
Green, Russell, Providence, R. I.
Green, David C., Providence, R. I.
Green, Arnold, Providence, R. I.
Green, Miss Frances Mary, Providence,
Green, Mrs. Mary, New York.
Green, Rev. John, Westfield, Mass.
Green, Rev. Charles H, Hydeville, Vt.
Green, Mrs. Sarah E., Hydeville, Vt.
Green, Spencer, Rutland, Vt.
Green, Ralph, Three Rivers, Mass.
Green, Rev. Thomas H., Ogdensburgh, N. Y.
Green, Alma C., Troy, N. Y.
Green, Miss Fanny, Saratoga Springs, N. Y.
Green, Rev. James W., Albany, N. Y.
Green, John A., New York.
Green, Edward F., Brookfield, Ohio.
Greene, Mrs. B., New Bedford, Mass.
Greene, William C., Providence, R. I.
Greene, Mrs. Catharine, Albany, N. Y.
Greenleaf, Rev. Calvin, Griggsville, Ill.
Greenleaf, Amos C., New York.
Greenleaf, John, Cambridge, Mass.
Greenleaf, Mrs. Elizabeth H. Cambridge, Mass.
Greenwood, Simeon A., Worcester, Mass.
Greenwood, Samuel, New London, N. H.
Greenwood, Mrs. Martha T., New London, N. H.
Greenwood, Walter, Templeton, Mass.
Grenell, Mrs. Eliza, Port Jarvis, N. Y.
Grenell, Mrs. C. Amelia, Honesdale, Pa.
Grenell, Rufus M., Rock Island, Ill.
Gregg, William Henry, Wilmington, Del.
Gregory, Miss Clarissa, New York.
Gregory, Rev. S., New Lisbon, N. Y.
Gregory, Uriah, Weston, Mass.
Gregory, Rev. Truman, Leo, Ill.
Griffee, Peter, Philadelphia, Pa.
Griffin, Rev. Charles, Wilmington, Del.
Griffin, Nathaniel L., Edgefield, S. C.
Griffin, Edwin, New York.
Griffin, James T., Rochester, N. Y.
Griffin, Reuben P., Boston, Mass
Griffis, Rev. P., Lodi Centre, N. Y.
Griffith, Rev. B., Philadelphia, Pa.
Griffiths, A.W., M.D., Philadelphia, Pa
Griffiths, John J., New York.
Griggs, David R., Brookline, Mass.
Griggs, Seth D., Belchertown, Mass.
Griggs, J. W., Boston, Mass.
Grimley, Rev. Joseph J., Unionville, N. Y.
Grimshaw, Miss Martha, Arcadia, N. Y.
Grinnell, Mrs. Mary B., New Bedford, Mass
Grinnell, Sylvia H., New Bedford, Mass.
Griswold, Harry, Racine, Wis.
Griswold, Aaron, ——, N. Y.
Grose, Rev. Henry L., Galway, N. Y
Gross, Rev. Alva, Brimfield, Ill.
Grout, Thomas J., New York
Grout, Edward, New York.
Grover, Joseph, Elmira, N. Y
Grow, Rev. James, Thompson, Ct
Grummon, William, Newark, N. J
Guild, Rev. J., Ellis, Newton, Iowa.
Guild, Mrs. Julia A., East Thompson, Ct
Guild, George M., Boston, Mass.
Guild, Reuben A., Providence, R. I
Gunn, Rev. Elihu, Keokuk, Iowa
Gunn, George, New Haven, Ct
Gunn, E., Montague, Mass

MEMBERS FOR LIFE.

[illegible]

Ingalls, Charles, Methuen, Mass.
Ingals, Mrs. Sarah H., Sublette, Ill.
Ingerson, Irad S., Woburn, Mass.
Inman, Rev. Thomas E., Salem, Ohio.
Ireson, Mrs. Parmelia C., Lynn, Mass.
Ireland, Miss Mary, Brooklyn, N. Y.
Irish, Peter D., New London, Ct.
Irish, Mrs. Sarah B., New London, Ct.
Irish, William O., New London, Ct.
Irish, Miss Sarah E., New London, Ct.
Irish, Jedediah R., New London, Ct.
Ivens, Mrs. Ann, Imlaystown, N. J.
Ivens, Miss Helena R., Imlaystown, N. J.
Ivers, Miss Mary, New York.
Ives, Eli, Meriden, Ct.
Ives, William J., Meriden, Ct.
Ives, John, Meriden, Ct.
Ives, Abram, Holyoke, Mass.
Jackson, Henry, Croton, N. Y.
Jackson, Mrs. M. T., Newport, R. I.
Jackson, Mrs. Jerusha A., Chelsea, Mass.
Jackson, Daniel, Westford, Vt.
Jackson, Rev. Aaron, Oyster Bay, N. Y.
Jackson, Mrs. Susan, Newton, Mass.
Jacobus, J. L., Chicago, Ill.
Jacobs, Charles P., Goshen, Ia.
Jacobs, William H., Williamsburgh, N. Y.
Jacobs, William, Oxford, N. Y.
Jacoby, Mrs. B. A., Davenport, Iowa.
James, Rev. Joshua J., Raleigh, N. C.
James, George, Zanesville, O.
James, Francis H., Philadelphia.
James, Rev. David, Osceola, Ill.
James, Thomas M., New Bedford, Mass.
James, John, Brookfield, O.
Jamison, Alexander, Wilmington, Del.

[redacted]

Johnson, Rev. George J., Fort Madison, Iowa.
Johnson, Mrs. George J., Fort Madison, Iowa.
Johnson, Rev. Benedict, West Woodstock, Ct.
Johnson, Rev. Hezekiah, Oregon City, Oregon.
Johnson, Albert B., Willistown, Pa.
Johnson, Edward, New York.
Johnson, Mrs. Mary, Albany, N. Y.
Johnson, Merrick, Willington, Ct.
Johnson, Miss Jane Ann, Wilson, N. Y.
Johnson, Oliver, Providence.
Johnson, Ralph, Norwich, N. Y.
Johnson, Mrs. Mary, Norwich, N. Y.
Johnson, Elias, Troy, N. Y.
Johnson, Mrs. Elizabeth, Philadelphia.
Johnson, Mrs. Catharine B., Haverhill, Mass.
Johnson, Mrs. Mehitable, Danversport, Mass.
Johnston, Andrew, Newark, N. J.
Johnston, Mrs. Andrew, Newark, N. J.
Johnston, James, Sing Sing, N. Y.
Johnston, John L., Sing Sing, N. Y.
Johonnet, Mrs. Andrew, Providence.
Jolls, John F., Providence.
Jones, Nathaniel, Jr., Homer, N. Y.
Jones, Rev. Stephen, Norwalk, Ohio.
Jones, Mrs. Stephen, Norwalk, Ohio.
Jones, Rev. John, Seaville, N. J.
Jones, Mrs. Deborah, Seaville, N. J.
Jones, Mrs. Ann T., Williamsburgh, Va.
Jones, Eliza T., Tavern, P. O., Pa.
Jones, Mrs. Margaret, New York.
Jones, Mrs. Eliza W., Noank, Ct.
Jones, Mrs. Elizabeth, Macedon, N. Y.
Jones, David, New York.
Jones, Mrs. Sarah, New York.
Jones, Mrs. Mary, New York.
Jones, Miss Catharine L., Philadelphia.
Jones, Rev. Joseph H., Frederick City, Md.
Jones, Rev. David N., Richmond Va.
Jones, Rev. Theophilus, Pughtown, Pa.
Jones, Rev. Isaac D., Wiltonville, N. Y.
Jones, John B., Roxbury, Mass.
Jones, William G., Wilmington, Del.
Jones, Washington, Wilmington, Del.
Jones, William M., New York.
Jones, Mrs. Margaretta V., New York.
Jones, Rev. J. W., Hyde Park, N. Y.
Jones, Rev. Howard M., Schoolcraft, Mich.
Jones, J. F., East Cambridge, Mass.
Jones, Rev. T., Rock Hill, Ohio.
Jones, Rev. Edward, Brookfield, Ohio.
Jones, Mrs. Abigail, New York.
Jones, Rev. A. B., Greene, N. Y.
Jones, Rev. H. S., Smyrna, N. Y.
Jones, Mrs. Clara A., Worcester Mass.
Jones, John M., West Troy, N. Y.
Jones, John, Philadelphia.
Jones, Mrs. Elizabeth, Dubuque, Iowa.
Jones, E., North Leverett, Mass.
Jones, George B., Pittsburg, Pa.
Jordan, Elder R. K., Moline, Ill.
Jordan, Philana D., Columbia, Ohio.
Jordon, Mrs. Esther, Brooklyn, N. Y.
Jordon, True P., Lowell Mass.
Joslin, Joseph, East Poultney, Vt.
Joyce, Miss Sarah W., Worcester, Mass.
Judd, Rev. Truman O., Fair Haven, Ct.
Judd, Mrs. L. A. H., Fair Haven, Ct.
Justice, David, Forestville, N. C.
Justin, Rev. Ira, Richmond, N. Y.
Kain, Mrs Sarah, Marlton, N. J.
Kain, Rev. Charles, Jr., Mullica Hill, N. J.
Kain, Mrs. Maria, Mullica Hill, N. J.
Kallock, Dea. M., Warren, Me.
Kallock, Rev. I. S., Boston, Mass.
Kasson, Marcus A., Warren, Ill.
Kauffman, Henry, Paoli, Pa.
Kauffman, Mrs. Sarah, Paoli, Pa.
Kavanagh, Michael, Lowell, Mass.
Keely, Mrs. George, Haverhill, Mass.
Keely, Mrs. John, Haverhill, Mass.
Keely, Rev. Thomas E., South Danvers, Mass.
Keen, Mrs. Susan B., West Philadelphia.
Keen, George B., West Philadelphia.
Keen, William W. J., West Philadelphia.
Keen, Charles B., West Philadelphia.
Keeney, John, New London, Ct.
Keeney, William H., New London, Ct.
Keeney, Rev. Curtis, New London, Ct.
Keith, Henry B., Worcester, Mass.
Keith, William, Boston, Mass.
Kelley, Mrs. Catharine, New York.
Kelley, Mrs. Eli, New York.
Kelley, Miss Georgiana, New York.
Kelley, James D., Pittsfield, N. H.
Kelley, Mrs. Electa M., Newport, N. H.
Kellogg, U. H., Utica, N. Y.
Kellogg, Moses S., Chicopee Falls, Mass.
Kelly, Mrs. Joan, Elmira, N. Y.
Kelly, Mrs. Mary M., Brooklyn, N. Y.
Kelly, Rev. Joshua, Muncy, Pa.
Kelsey, Rev. Daniel, Pittsgrove, N. J.
Kelton, George, Haddonfield, N. J.
Kemp, Sylvester A., Florida, Mass.
Kemp, Nathaniel P., Jamaica Plains. Mass.
Kempsey, Rev. M. C., Jersey City, N. J.
Kendall, H. N., St. Louis, Mo.
Kendall, Charles S., Boston, Mass.
Kendrick, Mrs. Fanny, Detroit, Mich.
Kendrick, Adin, East Poultney, Vt.
Kendrick, Rev A. C., D.D., Rochester, N. Y.
Kendrick, Mrs. Ann, Hamilton, N. Y.
Kendrick, Mrs. Caroline E. H., Albany, N. Y.
Keniston, Mrs. Gardner, Haverhill, Mass.
Kennan, Mrs. Eliza, Thompsonville, Va.
Kennard, Mrs. Spencer J., Bridgeton, N. Y.
Kenney, Rev. Silas, West Royalton, Mass.
Kenney, Mrs. Ellen B., Derby, Vt.
Kenower, John, Huntington, Ia.
Kent, Luther, Streetsboro, Ohio.
Kent, William, New Brunswick, N. J.
Kenworthy, Mrs. Mary, New York.
Kengon, P. W., Brooklyn, N. Y.
Kerr, John. Yanceyville, N. C.
Kerfoot, Mrs. Maria C., Upperville, Va.
Kerfoot, Mrs. Harriet E., Battletown, Va.
Ketcham, Charles F., Brooklyn, N. Y.
Ketcham, Rev. F., Panola, Ill.
Ketcham, Miss Sarah A., New York.
Ketcham, James, Dover Plains, N. Y.
Ketchum, Rev. Jonathan, Wayne, N. Y.
Keyes, Mrs. Lydia L., Portland, N. Y.
Keyes, Miss Sarah E., Portland, N. Y.
Keyes, Jesse, Almont, Mich.
Keyes Samuel, North Adams, Mass.
Kidder, Abner C., Boston, Mass.
Kidder, Horace, Dundee, N. Y.
Kimball, Abraham, Boston, Mass.
Kimball, Mrs. Edward, Haverhill, Mass.
Kimball, Rufus, Haverhill, Mass.
Kimball, Mrs. Rufus, Haverhill, Mass.
Kimball, Miss Mary W., Haverhill, Mass.
Kimball, Nathaniel T., Haverhill, Mass.
Kincaid. Rev. Eugenio, Ava, Burmah.
Kindel, Job, Pemberton, N. J.
King, Daniel K., Port Byron, N. Y.
King, Robert, New York.
King, Rev. William H., Owego, N. Y.
King, John N., Suffield, Ct.
King, Elias, Greenport, N. Y.
Kingman, Martin E., New York.
Kingman, Mrs. Eliza F., New York.
Kingman, Sumner A., New York.
Kingman, Miss Augusta E., New York.
Kingsbury, Rev. Arnold, Adrian, Mich.
Kingsford, Rev. Edward, D.D., Richmond, Va.
Kingsland, Mrs. Sarah Jane, New York.
Kingsland, E. J., Philadelphia, Pa.
Kingsley, Rev. A. C., Parma Centre, N. Y.
Kinne, Mrs. Orissa, Norwich, Ct.
Kinney, Mrs. Ellen B., Derby, Vt.

MEMBERS FOR LIFE.

Kirk, Robert, New York.
Kline, P. D., Marvin, Ill.
Knapp, H. W., New York.
Knapp, S. J., New York.
Knapp, Rev. Henry R., Greenport, N. Y.
Knapp, Mrs. Mary, Greenport, N. Y.
Knapp, John, Bridgeport, Ct.
Knapp, Rev. A., Otselic, N. Y.
Knapp, J. F., Camillus, N. Y.
Knight, Edward H., Salem, Mass.
Knight, Abram, Williamsburgh, N. Y.
Knight, Daniel N., Brooklyn, N. Y.
Knight, Mrs. D. N., Brooklyn, N. Y.
Knight, Jonathan, Worcester, Mass.
Knight, Mrs. Samuel, Haverhill, Mass.
Knight, Rev. Benjamin, Salem, Mass.
Knowles, Levi, Philadelphia.
Knowles, Susan E., Providence.
Knowles, Isaac, New London, Ct.
Knowlton, Miss Sarah L., North Chatham, N. Y.
Knowlton, D. A., Freeport, Ill.
Knowlton, Edward, Marion, Iowa.
Knowlton, Hezekiah, Beverly, Mass.
Knowlton, J. B., Cumberland, Ohio.
Knox, Miss Rachel, Hillsdale, N. Y.
Knudson, Mrs. Sarah Jane, Brooklyn, N. Y.
Kone, Louk, Maulmain, Burmah.
Kyle, Miss Mary, New York.
L'Amoureaux, Mrs. Nancy, Hadley, Mass.
Lacompt, Edwin A., Boston, Mass.
Ladd, Mrs. C. Ann, Williamsburgh, N. Y.
Ladow, John T., Dividing Creek, N. J.
Lafever, Reuben, Reading Centre, N. Y.
Lafferty, Mrs. Hannah, Exeter, N. H.
Lafleur, Rev. Theodore, Longueuil, C. E.
La Grange, Rev. John, St. Peter, Minn.
Laing, Miss Jane, New York.

[redacted]

Leach, Rev. Beriah N., Middletown, Vt.
Leach, Rev. D. F., Harpersville, N. Y.
Leach, Rev. William, Omaha City, Neb. Ter.
Leach, Mrs. Esther, Waterford, Ct.
Leask, Mrs. Margaret, New York.
Ledger, Mrs. Marion, Brooklyn, N. Y.
Lee, George, North Bristol, N. Y.
Lee, Mrs. Amanda, North Bristol, N. Y.
Lee, Miss Ann Mollan, New York.
Lee, J. A., New York.
Lee, Francis R., Trenton, N. J.
Lee, Francis R., Baptist Town, N. J.
Lee, Franklin, Philadelphia.
Leicester, Mrs. Mary, New York.
Leigh, James, Princeton, N. J.
Leggett, Rev. William, Owasco, N. Y.
Leland, J. A., Brooklyn, N. Y.
Leland Sarah A., Brooklyn, N. Y.
Lemont, Charles A., Chelsea, Mass.
Lemont, Mrs. Ann M., New York.
Leonard, Richard, Riceville, N. J.
Leonard, Thomas, Riceville, N. J.
Leonard, Mrs. Mahetable, Zanesville, O.
Leonard, Rev. Isaac, Burlington, Iowa.
Leonard, Mrs. Caroline F., Taunton, Mass.
Leonard, George E., Newton, Mass.
Leonard, George A., New York.
Leonard, Halsey, West Woodstock, Ct.
Lester, Samuel C., Auburn, N. Y.
Lett, James, Wharton, O.
Levy, Rev. Edgar M., Newark, N. J.
Lewis, William J., New York.
Lewis, Elijah, Brooklyn, N. Y.
Lewis, Mrs. Ann, Brooklyn, N. Y.
Lewis, Mrs. Mary B. S., Brooklyn, N. Y.
Lewis, Mrs. Asa, Worcester, Mass.
Lewis, Rev. Charles C., Westerly, R. I.

[redacted]

Lombard, Nathan, C.
Long, E. J., Boston, Mass.
Long, William, Shelburne Falls, Mass.
Long, William, Urbana, O.
Longstreet, Mrs. Mary L., Imlaystown, N. J.
Longstreet, J. H. Holmdel, N. J.
Longyear, Rev. Henry C., Westkill, N. Y.
Lord, Henry E., New York.
Loring, Samuel H., Boston, Mass.
Loring, Mrs. James, Boston, Mass.
Loring, Mrs. Eliza P., Boston, Mass.
Loring, Miss Sarah P., Boston, Mass.
Lothup, Ansel, Boston, Mass.
Louther, Rev. Thos., Duncansville, Pa.
Love, Rev. H. T., Brooklyn, N. Y.
Love, Mrs. Catharine W., Brooklyn, N. Y.
Love, John, New York.
Lovell, George, Osterville, Mass.
Lovell, Mrs. Lucy, Fall River, Mass.
Lovell, Rev. Andrew S., Bloomfield, Ct.
Low, Mrs. Eliza G., Haverhill, Mass.
Low, Mrs. Harriet N., Salem, N. J.
Lucas, Rev. Elijah, Stanford, N. Y.
Lucas, Mrs. Thirza, Bangall, N. Y.
Luckey, James E., Palo, Ill.
Luckey, Emma M., Palo, Ill.
Luddington, Samuel, Niverville, N. Y.
Ludlow, John R., New York.
Ludlow, Mrs. Clarisa Ann, Newport, R. I.
Ludlam, David, Jr., Sing Sing, N. Y.
Lull, Rev. Abner, Oshkosh, Wis.
Luther, Job, Providence, R. I.
Luther, Gardner, Seekonk, Mass.
Luther, Mrs. Mary, Seekonk, Mass.
Lyle, Robert, New Brunswick, N. J.
Lynch, Thomas, Philadelphia, Pa.
Lyon, Jesse, Fitchburg, Mass.
Lyon, Moses G., Fitchburg, Mass.
Lyon, Cyrus, York, N. Y.
Lyon, Mrs. Mary, York, N. Y.
Lyon, Miss Rebecca, Plainfield, N. J.
Lyon, Rev. Daniel D., Greenville, Ct.
Lyon, Rev. Joel, Owosso, Mich.
Lyon, Mrs. Caroline P., Chatham, Mass.
Lyon, Mrs. Merrick, Providence, R. I.
Lyon, Rev. A. S., Newport, Minn.
Lyons, Rev. John M., Columbus, N. J.
Lynt, Odell D., Hastings, N. Y.
Lytle, Andrew, Williamsburgh, Va.
McBride, Miss Jane Ann, New York.
McBride, Miss Eliza H., New York.
McBullen, Miss Sarah, New York.
McCarthy, Rev. William, Gorham, N. Y
McCless, Peter, Middletown, N. J.
McClung, Anthony, Kingston, N. Y.
McCormick, Mrs. Sarah M., New York.
McCoy, John, Charlestown, Ia.
McCune, John P., Salem, N. J.
McCutchen, Wm. G., Williamsburgh, N. Y.
McDade, Mrs. Jane, Morrisania, N. Y.
McDaniel, Randle, Fayetteville, N. C.
McFarland, Rev. D., Oswego, N. Y.
McGear, Daniel L.
McGonagal, George, New York.
McIntosh, Mrs. Mary, Philadelphia, Pa.
McIver, Mrs. Ann J., Society Hill, S. C.
McIver, A. M, Society Hill, S. C.
McJannett, Mrs. Elizabeth, Brooklyn, N. Y.
McKean, Rev. John A., Philadelphia, Pa.
McKean, Mrs. Eliza J., Philadelphia, Pa.
McKewan, John, New York.
McLallan, James, Trumansburg, N. Y.
McLallan, Mrs. Ellen, Trumansburg, N. Y.
McLean, Mrs. Mary, New London, Ct.
McLowth, Rev. Benjamin, Scipio, N. Y.
McMahon, Henry L., Philadelphia, Pa.
McNabb, Mrs. E., Fayetteville, N. C.
McTaggart, Mrs. Margaret, Reading, Pa.
McTaggart, Daniel, Reading, Pa.
Macdonald, Alexander, Williamsburgh, N. Y.
Macdonald, Mrs. E., Williamsburgh, N. Y.
Mack, Rev. Levi M., Casco, Wis.
Mack, Elisha H., Oswego, N. Y.
Maclay, Hon Wm. B., New York.
Maclay, Archibald, New York.
Maclay, Moses B., New York.
Macomber, John, Watertown, N. Y.
Mabbett, James K., Dover Plains, N. Y.
Mabbett, Mrs. Maria K., Dover Plains, N. Y.
Mabbett, T., Brooklyn, N. Y.
Mace, Rev. Jeremiah M., Middleboro', Mass.
Madison, Almond Z., Fredonia, N. Y.
Magee, Rev. Thomas, New Brunswick, N. S.
Magee, Thomas H., New York.
Maghee, Miss Frances, New York.
Magoon, Miss Ella Louise, Albany, N. Y.
Magoon, Frank N. L., Albany, N. Y.
Mahoney, Rev. Henry W., Piedmont, S. C.
Main, Randall W., New York.
Mair, Dudley, Boston, Mass.
Mallory, Rev. Almond C., Benton Centre, N. Y.
Mallory, Rev. James, Eden, N. Y.
Mandeville, Stephen, Batavia, Ill.
Mandeville, Mrs. Mary, Batavia, Ill.
Mandeville, Miss Phebe E., Batavia, Ill.
Mandeville, George, New York.
Mandeville, Henry, New York.
Mansfield, Edward, South Reading, Mass.
Mangam, William D., New York.
Mangam, Edgar B., New York.
Mangum, Rev. Daniel, Pagesville, S. C.
Mann, Rev. Levi L., Trout Creek, N. Y.
Manning, Rev. Edward, Cornwall, N. S.
Manning, William, Boston, Mass.
Manning, Melville M., Boston, Mass.
Manning, Mrs. Rachel D., Plainfield, N. J.
Manning, Francis H., Worcester, Mass.
Manning, M. C., Lorraine, N. Y.
Manro, Phillip A., Throopsville, N Y.
Manton, Rev. Joseph R., Providence, R. I.
Manwaring, C. S., East Lyme, Ct.
Maple, John E., Canton, Ill.
March, Peter S., New York.
Marchant, Henry, Jr., Providence, R. I.
Marchant, Miss Mary W., Providence, R. I.
Marchant, Henry C., Providence, R. I.
Marcley, Michael F., Morrisania, N. Y.
Marsall, Rev. J. F, Columbia, S. C.
Marsh, Rev. Asa, Austin, Minn.
Marsh, Benjamin, Newport, R. I.
Marsh, Enoch S., Hudson, N. H.
Marshall, Rev. Samuel, Ohio.
Marshall, Albert, Holden, Mass.
Marshall, Mrs. Maria, Holden, Mass.
Marshall, Mrs. Mary Ann, New York.
Marshall, Mrs. Mary, New York.
Marston, John, Saratoga Springs, N. Y.
Marston, Mrs. Marcia, Saratoga Springs, N. Y.
Marston, Rev. S. W., Greenville, Ill.
Marston, Mrs. S. H., Greenville, Ill.
Martin, William R., New York.
Martin, Mrs. Charles J., New York.
Martin, Franklin, New York.
Martin, Miss Emily, New York.
Martin, Miss Mary, New York.
Martin, Miss Sarah, New York.
Martin, A., New York.
Martin, Mrs. Mary C., New York.
Martin, Alfred, New York.
Martin, Mrs. Harriet W., New York.
Martin, Mrs. Mary Ann, New York.
Martin, Henry L., New York.
Martin, Reune, New York.
Martin, William H., Providence.
Martin, Mrs. James A., Providence.
Martin, Rev. Sandford S., Delavan, Ill.
Martin, Peter, Philadelphia.
Martin, M. D., Bristol, Ct.
Martin, Mrs. Sarah Ann, New York.
Martin, D., Brooklyn, N. Y.

Mason, Mrs. Arnold G., Jersey City, N. J.
Mason, R. B., Webster, N. Y.
Mason, Mrs. Sumner R., Cambridgeport, Mass.
Mason, Rev. J. T., Sterling, Ill.
Mason, Bethuel, Somerville, N. J.
Mason, Charles J., New York.
Mason, Mrs. Lavinia, New York.
Mason, Miss Sarah Elizabeth, New York.
Mason, James, Brooklyn, N. Y.
Mason, Rev. Eddy, Sennet, N. Y.
Mason, Joseph R., Providence.
Mason, George, Providence.
Mason, Miss Harriet, Boston.
Mason, William, Fall River, Mass.
Mason, Mrs. Lydia, Warren, R.
Massey, Mrs. Catharine, Bellingham, Mass.
Mastin, John S., New York.
Mather, Increase, Horse Heads, N. Y.
Mather, Mrs. Mary A., Deep River, Ct.
Mathews, Rev. George, Seekonk, Mass.
Mathews, Mrs. Elizabeth, Seekonk, Mass.
Mathewson, Nathan F., Providence.
Matteson, Rev. N. H., Preston City, Ct.
Maul, Rev. William, Greenwich, N. J.
Maul, Mrs. Sarah Ann, Greenwich, N. J.
Maxwell, B., Shelburne Falls, Mass.
Maxwell, Rev. J. M., Kingsbury, Ia.
Mayell, Mrs. Eliza, Albany, N. Y.
Maynard, Walter, Springfield, Mass.
Maynard, Mrs. Clarissa, Corning, N. Y.
Meacham, Miss Elizabeth, Brooklyn, N. Y.
Mead, John, Troy, N. Y.
Mead, Joshua, New York.
Mead, William, Lawrence, Mass.
Mead, John K., Amenia, N. Y.
Meads, Rev. George W., Vienna, N. Y.
Medbery, Andrew N., Seekonk, Mass.
Meech, Rev. Wm. W., Long Plain, Mass.
Meech, Mrs. Lydia, Preston, Ct.
Meech, Rev. Levi, Preston, Ct.
Meech, Levi W., Preston, Ct.
Medbury, Rev. Nicholas, Newburyport, Mass.
Medbury, Viall, Seekonk, Mass.
Meeker, Aaron B., Elizabeth, N. J.
Merron, Mrs. Caroline M., New Haven, Ct.
Meekins, Mrs. Harriet R. H., Northampton, Mass.
Meeson, Rev. J. D., Burlington, N. J.
Merchant, James H., New York.
Merchant, Mrs. Amanda M., New York.
Merchant, Miss Louise, New York.

Metc
Mers
Merv
Mico
Mier
Mike
Mike
Milbe
Milba
Milba
Milba
Milba
Milba
Milba
Milba
Milba
Milba
Middl
Middl
Miles,
Miles,
Miles,
Miles,
Miles,
Millar
Millar
Millar
Millar
Miller,
Miller,
Miller,
Miller,
Miller,
Miller,
Miller,
Miller,
Miller,
Miller,
Miller,
Miller,
Miller,
Miller,
Miller,
Miller,
Miller,
Mills, C
Mills, S
Mills, F
Milne,
Milne,

Mingus, Miss Julia Ann, New York.
Mintch, Mrs. Phebe, Shiloh, N. J.
Mitchell, Rev. George H., Wagontown, Pa.
Mitchell, Mrs. Phebe H., Wagontown, Pa.
Mitchell, Seth, Montrose, Pa.
Mitchell, Ellen E., Montrose, Pa.
Mitchell, Rev. Thomas, Troy, Pa.
Mitchell, Mrs. Maria M., Boston, Mass.
Mix, G. I., Meriden, Ct.
Mixter, Rev. George, Pequonoc Bridge, Ct.
Mixter, Mrs. Chloe, Pequonoc Bridge, Ct.
Mondon, Gilbert F., Port Jarvis, N. Y.
Monroe, Rev. William Y., Graham, Ia.
Montgomery, William, Danbury, Ct.
Montgomery, Mrs. Susan, Danbury, Ct.
Montgomery, S. P., Danbury, Ct.
Montgomery, Wm., Jr., Danbury, Ct.
Montgomery, Miss Susan, Danbury, Ct.
Montague, Rev. Oreb, Whitewater, Wis.
Moon, John, New York.
Moone, Lyman, Lyndonville, N. Y.
Moore, Dr. G. C., St. Johns, N. C.
Moore, Mrs. Julia, St. Johns, N. C.
Moore, Mrs. Theodosia M., St. Louis, Mo.
Moore, James, Old Mines, Mo.
Moore, Francis W., New York.
Moore, Rev. Lyman H., Lansing, Mich.
Moore, Rev. W. W., Albany, N. Y.
Moore, Rev. George C., Stratford, Canada.
Moore, James, Wilmington, Del.
Moore, Enoch, Danbury, Ct.
Moore, Rev. Farris, Lee, Mass.
Moore, Robert, Greencastle, Ia.
Moore, Rev. D., Jr., Le Roy, N. Y.
Moore, Joseph C., Dividing Creek, N. J.
Moore, Ezra, East Lynn, Ct.
Moore, Nathaniel W., New Haven, Ct.
Morgan, Gilbert E., Mystic River, Ct.
Morgan, William, Brooklyn, N. Y.
Morgan, Miss Harriet, Brooklyn, N. Y.
Morgan, David, Cleveland, O.
Morgan, David, Sen., Allegany City, Pa.
Morgan, Hiram, Blackwoodtown, N. J.
Morgan, Joshua, Philadelphia, Pa.
Morgan, Mrs. Mary Ann, Philadelphia, Pa.
Morgan, Augustus, Noank, Ct.
Morgan, Mrs. Jane E., North Becket, Mass.
Morgan, Avery, Hartford, Ct.
Morgan, Wm. P., Albion, N. Y.
Morgan, Mrs. Anne E., Groton Bank, Ct.
Morrell, Mrs. Sarah G., Savannah, Ga.
Morrill, Geo. W., Salisbury, Mass.
Morrill, Miss Mary, Salisbury, Mass.
Morrill, Joseph, Amesbury, Mass.
Morrill, Daniel, Amesbury, Mass.
Morris, Rev. J., Hamburg, S. C.
Morris, Rev. David, Cross River, N. Y.
Morrison, Jonathan, Brooklyn, N. Y.
Morrison, Mrs. A. Henrietta, Brooklyn, N. Y.
Morse, Mrs. Sophia A., Sturbridge, Mass.
Morse, Enoch R., Chelsea, Mass.
Morse, K. P., Greenville, Ill.
Morse, Mrs. Clara S., Charlestown, Mass.
Morse, Curtis G., South Dedham, Mass.
Morse, Benjamin, ——, Iowa.
Morse, Charles A., Brooklyn, N. Y.
Morse, Mrs. Eliza, New Market, N. J.
Mortimer, George W., Wilmington, Del.
Morton, Mrs. Susan, Corning, N. Y.
Morton, Miss Sarah B., Corning, N. Y.
Morton, Miss Matilda N., Corning, N. Y.
Morton, Miss Kate E., Corning, N. Y.
Morton, George, Brooklyn, N. Y.
Mosely, Green, Dupree's Store, Va.
Mosely, Miss S. A., Dupree's Store, Va.
Moss, Lemuel, Rochester, N. Y.
Moss, Mrs. Nancy, Upperville, Va.
Mott, Miss Elizabeth, New York.
Moulthrop, Major, New Haven, Ct.
Mount, David, Albany, N. Y.
Moxley, Rev. Oel W., Madrid, N. Y.
Mugg, Rev. John, Gosport, Ia.
Mulford, Charles, Salem, N. J.
Mulhern, Rev. Denis, De Sota, Wis.
Mumford, Rev. N., Desota, N. Y.
Munger, Rev. Washington, Waterford, Ct.
Munger, Mrs. Louisa N., Waterford, Ct.
Munger, Morgan, Schaghticoke, N. Y.
Munger, L. F., Leroy, N. Y.
Munn, Mrs. Mary, New York.
Murdock, Mrs. Martha B., Boston, Mass.
Murphy, Wm. D., New York.
Murphy, Samuel, Hoboken, N. J.
Murphy, Rev. John R., Marlton, N. J.
Murphy, Mrs. Sophronia S., Marlton, N. J.
Murray, Thomas S., New Hope, Pa.
Murray, Mrs. Margaret M., New Hope, Pa.
Murray, Miss Sarah L., Boston, Mass.
Mustin, John, Philadelphia, Pa.
Myers, Mrs. Ann R., Philadelphia, Pa.
Myers, James, Jr., New York.
Mylne, Rev. Wm., Louisa C. H., Va.
Myrick, Albert A., Gilbertsville, N. Y.
Napier, Rev. Robert, Mizpath, S. C.
Nash, Richard E., Webster, Mass.
Neale, Jeremiah, Plainville, Ct.
Neale, John, Southington, Ct.
Nearing, Alfred N., New York.
Nelson, Rev. Wm. F., Min.
Nelson, Simeon B., Menasha, Wis.
Newcomb, Butler, Cedarville, N. J.
Newcomb, Mrs. Thomas, Haverhill, Mass.
Newcomb, James, New London, Ct.
Newcomb, Mrs. Sarah A., Groton, Ct.
Newcomb, Josiah T., Newport, N. J.
Newel, James S., Essex, Ct.
Newell, Andrew H., Brookline, Mass.
Newell, Mrs. Asa, Providence, R. I.
Newhall, Rev. Charles, Stratham, N. H.
Newland, D., Stillwater, N. Y.
Newland, Rev. C. A., Phelps, N. Y.
Newland, Peabody, Lawrenceville, N. Y.
Newton, Mrs. Sally, Albany.
Newton, Wm., Worcester, Mass.
Newton, Rev. Baxter, Cazenovia, N. Y.
Newton, Miss Frances M., New York.
Newton, Mrs. Jane, Bridgeton, N. J.
Newton, Horace B., Albany, N. Y.
Nice, Mrs. Sarah R., Philadelphia.
Nice, Mrs. Elizabeth A., ——, Md.
Nichols, Reuben, Davenport, Iowa.
Nichols, Rev. D. A., Port Providence, Pa.
Nichols, Jonathan, Berlin, N. Y.
Nichols, Mrs. Eliza A., Boston.
Nichols, Luther W., Amherst, N. H.
Nichols, Walter S., Wickford, R. I.
Nicholas, Rev. Noah, Rutland, Vt.
Nicholson, A. M., Bostick Mills, N. C.
Nickerson, Harden, Providence, R. I.
Nickels, George, Rockhill, O.
Niel, James R., Brooklyn, N. Y.
Nilsson, Rev. Frederick O., Scandia, Min.
Nixon, George, Providence.
Noble, Mrs. Margaret, Brooklyn, N. Y.
Noble, Gorham, New York.
Nolton, Miss Sarah J., Petersburgh, N. Y.
Norman, Miss Arnoretta D., Elmira, N. Y.
Normandeau, Mrs. C. A., Quebec, C. E.
Northam, E., Rockingham, N. C.
Northam, George, Va.
Norton, Rev. Charles C., New York.
Norton, Rev. Noah, Brunswick, Me.
Norton, Newbury, Agawam, Mass.
Norton, M. F., Cleveland, O.
Norris, Mrs. F. Henrietta, Brooklyn, N. Y.
Norris, Mrs. Eliza D., Sanbornton, N. H.
Noyes, Henry, Chelsea, Mass.
Noyes, A. D., New London, Ct.
Noyes, Nathaniel, West Dedham, Mass.
Numan, Abraham, Troy, N. Y.

Nunn, James D., Raleigh, N. C.
Nye, Thomas, Littleton, Mass.
Ody, Mrs. Rebecca, Davenport, Mass.
Odell, Jonathan, Yonkers, N. Y.
Ogden, Joseph H., Greenwich, N. J.
Ogden, Horace [illegible], Greenwich, N. J.
Ogden, Elmer, Greenwich, N. J.
Oldring, Henry J., Williamsburg, N. Y.
Olin, Joseph, Lawrenceville, N. Y.
Olin, Benjamin, Canton, N. Y.
Oliver, Marcus, Bridgeport, Ct.
Olmstead, Rev. J. W., Boston.
Olney, Rev. David B., Weston, N. Y.
Olney, Rev. Philetus, Horse Heads, N. Y.
Olney, Mrs. P., Horse Heads, N. Y.
Olney, James, Pawtucket, R. I.
Olney, Rev. Lafayette W., [illegible], N. Y.
Olney, Edward A. M., Kalamazoo, Mich.
Olney, Wm., Malden, Mass.
Ombersen, Wm. J., New York.
Otis, Harvey, Kingston, N. Y.
O'Brien, Miss Mary, New York.
O'Brien, Mrs. Mary L., Concord, N. H.
O'Neal, Mrs. Jane, Brooklyn, N. Y.
Oncken, Rev. J. G., Hamburg, Germany.
Oncken, Mrs. Ann, Hamburg, Germany.
Oncken, Miss Marg't. A., Hamburg, Germany.
Onderdonk, Peter C., New Brunswick, N. J.
Osborn, Rev. J. W., Piqua, Ohio.
Osgood, Miss Sarah C., Salisbury, Mass.
Osgood, Miss Jane, Salisbury, Mass.
Osgood, John, Amesbury, Mass.
Osgood, Rev. S. M., Philadelphia.
Osgood, Miss Sarah Ann, [illegible], Mass.
Osgood, Miss Caroline W., Philadelphia.
Osgood, Rev. Howard, [illegible], N. Y.
Osgood, R. F., [illegible], Ohio.

Parker, Lydia P., Allen, Mich.
Parker, Rev. Harvey L., Fairfax, Vt.
Parker, Mrs. E. R., Norwich, N. Y.
Parker, Miss Susan E., Boston.
Parker, Jonathan, Boston.
Parker, Mrs. Sarah E., Malone, N. Y.
Parks, Rev. R. M., Bedford, Ind.
Parks, Mrs. Nancy J., Great Falls, N. H.
Parks, Mrs. Sarah J., Great Falls, N. H.
Parks, Mrs. Marianne C., South Berwick, Me.
Parkhurst, John, Fitchburg, Mass.
Parkhurst, G. R., Brooklyn, N. Y.
Parkhurst, Mrs. Fidelia, Brooklyn, N. Y.
Parkhurst, Mrs. M. W. Newton Centre, Mass.
Parmlee, Mrs. Syrena, New York.
Parmelee, Elias F., Essex, Ct.
Parmelee, Rev. J. H., Xenia, O.
Parmely, Rev. Levi, Elgin, Ill.
Parmely, Mrs. Catharine H., Elgin, Ill.
Parish, Warren, Mendon, N. Y.
Parshley, John, New Haven, Ct.
Parsons, Silas, Swanzey, N. H.
Parsons, Mrs. Patience, Swanzey, N. H.
Parsons, Wm., Medford, Mass.
Parsons, Rev. William M., Brooklyn, N. Y.
Parsons, Ralph, Granville, O.
Partridge, Henry A., Minneapolis, Min.
Pasco, Rev. Cephas, Egremont, Mass.
Passage, Adam, Weedsport, N. Y.
Patch, Rev. George W., Marblehead, Mass.
Patrick, Charlotte M., Saratoga Springs, N. Y.
Pattengill, Rev. C. N., Whitesboro, N. Y.
Patterson, Rev. Wm. C., East Dedham, Mass.
Patterson, Mrs. Mary, Chapel Hill, N. C.
Patterson, Mrs. Lucy A., Williamsburgh, N. Y.
Patton, John E.
Paulin, Mrs. Ann, Salem, N. J.

[redacted]

Perine, Mrs. Sarah, Plainfield, N. J.
Perley, John E., Boston.
Perkins, Jabez, Topsham, Me.
Perkins, Rev. Nehemiah M., Brookline, Mass.
Perkins, George, Amesbury, Mass.
Perkins, Russell B., Meriden, Ct.
Perkins, Schuyler, Little Mill Creek, O.
Perkins, Mrs. Eveline A., Meriden, Ct.
Perkins, Eliab, Fond du Lac, Wis.
Perkins, Samuel S., Boston.
Perkins, John, Moorestown, N. J.
Perrine, J. W., Freehold, N. J.
Perry, Mrs. Sarah, McWilliamstown, Pa.
Perry, Valentine, Macedon, N. Y.
Perry, Samuel S., Manchester, N. Y.
Perry, Wm. H., Brooklyn, N. Y.
Persons, Rev. R., Victory, N. Y.
Peterson, Rev. J. F., Richardson's, S. C.
Peterson, Richard E., New York.
Peterson, Mrs. Deborah V., New York.
Peterson, Samuel F., Philadelphia.
Pettingill, Daniel, Haverhill, Mass.
Pettingill, Mrs. Charlotte, Haverhill, Mass.
Petteys, Harvey E., Greenwich, N. Y.
Petteys, Mrs. Helen J., Greenwich, N. Y.
Pettit, Curtis, Wilson, N. Y.
Pettit, Rev. Harvey, Shelby, N. Y.
Pettigrew, Rev. W. J., Pittsburgh, Pa.
Pew, John, Gloucester, Mass.
Phares, Rev. M. B., Dupont, Ia.
Phelps, Humphrey, New York.
Phelps, John, Owego, N. Y.
Phelps, Mrs. Sophia Emelia, New Haven, Ct.
Phelps, Mrs. Mary S., New York.
Phelps, Miss Julia Adelaide, New York.
Phelps, Miss Sophronia E., New York.
Phelps, Miss Mary Amelia, New York.
Phelps, Willard, New York.
Phillio, Calvin, Providence.
Phillips, Mrs. James M., Mystic River, Ct.
Phillips, John M., Penningtonville, Pa.
Phillips, Geo. W., Penningtonville, Pa.
Phillips, George H., Troy, N. Y.
Phillips, Rev. W., Providence.
Phillips, Rev. David L., Jonesboro', Ill.
Phillips, Rev. W. F., Dodgeville, Wis.
Phillips, Rev. W. C., St. Cloud, Min.
Phillips, Mrs. Ann, New York.
Phillips, Mrs. Theodosia, Morristown, N. J.
Phillips, Peter, Rondout, N. Y.
Phillips, Mrs. Zilla, North Nassau, N. Y.
Phillips, Mrs. Lester S., New London, Ct.
Phillips, J. E., New London, N. H.
Philbrook, Rev. Abel, Pittsgrove, N. J.
Phippen, Rev. George, Tyringham, Mass.
Pier, Mrs. Deborah, New York.
Pierce, Rev. Sem, Londonderry, Vt.
Pierce, Philo, Bristol, Ct.
Pierce, Mrs. Patty B., Nunda, N. Y.
Pierce, John W., Boston.
Pierce, John N., Harvard, Mass.
Pierce, Mrs. Osgood, Beverly, Mass.
Pierce, Mrs. Rebecca Walker, Grafton, Vt.
Pierce, Rev. George, Manchester, N. H.
Pierce, J. O., Rochester, N. Y.
Pierson, David, East Avon, N. Y.
Pike, Jonathan, Providence.
Pike, Mrs. Jonathan, Providence.
Pike, Miss Ann E., Providence.
Pike, Albert B. H., Providence.
Pike, Benj., Jr., New York.
Pike, Mrs. Frances M., New York.
Pike, Miss Catharine E., New York.
Pike, Miss Mary Emma, New York.
Pike, Mrs. Abby C., Taunton, Mass.
Pike, Rev. William, Canton, N. J.
Pillsbury, Rev. Phineas, Ill.
Pillsbury, John G., Boston.
Pinder, Mary, Danversport, Mass.
Pinney, Mrs. Mary, Owego, N. Y.
Piper, John G., Canton, Ill.
Piper, David, Jay, N. Y.
Pitcher, Miss Elizabeth, Brooklyn, N. Y.
Pitman, Rev. Joseph M., Sutton, N. H.
Pixley, Rev. Joseph B., Hartwick, N. Y.
Plant, E. H., Plantsville, Ct.
Plant, A. P., Plantsville, Ct.
Plant, Mrs. Cornelia, Plantsville, Ct.
Platt, Alfred, Waterbury, Ct.
Platt, G. W., New York.
Platt, Mrs. Jane D., New York.
Platt, Rev. E. F., Toledo, Ohio.
Platt, Josiah, Stratfield, Ct.
Platt, Daniel, Amenia, N. Y.
Platt, Abraham, New Brunswick, N. J.
Platts, Daniel, Bridgeton, N. J.
Playford, Thomas, Stamford, Ct.
Plumb, William, Pomfret, Wis.
Plumb, Mrs. Cynthia G., Evansburgh, Pa.
Plymer, Mrs. Eliza, New York.
Pohlman, William, Albany, N. Y.
Poole, Rev. A. W., Woodland, La.
Pooler, Seth, Lowell, Mass.
Poland, W. C., Boston.
Poland, Rev. James W., Goffstown Center, N. H.
Pollard, Mrs. Elizabeth, Taunton, Mass.
Polhamus, H. A., New York.
Pomeroy, Rev. Samuel, West Stockbridge, Mass.
Pomeroy, Mrs. Betsey, West Stockbridge, Mass.
Pomeroy, Harvey S., York, N. Y.
Pomroy, William, Middlefield, Mass.
Pond, William, New York.
Pond, Joseph A., Boston.
Pond, Moses W., Boston.
Pope, Rev. J. D., St. Paul, Min.
Pope, Edward R., New Bedford, Mass.
Pope, Elizabeth Coggeshall, New Bedford, Mass.
Porter, Mrs. Welthea M., Pittsfield, Mass.
Porter, Miss Clara Maria, Pittsfield, Mass.
Porter, Miss Helen Gertrude, Pittsfield, Mass.
Porter, Timothy, Waterbury, Ct.
Porter, Miss Charlotte, Danvers, Mass.
Porter, Mrs. Rebecca P., Danvers Mills, Mass.
Porter, Eliza J., Danversport, Mass.
Porter, Henry S. M. D., Philadelphia.
Post, Mrs. Sarah, New York.
Post, Alanson H., Hinesburg, Vt.
Post, Levi, Pitcher, N. Y.
Post, Joy, Brooklyn, N. Y.
Post, John, Saline, Mich.
Post, Prof. John D., Oregon City, Oregon.
Post, Peter K., Somerville, N. J.
Post, Mrs. Susan A., Deep River, Ct.
Post, James T., Jerseyville, Ill.
Post, Rev. Charles B., Dover Plains, N. Y.
Potter, Henry, Cambridge, Mass.
Potter, James, Bridgeport, Ct.
Potter, Rev. Charles W., Cromwell, Ct.
Potter, Rev. Aaron, Centerville, Mich.
Powelson, Chas. G., Stamford, Ct.
Powell, Daniel L., Schenectady, N. Y.
Powell, Rev. Thomas, Davenport, Iowa.
Powell, Mrs. E., Davenport, Iowa.
Powell, William T., Ottawa, Ill.
Powell, Rev. Peter, Beverly, N. J.
Powell, Mrs. Nancy, Powelton, N. C.
Powell, William, Cincinnati, Ohio.
Powers, Miss Amelia, New London, Ct.
Powers, Charles W., Bloomfield, N. J.
Powers, Rev. Hiram, Thorn Hill, N. Y.
Powless, Mrs. Anna Maria, Hoboken, N. J.
Pratt, Rev. John, Newport, R. I.
Pratt, Rev. Samuel C., Lowell, Mass.
Pratt, Rev. James H., North Granville, N. Y.
Pratt, Mrs. James H., North Granville, N. Y.
Pratt, Daniel, Brooklyn, N. Y.
Pratt, Oliver T., New York.
Pratt, Eli, Johnstown, Ohio.
Pratt, John C., Boston.
Pratt, Rev. John, Granville, O.

Pratt, Paul, [illegible], N. Y.
Pratt, Mrs. Jessie H., [illegible], N. Y.
Pratt, Jeremiah, Burlington, N. Y.
Pratt, Mrs. Herman, Boston, Mass.
Prentiss, Mrs. Sarah, [illegible], N. Y.
Preston, Rev. George, [illegible], N. Y.
Preston, Mrs. [illegible], [illegible], Ct.
Probyn, Mrs. Ann.
[illegible], John R., [illegible], N. Y.
Prowitt, Henry M., Norwalk, Ct.
Preston, Mrs. Hannah S., New York.
[illegible], N. Y.
Purdy, Rev. [illegible], N. C.
Purdy, Mrs. [illegible], N. C.
Purdy, Rev. [illegible], Washington, D. C.
Purrington, Mrs. [illegible], Plattsburgh, N. Y.
Purviance, Rev. [illegible], Smithfield, Pa.
[illegible], Rev. J. M., [illegible]
Purington, Rev. Lewis M., Rensselaerville, N. Y.
[illegible], Miss Mary Ann, [illegible]
Parks, Mrs. [illegible]
[illegible], Jay, N. Y.
Putnam, Rev. [illegible], N. Y.
Putnam, Mrs. [illegible], N. Y.
Putnam, Rev. H. [illegible], Pa.
Putnam, John, Boston.
Putnam, Howard [illegible], Boston.
Putnam, Mrs. [illegible], Davenport, Mass.
Putnam, Mrs. [illegible], Davenport, Mass.
Putnam, Mrs. Mary B., Haverhill, Mass.
Quackenboss, Mrs. [illegible], Detroit, Mich.
[illegible], John V. [illegible], N. Y.
[illegible], Mrs. Ann, Philadelphia.
[illegible], Mrs. [illegible], Brooklyn, N. Y.
Quincy, Josiah, Rumney, N. H.
Quincy, Mrs. [illegible], Rumney, N. H.
Radcliff, Joshua, Haverhill, Mass.
[illegible]

[redacted]

Raymond, Charles P., South Norwalk, Ct.
Raynor, Samuel, New York.
Raynor, Mrs. Sarah D., New York.
Raynor, William P., New York.
Raynor, Miss Mary S., New York.
Raynor, James W., New York.
Rey, William A., Providence, R. I.
Read, Rev. Hiram W., Falls Church, Va.
Read, Mrs. Alzina A. J., Falls Church, Va.
Read, Rev. Daniel, Medina, N. Y.
Read, Rev. James S.
Read, Mrs. James H., Providence, R. I.
Read, George W., Fall River, Mass.
Read, Mrs. Hannah M., Deep River, Ct.
Read, Dr. Thomas H., Decatur, Ill.
Reading, George, New York.
Reading, Caezer, Flemington, N. J.
Reed, Mrs. Sarah, Deep River, Ct.
Reed, Evans H., Townsend, Vt.
Reed, Mrs. Fanny B., Townshend, Vt.
Reed, Daniel, Townshend, Vt.
Reed, Mrs. Sarah B. G., Bristol, R. I.
Reed, Mrs. Emeline, Chelsea, Mass.
Reed, Thomas B., New York.
Reed, Wm. B., North East, N. Y.
Reed, Mrs. Mary Ann, North East, N. Y.
Reed, Mrs. Eunice, North East, N. Y.
Reed, Miss Mary I., North East, N. Y.
Reed, Rev. E. D., Oneida, N. Y.
Reed, Mrs. E. D., Oneida, N. Y.
Reed, David, Utica, N. Y.
Reed, Enos, East Cambridge, Mass.
Reed, Lewis B., New York.
Reed, Rev. William, Raynham, Mass.
Reed, Rufus, Albion, N. Y.
Reed, G. Washington, Philadelphia.
Reed, Miss Henrietta A., Boston.

[redacted]

Richards, Truman, Brooklyn, N. Y.
Richards, Miss Isabel, New York.
Richards, James, Cleveland, Ohio.
Richards, A. R., Rochester, N. Y.
Richards, Rev. Samuel, Providence, R. I.
Richards, Mrs. Maria T., Providence, R. I.
Richards, Ebenezer T., Holyoke, Mass.
Richards, Mrs. Cornelia V. H., Providence.
Richardson, Rev. Daniel F., Hanover, N. H.
Richardson, Wm. T., Cambridge, Mass.
Richardson, Thomas S., Brooklyn, N. Y.
Richardson, Mrs. Ann, Boston.
Richardson, Freeman, Auburn, N. Y.
Richardson, Rev. John, South Berwick, Me.
Richardson, Mrs. Euphemia, Troy, N. Y.
Richardson, Mrs. Lydia, Salem, Mass.
Richardson, Leonard, Brooklyn, N. Y.
Richmond, Miss Maryetta, Harlemville, N. Y.
Richmond, Rev. Nathaniel, Pendleton, Ia.
Rider, Charles C., Roxbury, Mass.
Riddick, Jethro H., Sunbury, N. C.
Riddick, Nathan, Sunbury, N. C.
Rigley, Henry, Albany, N. Y.
Riley, Rev. G. W., Paris, Ill.
Riply, Rev. Thomas B., Portland, Me.
Ripley, Joseph, Hingham, Mass.
Ripley, Rev. S., Northboro', Mass.
Ripley, Rev. Henry J., D.D., Newton, Mass.
Ripley, Miss A. E. Newton, Mass.
Ripley, Rev. Nathaniel, South New Berlin, N. Y.
Ristine, Jacob, West Harford, Pa.
Roach, Rev. E. W., Harvey's Store, Va.
Robert, Rev. Joseph T., Zanesville, Ohio.
Roberts, E. G., Brooklyn, N. Y.
Roberts, Mrs. E. G., Brooklyn, N. Y.
Roberts, Rev. Thomas, Riceville, N. J.
Roberts, N. H., Riceville, N. J.
Roberts, Thomas, jr., Chanceville, N. J.
Roberts, Rev. Philip, jr., Malden Bridge, N. Y.
Roberts, Sarah, New Bedford, Mass.
Roberts, Mrs. Thyrza, Brooklyn, N. Y.
Robertson, Rev. Thomas N., Orleans, Ia.
Robbins, Lewis, Imlaystown, N. J.
Robbins, Mrs. Mary, Imlaystown, N. J.
Robbins, Mrs. Elizabeth, Littleton, Mass.
Robbins, Rev. Gilbert, Sterling, Mass.
Robbins, Austin, Smithville, N. Y.
Robbins, Oliver, Sacketts Harbor, N. Y.
Robbins, Ira, Boston.
Robbins, Rev. Gurdon, Hartford, Ct.
Robbins, Charles, Providence.
Robinson, Alfred, Cooperstown, N. Y.
Robinson, Rev. E. G., D.D., Rochester, N. Y.
Robinson, Rev. Samuel, St. John, N. B.
Robinson, Rev. Daniel, Sand Lake, N. Y.
Robinson, Benjamin, Providence.
Robinson, Mrs. Mary E., Providence.
Robinson, Demas.
Robinson, Wm., New York.
Robinson, Mrs. Catharine, New York.
Robinson, Mrs. Martha, Savannah, Ga.
Robinson, Reuben T., Boston.
Robinson, Edward, Arcadia, N. Y.
Robinson, Solomon, Webster, Mass
Robinson, Mrs. Barbara, Tremont, Ill.
Robinson, Henry M., Concord, N. H.
Robinson, Mrs. Ursula, Sand Lake, N. Y.
Robinson, Mrs. Eliza, Boston, Mass.
Rockafellow, George, Avoca, N. Y.
Rockwell, David, Plainfield, N. J.
Rockwood, Rev. Joseph M., New Eng. Vil., Mass.
Rockwood, Mrs. Lucretia, Brooklyn, N. Y.
Roe, Rev. Charles H., Belvidere, Ill.
Roe, Mrs. Mary, Belvidere, Ill.
Roel, Austin, Randolph, Mass.
Rogers, Rev. Joseph D., Berlin, N. Y.
Rogers, Enos, Chatham, Mass.
Rogers, Mrs. Eliza D., Providence.
Rogers, Miss Eleanor F., Providence.
Rogers, Richard, New London, Ct.
Rogers, Rev. J. B., Fond du Lac, Wis.
Rogers, Dr. Alexander W., Paterson, N. J.
Rogers, George W., New London, Ct.
Rogers, Richard, New London, Ct.
Rogers, Mrs. Sally, New London, Ct.
Rogers, Daniel, New London, Ct.
Rogers, Mrs. Phebe, Deep River, Ct.
Rogers, Gilbert, Waterford, Ct
Rogers, Archibald, Greenwich, N. Y.
Rollin, Rev. J. B., Tonawanda, N. Y.
Rollinson, Mrs. Sophronia, Rahway, N. J.
Rome, Mrs. Jane, Brooklyn, N. Y.
Roney, Rev. William, ——, N. Y.
Roof, Milton, New York.
Rose, William, Granville, O.
Rose, Mrs. Mary, Granville, O.
Rose, Daniel B., Troy, N. Y.
Rose, Mrs. Olive E., Troy, N. Y.
Rose, Northup, Amenia, N. Y.
Ross, Rev. Arthur A., Pawtucket, R. I.
Ross, Daniel V., Providence, R. I.
Ross, Mrs. Jerusha, Pawtucket, R. I.
Root, John A., Granville, Mass.
Rouse, Rev. Henry H., Chittenango, N. Y.
Rowan, Phineas, Philadelphia, Pa.
Rowe, John K., Baltimore.
Rowe, Edwin, Keeseville, N. Y.
Rowell, James, Salisbury, Mass.
Royal, Rev. Wm., Winterseat, S. C.
Rue, Rev. Joshua E., Louisville, Ky.
Rue, Joshua E., Jr., Hightstown, N. J.
Rue, Miss Mary, Hightstown, N. J.
Rugg, George W., Worcester, Mass.
Runyon, Richard E., New Brunswick, N. J.
Runyon, Hon. Peter P., New Brunswick, N. J.
Runyon, Mrs. Phebe, New Brunswick, N. J.
Runyon, Daniel, New Brunswick, N. J.
Runyon, Elias, New Brunswick, N. J.
Runyon, Reune D., New Market, N. J.
Runyon, Ephraim J., New Market, N. J.
Runyon, Mrs. Osee, New Market, N. J.
Runyon, Mrs. Isabella, New York.
Runyon, Isaac M., Plainfield, N. J.
Rupert, Benjamin, Dubuque, Iowa.
Russell, Rev. Philemon R., Rock, Mass.
Russell, William, Yanceyville, N. C.
Russell, Rev. Abm. A., Walworth, N Y.
Russell, Rev. Rutherford, Deep River, Ct
Russell, Samuel P., Chester, Ct.
Russell, Mrs. James, Haverhill, Mass.
Russell, Levi F., Cambridge, Mass.
Russell, Andrew W., Albany, N. Y.
Ryland, Rev. Robert, Richmond College, Va.
Sabin, Rev. Alvah, Georgia, Vt.
Sackett, Mrs. Eunice M., Stanford, N. Y.
Saddington, Thomas B., Williamsburgh, N. Y.
Safford, Mrs. Sarah B., Salem, Mass.
Safford, Morgan, Norwich, Ct.
Safford, Henry G., South Boston, Mass
Safford, Mrs. Eunice, South Boston, Mass.
Sage, Wm., Rochester, N. Y.
Sage, Orrin, Rochester, N. Y.
Salisbury, Wm. D., New York.
Samson, Mrs. Harriet H., Brooklyn, N. Y.
Samson, Rev. George W., Washington, D. C.
Samson, A. W., Brooklyn, N. Y.
Sams, Dr. Lewis R., Beaufort, S. C.
Sanborn, Seth J., Manchester, N. H.
Sanders, Henry, Warren, R. I.
Sanders, Jacob, Homer, N. Y.
Sands, Ezra, Philadelphia, Pa.
Sands, William H., Boston, Mass.
Sandys, Rev. Edwin, Pittsfield, Mass
Sanford, Mrs. Harriet E., Norwich, N. Y.
Sanxey, Mrs. Agnes, Brooklyn, N. Y.
Sargeant, Adaline A., N. England Village, Mass.
Sargeant, J., Amesbury, Mass.
Sargeant, Mrs. Betsey, Amesbury, Mass.
Sargent, Solon, Haverhill, Mass.
Satterlee, L. R., Rochester, N Y.

MEMBERS FOR LIFE.

Sault, Matthew, New Haven, Ct.
Saunders, Mrs. Harriet, Nuttsville, Va.
Saunders, Thomas L., Lowell, Mass.
Saunders, Miss Ann, Haverhill, Mass.
Saunders, Miss Martha A., Newton Corner, Mass.
Savage, Moses B., Brooklyn, N. Y.
Savage, Mrs. Moses B., Brooklyn, N. Y.
Savage, Rev. Edward, Columbus, O.
Savage, Mrs. Sarah F., Columbus, O.
Savage, E. Payson, Columbus, O.
Savage, Rev. Eleazer, Kendall, N. Y.
Savage, Mrs. Bridget, Bedford, N. Y.
Savage, Morgan, Little Mill Creek, O.
Sawin, Rev. Addison A., Lyons, Iowa.
Sawin, Mrs. C. A. Scott, Lyons, Iowa.
Sawin, Mrs. Sarah, Cambridge, Mass.
Sawyer, Rev. Wm., Ransomville, N. Y.
Sawyer, Moses W., Malden, Mass.
Sawyer, David, Haverhill, Mass.
Sawyer, Rev. Isaac, Allegheny City, Pa.
Sawyer, Mrs. H. S., Allegheny City, Pa.
Sawyer, Rev. Conant, Canton, N. Y.
Sawyer, Enoch, Salisbury, Mass.
Sawyer, Rev. A. W., Acadia, N. B.
Sawyer, Mrs. Mary G., Haverhill, Mass.
Sawyer, Mrs. Adelia P., Parma, N. Y.
Scarritt, Rev. Jas. J., Jackson, Mich.
Schaffer, Charles, Philadelphia, Pa.
Schoolcraft, John L., Albany, N. Y.
Schofield, Rev. James, Rossville, Iowa.
Scott, Robert, Amesbury, Mass.
Scott, John, Columbia, N. Y.
Scott, Mrs. Cornelia S., Newburgh, N. Y.
Scott, Alfred, Lowell, Mass.
Scott, Rev. Ebenezer J., Richburg, N. Y.
Scott, Rev. George, Strawberry Point, Iowa.
Scott, Rev. Jacob B., Yonkers, N. Y.
Shaw, James M., New York.
Shaw, Mrs. Rhoda, New York.
Shaw, Miss Mary A., New York.
Shaw, John, Wales, Mass.
Shaw, Edward, Nashua, N. H.
Shaw, Henry, Worcester, Mass.
Sheardown, Rev. T. S., Homerville, N. Y.
Shearman, Francis, New York.
Shed, Charles.
Sheffield, Mrs. Mary, Stamford, Ct.
Sheffield, Thomas S., Brooklyn, N. Y.
Shelden, Martin J., Suffield, Ct.
Sheldon, Gaylor, Albany, N. Y.
Sheldon, Frederick A., Troy, N. Y.
Sheldon, L. C., Suffield, Ct.
Sheldon, William, North East, N. Y.
Sheldon, Rev. C. P., Troy, N. Y.
Sheldon, Mrs. Ruth, Adams Centre, N. Y.
Sheldon, R. S., Troy, N. Y.
Shelley, Lewis E., Davenport, Iowa.
Shelley, Russell T., New Haven, Ct.
Shelmire, Mrs. Maria, Rochester, N. Y.
Shenston, Joseph W., New York.
Shepard, Russell R., Worcester, Mass.
Shepardson, Rev. John, Petersham, Mass.
Shepardson, Mrs. Maria A., Petersham, Mass.
Shepardson, Ansel, Fairfax, Vt.
Shepardson, Miss Julia H., Cincinnati, O.
Sheppard, Sylvanus B., Salem, N. J.
Sheppard, Isaac A., Bridgeton, N. J.
Sheppard, Miss Jane B., Bridgeton, N. J.
Sheppard, John M., Mintonsville, N. C.
Sheppard, Ephraim, Seaville, N. J.
Sheridan, John, Brooklyn, N. Y.
Sherman, William N., Wickford, R. I.
Sherman, Mrs. Mary M., Wickford, R. I.
Sherman, George J., Providence, R. I.

[redacted]

Sizer, Amasa, Jr., Meriden, Ct.
Skelding, A. Eugene, Mianus, Ct.
Skiff, James M., Greenwich, N. Y.
Skinner, E. B., Hertford, N. C.
Skinner, Charles W., Hertford, N. C.
Skinner, H. P., Hudson, N. Y.
Skinner, Miss Sarah R., Hudson, N. Y.
Skinner, Mrs. Phebe B., Hudson, N. Y.
Skinner, Rev. H. C., Wabash, Ia.
Skinner, Mrs. Louisa R., Wabash, Ia.
Skinner, Ebenezer, Brooklyn, N. Y.
Slack, Thomas, Brooklyn, N. Y.
Slade, Zacheus, Newbern, N. C.
Slate, Needham, Mansfield, Ct.
Slater, Mrs. S. J., Providence, R. I.
Slater, Rev. Franklin A., Keyport, N. J.
Slater, Mrs. Sophronia E. H., Keyport, N. J.
Slaughter, James M., Baltimore, Md.
Sleath, Samuel, South Ballston, N. Y.
Sleeper, Rev. George, Dividing Creek, N. J.
Sleeper, Mrs. Norcorsa, Dividing Creek, N. J.
Slote, Henry L., New York.
Slover, Mrs. Susan E., New Brunswick, N. J.
Smalley, Henry, New Brunswick, N. J.
Smalley, Mrs. Susan M., Brooklyn, N. Y.
Smart, James, Philadelphia, Pa.
Smart, Miss Mary A., Philadelphia, Pa.
Smart, Rev. M. M., Russia, N. Y.
Smiley, Mrs. William, Haverhill, Mass.
Smiley, Miss Betsey, Haverhill, Mass.
Smith, Rev. Francis, Providence, R. I.
Smith, Mrs. M. G., Providence, R. I.
Smith, Charles A., Providence, R. I.
Smith, Asa F., New England Village, Mass.
Smith, Mrs. B. S. W., New Eng. Village, Mass.
Smith, Rev. Harry, Valparaiso, Ia.
Smith, Mrs. Lydia W., Valparaiso, Ia.
Smith, Samuel, Salem, N. J.
Smith, Mrs. Sarah B., Salem, N. J.
Smith, Mrs. Ruth Ann, New York.
Smith, Mrs. William H., Brooklyn, N. Y.
Smith, Mordecai, Brooklyn, N. Y.
Smith, John H., Brooklyn, N. Y.
Smith, Henry W., Brooklyn, N. Y.
Smith, Augustus, Brooklyn, N. Y.
Smith, Mrs. Mary B., Brooklyn, N. Y.
Smith, Miss Ada Fanny, Providence, R. I.
Smith, William, Winsboro', S. C.
Smith, Jonathan, New London, Ct.
Smith, Rev. Alexander, Skaneateles, N. Y.
Smith, Mrs. Priscilla B., Clarkson, Va.
Smith, Mrs. Sally, Hancock, Mass.
Smith, Mrs. Mary E., Christianville, Va.
Smith, Rev. Joseph, Worcester, Mass
Smith, Mrs. Abigail M., Worcester, Mass.
Smith, Mrs. S. L., Fayetteville, N. C.
Smith, Hamilton E., Fowlerville, N. Y.
Smith, Rev. Samuel, New York.
Smith, Alvah, York, N. Y.
Smith, George H., Branchport, N. Y.
Smith, William, Port Rowan, Canada West.
Smith, Rev. C. Billings, Iowa City, Iowa.
Smith, John H., New York.
Smith, Rev. William W., Broadalbin, N. Y.
Smith, Rev. Andrew M., Hartford, Ct.
Smith, Rev. Justin A., Chicago, Ill.
Smith, Rev. William A., Groton, Ill.
Smith, Rev. Isaac, Foxboro', Mass.
Smith, Mrs. Harriet A., Amherst, Mass.
Smith, Shubael, Colchester, Ct.
Smith, Eliza, New London, Ct.
Smith, Mrs. Wm. M., New London, Ct.
Smith, Rev. Eli B., D.D., Fairfax, Vt.
Smith, Adam, Brooklyn, N. Y.
Smith, Rev. N. W., Vershire, Vt.
Smith, Ebenezer, East Tisbury, Mass.
Smith, Mrs. Sarah A., East Tisbury, Mass.
Smith, Rev. Dexter P., Iowa City, Iowa.
Smith, Gilbert D., New York.
Smith, Daniel, Worcester, Mass.
Smith, Rev. Lewis, Hightstown, N. J.
Smith, Jonathan, New York.
Smith, Rev. Rufus, West Swanzey, N. H.
Smith, Mrs. Mary E., West Swanzey, N. H.
Smith, Mrs. Annie, Worcester, Mass.
Smith, Henry D., Worcester, Mass.
Smith, William H., Brooklyn, N. Y.
Smith, E. M., East Meredith, N. Y.
Smith, Rev. Edgar, East Lansing, N. Y.
Smith, Capt. Leonard, New London, Ct
Smith, Mrs. Helen M., Greenwich, N. Y.
Smith, Allen, Gouverneur, N. Y.
Smith, Rev. C. B., Townsend, Vt.
Smith, Miss Emma F., Banksville, Ct.
Smith, Jesse H., New England Village, Mass.
Smith, Mrs. Mary White, Newton, Mass.
Smith, Mrs. Jane, Troy, N. Y.
Smith, Lucius E., Boston, Mass.
Smith, Mrs. Elizabeth, New York.
Smith, Charles E., Fall River, Mass.
Smith, B. M., Brooklyn, N. Y.
Smith, Rev. Levi, West Plattsburg, N. Y.
Smith, Mrs. Levi, West Plattsburg, N. Y.
Smith, Rufus, Shelburne Falls, Mass.
Smith, Rev. R. T., Lyndonville, N. Y.
Smith, Henry N., North Chatham, Mass.
Smith, Rev. Sherman G., East Greenwich, R. I.
Smith, Wm. B., Cherryville, N. J.
Smith, Albert, New York.
Smith, H. H., Davenport, Iowa.
Smith, Adoniram, North Randolph, Mass.
Smith, Edward T., Albany, N. Y.
Smith, Oliver, Worthington, Mass.
Smith, Rev. John B., Fayetteville, N. Y.
Smyth, Royal, Boston.
Snelling, Miss Priscilla, Chelsea, Mass.
Sniffin, Mrs. Sarah Ann, New York.
Snowdon, Mrs. Eliza, New York.
Snow, Mrs. Abby S., Stonebridge, R. I.
Snow, Edwin M., Providence, R. I.
Snow, Rev. Charles A., Fall River, Mass.
Snyder, Peter, Marietta, Ohio.
Snyder, Charles H., Freehold. N. J.
Sommers, Mrs. Eliza B., New York.
Souders, Mrs. Catharine B. L., Frazer's, Pa.
Southerland, Jonas, Burnt Hills, N. Y.
Southwick, Mrs. Cynthia, Grand de Tour, Ill.
Southwick, George, Kingston, N. Y.
Southwood, Rev. Wm., Aylett's, Va.
Southworth, James Adalbert, Brooklyn, N. Y.
Southworth, John, Penfield, N. Y.
Sowers, Mrs. Mary E., Battletown, Va.
Sowers, Mrs. Elizabeth, Milwood, Va.
Spafford, Rev. Lysander E., Morris, N. Y.
Spafford, Rev. Russel H., Charlotteville, N. J
Spalding, Miss H. M., Middletown, Ct.
Sparks, Rev. Peter, Newark, N. J.
Spaulding, Nathan, Tolland, Ct.
Spaulding, Isaiah, Chelmsford, Mass.
Spaulding, Daniel B., Stoningtonboro', Ct.
Spaulding, Rev. Silas, Clockville, N. Y.
Spaulding, Rev. Amos F., Calais, Me.
Spaulding, Mrs. Carrie E., Calais, Me.
Spaulding, D. A., St. Louis. Mo.
Spaulding, Edward, Billerica, Mass.
Spear, Rev. Prof. P. B., Hamilton, N. Y.
Spear, Abraham, Jeddo, N. Y.
Spear, William, Reading, Mass.
Spier, John, Brooklyn, N. Y.
Spier, Mrs. Elizabeth, Brooklyn, N. Y.
Spier, Miss Susan B., Brooklyn, N. Y.
Spier, A. D., Brooklyn, N. Y.
Spelman, Thomas, Alexandria, O.
Spelman, Mrs. Mary G., Granville, O.
Spencer, Robert, Little Plymouth, Va.
Spencer, Elijah, Moodus, Ct.
Spencer, Rev. Wm. H., Spencer, N. Y.
Spencer, Charles M., East Lyme, Ct.
Spencer, Thaddeus H., Suffield, Ct.
Spencer, Carnot O., Essex, Ct.

MEMBERS FOR LIFE.

[illegible]

Stimson, Mrs. Louisa, Binghamton, N. Y.
St. John, Edgar, Binghamton, N. Y.
St. John, Elwin, Yates, N. Y.
Stockbridge, Mrs. Maria, Dedham, Mass.
Stockbridge, Mrs. J. C., Boston, Mass.
Stocks, Thomas, Greensb[illegible], Ga.
Stockwell, [illegible]mes W., Chicopee, Mass.
Stockwell, [illegible] Q. A., Sennet, N. Y.
Stoddard, Mrs. Sarah Jane, New York.
Stoddard, Hon. A., Townshend, Vt.
Stokes, Mrs. Caroline, New York.
Stotes, Rev. Thomas S., Dennis Creek, N. J.
Stone, Rev. Marsena, Leban[illegible], Ohio.
Stone, Mrs. Damaris, Swanzey, N. H.
Stone, Eben, Newton, Mass.
Stone, Prof. J. A. B., D.D., Kalamazoo, Mich.
Stone, Rev. O. B., San Jose, Cal.
Stone, Miss Ann Judson, Worcester, Mass.
Stone, A. P., Millbury, Mass.
Stone, Nathan, Jamaica Plains, Mass.
Stone, Jacob T., Homer, N. Y.
Stone, Francis S., Salina, N. Y.
Storer, Mrs. Olive H., Fisherville, N. H.
Storer, Rev. Joseph, Fisherville, N. H.
Storey, Simeon N., Worcester, Mass.
Storey, James Arnot, Williamsburgh, N. Y.
Storms, Andrew, New York.
Storms, Anthony D., New York.
Story, Wm. F., Boston, Mass.
Story, Joseph, Boston, Mass.
Story, Harriet M., Norwich, Ct.
Story, Eunice M., Worcester, Mass.
Story, Clara, Worcester, Mass.
Story, Eunice H., Worcester, Mass.
Stout, Rev. D. B., Middletown, N. J.
Stout, Mrs. Jane, Middletown, N. J.
Stout, Mrs. J. M., Louisa C. H., Va.

[redacted]

Swain, Joshua, Dennis Creek, N. J.
Swallow, Mrs. Nancy F., Nashua, N. H.
Swallow, Mrs. Almira, Boston, Mass.
Swan, Mrs. Laura, New London.
Swany, Andrew F., New York.
Swany, Thomas, Brooklyn, N. Y.
Swartwout, Mrs. Margaret, Crescent, N. Y.
Sweet, Rev. Joel, Tivoli, Ill.
Sweet, Joel G., New Brunswick, N. J.
Sweet Mrs. Sarah A., Troy, N. Y.
Sweetser, Albert, South Reading, Mass.
Swepson, Mrs. V. B., Yanceyville, N. C.
Swick, Rev. Benj. R., Lima, N. Y.
Swick, Mrs. Harriet, Lima, N. Y
Swift, William A., Boston, Mass.
Sykes, Rev. James N., East Boston, Mass.
Sym, Rev. Wm., Towanda, Pa.
Symes, W. J., New York.
Symonds, Newton, Reading, Mass.
Symonds, Margaret, North Salem, Mass.
Taber, John, Portage, Mich.
Taft, Timothy, Clinton, N. Y.
Taft, Mrs. Mary, Anthony Village, R. I.
Taggart Mrs. Harriet M., Detroit, Mich.
Taggart, Wm M., Detroit, Mich.
Tainter, Daniel A., Watertown, Mass.
Tallman, W. M., Brooklyn, N. Y.
Talmage, I. A., Rochester, N. Y.
Tandy, Rev. Los., Barry, Mass.
Tanner, Mrs. Elizabeth F., Spring Garden, Va.
Tanner, Cyrus S., Sennet, N. Y.
Tanner, Mrs. C. S., Sennet, N. Y.
Tanner, William, Sennet, N. Y.
Tanner, Miss Margaret, Pembina, Min.
Tanner, John, Pembina, Min.
Tanner, Mrs. Margaret, Pembina, Min.
Tanner, Edward, Pembina, Min.
Tanner, Elijah, Pembina, Min.
Tapley, Joseph, Lowell, Mass.
Tapley, Joseph W., Boston, Mass.
Tattersall, Wm. K., New York.
Taylor, Wm. H., New York.
Taylor, John G., Holmdel, N. J.
Taylor, Mrs. Ann B., Holmdel, N. J.
Taylor, Miss Sarah, Holmdel, N. J.
Taylor, Mrs. Sophia, Holmdel, N. J.
Taylor, James C., Holmdel, N. J.
Taylor, Mrs. Laura, New York.
Taylor, Miss Emily, New York.
Taylor, Miss Ann Jane, New York.
Taylor, Miss Louisa, New York.
Taylor, Mrs. Sarah A., New York.
Taylor, Mrs. E. E. L., Brooklyn, N. Y.
Taylor, Miss Harriet Hill, Troy, N. Y.
Taylor, Mrs. Maria B., Lawtonville, S. C.
Taylor, Mrs. Dimis, York, N. Y.
Taylor, Rev. Thomas R., Alleghany City, Pa.
Taylor, Rev. Alfred H., Hollidaysburg, Pa.
Taylor, Rev. Thomas, Jacksonville, Ill.
Taylor, Samuel W. E., Bath, Me.
Taylor, Rev. O. D., Freeport, Ill.
Taylor, Henry C., Granville, O.
Taylor, Elvin, Albany, N. Y.
Taylor, John, East Cambridge, Mass.
Taylor, John, New York.
Taylor, J. R., East Cambridge, Mass.
Taylor, William, New York.
Taylor, Mrs. Jane B., Philadelphia, Pa.
Taylor, J. William, Springfield, Ohio.
Taylor, Rev. Malachi, Whitehall, N. Y.
Tefft, Willard, Greenwich, N. Y.
Tefft, Thomas A., Providence, R. I.
Temple, James H., Chillicothe, Ill.
Tennant, John, Keeseville, N. Y.
Terrell, Holland, Albany, N. Y.
Terrel, Edward, Waterbury, Ct.
Terry, Mrs. A. N., Spring Garden, Va.
Terhune, Frederick, Brooklyn, N. Y.
Thatcher, Mrs. Elizabeth R.
Thayer, Thomas M., Gouverneur, N. Y.
Thayer, Lewis, Worcester, Mass.
Thayer, James H., Cambridge, Mass.
Theall, Mrs. Jane, New York.
Theall, Miss Susan, New York.
Thigpen, Rev. Samuel, Raymond, Miss.
Thistle, Mrs. Hannah, New York.
Thomas, Thomas (architect), New York.
Thomas, James H., New York.
Thomas, Rev David E., Zanesville, Ohio.
Thomas, Griffith, New York.
Thomas, Rev. C. A., D.D. Brandon, Vt.
Thomas, Mrs. Eliza Ann, New York.
Thomas, Mrs. Mary, Brooklyn, N. Y.
Thomas, Mrs. Almira S., Brandon, Vt.
Thomas, Rev. Evan J., Atlanta, Ill.
Thomas, Osmar, Streetsboro', Ohio.
Thomson, Thos. M., Montreal, Can.
Thompson, Robert, Jr., New York.
Thompson, Mrs. Ann E., New York.
Thompson, Mrs. S. S., Pittsborough, N. C.
Thompson, Rev. Charles E., Iowa City, Iowa.
Thompson, L., Britton's Cross Roads, N. C.
Thompson, Benjamin M., Harlem, N. Y.
Thompson, Rev. Sherman B., Little Valley, N.Y.
Thompson, Mrs. Serena, New York.
Thompson, Mrs. Harvey, Norwich, N. Y.
Thompson, Joshua J., Salem, N. J.
Thompson, Richard H., Fisherville, N. H.
Thompson, Horace, New Haven, Ct.
Thurston, Henry, Brooklyn, N. Y.
Thurber, Edmund, Providence, R. I.
Thurber, Gurbam, Providence, R. I.
Thurber, Charles, Worcester, Mass.
Ticknor, William D., Boston, Mass.
Tiebout, Adam T., Brooklyn, N. Y.
Tiebout, Mrs. Jane, Brooklyn, N. Y.
Tiffany, Lyman, Newton Corner, Mass.
Tilden, Rev. Chester, North Lyme, Ct.
Tilley, Mrs. Elizabeth S., New York.
Tillinghast, Jefferson, Norway, N. Y.
Tillinghast, Charles E., Providence, R. I.
Tillinghast, Rev. J. A., Allenton, R. I.
Tilson, Rev. Jonathan, Hingham, Mass.
Tilton, Rev. Charles, Jefferson, Pa.
Tilton, Rev. Josiah H. Holden, Mass.
Tilton, Mrs. Abigail, S F., Sandbornton, N. H.
Timberman, Rev. Jacob, Mansfield, N. J.
Tindall, Samuel L., Wilmington, Del.
Tingley, Miss Nancy B., Valley Falls, R. I.
Tingley, Timothy C., North Scituate, Mass.
Tingley, Miss Emma S., North Scituate, Mass.
Tingley, Miss. Mary E., North Scituate, Mass.
Tinkham, Rev. D, Centre White Creek, N. Y.
Titchener, Henry, Binghamton, N. Y.
Tirrill, Jesse, Boston, Mass.
Titus, F. J., Middletown, O.
Titus, Rev. S. W., Oswego, N. Y.
Titus, Mrs. Annie C., Providence, R. I.
Todd, Rev. William, Stevensville, Va.
Todd, Drake, P., New York.
Todd, Mrs. Angeline M., New York.
Todd, William J., New York.
Todd, Thomas W., New York.
Tolan, Rev. William B., Stepney Depot, Ct.
Tolman, Rev. John N., North Shore, N. Y.
Tolman, Mrs. John N., North Shore, N. Y.
Tolman, Thomas, Philadelphia, Pa.
Tolman, Mrs. Mary, Philadelphia, Pa.
Tolman, Miss Martha, Boston, Mass.
Tolman, Mrs. Elizabeth A., Philadelphia, Pa.
Tolman Miss Martha J., Philadelphia, Pa.
Tonkin, Rev. Henry, Concord, N. H.
Toplif, Rev. C. H., Weston, Mass.
Torbet, Rev. Andrew M., Taylor's Falls, Min.
Torian, Elijah, Halifax C. H., Va.
Torrance, Riley, Jay, N. Y.
Tourtellot, Abraham, Nashua, N. H.
Tousley, Charles, New York.
Tower, Mrs. Elvira, Ira, Vt.
Towle, Miss Sarah G., Newburyport, Mass.

Townsend, S. P., New York.
Townsend, Mrs. [illegible], New York.
Townsend, Rev. [illegible], Mass.
Townsend, Mrs. Louisa L., [illegible], N. Y.
Townsend, Rev. H. C., [illegible], N. Y.
Townsend, [illegible], Mass.
Townsend, [illegible], R. I.
[illegible], New London, Ct.
Tracy, Rev. [illegible], Concord, N. H.
Tracy, Mrs. Martha [illegible], N. H.
Tracy, Mrs. Sarah M., [illegible], N. H.
Tracy, Mrs. A. S., Haverhill, Mass.
Travis, Simeon S., New York.
[illegible], Southbridge, Mass.
[illegible], Rochester, N. Y.
[illegible], Philadelphia, Pa.
[illegible] R. M., Pittsburgh, Pa.
[illegible], Mass.
[illegible] H., New York.
[illegible] H., New York.
[illegible], New York.
[illegible], William, [illegible]
[illegible], Rev. Augustus H., Montgomery, N. Y.
[illegible], William, [illegible] Falls, Wis.
[illegible] M., [illegible], N. H.
[illegible] Mrs. Hannah, [illegible], N. H.
[illegible] M.
[illegible], N. Y.
[illegible], Mass.
[illegible], N. Y.
Truman, [illegible], N. Y.
[illegible], N. Y.
[illegible] M., [illegible], N. Y.
[illegible], N. Y.
[illegible], N. J.
[illegible], N. Y.

Van De Boe, Adam, Claverack, N. Y.
Van De Werken, E., New York.
Van De Werken, Mrs. Janet, New York.
Van Derlip, George M., New York.
Van Derlip, Mrs. Grace, New York.
Van Dusen, Wm., Albion, N. Y.
Vanderveer, Mrs. Ann, Moorestown, N. J.
Van Pelt, Mrs. Harriet, Port Richmond, N. Y.
Vail, J. E., Brooklyn, N. Y.
Valentine, Rev. Andrew M., W. Henrietta, N. Y.
Valentine, Elijah F., Cambridge, Mass.
Van Brakle, John, New York.
Van Hoesen, T. C., Sing Sing, N. Y.
Van Horn, Hon. James, Newfane, N. Y.
Van Horn, Burt, Newfane, N. Y.
Van Pelt, Mrs. Mellona S., New York.
Van Sickler, Reuben N., Albany, N. Y.
Vanness, Christian, New York.
Vanest, Abraham, Hightstown, N. J.
Van Husen, Mrs. Rachel M., West Gilboa, N. Y.
Van Marter, John, Brooklyn, N. Y.
Van Marter, Mrs. Mary E., Brooklyn, N. Y.
Van Osdel, John M., Chicago, Ill.
Van, Samuel A., New Haven, Ct.
Vane, James, Albany, N. Y.
Vansant, T. J., Norwalk, Ct.
Van Sickler, R. M., Albany, N. Y.
Van Vleck, Rev. J., Lyndon, Ill.
Van Wagenen, W. Frederick, New York.
Van Wickle, Simon, New Brunswick, N. J.
Vassar, Matthew, Poughkeepsie, N. Y.
Vassar, Mrs. Matthew, Poughkeepsie, N. Y.
Vassar, Rev. T. E., Armenia, N. Y.
Vassar, Charles, Poughkeepsie, N. Y.
Veasey, Benjamin, Brentwood, N. H.
Ventres, W. H. S., Cambridge, Mass.

[redacted]

Walker, Mrs. Velina P., Trenton, N. J.
Walker, William, Clinton, Mass.
Walker, Rev. O. B., Foxcroft, Me.
Walker, Amos, Pontiac, Mich.
Walker, Francis, Pawtucket, R. I.
Walker, Rev. James, Greenbush, N. Y.
Wallace, William S., Brooklyn, N. Y.
Wallace, Mrs. Margaret, New York.
Wallace, Miss Eliza, Brooklyn, N. Y.
Wallace, Jonathan, Fort Covington, N. Y.
Walter, Rev. John P., General Wayne, Pa.
Walters, Jacob, Wilmington, Del.
Walton, Joel, Va.
Walton, Jesse, Augusta, Ga.
Ward, Willard, Worcester, Mass.
Ward, William, Worcester, Mass.
Wardner, Rev. Chauncey, Perry, N. Y.
Wardner, Mrs. Margaret A., Perry, N. Y.
Warfield, Mrs. Caroline, Manchester, N. Y.
Warford, Elijah, Cherryville, N. J.
Ware, Dr. R. J., Montgomery Co., Ala.
Waring, James Jr., Fall River, Mass.
Warn, Mrs. Sarah M., Sennet, N. Y.
Warn, Mrs. Mary, Sennet, N. Y.
Warner, Dr. Ransom, New York.
Warner, Benjamin I., Williamsburgh, N. Y.
Warnock, Miss Elizabeth, New York.
Warren, Mrs. Diantha O., West Potsdam, N. Y.
Warren, Rev Patrick, Baltimore, Md.
Warren, Rev. Benjamin, Chili, N. Y.
Warren, Rev. J. G., D.D., Boston, Mass.
Warren, Charles W., Utica, N. Y.
Warren, Rev. Edwin R., East Greenwich, R. I.
Warren, Moses, Cambridge, Mass.
Warren, Mrs. Grace, Cambridge, Mass.
Warren, Rev. H. S. P., Madrid, N. Y.
Warren, Horace, Norwich, Ct.
Warren, Rev. John, Easton, Ct.
Warren, Mrs. Emma, Burlington, Iowa.
Warren, Thomas, New York.
Warren, Miss Miriam, Chelmsford, Mass.
Warriner, Rev. Norman, Le Clair, Ill.
Warriner, Rev. R. L., Chaseville, N. Y.
Warriner, Mrs. Clarissa, Chaseville, N. Y.
Washburn, Nathan W., Mt. Pleasant, Ill.
Washburn, Rev. R. A., Andover, N. Y.
Washington, Mrs. Elizabeth, Newbern, N. C.
Wasson, Mrs. Clarissa, Albany, N. Y.
Waterbury, Miss Martha, Williamsburgh, N. Y.
Waterbury, Mrs. Mary, Saratoga Springs, N. Y.
Waterbury, Francis W., Saratoga Springs, N. Y.
Waterbury, N. H., Saratoga Springs, N. Y.
Waterman, Nathan, Jr., Providence, R. I.
Waterman, R. W., Covington, Ia.
Waters, Mrs. Elizabeth A., Brookline, Mass.
Waters, Horace, Brooklyn, N. Y.
Watkins, Mrs. Hannah, New York.
Watkins, Henry M., New York.
Watkinson, Rev. Wm. E., Manyunk, Pa.
Watkinson, Rev. Mark R., Portsmouth, Va.
Watrous, Richard, New York.
Watrous, Rev. E. H., Three Rivers, Mass.
Watson, William H., Albany, N. Y.
Watson, George, New York.
Watson, James, Brooklyn, N. Y.
Watson, W. W., Springfield, Ill.
Watson, John, New York
Watson, Rev. D. S., Cleveland, Ohio.
Watters, Miss Sarah A., Philadelphia, Pa.
Watts, Isaiah, New York.
Watts, Mrs. Emma, New York.
Watts, Charles Henry, New York.
Watts, John, Elmira, N. Y.
Wattson, Mrs. Mary B., Philadelphia, Pa.
Wattson, Miss Elizabeth, Philadelphia, Pa.
Wattson, Rev. W. H., West Acton, Mass.
Way, Rev. Samuel P., North Brookfield, N. Y.
Way, Mrs. Welthy A., North Brookfield, N. Y.
Wayland, Mrs. H. S. H., Providence, R. I.
Wayland, Francis, Jr., Worcester, Mass.

Wead, Mrs. Nancy M., Malone, N. Y.
Weaver, Rev. C. S., Norwich, Ct.
Weaver, Mrs. Diana, Norwich, Ct.
Weaver, Edwin H., Norwich, Ct.
Weaver, Mrs. Ann, Groton, Ct.
Weaver, C. Arnold, New London, Ct.
Weaver, Mrs. S. Augusta, New London, Ct.
Weaver, Daniel L., Albany, N. Y.
Webb, Joshua, Philadelphia, Pa.
Webb, Mrs. Maria, New Brunswick, N. J.
Webb, Moses F., New Brunswick, N. J.
Webb, Rev. Abner, Belleville, N. Y.
Webb, Rev. W. R., Dixon, Ill.
Webb, Daniel, Leroy, N. Y.
Webb, Mrs. J. N., Fort Covington, N. Y.
Webb, Rev. J. N., Fort Covington, N. Y.
Webb, John, Newtown, Ohio.
Webber, Rev. Julius S., Meridian, N. Y.
Webster, Phineas, Haverhill, Mass.
Webster, Mrs. Phineas, Haverhill, Mass.
Webster, Rev. Amos, Boston, Mass.
Webster, Rev. S. B., Norwalk, O.
Webster, Caleb, Lowell, Mass.
Webster, Rev. J. D., Green, N. Y.
Webster, John, Nashua, N. H.
Weckerly, Daniel, Philadelphia, Pa.
Weckerly, Mrs. Ann, Philadelphia, Pa.
Weddell, Rev. Peter M., Canton, Ohio.
Welch, Mrs B. T., Newtonville, N. Y.
Welch, Rev. James E., Hickory Grove, Mo.
Welch, Rev. James S., Lowell, Mass.
Weirick, Mrs. Sallie A., Logansport, Ia.
Weld, Nathaniel, Jamaica Plain, Mass.
Weld, Mrs. Lucy, New York.
Weld, Aaron D., Winchester, Mass.
Weldon, Asa W., New York.
Weller, R. F., Albany, N. Y.
Welling, Mrs. Sarah Jane, Princeton, N. J.
Wells, Mrs. Elizabeth, New York.
Wells, Rev. Alfred, Attica, N. Y.
Wells, Rev. Wm. A., Muscatine, Iowa.
Wells, Miss Mary E., Providence, R. I.
Wells, Henry E., Greenport, N. Y.
Wells, Daniel D., Greenport, N. Y.
Wemple, Abraham A., Schenectaday, N. Y.
Wemple, Mrs. Mary S., Schenectaday, N. Y.
Wescott, Rev. Isaac, Newburgh, N. Y.
Wescott, Jehiel, Bridgeton, N. J.
Wescott, Jehiel Jr., Bridgeton, N. J.
Wescott, Josiah S., Bridgeton, N. J.
Wescott, Rev. Henry, Warrenville, Ill.
Wescott, John, Bridgeton, N. J.
West, L. M., Rockford, Ill.
West, Mrs. Ann, Brooklyn, N. Y.
West, John G., Williamsburgh, N. Y.
West, Willoughby W., York, N. Y.
West, Rev. Hezekiah, Watkins, N. Y.
Weston, Rev. Henry G., New York.
Weston, Franklin L., Johnson's Creek, N. Y.
Weston, David, Providence, R. I
Westervelt, John, Williamsburgh, N. Y.
Westover, Rev. John T., East Troy, Wis.
Westover, Mrs. John T., East Troy, Wis.
Wetherbee, Ephraim, Broadalbin, N. Y.
Wetherbee, Miss Ruby, Broadalbin, N. Y.
Wethern, George M., Lowell, Mass.
Wetterau, Mrs. Frances, New York.
Whedon, C. H., Homer, N. Y.
Wheat, Mrs. Priscilla P., Philadelphia.
Wheaton, Reuben, Wilmington, Del.
Wheaton, Mrs. Elizabeth M., Columbus, O.
Wheaton, John M., Columbus, O.
Wheaton, William, Cohansey, N. J.
Wheelock, Mrs. E. M., Fredonia, N. Y.
Wheelock, S. B., Greenwich, N. Y.
Wheelock, Mrs. C. E. S., Milwaukee, Wis.
Wheeler, Mrs. Elizabeth H., Sacramento, Cal.
Wheeler, Miss Melvina P., Sacramento, Cal.
Wheeler, Mrs. Maria N., Grafton, Vt.
Wheeler, Rev. Benj., Randolph, Mass.

MEMBERS FOR LIFE.

[illegible — left column entries faded beyond reading]

White, [illegible]

White, [illegible], Newton, Mass.

White, [illegible] B., [illegible], N. Y.

White, Mrs. Mary, New York.

White, [illegible], N. J.

Wiggins, Rev. J. W., Throopsville, N. Y.
Wilbur, Rev. H. R., Galena, Ill.
Wilbur, Mrs. Sally, East Avon, N. Y.
Wilbur, Curtis, Troy, N. Y.
Wilbur, Rev. O., Lowville, N. Y.
Wilcox, Rev. J. F., Northfield, Min.
Wilcox, Abraham, Shelburne Falls, Mass.
Wilcox, Allen, Wing's Station, N. Y.
Wilder, Mrs. Delia A., Albany, N. Y.
Wilder, Rev. Sydney, Arcadia, N. Y.
Wildman, John, [illegible], N. Y.
Wildman, Mrs. Roxey S., Lebanon, Ct.
Wildman, Daniel, Lebanon, Ct.
Wildman, Mrs. Sally, Danbury, Ct.
Wiley, James, Philadelphia.
Wiley, Mrs. Martha, East Hillsdale, N. Y.
Wilkins, Rev. Andrew, Sennett, N. Y.
Wilkins, Mrs. Laura J., Sennett, N. Y.
Wilkinson, Rev. Wm., Drummondville, C. W.
Willard, Rev. Geo. A., Warwick Neck, R. I.
Willard, Lucius A., Providence.
Willard, Mrs. Polly, Pawlet, Vt.
Willard, Wm. B., Still River, Mass.
Willard, Mrs. Nancy, Jonesborough, Ill.
Willard, Rev. C. N., Eastport, Me.
Willard, Mrs. Anna F., East Needham, Mass.
Willett, Miss Sarah, New York.
Willett, Mrs. Charles, La Crosse, Wis.
Williams, Charles S., Mystic River, Ct.
Williams, Robert, Brookfield, Iowa.
Williams, Mrs. E. S., Fayetteville, N. C.
Williams, Mrs. Charity S., Fayetteville, N. C.
Williams, Mrs. Mary M., Fayetteville, N. C.
Williams, Polly M., Rockport, Ohio.
Williams, Francis B., New York.
Williams, Rev. David S., Cumberland, N. C.

[redacted]

Windust, Edward, New York.
Winn, Mrs. Meribah, Nashua, N. H.
Winship, Alfred, Henniker, N. H.
Winslow, Robert F., Fond du Lac, Wis.
Winslow, Rev. Octavius, Leamington, Eng.
Winston, Rev. Meriweather, Richmond, Va.
Winter, Rev. Thomas, Roxborough, Pa.
Winter, Rev. John, Knoxville, Ill.
Winterton, Mrs. Mary, New York.
Wise, Miss Clarissa R., New Russia, N. Y.
Wisner, Mrs. Sarah, Mount Morris, N. Y.
Wisham, Samuel, Philadelphia.
Wiswell, Mrs. C. A., West Troy, N. Y.
Witherwax, Mrs. Emeline B., Davenport, Iowa.
Witherwax, Miss Mary B., Davenport, Iowa.
Withall, John, Henrietta, N. Y.
Witherbee, John B., Jamaica Plains, Mass.
Withington, Mrs. M., Morrisania, N. Y.
Wolcott, Mrs. Mary S., New York.
Wolcott, Mrs. Naomi, Rochester, N. Y.
Wollaston, Joshua, Wilmington, Del.
Worrall, Rev. Thomas D., Lowell, Mass.
Wood, Lowell M., Boston.
Wood, George W., Brooklyn, N. Y.
Wood, Mrs. J. S., Hertford, N. C.
Wood, Mrs. Mary E., Hertford, N. C.
Wood, Rev. N. N., D.D., Upper Alton, Ill.
Wood, Jennings J., Speedwell, S. C.
Wood, George, Springfield, Ill.
Wood, Joseph T., Westboro', Mass.
Wood, Mrs. Amelia, Brooklyn, N. Y.
Wood, Eliphalet, Honesdale, Pa.
Wood, Ambrose, Albion, N. Y.
Woods, Gardner, Jersey, Ohio.
Woods, Hiram, Nashua, N. H.
Woodbridge, William A., Sag Harbor, N. Y.
Woodbury, William W., Suffield, Ct.
Woodbury, Rev. John, Templeton, Mass.
Woodbury, Miss Frances, Danvers, Mass.
Woodbury, Eliza A., Lynn, Mass.
Woodbury, Seth, Goffstown, N. H.
Woodman, Moses, New Gloucester, Me.
Woodruff, Mrs. Innocent, Albany.
Woodward, Rev. Jonas, Cedar Rapids, Iowa.
Woodward, Mrs. Eliza, Cedar Rapids, Iowa.
Woodward, Mrs. Mary D., Middlesex, Va.
Woodward, Sylvester, Lowell, Mass.
Woodward, Darwin W., Franklindale, N. Y.
Woodworth, Levi B., Canaan, O.
Woodston, Mrs. Keziah, Vincentown, N. J.
Worrall, Elwood P., Westchester, Pa.
Wooster, Mrs. Aurelia R., Deep River, Ct.
Wooster, Hinman, Charlotte, Vt.
Wooster, George P., New Haven, Ct.
Work, Rev. Perley, Omeo, Wis.
Worth, Rev. Edmund, Kennebunk, Me.
Worth, J. C., Hanover, N. H.
Worthington, S., Springfield, Mass.
Worthington, Gershom B., Colchester, Ct.
Wright, Rev. David, North Lyme, Ct.
Wright, Wm. J., Hardgrove's, Va.
Wright, Theodore, N. Y.
Wright, Asahel B., Lowell, Mass.
Wright, Harvey, Three Rivers, Mass.
Wright, Mrs. Julia A., Westport, N. Y.
Wright, Rev. Ansell T., Weart's Corners, N. J.
Wright, R. A., Rochester, N. Y.
Wright, James G., Canton, N. J.
Wright, B. H., Dover Plains, N. Y.
Wright, William S., Weartsville, N. J.
Wyckoff, Mrs. Cornelius R., Weedsport, N. Y.
Wyckoff, J. N., Woodbridge, N. J.
Wyckoff, Mrs. Elizabeth, Woodbridge, N. J.
Wyckoff, W. G., Middletown, N. J.
Wyckoff, Francis, Plainfield, N. J.
Wyckoff, Mrs. Sarah B., Brooklyn, N. Y.
Wyckoff, Jacob F., Boston, Mass.
Wyer, Rev. Henry O., Alexandria, Va.
Wynn, Mrs. Susan, Tuckahoe, N. J.
Wynn, Benjamin F., Tuckahoe, N. J.
Yale, Levi, Augusta, N. Y.
Yale, Mrs. Ruth, Augusta, N. Y.
Yale, H. C., Brooklyn, N. Y.
Yendall, Sarah, Boston.
Yeomans, Mrs. Olive, Providence.
Yeomans, Miss Mary Ann, Providence.
York, Mrs. Hannah, Haverhill, Mass.
York, C., Norwich, N. Y.
York, Mrs. Esther, Norwich, N. Y.
Young, Mrs. Sarah, Brooklyn, N. Y.
Young, Rev. George, N. J.
Young, Rev. Robert F., Chestnut Hill, Pa.
Young, Mrs. Maria Ann, Chestnut Hill, Pa.
Young, Robert McCarthy, New York.
Young, Rev. G. W., Antistown, Pa.
Young, William W., Stamford, Ct.
Yuran, Mrs S. S., Tunbridge, Vt.
Zebley, John F., New York.
Zimmerman, Edwin, New York.

MEMBERS FOR LIFE.

Wheeler, Lucius, New York.
Wheeler, Rev. S. S., Placerville, Cal.
Wheeler, Mrs. Mary B, Placerville, Cal.
Wheeler, Perry, South Dover, N. Y.
Wheeler, Russell, Utica, N. Y.
Wheeler, Mrs. Ann. New York.
Wheeler, Mrs. Mary E., North Randolph, Mass.
Wheeler, Rev. R., Grafton, Vt.
Wheeler, Charles H., New London, Ct.
Wheeler, Mrs. Mary G., Boston, Mass.
Whelden, Francis J., Greenwich, N. Y.
Whidden, Mrs. Sarah, Calais, Me.
Whilden, Rev. B W., Camden, S. C.
Whipple, Harvey, Malone, N. Y.
Whipple, Ethan, Providence, R. I.
Whipple, Mrs. Phœbe, Providence, R. I.
Whipple, Mrs. Hannah, New Boston, N. H.
Whipple, Mrs. Angelina, Nashua, N. H.
Whitaker, Alanson, Granville, Ill.
Whitaker, Wm. N., Philadelphia.
Whitcomb, Peter, Littleton, Mass.
White, Mrs. E., North Shore, N. Y.
White, Cyrus B., North Shore, N. Y.
White, Mrs. Martha D., Marcus Hook, Pa.
White, Miss Lydia, Haverhill, Mass.
White, Thomas, Brooklyn, N. Y.
White, Samuel S., Whiteville, N. Y.
White, Harvey, Mt. Holly, Vt.
White, Thomas P, Bridgeport, Ct.
White, Mrs. Thomas P., Bridgeport, Ct.
White, Joseph, Winchendon, Mass.
White, Beza L., Taunton, Mass.
White, Ebenezer, Newton, Mass.
White, Ebenezer B., Williamsburgh, N. Y.
White, Mrs. Mary, New York.
White, Samuel, Bordentown, N. J.
White, Mrs. Sylvanus, Brooklyn, N. Y.
White, Samuel, Littleton, Mass.
White, Miss Mary, New York.
White, Miss Emily J., Taunton, Mass.
White, Almeth, Rahway, N. J.
Whitehead, Samuel, Bound Brook, N. J.
Whitehead, Mrs. Emeline V., New York.
Whitehead, Artemas K., New York.
Whitehead, John W., New York.
Whitehead, Linus P., New York.
Whitehead, Rev. Wm. M., Spread Eagle, Pa.
Whitehead, Rev. J M., Westville, Ia.
Whitford, H. G., Willington, Ct.
Whitford, Mrs. Florilla, Willington, Ct.
Whiting, Rufus W., Boston.
Whitman, Charles S., Belvidere, Ill.
Whitman, Mrs. Matilda, Belvidere, Ill.
Whitman, Spencer, Belvidere, Ill.
Whitman, Alva, Mich.
Whitman, John C., Sennet, N. Y.
Whitney, Miss Harriet, New York
Whitney, Mrs. Betsey, Worcester, Mass.
Whitney, Bennet, Bridgeport, Ct.
Whitney, Raymond, North Fairfield, O.
Whitney, Mrs. E. S., Brooklyn, N. Y.
Whitney, Eben, Norwalk, Ct.
Whittemore, Joseph, New York.
Whittemore, Mrs. Elizabeth, Londonderry, N.H.
Whittier, Leonard, Haverhill, Mass.
Whittier, Mrs. Leonard, Haverhill, Mass.
Whittier, Miss Abby, Haverhill, Mass.
Whittier, Hannah, Haverhill, Mass.
Whittier, Mrs. Rebecca, Haverhill, Mass.
Whittier, Miss Sarah P., Haverhill, Mass.
Whittier, Mary Jane, Danversport, Mass.
Wiburg, Rev. Andreas, Stockholm, Sweden.
Wiburg, Mrs. Caroline, Stockholm, Sweden.
Wight, Leonard B., Wales, Mass.
Wightman, Asa, New London, Ct.
Wightman, Stillman K., New York.
Wightman, Frederick B., New York.
Wightman, Mrs. Emeline, East Lyme, Ct.
Wightman, Rev. J. C., Middletown, Ct.
Wightman, John, Colchester, Ct.
Wiggins, Rev. J. W., Throopsville, N. Y.
Wilbur, Rev. H. R., Galena, Ill.
Wilbur, Mrs. Sally, East Avon, N. Y.
Wilbur, Curtis, Troy, N. Y.
Wilbur, Rev. O., Lowville, N. Y.
Wilcox, Rev. J. F., Northfield, Min.
Wilcox, Abraham, Shelburne Falls, Mass.
Wilcox, Allen, Wing's Station, N Y.
Wilder, Mrs. Delia A., Albany, N. Y.
Wilder, Rev. Sydney, Arcadia, N. Y.
Wildman, John, Pitcher, N. Y.
Wildman, Mrs. Roxey S., Lebanon, Ct.
Wildman, Daniel, Lebanon, Ct.
Wildman, Mrs. Sally, Danbury, Ct.
Wiley, James, Philadelphia.
Wiley, Mrs. Martha, East Hillsdale, N. Y.
Wilkins, Rev. Andrew, Sennet, N. Y.
Wilkins, Mrs. Laura J., Sennet, N. Y.
Wilkinson, Rev. Wm., Drummondville, C. W.
Willard, Rev. Geo. A., Warwick Neck, R. I.
Willard, Lucius A., Providence.
Willard, Mrs. Polly, Pawlet, Vt.
Willard, Wm B., Still River, Mass.
Willard, Mrs. Nancy, Jonesborough, Ill.
Willard, Rev. C. N., Eastport, Me.
Willard, Mrs. Anna F., East Needham, Mass.
Willett, Miss Sarah, New York.
Willett, Mrs. Charles, La Crosse, Wis.
Williams, Charles S., Mystic River, Ct.
Williams, Robert, Brookfield, Iowa.
Williams, Mrs. E. S., Fayetteville, N. C.
Williams, Mrs. Charity S., Fayetteville, N. C.
Williams, Mrs. Mary M., Fayetteville, N. C.
Williams, Polly M., Rockport, Ohio.
Williams, Francis B., New York.
Williams, Rev. David S., Cumberland, N. C.
Williams, Rev. Wm. B., Williamsville, N. Y.
Williams, Mrs. Eunice, Deep River, Ct.
Williams, Rev. John, Princeton, N. Y.
Williams, Rev. C. C., Adams, N. Y.
Williams, Mrs. Marana, Adams, N. Y.
Williams, Rev. Lester, West Townsend, Mass.
Williams, Rev. B. S., Plymouth, N. Y.
Williams, Mrs. Wm. R., New York.
Williams, W. S., Hartford, Ct.
Williams, Rev. Philo J., Colchester, Ct.
Williams, Mrs. Catharine, New York.
Williams, Rev. N. M., Somerville, Mass.
Williams, George P., Albion, N. Y.
Williams, Edward, Trenton, N. J.
Williams, Rev. A. D., Chester, Pa.
Williamson, Mrs. Rachel, Plainfield, N. J.
Willingham, Thomas, Lawtonville, S. C.
Willington, Miss Catharine, Watertown, Mass.
Willis, Rev. Samuel B., Saugerties, N. Y.
Willis, J. D. K., Chelsea, Mass.
Willis, Benj. B., Philadelphia.
Wilson, Mrs. Catharine, New York.
Wilson, Miss Sarah E., New York.
Wilson, Mrs. Frances M., Catskill, N. Y.
Wilson, Isaac D., Society Hill, S. C.
Wilson, Clement A., Philadelphia.
Wilson, Rev Charles E., Holmdel, N. J.
Wilson, Mrs. Theresa, Holmdel, N. J.
Wilson, Rev. Adam, D.D., Paris, Me.
Wilson, Rev. W. V., Chanceville, N. J.
Wilson, Mrs. Martha, Chanceville, N. J.
Wilson, Jeremiah V. F., Hoboken, N. J.
Wilson, Mrs Grace, Elmira, N. Y.
Wilson, George W., Chelsea, Mass.
Wilson, Robert, New York.
Wilson, Rev. James E., Haddonfield, N. J.
Wilson, Miss Elizabeth, Brooklyn, N. Y.
Wilson, Garrett, Centre Bridge, N. J.
Wingate, Mary, Haverhill, Mass.
Wingate, Dexter B., New England Village, Mass.
Winans, Mrs. Marcy, Lima, N. Y.
Winans, Theodore, Plainfield, N. J.
Winchell, Miss Ann, New York.
Winchell, George R., North East, N. Y.

t, Edward, New York.
Mrs. Meribah, Nashua, N. H.
), Alfred, Henniker, N. H.
r, Robert F., Fond du Lac, Wis.
r, Rev. Octavius, Leamington, Eng.
1, Rev. Meriwether, Richmond, Va.
, Rev. Thomas, Roxborough, Pa.
. Rev. John, Knoxville, Ill.
on, Mrs. Mary, New York.
liss Clarissa R., New Russia, N. Y.
, Mrs. Sarah, Mount Morris, N. Y.
1, Samuel, Philadelphia.
l, Mrs. C. A., West Troy, N. Y.
wax, Mrs. Emeline B., Davenport, Iowa.
wax, Miss Mary B., Davenport, Iowa.
, John, Henrietta, N. Y.
ee, John B., Jamaica Plains, Mass.
gton, Mrs. M., Morrisania, N. Y.
:, Mrs. Mary S., New York.
:, Mrs. Naomi, Rochester, N. Y.
on, Joshua, Wilmington, Del.
., Rev. Thomas D., Lowell, Mass.
Lowell M., Boston.
George W., Brooklyn, N. Y.
Mrs. J. S., Hertford, N. C.
Mrs. Mary E., Hertford, N. C.
Rev. N. N., D.D., Upper Alton, Ill.
Jennings J., Speedwell, S. C.
George, Springfield, Ill.
Joseph T., Westboro', Mass.
Mrs. Amelia, Brooklyn, N. Y.
Eliphalet, Honesdale, Pa.
Ambrose, Albion, N. Y.
Gardner, Jersey, Ohio.
Hiram, Nashua, N. H.
idge, William A., Sag Harbor, N. Y.
ary, William W., Suffield, Ct.
ary, Rev. John, Templeton, Mass.
ary, Miss Frances, Danvers, Mass.
ary, Eliza A., Lynn, Mass.
ary, Seth, Goffstown, N. H.
an, Moses, New Gloucester, Me.
iff, Mrs. Innocent, Albany.
ard, Rev. Jonas, Cedar Rapids, Iowa.
ard, Mrs. Eliza, Cedar Rapids, Iowa.
ard, Mrs. Mary D., Middlesex, Va.
ard, Sylvester, Lowell, Mass.
ard, Darwin W., Franklindale, N. Y.
orth, Levi B., Canaan, O.
on, Mrs. Keziah, Vincentown, N. J.

Worrall, Elwood P., Westchester, Pa.
Wooster, Mrs. Aurelia R., Deep River, Ct.
Wooster, Hinman, Charlotte, Vt.
Wooster, George P., New Haven, Ct.
Work, Rev. Perley, Omeo, Wis.
Worth, Rev. Edmund, Kennebunk, Me.
Worth, J. C., Hanover, N. H.
Worthington, S., Springfield, Mass.
Worthington, Gershom B., Colchester, Ct.
Wright, Rev. David, North Lyme, Ct.
Wright, Wm. J., Hardgrove's, Va.
Wright, Theodore, N. Y.
Wright, Asahel B., Lowell, Mass.
Wright, Harvey, Three Rivers, Mass.
Wright, Mrs. Julia A., Westport, N. Y.
Wright, Rev. Ansell T., Weart's Corners, N. J.
Wright, R. A., Rochester, N. Y.
Wright, James G., Canton, N. J.
Wright, B. H., Dover Plains, N. Y.
Wright, William S., Weartsville, N. J.
Wyckoff, Mrs. Cornelius R., Weedsport, N. Y.
Wyckoff, J. N., Woodbridge, N. J.
Wyckoff, Mrs. Elizabeth, Woodbridge, N. J.
Wyckoff, W. G., Middletown, N. J.
Wyckoff, Francis, Plainfield, N. J.
Wyckoff, Mrs. Sarah B., Brooklyn, N. Y.
Wyckoff, Jacob F., Boston, Mass.
Wyer, Rev. Henry O., Alexandria, Va.
Wynn, Mrs. Susan, Tuckahoe, N. J.
Wynn, Benjamin F., Tuckahoe, N. J.
Yale, Levi, Augusta, N. Y.
Yale, Mrs. Ruth, Augusta, N. Y.
Yale, H. C., Brooklyn, N. Y.
Yendall, Sarah, Boston.
Yeomans, Mrs. Olive, Providence.
Yeomans, Miss Mary Ann, Providence.
York, Mrs. Hannah, Haverhill, Mass.
York, C., Norwich, N. Y.
York, Mrs. Esther, Norwich, N. Y.
Young, Mrs. Sarah, Brooklyn, N. Y.
Young, Rev. George, N. J.
Young, Rev. Robert F., Chestnut Hill, Pa.
Young, Mrs. Maria Ann, Chestnut Hill, Pa.
Young, Robert McCarthy, New York.
Young, Rev. G. W., Antistown, Pa.
Young, William W., Stamford, Ct.
Yuran, Mrs S. S., Tunbridge, Vt.
Zebley, John F., New York.
Zimmerman, Edwin, New York.

1833-4.

DIRECTOR.

Cobb, Nathaniel R., Boston, Mass.

MEMBERS.

Barrett, Rev. Thomas, Webster, Mass.
Chase, Rev. John, Brookfield, Mass.

1834-5.

MEMBER.

Lazell, Rev. J. E., Harvard Mass.

1835-6.

DIRECTORS.

Foster, Rev. E., Amesbury, Mass.
Freeman, Rev. E. W., Lowell, Mass.
Jacobs, Rev. Bela, Cambridge, Mass.

MEMBER.

Martin, Rev. A. R., Staten Island, N. Y.

1836-7.

DIRECTOR.

Trask, Rev. Wm. G., Taunton, Mass.

1837-8.

DIRECTOR.

Davis, Rev. Gustavus F., Hartford, Ct.

MEMBERS.

Blain, Miss Mary E., Syracuse, N. Y.
Holroyd, Rev. John, Danvers, Mass.

B
B
H
S
C
H
S
C
D
H
M
N
S
V
W
B
C
F

1843-4.

DIRECTORS.

Cooper, Thomas, Eatonton, Geo.
Linsley, Rev. James H., Stratford, Ct.
Middleton, Rev. John, Geneva, N. Y.

MEMBERS.

Pickins, Mrs. Margaret Eliza, Edgefield, S. C.
Rankin, Henry, Reading, Pa.
Wasson, J. G., Albany, N. Y.

1844-5.

DIRECTORS.

Armstrong, Rev. John, Columbus, Miss.
Coolidge, James D., Madison, N. Y.
Going, Rev. Jonathan, D.D., Granville, O.
Miller, Rev. Wm. George, Essex, Ct.

MEMBERS.

Adams, Mrs. Mary, New York.
Belden, Charles D., New York.
Birdsall, Rev. John O., Perrysburg, O.
Carney, Richard, Portsmouth, Va.
McIntosh, Mrs. Mary, Philadelphia, Pa.

1845-6.

MEMBERS.

Cauldwell, Mrs. Maria, New York.
Hall, Rev. Wilson, Beaufort, S. C.
Jones, Mrs. J. Leavitt, Bankok, Siam.
Lathrop, Rev. Lebbeus, Samptown, N. J.
Marshall, Joseph H., Nashville, Tenn.
Mitchell, Rev. John, Hoosick, N. Y.
Randall, Mrs. Mary E., Woburn, Mass.
Reynolds, Joseph, Norwich, Ct.

1846-7.

DIRECTORS.

Bacheller, Mrs. Mary, Lynn, Mass.
Devan, Mrs. Lydia, Canton, China.
Everts, Rev. Jeremiah B., Washington, N. Y.

MEMBERS.

Cooper, Mrs. Eliza A., New York.
Lee, Mrs. Olive, North Bristol, N. Y.
Rose, Richard, Parham's Store, Va.
Thurston, Rev. Peter, New York.

1847-8.

DIRECTORS.

Martin, John J., Montgomery, N. Y.
Orr, Rev. David, Reed's Creek, Ark.
Parkinson, Rev. William, New York.
Peck, Rev. Philetus B., Owego, N. Y.
Tryon, Rev. Wm. M., Houston, Texas.

MEMBERS.

Colby, Joseph, New London, N. H.
Evans, Rev. George, Manchester, N. H.
Gilbert, Joshua, New York.
Jeter, Mrs. Sarah A., Richmond, Va.
Leaver, Rev. Thomas, Newport, R. I.
Peck, Mrs. Sarah, New Woodstock, N. Y.
Peck, Rev. Linus M., Hamilton, N. Y.
Van Loon, Rev. Charles, Poughkeepsie, N. Y.
Wilson, Edwin C., Elizabeth City, N. C.
Wood, John, Hertford, N. C.

1848-9.

DIRECTORS.

Benedict, Rev. George, New York.
Child, George, New York.

MEMBERS.

Allen, Mrs. Eliza C., New York.
Brouner, Rev. Jacob H., New York.
Chamberlin, Hinds, Leroy, N. Y.
Jencks, Mrs. Caroline B., Bankok, Siam.
Ludlam, John H., New York.
Naylor, Rev. J. G., Portsmouth, N. H.
Peck, Rev. Abijah, Clifton Park, N. Y.
Shaw, Oliver, Providence, R. I.
Wayland, Rev. F., Saratoga Springs, N. Y.
Wildman, Rev. Daniel, Lebanon, Ct.
Williams, Rev. Daniel, New York.

1849-50.

DIRECTORS.

Allen, Rev. Ira M., New York.
Bradford, Rev. Z., Providence, R. I.
Estes, Rev. Elliott, Lower Three Runs, S. C.
Milbank, Charles W., New York.
Peck, Rev. John, New Woodstock, N. Y.
Train, Rev. Charles, Framingham, Mass.
Wilson, James, New York.

MEMBERS.

Baillie, Jonathan, Parham's Store, Va.
Barker, Rev. Luke, M.D., New York.
Brockway, C., Broadalbin, N. Y.
Brown, William, Parham's Store, Va.
Cate, Rev. George W., Barre, Mass.
Corning, Mrs. Nancy, Brooklyn, N. Y.
Cox, Charles, Rahway, N. J.
Crawford, Rev. D. B., Antioch, Miss.
Forrester, James M., New York.
Gale, Mrs. Phebe, East Bennington, Vt.
Harris, Rev. William, Nassau, N. Y.
Lewis, Rev. D. D., New Brunswick, N. J.
Lyman, Nathan, Andover, Ct.
Payne, Mrs. Betsey, Hamilton, N. Y.
Rogers, Rev. John, Paterson, N. J.
Roy, Rev. Wm. A., Charlotteville, Va.
Winchell, Rev. Reuben, Lockport, N. Y.
Yancey, Algernon, Yanceyville, N. C.

1850-1.

DIRECTORS.

Granberry, Rev. N. R., Meridian Springs, Miss.
Graves, Rev. Hiram A., Boston, Mass.
Judson, Rev. A., D.D., Maulmain, Burmah.

MEMBERS.

Bennett, Rev. Alfred, Homer, N. Y.
Bond, Levi, Windsor, N. C.
Briggs, Rev. Ebenezer, Middleboro', Mass.
Burdick, Miss E. M., New York.
Burke, Joshua A., Brooklyn, N. Y.
Cook, Rev. B., Jr., Jewett City, Ct.
Cornelius, Mrs. Rachel, Mount Holly, N. J.
Darrow, Rev. Francis, Waterford, Ct.
Davis, W., Strebane, N. C
Frey, Rev. J. C. F., Pontiac, Mich.
Going, Mrs. Lucy T., Columbus, O.
Horn, Turner, Britton's Cross Roads, N. C.
Humphrey, Mrs. Julia Ann, Albany, N. Y.
Jackson, Rev. Timothy, Piqua, O.
Kelley, Mrs. Elizabeth, New York.
Kendall, Josiah, Littleton, Mass.
Logan, Rev. John, Blandenville, Ill.
Lester, David, Brooklyn, N. Y.
McLaren, Finley, Le Roy, N. Y.
Munn, Mrs. Sarah P., New York.

Sherman, Rev. O. J., Peoria, Ill.

MEMBERS.

Anderson, J. S., Stonington, Ct.
Bolles, Rev. D. C., Southbridge, Mass.
Chase, Amos, Haverhill, Mass.
De Graffenried, Mrs. S., Crosbyville, S. C.
Downing, J., Colerain, N. C.
Farnsworth, Rev. B. F., Nashville, Tenn.
Gibbs, Mrs. Betsey H., Sullivan, N. H.
Goodell, A., Somersworth, N. H.
Hall, Rev. Daniel, New York.
Jones, Mrs. Susan, Newbern, N. C.
Lathrop, Mrs. Jane E., New York.
Manning, Rev. Benjamin, Brookfield, Mass.
Martin, Mrs. R. W., New York.
Miller, John B., Sumterville, S. C.
Morrill, Otis H., Lowell, Mass.
Remington, Mrs. Eliza Ann, New York.
Rider, Miss Olive P., Suffield, Ct.
Shuck, Mrs. Eliza G., Shanghai, China.
Stone, Mrs. Sarah A., New York.
Tucker, Mrs. Levi, Boston, Mass.
Whitman, Rev. S. S., Madison, Wis.

1852-3.

DIRECTORS.

Brown, Rev. O. B., Washington, D. C.
Crozer, Miss Sallie K., Chester, Pa.
Miller, Pardon, Providence, R. I.
Rhees, Rev. M. J., D.D., Williamsburgh, N. Y.

MEMBERS.

Adams, Mrs. Cornelia C., Cleveland, O.
Ashley, Mrs. Hannah, Poultney, Vt.
Bellamy, Mrs. Eliza, Arcadia, N. Y.
Boynton, Mrs. Ruth, North Springfield, Vt.
Brown, Mrs. O. B., Washington, D. C.
Carraway, Mrs. H., Kingston, N. C.
Cosner, Rev. Henry, Lyndon, Ill.
Fant, Rev. Ephraim, Halseville, S. C.
Goodliff, James, New York.
Haskell, Rev. Daniel, Hamilton, N. Y.
Haynes, Rev. Arus, M.D., New York.

Hill, Mrs. Matilda Pierce, Albany, N. Y.
Hill, Mrs. Lydia Ann, Carmel, N. Y.
Judson, Mrs. Emily C., Hamilton, N. Y.
Miner, Rev. Bradly, Providence, R. I.
Neale, Mrs. Melissa Y., Boston, Mass.
Oakley, Mrs. Cassandra, New York.
Pennypacker, John, Wilmington, Del.
Porter, Edwin, Lowell, Mass.
Richards, Rev. Humphrey, Dorchester, Mass.
Richards, Mrs. Eunice J., Dorchester, Mass.
Rodgers, Rev. Ebenezer, Upper Alton, Ill.
Sharp, J. Milton, Williamsburgh, N. Y.
Skinner, Mrs. Anna, Hertford, N. C.
Spencer, Rev. Horace, Reed's Corners, N. Y.
Spivey, Aaron J., Brownsville, Tenn.
Sweet, H. H., Fredonia, N. Y.
Taylor, Daniel Webster, New York.
Walker, Mrs. Jane P., Central Falls, R. I.
Waterbury, Rev. J. H., Elizabethtown, N. J.
Willard, Hon. Levi, Keene, N. H.

1855-6.

DIRECTORS.

Cone, Rev. Spencer H., D.D., New York.
Choules, Rev. J. O., D.D., Newport, R. I.
Crane, James C., Richmond, Va.
Germond, George C., Williamsburgh, N. Y.
Ives, Mrs. Hope, Providence, R. I.
Morse, Jacob, Sturbridge, Mass.
Munn, Stephen B., New York.
Pratt, Rev. D. D., Nashua, N. H.
Purser, Thomas, Brooklyn, N. Y.
Shaw, Thomas, Boston, Mass.

MEMBERS.

Ballard, Rev. John B., New York.
Belden, Rev. A. R., Iowa City, Iowa.
Bishop, William, Bloomington, Ill.
Bottum, Hon. N. H., Shaftsbury, Vt.
Brayton, Philip, Phenix, R. I.
Calam, Mrs. Mary N., Sing Sing, N. Y.
Challis, John, Salem, N. J.
Clapp, Mrs. Jane M., Danbury, Ct.
Colver, Mrs. Esther B., Worcester, Mass.
Cox, Miss Achsah, Imlaystown, N. J.
Davis, Rev. Jonathan, Monticello, S. C.
Davis, Rev. Joseph, Hebron, O.
Duff, Miss Mary, Boston, Mass.
Edwards, Miss Mary, New York.
English, Isaac, Salem, N. J.
Evans, Mrs. Mary, New York.
Hardin, Rev. Theodore, Horton, N. Scotia.
Harris, Isaac, New London, Ct.
Hazard, Simeon, Newport, R. I.
Hedden, Mrs. C. F., Manchester, N. H.
Hunt, Dr. George, Le Clair, Ill.
Jones, Mrs. Rhoda, Smithville, N. Y.
Jones, Rev. Matthew, Stephentown, N. Y.
Leland, Mrs. Caroline M., Brooklyn, N. Y.
Logan, Rev. John, Blandensville, Ill.
Mangam, Mrs. Sarah Ann, New York.
Miller, John B., Sumpterville, S. C.
Miner, Rev. Cyrus, Attica, N. Y.
Nelson, Rev. Caleb, Omego Creek, N. Y.
Nice, Rev. W. J., Imlaystown, N. J.
Nichols, Miss Hannah, Bridgeport, Ct.
Purser, Mrs. Mary, Brooklyn, N. Y.
Richards, Joel, Claremont, N. H.
Richmond, Rev. J. L. Indianapolis, Ia.
Scott, Rev. James, Newburg, N. Y.
Sheppard, Rev. Wm., Bridgeton, N. J.
Sheppard, Joseph, Bridgeton, N. J.
Smith, Z. L., Norwich, Ct.
Steadman, Rev. N. V., Evansville, Ia.
Stickney, Samuel, Watertown, Mass.
Sutton, George, New York.
Teasdale, Rev. John, St. Louis, Mo.
Thomas, Moses, Ballston Spa, N. Y.
Thornton, Rev. V. R., Public Square, Geo.
Tubbs, Benj. H., West Dedham, Mass
West, John, Brooklyn, N. Y.
Whitman, Hiram, Belvidere, Ill.
Wheeler, Nelson, Providence, R. I.
Wyckoff, Rev. Cornelius P., Weedsport, N. Y.

1856-7.

DIRECTORS.

Clarke, Rev. Elbert W., Arcade, N. Y.
Colgate, William, New York.
Collom, Rev. J. G., Mt. Holly, N. J.
Conant, John, Brandon, Vt.
Cramb, Rev. Augustus B., Metamora, Ill.
Flanders, Benjamin, Brooklyn, N. Y.
Granger, Rev. J. N., D.D., Providence, R. I
Kelly, Samuel R., Brooklyn, N. Y.
Wightman, Rev. F., Wethersfield, Ct.

MEMBERS.

Beebe, Alexander M., LL.D., Utica, N. Y.
Capern, Thomas, Moorestown, N. J.
Cone, Miss Amelia M., Philadelphia, Pa.
Danforth, Rev. G. F., South Dartmouth, Mass.
Edmond, Mrs. Emily S., Brookline, Mass.
Farnsworth, W. Fleming, N. Y.
Fish, Rev. Elisha P., Haddam, Ct.
Forsyth, Russell, Albany, N. Y.
Graham, James C., Jerseyville, Ill.
Guest, Rev. Pitney, Canton, O.
Green, Rev. Jonathan R., Derby, Vt.
Hayes, Seth, Colchester, Ct.
Harvey, Rev. Nathaniel, Westboro', Mass.
Hovey, Mrs. Elizabeth, Cambridge, Mass.
Ingals, Rev. Lovell, Akyab, Arracan.
Kain, Charles, Marlton, N. J.
Martin, Stelle R., Rahway, N. J.
Marsh, Rev. L. G., New York.
Marshall, Rev. Andrew, Savannah, Geo.
Marshall, William, Fitchburg, Mass.
Miller, Rev. Harvey, Meriden, Ct.
Perego, Mrs. Margaret, New York.
Phillips, Samuel B., M.D., New York.
Silliman, Rev. Gershom, Helena, Ill.
Smith, Mrs. Hannah B., Iowa City, Iowa.
Thomas, Thomas, New York.
Underhill, Rev. Charles H., Peekskill, N. Y.
Walder, Mrs. Grace W., Marcus Hook, Pa.
Woodruff, David, Bridgeton, N. J.

1857-8.

DIRECTORS.

Dale, Rev. Harvey S., Lebanon, Ohio.
Farquharson, Rev. James, Warren, Me.
Hatt, Rev. Josiah, Morristown, N. J.
Peck, Rev. John M., D.D., Shiloh, Ill.
Seaver, Rev. Horace, New York.
Welch, Rev. J. C., Providence, R. I.

MEMBERS.

Ashley, Elisha, Poultney, Vt.
Barnhurst, Joseph, Sr., Francisville, Pa.
Benedict, Uriah, Central Falls, R. I.
Benton, John, Saratoga, N. Y.
Brown, Mrs. Prudencia, Middletown, N. J.
Corning, Ephraim, Brooklyn, N. Y.
Cox, John W., Mt. Holly, N. J.
Crosby, Nathaniel, Janesville, Wis.
Cornwell, Rev. William E., Princeton, N. J.
Demming, Levi L., Honesdale, Pa.

Jerrard, Rev. Richard, Fond du Lac, Wis.
Kingman, Henry W., New York.
Lewis, Rev. Lester, Middletown, Ct.
McCormick, Richard C., New York.
Mallary, Rev. S. S., Pawtucket, R. I.
Marshall, William, Fitchburgh, Mass.
Mason, Mrs. Sarah R., Chelsea, Mass.
Mears, Elijah, Boston, Mass.
Miles, Rev. George I., Muscatine, Iowa.
Mulford, Mrs. Phebe, Roadstown, N. J.
Plumer, John, Goffstown Centre, N. H.
Powell, Miss Sarah P., Davenport, Iowa.
Rand, Rev. Thomas, Ireland, Mass.
Reed, Rev. James, Hamburg, N. Y.
Richards, William H., Philadelphia, Pa.
Russell, Rev. Caleb, Upper Middleton, Pa.
Sarles, Mrs. Cornelia A., Brooklyn, N. Y.
Scribner, Samuel T., Danbury, Ct.
Seeley, Mrs. Agnes Jane, New Erin, Ill.
Southworth, Mrs. James E., Brooklyn, N. Y.
Taylor, Rev. David, Terre Haute, Ia.
Thompson, Rev. Richard, Milton, Ct.
Todd, Mrs. William W., New York.
True, Osgood, Plainfield, N. H.
True, Reuben, Plainfield, N. H.
Twiss, Rev. Daniel F., Spottswood, N. J.
Van Valkenburgh, John, Williamsburgh, N. Y.
Weston, Mrs. Hetty, Lynn, Mass.
Weston, Mrs. Henry G., Peoria, Ill

Ne
Wi

Bo
Br
Bu
Bu
Ca
Ch
Cot
Cul
Du
Eat
Elki
Jan
Ken
Mal
Mul
Plu
Poi
Pre
Req
Spr
Tho
Tob
Vint
Wild

CONTENTS.

ANNUAL REPORT OF THE EXECUTIVE BOARD.

MISCELLANEOUS MATTER.

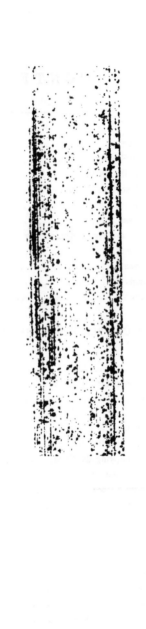

TWENTY-EIGHTH REPORT

OF THE

AMERICAN BAPTIST HOME MISSION SOCIETY,

PRESENTED BY THE

EXECUTIVE BOARD

AT THE

ANNIVERSARY HELD IN CINCINNATI,

MAY 24, 1860;

WITH

THE TREASURER'S REPORT AND OTHER DOCUMENTS.

NEW YORK:
PUBLISHED AT THE AMERICAN BAPTIST HOME MISSION ROOMS, No. 115 NASSAU STREET,
AND PRINTED BY THOMAS HOLMAN, CORNER CENTRE AND WHITE STS.
1860.

ACT OF INC

AN ACT TO INCORPORATE THE AMERICAN
APRIL 12, 1843, AND AMI

The People of the State of New York,
enact as

CONSTITUTION.

NAME.

I.—This Society shall be called the AMERICAN BAPTIST HOME MISSION SOCIETY.

OBJECT.

II.—The object of this Society shall be to promote the preaching of the Gospel in North America.

MEMBERSHIP.

III.—The Society shall be composed of Annual Delegates, Life Members, and Life Directors. Any Baptist church, in union with the denomination, may appoint a delegate for an annual contribution of ten dollars, and an additional delegate for each additional thirty dollars. Thirty dollars shall be requisite to constitute a Member for Life, and one hundred dollars, paid at one time, or a sum which, in addition to any previous contribution, shall amount to one hundred dollars, shall be requisite to constitute a Director for Life.

OFFICERS.

IV.—The officers of the Society shall be a President, two Vice-Presidents, a Treasurer, two Auditors, one or more Corresponding Secretaries, and a Recording Secretary.

MANAGERS.

V.—There shall be twelve Managers also, residing in the city of New York, or its vicinity, who shall be divided by lot among themselves into two classes of six members each. The term of service of the first class shall expire in one year, and that of the second class in two years. At each annual meeting of the Society after the first election under this amended Constitution, one class only shall be elected for the term of two years, to the end that the half of the whole number of Managers may be annually chosen; provided, however, that vacancies remaining in any class may be filled for the unexpired term. The Officers and Managers shall be elected by ballot, and continue to discharge their official duties, until superseded by a new election.

EXECUTIVE BOARD.

VI.—The Treasurer, Auditors, Recording Secretary, and Managers of the Society, shall constitute an Executive Board, to conduct the business of the Society; seven of whom shall be a quorum for that purpose. They shall have power to appoint their own meetings; elect their own Chairman and Recording Secretary; enact their own By-laws and Rules of Order, provided always, that they be not inconsistent with this Constitution; fill any vacancies which may occur in their own body, or in the offices of the Society during the year; and, if deemed necessary by two thirds of the members, convene special meetings of the Society. They shall establish such agencies as the interests of the Society may require; appoint agents and missionaries; fix their compensation; direct and instruct them concerning their particular fields and labors; make all appropriations to be paid out of the treasury; and present to the Society, at each annual meeting, a full report of their proceedings during the current year.

DESIGNATED FUNDS.

VII.—All moneys or other property contributed and designated for any particular missionary field or purpose, shall be so appropriated, or returned to the donors, or their lawful agents.

TREASURER.

VIII.—The Treasurer shall give bonds to such amount as the Executive Board shall think proper.

ELIGIBILITY TO APPOINTMENT.

IX.—All the Officers, Managers, Missionaries, and Agents of the Society, shall be members in good standing in regular Baptist churches.

ANNUAL MEETING.

X.—The Society shall meet annually for the election of Officers and Managers, and the transaction of other necessary business, at such time and place as the Executive Board shall appoint.

ALTERATIONS OF THE CONSTITUTION.

XI.—No alteration of this Constitution shall be made without an affirmative vote of two thirds of the members present at an annual meeting; nor unless the same shall have been proposed in writing, and the proposition sustained by a majority vote, at a previous annual meeting, or recommended by the Executive Board.

STATED MEETINGS FOR 1860-61.

Of the Executive Board.—Thursday before the first Wednesday in each month, at four o'clock P.M., during the Summer months; at three P.M., in the Winter months; and half-past three P.M. in the Fall and Spring months.

Of the Committee on Missions.—The day previous to that of the Board, at three o'clock P.M.

Of the Committee on Agencies and Finance.—The Tuesday preceding, at four o'clock P.M., in the Summer months; and at three P.M., in the Winter months.

Of the Committee on Church Edifice Fund.—The Monday preceding, at half-past nine A.M.

BY-LAWS OF THE BOARD.

1. All meetings shall be opened with prayer.
2. All Committees shall be nominated by the presiding officer and approved by the Executive Board, unless otherwise specially ordered.
3. No moneys shall be paid out of the treasury but by order of the Executive Board.
4. All resolutions, if required, shall be presented in writing.
5. Whenever a vacancy occurs in the Executive Board the fact shall be entered on the Minutes, and at the next stated meeting the Board shall proceed to fill such vacancy by ballot.
6. No By-law of the Board shall be suspended for any temporary purpose, unless by a vote of two thirds of the members of the Board.

ORDER OF BUSINESS.

1. Reading the Minutes of the last meeting.
2. Treasurer's Report.
3. Communications of Corresponding Secretary.
4. Reports of Standing Committees.
5. Reports of Select Committees.
6. Unfinished Business.
7. New Business.

STANDING COMMITTEES.

AGENCIES AND FINANCE.	MISSIONS.	CHURCH-EDIFICE FUND.
E. Cauldwell,	E. E. L. Taylor,	F. S. Miner,
S. Sheldon,	W. H. Parmly,	H. P. Freeman,
J. M. Bruce, Jr.,	H. G. Weston,	J. B. Peck.
L. Ballard,	E. Lathrop,	
D. M. Wilson.	J. S. Holme.	

LEGACIES.

A. B. Capwell, H. C. Fish, M. G. Hodge.

MINUTES OF THE TWENTY-EIGHTH ANNIVERSARY

OF THE

American Baptist Home Mission Society,

Held in Cincinnati, May 24, 1860.

The American Baptist Home Mission Society convened in the meeting-house of the Ninth Street Baptist Church, Cincinnati, at ten o'clock A.M., May 24, 1860.

The President, John P. Crozer, Esq., not being present, the Hon. J. M. Linnard, of Pa., called the Society to order, and nominated A. B. Capwell, Esq., of N. Y., as Chairman of the meeting; who was duly appointed.

After a few appropriate remarks by the Chairman, and the singing of the 888th hymn, prayer was offered by the Rev. G. S. Webb, D.D., N. J.

On motion of Rev. G. W. Anderson, Pa., Rev. W. H. Pendleton, of N. Y., was appointed Recording Secretary *pro tem*.

On motion of Rev. B. M. Hill, Corresponding Secretary, Rev. G. W. Anderson was appointed Assistant Recording Secretary.

On motion of Rev. G. W. Anderson, it was

Resolved, That, in all discussions, each speaker be limited to ten minutes.

On motion of Rev. Wm. C. Richards, of R. I., it was

Resolved, That ministers and other brethren present, not members of the Society, be invited to participate in our deliberations.

The invitation was accepted by Rev. Wm. M. Pratt, Lexington, Ky.; Rev. F. Tolhurst, Columbia, Ohio; Rev. Lyman Wilder,

Columbia, Ind.; Rev. P. P. Bish
B. Ewing, Burlington, Iowa; R
Rev. D. Read, LL.D., Upper Al
County, Ohio; Rev. J. G. Bowen
I. N. Carman, Ashland, Ohio.

On motion of G. C. Lee, Esq.,

Resolved, That the following be the hou
sessions of the Society: Commence at te
o'clock P.M. Closing at half-past twelve

Upon the nomination of the Ch
were appointed:

On Credentials of Delegates.—
H. Burlingham, N. Y.; Rev. C.
D. Fendall, N. J.; Rev. J. Shep

On Nomination of Officers.—Re
Rev. G. S. Webb, D.D., N. J.;
G. W. Anderson, Pa.; Rev. W

On Life Directors and Members.
Rev. J. S. Ladd, N. Y.; E. J. T

On motion, the proposed amendments to the fifth, sixth, and tenth Articles were each adopted by a two-thirds vote of the members present.

In accordance with a constitutional provision, Rev. B. M. Hill, D.D., N. Y., submitted for action at the next Annual Meeting the following proposition of amendment to Article five of the Constitution, which was sustained, viz.,

V.—There shall be fifteen Managers also, residing in the city of New York, or its vicinity, who shall be divided by lot among themselves into three classes of five members each. The term of service of the first class shall expire in one year, that of the second class in two years, and that of the third class in three years. At each Annual Meeting of the Society after the first election under this amended Constitution, one class only shall be elected for the term of three years, to the end that the third part of the whole number of Managers, as nearly as possible, may be annually chosen; provided, however, that vacancies remaining in any class may be filled for the unexpired term of that class. The Officers and Managers shall be elected by ballot, and continue to discharge their official duties, until superseded by a new election.

The hour of adjournment having arrived, after prayer by Rev. Howard Malcolm, D.D., Pa., the Society adjourned.

AFTERNOON SESSION.

The Chairman called the Society to order at half-past two o'clock P.M. After singing 896th hymn, prayer was offered by Rev. Ezra Going, Ohio.

The Treasurer, Ebenezer Cauldwell, Esq., being absent, his annual report was read by the Corresponding Secretary; and, after interesting addresses by Mr. G. C. Lee, Iowa, and Mr. Geo. F. Davis, Ohio, was adopted and ordered to be printed with the annual report. (See pages 12, 13.)

Rev. Jay S. Backus, D.D., N. Y., moved to appoint a committee to nominate the Board of Managers, required by the amended Constitution. Rev. E. Lathrop, D.D., N. Y., offered, as an amendment, that the nomination be referred to the Committee on Nomination of Officers. The amendment prevailed.

The Corresponding Secretary read a communication from the President, John P. Crozer, Esq., declining a re-election, which was referred to the Committee on Nominations.

Thereupon, the Committee on No
their report, which was accepted, an

On the nomination of the Chai
pointed as tellers: Mr. George F.
Jeffery, Penn.; Rev. J. S. Ladd, N. Y
as duly elected Officers and Manager
persons, viz., (See page 14.)

On motion of Rev. Sam'l White,
aries was appointed, consisting of
Henry Davis, D.D., Ohio; Rev. C. M

The Committee on Life Directors
report, through their Chairman, Rev.
ing forty-five Life Directors, and seve

The report was accepted, and the
in the Minutes, viz.,

LIFE DIRECTORS PR

Anderson, Rev. George W., West Haverford, Pa.	Ho
Backus, Rev. J. S., Syracuse, N. Y.	Ke
Burlingham, Rev. A. H., New York.	La
Bright, Rev. E., New York.	Le
Baker, B. P., Cincinnati, Ohio.	Lin
Challis, Rev. J. M., Roadstown, N. J.	Lat
Colver, Rev. N., Cincinnati, Ohio.	Ma
Cole, Rev. Jirah D., Barry, Ill.	Ma
Caldwell, Rev. S. L., Providence, R. I.	Mu
Clarke, Rev. M. G., Indianapolis, In.	Ma
Corey, Rev. D. G., Utica, N. Y.	Olc
Crozer, George K., Chester, Pa.	Per
Crozer, Robert H., Chester, Pa.	Re
Davis, Rev. Henry, Columbus, O.	[illegible]

LIFE MEMBERS.

Brown, John S., Fisherville, N. H.
Bailey, Rev. L., Bellevue, Ohio.
Brown, Rev. E. T., Wooster, Ohio.
Brandt, Rev. Thomas, Waukesha, Wis.
Bond, Rev. E. P., Lawrenceburg, Ia.
Brown, Rev. Joseph, Springfield, Ohio.
Burton, Rev. N. S., Granville, Ohio.
Church, Wm. C., New York.
Chambers, Rev. James, McConnellsville, Ohio.
Cummings, Rev. E. E., Concord, N. H.
Cressy, Rev. T. R., Hastings, Min.
Capwell, A. B., Brooklyn, N. Y.
Crane, Rev. D. M., Boston, Mass.
Carpenter, Rev. B. B., Griggsville, Ill.
Corwin, Rev. Ira, South Bend, Ia.
Duncan, J. H., Haverhill, Mass.
Dunlevy, A. H., Lebanon, Ohio.
Darrow, Rev. A., Norwalk, Ohio.
Everts, Rev. W. W., Chicago, Ill.
Eaton, Rev. Geo. W., Hamilton, N. Y.
Evans, J. T., New York.
Fish, Rev. J. W., Fox Lake, Wis.
Ferris, S. M., Columbia, Ohio.
Fletcher, Rev. H., Townshend, Vt.
Griffith, Rev. B., Philadelphia.
Going, Rev. Ezra, Granville, Ohio.
Goodno, Rev. W. S., Jacksonville, Ill.
Haynes, Rev. D. C., New York.
Ingalls, Charles, Methuen, Mass.
Jeffery, Rev. R., Philadelphia.
Johnson, Rev. George J., Fort Madison, Iowa.
Joslyn, Rev. A. J., Chicago, Ill.
Keely, Rev. Thomas E., South Danvers, Mass.
King, Mrs. Betsey B., Xenia, Ohio.
Lincoln, Rev. T. O., Utica, N. Y.
Lowry, Rev. Robert, New York.
Lincoln, Joshua, Roxbury, Mass.
Leonard, George E., Ironton, Ohio.
Miller, Rev. U. B., Fort Wayne, Ohio.
Mason, Rev. J. T., Stirling, Ill.
Marshall, Rev. Sam'l, Jamestown, Ohio.
Olmstead, Rev. J. W., Boston, Mass.
Osborne, Rev. J. W., Mansfield, Ohio.
Osgood, Rev. S. M., Philadelphia.
Platt, Rev. E. I., Toledo, Ohio.
Pope, Rev. J. D., St. Paul, Min.
Powell, W., Cincinnati, Ohio.
Powell, Rev. Benj. J., Chesterville, Ohio.
Phares, Rev. M. B., Dupont, Ia.
Raymond, Rev. Lewis, Peoria, Ill.
Randall, Rev. D. A., Columbus, Ohio.
Stelle, Rev. B., Klinesville, N. J.
Smith, Rev. J. A., Chicago, Ill.
Smith, Rev. Jesse H., New Engl'd Village, Mass.
Smith, Lucius E., Groton, Mass.
Scott, Rev. Ebenezer J., Richburg, N. Y.
Smith, Rev. J. Hyatt, Philadelphia.
Smith, Rev. Harry, Valparaiso, Ia.
Storer, Rev. Joseph, Fisherville, N. H.
Stone, Rev. Marsena, Lebanon, Ohio.
Shepardson, Rev. J., Petersham, Mass.
Stearns, Rev. O. S., Newton Centre, Mass.
Sedwick, Rev. Wm., Adamsville, Ohio.
Siegfried, Rev. B. Y., Georgetown, Ohio.
Spencer, Rev. Wm. H., Litchfield, Pa.
Thomas, Rev. C. A., Brandon, Vt.
Tytus, F. J., Middletown, Ohio.
Wilson, Rev. C. E., Holmdel, N. J.
Whitehead, Rev. J. M., Westville, Ia.
Walker, Rev. Joseph, Marcus Hook, Pa.
Wilson, Rev. W. V., New Monmouth, N. J.
Wood, Rev. N. N., Alton, Ill.
Warren, Rev. J. G., Boston, Mass.
Webster, Rev. S. B., Norwalk, Ohio.
Ward, Rev. Henry, Lafargeville, N. Y.
Watson, Rev. D. S., Cleveland, Ohio.

The Committee on Credentials of Delegates reported the names of Rev. I. J. Stoddard, as a delegate from the Baptist church at Oskaloosa, Iowa; and Rev. G. W. Fuller, delegate from the church in Chatfield, Min., upon the payment of ten dollars each.*

The report was accepted, the names to be entered upon the Minutes.

The Committee to whom was referred the proposed amendment to the third Article of the Constitution, made their report through their Chairman, Rev. E. E. L. Taylor, D.D., N. Y., submitting the following proposition of further amending the same, which, on motion, was sustained by a majority vote.

---

* Several other names were presented, but no record of the payment of the money necessary to the appointment of an annual delegate could be found, unless paid through Associations or Conventions.

Article third shall read as follows:

The Society shall be composed of such persons as shall be members or directors for life at the time of the adoption of this amended Constitution, and those who are entitled to become such on the completion of payments already commenced for that purpose, and of annual members. Any regular Baptist church, by contributing to the funds of the Society ten dollars annually, may appoint one annual member; for twenty-five dollars, in addition, a second annual member; and an additional annual member for each additional fifty dollars. Any individual may become an honorary member for life by the payment, during the financial year, of not less than thirty dollars; and every honorary member shall have a vote in the meetings of the Society so long as he continues to be an annual contributor to its treasury, and a member in good standing of a regular Baptist church.

The hour having arrived, the Society adjourned after prayer by Rev. Henry Davis, D.D., Ohio.

EVENING SESSION.

The Society reassembled, and was called to order by the Chairman at half-past seven P.M. Exercises commenced with singing the 664th hymn. Prayer was offered by Rev. N. A. Reed, N. J.

The Corresponding Secretary concluded the reading of the annual report of the Executive Board.

On motion, the annual report was accepted and ordered to be printed under the direction of the Executive Board.

Whereupon, the Society listened to interesting addresses from Rev. G. J. Johnson, of Iowa; Rev. T. R. Cressey, of Min.; Rev. A. J. Joslyn, Ill.; Rev. Lewis Raymond, Ill.; Rev. J. G. Warren, Mass.; Rev. A. H. Danforth, Assam; interspersed with songs of praise.

The Committee on Obituaries made their report, which was adopted.* Whereupon, the Society joined in prayer with Rev. James Delancy, of Wis.

On motion of Rev. G. W. Anderson, Pa., it was

Resolved, That the acknowledgments of this Society be and are herewith tendered to the brethren and friends in this city, who have welcomed us so heartily, and so generously extended their hospitalities during the anniversary services; also, to the

---

* This report was written with a pencil and has become illegible. We therefore refer our readers to *the list of deceased members.*

various Railroad Cos., who have furnished tickets over their roads at reduced rates; and to the proprietors of the several hotels, who have extended like courtesies in the accommodation of delegates.

On motion, it was unanimously

Resolved, That the thanks of this Society were due to the Chairman, A. B. Capwell, Esq., N. Y., for the judicious and impartial manner in which he has discharged the duties assigned him as the presiding officer.

The Minutes were read and duly approved, and the Society adjourned with prayer by Rev. H. G. Weston, D.D., N. Y.

W. H. PENDLETON,
Recording Secretary pro tem.

-- Cash paid on account Church-

-- Cash paid for Fuel, Station
incidental expenses........

-- Cash paid for Paper, Printing
Minutes Record, and incidenta

-- Cash paid for Paper and Pri
Certificates, Blanks, etc ....

-- Cash paid interest on condition

-- Cash paid for Taxes on Land d
including Surveying of Prop

-- Cash paid for Insurance.......

-- Cash paid for Rent of Rooms..

-- Cash paid for Exchange and
Money ....

-- Cash paid for Legal Services in

-- Bank Stock account...........

-- Balance.......................

IN ACCOUNT WITH EBENEZER CAULDWELL, TREASURER. Cr.

1860. March 31,	By Balance as per last Report........................		$4,803 86
	" Contributions since April 1, 1859........	$38,539 92	
	" Less Checks not due....................	100 00	
			38,439 92
	" Legacies same period in Cash.....................		9,598 92
	" Legacy of Margaretha Medera for Investment, charged with the Interest on the same as an Annuity to a Minister of the Gospel.........................		2,500 00
	" Contributions to Church-edifice Fund, and Interest...		1,664 90
	" Legacy of Rev. J. Drake, to same Fund............		300 00
	" Subscriptions to *Home Mission Record*		1,173 09
	" Interest on Legacies past due....................		49 63
	" " " Temporary Investment.................		30 00
	" " " Special Salary Fund		420 00
	" " " a Special Investment by direction of the Donor............................		175 00
	" " " Investment made to cover conditional donations, for which the Society is paying interest...........................		280 00
	" Dividends on Bank Stock, bequeathed by the late John Allen, R. I....................................		170 76
	" Bank Stock bequeathed by the late John Allen, of R. I., estimated at its par value, but not yet disposed of..		2,975 00
			$62,581 08
	By Balance to account..............................		$11,273 12
	Subject to drafts on Treasury outstanding..	$2,881 24	
	" " Salaries due Missionaries........	904 30	
	" " Funding Medera Legacy........	2,500 00	
		$4,285 54	4,285 54
			$6,987 58

E. Cauldwell, *Treasurer.*

OFFICERS OF THE SOCIETY,

AND

EXECUTIVE BOARD.

OFFICERS.

PRESIDENT.

J. E. SOUTHWORTH, Esq., New York.

VICE-PRESIDENTS.

J. W. MERRILL, Esq., Boston.
REV. ALEXIS CASWELL, D.D., Providence, R. I.

TREASURER.

EBENEZER CAULDWELL, Esq., New York.

AUDITORS.

SMITH SHELDON, New York.
JOHN M. BRUCE, Jr., "

CORRESPONDING SECRETARY.

REV. BENJAMIN M. HILL, D.D., New York.

RECORDING SECRETARY.

A. B. CAPWELL, Esq., New York.

MANAGERS.

FIRST CLASS, FOR ONE YEAR.

LOOMIS BALLARD,..........Brooklyn, N. Y.
REV. E. E. L. TAYLOR, D.D., "
" H. G. WESTON, D.D.,..New York.
F. S. MINER,................ "
D. M. WILSON,..............Newark, N. J.
REV. E. LATHROP, D.D.,.....New York.

SECOND CLASS, FOR TWO YEARS.

REV. H. C. FISH, D.D.,..Newark, N. J.
" M. G. HODGE,....Brooklyn, N. Y.
" W. H. PARMLY,..Jersey City, N. J.
H. P. FREEMAN,.......Williamsburgh, N. Y.
J. B. PECK,.............New York.
REV. J. S. HOLME,......Brooklyn, N. Y.

CHAIRMAN OF THE EXECUTIVE BOARD.

REV. M. G. HODGE.

RECORDING SECRETARY OF THE BOARD, AND CLERK.

JAMES M. WHITEHEAD, New York.

ANNUAL REPORT

OF THE AMERICAN BAPTIST HOME MISSION SOCIETY,

At its Twenty-eighth Anniversary, held in Cincinnati, May 24, 1860.

The Executive Board of the American Baptist Home Mission Society, in presenting the Annual Report of their proceedings, trust they are influenced by the same spirit that animated Barnabas and Paul, who, after preaching the Gospel in various places, returned to their brethren who had sent them forth, and "rehearsed all that God had done with them, and how he had opened the door of faith unto the Gentiles."

DEATHS.

Before entering upon this duty, however, it is proper to allude to the doings of death. So far as we have learned, five of the Directors and thirty-six of the Members of the Society have fallen by his afflictive visitation. Among their names (which are recorded in the list of the deceased) are those of thirteen ministers of the Gospel, and two ministers' wives, to which may be added those of the wives of four missionaries.

Among the names of deceased females, it is befitting us to mention particularly that of Miss Phebe Arnold, of the State of New York, who, though occupying a retired position in life, and unobtrusive in her habits, was, in more than an usual degree, a child of faith, and devoted to the cause of Christ. Her liberal benefactions of nearly all she possessed to this Society and others, while yet enjoying health and reasonable prospects of its continuance, reserving for herself its use for only a necessary subsistence, and practicing a rigid self-denial, prove her love of the Savior, and her strong desire to do what she could to promote His cause.

DIRECTORS AND MEMBERS FOR LIFE.

Fifty-eight persons have been constituted Directors for Life, of whom twelve had been previously members. Five Directors have died, making the present number six hundred and ninety-seven.

Three hundred and sixty-five persons have been constituted Members for Life. Thirty-six have died during the year, and the decease of eleven others in previous years has been ascertained, leaving the present number five thousand five hundred and eleven. The total number of both classes is six thousand two hundred and eight.

SECRETARIES OF CORRESPONDENCE.

At the last meeting of the Society, a measure was adopted for increasing the vigor and efficiency of its operations. In accordance with it, two Secretaries of Correspondence were elected. The Rev. D. B. Cheney, one of the number, soon after the meeting accepted an important pastorate in California, and removed to that State, where he has performed valuable service for the Society. As, however, by this removal, his *entire* services could not be obtained, as was contemplated in his election, the Board attempted, as they were instructed, to fill the vacancy by the appointment of some other person until the present meeting; but, for various reasons, they have failed of success, and the business of the year has been transacted, as ·eretofore, by one Secretary.

·r twenty-two years from the ganization of the Society, the Constitution provided for but one "Corresponding Secretary," and for three years afterward for "a Corresponding Secretary and a Financial Secretary;" since which, it has admitted of an indefinite number of "Secretaries of Correspondence." The practical bearings of a plurality of Secretaries, has engaged the attention of the Board for several years. A year ago, after a thorough discussion by a select committee of their appointment, and by the Board itself, a vote was passed recommending a restoration by the Society of the original phraseology. This was submitted to the Society at its last annual meeting, and was by them referred back to the Executive Board. A special committee also was appointed by the Society to consider the subject in connection with other changes, who made a report which has not been finally disposed of. At a recent meeting of the Board, the subject was again discussed, and without intending any interference with the action of the Society upon that report, but to allow of a choice of alterations, either of which may be immediately carried into effect; a vote was passed, recommending that, at this anniversary, the fourth article of the Constitution be altered, by the substitution of the words "a Corresponding Secretary," for the words "Secretaries of Correspondence;" and thus respectfully renew their recommendations of last year.

CHURCH-EDIFICE FUNDS.

Every year produces additional evidence of the necessity of means, in connection with the operations of the Society, to aid feeble churches to build suitable houses of worship. The past year has produced such evidence in great abundance, and the Board have been induced to revive, with some modifications, their plan of a Church-edifice Fund. The subject has received their attention, and they have submitted their views in general terms to the consideration of churches and individuals, with the hope that they will be disposed to co-operate in the measure. The report of the Committee of the Board upon the subject is herewith presented for the consideration of the Society, and for their decision whether such means of increasing their ability to establish the institutions of the Gospel shall be placed at their disposal.

COLLECTING AGENCIES.

The subject of collecting agencies for the Society has received attention. Inquiries have been made, with a view of ascertaining to what extent they may be safely dispensed with, and plans have been arranged, and partially executed, to render that branch of our operations at once more efficient and economical.

The members of the Executive Board are all members of churches, and several of them are pastors. They are annually elected to their positions, and render their official services gratuitously, while from them, individually, and from the churches with which they are connected, a considerable portion of the funds of the Society is annually obtained. In these facts, it is believed that the public have a good guarantee for the exercise of their official powers with due regard to economy. Thus far, collecting agents have been the main reliance of the Board for obtaining funds, and the experience of nearly thirty years confirms them in the opinion that they are yet indispensable for that purpose.

On the other hand, it has been noticed with satisfaction, that, for some years past, the missionary spirit has been increasing among the friends of Christ, and has now become so extensively operative, that some modification can be consistently made in the working of our agency department. The systematic arrangements adopted by many churches for the collection of missionary funds (a plan that has always been encouraged by the Board) has made it practicable and desirable to enlarge the agency fields, and reduce the number of the agents. To accomplish these objects without injury to important interests, considerable time has been necessary; but the business of collecting funds during the entire year has been conducted with one less on the list of agents than heretofore; and a further reduction of the number, soon, is contemplated; thus enabling the Board to apply a larger proportion of their means to increase the number of missionaries. How much farther this plan of reduction can be prosecuted will depend on the readiness of the Society and its friends to supply the treasury with adequate means for the performance of the work expected of the Board. With great satisfaction would we hail the advent of the period when voluntary offerings to the treasury will entirely supersede the collecting agencies, and we believe that none would more heartily rejoice in such a change than the devoted and estimable brethren who have faithfully and profitably labored in those agencies, when they were at all points deemed indispensable.

FINANCIAL AFFAIRS.

At the last annual meeting of the Society, a resolution, based upon the benevolence of warm and generous hearts, was passed, recommending that an effort be made to raise one hundred thousand dollars for the uses of the Board during the then current year. That amount was desirable and necessary, but, as the Treasurer's account shows, was not realized. In several individual cases, and by some churches, the recommendation was responded to nobly; but the country had not sufficiently recovered from the

recent financial revulsion to a
from the people generally ; an
yond the control of the Boa
rather than increase, our inco
things, the financial conditio
been more satisfactory than
covered, we trust, from the
past causes of depression.

The following is a general
condition on the 31st of Marc

Balance from last year's account...............	
Receipts from all sources during the year........	
Total amount of resources for the year...........	
Total amount of disbursements for the year.......	
Amount of cash in the treasury, April 1, 1860....	
Amount due missionaries, same date	
[illegible]	

an interest equal to that to be paid out. This amount, therefore, is not at present available for missionary purposes.

The balance of another legacy of $2975 was received in certificates of bank stock, which the Board think it more advantageous to hold than to dispose of at present, and is also unavailable till sold.

After making these deductions, there remains an available balance in the treasury of nearly $5000, by which the Board are unexpectedly in possession of means to commence some heavy operations at distant points, and appropriations have already been made for that purpose.

It may be interesting to learn, that more than 37 per cent. of the total amount of receipts into the treasury were paid in the months of February and March, which accounts for so large a surplus.

The discount from the total amount of resources paid in transacting the business of the year, including salaries and traveling expenses of agents and secretaries, printing, stationery, taxes on lands, insurance, discount on uncurrent funds, legal services, interest, rent, necessary incidentals, publication of the *Home Mission Record*, loss on uncurrent and counterfeit bank bills and bills of broken banks, was 20 per cent.

GRANDE LIGNE MISSION.

In the year 1849, a great change took place in the religious sentiments of the members of the Swiss mission in Canada. Until then, they had been Pedobaptists; but at that time they had become Baptists. In the near approach of a Canadian Winter, and trials consequent upon their pecuniary necessities, the change was announced to the Executive Board, with an appeal for sympathy and aid. These they promptly received, and since that period

to a great extent, those preach
our Society, have been subject
the connection complex, and so
cluding in its operations colport
cultural interests, with the erec
uses, all of which necessarily i
on Christian benevolence, the
the necessity of working by inc
in the estimation of the Chris
which they work is identical
plexity of the connection,
fuse the public mind.

MISSIONARY OPERATIONS.

The missionary operations of the year have been extended and improved. A greater number of places have been occupied, which, from their respective positions, promise rapid growth and importance, and able ministers have been appointed to labor in them as missionaries.

The increasing population of our country, and the growth of large towns at various points east and west of the Rocky Mountains, have caused many applications for aid from the Board. A deep religious feeling, also, in large sections of the Western States, has created an earnest desire among the people for the services of faithful preachers. The financial revulsion, which, three years ago, swept so fearfully over all the country; the destruction of harvests for two years, and, in some instances, three years in succession, and other providential visitations, fell distressingly upon many of the western churches, destroying their pecuniary resources, reducing multitudes to suffering, and entire communities to poverty; rendering them utterly unable to support their ministers. For these reasons, churches which had previously supported their pastors were compelled to seek the aid of the Society, as their only earthly hope of enjoying the institutions of the Gospel. Their applications could not be denied, but were met by the appointment of their pastors as missionaries, and by as liberal grants for their support as the state of the treasury admitted.

Experience has constantly taught us lessons of practical wisdom in the selection of places upon which our spiritual cultivation should be bestowed, and of ministers through whose agency that cultivation should be executed. Our system of Exploring Agencies is found to be well adapted

to these objects. Through tl
tions of the Board have been
sionary spirit has been kept al
what is far better, and a cause
God, is the evidence that the
the means employed. The L
his work in fields occupied by
souls have been won to Chris
the missionaries, published in
contains many details of the fr

SUMMARY OF LABOR

We present the following a
labors during the past year, an
they have been reported to us

The number of missionaries,
agents, who labored under the

and forty-four foreign Lutherans); the hopeful conversion of sixty-one others, who had not yet been baptized; the organization of fifty churches; the ordination of twenty-four ministers; the completion of seven church edifices, and the commencement of nineteen others.

The churches which were aided by the Society contributed to the usual objects of Christian benevolence $2,154 88, and for the support of the Gospel among themselves $16,985 10. Four churches aided by the Society, have acquired ability to sustain the Gospel without further dependence upon our treasury.

Many other items of labor, and their apparent results, have been reported, which are embodied in a note on this page,* and in the Missionary Table accompanying this report; to which we respectfully refer inquirers.

This summary we commend to the serious consideration of the Society and all its friends, believing that reasonable and candid minds will find abundant evidence of the usefulness of the Society, of the faithfulness and success of its missionaries, of the Divine approbation of their labors, of the necessity of continued effort in the same direction, of increased liberality on the part of individuals, and more fervent prayer by the friends of our Lord

---

* In addition to the above, the missionaries report the following:

Sermons preached	12,691
Lectures and addresses	1,337
Pastoral visits	28,278
Prayer and other meetings attended	9,073
Signatures to Temperance Pledge	365
Miles traveled in discharge of duty	124,581
Schools visited	467
Sabbath schools in the churches	156
Bible classes	112
Number of teachers	1,023
Number of scholars	8,391
Volumes in S. S. libraries	18,214
Stations where monthly concert of prayer is observed	56
Preparing for the ministry	41

Jesus, for the Divine blessing to rest upon the labors of the Society, its officers, its agents, and its missionaries.

PROSPECTIVE LABOR.

It was stated in the last annual report that Kansas was ready for the operations of the Society. Since then additional missionaries have entered that promising field, under appointments from the Board, and others would have followed if circumstances had favored our desire to send them. Valuable preliminary work has been performed there, and unless unexpected hindrances interpose, several important points in that territory will be added, ere long, to our list of missionary stations,* well supplied with pastors or itinerant preachers.

Recently, rich mineral deposits have been discovered in a spur of the Rocky Mountains, and thither a great [redacted] ka; and as soon as the secular interests of the country, generally, become more prosperous, and the tide of emigration begins again to flow in that direction, it will be necessary to add still others.

Circumstances seem to indicate the necessity of soon strengthening our mission in New Mexico. A missionary of special adaptation to that field should be sent out as soon as practicable; and it is desirable that he should be accompanied, or soon followed, by an assistant, to preach and teach a school, as necessity may require. The expense of the measure may be considerable, but the arrangement is none the less necessary or desirable on that account. The responsibilities of the Society in that territory originated in the special guidance of Divine Providence, and in no degree have they been removed from us. Many souls there have been rescued from the delusions of a false religion and converted to Christ; preachers of the Gospel have been raised up from among the converts; church edifices have been built; and every missionary report contains evidence of the progress of truth among the people. These things, instead of removing our responsibilities, serve to fasten them more strongly upon us. They can not be canceled in any way pleasing to God, or honorable to ourselves, but by vigorously following up our successes, already patent and hopeful, by the use of all the means we can consistently employ.

In the State of California there are upward of fifty Baptist churches, and about thirty ministers. The Society has had a few missionaries in that portion of the country from its first settlement by Americans, some of whom yet remain there. The great difficulty in inducing suitable men to enter that field in former years, the large expense attending the removal of missionary families, and their support after reaching the country, and certain untoward circumstances, which, at so great a distance, could not be averted, together with insufficient annual supplies for our treasury, have prevented more extensive arrangements for planting the cause of Christ there. During the past year, however, the renewal of our efforts has been urged and complied with. Three ministers residing in that State bear the commission of the Society, in as many places, and a fourth, residing at the East, has received an appointment, and will immediately proceed on his mission.* The number should be greater. Three or four other places should be supplied with experienced and able men, with as little delay as possible. Such men begin to look more favorably upon a residence in California than formerly; and it is to be hoped that sufficient means may be placed at the disposal of the Board to enable such as need aid to proceed, and enter at once upon evangelical work in that State.

Calls for missionaries are also renewed in Oregon. Baptist ministers are laboring at various points in that State, but at the two principal places, the commercial city and the seat of government, are churches destitute of pastors, whose loud cry now is, "come over and help us." The Board, understanding the importance of those places, have encouraged those churches to expect aid as soon as practicable.

At a yet more distant point, the territory of Washington, there is already a population of seven thousand souls, among whom are many members of Baptist churches, and not a single minister. Those people have a strong claim upon our Christian sympathy. They should be kindly remembered and cared for in their far-distant wanderings.

---

* He sailed with his family on the 5th of May.

This they ask of us. Two good, energetic men should be commissioned within the ensuing year to comply with the request.

ESTIMATES FOR THE NEW YEAR.

The adverse providences experienced by the people of the Western States the last three years leave but little ground of hope that many of the churches, now aided by the Society, will be able to dispense with that aid until a bountiful harvest shall have put them in possession of the means. If, therefore, our object were merely to prevent retrogression in our operations, our income for the ensuing year should be, at least, $55,000. But, we are persuaded, better things of the Society than such an object and things that accompany salvation to the multitudes who are interested in our movements. It is expected that we shall press toward the mark for the prize which is placed before us, the evangelization of North America; and that we so run that we may obtain.

Many missionaries in the valley of the Mississippi, find themselves oppressed with numerous claims for their services, at great distances from their proper stations. Settlements visited by them at first as out-stations, become populous and require increasing attention, which the missionaries find it beyond their power to bestow; and for their relief they urgently ask for additional laborers. Their requests are reasonable, and should be granted. The requisite amount to meet the necessities for the ensuing year, for this purpose is about $5000.

The estimated expense of placing the necessary number of missionaries at the more distant points, from New Mexico to the territory of Washington, and supporting them one year, is, at least, $20,000, making an aggregate of $80,000. As, however, there is an available balance in the treasury of some $5000, it follows that, to accomplish the objects proposed, it is necessary that the receipts of the Society from all sources, during the ensuing year, should be $75,000. While, therefore, the Board feel that, to prosecute the duties assigned to them with the greatest advantage, they would be justified in asking a larger amount, they can not withhold the expression of their opinion that to ask for less would be coming short of the duty which Divine Providence seems to require of us. The disposal of the subject we submit to every man's conscience in the sight of God.

The Executive Board, in surrendering to the Society the official trust conferred upon them a year ago, unite in fervent prayer for Divine wisdom to characterize all the deliberations and acts of the body.

By order of the Executive Board,

BENJAMIN M. HILL,

Corresponding Secretary.

EXPLANATION OF THE FOLLOWING MISSIONARY TABLE.

The parallel columns show—

1. The names of agents and missionaries, and the States in which they reside.
2. The post-office address of agents and missionaries.
3. The field of labor occupied by agents and missionaries.
4. The dates at which the appointments commence.
5. The number of months for which the appointments are respectively made.
6. The number of weeks' labor performed during the time reported.
7. The number of stations and out-stations supplied.*
8. The number of persons baptized by the missionaries within the time reported.
9. The number received by letter.
10. The number of scholars in Sabbath schools under the care of missionaries.†
11. The amount contributed to benevolent objects.
12. Additional facts reported concerning the state and progress of the churches.‡

---

* "Stations" are churches or villages regularly supplied on the Lord's day, and are indicated in column three. "Out-stations" are places where the missionaries have *stated* appointments for preaching more or less frequently.

† In new places, where Union schools are established, the number of scholars connected with Baptist families only are reported.

‡ In many cases, two lines appear for the same missionary, extending through all the columns. In such cases, the second line indicates a reappointment of the missionary, and the dates in column four determine to which appointment or year the statistics and remarks on the different lines belong. A particular notice of those dates is necessary to a proper understanding of certain changes which appear against the names of some individuals.

MISSIONARY TABLE.

POST-OFFICE ADDRESS.	FIELD OF LABOR.	Date of Commission.	Months Commis'd.	Weeks labor reported.	Stations supplied.	Baptized.	Received by Letter.	Schol's in S. S. & B. Class	Contrib. to Benevolent Objects.	
eal..............	Among the French in M....	Nov. 1, 1858	12	39	1	1	....	....	150 00	Labored a pa
....	" "	Nov. 1, 1859	12	13	....	..	....	....	100 00	More than us
e Ligne..........	Grande Ligne..............	Nov. 1, 1858	12	39	1	..	....	40	100 00	Revival amon
"	"	Nov. 1, 1859	12	13	....	..	....	55	25 00	A spirit of in
....	St. Pie and St. Marie...... ..	Nov. 1, 1858	12	39	....	6	....	....	88 90	Church at St
rie..............	St. Marie de Monnoir.......	Nov. 1, 1859	12	13	....	..	....	....	23 88	The priest in
iver..............	Pike River and Henryville...	Nov. 1, 1858	12	39	3	5	[illegible]	[illegible]	[illegible]	[illegible]
	" "									

Names of Agents and Missionaries.	Post-Office Address.	Field of Labor.	Date of Commission.	Months Commis'd.	Weeks labor reported.	Stations supplied.	Baptized.	Received by Letter.	Schol's in S. S. & B. Class	Contrib. to Benevolent Objects.	Additional Facts Reported.
MASSACHUSETTS.											
J. W. Parkhurst........	Newton Centre..........	Massachusetts......	April 1, 1859	12	52	....	..	....	....	......	Collecting agent for Massachusetts; and for Eastern Mass. and Rhode Island from Jan. 1.
J. V. Ambler..........	Lanesboro'....	Western Mass., Ct., and Eastern N. Y.	Jan. 1, 1860	3	13	....	..	....	....	......	Collecting agent for Western Mass., Eastern N. Y., and Connecticut.
CONNECTICUT.											
A. E. Denison...... ...	Clinton...............	Connecticut and R. Island..	April 1, 1859	12	39	....	..	....	....	......	Collecting agent for Ct. and R. I. Resigned from January 1.
NEW YORK.											
James S. Ladd.........	Williamsburgh.........	Southeast N. Y. & East N. J.	April 1, 1859	12	52	....	..	....	....	......	Coll. agent in Eastern N. Y. and Eastern N. J.
Charles Randall........	Auburn......	Central New York.........	April 1, 1859	12	52	....	..	....	....	......	Collecting agent in Central N. Y.
Charles Morton........	Corning...............	Western New York........	April 1, 1859	12	52	....	..	....	....	......	Collecting agent in Western N. Y.
NEW JERSEY.											
A. J. Hires............	Woodstown...........	Pennsylvania & South N. J..	April 1, 1859	12	52	....	..	....	...	......	Collecting agent in Pa. and Southern N. J.
PENNSYLVANIA.											
Demas L. Clouse.......	West Greenville........	West Greenville...........	Oct. 1, 1858	12	26	1	..	....	64	18 32	Encouraging progress.
"	" "	"	Oct. 1, 1859	12	26	....	4	1	58	......	Revival. Paid off entire debt on ch. edifice.
DELAWARE.											
Julius C. Haselhuhn...	Wilmington............	Germans in W. and vicinity.	Nov. 1, 1858	12	39	2	6	4	78	59 50	Church in peace and walking in love.
" " ...	"	" "	Nov. 1, 1859	12	13	....	1	4	77	35 00	Church revived. Pastor encouraged.

3

[redacted]

[illegible]	[illegible]	[illegible]	[illegible]	[illegible]	[illegible]	[illegible]	[illegible]
12	[illegible]	1		1	[illegible]	[illegible]	[illegible]
[illegible]	[illegible]	1			1		[illegible]
[illegible]	[illegible]			[illegible]	13	[illegible]	
12	[illegible]	[illegible]			[illegible]	[illegible]	
12	6	2	2	1	98	......	Many deaths and removals. Influence of the church increased. Pastor resigned.
12	30	3	3	2	168	19 50	Church paying their debt on meeting-house. Pastor leaves the field.
12	39	1	..	10	45	21 25	Finished meeting-house. Leaves the pastorate on account of the loss of one of his eyes.
12	39	3	1	7	116	3 00	Church more than doubled during the year. Pastor resigned.
12	13	2	..	1	59	......	Purchased a lot for meeting-house and will proceed in its erection.
12	....	....	..	....	....	......	A new appointment.
12	43	....	..	....	....	......	Exploring agent in Indiana.
3	....	....	..	....	....	......	
12	26	1	..	....	16	8 40	Congregation increasing.
12	26	....	..	....	60	......	Church united and harmonious.
12	26	4	11	3	90	31 00	Revival.
12	26	....	11	....	....	......	Revival at an out-station.
12	13	....	1	7	310	50 00	The Association will hereafter support a missionary without further aid.

NAMES OF AGENTS AND MISSIONARIES.	POST-OFFICE ADDRESS.	FIELD OF LABOR.	Date of Commission.	Months Commis'd.	Weeks labor reported.	Stations supplied.	Baptized.	Received by Letter.	Schol's in S. S. & B. Class.	Cont. to Benevolent Objects.	ADDITIONAL FACTS REPORTED.
J. L. McLeod	Columbia City	Columbia City	Dec. 1, 1858	12	39	3	..	4	77	29 50	Church active and efficient. Sunday school large, and in a prosperous condition.
" "	" "	" "	Dec. 1, 1859	12	13	....	4	5	....	3 00	Revival.
William M. Simons	Plymouth	Plymouth	May 1, 1859	12	39	4	2	7	8	117 50	Wife deceased. Need a house of worship.
James Goodrich	Huntington	Huntington	Nov. 1, 1859	12	13	3	1	....	50	......	Prospects encouraging.
J. H. Dunlap	Roanoke	Huntington Association	Jan. 1, 1860	12	13	5	..	....	....	75 00	Nothing special.
Chas. Ager	Goshen	Goshen and vicinity	M'ch 1, 1860	12	....	....	..	....	....	......	A new appointment. Report not due.
ILLINOIS.											
Irenius Foulon	Highland	Among the French at Sugar Creek, etc.,	Nov. 1, 1858	12	39	2	11	....	24	......	Building a meeting-house.
" "	"	"	Nov. 1, 1859	12	13	....	..	....	30	......	Embarrassed in building their meeting-house.
F. O. Nilsson	Rock Island	Scandinavians at Rock Island etc.,	Nov. 1, 1859	6	13	3	..	2	20	......	Putting things in order among the churches of his countrymen. Churches at Rock Island and Moline revived.
John H. Kruger	Peoria	Germans in Peoria	Feb. 1, 1860	12	....	....	..	....	....	......	A new appointment. Report not due.
WISCONSIN.											
C. M. Fuller	Delavan	Wisconsin	April 1, 1859	12	26	....	..	....	....	......	Exploring agent in Wisconsin.
James Delany	Horicon	Horicon and vicinity	Jan. 1, 1859	12	39	4	3	2	22	21 00	Some encouraging indications.
" "	"	" "	Jan. 1, 1860	12	13	....	..	1	....	7 00	Church revived.
Alex. Hamilton	Appleton	Appleton and vicinity	Dec. 1, 1858	12	39	1	2	2	66	......	Finished meeting-house. Church in encouraging circumstances.
" "	"	" "	Dec. 1, 1859	12	13	....	1	1	72	10 00	Sunday school interesting and profitable.
A. Gibson	River Falls	River Falls, etc.,	June 1, 1858	12	13	7	4	1	75	10 00	Nothing special.
" "	"	" "	June 1, 1859	12	26	....	1	1	....	......	Revival, converts not yet received into the church.
Abner Lull	Oshkosh	Oshkosh	Jan. 1, 1859	12	13	1	..	....	55	......	On account of a great fire, the church not able to sustain him. Leaves the field.
Theodore Ulbricht	Milwaukee	Germans in Milwaukee	Nov. 1, 1858	12	39	7	4	....	63	10 57	Building a meeting-house. Prospects very encouraging.
" "	"	" "	Nov. 1, 1859	12	13	....	..	....	52	4 00	Finished meeting-house.
I. P. Agenbroad	Prairie du Chien	Prairie du Chien	April 1, 1859	12	5	1	..	....	....	......	Resigned.

[redacted]

[illegible]							
12	5	1	..	..	40	.....	Leaves the field on account of ... health.
12	10	2	..	....	47	.....	Building a meeting house. Meetings of late more interesting.
12	15	...	...	....	72	.....	Progressing.
12	39	1	1	2	80	8 00	Exchanged their church property which will relieve them from pecuniary embarrassment. Pastor leaves the field.
12	39	3	5	12	51	27 00	Encouraging success and progress. Pastor retires from the field.
12	39	1	1	2	52	.....	Church not united. People pressed by the hard times.
12	26	3	1	2	30	.....	Wife deceased. Can not complete meeting-house for want of funds.
12	13	4	1	1	....	.....	Building a meeting house.
12	26	1	..	....	42	4 00	Church has been in a low state. System being introduced and good results hoped for.
12	....	....	....	....	....	.....	A new appointment. Report not due.
12	26	3	5	....	250	25 60	Revival at an out station.
12	13	1	..	....	38	5 00	Asks no further aid.
12	13	3	..	1	158	.....	
12	39	2	8	....	150	47 10	Revival at an out station. Leaves the field. Health of self and wife suffering.

NAMES OF AGENTS AND MISSIONARIES.	POST-OFFICE ADDRESS.	FIELD OF LABOR.	Date of Commission.	Months Commis'd.	Weeks labor reported.	Stations supplied.	Baptized.	Received by Letter.	Schol's in S. S. & B. Class	Cont. to Benevolent Objects.	ADDITIONAL FACTS REPORTED.
L. M. Newell	Wawkon	Wawkon	June 1, 1858	12	13	5	..	....	33	2 00	
Thomas M. Ind	Burlington	S. Burlington	May 1, 1858	12	13	1	2	2	169	......	
"	"	"	May 1, 1859	12	39	....	7	7	....	7 50	Sunday school in a prosperous condition. Religious declension in the city.
George Scott	Strawberry Point	Strawberry Point	May 1, 1858	12	13	9	2	1	137	......	Striving to preserve their meeting-house.
"	"	"	Jan. 1, 1860	12	13	6	3	4	....	......	
Charles E. Brown	Vernon Springs	Vernon Springs	Aug. 1, 1858	12	26	1	5	....	66	.....	
"	"	" & other places.	Aug. 1, 1859	12	26	3	..	....	40	44 88	Can not build a meeting-house until times are easier. Congregations never larger. Repaired the room in which the church meet. Organized two churches on his field.
P. P. Shirley	Le Clair Centre	Le Clair Centre	June 1, 1858	12	13	6	2	2	206	......	Need no further aid.
J. M. Coggeshall	Wapello	Wapello	July 1, 1858	12	13	3	16	1	142	......	Revival.
"	"	"	July 1, 1858	12	33	4	..	....	....	2 00	Resigned.
G. G. Edwards	Toledo	Toledo	Sept. 1, 1858	12	26	5	3	2	86	......	Need a meeting-house.
"	"	"	Jan. 1, 1860	12	13	4	8	3	60	......	Revival.
J. F. Childs	Oskaloosa	Oskaloosa	Aug. 1, 1858	12	26	3	2	5	132	......	Sunday school benefited by books from the East.
"	"	"	Aug. 1, 1859	12	26	...	12	1	....	4 00	Revival at an out-station.
O. A. Holmes	Webster City	Webster City	Nov. 1, 1858	12	39	3	11	2	55	5 00	Prospects encouraging.
"	"	"	Nov. 1, 1859	12	13	4	..	....	....	......	Increased encouragement.
A. G. Eberhart	Waterloo	Waterloo	Sept. 1, 1858	12	26	3	30	8	122	20 00	Congregation large.
"	"	"	Sept. 1, 1859	12	26	2	..	5	145	12 00	Encouraging indications.
S. H. Worcester	Ottumwa	Ottumwa	Nov. 1, 1858	12	39	4	..	5	50	6 00	Church in an improved condition.
"	"	"	Nov. 1, 1859	12	13	5	4	2	....	53 15	Prayer meetings give encouragement.
Joshua Currier	Monroe	Central Association	Dec. 1, 1858	12	29	8	14	6	....	53 50	Revival at two stations.
Alvah Bush	Strawberry Point	Strawberry Point	May 1, 1859	6	26	4	2	3	110	13 00	Church burdened by debt.
A. H. Starkweather	Lyons	Lyons and vicinity	July 1, 1859	12	39	3	3	2	72	......	Revival at an out-station.
John Fulton	Independence	Independence	Oct. 1, 1859	12	26	1	3	7	....	......	An increased religious interest.
A. W. Russell	Wintersett	Wintersett	Oct. 1, 1859	12	26	3	..	....	40	12 40	Building a meeting-house. An increase of religious interest. Embarrassed for funds for meeting-house.
F. D. Rickerson	Grinnell	Grinnell	Nov. 1, 1859	12	13	2	..	....	42	......	Encouraging progress.
L. L. Frisk	Mineral Ridge	Swede Bend, etc.	Oct. 1, 1859	12	26	7	1	2	....	5 00	
Morgan Edwards	Denmark	Burlington & Keokuk Assoc.	Oct. 1, 1859	6	26	5	18	7	....	100 00	Meeting-house nearly completed at one station. Revival at another station.
Wm. A. Eggleston	"	Denmark	Oct. 1, 1859	12	26	3	4	2	50	......	Been sick. Health very poor.
Isaac Butterfield	Davenport	Davenport	Oct. 1, 1859	12	26	1	..	77	350	30 00	The two churches in Davenport united.
U. R. Walton	Cedar Falls	Cedar Falls	Nov. 1, 1859	12	13	3	11	9	40	16 51	Spiritual condition of the church much improved.

Months Commiss'd.	Weeks labor reported.	
		Church have experienced great trials, but have preserved the order of the Gospel, and are now strongly united.
		A new appointment.
		A new appointment.
		Discipline been necessary. Congregations well sustained.
		A reappointment. Report not due.
		Exploring agent for that State.

Names of Agents and Missionaries.	Post-Office Address.	Field of Labor.	Date of Commission.	Months Commiss'd.	Weeks labor reported.	Stations supplied.	Baptized.	Received by Letter.	School's in S. S. & B. Class.	Contrib. in Benevolent Objects.	Additional Facts Reported.
Erastus Westcott	Rochester	Rochester	Aug. 1, 1858	12	26	1	12	7	87	27 50	Revival.
" "	"	"	Aug. 1, 1859	12	26	....	1	7	....	2 30	Several dismissed and others died. The remaining members active and not discouraged.
William C. Phillips	St. Cloud	St. Cloud	May 1, 1858	12	13	2	1	2	48	10 25	Congregation large.
" "	"	"	May 1, 1859	12	39	....	..	....	45	......	Struggling to inclose meeting-house. Embarrassments and difficulties in the church.
George W. Fuller	Chatfield	Chatfield	June 1, 1858	12	13	5	..	4	33	3 00	Embarrassed by debt on meeting-house and scarcity of money. A destitute field around him. Wife deceased.
" "	"	"	June 1, 1859	12	39	....	..	4	55	15 00	
J. F. Wilcox	Northfield	Northfield	Aug. 1, 1858	12	26	5	4	6	50	......	
" "	"	"	Aug. 1, 1859	12	26	3	..	1	68	......	Need a meeting-house.
A. M. Torbet	Taylor's Falls	Taylor's Falls	May 1, 1859	12	39	2	3	1	100	......	Organized a church at his station.
A. Smith Lyon	Newport	Newport	June 1, 1858	12	13	2	..	....	69		Church in a healthy and hopeful state.
" "	"	"	June 1, 1859	12	39	3	2	....	45	21 50	
Isaac Waldron	Cannon Falls	Zumbrota and Cannon Falls	Nov. 1, 1858	12	39	5	6	6	143	......	Revival at one station. Organized a church at another.
" "	Stanton	" "	Nov. 1, 1859	12	13	4	2	1	100	... ..	Churches prospering.
H. B. Slater	Saratoga	Saratoga	Oct. 1, 1858	12	26	6	..	1	72	......	Progressing, and is encouraged.
" "	"	"	Oct. 1, 1859	12	26	....	..	2	30	......	Revival at an out-station.
Moses Heath	Belle Plaine	Belle Plaine and Jordan	April 1, 1859	12	52	5	18	....	125	1 64	Revival at Jordan and at an out-station. Organized a church at Belle Plaine.
Lyman Palmer	Anoka	Anoka and vicinity	Sept. 1, 1858	12	26	3	3	2	60	......	Embarrassed by debt on meeting-house.
E. F. Gurney	Austin	Austin	M'ch 1, 1859	12	52	7	..	2	....	1 00	Declension in religious matters.
" "	"	"	M'ch 1, 1860	12	....	....	..	....	....	......	
R. F. Sheldon	Carimona	Carimona	April 1, 1859	12	30	3	2	....	60	......	Removed from the field.
R. H. Weeks	Monticello	Monticello	Nov. 1, 1859	12	11	5	..	4	....	......	A new field. Some encouragements, but need a meeting house.
S. S. Utter	Shakapee	Shakapee	Nov. 1, 1859	12	13	4	..	1	...	......	Organized a church at Chaska.
A. P. Graves	Lake City	Lake City	June 1, 1859	12	39	3	1	14	137	3 00	Finished meeting-house.
J. R. Ash	Mankato	Mankato and vicinity	Aug. 1, 1859	12	26	3	2	9	....	......	Organized a church at Mankato, where prospects are encouraging.
M. W. Hopkins	High Forrest	Hamilton and High Forrest	Jan. 1, 1860	12	13	7	12	....	....	......	Some encouragements.
O. O. Stearns	Winona	Winona	Dec. 1, 1859	12	13	2	..	1	85	......	Church embarrassed by debt on their meeting-house.
Elijah S. Smith	Wilton	Blooming Grove and Wilton	Jan. 1, 1860	12	13	4	..	...	12	......	People anxious for the Gospel, but can do but little for the support of a preacher.
D. L. Babcock	St. Charles	St. Charles and Utica	April 1, 1860	12	....	....	..	....	....	......	A new appointment.

[redacted]

12	52	3	1	1	75	12 &	General Itinerant for Kansas
12	...	...	...	...	...	......	
12	50	6	2	13	95	15 80	An unusual religious interest in his field.
12	39	1	1	5	75	......	Their house of worship become too strait for them, and need a larger house.
12	26	1	2	36	70	125 00	Religious interest encouraging. People very eager to hear the Gospel.
12	24	3	..	2	47	93 32	An increased religious interest among his people.
12	13	8	9	7	...	16 25	A new field. Been sick.
12	26	...	2	....	....	.....	Persecutors using more policy, but none the less annoying.
12	26	....	1	....	....	......	Preaches to attentive listeners, and sometimes to large congregations.
12	26	....	2	...	25	......	Baptized two persons and was mobbed at Manzana.
12	29	...	..	....	....	......	Accomplishing much good by teaching the young.

NAMES OF AGENTS AND MISSIONARIES.	POST-OFFICE ADDRESS.	FIELD OF LABOR.	Date of Commission.	Months Commis'd.	Weeks labor rep.rted.	Stations supplied.	Baptized.	Received by Letter.	Schol's in S. S. & B. Class.	Cont. to Benevolent Objects.	ADDITIONAL FACTS REPORTED.
Jose Senun	Albuquerque	Laguna	Oct. 1, 1858	12	26	....	..	....	....	......	Bitter persecution at Laguna. One converted Catholic died in consequence of excitement produced by persecution.
" "	"	"	Oct. 1, 1859	12	26	....	..	....	....	......	People driven by whips to Roman Catholic churches. The Missionary expects to be killed.
Jose Maria Chaves	Peralto	Peralto, etc.	April 1, 1859	12	52	....	..	....	....	......	Has much to encourage him.
Jose Santos Tayes	Socorro	Socorro, etc.	April 1, 1859	12	52	....	..	....	....	......	Labored with the people at his house, and by the way-side and at their houses.
Antonio Jose Garcia	Los Jarelles	Mongano, etc.	April 1, 1859	12	52	....	..	....	....	......	
Blas Chaves	Albuquerque		Oct. 1, 1858	12	26	....	..	....	....	......	Has an easy access to the people. Many give respectful attention to the Gospel, but some revile.
" "	Santa Fe	Santa Fe	Oct. 1, 1859	12	26	....	..	....	....	......	
CALIFORNIA.											
J. B. Saxton	San Francisco	San Francisco	July 1, 1858	12	9	1	2	....	90	......	Church dissolved.
" "	Oakland	Oakland & Brooklyn	June 1, 1859	12	39	2	7	8	66	......	Painting and improving meeting-house. The cause in the State in a more prosperous condition.
H. Holcombe Rhees	Marysville	Marysville	Jan 1, 1860	12	13	1	..	8	....	......	Need a meeting house. No Sunday school for the want of a room in which to hold it.
C. W. Rees	Petaluma	Petaluma	M'ch 1, 1860	12	....	....	..	....	....	......	A new appointment. Report not due.
Saml. Cornelius, Jr.				12	....	....	..	....	....	......	
NEW GRANADA.											
P. B. Livingston	San Andreas	San Andreas	April 1, 1859	12	52	....	1	....	141	....	Been very sick.

STATE CONVENTIONS

AND

GENERAL ASSOCIATIONS IN THE UNITED STATES,

[illegible] Corresponding Secretaries, the Time and Place of their Meetings [illegible], and amount of Receipts into their [illegible].

[illegible]	[illegible]	[illegible]	PLACE OF NEXT ANNIVERSARY.	Time of Anniversary.	Number of Missionaries.	Amount of Receipts for Dom. Miss. in 1859.
		[illegible]	Augusta	June [illegible]	27	$45[illegible]0 93
		[illegible]	Newport	Oct. 17	14	1542 67
		M[illegible]	[illegible]	Oct. [illegible]	2	[illegible] 72
		[illegible]	[illegible]	Oct. 31	44	[illegible] 31
		[illegible]	Providence	April 24	12	1122 [illegible]
		[illegible]	New Haven	June 12	9	16[illegible] [illegible]
		[illegible]	Albion	Oct. [illegible]	46	[illegible]442 10
		[illegible]	[illegible]	Oct. [illegible]	16	24[illegible]1 70
		[illegible]phia	Waverly		[illegible]0	[illegible]72 13
		[illegible]	W[illegible] D.C.	Nov. 11	42	3762 94
[illegible]		[illegible]mond	Staunton	May 31	58	11221 47
North Carolina	[illegible] Residence [illegible]	Warrenton		Oct. 31	5	1878 12

[redacted]

AGGREGATE CONTRIBUTIONS

FROM ALL THE STATES SINCE 1832.

STATES.	Total Amount to 1850.	1851–1855.	1856.	1857.	1858.	1859.	1860.
Canada	4,139 49	1,063 80	143 75	450 36	446 44	512 00	601 60
Maine	3,214 40	1,053 22	102 44	82 09	27 37	82 51	60 12
New Hampshire	4,874 52	6,519 01	1,608 22	1,627 09	1,377 14	2,157 71	1,744 89
Vermont	4,072 96	3,741 54	1,186 34	967 44	860 69	1,219 93	771 67
Massachusetts	41,291 55	43,460 77	10,467 62	10,176 01	11,620 96	10,667 47	10,639 29
Rhode Island	12,297 02	9,734 31	2,560 07	1,768 88	1,265 58	993 76	4,603 99
Connecticut	17,660 91	16,391 14	4,047 46	3,840 83	3,069 55	3,001 38	3,430 20
New York	100,644 16	79,584 59	14,796 88	14,855 15	13,050 00	13,615 68	20,763 89
New Jersey	14,990 78	15,414 29	2,985 34	2,498 44	2,637 69	3,427 97	4,519 63
Pennsylvania	9,449 57	12,388 36	2,507 89	1,894 36	2,277 41	3,512 17	3,354 30
Delaware	603 50	740 70	103 75	183 04	51 00	124 00	24 50
Maryland	2,055 06	15 50	200 00	......	......	......	......
District of Columbia	993 12	211 31	......	8 22	......	......	......
Ohio	1,369 57	7,616 25	2,708 28	1,665 00	864 54	398 28	946 61
Michigan	1,719 95	3,375 32	179 23	198 72	284 81	299 66	276 32
Indiana	104 86	7,142 33	656 72	1,317 29	1,013 79	456 88	812 62
Illinois	4,348 55	8,515 80	1,700 17	150 86	124 54	59 50	32 08
Wisconsin	378 79	1,802 48	418 43	179 19	186 06	667 49	476 47
Iowa	562 72	1,456 36	573 12	383 92	744 96	811 46	511 46
Minnesota	....	605 91	328 25	577 07	647 25	909 90	1,397 78
Nebraska	....	....	......	150 00	100 00	6 00	23 98
Kansas	....	....	......	5 00	98 00	40 15	649 17
Missouri	266 82	292 00	......	29 00	15 00	......	......
Kentucky	304 38	42 25	......	......	......	......	......
Virginia	9,325 15	28 75	......	7 00	......	6 02	......
North Carolina	5,391 69	....	......	......	......	......	......
South Carolina	8,498 10	30 00	30 00	20 00	......	......	......
Georgia	10,861 20	30 00	......	40 00	......	......	......
Alabama	493 08	30 00	......	......	......	......	......
Florida	172 82	....	......	......	......	......	......
Mississippi	1,399 66	....	......	......	......	......	......
Tennessee	486 10	....	......	......	......	......	......
Louisiana	79 00	....	......	......	......	1 00	......
Arkansas	69 20	....	......	......	......	......	......
Texas	....	....	......	......	......	......	......
California	....	515 50	105 00	......	10 00	25 00	.....
Oregon	....	299 95	44 98	17 60	10 00	......	......
New Mexico	....	183 90	......	30 00	5 00	......	......
U. S. Government	....	....	435 00	......	......	......	......
New Granada	....	....	39 60	25 20	......	......	......
Unknown	....	....	......	139 00	......	1 00	......
Aggregate for each period	262,618 68	222,285 33	47,928 54	43,286 76	41,707 82	42,997 02	55,640 47

LIST OF

PAID TO THE SOCIETY

1834 *Dea. Josiah Penfield, Savannah, Ga., per Rev
1835 Mrs. Clarissa Long, Shelburne, Mass., per W.
" William Powers, Hebron, N. H., per Rev. I.
" Miss Maria Curtis, Southbridge, Mass., per R
" Mrs. Jemima Elliott, Hampton, Ct., per Rev.
1836 Mrs. Betsey Sprague, Attleboro', Mass., per
" Robert Rodgers, Newport, R. I.................
" Ebenezer Boyd, Providence, R. I.............
1839 Mrs. Abigail Marshall, New York, per Mr. Sch
" Mrs. Margaret Pugsley, Dutchess Co., N. Y.,
" Mrs. Irene Coats, New York, per Alfred Deck
1841 Mrs. Elizabeth G. Moore, Hartford, Ct., per J.
1842 Nathaniel Tucker, Milton, Mass., per W. D. T
1843 Mrs. Margaret Martin, Montgomery, N. Y.,
" Miss Cynthia M. Wright, Suffield, Ct., per H.
1844 Mr. Zephaniah Eddy, New Bedford, Mass., pe
" Mr. Josiah Kendall, Groton, Mass., per F. E.
" Miss Jane McCall, Society Hill, S. C., per John
" Miss Lydia Sweetzer, South Reading, Mass., p
" Mrs. Elizabeth Griffin, New York, per one of

1849	John J. Martin, Montgomery, N. Y., per M. Bookstaver, Executor	$1000 00
"	Mrs. Martha Howe, West Boylston, Mass., per Messrs. E. J. Howe & Co.	50 00
"	A. H. Reed, Sweden, N. Y., per Rev. D. Searl	13 00
"	Asa H. Truman, Owego, N. Y., per E. Truman, Executor	248 00
1850	George D. James, Amenia, N. Y., J. K. Mead and N. Rose, Executors	100 00
"	John Everett, Manchester, Mich, per F. Everett	70 00
"	Jacob Whitman, Belvidere, Ill., in part, per N. Crosby, Esq	160 00
"	Jonas Taylor, Boston, Mass	12 50
"	Miss Rebecca Thompson, Amenia, N. Y., per A. B. Capwell, Esq	801 00
"	Joanna Minot, Boston, Mass., per E. Mears and I. Parker, Executors	100 00
"	Claudius F. Brown, Arkwright, N. Y., per David Barrell	150 00
"	Miss Anna Roe, Egremont, Mass., per R. B. Brown, Executor	50 00
1851	David Schauber, Burnt Hills, N. Y., per J. and D. M. Schauber, Executors	10 00
"	Woolcott Griffin, Gouverneur, N. Y., per O. L. Barnum, Executor	100 00
"	Joseph Flanders, Brooklyn, N. Y., per Mrs. Eliza A. Flanders and Benj. Flanders	500 00
"	William Williams, New York, per John Allen, Executor	400 00
"	Ely Wiley, South Reading, Mass	50 00
1852	Miss Pharozene C. Kelly, Hopkinton, N. H., per John Page	50 00
"	Jonathan W. Ford, Boston, Mass	100 00
"	Theron Fisk, Warsaw, N. Y., in advance	2500 00
"	Joshua A. Burke, Brooklyn, N. Y., per Messrs. E. and W. A. Burke	350 00
"	Eliza Skaats, New York, in part, per G. N. Bleecker, Executor	1000 00
"	Barnum M. Howard, Sweden, N. Y., per H. M. Howard, Executor	20 00
1853	Alanson Stewart, Liberty, N. Y., per W. W. Murphy	5 00
"	Mrs. Sarah B. Pierce, Middleboro', Mass	100 00
"	Arnold Whipple, Providence, R. I., per Mrs. P. Whipple, Executrix	200 00
"	Mrs. Fanny McGillvreay, Brookline, N.H. (Annuity), per H. A. Daniels, Administrator	40 00
"	Mrs Lucretia Goddard, Worcester, Mass., per Hon. I. Davis, Executor	300 00
"	P. F. Brayton, Providence, R. I., per A. K. Brayton and Rev. J. Brayton, in addition	594 87
"	Mrs. Elizabeth Gale, Washington, D.C	50 00
1854	Edward Rodgers, Chester, Ill, per Rev. M. B. Kelly	5 00
"	Miss Esther Ann Blakely, Pawlet, Vt., per Rev. J. J. Peck	73 00
"	Daniel Cummings, Chelsea, Mass., per Mr. Eaton, Executor	1000 00
"	Mrs. Mary Leuce, Bristol, R. I., per S. F. Baars	7 50
"	D. Valentine, Washington, Pa., per H. W. Wilson, Executor	230 80
"	Willis L. Eaton, East Weare, N. H., per J. L. Eaton, Executor	100 00
"	Asa Read, Attleboro', Mass., per Amos M. Read, Executor	1000 00
"	Friend Humphrey, Albany, per his son, Executor	106 30
"	George Corbett, Worcester, Mass	8 00
"	Mrs. Abby Arnold, Centreville, R. I., per Wm. Arnold	95 00
"	Garrat N. Bleecker, New York, per E. Cauldwell and W. F. Van Wagner, Executors	6000 00
"	Eunice Shepherdson, Belleville, N. Y	70 00
"	Mrs. Mary Johnson, Albany, N. Y., per Chas. Pohlman	10 00
"	Mrs. Olive Stowell, Le Roy, N. Y., per R. Bell	10 00
"	David Trull, Lowell, per J. Fox	542 00
1855	Roger Pegg, New York, per Mr. Coe, Executor	100 00
"	John Goodell, Jr., Woodstock, N. Y., in part, per Mrs. Maria H. Goodell, Executrix	268 26
"	Mrs. Frances Thompson, Alabama, N. Y	50 00
"	Miss Mercy Hayden, Grafton, Mass., per Rev. J. Smith	20 00
"	Joseph D. Murray, New Hope, Pa	30 00
"	W. S. Ward, Salem, Mass	100 00
"	Mrs. Lucy Bushnell, Monticello, N. Y., per Rev. Samuel White	50 00
"	W. Littlefield, Belleville, N. Y	30 00
"	Mary E. Bennett, Ludlow, Vt., per Rev. N Cudworth, Executor	111 00
"	Margaret Sherwood, New York, per E. J. Mattocks, Executor	50 00
"	Linus Austin, Akron, O	27 00
"	Mrs. —— Nelson, Peoria, Ill	3 00
"	Mrs. Margaret Davies, New York, per John M. Davies	20 00
"	Abijah Porter, Danvers, Mass., per Rev. J. W. Parkhurst	500 00

[illegible] Stephen A. Moore [illegible]	$400 00
[illegible] Albert R[illegible]	200 00
[illegible]	50 00
[illegible] Executor	327 24
[illegible] Nathan Botters, Executor	140 00
[illegible] P. B. Spear [illegible]	200 00
Rev. J. W. [illegible]	8 00
[illegible]	50 00
[illegible] Executor	50 00
[illegible] Executor	25 00
[illegible]	100 00
[illegible]	25 00
[illegible]	355 47
[illegible] Executor	1431 24
[illegible] Kelton, Executor	132 00
[illegible] A. M[illegible], Executor	219 38
[illegible] Executor	100 00
[illegible] Snow, Executor	15 00
[illegible] J. J. Babcock	4 75
[illegible]	100 00
[illegible] George Cum[illegible], Executor	3391 [illegible]
[illegible] W[illegible], Executor	10 00
[illegible] M[illegible]	100 00
[illegible] Stanley, Executor	50 00
[illegible] Brown and Joseph Be[illegible], Executors	402 13
[illegible] per A. L. Daniels	415 00
[illegible] Rev. H. [illegible]	149 47
[illegible] Stephen, Executor	2037 00

[redacted]

1859	John Tustin, Chester Springs, Pa.	$10 00
"	Ezra Reynolds, Benton, Pa., in part, Saml. Manchester, Executor	25 00
"	Henry Case, Sweden, N. Y., Rev. Z. Case, Executor	150 00
"*	Rev. Jacob Drake, Delaware, Ohio	544 22
"	Miss Mary True, Plainfield, N. H., Reuben True, Executor	200 00
"	Lucy A. Roberts, Cromwell, Ct., Mrs. Hubbard, Executrix	50 00
"	An aged sister, Thetford, Vt., per W. W. Baker	20 00
"	Lucy F. Gray, Chelmsford, Mass	60 92
"	Isaac Morse, New Woodstock, N. Y	50 00
"	Mrs. Mary E. Arnold, West Medway, Mass., per Rev. E. C. Messenger	100 00
"	Junia Freeman, Rushford, N. Y., E. B. Freeman, Executor	53 50
"	Thomas Wakefield, Waterville, N. Y., Henry Tower, Executor	200 00
"	Anna Crossman, Sheldon, Vt., Hon. George Green, Executor	65 00
"	Betsey Harrimon, Georgetown, Mass	152 53
"	Elijah Withington, Morrisania, N. Y., Saml. Wilde and others, Executors	100 00
1860	Tirza E. Gilman, Sanbornton, N. H., Benj. N. Smith, Executor	50 00
"	Rufus Fiske, Cambridge, Mass., Susan Fiske, Executrix	10 00
"	Mrs. J. W. Putnam, Chicopee Falls, Mass., Rev. R. K. Bellamy, Executor	300 00
"	Miss Phebe Arnold, Jay, N. Y	2300 00
"	Margaretha Medera, New York, Rev. Thomas T. Devan, Executor	2500 00
"	Harvey Tracy, Tunbridge, Vt., per Rev. Leonard Tracy	50 00
"	Miss Sarah Bartholomew, Pa., Jonathan Roberts, Executor	47 50

IMPORTANT WHEN WILLS ARE MADE.

LEGACIES are sometimes diverted from the purposes of testators on account of technical informalities especially in the devising clause. The form of bequest, which has been approved by high legal authority, and to which we solicit the careful attention of those friends who kindly intend to place the Society among their legatees, as one which, if followed, will secure to us the favors intended, may be found on the second page of cover.

FORM OF A BEQUEST TO THE SOCIETY.

I give and bequeath to the American Baptist Home Mission Society, formed in New York, in the year eighteen hundred and thirty-two, the sum of —— dollars, for the purposes of said Society.

ADDRESS OF G. C.

ON A MOTION TO ACCEPT

MR. CHAIRMAN,—I rise for the purpos
report just read; and, in doing so, I beg
for devout and grateful thanksgiving t
ments which have marked the efforts of y
edge of Jesus, but also for the gratifying
the report of your treasurer indicates.

It is surely a matter for profound and
ing the temporal reverses which for the p
ern and Northwestern States, whereby
elevated on the wave of prosperity, were
Christ and the promotion of his cause
their possessions and reduced from comp
notwithstanding *this*, the receipts of the
exceed, *by several thousand dollars*, thos
that, in the vigorous extension of her be

toward you, and asked for help. The appeal was not made in vain. Can a mother forget her helpless child? A cordial response was given, and to-day, despite the hopes and predictions of her malicious foes, surviving the assaults of the gates of hell, and the enemies of the cross, with a devoted pastor, "whose praise is in all the churches," she stands a firm and united brotherhood, welded together by common trials, persecutions, and sufferings, to battle valiantly for the truth, and to carry forward with resistless vigor the standard of the Lord Jesus.

What has been the history of this church, thus sustained by the timely aid of your Society, is, in part, the history of hundreds of churches scattered throughout the Western and Northwestern States. These vines of the Lord are yearly taking deeper and firmer root, they are beginning to send out "their boughs unto the sea, and their branches unto the river;" and, ere long, they will be laden with thick clusters of precious fruit, and repay a thousand-fold the abundant care you have bestowed upon them.

But, brethren in Christ, while with joyful lips I thank God to-day "for the great things he hath done for us, whereof we are glad," I, nevertheless, mourn that we have not yet attained to the full measure of our duty. Comparatively large as that sum is, what is sixty-two thousand dollars toward meeting the multiplied demands constantly made upon us? Fathers and mothers in Israel, your sons and daughters are weekly leaving the cherished scenes of childhood for new and untrodden fields, where the "joyful sound" is rarely, if ever heard. They need, and must have, the Gospel—a pure and unadulterated Gospel—and their appeals come to you with an impressiveness and power which can not and must not be denied. Instead of sixty-two thousand dollars, one hundred thousand dollars is the very *smallest sum*, which ought annually to be expended on the promising fields, and we are faithless to our great trust if we do not largely increase our efforts for sowing the Gospel seed upon soil, which is not only fully prepared for its reception, but which gives such cheering signs of yielding an ample harvest.

In the disposition and ability of my brethren rightly to comprehend the signs of the times, I have the firmest faith, and I can not doubt, but that we shall enter more efficiently than ever upon the great work which God has given us to do.

REP

Of a Committee appointed by the Board t which moneys contributed to assist the n worship, may be made available to the Cl tist Home Mission Society.

The Committee would suggest:

That, perhaps, in a majority of instanc guishing a debt upon their meeting-house immediate payment is demanded, the chur meet the demand, or even the high rate of save their property.

Most such churches could pay their be obtained, or they be relieved from

In view of these facts, we suggest—

First, That this Board advise churche or paying a debt, to refer the case to a co shall examine and report if there is a w such advice as the state of things requires

Comparatively few churches, however, are able to build their *first* house of worship without aid from abroad, or else incurring liabilities which unforeseen events may render exceedingly embarrassing, and, perhaps, serious.

Your Committee would, therefore, say that, in their judgment, it is alike the dictate of the truest benevolence and the soundest Christian economy for our churches to respond favorably to applications for aid from abroad, from churches which, in consequence of events alike unforeseen and beyond their control, find themselves in danger of losing their houses of worship—houses dear to them, not more by the labor already expended, and the *hopes* which have been inwrought in the structure, than by the *fact* that the question of life and death, or the prosperity of the church, is, to all human appearance, to be decided by the fate of their house.

But we must all know that there are sometimes presented for assistance, cases which are of such a character that a sound Christian discretion can not consider suitable objects of Christian benevolence. There are some cases in which, whatever is contributed, would be likely to be wasted, because of the extreme improbability of securing enough to redeem the property in peril.

There are, also, other cases, the position and prospects of which do not warrant the expenditure of the amount of money desired. While again there are others, which, from lack, hitherto, of the oversight of persons of skill and discretion, require, first of all, that, as we have suggested, some judicious business man or men examine their condition, so far as they can, and, if possible, put them in a position to secure success.

We confidently believe that such a course inaugurated and practically developed by a little experience, for which time would be required to afford the opportunity, there would thereupon be formed a proper basis, from which successfully to make an appeal to a benevolent Christian public.

Observation already had, in not a few instances, goes to show that, in many cases, the advice given by a man of skill and experience, or a committee of judicious men of business talent and habit, would be worth more to the needy church than a large gift of money without such advice.

We can but pleasurably believe that by some such plan as we here contemplate, we should be rendering essential aid to churches in their weakness and want; and by so doing, lift them up toward strength and durability—a state in which having attained to, they would become cheerful auxiliaries to a fund that would confer untold benefits, for years to come, on churches yet to arise in various parts of our vast and increasing population—a population we can not yet begin to estimate—destined to cover our country, North and South, East and West—demanding of us our share of the work in giving the knowledge of salvation which is by Jesus Christ our Lord.

A. D. GILLETTE,
H. G. WESTON,
D. M. WILSON.

THE WORK

The *Christian Secretary*, after sum
Mission Society, takes a broader view o
The good which this Society has
rapid growth of our country is unparallel
immigration as has been flocking to o
was never known before in the history o
without any apparent diminution of nu
ues, it will increase rather than diminis
bringing with them the morals, the corr
as it is, of the *old* world; consequently,
They need instruction, and, above all, th
to make them good and reliable citizen
immigrants, on their arrival, repair at o
cheap, but where there are no churches,
unless preachers are sent to them, they w
grow up in ignorance after them, fitted

DIRECTORS FOR LIFE,

Constituted during the Year ending March 31, 1860.

BY VIRTUE OF A CONTRIBUTION OF ONE HUNDRED DOLLARS OR MORE.

As a measure of economy, we omit the names of Directors and Members heretofore published, and propose to continue the plan hereafter, except once in four or five years, when the entire list will be printed.

Baker, Rev. Samuel, D.D., Williamsburgh, N. Y.
Bellamy, Rev. David, Rome, N. Y.
Bird, James M., Philadelphia.
Bliss, Elijah, Brooklyn, N. Y.
Blount, Rev. Elijah G., Fabius, N. Y.

Capon, E., Canton, Mass.
Carter, Cyrus L., New York.
Castle, Rev. John H., West Philadelphia, Pa.
Cleghorn, Rev. Adams, Belleville, N. Y.
Corey, Rev. Daniel G., D.D., Utica, N. Y.
Corey, Charles H., Newton, Mass.
Crosby, C. C. P., Brooklyn, N. Y.

Denike, Abraham, New York.

Ewell, Rev. H. B., Pavilion, N. Y.

Ford, John M., Philadelphia.
Frost, Mrs. Lydia, Middletown, N. J.

Gilmore, J. H., Newton Centre, Mass.
Grubb, William, Boston, Mass.

Hale, David, Suffield, Ct.
Hires, Rev. A. J., Moorestown, N. J.
Holme, Mrs. Anna M., Brooklyn, N. Y.

Johnson, Ralph, Norwich, N. Y.

Keen, George B., West Philadelphia, Pa.
Keen, Charles B., West Philadelphia, Pa.
Keen, William W., Jr., West Philadelphia, Pa.
Knapp, Rev. Samuel J., New York.

Latham, Miss Ellen, Groton, Ct.
Leland, Jeanison A., Brooklyn, N. Y.

McMasters, William, Toronto, Canada.
Mangam, Edgar B., New York.
Maples, Joseph, Philadelphia.
Mikels, Rev. William S., New York.

Pendleton, Rev. William H., New York.

Randall, John A. C., Boston, Mass.

Sawyer, Samuel A., Brooklyn, N. Y.
Smith, John H., Brooklyn, N. Y.
Smith, Rev. Edgar, East Lansing, N. Y.
Sparks, Jonas, New York.
Spier, John, Brooklyn, N. Y.
Stone, Samuel R., Newton Centre, Mass.
Stone, Jonas, Newton Centre, Mass.
Stone, Grafton Willard, Newton Centre, Mass.
Stone, Mary, Newton Centre, Mass.
Stone, Eben, Newton Centre, Mass.
Stone, Mrs. Minerva, Newton, Mass.
Swaim, Hon. Thomas, Pemberton, N. J.

True, Reuben, Plainfield, N. H.
True, Mrs. Hannah M., Plainfield, N. H.
Tucker, Stephen, Papineauville, Can.

VanSickler, Reuben M., Albany, N. Y.

Walraven, Lewis Y., Philadelphia.
Webster, Rev. George, North Orange, N. J.
Weston, Rev. Henry G., D.D., New York.
Weston, Mrs. Mary L., New York.
Wheelock, Mrs. Alonzo, Fredonia, N. Y.
Whitney, Salmon, Boston, Mass.
Winston, Rev. Meriweather, Philadelphia.

MEMBERS

Constituted during the Y

BY VIRTUE OF A CONTRI

Adams, Mrs. Angeline M., New York.
Adams, Mrs. Sarah, Deckertown, N. J.
Albright, J. G., Dorchester, Mass.
Allen, Elihu, Sandy Hill, N. Y.
Allen, John, South Gardner, Mass.
Andrews, Rev. Erastus, Suffield, Ct.
Armstrong, Miss Emma J., Lambertville, N. J.
Austin, Edward, Suffield, Ct.

Bailey, Rev. Alvin, McGrawville, N. Y.
Baker, Mrs. Anna M., Woodstown, N. J.
Baker, W. W., Thetford Hill, Vt.
Baker, Elias, New Brunswick, N. J.
Balcom, Rev. George, Milo, N Y.
Barber, Rev. Elijah N., Elmira, N. Y.
Barker, Richard, Hightstown, N. J.
Barstow, Samuel, New York.
Bartlett, Horace, New Haven, Ct.
Barton, Mrs. Susan S., Flemington, N. J.
Barton, John, Flemington, N. J.

Forbes, Mrs. M. Prattsburg, N. Y.
Foster, Mrs. Margaret, New York.
Francis J. Dwight, Pittsfield, Mass.
Franklin, Mrs. Mary Trenton, N. J.
Freeman, Arnold, Boston, Mass.
Fuller, Lewis, South Berlin, N. Y.

Gage, Mary, Central Falls, R. I.
Gage, Isaiah, Central Falls, R. I.
Gale, Mrs. Caroline E. Minneapolis, Min.
Geddes, Andrew A. Jersey City, N. J.
Gates, Rev. Oliver W Greenville, Ct.
Godfrey, Mrs. Polly Ann, Eaton, N. Y.
Goodnow, A. J., Sudbury, Mass.
Gordon, Selden S., Brooklyn, N. Y.
Gould, Silas, Exeter N. H.
Gould, John, Dover, N. H.
Gow Rev George B., South Groton, Mass.
Greeley, Mrs. Joanna C. M., Hudson, N. H.
Green, Mrs. Judith A K., Haverhill, Mass.
Griffiths, Mrs. Margaret, New York.
Grout, Paul, New York.
Grover, Mrs. Joseph Elmira, N Y.
Gurley, Miss Olive E , Troy, N. Y.

Haigh, Rev. W. M., Bristol, Ill.
Hale, Rev. Sumner, Fitchburg, Mass.
Halteman, Rev. D. E. Marengo, Ill.
Hammond Ruth H. Wickford, R. I.
Hanna, Samuel, Troy, N. Y.
Hansell, George H , New York.
Hardenbrook, Robert, Greenport, N. Y.
Harmon, Rev. G. N., Three Mile Bay, N. Y.
Harris, Douglass N., New London, Ct.
Harrison, Rev. T. Spencer, Dundee, N. Y.
Haskell Rev Joseph, Shutesbury, Mass.
Hazen, Rev. J. H., Brimfield, Ill
Higgins, Vandeveer, Flemington, N. J.
Higgins, Miss Sallie B. Flemington, N. J.
Hildreth Joseph Cheviot, Ohio.
Hill, Henry F. Livonia, N Y
Hillman, Miss Catharine, Hastings, N. Y.
Hires, Mrs. A. J., Woodstown, N. J.
Hedden, Mrs. Annie M., Mansfield, Ct.
Herrick, Mrs. Mary B., Watertown, N. Y.
Herrington, Miss Freelove, West Hoosick, N. Y.
Herrington, Nelson M. Corning N. Y.
Herrington. Ezekiel, Union Village, N. Y.
Hendrickson, Miss Mary, South Dover, N. Y.
Hoag, George W., Hoosick Four Corners, N. Y.
Hoff, Lewis, Rahway, N. J.
Holly, John, Greenville, N. Y.
Holt, Rev. R., Ashland, Mass.
Hopkins, Miss Ellen M., New York.
Hopkins, Samuel K., West Philadelphia, Pa.
Hooper, W. G., West Philadelphia, Pa.
Houple, Wm Henry, New York.
Hotchkiss, Mrs. Laura A., Southington, Ct.
Howard, Abby A., New London, Ct.
Hutchins, Mrs. Irene, Troy, N. Y.

Ingersoll, H. H., New York.
Irving, Rev. Peter, Romulus, N. Y.

Jemison, Lewis, M.D. Hightstown N. J.
Jewett, Mrs. Dorah P Minneapolis, Min.
Johnson, Robert P Great Bend, Ohio.
Johnson, Wallace, Buffalo, N. Y.
Johnson, George, West Philadelphia, Pa.
Jones, H. W., Troy, N. Y.
Jones, H. G., Philadelphia.
Jones, Mrs. Nathan L. Lower Merion, Pa.
Joslyn Rev. A. J., Chicago, Ill.

Keech, Jefferies, West Philadelphia, Pa.
Keeney Mrs. Wm. H. New London, Ct.
Kennedy Robert, New York.
Kenyon, Clark, Union Village, N. Y.
Keyes, Rev J. Judson, Penfield, N Y.
Keyser Mrs. Lizzie B. Providence R. I.
King, Mrs Betsey K. Xenia, Ohio.
King, Rufus S. Buffalo, N. Y
King, Mrs Harriet S. Windsor Vt.
Kirby, Charles, Worcester, Mass.
Knapp, Reuben D., Cold Spring, N. Y.
Knight, Miss Ann H., Haverhill, Mass.

Ladd, Ella Louisa, Brooklyn, N. Y.
Langworthy Henry D. Groton, Ct.
Lathrop Harry Stafford, N Y
Leaming, J. F. Seaville, N. J.
Lester, Gurdon New London, Ct.
Levisee, Rev Walter, New London, Wis.
Little, Rheuamah Stamford Ct.
Livingston, William Adamsville, Ohio.
Locke, Mrs. Wm. H. Jersey City N. J.
Lowry Rev. Robert, New York.
Lyon, James C., Cincinnati Ohio.

McCarten, Henry A E. New York.
Manning James W. Putnam, Ct.
Mack, Royal Oswego, N Y
Mallory, Rev. John C. Savona, N. Y.
McElroy G., Hiramsburg Ohio.
March, Delano, Watertown, Mass.
Marsh, Prof. F. O., Granville, Ohio.
Martin, Wooster Wallingford Ct.
Martin, Levi, Newtown, Ohio.
Mason, Mrs. Lydia Warren, R. I.
Mason, Warren, North Granville, N. Y.
Maynard, Rev. Abner, Mount Vision, N. Y.
Mears, Franklin Peterboro' N. H.
Meixell, Joseph Milton Pa.
Metcalf, George R. Greenfield, Mass.
Metcalf, Mrs. Whitman Nunda, N. Y.
Meylert, Asa P., Pittsburgh, Pa.
Miles, Rev. S. W. Plainfield, N. H.
Miller, Rev. J. C., Amboy, Ill.
Morgan, Rev. H. A. North Becket, Mass.
Moore, Rev. John G., Salisbury N. Y.
Morse, George E. Eaton, N Y
Mudge, Mrs. Sarah, Palmyra N. Y.
Munroe, John Elbridge, N Y
Mustin Anthony Sen., West Philadelphia, Pa.
McPherson, A. H., Jersey City, N. J.

Newton Rev. A. R., Farmington, Ill.
Noyes, Samuel, Watertown, Mass.

Olmstead, William, New Haven, Ct.
Olney, Mrs. Eunice C., Tirone, N. Y.
Olney, Mrs. Cynthera D., Castile, N. Y.
Onderdonk, Mrs. Eliza P., Yates, N. Y.

Paige, John F., New London, Ct.
Palmer, Israel C., Medway, N. Y.
Palmer, John, Noank, Ct.
Parker, Avery, Flemington, N. J.
Parker, Mrs. Joel R., Fredonia, N. Y.
Parmly, Mrs. Katharine D., Jersey City, N. J.
Parr, Jesse, Great Bend, Ohio.
Parks, Levi P., Passumpsic, Vt.
Parks, Rev. J. H., Bedford, N. Y.
Parks, Mrs. S. C., Bedford, N. Y.
Peabody, Mrs. Lucinda D., Salem, Mass.
Peck, Mrs. Electa, Nicholsville, N. Y.
Peck, E. L., Seekonk, Mass.
Peck, Eliza Ann, Exeter, N. H.
Peterson, Mrs. Rachael D., Woodstown, N. J.
Perkins, E., Kennebunk Port, Me.
Perkins, Ann, Newton, Mass.
Phillips, Rev. W. S., Wales, Mass.
Plant, Miss Emily C., Southington, Ct.
Pond, Mrs. Nancy, Boston, Mass.
Post, Peter J., New York.
Pratt, Rev. W. C., Delavan, Ill."
Price, Andrew, M.D., Valparaiso, Ia.
Puffer, Miss Jane M., Bangall, N. Y.

Quick, Charlotte A., Bowman's Corners, N. Y.

Wilbur, Mrs. Huldah Jane, Saxton's River, Vt.
Wiley, Francis, New York.
Wilkinson, Rev. Wm. C., New Haven, Ct.
Willetts, Miss Emily, New York.
Willetts, Miss Louisa, New York.
Williams, Rev. G. B., Kingston, Mass.
Winston, Mrs. Meriweather, Philadelphia.
Wixon, Sackett B., Barrington, N. Y.
Wixon, Mrs. Lyd'a, Wayne, N. Y.
Wording, William E., Racine, Wis.
Worthington, Gershom B., Colchester, Ct.

Yale, Rev. Luman B., Guilford, N. Y.
Yeager, George, West Philadelphia, Pa.
Young, Carlton, Racine, Ohio.
Young, Arnold A., Union Village, N. Y.

Zimmerman, Angeline, Norwalk, Ct.

LIST OF DECEASED

Directors and Members for Life, 1859—60.

DIRECTORS.

Belcher, Rev. Joseph, D.D., Philadelphia, Pa.
Hague, James, Newark, N. J.
Hartwell, Rev. J., D.D., Mt. Lebanon, La.
Nott, Rev. A. Kingman, New York.
Vanderveer, John, Moorestown, N. J.

MEMBERS.

Arnold, Miss Phebe, Jay, N. Y.
Bleecker, George W., Brooklyn, N. Y.
Boker, David A., Brooklyn, N. Y.
Bosworth, George H., Fall River, Mass.
Briggs, Sarah H., Fitchburg, Mass.
Colgate, Miss Sarah, New York.
Conover, Mrs. Rebecca M., Holmdel, N. J.
Cornell, William W., Plainfield, N. J.
Cotton, Mrs. Sarah McCullen, Mt. Vernon, N. Y.
Dixson, Rev. J. A., Evansville, Ia.
Dodson, Rev. Elijah, Woodburn, Ill.
Edwards, Robert, New York.
Fennell, Rev. George, Harrell's Store, N. C.
Fletcher, Rev. Leonard, Pennington, Pa.
Folwell, Job W., Defiance, Ohio.
Galusha, Truman, Jericho, Vt.
Green, Ralph, Three Rivers, Mass.
Greenwood, Samuel, New London, N. H.
Harrison, Rev. J. C., D.D., Kingston, N. Y.
Howe, James, East Washington, N. H.
James, Rev. David, Osceola, Ill.
Kain, Mrs. Maria, Mullica Hill, N. J.
Kelley, Mrs. Eli, New York.
Kingsford, Rev. Edward, D.D., Richmond, Va.
Newland, D., Stillwater, N. Y.
Pier, Mrs. Deborah, New York.
Pillsbury, Rev. Phineas, Greene, Me.
Silkworth, Samuel O., New York.
Spear, Abraham, Joddo, N. Y.
Swaim, Mrs. Mary, Pemberton, N. J.
Sweet, Rev. J., Tivoli, Ill.
Tillinghast, Rev. J. A., Tolland, Ct.
Wells, Mrs. Elizabeth, New York.
Wilson, Mrs. Francis N., Catskill, N. Y.
Willett, Mrs. Charles, La Crosse, Wis.
Wynn, Mrs. Susan, Tuckahoe, N. J.

DECEASED WIVES OF MISSIONARIES

For 1859-60.

Mrs. J. D. Rossier,	Grande Ligne,	Canada.
" Wm. M. Simons,	Plymouth,	Ia.
" Wm. J. Chapin,	Mauston,	Wis.
" G. W. Fuller,	Chatfield,	Min.

CONTENTS.

ANNUAL REPORT OF THE EXECUTIVE BOARD.

MISCELLANEOUS MATTER.

TWENTY-NINTH REPORT

OF THE

AMERICAN BAPTIST HOME MISSION SOCIETY,

PRESENTED BY THE

EXECUTIVE BOARD

AT THE

Anniversary held with the First Baptist Church,

IN BROOKLYN, N. Y.,

MAY 30, 1861;

WITH

THE TREASURER'S REPORT AND OTHER DOCUMENTS.

NEW YORK:

PUBLISHED AT THE AMERICAN BAPTIST HOME MISSION ROOMS, No. 115 NASSAU STREET,

AND PRINTED BY THOMAS HOLMAN, CORNER CENTRE AND WHITE STREETS.

1861.

CONSTITUTION.

NAME.

I.—This Society shall be called the American Baptist Home Mission Society.

OBJECT.

II.—The object of this Society shall be to promote the preaching of the Gospel in North America.

MEMBERSHIP.

III.—The Society shall be composed of Annual Delegates, Life Members, and Life Directors. Any Baptist church, in union with the denomination, may appoint a delegate for an annual contribution of ten dollars, and an additional delegate for each additional thirty dollars. Thirty dollars shall be requisite to constitute a Member for Life, and one hundred dollars, paid at one time, or a sum which, in addition to any previous contribution, shall amount to one hundred dollars, shall be requisite to constitute a Director for Life.

OFFICERS.

IV.—The officers of the Society shall be a President, two Vice-Presidents, a Treasurer, two Auditors, one or more Corresponding Secretaries, and a Recording Secretary.

MANAGERS.

V.—There shall be fifteen managers also, residing in the city of New York, or its vicinity, who shall be divided by lot among themselves into three classes of five members each. The term of service of the first class shall expire in one year, that of the second class in two years, and that of the third class in three years. At each Annual Meeting of the Society, after the first election under this amended Constitution, one class only shall be elected for the term of three years, to the end that the third part of the whole number of managers, as nearly as possible, may be annually chosen; provided, however, that vacancies remaining in any class may be filled for the unexpired term of that class. The officers and managers shall be elected by ballot, and continue to discharge their official duties, until superseded by a new election.

EXECUTIVE BOARD.

VI.—The Treasurer, Auditors, Recording Secretary, and Managers of the Society, shall constitute an Executive Board, to conduct the business of the Society; seven of whom shall be a quorum for that purpose. They shall have power to appoint their own meetings; elect their own Chairman and Recording Secretary; enact their own By-laws and Rules of Order, provided, always, that they be not inconsistent with this Constitution; fill any vacancies which may occur in their own body, or in the offices of the Society during the year; and, if deemed necessary by two thirds of the members, convene special meetings of the Society. They shall establish such agencies as the interests of the Society may require; appoint agents and missionaries; fix their compensation; direct and instruct them concerning their particular fields and labors; make all appropriations to be paid out of the treasury; and present to the Society, at each annual meeting, a full report of their proceedings during the current year.

DESIGNATED FUNDS.

VII.—All moneys or other property contributed and designated for any particular missionary field or purpose, shall be so appropriated, or returned to the donors, or their lawful agents.

TREASURER.

VIII.—The Treasurer shall give bonds to such amount as the Executive Board shall think proper.

ELIGIBILITY TO APPOINTMENT.

IX.—All the Officers, Managers, Missionaries, and Agents of the Society, shall be members in good standing in regular Baptist churches.

ANNUAL MEETING.

X.—The Society shall meet annually for the election of officers and managers, and the transaction of other necessary business, at such time and place as the Executive Board shall appoint.

ALTERATIONS OF THE CONSTITUTION.

XI.—No alteration of this Constitution shall be made without an affirmative vote of two thirds of the members present at an annual meeting; nor unless the same shall have been proposed in writing, and the proposition sustained by a majority vote, at a previous annual meeting, or recommended by the Executive Board.

STATED MEETINGS FOR 1861-62.

OF THE EXECUTIVE BOARD.—Thursday before the first Wednesday in each month, at four o'clock P.M., from June to October; and at three P.M. during the remaining months.

OF THE COMMITTEE ON MISSIONS.—The day previous to that of the Board, at the same hours as the Board.

OF THE COMMITTEE ON AGENCIES AND FINANCE.—The Tuesday preceding, at four o'clock P.M., in the Summer months; and at three P.M., in the Winter months.

OF THE COMMITTEE ON CHURCH-EDIFICE FUND.—The Monday preceding, at half-past nine A.M.

BY-LAWS OF THE BOARD.

1. All meetings shall be opened with prayer.
2. All Committees shall be nominated by the presiding officer and approved by the Executive Board, unless otherwise specially ordered.
3. No moneys shall be paid out of the treasury but by order of the Executive Board.
4. All resolutions, if required, shall be presented in writing.
5. Whenever a vacancy occurs in the Executive Board the fact shall be entered on the Minutes, and at the next stated meeting the Board shall proceed to fill such vacancy by ballot.
6. No By-law of the Board shall be suspended for any temporary purpose, unless by a vote of two thirds of the members of the Board.

ORDER OF BUSINESS.

1. Reading the Minutes of the last Meeting.
2. Treasurer's Report.
3. Communications of the Corresponding Secretary.
4. Reports of Standing Committees.
5. Reports of Select Committees.
6. Unfinished Business.
7. New Business.

STANDING COMMITTEES.

AGENCIES AND FINANCE.	MISSIONS.	CHURCH-EDIFICE FUND.
E. Cauldwell,	J. S. Holme,	H. P. Freeman,
A. N. Nearing,	E. E. L. Taylor,	J. B. Peck,
W. H. Chapman,	W. H. Parmly,	F. S. Miner.
Avery Bill, Jr.,	H. G. Weston,	
S. S. Constant,	E. Lathrop,	
D. M. Wilson.	E. T. Hiscox.	

LEGACIES.

J. Dowling,	C. C. Norton,
D. I. Yerkes,	J. G. Whipple.

MINUTES OF THE TWENTY-NINTH ANNIVERSARY

OF THE

American Baptist Home Mission Society,

Held in Brooklyn, New York, May 30, 1861.

The American Baptist Home Mission Society convened in the meeting-house of the First Baptist Church, in the City of Brooklyn, N. Y., on Thursday morning, May 30, 1861, at ten o'clock.

James E. Southworth, Esq., President, called the Society to order. After a song of praise, prayer was offered by Rev. W. Sym, N. Y.

The Society was then briefly addressed by the President. (See page 43.)

The following Committees were, upon the nomination of the President, duly appointed:

On Credentials of Delegates.—Rev. J. S. Ladd, N. Y.; Rev. J. W. Parkhurst, Mass.; Rev. O. Tracy, N. H.; Rev. J. V. Ambler, Mass.; Rev. A. J. Hires, N. J.

On Life Directors and Life Members present.—Rev. J. L. Hodge, D.D., N. Y.; Rev. Wm. H. Eaton, N. H.; Rev. A. Gale, Min.; Rev. D. I. Yerkes, N. Y.; H. Day, Esq., Ct.

On Nomination of Officers and Managers.—Rev. H. G. Weston, D.D., N. Y.; Rev. A. P. Mason, D.D., Mass.; Rev. H. M. Richardson, Ohio; Rev. Edward Bright, D.D., N. Y.; Rev. S. Dryden Phelps, D.D., Ct.

On motion of Rev. Wm. H. Parmly, N. J., the times for commencing and closing the sessions of the Society's meetings be as follows: Commence at half-past nine A.M., at half-past two and half-past seven P.M.; close at one and at five o'clock P.M.

On motion of Rev. E. K. Fuller, R. I.,

Resolved, That ministers and other brethren present, not members or delegates, be invited to participate in our deliberations.

Rev. W. H. Kelton Bluehill, Me., Rev. James Dixon, Ill., Rev. Joseph Tingley, N. J.; Rev. Chas. H. Malcom, R. I.; and Rev. T. S. Rogers, N. Y.; accepted this invitation.

The amendment to the Third Article of the Constitution, proposed by the Society at its last Anniversary, reading as follows:

III. The Society shall be composed of such persons as shall be members or directors for life at the time of the adoption of this amended Constitution, and those who are entitled to become such on the completion of payments already commenced for that purpose, and of annual members. Any regular Baptist church, by contributing to the funds of the Society ten dollars annually, may appoint one annual member; for twenty-five dollars in addition a second annual member; and an additional annual member for each additional fifty dollars. Any individual may become an honorary member for life by the payment, during the financial year, of not less than thirty dollars; and every honorary member shall have a vote in the meetings of the Society so long as he continues to be an annual contributor to its treasury, and a member in good standing of a regular Baptist church;

Was taken up, and, after remarks by several members, was, on motion of Rev. Thomas Armitage, D.D., N. Y., postponed indefinitely, on a division of 75 ayes to 51 nays.

The amendment to

AFTERNOON SESSION.

The Society was called to order at half-past two o'clock P.M. Prayer was offered by Rev. Silas Ilsley, Me.

Rev. Wm. H. Pendleton, N. Y., offered the following resolution, which was adopted:

Resolved, That the Committee on Nomination of Officers and Managers be instructed to present the name of but one person from any one church.

The annual report of the Board of Managers was presented, and an abstract therefrom read by the Corresponding Secretary, Rev. B. M. Hill, D.D.

On motion, the report was adopted and ordered to be printed with the minutes, under the direction of the Board of Managers.

The Committee on Credentials of Delegates present reported that there was one delegate present—P. A. Gladwin, R. I. Report adopted.*

The Committee on Life Directors and Life Members present, reported that there were present sixty-six Life Directors, and eighty-one Life Members, as follows:

LIFE DIRECTORS PRESENT.

Armitage, Rev. Thomas, D.D., N. Y.
Baker, Rev. Samuel, D.D., Williamsburgh, N. Y.
Baldwin, Rev. Geo. C., D.D., Troy, N. Y.
Bellamy, Rev. David, Rome, N. Y.
Boyce, James, Providence, R. I.
Brooks, Rev. Kendall, Fitchburg, Mass.
Bright, Rev. Edward, D.D., N. Y.
Bucknell, William, Philadelphia.
Burlingham, Rev. A. H., N. Y.
Capwell, A. B., New York.
Church, Rev. P., D.D., N. Y.
Denny, Mrs. Jane, Rochester, N. Y.
Devan, Rev. Thos. T., Nyack, N. Y.
Dodge, Rev. O., Brooklyn, N. Y.
Eaton, Rev. Joseph W., Chicago, Ill.
Evans, Rev. Charles, Brooklyn, N. Y.
Fish, Rev. H. C., D.D., Newark, N. J.
Freeman, Rev. A. L., Deposit, N. Y.
Fuller, Rev. E. K., Providence, R. I.
Gillette, Rev. A. D., D.D., N. Y.
Hallsted, Benjamin, Brooklyn, N. Y.
Hillman, Wm., N. Y.
Hires, Rev. A. J., Woodstown, N. J.
Hiscox, Rev. E. T., D.D., N. Y.
Hodge, Rev. J. L., D.D., N. Y.
Hodges, Rev. Joseph, Cambridge, Mass.
Holme, Rev. J. S., Brooklyn, N. Y.
Ilsley, Rev. Silas, Damariscotta, Me.
Keyser, Rev. Charles, Providence, R. I.
Ladd, Rev. James S., Bergen, N. Y.
Lathrop, Rev. Edward, D.D., N. Y.
Malcom, Rev. Howard, D.D., Leverington, Pa.
Mason, Rev. A. P., Chelsea, Mass.
Mikels, Rev. W. S., N. Y.
Miller, John A., Brooklyn, N. Y.
Miller, Rev. D. Henry, Meriden, Ct.
Murdock, Rev. J. N., D.D., Boston, Mass.
Parkhurst, Rev. J. W., Newton Centre, Mass.
Parmly, Rev. Wheelock H., Jersey City, N. J.
Peck, Rev. S., D.D., Roxbury, Mass.
Phelps, William, N. Y.
Phelps, Rev. S. D., D.D., New Haven, Ct.
Porter, Rev. Lemuel, D.D., Pittsfield, Mass.
Pendleton, Rev. Wm. H., N. Y.
Peltz, Rev. G. A., N. Y.
Reid, Rev. William, New London, Ct.
Remington, Rev. S., N. Y.
Richards, Rev. W. C., Providence, R. I.
Rollinson, Rev. Wm., Rahway, N. J.
Sanford, Rev. Miles, North Adams, Mass.
Swaim, Rev. S. B., West Cambridge, Mass.
Taylor, Rev. E. E. L., D.D., Brooklyn, Mass.
Thomas, C. W., Hastings, N. Y.
Tracy, Rev. O., Concord, N. H.

* Two others were presented but neither were furnished with credentials of appointment from any church, and no record of the payment of money necessary to the appointment can be found on the books of the Society.

Vogell, Rev. H. C., D.D., Utica, N. Y.
Webb, Rev. G. S., D.D., New Brunswick, N. J.
Welsh, Rev. B. T., D.D., Newtonville, N. Y.
Webster, Rev. George, Orange, N. J.
Weston, Rev. H. G., D.D., N. Y.
[illegible], Rev. Z. P., N. Y.
Wilson, D. M., Newark, N. J.
White, Rev. Samuel, North Shore, N. Y.
Whitehead, James M., N. Y.
Winterton, Rev. William, Ct.
Wright, Rev. L., Norwich, N. Y.
Wright, Rev. Thos. G., Roadstown, N. J.

LIFE MEMBERS PRESENT.

Adams, Rev. E. J., Wallingford, Ct.
Ambler, Rev. J. A., [illegible], Mass.
Ambler, Rev. E. C., Philadelphia.
Atkinson, Rev. Robert, Newark, N. J.
Baker, Rev. J. James, [illegible], N. J.
Barnes, Wm. A., North Shore, N. Y.
Bates, Rev. L. C., Groton, N. Y.
Bliss, Marcus H., Hamilton, N. Y.
Brackett, Rev. John B., Poughkeepsie, N. Y.
Brown, Jr., John M., N. Y.
Bromley, Henry, Norwich, Ct.
Brown, Rev. [illegible], N. J.
Brown, Rev. Amasa, Concord, N. H.
Brownson, Rev. I. K., Greenfield, Ohio.
Chase, Rev. C. N., Deep River, Ct.
Cheesbro, Rev. J. Smith, Waterford, N. Y.
Church, [illegible], N. Y.
Cook, Rev. [illegible], Mass.
Conant, Rev. [illegible], N. Y.
[redacted]

Hubbell, A., Utica, N. Y.
Jeffery, Rev. R., Philadelphia.
Jones, Rev. H. M. Racine, Wis.
Jones, Rev. J. F., Ware, Mass.
Lincoln, Rev. Heman, Providence, R. I.
Lowry, Rev. Robert, Brooklyn, N. Y.
Lyons, Rev. J. M., New Rochelle, N. Y.
Macdonald, A., Williamsburgh, N. Y.
Mallory, Rev. J. C., Savona, N. Y.
Mallory, Eld. A. C., Benton Centre, N. Y.
Mason, Pethuel, Somerville, N. J.
Mason, A. Francke, Barnstable, Mass.
Matthews, Rev. Geo., Groton Bank, Ct.
Meeson, Rev. J. D., Burlington, N. J.
Osgood, Rev. S. M., Chicago, Ill.
Page, Rev. E. H., Charlestown, Mass.
Parker, Rev. A., Agawam, Mass.
Parkhurst, G. R., Brooklyn, N. Y.
Parsons, Rev. Wm. M., Brooklyn, N. Y.
[redacted]

After remarks by Rev. John I. Fulton, N. Y., Rev. Peter Conrad, N. Y., and Rev. E. T. Hiscox, D.D., N. Y., the resolution was adopted.

The Committee on Nomination of Officers and Managers presented their report.

The report was accepted, and, on motion, the Society proceeded to ballot for Officers and Managers.

The President named the following tellers to collect the votes for Officers: Rev. L. Wright, N. Y.; J. M. Bruce, Esq., N. Y.; Rev. Lewis Smith, N. J.; and Rev. D. Henry Miller, Ct.

The tellers, having collected and counted the votes for Officers, announced that the officers, as presented by the Committee on Nomination, had each received a majority of the votes cast, and they were therefore declared duly elected.

The President named as tellers for the Board of Managers—E. Lewis, Esq., Brooklyn; Dr. A. C. Burke, Brooklyn; Samuel Hillman, Esq., N. Y.; and Rev. W. C. Richards, R. I.

Having collected and counted the votes for managers, the tellers announced that the names presented by the Committee had received a majority of the votes cast, and they were therefore declared duly elected. (For the names see page 11.)

Rev. R. Jeffery, Pa., moved a vote of thanks to this and the other churches of Brooklyn for their hospitalities, which was adopted.

The minutes were read and approved. After prayer by Rev. G. S. Webb, D.D., N. J., the Society adjourned.

EVENING SESSION.

The Society, accompanied by a large congregation of others, convened at half-past seven o'clock P.M.

After an anthem by the choir, and prayer by Rev. A. D. Gillette, D.D., the Rev. Walter R. Brooks, of Hamilton, N. Y., delivered the missionary sermon, founded upon the text in Genesis, 49th chap., and last part of 10th verse—" Unto Him shall the gathering of the people be." After which a liberal contribution was taken up for the treasury of the Society, a doxology was sung, and the Apostolic benediction was pronounced by Rev. D. I. Yerkes pastor of the church. The sermon was very appropriate and interesting, and it is hoped that the author will consent to a request of the Executive Board to furnish them a copy for publication.

MISSIONARY CONFERENCE.

June 31, 1861.

A large number of members of the Society, and its friends, assembled at ten o'clock A.M., for the purpose of listening to communications from missionaries respecting the operations of the Society on their respective fields. The Rev. O. Tracy presided, and the exercises were introduced with prayer by Rev. Wm. Sym, of N. Y. After which addresses were delivered by Rev. Peter Conrad, recently of Wisconsin; Rev. Amory Gale, exploring agent of the Society in Minnesota; and Rev. J. B. Simmons, of Ia., who were listened to with deep interest and attention. Rev. Mr. Gale, in his remarks, alluded to the great want of church edifices by the people throughout the West, but especially his field, and to the noble effort now being made by the Society to provide funds to aid them. He approved heartily of their plan, and commended it for the co-operation of the churches, as essential to speedy success in general missionary operations.

The dollar plan for raising funds was explained by the Corresponding Secretary, Rev. B. M. Hill, and a general offering of one dollar each was made by those present. After which the meeting was closed as usual. It was a delightful appendage to the usual exercises.

A. B. CAPWELL,
Recording Secretary.

OFFICERS OF THE SOCIETY,

AND

EXECUTIVE BOARD.

OFFICERS.

PRESIDENT.

HON. IRA HARRIS, Albany, New York.

VICE-PRESIDENTS.

J. W. MERRILL, Esq., Boston, Mass.
J. M. HOYT, Esq., Cleveland, Ohio.

TREASURER.

EBENEZER CAULDWELL, Esq., New York.

AUDITORS.

S. S. CONSTANT, New York.
F. S. MINER "

CORRESPONDING SECRETARY.

REV. BENJAMIN M. HILL, D.D., New York.

RECORDING SECRETARY.

REV. E. T. HISCOX, D.D., New York.

MANAGERS.

FIRST CLASS, FOR ONE YEAR.

REV. W. H. PARMLY,..Jersey City, N. J.
H. P. FREEMAN,........Williamsburgh, N. Y.
J. B. PECK,.............New York.
A. N. NEARING,........ "
REV. J. DOWLING, D.D.,. "

SECOND CLASS, FOR TWO YEARS.

D. M. WILSON,................Newark, N. J.
REV. E. LATHROP, D.D.,.....New York.
" D. I. YERKES,..........Brooklyn, N. Y.
W. H. CHAPMAN,............New York.
AVERY BILL, Jr.,............ "

THIRD CLASS, FOR THREE YEARS.

REV. E. E. L. TAYLOR, D.D.,............................Brooklyn, N. Y.
" H. G. WESTON, D.D.,..............................New York.
" J. S. HOLME,.......................................Brooklyn, N. Y.
J. G. WHIPPLE,.. "
REV. C. C. NORTON,...................... ....New York.

CHAIRMAN OF THE EXECUTIVE BOARD.

D. M. WILSON.

RECORDING SECRETARY OF THE BOARD, AND CLERK.

JAMES M. WHITEHEAD, New York.

Dr. THE AMERICAN BAPTIST HOME MISSION SOCIETY,

1861. March 30.	To Cash paid Missionaries' Salaries to this date	$36,518 39
	" Cash paid Agents for Salaries, Traveling Expenses, Postage, etc., to this date........................	7,325 72
	" Cash paid Secretary and Clerks for Salaries (of which amount there has been received from Special Salary Fund $420)................................	2,704 58
	" Cash paid on account Church-edifice Fund	2,785 72
	" Cash paid Investment of the Medera Legacy received last year..................................	2,500 00
	" Cash paid for Fuel, Stationery, Postage, and other incidental expenses..........................	433 89
	" Cash paid for Paper, Printing and Editing of *Home Mission Record*, and incidental expenses on same..	1,838 54
	" Cash paid for Paper and Printing Annual Report, Certificates, Blanks, etc......................	277 09
	" Cash paid interest on conditional donations.........	86 61
	" Cash paid interest on Legacy paid in advance.......	6 31
	" Cash paid Annuity on account of the Medera Fund..	87 50

[redacted]

IN ACCOUNT WITH EBENEZER CAULDWELL, TREASURER. *Cr.*

1861. March 30.	By Balance as per last Report........................		$11,273 12
	" Contributions since April 1, 1860..................		32,595 79
	" Legacies same period in Cash...........	$5,904 45	
	" " " " " Secured Notes payable in one, two, and three years..	625 00	
	" Legacies same period in Railroad Stock, estimated value....................	600 00	
			7,129 45
	" Contributions to Church-edifice Fund, and Interest on account of Loan paid..........................		4,082 03
	" Subscriptions to *Home Mission Record*..............		935 68
	" Avails of Bank Stock sold, bequeathed by the late John Allen, of Rhode Island..		3,170 92
	" Avails of Bills Receivable, contributed last year.....		100 00
	" Avails of Real Estate sold on foreclosure of Mortgage		1,000 00
	" Interest on Temporary Investment.................		30 00
	" " " Special Salary Fund		420 00
	" " " a Special Investment by direction of the Donor		175 00
	" " " Investment made to cover conditional donations, for which the Society is paying interest...........................		280 00
	" Dividends on Bank Stock, bequeathed by the late John Allen, Rhode Island...............		120 75
	" Dividends on Railroad Stock, bequeathed by the late William Souldin, of Albany, New York..........		18 00
	" Interest on an Investment, charged with an Annuity.		134 60
	" Cash designated for Sunday School Library.........		10 00
	" " " " Sufferers in Kansas............		527 65
			$62,002 99
	By Balance to account.....		$4,161 82
	Subject to demand for Liabilities due April 1, 1861...........................	$4,644 15	
	Deficiency in the Treasury to meet those Liabilities.....	482 33	

E. E. EBENEZER CAULDWELL, *Treasurer.*

This is to certify that we have carefully examined the foregoing account, together with the vouchers connected therewith, and find the same correct. The balance in the treasury is four thousand one hundred and sixty-one 82-100 dollars ($4,161.82).

(Signed) SMITH SHELDON, JOHN M. BRUCE, JR., } *Auditors.*

NEW YORK, March 30, 1861.

ACT OF INCORPORATION.

AN ACT TO INCORPORATE THE AMERICAN BAPTIST HOME MISSION SOCIETY, PASSED APRIL 12, 1843, AND AMENDED FEBRUARY 9, 1849.

The People of the State of New York, represented in **Senate and Assembly, do** *enact as follows:*

§ 1. All such persons as now are, or may hereafter become, members of the American Baptist Home Mission Society, formed in the city of New York in the year one thousand eight hundred and thirty-two, [redacted]

ANNUAL REPORT

OF THE AMERICAN BAPTIST HOME MISSION SOCIETY,

At the Twenty-ninth Anniversary, held in Brooklyn, May 30, 1861.

It has ever contributed to the happiness of the Executive Board, when presenting their annual report, to recognize the Divine hand in guiding them, and the Divine goodness and mercy which aided them in their progress. That happiness they experience on this occasion, as they remember all the way in which the Lord their God has led them safely to the close of another year.

DEATHS.

Yet is this happiness tempered by sorrow at the repeated bereavements of the past year. In the list of the dead for 1860–61, which accompanies this report, are found the names of cherished Christian friends, who have been fellow-laborers with us in spreading the Gospel of Jesus Christ, through the medium of this Society. Our consolation lies in the assurance of the efficacy of that Gospel in saving souls, and in preparing them for their entrance upon the eternal rewards which await the faithful servants of the Lord.

By reference to the "List of the Deceased" for the year ending March 31, it will be seen that twenty-four deaths have occurred. Of that number, ten were ministers of the Gospel, three of whom were formerly mis-

sionaries of this Society. Ano
Maclay, D.D., was elected a m
Board and its chairman, at the
formation of the Society in 1
was confirmed, at the regular
was re-elected to fill it for sever
was also one of the vice-preside
twelve years after its organizati
just previous to our last anniver
ments for the year had been ma
ceive the report of the Commit
anniversary makes it proper to
He was a good man, a faithful
servant of God.

DIRECTORS AND MEMB

In the course of the year, thir

gent view of its advance in the important elements of national prosperity, especially through religious and moral influences.

At the commencement of its publication, it was sent gratuitously to the Life Members and Life Directors of the Society, but the list of such became numerous, increasing the expense of publication much beyond what was originally contemplated, and absorbing too large a share of funds contributed for missionary purposes. In view of these facts the free list was suspended with the January number of the present year, and the support of the publication made to depend on its own income from subscribers. In the adoption of this policy the Board were encouraged by friends of the Society, and a somewhat increased subscription list has followed. But it is very important that the list should be still further increased, so that it shall be distributed in every church, carrying everywhere its rich illustrations of the grace of God in the salvation of souls, and the advance of the Redeemer's kingdom among men. For this purpose the Board invite the prompt and active co-operation of all their friends, especially those in the pastoral office.

TRACT AND BIBLE DISTRIBUTION.

The missionaries of the Society are instructed to interest themselves in the distribution of the Sacred Scriptures, and of religious tracts and books within their respective fields. This duty is performed efficiently by all, but especially by those who itinerate in large frontier districts, of whom there are many.

With great pleasure the Board acknowledge the continuance of the kind offices of the American Tract Society in gratuitously supplying each of the missionaries who have made application, with five thousand pages of excellent tracts for distribution, besides much larger and more extensive appropriations of Spanish tracts and books for those who labor in New Mexico. These have proved almost indispensable aids to those missionaries. With the same kindness the American and Foreign Bible Society have supplied them with Spanish Bibles and Testaments.

FINANCIAL AFFAIRS.

It is well known that the political troubles of the country have unfavorably affected all branches of mercantile business, and that the effects of general mercantile embarrassment are usually felt very soon by benevolent societies in their diminished revenues. Such has been the effect upon this Society the past year. The receipts into its treasury from ordinary donations for missionary pur-

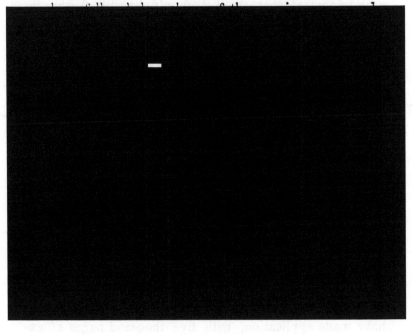

[redacted]

The following is a general statement of the financial condition of the Society on the 31st of March:

Balance from last year's account		$11,273 12
Receipts from all sources during the year		50,729 87
Total amount of resources for the year		$62,002 99
Total amount of disbursements for the year		57,841 17
Amount of cash in the treasury, April 1, 1861		$4,161 82
Amount of liabilities, chiefly to missionaries, same date		4,644 15
Showing the amount to be provided for		$482 33
Of the total amount received, there were, in ordinary contributions from churches and individuals		32,595 79
Being less than those of the previous year		5,844 13
The amount of cash received in legacies is	$5,904 45	
The amount received in securities from legacies	1,225 00	
		7,129 45
Being less than those of the previous year		2,819 10
The amount received for Church-edifice Fund, including a Loan for a Church-edifice repaid, and Interest on the same		4,082 03
Being an increase over that of the previous year of		2,118 93
Amount of Receipts, from all sources, last year		57,777 22
Amount of Receipts, from all sources, this year		50,729 87
Decrease of Receipts this year		$7,047 35
The amount of Receipts this year includes for sufferers in Kansas		452 90

CHURCH-EDIFICE FUND.

Since the last anniversary, facts have been communicated to the Board which confirm their opinion, heretofore expressed, relative to the necessity of a Church-edifice Fund, and that confirmation is strengthened by favorable notice of the subject in various periodicals, and the correspondence of judicious friends, showing the advantage which would accrue to the missionary cause, and especially to the Home Mission Society, by aiding young churches in early providing places of public worship. So far as such churches in the new Western States and Territories are concerned, their dependence upon the pecuniary liberalities of the older Eastern States during a few of the first years of their efforts to establish the institutions of the Gospel needs no argument. The only question really remaining is, whether the people will provide missionary funds for a series of years to support preachers on fields where they have no convenient houses of worship, or supply a sufficiency for the building of such houses, with a certainty that self-sustaining churches will be raised up in them in a much shorter period. The latter effect, it is believed, would, as a general rule, follow the early building of church edifices, leaving a much larger portion of our annual receipts to be used in a more extended diffusion of the Gospel among the destitute. With a view to such an object the plan of the Church-edifice Fund has been modified. It proposes to aid chiefly the incipient efforts of churches in new and growing villages, by loans of small sums for a few years; and

We are happy to state that a number of individuals and churches have patronized the plan, and there is reason to believe that, but for the specially embarrassed condition of financial interests in the country generally, very considerable additions would have been made to the amount already received for the purpose.

Accompanying this report will be published various documents, showing more in detail the practical importance and working of the plan. To these we invite attention; and for the success of the measure, ask the co-operation of all its friends.

MISSIONARY OPERATIONS.

The past fiscal year opened with the most encouraging prospects. The treasury had been liberally supplied during the previous year, especially in the last month of it, and important fields of usefulness invited the introduction of missionaries. With the hope that, at least, the usual amount of monthly supplies would promptly reach the treasury, a considerable expansion of missionary operations was commenced, chiefly in the newer and more distant portions of the country. An additional missionary was sent to California, whose designation was providentially changed to Oregon; two others, residents of California, and two in Oregon and Washington Territory, would have been added to the number there, and still others would have been appointed to occupy other important stations, but our hope was soon disappointed. The receipts from the beginning of the year, were insufficient to justify large appropriations, and during the last half of it, nothing more could be done than to meet the claims of missionaries already on the field, as their salaries became due, from month to month. With the exception of a few weeks this has been done, and all the missionaries have been retained

and provided for, except sucl
ceased to look to the Society

The names of missionaries
agents, the fields they occupy
appointment and labors, are
Table accompanying this repc

SUMMARY OF LABO

The number of missionaries
whole or a part of the year w
were in commission at the con
23 were appointed subsequen
in foreign languages.

The number of States and
viz., Canada, Pennsylvania,
Indiana, Illinois, Wisconsin,
Nebraska, New Mexico, Co

For various other items of labor, and its results, we refer inquirers to the foot-note on this page.*

This summary, while exhibiting many gratifying fruits of missionary effort, falls far short of the ardent hopes and expectations of the Board at the commencement of the year. It shows that, with a somewhat smaller force employed, a considerably larger amount of labor has been performed the past year than in the previous one, and that greater success attended that labor. On account of the comparatively small amount of means received, only a limited number of new appointments could be prudently made, while applications for them constantly increased, and finally became very numerous. That the Board should be enabled, by the liberality of the Society and its friends, to comply with such applications is obvious, from the fact that a large emigration continues to flow westward, filling more densely the older States, increasing the population of existing territories; and, by penetrating the wide wastes of the West still further, rendering necessary the formation of others. Kansas, which, last year, was only a territory, has passed to the dignity of a State. Nebraska and New Mexico will probably soon follow. In only a few years, Washington will be prepared for the

* In addition to the above, the missionaries report the following:

Sermons preached	14,122
Lectures and addresses	1,018
Pastoral visits	34,563
Prayer and other meetings attended	10,931
Signatures to Temperance Pledge	373
Miles traveled in discharge of duty	162,906
Schools visited	449
Sabbath schools in the churches	181
Bible classes	137
Number of teachers	1,271
Number of scholars	9,496
Volumes in S. S. libraries	21,703
Stations where monthly concert of prayer is observed	60
Preparing for the ministry	17

same change. Already Dak
are authorized by Congress to
of new territories.

REINFORCEMEN

In all the present States of
forcement of missionary streng
lost to us every month, in whi
Thousands of people are sc
among whom are many of
more, who are now attach
institutions, and advocate ou
gone away from old associatio
in altogether too large numb
the influence of the powers of
of our churches are recreant
cause they are so far remov

Macedonia, that we should come over and help them. And such appeals increase with every month. All that the Board have been able to do for months past has been to encourage new applicants to expect aid whenever it may be in their power; but until they are made able by the liberalities of their brethren, the hope of those anxious applicants must be deferred, though years pass over them unaided, though other hands than ours may, for good or evil, minister to their wants, or though they themselves pass away from all the wants and neglects of this world, and with them thousands of others, for whose immortal interests they pleaded, but pleaded in vain.

OUR NATION'S TIME OF TROUBLE.

The Board are not forgetful of the trying times which have come over the nation—of mercantile derangements, of financial embarrassments, and of civil war. Would that God would graciously remove those troubles, and avert the dangers, which threaten to grow out of them. Neither are we forgetful of the moral evils which, in times of peace, and much more in war, exist and spread their dark pall over the millions who are stricken with spiritual death—evils which threaten the stability of our free institutions, the usefulness, happiness, and even the existence of our churches—evils, which assail our sons and daughters, and the purity of our moral character; evils which would obstruct our advance in civilization, stealthily undermine the foundations of our national liberty, and destroy the rich advantages of our social compact.

OUR NATION'S GROUND OF HOPE.

On the other hand, we do not overlook the past history of our country, and the influence of pure Christianity in the formation of its character, nor the indispensable necessity for its perpetuation in the higher exaltation of that character, in increasing its civil and religious influence among the nations of the earth, and especially in preparing men for the great day of the Lord. Amid such considerations, we see in the times, which now try men's souls, no reason for relaxing the spirit of benevolence, but far weightier obligations, resting on all, to promote the cause of Jesus Christ, though the cost of the effort may assume the proportions of an actual sacrifice for his name's sake. The gold and silver are his, not ours. Our loved, but threatened country, its helpless churches, and endangered souls, need its expenditure, and Christ, the King of Zion, requires that we bring all our tithes into his storehouse. Shall we, because of grievous troubles, because even of civil

EXPLANATION OF THE FOLLOWING MISSIONARY TABLE.

The parallel columns show—

1. The names of agents and missionaries, and the States in which they reside.
2. The post-office address of agents and missionaries.
3. The field of labor occupied by agents and missionaries.
4. The dates at which the appointments commence.
5. The number of months for which the appointments are respectively made.
6. The number of weeks' labor performed during the time reported.
7. The number of stations and out-stations supplied.*
8. The number of persons baptized by the missionaries within the time reported.
9. The number received by letter.
10. The number of scholars in Sabbath schools under care of missionaries.†
11. The amount contributed to benevolent objects.
12. Additional facts reported concerning the state and progress of the churches.‡

---

* "Stations" are churches or villages regularly supplied on the Lord's day, and are indicated in column three. "Out-stations" are places where the missionaries have *stated* appointments for preaching more or less frequently.

† In new places, where Union schools are established, the number of scholars connected with Baptist families only are reported.

‡ In many cases, two lines appear for the same missionary, extending through all the columns. In such cases, the second line indicates a reappointment of the missionary, and the dates in column four determine to which appointment or year the statistics and remarks on the different lines belong. A particular notice of those dates is necessary to a proper understanding of certain changes which appear against the names of some individuals.

ST-OFFICE DDRESS.	FIELD OF LABOR.	Date of Commission.	Months Commis'd.	Weeks labor reported.	Stations supplied	Baptized.	Received by Letter	Schol's in S. S. & B. Class	Contrib. to Benevolent Objects.	ADDI
. City..........	Indiana	April 1, 1860	12	50	....	..	....	....	......	
....	Wabash........................	Oct. 1, 1859	12	13	1		1	50	20 00	Resigns on acc
....	Westville and vicinity	Aug. 1, 1859	12	26	4	38	7	155	51 00	Revival. Need
City..........	Columbia City...............	Dec. 1, 1859	12	39	1	..	....	85	19 75	Sunday school
....	Plymouth.....................	May 1, 1859	12	13	4	..	1	8	37 50	Health not goo
....	"	May 1, 1860	12	39	....	..	3	50	112 50	Resigned.
on	Huntington	Nov. 1, 1859	12	39	3	3	1	87	68 3	Prospects encou
....	"	Nov. 1, 1860	12	13	....	..	....	50	......	The faith of th
....	Huntington Association....	Jan. 1, 1860	12	39	5	1	....	....	300 00	Organized a ch
....	" "	Jan. 1, 1860	12	13	3	..	....	....	......	
....	Goshen and vicinity.........	M'ch 1, 1860	12	52	1	3	9	162	......	Some progress.
....	" "	M'ch 1, 1861	12	....	....	..	....	....	......	

Names of Agents and Missionaries.	Post-Office Address.	Field of Labor.	Date of Commission.	Months Commis'd.	Weeks labor reported.	Stations supplied.	Baptized.	Received by letter.	Schol's in S. S. & B Class.	Contrib. to Benevolent Objects.	Additional Facts Reported.
Theodore Ulbricht	Milwaukee	Germans in Milwaukee	Nov. 1, 1860	12	13	2	1	....	98	2 40	Sunday school prosperous. Is encouraged but feel the pressure of the hard times.
Ernest Tschirch	Racine	Germans in Racine	Jan. 1, 1860	12	39	2	1	....	48	43 00	Progressing. Sunday school increasing in interest.
" "	"	" "	Jan. 1, 1861	12	13	....	6	....	....	17 50	Some unconverted awakened.
D. H. Cooley	Stevens Point	Stevens Point	June 1, 1859	12	13	2	2	....	91	......	More respect for religion by the people generally.
" "	"	"	June 1, 1860	12	39	....	..	....	120	6 00	
A. W. Peck	Superior	Superior	Oct. 1, 1859	12	26	2	..	....	6	......	Prospects discouraging. The place much deserted by the people.
" "	"	"	Oct. 1, 1860	12	26	....	..	....	7	......	
Wm. Sturgeon	Dunnville	Waubeck and vicinity	Sept. 1, 1859	12	26	2	..	2	35	......	Slowly gaining ground.
"	Chippewa.	" "	Sept. 1, 1860	12	26	....	2	....	11	.....	
Denis Mulhern	Richland Centre	Richland Centre, etc.	April 1, 1860	12	26	2	..	1	....	......	Secured a good lot for a church edifice.
S. T. Catlin	Osceola Mills	Osceola and vicinity	Dec. 1, 1859	12	29	2	..	1	62	4 55	Religion in a low state.
" "	"	" "	Dec. 1, 1860	12	13	3	..	1	....	......	
J. B. Patch	Watertown	Watertown	May 1, 1859	12	13	3	6	....	40	12 00	Leaves the field.
Harmon Ellis	Amherst	Stanton and vicinity	June 1, 1859	12	18	1	2	4	16	......	Society in a formative state
W. J. Chapin	Mauston	Mauston, etc.	Sept. 1, 1859	12	26	3	..	...	40	2 10	Church discouraged. Pastor leaves the field.
D. A. Peck	Waupaca	Weyauwego	Nov. 1, 1859	12	39	5	2	2	....	......	Church dismissed their pastor in order to complete their church edifice.
W. F. Nelson	Hudson	Hudson	Oct. 1, 1859	12	4	1	3	....	42	7 75	Resigned.
Walter Levisee	Waupaca	Waupaca and N. London	M'ch 1, 1860	12	52	5	3	9	100	10 25	Declension of religion in the place.
Isaac J. Hoile	Oshkosh	Oshkosh	April 1, 1860	12	52	4	1	6	138	129 21	Improved religious feeling Leaves the field for health.
Wm. H. Card	La Crosse	Salem and vicinity	April 1, 1860	12	52	3	1	20	126	14 00	Finished church edifice. Need no further aid.
J. J. McIntire	Watertown	Watertown	May 1, 1860	12	39	1	4	4	86	71 00	Former prejudices against Baptists giving way.
" "	"	"	May 1, 1861	12		....	..	....	....	......	
T. B. Rogers	Richmond	Willow River Valley	May 1, 1860	12	39	4	12	1	31	......	Some progress.
W. H. Brisbane	Madison	Madison	Aug. 1, 1860	12	26	1	..	10	100	20 00	Harmonizing conflicting elements.
Benj. L. Brisbane	Monroe	Monroe	Nov. 1, 1860	12	13	2	..	....	45	......	Bought a church edifice.
IOWA.											
Jonas Woodward	Cedar Rapids	Kingston and vicinity	May 1, 1859	12	13	2	..	....	100	5 00	Leaves the place on account of ill health.
Thomas M. Ind	Burlington	South Burlington	May 1, 1859	12	13	1	1	....	124	......	General declension in the city.
"	"	"	May 1, 1860	6	9	....	..	....	139	4 50	Resigns on account of poor health. Paid debt on church edifice.
ge Scott	Strawberry Point	Strawberry Point	Jan. 1, 1860	12	39	6	1	3	137	6 50	Pecuniary prospects more encouraging.

Names of Agents and Missionaries.	Post-Office Address.	Field of Labor.	Date of Commission.	Months Commiss'd.	Weeks labor reported.	Stations supplied.	Baptized.	Received by letter.	Schol's in S. S. & B. Class.	Contrib. to Benevolent Objects.	Additional Facts Reported.
George Scott	Strawberry Point	Strawberry Point	Jan. 1, 1861	12	13	....	..	....	....	......	Paying off debt on church edifice.
Charles E. Brown	Vernon Springs	Vernon Springs and other places	Aug. 1, 1859	12	26	3	23	3	80	55 18	Revival.
"	"	Vernon Springs and other places	Aug. 1, 1860	12	26	....	1	2	30	59 00	Labor interrupted for want of a place of worship
G. G. Edwards	Toledo	Toledo	Jan. 1, 1860	12	31	4	10	6	150	......	Resigned.
J. F. Childs	Oskaloosa	Oskaloosa	Aug. 1, 1859	12	26	1	18	5	120	12 55	Congregations large and encouraging.
"	"	"	Aug. 1, 1860	12	26	....	..	7	....	43 10	
O. A. Holmes	Webster City	Webster City	Nov. 1, 1859	12	39	4	15	....	83	......	Revival. Church pecuniarily weak.
"	"	"	Nov. 1, 1860	12	13	3	..	....	....	......	Commenced building a church edifice.
A. G. Eberhart	Waterloo	Waterloo	Sept. 1, 1859	12	26	2	15	3	147	10 00	Will do without further aid.
"	Cedar Rapids	Cedar Rapids	Nov. 1, 1860	12	13	1	11	4	70	......	Religion in a low state.
S. H. Worcester	Ottumwa	Ottumwa	Nov. 1, 1859	12	39	5	5	2	40	7 00	Building a church edifice at an out-station.
"	"	"	Nov. 1. 1860	12	13	....	..	7	....	2 50	Sunday school very interesting.
A. H. Starkweather	Lyons	Lyons and vicinity	July 1, 1859	12	13	3	..	....	85	7 00	Building a church edifice.
"	"	"	July 1, 1860	12	39	....	6	....	70	......	Completed a church edifice. Revival.
John Fulton	Independence	Independence	Oct. 1, 1859	12	26	....	2	3	35	......	Need a place of worship.
"	"	"	Oct. 1, 1860	12	26	7	6	1	45	......	Revival at an out-station.
A. W. Russell	Winterset	Winterset	Oct. 1, 1859	12	26	3	3	....	40	......	A growing interest in the cause of Christ.
"	"	Western Iowa Association	Oct. 1, 1860	12	26	....	2	3	....	125 00	Is encouraged and strengthened.
F. D. Rickerson	Grinnell	Grinnell	Nov. 1, 1859	12	39	2	15	1	50	9 00	Revival. Pastor resigned.
L. L. Frisk	Mineral Ridge	Swede Bend, etc.	Oct. 1, 1859	12	26	7	5	....	20	5 00	Opposition from errorists.
"	" "	" "	Oct. 1, 1860	12	26	8	1	4	....	......	Severe snow-storms interfered with labors.
Wm. A. Eggleston	Denmark	Denmark	Oct. 1, 1859	12	26	3	4	....	60	12 00	Ch. in an improved condition. Pastor resigns.
Isaac Butterfield	Davenport	Davenport	Oct. 1, 1859	12	26	1	..	12	350	41 75	Ask for no further aid.
U. B. Walton	Cedar Falls	Cedar Falls	Nov. 1, 1859	12	39	5	13	2	115	28 14	Infidelity abounds. Pastor leaves the field.
Thomas S. Griffith	Keokuk	Keokuk	Sept. 1, 1859	12	26	1	..	3	105	27 00	Valuable members removing.
"	"	"	Sept. 1, 1860	12	26	....	13	2	140	77 50	Revival.
Lemuel Yarnal	Adel, Dallas Co.	Adel and Panora	Oct. 1, 1859	12	26	4	4	....	....	1 00	Progressing.
"	" "	" "	Oct. 1, 1860	12	26	5	9	....	....	......	Revival at Panora.
H. H. Burrington	Waverly	Waverly and Janesville	April 1, 1860	12	52	4	3	3	50	19 51	Churches revived.
"	"	" "	April 1, 1861	12	....	....	..	....	....	......	
J. Ellis Guild	Rising Sun	Iowa Central Association	April 1, 1860	12	52	....	4	2	....	76 44	Revival in his field. Several baptized besides those reported. Discontinues his labors in this field.
Samuel Pickard	Keokuk	Lee and other counties	Mar. 1, 1860	12	52	7	174	8	380	317 60	An interesting field. People anxious to have the Gospel.
"	"	" "	Mar. 1, 1861	....	....	....	..	....	....	......	
John Y. Aitchison	Delhi	Manchester and Delhi	June 1, 1860	12	39	3	5	2	99	14 50	Wife deceased. Improved state of religious feeling.

NAMES OF AGENTS AND MISSIONARIES.	POST-OFFICE ADDRESS.	FIELD OF LABOR.	Date of Commission.	Months Commis'd.	Weeks labor reported.	Stations supplied.	Baptized	Received by letter.	Schol's in S. S. & B. Class.	Contrib's to Benevolent Objects.	ADDITIONAL FACTS REPORTED.
J. Edminster	Camanche	Camanche	Aug. 1, 1860	12	26	1	..	1	....	......	Completed church edifice. Have facilities for success.
W. W. Moore	McGregor	McGregor	Dec. 1, 1860	6	13	1	..	1	126	75 00	Organized a church of eighteen members.
MINNESOTA.											
Amory Gale	Minneapolis	Minnesota	April 1, 1860	12	52	....	4	....	....	......	Exploring agent and general itinerant.
Timothy R. Cressy	Hastings	Hastings	Mar. 1, 1860	12	52	3	4	5	120	......	Purchased and paid for a convenient place of worship.
" "	"	"	Mar. 1, 1861	....	....	....	..	....	....	......	
John C. Hyde	St. Anthony	St. Anthony	June 1, 1859	12	13	3	..	....	40	8 15	Piety of the church increased.
" "	"	"	June 1, 1860	12	39	....	..	4	125	.....	Repairing their church edifice, but need a better one.
W. C. Shepard	Wasioja	Wasioja and vicinity	Oct. 1, 1859	12	26	3	..	5	70	10 00	Encouraging indications.
" "	"	Wasioja and Rice Lake	Oct. 1, 1860	12	26	....	..	....	....	2 00	
B. Wharton	Wabashaw	Wabashaw	May 1, 1859	12	13	....	5	1	35	......	
"	"	"	May 1, 1860	12	30	4	2	5	110	......	Resigned.
Edgar Cady	Dodge City	Owatonna	June 1, 1859	12	13	4	1	3	55	......	Resigned.
John LaGrange	St. Peter	St. Peter and Traverse	May 1, 1859	12	13	2	3	1	87	......	Encountered much opposition.
A. Norelius	Redwing	Swedes in Wastado and So. Minnesota	April 1, 1860	12	52	....	11	1	22	5 89	Church blessed with steadfastness.
"	Spencer	" "	April 1, 1861	12	....	....	..	....	....	......	
Enos Munger	Lakeland	Lakeland	April 1, 1860	12	52	3	7	....	60	6 55	Revival.
H. C. Hazen	Faribault	Faribault	Jan. 1, 1860	12	39	3	16	1	80	......	Good indications of spiritual progress.
" "	"	"	Jan. 1, 1861	12	13	....	..	....	85	17 00	
Erastus Westcott	Rochester	Rochester	Aug. 1, 1859	12	26	1	2	3	92	......	Church united and prosperous. Pastor resigned.
Wm. C. Phillips	St. Cloud	St. Cloud	May 1, 1859	12	13	2	2	....	42	8 00	Revival at an out-station.
" "	"	"	May 1, 1860	12	39	....	1	3	....	......	Prospects good. Commenced a church edifice at Silver Creek.
Geo. W. Fuller	Chatfield	Chatfield	June 1, 1859	12	13	5	11	4	70	17 00	Revival. Organized a church at an out-station.
" "	"	"	June 1, 1860	12	39	1	1	5	68	61 00	Progressing.
J. F. Wilcox	Northfield	Northfield	Aug. 1, 1859	12	26	3	..	5	42	......	
" "	"	"	April 1, 1860	12	26	....	2	2	35	......	Pastor encouraged.
A. M. Torbet	Taylor's Falls	Taylor's Falls and St. Croix Falls	May 1, 1859	12	13	2	..	....	100	3 00	Congregations attentive.
" "	"	" "	May 1, 1860	12	39	3	..	2	....	2 00	Depressed and discouraged at times.
A. Smith Lyon	Newport	Newport and Cottage Grove	June 1, 1859	12	13	3	..	....	50	67 50	
" "	"	Newport and other places	June 1, 1860	12	39	2	..	....	65	5 05	Need a church edifice.
Isaac Waldron	Stanton	Zumbrota and Cannon Falls	Nov. 1, 1859	12	39	4	8	2	175	18 00	Revival at Warsaw. Organized churches at two out-stations.

C

NAMES OF AGENTS AND MISSIONARIES.	POST-OFFICE ADDRESS.	FIELD OF LABOR.	Date of Commission.	Months Commis'd.	Weeks labor reported.	Stations supplied.	Baptized.	Received by letter.	Schol'rs in S. S. & B. Class.	Contrib's to Benevolent Objects.	ADDITIONAL FACTS REPORTED.
Isaac Waldron	Stanton	Cannon Falls and Valley	Nov. 1, 1860	12	13	4	..	1	76	......	Building a church edifice at Warsaw.
H. B. Slater	Saratoga	Saratoga and vicinity	Oct. 1, 1859	12	21	1	2	8	95	3 54	Will do without further aid.
Moses Heath	Belle Plaine	Belle Plaine and Jordan	April 1, 1860	12	52	6	7	....	65	......	Church in Jordan revived.
" "	" "	" "	April 1, 1861	....	....	....	..	....	....	......	
E. F. Gurney	Austin	Austin and vicinity	Mar. 1, 1860	12	52	5	6	12	10	2 00	Harmony and spirituality prevail in the church.
" "	"	" "	Mar. 1, 1861	....	....	....	..	....	....	......	
R. H. Weeks	Monticello	Monticello	Nov. 1, 1859	12	39	5	5	8	....	8 00	Revival at Silver Creek and a church organized.
" "	"	"	Nov. 1, 1860	12	13	....	..	....	....	9 00	Need a church edifice.
S. S. Utter	Shakapee	Shakapee and Chaska	Nov. 1, 1859	12	39	4	4	5	50	......	Is encouraged by progress made.
" "	"	" "	Nov. 1, 1860	12	13	5	7	2	....	......	Need a church edifice.
A. P. Graves	Lake City	Lake City	June 1, 1859	12	13	4	..	5	182	......	Wife deceased. Signs of advance in the cause of truth.
" "	" "	"	June 1, 1860	12	39	....	4	9	165	......	
J. E. Ash	Mankato	Mankato and vicinity	Aug. 1, 1859	12	26		4	3	....	100 00	Much religious interest in the church.
" "	"	Mankato and St. Peter	Aug. 1, 1860	12	26	4	1	1	15	......	Revival in Mankato. Declension at St. Peter.
M. W. Hopkins	High Forrest	Hamilton and High Forrest	Jan. 1, 1860	12	39	4	5	3	61	4 00	Congregations good, and is encouraged. Church at High Forrest commenced a church edifice.
O. O. Stearns	Winona	Winona	Dec. 1, 1859	12	39	7	2	2	116	3 14	Church united. Would be encouraged but for debt on church edifice.
" "	"	"	Dec. 1, 1860	12	13	4	..	4	140	5 66	Paying debt on church edifice.
Elijah S. Smith	Wilton	Blooming Grove and Wilton	Jan. 1, 1860	12	39	3	..	1	46	......	Organized a church at an out-station.
" "	"		Jan. 1, 1861	12	13	6	.	...	....	.....	
D. L. Babcock	St. Charles	St. Charles and Utica	April 1, 1860	12	52	3	1	8	56	10 00	Congregation falling off for want of a ch. edifice.
A. B. Green	Stillwater	Stillwater	May 1, 1860	12	39	7	1	....	....	35 00	People generally indifferent to religion.
J. A. Peterson	Scandia	Swedes in S. and other places	Sept. 1, 1860	12	22	3	2	....	62	......	Sunday school interesting and hopeful.
Frederick Hill	Bear Valley	Farmington and Chester	Sept. 1, 1860	12	26	 4	7	7	59	......	People anxious to hear the Gospel.
NEBRASKA.											
G. W. Barnes	Omaha	Omaha and vicinity	June 1, 1859	12	9	....	1	4	20	......	
" "	"	Omaha and Belleview	May 1, 1860	12	39	3	1	5	30	......	Revival of religion.
J. G. Bowen	Nebraska City	Nebraska City	Dec. 1, 1859	12	13	....	27	5	40	4 15	Revival.
John M. Taggart	Cuming City	Fontenelle & Cuming City	June 1, 1859	12	13	5	2	2	57	......	Increased attention to religion.
" "	" "	Cuming City	June 1, 1860	12	39	....	6	4	80	......	Ch. revived and prospects encouraging.
J. D. P. Hungate	Tekamah	Tekamah and vicinity	July 1, 1860	12	37	4	..	2	....	......	Good attention to the preaching of the Gospel.

NAMES OF AGENTS AND MISSIONARIES.	POST-OFFICE ADDRESS.	FIELD OF LABOR.	Date of Commission.	Months Commis'd.	Weeks labor reported.	Stations supplied.	Baptized.	Received by Letter.	Schol's in S. S. & B. Class.	Contrib. to Benevolent Objects.	ADDITIONAL FACTS REPORTED.
KANSAS.											
R. C. Brant	Lawrence	Kansas	April 1, 1860	12	52	....	2		....	......	People attentive to the preaching of the Gospel.
E. Allward	Wathena	Doniphan Co.	April 1, 1860	12	52	6	19	13	120	175 87	Revival.
W. O. Thomas	Lawrence	Lawrence	June 1, 1859	12	13	1	22	1	80	......	Church strengthened and encouraged. Many of the baptised united with another Baptist ch.
Wm. J. Kermott	Manhattan	Manhattan	Aug. 1, 1859	12	26	....	2	14	50	125 00	
" "	"	"	Aug. 1, 1860	12	26	1	21	7	70	2 00	Revival. Need a church edifice. Embarrassed by sufferings of the people generally.
C. C. Hutchison	Topeka	Topeka, etc.	Aug. 1, 1860	12	26	3	5	4	40	100 00	Organized a church. Building a church edifice.
J. M. Lackey	Olathe	Johnson Co.	Nov. 1, 1859	12	39	6	12	22	46	......	Progressing.
" "	"	"	Nov. 1, 1860	6	13	....	4	6	....	18 75	The sufferings of the people, and political troubles, give them but little time for religion.
Aaron Perkins	Lawrence	Lawrence	Dec. 1, 1860	6	13	1	..	....	....	......	
Nelson Alvord	Oskaloosa	Oskaloosa and Hebron	June 1, 1860	12	39	4	1	....	....	......	Famine very severe in his field.
William Hobbs	Mound City	Linn Co.	July 1, 1860	12	39	3	21	19	....	27 06	Organized a church at Green Valley. People suffering from famine.
H. S. Tibbits	Hiawatha	Brown and Lebanon Cos.	July 1, 1860	12	39	8	4	15	....	......	Organized a church at Irving. Great want among his people. Pastor lost his library by fire.
Israel Harris	Hartford	Neosha Valley	Sept. 1, 1860	12	26	4	..	2	140	18 50	Encouraging indications. Prevalence of error on this field.
NEW MEXICO.											
J. Milton Shaw	Socorro	Socorro, etc.	Oct. 1, 1859	12	26	....	6	....	....	......	Catholic priest at Toas acting independently of the bishop, teaching the people that the Bible is the only rule of faith and practice. Mr. Shaw well received by him.
" "	"	"	Oct. 1, 1860	12	13	....	..	....	....	......	Bibles and religious books much inquired for by the people.
Samuel Gorman	Santa Fe	Santa Fe	Oct. 1, 1859	12	26	....	..	....	15	......	Has a day school, which he finds advantageous. Sunday congregations generally composed of people of the best standing for intellect and virtue in the community.
" "	"	"	Oct. 1, 1860	12	26	....	..	....	20	......	Romanists endeavoring to break up his school. Distributed many books and tracts to good advantage.

NAMES OF AGENTS AND MISSIONARIES.	POST-OFFICE ADDRESS.	FIELD OF LABOR.	Date of Commission.	Months Commis'd.	Weeks labor reported.	Stations supplied.	Baptized.	Received by Letter.	Schol's in S. S. & B. Class.	Contrib. to Benevolent Objects.	ADDITIONAL FACTS REPORTED.
Jose Senun	Albuquerque	Indians at Laguna, etc.	Oct. 1, 1859	12	26						Taken sick.
" "	"	" "	Oct. 1, 1860	6	26						Health improved so as to talk to the people who visit him. Been elected Governor of the Pueblo by the same parties who formerly persecuted him.
" "	"	" "	April 1, 1861	12							
Jose Maria Chaves	Peralto	Peralto, etc.	April 1, 1860	12	52						People anxious to hear the Gospel.
" " "	"	"	April 1, 1861	12							
Jose Santos Tayes	Socorro	Socorro Co.	April 1, 1860	12	39						Some give encouraging attention, others maltreat him.
" " "	"	"	April 1, 1861	12							
Antonio Jose Garcia	Manzana	Manzana and vicinity	April 1, 1860	12	52						Encouraged by the willingness of the people to hear the truth.
Blas Chaves	Santa Fe	Santa Fe, etc.	Oct. 1, 1859	12	26						Work retarded for the want of religious books, Bibles, and Testaments.
" "	"	"	Oct. 1, 1860	6	26						People devoted to idolatry and vice, and but few listen to preaching.
" "	"	"	Oct. 1, 1861	12							
CALIFORNIA.											
J. B. Saxton	Oakland	Oakland and Brooklyn	June 1, 1859	12	13	2	1		66		Building a church edifice in Brooklyn.
" "	"	" "	June 1, 1860	4	17			2			Finished the church edifice, and will do without further aid.
H. Holcombe Rhees	Marysville	Marysville	Jan. 1, 1860	12	39	1		13			Need a church edifice.
" "	"	"	Jan. 1, 1861	12	13			1			A good feeling among the members of the ch.
C. W. Rees	Petaluma	Petaluma	M'ch 1, 1860	12	52	1	3	12	66		Finished a good church edifice, and gaining influence in the community.
Benjamin Brierly	Nevada	Nevada	May 1, 1860	12	26	4		5			Purchased a church edifice.
OREGON.											
Samuel Cornelius, jr.	Portland	Portland	July 1, 1860	12	39	1		6	65	9 00	Organized a church. Is encouraged.
NEW GRANADA.											
Philip B. Livingston	San Andreas	San Andreas	April 1, 1860	12	26		25		143	20 00	Revival.

STATE CONVENTIONS

AND

GENERAL ASSOCIATIONS IN THE UNITED STATES,

With the Names and Post-office Addresses of the Corresponding Secretaries; the Time and Place of their Anniversaries for 1861; *the number of Missionaries employed, and amount of Receipts into their Treasuries for* 1860, *including Balances of the previous year.*

STATES.	CORRESPONDING SECRETARIES.	POST-OFFICE ADDRESSES.	PLACES OF NEXT ANNIVERSARY.	Time of Anniversary.	Number of Missionaries.	Amount of Receipts for Dom. Miss. in 1860.
Maine*	N. M. Wood	Waterville	....	....	....	....
New Hampshire	K. S. Hall	Manchester	Lake Village	Oct. 16	16	$1612 25
Vermont	T. H. Archibald	Mount Holly	Factory Point	Oct. 2	12	2300 14
Massachusetts	J. Ricker	Boston	Boston	Oct. 30	40	4002 79
Rhode Island	A. H. Granger	Providence	Providence	April 30	9	1970 26
Connecticut	E. Cushman	West Hartford	Norwich	June 11	6	2014 25
New York	John Smitzer	Oneida	Albany	Oct. 9	48	9277 19
New Jersey	J. M. Carpenter	Jacobstown	Newark	Oct. 29	19	2212 53
Pennsylvania	Malachi Taylor	Philadelphia	Lower Merion	....	30	6570 72
Maryland	A. Fuller Crane	Baltimore	Baltimore	Nov. 13	13	3953 14
Virginia*	H. K. Ellyson	Richmond	....	....	....	....
North Carolina*	J. B. Solomon	Warrenton	....	....	....	....
South Carolina*	J. J. Brantly	Greenville	....	....	....	....
Georgia*	J. F. Dagg	Cuthbert	....	....	....	....
Alabama*	T. W. Tobey	....	....	....	....	....
Mississippi*	W. M. Farrar	Jackson	....	....	....	....
Louisiana*	B. Egan	Rehoboth	....	....	....	....
Texas*	F. J. Kelly	....	....	....	....	....
Tennessee*	G. W. Griffin	Knoxville	....	....	....	....
Arkansas*	John J. Harris	Tulip	....	....	....	....
Kentucky*	A. Broaddus	Louisville	....	....	....	....
Missouri*	Leland Wright	Fayette	....	....	....	....
Illinois	A. J. Joslyn	Chicago	Ottawa	Oct. 18	10	2435 76
Indiana	Gibbon Williams	Indianapolis	Greensburgh	Oct. 22	12	2464 23
Ohio	D. F. Carnahan	Zanesville	Mansfield	Oct. 24	12	3715 01
Michigan*	J. A. Clark	Adrian	....	....	....	....
Wisconsin	J. W. Fish	Fox Lake	Racine	Sept. 18	9	980 49
Iowa	J. F. Childs	Oskaloosa	Keokuk	Oct. 19	6	2925 55
Minnesota*	J. D. Pope	St. Paul	....	....	....	....
Kansas	E. Allward	Wathena	Lawrence	June 5	....	....
California	J. B. Saxton	Oakland	....	....	....	....
Oregon*	....	....	....	....	....	....

Amount of receipts reported above.................................$44,464 05
Amount of receipts of the H. M. Society.............................62,002 99

Total amount reported for Home and Domestic Mission purposes....$106,467 04

AGGREGATE CONTRI

FROM ALL THE STATES SINC

STATES.	Total Amount to 1850.	1851-1855.	1856.	1857.	
Canada	$1,139 49	$1,063 80	$143 75	36	$116
Maine	3,214 40	1,053 22	102 44	09	27
New Hampshire	4,874 62	6,519 01	1,608 22	1,627 09	1,377
Vermont	4,072 96	3,741 64	1,186 34	967 44	860
Massachusetts	41,291 55	43,460 77	10,467 62	10,176 01	11,620
Rhode Island	12,207 02	9,734 31	2,560 07	1,768 88	1,265
Connecticut	17,660 91	16,391 14	4,047 46	3,840 83	3,039
New York	100,644 16	79,584 59	14,796 65	14,835 15	13,020
New Jersey	14,990 78	15,414 29	2,985 34	2,498 44	2,637
Pennsylvania	9,449 57	12,388 36	2,507 69	1,894 36	2,277
Delaware	603 50	740 70	103 75	183 04	61
Maryland	2,055 06	15 50	200 00	....	......
District of Columbia	993 12	211 31	.. ....	9 22	......
Ohio	1,369 57	7,616 25	2,708 28	1,065 00	864
Michigan	1,719 95	3,375 32	179 23	199 72	284
Indiana	104 86	7,142 38	656 72	1,317 29	1,013
Illinois	4,348 55	8,516 80	1,700 17	150 80	124

LIST OF LEGACIES

PAID TO THE SOCIETY SINCE ITS ORGANIZATION.

1834	Dea. Josiah Penfield, Savannah, Ga., per Rev. H. O. Wyer.	$1250 00
1835	Mrs. Clarissa Long, Shelburne, Mass., per W. Wilder, Esq., Executor	37 50
"	William Powers, Hebron, N. H., per Rev. I. Merriam	100 00
"	Miss Maria Curtis, Southbridge, Mass., per Rev. E. Going	200 00
"	Mrs. Jemima Elliott, Hampton, Ct., per Rev. J. Payne, Executor	100 00
1836	Mrs. Betsey Sprague, Attleboro', Mass., per Mr. A. Beed, Executor	451 25
"	Robert Rodgers, Newport, R. I.	25 00
"	Ebenezer Boyd, Providence, R. I.	10 00
1839	Mrs. Abigail Marshall, New York, per Mr. Schofield, Executor	702 17
"	Mrs. Margaret Pugsley, Dutchess Co., N. Y., per Miss Cornelia Pugsley	280 00
"	Mrs. Irene Coats, New York, per Alfred Decker, Esq.	250 00
1841	Mrs. Elizabeth G. Moore, Hartford, Ct., per J. B. Gilbert	200 00
1842	Nathaniel Tucker, Milton, Mass., per W. D. Ticknor	200 50
1843	Mrs. Margaret Martin, Montgomery, N. Y., per Mr. J. J. Martin, Executor	100 00
"	Miss Cynthia M. Wright, Suffield, Ct., per H. Sheldon, Administrator	50 00
1844	Mr. Zephaniah Eddy, New Bedford, Mass., per Rev. H. Jackson, Executor	150 00
"	Mr. Josiah Kendall, Groton, Mass., per F. E. Wheelock and Rev. A. Sanderson, Executors	1150 00
"	Miss Jane McCall, Society Hill, S. C., per John McIver	20 00
"	Miss Lydia Sweetser, South Reading, Mass., per H. Sweetser	324 00
"	Mrs. Elizabeth Griffin, New York, per one of her heirs	83 34
"	Josiah Flint, Cornish, N. H., per Mr. A. Burnap	80 00
"	Thomas Cooper, Esq., Eatonton, Ga., per Hon. M. A. Cooper, Executor	2000 00
"	Miss Betsey Hutchinson, Passumpsic, Vt., per L. P. Parks	50 00
"	Rev. Amos Dodge, Brighton, Macoupin Co., Ill., by his widow	30 00
"	Mr. John Ward, Warren, N. Y., per J. Northrop and A. Ward, Executors	847 50
1845	Joseph H. Hayden, Saybrook, Ct., per H. L. Champlin, Executor	100 00
1846	John Allen, Centreville, R. I., per H. Hamilton, and Rev. E. K. Fuller, Executors	3805 00
"	Rev. Jesse Mercer, Wilks Co., Ga., per B. M. Saunders, Executor	1331 87
"	Miss Mary Bliven, McDonough, N. Y., per Rev. John Peck,	46 75
"	Mrs. Betsey Haykes, Cincinnatus, N. Y., per Trustees of the Baptist Society	100 00
"	Mrs. Charlotte Cole, Alexandria, Va., per Robert Ball, Executor	10 00
"	Dea. Medad Jackson, W. Meredith, N. Y., per H. Jackson and W. Stillson, Executors	1105 00
"	Mrs. Urania Grant, West Wrentham, Mass., per R. E. Eddy	20 00
"	Mr. Richard Dubois, Malta, N. Y., per H. J. Rodgers, Executor	50 00
1847	Dea. Saxton Bailey, Lebanon, Ct., per Executor	100 00
"	Mr. Lewis Porter, Covert, N. Y., in advance, per J. McLellan	250 00
"	Miss Mary Havens, St. Catharine, Canada West, per Rev. E. Savage	68 93
"	Miss Amanda Hadley, Brattleboro', N. H., per Rev. J. Z. Foster	25 00
"	James Shearer, Canada West, per Rev. E. Savage	151 00
"	L. Crossman, Elbridge, N. Y., in advance	30 00
1848	William Jones, Iowa City, Iowa, per G. W. Hampton, Executor	25 00
"	Hon. James Vanderpool, Newark, N. J., per B. Vanderpool, Executor	1000 00
"	Miss Susan Farrar, Keene, N. H., per G. Robins	10 00
"	Mrs. Eunice Nicholls, Cambridge, Mass., per E. Mansfield, Executor	500 00
"	Mrs. Hannah Carleton, Portland, Me., per Rev. G. J. Carleton, Administrator	500 00
1849	Mr. Samuel R. Stelle, Piscataway, N. J., per Lewis R. Stelle, Esq., Executor	200 00
"	Mrs. Phebe Gale, East Bennington, Vt., per Executor of Estate of S. Harmon	25 00
"	Mr. William Reynolds, Boston, Mass., per J. H. Duncan, Esq., and Mrs. Susan D. Reynolds, Executors, a part ($625) in secured notes	1500 00
"	Josiah Lyman, Andover, Ct., per N. B. Lyman, Executor	50 00
"	John J. Martin, Montgomery, N. Y., per M. Bookstaver, Executor	1000 00

1849 Mrs. Martha Howe, West Boylston, Mass., per Messrs. E. J. H
" A. H. Reed, Sweden, N. Y., per Rev. D. Searl ....
" Asa H. Truman, Owego, N. Y., per E. Truman, Executor....
1850 George D. James, Amenia, N. Y., J. K. Mead and N. Ross,
" John Everett, Manchester, Mich., per F. Everett............
" Jacob Whitman, Belvidere, Ill., in part, per N. Crosby, Esq..
" Jonas Taylor, Boston, Mass.......................................
" Miss Rebecca Thompson, Amenia, N. Y., per A. B. Capwell, I
" Joanna Minot, Boston, Mass., per E. Mears and I. Parker, Ex
" Claudius F. Brown, Arkwright, N. Y., per David Barrell......
" Miss Anna Roe, Egremont, Mass., per R. B. Brown, Executor
1851 David Schauber, Burnt Hills, N. Y., per J. and D. M. Schaul
" Woolcott Griffin, Gouverneur, N. Y., per O. L. Barnum, Exe
" Joseph Flanders, Brooklyn, N. Y., per Mrs. Eliza A. and Ben
" William Williams, New York, per John Allen Executor..
" Eli Wiley, South Reading, Mass..................................
1852 Miss Pharozene C. Kelly, Hopkinton, N. H., per John Page..
" Jonathan W. Ford, Boston, Mass.................................
" Theron Fisk, Warsaw, N. Y., in advance.........................
" Joshua A. Burke, Brooklyn, N. Y., per Messrs. E. and W. A.
" Eliza Skaats, New York, in part, per G. N. Bleecker, Executo
" Barnum M. Howard, Sweden, N. Y., per H. M. Howard, Exe
1853 Alanson Stewart, Liberty, N. Y., per W. W. Murphy.......
" Mrs Sarah B. Pierce, Middleboro', Mass. ....
" Arnold Whipple, Providence, R. I., per Mrs. P. Whipple, Exe
" Mrs. Fanny McGilvreay, Brookline, N. H. (Annuity), per H.
" Mrs. Lucretia Goddard, Worcester, Mass., per Hon. I. Davis,
" P. F. Brayton, Providence, R. I., per A. K. and Rev. J. Bray

1855	Andrew McCleary, Frederick City, Md., per Albert Ritchie	$200 00
1856	Miss Hannah Briggs, Rock Island, Ill., per Rev. A. Briggs	50 00
"	Eunice Upham, West Woodstock, Ct., P. Corbin, jr., Executor	327 34
"	Hon. Nathan H. Bottum, Shaftsbury, Vt., per Norman Bottum, Executor	180 00
"	Miss Eliza Jackson, Hamilton, N. Y., per Prof. P. B. Spear	100 00
"	Mrs. M. W. Denison, Rock Island, Ill., per Rev. J. W. Denison	8 00
"	Miss Achsah Cox, Imlaystown, N. J.	50 00
"	Samuel Stone, Dundee, Mich., T. Babcock, Executor	30 00
"	Louisa S. Platt, Haverhill, Mass., S. Peaslie, Executor	35 00
"	Mrs. Hannah Kent, Danversport, Mass.	100 00
"	Manley Street, Holyoke, Mass.	25 00
"	Mrs. Lorain Sheldon, Suffield, Ct.	355 47
"	Mrs. Abigail Hatch, Boston, Mass., per Thomas Mair, Executor	1491 24
"	David Stanton, Penn's Neck, N. J., per George Kelton, Executor	165 00
"	Rev. Azel Waters, Miama, Ia., per C. W. Morgan, Executor	219 38
1857	Mrs. Rachael Prescott, per John Crockett, Executor	100 00
"	Azariah Snow, Lunenburgh, Vt., per John Snow, Executor	15 00
"	Mrs. E. K. Babcock, Jay, N. Y., per Rev. J. J. Babcock	4 75
"	Wm. Cook, Worcester, N. Y.	100 00
"	Mrs. Elizabeth Hovey, Cambridge, Mass., George Cummings, Executor	3000 00
"	Hannah Godfrey, Hastings, N. Y., C. A. Wilson, Executor	10 00
"	Betsey Miller, Eariville, N. Y., per L. H. Miller	100 00
"	Mrs. Phebe Mulford, Roadstown, N. J., per I. Smalley, Executor	50 00
"	Hannah S. Trask, Fall River, Mass., R. C. Brown and Joseph Borden, Executors	402 13
"	Miss Catharine Sharp, Barre, N. Y., in part, per A. L. Daniels	415 00
"	Miss Achsah Pierce, Mohawk, N. Y., per Rev. H. T. Love	149 47
"	Michael Shepherd, Salem, Mass., per H. F. Shepherd, Executor	2957 60
"	Cornelia A. Perry, Centre White Creek, N. Y., per Nathaniel Cottrell, Executor	300 00
"	Mrs. Eleanor Willard, Harvard, Mass.	100 00
"	Sabina Bennett, West Eaton, N. Y.	14 00
"	James Nickerson, Cazenovia, N. Y., Benj. T. Clark, Executor	100 60
1858	Jabez Keep and wife, Cortlandville, N. Y., per Rev. Henry Bowen	789 68
"	Aaron Treat, North Stonington, Ct.	5 00
"	Mrs. Martha Straton, Woburn, Mass., per B. Millett, Executor, in part	575 42
"	Mrs. Franklinia E. Aikman, Burlington, N. J.	508 68
"	J. B. Jones, Roxbury, Mass., per S. Walker and G. B. Jones, Executors	1000 00
"	Mrs. Sarah H. Canfield, Stanford, N. Y., per Cor. N. Campbell, Executor	505 90
"	Mrs. Jane B. Dustin, Concord, N. H., Enos Blake, Executor	800 00
"	Miss Martha Whiting, Charlestown, Mass., Interest on her Legacy, per A. J. Bellows, Ex.	490 00
"	Mrs. Susan Hull, Adams, N. Y., per Abram Sheldon, Executor	100 00
"	Benjamin Porter, Danvers, Interest on his Legacy	232 50
"	Miss Deborah Flock, Lawrence, N. J., per James B. Coleman, Executor	100 00
"	Elisha Ashley, Poultney, Vt., per J. Joslin, Executor	500 00
1859	Miss Hannah Spaulding, Chelmsford, Mass.	100 00
"	Joel Hayford, Farmersville, N. Y., per Jarvis Leonard, Executor	50 00
"	Miss Amelia M. Cone, Philadelphia, per O. W. Davis	51 13
"	Daniel Flagg, Littleton, Mass.	50 00
"	Lucy F. Granger, Mass., per B. J. Spaulding	50 00
"	Interest on legacy of Polly Browning, Waterford, Ct.	39 09
"	Mrs. Abigail Lamb, Newton, Mass., Eben Stone, Executor	800 00
"	Micajah Reynolds, Newark, N. J., Messrs. Hollyer and Kitchell, Executors	2131 00
"	Miss Betsey Harriman, Georgetown, Mass., in part	500 00
"	Mrs. Lucy Johnson, West Medbury, Mass., per Rev. E. C. Messenger	200 09
"	Miss Catharine Orcutt, Cambridgeport, Mass.	284 00
"	Miss Anna Marchant, Barnstable, Mass., Freeman Marchant, Executor	225 00
"	Joseph McCulloch, Newport, R. I., W. D. Southwick, Executor	200 00
"	Mrs. Phebe Taylor, Syracuse, N. Y., in part	5 00
"	Sarah S. T. Davis, Gaines, N. Y., per Jesse S. Wetmore	295 00
"	John Tustin, Chester Springs, Pa.	10 00

1859	Ezra Reynolds, Benton, Pa.; in part, Saml. Manchester, Executor	$50 00
"	Henry Case, Sweden, N. Y., Rev. Z. Case, Executor	150 00
"	Rev. Jacob Drake, Delaware, Ohio	544 22
"	Miss Mary True, Plainfield, N. H., Reuben True, Executor	200 00
"	Lucy A. Roberts, Cromwell, Ct., Mrs. Hubbard, Executrix	50 00
"	An aged sister, Thetford, Vt., per W. W. Baker	20 00
"	Lucy F. Gray, Chelmsford, Mass	60 92
"	Isaac Morse, New Woodstock, N. Y	50 00
"	Mrs. Mary E. Arnold, W. Medway, Mass, per Rev. E. C. Messenger, a part in Bank Stock.	425 00
"	Junia Freeman, Rushford, N. Y., E. B. Freeman, Executor	53 50
"	Thomas Wakefield, Waterville, N. Y., Henry Tower, Executor	200 00
"	Anna Crossman, Sheldon, Vt., Hon. George Green, Executor	65 00
"	Betsey Harrimon, Georgetown, Mass	152 53
"	Elijah Withington, Morrisania, N. Y., Saml. Wilde and others, Executors	100 00
1860	Tirza E. Gilman, Sanbornton, N. H., Benj. N. Smith, Executor	50 00
"	Rufus Fiske, Cambridge, Mass., Susan Fiske, Executrix	10 00
"	Mrs. J. W. Putnam, Chicopee Falls, Mass., Rev. R. K. Bellamy, Executor	300 00
"	Miss Phebe Arnold, Jay, N. Y.	2300 00
"	Margaretha Medera, New York, Rev. Thomas T. Devan, Executor	2500 00
"	Harvey Tracy, Tunbridge, Vt., per Rev. Leonard Tracy	50 00
"	Miss Sarah Bartholomew, Pa., Jonathan Roberts, Executor	47 50
"	Estate of Lydia Sherwood, Bridgeport, Ct., per Dea. A. Day	278 88
"	Dea. Benjamin Warren, Augusta, N. Y., in part,	89 55
"	Catharine Westgate, Plainfield, N. H., Earl Westgate, Executor	200 00
"	Joseph McCracken, New York, per A. B. Capwell	423 15
"	Mrs. Huldah B. Slosson, Pitcher, N. Y., per E. A. Fish, Executor	25 00
"	Fanny C. Randall, Oneida Castle, N. Y., O. P. Root, Administrator	50 00
"	Johnson N. Reynolds, Pulteney, N. Y., J. J. Reynolds and David Armstrong, Executors	500 00
"	Mrs. Willard Putnam, Danverse, Mass	100 00
"	Elijah Carey, Brookline, Mass., with interest	537 50
"	John Benton, Saratoga Springs, N. Y., with interest, per A. B. Capwell	341 53
"	Catharine Burd, Baptist Town, N. J., per Elder Thomas Barrass	10 00
"	Caleb Hobart, Milton, Mass	395 81
"	Robert Edwards, New York, Horace Holden, Esq., Executor	500 00
"	Mercy Winans, Ogden, N. Y., per M. P. Winans, Executor,	100 00
1861	Mrs. Sophia F. Macomber, Dracut, Mass	102 97
"	Abigail Crouch, West Swanzey, N. H.	8 50
"	William Clark, Syracuse, N. Y., Mrs. Sally Clark, Administratrix	100 00
"	Ebenezer Pearson, Milford, N. H., James Pearson Executor	502 80
"	Rev. Gershom Lane, Moriah, N. Y., in part, per J. F. Havens	100 00
"	Susan M. Lewis, Federal Store, N. Y., Wm. S. Thompson, Executor	50 00
"	Rufus Fisk, Annuity, Cambridge, Mass	10 00
"	William Souldin, Albany, N. Y., per W. S. McIntosh, Executor, in Railroad Stocks, value not known.	

IMPORTANT WHEN WILLS ARE MADE.

Legacies are sometimes diverted from the purposes of testators on account of technical informalities especially in the devising clause. The form of bequest, to which we solicit the careful attention of those friends who kindly intend to place the Society among their legatees, as one which, if followed, will secure to us the favors intended, is as follows:

FORM OF A BEQUEST TO THE SOCIETY.

"I give and bequeath to the American Baptist Home Mission Society, formed in New York, in the year eighteen hundred and thirty-two, the sum of —— dollars, for the purposes of said Society."

Please remember to use the word "Baptist," and to write "Mission," instead of "Missionary."

ADDRESS

OF THE

PRESIDENT OF THE SOCIETY,

ON THE OCCASION OF ITS ANNIVERSARY, MAY 30, 1861.

DEAR BRETHREN,—I was deprived of the pleasure of attending the last Anniversary held at Cincinnati, Ohio, at which time you elected me as your presiding officer, and this is the first opportunity I have had to acknowledge the honor then conferred.

I appreciate this mark of distinction as one I am unworthy to bear, or have the ability to sustain; yet, as you have placed me here, by God's help and your co-operation, I will endeavor to discharge the duties of the office according to my best ability, praying for that "wisdom which cometh down from above," and is able to direct at all times and under all circumstances.

Fifteen years ago you met with this church, to celebrate the fourteenth anniversary of this Society; it was at that anniversary, in 1846, when radical changes were made in the Constitution of the Society, by which it dissolved its auxiliary relations with all the State organizations and became a distinct and independent body, with properly defined character and powers, which have since that period governed its action. An interesting and detailed account of those changes may be found in the Decennial Review of the Executive Board, published in the Twentieth and Twenty-fifth Reports of the Society, 1852 and 1857. To-day, in the providence of God, we are again permitted to meet with this same church, which was once the spiritual home of Dr. Going, the founder of the Society, and of Luther Crawford, his successor in the Secretaryship, to hold our Twenty-ninth Anniversary.

While we would thank God for the continuance of this our beloved Society, and for his fostering care which has ever been over it, we have to mourn the loss, by death and removal, of most of those who then composed the Executive Board; there are present with us to-day *only* one officer and two of the managers, who occupied those positions at that time. These changes are incidents in human life which should prompt us all to work diligently in our Master's service while we have opportunity.

I have ever esteemed my twelve years' service in the Executive Board, as one of the greatest privileges of my life—that of laboring with my brethren in the glorious cause of Home Missions—a work commenced by our Savior when here upon earth, and committed to his apostles, saying, begin at Jerusalem, and from thence go forth throughout the whole world preaching my Gospel to every creature. This is emphatically the work which this Society is now, and ever has been doing, and God grant it may continue to do until the end of time.

The Treasurer will report to you the financial condition of the Society, and the Corresponding Secretary will give a detailed account of the management and operations of the Society for the past year, which precludes the necessity of any further remarks from me.

ıne Uommittee on Home Missions an
That they regard the American Bapti
a position of primary importance amonį
world. Their aim is single, and their fi
means are furnished, they aim to give th
This field is large enough to tax the ener
of American Baptists. Considered with
other portions of the great family of mar
measurable importance. If we confin
Territories, it is obvious that not only t
great extent, the welfare of the world, it
the work of Home Missions. Our hope
Christianity. Let our native and forei
and consecrated to his service, and all o
Christianity triumph here, and we shall
the nations of the earth. We shall be st
spirit of true religion shall live and pre
view of the subject, we must say, with P
world does not present another such missi
are urged to cultivate this field by every
our nation—by the millions of foreigners
population—by the wants of the new an
the intimate connection we have with oth
tion, and missions, and, above all, by the
God by his most precious blood. Shall t
of Home Missions be sustained and carri
and members of the Baptist churches in
will give us increased sympathy and aid i

Territories, or Provinces: Pennsylvania, Delaware, Ohio, Michigan, Indiana, Illinois, Wisconsin, Iowa, Minnesota, Kansas, Nebraska, New Mexico, California, Canada, and New Granada.

The Missionaries reported, as some of the good results of their labors during the year, the organization of fifty churches, the ordination of twenty-four ministers, the baptism of four hundred and ninety-six persons on a profession of their faith in Christ, and the hopeful conversion of sixty others who had not been baptized.

When we consider the rapid increase of population in our new States and Territories, the poverty and temptation in connection with many of the new settlers, and the recklessness and error abounding among residents of good pecuniary conditions; we say not, "there are four months, and then cometh harvest;" but look on the fields, for they are white, all ready to harvest.

We ask for our "Home Mission Society" the earnest prayers and generous contributions of the churches of this Convention; for, in the language of the last annual report, all candid minds will find abundant evidence of the usefulness of the Society, of the faithfulness and success of its missionaries, of the Divine approbation of their labors, and of the necessity of increased prayer and liberality in behalf of this great and good work.

CONNECTICUT.

REPORT ON HOME MISSIONS.

The field which the friends of Home Missions in America are endeavoring to cultivate has been steadily and rapidly increasing in importance from year to year, until it has come to be regarded second to no other, as a missionary field. And, though our efforts in this cause have been somewhat increased, still they are far from being commensurate with its importance. To meet the religious wants of the heterogeneous mass of foreigners cast among us by Divine Providence, coming from every quarter of the globe, and representing every false religion, as well as the wants of the numerous thousands of our own countrymen who have taken up their residence in the West, we must, in harmony with the urgent appeal of Rev. John Angel James to American Christians, concentrate our religious efforts more fully upon our own country. Christian patriotism, the safety of our free institutions, as well as the commission of Christ, seem to demand this at our hands. While, therefore, we rejoice that the amount contributed to the funds of the American Baptist Home Mission Society has been considerably increased the past year, giving evidence of a more enlarged view of the importance of the object generally, we earnestly recommend a still more energetic and adequate co-operation of every friend of the cause in Connecticut.

INDIANA.

REPORT ON HOME MISSIONS.

Your Committee would beg leave to report, that, in their judgment, the American Baptist Home Mission Society is entitled to a large place in the hearts of the

Baptists of this State, and to their steady and hearty co-operation. The Society this year is expending some twelve hundred dollars, and is ready to do all its funds will allow to help feeble churches in the State.

Its history is already most gratifying, and its converts are more than 26,000. Everywhere throughout this whole western country, churches exerting an extensive influence have been built up, and every religious and moral enterprise has been helped forward by the persevering labors of its devoted, self-sacrificing missionaries.

In the year 1836, the whole number of Baptist churches in all the western States was about 1817. There are now more than 6000. We must all acknowledge that the Home Mission Society, under God, has been one of the most efficient instrumentalities in the accomplishment of this glorious result.

While we will unitedly labor for the success of our Domestic Mission enterprise, let us not forget that as in former years we received largely of the Home Mission Society, so now, in our prosperity and enlargement, we should freely give, that the comprehensive plans and noble purposes of the Society may be carried out and accomplished.

IOWA.

The Committee on American Baptist Home Mission Society reported the following, which was unanimously adopted, after remarks by a number of brethren, and a special contribution of $23.50, and $400 pledged:

We regard the purposes, plans, and labors of the American Baptist Home Mission Society with undiminished interest, and consider it entitled to the warmest sympathies and patronage of our churches throughout the State;

1. Because we have the monuments and mementoes of its wise and benevolent aid before us, in the churches and ministers which so largely share in the labors of this Convention;

2. Because its fostering influence has called into being many of the churches, and has induced the erection of many church edifices, which are consecrated to the exhibition of the truth and ordinances of Christ, by the 12,000 Baptists of Iowa;

3. Because it is still engaged in doing good to our State by sustaining valuable laborers in important and commanding positions;

4. Because the "Macedonian cry" from the new and opening settlements of the "regions beyond" us in the vast West, can only be adequately responded to by the vigilance, zeal, and prosperity of the Society;

5. Because hearty co-operation with it affords the best means of promoting the interests of our own Convention, as well as those of Foreign Missions, Bible distribution, Sunday schools, and every great and good work in which our hearts and hands are, and ought to be, employed.

THE STATIONS IN NEW MEXICO.

From Rev. J. M. Shaw.

SOCORRO, N. M., January 5, 1861.

We have been permitted by a good Providence to prosecute our duties and labors another year without any material interruption by sickness or other cause; it is the lot of but few, if any, missionaries to labor in as unpromising and laborious a field as your missionaries in New Mexico; the bitter prejudices of the people against all Americans, and especially Protestants and Protestant missionaries, and the ignorance and vice of the people, make it more laborious and less inviting than the mission fields of our more distant brethren. But a brief review of the past gives us encouragement to hope for the future; and we have to ask, Why have we so little faith? and I often think of a remark I made, when giving a farewell address, before leaving for New Mexico, "that if I was permitted to see a native church gathered of twenty members, at the close of twenty years' labor, I should be amply rewarded for the undertaking." I have not been here half that time yet, and now have gathered around me more than twice that number of devoted brethren and sisters, who are not only willing to lay down their lives, if necessary, for the Gospel, but for us also; taking a stand-point where I stood nine years ago, when I came to this field, and the change appears such as only God can make. It is only four years since we organized our church here of eleven members, since then I have baptized more than twice the original number here, all converted Romanists, besides six I baptized into the fellowship of the church at Peralta, which now constitutes a part of my field of labor. The present number of our church here is thirty-six, two having died, and three which are not in the fellowship of the church. We should ere this, have been worshiping in our new house of worship, but for the impossibility of getting lumber to complete it, having paid for it twice, and failing in both cases to get the lumber; for the want of our house we have not been able to concentrate our efforts as much as I would desire. My congregations are small, varying from five to one hundred, according to circumstances; in Socorro we have (except on funeral occasions) from ten to twenty; in Escondida, an out-station three miles distant, from twenty to thirty; in San Antonito, another out-station, twelve miles distant, about twenty; in Tajo, another out-station, from ten to twenty; at Peralta, another station, from forty to one hundred, this is sixty miles from here, making one hundred and twenty miles' travel to and from my appointments, gathering small congregations on the way; Pulvedero is another out-station ten miles distant, where we have from eight to twelve, on baptismal occasions many more; at Lajollita I have now a house offered for another station, and the family expect soon to be baptized, this is fifteen miles distant, and will be the nucleus for another congregation. I have other places where occasionally I have congregations of from five to ten or fifteen, but not reliable; at all of the others we have members, and their congregations established, and devotion properly conducted, whether I am present or not; all of these are centres of influence, and the membership is of such material that we hope they are permanent. I have a native laborer to assist me in this field, brother Santos Tejea, a man of good

morality; their religion being consistent
much love—hundreds acknowledge the fa
embrace and practice the Christian virtues;
instances has been burned by the priests is
book in a majority of the better families of t
them to study, not to accumulate dust. Re
much interest; box after box of Bibles an
from the tree of life, which are for the heali
so powerful for good, it is not extravagant t
enter into our labors, and see the fruit of
unfold the untold good that has been ar
Mission Society in this dark portion of c
results already attained, and the hope of th
Missions to renewed effort, zeal, and prayer
deluded by false teachers; they are a reli
they will even eat the dust that collects on
rooms, to which they pay their devotion as
minds imbittered against the Gospel by th
idolatry and superstition to the truth as it i
they are told that it is heresy and a da
intimidated by the threats and anathemas
called we trust a few will be chosen.

From Rev. S.

S

Dear Brother,—As you request me to w
of labor, I now endeavor to comply.

My report includes all the field within the

present only a part of the time. When we began Sabbath school we had eight teachers and twenty-five to thirty scholars. But some moved away, and some grew weary of the work, and left us to work alone.

I have taught day school eleven months of the year, and night school about six months. My labors in the school have been exceedingly toilsome, on account of the differences of ability in the scholars, and a want of uniformity in text-books.

Have had in my school during the year sixty scholars. But the average attendance has only been about twenty-five, owing to frequent changes. But, all things considered, we have held our own against the opposition and competition of the Romanists very well. They have now a convent for girls, and what they call a *college* for boys. This last they started since I began my school. And then to catch up what could not or would not enter these schools, they began outside day schools for boys and for girls; and, finally, to get away some of our girls that were farthest advanced, they opened their convent doors to receive outsiders, as day scholars in the convent. This last move on their part, we believe, is very unusual, and it was refused to some of those who came to my school, and who had asked to be received there before they came to me, but afterward they were invited into the convent. And as we did not have teachers in some of the higher female branches, they left us, and went to the convent. But, in return, we have received quite as many boys from their schools as they have girls from ours. In a little time, if we can have means to put up buildings, and procure suitable apparatus and teachers, we shall have a good school, if the Lord bless us.

With fond hope that we shall yet get help, as soon as the financial pressure shall have passed a little, we toil on against wind and tide. We did hope that I could visit the States, to secure this point during the present year, but circumstances seem at present to forbid it. During the year our congregations have been varied. Sometimes we would have as high as seventy-five persons at preaching; at others not over a dozen. But we have not known of any conversions, or even lasting seriousness. The community, generally, high and low, Americans and Mexicans, are so ensnared in vice and sin, that, humanly speaking, there is very little hope, for years to come, of doing any thing like reaping precious grain. Yet we hope that the seed of the Gospel will fall on some good spots, and bear fruit to the glory of God. We have been able to circulate as many books and tracts as we could get, till the last part of the year a box came, that is not quite gone yet. And indeed we had many calls that we could not supply.

Our work is not confined to Santa Fé. We come in contact with people from all parts of the territory. And often they bear away to their distant homes Bibles and other books, that will work for the enlightenment and salvation of precious souls when we are in our graves.

Brother Blas Chaves, our assistant here, is daily addressing groups of people on the streets and in the houses, and he gets a great many to hear him. Some revile, some ask questions, some listen seriously, and we believe that good is being done.

We do not have a church organized here yet. We labor in the name of the

members. At Laguna, forty-five miles wes
one of whom is a licensed preacher, who is
of the congregation and of the church edif
months, and not able to preach. He report
and who wish to be baptized, and before his

At Manzana, one hundred miles southeast
of Peralto, we have several members and on
us missionaries have been able to visit that
any ingathering there. Nor do we know
assistant seems encouraged.

The statistics of the Albuquerque Churc

Baptized within the year *three*, died
present number twenty-eight members.

There are two licensed preachers, one
studying for the ministry, one assistant
belonging to the church.

THE WORK O

The following statement of the labors of
in Iowa, will interest our readers:

In rendering my last quarter's report for
been serving the Society as missionary in
proper for me to give you a kind of a
account of my field and various interestin
nection therewith. That portion of South
more properly my field, contains a populati
larger towns, such as Keokuk, Fort Mad
This section is now traversed by at least

spiritual infancy. It is true, that, within a very short period past, the cause ot Christ has greatly prospered here. Many new churches have been organized, and new laborers raised up on the field, and a few valuable ones brought into it from abroad. This is all especially true of the Baptist denomination. Our numbers and strength, within the past two years, have wonderfully increased, and increased in many instances far beyond those of our brethren of other names. I could mention at least two important localities where a few years since were quite strong churches, and where the field was entirely controlled by them, where now that denomination has almost entirely disappeared, and now strong Baptist churches exist. In Lee County, which embraces the very southeasternmost corner of the State, our membership and churches and ministry have so rapidly and largely multiplied within the past two years as to become the frequent subject of remark by outside observers. It was but a few months since that a Quaker friend met one of our brethren, and addressed him somewhat thus, "Well, friend, I do believe that dog-fennel and the Baptists are going to take Lee County." But still, notwithstanding all this prosperity and increase which our cause has enjoyed, we are yet weak, and in the important and critical condition of infancy. Every thing depends upon our being able and zealous to follow up advantages now coming under our control. Should the present opportune state of affairs fail to be improved, the like favorable state of things, for building up the Baptist cause and saving the souls of sinners in this region, may never come again.

In addition to all this, which speaks loudly to the Home Mission Society for their continued help in this field, is the fact of the present comparative poverty of most of our churches. Not only are these churches young and yet weak, even in times of prosperity, but the West almost universally, and especially Iowa, has been a great sufferer by the pecuniary reverses of the past three years. The crash of 1857 came upon us all burdened with debt, and though the late harvest was a most bountiful one, and vast quantities of wheat, corn, grass, potatoes, pork, and beef, which are the great staples of our section, have gone to the market, or are ready, on the opening of spring trade, to be shipped to the East and the South, still the large returns coming in and expected for all this will fall far short of settling the immense balances which for the past three years have been standing and accumulating against the country. Our churches, therefore, can not yet undertake their own support, and that of the home missionary work which is opening and inviting us to labor on every hand. Should, therefore, the aid of the Home Mission Society at this critical juncture be withdrawn, or even their enlarged appropriations be withheld, most serious and calamitous would be the result. We therefore entreat the continued and enlarged operations of the American Baptist Home Mission Society in Southeastern Iowa.

As your missionary for the past year, I have labored 52 weeks, preached 288 sermons, attended 159 prayer meetings, visited 693 families, and 7 public schools; baptized 180 converts, received 16 on experience, and 3 by letter; organized 3 new churches; attended the ordination of 1 minister; and traveled in the discharge of my duties 3026 miles. Also there have been paid me on my field for the Home Mission Society $200.10; for Domestic Missions $46; and for the Iowa Baptist

Education Society $65. Also, I may say that, during the year, I have myself conducted or aided in eleven different protracted meetings; and two of the churches organized by myself already have pastors, and are self-sustaining. In conclusion, I have only to say, the Lord has been wonderfully good to his servant, and crowned his labors with far more abundant success than his feeble faith anticipated, or his own sense of the unworthiness of his efforts deserved. To God alone be all the praise for his salvation so richly bestowed.

DOCUMENTS RELATIVE TO THE CHURCH-EDIFICE FUND.

REPORT OF A COMMITTEE OF THE EXECUTIVE BOARD.

A Committee appointed by the Executive Board to consider and suggest some method by which moneys contributed to assist the needy in erecting houses of worship, or paying for such as are erected, may be made available to the Church-edifice Fund of the Society, made their report, which was accepted and ordered to be printed. Among many other judicious suggestions it contains the following:

First, That this Board advise churches applied to for aid in erecting edifices, or paying a debt, to refer the case to a Committee of *judicious* business men, who shall examine and report if there is a warrantable prospect of success, and give such advice as the state of things requires.

Secondly, We suggest that this Board advise *churches*, contributing either to the paying a debt or erecting an edifice for worship, to do so with the *express stipulation* with said church that the amount given is to be credited to the Church-edifice Fund of the American Baptist Home Mission Society; said church giving said Society security to refund the same as soon, and in such sums, as they are able.

This plan has been acted upon to some extent with good effect. The givers, the receivers, and the Board have been gratified.

In order to effect uniformity in such action, we respectfully propose the following system for such as are disposed to favor the plan:

1. That, in all cases, when a church is disposed to admit an application for aid to build a church edifice, or to pay a debt for one already built, a Committee be appointed, as recommended above.*

2. If the case is favorably entertained, that the necessary traveling expenses of the visiting agent be paid him, and the balance of his collections be transmitted to the Treasurer of the Home Mission Society for the Church-edifice Fund, and designated for the aid, first, of the church for which it was contributed. If any

* In cities where there are several churches, a standing Committee, consisting of members from each church, might prove a convenience and advantage.

number of years* is agreed upon for the repayment of the loan, or any amount of interest which the people are to pay for the use of the money, let a specific statement of it be made to the Treasurer, in the letter accompanying the money, and let the agent be supplied with a certificate of the amount sent to the Treasurer, and the terms of the loan.

3. If the contributors have no special wish to fix the terms of such loans, they will be fixed by mutual agreement between the Board and the church aided, according to the fixed plans and rules of the Church-edifice Fund, as set forth in accompanying documents.

SPECIAL CIRCULAR.

American Baptist Home Mission Rooms,

No. 115 Nassau Street, New York, November, 1860.

The annexed plan of the Church-edifice Fund of the American Baptist Home Mission Society is respectfully submitted to your examination, with the hope that it will meet your approval and secure your kind co-operation. Years of close observation and largely accumulated correspondence on the subject, have convinced the Executive Board that much greater economy in the use of missionary funds would be secured by the adoption of the proposed measure.

A large amount of money has been collected for church edifices, by agents of soliciting churches, which, from various causes, has been expended with but little profit. Some of those edifices might have been built without the aid of foreign contributions; some have been built in comparatively obscure and unimportant places; some without regard to legal enactments in the organization or election of a Board of Trustees; some with no trustees, and, of course, no legal hold of the property; some without proper attention to titles to their property; some on sites inconvenient of access to the inhabitants of the villages; some without proper regard to the pecuniary ability of the churches, thus contracting embarrassing debts, and from these and similar causes, serious consequences, and, in not a few instances, the total loss of the property, have followed. These points are seldom, if ever, investigated, or even alluded to, by those who donate the funds. The Executive Board propose to attend to all those matters; to supply themselves with copies of the laws of the different States, relating to the organization of religious societies and their powers, and to obtain all needful evidence of the correctness of the proceedings of applicants for aid, in all important respects. This, they feel confident, can be effected by the application of fixed and uniform rules, and through the numerous agencies now at their disposal. They propose to aid, as far as they have ability, all who produce satisfactory evidence of their actual necessity, and of the probable establishment, within a reasonable period, of an efficient church by such aid, and this they will do in a fraternal, Christian spirit, and with a view to secure to the applicants the undisputed ownership and enjoyment of a plain, comfortable, and well-located church edifice, free from debt. It is believed that the

* Five years, at longest, is generally thought to be ample time.

success of the proposed measure will, within a few months, produce the means necessary for a prosperous commencement of operations, rendering the ordinary applications for aid unnecessary, and in a reasonable time the system would become so perfected, that a case could only rarely occur to justify such an application at all.

Many facts could be given to illustrate the advantages of the plan. We offer, however, only one, in which it is ascertained that the systematic expenditure of only two thousand dollars in a single State (Minnesota) would secure the immediate construction of fifteen church edifices, and the probable establishment of as many self-sustaining churches at an early period. Where or how could so small an amount of money be expended to produce so great and good a result?

In view of the whole subject, your kind and liberal co-operation and contribution at the earliest practicable day are earnestly invited.

PLAN OF THE CHURCH-EDIFICE FUND.

1. The Church-edifice Fund of the American Baptist Home Mission Society is intended to aid feeble churches in their incipient efforts to establish the institutions of the Gospel.

2. The amount of aid granted in each case will be small; it will depend much upon the amount raised by the applicants themselves; and will be intended as the final payment on the cost of the edifice.

3. The lot on which the edifice is erected must be of ample dimensions, centrally situated for the purpose of public worship, and the title of the applicants to it must be free of all encumbrances.

4. When aid is granted, it will be in the form of a loan for a reasonable term of years, to be properly secured and drawing a moderate annual interest. Donations will be made, if money is contributed to the treasury, and designated by the donors for the purpose.

5. Loans granted will be transmitted in installments as the building progresses, unless otherwise ordered.

6. Applications for aid must be made by the trustees of the churches or societies, according to the laws of their respective States or Territories, and be accompanied by evidence of the regular organization of the church and of the Board of Trustees; of the concurrence of the church in the measure of building; of the actual unencumbered ownership of the property; and of the entire proceedings relative to the loan having been according to the laws of their respective States.

7. The arrangements with the borrowers will be made with all reasonable reference to their convenience in the repayment of loans; and loans repaid will be immediately loaned to others on the same principles, thus creating a perpetual source of aid for churches in similar circumstances.

Necessity for a Fund.

It is unnecessary to present arguments in support of the necessity or utility of suitable houses of worship for the use of churches in planting the Gospel in new places. A thousand facts speak conclusively on the subject, and a thousand more clearly show that provision for the support of ministers by missionary funds must be prolonged two or three years, and sometimes longer, where there is no convenient place of worship, than at those places where such accommodations are offered. The value of missionary funds bestowed upon such places, therefore, is diminished.

The Desire of Feeble Churches for a Fund.

The amount of aid indispensable to success in ordinary cases in the new States of the Home Mission field is comparatively small. The houses actually necessary in the commencement of operations need not be large, but comfortable and neat. The people can manage to secure a good site and procure most of the materials, but money they can not raise until their farms are paid for, and their business sufficiently advanced. The years for accomplishing this, however, are just those when the incipient arrangements for gathering and establishing the churches should be made, and to pass them unimproved is fatal to early success. A few hundred dollars—in most cases from one hundred to five hundred—for the purchase of materials and labor, which can not be obtained without cash, would be sufficient. This the people can not obtain near them, except by paying exorbitant and ruinous rates of interest. They would gladly borrow the needful amount at the legal rates of interest in eastern States, and in any place of ordinary importance they would be abundantly able to pay such interest, and, in a reasonable term of years, to refund the amount borrowed.

Plans for easily raising a Fund.

To obtain the amount necessary for such operations, the Executive Board do not wish to subject their friends to a burdensome extra effort. As yet, they hope, it is not necessary. Their plans have been published in the *Home Mission Record*, and a general co-operation with them on those plans, it is believed, will speedily supply them with the means in an easy and pleasant way. The contribution of one dollar from each member of Baptist churches, previous to April 1, 1861, will fully accomplish the object, and render further application to those churches by agents from abroad unnecessary.

If there be churches not yet ready for such a measure, and disposed to encourage the old plan of contributing on the application of church agents still longer, it would aid the promotion of our object by their depositing the amount of their contributions in our treasury, to be loaned to the church for which it was contributed on the foregoing terms—the contributing church directing the number of years in which it should be repaid, and the rate of interest to be required for its use. The former, however, would be the speedier, the better, the more efficient method, and would enable the Board immediately to expand their usefulness and bless large numbers of waiting churches in the wilderness.

Shall the Needful Amount be Raised?

We commend to our friends the perusal of the numerous articles in the *Home*

First.—The Church-edifice Fund is empl
incipient efforts to establish the institutions

Second.—The churches aided must own a
which the proposed house of worship is to b
for the purpose of public worship, the churc
cumbrances, and the church edifice, when op
from debt.

Third.—The amount loaned in each ca
depend much on the amount raised by the a

Fourth.—When aid is granted it will be
drawing a moderate annual interest, and to
nations can be made only when money has b
designated by the donors for that purpose.

Fifth.—Loans made by the Board will
building progresses, unless otherwise ordered

Sixth.—Applications for aid, and the tr
pletion, must be by the trustees of the churc
of their respective States or Territories, an
tions by documents, as follows: A copy of
Council at the organization of the church, c
was regularly organised and is in the fellows
tion. A copy of the vote of the church
make the loan. A certificate of the clerk o
signed by the deacons, showing that the sai
pointed meeting of the church; and an "
title of the lot on which the church edifice i

The Dollar Plan.

Subscriptions of one dollar for the Church-edifice Fund have been voluntarily sent to our treasury by persons in different sections of the country, with expressions of the wish that the example should be generally followed; and we are certain that if it were followed an amount would be realized that, with proper management, would relieve all *real* necessities likely to occur from year to year, from the erection of houses of worship by feeble churches. One hundred thousand dollars would be sufficient. That amount can be raised easily, if the Baptists are disposed to do it.

In the northern and northwestern States alone, the number of Baptist church members is about 383,000. After making every reasonable allowance, at the very least one quarter of the number, or say in round numbers 100,000, could give without inconvenience one dollar each for the above purpose. But it is not indispensable to raise the whole amount at once. From ten to twenty thousand dollars per annum, for a few years, would meet all really important demands. The money thus annually raised, being loaned in greater or less amounts, from $100 to $500, would be repaid in most cases within five years, and would then be loaned to other needy churches, to be repaid again and again perpetually.

The money would be placed at the disposal of a responsible Society, having the whole field under its observation, and no new organization would be necessary.

The success of the plan would soon relieve the people from incessant and annoying applications. It would secure them against imposition. It would save large sums, which, on the present method of indiscriminate giving, often go to places of comparative unimportance, and in many instances where the applicants are able to dispense with such aid. It would save hundreds of dollars, annually expended for salary and traveling expenses of agents who solicit funds for building church edifices; and, with the efforts of the churches which it would stimulate, would build and pay for a great many suitable houses of worship, where they are truly needed, and where they would strengthen active devoted churches, and impart stability to the cause of Jesus Christ—all by one dollar each from about a quarter of the church members of the Free States.

The Cost of Home Missionary Churches—Missionary Labors of an Agent.

From Rev. O. Tracy, Concord, March 31.

You know my field is a hard field to cultivate. The past year an effort has been made to raise some $2500 to $3000 among the churches in Vermont, to build a house of worship in Bellows Falls. Where churches have contributed $50, $100, or $300, and I have *been told* it was for the same object as Home Missions, we *can not* bring up our subscriptions as usual. But really the Home Mission Society will gather few churches, or build few houses of worship, if they cost as much as they do in Vermont and New Hampshire. How much has each church, gathered by the Home Mission Society, cost them? Why, God has given us *one church* for every $600 or $650 put into the Home Mission treasury. Then, if, as you suppose, that the hopeful conversions are about double the number of the baptisms reported, then God has given us *one hopeful convert* for every $12 put into our treasury. I say nothing of the many feeble churches that have been fostered and become strong by your aid. Such results are encouraging. I have now been in your service nine years. About one half of my time has been spent in New Hampshire. I have done considerable missionary work. More than half of my Sabbaths have been spent with destitute churches, or with churches whose pastors were sick, or from home, or I have sent him out to supply some feeble church. For nineteen years before I came into New Hampshire, the churches in the State collected on an average some $265 annually. The last nine years they have averaged $1660. I have pursued a similar course in Vermont; average collections prior to 1851 were a little less than they were in New Hampshire. For nine years past we have collected nearly $1000 a year, and yet I have been in the State *less* than one half of the time, and more than one half of my Sabbaths have been spent with feeble churches, so that at least one half of my Sabbaths I have been doing missionary work. I state these facts that the Board may know how I am laboring, and what are the results of such efforts.

Build Church Edifices, or let Churches die.

From Rev. C. Willett, La Crosse, March 26.

Many of our churches must have houses of worship, or die. Appropriating money to be preached out in cabins and in miserable log school-houses, that belong to any body or every body or nobody, is about as profitable as the last few years' land speculation. *Every thing is nowhere.* Baptists and Methodists break ground; toil early and late; in season, out of season; and begin to gather a harvest, when Congregationalists, or Presbyterians come in with their building fund and erect a very neat house of worship, and gather into it much of the best fruit of other's self-denying toil, leaving little more than the refuse for others. The fact is, creeds hang very lightly on many in these parts. A comfortable slip for a family outweighs, with many, all that Fuller or Dwight, or even Paul or John, ever wrote. Whatever danger of consolidation may exist about New York or Boston, be assured there is none this way; we living together much like the waves of the sea, not anywhere in particular, or for any particular length of time. Must one half that has been done on the frontiers within the last five years be lost, and a much larger proportion of present and future labors, for the want of church homes? I confess a degree of feeling on this subject, that, at times, reaches an intensity hardly wise.

The mild brilliant nights of the present month have been illuminated by vast areas of fires in all directions, burning over marsh, prairie, and bluff, and as I have gazed upon them, oh! how I have wished that the whole field from which funds for our Home Mission work come might be warmed and illuminated with this crying necessity of which I write, and not a dark cold heart remain. If the material for combustion were here at home, most quickly would I apply the torch (if I could), and then devotedly fan the flame. What intelligent mechanic would employ a gang of hands to carry on his work without suitable buildings in which to labor? What merchant would forward large invoices of goods for sale and provide no store where they could be disposed of? Not one. And yet, just that thing is done by the patrons of Home Missions. Oh! if the intelligent portion of our brethren east, would see this matter in its true light, they would quickly set themselves to rights. The relation of building to sustaining public worship is just the reverse here to what it is east. I am not sure but it would be wisdom to stop appropriations for a year or two, and devote all that could be gathered up to this business, securing, as we ought to have, a fund of $100,000, to be loaned with just interest enough to cover inevitable losses on ordinarily good securities.

Many of our brethren would willingly go to the extent of human endeavors to secure a place of worship, and thus prevent the fruits of their self-denying toils being ungraciously taken from them by their well-furnished and not reluctant neighbors. How much I should be prompted to do, if a loan could be secured to erect a house here, I am not prepared to say, except that it should exceed that of any other man of equal means, though I might not preach in it a single day. Here, we are dead-locked in our *tomb*, and here, so far as growth is concerned, we must be, until we have a different place to meet in.

DIRECTORS FOR LIFE,

Constituted during the Year ending March 31, 1861,

BY VIRTUE OF A CONTRIBUTION OF ONE HUNDRED DOLLARS OR MORE.

Baker, B. P., Cincinnati, Ohio.
Beebe, William J., Brooklyn, N. Y.

Carpenter, Cyrus, Boston, Mass.
Denny, Mrs. Jane, Rochester, N. Y.

Gow, Rev. George B., South Groton, Mass.

Hammond, Timothy, Bow, N. H.
Harkness, Prof. Albert, Providence, R. I.

Hill, Nathaniel, Boston, Mass.
Hubbard, jr., Rev. John, Lowell, Mass.

Jones, M. M., Utica, N. Y.

Mosman, Rufus, Boston, Mass.
Moss, Rev. Lemuel, Worcester, Mass.

Neale, Alonzo F., Boston, Mass.

Peck, Rev. Solomon, D.D., Roxbury, Mass.

Rand, Ransom R., Boston, Mass.
Randall, Rev. Charles, Auburn, N. Y.
Raymond, John H., LL.D., Brooklyn, N. Y.
Reed, Rev. Edwin D., Caseville, N. Y.

Scott, Lieut. Gen'l Winfield, New York.
Sheldon, Isaac E., New York.

[redacted]

Canfield, Mrs. Mary R., Shortsville, N. Y.
Carpenter, Mrs. Weltham, Wickford, R. I.
Carter, Cyrus, Troy, N. Y.
Caswell, Edward F., Providence, R. I.
Chamberlin, David, Garrettsville, Ohio.
Chapman, Nathan, North Marshfield, Mass.
Cheshire, Mrs Philenah, Williamsburgh, N. Y.
Clark, Mrs. William, Syracuse, N. Y.
Clapp, Frederic, Cambridgeport, Mass.
Churchill, Samuel, Lowell, Mass.
Cole, Austin H., Rochester, N. Y.
Collins, Rev. D. B., Sloansville, N. Y.
Coombs, A. Amelia, Ohio.
Cooper, D. S., New Haven, Ct.
Cornell, Joseph M., Albion, N. Y.
Cornwell, Rev. W. E. Woodstown, N. J.
Craig, Edmund, Cheviot, Ohio.
Crane, Rev. C. B., Hartford, Ct.
Craft, Mrs. Nancy C., New London, N. H.
Cressy, Mrs. Timothy R., Hastings, Min.
Crocker, Isaac F., Central Falls, R. I.
Crowell, Mrs. Sarah M., Rome, N. Y.
Cudworth, S. S., Boston, Mass.
Curry, Samuel, Providence, R. I.
Cutler, Mrs. J., Brattleboro', Vt.
Cutting, Mrs. Hannah, Mason Village, N. H.

Davis, Mrs. Susan, Adams Centre, N. Y.
Davis, William, M D., Chester Springs, Pa.
Dawson, Mrs. Ann C., Philadelphia.
Dare, Rev. S. C, Canton, N. J.
Dean, Willard L., Poughkeepsie, N. Y.
Dean, Hiram G., Milton, Ct.
Dean, Charles H., Fall River, Mass.
De Land, Daniel B., Fairport, N. Y.
Dibble, Sherman, Hindsburgh, N. Y.
Dix, Benj. H., Mason Village, N. H.
Dodge, Frank W., Brooklyn, N. Y.
Dodge, Miss Emeline C., Brooklyn, N. Y.
Dodge, Miss Frances M., Brooklyn, N. Y.
Doron, John, Vincentown, N. J.
Douglass, William W., Providence, R. I.
Douglass, Mrs. Sarah P., Hamilton, N. Y.
Dowers, Theodore, Sheldrake, N. Y.
Dunsby, William, New York.
Durham, Mrs. Mary, Wearts' Corners, N. J.

Earle, Abby P., Philadelphia, Pa.
Easterbrook, Rev. Isaac, Big Flatts, N. Y.
Elliot, Moses, Petersham, Mass.
Ellis, Zenas, Chaumont, N. Y.
Ely, Mrs. Mary T., Holmdel, N. J.
Emerson, Mrs. Celenda, Haverhill, Mass.
Evans, Miss Mary C., South Reading, Mass.
Evans, William, North Marshfield, Mass.

Fargo, Mrs. Elizabeth, Fairport, N. Y.
Farr, Rev. A. L., York, N. Y.
Ferguson, Thomas, Manyunk, Pa.
Ferris, Rev. James M. Lowville, N. Y.
Ferry, Mrs Emeline, Preston, N. Y.
Ford, John, Cambridgeport, Mass.
Forrest, John, Brooklyn, N. Y.
Foster, Mrs. Sophia, Hudson, N. H.
Freeman, Jonathan, Camillus, N. Y.
French, Job B., Fall River, Mass.
Funk. Angeline, Philadelphia.

Gibbs, Mrs. Julia A., Batavia, N. Y.
Gillet, J. Laroy, Cortland, N. Y.
Gimbry, Lewis S., Chester Springs, Pa.
Goddard, Emily A., Philadelphia.
Goddard, Ellen M., Philadelphia.
Goodrich, Rev. Washington, Gilboa, N. Y.
Goodsell, Mrs. Christiana W., Hornby, N. Y.
Gordon, Adoniram J., Providence, R. I.
Gould, Mrs. Sarah S., Dover, N. H.
Gray, Rev. Isaac, Frankford, Pa.
Green, Luke, Providence, R. I.
Green, Hon. George, Swanton, Vt.
Green, Mrs. Polly, Swanton, Vt.
Gregory, Rev. Silas B., Little Falls, N. Y.

Hagar, John, Brooklyn, N. Y.
Haigh, Miss Emily, New York.
Hammond, Simeon, Corning, N. Y.
Hanchett, Carlton, Twinsburg, Ohio.
Hale, Mrs. Rebecca S, Haverhill, Mass.
Harmon, Samuel, Adams, N. Y.
Harwood, Frances R., East Canaan, N. Y.
Haskell, Hosee C., Troy, N. Y.
Hathaway, Mrs. Mary A., Green Point, N. Y.
Hayden, Mrs. Mary J. P., New London, N. H.
Henderson, J. J., Covington, Ia.
Herrick, Ira N., Watertown, N. Y.
Higbie, Abijah P., Penfield, N. Y.
Hill, David, Wearts' Corners, N. J.
Hill, Harvey D., Lower Newport, Ohio.
Hill, Isaac, Syracuse, N. Y.
Hill, Reuben, Cuba, N. Y.
Hills, Thomas W., Eldridge, N. Y.
Hinds, Amasa, East Brookfield, Mass.
Hodges, Mrs. Ruth, Torrington, Ct.
Holman, Miss Mary L., New York.
Houston, Andrew, Elmira, N. Y.
Howe, Mrs. Phebe, Haverhill, Mass.
Howe, Samuel B., Penn Yan, N. Y.
Hughes, Miss Mary Ann, New York.
Hull, Daniel South Onondaga, N. Y.
Humphrey, Benj., Lower Merion, Pa.
Hunt, E. T., South Adams, Mass.
Hunt, Mrs. Eunice O., Eaton Village, N. Y.
Hunter, Rev. D. W., McWilliamstown, Pa.

Jackson, Josiah M., Altay, N. Y.
Johnson, Chas. R., Norwich, N. Y.
Johnson, Rev. George, Greece, N. Y.
June, Morris W., Syracuse, N. Y.
June, Clarissa L., Syracuse, N. Y.

Kelly, Mrs. Mary, Haverhill, Mass.
Kennedy, Archibald, Providence, R. I.

Longstreet, Mrs. Mary, Holmdel, N. Y.
Look, Rev. W., Forestville, N. Y.
Lott, Samuel, Reading Centre, N. Y.
Lung, Rev. A. H., Canandaigua, N. Y.
Luther, Benjamin C., Fall River, Mass.
Lynes, Frederick S., Catskill, N. Y.

Madison, John R., Fredonia, N. Y.
Malcom, Mrs. Ann R., Leverington, Pa.
Manchester, Mrs. Fidelia P., Benton, Pa.
Mangam, Mary E., New York.
Mangam, Laura M., New York.
Mangam, Sarah R., New York.
Manning, Mrs. Sarah A., Elmira, N. Y.
Marsh, Rev. Stephen V., Lodi, N. Y.
Mason, Rev. Horace G., Plainfield, N. J.
Mason, Mrs. S. Eugenia, Plainfield, N. J.
Mathewson, Parley M., Providence, R. I.
Merz, John, Greenport, N. Y.
McGenniss, George W., Princeton, N. J.
McMaster, Charles, Amherst, Mass.
Miller, Mrs. Martha, Burnt Hills, N. Y.
Miller, Friend, Wallingford, Ct.
Miller, Mrs. Gilbert W., Bedford, N. Y.
Miller, John, Duncan's Fall, Ohio.
Mills, Rev. Ephraim, North East, Pa.
Mitton, William H., Brooklyn, N. Y.
Morgan, S. A., Pequonoc, Ct.
Moulton, Charles H., Boston, Mass.
Moody, Miss Marianne, Bridgeport, Ct.
Moody, Miss Jane, New York.
Moore, Ezekiel, Bridgeton, N. J.
Morey, Rev. Reuben, Wyoming, N. Y.
Munger, Rev. Daniel B., Mumford, N. Y.
Murdock, Hiram, M.D., Stillwater, Min.
Murray, Miss Mary Ann, New Hope, Pa.

Thompson, Chester, Stockton, N. Y.
Tilden, Rev. Alanson, Woodhull, N. H.
Tilton, Mrs. Abby R., North Sanbornton, N. H.
Tinklepaugh, Peter, Preston Hollow, N. Y.
Tolman, Jennie, Philadelphia.
Townsend, William C., Providence, R. I.
Townsend, Almon H., Providence, R. I.
Truman, Mrs. Sophia, Greenport, N. Y.
Tuck, Rev. Jacob, Hanover, Mass.

Underhill, Isaac, Norwalk, Ohio.
Updike, Miss S. Lizzy, New York.
Updike, Miss M., New York.
Upham, Abijah, Weston, Mass.

Van Buren, James, New York.
Vanduyne, V. S., Sennett, N. Y.
Van Kleeck, E. A., Poughkeepsie, N. Y.
Van Meter, Rev. W. C., Williamsburgh, N. Y.
Vose, Miss Harriet B., Boston, Mass.

Walsworth, Arvin C., Preston, N. Y.
Waltermire, Prudence H., Troy, N. Y.
Warner, Ralph, Boston, Mass.
Washington, Rev. S., Aurora, Ill.
Webb, Orange S., Greenport, N. Y.
Westgate, Martha E., Plainfield, N. H.
Weston, Mrs. Sarah S. H., Lynn, Mass.
Weston, Miss Lucy E., New York.
Westover, Henry W., Galva, Ill.
Westover, Frank A., Galva, Ill.
Wheat, Alfred, Horse Heads, N. Y.
Wheeler, Thomas, South Dover, N. Y.
White, H. J., Newton, Mass.
White, Samuel P., North Shore, N. Y.
White, Sylvanus, Brooklyn, N. Y.
Whiting, Adna, Plainville, Ct.
Wier, John, Grafton, Vt.
Wilcox, Mrs. Harriet, Hartford, Ct.
Wilcox, Mrs. Rosalinda, Rome, N. Y.
Wilkinson, Rev. Israel, Port Byron, N. Y.
Williams, Miss Lavinia, Boston, Mass.
Willson, Rev. Rodolphus, Somerset, N. Y.
Wilson, Miss Mary Anna, Port Monmouth, N. J.
Wilson, H. W., Washington, Pa.
Winter, Andrew, Chapel Hill, N, J.
Winterton, Miss Ruth, New York.
Woods, Leonard B., Johnstown, Ohio.
Woodworth, Mrs. Hattie B., North East, N. Y.
Wr ght, Rev. Wm. D., Huntington, N. Y.

Young, Miss Jeanette, New York.
Young, Chas. L. Stamford, Ct.
Young, Mrs. Mary, Stamford, Ct.

LIST OF DECEASED

Directors and Members for Life, 1860-61.

DIRECTORS.

Corwin, Rev. Jason, Washington, Ill.
Crane, Rev. Origen, New England Village, Mass.
Edmunds, James, Louisville, Ky.
Leighton, Rev. Samuel S., West Townsend, Mass.
Maclay, Rev. Archibald, D.D., New York.
Prevaux, Rev. F. E., Amesbury, Mass.

MEMBERS.

Baber, Alfred, Keeseville, N. Y.
Condit, Miss Sarah E., New York.
Dean, Rev. Myron M., Boston, Mass.
Germond, Mrs. Juliana, Washington, N. Y.
Hatt, Joel, Orange, N. J.
Lewis, Elijah, sen., Brooklyn, N. Y.
Luddington, Samuel, Niverville, N. Y.
Magoon, Miss Ella Louisa, Albany, N. Y.
Miller, Rev. U. B., Indianapolis, Ia.
Munro, John, Eldridge, N. Y.
Olney, Rev. D. B., Bath, N. Y.
Rogers, Rev. Joseph D., Berlin, N. Y.
Schoolcraft, John L., Albany, N. Y.
Tefft, Thomas A., Providence, R. I.
Walker, Rev. Wareham, Flint, Mich.
Wallace, Mrs. Sarah P., Sanbornton, N. H.
Woodbury, W. W., Suffield, Ct.

CONTENTS.

ANNUAL REPORT OF THE EXECUTIVE BOARD.

[redacted]

THIRTIETH REPORT

OF THE

AMERICAN BAPTIST HOME MISSION SOCIETY,

PRESENTED BY THE

EXECUTIVE BOARD

AT THE

Anniversary held with the Brown St. Baptist Church,

IN PROVIDENCE, R. I.,

MAY 29, 1862;

WITH

THE TREASURER'S REPORT AND OTHER DOCUMENTS.

NEW YORK:
PUBLISHED AT THE AMERICAN BAPTIST HOME MISSION ROOMS, NO. 132 NASSAU STREET,
AND PRINTED CORNER CENTRE AND WHITE STREETS.
1862.

CONTENTS.

ANNUAL REPORT OF THE EXECUTIVE BOARD.

MISCELLANEOUS MATTER.

CONSTITUTION.

NAME.

I.—This Society shall be called the AMERICAN BAPTIST HOME MISSION SOCIETY.

OBJECT.

II.—The object of this Society shall be to promote the preaching of the Gospel in North America.

MEMBERSHIP.

III.—The Society shall be composed of Annual Delegates, Life Members, and Life Directors. Any Baptist church, in union with the denomination, may appoint a delegate for an annual contribution of ten dollars, and an additional delegate for each additional thirty dollars. Thirty dollars shall be requisite to constitute a Member for Life, and one hundred dollars, paid at one time, or a sum which, in addition to any previous contribution, shall amount to one hundred dollars, shall be requisite to constitute a Director for Life.

OFFICERS.

IV.—The officers of the Society shall be a President, two Vice-Presidents, a Treasurer, two Auditors, one or more Corresponding Secretaries, and a Recording Secretary.

MANAGERS.

V.—There shall be fifteen managers also, residing in the City of New York, or its vicinity, who shall be divided by lot among themselves into three classes of five members each. The term of service of the first class shall expire in one year, that of the second class in two years, and that of the third class in three years. At each Annual Meeting of the Society, after the first election under this amended Constitution, one class only shall be elected for the term of three years, to the end that the third part of the whole number of managers, as nearly as possible, may be annually chosen; provided, however, that vacancies remaining in any class may be filled for the unexpired term of that class. The officers and managers shall be elected by ballot, and continue to discharge their official duties, until superseded by a new election.

EXECUTIVE BOARD.

VI.—The Treasurer, Auditors, Recording Secretary, and Managers of the Society shall constitute an Executive Board, to conduct the business of the Society, seven of whom shall be a quorum for that purpose. They shall have power to appoint their own meetings, elect their own Chairman and Recording Secretary, enact their own By-laws and Rules of Order, provided, always, that they be not inconsistent with this Constitution, fill any vacancies which may occur in their own body, or in the offices of the Society during the year, and, if deemed necessary by two thirds of the members, convene special meetings of the Society. They shall establish such agencies as the interests of the Society may require, appoint agents and missionaries, fix their compensation, direct and instruct them concerning their particular fields and labors, make all appropriations to be paid out of the treasury, and present to the Society, at each annual meeting, a full report of their proceedings during the current year.

DESIGNATED FUNDS.

VII.—All moneys or other property contributed and designated for any particular missionary field or purpose shall be so appropriated, or returned to the donors or their lawful agents.

TREASURER.

VIII.—The Treasurer shall give bonds to such amount as the Executive Board shall think proper.

ELIGIBILITY TO APPOINTMENT.

IX.—All the Officers, Managers, Missionaries, and Agents of the Society shall be members in good standing in regular Baptist churches.

ANNUAL MEETING.

X.—The Society shall meet annually for the election of officers and managers and the transaction of other necessary business at such time and place as the Executive Board shall appoint.

ALTERATIONS OF THE CONSTITUTION.

XI.—No alteration of this Constitution shall be made without an affirmative vote of two thirds of the members present at an annual meeting; nor unless the same shall have been proposed in writing, and the proposition sustained by a majority vote, at a previous annual meeting or recommended by the Executive Board.

STATED MEETINGS FOR 1862-63.

OF THE EXECUTIVE BOARD.—On the last Tuesday in each month, at three o'clock P.M.

OF THE COMMITTEE ON MISSIONS.—At eleven o'clock A.M., on the same day.

OF THE COMMITTEE ON AGENCIES AND FINANCE.—On Saturday preceding, at three o'clock P.M.

OF THE COMMITTEE ON CHURCH-EDIFICE FUND.—The Monday preceding the meeting of the Board, at half-past nine A.M.

BY-LAWS OF THE BOARD.

1. All meetings shall be opened with prayer.
2. All Committees shall be nominated by the presiding officer and approved by the Executive Board, unless otherwise specially ordered.
3. No moneys shall be paid out of the treasury but by order of the Executive Board.
4. All resolutions, if required, shall be presented in writing.
5. Whenever a vacancy occurs in the Executive Board the fact shall be entered on the Minutes, and at the next stated meeting the Board shall proceed to fill such vacancy by ballot.
6. No By-law of the Board shall be suspended for any temporary purpose, unless by a vote of two thirds of the members of the Board.

ORDER OF BUSINESS.

1. Reading the Minutes of the last Meeting.
2. Treasurer's Report.
3. Communications of the Corresponding Secretary.
4. Reports of Standing Committees.
5. Reports of Select Committees.
6. Unfinished Business.
7. New Business.

STANDING COMMITTEES.

AGENCIES AND FINANCE.	MISSIONS.	CHURCH-EDIFICE FUND.
E. Cauldwell,	J. S. Holme,	J. B. Peck,
Avery Bill, Jr.,	E. E. L. Taylor,	E. T. Hiscox,
Smith Sheldon,	H. G. Weston,	J. B. Durbrow,
John Westervelt,	T. D. Anderson,	D. M. Wilson.
William Phelps.	Howard Osgood,	
	H. C. Fish.	
	E. Lathrop.	

LEGACIES.

D. I. Yerkes, C. C. Norton, J. G. Whipple.

MINUTES OF THE TWENTY-NINTH ANNIVERSARY

OF THE

American Baptist Home Mission Society,

Held in Providence, R. I., May 29, 1862.

THE American Baptist Home Mission Society convened in the Meeting House of the Brown Street Baptist Church, Providence, R. I., on Thursday, May 29, 1862, at nine o'clock A.M.

J. W. Merrill, Esq., first Vice-President, called the meeting to order; and, after singing, prayer was offered by Rev. Dr. Backus of Syracuse.

The Chairman briefly addressed the Society, after which a letter from the Corresponding Secretary, was read by Dr. Hill, from Hon. Ira Harris. President of the Society, giving as the reason of his absence pressing duties in the Senate of the United States.

The following Committees were nominated by the Chairman, and duly appointed:

On Credentials of Delegates.—Rev. O. Tracy, N. H.; Rev. J. V. Ambler, Mass.; Rev. J. W. Parkhurst, Mass.; Rev. J. S. Ladd, N. Y.; Rev. Geo. W. Barnes, Neb. Ter.

On Life Directors and Life Members.—Rev. M. Wilbour, Vt.; Rev. B. Stelle, N. J.; Rev. G. W. Gorham, Mass.; Rev. W. H. Pendleton, N. Y.; Rev. Geo. W. Young, Pa.

On Nomination of Officers and Managers.—Rev. J. S. Backus, N. Y.; Rev. Henry Jackson, R. I.; Rev. S. R. Mason, Mass.; Rev. G. A. Peltz, N. Y.; J. E. Southworth, Esq., N. Y.; Rev. Geo. W. Anderson, Pa.; M. J. Amsden, Vt.

On Arrangements for the Present Session.—Rev. Wm. C. Richards, R. I.; Rev. B. M. Hill, N. Y.; Rev. J. P. Hill, Mass.

On motion of Rev. T. O. Lincoln, D.D., the usual invitation was extended to visiting brethren, which was accepted by Rev. J. N.

The Treasurer's report was rec
motion, adopted and ordered t
(See Treasurer's Report.)

Portions of the annual report
Secretary.

On motion of Dr. Lincoln, so
agencies was referred to a Speci
T. O. Lincoln, N. Y.; Rev. A. F.
er, Vt.; Rev. W. H. Eaton, N. I

On motion of Dr. Welch, so m
re-occupation of southern fields v
tee, consisting of Rev. B. T. We
Rev. G. B. Ide, Mass.; Rev. B. I
son, Mass.

On motion of Dr. Corey, so m
subject of Finance was referred t
of Rev. D. G. Corey, N. Y.; Re
R. H. Neal, Mass.; Rev. S. R. M
R. I.; Rev. N. M. Williams, Me.

While the list of Committees w
tion sang the hymn, "Come Hol

Rev. O. Tracy reported on be

On motion of Rev. M. Willis, the following were appointed a Committee on Obituaries: Rev. S. P. Willis, N. Y.; Rev. J. T. Seeley, N. Y.; Rev. Wm. Phillips, R. I.; Rev. O. W. Gates, Ct.; Hon. H. Lincoln, Mass.

Mr. Davis, a deacon in the Colored Baptist Church at Hampton, Va., near Fortress Monroe, being present, was invited to make remarks, which he did.

Committee on Life Members and Life Directors present reported through their Chairman, showing eighty-eight Life Directors and one hundred and twenty-seven Life Members present. Their names are as follows:

LIFE DIRECTORS PRESENT.

Averill, Rev. A. M., Holyoke, Mass.
Ayer, Rev. Oliver, Claremont, N. H.
Ambler, Rev. J. V., Lanesborough, Mass.
Anderson, Rev. Geo. W., West Haraford, Pa.
Alden, Rev. W. H., Lowell, Mass.
Brooks, Rev. Kendall, Fitchburg, Mass.
Blain, Rev. John, Mansfield, Mass.
Blain, Mrs. Amy Ann, Mansfield, Mass.
Boyce, James, Providence, R. I.
Backus, Rev. Jay S., Syracuse, N. Y.
Bailey, Rev. Joseph A., Waterbury, Ct.
Banvard, Rev. Joseph, Mass.
Borden, Jefferson, Fall River, Mass.
Colgate, Samuel, New York.
Chaplin, Rev. A. J., Catskill, N. Y.
Corey, Rev. D. G., Utica, N. Y.
Colver, Rev. Nathaniel, Chicago, Ill.
Corey, Charles H., New Hampshire.
Cauldwell, E., New York.
Denike, Abram, New York.
Day, Albert, Hartford, Ct.
Dowling, Rev. John, New York.
Dodge, Rev. O., Brooklyn, N. Y.
Dunn, Rev. Lewis A., Fairfax, Vt.
Doolittle, Rev. Horace D., Wappinger's Falls, N.Y.
Eddy, Rev. E. B., New Hampshire.
Everett, E., Brooklyn, N. Y.
Fletcher, Rev. Joshua, Southington, Ct.
Field, Rev. S. W., Providence, R. I.
Field, Alfred, Taunton Green, Mass.
Fish, Rev. H. C., Newark, N. J.
Fuller, Rev. Edward K., Providence, R. I.
Gray, Rev. E. H., N. Y.
Gallatly, W. A., Brooklyn, N. Y.
Gillette, Rev. A. D., New York.
Girdwood, Rev. John, New Bedford, Mass.
Hunt, Samuel, Providence, R. I.
Hiscox, Rev. E. T., New York,
Hill, Benj. M., New York.
Hodges, Rev. Joseph, Cambridge, Mass.
Ilsley, Rev. Silas, Maine.
Ide, Rev. G. B., Springfield, Mass.
Jameson, William H., Melrose, Mass.
Jackson, Rev. Henry, Newport, R. I.
Keyser, Rev. Charles, Providence, R. I.
Lincoln, Rev. T. O., Elmira, N. Y.
Lincoln, Heman, Boston, Mass.
Ladd, Rev. James S., Bergen, N. J.
Mason, Rev. S. R., Cambridgeport, Mass.
Mason, Rev Alanson P., Chelsea, Mass.
Miller, Rev. D. Henry, Meriden, Ct.
Mills, Rev. Robert C., Salem, Mass.
Malcom, Rev Howard, Philadelphia.
Murdock, Rev. J. N., Boston, Mass.
Moss, Rev. Lemuel, Worcester, Mass.
Neale, Rev. R. H., Boston, Mass.
Patton, Rev. A. S, Roxbury, Mass.
Parkhurst, Rev. John, Chelmsford, Mass.
Peltz, Rev. Geo. A., New York.
Phillips, Rev. Daniel W., South Reading, Mass.
Phelps, William, New York.
Pollard, Rev. Andrew, Taunton, Mass.
Pendleton, Rev. W. H., New York.
Phelps, Rev. S. D., New Haven, Ct.
Ricker, Rev. Joseph, Charlestown, Mass.
Richards, Rev. W. C., Providence R. I.
Reid, Rev. William, Greenpoint, N. Y.
Randall, Rev. S. B, Mystic River, Ct.
Richardson, Rev. John G, Valley Falls, R. I.
Reed, Rev. E. D., Cassville, N. Y.
Reding, Rev. C. W., Manchester, Mass.
Swaim, Rev. Samuel B., West Cambridge, Mass.
Stockbridge, Rev. J. C., Boston, Mass.
Seely, Rev. John T., Lima, N. Y.
Shailer, Rev. W. H., Portland, Me.
Smith, Rev. Henry F., Bloomfield, N. J.
Stearns, Rev. O S., Newton Centre, Mass.
Stone, Rev. James R., Worcester, Mass.
Smith, Rev. J. T., Amherst, Mass.
Sheldon, Rev. C. P., Troy, N. Y.
Tingley, Rev. T. C., North Scituate, Mass.
Tracy, Rev. Leonard, Keene. N. Y.
Tracy, Rev. O., Concord, N. H.
Welch, Rev. B. T., Newtonville, N. Y.
Weston, Rev. H. G., New York.
Wilson, D. M., Newark, N. J.
Webb, Rev. Geo. S., New Brunswick, N. J.
Winterton, Wm., New York.

Beck, Rev. L. G., Pemberton, N. J.
Brigham, Rev. J. H., Homer, N. Y.
Bigelow, Rev. J. F., Keesville, N. Y.
Bickford, Rev. N. L., Waltham, Mass.
Ballou, Alexander, Blackstone, Mass.
Buyrn, Rev. E. M., Cross River, N. Y.
Bronson, Rev. A. C., Mystic River, Ct.
Brown, Rev. Joseph P., Moosup, Ct.
Benedict, Rev. David, Pawtucket, R. I.
Clark, Rev. N. J., South Abington, Mass.
Clark, Rev. G. W., Elizabeth, N. J.
Crane, Rev. C. B., Hartford, Ct.
Cordo, Rev. H. A., Lambertville, N. J.
Colesworthy, Rev. Geo., Greenfield, Mass.
Chase, Rev. J. N., Deep River, Ct.
Colgate, Edward, New York.
Chaffin, Rev. A. W., Danverse, Mass.
Dalrymple, Rev. W. H., Nashua, N. H.
Dowling, Rev. Thomas, New London, Ct.
Dyer, Rev. Sidney, Pa.
Daniels, Horace, Central Falls, R. I.
Durbrow, J. B., New York.
Davis, Stilman S., Nashua, N. H.
Decker, Alfred, New York.
Eddy, John S., Providence, R. I.
Elliott, Rev. S. L., Fairfax, Vt.
Eaton, Rev. Geo. W., Hamilton, N. Y.
Felton, George D., Granville, Mass.
Foljambe, Rev. S. W., Boston, Mass.
Fairbanks, Rev. Geo. G., Somerville, Mass.
Foster, J. C., Beverly, Mass.
Forbes, Rev. M., Prattsburgh, N. Y.
Fish, J. L. A., Webster, Mass.
Fletcher, Rev. H., Townshend, Vt.
Fletcher, Rev. C., Tewksbury, Mass.
Fitts, Rev. Harvey, Middleboro, Mass.
French, Job, Fall River, Mass.
Fitz, Rev. William, R. I.
Gammell, A. M., Warren, R. I.
Goodnow, Rev. A. W., Vt.

At the suggestion of Hon. H. Lincoln, Dr. Webb of N. J. engaged in prayer.

Committee on the re-occupation of southern fields reported; pending the discussion of which the Society adjourned. Prayer by Dr. Warren of Mass.

AFTERNOON SESSION.

Society convened at three o'clock. After singing, prayer was offered by Rev. Mr. Blain of Mass.

The Corresponding Secretary read the remaining portions of the annual report, when the whole was adopted, and ordered to be printed with the Minutes.

Committee on Agencies reported. (See Document No. 1.) Report adopted.

Report on the re-occupation of southern fields was called up, and after discussion was adopted. (See Document No. 2.)

Committee of Nominations reported a list of Officers and Managers, for the First Class, for the ensuing year, when, after considerable and spirited discussion, it was voted to proceed to an election.

Tellers reported the result of the ballot, and the following Officers and Managers, for the Third Class, were declared elected: (See page 11.)

Committee on Obituaries reported. Report adopted. (See Document No. 3.)

On motion, the following resolution was passed:

Resolved, That we tender our thanks to the Brown Street Church, and to the other Baptist Churches of this City, and, also to the families of other denominations, who have so generously entertained the delegates of the Society, during the present Anniversary.

On motion, the following resolution was passed:

Resolved, That we gratefully acknowledge the reduction of fare of the several railroad and steamboat companies, to those in attendance on our meeting.

On motion, the following resolution was passed:

Resolved, That the thanks of this Society be tendered to our late Corresponding Secretary, for his long and faithful services to the cause of Christ, in connection with this organization.

Committee on Finance reported. Report adopted. (See Document No. 4.)

Society adjourned by prayer.

EVENING SESSION.

Society met at seven and a half o'clock, when, after singing, prayer was offered by Rev. Dr. Eaton of N. Y., Dr. Murdock of Mass. read the Scriptures.

Rev. William R. Williams, D.D., of N. Y., preached the annual sermon before the Society, from Jer. xxvii., 7. Closing prayer was offered by Dr. Welch of N. Y.

On motion, it was

Resolved, That the thanks of this Society be tendered to Dr. Williams for the sermon delivered this evening, and that a copy be requested for publication.

The doxology was then sung, and the benediction pronounced, when the Society adjourned.

E. T. HISCOX,

Recording Secretary.

OFFICERS OF THE SOCLETY,

AND

EXECUTIVE BOARD.

OFFICERS.

PRESIDENT.

J. W. MERRILL, Esq., Boston.

VICE-PRESIDENTS.

J. M. HOYT, Esq., Cleveland, Ohio.

M. B. ANDERSON, LL.D., Rochester, N. Y.

TREASURER.

EBENEZER CAULDWELL, New York.

AUDITORS.

WILLIAM PHELPS, New York.

JOHN B. DURBROW, New York.

CORRESPONDING SECRETARY.

REV. J. S. BACKUS, D.D., Syracuse, N. Y.

RECORDING SECRETARY.

REV. E. T. HISCOX, D.D., New York.

MANAGERS.

FIRST CLASS.

D. M. WILSON,............. Newark, N. J.
REV. D. I. YERKES,..........Brooklyn, N. Y.
REV. HOWARD OSGOOD,.....New York.
AVERY BILL, Jr.,............New York.
REV. EDWARD LATHROP, D.D.,..New York.

SECOND CLASS.

REV. E. E. L. TAYLOR, D.D,..Brooklyn, N. Y.
REV. H. G. WESTON, D.D.,....New York.
REV. J. S. HOLME,...........Brooklyn, N. Y.
J. G. WHIPPLE,............... "
REV. C. C. NORTON,..........New York.

THIRD CLASS.

J. B. PECK,...New York.
REV. H. C. FISH,...Newark, N. J.
JOHN WESTERVELT,......................................Williamsburgh, N. Y.
REV. T. D. ANDERSON, D.D.,...............................New York.
SMITH SHELDON,...New York.

CHAIRMAN OF THE EXECUTIVE BOARD.

D. M. WILSON.

RECORDING SECRETARY OF THE BOARD, AND CLERK.

JAMES M. WHITEHEAD, New York.

ry Fund $574.56)........
" Cash paid on account Churcl
" Cash paid for Fuel, Station
incidental expenses......
" Cash paid for Paper, Printir
Mission Record, and incidei
" Cash paid for Paper and P
Certificates, Blanks, etc..
" Cash paid interest on conditi
" Cash paid Annuity on accou
" Cash paid for Sunday School
" Cash paid for Taxes on Land
" Cash paid for Insurance
" Cash paid for Rent of Rooms
" Cash paid for Exchange a
Money ....
" Real Estate account.......
" Bills Receivable account...
" Railroad Stock account....
" Cash paid Anniversary expe
" Cash paid for Sufferers in Ka
" Cash paid for Investment, b
tion on which the Society j
" Balance..................

IN ACCOUNT WITH EBENEZER CAULDWELL, TREASURER. *Cr.*

1862. March 31.	By Balance as per last Report		$4.161 82
	" Contributions since April 1, 1861, in Cash	$25,976 88	
	" " " in Land in Wis	60 00	
			26,036 88
	" Legacies same period		3,884 08
	" Contributions to Church-edifice Fund	$660 15	
	" " " in Land in Wis	100 00	
	" Received on account of Loan	107 98	
	" Interest on Loans	43 71	
			911 84
	" Subscriptions to *Home Mission Record*		522 49
	" Cash designated for Sunday School Library		10 00
	" " " " Sufferers in Kansas		30 42
	" Avails of Bills Receivable	$258 33	
	" Interest on the same	6 24	
			264 57
	" Avails of Bond sold		500 00
	" Avails of Railroad Stock sold, bequeathed by the late William Souldin, of Albany, New York	$561 75	
	" Dividend on the same	21 00	
			582 75
	" Interest on an Investment, charged with an Annuity		210 00
	" " " Temporary Investment		15 00
	" " " Special Salary Fund		574 56
	" " " a Special Investment by direction of the Donor		175 00
	" " " Investment made to cover contingent donations, for which the Society is paying interest		15 00
			$37,894 41
	By Balance to account	$4,264 02	
	Subject to demand for Liabilities due April 1, 1862	4,118 11	
	Balance in the Treasury	$145 91	

EBENEZER CAULDWELL, *Treasurer.*

This is to certify that we have carefully examined the foregoing account, together with the vouchers connected therewith, and find the same correct. The balance in the treasury is four thousand two hundred and sixty-four 02-100 dollars ($4264.02).

(Signed) FRANCIS S. MINER, SAMUEL S. CONSTANT, } *Auditors.*

NEW YORK, April 1, 1862.

ACT OF INCORPORATION.

AN ACT TO INCORPORATE THE AMERICAN BAPTIST HOME MISSION SOCIETY, PASSED APRIL 12, 1843, AND AMENDED FEBRUARY 9, 1849.

The People of the State of New York, represented in Senate and Assembly, do enact as follows:

§ 1. All such persons as now are, or may hereafter become, members of the American Baptist Home Mission Society, formed in the City of New York, in the year one thousand eight hundred and thirty-two, shall be, and hereby are, constituted a body corporate, by the name of the American Baptist Home Mission Society, for the purpose of promoting the preaching of the Gospel in North America.

§ 2. This Corporation shall be capable of taking, holding, or receiving any property, real or personal, by virtue of any devise or bequest contained in any last will or testament of any person whomsoever, the clear annual income of which devise or bequest shall not exceed the sum of ten thousand dollars; Provided no person leaving a wife, or child, or parent, shall devise or bequeath said Corporation more than one fourth of his or her estate, after the payment of his or her debts; and such devise or bequest shall be valid to the extent of such one fourth, and no such devise or bequest shall be valid in any will which shall not have been made and executed, at least two months before the death of the testator; and provided that no verbal mistake in the name of the said Corporation shall invalidate any gift, grant, devise, or legacy intended for it. The net income of said Society, arising from their real estate, shall not exceed the sum of ten thousand dollars annually.

§ 3. This Corporation shall possess the general powers, and be subjected to the provisions contained in title third of chapter eighteen of the first part of the Revised Statutes, so far as the same are applicable and have not been repealed.

§ 4. This Act shall take effect immediately.

§ 5. The Legislature may at any time modify or repeal this Act.

ANNUAL REPORT

OF THE

American Baptist Home Mission Society,

AT THE

Thirtieth Anniversary, held in Providence, R. I., May 29, 1862.

The Executive Board of the American Baptist Home Mission Society, in presenting their Thirtieth Annual Report, feel that they have fresh reason to adore the Divine goodness which allows them the opportunity for such service undisturbed by the calamitous events which in certain portions of our common country prevent such convocations. We experience some of the afflictions incident to a state of civil war, perhaps suffer some of its sore bereavements, but the clang of opposing arms and the thunder of death-dealing artillery are not heard by us; we are not compelled to look upon garments rolled in blood, nor do we bear the guiltiness of political treason on our souls, or the madness of rebellion against a beneficent government in our acts. We are here in peace and quiet, upon ground once pressed by the footsteps, and still consecrated by the privations and sufferings of Roger Williams, the earliest apostle of civil and religious liberty in our country. We have reason to thank God to-day for the inestimable blessings which he has bestowed upon us through our fathers' conflicts, which are now so successfully maintained by our brothers and sons, and for the perpetuation of which he has granted our nation unanimity of mind and cheerfulness of heart. Let us thank Him, because we may here bring our offerings of religious knowledge and experience, and love, and zeal, and lay them humbly at his feet, as means of counteracting the wickedness of those who have so violently assailed our free institutions, and the greater wickedness of man's rebellion against the government of God.

DEATHS.

Since our last anniversary six Directors and twenty-three Members of the Society have died;* eleven of them were ministers of the Gospel. With almost a certainty that some of us will follow them before another anniversary, and the serious uncertainty as to whom it shall be, should we not all work diligently in the vineyard of our Lord, turning from our labor neither to the right hand nor to the left?

DIRECTORS AND MEMBERS FOR LIFE.

Twenty-one persons were constituted Life Directors during the year, six of whom had previously been Members. Six have died, making the present number 735.

One hundred and eighty-six were constituted Life Members,† and twenty-three have died. The present number is 5957. The total number of Directors and Members is 6692.

FINANCIAL AFFAIRS.

In one respect the financial affairs of the Society present an unfavorable comparison with those of the previous year. The amount of receipts into the treasury has been much smaller, the principal cause of which, it is almost unnecessary to say, is easily traced to the existence of our national troubles, by which the means of a large proportion of our contributing friends have been diminished.

---

* See list of deceased Directors and Members.

† See list of Directors and Members constituted during the year.

This was anticipated at the commencement of the fiscal year. It was then feared that the Board would not be able, promptly, to meet the claims of the missionaries for their salaries. A reduction of the aggregate amount of those claims, therefore, became necessary, and has been accomplished by the voluntary resignation of some missionaries, the expiration of the appointment of others, without renewal, and the discontinuance of new appointments. By these means all the liabilities of the Society have been canceled, and, on account of larger receipts at the close of the year, the Board is in good condition to proceed with its present amount of business, and to expand it in due proportion to any increase of funds in the treasury, beyond the amount received last year.

The general statement of the financial condition of the Society on the 31st of March is as follows: *

Balance from last year's account	$4,161 82
Receipts from all sources during the year	33,732 59
Total amount of resources for the year	$37,894 41
Total amount of disbursements for the year	33,630 39
Amount of cash in the treasury, April 1, 1862	$4,264 02
Amount of liabilities, chiefly to missionaries, same date	4,118 11
Showing a balance over amount due, April 1, 1862, of	$145 91
Of the total amount received, there were in ordinary contributions	$26,036 88
Being less than the previous year	6,558 91
Amount received in legacies	$3,884 08
Being less than those of the previous year	3,245 37
Amount received for Church-edifice Fund, including a loan repaid and interest	$811 84
Being less than the previous year	3,270 19
Amount of receipts from all sources last year	$50,729 87
Amount of receipts from all sources this year	33,732 59
Decrease	$16,997 28

* See note A, page 30.

COLLECTING AGENCIES.

Two years ago, it was stated that plans had been arranged and partially executed, to reduce the number of collecting agents. Those plans have been followed up as far as practicable ; but the further adherence to them will depend much upon the development of the Society's views at its present meeting. The plan of reduction was based, in a considerable degree, upon arrangements of certain churches, adopted by themselves, for the collection of missionary funds; and it was stated at the time, that the extent of reduction would depend on the success of such arrangements in supplying our treasury with adequate means for the performance of the Society's work. Systematic arrangements, by the churches, have long been encouraged by the Board, and, if they were generally adopted, and conscientiously, vigorously, and regularly pursued, they would simplify their business, relieve them of no small expense, responsibility, and anxiety, and, of course, enable them to apply a larger proportion of their means to the increase of missionaries on the field. With such results they would rejoice to surrender the business of collecting funds into the hands of the churches. Thus far, however, the results have not been sufficiently encouraging to justify further change, without a more perfect understanding of the wishes and intentions of the Society. If all the benevolent societies should discontinue their collecting agencies, as many persons seem desirous of having done, and if churches, and ministers, universally, assume the responsibility of providing the means necessary for the purposes of those societies, a few years would show the actual advantage or disadvantage of such a policy.

CHURCH-EDIFICE FUND.

The Church-edifice Fund has suffered in common with

other financial interests of the Society, though it has enjoyed some favor, and by it the Board have been enabled to encourage churches which, otherwise, would have been destitute of even scarcely comfortable places of worship. The fund, as now managed, is a noble feature of the Society's operations; and if, on the return of more prosperous times, it should be endowed in fair proportion to its merits, it will be found to be a cheap and efficient auxiliary in promoting the great object of the Society—the preaching of the Gospel in North America.

MISSIONARY OPERATIONS.

The missionary operations of the Board have been graduated strictly by the amount of means actually supplied to the treasury. Because that amount has been comparatively small the number of missionaries has been reduced, and, consequently, the amount of labor has been proportionably small. The existing national troubles, also, have made great changes in the condition of the missionary field. Large numbers of people in the western States, of whom a fair proportion are from the churches and congregations of our missionaries, have been absent at the seat of war nearly all the year. For this reason, the ability of the churches to support the Gospel became diminished, and, as the means of the Board to aid them were also insufficient, many of those missionaries, at the termination of their appointment, experienced a necessity for leaving their respective fields of labor. A considerable number of them, with patriotic devotion to the cause of the country, entered the army as chaplains, where they have been most usefully employed in their appropriate duties. Much of the demoralizing influence of camp life has been counteracted by their efficient and timely labors among the soldiers. Their churches and families, however, have suffered by the absence of their friends and protectors, the alarms and anxieties growing out of their dangerous employment, the grief of sudden bereavement upon the battle field, and destitution of the blessings of the sanctuaries where they have been accustomed to find consolation in their times of trouble. The Board did what they could to relieve them, but they dared not transcend the bounds of financial caution. The vacancies created could not be prudently filled by the appointment of new men, but as many as practicable have been retained who were previously under appointment.

SUMMARY OF LABORS AND RESULTS.

During the past year ninety missionaries labored under the appointment of the Executive Board. Of this number, eighty-eight were in commission at the close of the previous year, and two were subsequently appointed. Twelve of the number preached in foreign languages.

The number of States and Territories occupied was fourteen, viz., Pennsylvania, Delaware, Ohio, Michigan, Indiana, Illinois, Wisconsin, Iowa, Minnesota, Kansas, Nebraska, New Mexico, California, and Oregon.

Two hundred and fifty-two stations and out-stations were supplied. The aggregate amount of time bestowed in labor is equal to that of one man for about seventy-one years.

Revivals of religion were reported from seven places. Four hundred and seventy-three persons were baptised (of whom twelve had been Roman Catholics, and ten foreign Lutherans); thirty churches were organized; twenty-eight ministers were ordained; three church-edifices were completed, and six were commenced.

The churches aided contributed to the usual objects of Christian benevolence $2074.10, and for the support of the Gospel among themselves $14,167.77. Eight churches. which had been aided a few years, became self-sustaining.*

OLD FIELDS TO BE REOPENED.

As one of the effects of the civil war, fields once open for the cultivation of the Society, and subsequently closed on account of the slavery controversy, are now opening again. Applications are already on file for the appointment of missionaries in slave States. Steps have been taken to ascertain how far it might be the duty of the Board to act in those cases, but with means inadequate to the necessities of any new territory, and even of ministers and churches already under the patronage of the Society, there would have been no justification for attempting such an extension of operations. Hence, no missionary has been sent to either of those old fields nor to the new Territories, and no addition has been made to the number in any other Territory or State. In all, there has been a decrease.

A SOLEMN INQUIRY.

The inquiry arises with solemn interest: why has this decrease been allowed? Is the Gospel the power of God unto salvation to those who believe, and are the disciples

---

* In addition to the above, the missionaries report the following:

Sermons preached	10,240
Lectures and addresses	698
Pastoral visits	15.951
Prayer and other meetings attended	9,665
Signatures to Temperance Pledge	61
Miles traveled in discharge of duty	92,666
Schools visited	274
Sabbath schools in the churches	126
Bible classes	80
Number of teachers	692
Number of scholars	5,563
Volumes in S. S. libraries	14,446
Stations where monthly concert of prayer is observed	30
Preparing for the ministry	10

of our Lord Jesus Christ under paramount obligations to send it to the poor and the perishing? And may not other inquiries, long since first uttered, be repeated here? How can they believe in him of whom they have not heard; and how can they hear without a preacher; and how can they preach except they be sent; and, we add. who will send them if the friends of Jesus, whose Gospel it is, do not? The Board admit the vast importance of our present national struggle, to maintain the integrity of our beneficent government, our civil and religious freedom: our moral and social influence. and the necessity for personal sacrifice for their perpetuation; but the already large amount of financial sacrifice and personal effort for that purpose, would require an almost unbounded increase. if they were unaccompanied and unsustained by the religious influences to which the people have been accustomed. If large voluntary offerings of wealth are necessary for the benefit of our young men who encounter the dangers of military life, a proper proportion should be bestowed in fostering the religious influences by which they may be the more perfectly fitted to meet them. If their beloved ones at home must surrender them to the hardships and dangers of such a life, they should at least be aided to enjoy. in the institutions of the Gospel, support in their alarms and consolation in their sorrows. Surely, when the utterances of their desolated hearts come wailing upon our ears, "Have pity upon me, O ye, my friends, for the hand of God hath touched me," there should be a soothing response from evangelical lips, in the sanctuary where such sorrowing ones seek the solace of Christian sympathy.

DECENNIAL REVIEW.

The Society has now completed the third decade of its history. At the close of the second decade, its missionary labors had been prosecuted in Canada, from Montreal and its vicinity in the Eastern Province to Paris in the Western section, and in the United States, in the region of the great lakes as far as Green Bay in Wisconsin. Up the Mississippi River they had reached the Falls of St. Anthony, though above Dubuque, in Iowa, they were limited to short distances from that stream. Below Dubuque, a few stations had been occupied to the distance of fifty miles westward, and missionaries had been introduced into New Mexico, California, and Oregon. Within those limits were sections of inhabited .territory, where our missionaries had not labored, and in nearly all the Atlantic States, and all the slave States, in fields once occupied, they had ceased to labor. In northern Wisconsin and Michigan, and in western Iowa, the sparsely settled condition of the country did not seem to require those labors except at a few points.

Within the past decade some additional territory, known as Arizona, has been purchased from the Mexican Government, and added to the domain of the United States, The population of the country has extended widely in different directions, and several political divisions and subdivisions have been made. Kansas, Nebraska, Washington, Dakota, Nevada, and Colorado have been organized as Territories—the last three only one year ago—and California, Oregon, Minnesota, and Kansas have been admitted as States into the Federal Union.

The total population of the United States in 1860 was upward of thirty-one million, of which nearly 11,000,000 occupied the region beyond the Alleghany Mountains, including those in Missouri and Kentucky. The population of the new States and Territories named is nearly 922,000.

Of the total population, 1,036,756 were Baptist com-

tories, nor into Arizona or Utal
ful efforts were made for th
Nebraska, so soon as it seemed
ization would not rest on a bas
sion to any of their inhabita
missionaries to the Territory of
plated, but postponed till a mo
the country shall warrant the e

It was deemed inconsistent ar
the complicated arrangement
years for aiding the Grande I
Canada; and as our brethren
sustain a missionary organiza
further labors in that region, al
specially necessary.

Comparatively little was done
chiefly because of the heavy ex
points, and the continuous succe
in the country during the last
for these our missionary force i

idential government of God, call upon us, also, for deep humility at his feet. As a historical event, connected in certain respects with missionary operations at home, it is proper to mention the sudden and appalling disturbance of our once happy National Union, which, commencing in one of the Southern States, and spreading with great rapidity from State to State south of the Potomac River, soon reached the extended proportions of a gigantic rebellion against the general government; requiring for its overthrow nearly a million of armed men, and hundreds of millions of money. The effects upon our Society, and the religious interests of the people whom it is its principal object to benefit, have been disastrous. The business of the country being prostrated, the resources of the Society became impaired, so that comparatively little could be done in spreading the Gospel. The mouth of the Mississippi River and its great commercial City being in the hands of the rebels, the States nearest its sources became specially interested in the strife, and their people in large numbers engaged in it for the defense of the government. Those who remained at home, in some of the States, remained to experience the horrors of border warfare, and those of others, being comparatively new settlers in frontier positions, suffered much from the effects of warlike operations. It is cause of gratitude to God that those troubles have been in no small degree ameliorated by the labors of the missionaries who remained upon the field, but it is reason for heartfelt sorrow that, as one of the sad fruits of the wicked revolt, the missionary cause has received a serious check.

ACTUAL PROGRESS.

Notwithstanding the numerous obstacles to the advance of the Society, good progress has been made in its appropriate work. During the last ten years that work has been extended up the Mississippi River some fifty miles above the Falls of St. Anthony, and west, up the Minnesota River, nearly a hundred miles, and reaching to considerable distances on either side of both. It has passed in the same direction beyond the Missouri River in the State of Kansas and the Territory of Nebraska, and up that river about one hundred and sixty miles above the border line of Kansas. It has been prosecuted up the River St. Croix, which separates Minnesota from Wisconsin, as far as the Falls of St. Croix, some forty-five miles above its confluence with the Mississippi, and it has been commenced beyond the sources of the St. Croix, at the very head of Lake Superior. Previous efforts in the Valley of the Mississippi and the vicinity of the great lakes have been followed up by strengthening churches already formed, and organizing others at points of importance where the State Conventions were unable to bestow the necessary aid. In the northwestern portion of Wisconsin the cause has made considerable advance, and no particular decline has been perceptible at any other point. In Iowa, portions of which have been considerably settled as far west as the Missouri River, and in Minnesota a very rapid advance is exhibited in all the elements of efficiency among the churches. In the last named State our labors commenced in 1849, soon after its organization as a Territory. The fruits are upward of one hundred churches, about four thousand members, and not far from eighty ministers, a large proportion of whom have been aided by the Society. The work commenced in New Mexico, toward the close of the second decade, has been steadily prosecuted amidst many discouragements. There, the tone of moral and religious feeling among the people has been much improved, and the true conception of civil and religious liberty has been widely imparted and is appreciated among them. Many conversions have occurred, churches have been organized, church-edifices have been erected, and the sacred Scriptures have been distributed and freely and extensively read. In the Pacific States the cause has taken deeper root, through the cultivation of ministers commissioned by the Society, and by others who have more recently emigrated to that region without its aid. In some of the older States, west of the Alleghany Mountains, which were aided by the Society in previous decades, the Conventions have undertaken to supply their own destitution. Contributions have been received from nearly all those States, to aid the Society in sending the gospel to regions beyond them; thus beginning to redeem the pledges of their ecclesiastical infancy, and imparting assurance that in more prosperous times they will not forget their early benefactors, nor fail to strengthen our hands by liberal supplies. Such, and similar results, were numerous and encouraging, until causeless and reckless insurrection arrested the good work.

DECENNIAL RESULTS.

In the course of the third decennial period one thousand three hundred and fourteen ministers labored under the commission of the Society. The aggregate of time bestowed by them is equal to that of one man for more than nine hundred and seventy years. They baptised seven thousand four hundred and forty-four persons (of whom three hundred and ninety-three were previously Roman Catholics or foreign Lutherans), organized four hundred and fifty-seven churches, ordained two hundred and seventy-three ministers, and, aside from general labors in the cause of temperance, obtained three thousand eight hundred nine churches, aided by the

came self-sustaining.

TOTAL R

These statistics, added to t
that the total number of m
under the commission of the
hundred and forty-seven ; th
ed the labor of one man f
hundred and ninety-eight ye
twenty-seven thousand nine h
organized one thousand tv
churches, ordained six hund
ters, and the people amon
built at least two hundred and
and contributed more than
of Christian benevolence.

These, though the most ap
labors, are, by no means, a
to illustrate the beneficence
ness of its acts. We might

influence among the heterogeneous crowds of our distant West. To these we point as real tangible evidence of the Society's pre-eminent usefulness in the formation of a proper social and moral character to the new communities of our country, in the promotion of Christ's kingdom on earth, and the spiritual interests of mankind wherever its benign influence is extended.

COST OF THE WORK.

It is not the least interesting fact connected with this decennial statement, that the entire cost of all this labor and all these benefits, during the whole thirty years, has been only about $791,418; which shows an average of $26,238 per annum, and an average expenditure of $267 per annum for each missionary employed.

In all these may be seen the exceeding great value and economy of the Society as an instrumentality for religious ends. What other organization is more economical? What other is more beneficial? What other deserves more serious interest and liberal support from the churches?

By order of the Executive Board,

BENJAMIN M. HILL,

Corresponding Secretary.

MISSIONARY TABLE.

:	FIELD OF LABOR.	Date of Commission	Months Commis'd.	Weeks' labor reported.	Stations supplied.	Baptized.	Received by Letter	School's in S. S. & B. Class	Contrib. to Benevolent Objects	ADDR
.....	New Hampshire & Vermont.	April 1, 1861	12	52	..	..	....	....	.....	Collecting agent
....	Eastern Mass. and R. I......	April 1, 1861	12	52	....	.	....	....	....	Collecting agent
....	Mass., Ct., & Eastern N. Y.	April 1, 1861	12	52	....	.		...	......	Collecting agent

Names of Agents and Missionaries.	Post-Office Address.	Field of Labor.	Date of Commission.	Months Commis'd.	Weeks' labor reported.	Stations supplied.	Baptized.	Received by Letter.	Schol's in S. S. & B. Class.	Contrib. to Benevolent Objects.	Additional Facts Reported.
DELAWARE.											
Julius C. Haselhuhn	Wilmington	German Church	Nov. 1, 1860	12	39	1	4	....	89	111 00	Progressing amidst opposition.
" "	"	" "	Nov. 1, 1861	12	10	....	..	....	98	10 00	Resigned.
MICHIGAN.											
J. S. Goodman	East Saginaw	East Saginaw	June 1, 1860	12	13	2	..	....	42	18 50	Church spiritually improved.
" "	" "	" "	June 1, 1861	12	39	....	..	12	65	6 00	Sunday school flourishing. Church united and strengthened by additions by letter.
INDIANA.											
J. L. McLeod	Pierceтown	Elkhart River Association	April 1, 1861	12	52	8	6	5	....	......	People pecuniarily embarrassed.
James Goodrich	Huntington	Huntington	Nov. 1, 1860	12	39	1	4	4	100	13 40	Need no further aid.
J. H. Dunlap	Roanoke	Huntington Association	Jan. 1, 1861	12	39	3	..	....	....	225 00	No further aid asked for.
Charles Ager	Goshen	Goshen	M'ch 1, 1861	12	52	1	3	7	120	......	Influence of the church increased.
" "	"	"	M'ch 1, 1862	12	....	....	..	....	....	......	
ILLINOIS.											
Irenius Fouion	Highland	French at Sugar Creek and Beaver Creek	Nov. 1, 1861	12	39	2	15	9	30	......	People pecuniarily embarrassed. Religious indications encouraging.
" "	"	" "	Nov. 1, 1862	12	13	....	..	....	....	......	Nothing special.
WISCONSIN.											
A. Gibson	River Falls	River Falls and vicinity	June 1, 1860	12	13	7	..	....	75	......	Nothing special.
Theodore Ulbricht	Milwaukee	German Church	Nov. 1, 1860	12	12	2	..	....	97	......	Church suffering by divisions. Pastor quits the ministry.
Ernest Tschirch	Racine	German Church	Jan. 1, 1861	12	39	2	3	4	42	58 50	Some encouragement.
" "	"	" "	Jan. 1, 1862	12	13	....	..	....	31	17 00	

	FIELD OF LABOR.	Date of Commission.	Months Commis'd.	Weeks' labor reported.	Stations supplied.	Baptized.	Received by Letter.	Schol's in S. S. & B. Class.	Contrib. to Benevolent Objects.	ADDITIO
.....	Stevens' Point............	June 1, 1860	12	13	2	..	....	110	......	Paid debt on chur station.
.....	Appleton.....	June 1, 1861	12	39	1	2	6	103	74 25	Pastor encourage
.....	Superior................	Oct. 1, 1860	12	13	2	..	....	9	......	Resigned.
.....	Waubeck and vicinity... ..	Sept. 1, 1860	12	26	5	1	....	30	2 00	Nothing special.
.....	" "	Sept. 1, 1861	12	17	....	1	....	....	......	Resigns for anotl
.....	Osceola and vicinity........	Dec. 1, 1860	12	39	3	2	2	94	......	Church exerting
.....	Watertown...............	May 1, 1860	12	13	1	..	1	97	28 00	Congregation gre interest.
.....	"	May 1, 1861	12	39	2	2	3	115	53 25	S. school in an e
.. ..	Willow River Valley...	May 1, 1860	12	13	4	..	....	27	......	Nothing special.
.....	" "	May 1, 1861	12	39	5	..	1	30	150 00	Religion in a low
.....	Madison.................	Aug. 1, 1860	12	26	1	..	5	115	62 59	Ask for no furthe
.....	Eau Claire & Chippewa Falls	May 1, 1861	12	39	4	4	19	30	......	People very anxi
.....	Oshkosh.................	Sept. 1, 1861	12	26	3	..	3	60	.....	Prospects encour

Names of Agents and Missionaries.	Post-Office Address.	Field of Labor.	Date of Commission.	Months Commis'd.	Weeks' labor reported.	Stations supplied.	Baptized.	Received by Letter.	Schol's in S. S. & B. Class.	Contrib. to Benevolent Objects.	Additional Facts Reported.
A. W. Russell	Winterset	Western Association	Oct. 1, 1860	12	26	....	...	16	....	133 50	Indians committing depredations on the white settlements.
L. L. Frisk	Mineral Ridge	Swedes in Bond and other counties	Oct. 1, 1860	12	26	8	...	....	35	.....	
Thomas S. Griffith	Keokuk	Keokuk	Sept. 1, 1860	12	26	1	60	8	120	33 50	Revival.
" "	"	"	Sept. 1, 1861	12	26	....	2	24	95	27 00	Many of the members of the church gone to the war. Considerable religious interest in the congregation.
Lemuel Yarnall	Adel	Adel and Panora	Oct. 1, 1860	12	13	5	...	....	....	......	Resigned on account of poor health.
H. H. Burrington	Waverley	Waverley and Janesville	April 1, 1861	12	52	4	4	11	45	.....	Has been sick.
Samuel Pickard	Keokuk	South Eastern Iowa	Mar. 1, 1861	12	52	....	126	4	154	10 00	Continuous revival. Resigned and joined the army.
John Y. Aitchison	Delhi	Manchester and Delhi	June 1, 1860	12	13	3	16	1	104	10 00	Revival at Delhi.
" "	"	" "	June 1, 1861	12	29	....	2	1	117	13 75	The war engrosses the minds of the people.
James Elminster	Camanche	Camanche	Aug. 1, 1860	12	26	1	10	....	66	9 10	Revival.
W. W. Moore	McGregor	McGregor	Dec. 1, 1860	12	11	....	...	1	176	78 07	Congregation gradually increased. Pastor leaves the field.
L. M. Whitman	"	"	Sept. 1, 1861	12	26	1	2	7	190	5 00	Finished church-edifice. Declension in religious matters.
MINNESOTA.											
Amory Gale	Minneapolis	General itinerant	July 1, 1861	12	30	...	...	....	....	......	Labored in revivals.
Timothy R. Cressy	Hastings	Hastings and vicinity	Mar. 1, 1861	12	21	4	5	6	....	......	Resigned, and entered the army as chaplain.
John C. Hyde	St. Anthony	St. Anthony	June 1, 1860	12	13	4	...	....	60	.....	Resigned.
W. C. Shepard	Wasioja	Wasioja and Rice Lake	Oct. 1, 1860	12	26	8	25	2	75	60 00	Revival.
" "	"	" "	Oct. 1, 1861	12	26	....	...	2	65	3 00	Some valuable members enlisted in the army.
A. Norelius	Spencer	Swedes in Goodhue County	April 1, 1861	12	52	2	2	4	35	9 96	Need no further aid.
Enos Munger	Lakeland	Lakeland	April 1, 1861	12	52	2	...	....	52	10 15	Church weakened by deaths and removals.
H. C. Hazen	Faribault	Faribault	Jan. 1, 1861	12	39	1	1	1	95	......	People excited by the war. Church firm.
" "	"	"	Jan. 1, 1862	12	13	2	3	1	90	3 00	Church revived. Some conversions in congregation and S. school.
Wm. C. Phillips	St. Cloud	St. Cloud	May 1, 1860	12	38	2	...	....	85	10 25	Nothing special.
" "	"	"	May 1, 1861	12	39	2	...	....	95	5 00	Church at Maine Prairie commenced a meeting house. Prospects encouraging.
George W. Fuller	Chatfield	Chatfield	June 1, 1860	12	13	1	...	....	30	7 00	
" "	"	"	June 1, 1861	12	39	3	2	4	50	67 00	Church revived. Some conversions in the cong.
J. F. Wilcox	Northfield	Northfield and vicinity	Aug. 1, 1860	12	26	2	...	....	53	......	
" "	"	" "	Aug. 1, 1861	12	26	....	...	1	....	......	Organized a church at one of his stations.

FIELD OF LABOR.	Date of Commission.	Months Commis'd.	Weeks' labor reported.	Stations supplied.	Baptized.	Received by Letter	School's in S. S. & B. Class.	Contrib. to Benevolent Objects.	ADDITIONA
Taylor's Falls, etc.	May 1, 1860	12	13	3	..	....	100	.....	Some encouragemen
" "	May 1, 1861	12	39	....	1	1	....	......	Aspects encouraging in his family.
Newport and other places	June 1, 1860	12	13	4	..	....	100	5 05	Churches progressin
" "	June 1, 1861	12	39	....	..	....	....	......	War has engrossed
Cannon Falls and Valley	Nov. 1, 1860	12	39	4	2	2	84	27 00	Some members of t schools flourishin
" " and Warsaw	Jan. 1, 1862	12	13	5	..	3	76	......	Severe weather kep
Belle Plaine and Jordan	April 1, 1861	12	52	5	2	....	75	......	Congregation lessen Finished church-
Austin and vicinity	M'ch 1, 1861	12	52	7	..	1	....	13 00	Building a church-e of protracted poo
Monticello and vicinity	Nov. 1, 1860	12	39	3	1	4	25	15 00	Church feels the eff
" "	Nov. 1, 1861	12	13	....	..	....	....	......	Some encouraging
Shakapee, etc	Nov. 1, 1860	12	33	5	2	....	....	......	Suffers from poor h

Names of Agents and Missionaries.	Post-Office Address.	Field of Labor.	Date of Commission.	Months Commis'd.	Weeks' labor reported.	Stations supplied.	Baptized.	Received by Letter.	Schol's in S. S. & B. Class.	Contrib. to Benevolent Objects.	Additional Facts Reported.
J. D. P. Hungate	Tekamah	Tekamah and vicinity	July 1, 1860	12	13	4	..	....	....	......	
" "	"	" "	July 1, 1861	12	39	....	6	....	....	7 00	War engrosses the attention of the people.
KANSAS.											
R. C. Brant	Lawrence	Kansas	April 1, 1861	3	13	....	7	....	....	......	Enlisted in a Kansas Regiment as Chaplain.
E. Alward	Wathena	Doniphan Co.	April 1, 1861	12	52	9	15	1	60	......	Revival at [illegible], and a church organized there. Other churches doing well, [illegible]standing the war.
W. J. Kermott	Manhattan	Manhattan and vicinity	Aug. 1, 1860	12	26	....	3	5	100	......	[illegible] building a church-edifice. Encouraged in view of progress [illegible].
" "	"	" "	Aug. 1, 1861	12	26	....	1	....	....	......	Many [illegible] of the church gone to the war. Pastor narrowly [illegible] assassination by the Jayhawkers.
J. M. Lackey	Olathe	Johnson Co	Nov. 1, 1860	12	13	....	12	1	...	18 75	[illegible] relative to the national troubles. [illegible] resigned and gone into the army.
Aaron Perkins	Lawrence	Lawrence	Dec. 1, 1860	12	13	1	..	...	...	....	Removed to Atchison.
" "	Atchison	Atchison	June 1, 1861	12	39	....	..	7	65	......	Some favorable indications.
Nelson Alvord	Oskaloosa	Oskaloosa and Hebron	June 1, 1860	12	13	4	2	10	...	......	Church financially reduced by the famine.
" "	"	" "	June 1, 1861	12	39	....	2	3	....	......	The war distracts the minds of the people. Cold weather and the want of proper places to hold meetings prevented the people coming together for worship.
Wm. Hobbs	Mound City	Linn Co.	July 1, 1860	12	13	3	2	3	46	25 50	War excitement very high. The fear of being murdered, or driven off by the secessionists and Indians, has paralyzed every effort for permanent good.
" "	"	Linn and Allen Cos.	July 1, 1861	12	27	5	..	....	....	155 77	The recent success of the national arms calmed the people, and prospects religiously more encouraging.
H. S. Tibbits	Hiawatha	Brown and Nehama Cos	July 1, 1860	12	13	8	1	1	9	......	Some encouraging indications.
" "	"	" "	July 1, 1861	12	26	....	..	8	....	25 00	Organized a church at one station. Most of the able bodied men in this field enlisted for the war. Pastor been sick.
Israel Harris	Hartford	Neosha Valley	Sept. 1, 1860	12	26	4	..	9	140	81 50	Progressing.
" "	"	" "	Sept. 1, 1861	12	26	...	..	....	....	41 74	Church at Italia commenced building a meeting house.

	FIELD OF LABOR.	Date of Commission.	Months Commis'd.	Weeks' labor reported.	Stations supplied.	Baptized	Received by Letter.	Schol's in S. S. & B. Class.	Contrib. to Benevolent Objects.	ADDITIO
...	Socorro and other places...	Oct. 1, 1860	12	39	....	..	....	....	......	Work progressing
...	" " ...	Oct. 1, 1861.	6	13	....	2	....	....	......	Mission never
...	Santa Fe and other places..	Oct. 1, 1860	12	16	....	..	....	15	......	Famine prevailing diminished a
....	" " ..	Oct. 1, 1861	6	26	....	..	....	....	......	War unfavorable some interest sh
...	Laguna, etc.....	April 1, 1861	12	13	....	..	....	....	......	Bro. S. the Mexico, and lab Missionary, and
...	Peralto district............	April 1, 1861	12	39	....	..	....	....	......	Opposed by the pr
...	Socorro district............	April 1, 1860	12	13	....	..	....	....	.....	Cause of Christ ga Scarcity of prov mals lessen his
...	" "	April 1, 1861	12	39	....	..	....	....	......	Truth making pro
...	Santa Fe and vicinity.......	April 1, 1861	12	39	....	..	....	....	......	Labored with a la families with

LIST OF LEGACIES

PAID TO THE SOCIETY SINCE ITS ORGANIZATION.

1834	Dea. Josiah Penfield, Savannah, Ga., per Rev. H. O. Wyer	$1250 00
1835	Mrs. Clarissa Long, Shelburne, Mass., per W. Wilder, Esq., Executor	37 50
"	William Powers, Hebron, N. H., per Rev. I. Merriam	100 00
"	Miss Maria Curtis, Southbridge, Mass., per Rev. E. Going	200 00
"	Mrs. Jemima Elliott, Hampton, Ct., per Rev. J. Payne, Executor	100 00
1836	Mrs. Betsy Sprague, Attleboro', Mass., per Mr. A. Reed, Executor	451 25
"	Robert Rodgers, Newport, R. I	25 00
"	Ebenezer Boyd, Providence, R. I	10 00
1839	Mrs. Abigail Marshall, New York, per Mr. Schofield, Executor	702 17
"	Mrs. Margaret Pugsley, Dutchess Co., N. Y., per Miss Cornelia Pugsley	280 00
"	Mrs. Irene Coats, New York, per Alfred Decker, Esq	250 00
1841	Mrs. Elizabeth G. Moore, Hartford, Ct., per J. B. Gilbert	200 00
1842	Nathaniel Tucker, Milton, Mass., per W. T. Ticknor	200 50
1843	Mrs. Margaret Martin, Montgomery, N. Y, per Mr. J. J. Martin, Executor	100 00
"	Miss Cynthia M. Wright, Suffield, Ct., per H. Sheldon, Administrator	50 00
1844	Mr. Zephania Eddy, New Bedford, Mass., per Rev. H. Jackson, Executor	150 00
"	Mr. Josiah Kendall, Groton, Mass., per F E. Wheelock and Rev. A. Sanderson, Executors	1150 00
"	Miss Jane McCall, Society Hill, S. C, per John McIver	20 00
"	Miss Lydia Sweetzer, South Reading, Mass., per H. Sweetzer	324 00
"	Mrs. Elizabeth Griffin, New York, per one of her heirs	83 34
"	Josiah Flint, Cornish, N. H., per Mr. A. Burnap	80 00
"	Thomas Cooper, Esq., Eatonton, Ga., per Hon. M. A. Cooper, Executor	2000 00
"	Miss Betsy Hutchinson, Passumpsic, Vt., per L. P. Parks	50 00
"	Rev. Amos Dodge, Brighton, Macoupin Co., Ill., by his widow.	30 00
"	Mr. John Ward, Warren, N. Y., per J. Northrop and A. Ward, Executors	847 50
1845	Joseph H. Hayden, Saybrook, Ct., per H. L. Champlin, Executor	100 00
1846	John Allen, Centreville, R. I., per H. Hamilton and Rev. E. K. Fuller, Executors	3805 00
"	Rev. Jesse Mercer, Wilks Co., Ga., per B. M. Saunders, Executor	1331 87
"	Miss Mary Bliven, McDonough, N. Y., per Rev. John Peck	46 75
"	Mrs. Betsey Haykes, Cincinnatus, N. Y., per Trustees of the Baptist Society	100 00
"	Mrs. Charlotte Cole, Alexandria, Va., per Robert Bell, Executor	10 00
"	Dea. Modad Jackson, West Meredith, N. Y, per H. Jackson and W. Stilson, Executors	1105 00
"	Mrs. Urania Grant, West Wrentham, Mass., per R. E. Eddy	20 00
"	Mr. Richard Dubois, Malta, N. Y., per H. J. Rodgers, Executor	50 00
1847	Dea. Saxton Bailey, Lebanon, Ct., per Executor	100 00
"	Mr. Lewis Porter, Covert, N. Y., in advance, per J. McLellan	250 00
"	Miss Mary Havens, St. Catharine, Canada West, per Rev. E. Savage	68 93
"	Miss Amanda Hadley, Brattleboro', N. H., per Rev. J. Z. Foster	25 00
"	James Shearer, Canada West, per Rev. E. Savage	151 00
"	L. Crossman, Elbridge, N. Y., in advance	30 00
1848	William Jones, Iowa City, Iowa, per G. W. Hampton, Executor	25 00
Hon.	James Vanderpool, Newark, N. J., per B. Vanderpool, Executor	1000 00
"	Miss Susan Farrar, Keene, N. H., per G. Robins	10 00
"	Mrs. Eunice Nicholls, Cambridge, Mass., per E Mansfield, Executor	500 00
"	Mrs. Hannah Carleton, Portland, Me., per Rev. G J. Carleton, Administrator	500 00
1849	Mr. Samuel R. Stelle, Piscataway, N. J., per Lewis R. Stelle, Esq., Executor	200 00
"	Mrs. Phebe Gale, East Bennington, Vt., per Executor of Estate of S. Harmon	25 00
"	Mr. William Reynolds, Boston, Mass., per J. H. Duncan, Esq., and Mrs. Susan D. Reynolds, Executors, a part in secured notes,	1500 00
"	Josiah Lyman, Andover, Ct., per N. B. Lyman, Executor	50 00
"	John J. Martin, Montgomery, N. Y., per M. Bookstaver, Executor	1000 00
"	*Mrs. Martha Howe, West Boylston, Mass., per Messrs. E. J. Howe & Co.*	250 00
"	*A. H. Reed, Sweden, N. Y., per Rev. D. Searl*	[illegible]

" Joseph Flanders, Brooklyn, N. Y., per Mrs. Eliz
" William Williams, New York, per John Allen, E
" Eli Wiley, South Reading, Mass...............
1852 Miss Pharozine C. Kelly, Hopkinton, N. H., per
" Jonathan W. Ford, Boston, Mass..............
" Theron Fisk, Warsaw, N. Y..................
" Joshua A. Burke, Brooklyn, N. Y., per Messrs.
" Eliza Skaats, New York, in part, per G. N. Blee
" Barnum M. Howard, Sweden, N. Y., per H. M.
1853 Alanson Stewart, Liberty, N. Y., per W. W. Mu
" Mrs. Sarah B. Pierce, Middleboro', Mass.. ....
" Arnold Whipple, Providence, R. I., per Mrs. P.
" Mrs. Fanny McGilvreay, Brookline, N. H., Annu
" Mrs. Lucretia Goddard, Worcester, Mass., per H
" P. F. Brayton, Providence, R. I., per A. K. and
" Mrs. Elizabeth Gale, Washington, D. C.........
1854 Edward Rodgers, Chester, Ill., per Rev. M. B. K
" Miss Esther Ann Blakely, Pawlet, Vt., per Rev..
" Daniel Cummings, Chelsea, Mass., per Mr. Eaton
" Mrs. Mary Leuce, Bristol, R. I., per S. F. Baars.
" D. Valentine, Washington, Pa., per H. W. Wilso
" Willis L. Eaton, East Weare, N. H., per J. L. E
" Asa Reade, Attleboro', Mass., per Amos M. Rea
" Friend Humphrey, Albany, per his son, Execut
" George Corbet, Worcester, Mass.................
" Mrs. Abby Arnold, Centreville, R. I., per Wm. A
" Garrat N. Bleecker, New York, per E. Cauldwell
" Eunice Shepherdson, Belleville, N. Y...........
" Mrs. Mary Johnson, Albany, N. Y., per Charles I
" Mrs. Olive Stowell, Le Roy, N. Y., per R. Bell ..
" David Trull, Lowell, per J. Fox.................
1855 Roger Pegg, New York, per Mr. Coe, Executor...
" John Goodell, Jr., Woodstock, N. Y., in part, per
" Mrs. Frances Thompson, Alabama, N. Y........

1856	Hon. Nathan H. Bottum, Shaftsbury, Vt., per Norman Bottum, Executor, Annuity.....	$200 00
"	Mrs. Eliza Jackson, Hamilton, N. Y., per Prof. P. B. Spear..........................	100 00
"	Mrs. M. W. Denison, Rock Island, Ill., per Rev. J. W. Denison.......................	8 00
"	Miss Achsah Cox, Imlaystown, N. J..	50 00
"	Samuel Stone, Dundee, Mich., T. Babcock, Executor..................................	30 00
"	Louisa S. Platt, Haverhill, Mass., S. Peaslie, Executor.............................	35 00
"	Mrs. Hannah Kent, Danversport, Mass...	100 00
"	Manley Street, Holyoke, Mass..	25 00
"	Mrs. Lorain Sheldon, Suffield, Ct...	355 47
"	Mrs. Abigail Hatch, Boston, Mass., per Thomas Mair, Executor........................	1491 24
"	David Stanton, Penn's Neck, N. J., per George Kelton, Executor, Annuity.............	198 00
"	Rev. Azel Waters, Miama, Iowa, per C. W. Morgan, Executor...........................	219 38
1857	Mrs. Rachael Prescott, per John Crockett, Executor..................................	100 00
"	Azariah Snow, Lunenburgh, Vt., per John Snow, Executor..............................	15 00
"	Mrs. E. K. Babcock, Jay, N. Y., per Rev. J. J. Babcock..............................	4 75
"	Wm. Cook, Worcester, N. Y...	100 00
"	Mrs Elizabeth Hovey, Cambridge, Mass., George Cummings, Executor....................	3000 00
"	Hannah Godfrey, Hastings, N. Y., C. A. Wilson, Executor.............................	10 00
"	Betsey Miller, Earlville, N. Y., per L. H. Miller....................................	100 00
"	Mrs. Phebe Mulford, Roadstown, N. J., per I. Smalley, Executor......................	50 00
"	Hannah S. Trask, Fall River, Mass., R. C. Brown and Joseph Borden, Executors.........	402 13
"	Miss Catharine Sharp, Barre, N. Y., in part, per A. L. Daniels.......................	415 00
"	Miss Achsah Pierce, Mohawk, N. Y., per Rev. H. T. Love..............................	149 47
"	Michael Shepherd, Salem, Mass., per H. F. Shepherd, Executor........................	2957 60
"	Cornelia A. Perry, Centre White Creek, N. Y., per Nathaniel Cottrell, Executor.......	300 00
"	Mrs. Eleanor Willard, Harvard, Mass...	100 00
"	Sabina Bennett, West Eaton, N. Y..	14 00
"	James Nickerson, Cazenovia, N. Y., Benj. T. Clark, Executor.........................	100 00
1858	Jabez Keep and wife, Cortlandville, N. Y., per Rev. Henry Bowen......................	789 65
"	Aaron Treat, North Stonington, Ct...	5 00
"	Mrs. Martha Straton, Woburn, Mass., per B. Millett, Executor, in part................	575 42
"	Mrs. Franklinia E. Aikman, Burlington, N. J..	508 68
"	J. B. Jones, Roxbury, Mass., per S. Walker and G. B. Jones, Executors................	1000 00
"	Mrs. Sarah H. Canfield, Stanford, N. Y., per Cor. N. Campbell, Executor..............	505 90
"	Mrs. Jane B. Dustin, Concord, N. H., Enos Blake, Executor...........................	800 00
"	Miss Martha Whiting, Charlestown, Mass., Interest on her Legacy, per A. J. Bellows, Ex.	550 00
"	Mrs. Susan Hull, Adams, N. Y., per Abram Sheldon, Executor..........................	100 00
"	Benjamin Porter, Danvers, Annuity...	282 50
"	Miss Deborah Flock, Lawrence, N. J., per James E. Coleman, Executor..................	100 00
"	Elisha Ashley, Poultney, Vt., per J. Joslin, Executor,..............................	500 00
1859	Miss Hannah Spaulding, Chelmsford, Mass...	100 00
"	Joel Hayford, Farmersville, N. Y., per Jarvis Leonard, Executor......................	50 00
"	Miss Amelia M. Cone, Philadelphia, per O. W. Davis..................................	51 13
"	Daniel Flagg, Littleton, Mass...	50 00
"	Lucy F. Granger, Mass., per P. J. Spaulding...	50 00
"	Polly Browning, Waterford, Ct., Annuity...	47 84
"	Mrs. Abigail Lamb, Newton, Mass., Eben Stone, Executor..............................	800 00
"	Micajah Reynolds, Newark, N. J., Messrs. Hollyer and Kitchell, Executors.............	2131 00
"	Miss Betsey Harriman, Georgetown, Mass., in part.....................................	500 00
"	Mrs. Lucy J. Johnson, West Medbury, Mass., per Rev. E. C. Messenger..................	575 00
"	Miss Catharine Orcutt, Cambridgeport, Mass...	284 00
"	Miss Anna Marchant, Barnstable, Mass., Freeman Marchant, Executor.....................	225 00
"	Joseph McCulloch, Newport, R. I., W. D. Southwick, Executor..........................	200 00
"	Mrs. Phebe Taylor, Syracuse, N. Y., in part..	5 00
"	Sarah S. T. Davis, Gaines, N. Y., per Jesse S. Wetmore...............................	235 00
"	John Tustin, Chester Springs, Pa...	10 00
"	Ezra Reynolds, Benton, Pa., in part, Saml. Manchester, Executor......................	50 00
"	Henry Case, Sweden, N. Y., Rev. Z. Case, Executor....................................	150 00
"	*Rev. Jacob Drake, Delaware, Ohio*..	541 83
"	*Miss Mary True*, Plainfield, N. H., Reuben True, Executor...........................	200 00

1859 Lucy A. Roberts, Cromwell, Ct., Mrs. Hubbard, I
" An aged sister, Thetford, Vt., per W. W. Baker..
" Lucy F. Gray, Chelmsford, Mass..................
" Isaac Morse, New Woodstock, N. Y...............
" Mrs. Mary E. Arnold, W. Medway, Mass., per Re
" Junia Freeman, Rushford, N. Y., E. B. Freeman
" Thomas Wakefield, Waterville, N. Y., Henry To
" Anna Crossman, Sheldon, Vt., Hon. George Gree
" Betsey Harrimon, Georgetown, Mass............
" Elijah Withington, Morrisania, N. Y., Saml. Wi
1860 Tirza E. Gilman, Sanbornton, N. H., Benj. N. S
" Rufus Fiske, Cambridge, Mass., Susan Fiske, Ex
" Mrs. J. W. Putnam, Chicopee Falls, Mass., Rev.
" Miss Phebe Arnold, Jay, N. Y..................
" Margaretta Meslers, New York, Rev. Thomas T.
" Harvey Tracy, Tunbridge, Vt., per Rev. Leonar
" Miss Sarah Bartholomew, Pa., Jonathan Robert
" Estate of Lydia Sherwood, Bridgeport, Ct., per I
" Dea. Benjamin Warren, Augusta, N. Y., in par
" Catharine Westgate, Plainfield, N. H., Earl Wes
" Joseph McCracken, New York, per A. B. Capwel
" Mrs. Huldah B. Slosson, Pitcher, N. Y., per E.
" Fanny C. Randall, Oneida Castle, N. Y., O. P. R
" Johnson N. Reynolds, Pulteney, N. Y., J. J. Rey
" Mrs. Willard Putnam, Danverse, Mass..........
" Elijah Carey, Brookline, Mass., with interest....

IMPORTANT WHEN WILLS ARE MADE.

Legacies are sometimes diverted from the purposes of testators on account of technical informalities, **especially** in the devising clause. The form of bequest, to which we solicit the careful attention of those **friends** who kindly intend to place the Society among their legatees, as one which, if followed, will secure **to us** the favors intended, is as follows:

FORM OF A BEQUEST TO THE SOCIETY.

"I give and bequeath to the American Baptist Home Mission Society, formed in New York, in the year eighteen hundred and thirty-two, the sum of ...... dollars, for the purposes of said Society."

Please remember to use the word "Baptist," and to write "Mission," instead of "Missionary."

AGGREGATE CONTRIBUTIONS

FROM ALL THE STATES SINCE 1832.

STATES.	Total Amount to 1850.	1851-1855.	1856.	1857.	1858.	1859.	1860.	1861.	1862.
Canada....	$4,139 4[illegible]	$1,0[illegible]	$143 77	$470 36	$446 44	$512 [illegible]	$401 [illegible]	$334 26	....
Maine......	3,214 40	1,05[illegible] 22	102 44	82 0[illegible]	27 57	82 51	60 1[illegible]	16 00	$[illegible]5 00
N. Hamp....	4,874 5[illegible]	6,519 01	1,008 22	1,627 00	1,877 14	2,157 71	1,744 8[illegible]	2,344 22	1,480 26
Vermont....	4,072 90	3,741 54	1,[illegible]86 54	967 44	860 69	1,219 9[illegible]	771 67	586 97	1,345 64
Mass.	41,291 5[illegible]	43,400 77	10,467 6[illegible]	10,176 01	11,020 98	10,667 47	10,620 2[illegible]	9,523 96	6,163 79
Rh. Island..	12,297 0[illegible]	9,754 [illegible]	2,500 07	1,768 88	1,265 58	903 70	4,003 9[illegible]	1,393 96	1 044 07
Conn	17,[illegible]20 9[illegible]	16,391 14	4 047 40	3,840 8[illegible]	3,089 55	3,001 58	3,439 2[illegible]	4,[illegible]53 25	3,132 96
New York .	100 644 16	79,584 59	14,766 88	14,855 15	13 959 [illegible]	13,615 68	10,7[illegible]3 8[illegible]	10,390 50	10,677 37
New Jersey.	14,990 78	15,414 29	2,085 54	2,498 44	2,667 60	3 427 97	4 519 6[illegible]	2,344 57	1,745 07
Penn	9,449 57	12,388 30	2,507 8[illegible]	1,804 [illegible]	2,277 41	3 512 17	3,354 3	2,326 97	1,982 91
Delaware ..	683 50	740 70	103 77	18[illegible] 04	31 0[illegible]	124 00	24 50	105 50	100 00
Maryland...	2 055 0	15 50	200 00	....	....	....	....	....	....
Dist of Col.	993 12	211 81	....	8 22	....	....	....	....	....
Ohio.......	1,369 57	7,616 25	2,708 28	1,065 01	804 50	598 28	946 61	289 50	94 91
Michigan..	1,719 9[illegible]	3,375 52	179 2[illegible]	198 72	284 81	200 60	276 52	57 27	139 24
Indiana.....	104 80	7,142 3[illegible]	656 7[illegible]	1,317 29	1,01[illegible] 79	456 88	812 62	1,182 95	622 96
Illinois	4,348 55	8,515 80	1,700 17	150 80	124 54	54 50	32 98	311 01	190 10
Wisconsin..	578 72	1 802 48	418 4[illegible]	179 19	18[illegible] 08	667 40	476 47	623 79	224 01
Iowa........	562 72	1,456 55	573 12	683 92	744 90	811 40	511 40	757 84	319 34
Minnesota..	....	605 91	328 25	377 07	647 2[illegible]	[illegible] 90	1 397 78	606 31	583 11
Nebraska...	....	....	....	150 00	100 0[illegible]	6 00	23 50	....	6 58
Kansas	....	....	....	5 00	98 00	40 17	649 17	589 23	553 26
Missouri ...	266 8[illegible]	262 00	....	20 00	15 00	....	....	120 05	....
Kentucky..	344 38	42 25	....	....	....	....	....	....	....
Virginia....	9,325 15	28 75	....	7 00	....	6 02	....	....	....
N. Carolina.	5,591 60	....	....	....	....	....	....	....	....
S. Carolina.	8,408 10	50 00	50 0	20 0	....	....	....	....	....
Georgia....	10,861 20	30 0	....	40 00	....	....	....	....	....
Alabama ...	493 08	59 00	....	....	....	....	....	5 00	....
Florida	172 82	....	....	....	....	....	....	....	....
Mississippi .	1,899 00	....	....	....	....	....	....	....	....
Tennessee..	466 10	....	....	....	....	....	....	....	....
Louisiana ..	70 0	....	....	....	....	1 00	....	50 00	....
Arkansas ..	60 2[illegible]	....	....	....	....	....	....	....	....
Texas......	....	....	....	....	....	....	....	....	....
California ..	....	515 50	105 00	....	10 00	25 00	....	....	....
Oregon	....	200 65	44 90	17 00	10 00	....	....	9 00	420 53
N. Mexico..	....	183 90	....	50 00	5 00	....	....	....	....
U. S. Gov ..	....	....	4 50	....	....	....	....	....	....
N. Granada.	....	....	30 00	25 20	....	....	....	....	....
Unknown...	....	....	....	159 00	....	1 00	....	....	....
Aggregate for each pd.	202,618 68	222,285 3[illegible]	47,028 54	43,280 70	41,707 82	42,997 0[illegible]	[illegible]5,040 47	44,282 19	[illegible]0,891 11

STATE CO

GENERAL ASSOCIATIO

With the Names and Post office Addresses of the
Anniversaries for 1862 ; *the number of*
Treasuries for 1861, *including Balances of*

STATES.	CORRESPONDING SECRETARIES.
Maine..............	N. M. Wood.........
New Hampshire......	K. S Hall...........
Vermont............	T. H. Archibald......
Massachusetts.	J. Ricker............
Rhode Island*.......	A. H. Granger.......
Connecticut.........	E. Cushman.........
New York...........	John Smitzer........
New Jersey..........	J. M. Carpenter......
Pennsylvania*.......	Malachi Taylor ......
Maryland	A. Fuller Crane. ....
Virginia*............	H. K. Ellyson........
North Carolina*......	J. B. Solomon. ......

DECENNIAL CENSUS FOR MINNESOTA.

Showing the names and number of Counties in the State and their Population, the number of churches organized, their number of members, the number of church-edifices in each County, from 1850 to 1861, inclusive, etc., etc.

1861.

COUNTIES.	Population.	Churches.	Members.	Baptized.	Ministers.	Ch. Edifices.
Aitken	2					
Anoka	2,106	1	42	19	1	1
Becker	386					
Benton	627					
Blue Earth	4,802	3	64	8	4	
Breckenridge	79					
Brown	2,339					
Buchanan	26					
Carlton	51					
Carver	5,106	4	123	89	4	1
Cass	150					
Chisago	91	2	18	27	1	
Cottonwood	12					
Crow Wing	269					
Dakota	9,093	1	3[illegible]	11	1	1
Dodge	3,797	2	53	1	2	1
Douglass	195					
Faribault	1,338	1	12	1	1	
Fillmore	13,543	10	304	104	5	1
Freeborn	3,567	3	35	6	1	
Goodhue	8,977	8	227	30	3	
Hennepin	12,849	5	218	61	5	3
Houston	6,645	4	62	32	3	
Isanti	284	1	19			
Itasca	51					
Jackson	181					
Kandiyohi	76					
Kanebeck	30					
Lake	248					
La Seuer	5,318	3	60	7	4	1
Manomin	136					
Martin	151					
McLeod	1,286					
Carried forward,	83,608	48	1270	396	35	9
Brought forward,	83,608	48	1270	396	35	9
Meeker	928					
Mille Lac	72					
Monogalia	350					
Morrison	618					
Mower	3,217	2	45	5	4	
Murray	29					
Nicolet	3,773	2	34	17	1	
Nobles	35					
Olmstead	9,527	3	87	19	3	1
Otter Tail	240					
Pembina	1,612					
Pierce	10					
Pine	1,741					
Pipestone	23					
Polk	245					
Ramsey	12,150	1	118	61	2	1
Rensville	245	1	21	7		
Rice	7,543	3	116	34	2	
St. Louis	406					
Scott	4,594	4	73	27	3	1
Sherburn	724					
Sibley	3,609					
Stearns	4,505	3	72	3	2	1
Steel	2,863	5	73	34	2	
Todd	430					
Toombs	40					
Wabashaw	7,228	2	61	9	4	1
Waseca	2,601				1	
Washington	6,123	2	40	9	2	
Winona	9,208	5	183	56	7	1
Wright	3,729	2	35	7	1	
Total,	172,022	83	2238	684	69	15

This table was prepared by Rev. A. Gale, of Minneapolis, Minnesota. Statistics for 1850 accompanied it, but they showed a population of only 6077, in seven counties, viz., Benton, Dakota, Pembina, Ramsey, Wabashaw, and Washington. In Hennepin County there was 1 church and 10 members; in Ramsey County, 1 church, 18 members, and 1 minister; in Washington County, 1 church, 9 members, and 1 minister. Total, 3 churches, 37 members, and 3 ministers.

DEC[illegible]IAL CENSUS FOR IOWA.

Counties in the State, and their population; the number of churches organized; their
mber of church-edifices erected in each County from 1851 to 1861, inclusive, etc.

	1850.							1861.						
	Churches.	Members.	Baptized.	Ministers.	Ordinations.	Meeting-houses.	Cost of church property.	Population.	Churches.	Members.	Baptized.	Ministers.	Ordinations.	Meeting-houses.
...	....	....	....	....	....	....	....	1,523	2	44	14	1	...	....
7	....	....	....	....	....	....	....	12,236	4	132	61	2	...	1
[illegible]	1	78	21	1	....	....	....	11,933	15	673	646	7		1
2	....	....	....	....	....	....	....	8,502	4	168	85	2	...	2
35	....	....	....	....	....	....	....	8,244	3	197	165	3		1
35	....	....	......	....	....	....	....	4,231	3	93	72	1		....
..	....	....	....	....	....	....	....	4,915	4	119	50	3		....
7	....	....	....	....	....	....	....	7,106	4	127	25	3		....
..	....	....	....	....	....	....	....	3,724	2	67	34	1	1	....
..	....	....	....	....	....	....	....	147	1	6	1	....	....	...
..	....	....	....	....	....	....	....	1,612	2	74	41	1	....	...
[illegible]	1	17	4					[illegible]						

COUNTIES.	1850. Population.	Churches.	Members.	Baptized.	Ministers.	Ordinations.	Meeting-houses.	Cost of church property.	1861. Population.	Churches.	Members.	Baptized.	Ministers.	Ordinations.	Meeting-houses.	Cost of church property.	Increase.	Ratio.
Johnson,	4,472	1	54	¶28	1		1	$5,000	17,572	2	172	81	2	1	1	$5,100	118	1 in 103
Jones,	3,007	1	18	¶3	1				13,305	4	114	33	3	1	1	1,000	96	1 in 125
Keokuk,	4,822	2	55	¶14	1				13,284	4	211	194	5	1	2	1,600	156	1 in 63
Kossuth,									416	1	18	1					18	1 in 23
Lee,	18,861	6	254	¶123	3	1	3	4,600	29,232	11	893	1,025	9	3	5	13,500	637	1 in 33
Linn,	5,444	1	62	¶9	1		1	1,500	18,950	9	374	214	3	1	2	3,000	152	1 in 51
Louisa,	4,939	1	†						10,370	2	125	75	1		1	1,500	125	1 in 75
Lucas,	471								5,766	4	212	163	2	2	†		212	1 in 27
Madison,	1,179								7,338	2	114	72	2		1	3,000	114	1 in 64
Mahaska,	5,989	1	33	2	1				14,816	8	455	274	6	3	2	2,500	314	1 in 33
Marion,	5,482								16,815	7	847	320	5	3	2	8,500	347	1 in 48
Marshall,	338								6,015	¶2	49	12	1				49	1 in 133
Mitchell,									3,409	2	26		1	1			26	1 in 133
Monroe,	2,884	1	†						8,611	5	139	51	1		1	800	139	1 in 62
Mills,									4,480	2	54	34	1				54	1 in 83
Muscatine,	5,731	1	22	¶14	1		1	2,000	16,444	4	265	201	3	1	1	2,000	243	1 in 62
Page,	551								4,419	3	102	57	2				102	1 in 42
Polk,	4,513								11,625	3	123	38	3		1	4,000	123	1 in 95
Pottawottomie,	7,828	‡							4,962									
Poweshiek,	615								5,670	5	154	88	5	3			154	1 in 37
Ringold,									2,923	1	15	4	1				15	1 in 195
Sac,									246	1	19	3	1	1			19	1 in 13
Scott,	5,986	5	142	*¶92	4		2	5,000	25,960	8	580	514	7	7	6	29,700	237	1 in 44
Story,									4,052	2	60	21	2		1	2,500	60	1 in 68
Tama,	8								5,285	§2	74	24	1	1	1	800	74	1 in 71
Taylor,	204								3,589	5	319	171	3	2	1	†	319	1 in 11
Van Buren,	12,270	4	155	¶160	1	1			17,083	7	238	243	4	1	2	4,000	183	1 in 51
Wapello,	8,471	2	77	¶123	1				14,518	13	562	515	5	2	2	2,500	475	1 in 26
Warren,	961								10,282	7	217	97	2	1	1	1,500	217	1 in 48
Washington,	4,957	2	31	55	1		1	600	14,233	4	175	160	1		3	2,500	144	1 in 81
Wayne,	340								6,411	6	169	80	1	2	1	500	169	1 in 39
Webster,									2,504	3	68	16	2				68	1 in 37
Winneshiek,	546								13,942									
Woodbury,									1,119	1	13						13	1 in 86
27 other Counties, no churches.									10,998									
	192,214	54	1,654	1,095	32	4	13	$23,700	674,948	26[illegible]	11,403	8,713	170	78	67	$147,900	10,224	1 in 59

* 1 house burned. † Unknown. ‡ Parsonage. § Church-lots. ¶ Imperfect.—At the foot of the Columns, is put the *total* of Baptisms for the *whole* period, gathered from various sources; minutes being lost, baptisms for each church can not be gathered.

The above table was furnished by Rev. T. S. Griffith of Keokuk, Iowa, who was assisted by other ministers. There are some deficiencies which could not be supplied, put the statistics are as perfect as they could be made.

PROGRESSION TABLE,

tates, each ten years, from 1800, together with the number of regular Baptist Churches, Ministers, and . . . 's of which year could not be found. The first two Decades extend two years over the regular periods for

1820. Population.	1830. Population.	1840. Population.	1850. Population.	1860. Population.	1812.			1832.				1840.		
					Churches.	Ordained Ministers.	Members.	Churches.	Ordained Ministers.	Licentiates.	Members.	Churches.	Ministers.	Members.
298,335	399,955	501,793	583,188	628,276	123	92	5,870	222	145	23	15,000	258	183	19,4
214,161	269,328	284,574	317,964	326,072	41	31	2,285	90	64	14	6,505	75	71	9,3
235,764	280,652	291,948	314,120	315,116	121	87	9,197	125	78	9	10,525	123	85	9,9
523,287	610,408	737,699	994,499	1,231,065	91	85	8,542	189	160	60	20,290	194	186	22,2
83,059	97,199	108,830	147,544	174,621	63	63	6,083	20	17	3	3,271	32	25	5,1
275,202	297,665	310,015	370,791	460,151	66	50	6,350	92	77	20	10,039	96	77	11,0
372,812	1,918,608	2,428,921	3,097,394	3,887,542	268	179	18,940	580	435	93	59,068	776	633	81,5
277,575	320,823	373,306	489,555	672,031	21	16	1,943	56	49	5	3,739	49	49	6,3
049,458	1,348,233	1,724,022	2,311,786	2,906,370	72	65	4,616	134	83	23	10,213	251	165	20,1
72,749	76,748	78,085	91,535	112,218										
407,350	447,040	469,232	583,035	687,034	32	15	1,336	10	12	.	1,065	44	26	1,5
33,039	39,834	43,712	51,687	75,076										
065,379	1,211,405	1,239,797	1,421,661	1,596,083	283	283	35,164	338	183	34	49,844	463	235	40,4
638,829	737,987	753,110	[illegible]	[illegible]	[illegible]	[illegible]	[illegible]	[illegible]	[illegible]	[illegible]	[illegible]	[illegible]	[illegible]	[illegible]

DECENNIAL CENSUS FOR WISCONSIN.

Showing the names and number of Counties in the State and their Population, the number of churches organized, their number of members, the number of church-edifices in each County, from 1850 to 1861, inclusive, etc., etc.

COUNTIES.	1850. Population.	1850. Churches.	1850. Members.	1850. Pastors.	1850. Ch. Edifices.	1860. Population.	1860. Churches.	1860. Members.	1860. Pastors.	1860. Ch. Edifices.	Baptized from 1850 to 1860.
Adams	181					6,492	3	74	1	1	50
Brown	6,215					11,795	1	22			7
Crawford	2,496					8,068	1	36		1	
Calumet	1,743					7,892	3	70	2		13
Columbia	9,561	2	41	1		24,442	8	259	5	2	152
Chippewa	615					1,895					
Dane	16,639	7	237	2		43,857	16	507	11	5	260
Dodge	19,138	3	120	3	1	42,819	8	837	6	6	226
Fon du Lac	14,510	3	119	1	1	34,157	5	391	5	3	144
Grant	16,198	3	75	1		31,198	5	153	4	1	117
Green	8,566	2	104	1	1	19,809	3	458	2	3	219
Iowa	9,522	1	40		1	18,968	3	57	2	1	25
Jefferson	15,317	3	108	2	1	30,438	2	108	2	1	81
Kenosha	10,734	6	208	4	2	13,904	5	156	2	2	128
Lafayette	11,531	3	85			18,133	6	222	3	1	64
Lapointe	489					672					
Manitowoc	7,302					22,416	1	17			4
Marathon	508					2,894					
Marquette	8,641	2	56	2		8,233	10	229	4	2	160
Milwaukee	31.077	4	270	2	1	62,528	5	348	4	3	164
Portage	1,250					7,509	5	152	3	1	59
Racine	14,973	4	236	2	2	21,363	7	310	6	4	189
Richland	903					9,733	7	115	4		11
Rock	20,750	8	470	4	2	36,691	13	1,082	11	7	724
Saint Croix	624					5,393	2	78	1		6
Sauk	4,371	2	59	1		18,965	8	361	7	1	141
Sheboygan	8,379	3	125	2	1	26,876	7	319	4	2	154
Walworth	17,862	10	747	10	9	26,498	12	1,002	10	12	555
Washington	19,485	3	48	2		23,621	2	108	1	1	80
Waukesha	19,258	3	198	2	2	26,836	4	227	3	3	106
Winnebago	10,167					23,773	9	395	3	4	130
Total in 1850....31.	305,391	72	3,341	42	22						
COUNTIES ORGANIZED SINCE 1850.											
Ashland						196					
Bad Ax						1,109	4	81	2		10
Buffalo						3,864					
Burnett						12					
Clark						789					
Dallas						13					
Door						2,948					
Douglass						819	1	15			
Dunn						2,705					
Eau Claire						3,161					
Green Lake						12,663	5	221	2	1	98
Jackson						4,192	2	16			1
Juneau						8,771	3	132	1	1	95
Kewaunee						5,530					
La Crosse						12,152	6	379	6	2	217
Monroe						8,410	2	168	1	1	49
Oconto						3,593					
Ontagamie						9,587	2	61	2	1	9
Ozaukee						15,682	1	7			26
Pepin						2,392					
Pierce						4,674	1	17	1		1
Polk						1,400					
Shawano						829					
Trempeleau						2,560	2	24	1		
Waupacca						8,855	4	105	3		20
Waushava						8,777	3	63	2	1	23
Wood						2,425					
Grand Total....31 + 27 = 58.						775,873	196	9,071	127	74	4,519

The above Table was prepared By Rev. J. T. Westover, of Iowa City, Iowa, (formerly of Wisconsin,) is believed to be as correct as it can be made with present means of information.

REPORTS OI

ON TOPICS PRESENTED IN
EXECUT

REPORT OF COM

The Committee upon Agencies repo
agency as indispensable to the successf
they yet are gratified with the result of
ber of collecting agents, and would rec
with safety. In attempting it, howeve
labor assigned to different individuals,
the detail of collection by training the
nection they would suggest the inqui

pated slaves—whether in the District of Columbia or in other places now held by our forces—and also to inaugurate a system of operations for carrying the Gospel alike to free and bond throughout the whole southern section of our country, so fast and so far as the progress of our arms, and the restoration of order and law shall open the way.

B. T. WELCH, *Chairman.*

NO. 3.

REPORT OF COMMITTEE ON OBITUARIES.

Your Committee on Obituaries respectfully report: That the number of Directors, Life Members, and friends of this Society, called to their home and reward during the past year is unusually large. Of Directors we find the names of Rev. JONATHAN ALDRICH, Rev. C. C. P. CROSBY, THERON FISK, SYLVESTER PIER, and REUBEN POST.

These were brethren of whose virtues we might say much in honor of the grace of God; they were men whose wisdom in counsel, and devotion to the interests of the Kingdom of the Redeemer, will long be had in grateful remembrance.

We also record the death of twenty-two Life Members, eight of whom were ministers of the Gospel. Other beloved fellow-helpers have been called away from this scene of toil to the rest of heaven, among whom was our beloved sister Gorman, wife of Rev. Samuel Gorman, our missionary in New Mexico, whose very life and being were most fully identified with the cause of Home Missions. For nine years she was engaged in Missionary labor in that distant Territory, laboring much of that time among the Puebla Indians, until by excessive toil her health became impaired, and she was called to rest from her labors. Her works do follow her.

While with deep sorrow we record the removal of so many of the friends of missions, we would not be discouraged, but by more diligence and zeal, evince our interest in His kingdom, as followers of those who, through faith and patience, inherit the promises.

SAMUEL B. WILLIS, *Chairman.*

To the above should be added the name of Josè Senun. He was a Puebla Indian of much more than ordinary intelligence, and in his early life was a devotee of the pagan worship of the Pueblas, and subsequently a Roman Catholic. After Bro. Gorman commenced his labors in New Mexico, in 1852, Senun commenced the study of the Bible, and in 1854 abandoned both his idolatrous worship and his Romanism, and gave evidence of true conversion. Possessing good gifts and a very well cultivated mind, he was, in January, 1855, appointed an assistant missionary of the Home Mission Society, and labored zealously among his people to bring them to Christ. He preached with much fluency, and though never ordained, such confidence was felt by our missionaries in his judgment and discretion, that he was left by Bro. Gorman in charge of the mission station at Laguna, while Bro. Gorman took up his residence at Santa Fé. His life, after his conversion, was one of blameless integrity, and though at first bitterly opposed, persecuted, and reviled by the Romanists and by his own people, his exemplary conduct so won upon them, that last winter the Indians of the Puebla town of Luguna, which contained about 1000 inhabitants, unanimously elected him their Governor, which office he held till his decease. At the time of his death he was forty-six years of age. Bro. Gorman in communicating the sad intelligence says, "We have lost one of our best, very best, brethren and laborers; as near the 'noblest work of God' as men are apt to be in this world. He was a good and honest man, and though dead he yet speaketh."

NO. 4.

REPORT OF COMMITTEE ON FINANCE.

The Committee on Finance beg to report: According to the report of your Treasurer, the receipts of the Society from all sources during the past year have been $33,732.59. Of this amount $26,036.88 have been contributed directly from the churches. Thus making a deficiency, as compared with the previous year, of more than $6000 in ordinary contributions. We also find, that in the total amount of resources, there is a difference of nearly $17,000 in favor of the preceding financial year of the Society.

With these facts before them, your Committee have very naturally been led to inquire as to the cause of this decrease. They are well aware that we have fallen upon no ordinary times in the history of our country, and that during a portion of the past year, at least, it has been comparatively difficult to secure money from the churches. But in view of the magnitude of the object, the relation this Society sustains to the spiritual welfare of thousands who are perishing for the bread of life in the home-field, your Committee are of the opinion that a much larger amount might and should have been raised. Certain it is, that the American Baptist Home Mission Society is second to no organization existing among us. Nor in all its past history have more extended and promising fields of labor called for religious culture. In addition to the sphere of its operations for years past, the civil war now raging is opening new fields, and the cry is already heard, "Come over and help us." From the present hour this Society will need more money and men to meet the claims of the destitute than at any former period. We ask brethren to look this subject fully in the face, and then inquire as to the means of infusing a new life and vigor into this organization dear to all our hearts. One thing is obviously necessary to our increased efficiency. By some means, larger pecuniary contributions must be secured from the churches, and to accomplish this, new and increased enterprise and energy are required in money.

Your Committee, therefore, wou'd recommend to the Society and Board the adoption of such measures, as in their opinion, are adapted to secure this object.

D. G. Corey, *Chairman.*

TESTIMONIALS FROM STATE CONVENTIONS.

CONNECTICUT.

REPORT ON HOME MISSIONS.

The Committee on Home Missions would report the following :

The purpose of this Society, as its Constitution declares, is "to preach the Gospel throughout North America." This purpose it has steadily pursued since its organization, employing, for the last year, one hundred and thirty-one laborers, in the Canadas and in fifteen States and Territories of the Union, at an expense of between fifty and sixty thousand dollars; and whose labors have been blest by revivals of religion in twenty-one places, and by the baptism of eighteen hundred and sixty-seven persons.

No field of Christian effort has claims upon us for earnest and sacrificing labor, none appeals to the instinct of self-preservation, in addition to all other motives which Christian men feel and acknowledge, as this field and work of home evangelization.

The growth which we, as a people, are experiencing in numbers, in wealth, in influence, the energy of our national character, the vigor of Anglo-American ideas, and the part which God, in his providence, seems preparing for us to act in the history of the world, are reasons, which all must feel to be of great weight, for enlarged and persevering efforts to diffuse throughout the land the Gospel of Jesus Christ, and so to season our cherished institutions with this only preservative.

And, especially in these troublous times, when the progress of a Christian civilization is violently arrested, and institutions, the wonder and hope of the world, are threatened with destruction by the evil genius of our age and nation, in these times we should seek to increase the power and appliances of the Home Mission Society. Wars, while they are divine chastisements for the sins of a people, are God's method of ploughing the nations, that the seeds of better things may be cast into the softened soil; and to withhold from this Society what is due, because the state of the country has rolled unwonted burdens upon us, would be to enact in spiritual husbandry the folly of the farmer who should think his ploughing so expensive that he could not follow it by seeding.

We especially commend that feature of the Society's work which looks toward rendering direct aid to feeble churches, in erecting suitable houses of worship, and we would urge upon the churches of the State to do their part to make this, and all the good works in which this Society is engaged, efficient for the current year.

early day, there were about 15 or 20 ch
are there 265 churches, sixteen associa
12,000. The brethren who formed tha
some to other Territories and States, an
one" has become many "thousand." It
band had any idea of the results of th
sad changes which were in store for ou
in civil war, occasioned by an attempt, t
overthrow our Government, and which, i
despotism more at variance with civil a
ment that ever existed. This will be the re
this rebellion is put down, treason crushed
sustained.

But while the state of our country is th
hundreds of families are mourning the fall,
who have died defending our liberties, it is
that he has spared *our* ranks with so few ex
past year. It has not, however, been a year
and fear; of faith and anxiety. The sad ch
fected our operations. Another calamity, m
west, has crippled our efforts most seriously,
The "great currency panic," caused untol
closing avenues of trade, stopping public im
ing bankruptcy and ruin into all circles of l
have been against us, and greatly curtailed c

titute field, except some favored portions already attended to. There are important centres, rapidly increasing in numbers, county-seats, railroad towns, and rural settlements, which are looking to the Convention for help to *begin*, in many instances, the work of the gospel in them. And, while the times have been changing from bad to worse, as affecting our missionary operations, the field has increased in size and in its needs. Probably at no previous period in our history as a Convention, have there been so many and urgent demands made upon its treasury as at present, and which the unhappy state of our country and other causes beyond our control will not justify the attempt to meet.

...aldwin, A. T., Brooklyn, N. Y.

Capwell, Albert B , Brooklyn, N. Y.
Clarke, Rev. John C. C , Yonkers, N. Y.

Davis, John F , Brooklyn, N. Y.
Davis, George F., Burlington, Vt.
Doolittle, Rev. Horace D., Wappinger's Falls, N.Y.

Fish, Rev. J. L. A., Webster, Mass.
Ford, William, Philadelphia.
Ford, William, Jr., Philadelphia.
Funk, Cyrus, Holyoke, Mass.

Hanna, William B , Philadelphia.
Hoag, Foster, Amenia, N. Y

MEMBERS F

Constituted during the Year

BY VIRTUE OF A CONTRIBUTIO

Adams, Austin, Williamsburgh, N. Y.
Allen, George A , Brooklyn, N. Y.
Alderson, Rev. L. A , Atchison, Kansas.
Ambler, A. S , Brooklyn, N. Y.
Amsden, M. J. Saxton's River, Vt.
Andrews, Miss Kate, Williamsburgh, N. Y.
Applegate, John D. Penn Yan, N. Y.
Armstrong, Mrs. Abigail L., Rome, N. Y.
Atkinson, John H., Newburgh, N. Y.
Atkinson, Rev. Robert, Newark, N. J.
Atwater, Mrs Hannah S. B., So. Ab...

Daniels, Mrs. Lucy E., Fitchburgh, Mass.
Daniels, Mrs. Sophia, Brooklyn, N. Y.
Davenport, Jonathan G., New York.
Davis, Mrs. Sarah W., Brooklyn, N. Y.
Davis, Mrs. Charlotte M., Brooklyn, N. Y.
Deats, Miss Emily O., Cherryville, N. J.
Demonet, J. B., Brooklyn, N. Y.
Dingler, T. C., Jersey Shore, Pa.
Dodge, Mrs. Mary T., New Boston, N. H.
Doolittle, Mrs. S. W., Wappinger's Falls, N. Y.
Dunham, Nelson, New Brunswick, N. J.
Durando, Charles P., Brooklyn, N. Y.

Eaton, Eben, Boston, Mass.
Eddy, Thomas J., Waterford, N. Y.
Eddy, Mary E., Waterford, N Y.
Edgerton, L. P., Brooklyn, N. Y.
Eldridge, John J., Aurora, Ohio.
Elmore, Rev. Jerome B., Bedford Station, N. Y.
Ely, William M., Holmdel, N. J.

Farley, Rev. R. G., Morristown, N. J.
Farren, John S., Brooklyn, N. Y.
Fenn, Wallace B., New Haven, Ct.
Fisher, Mrs. Mary, New London, Ct.
Fisk, Lewis, North Tewksbury, Mass.
Forst, D. P., Trenton, N. J.
Fox, William B., Poughkeepsie, N. Y.
Fredericks, Miss Sarah, Williamsburgh, N. Y.
Frobos, Charles L., New York.

Galusha, Mrs. Mary, Fort Edward, N. Y.
Garrett, Anson B., Ballston Spa, N. Y.
Genther, Miss Malissa, Williamsburgh, N. Y.
Gilmore, Mrs. M. Josephine, Newton Cent., Mass.
Gladding, George F., Providence, R. I.
Gladding, Benjamin H., Providence, R. I.
Gladding, John H., Providence, R. I.
Gladding, Mrs. Rebecca M., Providence, R. I.
Gladding, Munro H., Providence, R. I.
Gonsalves, Mrs. Sarah, Philadelphia.
Goodwin, Mrs. Lydia M., East Greenwich, R. I.
Goodrich, Justus H., Stephentown, N. Y.
Green, Mrs. Judith, Plymouth, N. H.
Guild, Rev. H. A., Berlin, N. Y.

Hall, David, Adamsville, N. Y.
Hall, Rev. Silas.
Hall, Mrs. Ann E., Manchester, N. H.
Hammond Thomas, Dover Plains, N. Y.
Hancock, Miss Martha W., Cambridgeport, Mass.
Haskell, Henry L., South Reading, Mass.
Heart, Abraham G., Fall River, Mass.
Heath, Mrs. Sarah C., Brooklyn, N. Y.
Herrick, John, Chicopee Falls, Mass.
Herrick, Henry S., Chicopee Falls, Mass.
Higgins, Judiah, Flemington, N. J.
Hill, Mrs. Annie M., New Market, N. J.
Hires, I. Clawson, Woodstown, N. J.
Hobart, Mrs. Maria R., Adams, N. Y.
Hopkins, Ira, Towner's Station, N. Y.
Hopkins, Miss Biah O., Williamsburgh, N. Y.
Hopkins, *Miss Lillie R.*, Williamsburgh, N. Y.

Hovey, Mrs. Mary H., Cambridgeport, Mass.
Howard, Mrs. Annie E., Hartford, Ct
Howe, Mrs. Annie C., Covert, N. Y.
Howe, A. H., Brooklyn, N. Y.
Hoyt, Mrs. Arabella, Brooklyn, N. Y.
Hunt, Eddie T., Brooklyn, N. Y.
Huntington, Charles R., Brooklyn, N. Y.

Jackson, Rev. J. B.
Johnson, William, Farmer, N. Y.
Johnston, Mrs. Amelia M., Philadelphia.

Keith, Mrs. Orpah, Newport, N. H.
Keller, Gilbert A., North Manlius, N. Y.
Kinney, George W., Preston, Ct.

Langdell, Mrs. Fanny, New Boston, N. H.
Latham, Elias, Greenport, N. Y.
Leach, Almon, Utica, N. Y.
Lecount, John, New York.
Letts, John, Utica, Ohio.
Lentell, Mrs. Louisa R., Montville, Mass.
Linda, Mrs. Margaret, New York.
Lines, Mrs. Louisa R., Utica, N. Y.
Lott, Mrs. Betsey, Reading, N. Y.
Ludlam, Mrs. Elizabeth F., Brooklyn, N. Y.
Ludlam, Mrs. Phebe R., Sing Sing, N. Y.
Lyon, Benjamin F., Fitchburgh, Mass.

Mahoney, Mrs. Rebecca M., Providence, R I.
Manwaring, Mrs. Calvin S., Niantic, Ct.
Martin, G. W., New York.
Martin, Arthur, Orange, N. J.
Mason, Miss Maria P., Milwaukee, Wis.
Matteson, Rev. L. Jerome, Watertown, N. Y.
McFarland, Walter, Philadelphia.
Merrifield, Miss Chrissie E., Brookline, Vt.
Mootey, Mrs. Phebe, Williamsburgh, N. Y.
Mootey, Miss Ellen, Williamsburgh, N. Y.
Moreley, Mrs. Priscilla, Centre White Creek, N Y.
Morgan, Thomas N., Brooklyn, N. Y.
Muzzy, E. R., Cumberland, Ohio.

Newton, John, Kingsbury, N. Y.
Nugent, George, Philadelphia.

Osgood, J. W., Chicopee Falls, Mass

Peck, George, Brooklyn, N. Y.
Perkins, Charles R., Meriden, Ct.
Pool, John, Matamoras, Ohio.
Post, Mrs. Mary Ann, Dover Plains, N. Y.
Pratt, E. R., Brooklyn, N. Y.
Reed, Mrs. L. B., New York.
Richards, Humphrey, New York.
Roberts, O. E., Brooklyn, N. Y.
Roper, Tonsdale J., Morristown, N J.
Rorer, Daniel, Hatboro, Pa.

Saddington, Miss Susan E., Williamsburgh, N. Y.
Sanborn, Mrs. Ann C., Danville, N. H.
Sandford, James, Tarrytown, N Y.
Sawyer, Mrs. Samuel A., Brooklyn, N. Y.
Sawyer, Albert, Brooklyn, N. Y.

Silliman, Mrs. Martha Frances, Easton, Ct.
Simpson, Mrs. Gertrude, Freehold, N. J.
Simons, Mrs. Sarah P., Stepney, Ct.
Skerry, Robert, Salem, Mass.
Skerry, Sarah M., Salem, Mass.
Smith, Lewis M., Newburgh, N. Y.
Smith, Miss Eliza P., Brooklyn, N. Y.
Smith, Henry, Holley, N. Y.
Smith, Martin L., Cambridgeport, Mass.
Spalding, Miss Harriet M., Hopewell, N. Y.
Sparks, Jonas, Jr., New York.
Sparks, Peter B., New York.
Spencer, Miss Sarah A., East Greenwich, R. I.
Standiford, Mrs. Hannah, Greencastle, Ia.
Stanley, Miss Mary A., Concord, N. H.
Stebbins, Mrs. Esther M., Utica, Min.
Stetson, T. P., Brooklyn, N. Y.
Stone, Mrs. Sarah M., Scriba, N. Y.
Stoddard, Miss Lizzie A., Williamsburgh, N. Y.
Skerry, Robert, Salem, Mass.
Skerry, Sarah M., Salem, Mass.
Story, Rupert, Brooklyn, N. Y.
Swain, Rev. E. Y., Seaville, N. J.
Swallow, Mrs. Hannah Eliz., Flemington, N. J.
Taylor, Mrs. Lydia, Holmdel, N. J.
Taylor, Miss Emma C., Holmdel, N. J.

LIST OF DE

Directors and Members

DIRECTORS.

Aldrich, Rev. Jonathan, Worcester, Mass.
Crosby, Rev. C. C. P., Brooklyn, N. Y.

CONTENTS.

ANNUAL REPORT OF THE EXECUTIVE BOARD.

MISCELLANEOUS MATTER.

Lightning Source UK Ltd.
Milton Keynes UK
UKHW020601270219
338007UK00009B/1051/P

9 781528 106832